THE ROUTLEDGE COMPANION TO SEVENTEENTH CENTURY PHILOSOPHY

The Routledge Companion to Seventeenth Century Philosophy is an outstanding survey of one of the most important eras in the history of Western philosophy – one which witnessed philosophical, scientific, religious, and social change on a massive scale.

A team of twenty international contributors provide students and scholars of philosophy and related disciplines with a detailed and accessible guide to seventeenth century philosophy. The *Companion* is divided into seven parts:

- Historical Context
- Metaphysics
- Epistemology
- Mind and Language
- Moral and Political Philosophy
- Natural Philosophy and the Material World
- Philosophical Theology.

Major topics and themes are explored and discussed, including the scholastic context that shaped philosophy of the period, free will, skepticism, logic, mind-body problems, consciousness, arguments for the existence of God, and the problem of evil. As such *The Routledge Companion to Seventeenth Century Philosophy* is essential reading for all students of the period, both in philosophy and related disciplines such as literature, history, politics, and religious studies.

Dan Kaufman is Associate Professor of Philosophy at the University of Colorado, Boulder, USA. He has published extensively on issues in seventeenth century philosophy, especially on modality, substance, individuation, and identity.

Routledge Philosophy Companions

Routledge Philosophy Companions offer thorough, high-quality surveys and assessments of the major topics and periods in philosophy. Covering key problems, themes, and thinkers, all entries are specially commissioned for each volume and written by leading scholars in the field. Clear, accessible, and carefully edited and organised, *Routledge Philosophy Companions* are indispensable for anyone coming to a major topic or period in philosophy, as well as for the more advanced reader.

Recently published

The Routledge Companion to Feminist Philosophy
Edited by Ann Garry, Serene J. Khader, and Alison Stone

The Routledge Companion to Philosophy of Social Science
Edited by Lee McIntyre and Alex Rosenberg

The Routledge Companion to Sixteenth Century Philosophy
Edited by Benjamin Hill and Henrik Lagerlund

The Routledge Companion to Free Will
Edited by Kevin Timpe, Meghan Griffith, and Neil Levy

The Routledge Companion to Philosophy of Medicine
Edited by Miriam Solomon, Jeremy R. Simon, and Harold Kincaid

The Routledge Companion to Philosophy of Literature
Edited by Noël Carroll and John Gibson

The Routledge Companion to Islamic Philosophy
Edited by Richard C. Taylor and Luis Xavier López-Farjeat

The Routledge Companion to Virtue Ethics
Edited by Lorraine Besser-Jones and Michael Slote

The Routledge Companion to Bioethics
Edited by John Arras, Rebecca Kukla, and Elizabeth Fenton

The Routledge Companion to Hermeneutics
Edited by Jeff Malpas and Hans-Helmuth Gander

The Routledge Companion to Eighteenth Century Philosophy
Edited by Aaron Garrett

The Routledge Companion to Ancient Philosophy
Edited by Frisbee Sheffield and James Warren

The Routledge Companion to Social and Political Philosophy
Edited by Gerald Gaus and Fred D'Agostino

For a full list of published *Routledge Philosophy Companions*, please visit www.routledge.com/series/PHILCOMP

THE ROUTLEDGE COMPANION TO SEVENTEENTH CENTURY PHILOSOPHY

Edited by Dan Kaufman

LONDON AND NEW YORK

First published 2018
by Routledge
2 Park Square, Milton Park, Abingdon, Oxon OX14 4RN

and by Routledge
711 Third Avenue, New York, NY 10017

Routledge is an imprint of the Taylor & Francis Group, an informa business

© 2018 selection and editorial matter, Dan Kaufman; individual chapters, the contributors

The right of Dan Kaufman to be identified as the author of the editorial material, and of the authors for their individual chapters, has been asserted in accordance with sections 77 and 78 of the Copyright, Designs and Patents Act 1988.

All rights reserved. No part of this book may be reprinted or reproduced or utilised in any form or by any electronic, mechanical, or other means, now known or hereafter invented, including photocopying and recording, or in any information storage or retrieval system, without permission in writing from the publishers.

Trademark notice: Product or corporate names may be trademarks or registered trademarks, and are used only for identification and explanation without intent to infringe.

British Library Cataloguing-in-Publication Data
A catalogue record for this book is available from the British Library

Library of Congress Cataloging-in-Publication Data
Names: Kaufman, Daniel, 1968- editor.
Title: The Routledge companion to seventeenth century philosophy / edited by Dan Kaufman.
Description: 1 [edition]. | New York : Routledge, 2017. | Series: The Routledge companion to feminist philosophy | Includes bibliographical references and index.
Identifiers: LCCN 2017001643 | ISBN 9780415775670 (hardback : alk. paper) | ISBN 9781315771960 (e-book)
Subjects: LCSH: Philosophy, Modern—17th century.
Classification: LCC B801 .R69 2017 | DDC 190.9/032—dc23
LC record available at https://lccn.loc.gov/2017001643

ISBN: 978-0-415-77567-0 (hbk)
ISBN: 978-1-315-77196-0 (ebk)

Typeset in Goudy
by Apex CoVantage, LLC

For those who taught me seventeenth century philosophy: Vere Chappell, Eileen O'Neill, and Robert C. Sleigh, Jr.

In memory of Gareth Matthews and Sophie Charlotte Lovetron.

CONTENTS

Contributors   x
Acknowledgment   xiv
Foreword by Steven Nadler   xv

PART 1
Historical context   1

1 The Scholastic background   3
  DAVID CLEMENSON

PART 2
Metaphysics   33

2 Theories of substance   35
  TAD M. SCHMALTZ

3 Qualities   60
  SAMUEL C. RICKLESS

4 Causation   87
  SUKJAE LEE

5 Free will and determinism   117
  C. P. RAGLAND

PART 3
Epistemology   143

6 Skepticism   145
  GIANNI PAGANINI

7 Theories of ideas   195
  LEX NEWMAN

8 Logic and knowledge   224
  ALAN NELSON

PART 4
Mind and language — 251

9 Mind-body problems — 253
   DAVID CUNNING

10 Theories of sense perception — 287
   ANTONIA LOLORDO

11 Consciousness — 310
   STEVEN NADLER

12 Power and passion in Hobbes, Descartes and Spinoza — 334
   DEBORAH BROWN

13 Philosophy of language — 354
   WALTER OTT

PART 5
Natural philosophy and the material world — 383

14 Natural philosophy — 385
   ANDREW JANIAK

15 The theory of matter — 410
   ANDREW PYLE

PART 6
Moral philosophy and political philosophy — 447

16 Moral philosophy — 449
   MICHAEL LEBUFFE

17 Political philosophy — 476
   SUSANNE SREEDHAR

PART 7
Philosophical theology — 503

18 Arguments for the existence of God — 505
   MARCY P. LASCANO

19 The problem of evil — 536
   SAMUEL NEWLANDS

CONTENTS

20 The rise of religious skepticism   **563**
    MICHAEL W. HICKSON AND THOMAS M. LENNON

Index of names   583
Index of subjects   587

CONTRIBUTORS

Deborah Brown is associate professor in philosophy at the University of Queensland, Australia. She has written many articles on early modern philosophy, especially on Descartes's theory of mind, and she is the author of the book *Descartes and the Passionate Mind* (Cambridge, 2006). She is currently working on a book project, *Descartes' Ontology of Everyday Life* (with Calvin Normore), as well as articles on the history of animals, Hume's nominalism, and the *conatus* principle in the philosophy of Hobbes and Descartes.

David Clemenson is associate professor of philosophy at the University of St. Thomas (St. Paul) and is the author of *Descartes's Theory of Ideas* (Continuum, 2007), as well as articles on *early* early modern philosophy. He is currently the editor of *American Catholic Philosophical Quarterly*. His current interests in the history of philosophy include the theory of universals in the Conimbricenses's *Dialectic* and related topics in the history of logic.

David Cunning is associate professor of philosophy at the University of Iowa and the author of *Argument and Persuasion in Descartes' Meditations* (Oxford, 2010), as well as the forthcoming volume on Margaret Cavendish, for the *Routledge Arguments of the Philosophers* series. He is also the editor of *The Cambridge Companion to Descartes' Meditations* (Cambridge, 2014).

Michael W. Hickson is assistant professor of philosophy at Trent University, Canada. He has published several papers on Pierre Bayle and on Descartes in the *Journal of the History of Philosophy*, the *British Journal for the History of Philosophy*, and other venues. He and Thomas Lennon wrote a chapter on skepticism in Descartes's First Meditation for *Descartes' Meditations: A Critical Guide*, edited by Karen Detlefsen (Cambridge, 2013).

Andrew Janiak is Creed C. Black Associate Professor of Philosophy and a member of the Bass Society of Fellows at Duke University, as well as the director of graduate program in history and philosophy of science, technology, and medicine. His work has focused on Newton and on Kant. He is the author of *Newton as Philosopher* (Cambridge, 2008), the forthcoming *Isaac Newton*, in the *Blackwell Great Minds* series edited by Steven Nadler, and the editor of *Newton: Philosophical Writings* (Cambridge, 2014, second edition) and the co-editor (with Eric Schliesser) of *Interpreting Newton: Critical Essays* (Cambridge, 2012).

Marcy P. Lascano is associate professor of philosophy, California State University, Long Beach. She has published on a wide variety of topics and authors in early modern philosophy, including papers on Locke, Leibniz, Conway, Astell, Damaris Masham, and Elisabeth of Bohemia. She is also the co-editor (with Eileen O'Neill) of the forthcoming *Feminist History of Philosophy: The Recovery and Evaluation of Women's Philosophical Thought* (Springer). She is currently working on a book manuscript titled *Early Modern Women: Cosmology to Human Nature*.

Michael LeBuffe is professor and Baier Chair of Early Modern Philosophy at the University of Otago, New Zealand. He is the author of *From Bondage to Freedom: Spinoza on Human Excellence* (Oxford, 2010), as well as many articles on Spinoza and on Hobbes, including "Theories of Consciousness in Spinoza's *Ethics*," *Philosophical Review* (2010). He is currently working on several essays on Hobbes and Spinoza, and finishing a book, *Spinoza on Reason* (Oxford, forthcoming).

Sukjae Lee is associate professor of philosophy at Seoul National University, where he did his undergraduate studies. For many years, he was faculty at the Ohio State University. His research has focused primarily on early modern theories of causation, especially in Leibniz, Malebranche, and Berkeley; and his papers include "Leibniz on Divine Concurrence," *Philosophical Review* (2004), and "Necessary Connections and Continuous Creation: Malebranche's Two Arguments for Occasionalism," *Journal of the History of Philosophy* (2007). He was awarded the Rogers Prize for the best article published in the *British Journal for the History of Philosophy* in 2012 for his "Berkeley on the Activity of Spirits."

Thomas M. Lennon is professor emeritus at the University of Western Ontario. He is the author of, among other publications on the history of early modern philosophy, *The Battle of the Gods and Giants: The Legacies of Descartes and Gassendi, 1655–1715* (1993), *Reading Bayle* (1999), and *The Plain Truth: Descartes, Huet, and Skepticism* (Leiden: Brill, 2008).

Antonia LoLordo is professor of philosophy at the University of Virginia; has authored two books: *Locke's Moral Man* (Oxford, 2012) and *Pierre Gassendi and the Birth of Early Modern Philosophy* (Cambridge, 2006); and co-edited (with Stewart Duncan) a collection of essays, *Debates in Modern Philosophy: Essential Readings and Contemporary Responses* for the Routledge Key Debates in the History of Philosophy series (2013). She has also written articles on Descartes, Edwards, Gassendi, Hume, Locke, Malebranche, and early modern Epicureanism.

Steven Nadler is the William H. Hay II Professor of Philosophy at the University of Wisconsin-Madison. His books include *Arnauld and the Cartesian Philosophy of Ideas* (Princeton University Press, 1989), *Malebranche and Ideas* (Oxford University Press, 1992), *Spinoza: A Life* (Cambridge University Press, 1999), *Spinoza's Heresy: Immortality and the Jewish Mind* (Oxford University Press, 2002), *Spinoza's Ethics: An Introduction* (Cambridge University Press, 2006), *The Best of All Possible Worlds: A Story of Philosophers, God and Evil* (Farrar, Straus & Giroux, 2008), *Occasionalism: Causation Among the Cartesians* (Oxford University Press, 2011), *A Book Forged in Hell: Spinoza's Scandalous Treatise and the Birth of the Secular Age* (Princeton, 2011), and *The Philosopher, the Priest, and the Painter: A Portrait of Descartes* (Princeton, 2013).

CONTRIBUTORS

Alan Nelson is professor of philosophy at the University of North Carolina at Chapel Hill. He has also taught at UCLA, USC, Pittsburgh, Stanford, and UC Irvine. He edited *A Companion to Rationalism* (Blackwell, 2005) and has recently published or has forthcoming articles on historical methodology, Descartes, Spinoza, and Hume. Nelson has won several awards for mentoring doctoral students. He is currently working on neo-Platonic thinking in early modern philosophy.

Samuel Newlands is the William J. and Dorothy K. O'Neill Associate Professor of Philosophy at the University of Notre Dame. His research focuses on early modern philosophy, metaphysics, and philosophy of religion. He has received an NEH fellowship for his work on Spinoza, and he has published more than two-dozen pieces on early modern philosophy in venues ranging from *The Philosophical Review* to *The Wall Street Journal*. He is the co-editor of *Metaphysics and the Good* (Oxford, 2009) and *New Essays on Leibniz's Theodicy* (Oxford, 2014). He co-directed *The Problem of Evil in Modern and Contemporary Thought*, a three-year research initiative. Beginning in 2014, he will co-direct *Hope and Optimism: Conceptual and Empirical Investigations*, a large, multidisciplinary investigation into the nature and norms of hope and optimism.

Lex Newman is associate professor of philosophy at the University of Utah. He is the author of many articles, including "Descartes on Unknown Faculties and Our Knowledge of the External World," *Philosophical Review* (1994); and "The Fourth Meditation," *Philosophy and Phenomenological Research* (1999). He is also the editor of *The Cambridge Companion to Locke's* Essay Concerning Human Understanding (2007).

Walter Ott is associate professor of philosophy at the University of Virginia and the author of *Locke's Philosophy of Language* (Cambridge, 2004) and *Causation and Laws of Nature in Early Modern Philosophy* (Oxford, 2009). Recent papers include "What Is Locke's Theory of Representation?" *British Journal for the History of Philosophy*; and "Malebranche and the Riddle of Sensation," *Philosophy and Phenomenological Research*.

Gianni Paganini is professor of history of philosophy at the Università del Piemonte Orientale "Amedeo Avogadro," department of humanities, Vercelli. Among his many publications are *Pierre Bayle* (1991), and a two-volume critical edition of the previously unpublished *Theophrastus redivivus* (with Guido Canziani; 1981–82). His book *Skepsis: Le débat des modernes sur le scepticisme* (2008) won the La Bruyère Award for Philosophy in 2009 from the Académie Française. He published many articles on Montaigne, Descartes, Hobbes, Hume, Condillac, besides two annotated Italian translations: Hobbes, *De motu, loco et tempore* (2010) and Hume, *Dialogues Concerning Natural Religion* (2013). In 2011 he won the prize for philosophy given by the Italian Academy (Accademia dei Lincei).

Andrew Pyle was reader in early modern philosophy at the University of Bristol, UK, until the summer of 2017. His extensive list of publications includes *Atomism and Its Critics*, *Malebranche* (in the Routledge *Arguments of the Philosophers* series, 2003), and *Locke* (in the Polity Press *Classic Thinkers* series, 2013).

CONTRIBUTORS

C. P. Ragland is associate professor of philosophy at Saint Louis University. His papers include "Descartes on Degrees of Freedom: A Close Look at a Key Text," *Essays in Philosophy* 14:2 (July 2013), 239–268; "Descartes' Theodicy," *Religious Studies* 43:2 (2007), 125–44; and "Descartes on Divine Providence and Human Freedom," *Archiv für Geschichte der Philosophie* 87 (2005), 159–188. His book, *The Will to Reason: Theodicy and Freedom in Descartes*, was published by Oxford University Press in 2016.

Samuel C. Rickless is professor of philosophy at the University of California, San Diego. His areas of research include early modern philosophy, ancient philosophy (particularly Plato), nonconsequentialist ethics, the philosophy of law, and the philosophy of language. He is the author of three books: *Plato's Forms in Transition: A Reading of the Parmenides* (Cambridge University Press, 2007), *Berkeley's Argument for Idealism* (Oxford University Press, 2013), and *Locke* (Wiley-Blackwell, 2014). In the history of philosophy, he has published on the following topics: Plato's *Protagoras, Parmenides,* and *Sophist*; the Cartesian circle; Locke's anti-innatism and his theories of qualities, personhood, freedom, and knowledge; Berkeley's antiabstractionism and theism; Hume's theory of the passions; and Kant's argument for the categorical imperative. Current history-focused research projects include an article on Locke's theory of freedom for the *Stanford Encyclopedia of Philosophy*, and an article on Berkeley's continuity argument for the existence of God for a critical guide to *Three Dialogues Between Hylas and Philonous* (Cambridge University Press).

Tad M. Schmaltz is professor of philosophy and James B. and Grace J. Nelson Fellow at the University of Michigan, Ann Arbor. He has published on various topics in early modern philosophy. His books include *Descartes on Causation* (Oxford, 2008), *Radical Cartesianism* (Cambridge, 2002), and *Malebranche's Theory of the Soul* (Oxford, 1996). He also is editor of *Receptions of Descartes* (Routledge, 2005), and co-editor of *Integrating History and Philosophy of Science* (Springer, 2011) and the *Historical Dictionary of Descartes and Cartesian Philosophy* (Scarecrow, 2003). His edited volume, *Efficient Causation*, a collection of essays on the history of this concept, is the first volume published (2014) in the *Oxford Philosophical Concepts* series.

Susanne Sreedhar is associate professor of philosophy at Boston University. Her research addresses the moral and political questions that arise within the history of the social contract tradition. She is the author of *Hobbes on Resistance: Defying the Leviathan* (Cambridge University Press, 2010). She has received fellowships from the Boston University Center for the Humanities and the National Humanities Center in North Carolina to support her research.

ACKNOWLEDGMENT

Thanks to Adam Johnson and Tony Bruce for their nearly infinite patience; to Steven Nadler for invaluable help precisely when the most help was needed; to Michael Sechman, Ben Kultgen, Noel Saenz, and Joseph Stenberg for help with proofreading and so forth; and most of all, to Mary Katrina Krizan, who has been selflessly working with me on this project every step of the way, doing more to get this volume to the light of day than anyone else. Thanks so much.

FOREWORD

Scholarship on early modern European philosophy – that is, in the seventeenth and eighteenth centuries – has undergone significant changes over the past quarter-century, all for the better. Once upon a time, most studies, especially in Anglo-American research, were confined to a relatively small number of thinkers and philosophical problems. The so-called canon consisted mainly of René Descartes, Bento (Benedictus) Spinoza, Gottfried Wilhelm Leibniz, John Locke, George Berkeley, and David Hume. And the topics that most interested scholars were primarily in the areas of epistemology and metaphysics. Political philosophy in the period was often treated as a separate subject altogether, and moral philosophy was rarely addressed at all.

Today, the best work by historians of early modern philosophy is much more inclusive, in many different ways, and for that reason more sophisticated and interesting. Philosophically relevant figures once dismissed as "minor" and thus ignored now occupy a central place in the story. Not just thinkers who qualify as "philosophers" in our narrow contemporary sense but also theologians, natural scientists, mathematicians, and political theorists are now all seen to have played an important role – a *philosophical* role – in the rise of modern philosophy. On the Continent, this includes the likes of Nicolas Malebranche, Antoine Arnauld, Pierre Gassendi, Pierre Bayle, Marin Mersenne, Hugo Grotius, and Samuel Pufendorf, among others. In Great Britain, there is Henry More, Ralph Cudworth, and Robert Boyle, as well as other members of the Royal Society, Anthony Cooper (the third earl of Shaftesbury), and Francis Hutcheson. More attention is now also paid to the essential contributions made by women philosophers in the period, including Elisabeth of Bohemia, Anne Conway, Anna Maria van Schurman, Damaris Cudworth (Lady Masham), and Mary Astell.

Another important development in recent scholarship is the focus on the varieties of philosophizing in these centuries and the different contexts in which they took place. Modern philosophy was not a monolithic enterprise. There were competing philosophical traditions throughout the period, and even partisans who shared the basic goals of the "new philosophy" differed fundamentally in terms of both method and content. Moreover, the ways in which early modern philosophers addressed even problems narrowly conceived as "epistemological" and "metaphysical" cannot be truly understood outside of their broader historico-philosophical setting (including the legacies of medieval thought, the influence and opposition represented by late Scholasticism, and robust brands of skepticism). Just as important is the relationship between philosophy and what are today regarded as separate disciplines. Topics once dismissed by scholars as not sufficiently "philosophical" are now seen as in fact central to early modern philosophizing. After all, in the seventeenth century the line between "philosophy" and "science" did not exist; what we now think of as science was then simply natural philosophy. Similarly, there was no hard boundary between philosophy and theology or religious thought or between philosophy and jurisprudence.

Finally, it is now commonplace that philosophy did not suddenly become "modern" because of this or that thinker or treatise or even movement. The development of what stands as modern philosophy occurred in fits and starts and even some backsliding. Philosophers such as Descartes and Spinoza did not totally abandon the vocabularies and conceptual frameworks of their forebears; Leibniz, in fact, explicitly and unashamedly embraced aspects of ancient and medieval thought. Even intellectual revolutions and "paradigm shifts" maintain some engagement with the past, and the divisions between periods of philosophy are always much cleaner in hindsight. A lot of philosophy of the seventeenth century, as recent scholarship has shown, sought to assimilate, modify, or update Scholastic thought rather than reject it outright. At the same time, these early modern thinkers were, quite self-consciously, out to transform philosophy and set it on a new course.

The chapters in this volume are representative of the outstanding work now being done in the historiography of early modern philosophy. The range of thinkers and topics addressed by these leading scholars provides a superb introduction to two centuries of philosophizing and an excellent survey of the state of the field. The chapters are organized thematically, rather than simply by philosophical names, to give the reader a greater sense of the broad "conversation" that was going on in the period. No philosopher does his or her work in an intellectual and historical vacuum. One thinker's views on substance or causation or free will are best understood in the context of what others thought as well. Philosophy, as Plato recognized, is essentially a dialogue, and the chapters here provide the reader with a good sense of what was being said by whom, to whom, and why. The result, we hope, is a deeper understanding of the many dimensions of philosophy in what is arguably its most brilliant era.

Steven Nadler, January 2017

Part 1

HISTORICAL CONTEXT

1
THE SCHOLASTIC BACKGROUND

David Clemenson

Almost every major seventeenth century philosopher studied Scholastic philosophy at college or university.[1] Scholastic philosophical training of the period typically concentrated on the reading of textbooks, which usually took the form of commentaries on Aristotle's major works. Some of the most influential of these textbooks were composed in the sixteenth and seventeenth centuries by Jesuits or by Protestants indebted to their works.[2]

Baroque Scholasticism produced a plethora of lengthy and closely reasoned texts covering a wide range of fields. No brief study can do justice to the tradition and its effects on early modern thought. In this chapter's first section, I have chosen to discuss a few doctrines and controversies characteristic of Scholastic metaphysics and philosophy of cognition in this period. The chapter's second section lists some salient points of contact between particular seventeenth century philosophers and Baroque Scholasticism.[3]

1. Selected themes in Baroque Scholastic metaphysics and philosophy of cognition

1.1. *Philosophy of cognition 1: the conceivability of individuals*

Scholastics, following Aristotle, taught that all human knowledge is ultimately derived from the senses. On the standard Aristotelian account, the external senses perceive material individuals according to a particular sensory modality (e.g. the visual faculty perceives an individual such as Socrates simply *qua* colored, not *qua* human, or *qua* material substance).[4] Sensations of different modalities are discriminated and coordinated into complexes (e.g. Socrates *qua* visible and audible) by an internal sense-perceptual faculty called the "common sense." These complexes are stored in the "phantasy" (sense memory and imaginative power) as "phantasms" (images).[5] The phantasy, a corporeal power like the senses, is able to divide and recombine images received from the common sense (e.g. of pink and of elephant) to form new, complex images (e.g. that of a pink elephant) not derived from the common sense or external senses. Phantasms are used by one of two incorporeal intellectual powers, the "agent intellect" (*intellectus agens*), to fashion "intelligible species" (roughly, concepts, whether in actual use or merely stored in the intellectual memory) that are received and stored in the other intellectual power, the "passive intellect" (*intellectus patiens*, also called the *intellectus possibilis* or "possible" intellect). This second incorporeal power is called "passive" because it is acted on by the agent intellect, but that does not mean that it is incapable of any productive activity of its own. On the contrary, the passive intellect divides and recombines the contents it receives to form new concepts not produced by the agent intellect, just as the imagination does with images it receives from the common sense.[6]

The intellect's intelligible species or concepts exhibit material things' natures, for example the nature of red or of horse, or of "metaphysical parts" of those natures (e.g. the genus of accident, for red, or of substance, for horse). It was a widespread view, derived from the Muslim philosopher Avicenna (ibn Sina), that in themselves natures are neither universal nor individual but susceptible of receiving either individuality (outside the intellect) or universality (in the intellect's concept).[7] There was thought to be no contradiction here: one and the same thing can be simultaneously individual and nonindividual, provided it is so in different respects, namely, outside the intellect versus inside it. (The notion of the "reduplicative sense," formed by restricting a concept via some qualifying term such as "*qua*" or "insofar as," was often used to block paradoxes that would otherwise result from application of the principle "identicals are indistinguishable"; cf. medieval discussions of the fallacy *secundum quid et simpliciter*, discussed in Novaes and Read 2008).

Scholastics commonly believed that universals are conceived only by the intellect. Jesuits and other Scholastics directly influential on the early moderns held, in addition, that some of the human intellect's concepts exhibit individuals. Not all Scholastics agreed. St. Thomas Aquinas (1224/25–1274) and his more conservative followers held that the intellect cannot represent individuals through its own concepts but knows them only indirectly, by a "reversion to the phantasms" present in the corporeal phantasy (commentators disagree about what this reversion amounted to).[8]

The Jesuits, and others who disagreed with Aquinas and his followers on this point, were obliged to argue for their position.[9] Among their arguments were the following. If the human intellect had no proper concepts of individuals, how could it form judgements such as "Socrates is human," which obviously concern an individual? How could it refer to nonsensible individuals such as God? Without direct perceptions of individuals, how could the human intellect be superior to the senses, or akin to the intellects of angels, since (as was generally admitted) the senses and the angelic intellects do have such perceptions? Arguments of this sort were repeated by the Jesuit philosopher Manuel de Góis (1542–1597), author of the *De anima* portion of the widely read Coimbra series of commentaries on the works of Aristotle.[10]

> The . . . view of those who say that sensible singulars are intellectually known (*intelligi*) by us, by means of a concept proper and peculiar to them, is true. This is accepted by Scotus (*in 4, dist. 45, q. 3*), Gregory [of Rimini] (*in 2, dist. 3, q. 7*), Durand [de Saint-Pourçain] (*in 2, dist. 3, q. 7*), Richard [of Middleton?] (*in 2, dist. 24, q. 4, circa 3, principale*), [Walter] Burley (*1 Physics*) and others. It is proved, first, by the fact that if sensible singulars could not be known (*cognosci*) in themselves (*per se*), and by a concept proper to them, this would be due either to their being singulars, or to their being sensibles. It cannot be because they are singulars; otherwise, no singular, not even one that was intelligible and non-material, would in itself (*per se*) fall under the scope of our intellect – not even in theology. Nor can it be because they are sensibles; otherwise, not even the common natures endowed with matter [e.g. the common nature of horse or

of any other species of material object] would be intelligible in themselves. ...
Secondly, our intellect posits a difference or an agreement between the singular
and the universal, through understandings (*rationes*) proper and peculiar to
them, as when it judges that [the universal nature] man has a wider extension
than [the individual nature] Socrates, or that outside the mind (*in re*) Socrates
is the same as man: thus each, the universal and the singular, is properly and
distinctly perceived by our intellect.

(Coimbra 1604, 441)[11]

All the authorities cited in the previous passage are late thirteenth or early fourteenth century writers (an example of Baroque Scholastics' reliance on their late medieval predecessors). Góis argues for the same view, with some additions, in his commentary on Aristotle's *Physics*, published, like his *De anima* commentary, as part of the Coimbra series (Coimbra 1594, 1: 74–5). As authorities for the opposing view, which was that of St. Thomas Aquinas, Góis cites the Thomists Giles of Rome, Capreolus, and Cajetan, together with the Spanish Muslim commentator Averroes (ibn Rushd) and the Greek Aristotelian commentators John Philoponus and Themistius (Coimbra 1594, 440).[12]

Arguments similar to those of Góis may be found in the writings of the influential Jesuits Pedro da Fonseca (1528–1599), Francisco Toledo (1532–1596), and Antonio Rubio (1548–1615) – each of whom was read by Descartes during his college years (references to specific texts are given in Clemenson 2007, 7–13, 42–3). Jesuits were not the only ones to hold this position. The widely read Paduan philosopher Giacomo (or Jacopo) Zabarella (1533–1589) wrote, in his "De anima" (part of his larger work *De rebus naturalibus*),[13]

I, however, together with many others, judge that our intellect can also [i.e. in addition to knowing universals] know singulars. In support of this I bring the very powerful argument that in the soul's faculties the higher faculty cognizes whatever the lower faculty does, and wherever the lower faculty leaves off, there the higher faculty begins; to deny this is to destroy the order and unity of the parts of the ensouled thing (*animal*). This is manifest in the phantasy, in relation to the external senses, for it can imagine all things which the senses can sense, but they differ in that the external senses do not sense an absent object, but only one that is present, while the phantasy imagines even absent things. Now, this difference is not to be understood to imply that the senses sense only present things, while the phantasy senses only absent things; rather, the phantasy senses both present and absent things. ... And so, as the senses are directed to the phantasm, so the phantasy to the intellect. The difference between the intellect, phantasy, and all the senses must be of this kind: that the intellect can cognize (*cognoscere*) everything that the phantasy and senses cognize, and more besides, so that just as the senses and phantasy cognize singulars, so too must the intellect cognize singulars, and, in addition to them, universals, which neither the senses nor the phantasy cognize.

(Zabarella 1602, 950)

Among Zabarella's other arguments for this view are that (1) that the soul can only know its own individual acts of intellection by the intellect, because such acts cannot be sensed, and (2) that the intellect must know individuals in order to know what individuality is, because (in the Aristotelian view) no property can be known except by abstraction based on knowledge of individual instances of that property (Zabarella 1602, 950–2).

The doctrine of the direct intellection of individuals seems to have been stoutly defended by Scholastics of the Baroque period – outside conservative Thomist circles.

1.2. General metaphysics: being as possibility

The claim that the human intellect's concepts exhibit individuals is closely related to the claim that not all individuals are actual (where "all" does not, of course, range over actuals, but over possibles).[14] Aristotelians agreed that any intellectual concept exhibiting an individual was indifferent to the actuality of that individual – the actuality of the cognized individual might be necessary to sensation, but not to intellection (for many Jesuits, not even sensation absolutely required the object's actuality; see Clemenson 2007, 38–42).

(For the remainder of this chapter, the term "actuality" will be taken as synonymous with "existence either outside time or at some time"; "existence" will be taken as synonymous with "existence that does not consist simply in being the object of some cognition"; and the domain of quantifiers such as "all," "every," and "some" will be the class of all possible things or essences, whether actual or not, whether individual or not.[15] In most contexts, "actuality" and "existence" will be interchangeable.)

Just as the views of the Jesuits and their followers on the intellection of individuals were at variance with those of conservative Thomists, so were their views on nonactual individuals. For Aquinas, there could be no nonexistent, merely possible individuals, but only nonexistent, hence nonindividual, complexes of common natures: individuality entailed actuality.[16] Aquinas's thinking on these matters seems to have had no effect on that portion of Baroque Scholasticism directly influential on the early moderns.

The ontological commitment of the Jesuits and their followers to nonactual individuals manifested itself in several ways: (1) a metaphysics in which the essence of a created or creatable thing was, in a sense to be explained, ontologically prior to its actuality; (2) a general philosophy of cognition in which nonactual things can be objects of direct cognition;[17] and (3) the middle-knowledge theory of divine foreknowledge and providence (a theory held by all major Jesuit writers of the time, though rejected by many of the Jesuits' Scholastic contemporaries, Catholic and Protestant alike). The first two of these are the subject of the present subsection and the next; the third is beyond the scope of this chapter.

Actuality or existence was considered only one of many "modes of *esse*" or "*esse-modes*" (*modus essendi*). Being (*ens*) was identified with essence, the possible as such.[18] (Here and throughout, *esse*, the infinitive of the finite copula *est* ["it is"] is left untranslated. Translating it as "being" or "existence" would risk confusing it either with *ens*, a verbal noun orthographically identical to the present participle of *esse*, or with *existentia*; as will be seen, *ens* and *existentia* are not in general synonymous with *esse*.[19] Translating *esse* as "to be" would yield such monstrosities as "to-be-modes.")[20]

> The name "being" (*ens*), considered generally, can be understood in two ways: (1) as signifying an act of *esse*, which is the same as [an act] of existing; in this sense it is the participle of the verb "am," or (2) as signifying the *nature* itself of the existing thing.... What is signified by "being," in the second and *far more*

common [my emphasis] sense, is typically labeled by the following three names: "nature," "quiddity," and "essence." It is called "nature" . . . because there is no entity that does not have some property – for "nature" is here taken as that from which some property comes forth, as it were. It is called "quiddity" insofar as it is signified through a definition, because only a definition explicates what (*quid*) a thing is. And it is called "essence" insofar as through it and in it each thing has the act of *esse* that we call existence.

(Fonseca 1615, 1: 739–41)

Whatever shares in real entity shares . . . in that common description of real being, by which it is called "that which is *able* to exist."

(Coimbra 1607, 1: 108, my emphasis)

Before considering further the Jesuits' views on essence's relation to existence, it is necessary to discuss their notion of essence as such.

Jesuit philosophers took *esse* in the pure sense to be not existence but the fact or status of being an essence (or "nature"). The various *esse-modes* (*modi essendi*) were various ways of being an essence. The principal way was existence or actuality (more on this later). The Scholastics were bound to assert that many creatable essences never acquire existence. To deny this would have been to deny the contingency of creation, a cardinal point of Christian doctrine. Creatures' *esse*, on the other hand, was necessary and eternal:

the natures of things can be viewed in two ways: with respect to essence, and with respect to existence; taken in the second way [natures] are subordinate to the divine will . . . but [taken in the first way] they can hardly be said to receive *esse* from God's will; they receive it [*esse*] from ideas existing in the divine essence prior to every act of will (as is taught by Cajetan, among others, in the final section of his commentary on q. 14, a. 16, in the First Part of the *Summa theologiae*). And the reason for this is that existence is a contingent predicate, which is communicated to things by a real influx in time, which God can apply at will, but essence is eternal, and in no way separable from the thing of which it is the essence, and so does not depend on free will.

(Coimbra 1607, 2: 20)

The existence neutrality of *esse* and related terms is a potential source of confusion when reading the Baroque Scholastics, whether in Latin or in translation. A being or essence was often referred to as a "thing," *res*; abstract *realitas* was to concrete *res* as abstract *albedo*, "whiteness," was to concrete *album*, "white": the abstract term signifies a condition or property, whereas the concrete term signifies an item *qua* having that condition or property. In consequence, *realitas*, strictly speaking, was not existence; it was the condition of being a thing or essence. Because the English term "reality" generally connotes existence or actuality, it can be misleading when used to translate *realitas* in English translations of the Latin works of Jesuits or Jesuit-influenced Scholastics, or of early moderns influenced by them. "Essence-hood" might be a better choice (but here I will translate it by the customary term "reality").

Scholastics inherited from Aristotle a theory in which essences or things are distributed into ten highest classes or genera of "predicates" (understood not as inscriptions, such as "red" or "man," but as the essences that, for Scholastics, are the ultimate meanings of such inscriptions): "substance" (that which cannot be "in" another, as properties are in subjects) and the nine kinds of "accident" (that which can be in another as a property in a subject), namely quantity, quality, relation, action, being acted on (*passio*), "where" (*ubi*), "when" (*quando*), orientation or posture (*situs*), and vesture (*habitus*). In general, each essence or being belonged to exactly one of these categories ("transcendentals" such as being or unity, which are predicable of things in every category, were recognized to be a special case).

Because a thing's "reality," in Baroque Scholastic terms, comprised its condition of being the essence that it is, any two essences, whether in the category of substance or in one of the accidental categories, were said to be *realiter* or "really" distinct from each other – for example a corporeal substance's quantity was really distinct from the substance of which it was the quantity (it was generally agreed that within any pair of really distinct items, one of the two could, at least through the absolute power of God, exist without the other).[21] Fictional or mind-dependent distinctions (distinctions *rationis*) obtained between different ways of considering a single thing – for example Peter considered as subject and as predicate of the judgement "Peter is Peter."[22]

It was noted previously that for the metaphysics under discussion here, actuality was only one of a number of modes of *esse* that an essence might have. Some of these modes were considered necessary to the essence; others were not (except in the trivial sense that the mode is necessary to the essence *qua* possessing that mode).[23]

> There are three kinds of *esse-mode*. Some [the first kind] are beings in the strict sense (*sunt formaliter entia*), and are non-fictionally distinct (*distinguuntur ex natura rei*) from the things [*rebus*] of which they are the *esse-modes*; often, indeed, they are distinct as one thing from another (*realiter*). [Examples of nonfictionally distinct *esse-modes*] are being-this-or-that-shape (*esse huius vel illius figurae*), being-white, being-sweet, etc. Others [the second kind], although they are beings in the strict sense, are only fictionally distinct from the things of which they are the *esse-modes*, the distinction arising only from our imperfect mode of understanding. Such are the *esse-modes* through which being (*ens*) is divided into substance, quantity, and the other highest genera. . . . Others [the third kind], finally, are quite different (*contra se habent*). For even though they are non-fictionally (i.e. independently of any operation of the intellect) distinct from the things of which they are the *esse-modes* nevertheless they are not beings in the proper sense of the word – unless "being" is taken very broadly for that which is not nothing (*quod non est nihil*). Such are the modes of being-in-a-subject and being-without-a-subject.
>
> (Fonseca 1615, 2: col. 400)

For Fonseca in this passage the term "mode" seems to apply to virtually anything expressible by any word or phrase that grammar permits to be immediately affixed to the copula "is" (*est*) in a possibly true sentence (i.e. a sentence that God could cause, or could have caused, to be literally and nonperiphrastically true) – whether the predicate is "a circle" or "sweet" (expressing modes of the first kind), "a substance" (expressing a mode of the second kind), or "in a subject" (expressing a mode of the third kind). It is also notable that for Fonseca accidents such as being-white and being-sweet count as *esse-modes*.

Subsequent Scholastics' conceptions of modes and modal distinctions departed from Fonseca's in nontrivial ways; for example, Francisco Suárez (1548–1617), in his widely read *Disputationes metaphysicae* (1597), restricts the term "mode" to what Fonseca calls a mode of the third kind (*DM* 7.1.19). Like Suárez, many early modern philosophers employed a pared-down concept of mode. Descartes considers that x is mode of a substance y just in case y can be clearly and distinctly conceived without x (and thus can be made by an omnipotent God to exist without x) but not vice versa (AT VIIIA 29–30; CSM I 213–14). Following Suárez rather than Fonseca, early moderns did not label accidents (as the Scholastics understood them)[24] "modes."

In their philosophy of nature, early moderns went even further and dispensed with accidents – in the Jesuits' sense[25] – altogether (cf. Des Chene 1996, 131–2). Continuous quantity or extension, which the Scholastics had treated as an accident, is elevated by Descartes and his followers to the rank of substance, whereas it (or an infinite "space" of which finite continuous quantities are parts) is taken by some other early moderns as ontologically prior to all corporeal substance.[26] The other eight Scholastic accidental categories were usually relegated to the status of phenomena (as in the case of sensible qualities such as colors, smells, etc.) or conceptual fictions (as in the case of relations).

The notion of modes (whether Fonsecan or Suárezian) that were not properly things (or essences), but nonfictional ways in which an essence might have its *esse*, required the notion of a nonfictional "modal distinction," over and above the *realis* ("real" or thinglike) distinction described previously. This distinction was rejected by conservative Thomists, who recognized only one nonfictional distinction, the real.[27]

> The modal distinction is that by which (a) beings (*entia*) are distinguished through (*per*) modes that are not themselves beings, strictly speaking (*formaliter*), or by which (b) the modes themselves are distinguished both from each other and from the beings [of which they are the modes]. It is in this way that a quantity that exists at one time in a subject and at another time outside of all subjects[28] is distinguished from itself, via diverse modes that are not themselves beings, in the proper sense of the word. And it is in this way that these modes themselves are distinguished from each other, and from the quantity.
> (Fonseca 1615, 2: col. 400)

Fonseca's phrase "that are not themselves beings, strictly speaking" in clause (a) is intended to exclude both accidents (which, though really – hence, not merely modally – distinct from their subjects, were still "modes," on Fonseca's definition of the term) and metaphysical parts (e.g. the genus animal in Peter, which is only fictionally distinct from Peter). By this exclusion, the termini of the modal distinction are reduced to precisely those "modes" recognized by Suárez and the early moderns. Accordingly, Suárez and the early moderns are able to adopt definitions of "modal distinction" extensionally identical to Fonseca's (cf. Descartes, AT VIIIA 29–30; CSM I 213–14). But given their more restricted definition of "mode," they are able to say (as Fonseca cannot) that every mode is modally (neither *realiter* nor merely fictionally) distinct from its subject.

The notion of an *esse-mode* and the modal distinction furnished the means for answering the metaphysically central question "what sort of distinction obtains between a created essence and its own existence or actuality?"

In Fonseca's account, no *esse-mode* of the first kind is metaphysically necessary to its subject: no shape is necessary (in the metaphysical sense) to the quantity it modifies; no color is necessary to the substance that has it. The reverse is true of *esse-modes* of the second kind (e.g. Caesar's *esse-mode* of being a substance, or red's *esse-mode* of being a quality): all such *esse-modes* are necessary to the things of which they are the modes. For *esse-modes* of the third kind, things are more complicated. Some clearly are necessary to the things that have them: Caesar can never lose his *esse-mode* of being-without-a-subject, for to be within a subject is to be a nonsubstance, hence a non-Caesar. Other modes of the third kind, however, are not necessary to the things that have them: bread's quantity can (by a miracle) lose its *esse-mode* of being-in-a-subject (see note 24).

Because actuality or existence is not necessary to creatable essences, it cannot (in such essences) be an *esse-mode* of the second kind. Nor is it an *esse-mode* of the first kind, because it is not (strictly speaking) an essence but is instead the actuality of essences. It must therefore be an *esse-mode* of the third kind:

> To this same [the third] class of *esse-modes* belongs the very existence of things that are inferior to God – both the actual existence of things that are in themselves, and the potential existence of things that are in their causes – as well as necessary-esse, contingent-esse, complete-esse, incomplete-esse, and a host of others of this kind.
> (Fonseca 1615, 2: col. 401)

As an *esse-mode* of the third kind, like simplicity or composition, singularity or universality, modally distinct from what has it, actuality was not keyed to a single kind of essence (as shape is to quantity) but ranged freely across (or "transcended") the categories.

Something like Fonseca's view on existence or actuality as a mode of essence seems to have been held as a matter of course among Jesuits and Protestant Scholastics.[29] This general agreement has been obscured by the Jesuit Francisco Suárez's (1548–1617) denial, in Disputation 31 of the *Disputationes metaphysicae* (1597), of any nonfictional distinction, even modal, between essence and existence (*DM* 31.1.13 and *DM* 31.6.9). But in that disputation the primary sense of "essence" seems to be "essence *qua* actual," whereas in the passage just quoted Fonseca takes "essence" without any such "reduplicative" restriction (see section 1.1) As Suárez himself says, his disagreement with Fonseca on this point seems to be merely verbal: "Fonseca, in book 4, chapter 3, question 4 of his *Metaphysics*, seems to have no substantive disagreement with [my] opinion, in the form in which [I] am about to explain it, although his words seem to favor [a modal distinction between existence and essence]" (*DM* 31.1.12).

Fonseca's granting of the term "mode" to existence, and Suárez's refusal to do so, occur in different contexts. Fonseca is considering the modes that belong to essences *simpliciter*, neither *qua* actual nor *qua* nonactual, whereas Suárez is considering them *qua* actual. Fonseca would surely have agreed with Suárez that an essence precisely qua actual is only fictionally distinct from its own actuality (just as Socrates *qua* sitting is only fictionally distinct from his sitting, though Socrates *simpliciter* and his sitting are nonfictionally distinct). By the same token, Suárez would surely have agreed with Fonseca that an essence *simpliciter* (essence neither *qua* actual nor *qua* nonactual) is nonfictionally distinct from its own actuality. The difference between them turns on how each of them understands the term "essence," in his own discussion of the essence-existence distinction.[30]

To view actuality as one of a multitude of *esse-modes*, modally distinct from its essence (essence *simpliciter*, I mean, not Suárez's essence *qua* actual), is evidently to see it as subordinate – in one sense of that term – to essence (*simpliciter*). Not, of course, that Fonseca and other Baroque Scholastics influential on the early moderns were blind to existence. They did not deny that actual essences are much more valuable than (and, in that sense, superior to) nonactual ones. The subordination of existence to essence in their metaphysics lies not in the order of value, but in the order consequent upon the modal distinction. If x has a mode y (understanding the term "mode" to include such nonessences as existence, contingent-esse, incomplete-esse, etc.) that is not necessary to x, then x is prior to y in the order of modal distinction, as quantity is prior, in the order of modal distinction, to shape. It is in this sense that Fonseca and like-minded Baroque Scholastics took essence (*simpliciter*) to be ontologically prior to existence or actuality.

The just-explained priority of essence to existence and the closely associated notion of *esse-modes* play a role in the sort of direct realism that was held by Baroque Scholastics and transmitted to Descartes.

1.3. Philosophy of cognition 2: essentialist direct realism and beings of reason

One of the most important esse-modes discussed by Scholastics was object-esse (esse objectivum, often translated "objective being"), the status of being an immediate object of cognition. This *esse-mode* consisted in "being inside the mind," but not in the way that an accidental feature is in a substance (e.g. as heat is in a rock). To have object-esse was to be in the mind as an object of thought.[31]

Certain items could only have object-esse, not actuality. These were the impossibles, or nonthings. Because they could have *esse* only in the intellect, they were called "beings of reason" (*entia rationis*), as opposed to "real beings" (*entia realia*).[32] Because metaphysics was supposed to be properly concerned with reality, it was thought to contain only improperly or incidentally the study of beings of reason. But metaphysicians could not altogether ignore them, because they included the philosophically important class of universals.[33]

Some Scholastics held that object-esse, insofar as it was predicated of the object of cognition, was itself a fiction. More precisely, it was held (by some) to be an "extrinsic denomination." A predicate was said to be extrinsic when it failed to name an accident or mode of the subject but could still be licitly predicated – nonliterally and periphrastically – of the subject. A classic example was the extrinsic denomination of standing to the left of something, say a pillar. No accidental form or mode in a thing is named by the predicate "to the left of the pillar," yet the claim that Peter is standing to the left of the pillar can still be true, if taken as paraphrasing a more complicated proposition specifying the places (*loci*, in the accident category of *ubi*) and orientations or postures (in the accident category of *situs*) of Peter, the pillar, and the one who makes the judgement expressed by the proposition. Similarly, some maintained, the propositions "the sun has object-esse" or "the sun is an object of thought" are true if taken as paraphrases of propositions about some mind, but the predicates "has object-esse" and "is an object of thought" signify no accident or mode.

The Louvain-educated priest and theologian Jan de Kater (Caterus, 1590–1655), author of the first set of objections to Descartes's *Meditations*, seems to have been among the Scholastics who considered "object-esse" to be an extrinsic denomination:

> what is it to be objectively in the intellect? According to what I learned, it is to terminate the intellectual act itself, through the mode of an object. This is

clearly an extrinsic denomination . . . what cause therefore will I seek of that which is not in act, and which is a bare denomination, and nothing?

(AT VII 92; CSM II 66–7)

Descartes held the opposite view. Or rather, he draws a distinction. De Kater is right in the sense that object-esse is indeed an extrinsic denomination when predicated of the essence *qua* actual (outside the mind). But not when it is predicated of the essence *simpliciter*. Predicated of the essence *simpliciter*, the term "object-esse" signifies a genuine *esse-mode* of the essence – an *esse-mode* that, although less perfect than actuality (cf. section 1.2), still suffices to constitute the essence as a concept (specifically, an "objective" concept) or "idea" in the mind.

> [De Kater] refers to the thing itself qua posited outside the intellect, and under that description (*ratio*) it certainly is an extrinsic denomination that a thing is objectively in the intellect, but I was speaking about an idea, which is never outside the intellect, and under whose description (*ratio*) "objective *esse*" signifies nothing but *esse* in the intellect, in that mode in which objects are usually there. . . . [C]ertainly this *esse-mode* is far more imperfect than that by which things outside the intellect exist, but it is not on that account completely nothing.
>
> (AT VIII 102–3; CSM II 74–5)

This is an echo of the *esse-mode* theory of Fonseca. In systems like Fonseca's, in which *esse-modes* were modally distinct from the essences that have them, object-esse served as the foundation of a modal distinction between a thing and itself. Just as a thing *qua* actually existent in itself was only modally distinct from itself *qua* potentially existent in its causes, it was only modally distinct from itself *qua* objectively existing in the mind of a knower.[34] Hence one and the same thing might have either object-esse, inside the mind, or actual *esse*, that is existence, outside it. Or it might have only object-esse, without existence. Thus, both existent individuals and nonexistent individuals could be immediate objects of cognition.

As early as the turn of the fourteenth century, the notion of object-esse had been used by Peter Aureol and others to formulate a version of direct realism capable of accommodating erroneous perceptions (Tachau 1988). To be directly perceived a thing required only object-esse; actuality was superfluous. So, erroneous perception was accounted for: a perception was false if and only if its immediate object lacked actuality. And it was accounted for without introducing any "veil of ideas" between the mind and the world. For if the thing with object-esse happened to have existence outside the mind, the mind's immediate object would have not only object-esse but also actual existence. In such a case, the mind's perception of the extramental existent would be immediate.[35]

The Scholastic theory of cognition developed in the early fourteenth century, and taken up by the Jesuits and their Protestant followers, may be labeled an "essentialist direct realism." It is a direct realism in two respects: (1) essences, whether actual or not, are perceived – whether by the senses (in the case of sensible essences, such as this or that individual red) or by the intellect (in the case of intelligible essences, such as man, or intelligible individual substances, such as Peter) – in themselves, not in some representation that is really distinct from them; and (2) some of these directly perceived essences have actuality, existence out in the world, in addition to the object-esse that qualifies them as objects of direct cognition. For example, when we see or think of the sun, it is the sun itself, not merely some mental item really distinct from the sun, that is directly perceived.[36]

The theory is essentialist inasmuch as it teaches that not existence but being-an-essence (*esse* or *entitas*) constitutes a thing or essence as perceivable directly or "in itself." This seemed to the seventeenth century Dominican John of St. Thomas (Jean Poinsot, 1589–1644) to entail skepticism: for if nonexistents can be directly perceived, how can we be sure that the objects of sensation exist (John of St. Thomas 1930–37, 3:173–4)? But this criticism seems unjust. An "existentialist" direct realism, in which existence or actuality is a necessary condition for a thing's being perceived directly or "in itself," is subject to the same epistemological challenges as an essentialist direct realism is. Anyone claiming to have a direct perception may always be challenged to produce a justification for that claim, and the job of finding such a justification is not made any easier by the assumption that only existents may be directly perceived.

2. Some seventeenth century philosophers' links to Baroque Scholasticism

2.1. Descartes

The "novators" of the seventeenth century rejected many of Scholasticism's characteristic concepts, doctrines, and methods. Descartes (1596–1650) was at the forefront of this anti-Scholastic movement. Yet, as Gassendi noted, he seems to have been indebted to his opponents in ways he did not acknowledge:

> When you conclude that "one of the things manifest by the natural light is that conservation differs only fictionally from creation," one is left speechless – except to say how fortunate you are, to whose natural light everything is so manifest. To you, stripped of all previous knowledge [by the methodical doubt], things occur in a completely spontaneous way that occur to the subtlest and most learned philosophers and theologians only after long studies and profound scrutiny of matters human and divine. What an incomparable felicity. But tell me, please: would you have expressed yourself in such terms, had you not received them from the Scholastics?
>
> (1962 [1644], 353)

The notion of fictional distinction (discussed in the last section) that Descartes invokes here and the question of how, or whether, God's act of creation differs from his act of conserving creatures in existence were, Gassendi knew, characteristically Scholastic.

Descartes learned his Scholasticism at the Jesuits' college at La Flèche, which he attended from his eleventh to his nineteenth year (spring 1607 to summer 1615).[37] His last three years there were devoted to the study of philosophy and allied fields, such as mathematics. The philosophy course was based on commentaries on the works of Aristotle (and Porphyry's *Isagoge*), principally the *Categories* (supplemented by Porphyry's *Isagoge*), *De interpretatione*, *Prior Analytics*, *Posterior Analytics*, *Topics*, and *Sophistical Refutations*, plus the *Physics*, *De Generatione*, *De anima*, *Metaphysics*, and *Nicomachean Ethics*.[38] All the commentaries assigned to Descartes seem to have been the work of

Iberian (Portuguese or Spanish) Jesuits: primarily Fonseca; Rubio; Toledo; Góis; and Góis's colleague at the faculty of arts at Coimbra, Sebastião do Couto (1567–1639).[39]

Many studies of Scholastic influence on Descartes have focused on his theory of ideas. Descartes was long read as claiming that the mind has immediate awareness of nothing but its own ideas, which are (on this reading) simply modes of itself. These ideas were supposed to furnish indirect knowledge of extramental things by "representing" them in some way analogous to the way pictures represent the things they depict. But it has recently been argued that – at least in some contexts – Descartes was not a "representationalist" (in the foregoing sense) but instead embraced a direct realism that owes much to the Scholastics. As seen in the preceding section, Descartes embraced the Jesuit theory of object-esse as a genuine *esse-mode* alternative to actuality. Because the concept of object-esse served to ground an "essentialist direct realism" in Baroque Scholasticism, it seems reasonable to assume that it performs the same service in Descartes's philosophy. This explains why Descartes thinks that in understanding the term "God" in the Third Meditation we intellectually perceive not a (finite) representation in our (finite) minds, but the infinite divine essence itself (Descartes is careful to point out that to perceive a thing is not to understand it comprehensively, just as to touch the ocean is not to embrace it in its entirety). It also explains how, in the "wax example" of the Second Meditation, he can claim that the intellect (as distinct from the imagination) perceives not just the common nature of bodies, but the individual essence (which, for him, is this or that shaped finite quantity) of this or that individual body. But unlike the Jesuits, Descartes employs the object-esse concept only for intellectual cognition. For this and other reasons, it seems safe to say that he restricted essentialist direct realism to intellectual cognition.[40] Relevant literature on Descartes's direct realism and its relationship to Scholastic views includes Dalbiez 1929; Cronin 1966; O'Neil 1974; Yolton 1975, 148–53; Cook 1975; 1987; Nadler 1989; and my own 2007 study. For an argument against the direct realist reading see Secada 2000, 86–91.

Other debts Descartes may have owed to his Scholastic background include his theory of identity and distinction (AT VIIIA 28–30; CSM I 213–15), which bears clear traces of Baroque Scholastic views discussed in the previous section. Paul Hoffman 1986 (esp. pp. 354 and 363–4) has argued for a "Cartesian hylomorphism"[41] with antecedents in Scotist and Ockhamist accounts of the *per se* unity of collections of actual individuals (cf. Hoffman 1990, 1999, 2002; for a critique see Rozemond 1998, 138–71). It has also been suggested that Descartes's views on causation, or on mind-body interaction (a topic related but different to that of mind-body distinction), or both, owe much to his Jesuit teachers (see Des Chene 1996, esp. pp. 324, 331; and Hattab 1998, 2001, 2003). His concept of space has been related to that of Francisco Toledo by Echarri 1950, who offers a detailed comparison of parts of Toledo's *Physics* commentary and Descartes's *Principles of Philosophy*.[42] Anticipations of the Cartesian *cogito* and ontological argument by (respectively) Augustine and St. Anselm of Canterbury were acknowledged by Descartes himself; the case for a more far-reaching indebtedness to Augustine is made in Menn 1998a.[43] The Aristotelian notion of teleology, which Descartes is widely thought to have expelled from his account of the physical world, is claimed by Simmons 1999, 2001 to have made a cautious reappearance in his account of sensation. A comparison of Descartes's views on human freedom to Baroque Scholastic discussions, stressing the underlying nonlibertarian character of his theory of human volition, is given in Sleigh, Chappell, and Della Rocca 1998, 1195–211. Extensive discussion of Baroque Scholastic metaphysics and the philosophy of knowledge and their relationship to Descartes's philosophy (but with an accent on differences rather than similarities) may be found in Secada 2000. Gilson's *Index Scolastico-Cartésien*, first published in 1913, remains a valuable source of comparisons between Scholastic and Cartesian texts, as does his *La Liberté chez Descartes at la théologie*.

2.2. Bacon, Hobbes, and Locke

Bacon (1561–1626) studied at Trinity College, Cambridge, for only two years, from 1573 to 1575 (he did not take his degree); Hobbes (1588–1679) was at Magdalen Hall, Oxford, from 1603 to 1608, graduating with a bachelor of arts degree; Locke (1632–1704) entered Christ Church, Oxford, in 1652, took both the B.A. and the M.A. there and retained an association with the college for many years. During their student years, Bacon, Hobbes, and Locke would have been expected to study Scholastic logic and to take part in the logical exercise of disputation, in which a "respondent" was expected to defend a given thesis against the criticisms of "objectors," using standard argument forms. They were no doubt exposed to much Scholastic philosophy of nature and of cognition along with it. Locke, at least, seems to have had a good dose of metaphysics as well.[44]

Some of this Scholastic instruction seems to have stuck with them. In point 259 of Bacon's posthumously published *Sylva sylvarum*, the Scholastic theory of intentional representation (briefly described in the preceding section) is employed to account for the propagation of light and sound: "[b]oth of them, in their virtue and working, do not appear to emit any corporeal substance into their mediums, . . . but only to carry certain spiritual species" (Bacon 1862, 4: 288).[45] It has been claimed (Leijenhorst 2002a, 24) that Bacon's separation of "first" philosophy or metaphysics from natural theology (cf. *The Advancement of Learning* bk. 3, chs. 1–2) owes something to Jesuit and Protestant Scholastic views on the nature and object of metaphysics. On the other hand, the Aristotelian-sounding term "form" seems to have carried, in Bacon's works, a non-Aristotelian sense (Fletcher 2005).

Hobbes is known to have read parts of Suárez's *Disputations* (Leijenhorst 2002a, 10). His views on "imaginary space" in *De corpore* (1655) appear to owe much to Baroque Scholastic discussions, especially those of Suárez and (perhaps) Toledo.[46] Cees Leijenhorst has recently argued that although Hobbes's doctrine of space is indebted to non-Scholastic sources, notably the Renaissance humanist and naturalist Francesco Patrizi (1529–1597), it was from the Jesuits that he learned to think of space as a pure nonbeing (*non ens*) and as an inadequate, merely human way of understanding a reality outside the human mind (Leijenhorst 2002a, 115–16, 119–21).

Very little is known about which Baroque Scholastic texts Bacon and Hobbes read; in reconstructing their relations to Scholasticism, one must rely on textual similarities and educated guesswork. Things are somewhat clearer for Locke, who pursued the Oxford arts course to its terminus, the M.A., and maintained an association with the college of Christ Church for over two decades. His account books for his tutorship at Christ Church (Kenney 1959) list books purchased (presumably on his recommendation) by his students. These include logic texts by Zabarella, the Jesuits Marcin Śmiglecki (Martinus Smiglecius, 1564–1618) and Philippe du Trieu (1580–1645), and the Englishmen Robert Sanderson (1587–1663) and Samuel Smith (1587–1620), as well as works on metaphysics by the Protestant Scholastics Christof Scheibler (1589–1653), Johann Combach (1585–1651), and Franco Burgersdijk (Burgersdicius, 1590–1635).[47]

Although for the most part the account book lists only authors, not titles,[48] reliable guesses about the titles can be made. For the logic authors on Locke's list, we may be reasonably sure of the following author-to-title assignments: Zabarella, *Opera logica*; du Trieu, *Manductio ad logicam*; Smiglekci, *Logica*; Sanderson, *Logicae artis compendium*; and Smith, *Aditus ad logicam*. The metaphysics texts Locke had in mind were probably Combach, *Metaphysicorum libri duo*; Burgersdijk, *Institutionum Metaphysicarum libri duo*; and Scheibler, *Opus metaphysicum*. In this and similar lists of texts used at seventeenth century Oxford or Cambridge, comparatively recent authors predominate: Locke's list contains no text whose first edition appeared before 1578 (the date of the first edition, at Venice, of Zabarella's *Opera logica*). It was primarily Baroque Scholastics, not their medieval predecessors, whose works Locke read as a student and teacher Oxford.[49]

Consideration of Locke's Scholastic training has led some scholars to question the traditional reading of his idea theory as representationalist: John Yolton 1970, 1975, 1984, 2000 has maintained that Locke was a kind of direct realist (for a criticism, see Ayers 1998). Locke's theory of language and logic too, it has been argued, contained important Scholastic elements. According to Jennifer Ashworth 1981, his doctrine that words immediately and directly signify ideas, not extramental things (cf. *Essay* 3.2.1–2), was derived from Baroque philosophers such as Burgersdijk (but this claim must be brought into dialogue with the "direct realist" reading of Locke and Baroque Scholastics such as Burgersdijk, which might be thought to contradict it). And Paul Schuurman 2001 claims analogies in structure and content between Robert Sanderson's *Logicae artis compendium* and Locke's *Essay* (supplemented by his posthumously published *Of the Conduct of the Understanding*).[50]

2.3. *Spinoza, Gassendi, Malebranche, and Arnauld*

Parallels between some of Spinoza's (1632–1677) concepts and doctrines and those of certain Baroque or medieval Scholastics were noted by several nineteenth and twentieth century scholars.[51] His knowledge of the Scholastic tradition was not acquired in the usual way, by matriculating at a university or college. In his early twenties, he attended an Amsterdam school run by the Antwerp native Frans van den Enden (van Eynde, van den Eynden, 1602–1674), a reputed "freethinker" and pantheist – but also a former Jesuit, who taught Spinoza the rudiments of Scholasticism.[52] In this instruction, van den Enden might well have used the Jesuit texts with which he himself was familiar, though this must remain a matter for speculation. Spinoza may also have audited lectures at the university of Leiden by Adrian Heereboord (1613/14–1661), an eccentric Scholastic who tried to blend Aristotelian philosophy with elements of Cartesianism.[53] Spinoza's early work,[54] *Cogitata metaphysica*, includes some passages from Burgersdijk's *Institutionum metaphysicarum* (which, as noted previously, was known to Locke as well; Burgersdijk, incidentally, was a teacher of Heereboord).[55] His small library included a number of works by Baroque Scholastic authors, including Bartholomew Keckerman (1571–1609), Johann Clauberg (1622–1665) – like Heerebord, a Cartesian Aristotelian – Joannes à Bononia,[56] the Jesuit Benito Pereira (Benedictus Pererius, Pererio, Perera, 1535–1610), and Huig de Gruit (Hugo Grotius, 1583–1645).[57] Spinoza is said to have used Jakob Reefsen's (Jacobus Revius, 1586–1658) *Suarez repurgatus* (1643) as a handbook of Scholasticism (Dunin-Borkowski 1910, 259). Spinoza's use of Scholastic terms such as "mode" and "*natura naturans/naturata*" suggests notable debts to Scholasticism, but their nature and extent are still unclear.[58]

Gassendi (1592–1655), Arnauld (1612–1694), and Malebranche (1638–1715) constitute the main exception to the generalization that it was the Jesuits (ex-Jesuit, in Spinoza's case), or Protestants influenced by them, from whom the early moderns learned the elements of Scholasticism. All three were Catholic priests; each received advanced training in Scholastic philosophy and theology, but there is no reason to posit a significant Jesuit (much less Protestant) influence on any of them. Following elementary education at the Collège de Digne, Gassendi matriculated at the university of Aix-en-Provence, where he received training in Scholastic philosophy (under one Philibert Fesaye, a Carmelite priest), theology, Greek, and Hebrew. In 1614, at Avignon, he became doctor of theology; in 1616 he was ordained priest in Aix and took up a teaching post in philosophy there (according to some, in the following year, 1617), which he occupied until 1622 (or possibly 1623), when the diocese of Aix entrusted the university to the Jesuits. He is not known to have taught Scholastic philosophy or theology thereafter.[59] Arnauld taught philosophy at the Collège de Mans, received his doctorate in theology at the Sorbonne in 1641 (at about the time he composed the Fourth Objections to Descartes's *Meditations*), and was admitted to the theology faculty in 1643. With Pierre Nicole (1625–1695), he published the widely read *Logique, ou l'art de penser* (first edition, 1662; it has come to be known as the *Port-Royal Logic*), a work that, in spite of its Cartesian elements and other innovative features, owes significant debts to its Scholastic predecessors (Schuurman 2001, 451). Malebranche received his early schooling at home; at the age of sixteen he entered the Collège de la Marche (Paris), where he gained an M.A. (1656) in philosophy.[60] He then pursued a course in theology, leading to a doctorate in 1669 at the Sorbonne. Though it is not known what Scholastic texts Gassendi, Arnauld, and Malebranche read, it is likely that their philosophical studies were based mainly on Baroque Aristotelian commentaries of some sort.

The details of Scholasticism's influence on Gassendi, Arnauld, and Malebranche are still unclear. Pendzig 1908 claims that among the Scholastic concepts or terms that Gassendi adapted to his own use are sensible and intelligible species, prime matter, substance, substantial and accidental form, and act and potency (Pendzig 1969 [1908], 175). Osler 2002 identifies some textual similarities between the second part ("Physica") of Gassendi's 1658 *Syntagma Philosophicum* and Aristotelian natural philosophy works of the day, for example the 1642 *Physiologiae Peripateticae Libri Sex* of Johannes Magirus (most of these similarities are, however, at the rather superficial level of textual organization). Cook 1974 and Nadler 1989, 143–78, compare Arnauld's (and, in Nadler's case, Malebranche's) idea theories to Suárez's and Aquinas's views on intentional species, opening up promising lines of inquiry that have yet to be pursued to their conclusion.

In their famous dispute over the natures of ideas, Arnauld and Malebranche each claimed to follow Descartes's notion of "idea," which (see subsection 2.1) has been linked to Scholastic theories of intentionality. Cook 1974, Wahl 1988, and Nadler 1989 have argued that Arnauld was a direct realist; Wahl 1988, 568, draws an interesting comparison between Arnauld and Scotus in this regard (and compares Malebranche's "vision in God" doctrine with the Augustinian views of the late thirteenth century Scholastic Henry of Ghent), whereas Nadler turns to Suárez for elucidation of Arnauld's views. As Scholastically trained theologians, Arnauld and Malebranche would have had a thorough understanding of the controversies over providence and predestination – matters about which, during the Jansenist controversy, they held sharply conflicting views. The links between their theological disagreements and their debate over the nature of ideas probably deserves more attention that it has received (Nadler 1989, 179–84, makes some remarks on this subject).[61]

2.4. Leibniz

It is a commonplace that Leibniz (1646–1716) was better disposed toward Aristotle than any other major non-Scholastic philosopher of the early modern period. Less frequently remarked is his lifelong interest in Baroque Scholasticism.

At the age of fifteen (1661) Leibniz entered the university of Leipzig, where his father Friedrich, who had died nine years before, had served as professor of (Scholastic) moral philosophy. There he studied philosophy under Jakob Thomas (Thomasius, 1622–1684);[62] the topic of his 1663 dissertation for the master of arts degree, the principle of individuation, was standard Scholastic fare. His precocity in the subject (a master of arts at the age of seventeen) was surely due in part to his having struck up an acquaintance with it very early in life. While still a child he began to read works by Francisco Suárez (1548–1617), Rubio, Fonseca, and Zabarella that he found in his deceased father's library (Petersen 1921, 341). Decades after leaving university, he maintained substantive philosophical contacts with Scholastics, including the Jesuit Bartholomew Des Bosses (1663–1738).[63]

Notes and treatises by Leibniz unpublished in his lifetime contain a wealth of references to Scholastic authors. Only a few will be listed here: the Lutheran Scholastic Jakob Werenberg (1582–1623?); the Dominican Diego Álvarez (1550–1635); the Jesuits Fonseca, Gabriel Vázquez (1549–1604), Paolo Valla (Paulus Vallius, 1561–1622), Sebastián Izquierdo (1601–1681), Richard Lynch (or Lyncaeus, 1610–1676), Andrés Mendo (or Mendus, 1608–1684), and "Aloysius Temmik" (a pseudonym of Gaspar Kuemmet or Kuemmeth);[64] the ex-Jesuit member of the Cistercian order Francisco à Sancto Augustino Macedo (1596–1681); and the multifaceted Cistercian philosopher and theologian Juan Caramuel y Lobkowitz (1606–1682). He seems to have maintained a lifelong interest in the *Labyrinthus, sive de compositione liber unus, philosophis, mathematicis, theologicis utilis ac jucundus* (Antwerp 1631) of the Louvain theologian Libert Froidmont (or Fromondus, 1587–1653); he mentions it in unpublished manuscripts of 1671 and 1686, and again in his 1710 *Theodicy*.[65]

Parts of the *Theodicy*, as well as the opuscules "Middle Knowledge" and "Conversation with Bishop Steno on Liberty,"[66] and the note "Concerning Luis à Dola's *Disputatio quadrapartita de modo coniunctionis concursuum Dei et creaturae ad actus liberos ordinis naturalis* [1634]"[67] testify to his interest in Baroque Scholastic discussions of freedom, foreknowledge, and predestination. The Jesuits' famous middle-knowledge theory was associated with the view that there is a "moral" necessity (lesser than metaphysical necessity or necessity relative to God's will) concerning what a possible human being would freely choose in a given set of circumstances, which enables God to have infallible knowledge of what the free choices of existing created agents will be. In a 1708 letter to Des Bosses, Leibniz mentions that in his youth he read works on moral necessitation composed by the Jesuits Antonio Pérez (1599–1649) and Martín de Esparza y Artieda (1606–1689).[68]

In addition, Leibniz's interest in a universal language or "characteristic" may be linked to the views of certain Jesuit Scholastics, for example Śmiglecki, who considered the possibility of a prelapsarian Adamic perfect language, the terms and syntax of which exhibited the essences and essential structure of natural objects.[69] Leibniz's relation to the *philosophia perennis* tradition, which (like theories of naturally signifying languages) had links both to Scholastic and to neo-Platonist and Hermetic thought, is briefly discussed in Schmitt 1966, 530–1. Weier 2000 makes the case that some of Leibniz's views (e.g. on the distinction between real and nominal definitions, and on *petites perceptions*) are "extensions and unfoldings" of the views of Johannes Clauberg (already mentioned in connection with Spinoza). Finally, the effect of the essentialist aspect of Baroque Scholastic metaphysics (see section 1) on Leibniz's notion of "entity" is noted in Angelelli 1994.[70]

Further reading

Literature on the main topics of this chapter is cited in the body of the text or in the notes. The French-language site "Scholasticon" (ed. Jacob Schmutz) is a helpful online resource for all matters pertaining to Baroque Scholasticism (http://www.scholasticon.fr); the bibliographies in its "Nomenclator" section will be useful even to those who read no French. Especially noteworthy recent works devoted in whole or in part to Renaissance or Baroque Scholasticism, or to their influence on the early moderns, include Ferrater Mora 1953; Schmitt 1973; 1988; Trentman 1982; Lohr 1988b; 1988c; Kessler 1990; Murdoch 1990; Gracia 1993a; Mercer 1993; articles by Jill Kraye and Stuart Brown in Parkinson 1993; Menn 1998b; Tuck 1998; Stone 2002; Friedman and Nielsen 2003; Pozzo 2004; White 1997; and Novotný 2013. Late Scholastic logic and philosophy of language is the subject of Ashworth 1974; 1988a; 1988b; Nuchelmans 1998; and Risse 1964–70; 1965–79. Iberian Scholasticism, of central importance for Baroque Scholasticism as a whole, is surveyed in Gracia 1993a; White 1997; and Doyle 2007. Detailed studies include Solana 1928; 1941. The best studied of all Baroque Scholastics is undoubtedly Suárez; extensive and up-to-date bibliographies of works dealing with all aspects of his philosophy may be found in Pereira 2007 and in "Scholasticon." The best studied of all real or alleged early modern debts to Scholasticism are those of Descartes; valuable discussions and copious references are available in Ariew 1992; 1999; 2002; and Secada 2000. Renaissance and Baroque Aristotelian natural philosophy is the subject of Di Liscia, Kessler, and Methuen 1997. The post-nineteenth century distinction between philosophy of nature and natural science cannot be applied to the seventeenth century without anachronism, with the result that much of the history of Baroque natural philosophy, Scholastic and non-Scholastic alike, has been written by historians of science. Lüthy 2000 provides an introduction to some of this literature. Two of the most notable authors writing at the intersection of the history of early modern science and the history of Baroque Scholastic natural philosophy are Dennis Des Chene and William A. Wallace. Des Chene 1996 contains a wealth of information on Baroque Scholastic natural philosophy and comparisons to important aspects of Descartes's physics, whereas his *Life's Form: Late Aristotelian Conceptions of the Soul* (Cornell 2000) concerns Baroque Scholastic philosophy of organic substance; Wallace has established links from Galileo to Scholastic natural philosophers (see Wallace 2006 and his other works cited there). The literature on Baroque Scholastic ethics and political philosophy is too large even to be summarized here, but an entry to the literature is provided by parts of Doyle 2007 and of White 1997. A more extensive treatment of selected Baroque Scholastic moral and political philosophers may be found in volumes 2 and 3 of Giacon 1944–50. Sommervogel et al. 1960 (1st ed., 1890–1932) contains titles of works by Jesuits of the sixteenth and seventeenth centuries (and later), collected by author (individual or corporate, e.g. the Coimbrans).

DAVID CLEMENSON

Acknowledgments

Research for this chapter was funded in part by a generous grant from the Czech Academy of Science's Institute of Philosophy (Department for the History of Older Czech and European Philosophy) in Prague, Summer 2008. I am greatly indebted to the staff, members, and friends of the institute for their hospitality. Thanks are due to the staff of the National Library (Klementinum) of the Czech Republic; to the O'Shaugnessey-Frey Library's Interlibrary Loan Office at the University of St. Thomas (St. Paul); and to a diligent student assistant, Steven Winkelman, who transferred many pages of microfilmed text to legible hard copy.

Notes

1 Pascal was one exception. Spinoza studied Scholasticism, but not at a university.
2 Late sixteenth and early seventeenth century Jesuit texts were very popular throughout Europe, even in Calvinist and Lutheran universities and schools. Many Protestant Scholastics (e.g. Scheibler and Burgersdijk, cited by Locke) make frequent favorable references to Jesuit authors – especially to Suárez, whom the seventeenth century Oxford tutor Timothy Halton described as "incomparably the ... best author that ever wrote upon" metaphysics (Kenney 1959, 36). Halton ranked Suárez's skills as a metaphysical expositor higher than those of Aristotle, whose *Metaphysics* he called "a rapsody [sic] of logical scraps." Suárez's influence on Calvinist philosophy is discussed in Krop 1993 and van Ruler 1993. Describing his university education at Marburg in the late 1620s, the man of letters and pedagogue Johann Balthasar Schuppe wrote (Petersen 1921, 289) that all the talk was of the (Jesuit) Coimbra College, Rubio, Suárez, and the Aristotelian syllogistic moods Darapti and Felapton. Jesuit influence on Lutheran philosophers, in particular, is examined in Karl Eschweiler 1928 and Ernst Lewalter 1935, and in the works cited in Telkamp 1927, 10–11. Comparatively little direct influence outside the Catholic world seems to have been exerted by the older religious orders that had played so important a role in medieval Scholasticism – notably the Dominicans and Franciscans. Although these religious societies continued to produce important theologians and philosophers throughout the Renaissance and Baroque period, some of whom may have exerted an indirect influence on early modern philosophy by having taught (or been read by) Jesuits or other Scholastics directly influential on the early moderns, those interested mainly in Baroque Scholasticism's relationship to early modern philosophy must concentrate mainly on the Jesuits, and on the Protestant Scholastics influenced by them.
3 Some general studies of Scholasticism are listed at the end of the chapter, under "Further reading." The Scholastic revival of the sixteenth and seventeenth centuries has been variously labeled "Second," "Silver Age," "Renaissance," "Neo-," and (for its Catholic branch) "Iberian" or "Hispanic." The suitability of "Baroque," as a general term covering Catholic and Protestant Scholasticism of the period covered here, is well argued by Novotný 2013.
4 More precisely, there is an individual color x in Socrates such that x is the visual faculty's proper object. Strictly speaking, the content expressed by the phrase "Socrates *qua* colored" is not the object of the visual sense, for on Aristotelian theory the sense does not frame the universal concept expressed by the word "color."
5 Baroque Scholastic authors disagreed on the question of whether the sense memory and imaginative power constituted a single faculty or two (or more). Many other such disagreements (e.g. the question of the "agent sense") are passed over here.
6 A wide-ranging review of Scholastic views on cognitive "species" may be found in Spruit 1994–95.
7 Most analytic philosophers treat "singular," "particular," and "individual" as synonyms, but the Scholastics did not. As explained in Coimbra 1607, 1:176, the terms "singular" and "individual" were extensionally equivalent but had different connotations, the first connoting lack of the commonality that is proper to universals, and the second, lack of the universal's division-into-many. The term "particular" had wider extension than "singular" and "individual": the species horse was particular (but not individual or singular) with respect to the genus animal. For a specimen of Baroque Scholastic treatments of universality, see Coimbra 1607, 1:78–163 (In Praefat. Porphyr., qq. 1–6).
8 Conservative Thomism was centered in Aquinas's Dominican order, which officially adopted his doctrine in the late thirteenth century. That the intellect perceives only universals seems to be asserted by

THE SCHOLASTIC BACKGROUND

Aristotle at *Physics* 1.5 (189a1–2), and also at *De anima* 2.5 (417b22–23). Aquinas discusses the *De anima* text in his commentary on *De anima* 2, lectio 12; an English translation of the relevant passages is given in Foster and Humphries 1951, 249–51.

9 Controversy over Aquinas's position on this point can be traced back to (at least) the aftermath of the 1277 condemnations at Paris, notably the *Correctorium fratris Thomae* ("Correction of Brother Thomas") of the late thirteenth century Franciscan William de la Mare, and the Dominican responses it provoked. Cf. Glorieux 1927, 12–17, 381–3.

10 The Coimbra series of Aristotle commentaries were so-called because they were published not as the works of individuals but under the corporate authorship of the Faculty of Arts of the University of Coimbra (Portugal), instruction at which had been entrusted to the Jesuits. These commentaries covered all the major works of Aristotle treated in Jesuit colleges, save one: the *Metaphysics*. Pedro da Fonseca, who for a time taught at Coimbra, was the author of a widely used commentary on Aristotle's *Metaphysics* and was the mastermind behind the Coimbra commentary series. According to Lewalter 1939, 24, Fonseca's commentary was used "throughout all the Jesuit colleges, and soon afterward in all the universities," even Protestant ones such as Helmstedt, where Cornelius Martini used it in his lectures on metaphysics. Evidently the Coimbrans considered it unnecessary to try and improve on their own leader's magisterial commentary on that work; in fact, Fonseca's *Metaphysics* may be considered part of the Coimbra series (cf. Secada 2000, 29, where Fonseca is counted as one of the Combrans).

11 Coimbra 1604, 441 (bk. 3, ch. 8, q. 5, a. 2). All translations are my own, unless otherwise noted (e.g. by citation of an English translation in the "References" section). Gregory of Rimini (ca. 1300–1358) was a member of the Augustinian order. Durand de Saint-Pourçain (1270/75–1334) was a Dominican investigated by his order on charges of having departed from Aquinas's doctrine (see Friedman 2005, who emphasizes the Platonic and Augustinian elements in Durand's views on cognition). Richard of Middleton (fl. 1270s–1280s) was a Franciscan. Walter Burley (ca. 1275–1344/45) was an important member of the "Oxford calculators" school.

12 He also cites "Mirandulanus" (presumably Giovanni Pico della Mirandola, 1463–1494, not his nephew and fellow philosopher Giovanni Francesco) and Peter Aureol (1280–1322?). On Aureol's notion of how the intellect makes use of the phantasm in order to cognize singulars, see Friedman 2000 and parts of Tachau 1988.

13 For a summary of Zabarella's life and works, as well as an entrée to the extensive literature on Zabarella and the Paduan Aristotelians, see Grendler 2002, 252–3, 263–6.

14 Here and throughout, the term "possible" carries the sense it normally has today, namely "not of necessity nonactual"; on this usage, the claim "actuals are possible" is counted true. But in many Scholastic texts, "possible" meant "nonactual, but not so by necessity"; on this usage, "actuals are possible" is counted false. In such texts, actuals that are not of necessity actual (namely all and only created things) were called "contingent."

15 These are not intended as proper definitions (the term "existing" cannot properly be defined by a phrase that contains the term); they merely signal the equivalence, for the purposes of this chapter, of the relevant terms and phrases.

16 Here I follow Kenny 2002, 89, 116 (for a contrasting view, see Normore 2007, 113). References to some recent literature concerning Aquinas's thoughts on merely possible (nonindividual) natures are given in Doolan 2008, 139 nn. 43, 44. The converse, that actuality entails individuality, was common Scholastic Aristotelian teaching. See, for example, Aquinas's commentary on Aristotle's *De interpretatione* I, lect. 10, n. 12 (Oesterle 1962, 82).

17 Some Jesuit Scholastics, but not all, were willing to apply the term "intuition" to cognitions of this kind. See Clemenson 1991.

18 Most Baroque Scholastics took metaphysics or "first philosophy" to be the science whose subject (or "formal object," as it was called; cf. Coimbra 1607, 2:130, 667) is *ens qua ens*, "being *qua* being." The term *ens* was sometimes predicated even of impossibles such as circular squares, which, if they exist in any sense, exist only as objects of thought. But few took "being" in this sense to be metaphysics' proper subject (some logic authors preferred the term "*thema*" to convey this widest sense of *ens*; cf. Burgersdijk, *Institutionem logicarum libri duo*, ch. 2 [1666, 5], who defines *thema* as "whatever can be proposed for cognition"). One of these few was Clemens Timpler (or Tümpler, 1563?–1624), a Calvinist metaphysician who took the object of metaphysics to be the conceivable as such (Wundt 1939, 177). The question of metaphysics' formal object was complicated by the fact that Aristotle himself had conceived of it not only as the science of being *qua* being but also as the science of immaterial being – God and the separate intelligences. Perhaps in an effort to unify these distinct notions of metaphysics, Burgersdijk claimed that its proper object is immaterial being as such (Wundt 1939, 165).

19 Suárez, at the beginning of Disputation 31 (*DM* 31.1.2) of his *Disputationes metaphysicae*, declares that he will take *esse* and *existentia actualis rerum* as synonyms. But in that same place he notes the many other uses to which the term *esse* is customarily put. He himself reverts to such customary uses (e.g. *esse essentiae* and *esse existentiae*) later in the disputation.

20 For Latin terms that are italicized even when used, I do not bother to distinguish mention from use by the customary device of enclosing the italicized term in (single or double) quotation marks. Context will make it clear whether the term is being used or mentioned (i.e. whether it bears its usual semantic value or refers to itself as the bearer of that semantic value).

21 "Thing-wise" might be a better translation of *realiter*; it conveys the idea that the "real" distinction is that which obtains between two things or essences.

22 Some such fictional distinctions had, and others lacked, a "foundation in reality," in virtue of which an assertion of distinction might be considered a paraphrase of some other assertion (one not involving the distinction in question) that was literally, nonperiphrastically true. Those (like the distinction of Peter as subject from himself as predicate) without such foundation were called distinctions *rationis sine fundamento in re*, or *rationis ratiocinantis*; those with such foundation were called *rationis cum fundamento in re*, or *rationis ratiocinatae*. Scholastics disagreed over what sorts of distinctions to include in the latter category. Those who admitted non-realis nonfictional distinctions (e.g. the Scotist's formal distinction, or the Jesuits' "modal" distinction) assigned to these categories of distinction items that conservative Thomists, who admitted no nonfictional distinction but the *realis*, considered to be fictional distinctions *cum fundamento in re*. An example is the distinction between an extended quantity and its shape. In this case, the "foundation" for the fictional distinction might be considered the potency of the quantity (or of the substance in which it inheres) to assume shapes different from the one that it "has" (or "is," contingently and partially).

23 For example, the essence of Caesar, *qua* actual, must have the *esse-mode* of actuality (though actuality is not necessary to the essence of Caesar "*simpliciter*" – neither taken as actual nor as nonactual. Cf. Suárez and Fonseca on the essence-existence distinction.

24 More precisely, as Catholic Scholastics did. See the next note.

25 Owing to differences over the doctrine of the Eucharist, Jesuits and other Catholic Scholastics conceived of accidents differently than their Protestant counterparts. Traditional Catholic understanding of the Eucharist (cf. Aquinas, *ST* part 3, q. 77) requires that the accidents of bread and wine be capable of persisting in the absence of their subjects (the substances of bread and wine). This is why Fonseca considered the *esse-mode* of being-in-a-subject to be nonessential to accidents. Accidents are "disposed" by their nature to exist in a subject but can be miraculously preserved without them. Protestants, on the other hand, were free to maintain that accidents cannot be clearly and distinctly conceived apart from a subject.

26 Leibniz, and in the eighteenth century Berkeley, went even further, transferring (continuous) quantity itself to the phenomenal realm. (The idealist reading of Leibniz on which this interpretation of Leibniz's remarks on space is based, cf. Adams 1994, is not universally accepted.)

27 They did, however, accept that some fictional distinctions had a "foundation in reality." See note 21.

28 See note 24.

29 See Wundt 1939, 180–1, on seventeenth century Protestant Scholastics' notion of existence as a certain mode of beings.

30 The Lutheran Scholastic Christof Scheibler (1589–1653), nicknamed "the Protestant Suárez," held a similar view of the essence-existence distinction. He agrees with Suárez that there is no nonfictional distinction between existence, actuality, and the essence *qua* actual and also agrees with Fonseca that existence is mode. See Scheibler (1617, 1:325–6, 329–30; lib. 1, cap. 15). Suárez scholars have long debated whether his views are "essentialist" and what it would mean to say that they are; there is not enough space here to treat adequately the question and its history. An early "essentialist" interpretation is given in Gilson 1949. For a recent contribution to this debate, together with a polemical review of the contributions of Gilson and others, see Pereira 2007, 13–39.

31 The concept of object-esse – which Scotus has sometimes been credited with originating – is not obviously equivalent to that of intentional *esse*, with which Aquinas was familiar (though some Baroque Scholastics seem to have treated the two as equivalent). Intentional *esse*, for Aquinas, seems to have been a nonmaterial yet actual way of existing. A rose's red color, for example, was supposed to exist "intentionally in," that is without informing the matter of, the eye that sees the red. Tommaso da Vio, Cardinal Cajetan (1469–1534), was among the Thomists who criticized Scotist object-esse (cf. Dalbiez 1929).

32 *Res* and *ens reale* (plurals: *res* and *entia realia*) were commonly taken as synonyms, but not always. Cf. Scheibler 1617, 1:71. (lib. 1, cap. 2, n. 4).
33 Cf. Coimbra 1607, 1:155–61 ("In Praefat. Porphyr." q. 6, aa. 2, 3). An up-to-date discussion of Baroque Scholastic views on beings of reason, including a wealth of references to the literature on the topic, may be found in Novotný 2013.
34 It was, however, really distinct from itself *qua* actual (Clemenson 2007).
35 The Coimbra logic goes so far as to say that in such cases the thing's object-esse becomes its actual *esse* (Coimbra 1607, 2:61).
36 The nature of object-esse in Suárez's metaphysics is debated by Gracia 1991; 1993b; Wells 1990; and 1993.
37 The dates of Descartes's stay are disputed. I have followed Rodis-Lewis 1998, 8–9. In his thirties, Descartes matriculated at two universities in the Netherlands, at the University of Franeker in 1629 and at the University of Leiden in 1630 (Gaukroger 1995, 195, 210; Vrooman 1970, 83); at Franeker he was registered as "Renatus des Cartes, Frenchman, philosopher." But the extent of his contacts with Scholasticism while at these universities is unknown.
38 Rodis-Lewis 1998, 9–12. A student at a Jesuit college typically had the same professor for all three years of his philosophical studies; a professor would teach logic for a year, then physics, then metaphysics (including metaphysics of the soul) and ethics. On p. 9, Rodis-Lewis summarizes the reasons for taking Étienne Noël to have been Descartes's philosophy teacher. The study of ethics seems not to have been as prominent a part of the Jesuit philosophy triennium as one might expect (though it was mandated for the third and final year, with the *Nicomachean Ethics* as the prescribed text: Lukács 1986, 401). Ethical questions may have received more attention in the theology curriculum, which was ordinarily pursued only by Jesuit novices, following completion of the philosophy triennium. The comparative influence of Aristotle's ethics on seventeenth century moral philosophy as a whole – as compared to Stoic ethics, for example – is an interesting but little explored topic. Schmitt 1979, 103, has a few words so say ("[in the sixteenth century] interest in the 'Nicomachean Ethics' was enormous").
39 In a letter to Mersenne (30 Sep. 1640), Descartes recalls having read "the Coimbrans" (this may have been meant to include Fonseca), Rubio, and Toledo. In other letters, and in published and unpublished works, Descartes sometimes mentions Aquinas's *Summa* and Suárez's *Disputationes*, but not in such a way as to demonstrate extensive acquaintance with these texts. The Jesuit commentaries would have been his constant companions during the philosophy triennium at La Flèche. Brief prosopographies for the aforementioned Jesuits are given in Lohr 1988a, 105, 150–1, 170, 395–6, and 458–61. For a list of the texts from which Descartes's La Flèche textbooks are likely to have been drawn, see Clemenson 2007, 7–13, 98–103. Descriptions of student life and curricula at La Flèche or other Jesuit colleges of the day are provided by Rodis-Lewis 1998, 9–19, 232–3 (esp. nn. 18–21); and Wallace 2006 (esp. pp. 315 ff.).
40 And to that "third level" of "sensation" spoken of in the Sixth Replies, which actually consists in intellectual interpretation of sensory data. Descartes calls such interpretation "sensation" only because it is executed habitually, quasi-automatically, on the occasion of the intellect's reception of sense images.
41 Hylomorphism (literally, "matter-form-ism") was the Aristotelian theory that corporeal substances are composed of prime matter (an immanent principle of continuity through substantial change) and substantial form (an immanent principle of belonging to this or that substance-kind, e.g. horse or dog). On some versions of hylomorphism, there was a nonfictional distinction between matter and form; on others, a fictional distinction *cum fundamento in re*.
42 Though some would say it pertains to the history of science, not to the history of philosophy, mention may also be made of Gilson's comparison between the structure of Descartes's *Météores* and that of the corresponding Coimbra commentary (Gilson 1951).
43 Descartes's doctrine of God's creation of the eternal truths is one of the topics discussed. According to Menn, Descartes ascribed this view to Augustine, arriving at it by a "radicalization of Augustine's conception of God as the source of truth" (Menn 1998a, 340).
44 Martinich 1999, 11–13; Peltonien 1996, 3. Attacks on Scholastic logic by Bacon, Hobbes, and Locke appear in Feingold 1984, 278–83, 300 (but these philosophers may well have been influenced by what they criticized). On the arts curriculum in late sixteenth century Oxford, see Fletcher 1986, esp. 159–60, 178–81.
45 Cf. Brandt 1928, 58–62. But perhaps Bacon's immediate source for this view was not Scholasticism. Hobbes, it has been argued, advances a theory of sensible species *in medio* that he received not immediately from the Scholastics, but from the physician Girolamo Fracastoro, one of several Italian philosophers of the late Renaissance and Baroque periods whose writings were known to English anti-Aristotelians of the time (Leijenhorst 2002a, 63–8, 97).

46 See Leijenhorst 2002a, 102–28, on the Baroque Scholastic antecedents of Hobbes's views on imaginary space. Leijenhorst 2002a in its entirety contains a wealth of information on Hobbes's relationship to Scholasticism. See also Leijenhorst 1996 and 2002b. Brandt's 1928 study of Hobbes's natural philosophy notes but does not explore in detail the possibility of important Scholastic influences. Prins 1987 notes some points in the theory of light and the philosophy of science in which Hobbes is closer to the Scholastics than to Descartes.

47 For information on other Scholastic authors with whose works Locke may have been acquainted, see Ashworth 1981, 304. A few details on the life and works of Sanderson may be found in Tyacke 1984, 591–2; 1987, 261, 263; as well as in Matthew and Harrison 2004, 48:878–80. A modern edition of Sanderson's *Logicae artis compendium* exists (edited by Jennifer Ashworth). For information on Smith, Combach, and Scheibler, see (respectively) Matthew and Harrison 2004, 51:297; and Wundt 1939, 84, 119. Brief *curricula vitae* for Śmiglecki, du Trieu, and Burgersdijk are provided in Lohr 1988a, 66–7, 129–30, 427; in addition, Burgersdijk is the main subject of Bos and Krop 1993 (this work also contains articles on broader topics in Calvinist Scholasticism). The literature contains discrepancies concerning biographical details for some Scholastic authors; for example, some sources list du Trieu's year of birth as 1585, not (with Lohr 1988a, 129) as 1580.

48 The account book is listed as Bodleian MS Locke f11 in Kenney 1959, 31. According to Kenney (1959, 32) Locke mentions the *Opera* of Scheibler and Ringelberg (presumably the Flemish humanist and philosopher Joachim Sterck van Ringelberg, 1499–1531), as well as the *De virtute* of Grotius. Other sources on Locke's relationship to Scholasticism or to the Oxford of his day consulted here include Schuurman 2004, Hargreaves-Mawdsley 1973, Telkamp 1927, Küppers 1895, and Krakowski 1915. Krakowski argues for the influence of Scholastic nominalism on Locke, but he also calls seventeenth century Oxford "generally Ramist," a claim not supported by Feingold 1993. Scholastic influences on Locke's views on language are discussed in Ashworth 1981.

49 Kenney (1959, 35–6) also reproduces part of a catalogue of texts "fit to furnish a library for young (yet academical) scholars," compiled by one Timothy Halton, tutor at Queen's College, Oxford, in 1652 (the year Locke entered Christ Church). The catalogue, evidently intended to help tutors choose books to recommend to their students, lists several Scholastic authors or titles Locke might have used, in addition to those listed here. A few other lists of texts compiled by seventeenth century Oxford students or tutors may be found in Feingold 1984, 294–6. A catalogue of Locke's library is given in Harrison and Laslett 1965.

50 Schuurman 2001, 457 (cf. Schuurman 2001, 453), also claims structural analogies to Scholastic logic texts for Gassendi's *Institutio Logica* (1658) and the logic portion of Hobbes's *De corpore* (1655).

51 See especially Freudenthal 1887, Dunin-Borkowski 1910, and Gueroult 1968 ("Index des noms propres cités," s.v. "Aristote," "Burgersdijck," "Eustache de Saint-Paul," "Heereboord," "Keckermann," and "Thomas (saint).")). Lewkowitz 1902 should perhaps be added to this list, but I have not been able to examine this work.

52 Cf. Dunin-Borkowski 1910, 468–78. According to this source, Spinoza attended van den Enden's school for two or three years, from 1654 to 1656 or 1657. Van den Enden, having entered the novitiate of the Society of Jesus in 1619, studied philosophy under the Jesuits for at least two years in Louvain and possibly for a third year in Antwerp. He began studies in theology at Louvain in 1629, but was not ordained a priest, and in 1633 was expelled from the society for alleged errors (Dunin-Borkowski 1910, 469).

53 Wundt 1939, 90; Gullan-Wuhr 1998, 87, 90, 107, 110. Van Ruler 1993, 41, gives his year of birth as 1613; other sources give it as 1614.

54 Dated by Mignini 1987 to around 1660 or 1661.

55 Freudenthal 1887, 111–12, notes close resemblances between several texts from Burgersdijk's *Institutiones metaphysicarum* and parts of the *Cogitata metaphysica* in which Spinoza summarizes Scholastic teaching. Heereboord's relationship to Burgersdijk is remarked in Van Ruler 1993, 41.

56 Some details on Joannes à Bononia, a sixteenth century professor of theology at Louvain and chaplain to Emperor Charles V, are given in Dunin-Borkowski 1910, 452 (it is unclear whether Joannes à Bononia is to be identified with Hieronymus à Bononia, a participant at the Council of Trent mentioned in Schneeman 1879, 82). According to Dunin-Borkowski, his text is a good source of information about the deliberations of the council fathers at Trent, and, in its positive doctrine, anticipates the Jesuit theory of middle knowledge. Another Scholastic work on divine providence, the anti-Pelagian *De causa Dei contra Pelagium et de virtute causarum* of the Merton College (Oxford) philosopher and theologian Thomas Bradwardine (1290?–1349) was, Dunin-Borkowski says, well known in Calvinist Holland (having been republished in London in 1618) and contains some "striking" anticipations of Spinoza, laying

"the philosophical foundation of determinist predestination." For Bradwardine, the human will is at liberty relative to all physical and (even) psychological preconditions, but not relative to God's predetermination (Dunin-Borkowski, 452–3).

57 The library also contained a 1548 edition of the works of Aristotle. The catalogue of Spinoza's library appears in Freudenthal 1899, 160–64 (cf. Dunin-Borkowski 1910, 450–52). For an account of how it was compiled, see Offenberg 1973, 309–10. Brief *curricula vitae* for Keckermann and Pereira may be found in Lohr 1988a, 209–10, 313–20. Like Heereboord, Clauberg was a Dutch thinker who tried to meld Aristotelian and Cartesian thought (Wundt 1939, 93–94).

58 See Freudenthal 1887, Lewkowitz 1902, Weijers 1978, and Coppens 2003. Max Wundt 1939, 90, noting Freudenthal 1899, also remarks similarities between Spinoza's *Cogitata metaphysica* and a roughly contemporary work (1662) by the Utrecht Cartesian Lambert Velthuysen (1622–1685), who, like Heereboord, tried to reconcile elements of Scholasticism with Cartesianism. For information on philosophical instruction at colleges and universities in the Netherlands during the seventeenth century, see Dibon 1954. On the Scholastic provenance of the terms *natura naturans* and *natura naturata* (including citations from Clauberg and Heereboord), see Hedwig 1984, 6: cols. 504–6; and Steenbakkers 2003. Wolfson 1934 draws a number of comparisons between Spinoza and "the medievals" (e.g. "Spinoza operates on the whole with mediaeval conceptions and uses mediaeval terms," Wolfson 1934, 1:253) and, in addition, to the Baroque Scholastics Burgersdijk, Eustache of St. Paul, Heereboord, Suárez, and Marcus Antonius Galitius de Carpenedulo, O.F.M., Cap. (fl. 1630?). Piero di Vona's work on Spinoza's relationship to the Baroque Scholastics (and on Baroque Scholasticism in general) came to my attention too late to be taken into account here. Di Vona 1988 includes references to some of his works relevant to the foregoing; interested readers will no doubt wish to consult his more recent works as well, for example *L'ontologia dimenticata: dall'ontologia spagnola alla "Critica della ragion pura"* (Naples: La Città del Sole, 2009).

59 This synopsis of Gassendi's education is based on Lolordo 2007, 7–9; Rochot 1955a, 13; 1955b, 183; and Joy 1987, 25–9 and 238 n. 2. Lolordo and Rochot disagree about the year in which Gassendi took minor orders; Lolordo says 1614; Rochot, 1612. This is not the only disagreement one will find in the literature concerning Gassendi's early life; cf. Joy 1987, 238 n. 2.

60 In his article on Malebranche for the *Dictionnaire de théologie catholique*, J. Wehrlé claims that Malebranche studied "un zélé péripatéticien, M. Rouillard" (Wehrlé 1927, col. 1776). I have not found any other information on this Rouillard.

61 Little seems to have been written about Scholastic or other Aristotelian influences on Gassendi, Arnauld, or Malebranche. One recent exception is Gventsadze 2007, who, however, cites no Scholastics but simply compares Gassendi to Aristotle. A few details on Arnauld's education appear in Brucker 1903, cols. 1978–79, and Kremer 1996, viii; on Malebranche, see Nadler 2000, 1–7; André 1886/1970; and Wehrlé 1927. Both the Collège de la Marche and the Sorbonne were originally residence halls of the university of Paris; the Sorbonne was home to the theology faculty.

62 His other teachers included Johann Adam Scherzer (1628–1683), Leipzig professor of (successively) philosophy, Hebrew, and theology, and Erhard Weigel (1625–1699), professor of mathematics at Jena, where Leibniz spent the summer of 1663 (Mercer 2001, 38). A few details on Scherzer and Weigel may be found in Wundt 1939, 141–2 and 130.

63 Leibniz makes some guardedly favorable comments about Scholasticism in *New Essays*, Ak 6.6:431 and also Ak 6.4:707 (here and elsewhere in citations of Leibniz's works, "Ak" signifies Leibniz 1923–, the still incomplete "Akademie" edition of Leibniz's works; the numerals immediately following signify series, volume, and page numbers in that edition). Discussions of Leibniz's relationship to Scholasticism – as distinct from Aristotle's own views (as Leibniz understood them) and from non-Scholastic Aristotelianism – may be found in Eschweiler 1928, 252–61; Murray 1995; 1996; Mercer 2001; Mercer 2002; and Greenberg 2005. More citations may be found in the works of Sven Knebel in the list of references. Friedman 1993 gives an overview of philosophy instruction in German universities during the century and half before Leibniz.

64 Angelelli 1967, 98 n. 13; Burkhardt 1980, 235.

65 Sources for the foregoing: Ak 2.1:179, 6.4:1334–43, 6.4: 2466, and 6.6:1211–99. Details on Werenberg's life and works may be found in Wundt 1939, 112–13. Lohr 1988a, 441–5, 470, 472–3, 491–2, contains brief *curricula vitae* for Suárez, Valla, Vázquez, and Werenberg. The secondary literature on Suárez is enormous; see, for example, the forty-five-page bibliography in Pereira 2007. Brief biographies and bibliographies for Caramuel y Lobkowitz, Izquierdo, Álvarez, Macedo, Mendo, and Lynch (as well as on many of the other Baroque Scholastics mentioned in this chapter) may be found, under these authors' names, in the "Nomenclator" section of "Scholasticon," ed. Jacob Schmutz. (http://www.scholasticon.

fr). Werenberg (whose year of death is reported by Petersen 1921 as 1625, but by Wundt 1939, 112, as 1623) taught philosophy first at Wittenberg and then as professor of logic and metaphysics at Hamburg's *Gymnasium*. Valla or Vallius (also "de la Valle"), whose *Logica* was published in Leiden in 1622, is mentioned by Wallace as a source of Galileo's "discovery" of the law of acceleration of falling bodies (cf. Wallace 2006). Brown 1995, 51, 63 n. 46, suggests that the title of Froidmont's work may have been the source of Leibniz's use of the "labyrinth" metaphor to characterize the problem of the continuum; I have relied on him for Froidmont's year of birth (the year of death is confirmed by the Akademie editors as 1653). In view of the connection that Leibniz himself drew between the problems of infinity and the continuum on the one hand, and problems of free will, contingency, and divine foreknowledge on the other (cf. Brown 1995), it is noteworthy that Froidmont (who was known to Descartes also; see his letter to Plempius for Froidmont [Fromondus], AT I 413; CSMK 61) is described by Leibniz (*Theodicy*, Prelim. 24) as a "great friend of" Jansen, the Louvain theologian whose work *Augustinus* sparked the Jansenist controversy in which Arnauld, Pascal, and Malebranche were embroiled. Froidmont is listed by Meyer 1715 as one of the parties to the sixteenth and seventeenth century controversy over middle knowledge that began with the *De auxiliis* affair at the turn of the seventeenth century and continued in the Jansenist–Port-Royal troubles (Meyer, "Index," after p. 448).
66 Ak 6.4:1373–83.
67 Ak 6.6:1789–92. Dola seems to have been a Capuchin Franciscan who was critical of Jesuit attempts to reconcile the doctrine of middle knowledge with God's immediate causal concourse with human sins; I have not been able to discover anything more about him. Murray 2005 claims that Dola's work was the source of Leibniz's view that God's foreknowledge is grounded in his knowledge of the human will's inclinations.
68 The theory of moral necessity (as distinct from the theory of middle knowledge, whose authors were Fonseca and Luis de Molina, 1536–1600) is said to have originated with the Jesuits Diego Ruiz de Montoya (1562–1632) and Diego Granado (1571–1632). Knebel has even claimed that Leibniz was himself a kind of middle-knowledge theorist, in spite of his opposition to certain standard versions of the theory (Knebel 1996, 200–1). A less-unconventional view of Leibniz's relationship to middle-knowledge theory (specifically, to Molina's libertarian view of free will) is given in Sleigh, Chappell, and Della Rocca 1998, 1256–9. The topic of God's concurrence with the human will (and with other finite causes) seems to have interested Leibniz from an early age; cf. Brown 1995, 63 n. 48.
69 I do not mean to imply that Leibniz held that there are terms that signify naturally rather than by convention. But this view, associated with Renaissance neo-Platonism and Hermeticism, is linked to a hope, which Leibniz shared (Rutherford 1995), that a suitably reformed human language might express the essences of things more clearly and distinctly than do present languages.
70 Ferrater Mora 1953 references several late nineteenth century or early twentieth century works in German on Leibniz's relationship to Baroque Scholasticism.

Bibliography

André, Y. M. 1970 [1886]. *La Vie du R. P. Malebranche prêtre de l'oratoire avec l'historire de ces ouvrages*. Geneva: Slatkine Reprints [Paris: Ingold].
Angelelli, I. 1967. "On Identity and Interchangeability in Leibniz and Frege." *Notre Dame Journal of Formal Logic* 8: 94–100.
———. 1994. "The Scholastic Background of Modern Philosophy: *Entitas* and Individuation in Leibniz." Pp. 535–42 of J. J. E. Gracia, ed. *Individuation in Scholasticism: The Later Middle Ages and the Counter-Reformation 1150–1650*. Albany: State University of New York Press.
Ariew, R. 1992. "Descartes and Scholasticism." Pp. 58–90 of J. Cottingham, ed. *The Cambridge Companion to Descartes*. Cambridge: Cambridge University Press.
———.1999. *Descartes and the Last Scholastics*. Ithaca, NY: Cornell University Press.
———. 2002. "Descartes and the Jesuits: Doubt, Novelty, and the Eucharist." Pp. 157–94 of M. Feingold, ed. *Jesuit Science and the Republic of Letters*. Cambridge, MA: M.I.T.
Ariew, R. and Grene, M. 1995. "Ideas, in and Before Descartes." *Journal of the History of Ideas* 56: 87–106 (reprinted in Ariew 1999).
Ashworth, E. J. 1974. *Language and Logic in the Post-Medieval Period*. Dordrecht: D. Reidel.
———. 1981. "Do Words Signify Ideas or Things? The Scholastic Sources of Locke's Theory of Language." *Journal of the History of Philosophy* 19: 299–326.

———. 1982. "The Eclipse of Medieval Logic." Pp. 787–96 of Kretzmann, Kenny and Pinborg.
———. 1988a. "Traditional Logic." Pp. 143–72 of Schmitt and Skinner.
———. 1988b. "Changes in Logic Textbooks From 1500 to 1650: The New Aristotelianism." Pp. 75–87 of E. Kessler, C. H. Lohr, W. Sparn, ed. *Aristotelismus und Renaissance: In Memoriam Charles B. Schmitt.* Wiesbaden: Otto Harrassowitz.
———. 1997. "Petrus Fonseca on Objective Concepts and the Analogy of Being." Pp. 47–63 of P. A. Easton, ed. *Logic and the Workings of the Mind.* Atascadero, CA: Ridgeview.
Ayers, M. 1998. "Ideas and objective being." P. 1062–1107 of D. Garber and M. Ayers, eds. *The Cambridge History of Seventeenth-Century Philosophy* vol. 2. Cambridge: Cambridge University Press.
Bacon, F. 1670. *Sylva sylvarum.* London: Printed by J. R. for William Lee.
Bos, E. P. and Krop, H. A. (eds.) 1993. *Franco Burgersdijk (1590–1635): Neo-Aristotelianism in Leiden.* Rodopi: Amsterdam.
Brandt, F. 1928. *Thomas Hobbes' Mechanical Conception of Nature.* Copenhagen: Levin & Munksgaard.
Brown, S. 1995. "The Seventeenth-Century Intellectual Background." Pp. 43–66 of N. Jolley, ed. *The Cambridge Companion to Leibniz.* Cambridge: Cambridge University Press.
Brucker, J. 1903. "Arnauld." Cols. 1978–83 of Vacant et al. 1903–67.
Burkhardt, H. 1980. *Logik und Semantik in der Philosophie von Leibniz.* Munich: Philosophia Verlag.
Burgersdijk, F. 1666. *Institutionum logicarum libri duo.* Cambridge: J. Field.
Centre International de Synthèse [corporate author] 1955. *Pierre Gassendi 1592–1655: Sa Vie et Son Oeuvre.* Paris: Albin Michel.
Clemenson, D. 1991. *Seventeenth Century Scholastic Philosophy of Cognition and Descartes' Causal Proof of God's Existence.* Ph.D. dissertation, Harvard University.
———. 2007. *Descartes' Theory of Ideas.* London: Continuum.
Coimbra, Universidade de [Colégio das Artes; corporate author] 1594. *In octo libros Physciorum Aristotelis.* Lyons: J.-B. Buysson. Reprint, Hildeshiem: G. Olms, 1984.
———. 1604. *In tres libros De anima Aristotelis.* Lyons: H. Cardon.
———. 1607. *In Universam Dialecticam Aristotelis.* Cologne: B. Gaultherium. Reprint, Hildesheim: G. Olms, 1976.
———. 2001. *The Conimbricenses: Some Questions on Signs.* Ed. and transl. J. Doyle. Milwaukee, WI: Marquette University Press.
Cook, M. 1974. "Arnauld's Alleged Representationalism." *Journal of the History of Philosophy* 12: 53–62.
———. 1975. "The Alleged Ambiguity of "Idea" in Descartes' Philosophy." *Southwestern Journal of Philosophy* 6: 87–94.
———. 1987. "Descartes' Alleged Representationalism." *History of Philosophy Quarterly* 4: 179–95.
Coppens, G. 2003 (ed.). *Spinoza en de Scholastiek.* Leuven [Louvain]: Academische Coöperatieve Vennootschap.
Cronin, T. 1966. *Objective Being in Descartes and in Suarez* (Analecta Gregoriana v. 154). Rome: Gregorian University Press.
Dalbiez, R. 1929. "L'Être objectif chez Descartes." *Revue d'histoire de la philosophie* 3: 464–72.
Descartes, René. 1964–76. *Oeuvres de Descartes.* 11 vols. Ed. C. Adam and P. Tannery. Revised edition. Paris: Vrin.
———. 1984–91. *The Philosophical Writings of René Descartes.* 3 vols. Ed. J. Cottingham, R. Stoothoff, D. Murdoch, and A. Kenny. Cambridge: Cambridge University Press.
Des Chene, D. 1996. *Physiologia: Natural Philosophy in Late Aristotelian and Cartesian Thought.* Ithica: Cornell University Press.
———. 2000. *Life's Form: Late Aristotelian Conceptions of the Soul.* Cornell: Cornell University Press.
de Rochemonteix, C. 1889. *Un Collège de Jésuites aux XVIIe et XVIIIe Siècles: Le Collège Henri IV de la Flèche.* 4 v. Le Mans: Leuicheux.
Dibon, P. 1954. *La Philosophie néerlandaise au siècle d'or.* Volume 1: *L'enseignement philosophique dans les universités à l'époque précartésienne (1575–1650).* Amsterdam: Elsevier. [3 volumes were projected; the second and third seem never to have appeared.]
Di Liscia, D. A., E. Kessler, and C. Methuen. 1997. *Method and Order in Renaissance Philosophy of Nature.* Aldershot: Ashgate.
Di Vona, P. 1988. "Il Problema della distinzioni nella filosofia di Spinoza." *Studia Spinoziana* 4: 147–64.
Doolan, G. 2008. *Aquinas on the Divine Ideas as Exemplar Causes.* Washington, DC: Catholic University of America Press.

Doyle, J. P. 2007. "Hispanic Scholastic Philosophy." Pp. 250–69 of J. Hankins, ed. *The Cambridge Companion to Renaissance Philosophy*. Cambridge: Cambridge University Press.

Dunin-Borkowski, S. [Grav von, S.J.] 1910. *Der junge De Spinoza: Leben und Werdegang im Lichte der Weltphilosophie*. Münster: Aschendorff.

Echarri, J. 1950. "Un influjo español desconocido en la formación del sistema cartesiano (Dos textos paralelos de Toledo y Descartes sobre el espacio)." *Pensamiento* 6: 291–323.

Edwards, M. 2007. "Aristotelianism, Descartes, and Hobbes." *The Historical Journal* 50: 449–64.

Eschweiler, K. 1928. "Die Philosophie der spanischen Spätscholastik auf den deutschen Universitäten des siebzehnten Jahrhunderts." Pp. 251–325 of H. Finke, ed., vol. 1, *Gesammelte Aufsätze zur Kulturgeschichte Spaniens*. Münster: Aschendorff.

Feingold, M. 1984. "'The Humanities.' *The History of the University of Oxford*. Ed. T. Aston." Pp. 211–357 of N. Tyacke, ed., vol. 4, *Seventeenth-Century Oxford*. Oxford: Oxford University Press.

———. 1993. "The Ultimate Pedagogue. Franco Burgersdijk and the English Speaking Academic Learning." Pp. 151–65 of Bos and Kop.

Ferrater Mora, J. 1953. "Suarez and Modern Philosophy." *Journal of the History of Ideas* 14: 528–47.

Fletcher, A. 2005. "Francis Bacon's Forms and the Logic of Ramist Conversion." *Journal of the History of Philosophy* 43: 157–69.

Fletcher, J. M. 1986. "'The Faculty of Arts.' *The History of the University of Oxford*. Ed. T. Aston." Pp. 157–79 of J. McConica ed., vol. 3, *The Collegiate University*. Oxford: Clarendon Press.

Fonseca, P. 1615. *Commentariorum in Libros Metaphysciorum Aristotelis Stagiritae*. 4 vols. Cologne: L. Zetznerus. Reprint, 2 vol., Hildesheim: G. Olms, 1964.

Forget, J. 1920. "Gomar et Gomarisme." Cols. 1477–86 of Vacant et al. v. 6.

Foster, K. and S. Humphries. 1951. *Aristotle's De Anima in the Version of William of Moerbeke and the Commentary of St. Thomas Aquinas*. New Haven: Yale University Press.

Freudenthal, J. 1887. "Spinoza und die Scholastik." *Philosophische Aufsätze: Eduard Zeller zu seinem fünfzigjährigen Doctor-Jubiläum gewidmet*. Leipzig: Fues's Verlag.

———. 1899. *Die Lebensgeschichte Spinoza's in Quellenschriften, Urkunden und nichtamtlichen Nachrichten*. Leipzig: Verlag Von Veit.

Friedman, J. 1993. "Aristotle and the Content of Philosophy Instruction at Central European Schools and Universities During the Reformation Era (1500–1650)." *Proceedings of the American Philosophical Society* 137: 213–53.

Friedman, R. L. 2000. "Peter Auriol on Intellectual Cognition of Singulars." *Vivarium* 38: 177–93.

———. 2005. "Durand of St.-Pourçain." Pp. 249–53 of J. J. E. Gracia and T. B. Noone eds., *A Companion to Philosophy in the Middle Ages*. Malden, MA: Blackwell.

Friedman, R. and Nielsen, L., eds. 2003. *The Medieval Heritage in Early Modern Metaphysics and Modal Theory, 1400–1700*. Dordrecht: Kluwer.

Garber, D. and Ayers, M. 1998. *The Cambridge History of Seventeenth-Century Philosophy*. 2 vols. Cambridge: Cambridge University Press.

Gassendi, P. 1962. *Disquisitio Metaphysica*. Ed. and transl. B. Rochot. Paris: Vrin.

Gaukroger, S. 1995. *Descartes: An Intellectual Biography*. Cambridge: Cambridge University Press.

Giacon, C. 1944–1950. *La Seconda Scolastica*. 3 vols. Milan: Fratelli Bocca.

Gilson, É. 1949. *Being and Some Philosophers*. Toronto: Pontifical Institute of Mediaeval Studies.

———. 1951. *Études sur la rôle de la Pensée médiévale dans la formation du système cartésien*. Paris: J. Vrin.

———. 1979. *Index scolastico-cartésien*. 2nd ed. Paris: J. Vrin.

———. 1987. *La Liberté chez Descartes et la théologie*. Paris: J. Vrin.

Glorieux, P. (ed.). 1927. *Le Correctorium Corruptorii "Quare."* Kain: Le Saulchoir.

Göckel, R. [Goclenius] 1967 [1597]. *Problemata Logica*. Marburg 1597; Olms reprint 1967.

Gracia, J. J. E. 1991. "Suárez's Conception of Metaphysics: A Step in the Direction of Mentalism?" *American Catholic Philosophical Quarterly* 65: 287–309.

———. 1993a. "Hispanic Philosophy: Its Beginning and Golden Age." *Review of Metaphysics* 46: 475–502.

———. 1993b. "Suarez and Metaphysical Mentalism: The Last Visit." *American Catholic Philosophical Quarterly* 67: 339–48.

Greenberg, S. 2005. "Leibniz Against Molinism." Pp. 217–33 of D. Rutherford and J. A. Cover eds., *Leibniz: Nature and Freedom*. Oxford.

Grendler, Paul, 2002. *The Universities of the Italian Renaissance*. Baltimore: Johns Hopkins University Press.

Grene, M. 1985. *Descartes*. Minneapolis: University of Minnesota Press.

Gueroult, M. 1968. *Spinoza I: Dieu (Ethique, I)*. Paris: Aubier-Montaigne.

Gullan-Wuhr, M. 1998. *Within Reason: A Life of Spinoza*. London: Jonathan Cape.

Gventsadze, V. 2007. "Aristotelian Influences in Gassendi's Moral Philosophy." *Journal of the History of Philosophy* 45: 223–42.
Hargreaves-Mawdsley, W. N. 1973. *Oxford in the Age of Locke*. Norman: University of Oklahoma Press.
Harrison, J. and P. Laslett. 1965. *The Library of John Locke*. Oxford: Oxford University Press.
Hattab, H. 1998. "One Cause or Many?: Jesuit Influences on Descartes's Division of Causes." Pp. 105–20 of Stephen F. Brown, ed. *Meeting of the Minds: The Relations Between Medieval and Classical Modern European Philosophy*. Tournhout: Brepols.
———. 2001. "The Problem of Secondary Causation in Descartes: A Response to Des Chene." *Perspectives on Science* 8: 93–118.
———. 2003. "Conflicting Causalitites: The Jesuits, their Opponents and Descartes on the Causality of the Efficient Cause." Pp. 1–22 of D. Garber and S. Nadler ed., vol. 1, *Oxford Studies in Early Modern Philosophy* Oxford: Oxford University Press.
Hedwig, K. 1984. "Natura Naturans/Natura." Pp. 504–99 of Joachim Ritter and Karlfried Grunder ed., vol. 6, *Historisches Wörterbuch der Philosophie*. 6th ed. Basel: Schwabe. 1971–2007. 13 vols.
Henry, J. and S. Hutton (eds.). 1990. *New Perspectives on Renaissance Thought: Essays in the History of Science, Education and Philosophy, in Memory of Charles B. Schmitt*. London: Duckworth.
Hoffman, P. 1986. "The Unity of Descartes's Man." *Philosophical Review* 95: 339–70.
———. 1990. "Cartesian Passions and Cartesian Dualism." *Pacific Philosophical Quarterly* 71: 310–33.
———. 1999. "Cartesian Composites." *Journal of the History of Philosophy* 37: 251–70.
———. 2002. "Descartes's Theory of Distinction." *Philosophy and Phenomenological Research* 64: 57–78.
Honnefelder, L. 1990. *Scientia transcendens: Die formale Bestimmung der Seiendheit und Realität in der Metaphysik des Mittelalters und der Neuzeit (Duns Scotus – Suárez – Wolff – Kant – Peirce)*. Hamburg: Felix Meiner.
John of St. Thomas 1930–37. *Cursus Philosophicus*. Ed. B. Reiser. 2nd ed., 3 vols. Rome: Marietti.
Joy, L. 1987. *Gassendi the Atomist*. Cambridge: Cambridge University Press.
Kenney, W. H. 1959. *John Locke and the Oxford Training in Logic and Metaphysics*. Ph.D. dissertation, St. Louis University.
Kenny, A. 2002. *Aquinas on Being*. Oxford: Oxford University Press.
Kessler, E. 1990. "The Transformation of Aristotelianism During the Renaissance." Pp. 137–47 of J. Henry and S. Hutton, eds.
Kessler, E., C. H. Lohr, and W. Sparn (eds.). 1988. *Aristotelismus und Renaissance: In Memoriam Charles B. Schmitt*. Wiesbaden: Otto Harrassowitz.
Knebel, S. 1991. "Necessitas moralis ad optimum (I). Zum historischen Hintergrund der Wahl der besten aller möglichen Welten." *Studia Leibnitiana* 23: 3–24.
———. 1992a. "Necessitas moralis ad optimum (II): Die früheste scholastische Absage an den Optimismus. Eine unveröffentlichte Handschrift Jorge Hemelmans SJ von 1617." *Theologie und Philosophie: Vierteljahresschrift* 67: 514–35.
———. 1992b. "Necessitas moralis ad optimum (III): Naturgesetz und Induktionsproblem in der Jesuitenscholastik während des zweiten Drittels des 17. Jahrhunderts." *Studia Leibnitiana* 24: 182–215.
———. 1993. "Necessitas moralis ad optimum (IV): Reportarum zur Optimismusdiskussion im 17. Jahrhunderts." *Studia Leibnitiana* 25: 201–8.
———. 1996. "Leibniz, Middle Knowledge, and the Intricacies of World Design." *Studia Leibnitiana* 28: 199–210.
———. 2000. *Wille, Würful, und Wahrscheinlichkeit: Das System des moralischen Notwendigkeit in der Jesuitenscholastik 1550–1770*. Hamburg: Felix Meiner.
———. 2003. "The Renaissance of Statistical Modalities in Early Modern Scholasticism." Pp. 231–51 of R. Friedman and L. Nielsen 2003.
Krakowski, É. 1915. *Les Sources médiévales de la Philosophie de Locke*. Paris: Jouve.
Kremer, E. J. (ed.). 1996. *Interpreting Arnauld*. Toronto: University of Toronto Press.
Kretzmann, N., A. Kenny, and J. Pinborg. 1982. *The Cambridge History of Later Medieval Philosophy*. Cambridge: Cambridge University Press.
Krop, H. A. 1993. "Natural Knowledge of God in Neo-Aristotelianism. The Reception of Suarez's Version of the Ontological Argument in Early Seventeenth Century Leiden." Pp. 67–82 of Bos and Krop.
Küppers, W. 1895. *John Locke und die Scholastik*. Berlin: H. S. Hermann.
Leibniz, G. 1923– . *Gottfried Wilhelm Leibniz: Sämtliche Schriften und Briefe*. Multiple volumes. Ed. Deutsche Akademie der Wissenschafter. Darmstadt and Berlin: Akademie Verlag.
Leijenhorst, C. 1996. "Jesuit Concepts of *Spatium Imaginarium* and Thomas Hobbes's Doctrine of Space." *Early Science and Medicine* 1: 355–80.

———. 2002a. *The Mechanisation of Aristotelianism: The Late Aristotelian Setting of Thomas' Hobbes' Natural Philosophy*. Leiden: Brill.

———. 2002b. "'Insignificant Speech': Thomas Hobbes and Late Aristotelianism on Words, Concepts and Things." Pp. 337–67 of E. Kessler and I. MacLean, eds. *Res et verba in der Renaissance*. Wiesbaden: Harrassowitz in Kommission (Wolfenbütteler Abhandlungen zur Renaissanceforschung, vol. 21).

Leinsle, U. G. 1985. *Das Ding und die Methode: Methodische Konstitution und Gegenstand der frühen protestantischen Metaphysik*. Augsburg: Maro Verlag. 1 Vol. in 2.

Lewalter, E. 1935. *Spanisch-jesuitische und deutsch-lutherische Metaphysik des 17. Jahrhunderts*. Hamburg: Ibero-amerikanisches Institut. Repr. 1967, Darmstadt: Wissenschaftliche Burchgesellschaft.

Lewkowitz, J. 1902. *Spinoza's Cogitata metaphysica und ihr Verhaeltnis zu Descartes und zur Scholastik*. Breslau: T. Schatzky.

Lohr, C. 1988a. *Latin Aristotle Commentaries II: Renaissance Authors*. Florence: Olschki.

———. 1988b. "The Sixteenth-Century Transformation of the Aristotelian Natural Philosophy." Pp. 89–99 of Kessler et al.

———. 1988c. "Metaphysics." Pp. 537–638 of Schmitt and Skinner.

Lolordo, A. 2007. *Pierre Gassendi and the Birth of Early Modern Philosophy*. Cambridge: Cambridge University Press.

Lukács, L. (ed.). 1986. *Ratio atque institutio studiorum Societatis Iesu (1586, 1591, 1599)*. Vol. 5 of *Monumenta Paedagogica Societatis Iesu*, and Vol. 129 of *Monumenta Historica Societatis Iesu*. Rome: Institutum Historicum Societatis Iesu.

Lüthy, C. 2000. "What to Do With Seventeenth-Century Natural Philosophy? A Taxonomic Problem." *Perspectives on Science* 8: 164–95.

Martinich, A. P. 1999. *Hobbes: A Biography*. Cambridge: Cambridge University Press.

Matthew, H. C. G. and B. Harrison (eds.). 2004. *Oxford Dictionary of National Biography*. Oxford: Oxford University Press.

Menn, S. 1998a. *Descartes and Augustine*. Cambridge: Cambridge University Press.

———. 1998b. "The Intellectual Setting." Pp. 33–86 of Garber and Ayers, vol. 1.

Mercer, C. 1993. "The Vitality and Importance of Early Modern Aristotelianism." Pp. 33–67 of T. Sorrell, ed. *The Rise of Modern Philosophy*. Oxford: Oxford University Press.

———. 2001. *Leibniz's Metaphysics: Its Origins and Development*. Cambridge: Cambridge University Press.

———. 2002. "Platonism and Philosophical Humanism on the Continent." Pp. 25–44 of S. Nadler (ed.).

Meyer, L. [ivino de]. 1715. *Historia controversiarum de divinae gratiae auxiliis . . . accendunt dissertations quatuor de mente S Concilii Tridentini*. Brussels: A. Claudinot.

Mignini, F. 1987. "Données et problèmes de la chronologie spinozienne entre 1656 et 1665." *Revue des Sciences Philosophiques et Théologiques* 71: 9–21.

Murdoch, J. E. 1990. "From the Medieval to the Renaissance Aristotle." Pp. 163–76 of J. Henry and S. Hutton (eds.).

Murray, M. 1995. "Leibniz on Divine Knowledge of Conditional Future Contingents." *Philosophy and Phenomenological Research* 55: 75–108.

———. 1996. "Intellect, Will, and Freedom: Leibniz and His Predecessors" *Leibniz Society Review* 6: 25–59.

———. 2005. "Spontaneity and Freedom in Leibniz." Pp. 194–216 of D. Rutherford and J. A. Cover, eds. *Leibniz: Nature and Freedom*.

Nadler, S. 1989. *Arnauld and the Cartesian Philosophy of Ideas*. Princeton, NJ: Princeton University Press.

———. (ed.). 2000. *Cambridge Companion to Malebranche*. Cambridge: Cambridge University Press.

———. (ed.). 2002. *A Companion to Early Modern Philosophy*. Oxford: Blackwell.

Normore, C. 2007. "The Invention of Singular Thought." Pp. 109–28 of H. Lagerlund, ed. *Forming the Mind: Essays on the Internal Senses and the Mind/Body Problem From Avicenna to the Medical Enlightenment*. Dordrecht: Springer.

Novaes, C. D. and S. Read. 2008. "*Insolubilia* and the Fallacy *Secundum Quid et Simpliciter*." *Vivarium* 46: 175–91.

Novotný, D. 2013. *Ens Rationis From Suárez to Caramuel*. Bronx, NY: Fordham University Press.

Nuchelmans, G. 1998. "Logic in the Seventeenth Century: Preliminary Remarks and the Constituents of the Proposition." Pp. 103–17 of Garber and Ayers.

Oesterle, J. (ed., transl.). 1962. *Aristotle: On Interpretation. Commentary by St. Thomas and Cajetan*. Milwaukee, WI: Marquette University Press.

Offenberg, Adri K. 1973. "Spinoza's Library. The Story of a Reconstruction." *Quaerendo* 3(4): 309–21.

O'Malley, J., G. A. Bailey, S. J. Harris, and T. F. Kennedy (eds.). 2006. *The Jesuits II: Cultures, Sciences, and the Arts, 1540–1773*. Toronto: University of Toronto Press.

O'Neil, B. 1974. *Epistemology and Direct Realism in Descartes' Philosophy*. Albuquerque: University of New Mexico Press.
Osler, M. J. 2002. "New Wine in Old Bottles: Gassendi and the Aristotelian Origin of Physics." *Midwest Studies in Philosophy* 26: 167–84.
Parkinson, G. H. R. (ed.). 1993. *The Renaissance and Seventeenth-Century Rationalism* of G. H. R. Parkinson and S. G. Shanker, eds. vol. 4, *Routledge History of Philosophy*. London: Routledge.
Peltonien, M. 1996. "Introduction." Pp. 1–24 of M. Peltonien, ed. *The Cambridge Companion to Bacon*. Cambridge: Cambridge University Press.
Pendzig, P. 1969. *Pierre Gassendis Metaphysik und ihr Verhältnis zur scholastischen Philosophie*. (reprint of Bonn: P. Hanstein, 1908 edition). New York: Burt Franklin.
Pereira, J. 2007. *Suárez: Between Scholasticism and Modernity*. Milwaukee: Marquette University Press.
Petersen, Peter. 1921. *Geschichte der aristotelischen Philosophie im protestantishcen Deutschland*. Leipzig: Felix Meiner.
Pozzo, R. (ed.). 2004. *The Impact of Aristotelianism on Modern Philosophy*. Washington, DC: Catholic University of America Press.
Prins, J. 1987. "Kepler, Hobbes and Medieval Optics." *Philosophia Naturalis* 24: 287–310.
Risse, W. 1964–70. *Die Logic der Neuzeit*. 2 vols. Cologne. Reprint, vol. I: 150–1640 vols. 2: 1640–1780. Stuttgart-Bad Cannstatt: Frommann-Hozboog.
———. 1965–79. *Bibliographia Logica*. Hildesheim: Olms.
Rochot, B. 1955a. "La vie, le caractère, et la formation intellectuelle." Pp. 11–54 of Centre International de Synthèse [corporate author] 1955.
———. 1955b. "Chronologie de la Vie et des Oeuvrages de Pierre Gassendi." Pp. 183–91 of Centre International de Synthèse [corporate author] 1955.
Rodis-Lewis, G. 1998. *Descartes: His Life and Thought*. Ithaca: Cornell University Press.
Rozemond, M. 1998. *Descartes's Dualism*. Cambridge, MA: Harvard University Press.
Rubio, A. 1620. *Commentarii in libros Aristotelis de Anima*. Lyons: Ioannis Pillehotte.
Rutherford, D. 1995. "Philosophy and Language in Leibniz." Pp. 224–69 of N. Jolley, ed. *The Cambridge Companion to Leibniz*. Cambridge: Cambridge University Press.
Scheibler, C. 1617. *Opus metaphysicum*. Giessen: Typis Nicolai Hampelii.
Schmitt, C. 1966. "Perennial Philosophy: From Augustino Steuco to Leibniz." *Journal of the History of Ideas* 27: 505–32 (reprinted as chapter 1 of Schmitt 1984).
———. 1973. "Towards a Reassessment of Renaissance Aristotelianism." *History of Science* 11: 159–93 (reprinted as chapter 6 of Schmitt 1981).
———. 1979. "Aristotle's Ethics in the Sixteenth Century: Some Preliminary Considerations." Pp. 87–112 of W. Rüegg and D. Wuttke, eds. *Ethik im Humanismus*. Boppard: Harald Boldt (reprinted as chapter 7 of Schmitt 1984).
———. 1981. *Studies in Renaissance Philosophy and Science*. London: Variorum Reprints.
———. 1983. *John Case and Aristotelianism in Renaissance England*. Kingston, Ontario: McGill-Queen's University Press.
———. 1984. *The Aristotelian Tradition and Renaissance Universities*. London: Variorum Reprints.
———. 1988. "The Rise of the Philosophical Textbook." Pp. 792–804 of Schmitt and Skinner 1988.
Schmitt, C. and Q. Skinner (eds.). 1988. *Cambridge History of Renaissance Philosophy*. Cambridge: Cambridge University Press.
Schneeman, G. (S. J.). 1879. *Die Entstehung der thomistisch-molinistichen Controversie. Ergänzungshefte zu den "Stimmen aus Maria-Lach"* 9. Freiburg: Herder.
Schuurman, P. 2001. "Locke's Logic of Ideas in Context: Content and Structure." *British Journal for the History of Philosophy* 9: 439–65.
———. 2004. *Ideas, Mental Faculties and Method: The Logic of Ideas of Descartes and Its Reception in the Dutch Republic, 1630–1750*. Leiden: Brill.
Secada, J. 2000. *Cartesian Metaphysics: The Scholastic Origins of Modern Philosophy*. Cambridge: Cambridge University Press.
Simmons, A. 1999. "Are Cartesian Sensations Teleological?" *Nous* 33: 347–69.
———. 2001. "Sensible Ends: Latent Teleology in Descartes' Accounts of Sensation." *Journal of the History of Philosophy* 39: 49–75.
Sleigh, R., V. Chappell, and M. Della Rocca. 1998. Pp. 1195–1278 of Garber and Ayers, v. 2.
Solana, M. 1928. *Los Grandes Escolásticos Españoles de los Siglos XVI y XVII: sus doctrinas filosóficas y su signification en la Historia de la Filosofia*. Madrid. J. Ratés.

———. 1941. *Historia de la Filosofía Española: Epoca del Renacimiento (Siglo XVI)*. 3 v. Madrid: Real Academia de Ciencias Exactas, Físicas y Naturales.

Sommervogel, C., Aloys de Backer, Augustin de Backer, and A. Carayon. 1960. *Bibliothèque de la Compagnie de Jésus*. 2nd ed. 12 vols. Héverlé-Louvain: Editions de la Bibliothèque S. J.

Spruit, L. 1994–95. *Species Intelligibilis: From Perception to Knowledge*. 2 v. (vol. 1: *Classical Roots and Medieval Discussions*; Vol. 2: *Renaissance Controversies, Later Scholasticism, and the Elimination of the Intelligible Species in Modern Philosophy*). Leiden: Brill.

Steenbakkers, P. 2003. "Een vijandige overname: Spinoza over *natura naturans* en *natura naturata*." Pp. 35–52 of Coppens, G., ed. *Spinoza en de Scholastiek*. Louvain: Acco.

Stone, M. F. W. 2002. "Aristotelianism and Scholasticism in Early Modern Philosophy." Pp. 7–24 of Nadler.

Tachau, K. 1988. *Vision and Certitude in the Age of Ockham. Optics, Epistemology and Semantics in the Age of Ockham 1250–1345*. Leiden: E. J. Brill.

Telkamp, A. 1927. *Das Verhältniss John Locke's zur Scholastik*. Münster in Westfallen: Verlag der Aschendorfschen Verlagsbuchhandlung.

Toledo, F. 1985. *Opera omnia*. Hildesheim: G. Olms. Reprint of 1615/16 Cologne edition.

Trentman, J. A. 1982. "Scholasticism in the Seventeenth Century." Pp. 818–37 of Kretzmann, Kenny and Pinborg.

Tuck, R. 1998. "The Institutional Setting." Pp. 9–32 of Garber and Ayers, v. 1.

Tyacke, N. 1984. *The History of the University of Oxford*. Vol. 4: *Seventeenth–Century Oxford*. Oxford: Oxford University Press.

Tyacke, N. 1987. *Anti-Calvinists: The Rise of English Arminianism, c. 1590–1640*. Oxford: Clarendon Press.

Vacant, A., Mangenot, E., and Amann, É. (eds.). 1903–1967. *Dictionnaire de théologie catholique*. Paris: Letouzey et Ané. 16 vols in 24.

Van Ruler, J. A. 1993. "Franco Petri Burgersdijk and the Case of Calvinism Within the Neo-Scholastic Tradition." Pp. 37–66 of Bos and Krop.

Viller, M., Cavallera, and F. J. de Guibert. 1932–95. *Dictionnaire de spiritualité ascetique et mystique* 17 volumes in 21. Paris: Beauchesne.

Vrooman, J. 1970. *René Descartes: A Biography*. New York: G. P. Putnam's Sons.

Wahl, R. 1988. "The Arnauld-Malebranche Controversy." *The Monist* 71: 561–72.

Wallace, W. 2006. "Jesuit Influences on Galileo's Science." Pp. 314–35 of O'Malley et al.

Wehrlé. J. 1927. "Malebranche." cols. 1775–1804 of Vacant et al. 1903–67.

Weier, W. 2000. "Leibnitiana bei Johannes Clauberg". *Studia Leibnitiana* 32: 21–42.

Weijers, O. 1978. "Contribution à l'histoire des terms 'natura naturans' et 'natura naturata' jusqu'à Spinoza." *Vivarium* 16: 70–80.

Wells, N. 1990. "Objective Reality of Ideas in Descartes, Caterus, and Suárez." *Journal of the History of Philosophy* 28: 33–61.

———. 1993. "'Esse cognitum' and Suarez Revisited." *American Catholic Philosophical Quarterly* 67: 339–48.

White, K. (ed.). 1997. *Hispanic Philosophy in the Age of Discovery*. Studies in Philosophy and the History of Philosophy 29. Washington, DC: Catholic University of America Press.

Wundt, M. 1939. *Die deutsche Schulmetaphysik des 17. Jahrhunderts*. Tübingen: J.C.B. Mohr; rept. Hildesheim: Olms, 1992.

Yolton, J. 1970. *Locke and the Compass of Human Understanding*. Cambridge: Cambridge University Press.

———. 1975. "Ideas and Knowledge in Seventeenth-Century Philosophy." *Journal of the History of Philosophy* 13: 145–65.

———. 1984. *Perceptual Acquaintance From Descartes to Reid*. Minneapolis: University of Minnesota Press.

———. 2000. *Realism and Appearances: An Essay in Ontology*. Cambridge: Cambridge University Press.

Zabarella, J. 1602. *De Rebus Naturalibus Libri XXX*. 4th ed. Cologne: Lazarus Zetznerus.

Part 2

METAPHYSICS

2
THEORIES OF SUBSTANCE
Tad M. Schmaltz

Aristotle (384–322 BCE) established broad parameters for subsequent discussions of the notion of substance, including of course the consideration of this notion that is such a dominant aspect of seventeenth century thought. There are two main sources for Aristotle's account of substance (*ousia*), namely the *Categories* and book Zeta of the *Metaphysics*. In the *Categories*, a primary substance, or substance "strictly speaking," is said to be that which is neither said of a subject nor in a subject, such as an individual human being (2a14–18; Aristotle 1984, 1:4). The contrast here is, on the one hand, with species and genera such as humanity and animality, which are "secondary substances" that are said of a subject but are not in a subject, and, on the other hand, with quantities, qualities, and relations such as volume, color, and position, which are accidents that exist in a subject.

In *Metaphysics* Zeta, however, Aristotle offers a discussion of substance in terms of his "hylomophism," which takes material beings to be composites of form and matter. Of the three candidates for substance – namely matter, form, and the form-matter composite – the conclusion seems to be that form is the most paradigmatically a substance, insofar as it is identified with the essence that causes an individual to be what it is (1041a5–30; Aristotle 1984, 2:1643–4). There are obvious questions regarding the compatibility of this conclusion with the account of substance in the *Categories*.[1] But what is most relevant here is simply that Aristotle introduced two different defining features of substance: the first, that it is the ultimate subject of predication, and the second, that it is the ultimate cause that constitutes the essence of a thing.

Two millennia separate Aristotle's account of substance from early modern thought, so it is perhaps not surprising that this account did not influence such thought directly. Rather, it was this account as articulated and modified by centuries of later Scholastic commentary that had an impact. I therefore begin my consideration of early modern theories of substance with a treatment of Scholastic views on this topic, taking as my representative the late Scholasticism of Francisco Suárez (1548–1617). We will see that Suárez offers a hylomorphic account of substance in terms of the union of matter and form that was a subject of ridicule in the early modern period. However, Suárez also provides an analysis of the distinction between infinite and finite substance, on the one hand, and between finite substance and mode, on the other, that conditions discussions of substance in early modern writings.

My discussion of the positive theories of substance in the early modern period focuses on the writings of René Descartes (1596–1650), Benedict de Spinoza (1632–1677), and

Gottfried Wilhelm von Leibniz (1648–1716).[2] The emphasis here is on the different, though in varying degrees interrelated, lines of reasoning that led these thinkers to their particular theories. In the case of Descartes, the result is both infinite-finite and mind-body substance dualisms, with the latter involving a plurality of substances of both kinds.[3] In the case of Spinoza, we end up with a substance monism that eliminates both forms of Descartes's substance dualism but that retains some distinction between thought and extension, on the one hand, and between infinite substance-attribute and its infinite and finite modes, on the other. In the case of Leibniz, there is an evolution toward a substance pluralism that distinguishes simple soul-like substances and their modes both from God and from the bodily phenomena that result from these substances and modes. In the course of our discussion of these accounts, we discover various uses of the two Aristotelian conceptions of substance as ultimate subject and as ultimate essential cause.

I close with a consideration of the more skeptical theory of substance offered toward the end of the seventeenth century in the work of John Locke (1632–1704). This theory – which is anticipated somewhat in Pierre Gassendi's critique of Descartes – emerges from Locke's account of our complex ideas of "pure substance in general" and of particular sorts of substances, an account that is informed by a critique of both Scholastic and early modern conceptions of substance.

1. Suárez

In his *Metaphysical Disputations* (1597), Suárez considers the question – which cannot be found in Aristotle – of whether being (*ens*) can be divided into infinite and finite (*DM* 28).[4] His answer is that being can be so divided, because we must distinguish between something that has being from itself (*ens a se*) and something that has being from another (*ens ab alio*). God, as something that has being from itself, is infinite, uncreated, necessary, and purely active, whereas creatures, as things that have being from another, are finite, created, contingent, and include passivity (*DM* 28.1.3–17). Though John Duns Scotus had earlier argued that the term *ens* applies univocally, or in the same sense, to God and creatures, officially, at least, Suárez subscribes to the more traditional position in Thomas Aquinas that this term applies only analogically, with God possessing being absolutely and essentially, and creatures possessing it only secondarily and "by participation" (*DM* 28.3.6).[5]

As it is with being, so it is with substance. Both God and created substances are substantial in the sense that they exist "in themselves and through themselves" (*in se ac per se*), in distinction from accidents, which exist in and through others (*DM* 33.1.1). However, God, as uncreated substance, is "through himself substantially and essentially subsisting," whereas created substances are "not essentially the act of subsisting, but by aptitude [*aptitudine*]" (*DM* 32.1.7). Thus, the term 'substance' applies primarily to uncreated substance, which essentially subsists substantially, and only by analogy to created substances, which merely have an aptitude so to subsist.

Suárez holds further that created substances have a kind of complexity that serves to distinguish them from uncreated substance. Most basically, created substances are complex by virtue of the fact that they can receive, and thus be the ultimate subject of, accidents. This sort of complexity is ruled out in the case of uncreated substance not only by the fact that it is purely active, and thus cannot have a passive receptivity to change, but also by the fact that it is perfectly simple, and so cannot be the subject of accidents distinct in nature from it. Interestingly, then, the Aristotelian criterion of being the ultimate subject of accidents cannot apply to what for Suárez is primarily a substance, namely God as uncreated substance.

Suárez holds that there is an additional complexity in the case of material substances. His account of this sort of complexity is informed by his theory of distinctions. According to this theory, there are three sorts of distinctions, typically connected to the separability of the items being distinguished. The first is a 'real distinction' (*distinctio realis*) between (created) things (*res*) that in many cases can exist apart from each other.[6] The second is a "modal distinction" (*distinctio modalis*) between a thing and a "mode" (*modus*) of it that cannot exist apart from that thing, though the thing can exist apart from it. Finally, there is a "distinction of reason" (*distinctio rationis*) between the same thing conceived in two different ways, in which case there is no possibility of separate existence. Thus, the real distinction usually requires the mutual separability of distinct *res*,[7] the modal distinction always requires a one-way separability of a *res* from its *modus*, and the distinction of reason always requires the inseparability of a *res* under different descriptions.[8]

On Suárez's version of an Aristotelian hylomorphic account of material substance, each such substance is composed of prime matter, the passive recipient of the generation of a composite substance, and substantial form, the active principle of this generation. This account in effect combines the two Aristotelian criteria for substantiality, with prime matter playing the role of the ultimate subject and substantial form the role of the active cause that gives the individual the distinctive sort of being that it has. Suárez invokes his theory of distinctions in claiming that prime matter and substantial form are really distinct *res* that unite to form a further *res* that is itself an essential unity (*unum per se*), namely the composite material substance.

In holding that prime matter is a *res* that can exist, at least miraculously, apart from substantial form, Suárez departs from the view of Thomas and his more orthodox followers, according to which prime matter depends essentially on substantial form for its being, and so cannot exist by itself, even miraculously. In contrast, Suárez insists that because prime matter is a *res* with its own essence, there is reason to conclude that it also is something that can exist apart from any other created *res*, including substantial form.

Suárez also posits various accidents of material substance, such as the qualities of sound, taste, and color, which he takes to be *res* that are distinct from substantial form, prime matter, and the form-matter composite, and that can exist apart from them, even though they naturally inhere in material substances.[9] In addition to substances and their really distinct accidents, Suárez posits "modes" of the substances and accidents that cannot exist, even miraculously, apart from what they modify. For instance, a shape that modifies the accident of quantity is a mode of this accident rather than a *res* distinct from it and thus is something not even God can cause to exist apart from quantity.[10] In material substance, then, there is the initial composition of the substance through the union of the really distinct constituents of substantial form and prime matter, which union is a mode of the composite substance. Then there is the inherence of accidents really distinct from the material substance in that substance, and the presence in the accidents of various modes, such as the mode of inherence itself, that cannot exist apart from these accidents, though the accidents can exist apart from them.

Perhaps the most controversial aspect of Suárez's theory of substance in the context of the early modern critique of Scholasticism is his appeal to substantial forms in the explanation of the composition of material substance.[11] Thus, in his *Origin of Forms and*

Qualities, Robert Boyle judges the notion of substantial forms to be "incomprehensible" and the positing of such forms to depend on arguments that are "rather metaphysical or logical, than grounded upon the principles and phenomena of nature, and respect words rather than things" (*OFQ*; Boyle 1979, 57–8). And across the Channel, we find Descartes claiming in correspondence several decades earlier that when the Scholastics "say that some action proceeds from a substantial form, it is the same as if they were to say that it proceeds from something they do not understand, which explains nothing" (AT III 506; CSMK 208–9).[12] We will discover that Leibniz nonetheless attempted to revive a modified version of the doctrine of substantial forms. Moreover, the view in Suárez of the basic metaphysical distinctions between uncreated and created substance, on the one hand, and created substance and its modes, on the other, provides an essential frame of reference for the alternative theories of substance in the early modern period, and in particular the theory we find in Descartes.

2. Descartes

The relevance of Suárez's theory of substance to Descartes's theory is evident from the claim in article 51 of the first part of Descartes's *Principles of Philosophy* (1644) that the term 'substance' does not apply "univocally" (*univoce*) to God and creatures (AT VIIIA 24; CSM I 210).[13] The reasoning here depends on the stipulation that a substance is "a thing [*res*] that so exists that it depends on no other thing to exist" (AT VIIIA 24; CSM I 210). Though God depends only on himself for his existence, and thus exists *a se*, all creatures depend on God not only for their initial creation but also for their continued existence.[14] Thus, no creature can be said to be a substance in the same sense in which God is a substance.

Some commentators take Descartes's denial that the term 'substance' applies univocally to God and creatures to indicate that he thinks there is merely what the Scholastics called an "equivocal" relation, or a mere similarity in name with no underlying metaphysical similarity.[15] However, in the *Meditations* (1641), Descartes speaks in Suárezian terms of a substance as "what has the aptitude to exist by itself [*rem quae per se apta est existere*]" (AT VII 44; CSM II 30). God alone is a substance in the primary sense, because he not only exists *per se* but also uniquely derives his existence from himself, and so exists *a se*. In contrast, creatures depend on God for their existence, and so instead of existing *a se*, they have merely an aptitude to exist. Nonetheless, creaturely substances share with God the attribute of existing *per se* when they do exist. This point is reflected in the version of *Principles* I.51 in the French edition (1647), which adds to the original version the claim that those creatures that "need only the ordinary *concursus* of God"[16] can be called substances, in distinction from those creatures (which, as we will discover, Descartes identifies with modes) that in addition to the divine *concursus* require other creatures through which they exist (AT IXB 47). As in Suárez, the analogy between divine substance and created substances is supported by the fact that both exist *per se*, as opposed to existing through another, when they exist (with God existing *a se*, and creaturely substances existing by means of God's "ordinary *concursus*").[17]

With respect to created substances, Descartes famously adopts a substance dualism, according to which (1) mind as thinking substance is really distinct from body as extended substance, and (2) mind and body are the only kinds of created substances.[18] The notion of a real distinction is drawn from Suárez and relies on the claim that because thinking substance (*res cogitans*) and extended substance (*res extensa*) can exist apart from each other, they are distinct *res*.[19] For Suárez, it does not follow from the fact that two things are distinct *res* that they are distinct substances; we have seen, for instance, that he allowed that certain accidents are really distinct from the substances in which they inhere. However, Descartes rejects the whole category of "real accidents" on the grounds that something that can exist on its own, even if only by God's miraculous power, must be a substance rather than an accident.[20] He concludes that accidents must be modes of either thinking or extended substance, which, given Suárez's own conception of modes and the modal distinction, cannot exist even miraculously apart from the substance they modify.[21]

In line with his hylomorphism, Suárez takes the human soul to be the substantial form of a composite substance, the human being. Descartes also speaks of the human soul as a substantial form (e.g. in AT III 505; CSMK 208). Nevertheless, he does not accept the view in Suárez that this soul unites with matter to form a single substance.[22] Moreover, Suárez follows more orthodox Scholastics in positing the rational human soul as the source of all of the vegetative and sensory powers of the living human body.[23] In contrast, Descartes conceives of the human body as a machine with vegetative and sensory powers that can be explained mechanistically entirely in terms of the motion of its parts, without any appeal to the human soul. As he explains in correspondence, the vegetative and sensory powers of animals and humans alike are merely a species of "locomotive power." No actions can be attributed to the human soul, Descartes says, "unless they depend on reason" (AT III 371; CSMK 182). Descartes's human soul is therefore the principle of reason – or, more accurately, of thought – as opposed to features that pertain to body alone.

In the dedicatory letter to the Sorbonne appended to the *Meditations*, Descartes emphasizes his attempt to follow the dictates of the Fifth Lateran Council (1512–17) in providing rational support for the belief in personal immortality. This support depends on his claim that each person has a soul or mind that is a substance and so requires only God's "ordinary *concursus*" in order to continue to exist.[24] Descartes therefore accepts a pluralism on which there are really distinct mental substances. He simply assumes that reflection on his thought reveals that his mind is a substance distinct from other finite thinking things (an assumption, as we will discover, that Spinoza challenges). As he put the point in correspondence with Arnauld, 'thought' in his case signifies a particular "thinking nature" that "constitutes the essence" of his particular mind (AT V 221; CSMK 357).

Descartes also offers an account of material substance at odds with Suárezian hylomorphism. In place of a substantial being composed of the really distinct *res* of prime matter and substantial form, all of which are in turn really distinct from the accident of quantity, Descartes offers a *res* that differs only with a distinction of reason from its extension or quantity. There is a recurring claim in the literature that Descartes also rejects the assumption in Suárez that there is a plurality of material substances, proposing instead that bodies are modes of a single material substance.[25] Some support for this claim may seem to be provided by Descartes's statement in the Synopsis to the *Meditations* that it is only body "taken in general" (*in genere sumptum*), as opposed to particular bodily configurations, that is a substance (AT VII 14; CSM II 10). However, it is far from evident that by the talk of corporeal substance taken "in general" (*in genere*), Descartes means matter taken "as a whole" (*in globo*). Indeed, in other passages that use similar terminology, he has in mind delimited portions of spatial extension rather than spatial extension as a whole. In the *Principles*, for instance, Descartes indicates that "extension in general" consists not of the whole of extension but rather of particular parts of space conceived generically.[26] Additionally, in a 1645 letter he uses 'a body in general' (*un corps en general*) to mean not the whole of matter but rather "a determined part" (*une partie determinée*) of it (AT IV 166; CSMK 242–3).

The evidence in fact indicates that Descartes accepts a pluralistic conception of material substance that complements his pluralistic conception of thinking substance. Thus, in the *Principles* he illustrates the nature of a real distinction by noting that our idea of material substance reveals that "if it exists, each and every part of it, as delimited in us by our thought, is really distinct from the other parts of the same substance" (AT VIIIA 28–9; CSM I 213). Elsewhere Descartes notes that his rejection of indivisible atoms depends on the claim that every corporeal substance is divisible into parts that are themselves corporeal substances. In correspondence with Gibieuf, for instance, he writes that the claim that there can be parts of matter that are indivisible is contradictory because "from the simple fact that I consider the two halves of a part of matter, however small it may be, as two complete substances, . . . I conclude with certainty that they are really divisible" (AT III 477; CSMK 202–3). Here the parts of material substance are conceived not as modes of that extension but rather as really distinct substances.

Descartes's view that material parts are substances rather than modes is further reinforced by his claim in the Sixth Replies that the surface of a body "is merely a mode and hence cannot be a part of a substance. For body is a substance, and a mode cannot be a part of a substance" (AT VII 433; CSM II 292). He explains that because a surface has no depth, and thus is completely two-dimensional, it cannot be a three-dimensional part of a body but must be a mode of such a part. The clear indication, however, is that the three-dimensional parts are not themselves modes but rather are substantial parts that compose a larger bodily substance.

Descartes's account of the difference between modes and parts is informed by his claim in the Second Replies that substance is that "in which whatever we perceive immediately resides, as in a subject." He offers as an illustration the fact that "the substance that is the immediate subject of local extension and of the accidents that presuppose extension, such as shape, position, local motion, and so on, is called *body*" (AT VII 161; CSM II 114). The immediate subject of particular shapes or motions would seem to be not the whole of matter but rather delimited parts of it. If so, then by this definition these parts, as well as the whole of matter that comprises all such parts, count as substances.

To be sure, Descartes does allow that a mode can be the subject of further modes. For instance, his physics presupposes that motion can be the subject of the further modes of speed and directional determination. When a correspondent protested that the presupposition must be rejected because determination cannot be in motion "as in a subject" given that motion is itself a mode, Descartes writes that "there is no awkwardness or absurdity in saying that an accident is the subject of another accident." Yet in this same letter he cautions that when he says that "motion is to its determination as a flat body is to its top or surface," he means not that motion is like the body in being a substance, but merely that they are both "concrete things" rather than "abstractions" (see AT III 355–6; CSMK 178). There remains a difference between the two concrete entities insofar as the flat body is the ultimate three-dimensional subject of its surface, whereas motion is a subject of determination that requires a further three-dimensional subject.

At this point, there is the obvious question of whether the notion of substance that is prominent here – according to which it is the ultimate subject of modes – is consistent with the implication of his theory of distinctions that a substance can exist *per se* apart from all other created substances.[27] And here it must be admitted that such an implication is in some tension with Descartes's account of the substantial parts of matter. For it seems that the substantial parts cannot exist apart from the parts that constitute them. In the case of finite minds there is no similar problem, because different minds do not constitute a whole in the same manner in which material parts do. Rather, each finite mind is an indivisible whole considered in itself or, as Descartes says in the Sixth Meditation, something that is "single and complete on its own." In contrast, body as an extended thing is something that is divisible into parts and thus not something that can exist on its own in the same manner (AT VII 85–6; CSM II 59).[28]

In order to hold that each portion of extension is composed of really distinct parts, then, Descartes must employ a concept of the real distinction that, in contrast to the concept that applies to the case of created minds, does not require the possibility of existence apart from all other substances of the same type. But this difference in the understanding of the real distinction carries with it a difference in the concepts of substance that apply to minds and bodies. Though we have seen Descartes's admission in the *Principles* that the term 'substance' does not apply univocally to God and creatures, he claims in this same text that this term "applies univocally to mind and body" because both "need only the *concursus* of God to exist" (AT VIIIA 24–5; CSM I 110). Descartes can allow that the substantial parts of spatial extension share with finite minds the property of depending only on God's concurrence for existence, and thus of being naturally incorruptible.[29] However, it seems that he ultimately is committed to some fundamental difference between the kinds of substantiality involved in the two cases given his view of the essential difference between mind and body. Whereas the mind is indivisible, and so single and complete on its own, body is by its nature divisible into distinct parts, and so cannot exist on its own apart from those parts. In order to accommodate this difference, Descartes needs to admit that the substantiality of bodily parts, unlike the substantiality of minds, does not require the possibility of existence apart from any other created substance. It turns out, then, that the term 'substance' cannot apply univocally to mind and body given the idiosyncratic nature of the spatial extension he posits.

To my knowledge, Descartes never confronted the difficulties that derive from the application of the notion of a real distinction that he borrowed from Suárez to the case of the parts of material substance. However, we will discover that this is a problem that Spinoza confronts – indeed, exploits – in defending his theory of substance.

3. Spinoza

Toward the start of his *Ethics* (1677), Spinoza stipulates that substance is "what is in itself and conceived through itself [*in se est et per se concipitur*]: that is that the concept of which does not require the concept of another thing from which it must be formed" (*E* 1d3; Geb II 45; C 408).[30] This may seem to be similar to Suárez's claim that substance exists *in se* and *per se* and Descartes's claim that a substance is at least apt to exist *per se*. However, these similarities are deceptive, because Spinoza has a distinctive understanding of existence *in se* and conception *per se*. For instance, his understanding of what it means for something to be conceived *per se* is informed by his axiom that "the cognition of the effect depends on the cognition of the cause, and involves the same" (*effectus cognitio a cognitione causae dependet, et eandem involvit*) (*E* 1a4; Geb II 46; C 410). Given this axiom, something that is conceived *per se* cannot be produced by something other than itself, because in that case it would have to be conceived through another. Thus, Spinoza concludes, as Suárez and Descartes would not, that anything that is conceived *per se* must have existence from itself and so exist *a se*.[31] Moreover, because for Spinoza only that which can be conceived *per se* can be said to exist *in se*, anything that exists *in se* as a substance, as opposed to existing in another as a mode of substance, must also exist *a se*.

A central conclusion of the first part of the *Ethics*, "On God," is that "whatever is, is in God, and nothing can be conceived without God" (*E* 1p15; Geb II 56; C 420). This conclusion is said to follow from the fact that "except God, no substance can be or be conceived" (*E* 1p14; Geb II 56; C 420), from the definition of a substance as "what is in itself and conceived through itself" (*E* 1d3; Geb II 45; C 408), and from the definition of modes as "the affections of substance, or that which is in another through which it is also conceived" (*E* 1d5; Geb II 45; C 409). Thus, according to Spinoza, whatever is not identical to God considered as the one substance must be a mode of God.

What would be objectionable to the Cartesian substance pluralist, of course, is the claim that no substance can be conceived except God. Spinoza's demonstration of this claim (*E* 1p14d; Geb II 56; C 420) depends on his version of the ontological argument for the existence of God (*E* 1p11d; Geb II 52–3; C 417–9), his stipulation that God is a being that consists of "an infinity of attributes" (*E* 1d6; Geb II 45; C 409), and his result that different substances cannot have the same attribute (*E* 1p5; Geb II 48; C 411). Because God has all of the attributes, and substances cannot share attributes, there can be no substance other than God.

However, an initial difficulty for this sort of substance monism may seem to be the fact that Spinoza accepts Descartes's view that thought and extension are conceptually irreducible attributes. Indeed, in commenting on an early draft of the *Ethics*, a member of Spinoza's Amsterdam circle, Simon de Vries objects, "If I should say that each substance has only one attribute, and if I had the idea of two attributes, I could rightly conclude that, where there are two different attributes, there are two different substances" (Ep 8; Geb IV 41). This objection is in line with Descartes's own view that it follows from the fact that thought and extension can be conceived completely on their own apart from each other that a thinking thing and an extended thing are really distinct substances.[32]

In response to De Vries, Spinoza claims that "the more attributes I attribute to a being the more I am compelled to attribute existence to it" (Ep 9; Geb IV 45). Though initially it may not seem to be entirely clear how this claim addresses the Cartesian objection that a substance can have only one principal attribute, Spinoza's point is ultimately that we must be able to conceive a substance with more than one attribute because we can conceive of a substance that necessarily has all attributes within itself. In fact, Spinoza takes God to be precisely such a substance, defining him as "a being absolutely infinite, that is, a substance consisting of an infinity of attributes, of which each one expresses eternal and infinite essence" (*E* 1d6; Geb II 45; C 409). Because God is "absolutely infinite," whatever "expresses essence and involves no negation" must also be an attribute of God (*E* 1d6ex; Geb II 46; C 409). But thought and extension, as "infinite in their own kind," do not involve negation and thus are equally attributes of God as substance.

In his letter, however, De Vries cites a passage from the draft of the *Ethics* that suggests a somewhat different – and, in a sense, more direct – response to his objection. In this passage, the claim is that attributes that are "really distinct" (*realiter distincta*) in the sense that they are conceived separately still do not "constitute two things [*entia*] or two diverse substances" insofar as they "are found together in" one and the same substance (Geb IV 41). Here the argument is not that we can conceive a substance that has the most reality, and thus all the attributes, but rather that attributes cannot exist apart from each other. The passage as expanded in the published version of the *Ethics* offers the intriguing argument that the fact that each of the attributes can be completely conceived apart from other attributes shows that each of the attributes exists necessarily and so must exist together with all of the other attributes (see *E* 1p10s). In essence, Spinoza is rejecting the assumption, essential for Descartes's argument for mind-body distinctness, that a real distinction between entities requires that such entities can exist apart.

There has been a vigorous debate in the literature between a "subjective interpretation" of the distinction between Spinoza's attributes, on which such attributes are only "subjectively" or "ideally" distinct, and an "objective interpretation" of the distinction, on which the attributes are distinct in reality, and thus objectively.[33] On the side of the subjective interpretation is the fact that Spinoza defines attribute as "what intellect perceives of substance, as constituting its essence" (*E* 1d4; Geb II 45; C 408), rather than simply as that which constitutes the essence of substance. Yet on the side of the objective interpretation is the fact that Spinoza takes as axiomatic that "a true idea must agree with its object" (*E* 1a6; Geb II 45; C 410), as well as the fact that he holds that we have a true and adequate idea of God's essence, including the attributes that express this essence (see *E* 2p46; Geb II 127–8; C 482).[34]

One way to start to settle this issue is by remembering that, in Suárezian terms, Spinoza's real distinction between attributes amounts to a distinction of reason between different aspects of one and the same thing. Because the distinction here is merely a conceptual one, there is a need for the reference in the definition of attribute to "what the intellect perceives of substance."[35] However, this sort of distinction is not merely an artifact of our or any other mind; ultimate reality is such that it can be conceived in infinitely many self-contained ways, among which our mind can conceive only the two ways reflected in the attributes of thought and extension.[36]

The claim that God has the attribute of thought is, in the context of seventeenth century thought, relatively uncontroversial. In his 1663 summary of portions of Descartes's *Principles* – the only text he published under his own name during his lifetime – Spinoza presents the argument that because God has all perfections, he must have the perfection of understanding in the highest degree, which perfection presupposes thought (*DPP* 1p9d; Geb I 167–8; C 253–4). However, in this same text he draws on Descartes's own view that extension cannot be an attribute of God insofar as extension has the imperfection of divisibility into parts, an imperfection that cannot pertain to God as a supremely perfect being (*DPP* 1p16d; Geb I 176–7; C 260).[37] Spinoza does add that "all the perfections of extension are not to be denied" God, and that "extension is to be rejected only insofar as its nature and properties involve some imperfection" (*DPP* 1p9s; Geb I 168; C 254). However, when speaking on behalf of Descartes – which is what he is doing in this text – Spinoza is reluctant to claim that extension is an attribute of God.

There is no such reluctance in the *Ethics*, where Spinoza is speaking on his own behalf. He clearly recognizes that the conclusion that God is extended substance is controversial from a more orthodox Cartesian perspective and indeed addresses the main Cartesian objection that because corporeal substance can be divided into parts, it cannot be identified with God as absolutely infinite being (*E* 1p15s; Geb II 57–8; C 421–2). Spinoza's response to this objection draws directly on the Cartesian argument against the vacuum that he had earlier presented in his summary of the *Principles* (see

DPP 2p3d; Geb I 188; C 268). His claim in the *Ethics* is that those "who deny that there is a vacuum" – in particular, the Cartesians – must deny that corporeal substance can be divided into really distinct parts, because if this substance could be so divided, "why could one of the parts not be annihilated, the rest remaining, connected among themselves as before? And why must they all be so fitted together, so that there is no vacuum?" Because there can be no vacuum, it follows that the parts of matter "cannot be really distinguished, that is, that corporeal substance, insofar as it is substance, cannot be divided" (*E* 1p15s; Geb II 59; C 423).[38]

This profound argument is not working with the sort of "real distinction" that Spinoza invokes with respect to the attributes.[39] Rather, the real distinction is the Cartesian version of the Suárezian one, according to which "of things that are really distinct, one can be, and remain in its state, without the other" (Geb II 59; C 423). And this sort of real distinction is ruled out in the case of material parts by the fact that all the parts of matter must exist together, without any gap that would create a vacuum.

In this portion of the *Ethics*, Spinoza admits that we can conceive the divisibility of a certain body, such as water, but only "insofar as it is water, but not insofar as it is corporeal substance" (Geb II 59; C 423). In particular, his view is that bodies are divisible into parts only insofar as they are modes of substance, and that "the whole of nature" can be conceived as "one Individual, whose parts, that is, all bodies, vary in infinite ways, without any change of the whole Individual" (*E* 1p13s, lem7s; Geb II 102). Whereas Descartes denies that parts are modes, Spinoza in effect argues that the inability of parts to exist on their own reveals, on Descartes's own Suárezian account of the real distinction, that these parts are modes rather than substances in their own right.

The "infinite individual" that Spinoza identifies with "the whole of nature" might seem to be the one ultimate subject of the predicates attributed to its parts and so count as substance according to the Aristotelian criterion of substantiality in the *Categories*. Indeed, one commentator has suggested that Spinoza identified the infinite individual with "God or nature" considered as substance.[40] However, Spinoza himself indicates otherwise. Thus, when his correspondent Walther von Tschirnhaus asked for examples of the immediate and mediate infinite modes mentioned in the *Ethics* (Ep. 63; Geb IV 276),[41] Spinoza offers for the immediate infinite mode of extension "motion and rest," and for the mediate infinite mode the "face of the whole Universe" (*facies totius Universi*), as described in the section of the *Ethics* that concerns the infinite individual (Ep. 44; Geb IV 278).[42]

Of course, Spinoza holds that God as extended substance is the subject of the infinite individual that modifies that substance. However, the conception of substance as ultimate subject of predication does not capture the full sense of the manner in which this mode is in that substance. In particular, it does not capture Spinoza's emphasis in the *Ethics* on the identification of God's substance with "the power by which he and all things are and act," a power that is "his essence itself" (*E* 1p34d; Geb II 77; C 439). In terms of this emphasis, the claim that all things other than God exist in the divine substance as modes requires that all such things derive from, and thus must be conceived in terms of,[43] God's power.

The causal aspect of substance is prominent in a critique of Descartes's conception of material substance that Spinoza offered toward the end of his life in correspondence with Tschirnhaus. Tschirnhaus opens the exchange by asking how Spinoza can claim to demonstrate *a priori* the existence of bodies with particular shapes and motions given that "there is nothing of this kind to be found in Extension, taken in the absolute sense"

(Ep 80; Geb IV 331).[44] Spinoza initially responds that it is in fact impossible to provide the demonstration from "Extension as Descartes conceives it," which reveals that "the Cartesian principles of natural things are useless, not to say absurd" (Ep 81; Geb IV 332). When Tschirnhaus then insists that bodies derive not from "inert matter" but in an inconceivable manner from "God as mover" (Ep 82; Geb IV 334), Spinoza repeats that "Descartes badly defined matter through Extension" and claims that it must be defined instead "through an attribute that expresses eternal and infinite essence" (Ep 63; Geb IV 354).[45] In the words of one commentator, Spinoza is offering, in place of Descartes's appeal to inert extension, an "ontology of power" (*ontologie de la puissance*) that takes material substance to be the ultimate internal causal source of all effects in material world.[46]

Spinoza's discussion of material substance thus reveals two essential aspects of substance that he takes Descartes to overlook: (1) this substance must be absolutely indivisible and unified, and therefore not be divisible into distinct parts, and (2) it must be a self-contained cause of all of its modes. Both aspects turn out to play a central role in Leibniz's theory of substance.

4. Leibniz

Leibniz's views on substance – and indeed, his philosophical views generally – are difficult to summarize not only because he never produced a systematic work akin to Suárez's *Metaphysical Disputations*, Descartes's *Principles of Philosophy*, or Spinoza's *Ethics* but also because, as scholars are well aware, there was considerable development in his thought over the course of his intellectual career.[47] However, a good place to start for an introduction to his theory of substance is with his *Discourse on Metaphysics* (1686), composed during his so-called middle period. In this text, the nature of an "individual substance" is defined as that which has "a notion so complete that it is sufficient to contain and to allow us to deduce from it all the predicates of the subject to which it is attributed" (*Discourse* §8; G IV 433; AG 41).[48] Thus substance is not only an ultimate subject of predicates, as Aristotle had insisted in the *Categories*, but also something the concept of which "contains" all of the predicates attributed to it. This stronger condition of substantiality is reminiscent of Spinoza's claim that all modes must be "conceived through" the substance they modify. And indeed, in Leibniz, as well as in Spinoza, there is a version of the position that substance is causally, as well as conceptually, self-contained. In the *Discourse on Metaphysics*, Leibniz defends a "complete concept theory," according to which for each individual substance there is a complete concept that contains all of the predicates that can be attributed to that substance (*Discourse* §8; G IV 433; AG 41). One of the "paradoxes" that is said to follow from the complete concept theory is that each substance is "a complete world" that is "perfectly spontaneous" in the sense that "everything that happens to it is a consequence of its idea" (*Discourse* §§9, 33; G IV 434, 458; AG 42, 64). In a way, Leibniz can be seen as offering an account of individual substance on which it is a kind of mini-Spinozistic substance, something that is causally independent of any other being (with the notable – and, for Spinoza, problematic – exception of God).[49]

We have seen in Spinoza's remarks on the vacuum in the *Ethics* an emphasis on the indivisible unity of substance. So also, Leibniz claims in the *Discourse* that "substance is not divisible into two" and that "one substance cannot be constructed from two" (*Discourse* §9; G IV 433–4; AG 42). Nevertheless, whereas Spinoza defended the indivisibility of extended substance by arguing implicitly against Descartes's position that substantial extension is divisible into really distinct parts, Leibniz argues against the Cartesians that the divisibility of extension precludes it from constituting the nature of a substance. In the *Discourse*, this point is expressed somewhat obliquely in terms of the claim that notions involving extension such as those "of size, shape, and motion are not as distinct as is imagined and that they contain something imaginary and relative to our perception" (*Discourse* §12; G IV 436; AG 44). However, the point that extension does not provide a sufficient basis for substantiality is somewhat clearer in an exchange concerning the *Discourse* that Leibniz had with Antoine Arnauld. The relevant exchange starts with Arnauld's objection that one cannot conclude that "extension is not the essence of matter, because it would have no true unity if it had extension as an essence, since it may be of the essence of matter not to have a true unity" (G II 87; LA 108).[50] In response, Leibniz initially insists that "one will never find any fixed principle for making a genuine substance from many entities by aggregation" (G II 101; LA 127). He then explains in a later letter that "many entities do not exist where there is not a single one that is genuinely an entity" because "every multiplicity presupposes unity" (G II 118; LA 151). Insofar as there is no true unity underlying infinitely divisible extension, then, there cannot be anything substantial in extension.

Whereas the insistence on the unity of substance can be found in Spinoza, what cannot be found in his writings – and indeed distinguishes Leibniz from most of the partisans of the new "mechanical philosophy" – is the claim in the *Discourse* that reflection on the nature of substance reveals that those who have "introduced and maintained the substantial forms that are so decried today . . . are not so ridiculous as the common lot of our new philosophers imagines." Leibniz grants that these forms "must not be used to explain particular phenomena." In physics, such phenomena are to be explained rather in terms of "geometric and mechanical demonstrations" (*Discourse* §10; G IV 434–5; AG 42–3). However, in the realm of metaphysics, the fact that extension cannot provide a basis for the substantiality of body shows that "we must necessarily recognize in body something related to souls, something we commonly call substantial form" (*Discourse* §11; G IV 435; AG 44).

In both the *Discourse* and his correspondence with Arnauld, Leibniz sometimes gives the impression that he takes souls or substantial forms to join with matter to form "quasi-Aristotelian" corporeal substances.[51] This is especially so in the case of the human being, which Leibniz claims to be an *unum per se* formed by the union of the human soul with a human body.[52] The theological motivations for this position are clear, given the declaration of the Fifth Lateran Council that the human soul is the substantial form of a unified human being.[53] However, in the *Discourse* the union of the human soul and its body is said to involve only the agreement (later called the "preestablished harmony") of the perceptions of the soul with what occurs in its body (*Discourse* §33; G IV 458–9; AG 64), and as we will see, doubts were later raised that this sort of union provides a sufficient basis for the substantiality of the human being. Moreover, there are intimations even in the *Discourse* of the more idealistic view of bodies that emerges in Leibniz's later writings. We have seen the claim in this text that notions involving extension "contain something imaginary." But when he attempts later to find something passive in substance, he does not follow Scholastics such as Suárez in appealing to the matter that unites to substantial form to constitute the corporeal substance. Rather, he invokes particular features that seem to be internal to the soul or substantial form, such as the decrease in the clarity of the manner in which it perceives the universe (*Discourse* §15; G IV 410–11; AG 48).[54]

In fact, there is some reason to think that at the time of the *Discourse*, Leibniz had not clearly distinguished the claim that a substance must *have* a principle of unity from the claim that a substance must *be* a principle of unity.[55] However, in his later writings he for the most part comes down on the side of the latter claim.[56] Thus in his *New System of the Nature and Communication of Substances, and of the Union of Soul and Body* (1695), Leibniz states unequivocally that "only metaphysical points or points of substance (constituted by forms or souls) are exact and real" (G IV 483; AG 142). Perhaps the clearest expression of his mature position is in his correspondence with the Cartesian Burcher de Volder, in which he claims that "there is nothing in things except simple substances, and in them perception and appetite" (G II 270; AG 181). In his *Monadology* (1714), these simple substances are called "monads"; are said to be devoid of parts, and thus of any extension, shape, or divisibility (M §§1, 3; G VI 598–9; AG 213); and are said to have both perceptions, which may or may not be conscious, and "appetitions," which bring about the change from one perception to another (M §§14–15; G VI 604–5; AG 214–15).

Another, though somewhat less substantive, shift in Leibniz's later thought is reflected in the fact that the complete concept theory, which was so central to the analysis of substance in the *Discourse*, disappears from his post-1690 writings. This theory is replaced by the notion of force, which was prominent in Leibniz's work in physics during the 1690s. In a 1694 essay, *On the Improvement of First Philosophy and on the Notion of Substance*, he claims that "the concept of forces or powers, which the Germans call *Kraft* and the French *la force*, and for whose explanation I have set up a distinct science of *dynamics*, brings the strongest light to bear on our understanding of the true concept of substance" (G IV 469). Likewise, in his *New System*, Leibniz asserts that the nature of substantial forms "consists in force" and that they are in fact "*primitive forces*, which contain not only *act* or the completion of possibility, but also an original *activity*" (G IV 478; AG 139). He further holds that God gave each created substance

> from the beginning, a nature or an internal force that can produce in it, in an orderly way (as would happen in a spiritual or formal automaton [. . .]), everything that will happen to it, that is, all the appearances or expressions it will have, without the help of any created being.
>
> (G IV 484; AG 144)

Despite differences in terminology, there is a reaffirmation here of the view in the *Discourse* that each created substance is as if it were a "complete world" unto itself.

In his mature thought, Leibniz holds that primitive forces pertaining to monads provide the foundation for the various derivative forces that, in his polemic against the Cartesians, he takes to be required for physics.[57] Likewise, the bodies that the physicist studies are themselves held to be "well founded phenomena" that "result from" monads and their perceptual states. However, the sort of "phenomenalist" account of bodies that Leibniz offers must be distinguished from the phenomenalism of George Berkeley, who argued that there are no material substances and that bodies are mere constructs from the coordinated perceptions of immaterial spirits.[58] Indeed, Leibniz distinguishes his position from Berkeley's in a brief comment on the latter's *Treatise of the Principles of*

Human Knowledge (1710). Leibniz begins by noting that "there is much that is correct and close to my view," a reflection of his rejection of any perceiver-independent extension. However, he also cautions that

> we have no need to say that matter is nothing; but it suffices to say that it is a phenomenon like the rainbow; and that it is not a substance, but a result of substances; . . . True substances are monads, that is perceivers. But the author should have gone further, to the infinity of monads, constituting everything, and to their preestablished harmony.
> (Leibniz 1849–55 II 184–5; AG 307)

For Leibniz, bodies are not merely coordinated perceptions but are aggregates of monads that are represented as composing a single body that is itself composed of other bodies, to infinity.[59]

We have seen that in the *Discourse*, Leibniz appealed to the harmony of perceptions in order to explain how the soul unites with a body to form a single *unum per se* (*Discourse* §34; G IV 459; AG 65). In the remarks on Berkeley, however, the suggestion is that the preestablished harmony explains how aggregates of monads can be taken to form a body, now conceived to be a phenomenon grounded in an aggregate of monads as opposed to an *unum per se*. This shift is significant in light of the criticism of the theory of preestablished harmony, as explicated in the *New System*, that the Jesuit Father René-Joseph de Tournemine offers in a 1703 article. For there Tournemine objects that Leibniz's invocation of the harmony between the operations of the soul and body fails to do better than the views of the Cartesians in explaining how these two can form a single human being. In response, Leibniz concedes that he can do no better than the Cartesians in showing how the soul and body form "a true union" and indeed forswears any attempt to provide an account of a "metaphysical union" that goes beyond what is revealed by the phenomena (G VI 595; AG 196–7). Though he seems to leave open the possibility of this sort of metaphysical union, his claim that "no one has given an intelligible notion of it," and thus that he "did not take it upon myself to seek a reason for it," seems to indicate that he sees no reason to take it seriously.[60]

However, the issue of the substantial unity of the soul-body composite did not disappear. In a ten-year correspondence with the Jesuit Bartholomew Des Bosses that lasted until the end of his life (1706–16), Leibniz introduces the possibility of a "substantial bond" (*vinculum substantiale*) that serves to join different monads into an *unum per se*.[61] He appeals to this possibility primarily to address concerns about the compatibility of his monadological system with the Catholic doctrine of the Eucharist.[62] But though these remarks seem to offer a more positive account of the metaphysical union than one finds in his response to Tournemine, Leibniz clearly is not comfortable with this addition to his metaphysical system. Indeed, he tells Des Bosses at one point that "I consider the explanation of all phenomena solely through the perceptions of monads functioning in harmony with each other, with corporeal substances rejected, to be useful for a fundamental investigation of things" (G II 450). Admittedly, one can also find more positive comments concerning the substantial bond from the Des Bosses correspondence.[63] However, the overall impression is that in the end Leibniz was most comfortable with a material world that ultimately consists only of monads and their states (perception and appetition), everything else being phenomena resulting from these.

5. Locke

To this point we have focused on the main positive accounts of substance in the early modern period that their authors proposed as replacements for the Aristotelian accounts in the work of the Scholastics. However, during this period there was also a more negative attack on the Scholastic presumption, found also in some early modern critics of Scholasticism, to have uncovered a concept of substance that reveals deep features of extraconceptual reality. We find particularly in Locke's *Essay Concerning Human Understanding* (1st ed., 1689) an emphasis on the fact that the experiential material from which we construct our various ideas of substance reveals little about the nature of substance itself. But even before Locke, there were other early modern thinkers who stressed that experience provides only very limited access to substances.

For instance, Pierre Gassendi offered an important critique of Descartes's thesis in the Second Meditation that the nature of mind is better known than that of body. In his Fifth Set of Objections to the *Meditations*, Gassendi protests that Descartes cannot claim to understand the nature of his mind simply by listing the various kinds of thoughts revealed by introspection. Rather, "what we are unclear about, what we are looking for, is that inner substance of yours whose property is to think." Just as knowledge of the nature of a particular body requires an investigation of its inner structure, and not simply a listing of its observable properties, so too in order to know his mind, Gassendi tells Descartes, "you should carefully scrutinize yourself and conduct a kind of chemical investigation of yourself, if you are to succeed in uncovering and explaining to us your internal substance" (AT VII 276–7; CSM II 92–3).

Gassendi's suggestion in this passage is that we know less about the nature of mind than we do about body, "the nature of which we know so much about through anatomy, chemistry, so many other sciences, so many senses and so many experiments" (AT VII 277; CSM II 193).[64] However, he offers an objection to the discussion in the Second Meditation of the example of the piece of wax that seems to cast doubt equally on our knowledge of mental and bodily substances. This objection is directed to Descartes's claim that we can better understand the nature of the wax once we strip away its accidents. Gassendi responds that though this kind of abstraction allows us to conceive "that there is something that is the subject of the accidents and changes we observe," still "what this subject is, or what its nature is, we do not know" (AT VII 271; CSM II 189). In the cases of both body and mind, experience does not reveal the underlying subject of the accidents we perceive.

It is this second objection that is prominent in Locke's discussion in the chapter of the *Essay* devoted to our ideas of substances. There he claims that our notions of the substance of body and spirit are equally obscure, because the one is "supposed to be (without knowing what it is) the *Substratum* to those simple *Ideas* we have from without," whereas the other is "supposed (with a like ignorance of what it is) to be the *Substratum* to those Operations, which we experiment in our selves within" (*Essay* 2.23.5, 297–8).[65] Just as we do not know what it is that thinks in us, so too we do not know "how the solid parts of Body are united, or cohere together to make Extension" (*Essay* 2.23.23, 308).

This skepticism concerning our knowledge of spiritual and body substance is informed by Locke's view that an individual who examines his idea of "*pure substance in general*" will discover that it is nothing more than "a Supposition of he knows not what support of such Qualities, which are capable of producing simple *Ideas* in us; which Qualities are commonly called Accidents" (*Essay* 2.23.2, 295). In a later correspondence with the Bishop of Worcester, Edward Stillingfleet, Locke explains that we form our complex idea of substance from "the general *Idea* of something, or being, with the Relation of a Support of Accidents" (*W* IV 19).[66] Locke further insists, in response to Stillingfleet's charge that he is deviating from a traditional understanding of substance, that he is simply following "the Authority of the Schools" in allying the idea of substance with the logical notion of a substratum that supports the qualities that inhere in it (*W* IV 23–4).

It is clear, however, that in holding up the Scholastic conception of substance, Locke means to expose its limitations. Thus, in the *Essay* he emphasizes that in the case of substance, "we have no *Idea* of what it is, but only a confused obscure one of what it does" (*Essay* 2.13.19, 175). Here we must keep in mind Locke's project of working as an "Under-Labourer" for the new corpuscularian science, found in the work of "Master-Builders" such as Boyle and Newton, by "clearing the ground a little, and removing some of the Rubbish, that lies in the way to Knowledge" (*Essay*, Epistle to Reader, 9–10). Among the rubbish is a Scholastic understanding on which substance requires a 'substantial form' that unites with matter. For Locke, we can clear away this understanding once we realize that the only intelligible content to our idea of substance is that of an unknown support of qualities. Such an idea is simply too thin to provide any barrier to corpuscularian explanations of bodies in terms of the sizes, shapes, solidity, and motion or rest of their insensible parts.

In the *New Essays Concerning Human Understanding* (1704; pub. 1765), his commentary on Locke's *Essay*, Leibniz objects that Locke's idea of substance is also too thin to be intelligible. Through the character Theophilus, he protests that to require that substance be only a "pure subject in general," abstracted from all other attributes, "is to demand the impossible" (*NE* 2.23.2). The suggestion here is that Locke equates substance with what has come to be called a "bare particular," an entity that has no qualities beyond bare subsistence.[67] However, this objection confuses epistemological and ontological issues. In saying that we do not know substance to be anything but a substratum that supports accidents, Locke is not committing himself to the view that there is nothing more to substance, as it exists external to mind, than being a substratum that supports accidents.[68]

In addition to our idea of pure substance in general, Locke holds that we have complex ideas of "particular sorts of substances" that are constructed by

> collecting such Combinations of simple *Ideas*, as are by Experience and Observation of Men's Senses taken notice of to exist together, and are therefore supposed to flow from the particular internal Constitution, or unknown Essence of that Substance.
>
> (*Essay* 2.23.3, 296)

In a later chapter on "the names of substances," Locke identifies this "unknown essence" as the "real essence," which he contrasts with the "nominal essence," defined as "*the abstract* Idea *to which the Name is annexed*" (*Essay* 3.6.2, 439). In this chapter, Locke is concerned to argue against the view that "the several Species of Substances had their distinct internal *substantial Forms*; and that it was those *Forms*, which made the distinction of Substances into their true *Species* and *Genera*" (*Essay* 3.6.10, 445). One line of argument against this position is that we do not have access to the real essence, or internal constitution, and so must classify substances according to their observable properties instead. Thus, he insists that in fact "our *distinguishing Substances into Species* by Names, *is not at all founded on their real Essences*; nor can we pretend to range, and determine them exactly into Species, according to internal essential differences" (*Essay* 3.6.20, 449).[69]

However, there is another, and in some ways more radical, argument against the view that we can distinguish substances simply by appealing to differences in their internal constitutions. This argument depends on the characterization of real essence as "that real constitution of any Thing, which is the foundation of all those Properties that are combined in, and are constantly found to co-exist with the *nominal Essence*" (*Essay* 3.6.6, 442). Thus, even if, contrary to the first line of argument, we did have access to the internal constitutions of bodies, there still would be issues about the classification of those bodies because the real essence depends not only on those constitutions but also on the observable properties included in the nominal essence. Indeed, a constitution is a real essence only by virtue of the fact that the observable properties we identify as essential to a species 'flow from' – that is depend causally upon – that constitution.

There is some question concerning Locke's understanding of the relation of real essence to substance. One finds in the literature a reading on which he holds that the notion of substance as substratum and the notion of real essence as inner constitution denote the same thing. Because the observable qualities of a substance flow from its real essence, according to this reading, the real essence can be said to be the substratum that stands under and supports those qualities.[70]

However, Locke himself seems to distinguish real essence from substance in his correspondence with Stillingfleet. Whereas Stillingfleet explicitly identifies the essence of a thing with its substance, Locke notes that on his view the essence is "in every thing that *internal Constitution*, or Frame, or Modification of the *Substance*, which God in his Wisdom and good Pleasure thinks fit to give to every particular Creature, when he gives it a Being; and such *Essences* I grant there are in all Things that exist" (*W* IV 82). The indication here is that the real essence is a modification of substance rather than the substance itself. In the case of bodies, the idea of substance picks out rather the matter that, when arranged in a particular manner, constitutes a particular internal constitution. Thus, in the chapter of the *Essay* on "identity and diversity," Locke notes that the identity of bodily substance consists in the fact that "the Mass, consisting of the same Atoms, must be the same Mass, or the same Body, let the parts be never so differently jumbled" (*Essay* 2.27.3, 330). The mass itself is the substance, whereas the inner constitution derives from the manner in which the mass is "jumbled."[71]

One further distinction between substance and real essence is relevant to the two Aristotelian criteria for substance with which we started. The qualities pertaining to the nominal essence clearly "flow from" the real essence in a causal sense. In this way, real essences would seem to satisfy the criterion of substantiality in Aristotle's *Metaphysics*, according to which substance is the essence that causes an individual to be what it is. In his discussion of the idea of "pure substance in general," however, what Locke emphasizes is that substance is that in which the qualities "subsist," where subsistence involves logical as opposed to causal dependence. Thus, the criterion of substantiality in Aristotle's *Categories*, according to which substance is the ultimate subject of predication, is most relevant to Locke's account of the idea of substance. We have seen that Spinoza and Leibniz each attempted in different ways to combine the two Aristotelian criteria, offering views on which substance is both an ultimate subject and an ultimate cause of the qualities or modes of that substance. However, it was an important task for Locke as underlaborer to detach the logical notion of substance as substratum from notions that the "Master-Builders" of the new science use in their causal explanations of the material world.[72]

Notes

1. For further discussion of Aristotle's accounts of substance in the *Categories* and *Metaphysics*, see Wedin 2000.
2. Cf. the discussion of the theories of substance in these three early modern philosophers in Woolhouse 1993.
3. But see note 25 for scholarly dissent from the claim that Descartes allowed for a plurality of extended substances.
4. *DM* will be used for Suárez 1965.
5. Cf. the claim in Marion that Suárez is committed to a univocal notion of being (Marion 1991, ch. 7). Marion's analysis is based on a subtle consideration of the purported implications of Suárez's account of the concept of being, but here I stick more closely to Suárez's actual statement of his account of the relation between being in God and creatures.
6. Rozemond has insisted, correctly, that for Suárez separability is merely sufficient for a real distinction and thus cannot constitute such a distinction (Rozemond 1998, 6). Indeed, in Disputation VII, Suárez mentions that merely existing apart from a "real union" with another can be a sign of a real distinction. Nevertheless, he also indicates as a general principle that "if things are really distinct, they can be really disjoined; and if they are really disjoined, there is no repugnance or contradiction involved in God conserving the one without the other" (*DM* 7.2.24; English translation of this Disputation, see Suárez 1947). Suárez does go on to note three exceptions to this principle. Two of these exceptions involve the special case of God, namely the real distinction of God from creatures (which involves only one-way separability) and the real distinction of the persons of the Trinity (which involves mutual inseparability; *DM* 7.2.25, 27). Suárez's third exception is a "real categorical relation" that is really distinct from its terminus even though it cannot exist without that terminus (*DM* 7.2.26). Because this sort of a relation is an accident, and because God can have no accidents, this case pertains to creatures alone. Even so, this third exception seems to prove the rule that in the case of creatures the real distinction requires separability. For in the section of his *Metaphysical Disputations* on real relations, Suárez indicates that a relation that is real and categorical (as opposed to one that is merely "of reason" or that is transcendental) is really distinct from its terminus only in the sense that the quality or substance that serves as the "absolute foundation" of the relation is really distinct from, and can exist apart from, the quality or substance that serves as the terminus of that relation (*DM* 47.9.3; for an English translation of this Disputation, see Suárez 2006). Thus, for instance, the whiteness in Socrates that serves as the absolute foundation for the relation of similarity in color to Plato is really distinct from, and can exist apart from, the whiteness in Plato that serves as the terminus of the relation. Even though this real relation cannot exist apart from its terminus, the absolute foundation of that relation, from which the relation differs only in reason (see *DM* 47.2.22), can so exist. Even in the case of real categorical relations, then, the real distinction requires separability.
7. But see note 6.
8. For further discussion of the significance of Suárez's theory of distinctions in the context of Scholastic thought, see Schmaltz 2008, 25–8.
9. Suárez needs to allow for the possibility that these qualities can subsist miraculously apart from substance in part to accommodate the Catholic doctrine of the Eucharist, according to which the qualities of the bread and wine miraculously subsist apart from the substance of these elements after consecration.
10. Suárez departs from Thomistic orthodoxy again in claiming that quantity inheres directly in prime matter rather than in the composite material substance. Thus, Suárez denies, what the Thomists assert, that the natural replacement of one material substance with another also involves the replacement of the quantity that inheres in and thus is bound to the first substance with a qualitatively indistinguishable but numerically distinct quantity that inheres in the second substance. For further discussion of the differences between the Thomists and Suárez on this point, see Des Chene 1996, 145–51.
11. For Suárez's account of substantial form and its causality, see *DM* 40. There is an English translation of this Disputation in Suárez 2000.
12. AT will be used for Descartes 1964–74; CSMK will be used for Descartes 1991. For more on the Scholastic account of substantial forms and the early modern reaction to it, see Pasnau 2004.
13. CSM will be used for Descartes 1984–85.
14. In the Third Meditation, Descartes claims that it is evident by the "light of nature" that "a work of the same force and action is needed for conserving a thing at each singular moment it endures, as the work to create it anew if it did not yet exist" (AT VII 49; CSM II 33). In the First Replies, he adds that "a cause

that possesses such great power that it can conserve something posited outside of itself must conserve itself by its own power, and so be *a se*" (AT VII 111; CSM II 80). Thus, any substance that is not *a se* must be conserved in existence by a substance that exists *a se*, that is by God.

15 See, for instance, Secada 2006, 77. In this paragraph, I offer some textual evidence that I take to provide a counterexample to Secada's claim that Descartes does not in the *Principles*, "or anywhere else, indicate that the term ['substance'] is applied analogically" (Secada 2006).

16 Following the Scholastics, Descartes holds that God's ordinary *concursus* involves God's nonmiraculous contribution to causal interactions in nature. However, whereas the Scholastics typically distinguished God's *concursus* with the *action* of creatures from his *conservatio* of the *being* of creations, there is not a clear distinction in Descartes between *concursus* and divine conservation. For further discussion of this difference between Descartes's view and the common Scholastic position, see Schmaltz 2008, esp. §3.1.3.

17 The claim that Descartes takes the term 'substance' to apply primarily to God and only secondarily to created things receives further support from his remark in correspondence:

> By 'infinite substance' I understand a substance having true and real, actually infinite and immense, perfections. This is not an accident added to the notion of substance, but the very essence of substance taken absolutely and qualified by no defects, for in relation to substance these defects are accidents while infinity or infinitude are not.
>
> (AT V 355–356; CSMK 377)

18 Point (2) has been the subject of some controversy, because there is the scholarly opinion that Descartes accepts a third kind of created substance, the mind-body union. See, for instance, Gueroult 1953, 2:147; Rodis-Lewis 1971, 1:353, 543; Hoffman 2009b, 18; Laporte 1988, 318. This view is sometimes characterized as 'trialism,' following Cottingham 1985, though Cottingham himself does not endorse the conclusion that the mind-body union constitutes a distinct kind of substance. I myself accepted a trialistic reading of Descartes at one point (see Schmaltz 1992, 288–9) but now see this reading as untenable. In particular, the view that the union constitutes a substance conflicts with the claim in the *Principles* that a (created) substance needs only the "ordinary *concursus*" of God in order to exist, because the union can be destroyed in the course of nature, to which God lends his ordinary *concursus* (see note 16). For other critiques of a trialistic reading of Descartes, see Voss 1994; Rozemond 1998, ch. 5; Secada 2000, 259–63; Kaufman 2008.

19 Descartes was initially prompted to consider the Scholastic theory of distinctions in the First Replies, where he adopts the Scotistic view of his critic Caterus that there can be a "formal" or "modal" distinction between inseparable items that is intermediate between a real distinction and mere distinction of reason (AT VII 120–121; CSM II 85–86; cf. AT VII 100; CSM II 72–73). There is a reference to Suárez's *Metaphysical Disputations* in the Fourth Replies (AT VII 235; CSM II 164), which was composed after the First Replies, and there is reason to think that Descartes's reading of this text led him to reject the Scotistic account of the modal distinction and to accept Suárez's position that a modal distinction requires one-way separability. This Suárezian position can be found in the *Principles* (PP I.62; AT VIIIA 30; CSM I 214–15), where Descartes explicitly corrects his remarks in the First Replies. For a complex account of Descartes's theory of distinctions that differs in some respects from the account I offer here, see Hoffman 2009c.

20 See Descartes's claim in the Sixth Replies that

> it is completely repugnant that there be given real accidents, since whatever is real, can exist separately from all other subjects; however whatever can so exist separately is substance, not accident.... [I]f everything that can exist naturally without a substance is substance, whatever can be by the extraordinary power of God without a subject should also be called substance.
>
> (AT VII 434–5; CSM II 293)

21 As indicated in note 9, one reason Suárez accepts the doctrine of real accidents is to accommodate the Catholic doctrine of the Eucharist. Because Descartes, as a Catholic, is bound to accept this doctrine, he needs to show how the denial of real accidents is compatible with the doctrine. For his attempt to do so, see his discussion of the Eucharist in the Fourth Replies, in a section concerning "points that may cause difficulty to theologians" that were raised by Antoine Arnauld in his set of objections to the *Meditations* (AT VII 248–56; CSM II 173–8; cf. Arnauld's remarks at AT VII 217–18; CSM II 152–3).

22 Though see the scholarly controversy on this point indicated in note 18.

23 More orthodox, that is, than Scholastics who deviated from the Thomistic line that there is only one substantial form of the human composite by claiming that there are vegetative and sensory souls of the human body that are distinct from the rational soul. In correspondence, Descartes tells Regius that his claim that human beings have a threefold soul "is a heretical thing to say" (AT III 371; CSMK 182).

24 In the Second Replies, Descartes admits that he cannot demonstrate the immortality of the soul because he cannot preclude the possibility that God annihilates the soul by means of his "absolute power" (AT VII 153–4; CSM II 108–9; cf. AT III 266; CSMK 163).

25 See, for instance, Gueroult 1953, 1:107–18; Williams 1978, 126–9; Secada 2006, 83; Lennon 2007.

26 In *PP* II.12, Descartes offers as an example of "extension considered in general" the extension successively occupied by a stone, wood, water, and air (AT VIIIA 46–7; CSM I 228), whereas in *PP* II.18, he offers as an example of "extension taken in general" the interior of a vessel conceived as having no necessary connection to any particular body the fills it (AT VIIIA 50; CSM I 230–1).

27 In comparing Descartes's view of the real distinction to Suárez's (see note 6), Rozemond seems to suggest that Descartes takes two-way separability to be a "sign" that is merely sufficient for such a distinction (Rozemond 1998, 5–6). However, she later indicates that Descartes takes separability to be necessary as well (see, e.g., Rozemond 1998, 28, where she claims that the real distinction entails separability) and is in any case more interested in the question of whether for Descartes separability *constitutes* the real distinction. But even if Descartes recognized a weaker notion of the real distinction that does not require separability, it still seems that he took a stronger notion of the real distinction to be involved in the case of the relation of finite minds to each other and to both extension as a whole and particular bodies.

28 This point is connected to Descartes's claim that mind is "more noble" than body; see, for instance, AT IV 292; CSMK 265–6.

29 We need to distinguish here between the incorruptible parts of matter and particular bodies marked out by motion. Descartes indicates in correspondence that the latter are subject to natural destruction due to division (see AT IV 166; CSMK 242–3). It is only the quantity that constitutes such bodies that remains after such division.

30 Geb will be used for Spinoza 1925, and C for Spinoza 1985.

31 See *E* 1p7, "it pertains to the nature of substance to exist" (Geb II 49; C 412), which is said to follow from *E* 1p6, "one substance cannot be produced by another substance" (Geb II 48; 411). The possibility that there is no cause of the existence of substance is precluded by the axiom that "what cannot be conceived through another, must be conceived through itself" (*E* 1a2; Geb II 46; C 410).

32 For discussion of Descartes's argument, see Rodriguez-Pereyra 2008.

33 The *locus classicus* of the subjective interpretation is Wolfson 1934, 142–57. For a critique of this interpretation that defends the objective interpretation, see Gueroult 1968, 50. One commentator has claimed that "it is as certain as anything disputed in Spinoza's *Ethics* can be, that Wolfson's interpretation of these passages [concerning the status of the attributes] in mistaken" (Donagan 1973, 171).

34 Cf. the summary of the debate in Shein 2009, 507–11.

35 Cf. the following passage from the draft of the *Ethics* that Spinoza quoted to De Vries:

> By substance I understand what is in itself and is conceived through itself, that is, whose concept does not involve the concept of another thing. I understand the same by attribute, except that it is called attribute in relation to the intellect, which attributes such and such a definite nature to substance.
>
> (Ep 9; Geb IV 46; C 195)

36 Cf. the related but differing attempts to accommodate elements of the two interpretations in Lennon 2005, 19–27, and Shein 2009, 525–31.

37 Cf. Descartes's remarks in *PP* I.23; AT VIIIA 13; CSM I 200–1.

38 I discuss Spinoza's "vacuum argument" further in Schmaltz 1999.

39 Moreover, the parts are not really distinct in the sense that applies to attributes either, because these parts cannot be conceived completely through themselves, apart from any consideration of their relation to the rest of material nature. For this point, see Spinoza's remarks to Oldenburg in Ep 32; Geb IV 171–4.

40 I find this suggestion in Bennett 1984, 208–9. Moreover, Bennett's "field metaphysic" interpretation of Spinoza, according to which finite bodily modes are qualitative alterations of space (see Bennett 1984, 88–106), would seem to be easily restated as the view that such modes are qualitative alterations of the one infinite individual.

41 Here Tschirnhaus has in mind *E* 1p21–3 (Geb II 65–7; C 429–30), in which Spinoza distinguishes two kinds of "infinite modes," the first of which follows "immediately" from the "absolute nature" of some

attribute of God, and the second of which follows from this nature by modifying a "mediating modification" that follows immediately from the attribute (E 1p23d; Geb II 67; C 430–1). The contrast here is with "any thing that is finite and has a determinate existence," which follows not from the absolute nature of a divine attribute, but rather from that attribute "insofar as it is modified by a modification that is finite and has a determinate existence" (E 1p28; Geb II 69; C 432).

42 For more on Spinoza's account of the mediate infinite mode, see Schmaltz 1997. In identifying this infinite mode with the particular "ratio of motion and rest" that modifies the immediate infinite mode of "motion and rest" in nature, this article takes issue with the position – popular in the literature – that the infinite modes are to be identified with laws of nature. For such a position, see, for instance, Curley 1988, 45–7.

43 Given Spinoza's axiom, cited earlier, that cognition of an effect depends on and involves the cognition of its cause (E 1a4; Geb II 46; C 410).

44 Tschirnhaus no doubt has in mind the proposition in the *Ethics* that "from the necessity of the divine nature, an infinity of infinite modes (that is, all that can fall under infinite intellect) must follow" (E 1p16; Geb II 60; C 424).

45 Spinoza ends the comment by noting that he "perhaps, if life endures, will some time discuss this with you more clearly" (Geb IV 334). In fact, Spinoza died seven months after writing this letter.

46 Matheron 1991.

47 For a summary of the main developments, see Mercer and Sleigh 1995, which covers Leibniz's writings from the so-called early and middle periods, from 1668 to the time of the *Discourse on Metaphysics*, and Rutherford 1995a, which covers Leibniz's writings from the "later" period, that is, from the 1690s until his death in 1716.

48 G will be used for Leibniz 1978, and AG for Leibniz 1989.

49 Of course, Spinoza would claim that because Leibniz's created substances are caused by God, they must also be conceived through God, and so be modes of the divine substance rather than substances themselves. It seems that Leibniz is relying on the distinction – familiar from Suárez and Descartes – between infinite substance, which exists both *per se* and *a se*, and finite substances, which exist *per se* but essentially depend for their existence on God, and thus do not exist *a se*. However, a further condition of *per se* existence in Leibniz – not found in either Suárez or Descartes – is that there be causal independence from anything else that exists *per se* but not *a se*.

50 LA will be used for Leibniz 1985. The suggestion here, in line with my discussion of Descartes in section 2, is that it cannot be assumed that extended substance must have the same sort of unity that thinking substance does, because the two kinds of substances may not be substantial in precisely the same manner.

51 Garber emphasizes such passages in defending the view that Leibniz accepted a more "realistic" account of corporeal substance during the 1680s (as opposed to the more "idealistic" account in his later writings); see Garber 2009, esp. chs. 2–6. See also Broad 1975 and Wilson 1989. For criticisms of this reading, see Sleigh 1990, ch. 5, and Adams 1994, ch. 11.

52 See the indication at the beginning of *Discourse* §34 that the human being is a paradigmatic case of an *unum per se* (G IV 459; AG 65). In this passage, Leibniz does not explicitly commit himself to the conclusion that there are corporeal substances other than humans. However, in his correspondence with Arnauld, he is increasingly confident that the doctrine of corporeal substance can be applied beyond this case. Cf. the more guarded remarks in the letter of 8 December 1686 (G II 77; LA 95) and the more confident remarks in the letters of 30 April and 9 October 1687 (G II 99–100, 118–20/LA 124–5, 151–2).

53 Leibniz cites this declaration in a 1686 letter to Arnauld (G II 75; LA 93).

54 It must be granted that Leibniz equates action and passion with the increase and decrease, respectively, of the expression of the *finite substance*, rather than the substantial form or soul (*Discourse* §15; G IV 410–11; AG 48). Nonetheless, he also says that the action involves pleasure, and the passion pain, which seems to indicate that the expression he has in mind is the soul's perceptual expression of the universe. See also Leibniz's claim in the previous article that "nothing can happen to us except thoughts and perceptions, and all our future thoughts and perceptions are merely consequences, though contingent, of our preceding thoughts and perceptions" (*Discourse* §14; G IV 439; AG 47).

55 For this point, see Rutherford 1995b, 269–70.

56 The 'for the most part' qualifier is required primarily due to Leibniz's discussions of the "substantial bond," to be discussed in the final paragraph of this section.

57 In the "Brevis Demonstratio Erroris memorabilis Cartesii et aliorum circa Legem Naturalem" (1686), his first published critique of Cartesian physics, Leibniz argues that Descartes's law of the conservation of the

quantity of motion must be replaced by a law of the conservation of force. In his "Specimen Dynamicum" (1695), Leibniz further distinguishes four different kinds of forces: primitive active, primitive passive, derivative active, and derivative passive. The primitive forces are considered to be the substantial form (active) and matter (passive) that constitutes the simple substance. Derivative forces are attributed to bodies as phenomena to explain the production of (active) or resistance to (passive) motion. See, for instance, Leibniz claim in correspondence with De Volder that

> I relegate derivative forces to the phenomena, but I think that it is obvious that primitive forces can be nothing but the internal strivings of simple substances, striving by means of which they pass from perception to perception in accordance with a fixed law of their nature.
> (G II 275; AG 181)

For a discussion of Leibniz's account of forces, which nonetheless concludes that the view presented to De Volder "may not have been Leibniz's considered opinion," see Garber 1995, 284–98.

58 But cf. the view in Furth 1967 that Leibniz offers "a reductive explication of statements about material things as translations or abbreviations of statements about perceptions" (184).
59 Leibniz holds that the aggregates that constitute a body have a "dominant monad," and that parts of that body have their own dominant monads, and those parts have their own parts with dominant monads, and so on without end.
60 See also his claim in a 1706 letter to De Volder, which concerns the exchange with Tournemine, that "this metaphysical union, I know not what, that the schools add, over and above agreement, is not phenomenon, and we do not have any notion of it or acquaintance with it. And so I could not have intended to explain it" (G II 281; AG 184). However, Leibniz also claims in the *Theodicy* (1710) to "admit a true union between the soul and the body, which makes a *suppositum* of them," a union that "belongs to the metaphysical" ("Preliminary Discourse," §55; G VI 81).
61 For more on the Des Bosses correspondence, including the discussion there of the substantial bond, see the introduction to Leibniz 2007. See also the discussion of Leibniz's view of the substantial bond in Look 2000.
62 In brief, Leibniz's suggestion is that transubstantiation can be explained in terms of the divine replacement of the substantial bond that constitutes the substance of the Eucharistic elements with the substantial bond that constitutes the substance of Christ's body.
63 As well as remarks that seem to endorse the existence of a "metaphysical union" that constitutes a corporeal substance over and above monads; see, for instance, the passage from the *Theodicy* quoted in note 60. One difficulty in interpreting Leibniz is that he may well tailor his message to his audience, expressing one thing in more popular works or in theologically or politically sensitive responses to criticisms, and another in writings directed to those more willing and able to grasp the subtleties of his metaphysical system. For this point, see Rutherford 1995b, 281–2.
64 There is a related line of argument against Descartes in the work of his later follower, Nicolas Malebranche. In Malebranche's case, the claim is that whereas we know body through a "clear idea" of extension, we have only a confused awareness (*sentiment*), and no clear idea, of the soul. For a comparison of the critiques of Descartes in Gassendi and Malebranche, see Schmaltz 1996, 35–43.
65 *Essay* will be used for Locke 1975.
66 *W* will be used for Locke 1963.
67 This, of course, does not exhaust Leibniz's objections to Locke's account of substance. However, it should be clear from my discussion of Leibniz in section 4 that his approach to the topic differs fundamentally from Locke's. This difference perhaps explains why Leibniz sometimes fails to make contact with Locke's skepticism concerning substance. For a comparison of Locke and Leibniz on this issue, see Jolley 1984, ch. 5.
68 As plausibly argued in McCann 2007, which defends the sort of "traditional" interpretation of Locke on substance that informs my discussion here. Cf. the critique in Ayers 1977 of a Leibnizian reading of Locke on substance, as well as the comprehensive consideration of Locke's views on substance in Ayers 1991, 2:15–128.
69 On Locke's view of the role of nominal essences in classifying species of substances, see Ayers 1981; Atherton 2007; Kaufman 2007.
70 For this reading, see Mandelbaum 1964b; Yolton 1970; Bolton 1976. Here I follow the critique of this reading in McCann 2007, 185–90.
71 Alexander argues that there is in fact no general idea of substance common to body and spirit; rather, there are two different kinds of substance-in-general: "solid stuff," in the case of bodies, and stuff with

the power of perception and thinking, in the case of spirits (see Alexander 1985, ch. 11). However, in his correspondence with Stillingfleet, Locke seems to assume that there is an idea of substance common to both cases when he says that

> the general idea of substance being the same everywhere, the Modification of *Thinking*, or the Power of *Thinking* joined to it, makes it a *Spirit*, without considering what other Modifications it has, as whether it has the Modification of *Solidity* or no. As on the other side *Substance*, that has the Modification of *Solidity*, is Matter, whether it has the Modification of *Thinking* or no.
>
> (W 4:33)

As I read this passage, Locke is saying that the general idea of substance is the same everywhere in the sense that it everywhere picks out the substratum to qualities: in the case of matter, to the quality of solidity, and in the case of spirit, to the quality of thinking. The fact that Locke restricts the idea of substance to its logical content allows him to avoid the problematic position – which he mentions in the *Essay* in connection to disputes over the ontological status of space – that "God, Spirits, and Body, agreeing in the same common nature of *Substance*, differ not any otherwise than in a bare different modification of that *Substance*" (Essay 2.13.18, 174).

72 Thanks to Dan Kaufman and Marleen Rozemond for helpful comments on this chapter.

Bibliography

Adams, Robert M. 1994. *Leibniz: Determinist, Theist, Idealist*. Oxford: Oxford University Press.
Alexander, Peter. 1985. *Ideas, Qualities and Corpuscles: Locke and Boyle on the External World*. Cambridge: Cambridge University Press.
Aristotle. 1984. *The Complete Works of Aristotle*. Ed. J. Barnes. 2 vols. Princeton: Princeton University Press.
Atherton, Margaret. 2007. "Locke on Essences and Classification." In Newman 2007, 258–85.
Ayers, Michael R. 1977. "Ideas of Power and Substance in Locke's Philosophy." In *Locke on Human Understanding*, ed. I. Tipton, 77–104. Oxford: Oxford University Press.
———. 1981. "Locke Versus Aristotle on Natural Kinds." *Journal of Philosophy* 78:247–71.
———. 1991. *Locke: Epistemology and Ontology*. 2 vols. London: Routledge.
Bennett, Jonathan. 1984. *A Study of Spinoza's Ethics*. Indianapolis, IN: Hackett.
Bolton, Martha Brandt. 1976. "Substances, Substrata, and Names of Substances in Locke's *Essay*." *Philosophical Review* 85:488–513.
Boyle, Robert. 1979. *Selected Philosophical Papers of Robert Boyle*. Ed. M. A. Stewart. Manchester: Manchester University Press.
Broad, C. D. 1975. *Leibniz: An Introduction*. Cambridge: Cambridge University Press.
Cottingham, John. 1985. "Cartesian Trialism." *Mind* 94:218–30.
Curley, Edwin. 1988. *Behind the Geometrical Method: A Reading of Spinoza's Ethics*. Princeton, NJ: Princeton University Press.
Descartes, René. 1964–74. *Œuvres de Descartes*. Ed. Ch. Adam and P. Tannery. 11 vols. Paris: Vrin.
———. 1984–85. *The Philosophical Writings of Descartes*. Trans. J. Cottingham, R. Stoothoff, and D. Murdoch. 2 vols. Cambridge: Cambridge University Press.
———. 1991. *The Philosophical Writings of Descartes*, vol. III: *The Correspondence*. Trans. J. Cottingham, R. Stoothoff, D. Murdoch, and A. Kenny. Cambridge: Cambridge University Press.
Des Chene, Dennis. 1996. *Physiologia: Natural Philosophy in Late Aristotelian and Cartesian Thought*. Ithaca, NY: Cornell University Press.
Donagan, Alan. 1973. *Spinoza*. Chicago: University of Chicago Press.
Furth, Montgomery. 1967. "Monadology." *Philosophical Review* 76:169–200.
Garber, Daniel. 1995. "Leibniz: Physics and Philosophy." In Jolley 1995, 270–352.
———. 2009. *Leibniz: Body, Substance, Monad*. Oxford: Oxford University Press.
Gueroult, Martial. 1953. *Descartes selon l'ordre des raisons*. Vol I: *L'ame et Dieu*. Paris: Aubier.
———. 1968. *Spinoza*. Vol I: *Dieu*. Paris: Aubier.
Hoffman, Paul. 2009a. *Essays on Descartes*. New York and Oxford: Oxford University Press.
———. 2009b. "The Unity of Descartes' Man." In Hoffman 2009a, 15–32.
———. 2009c. "Descartes's Theory of Distinction." In Hoffman 2009a, 51–70.
Jolley, Nicholas. 1984. *Leibniz and Locke: A Study of the New Essays on Human Understanding*. Oxford: Clarendon Press.

———, ed. 1995. *The Cambridge Companion to Leibniz.* Cambridge: Cambridge University Press.
Kaufman, Dan. 2007. "Locke on Individuation and the Corpuscular Basis of Kinds." *Philosophy and Phenomenological Research* 75:449–534.
———. 2008. "Descartes on Composites, Incomplete Substances, and Kinds of Unity." *Archiv für Geschichte der Philosophie* 90:39–73.
Laporte, Jean. 1988. *Le rationalisme de Descartes.* Paris: Presses Universitaires de France.
Leibniz, G.W.F. 1849–55. *Mathematische Schriften.* Ed. C. I. Gebhardt. 7 vols. Berlin: von Asher und Comp.
———. 1978 [1875]. *Die Philosophischen Schriften.* Ed. C. I. Gebhardt. 7 vols. Reprint, Hildesheim: Georg Olms.
———. 1985. *The Leibniz-Arnauld Correspondence.* Ed. and trans. H. T. Mason. New York and London: Garland.
———. 1989. *G. W. Leibniz: Philosophical Essays.* Trans. R. Ariew and D. Garber. Indianapolis, IN: Hackett.
———. 2007. *The Leibniz-Des Bosses Correspondence.* Trans. B. Look and D. Rutherford. New Haven, CT: Yale University Press.
Lennon, Thomas. 2005. "The Rationalist Conception of Substance." In Nelson 1995, 12–30.
———. 2007. "The Eleatic Descartes." *Journal of the History of Philosophy* 45:29–47.
Locke, John. 1963 [1823]. *The Works of John Locke.* 10 vols. Reprint, Amsterdam: Scientia Verlag.
———. 1975. *An Essay Concerning Human Understanding.* Ed. P. H. Nidditch. Oxford: Clarendon Press.
Look, Brandon. 2000. "Leibniz and the Substance of the *Viniculum Substantiale.*" *Journal of the History of Philosophy* 38:203–20.
Mandelbaum, Maurice. 1964a. *Philosophy, Science, and Sense Perception: Historical and Critical Studies.* Baltimore, MD: Johns Hopkins University Press.
———. 1964b. "Locke's Realism." In Mandelbaum 1964a, 1–60.
Marion, Jean-Luc. 1991. *Sur la théologie blanche de Descartes.* 2nd edn. Paris: Presses Universitaires de France.
Matheron, Alexandre. 1991. "Physique et ontologie chez Spinoza: L'énigmatique réponse à Tschirnhaus." *Cahiers Spinoza* 9:83–109.
McCann, Edwin. 2007. "Locke on Substance." In Newman 2007, 130–56.
Mercer, Christia, and R. C. Sleigh, Jr. 1995. "Metaphysics: The Early Period to the *Discourse on Metaphysics.*" In Jolley 1995, 67–123.
Nelson, Alan, ed. 1995. *A Companion to Rationalism.* Oxford: Blackwell.
Newman, Lex, ed. 2007. *The Cambridge Companion to Locke's "Essay Concerning Human Understanding."* Cambridge: Cambridge University Press.
Pasnau, Robert. 2004. "Form, Substance, and Mechanism." *Philosophical Review* 113:31–88.
Rodis-Lewis, Geneviève. 1971. *L'œuvre de Descartes.* 2 vols. Paris: Vrin.
Rodriguez-Pereyra, Gonzalo. 2008. "Descartes's Substance Dualism and His Independence Conception of Substance." *Journal of the History of Philosophy* 46:69–89.
Rozemond, Marleen. 1998. *Descartes's Dualism.* Cambridge, MA: Harvard University Press.
Rutherford, Donald. 1995a. "Metaphysics: The Late Period." In Jolley 1995, 124–75.
———. 1995b. *Leibniz and the Rational Order of Nature.* Cambridge: Cambridge University Press.
Schmaltz, Tad M. 1992. "Descartes and Malebranche on Mind and Mind-Body Union." *Philosophical Review* 101:281–325.
———. 1996. *Malebranche's Theory of the Soul: A Cartesian Interpretation.* Oxford and New York: Oxford University Press.
———. 1997. "Spinoza's Mediate Infinite Mode." *Journal of the History of Philosophy* 35:199–235.
———. 1999. "Spinoza on the Vacuum." *Archiv für Geschichte der Philosophie* 81:174–205.
———. 2008. *Descartes on Causation.* Oxford and New York: Oxford University Press.
Secada, Jorge. 2000. *Cartesian Metaphysics: The Late Scholastic Origins of Modern Philosophy.* New York: Cambridge University Press.
———. 2006. "The Doctrine of Substance." In *The Blackwell Guide to Descartes' Meditations,* ed. S. Gaukroger, 67–85. Oxford: Blackwell.
Shein, Noa. 2009. "The False Dichotomy Between Objective and Subjective Interpretations of Spinoza's Theory of Attributes." *British Journal for the History of Philosophy* 17:505–32.
Sleigh, R. C., Jr. 1990. "Leibniz on Malebranche on Causality." In *Central Themes in Early Modern Philosophy,* ed. J. A. Cover and M. Kulstad, 161–94. Indianapolis, IN: Hackett.
Spinoza, Benedict de. 1925. *Spinoza Opera.* Ed. C. Gebhardt. 4 vols. Heidelberg: Carl Winter.
———. 1985. *The Collected Works of Spinoza.* Vol. I. Ed. and trans. E. Curley. Princeton, NJ: Princeton University Press.

Suárez, Francisco. 1965 [1866]. *Disputationes Metaphysicae*. 2 vols. Reprint, Hildesheim: Georg Olms.

———. 1947. *On the Various Kinds of Distinctions* (Disputationes Metaphysicae, Disputatio VII). Trans. C. O. Vollert. Milwaukee: University of Wisconsin Press.

———. 2000. *On the Formal Cause of Substance* (Metaphysical Disputation XV). Trans. J. Kronen. Milwaukee: Marquette University Press.

———. 2006. *On Real Relation* (Disputatio Metaphysica XLVII). Trans. J. P. Doyle. Milwaukee: Marquette University Press.

Voss, Stephen. 1994. "Descartes: The End of Anthropology." In *Reason, Will, and Sensation: Studies in Descartes's Metaphysics*, ed. J. Cottingham, 273–306. New York and Oxford: Oxford University Press.

Wedin, Michael. 2000. *Aristotle's Theory of Substance: The Categories and Metaphysics Zeta*. New York and Oxford: Oxford University Press.

Williams, Bernard. 1978. *Descartes: The Project of Pure Inquiry*. Atlantic Highlands, NJ: Humanities Press.

Wilson, Catherine. 1989. *Leibiniz's Metaphysics: A Comparative and Historical Study*. Princeton, NJ: Princeton University Press.

Wolfson, Harry. 1934. *The Philosophy of Spinoza*. 2 vols. Cambridge, MA: Harvard University Press.

Woolhouse, Roger. 1993. *Descartes, Spinoza, Leibniz: The Concept of Substance in Seventeenth-Century Metaphysics*. London: Routledge.

Yolton, John. 1970. *Locke and the Compass of Human Understanding*. Cambridge: Cambridge University Press.

3
QUALITIES
Samuel C. Rickless

1. Introduction[1]

One of the more interesting philosophical debates in the seventeenth century concerned the nature and explanation of qualities. In order to understand these debates, it is important to place them in their proper historical-philosophical context.

In the Aristotelian metaphysics inherited by seventeenth century philosophers from their late medieval Scholastic predecessors, the natural world is a world of substances (human beings, sheep, geraniums, statues, rocks), themselves combinations of matter and substantial form. A human being is made of flesh, blood, and bone (its matter) and is made into the kind of thing that it is by its rational soul (its substantial form); a statue is made of, say, bronze (its matter) and is made into the kind of thing that it is by its shape (its substantial form). A human body without a form is not a human being; a lump of bronze without its distinctive shape is not a statue. On the Scholastic picture, human beings and statues also possess accidental forms (or simply, accidents), namely characteristics of substances that are not substantial. But what exactly are the accidents of substances?

Accidents divide into two main categories: the manifest and the hidden. There are, first, the sensible qualities of substances, qualities that can be perceived by means of the five senses (sight, hearing, smell, taste, and touch). These qualities include motion (and rest), shape, size, position, texture, color, sound, odor, flavor, and tangible qualities (including heat, cold, dryness, wetness, roughness, and smoothness). But there are also occult characteristics of substances, qualities that cannot be perceived by means of the senses. The most important occult qualities were thought to be gravity (or weight, the tendency to fall toward the center of the earth), magnetism, and (static) electricity. Aristotelians had fairly well worked out accounts of the nature and explanation of sensible qualities but struggled (understandably) to account for occult phenomena. In the seventeenth century, the opponents of Aristotle offered competing accounts of sensible qualities and thought it might be possible to vindicate their theories by accounting for occult phenomena as well.

The story of the seventeenth century is the story of a scientific revolution, prompted in part by the gradual replacement of the fundamental presuppositions of Aristotelian science by the basic principles of corpuscularian mechanism, namely matter and motion. Although the mechanists did not do away with substances, they either did away with immaterial substantial forms or found the need to appeal to such entities explanatorily redundant. But the elimination of substantial forms does not automatically translate into the elimination of accidental qualities: from the fact that a material substance (such as a statue) does not (or need not be understood to) consist in a composite of matter and substantial form, it does not follow that the statue does not have a shape, or size, or color, or smell. The new mechanists of the seventeenth century were therefore left with the following question: what is the place of accidental qualities in a mechanistic ontology?

In order to answer this question, mechanists needed to decide where, if anywhere, in the world accidental qualities exist. Are they in or on the material objects of perception (such as flowers and statues)? Are they in or on some perceptual medium (such as air or water) that lies between perceivers and the objects they perceive? Are they in the perceiving body's sense organs? Or are they in the (incorporeal) minds of perceivers themselves? Given their shared assumptions about the ultimate furniture of the physical world and the proper form of scientific explanation, one might have expected the mechanists to converge on one answer (or, at least, on a small number of similar answers) to these questions. But, perhaps surprisingly, there was no convergence; indeed, there was a veritable explosion of alternatives.

On some, but by no means all, of these alternatives, the realm of sensible qualities divides neatly into two: there are primary qualities (such as shape, size, motion, and position) and secondary qualities (such as color, sound, odor, taste, and tangible characteristics). For those who make this distinction, primary qualities are explanatorily basic: the existence of any secondary quality associated with a material object (and, indeed, the existence of any occult quality) is to be explained by the existence and arrangement of the object's primary qualities (or by the existence and arrangement of the primary qualities of the object's insensible material parts),[2] but not vice versa. It is widely believed that because mechanists were the first to distinguish between primary and secondary qualities, the distinction is a consequence or natural outgrowth of mechanism. But this, as we will see, is a mistake.

The purpose of this chapter is to articulate, and reconstruct some of the main reasons for and against, the various positions taken by seventeenth century philosophers on the question of the nature, location, and explanation of sensible qualities.[3] Part of my aim is to understand why there was so much disagreement in the context of widespread agreement on fundamentals.

This chapter is divided into the following sections. In section 2, I discuss the Aristotelian picture in opposition to which the new mechanists of the seventeenth century defined their theories of sensible qualities. In section 3, I discuss the intellectual seeds of mechanism that lie in ancient Greek and Roman atomism (as represented by Democritus, Epicurus, and Lucretius). In section 4, I explain how the new mechanists understood motion and rest (with some brief discussion of shape and size), and how their views contrast with the corresponding Aristotelian picture. In section 5, I focus on the new mechanists' theories of light, in large part because these theories shape their theories of color. In section 6, I discuss the new mechanists' theories of color. In section 7, I turn to the new mechanists' theories of sound, noting that their theories of other sensible qualities (such as odor, flavor, and tangible qualities) are modeled in large part on their theories of color and sound. In section 8, I explain how some, but not all, of the new mechanists thought that primary qualities (motion, shape, size, position, texture) are ontologically distinct from secondary qualities (color, sound, odor, flavor, and tangible qualities). In section 9, I outline and evaluate the reasons for the primary-secondary quality distinction advanced by two of its influential proponents. And in conclusion, I summarize and explain the significance of the seventeenth century debate about the nature, location, and proper explanation of sensible qualities.

2. The theoretical background: Aristotle

The idea of dividing the world into substances and their various characteristics derives from Aristotle. In the *Categories*, Aristotle claims that there are two fundamentally different kinds of entities. There are, in the first place, entities that are not in (that do not inhere in) any other entity: these are substances (*Cat.* 3a; *Phys.* I.2, 185a). And there are, in the second place, entities that are in (that do inhere in) other entities: these are (following the Scholastic tradition) accidents. Thus, Socrates is a substance, inasmuch as he does not inhere in anything else. But the paleness and size of Socrates are accidents inasmuch as they inhere in Socrates.

Seventeenth century philosophers were well aware of Aristotle's theories of the nature and explanation of sensible qualities and, within the category of occult qualities, of gravity.[4] Perhaps the most important sensible quality within the burgeoning mechanism of the seventeenth century is motion. For Aristotle, local motion, which is an accident of body, is a species of the more general category of motion (or change). Change is always with respect to one of the four main categories: substance, quantity, quality, or place. Change with respect to substance is coming-to-be (as in the building of a house), change with respect to quantity is increase or decrease, change with respect to quality is alteration (as in the change from white to black), and change with respect to place is local motion (or locomotion). Striving for a characteristic that all of these forms of change have in common, Aristotle arrives at a general definition of change as the fulfillment (or actualization) of what is potential as potential (*Phys.* III.1, 200b–201b); so, for example, building, which is a kind of change with respect to substance, is the putting together of (say) bricks and mortar, insofar as they are potentially a house.

Famously, Aristotle claims that there are two kinds of local motion: natural and violent. A body moves naturally when it derives its motion from itself; it moves violently when it derives its motion from something else, as when it is pushed, pulled, carried, or twirled (*Phys.* VIII.4, 254b; *Phys.* VII.2, 243a). In Aristotle's view, everything in the sublunary world is composed of four elements: earth, water, air, and fire (GC II.3, 330a–b). The superlunary world is composed of a fifth element: ether. Each of the four sublunary elements has a natural place, a place in which it naturally belongs and to which it naturally moves without being pushed or pulled, in a straight line. (Ether's natural motion is circular.) Earth and water naturally move downward, air and fire naturally move upward (*DC* I.2, 268b–269b).[5]

Aristotle's account of light and color, sound, odor, flavor, and tangible qualities (hot and cold, wet and dry, smooth and rough, etc.) was also very influential. For Aristotle, sensible qualities do not differ in ontological status. Just as shape and size belong to the body with that shape and size, so too does redness belong to the red body and sweetness belong to the sweet body, regardless of whether it is perceived to be red or sweet. Sensible qualities do differ epistemically, but only in the sense that some qualities (the "common sensibles," motion, rest, shape, and size) can be perceived by more than one sense (e.g. motion and shape can be both seen and felt), whereas other qualities (the "proper sensibles," color, sound, odor, flavor, and heat, wetness, and roughness) can be perceived by no more than one sense (color by sight; sound by hearing; odor by smell; flavor by taste; and heat, wetness, and roughness by touch).

Let us begin with Aristotle's theory of light. According to Aristotle, some media (such as air and water) are potentially transparent. That is, they have the capacity to become transparent under certain conditions. Light, as Aristotle defines it, is no more than the actuality of what is potentially transparent, an actuality that is itself brought about (or constituted) by the presence of a fiery element in the relevant medium (*DA* II.7, 418a–419a; *DS* 3, 439a). But Aristotle is adamant that light is to be identified neither with this fiery element nor with any kind of body, including purported corporeal emanations or effluvia, and criticizes Empedocles's doctrine that light travels on the grounds that we do not see it move, not even across vast distances (*DA* II.7, 418b). Indeed, it is an important aspect of Aristotle's theory that light is incorporeal.

Consider now Aristotle's theory of color. A body's color exists whether the body is illuminated or not, but its color is not visible in the absence of light (*DA* II.7, 418b, 419a). For Aristotle, color is to be defined as the limit of the transparent in determinately bounded body (*DS* 3, 439b), and color makes itself seen by setting the actually transparent medium (e.g. air) in motion, motion that extends continuously from the colored body to the organ of sight, thereby setting the latter in motion (*DA* II.7, 419a). In some places, Aristotle characterizes light as the proper color of what is transparent (*DA* II.7, 418b) or the color of the transparent incidentally (*DS* 3, 439a). Although it is not clear that these definitions are mutually coherent, seventeenth century Aristotelians did not much mind. So, for instance, the Aristotelian corpuscularian physician, Daniel Sennert, writes both that "light it self inasmuch as it is said to be seen, is comprehended under colour, and is as it were a whiteness," and that color is "*the Extremity of a transparent thing terminated*" (*TBNP* VII.2, 372).

Aristotle's theory of sound is quite modern inasmuch as he identifies sound with the motion of air when its dissipation is prevented, as occurs in the ear canal (*DA* II.8, 420a). But his theory of odor is less modern. As he sees it, odor is an immersion or washing of dryness in the moist and fluid (*DS* 5, 445a). Aristotle even criticizes his predecessors for having proposed that odor is constituted by a vaporous or smoky exhalation or emanation from odoriferous bodies. For, on the one hand, water does not have an odor (as anyone can tell by smelling it), and aquatic creatures can smell odors in the absence of any smoky emanation (itself a combination of air and earth; *DS* 5, 443a–b). Flavor is similar to odor, for it is produced (or constituted) by washing the dry and earthy in the moist and moving the moist by means of heat through the dry and earthy (*DS* 4, 441b).

Aristotle makes it quite clear that the qualities perceived by the sense of touch are manifold. They include the following pairs of contraries: hot-cold, dry-moist, heavy-light, hard-soft, viscous-brittle, rough-smooth, and coarse-fine (*GC* II.2, 329b). Heat and cold are defined, not by what they are in themselves, but rather by what they *do*: heat is what brings together homogeneous things, and cold is what brings together homogeneous and heterogeneous things alike (*GC* II.2, 329b). Dryness is defined as what is readily determinable by its own limit, whereas moistness is defined as what, though adaptable in shape, is not determinable by any limit of its own (*GC* II.2, 329b). All other tangible qualities are derivable from these four basic qualities – the fine, the viscous, and the soft from the moist, and the coarse, the brittle, and the hard from the dry (*GC* II.2, 330a). Indeed, these qualities are basic, not only in being those from which other tangible qualities are derived, but also in being the factors that differentiate the four elements, fire being hot and dry, air being hot and moist, water being cold and moist, and earth being cold and dry (GC II.2, 330b). Indeed, it is the gaining and losing of these qualities that explains the cyclical conversion of elements. Thus, air results from fire when the dry is overcome by the moist, water results from air when the hot is overcome by the cold, earth results from water when the moist is overcome by the dry, and fire results from earth when the cold is overcome by the hot (GC II.4, 331a–b).

3. The theoretical background: atomism

Even before Aristotle, various atomists had articulated an influential account of the nature, structure, and properties of the physical universe. Democritus had argued that because nothing comes from nothing and because it is impossible for nothing to come from something (material), it follows that there has always been and there will always be something (material). Because matter cannot be dissolved into nothing, there must be indestructible material substances. Democritus called these indestructible substances "atoms" (from the Greek word meaning "uncuttable"). In addition to atoms (tangible, solid substance), Democritus reasoned that there must also be intangible substance (empty space, void, vacuum) for otherwise the universe would be packed solid and motion would be impossible. Atoms, which are invisible, form the building blocks of compound, visible bodies. They are infinitely many and possess shape, size, and motion, but no color, sound, odor, flavor, or tangible qualities. Indeed, Democritus is famously quoted as having said that "by convention sweet and by convention bitter, by convention hot, by convention cold, by convention color; but in reality atoms and void."[6] In this view, atoms have no color, sound, and so on, but also compound bodies only possess such qualities "by convention." This strongly suggests that compound bodies possess color, sound, and so on, only insofar as humans ascribe these qualities to them. In the absence of "convention," and so in the absence of human perceivers, compound bodies would have no color, sound, odor, flavor, heat, or cold, and thus do not possess these qualities in themselves.

Later atomists, most notably Epicurus and Lucretius, agree with Democritus that atoms have no color, sound, odor, flavor, heat, or cold (*DRN* 2, 734–738). In order to possess any of these qualities, a body must emit particles that strike the organs of sense, and yet atoms, being indivisible, are incapable of emitting anything from themselves (*DRN* 2, 845–865). Unlike Democritus, however, Epicurus and Lucretius are not conventionalists about the proper sensibles, for they take all the qualities of compound bodies (including the proper sensibles) to be reducible to, and explicable by means of, the qualities possessed by their constituent atoms. Thus, for example, Lucretius claims that pleasant proper sensibles are produced by smooth and round atoms, that unpleasant proper sensibles are produced by rough and irregularly shaped atoms, and that hardness is produced by atoms that are hooked together (*DRN* 2, 381–477).

Indeed, part of the power of atomism lies in its ability in principle to explain a wide variety of different phenomena. Rare bodies are simply those that possess a great deal of void within their boundaries, whereas the atoms of dense bodies are more closely packed together. Heat and cold are both "continual streams of particles" (*DRN* 6, 924), particles of heat in the case of heat (*DRN* 5, 599), particles of cold in the case of cold. Lightning is produced when the clashing of clouds causes them to emit particles of fire (*DRN* 6, 160–161). Light itself is "composed of minute particles that hammer one another forward and, under the impulsion of blows from behind, unhesitatingly pass through the intervening air" (*DRN* 4, 185–190).

Unlike Democritus, Epicurus and Lucretius also postulate that atoms have weight that carries them downward through the void, for otherwise it would be impossible to explain how they come to be in motion (*DRN* 2, 184–215). (If all atoms were at rest and possessed no more than shape and size, there would be no reason for them to move.) Atoms therefore move (downward) of themselves, and exhibit a kind of natural motion (in Aristotle's sense), even if they are not drawn toward anything. (For the atomists, the infinite extension of the universe guarantees that the universe has no center.)[7]

Given that all bodies are combinations of atoms, it follows that the four elements of Aristotelian physics (namely earth, water, air, and fire) are not the ultimate building blocks of material substances. Indeed, for the atomists it is a point in favor of their theory that it provides an explanation for the Aristotelian doctrine of cyclical conversion (*DRN* 1, 783–829). And the basic pairs of opposite tangible characteristics that differentiate between the elements in Aristotle's theory (namely hot-cold and wet-dry) are also explicable on the atomists' theory as the outgrowth of atoms of different shapes, sizes, and weights.

Despite the considerable theoretical virtues of atomism, Aristotle's theory of substance and accidents reigned supreme in the learned world until the seventeenth century. Part of the reason for this was the considerable empirical support for Aristotelian hypotheses, though the alliance of Aristotelian metaphysics and science with Catholic doctrines also played an important role in explaining Aristotle's theoretical dominance. But by the dawn of the seventeenth century, natural philosophers had become increasingly aware of the limitations of Scholastic Aristotelianism. Aristotle's conception of the earth remaining motionless at the center of the universe had been forcefully countered by Copernicus's heliocentrism. His account of bodily motion as inversely proportional to the resistance of the relevant medium was known to be contradicted by free-fall experiments in which bodies of different weights (and thus bodies incurring different grades of air resistance) left to fall from the same height at the same time were observed to hit the ground at the same time. And his distinction between natural and violent motion was known to be contradicted by the observation of projectile motion (in which heavy bodies that are thrown move upward despite the fact that they appear to be neither pushed nor pulled). The limitations of Aristotelianism made the relative advantages of Lucretian atomism shine forth more brightly. Philosophers were well aware of the problem of explaining the possibility of motion in the absence of a void, of the fact that various phenomena (including evaporation and erosion) testify to the existence of insensible material particles, and of the fact that other phenomena (including the porous consistency of many bodies and variations in corporeal density) testify to the existence of a void. At the same time, philosophers were attracted to the relative simplicity of the basic form of atomic explanation in terms of the motion of particles of different shapes and sizes.

So it is against the background of the gradually diminishing influence of Aristotelian physics and the gradually increasing influence of atomic physics that the mechanists of the seventeenth century contributed some notable theories of sensible qualities.

4. Motion and rest

Aside from philosophers who, like Sennert, rested many of their own views on the authority and arguments of Aristotle (see *TBNP* I.9), seventeenth century philosophers tended to ridicule Aristotle's general definition of change as the actualization of what is potential as potential. In *The World*, for example, René Descartes writes, "[Aristotelians] have not yet been able to explain [motion] more clearly than in these terms: *Motus est actus entis in potentia, prout in potentia est.* For me these words are so obscure that I am compelled to leave them in Latin because I cannot interpret them" (AT XI 39; CSM I 93–94). Similarly, Walter Charleton writes that "nothing can be more obscure than" Aristotle's definition of motion (PEGC IV.2, 438). And John Locke is, if possible, even more dismissive:

> What more exquisite *Jargon* could the Wit of Man invent, than this Definition, *The Act of a being in Power, as far forth as in Power*, which would puzzle any rational Man, to whom it was not already known by its famous absurdity, to guess what Word it could ever be supposed to be the Explication of.
> (E 3.4.8, 422)

Many of Aristotle's opponents agreed with the atomists, who reduced all motion to *local* motion, namely change of place. Thomas Hobbes, for example, identifies motion as "*a continual relinquishing of one place, and acquiring of another*" (DCo 8.10). Charleton claims that Aristotle's definition of motion is "much inferior in Perspicuity to that most natural and familiar one of *Epicurus*; that Motion is *the migration or Remove of a body from one place to another*" (PEGC IV.2, 439). And early in his career, Descartes agrees:

> For my part, I am not acquainted with any motion except that which is easier to conceive than the lines of the geometers – the motion which makes bodies pass from one place to another and successively occupy all the spaces which exist in between.
> (AT XI 40; CSM I 94)

But several years later, Descartes, who by this point had become more hostile to atomism, changed his mind. In the *Principles*, he distinguishes between two senses of the term "motion": the ordinary sense, which is in accordance with what we can imagine and is appropriately captured by the atomists' definition, and the strict sense, which is "in accordance with the truth of the matter." To understand the strict sense of "motion," it is important to note that, like most of his contemporaries, Descartes treats motion as a mode of substance, that is as a way for substance to be. Motion is therefore something in the world, not something that is relative to one's perception of the world. But Descartes recognizes that whether one counts as moving in the ordinary sense depends on the frame of reference on which one chooses to focus. Thus, "a man sitting on board a ship which is leaving port considers himself to be moving relative to the shore which he regards as fixed; but he does not think of himself as moving relative to the ship, since his position is unchanged relative to its parts." In order to avoid the relativity of motion that is the natural corollary of the ordinary sense and that is inconsistent with the claim that motion is a mode of material substance, Descartes claims that, in the strict sense, "motion" should be defined as "*the transfer of one piece of matter, or one body, from the vicinity of other bodies which are in immediate contact with it, and which are regarded as being at rest, to the vicinity of other bodies*" (AT VIIIA 53; CSM I 233). This definition avoids the relativity problem Descartes discusses because it tells us that, strictly speaking, the man who is sitting on the ship is absolutely (nonrelatively) at rest, given that he is not being transferred from the vicinity of the ship (even if he is being transferred from the vicinity of the shore).[8]

But not all philosophers were happy with the atomists' definition of motion or with the epicycle Descartes added to it. Locke in particular faults both definitions for being circular and uninformative:

> The *Atomists*, who define Motion to be a *passage from one place to another*, What do they more than put one synonymous Word for another? For what is *Passage* other than *Motion*? And if they were asked what Passage was, How would they better define it than by *Motion*? . . . [This] is very far from a *Definition*, unless we will say, every English Word in the Dictionary, is the definition of the Latin Word it answers, and that Motion is a definition of *Motus*. *Nor will the successive Application of the parts of the Superficies of one Body, to those of another*, which the *Cartesians* give us, prove a much better definition of Motion, when well examined.
>
> (E 3.4.9, 423)

Locke's own view is that the idea of motion is simple, and hence incapable of definition. What the motion of a body is in itself is something to be apprehended by sense experience, rather than by abstract ratiocination.

Many philosophers of the seventeenth century ridiculed not only Aristotle's definition of motion but also his distinction between natural and violent motion. Natural motion is motion that has an internal cause and that tends toward a natural place. Thus, earth and water tend to move of themselves (without being pushed or pulled) toward the center of the universe, whereas air and fire tend to move upward (again without being pushed or pulled) away from the center of the universe. Violent motion is motion that has an external cause, as in the motion of a cart that is pushed or pulled along a road. It follows from Aristotle's theory that were an earthy object to move in a straight line toward the center of the universe, it would stop and remain at rest there.[9] For Francis Bacon, this consequence was too much to bear:

> Philosophers talk nonsense when they say if a hole were made through the earth, heavy bodies would stop when they came to the earth's centre. For it would surely be a wonderfully powerful and effective kind of nothing or mathematical point which had an effect on other things and which other things would seek; for body is acted on only by body.
>
> (*NO* II.35, 158)[10]

Bacon here makes clear that the absurdity of the Aristotelian prediction stems from the assumption that bodies can be set in motion *of themselves* without an external material cause. The thesis that local motion (which, as most anti-Aristotelians agreed, is the only kind of motion there is) can only be produced by contact, and that there can therefore be no such thing as action at a distance, was one of the defining features of the new mechanism of the seventeenth century. Indeed, the thesis distinguished the new mechanists not only from Aristotle but also from Epicurus and Lucretius, for whom atomic motion through the void is a natural result of their intrinsic weight.

Hobbes emphasizes the fact that no body can move of itself: "Whatsoever is at rest, will always be at rest, unless there be some other body besides it, which, by endeavouring to get into its place by motion, suffers it no longer to remain at rest" (*DCo* 8.19). His reason for this is that a body that is initially at rest in empty space cannot begin to move unless it is moved and that it must be moved by something external to it, given that "there was nothing in the body which did not dispose it to rest" (*DCo* 8.19). This argument is unsatisfactory because it simply begs the question against Aristotle (and, for that matter, against the atomists too). After all, why suppose that a body that is initially at rest is *not* disposed to move of its own accord?[11]

No doubt aware of this problem, Descartes attempts to *prove*, as his first law of nature, that "everything, in so far as it can, always continues in the same state," from which it follows directly that "if [a particular piece of matter] is at rest, . . . it will never begin to move unless it is pushed into motion by some [external] cause" (AT VIIIA 62; CSM I 241). The argument depends on Descartes's proof of the existence of God, who is the general cause of all motions in the world, and who, by reason of his immutability, operates "in a manner that is always utterly constant" (AT VIIIA 61; CSM I 240; see also AT XI 37–38; CSM I 92–93). Here, too, the proof leaves something to be desired, for it is unclear why, if God's action is constant, there is any motion (or rest) at all. Isn't it more consistent with God's constancy to suppose (along with Heraclitus) that everything is always in motion or (along with Parmenides) that everything is always at rest?

The problematic proofs of the fundamental principle of mechanism suggest that the new mechanists ought to have taken it as an axiom, rather than as a theorem, of their system. Had they done so, it would have become clearer to all that mechanism is best vindicated by how well it explains and predicts natural phenomena.[12]

Before we leave the topic of motion, it is worth taking note of the fact that although there was widespread agreement among seventeenth century mechanists that all motion is local motion and that all motion requires an external cause, differences arose over the nature of the external agent(s) of bodily motion. Most assumed that the motion of bodies can be produced by the motion of other bodies (as occurs in collisions). But there were naysayers on this issue, most notably Nicolas Malebranche, according to whom "no [bodies], large or small, [have] the power to move [themselves]," and who concludes from this that "it is minds which move them" (*Search* 6.2.3/LO 448). Indeed, Malebranche goes so far as to embrace occasionalism, the doctrine that God (a perfect, infinite mind) is the only true cause, and hence all other things, including bodies and finite minds, are causally impotent (*Search* 6.2.3/LO 449–451).

So much for motion. But what did seventeenth century philosophers say about *rest*? According to Aristotle, rest is simply a privation, or lack, of motion (*Phys.* VIII.1, 251a). In this view, rest (like blindness, which is the privation of sight) is not a real and positive characteristic of a body. So if, as was widely accepted, everything that is real and positive has a cause, it follows that motion must have a cause, but it does not follow that rest must have a cause. Indeed, if rest is a privation, it becomes easier to understand how, in Bacon's thought experiment, it might be possible for a body to come to rest at the center of the earth without being impeded in its motion. For the existence of an external, impeding cause need not be posited in order to explain the existence of a lack.

It is therefore no surprise to see that the doctrine of rest as privation came under concerted attack by anti-Aristotelians. And no attack was more significant than Descartes's. Already in *The World*, Descartes writes, "[Aristotelians say that rest] is nothing but the privation of motion. For my part, I conceive of rest as a quality too, which should be attributed to matter while it remains in one place, just as motion is a quality attributed to matter while it is changing place" (AT XI 40; CSM I 94). Later, in the *Principles*, Descartes emphasizes that "motion and rest are nothing else but two different modes of a body." His argument for this rests on his definition of motion as the transfer of a body away from its immediate vicinity. For, as he argues,

> it is clear that this transfer cannot exist outside the body which is in motion, and that when there is a transfer of motion, the body is in a different state from when there is no transfer, i.e., when it is at rest.
> (AT VIIIA 55; CSM I 234)

If rest is, as Descartes insists, a mode of corporeal substance, it follows directly that an explanation (in the form of an impeding cause) is required for a body's coming to rest from a state of being motion, and similarly, that an explanation (in the form of a motive cause) is required for a body's coming to move from a state of being at rest. The claim that rest is not a privation is therefore no mere anti-Scholastic curiosity, but in a very real sense one of the foundations of the new mechanistic physics.

Motion and rest represent the fundamental currency of the mechanistic physics of the seventeenth century. Natural philosophers from Galileo Galilei to Robert Boyle accepted that the explanation of natural phenomena depends entirely on the motion (and rest) of insensible material corpuscles of varying shapes and sizes. It is largely because of the perceived fruitfulness of mechanistic explanation in terms of matter and motion that atomism experienced such a profound and wide-ranging revival. Once Aristotelian forms (whether substantial or accidental) were no longer needed to explain natural phenomena, the stage was set for a battle between mechanistic proponents and mechanistic opponents of atomism. And it was largely in the context of this battle that philosophers of the seventeenth century proposed and defended new accounts of the nature and explanation of sensible qualities, both proper and common. However, aside from motion and rest, there was no disagreement among working philosophers over the nature of the common sensibles of shape and size. All were agreed that these are modes of body, inasmuch as a body's shape or size cannot exist independently of the body whose shape or size it is. For Descartes and many others, shape and size are merely different ways for a body to be extended (in length, breadth, and depth; see AT VIIIA 25; CSM I 210–211).

Locke makes clear, however, that, like the fact of being extended, the fact of having some shape or other, as well as the fact of having some size or other, is an essential property of every body (E 2.8.9, 134–135). The claim that shape, size, and mobility are essential to (inseparable from) bodies captures part of Descartes's claim that extension is the principal attribute of material substance (AT VIIIA 25; CSM I 210–211). But it is important to note, as will become clear when we come to discuss the nature of the distinction between primary and secondary qualities, that the essentiality or inseparability of shape, size, and mobility is true of them as determinable, but not as determinate, qualities. It is shape *as such* (size *as such*, mobility *as such*), not the particular shape (size, motion, or rest) that it happens to have, that a body cannot lose. Importantly, it is possible for a body to lose the determinate shape, size, and motion (or rest) it possesses, as when a block of putty is flattened or thrown across the room.[13]

5. Light

Recall the Aristotelian account of light as the (incorporeal) actuality of what is potentially transparent (through the presence of a fiery element in the relevant medium). Opposed to it is the atomist account, according to which light is nothing but a stream of light atoms. For the new mechanists of the seventeenth century, the Aristotelian account is profoundly mistaken. But this agreement masks significant disagreement on the nature of light.

According to some, the atomist account is essentially correct and only requires defense against alternatives. This is the view of Pierre Gassendi and his followers (including Charleton). According to Gassendi, light is a flux of very subtle (fluid, violently agitated, and tiny) corpuscles of a particular shape that are transmitted through air (or some other medium) with ineffable speed (OO 422; APG 149). Charleton's account is substantially the same.[14] Gassendi and Charleton are most concerned to establish the corporeality of light. In defense of this claim, they adduce the following phenomena (OO 427–430, PEGC III.5.2, 204–205): (1) locomotion, that is that light is "deradiated" from the lucid body to the eye; (2) resilition, that is reflection; (3) refraction; (4) coition, that is union, of rays that "become so violent as to burn any thing applied"; (5) disgregation, that is dispersal, and debilitation as a result of diffraction; and (6) igniety, "since Light seems to be both the Subject, and Vehicle to Heat, and those speak incorrigibly, who call Light, Flame attenuated.[15]

On the Gassendist picture, light exists between the luminous (or illuminated) body and the eye. But others, as hostile to Aristotle's theory as Gassendi and Charleton, locate light in the organ of sight itself. Hobbes, a materialist but also an opponent of the atomist doctrine of the existence of the void (DCo 26.2–4), argues that light is "the proper phantasm of sight" (DCo 25.10). Here Hobbes helps himself to an Aristotelian term, "phantasm," meaning a perceptual trace in the imagination, but gives it his own special materialistic twist. Hobbes claims that there is such a thing as "endeavour," namely "*motion made through the length of a point, and in an instance or point of time*" (DCo 15.2), where motion is "*a continual relinquishing of one place, and acquiring of another*" (DCo 8.10). Some endeavors are actions, but others reactions, where a reaction is an "endeavour in the patient to restore itself to that situation from which it was forced by the agent" (DCo 22.18). On Hobbes's account, luminous bodies (such as the sun) by their motion cause circumambient substances to move, and this motion is propagated straight to the eye, and thence to "the innermost part of the organ of sight, namely, to the heart" (DCo 27.2). Being acted upon in this way, the heart then reacts, and the resulting endeavor proceeds back toward the eye, "ending in the endeavour outwards" of the retina, which is "the thing which is called light, or the phantasm of a lucid body" (DCo 27.2).[16]

Yet others, as Gassendi aptly notices (OO 423), attempt to find a middle ground between Aristotelianism and atomism. Descartes likens light (as it exists outside the mind) to the action of a blind man's stick:

> I would have you consider the light in bodies we call "luminous" to be nothing other than a certain movement, or very rapid and lively action [i.e. tendency to move], which passes to our eyes through the medium of the air or other transparent bodies, just as the movement or resistance of the bodies encountered by a blind man passes to his hand by means of his stick.
>
> (AT VI 84; CSM I 153)

Descartes's picture of the physical relationship between the luminous body and the organ of sight is similar to Hobbes's. But whereas Hobbes locates light in the eye, Descartes locates it as a quality of luminous bodies. Descartes agrees with the atomists that light is not incorporeal, but agrees with Aristotle that "there is no need to suppose that something material passes from objects to our eyes to make us see . . . light" (AT VI 85; CSM I 153).[17]

Yet others split the difference between Hobbes on the one hand and the atomists on the other. Jacques Rohault, a follower of Descartes whose physics textbook was widely relied on before Isaac Newton's *Principia* displaced it, claims that the word "light" is ambiguous: it can mean either the sensation we have when we perceive a luminous or illuminated body or it can mean whatever it is on the part of external objects by means of which they are able to excite this sensation in us (*TP* I.27.1–2, 291–292).[18] In the second sense, Rohault agrees with Descartes that light consists in "a certain motion of the parts of luminous bodies that renders them capable of pushing in all directions the subtle matter that fills the pores of transparent bodies" (*TP* I.27.15, 298).[19] This way of approaching the matter appeals to Locke, who notes that "the *Cartesians* very well distinguish between that Light which is the Cause of that Sensation [of light] in us, and the *Idea* which is produced in us by it, and is that which is properly Light" (*E* 3.4.10, 424).

Yet Locke also identifies light with a capacity possessed by the luminous or illuminated body. As he puts it, "[Light is] nothing, in truth, but [a power] to excite [the sensation of light] in us" (*E* 2.31.2, 375–376). This view differs from the view that light is the cause of sensations of light inasmuch as the cause of something is not to be identified with the power (or possibility) of causing it (see *E* 2.21.1, 233). It is, in fact, a different, specifically dispositionalist, "third way" between Hobbesianism and atomism. As Locke sees it, light is in the world, not in the eye (and not in the mind or soul). But it is not a body, or even a property of body: it is a dispositional relation between luminous and illuminated bodies and the creatures that perceive them.

6. Color

Recall Aristotle's claim that color is the limit of the transparent in a determinately bounded body. In this view, color is on (or in) the bodies that are seen as colored, and the existence of light is required, not for the *existence* of color, but rather for its *visibility*. This picture is opposed both by the Democritean (subjectivist) view, according to which colors exist "by convention," and the Epicurean-Lucretian view, according to which bodies are colored inasmuch as they emit streams of atoms of a certain kind. On the Democritean picture, colors depend for their existence on the existence of *perceivers*; on the Epicurean-Lucretian picture, colors depend for their existence on the existence of *light*. As Lucretius asks, rhetorically, "What color can there be in blinding darkness?" (*DRN* 2, 799–800). Because many seventeenth century mechanists tied their theories of color to their theories of light, it is no surprise that they disagreed with Aristotle, some allying themselves with the atomists, others not.

Galileo and Hobbes were the most prominent Democriteans. According to Hobbes, the relationship between color and light is that between species and genus, and hence color is no more than a kind of endeavor (instantaneous outward motion) in the retina: "*Colour* is light, but troubled light, namely, such as is generated by perturbed motion" (*DCo* 27.13). For example, "*Whiteness* is light, but light perturbed by the reflections of many beams of light coming to the eye together within a little space" (*DCo* 27.15). Blackness, on the other hand, is no more than the privation of light (*DCo* 27.16). Thus Hobbes's color is no less perceiver dependent than is Hobbes's light. Color, for Hobbes, is in the eye, not in or on the objects seen.

Galileo's Democriteanism extends to all the proper sensibles, including colors, sounds, odors, tastes, and heat and cold. His view is that these qualities, "so far as their objective existence is concerned, are nothing but mere names for something which resides exclusively in our sensitive body" (*Assayer*, 57). For Galileo, there is no more reason to believe that redness is a property of the body that causes in us a sensation of red than there is to believe that "ticklingness" is a property of the body that causes in us a tickling sensation (*Assayer*, 57).

On the side of objectivist atomism, we find Gassendi (and, of course, Charleton). Like Hobbes, Gassendi identifies color with light (OO 432; APG III.1.14, 173). But Gassendi's light is not a phantasm in the sentient, but rather a stream of light particles. So Gassendi's position is essentially the same as the one taken by Epicurus and Lucretius. Gassendi therefore admits that bodies have no color in the dark. But he goes on to point out that bodies in the dark remain *disposed* to appear colored when illuminated (OO 434; APG III.1.14, 174).

Descartes and his followers split the difference. Descartes distinguishes between "what is called colour in objects" and "the colour of which we have sensory awareness" (AT VIIIA 34–35; CSM I 218). The latter is merely a sensation of a particular kind in the incorporeal mind. But colors in the former sense "are nothing other than the various ways in which . . . bodies receive light and reflect it against our eyes" (AT VI 85; CSM I 153).[20] Black bodies "break up the light-rays that meet them and take away all their force"; white bodies "cause the rays to be reflected without bringing about any other change in their action"; and bodies of other colors (red, yellow, blue, etc.) "bring about an additional change similar to that which the movement of a ball undergoes when we graze it" (AT VI 91–92; CSM I 156).

What is the ontological status of these ways of receiving and reflecting light rays? Descartes does not say. On one interpretation, his view is that colors are causal *powers* that belong to bodies. Some have thought this interpretation confirmed by the following passage:

> The properties in external objects to which we apply the terms light, colour, smell, taste, sound, heat and cold . . . are, so far as we can see, simply various dispositions (*dispositiones*) in those objects [in the shapes, sizes, positions and movements of their parts][21] which make them able to set up various kinds of motions in our nerves [which are required to produce all the various sensations in our soul].[22]
>
> (AT VIIIA 322–323; CSM I 285)

But the word "disposition," in both Latin and French, is ambiguous: it can mean "power" or "arrangement." Descartes could be saying that the red color of an apple, say, is a power (call it P) in the apple, grounded in the shapes, sizes, positions, and movements of its parts, to produce the sensation of red in us; but he could also be saying that this color is nothing but the arrangement of corpuscles at the apple's surface (with their various shapes, sizes, positions, and motions) that grounds P. Indeed, his intellectual successor, Rohault, takes the latter, rather than the former, position. For example, Rohault claims that "the essence of whiteness consists only in the asperity [i.e. surface roughness] of the body one calls white" (*TP* I.27.55, 323).

There is evidence that Descartes and his contemporaries did not draw a sharp distinction between a disposition or power and its grounds. Witness, for instance, Kenelm Digby:

> [T]he colour of a body, is nothing else, but the power which that body hath of reflecting light unto the eye, in a certaine order and position: and consequently, is nothing else but the very superficies [i.e. surface] of it, with its asperity, or smoothnesse; with its pores, or inequalities; with its hardnesse, or softnesse; and such like.
>
> (*TT* I.29.6, 262)

This refusal to distinguish extends at least to Boyle. Boyle claims that the proper sensibles "are not in the bodies that are endowed with them any real or distinct entities [as the Scholastics believe], or differing from the matter itself furnished with such a determinate bigness, shape, or other mechanical modifications" (*OFQ* 3). But Boyle also likens the proper sensibles to the power that gold has of being dissoluble in *aqua regis* (a combination of nitric acid and hydrochloric acid) but not dissoluble in *aqua fortis* (a solution of nitric acid in water), which properties "are not in the gold anything distinct from its peculiar texture [i.e. arrangement of insensible parts]" (*OFQ* 3). So for Boyle, as for Digby (and possibly also for the Cartesians), there is no sharp distinction to be drawn between powers and their grounds.[23]

But there are also reasons for thinking that Boyle *should* have drawn this distinction, especially in the case of colors. For Boyle, like his Democritean contemporaries, assumes that bodies would have no proper sensibles (including color) if there were no perceivers in the world.[24] But Boyle *also* assumes (along with everyone else) that bodies would retain their common sensibles (shape, size, motion, position, and texture) if all perceivers were annihilated. Boyle's position is therefore incoherent. It is left to Locke to clear up the potential confusion, by making it clear that colors (and other proper sensibles) are powers in bodies to produce certain sorts of sensations in us, powers that are grounded in, but distinct from, the textures of those bodies (*E* 2.8.9–26, 134–143).

There is therefore a plethora of different mechanist theories of color in the seventeenth century. Some think that colors are instantaneous outward motions in our eyes, some that colors are streams of corpuscles emitted by bodies, and others that colors are textures of the surfaces of those bodies; some think that colors are merely sensations in incorporeal minds, and others that colors are powers in bodies to cause these sensations. Some think the word "color" sometimes means one of these things, and sometimes another; and some simply fail to distinguish between powers and textures. One would think that this is enough metaphysical variety in the midst of widespread agreement on the basic principles of scientific explanation. But there is one more view, crucial to posterity and the development of optics that we have not yet considered.

In 1671/72, Newton published a letter in the *Philosophical Transactions of the Royal Society* detailing his experiments with light and prisms. From these experiments, he drew several conclusions: first, that "[l]ight it self is a *Heterogeneous mixture of differently refrangible Rays* [i.e. rays differently susceptible of refraction]"; second, that "as the Rays of light differ in degrees of Refrangibility, so they also differ in their disposition to exhibit this or that particular colour"; third, that consequently "[c]olours are not *Qualifications of Light*, derived from Refractions, or Reflections of natural Bodies (as 'tis generally believed), but *Original* and *connate* properties, which in divers Rays are divers"; and fourth, that because "[c]olours are the *qualities* of Light" and no quality "may be the subject of and sustain another," it follows (1) that there are no colors in the dark, and (2) that light is a body. So this is yet another view. Color, for Newton, is not a body, but an accident of body. But it is not an accident of the perceiver's body (or any of its parts), nor an accident of bodies that are perceived as colored, nor a power in those bodies to produce a sensation of color: it is, rather, an accident of light itself, indeed an accident of the individual rays of which (white) light is quite literally composed.

7. Sound

There are almost as many disagreements among seventeenth century mechanists on the nature of sound as there are on the nature of color. The main difference consists in the somewhat greater receptiveness to Aristotle's theory of sound. Aristotle's view is that sound is the motion of air when its dissipation is prevented, whereas Lucretius's picture is that sound is a stream of particles emitted by sonorous bodies (see, e.g., *DRN* 1, 354–355, 490; *DRN* 2, 854–859). This disagreement reappears quite neatly in the works of seventeenth century philosophers. Digby, for example, agrees with Aristotle: "*motion* and *sound* are in themselves one and the same thing, though expressed by different names, and comprised in our understanding under different notions" (*TT* I.28.9, 257). Gassendi, on the other hand, follows Lucretius in thinking that sound is "nothing other than corpuscles of a particular shape transported at great speed from the sonorous body to the ear, moving the organ, and causing the sensation we call *hearing*" (*OO* 414; *APG*, III.1.12, 131).[25]

But there are also other views, similar to views already discussed in conjunction with light and color. Hobbes, for instance, claims that "the motion of the medium is not the sound itself, but the cause of it." Sound itself is but the outward reaction of the organ of hearing, or phantasm, produced by the motion of the medium created by the sonorous body (*DC* 485). Descartes splits the difference again, claiming that there is on the one hand the sensation of sound and on the other "a certain vibration of air which strikes our ears" (AT XI 5; CSM I 82).[26] Descartes also characterizes sounds, as he does all other proper sensibles, as "dispositions in those objects [in the shapes, sizes, positions, and movements of their parts] which make them able to set up various kinds of motions in our nerves" (AT VIIIA 322–323; CSM I 285). Rohault claims that the word "sound" is ambiguous in roughly the way Descartes suggests, though he makes clear that what causes in us the sensation of sound (and, so, the referent corresponding to one sense of the word "sound") is, as Aristotle suggests, a particular sort of motion in the sonorous body and in the air surrounding it (*TP* I.26.1–12, 270–274).[27] However, Locke thinks of sound on the model of all the other proper sensibles, namely as a power in sonorous bodies to cause auditory sensations in our minds (*E* 2.8); and Boyle treats sound, as he does all the proper sensibles, indifferently as Lockean powers or as textures (*OFQ* 5–6). And substantially the same pattern of disagreement recurs for the other sensible qualities, namely odor, flavor, and the tangible qualities (including heat and cold).

8. The primary-secondary quality distinction

The question now arises whether there is, for the philosophers of the seventeenth century, a distinction to be drawn between different kinds of qualities. Aristotle had distinguished between the proper sensibles and the common sensibles on *epistemic* grounds. For many of the new mechanists, this distinction is no more. Digby, for instance, emphasizes "that odors may be tasted; that the relish of meates may be smelled; that magnitude and figure may be heard; that light may be felt; and that soundes may be seene" (*TT* I.28.9, 256). And, indeed, if any quality is reduced to motion, or to a stream of particles, or to texture (e.g. roughness), then it follows that it is no longer a *proper* sensible, for it is either unperceived or perceivable (at least in principle) by more than one sense. But the lack of an epistemic distinction does not entail the lack of a *metaphysical* distinction. And, indeed, at least some seventeenth century mechanists favored the making of such a distinction. But, naturally, they did not all characterize the distinction in the same way.

Let us then divide up the qualities into two groups. Let us count shape, size, motion and rest, position, and texture as *primary qualities*; and let us count color, sound, odor, flavor, and tangible qualities (e.g. heat and cold, roughness and smoothness) as *secondary qualities*. Is there any metaphysical difference between the primary qualities and the secondary qualities? If so, what is the proper criterion for the primary-secondary quality distinction? If there is such a distinction, does it make a difference? If so, what kind of difference?

There are some seventeenth century philosophers for whom there is really no metaphysical difference between the primary qualities and the secondary qualities. Hobbes, for example, thinks of secondary qualities as just particular kinds of primary qualities, for he identifies all secondary qualities with phantasms, that is with outward-directed motions in the sense organs or perceivers. There is, of course, a difference in the *location* of these qualities: many primary qualities (though not all) are in the world external to perceivers, whereas all secondary qualities are in perceivers' sense organs, and hence inside their own bodies. Digby, who identifies colors with the surfaces of colored bodies and who identifies sounds with motions, is also someone for whom there is no metaphysical primary-secondary quality distinction.

At the same time, the difference in location could be taken as the source of one criterion for the distinction. For, in Hobbes's view if not in Digby's, secondary qualities are in perceivers, and depend for their existence on the existence of the perceivers they are in. Hobbes is committed to the view that if all perceivers were annihilated, there would be no color (sound, odor, flavor, etc.) in the world, though shape (size, motion, position, and texture) of corporeal substances other than perceivers would continue to exist. So it is possible to construct a primary-secondary quality distinction for Hobbes, one that is founded on the criterion of perceiver dependence. It is exactly in this sense that there is a primary-secondary quality distinction for Galileo, who insists that, unlike primary qualities, secondary qualities "are nothing but mere names for something which resides in our sensitive body, so that if the perceiving creatures were removed, all of these qualities would be annihilated and abolished from existence" (*Assayer*, 57).

The Cartesians (Descartes, Rohault, Desgabets, Cordemoy, and Malebranche) are clearly a more complex case, for they distinguish between two senses of each word that is commonly thought to designate a single secondary quality. In one sense, secondary qualities are merely modes of incorporeal mental substance (i.e. sensations); in the other, secondary qualities are the corporeal (for Cordemoy and Malebranche, the occasional) causes of these sensations. In the latter sense, then, the Cartesians (despite their disagreements on the details) understand secondary qualities to be nothing but a subset of the primary qualities. In this way, the Cartesians and Hobbes find common ground. But in the former sense, the Cartesians and Hobbes part ways. For the Cartesians understand secondary qualities in the former sense to be sensations, and, in this approach, secondary qualities (in the relevant sense) are not in the external world at all, but in the mind.

Indeed, this is the most radical way of distinguishing between primary qualities and secondary qualities: secondary qualities are in immaterial substances, whereas primary qualities are in material substances. Insofar as material and immaterial substances are distinct, primary qualities and secondary qualities are distinct. For Descartes, primary qualities are modes of extension, different ways for bodies to be extended in length, breadth, and depth, whereas secondary qualities (in one sense) are modes of thought, different ways for minds to ideate. It follows, of course, that the annihilation of perceiving *minds* (though not of perceiving *bodies* or *sense organs*) would result in the annihilation of secondary qualities (in the relevant sense) but would not result in the annihilation of primary qualities. Thus, despite their fundamental disagreement over the nature of mind – Hobbesians being materialists, the Cartesians dualists – both sets of philosophers converge on the view that some sense of perceiver dependence distinguishes the secondary qualities (in one sense) from the primary qualities.

There is also a metaphysical primary-secondary quality distinction to be drawn within the atomist worldview. For Gassendi and Charleton, secondary qualities are streams or arrangements of atoms of different determinate primary qualities, atoms that themselves possess none of the secondary qualities inasmuch as they neither emit such atom streams nor possess other atoms as parts. On the atomist picture, secondary qualities are therefore *substances* or *arrangements of substances*, rather than accidents (or properties, or modes) of substance. This is a metaphysical distinction of first importance, but it is completely unrelated to the criterion of perceiver dependence that matters to Hobbes, Descartes, and Galileo. Indeed, it is an important aspect of the atomist picture that secondary qualities, like primary qualities, would not disappear if perceivers were annihilated.

There are other ways of drawing a metaphysical distinction between primary qualities and secondary qualities, ways that are commonly, though – I believe – mistakenly, attributed to Locke. Locke begins his discussion by distinguishing between ideas, namely the mind-dependent immediate objects of perception, and qualities, namely the powers to produce these ideas in our minds. Locke then characterizes primary qualities as "utterly inseparable from the Body, in what estate soever it be," and secondary qualities as "nothing in the Objects themselves, but Powers to produce various Sensations in us by their *primary Qualities*" (E 2.8.8–10, 134–135).

At first, the picture seems straightforward. Primary and secondary qualities are both powers to produce ideas in minds; secondary qualities are *mere* powers, in that they are *separable* from the objects that have them; primary qualities are *more than mere* powers, in that they are *inseparable* from the objects that have them. But this is almost certainly *not* the picture that Locke favors. Consider the difference between determinate and determinable qualities. Anything that has any shape at all possesses the *determinable* quality, Shape; the particular shape that anything with Shape possesses is its *determinate* shape. So, Shape is the determinable of which roundness and squareness are determinates. The basic problem with the separability criterion for the primary-secondary quality distinction is that, even though it works at the level of the determinables, it fails at the level of the determinates. On Locke's view, primary-quality determinables are inseparable, whereas secondary-quality determinables are separable, from bodies: every body must have Shape, but not every body must have Color (or Sound, or Odor, etc.). (After all, as Locke emphasizes, " 'tis plain [*Porphyre*] *has no colour in the dark*"; E 2.8.19, 139). Unfortunately, primary-quality determinates are just as separable as secondary-quality determinates: just as an object can lose its particular color (as an almond can lose its white color when it is pounded; E 2.8.20, 139), so an object can lose its particular shape (think of the same pounded almond). But Locke clearly holds that the distinction between primary and secondary qualities holds as much for determinates as it does for determinables. So it is unlikely that Locke's distinction is grounded in the separability criterion.

Locke is also commonly thought to have distinguished between primary and secondary qualities on grounds of *resemblance*. For he writes,

> [T]he *Ideas of primary Qualities* of Bodies, *are Resemblances* of them, and their Patterns do really exist in the Bodies themselves; but the *Ideas, produced* in us by these *Secondary Qualities, have no resemblance* of them at all. There is nothing like our *Ideas*, existing in the Bodies themselves.
>
> (E 2.8.15, 137)

Locke is here picking up on a strong and continuous strand of seventeenth century opposition to Scholastic theories of perception. Even before Locke, Descartes had made a point of emphasizing the fact that there is no resemblance between secondary qualities (thought of as sensations) and their causes in the external world (see AT XI 3–6; CSM I 81–82, AT VI 85 and 130–131; CSM I 153–154 and 167–168, and AT VIIIA 34–35; CSM I 218). This was important to Descartes, because it is one of the hallmarks of Scholastic theories of perception that there is such a resemblance. For the Scholastics, perception occurs in the soul when it receives an accidental form that is propagated through the relevant medium from a body that possesses that form. Indeed, on the Scholastic picture, there is not merely resemblance, there is also *identity*, between the immediate object of perception and its external cause.

In characterizing the primary-secondary quality distinction in terms of resemblance, Locke is therefore making a point to distance himself from the Scholastics. But what is significant about this way of drawing the distinction is that Locke takes it to follow immediately[28] from the following statement: "[Secondary qualities], whatever reality we, by mistake, attribute to them, are in truth nothing in the Objects themselves, but Powers to produce various Sensations in us, and *depend on those primary Qualities*" (E 2.8.14, 137). Locke is telling us here that we mistakenly take secondary qualities to be *real* qualities, that it is in this sense that we take secondary qualities to be more than mere powers. The nub of the distinction, then, is that primary qualities are real whereas secondary qualities are not. And the resemblance criterion, properly understood, is that ideas of primary qualities resemble *real* qualities in objects, whereas ideas of secondary qualities do not.

But what is it for a quality to be real? Locke writes that primary qualities "*are really in them*, whether any ones Senses perceive them or no: and therefore they may be called *real Qualities*, because they really exist in those Bodies" (E 2.8.17, 137–138); that "*Motion and Figure are really in the Manna*, whether we take notice of them or no" (E 2.8.18, 138); and that size, shape, texture, and motion "may properly be called *real Original*, or *primary Qualities*, because they are in the things themselves, whether they are perceived or no" (E 2.8.23, 141). For Locke, then, a quality is *real* when its existence in an object is independent of its being perceived to exist in that object. And Locke's fundamental way of distinguishing between primary and secondary qualities is that the latter are perceiver dependent whereas the former are not.

Locke's way of drawing the primary-secondary quality distinction is therefore similar to the way in which Hobbes, Descartes, and Galileo draw it. But this agreement also masks significant differences of opinion with respect to the metaphysical facts that ground the distinction. For Hobbes and Galileo, secondary qualities exist in perceivers' sense organs; for Descartes, such qualities (in one sense) exist in perceivers' immaterial minds. But for Locke, secondary qualities are (or include) *relations* between perceivers and the objects of perception. This is because secondary qualities are powers in the objects of perception to cause sensations in perceivers' minds, and, as Locke later points out, "*Power includes in it some kind of relation*" (E 2.21.3, 234). From the metaphysical point of view, the important thing about relations is that they cannot exist in the absence of their relata: just as Sophie can't be to the left of Alice if Sophie or Alice doesn't exist, so too does a piece of chalk not have the power to cause an idea of white in Dana's mind if Dana or the chalk doesn't exist (see note 24). Indeed, it is the latter metaphysical fact that explains *why* Locke is adamant that secondary qualities would disappear if all perceivers were annihilated (see E 2.31.2, 376).[29]

As we have seen, there is some evidence that Boyle, in some moments at least, thinks of secondary qualities as textures, and the explanation for this is probably that he does not distinguish between powers and their grounds. There are also a few passages in which Locke makes the same identification, quite possibly for the same reason. For he writes that "whiteness or redness are not in [porphyry] at any time, but such a texture, that hath the power to produce such a sensation [of whiteness or redness] in us" (E 2.8.19, 139). But this is not likely to be Locke's considered view. For textures are non-relational, perceiver-independent arrangements of corpuscles, and thus *real* (in Locke's technical sense) and hence metaphysically on a par with primary qualities. Indeed, Locke himself makes a point of including "texture" several times in his list of primary qualities (E 2.8.10, 135; 2.8.14, 137; 2.8.18, 138).

The most widely recognized criterion for distinguishing between primary and secondary qualities in the seventeenth century, then, is the reality (or perceiver-dependence) criterion. But does this distinction among qualities *make a difference*? Some think that the significance of the distinction lies in the thought that secondary qualities are not proper objects of scientific investigation. This is certainly true of the Cartesians, who think of the world as divided into corporeal substances (the behavior of which is governed by immutable laws) and incorporeal substances (the behavior of which is often subject to the will, which is free and undetermined). But this difference stems not from the reality criterion itself, but rather from the specific Cartesian metaphysics underlying the reality criterion. The fact that secondary qualities are perceiver dependent does not entail that they are beyond the reach of scientific enquiry. Indeed, for Hobbes, or Galileo, or Locke, or Boyle, it is in principle possible for science to tell us a great deal more about the nature of the secondary qualities. The significance of the distinction between primary and secondary qualities, then, does not concern the conduct of science, but rather concerns its impact on the demise of Scholastic theories of perception. For if there is one principle on which all advocates of the distinction are agreed, it is that the lack of resemblance between secondary qualities and their causes dooms the Scholastic picture of the relation between mind and world.

9. Arguments for the primary-secondary quality distinction

Did any of the seventeenth century mechanists who distinguished explicitly between primary and secondary qualities provide any arguments for the distinction independent of the arguments for their accounts of the nature of individual sensible qualities? Galileo and Locke did so, and it is instructive to consider their reasoning.

Galileo's view is that secondary qualities, unlike primary qualities, are radically perceiver dependent in that they are merely states of the sensing body. Galileo provides two reasons for taking this position. The first is that "if the perceiving creatures were removed, all [secondary] qualities would be annihilated and abolished from existence," whereas the same is not true of any of the primary qualities (*Assayer*, 57). Although this argument establishes at best a kind of perceiver dependence, it does not establish that the secondary qualities are *in perceivers*. For it is possible to conceive of secondary qualities as Locke does, namely as *relations* between perceivers and external objects. But the argument's most notable weakness, from our own point of view, is that few would now accept Galileo's assumption that colors, sounds, odors, flavors, and tangible qualities would disappear if all perceivers were annihilated. Still this is an assumption that was shared by a number of seventeenth century mechanists, who took the truth of the relevant counterfactual as a point in favor of their theories of qualities.

Galileo's second reason for accepting Democriteanism is that we are not "compelled to conceive of bodies as necessarily conjoined with such further conditions as being red or white, bitter or sweet, having sound or being mute, or possessing a pleasant or unpleasant fragrance" (*Assayer*, 56). But this argument is unpersuasive, for the most that could be concluded from the fact that *it is possible to conceive* of a body without color (flavor, sound, etc.) is that it is *possible* for a body to exist without color (flavor, sound, etc.), that is that color (flavor, sound, etc.) is not *essential* to bodies. But from the fact that it is possible for a body to exist without color (flavor, sound, etc.), it simply doesn't follow that color (flavor, sound, etc.) is perceiver dependent, any more than it follows from the fact that it is possible for a body to exist without its particular shape that that shape is perceiver dependent. Now if primary qualities were essential to bodies whereas secondary qualities were not, this would establish the existence of some distinction between the two kinds of qualities. Unfortunately, as we have seen, this kind of argument works at best at the level of the determinables, and not at all at the level of the determinates. This is because primary-quality determinates are no more essential to the bodies that have them than their secondary-quality determinate counterparts.

What of Locke's reasons? Locke provides three separate arguments for the conclusion that secondary qualities are not real (in the technical sense). Assuming, as Locke does, that primary qualities are real, these arguments, if successful, would indeed establish the existence of an important distinction.

Here is Locke's first argument:

> Let us consider the red and white colours in *Porphyre*: Hinder light but from striking on it, and its Colours vanish; it no longer produces any such *Ideas* in us: Upon the return of Light, it produces these appearances on us again. Can any one think any real alterations are made in the *Porphyre*, by the presence or absence of Light; and that those *Ideas* of whiteness and redness, are really in *Porphyre* in the light, when 'tis plain *it has no colour in the dark*?
>
> (E 2.8.19, 139)

Locke here tries to show that the redness and whiteness of porphyry are neither real in the dark nor real in the light. Assume first that redness is a real quality of porphyry in the dark. In being real, redness is such that its existence does not depend on its being perceived. So, porphyry must be red in the dark. But, as Locke insists, porphyry is colorless in the dark. By *reductio*, then, redness is not a real quality of porphyry in the dark.

(*Mutatis mutandis* for whiteness.) Now assume that redness is a real quality of porphyry in the light. But, as Locke also insists, the presence or absence of light does not produce any *real* alterations in porphyry. Consequently, if redness is a real quality in the light, then it must be a real quality in the dark. But, as has just been established, redness is not a real quality in the dark. By *reductio*, then, redness is not a real quality of porphyry in the light. (*Mutatis mutandis* for whiteness.) *Ergo*, redness and whiteness are not real qualities of porphyry, whether in the dark or in the light.

This argument, though valid, is only as persuasive as the assumption, shared, as we've seen, by several of Locke's contemporaries, that bodies have no color in the dark. Unfortunately, it is also an assumption that few of us take for granted nowadays. Locke's first argument, then, is dialectically ineffective.

Locke's second argument is brief:

> Pound an Almond, and the clear white *Colour* will be altered into a dirty one, and the sweet *Taste* into an oily one. What real Alteration can the beating of the Pestle make in any Body, but an Alteration of the *Texture* of it?
> (E 2.8.20, 139)

The reasoning here is simple. The pounding of an almond changes its color and taste, but the only real quality in an almond that it is possible to change by pounding it is its texture. So the color and taste of an almond are either textures or not real qualities; but neither the color nor the taste of an almond is identical to its texture. Therefore, the color and taste of an almond are not real qualities.

The problem with the argument is also simple. For it begs the question against his opponents for Locke to assume that texture is the only real quality in an almond that can be changed by pounding it. Now it might be thought that this assumption is a consequence of mechanism. But it isn't. Mechanists are committed to the view that pounding changes the texture of the almond, inasmuch as pounding produces a rearrangement of the almond's constituent corpuscles. But mechanists are not *ipso facto* committed to the view that texture is the *only* real quality that the pounding can change, unless they assume what Locke is trying to prove, namely that colors and tastes are not real qualities.

Locke's third and final argument is also straightforward:

> *Ideas* being thus distinguished and understood, we may be able to give an Account, how the same Water, at the same time, may produce the *Idea* of Cold by one Hand, and of Heat by the other: Whereas it is impossible, that the same Water, if those *Ideas* were really in it, should at the same time be both Hot and Cold.
> (E 2.8.21, 139)

The reasoning here is simple too. The same water (call it W), at the same time, produces an idea of heat when touched by one hand and produces an idea of cold when touched by the other hand; but anything that produces an idea of heat when touched by a hand has the quality, heat, and anything that produces an idea of cold when touched by a hand has the quality, cold. So W, at the same time, has heat and cold; but heat and cold are opposites, and it is impossible for opposite real qualities to exist in the same substance at the same time. So heat and cold are not both real qualities; but heat is a real quality if and only if cold is a real quality; consequently, neither heat nor cold is a real quality.

The problem with this argument, as George Berkeley points out, is that it proves too much:

> Now, why may we not as well argue that figure and extension are not patterns or resemblances of qualities existing in matter, because to the same eye at different stations, or eyes of a different texture at the same station, they appear various and cannot, therefore, be the images of anything settled and determinate without the mind?
>
> (PHK 14)

Berkeley's point is that if Locke's argument succeeds in showing that heat and cold are not real qualities, then it also succeeds in showing that figure and extension are not real qualities. But, as everyone agrees, figure and extension are real qualities. Therefore, Locke's third and final argument fails.

The result of Galileo's and Locke's efforts is that the reasoning in favor of a primary-secondary quality distinction based on the reality criterion of perceiver dependence is inconclusive. This should not surprise us. For even now there is a live debate on the metaphysical status of secondary qualities, a debate in which many of the most influential positions are identical to, or direct descendants of, positions taken by many of the mechanists of the seventeenth century.

10. Conclusion

Philosophers of the seventeenth century who offered theories of sensible and occult qualities found their intellectual bearings within the background legacies of ancient atomism and Scholastic Aristotelianism. The gradual ascendancy of atomism and corresponding decline of Aristotelianism shaped the debate and gave birth to a new mechanism that embraced the explanatory primacy of primary qualities over secondary qualities. Although divided over the question of the existence of physically indivisible bodies and the possibility of empty space, the mechanists of the seventeenth century abandoned the Aristotelian conception of natural motion, reduced all motion to local motion, and strove to explain all natural phenomena, both manifest and occult, much as the ancient atomists had, namely as the result of collisions among insensible corpuscles and their agglomerations. But this agreement on the proper model of scientific explanation masked serious metaphysical disagreements over the nature and location of the qualities of corporeal substances. Mechanism itself did not constrain the multiplication of proposals, and the speculative ingenuity of its numerous proponents filled the space of logical possibilities canvassed previously.

Mechanism is now a defunct explanatory research program, but the dream of mechanism lives on in the shape of the hope for a unified physics based on a finite number of general principles. Interestingly, the abandonment of mechanism and its replacement by quantum mechanics and general relativity has not created any greater convergence on a single theory (or family of theories) of sensible qualities. Indeed, secondary-quality theorists have carved new positions in logical space that the mechanists of the seventeenth century could not have dreamed of. Perhaps the moral of the story is that metaphysics does not walk in the shadow of science; rather science and metaphysics walk hand in hand.[30]

Notes

1. For my abbreviations of particular works, please see my bibliography.
2. Or by the existence and arrangement of the primary qualities possessed by other objects, whether sensible or insensible.
3. Detailed consideration of occult qualities is beyond the scope of this chapter. Mechanists approached the problem of explaining the nature of occult qualities by reducing them to the motion or arrangement of insensible material particles of various shapes and sizes. Gravity was to be understood as a body's being pushed or pulled by a very large number of insensible corpuscles (of light, or of subtle, fluid matter). Similar explanations were proposed to account for magnetism and (static) electricity.
4. Aristotle did not provide a theory of magnetism or static electricity, though he was well aware of (Thales's theories of) magnetic and electrostatic phenomena (in the form of the existence of lodestones, and in the form of rubbed amber attracting pieces of chaff and hair; see *DA* 405a, 411a; see also Plato, *Timaeus*, 80c). He did have a theory of lightning but did not connect it with the phenomenon of static electricity. In Aristotle's view, lightning is constituted by the burning of a dry wind that is squeezed out of contracting clouds (*Met.* II.9, 369b).
5. Material substances that fall to earth are composed predominantly of earth or water. This is the nature of gravity. For Aristotle, gravity is not produced by pushing, pulling, or by some attractive force possessed by Earth: it is simply the action of a body moving toward its natural place, namely the center of the world.
6. Sextus Empiricus, *Against the Mathematicians* VII, 135; translated by C.C.W. Taylor.
7. Epicurus and Lucretius recognized that a state of affairs in which atoms naturally move in the same direction (downward) through the void at the same (breakneck) speed would produce no collisions, hence no grouping of atoms, hence no visible bodies. To account for the phenomena, they therefore postulated that some atoms move unpredictably ever so slightly off course (the "swerve"), thereby colliding with, and thence combining with, each other (*DRN* 2, 216–224).
8. Descartes's definition of motion in the strict sense is taken up by his intellectual successors, including most notably Jacques Rohault (see *TP* I.10, 62).

    As Garber (1992: 170–171) notes, Descartes's definition of motion in the strict sense lands him in hot water when it comes to articulating the laws of physics. For it is difficult to make sense of the direction or speed of a body when it is in motion and its immediate vicinity is constantly changing. Part of the problem here is that what counts as the "immediate vicinity" of a body is essentially arbitrary. If the man on the ship starts walking toward the bow, he is being transferred away from the chair in which he is sitting; but he is not being transferred away from the clothes he happens to be wearing. And yet both the chair and the clothes have equal title to be considered part of the man's immediate vicinity.
9. Galileo Galilei uses the *Dialogue Concerning the Two Chief World Systems* to criticize Aristotle's account of the natural motion of material substances. As Galileo points out, the observation that unsuspended bodies fall to earth of their own accord is consistent, not only with Aristotle's own hypothesis that earth is naturally drawn to the center of the universe, but also with the competing Copernican hypothesis that smaller bits of earth are drawn to larger bits of earth. The first hypothesis, unlike the second, predicts that if the earth were pushed away from the center of the universe and left there, it would naturally move toward the center.
10. Galileo too makes use of this thought experiment in the *Dialogue Concerning the Two Chief World Systems*, except that there his Aristotelian character, Simplicio, admits that a body that moved through a hole in the earth toward its center would simply keep going past the center if it were unimpeded.
11. Other attempts to prove the proposition that bodies at rest cannot move of themselves fare no better than Hobbes's. Kenelm Digby, for example, urges that to suppose that a body "can moove it selfe towards any determinate part or place of the universe, of its owne intrinsecall inclination" is to suppose, absurdly, that it "by a quality in it can worke upon it selfe" (*TT* I.9.8, 70). Digby's idea here is that only substances can "worke upon" other substances, and thus modes, including the "intrinsecall inclinations" of bodies, cannot cause substances to move. But this assumption, too, simply begs the question against the Scholastics.
12. The widespread hostility toward the Aristotelian distinction between natural and violent motion did not automatically translate into hostility toward *any* distinction between kinds of motion that might legitimately be classified by means of the same vocabulary. Digby, for example, claims that "wee may determine those motions to be naturall unto bodies which have constant causes, or percutients to make them alwayse in such bodies; and those violent, which are contrary to such naturall motions" (*TT* I.10.1, 76). And Charleton, following Pierre Gassendi (*OO* 343), understands "a *Natural* Motion to be that, *which is made either of Natures own accord, or without any Repugnancy*; and a *Violent* to be that, *which is made either Praeternaturally, or with some Repugnancy*" (*PEGC* IV.2, 444).

13 Notice that Locke identifies solidity as one of the inseparable determinable qualities of body. Indeed, for Locke, as for the atomists, solidity is understood to be an essential property of every body: according to the common conception of body, nothing that fails to be solid could be a body (*E* 2.13.11, 171–172). Locke here disagrees with Descartes, for whom the essence of body consists in its being extended (AT VIIIA 25; CSM I 210; see also AT VIIIA 42; CSM I 224). This would be a tempest in a teapot were it not for the fact that Descartes uses the doctrine that the nature of body is extension to prove, against the atomists, that a vacuum (namely an extended, intangible substance devoid of body) is impossible (AT VIIIA 49; CSM I 229–230). In denying that the nature of body is extension, Locke is in effect defending the *possibility* of a vacuum in nature (*E* 2.13.21, 176–177).

14 "By the *Rayes of Light*, we understand, *certain most tenuious streams of Igneous Particles, in a continued fluor* [i.e. stream], *and with ineffable pernicity* [i.e. swiftness] *succeding each other in direct lines . . . towards the eye, and sensibly affecting the same*" (*PEGC* III.5.1, 198).

15 With respect to the identification of light with a kind of fire, Charleton is thinking of Gassendi (*OO* 424–425), but he also agrees with Digby, who defines light to be "fire extremely dilated, and without mixture of any other grosse body" (*TT* I.6.4, 43).

Gassendi and Charleton are also interested in rebutting Aristotle's arguments for light's incorporeality (*OO* 430–432; *PEGC* III.5.2, 206–207). Objection 1: If light were a body, it would be one that travels through transparent bodies (e.g. air and water), and hence it would follow, absurdly, that there could be two bodies in the same place at the same time (*DA* II.7, 418b). Reply 1: Light travels through the pores and empty spaces that exist in all compound bodies. Objection 2: If light were a body, it could not move instantaneously (for all motion takes time); but we observe light moving instantaneously from sky to earth and from east to west (*DA* II.7, 418b). Reply 2: Light particles move with a speed that surpasses anything we can imagine. Objection 3: The rays of light are invisible and hence incorporeal. Reply 3: Invisibility (as in the case of wind) does not entail incorporeality. Objection 4: If the sun were continually expelling fiery particles, it would have long since died out. Reply 4: The sun is huge and the fiery particles emitted very small. Objection 5: If light were a kind of fire, it would heat and burn everything it touches; but it doesn't. Reply 5: Light doesn't burn because of the attenuation of its rays. For similar replies to similar objections, see Digby (*TT* I.7–8, 45–63).

16 Hobbes sees it as an advantage of his theory that it can explain the widespread but mistaken belief that light is in the world external to the perceiver. For it is "by reason that the endeavour [of which the relevant phantasm consists] is now outwards [that the phantasm] doth always appear as something situate without the organ" (*DC* 391).

17 Gassendi offers trenchant criticisms of Descartes's theory in the *Syntagma* (*OO* 423–424; *APG* III.1.13, 150–154).

18 Pierre-Sylvain Régis, a fellow Cartesian, takes the claim of ambiguity one step further, alleging three-way polysemy. For Régis, there are two kinds of corporeal light: primary or radical light, which belongs to luminous bodies themselves, and secondary or derived light, which is the quality of the relevant medium (whether air, water, glass, etc.) that is impressed by primary light and causes the sensation of light in our minds (*Cours* 8.2.9, 137–138).

Rohault and other Cartesians, unlike Hobbes, locate the sensation of light, not in the eye (or any other part of the perceiver's body), but rather in the perceiver's incorporeal soul. Still, like Hobbes, they locate light (in one sense) on the side of the perceiver, rather than on the side of the external world.

19 According to Rohault's hypothesis, we should find some philosophers sometimes locating light in the perceiver and sometimes locating light in the external world. And, indeed, Malebranche does exactly this. On the one hand, we find him saying "that light is not and cannot be a property or a modification [i.e. mode] of matter and that it is in fact within the soul itself" (*Search* 1.12.5/*LO* 59). But on the other hand, we also find him saying that light consists in a pressure vibration of a particular frequency that subtle matter produces on the retina (*Eluc*. 16/*LO* 689). The Cartesian, Gerauld de Cordemoy, also distinguishes between (1) what causes the bodies we call "luminous" to excite in us the sensation (*sentiment*) that makes us perceive them and (2) that very sensation (*OP* 260).

20 See Rohault (*TP* I.27.1–2, 291–292). Robert Desgabets, whose work is heavily influenced by Descartes, agrees, extending the ambiguity thesis to all words used to designate the proper sensibles. The right method, he says,

> teaches us the true nature of all sensible qualities, namely that when considered in external objects, they are nothing other than the modes and local dispositions of the parts of matter, by which means they become able of making all sorts of impressions on our senses, . . . [but]

> when considered as in ourselves, they are nothing other than the proper perceptions and sensations [*sentiments*] in our souls, excited on the occasion of what happens outside us and subsequently in our own bodies.
>
> (GRN 1, 110)

Régis claims that the word "color" is three-way polysemous in just the way that the word "light" is (see note 18 and *Cours* 8.2.16, 173–174).

21 Added in the French version.
22 Added in a subsequent translation approved by Descartes.
23 Further evidence for this comes from the fact that Boyle claims that the poisonous power of beaten glass "is really nothing distinct from the glass itself . . . as it is furnished with that determinate bigness and figure of parts which have been acquired by comminution [i.e. pulverization]" (*OFQ* 3). As for the Cartesians, Rohault himself claims that

> the nature of all sensible qualities, or of all these different powers that various bodies have to make us sense as they do, consists only in the various sizes, the various shapes, and the different motions of the small parts of which these bodies are composed.
>
> (Entretiens, 58)

24 As Boyle puts it, "[I]f there were no sensitive beings, those bodies that are now the objects of our senses would be but *dispositively*, if I may so speak, endowed with colours, tastes, and the like, and *actually* but only with those more catholic [i.e. universal] affections of bodies – figure, motion, texture, &c." (*OFQ* 6). Boyle's point is that, in the absence of any perceivers, a body would not have any proper sensible but would have "such a disposition of its constituent corpuscles that, in case it were duly applied to the sensory of an animal, it would produce . . . a sensible quality" (*OFQ* 6).

It might be thought that, even in the absence of any perceivers, bodies retain the disposition or power to produce ideas in their minds. In the sense in which the words "disposition" and "power" are used today, this is true. But Boyle is clearly using these words in a different sense. For Boyle, it is impossible for A to have a power in relation to B unless both A and B exist. In other words, powers are relations, and relations can exist only if their relata exist. This is the point of Boyle's famous analogy of the lock and key. Before the invention of the key, a lock "was only a piece of iron of such a determinate figure." It is only after the invention of the key that the lock obtains "a new capacity . . . of being made to lock or unlock by" the key (*OFQ* 3). This point is important to the discussion of the primary-secondary quality distinction in section 8. (For further details, see Anstey [2000: 102–105] and Kaufman [2006].)

25 Charleton agrees with Gassendi, taking great pains to establish the "CORPORIETY of Sounds" (*PEGC*, III.6.2, 213–222). His argument for this conclusion is similar to his argument for the corporeality of light (see section 5).
26 Malebranche agrees (*Search*, Elucidation 16, 690), as do Desgabets (*GRN* 1, 110), as we've seen, and Cordemoy (*OP* 234).
27 Régis puts all this together, alleging three-way polysemy: "[the word 'sound'] signifies sometimes a sensation in the soul, sometimes a certain motion in sonorous bodies, and sometimes a certain air turbulence that depends on the motion of sonorous bodies" (see notes 18 and 20, and *Cours* 8.2.7, 123).
28 Locke introduces the resemblance criterion with the words "From whence I think it is easie to draw this Observation" (*E* 2.8.15, 137).
29 Interestingly, if this reading of Locke is correct, then primary qualities are not qualities in Locke's technical sense of "quality." For *in the technical sense* qualities are powers to cause ideas in minds, and all powers are (or include) relations. So, if primary qualities were qualities *in the technical sense*, then, as relations between perceived objects and perceivers, they too would disappear if all perceivers were annihilated. But Locke clearly thinks that the annihilation of all perceivers would not cause an apple's shape, size, motion, or texture to go out of existence.
30 I would like to thank the following for their useful comments and other helpful contributions to this project: David Foldi, Monte Johnson, Dan Kaufman, Antonia LoLordo, Dana Nelkin, Margaret Osler, Don Rutherford, and Dan Schwartz. I talked through some of the issues relating to Locke's version of the primary-secondary quality distinction at a miniconference in honor of Nicholas Jolley at UC Irvine in June 2009. I would like to thank all the conference participants for their constructive comments and suggestions, particularly Sven Bernecker, Sean Greenberg, Paul Hoffman, Nick Jolley, Jan-Erik Jones, Ed McCann, Larry Nolan, Don Rutherford, and Martin Schwab.

Bibliography

Further reading

Alexander, P., *Ideas, Qualities and Corpuscles: Locke and Boyle on the External World*, Cambridge: Cambridge University Press, 1985.

Allen, K., "Mechanism, Resemblance and Secondary Qualities: From Descartes to Locke," *British Journal for the History of Philosophy* 16 (2008): 273–291.

Anstey, P.R., *The Philosophy of Robert Boyle*, London: Routledge, 2000.

Ayers, M.R., *Locke*, London: Routledge, 1991.

Bolton, M.B., "Locke and Pyrrhonism: The Doctrine of Primary and Secondary Qualities," in *The Skeptical Tradition*, edited by M. Burnyeat, Berkeley: University of California Press, 1983, 353–376.

Clarke, D., *Occult Powers and Hypotheses: Cartesian Natural Philosophy Under Louis XIV*, Oxford: Clarendon Press, 1989.

Cottingham, J., "Descartes on Colour," *Proceedings of the Aristotelian Society* 90 (1990): 231–246.

Curley, E.M., "Locke, Boyle, and the Distinction Between Primary and Secondary Qualities," *Philosophical Review* 81 (1972): 438–464.

Fisher, S., *Pierre Gassendi's Philosophy and Science: Atomism for Empiricists*, Leiden: E.J. Brill, 2005.

Garber, D., *Descartes' Metaphysical Physics*, Chicago: University of Chicago Press, 1992.

Garber, D., J. Henry, L. Joy, and A. Gabbey, "New Doctrines of Body and Its Powers, Place, and Space," in *The Cambridge History of Seventeenth Century Philosophy*, edited by D. Garber and M. Ayers, Cambridge: Cambridge University Press, 1998, 553–623.

Jacovides, M., "Locke's Resemblance Theses," *Philosophical Review* 108 (1999): 461–496.

Jacovides, M., "Cambridge Changes of Color," *Pacific Philosophical Quarterly* 81 (2000): 142–163.

Jacovides, M., "Locke's Distinctions Between Primary and Secondary Qualities," in *The Cambridge Companion to Locke's Essay*, edited by L. Newman, Cambridge: Cambridge University Press, 2007.

Johnson, M.R., "Was Gassendi an Epicurean?" *History of Philosophy Quarterly* 20 (2003): 339–360.

Kaufman, D., "Locks, Schlocks, and Poisoned Peas: Boyle on Actual and Dispositive Qualities," *Oxford Studies in Early Modern Philosophy* 3 (2006): 153–198.

Keating, L., "Un-Locke-ing Boyle: Boyle on Primary and Secondary Qualities," *History of Philosophy Quarterly* 10 (1993): 305–323.

Keating, L., "Reconsidering the Basis of Locke's Primary-Secondary Quality Distinction," *British Journal for the History of Philosophy* 6 (1998): 169–192.

Keating, L., "The Role of the Concept of Sense in *Principles* IV, 189–98," *British Journal for the History of Philosophy* 12 (2004): 199–222.

Lennon, T.M., *The Battle of the Gods and Giants: The Legacies of Descartes and Gassendi, 1655–1715*, Princeton: Princeton University Press, 1993.

LoLordo, A., *Pierre Gassendi and the Birth of Early Modern Philosophy*, Cambridge: Cambridge University Press, 2006.

Menn, S., "The Greatest Stumbling Block: Descartes' Denial of Real Qualities," in *Descartes and His Contemporaries: Meditations, Objections, and Replies*, edited by R. Ariew and M. Grene, Chicago: University of Chicago Press, 1995, 182–207.

Osler, M.J., *Divine Will and the Mechanical Philosophy: Gassendi and Descartes on Contingency and Necessity in the Created World*, Cambridge: Cambridge University Press, 1994.

Osler, M.J., "Early Modern Uses of Hellenistic Philosophy: Gassendi's Epicurean Project," in *Hellenistic and Early Modern Philosophy*, edited by J. Miller, Cambridge: Cambridge University Press, 2003.

Rickless, S.C., "Locke on Primary and Secondary Qualities," *Pacific Philosophical Quarterly* 78 (1997): 297–319.

Sabra, A.I., *Theories of Light From Descartes to Newton*, London: Oldbourne, 1967.

Schmaltz, T.M., "Malebranche's Cartesianism and Lockean Colors," *History of Philosophy Quarterly* 12 (1995): 387–403.

Stuart, M., "Locke's Colors," *Philosophical Review* 112 (2003): 57–96.

Watson, R.A., *The Downfall of Cartesianism, 1673–1712: A Study of Epistemological Issues in Late 17th Century Cartesianism*, The Hague: Martinus Nijhoff, 1966.

Watson, R.A., *The Breakdown of Cartesian Metaphysics*, Atlantic Highlands, NJ: Humanities Press International, 1987.

Primary sources

Bacon, F., *The New Organon*, edited by L. Jardine and M. Silverthorne, Cambridge: Cambridge University Press, 2000.

Barnes, J. (ed.), *The Complete Works of Aristotle, Vol. 1: The Revised Oxford Translation*, Princeton: Princeton University Press, 1984. Abbreviations of Aristotle's works mentioned in the text are as follows: *Categories* (*Cat.*), *Physics* (*Phys.*), *On Generation and Corruption* (*GC*), *On the Heavens* (*DC*), *On the Soul* (*DA*), *Sense and Sensibilia* (*DS*), and *Metereology* (*Met.*).

Berkeley, G., A Treatise Concerning the Principles of Human Knowledge, in *The Works of George Berkeley, Volume 1*, edited by A. A. Luce and T. E. Jessop, London: Thomas Nelson and Sons, 1948. Abbreviated as *PHK*.

Boyle, R., The Origin of Forms and Qualities According to the Corpuscular Philosophy, in *Selected Philosophical Papers of Robert Boyle*, edited by M. A. Stewart, Indianapolis: Hackett Publishing Company, 1991. Abbreviated as *OFQ*.

Charleton, W., *Physiologia Epicuro-Gassendo-Charltoniana*, London: Newcomb, 1654. Abbreviated as *PEGC*.

Cordemoy, G. de, *Oeuvres Philosophiques*, edited by P. Clair and F. Girbal, Paris: Presses Universitaires de France, 1968, 257–276. Abbreviated as *OP*.

Cottingham, J., R. Stoothoff, and D. Murdoch (eds.), *The Philosophical Writings of Descartes, Volume 1*, Cambridge: Cambridge University Press, 1985.

Desgabets, R., Le Guide de la Raison Naturelle, in *Oeuvres Philosophiques Inédites, Analecta Cartesiana 5*, edited by J. Beaude, with an introduction by G. Rodis-Lewis, Amsterdam: Quadratures, 1985, 101–150.

Digby, K., *Two Treatises*, Paris: Blaizot, 1644. Abbreviated as *TT*.

Galilei, G., The Assayer, in *The Scientific Background to Modern Philosophy*, edited by M. R. Matthews, Indianapolis: Hackett Publishing Company, 1989.

Galilei, G., *Dialogue Concerning the Two Chief World Systems, Ptolemaic and Copernican*, Second Revised Edition, translated by S. Drake, Berkeley: University of California Press, 1967.

Gassendi, P., *Opera Omnia*, Lyon: Anisson and Devenet, 1658. Abbreviated as *OO*. Part of Gassendi's work was translated into French by François Bernier, *Abrégé de la Philosophie de Gassendi*, Lyon: Anisson, Posuel, and Rigaud, 1684. This work is abbreviated as *APG*.

Hobbes, T., Elements of Philosophy: The First Section, Concerning Body, in *The English Works of Thomas Hobbes*, edited by W. Molesworth, London: John Bohn, 1839. Abbreviated as *DCo*.

Locke, J., *An Essay Concerning Human Understanding*, edited by P. H. Nidditch, Oxford: Clarendon Press, 1975. Abbreviated as *E*.

Lucretius, *On the Nature of Things*, translated by M. F. Smith, Indianapolis: Hackett Publishing Company, 1969. Abbreviated as *DRN*.

Malebranche, N., *The Search After Truth*, edited by T. M. Lennon and P. J. Olscamp, Cambridge: Cambridge University Press, 1997. Abbreviated as *ST*.

Newton, I., A Letter of Mr. Isaac Newton, Containing His New Theory About Light and Colours, in *Philosophical Transactions of the Royal Society* 80 (19 February 1671/2), 3075–3087. Accessible online through The Newton Project at www.newtonproject.sussex.ac.uk/view/texts/normalized/NATP00006

Régis, P. S., *Cours Entier de Philosophie, ou Système Général Selon les Principes de M. Descartes*, Final Edition, Amsterdam: Aux dépens des Huguetan, 1691. Abbreviated as *Cours*.

Rohault, J., *Entretiens sur la Philosophie*, Paris: Le Petit, 1671. Abbreviated as *Entretiens*.

Rohault, J., *Traité de Physique*, Paris: Vve Savreux, 1671. Abbreviated as *TP*.

Sennert, D., *Thirteen Books of Natural Philosophy*, London: Peter Cole, 1660. Abbreviated as *TBNP*.

4
CAUSATION
Sukjae Lee

1. Introduction

The intellectual climate of seventeenth century Europe made for an exciting, if turbulent, setting for the philosophical understanding of causation. Scientific discoveries that fundamentally challenged the way we view the world were rapidly taking center stage. *The Assayer*, Galileo's work that included his famous claim that the book of nature is written in the language of mathematics, surfaced in 1623. Newton's monumental *Philosophiae Naturalis Principia Mathematica* emerged in 1687. This "new" science emphasized a mechanistic understanding of the universe governed by simple, quantifiable laws of nature, and clashed with the traditional "Aristotelian-Scholastic" model of scientific enquiry, which relied heavily on such notions as "substantial forms" and "final causes." Taking the contact-collision model of interaction between bodies as paradigmatic, the new mechanistic worldview shunned attempts to incorporate formal and final causal elements in accounting for ordinary events like bodies falling toward the center of the earth.

But although this current of the new science was undeniably strong, other traditional metaphysical and theological principles kept their ground, still very much at the core of the philosophical outlooks of this time period. For instance, while honing their distinctive responses to the challenges raised by the new science, all of the philosophers whose views on causation we will be examining in this section – Descartes, Locke, Malebranche, and Leibniz – still viewed the world through an ontological framework that was fundamentally Aristotelian and Scholastic: the world, according to this scheme, basically consists of substances and their properties, some essential ('attribute') and others accidental ('mode'). That is, this substance-based ontological framework persisted despite disagreements as to the true natures of substances and their fundamental properties. Moreover, all of these philosophers were also theists in the Judeo-Christian tradition, embracing the view that the finite substances of this world depended, in a fundamental manner, on the ultimate, infinite substance, God. Thus, a central reason why the philosophical discussion surrounding causation is so interesting and lively in this period is that the philosophers faced the task of accommodating and making room for each of these divergent approaches, which at times collided with each other. One can imagine the scope, diversity, and ingenuity of the views that would emerge when philosophers are faced with such a difficult task of reconciling such distinct and competing intuitions.

There are a variety of ways of organizing the divergent views about causation of this time period. Given our opening discussion, however, let us consider two particular issues, or what we might call the "two axes" of causal relations, to set up a framework of the overall landscape. Reconsider the principle that all finite (i.e. created) substances are fundamentally dependent on God – the unique infinite substance – in some way or another. The exact type of dependence will turn out to be an important issue later on, but even without the details, we can anticipate that there will be implications for our understanding of causality in general. A natural question is whether created substances are dependent on the divine substance when they exercise their causal powers. That is, is the causal power of finite substances somehow dependent on the causal power of God? If dependent, how much of a causal role does the finite substance actually play, and how stable is the assessment that the finite substance is a cause in its own right? Behind these questions is the worry whether finite substances can rightfully be said to have their *own* powers, if divine causation is playing a prominent role. Moreover, how exactly are we to understand the relation between divine causation and creaturely causation in the occurrence of natural events? This cluster of questions concerning the relationship between God and finite substances with respect to their causal powers and their exercise will, following Freddoso, be referred to as "the general problem of divine action in nature."[1] This problem is the first axis of causal relations in our time period.

The second axis concerns the causal relations that hold horizontally, as it were, across the multitude of finite substances in the world. When a red billiard ball hits a white ball and moves it across the table, what type of causality is at play here, if at all? Do physical objects possess causal powers and, if so, where do such powers fit on the list of other, paradigmatic extensional properties such as figure, size, and impenetrability? And when a pin pricks my finger and I feel pain, is the pin causing this pain? If this is indeed the case, how is this causal interaction to be explained? Moreover, if we follow Descartes in thinking that bodies and minds are fundamentally heterogeneous and do not share their essential attributes, the question takes on a higher level of urgency. As Princess Elisabeth had famously raised,[2] it is not obvious that the two "really distinct" substances can stand in genuine causal relations. Let us call this cluster of issues that concerned the alleged causal relations that hold between finite substances "the problem of intersubstantial causation." In the subsequent sections, we will examine what the philosophers of the seventeenth century had to say about the two sets of issues and their reasons for these views.

2. The general problem of divine action in nature

As we noted, the main intuition behind this cluster of issues is the theologically motivated principle that finite substances are fundamentally dependent on God. A prominent way in which this dependence was understood more concretely was to regard God as ultimately the first and direct cause of everything, including whatever occurs and exists in nature.[3] But depending on how one understands the scope and nature of this immediate and direct causality of God, one would think differently in specifying the scope and nature of the causal efficacy of finite substances as well. Historically speaking, three positions emerged in response to the challenge of satisfying this theological demand while attempting to secure a genuine causal role for finite substances: "conservationism," "concurrentism," and "occasionalism."

As one might suspect, these three positions reflect the different ways in which the philosophers tried to balance the relevant desiderata. On one end is conservationism (or "mere conservationism"), according to which divine causal activity is limited to God's keeping the substance and its powers in existence when natural events occur. That is, when a given effect, for instance the heating of water, occurs, fire alone is *directly* and *immediately* causing the heating. God's causal contribution is *mediated* or *indirect* in that God's activity conserves the fire and its power in existence, which allows the fire to do its causal work of heating. That is, the conservationist view is that the fire's power alone is the direct cause of the heating, because God's contribution is indirect or mediated in that God's power keeps the fire and its power in existence so that the fire can exercise this power directly. God's direct causal activity is exhausted by his keeping the creature and its power in existence (hence the term "mere conservationism").[4] Given that conservationism holds that the fire is the sole direct cause of the heating of the water, of the three positions aforementioned, conservationism carves out the most robust causal role for created substances, while minimizing divine causal activity.

From our contemporary perspective, this assessment of the situation might seem somewhat surprising. Can divine causal activity be described as *minimized* when God is said to keep the creature and its power in existence in conserving it?[5] This puzzlement, however, reveals our distance from how deeply embedded the philosophers of the seventeenth century took divine causality to be in the natural world. The vast majority of the theistic philosophers of our time period took it to be nonnegotiable that divine causal activity is directly and immediately operative in every aspect of the natural world, including the effects allegedly caused by the finite substance. In fact, the views of the sole proponent of conservationism mentioned commonly in the relevant literature, Cardinal Durandus, were deemed theologically suspect: limiting divine contribution to the mere conservation of substances was regarded as insufficient to secure the proper degree of divine causal involvement in the natural world.

Concurrentism and occasionalism share common ground in their rejection of conservationism. That is, both positions take divine causal activity to be operative directly and immediately in bringing about ordinary events. Their difference lies in how they respectively understand the nature of the causal contribution on the part of finite substances. Let us first consider occasionalism, which takes up the other end of the spectrum in opposition to conservationism. Occasionalism holds that there is one and only one real genuine cause, namely God. Finite substances do not contribute to the occurrence of natural events because they are not real causal agents. Rather their states are just occasions on the occurrence of which the real cause produces the relevant states. As Nicolas Malebranche, the most prominent occasionalist of our time period, put it, "[a] natural cause is . . . not a real and true but only an occasional cause, which determines the Author of nature to act in such and such a manner in such and such a situation" (OC II 312/*Search* 6.2.3/LO 448). Thus, if conservationism might be thought to maximize creaturely causal contribution by limiting divine causal activity, occasionalism might be thought of as maximizing divine causal activity by denying any genuine causal activity on the part of creatures.

The third and last position, concurrentism (or divine concurrentism), can be thought of as occupying the middle ground between conservationism and occasionalism. According to concurrentism, when a natural effect occurs, the finite substance and God are both causally active in bringing about the effect in question. Hence, the theological commitment that God is directly involved in every natural event is satisfied, and our commonsense intuition that finite substances are real causes in their own right is also satisfied on this account. That these two intuitions are supposedly satisfied explains why the majority of the philosophers of the Scholastic period took themselves to be concurrentists. But although concurrentism seems to be the most reasonable position to take, providing the details of *how* God and creature *concur* was fraught with difficulty, making concurrentism a target for both the occasionalists and the conservationists.[6]

3. The problem of intersubstantial causation

As noted earlier, this cluster of issues revolves around the topic of how to understand the causal interaction between finite substances that seems to be an everyday occurrence. If we take the general landscape of seventeenth century metaphysics to consist of the dual Cartesian substances of minds and bodies, then four types of causal relations emerge: body-body, mind-body, body-mind, and mind-mind causation.[7] But among these four, mind-body and body-mind causation received particular attention even in the seventeenth century. Let us see why.

That one's mind and body interact causally seems to be a common enough experience. The volition to raise my arm appears to cause my arm to rise up. The pricking of my finger appears to cause pain in my mind. This common experience notwithstanding, there were serious questions as to whether the two substances *could* interact, given their completely different natures as specified by Descartes. A prominent instance of this concern is raised by Princess Elisabeth in the following letter of 6 May 1643:

> I ask you please to tell me how the soul of a human being (it being only a thinking substance) can determine the bodily spirits, in order to bring about voluntary actions. For it seems that all determination of movement happens through the impulsion of the thing moved, by the manner in which it is pushed by that which moves it, or else by the particular qualities and shape of the surface of the latter. Physical contact is required for the first two conditions, extension for the third. You entirely exclude the one [extension] from the notion you have of the soul, and the other [physical contact] appears to me incompatible with a material thing.[8]

Princess Elisabeth's reasoning here is straightforward. If bodily change requires some type of contact, and contact presupposes extension, then souls cannot bring about bodily change. For souls are thinking substances and lack extension. That is, whatever brings about change in a body must come into contact with it, but souls in principle are not things that come into contact with anything. Elisabeth's penetrating question here focuses on one direction, namely the causal influence from souls to bodies. But a mirror argument can easily be constructed for the other direction as well: if a body needs to come into contact with that which it affects, then no body could bring about change in souls, because souls in principle cannot be "touched." These are tough questions indeed, and we can appreciate why heated discussions arouse in response to this challenge, including Descartes's own response, which we will consider later.

Last, we note that some have taken this criticism to be an instance of a broader, more general objection, which, following Richardson, we will call the "problem of heterogeneity."[9] This objection states that causal interaction requires some common property or attribute between the relevant causal relata, and given the absence of such commonality between minds and bodies, there cannot be any causal interaction between them.[10]

It is unclear from the text whether Elisabeth meant to endorse this general principle. Noticeable here is that she does not explicitly state such a principle, nor does she need it to advance her criticism.

A different worry was raised against the prospect of the soul bringing about bodily changes. It concerned whether the causal closure of the physical could be maintained if minds were capable of increasing or diminishing the motion of bodies. Descartes himself had propounded the conservation of the total quantity of motion in his *Principles*,[11] and this idea, that some constant quantity is maintained throughout the multifarious changes in the physical world, was rapidly emerging as a central feature of the new modern science. But the intrusion of mental powers on the physical raised worries about whether this constant quantity could be maintained. Suppose my soul is capable of making my arm move at time t_2, whereas it was not in motion at time t_1. Other things being equal, this would imply an increase in the total quantity of motion at t_2, a violation of the conservation of the total quantity of motion. Of course, it could be the case that at the instant my arm starts moving, a body which had possessed an identical quantity of motion somewhere in the world comes to a stop. But this suggestion does not seem to go that far to ameliorate the difficulty. Not only does the suggestion sound improbable in itself, given that some random body would have to stop in order for my arm to move, it also was thought that such a state of affairs would imply that God intervenes in the physical world by means of perpetual miracles, simply to allow for human souls to continue on with their bodily movements.

In this context, it is interesting to note Leibniz's claim that Descartes took souls to be capable of changing the direction of bodies while not being able to change the velocity.[12] This solution has the advantage of rendering the causal efficacy of souls consistent with the conservation of the total quantity of motion in Descartes's physics, because Descartes's conception of motion was scalar and hence did not make use of vectors in his physics. A key issue with this interpretation is that Leibniz is unique in providing testimony that Descartes actually held such a view, and we have no other textual evidence to corroborate Leibniz's testimony.

In response to this quandary concerning mind-body interaction, a variety of responses emerged, as we might imagine. The three main positions were "Cartesian interactionism," "occasionalism," and "preestablished harmony." Although the term "Cartesian Interactionism" suggests that this was Descartes's own position, and though there definitely is textual evidence to suggest this interpretation, we should be cautious in attributing this position to Descartes. For, as we will see, there is a considerable amount of controversy as to what Descartes's actual views were. Regardless of what Descartes's actual views were, let "Cartesian Interactionism" refer to the view that accepts as undeniable the causal interaction between the dual Cartesian substances of mind and body, despite the various problems facing the endorsement of such interaction. Even if one falls short of explaining in a sufficiently satisfactory manner *how* they interact, *that* they interact is firmly endorsed by Cartesian interactionism. In taking a closer look at Descartes, we will consider this position in more detail later and see what type of actual textual evidence there might be for attributing this position to Descartes.

Let us use the remaining space in this section to acquaint ourselves briefly with the other two responses, occasionalism and preestablished harmony. Occasionalism denies that mind and body interact, because, according to occasionalism, neither of the dual Cartesian substances possess any genuine causal efficacy. So, what happens when I will to raise my arm and it goes up? For the occasionalist, on the occurrence of my volition to raise my arm, God as the sole causal agent causes my arm to go up. And on the occurrence of the pricking of my finger, it is again God who causes pain in my soul on this occasion. Although such divine intervention might seem rather arbitrary, Malebranche, the main proponent of occasionalism in our time period, is careful to point out that the majority of occurrences in this world are not arbitrary in that they are governed by God's general volitions. That is, the causal activity in such regular occurrences is governed by God's general volitions, which correspond to general laws that link event types of a certain kind to event types of another kind, and hence is regular and predictable. Such regularity, however, does not imply that God *must* act in such a regular manner. According to Malebranche, God can and, at times, does eschew such general volitions and intervenes through particular volitions. These are the cases that we typically regard as miraculous.

Preestablished harmony also denies causal interaction between mind and body. However, Leibniz, the central proponent of preestablished harmony, finds the occasionalist claim that finite substances lack all causal powers to be seriously problematic and affirms genuine causal powers within creatures. How can one consistently hold that there are such genuine causal powers in finite substance while also denying causal interactions between mind and body? The causal powers of finite substances, according to Leibniz, are capable of bringing about changes in their own respective states but not in other substances. That is, Leibniz denies that finite substances have causal powers that can bring about changes in other, distinct substances – thus, he denies *intersubstantial* causal powers – but he firmly endorses causal forces that are operative within each substance, effective in bringing about changes within the substance itself – that is he endorses *intrasubstantial* causal powers. But if finite substances merely bring about changes to their own states, respectively, what accounts for the fact that they appear to be causally interacting with each other? That is, what accounts for the apparent correlation between the volition to raise my arm and my arm rising? This is explained by the fact that the substances bring about their respective changes in a manner that harmonizes the changes with each other. As I will to move my arm, the substances that make up my arm move upward spontaneously. The events of my soul, such as the willing to move my arm, and the events of my arm, such as its rising, each occur in isolation solely in accordance to their internal causal laws. Nonetheless, they are so well synchronized that they appear to be causally connected. This harmonization we mistakenly take as evidence of interaction, but in fact it is a feature of how perfect this world is, according to Leibniz.

4. Descartes

We are now in the position to consider in more detail the actual views of the relevant philosophers. Let us begin with Descartes on the issue of secondary causation in nature. What position can be reasonably attributed to him? The question is straightforward, but the answer is not. The secondary literature on this issue is divided, and all three positions of conservationism, concurrence, and occasionalism are currently being attributed to Descartes. A further complication is that there are reasons to think that Descartes's position differs depending on the type of substance under consideration. For instance, some think that, whereas Descartes was an occasionalist in the case of bodies or extended substances, he was not when it came to souls or thinking substances.[13]

At the center of the controversy is Descartes's understanding of bodies or extended substances, which emerges as a crucial aspect of his new physics. As Descartes states in the summary of section 4 of part II of the *Principles of Philosophy*, "[t]he nature of body consists not in weight, hardness, color, or the like, but simply in extension."[14] Many readers have taken statements such as this to express the view that for Descartes the fundamental properties of physical objects are exhausted by their extensional properties, such as size, figure, and motion (or rest). As his letter to Mersenne makes clear,[15] Descartes took it to be an important part of his overall project to present a new physics, one that does not rely on the traditional conceptions of substantial forms or final causes, which many of this time period took to be either explanatorily superfluous or obscure. The new, geometrical conception of matter enabled Descartes to divest these antiquated elements from the basic makeup of bodies. The resulting, rather sparse conception of extended substance, however, has suggested to many interpreters that Cartesian bodies thus are in principle not the type of thing that can possess forces or powers as a "mode" or property. For neither forces nor powers seem to have a natural place on the list of the official modes of extension, such as figure, size, or motion (or rest). To assign forces to Cartesian bodies would seem as much of a category mistake as to assign powers or forces to a Euclidean isosceles triangle. This line of reasoning has led many interpreters to conclude that Cartesian bodies are fundamentally passive and hence causally inert. That is, Cartesian bodies need an external causal source, an efficient causal power from the outside to move them around, because they themselves lack powers. But this basic picture of the physical world consisting of inert, passive bodies nonetheless needs some further elaboration. For, as we commonly experience, the physical world is brimming with bodies in motion, which collide with each other, seemingly imparting and receiving motion. How does such movement and collision of bodies fit into this basic Cartesian picture?

Descartes's main account of motion emerges in part II of the *Principles*. We turn to section 36, which has the rather informative title of "God is the primary cause of motion; and he always preserves the same quantity of motion of in the universe." Descartes goes on to elaborate:

> After this consideration of the nature of motion, we must look at its cause. This is in fact twofold: first, there is the universal and primary cause – the general cause of all the motions in the world; and second there is the particular cause which produces in an individual piece of matter some motion which it previously lacked. Now as far as the general cause is concerned, it seems clear to me that this is no other than God himself. In the beginning he created matter, along with its motion and rest; and now, merely by his regular concurrence, he preserves the same amount of motion and rest in the material universe as he put there in the beginning.
>
> (AT VIIIA 61–62; CSM I 240)

Passages like these have led many an interpreter to the occasionalist reading. Moreover, it is not difficult to find further textual evidence that appears to support occasionalism. For instance, consider how Descartes ends section 36: "God imparted various motions to the parts of matter when he first created them, and he now preserves all this matter in the same way, and by the same process by which he originally created it." If it is God that imparted motion to matter when he first created it, and he preserves matter *in the same way*, it seems to follow that if bodies are in motion at all, it is God who is imparting motion to them, whether the motion be that of the initial state of creation, or that of subsequent conserved instances.

Another passage cited widely in support of the occasionalist reading comes from the Third Meditation:

> [I]t does not follow from the fact that I existed a little while ago that I must exist now, unless there is some cause which as it were creates me afresh at this moment – that is, which preserves [i.e. conserves] me. . . . [T]he same power and action are needed to preserve anything at each individual moment of its duration as would be required to create that thing anew if it were not yet in existence. Hence the distinction between preservation [i.e. conservation] and creation is only a conceptual one.
>
> (AT VII 49; CSM II 33)

Most interpreters have taken this passage to be expressing Descartes's endorsement of the "conservation is but continuous creation" principle, which was widely affirmed by the majority of the theistic philosophers of this time period. And one way of reading this principle suggests that occasionalism is the right way to go. For if God's conserving activity is exactly like his creative activity, then God would be the sole causal agent in conservation just as God is the sole causal agent in creation. And, as we shall see, Malebranche pretty much argues for occasionalism in this manner in his *Dialogues on Metaphysics and on Religion*.

As a reading of Descartes, however, occasionalism faces challenges as well. Let us return to section 36 of *Principles* II. This very passage presents conflicting textual evidence, pushing us to reconsider the occasionalist reading. First, Descartes here explicitly mentions "particular causes," which produce "in an individual piece of matter some motion which it previously lacked." If God is the "primary cause" with "particular causes" in operation, the standard concurrentist setup, which typically invokes God as the general cause and the creature as the particular cause, seems to be in the background. Moreover, we note that Descartes explicitly invokes the term "concurrence" here. Descartes states that it is through God's "regular *concurrence*" (my emphasis) that he preserves the same amount of motion and rest. If Descartes is not using this term loosely, it would be odd for Descartes to hold that God *concurs* when there were no causal powers in bodies, as occasionalism holds. For concurrence conceptually requires causality from both sides, divine and creaturely. Last, with regard to Descartes's endorsement of the continuous creation principle, we are well aware that the majority of the theistic philosophers of this period all accepted some version of the continuous creation principle without committing themselves to occasionalism. That is, these philosophers understood the continuous creation principle in a way that was consistent with positing genuine causal powers in secondary substances. If so, it would be too quick to conclude that Descartes was an occasionalist simply from the fact that he endorsed the continuous creation thesis.

What then of the case for taking Cartesian bodies to be causally efficacious? Although there is disagreement as to whether Descartes was a divine concurrentist or mere conservationist,[16] causal realists about bodily forces all agree, against the occasionalist reading, that Cartesian bodies genuinely contribute to changes in the world as real causes. Most realist interpretations make their case by focusing on the particular laws that Descartes mentions as secondary causes in *Principles* II.37:

Indeed, from the same immutability of God can be known certain rules or laws of nature, which are the secondary and particular causes of the diverse motions that we perceive in individual bodies.

(AT VIIIA 62; CSM I 240)

The exact nature of the "rules or laws of nature" is at the crux of the issue and needs clarification. But the natural reading of this passage would be to take Descartes as aiming to distinguish God – described earlier as the "universal and primary cause," the general cause of all the motion in the world – from the "particular cause which produces in an individual piece of matter some motion which it previously lacked" (AT VIIIA 61, CSM I 240). Descartes goes on to describe the "first of these laws":

each thing, in so far as it is simple and undivided, always remains in the same state, as far as it can, and never changes except as a result of external causes.

(AT VIIIA 62; CSM I 241)

Some scholars have taken passages like this to support the view that Cartesian bodies possess certain durational tendencies over and above their geometrical and kinematic properties. On this reading, such tendencies are what ground the causal forces of bodies.[17] The intuition here seems to be that Cartesian bodies have an intrinsic tendency to endure in the same state, one that is distinct from God's inclination to maintain the same state of affairs unless a sufficient reason is provided, an inclination stemming from divine immutability and rationality. Thus, on this view, even if the laws are indicative of how God is causally involved in bringing about particular motions in the world, the laws themselves are grounded in the natures of bodies. It is in this sense that bodies can rightfully be thought to be genuine causal sources, or so some realists argue. Other realists about bodily forces suggest that Descartes holds a distinctive view of how the secondary laws work in conjunction with the particular states of individual substances, while granting that this understanding might seem rather foreign to our contemporary perspective. In this approach, it is the laws of nature themselves that are causally operative.

Up to this point, our focus has been on cases of body-body causation. Let us now turn our attention to other possible cases of intersubstantial causation in Descartes. For instance, what does Descartes think about cases where bodies appear to be bringing about changes in the mind, such as when a pin pricks my finger, and I feel pain? Does Descartes think that physical objects have the power to affect the mind? And what happens when I will to raise my arm and my arm goes up? Do minds have the power to affect bodily changes? As noted earlier, in addition to the question of whether bodies or minds possess causal powers at all, there is a more specific worry that can be raised in such cases where the alleged causal relata are of different types. For as we saw earlier, the problem of heterogeneity raised the issue of whether mind and body can affect each other when the two substances lack some common feature.

With regard to the heterogeneity objection, there is some textual evidence that Descartes would not accept the underlying assumption that there has to be some common feature shared by the substances of different types. For in the 1647 French edition of the *Meditations*, he adds the following response:

the whole difficulty . . . proceeds solely from a supposition that is false and cannot in any be proved, namely that, if the soul and body are two different substances with diverse natures, this prevents them from being able to act on each other.

(AT IX 213)[18]

Although this might be an acceptable response to the general worry stemming from heterogeneous natures, we are still left with the original, penetrating question raised by Princess Elisabeth. Her question had raised a more specific worry about whether any interaction between mind and body requires some type of physical contact between the two. But such contact seems ruled out in principle, because Cartesian minds are not extended in space.

Descartes seems more sensitive to this worry, and it is in response to this concern that he explicitly invokes his famous account of the 'primitive notion' of the union between mind and body:

> I can say with truth that the question your Highness proposes seems to me that which, in view of my published writings, one can most rightly ask me. For there are two things about the human soul on which all the knowledge we can have of its nature depends: one of which is that it thinks and the other is that, being united to the body, it can act on and be acted upon by it. I have said almost nothing about the latter. . . . I will try here to explain the manner in which I conceive of the union of the soul with the body and how the soul has the power to move it.
>
> First, I consider that there are in us certain primitive notions that are like originals on the pattern of which we form all our other knowledge. There are only very few of these notions; . . . we have, for the body in particular, only the notion of extension . . . and for the soul alone, we have only that of thought . . . and finally, for the soul and the body together, we have only that of their union, on which depends that of the power the soul has to move the body and the body to act on the soul, in causing its sensations and passions.
>
> (AT III 665; CSMK 218)

Not surprisingly, scholars are divided as to how to understand Descartes's views on the union of the soul and body. There seem to be two broad approaches to this issue. One is to regard the union to be nothing more than a set of correlations that hold regularly between certain bodily states and certain mental states, correlations that might be best thought of as underwritten by occasionalistic laws. The other is to take Descartes's claim about causal powers in this passage more literally. The soul is said to have the "power" to move the body, and the body to have the power to "act on the soul," but, more importantly, such powers are said to depend on the union. The critical questions would be (1) what it is about the union that allows the soul and body to have such powers, and (2) how should such powers, given the fact that physical contact, which seems required for genuine interaction, is lacking, be understood? Some interpreters at this juncture have focused on Descartes's claims about how the soul or mind can have an "extension of power," which emerge most prominently in his correspondence with More:

> in God and angels and in our mind I understand there to be no extension of substance, but only extension of power. An angel can exercise power now on

a greater and now on a lesser part of corporeal substance; but if there were no bodies, I could not conceive of any space with which an angel or God would be co-extensive.

(Letter to More, 15 April 1649, AT V 342; CSMK 372–373)

How is Descartes understanding this "extension of power," and how is it different from extension proper, the basic attribute of physical substances? In an earlier letter, Descartes had first brought out this idea as follows:

we easily understand that the human mind and God and several angels can all be at the same time in one and the same place. So we clearly conclude that no incorporeal substances are in any strict sense extended. I conceive them as sorts of powers or forces, which although they can act upon extended things, are not themselves extended – just as fire is in white-hot iron without itself being iron.

(Letter to More, 5 February 1649, AT V 270; CSMK 361)

Here Descartes infers from the fact that there can be multiple minds or souls in one and the same place that incorporeal substances are not extended in any strict sense. Why would he draw this inference? Given that the geometrical, extensional properties are constitutive of the identity conditions of a body that possesses these properties, any two extended substances that share the exact same extensional properties are for Descartes numerically identical. So, if two distinct souls are in one and the same place in the literal sense that they possess the exact same extensional properties, this would entail that they are numerically the same body. But presumably if substance A *qua* body is numerically identical to substance B *qua* body, then A *qua* soul would be numerically the same as B *qua* soul. But this goes against the original hypothesis that A and B are numerically distinct souls. Hence the assumption to reject in this inference is that the two distinct souls are extended in any strict sense. We are then left with the following explanation of "extension of power": two distinct souls while *being in one and the same place* are not extended in the sense of possessing extensional properties. But then in what sense are these souls in a place? Descartes's answer appears to be that they are in a place in the sense that *they can act on extended things*. It does not seem unlikely that Princess Elisabeth would have been dissatisfied with this answer, given that her original question concerned how souls and bodies could interact if they are not in physical contact. Insofar as the claim that souls are "extended in power" grants that souls are not literally extended and hence cannot come into physical contact with bodies, but merely holds that souls are extended in the sense that they can act on and be acted upon extended substances, the move to grant "extension of power" to souls appears to be nothing more than a bald statement that souls and bodies can interact without physical contact, the very possibility and intelligibility Elisabeth questioned.

In concluding this discussion about causation among Cartesian substances, let us bear the following point in mind. As we have seen, there are many different interpretations of Descartes's views. In order to properly evaluate the various interpretations, we need to distinguish what Descartes actually thought and what he was entitled to think given his other commitments. That is, given his understanding of the nature of souls and bodies and the nature of God's causal involvement in the physical world, we might rightfully argue that Descartes would have been inconsistent to have held that bodies are genuine causes. And charity might suggest that we read him as not committing such inconsistencies. Nonetheless, it is also possible that Descartes was indeed committed to bodies being real causes, despite the burden of inconsistency.

5. Locke

Of the four seventeenth century philosophers we are examining, John Locke mostly likely proves to provide the biggest challenge in our attempts to reach the bottom of his views about causality. The main reason for the difficulty is not due to Locke's lack of interest in the issues being discussed (though admittedly it does seem difficult to find any professed views in his works about divine causal activity in nature).[19] Rather the difficulty is tied to what seems to be the deep and interesting tension between Locke's substantive metaphysical theses and "his devout epistemic modesty," a tension remarked upon by many commentators.[20] For instance, although it is fairly clear that Locke did subscribe to what is generally known as the corpuscularian hypothesis – that is the view that bodies are fundamentally indivisible atoms or corpuscles, whose properties are exhausted by those of size, shape, location, motion or rest, and solidity (or impenetrability) – he is also very much against and rather suspicious of attempts to "engage in what Aristotelians and Cartesians would call 'first philosophy'; the Aristotelian-Scholastic and the Cartesian grounding of natural philosophy in *a priori* epistemological and metaphysical doctrines set out in systematic fashion."[21] As readers are well aware, the driving impetus behind the *Essays* is to determine the limits of our understanding, and Locke's findings are "epistemically pessimistic, even skeptical; when it comes to questions about how the world is constituted, our understandings cannot penetrate very far."[22] That is, if "first philosophy" expresses a confidence that we are able to get to the bottom of things with the subtle and careful use of our rational capacities, Locke is rather suspicious of such optimism, and, as a general tendency, he refrains from making definitive claims about the true nature of things.

There have been many interesting proposals as to how we might understand and resolve this tension between his corpuscularianism and epistemic modesty. Moreover, the common sentiment that it is this tension that makes Locke's work all the more interesting and worth reading seems appropriate. In this spirit, insofar as his readers bear in mind his overall reservation, Locke would seem to be comfortable in providing us with suggestive accounts as to how the world works causally speaking, to which we now turn.

A good place to start is Locke's well-known discussion of primary and secondary qualities. Recall Locke's description of "secondary qualities":

> such qualities which in truth are nothing in the objects themselves but power to produce various sensations in us by their primary qualities, i.e. by the bulk, figure, texture, and motion of their insensible parts, as colours, sounds, tastes, &c. These I call secondary qualities.
>
> (*Essay* 2.8.11)

Given our current focus on causation, it is somewhat striking that Locke seems to be taking for granted that the secondary qualities of bodies are "powers" that are capable of producing various sensations in us by their "bulk, figure, texture, and motion." This suggest that bodily qualities for Locke are fundamentally causal in character, capable of and, in fact, actually bringing about various sensations in our minds. But Locke is also too good of a philosopher not to consider the natural question that emerges at this point. Thus, after presenting his account of what the two qualities are and how they differ, Locke goes on to address the all-important question of "how bodies produce ideas in us": "The next thing to be considered is, how bodies produce ideas in us; and that is manifestly by impulse, the only way which we can conceive bodies to operate in" (*Essay* 2.8.11). That impulse is singled out is not surprising, because, as a corpuscularian, Locke is committed to the fact that all bodily changes occur through impact or contact action.[23] But given our earlier discussion of Descartes, we cannot but wonder how it is that bodily motion can affect the soul or mind through impulse, assuming that ideas are regarded as modifications of a soul. For it seems as though in order for souls to be affected through impulse, they must be spatially located. The difficulty for Descartes, we recall, had been that souls were in principle nonspatial, hence ruling out the possibility that they come into physical contact with bodies.

Fortunately, Locke's situation is somewhat better than Descartes's. Locke's views about the nature of bodies or corpuscles are significantly distinct from the Cartesian view, and solidity plays a prominent role. Solidity, as understood by Locke, is a noteworthy entry on the list of primary qualities, in that it is a property of bodies that bodies have over and above that of being extended. In fact, Locke finds the Cartesian identification of extension with bodies to be rather problematic:

> There are some that would persuade us, that body and extension are the same thing, who either change the signification of words, which I would not suspect them of, they having so severely condemned the philosophy of others, because it hath been too much placed in the uncertain meaning, or deceitful obscurity of doubtful or insignificant terms. If, therefore, they mean by body and extension the same that other people do, viz. by body something that is solid and extended, whose parts are separable and movable different ways; and by extension, only the space that lies between the extremities of those solid coherent parts, and which is possessed by them, they confound very different ideas one with another.
> (*Essay* 2.13.11)

He goes on to argue,

> And if it be a reason to prove that spirit is different from body, because thinking includes not the idea of extension in it; the same reason will be as valid, I suppose, to prove that space is not body, because it includes not the idea of solidity in it; space and solidity being as distinct ideas as thinking and extension, and as wholly separable in the mind one from another.
> (*Essay* 2.13.11)

One might think that relying on the contrast between thinking and extension to draw a distinction between space and solidity is rather exaggerated, even problematic. For although solidity is intimately connected to extension or space, thinking is not, and thus the ontological gap between thinking and extension is significantly wider than that between solidity and extension, or so it might seem. Such an objection, however, would reveal one's intuitive inclinations as leaning toward Descartes, because Locke explicitly states that souls or spirits are as mobile as bodies are:

> There is no reason why it should be thought strange, that I make Mobility belong to Spirit: For having no other Idea of Motion, but change of distance, with other Beings, that are considered as at rest; and finding that Spirits, as well as Bodies, cannot operate, but where they are; and that Spirits do operate at several times in several places; I cannot but attribute change of place to all finite Spirits.
> (*Essay* 2.23.19)

Spatiality in the sense of having a spatial location and being causally operative at this place is not a distinctively physical feature for Locke. Thus, he does not need to engage in the type of contorted efforts evidenced in Descartes's correspondence to More – recall the "extension in power" – to find some way to accommodate minds within space. As Locke states, spirits are not only in places but are operating there. In fact, it seems as though he thinks that being spatial is a necessary condition of being causally operative, because he finds "that Spirits, as well as Bodies, cannot operate, but where they are." In this way, because both bodies and spirits are spatial for Locke, he does not face the worry that confronted Descartes, in which the way spirits were fundamentally ruled out from being spatial is in any way common to that of bodies, lest they become bodies.

This advantage does not, however, imply that Locke is completely free from worries. One might wonder whether being spatial is enough to be causally affected through impulse. For does not contact action require impenetrability or solidity in addition to being in space? How could a corpuscle come into contact with an immaterial spirit, if the spirit in question does not offer any resistance? For, as Locke himself notes, "extension includes no solidity, nor resistance to the motion of body, as body does" (*Essay* 2.13.12).

At this point, we are naturally drawn to the famous passage of *Essay* 4.3.6, which includes Locke's discussion of the possibility that God "can, if he pleases, superadd to Matter a Faculty of Thinking." The interpretation of Locke on superaddition is a controversial topic,[24] and this is not the place to engage this issue fully. But we cannot help but turn our attention to the following section where Locke seems well aware of the difficulty just raised – how immaterial spirits that lack solidity might engage in contact – and, in fact, fully embraces it:

> What certainty of knowledge can any one have, that some perceptions, such as, v.g., pleasure and pain, should not be in some bodies themselves, after a certain manner modified and moved, as well as that they should be in an immaterial substance, upon the motion of the parts of body: Body, as far as we can conceive, being able only to strike and affect body, and motion, according to the utmost reach of our ideas, being able to produce nothing but motion; so that when we allow it to produce pleasure or pain, or the idea of a colour or sound, we are fain to quit our reason, go beyond our ideas, and attribute it wholly to the good pleasure of our Maker. For, since we must allow He has annexed effects to motion which we can no way conceive motion able to produce, what reason have we to conclude that He could not order them as well to be produced in a

subject we cannot conceive capable of them, as well as in a subject we cannot conceive the motion of matter can any way operate upon?

(*Essay* 4.3.6)

Note that what Locke here concedes as inconceivable is twofold. One is that we find it inconceivable how bodies could literally strike or come into contact with an immaterial spirit, the concern we just mentioned. The other is related but, in fact, different: if motion can only produce motion, then it is inconceivable to us how bodily motion could bring about an effect that is radically dissimilar, like sensations and ideas. And here we get a glimpse of Locke's astuteness cloaked behind his humility, in his distinguishing two separate worries concerning body-to-mind causation. Distinct from the issue of how bodies can come into contact with immaterial spirits, there is the further question of how bodily motion brings about effects that are so completely qualitatively dissimilar. Seen with this distinction in mind, we can speculate whether the possibility of superadded matter was actually intended to help with the first inconceivability. If a body that is affected through impulse itself were endowed with the faculty of thinking, so that the body ends up having certain sensations upon certain impulses, then although we might still wonder how it is that motion can bring about something utterly dissimilar, that this thinking body can be and is actually being affected through impulse is, *ex hypothesis*, fully accounted for, and conceivable. That is, the hypothesis of superadded matter could be serving a rather limited and nuanced purpose. Locke might be taken to be suggesting that the possibility of superadded matter makes things more intelligible for us, by addressing one of the inconceivabilities – that is the unintelligibility of causation without contact.

As for the latter, "dissimilarity" worry, Locke had brought it up earlier in his discussion of secondary qualities, and had addressed it in similar fashion:

let us suppose at present that the different motions and figures, bulk and number, of such particles, affecting the several organs of our senses, produce in us those different sensations which we have from the colours and smells of bodies; v.g. that a violet, by the impulse of such insensible particles of matter, of peculiar figures and bulks, and in different degrees and modifications of their motions, causes the ideas of the blue colour, and sweet scent of that flower to be produced in our minds. It being no more impossible to conceive that God should annex such ideas to such motions, with which they have no similitude, than that he should annex the idea of pain to the motion of a piece of steel dividing our flesh, with which that idea hath no resemblance.

(*Essay* 2.7.13)

So here is the picture Locke presents us with. Given our conception and understanding of bodies and immaterial spirits, we find it difficult to comprehend how bodies can affect our spirits to bring about various sensations and ideas. But this inconceivability is fully compatible with the omnipotent divine agent setting up various causal connections between certain bodily movements and various sensations. How does God establish such causal connections? Locke's epistemic modesty actually comes in as a supporting plank in his overall position, because, unlike Descartes, Locke is not committed to our ideas of bodies or spirits being clear and distinct in such a way to guarantee their capturing the real essences of the things in question. Given that our ideas are literally only ours, expressing the limited way in which we understand the world, that the various causal connections that seem inconceivable to us obtain in the world is perfectly intelligible and an accepted implication of Locke's overall outlook.

Before we end this section on Locke, let us briefly note that Locke also clearly affirms the power of our souls to

> begin or forbear, continue or end several actions of our minds, and motions of our Bodies, barely by the thought or preference of the mind ordering . . . the doing or not doing such or such a particular action.
>
> (*Essay* 2.21.5)

That is, we, in possessing willpower, are capable of producing ideas and willing the movement of our bodies. But again, the metaphysical underpinnings of such causal powers will most likely get similar treatment insofar as it is conceded that how immaterial souls might impact bodies to initiate or change motion is unintelligible for us.

6. Malebranche

In contrast to Locke, Nicolas Malebranche was decidedly less hesitant in professing his causal metaphysics to the world, and in so doing was arguably the most influential writer on the topic of causation in this time period.

Malebranche was an occasionalist. Thus, with regard to the issue of secondary causation in nature, he denied that creatures possessed any genuine causal power and held that God directly causes all the events in the world. With regard to the question of whether and how creatures causally interacted with each other, Malebranche held that they did not causally interact at all. Rather they are "occasional causes" in that a given state of a creature serves as an occasion for God to bring about its subsequent, corresponding state. As he famously states in the *Search*,

> there is only one true cause because there is only one true God; . . . the nature or power of each thing is nothing but the will of God; . . . all natural causes are not *true* causes but only *occasional* causes.[25]

In this section, we will canvass Malebranche's various arguments for occasionalism, and examine his account of "occasional causation," with a focus on how creaturely states fit into this picture.

Although there is disagreement as to how the arguments relate to each other, most commentators appear to agree that there are four main arguments for occasionalism that Malebranche presents through his works. Two of the arguments seemed to be tailored to each of the two Cartesian substances respectively, intended to establish the occasionalist conclusion for mind and body on the basis of their distinctive features. They are the "passive nature" argument (hereafter PN) and the "no knowledge" argument (hereafter NK). The major contours of the PN argument can be easily anticipated, given our earlier discussion of the Cartesian conception of bodies as consisting of purely extensional properties. If geometrical, extensional properties are said to exhaust the features that bodily substances possess, then forces or powers will not be included in the ontological makeup of Cartesian bodies. Malebranche endorses this understanding of bodies in a number of passages, including the following from the *Dialogues*:

> Consult the idea of extension and decide by this idea which represents bodies . . . whether they can have any property other than the *passive faculty* of receiving various figures and movements. Is it not entirely obvious that all the properties of extension can consist only in relations of distance?
> (OC XII 150–151/*Dialogues* 106, my emphasis)

Note the focus on the passivity of bodies, which, he argues, follows from the fact that all properties consist only in relations of distance. Insofar as force or power is something over and above mere relations of distance, it cannot be placed among bodily properties, and Malebranche accordingly identifies force or power with the will of God:

> When I see one ball strike another, my eyes . . . seem to tell me, that the one is truly the cause of the motion it impresses on the other. . . . But when I consult my reason I clearly see that since bodies cannot move themselves, and since their motor force is but the will of God that conserves them successively in different places, they cannot communicate a power they do not have and could not communicate even if it were in their possession. For the mind will never conceive that one body, a purely passive substance, can in any way whatsoever transmit to another body the power transporting it.
> (OC III 208–209/*Eluc.* 15/LO 660)

When a body meets a body and they collide, it is God who moves the bodies in accordance with certain general laws. The PN argument aims to establish the occasionalist conclusion for extended, bodily substances alone, with no implications for whether minds are causally active or not. Malebranche himself thought that the occasionalist thesis holds "globally," in that he held that no finite substance, be it a body or a soul, possessed any genuine causal powers. But the PN argument does not aim to establish occasionalism on this global level, because the focus is on the nature of extension and its implications. As we have seen, however, whether the Cartesian notion of extension indeed leads in such a straightforward manner to occasionalism is arguable.

The NK argument's basic strategy is to present an interesting, if controversial, requirement for volitional agency. As we can see from the following passage, the main idea is that for an intentional agent to bring about an effect, the agent has to know, in some sense, what is involved in bringing about the effect:

> I deny that my will is the true cause of my arm's movement, of my mind's ideas, and of other things accompanying my volitions, for I see no relation whatever between such different things. I even see clearly that there can be no relation between the volition I have to move my arm and the agitation of the animal spirits, i.e., of certain tiny bodies whose motion and figure I do not know and which choose certain nerve canals from a million others I do not know in order to cause in me the motion I desire through an infinity of movements I do not desire.
> (OC III 226/*Eluc.* 15/LO 669)

If the case of agitating the animal spirits seems less than straightforward, consider the following example. If I wish to be at a dinner party north of the Han River in Seoul, and getting there involves my taking the Banpo Bridge across the river, then it would seem that my making it successfully to the dinner without guidance would warrant the inference that I knew that the bridge had to be crossed. That is, I knew what was involved in bringing about this state of affairs.

Malebranche was not alone in holding such a view. Arnold Geulincx, a contemporary of Malebranche, had argued for the causal impotency of souls explicitly on the grounds that they fail to satisfy the "knowledge principle": you are not the cause of that which you do not know how to bring about.[26] Then, in like spirit, let us take this river-crossing case as paradigmatic and suppose Malebranche generalized in the following manner: insofar as the agent in question is an intentional volitional agent, then such knowledge can be assumed when the agent is successful in bringing about the effect. Taken this way, it does not seem too farfetched to uphold such a requirement for causal agency, as long as the agency in question is limited in this manner.

This qualification on the type of causal agent naturally raises a question about the scope of the NK argument. Some have argued that Malebranche had intended to apply the argument more broadly, to all causes in general, not just to intentional, volitional agents.[27] There is some textual evidence for this interpretation, as presented in the *Dialogues* and the *Conversations Chrétiennes*,[28] but the textual evidence is not conclusive. Moreover, given Malebranche's likely commitment to a core feature of Cartesian dualism, namely that the attributes of thought and extension are mutually exclusive, one would think that there is pressure on the part of Malebranche to deny that bodies are capable of possessing a certain type of awareness or thought-like property, which would then in principle rule out bodies from the domain of potential causes.

Let us now turn to Malebranche's "global" arguments for occasionalism. Most interpreters agree that Malebranche presents two such "global" arguments, the "no necessary connection" argument (hereafter NNC) and the "conservation is but continuous creation" argument (hereafter CCC).[29] NNC emerges prominently in the following famous passage from the *Search*:

> A true cause as I understand it is one such that the mind perceives a necessary connection between it and its effect. Now the mind perceives a necessary connection only between the will of an infinitely perfect being and its effects. Therefore, it is only God who is the true cause and who truly has the power to move bodies.
>
> (OC II 316/*Search* 6.2.3/LO 450)

Given Hume's influential discussion, readers most likely will find Malebranche's identification here of causation with necessary connection rather natural and intuitive.[30] In contrast to our affinity with this conception of causation as necessary connection, it is unclear whether the proponents of genuine creaturely causation in the seventeenth century would have felt the same. Much depends on how Malebranche's conception of necessary connections here is to be understood. Does Malebranche have in view the fact that all exercises of divine will are sufficient in themselves to bring about their effects? And is he therefore requiring that *any* instance of genuine causation meet such causal self-sufficiency? If so, the proponents of genuine secondary causation in our time period, be it the conservationist or concurrentist, would find this conception of causation unacceptable. For, as we have seen, neither the conservationist nor the concurrentist grants that a finite substance is sufficient on its own to bring about an effect. Even if a creature is a genuine cause, divine assistance, whether in the form of divine conservation or concurrence, is necessary. That is, the proponents of genuine creaturely causation fully accept that God is unique in terms of causal self-sufficiency. Their endorsement of creaturely causation is not meant to encroach upon this divine prerogative. Hence, under this understanding of necessary connection, Malebranche's conception would have been rejected as unacceptably narrow. Malebranche's insistence that creatures are not genuine causes because they fail to meet this requirement would be met by complaints that this strategy is in effect one that establishes occasionalism by stipulation, hence question begging. For no proponent of genuine creaturely causation would venture so far as to accept that creaturely causes are sufficient in themselves to bring about their effects, and any conception of causation that demands such causal self-sufficiency ought to be rejected.

This has led other interpreters to think that necessary connection for Malebranche should be understood differently as rejecting a certain type of essentialism with regard to causal powers. Consider the traditional Aristotelian essentialist model, according to which finite substances are typically characterized by certain essential powers, which enable them to bring about specific effects. In this model, fire, for instance, might be thought to have the power to burn flesh essentially in that fire would not be fire should it come into direct contact with flesh and not burn the flesh. This approach, that takes created substances to have essential causal powers, however, does not endorse the further claim that created substances are causally sufficient to bring about their effects. For instance, a concurrentist would hold that fire is not itself sufficient to burn flesh and thus requires the concurring causal activity of God, but, once all causal requirements are met, it cannot be the case that the flesh not burn. In this view, the necessary connection in question would be a logical connection in the sense that it would be contradictory for there not to be the effect, given the exercise of the causal power of the creature along with the other requisites such as divine concurrence or conservation being met. Might Malebranche have had such a conception of necessary connection in mind? And, if so, on what grounds would Malebranche think that such necessary connections fail to obtain between creatures and their alleged effects?

There seems to be some textual evidence that something like this was what Malebranche had in mind. Consider the following case, where Malebranche envisions the case of demons, where God wills to bring about a state of affairs contrary to what demons will:

> [L]et us suppose that God wills to produce the opposite of what some minds will, as might be thought in the case of demons . . . that deserve this punishment. One could not say in this case that God would communicate His power to them, since they could do nothing they willed to do.
> (OC II 316/Search 6.2.3/LO 450)

Here Malebranche seems to be attempting to weaken the link between the creature's power and its alleged effect by showing that God could always will some event contrary to what the creature brings about. Malebranche takes such cases of divine intervention to show that it is possible for a creature to fail to bring about the effect, which allegedly follows essentially from the creature's power. To deny such a possibility would entail a problematic restriction on divine omnipotence, or so Malebranche appears to be thinking.

But whether such cases of divine intervention are sufficient to weaken the Aristotelian essentialist's case is far from clear. For, as we have seen, the Aristotelian essentialist need not deny this possibility of divine intervention overriding the creaturely powers. And that such creaturely powers can be overridden in such intervention cases also is consistent with there being genuine creaturely causal connections when divine assistance is not that of intervention but rather that of concurrence or conservation. That is, when the divine concurring activity and other causal requisites are not that of overriding the creaturely powers in question but rather that of assisting the creature, the Aristotelian essentialist might still claim that it is logically inconsistent for the effect not to follow. Thus, if necessary connections are understood in this logical sense, then the critical premise of the NNC argument turns out to the claim that there are necessary connections only between the divine will and its effect, and this premise would emerge as questionable by the proponents of genuine secondary causation. For, as we have seen, the Aristotelian essentialists would deny that God's volition is unique in this respect.

On either reading of necessary connections, therefore, the NNC argument seems unlikely to persuade the proponents of secondary causation to abandon their position for occasionalism. Nonetheless, the significance of Malebranche's attempt here is not lost to us. Viewed against the traditional Aristotelian model with its somewhat dizzying array of distinct causes, Malebranche is attempting to present a clear, unified conception of causation that focuses on the necessary connections between the cause and effect.[31]

In his later major work, *Dialogues on Metaphysics and on Religion*, Malebranche tries a different approach to establish occasionalism across the board. In the Seventh Dialogue, Malebranche's opponent, Aristes, concedes that at the moment of creation, in willing a body to exist, God not only brought the body into existence but also created it in a particular place, thus making God the unique, full cause of the body and its state. But Aristes continues on to remark that such a dominant causal role by God need not be the case now because the moment of creation has naturally passed, to which Philonous, Malebranche's mouthpiece, responds:

> "The moment of creation has passed!" But if this moment does not pass, then you are in a spot, and will have to yield. . . . God wills that a certain kind of world exist. His will is omnipotent, and this world is thus created. Let God no longer will there to be a world, and it is thereby annihilated. For the world assuredly depends on the will of the creator. If the world subsists, it is because God continues to will its existence. Thus, the conservation of creatures is, on the part of God, nothing but their continued creation.
> (OC XII 156–157/*Dialogues* 112)

Note that Malebranche here is not attempting to provide a reductive analysis of causation. Rather it is from the broadly accepted theological principle that "conservation is but continuous creation" that Malebranche attempts to draw out the occasionalist thesis.[32] The basic idea appears to be simple: because God conserves the world by continuously creating it, just as it was God that had been the unique cause in the initial act of creation *ex nihilo*, it is God alone that is causally operative in all subsequent instances of conservation.

Malebranche's strategy in advancing this argument relies on the fact that the majority of the theistic philosophers of the time were committed to the CCC thesis. If many had previously taken the CCC thesis to be compatible with genuine creaturely causation, Malebranche's contribution was to create a tension between the acceptance of the CCC thesis and a commitment to genuine creaturely causation. That is, with this argument Malebranche was able to suggest, rather persuasively, that what might seem like an innocuous commitment to the CCC thesis is in fact a clear step toward occasionalism. A way to understand the force of the argument is to think of Malebranche as redefining or clarifying the identity relation between creation and conservation central to the CCC thesis. If previous endorsements of CCC took the identity to be numerical, in that the acts of creation and conservation are a numerically single, uninterrupted act, Malebranche here is suggesting that the identity should be thought of more as qualitative – that is in the sense that there is no qualitative difference in terms of the divine causality involved.[33]

If the identity between creation and conservation is merely numerical, then this identity appears to be consistent with the possibility that God is not as causally involved in the act of conservation as in the case of creation. Even if one starts a walk at a brisk seven-kilometers-per-hour pace and later slows down to four kilometers per hour, one would still be engaged in the same walk, numerically speaking, though the walker would not be exerting the same amount of effort throughout the walk. Contrast this to a walk where the walker maintains the speed of seven kilometers per hour throughout her walk such that the amount of physical exertion is qualitatively identical throughout the walk. Malebranche's ingenuity is to stress that the proper understanding of the CCC thesis is closer to the latter model, where the divine causal work is qualitatively uniform across creation and conservation. And given that God is the sole causal contributor at the moment of creation, it follows that God is the sole causal contributor in subsequent moments of conservation.

Let us end our discussion of occasionalism with a brief consideration of the following question: what role do creatures play, if any? Here is Malebranche's response: "A natural cause is . . . not a real and true but only an occasional cause, which determines the Author of nature to act in such and such a manner in such and such a situation" (OC II 312/*Search* 6.2.3/LO 448). So, creatures do have some role to play in the causal story of the world, though obviously it cannot be one that is causal in character. According to Malebranche, creaturely states are "occasional" causes, which figure into how divine volitions get exercised to bring about the changes in the natural world.

For Malebranche, all the events that occur naturally in the world are due to God's general volitions that serve as general laws that connect distinct types of events. For instance, when my arm regularly rises when I will to raise it, this is due to God's general volition that arms rise when willed by the agent. So, say I will to raise my arm at this instance, and my arm goes up. It is this willing on my part in this particular instance that Malebranche regards as an "occasion" for God to bring about the event of my arm rising. This is the sense in which the creaturely state "determines [God] to act in such and such a manner in such and such a situation." Given that all nonmiraculous events of nature, according to Malebranche, are governed by such general laws and volitions, any natural event would always be preceded by its occasional cause. In this respect, these general laws and volitions are sufficient to underwrite such counterfactual claims as my arm would not have risen had I not willed it. Unlike Hume, however, for Malebranche, neither such counterfactual dependence nor regularity between the occasional cause and its correlate are indicative of genuine causation. The only real causal connections hold directly between the divine will and its effects. Counterfactual dependence or regularity between natural events merely reveal that the preceding event is an occasional cause of the ensuing event.

7. Leibniz

Our preceding discussion of Descartes and Malebranche will come in handy as we set up the basic contours of Leibniz's views on causation. Let us begin with Leibniz's response to the problem of intersubstantial causation between created substances. On this issue, Leibniz in part agrees with Malebranche: Leibniz also denies that finite substances causally interact with each other. The criticisms directed against Cartesian interactionism noted earlier appears to have partly weighed on Leibniz's mind, but Leibniz also seems to have had other reasons against intersubstantial causal interaction, as the following, famous passage from the *Monadology* shows:

> There is also no way of explaining how a monad can be altered or changed internally by some other creature, since one cannot transpose anything in it, nor can one conceive of any internal motion that can be excited, directed, augmented, or diminished within it, as can be done in composites, where there can be change among parts. The monads have no windows through which something can enter or leave. Accidents cannot be detached, nor can they go outside of substances, as the sensible species of the Scholastics once did. Thus, neither substance nor accident can enter a monad from without.
> (AG 213–214)

Here Leibniz first appears to be arguing that the fact that monads or simple substances are not composites prevents them from being causally influenced from without. The assumption that change triggered externally requires that the subject of change be composed of parts is playing a crucial role in the argument, but this principle is far from self-evident. Furthermore, even if one were to grant that this principle might be plausibly applied to cases of bodily change, it is not clear that the same should hold for changes in thinking substances or souls. For the proponents of body-to-mind causation presumably would not deny that minds are without parts, but they would still insist on minds being influenced by external causes. Thus, unless Leibniz provides additional reasons for why being composed of parts is a prerequisite for being acted upon by external causes, this argument faces the danger of being question begging against the proponent of body-mind causation.

A second, different argument emerges in the passage just quoted as well. This argument suggests that genuine intersubstantial causation implies that the modes (or modifications) of substances are detached and move from one substance to another, which, Leibniz argues, is implausible. Given the Scholastic precedent of "intelligible species" migrating between substances, as Leibniz himself notes, the rejection of free-floating modifications is not to be taken for granted. However, there are reasons to think that Leibniz is on firmer ground in this case. Leibniz seems to be thinking that modifications are critically dependent on the substance of which they are modes, and, as such, the very idea that a mode could survive detachment, however brief, and exist on its own is unacceptably problematic.

As we can see, Leibniz's denial of intersubstantial causation between finite substances does not rely on occasionalistic principles. This is noteworthy but not surprising, for Leibniz famously affirms the causal powers of creatures, never wavering in his causal realism. As he states in *On Nature Itself*, for Leibniz, "the substance of things itself consists in the force of acting and being acted upon" (*PPL* 502). But this then raises a natural question: how can one deny causal interaction between substances and yet affirm their causal powers? Leibniz's answer is to restrict the causal powers of created substances to that of bringing about changes internally within each respective substance. That is, Leibniz affirms intrasubstantial causal powers (genuine causal powers that bring about changes to its own states), but he denies that these powers have intersubstantial effects (these powers do not bring about changes in states of distinct substances). The operation of Leibnizian forces is restricted to the confines of each individual substance, responsible only for bringing about change in each substance respectively. The exact nature of the causal forces within Leibnizian substances is a topic of some controversy and will be discussed in more detail in conjunction with the issue of secondary causation in nature. Let us first take a closer look at 'preestablished harmony,' Leibniz's well-known attempt at explaining the apparent causal relations that hold between finite substances.

If Leibniz is right to think that finite substances only possess powers to cause changes in their own states, how are we to make sense of the common phenomena whereby one substance *appears* to bring about change in another, distinct substance? What type of causal story is to be told, say, about a piece of cotton burning when coming into contact with fire? In a work that editors have dated to 1686, Leibniz gives us the following explanation:

> Strictly speaking, one can say that *no created substance exerts a metaphysical action or influx on any other thing*. For, not to mention the fact that one cannot explain how something can pass from one thing into the substance of another, we have already shown that from the notion of each and every thing follows all of its future states. What we call causes are only concurrent requisites, in metaphysical rigor. . . . *Also, assuming the distinction between soul and body, from this we can explain their union* without the common hypothesis of an influx, which is unintelligible, and without the hypothesis of an occasional cause, which appeals to a *Deus ex machina*. For God from the beginning constituted both the soul and the body with such wisdom and workmanship that, from the first constitution or notion of a thing, everything that happens through itself [*per se*] in the one corresponds perfectly to everything that happens in the other, just as if something passed from one to the other. This is what I call the hypothesis of concomitance. This hypothesis is true in all substances in the whole universe but cannot be sense in all of them, unlike the case of the soul and body.
>
> (Primary Truths, 1686?/AG 33)

In this passage, Leibniz rejects both interactionism and occasionalism and, as an alternative, presents his "hypothesis of concomitance," according to which what happens in one thing corresponds perfectly to what happens in other things "just as if something passed from one to the other." Returning to our example of cotton burning when coming into contact with fire, preestablished harmony holds that although it may seem to us that the fire burns the cotton, it is actually the cotton itself that burns spontaneously just at the moment it comes into contact with fire. Each thing acts through its own internal causal powers to bring about the changes in its states such that the changes that occur in any given substance are caused by its power alone, but the changes are mutually so well coordinated that it looks as if the substances are interacting.

It might be helpful at this point to contrast preestablished harmony with the occasionalist account presented earlier. Return again to our example of the burning cotton, and consider how Malebranche might account for such phenomena. For Malebranche, because God is the unique genuine cause that brings about real change in the world, it is God who burns the cotton on the occasion that it comes into contact with fire. There is a correlation between cotton coming into contact with fire and its combustion, but it is merely a correlation, one that is grounded in God's general volition. Furthermore, it is this divine general volition that cotton should burn when coming into contact with fire that is doing the causal work. For Malebranche, divine volitions are the paradigmatic causes; they are necessarily efficacious in bringing about the content of the volitions.

In contrast, for Leibniz, created substances are not devoid of causal powers, but are rather chock full of them, albeit forces that are limited to causing changes within the substance itself. Thus, on Leibniz's account, it is neither the fire nor God that burns the cotton when it burns. Rather it is the cotton itself that spontaneously burns when it comes into contact with fire. Thus, in the case of preestablished harmony the correlation between cotton coming into contact with fire and its combustion is grounded in the agreement or correspondence between the changes that are caused spontaneously to each substance by its intrasubstantial powers. Leibniz crystalizes this picture by presenting the famous clock analogy, as the following contained in the postscript of a letter to Basnage de Beauval from January 1696:

> You say that you do not understand how I can prove what I have suggested about the communication or harmony of two substances as different as the soul and the body. It is true that I thought I provided a way to do so. And this is how I propose to satisfy you. Imagine two clocks or watches which are in perfect agreement. Now this can happen in three ways. The first is that of a natural influence. . . . The second way of making two clocks, even poor ones, agree always is to assign a skilled craftsman to them who adjusts them and constantly sets them in agreement. The third way is to construct these two timepieces at the beginning with such skill and accuracy that one can be assured of their subsequent agreement.
>
> (PPL 459/G IV 498–500)

Note that this particular instance of preestablished harmony is not guaranteed to hold in all possible configurations of possible finite substances. Leibniz holds that there could easily be a piece of cotton the internal forces of which are such that they bring about its combustion without coming into contact with fire but rather when a firefly bumps into it. There could also be possible configurations of rational creatures such that volitions and bodily movements are inverted, as it were, so that one's left arm moves when one wills one's right arm to move. A world in which one's volition to raise one's left arm is followed by an alternation between one's right arm going up and one's left arm going up would be an even more disorderly world. In countenancing such scenarios, we can see that Leibniz takes the preestablished harmony that holds in our world as a particular feature of this possible world, a feature that he takes to be one of the reasons why this world is the best of all possible worlds. And this mutual correspondence distinctive of our world is what makes the world intelligible to us, allowing us to identify lawful regularities and make useful predictions, as Leibniz notes in section 14 of his *Discourse on Metaphysics*[34]:

> [E]ach substance is like a world apart, independent of all other things, except for God; thus all our phenomena, that is, all the things that can ever happen to

us, are only consequences of our being. And since these phenomena maintain a certain order in conformity with our nature or, so to speak, in conformity with the world which is in us, an order which enables us to make useful observations to regulate our conduct, observations justified by the success of future phenomena, an order which thus allows us often to judge the future from the past without error, this would be sufficient to enable us to say that these phenomena are true without bothering with whether they are outside us and whether others also perceive them. Nevertheless, it is very true that the perceptions or expressions of all substances mutually correspond in such a way that each one, carefully following certain reasons or laws it has observed, coincides with others doing the same – in the same way that several people who have agreed to meet in some place at some specified time can really do this if they so desire. But although they all express the same phenomena, it does not follow that their expressions are perfectly similar; it is sufficient that they are proportional. In just the same way, several spectators believe that they are seeing the same thing and agree among themselves about it, even though each sees and speaks in accordance with his view.

(AG 47)

Here we see that the mutual correspondence or harmony among the states of substances is what grounds the lawful relations we observe in this world and what allows us to make successful predictions to guide our behavior. This correspondence, then, is a beneficial feature of our world, and different possible worlds turn out to possess different degrees of goodness in terms of their overall harmony. That the goodness of this world is the primary reason behind God's decision to create it brings to the fore the fundamental role of final causation in Leibniz's system. The causal activity of the finite substances that make up this world exhibits a goodness or value, expressed in their mutual harmony, a goodness that is a critical causal factor in its coming into existence. The divine agent responsible for the actualization of a world is sensitive to such features of goodness, and this sensitivity is due to divine causality itself being teleological in a fundamental way. For God's causal activity is directed toward the end of bringing about the best, thus demanding that the various possible worlds be considered with regard to their varying degrees of goodness.

Given this understanding of preestablished harmony, let us now turn our attention to the topic of the nature of the internal forces that are responsible for such harmony. What type of causality did Leibniz have in mind as he advanced his causal realism? This is a complex issue, and different views have emerged. Several commentators have propounded the view that the Leibnizian powers are to be thought of as fundamentally efficient in character,[35] whereas others have argued that Leibnizian forces are better characterized as primarily formal and final causes.[36] A central dividing point in the debate appears to be whether one takes formal and final causation to be sufficiently robust to underwrite Leibniz's causal realism. As we noted in the beginning, many of the philosophers of our period shied away from adopting the key Aristotelian causal notions of 'substantial forms' and 'final causes' into their accounts of causation. For instance, neither Descartes nor Malebranche appear to place formal or final causality centrally in their accounts, especially when created substances are concerned. Among the four Aristotelian causes, for the philosophers of the seventeenth century, it seems as though efficient causality stands out easily as the paradigmatic type of genuine causality.

Interpreters who aim to anchor Leibnizian forces in efficient causality appear to agree with this privileging of efficient causality. But whether Leibniz also accepts this privileging of efficient causality is a different issue. Opponents of the efficient-causality reading point to Leibniz's frequent statements that express his willingness to accommodate Scholastic causal notions. For instance, in section 11 of the *Discourse on Metaphysics*, after subtitling the section "That the thoughts of the theologians and philosophers who are called scholastics are not entirely to be disdained," Leibniz goes on to profess,

> I know that I am advancing a great paradox by attempting to rehabilitate the old philosophy in some fashion and to restore the almost banished substantial forms to their former place. . . . [O]ur moderns do not give enough credit to Saint Thomas and to the other great men of his time and that there is much more solidity than one imagines in the opinions of the Scholastic philosophers and theologians, provided that they are used appropriately and in their proper place.
>
> (AG 43)

Leibniz's rehabilitation of substantial forms is an interesting and complex topic, which requires a fuller discussion than this section can permit. But we can minimally note that critical to Leibniz's adoption of this Scholastic notion is his identification of substantial forms with the 'primitive forces' of each individual substance. According to Leibniz, primitive forces are "internal tendencies of simple substances, by which according to a certain law they pass from perception to perception" (G II, 275/AG 181). That the basic causal forces are located in substantial form as primitive forces, which operate in a lawlike manner, does not itself imply that primitive forces for Leibniz are not somehow efficient in character. For, traditionally speaking, the substantial forms of individual substances were the seat of their efficient causal powers as well. But we also note that for Leibniz the connection between forces and laws are particularly tight, and, as Adams points out, Leibniz goes so far as to identify these forces with laws: "the primitive force is as it were the law of the series" of the successive states that make up the simple substance.[37] That primitive forces as the causal nexus of the simple substance, responsible for its series of perceptual changes, is lawful in such a fundamental manner highlights how causal and conceptual relations coalesce within Leibniz's system. For Leibniz also takes primitive forces to constitute the concrete correlate of the complete individual concept, the concept of the individual substance in virtue which of all predications of a substance are uniquely true of it. That the lawlike primitive forces make up the particular, concrete causal nexus that corresponds to the complete individual concept underwrites an isomorphism between the conceptual structure inherent in the complete individual concept of the simple substance and the substance's concrete causal structure as expressed in its primitive forces. Thus, formal and conceptual relations seem to be equally fundamental to the causal structure of Leibnizian substances.

But it was not only substantial forms that Leibniz adopted into this project of rehabilitation. As we saw earlier, Leibniz also regarded final causality to be a critical component of his basic metaphysical landscape. Divine causality itself is goal oriented, directed toward the end of bringing about the best of all possible worlds. But final causation is not exclusive to divine causality but also permeates the natural, created realm for Leibniz. As he states in his 30 June 1704 letter to de Volder, for Leibniz, "there is nothing in things but simple substances, and in them perception and appetite" (G II, 270/

AG 181). We see that appetites are as fundamental to simple substances as perceptions, and later on Leibniz describes appetites as "the action of the internal principle which brings about the change or passage from one perception to another" (Mon 15/AG 215). Thus, appetites emerge as the key causal principles within simple substances, strongly suggesting that for Leibniz the primitive forces mentioned earlier also have some type of final causality built into them. This assessment is consistent with Leibniz's numerous remarks throughout his mature metaphysics that the operation of simple substances is best thought of as belonging to the "kingdom of final causes" (Mon 87/AG 224). The foregoing considerations, both philosophical and textual, lead us to believe that the proper understanding of Leibniz's views on intrasubstantial causality requires a nuanced approach, one that incorporates his complex commitments to the efficient, formal, and final causation.

Equally important to this proper understanding of intrasubstantial forces is Leibniz's position with regard to the relation between divine and creaturely causation, the last topic of this section. Eschewing both occasionalism and conservationism, Leibniz holds that God and created substances concur in bringing about the natural effects of our world. Given his unwavering commitment to the intrasubstantial causal forces so fundamental to his conception of simple substances – "[t]he very substance of things consists in the force of acting and being acted on" (G IV, 508/PPL 502) – we are not surprised that Leibniz rejects occasionalism. Moreover, given his explicit endorsement of the CCC thesis, that he would regard mere conservationism too extreme in minimizing divine causal contribution is also understandable. Thus, Leibniz's concurrentism appears to be a natural position for him to take. But exactly how Leibniz's model of concurrence should be understood is unclear and has also been the topic of some controversy in the recent literature.

A focal point in this debate is Leibniz's commitment to the CCC thesis. As we have seen, Malebranche argued that the proper understanding of this thesis leads one straightforwardly to deny that created substances possess genuine causal powers, and Leibniz was not only well acquainted with Malebranche's works but also engaged in extensive correspondence with him.[38] Moreover, Leibniz himself endorses the continuous creation thesis, and his various statements concerning the role of divine causation in producing the perfections have appeared to many interpreters as coming dangerously close to occasionalism.[39] For instance, Leibniz writes to Des Bosses in his 2 February 1706 letter that "I hold, in general, that however much perfection there is in things, it flows forth from God by a continual operation" (G II, 295). This claim, that whatever perfection there is in created substances "flows forth" or emanates from God, easily brings to mind Malebranche's rendition of the continuous creation thesis. Nor is such a statement an aberration or isolated occurrence. In section 10 of the *Causa Dei*, Leibniz claims, "In acting, things depend on God, since God concurs in the actions of things, insofar as there is something of perfection in their actions, which, at least, must emanate from God" (G VI, 440, my emphasis; translation is from Sleigh 184). The central claim that whatever perfection that is in the action of creatures emanates from God is reaffirmed in the following passage from the *Theodicy*:

> And when it is said that the creature depends upon God insofar as it exists and insofar as it acts, and even that conservation is a continual creation, this is true in that God gives ever to the creature and produces continually all that in it is positive, good, and perfect, every perfect gift coming from the Father of lights.[40]

As we can see, Leibniz in these texts clearly asserts that whatever causal contribution creatures make, it is not in the form of producing perfections. But if this is the case, then we cannot but wonder what options Leibniz has to maintain causal efficacy on the part of creature.

A variety of interpretations have appeared to present a viable account of divine concurrence, one that presumably satisfies two desiderata. One is that of securing genuine causal activity in a simple substance. The other is that of rendering this activity consistent with Leibniz's claims about the divine production of all perfections within the creaturely realm. That Leibniz himself believed that such an account is possible is evident from the following:

> I grant in some way . . . that God continually produces all that is real in creatures. But I hold that in doing it he also continually produces or conserves in us that energy or activity which according to me constitutes the nature of substance and the source of its modifications. And so I do not grant that God alone acts in substances, or alone causes their changes, and I believe that that would be to make the creatures totally futile and useless.
> (G IV, 588f.; see also G III, 566)

The difficulty of the present task stems from the fact that the two requirements appear to be in tension, because, despite Leibniz's confidence, it is not clear that if God in some way "continually produces all that is real in creature," we can nonetheless be causally active. Recent interpretations have roughly fallen into two camps. One reading holds firm to the view that Leibniz's causal realism with regard to intrasubstantial powers requires a commitment on his part to efficient, productive powers in creatures.[41] The other view holds that the genuine efficacy of created substances consist in their formal and final causal powers rather than any direct efficient powers to produce perfections.[42] Both interpretative strategies agree that despite his endorsement of the continuous creation thesis, occasionalism is not a real option, and that Leibniz has a coherent account of concurrence. Their disagreement rests on the issues of how fundamental, productive, efficient causal powers are related to the makeup of Leibnizian simple substances, how we are to understand Leibniz's endorsement of the continuous creation thesis, and whether formal and final causes are sufficient to underwrite Leibniz's causal realism with regard to the intrasubstantial powers of created substances.

Notes

1. Alfred Freddoso 1994, 131–5 (*American Catholic Philosophical Quarterly*, Vol. LXVIII, No. 2).
2. AT III 660. Translation from *The Correspondence Between Princess Elisabeth of Bohemia and René Descartes*, ed. and trans. by Lisa Shapiro, University of Chicago Press, 2007.
3. Freddoso 1994, 131.
4. Freddoso 1994, 133–4.
5. One might envision an account according to which the initial creation of substances is the result of God's direct causal activity, but that subsequent, conserved states of the world are not directly dependent on divine causal activity, in contrast to what conservationism espouses. Such a position would secure an even more robust position for finite substances. Although philosophically coherent, theologically speaking, the account would have been unacceptably deistic. For this position would entail that the world would continue to exist even if, *per impossibile*, God were to cease existing.
6. For Durandus and Malebranche, for instance.

7 Of these four, the last relation, namely that concerning what kind of causal relation holds between numerically distinct minds or soul, does not appear to have received much attention at all by the philosophers of our period. It does not seem farfetched to suppose that "telepathic" causal powers – powers underwriting direct causal influence between minds without the involvement of sensory organs or our bodies – were taken by the philosophers of the seventeenth century to be as mysterious as we typically consider them to be.
8 AT III 661.
9 R. C. Richardson, "The 'Scandal' of Cartesian Interactionism," *Mind*, New Series, Vol. 91, No. 361 (January, 1982), p. 21.
10 E. O'Neill, "Mind-Body Interaction and Metaphysical Consistency: A Defense of Descartes," *Journal of the History of Philosophy*, Vol. 25 (April, 1987), pp. 227–45.
11 AT VIIIA 61–62; CSM I 240.
12 *NE* 1.1.
13 Dan Garber, *Descartes' Metaphysical Physics*, Chicago: University of Chicago Press, 1992; see also "How God Causes Motion: Descartes, Divine Sustenance and Occasionalism," in *Descartes Embodied*, Cambridge: Cambridge University Press, 2001, 189–220.
14 AT VIIIA 42; CSM I 224.
15 AT I 241–244; CSMK 36–37.
16 For the divine concurrentist reading, see Helen Hattab, "Concurrence or Divergence? Reconciling Descartes's Physics With His Metaphysics," *Journal of the History of Philosophy*, Vol. 45, No. 1 (2007), pp. 49–78; "One Cause or Many? Jesuit Influences on Descartes's Division of Causes," *Rencontres de Philosophie Médiévale*, Vol. 7, Société Internationale pour l'Étude de la Philosophie Médiévale (1998); and "The Problem of Secondary Causation in Descartes: A Response to Des Chene," *Perspectives on Science*, Vol. 8, No. 2 (2000), pp. 93–118; Andrew Pessin, "Descartes's Nomic Concurrentism: Finite Causation and Divine Concurrence," *Journal of the History of Philosophy*, Vol. 41, No. 1 (2003), pp. 25–49; and Denis Des Chene, "On Laws and Ends: A Response to Hattab and Menn," *Perspectives on Science*, Vol. 8, No. 2 (2000), pp. 144–163. For the conservationist reading, see Tad Schmaltz, *Descartes on Causation*, Oxford and New York: Oxford University Press, 2008.
17 For instance, Martial Gueroult, Alan Gabbey, and Tad Schmaltz appear to hold this view. See Martial Gueroult, "The Metaphysics and Physics of Force in Descartes," and Alan Gabbey, "Force and Inertia in the Seventeenth Century: Descartes and Newton," both in *Descartes: Philosophy, Mathematics and Physics*, ed. Stephen Gaukroger, Sussex: Harvester Press, 1980, 196–229 and 230–320, respectively. See Schmaltz 2008 for his view. Helen Hattab 2007 presents a nice summary of secondary literature.
18 Quoted in Schmaltz 2008, 130.
19 McCann provides an interesting account here about how Locke's corpuscularianism is much more theistically oriented than other proponents. See Edwin McCann, "Lockean Mechanism," *Philosophy, Its History and Historiography*, Vol. 3 (1985), pp. 209–231; see also "Locke's Philosophy of Body" in Vere Chappell, ed. *The Cambridge Companion to Locke*, Cambridge: Cambridge University Press, 1994, 56–88. There is of course the difficult issue of superaddition, about what God could do.
20 This thoroughly apt description I borrow from Downing 2007, 352. See Lisa Downing, "Locke's Ontology," in Lex Newman, ed. *The Cambridge Companion to Locke's Essay*, Cambridge: Cambridge University Press, 2007, 352–380. For an illuminating discussion for how this tension might be resolved in Locke's favor, see Downing's piece. Also see Margaret Wilson, "Superadded Properties: The Limits of Mechanism in Locke," *American Philosophical Quarterly*, Vol. 16 (1979), pp. 143–150.
21 McCann 1994, 58.
22 Downing 2007, 352.
23 McCann 1994, 56.
24 See McCann 1994; Downing 2007; Wilson 1979; and Michael Ayers, "Mechanism, Superaddition, and the Proof of God's Existence in Locke's Essay," *Philosophical Review*, Vol. 90 (1981), 210–251.
25 Nicolas Malebranche, *De la recherche de la vérité* (1678), VI, ii, 3 in *Oeuvres complètes de Malebranche*, ed. André Robinet (Paris: Vrin, 1958–84), vol. II, 312. The works of Malebranche will be cited by volume and page in *Oeuvres completes*, hereafter referred to as OC, and by the relevant English translations. In the case of the *Recherche* and the *Elucidations*, I follow Lennon and Olscamp, trans., *The Search for Truth and Elucidations of the Search for Truth*, Cambridge: Cambridge University Press, 1997, hereafter referred to as LO. For the *Entretiens sur la métaphysique et sur la religion*, I use Jolley, ed., Scott, trans., *Dialogues on Metaphysics and on Religion [Dialogues]*, Cambridge: Cambridge University Press, 1997, hereafter referred to as *Dialogues*.

26. This principle does not have its origins in Malebranche but is associated with Arnold Geulincx, who stated, "*Quod nescis quomodo fiat, id non facis.*" See *Metaphysica vera*, part I, Quinta Scientia, in *Arnoldi Geulincx Antverpiensis Opera Philosophica*, 3 vols., edited by J.P.N. Land, The Hague: Martinus Nijhoff, 1893, vol. 2, 150–151. For further discussion, see Stephen Nadler, "Knowledge, Volitional Agency and Causation in Malebranche and Geulincx," *British Journal for the History of Philosophy*, Vol. 7, No. 2 (1999), pp. 263–274; see also Nicholas Jolley, "Occasionalism and Efficacious Laws in Malebranche," *Midwest Studies in Philosophy*, Vol. 26 (2002) pp. 245–257; and Jolley 1997, in his introduction to the translation of Malebranche's *Dialogues*.
27. See Nadler 1999, p. 267. He duly notes that this broader reading is a minority view and also points out that "Malebranche's texts do not strongly support this broader reading of his argument."
28. Nadler also present the following passage from the *Conversations Chrétiennes*, which seems to support his suggestion that Malebranche at times thought something like the NK argument to be "an epistemic condition on causality *tout court*": "Can the fire act upon you? Can it cause in you pleasure that it does not possess, that it does not feel, pleasure of which it has no knowledge?" (OC IV, 15–6).
29. I follow Steven Nadler's description of this argument, presented in his " 'No Necessary Connection': The Medieval Roots of the Occasionalist Roots of Hume," *The Monist*, Vol. 73 (1996), pp. 448–466.
30. See Hume, *Treatise*. Malebranche did not merely anticipate Hume. There is strong evidence of an ancestral relation between the two. For Malebranche's influence on Hume, see Charles McCracken, *Malebranche and British Philosophy*, Oxford: Oxford University Press, 1983.
31. Does this prominence of efficient causation in Malebranche suggest that he rejects formal and final causation across the board? A brief answer will not do justice, but it does seem as though that final causation survives in Malebranche as well in that final causal elements are retained in Malebranche's explanation of God's selection of this world among many possible worlds. However, substantial forms seem to be more fully banished from the realm of created substance, at least in the case of extended substances. For Malebranche clearly rejects such fonts of causal powers in extended substances. The case of thinking substances is more complicated, because Malebranche does not deny that souls possess free will, and it is not clear whether he takes our free will to require something akin to substantial forms.
32. The *Elucidations* also contains passages which seem to suggest the main idea of the CCC argument.
33. For a more detailed presentation of this interpretation, see Sukjae Lee, "Necessary Connections and Continuous Creation: Malebranche's Two Arguments for Occasionalism," *Journal of the History of Philosophy*, Vol. 46, No. 4 (2008), pp. 539–566.
34. The *Discourse* is typically regarded as the first full presentation of Leibniz's mature metaphysics, including his views on preestablished harmony.
35. For example, Robert Sleigh, *Leibniz and Arnauld: A Commentary on Their Correspondence*, New Haven: Yale University Press, 1990; "Leibniz on Malebranche on Causality," in J. Cover and K. Kulstad, eds. *Central Themes in Early Modern Philosophy*, Indianapolis: Hackett Press, 1990; Donald Rutherford, *Leibniz and the Rational Order of Nature*, Cambridge: Cambridge University Press, 1995; and Jeffrey McDonough, "Leibniz: Creation and Conservation and Concurrence," *The Leibniz Review*, Vol. 17 (2007), pp. 31–60.
36. Sukjae Lee, "Leibniz on Divine Concurrence," *The Philosophical Review*, Vol. 113, No. 2 (2004), pp. 203–248. Julia von Bodelschwingh has an interesting mix; see Julia von Bodelschwingh, "Leibniz on Concurrence, Spontaneity, and Authorship," *The Modern Schoolman*, Vol. 88, No. 3/4 (2011), pp. 267–297.
37. Robert Adams, *Leibniz: Determinist, Theist, Idealist*, Oxford and New York: Oxford University Press, 1994, 80.
38. André Robinet, *Malebranche et Leibniz; relations personnelles présentées avec les textes complets des auteurs et de leurs correspondants*, Paris: Vris, 1955.
39. Sleigh 1990.
40. *Essais de Theodicée* G VI section 31; trans. by E. Huggard, La Salle, IL: Open Court, 1985 (hereafter abbreviated as T followed by section number). Also see A. Robinet, 1955, p. 421.
41. Sleigh 1990; McDonough 2007.
42. Lee 2004; von Bodelschwingh 2011.

5
FREE WILL AND DETERMINISM
C. P. Ragland

People typically regard one another as *morally responsible*: we believe that we deserve praise or reward for our morally good actions, and blame or punishment for our bad actions. Our moral responsibility seems to depend on our "free will" – our capacity to control or govern our actions in accordance with moral rules. All of the most important seventeenth century philosophers addressed the nature of freedom, as well as the perennial question of how freedom relates to determinism.

An event is *determined* just in case it results necessarily from its causes: given those causes (e.g. past history and the laws of nature), the event could not have failed to occur. *Determinism* is the thesis that *every* event is determined. The difference between a deterministic world (a world in which determinism is true) and an indeterministic world is similar to the difference between a standard novel and a "choose your own adventure" book. The latter has built into it several different possible endings to the story (though on any given reading, the reader can only get to one of them), whereas in a traditional novel, there is only one way the story can go. Similarly, if the world is indeterministic, then given how it began, there are many different paths history could take – the way it actually turns out is only one possibility among many. On the other hand, if determinism is true, then there is only one possible way things can go, given how the world began.

Can anyone be free and morally responsible if determinism is true? *Compatibilists* say yes: freedom is compatible with determinism, in the sense that both can exist at the same time. *Incompatibilists* say no. In their view, if determinism is true, then people cannot be legitimately rewarded or punished for their actions. *Hard determinists* are incompatibilists who believe in determinism and conclude that no one is free. *Libertarians* are incompatibilists who believe that because humans are free, determinism must be false. As we shall see, all of these positions are represented in the views of influential seventeenth century philosophers.

1. Bramhall (1594–1663)

The Anglican cleric John Bramhall is probably the least important and original thinker to be considered here, but his position on freedom deserves attention because it is a paradigmatic example of late medieval and early modern libertarianism, a view which deeply informed (often as an object of derision) the thinking of all the figures discussed here.

His understanding of freedom is extremely similar to that of the influential Scholastics Molina and Suárez,[1] and his writings on freedom are notable for their clear explanations of Scholastic terms and concepts. These writings, a source of inspiration for some contemporary libertarian philosophers,[2] grew out of a debate Bramhall had with Thomas Hobbes at the Paris home of the Marquess of Newcastle in 1645.[3]

Bramhall's view of freedom is rooted in his Aristotelian-Scholastic understanding of human nature. In this view, humans occupy an exalted place in a hierarchy of natural beings. Inanimate things and vegetative organisms do what they do automatically, with absolutely no understanding of why they act. Animals act from desire, which gives them a confused or imperfect grasp on why they act as they do. As rational animals, humans can evaluate their desires from the point of view of reason and decide which of their desires to pursue. This capacity for free choice gives humans "a more perfect knowledge of the end" for which they act and renders them morally responsible (*HBLN* 47–48).[4]

In the Scholastic picture, freedom of choice results from the interaction of two faculties in the rational soul: intellect (the power of understanding) and will (the power of choice). The intellect "proposes" various possible courses of action to the will and evaluates their relative goodness. The will, which is an appetite for the good in general (*HBLN* 46), can pursue any course of action that appears good to the intellect. This pursuit involves two stages. First, the will "elicits" or directly causes a volition (i.e. a choice, or instance of willing) to perform some physical or spiritual action (e.g. to open one's eyes, or add up some numbers). Next, the volition causes the relevant faculty (the body in the case of eye opening, the intellect in the case of addition) to produce the willed action. Volitions themselves are called "*elicited* acts of will." Their immediate effects (eye openings, computations, etc.), though strictly speaking the acts of other faculties, are called "*commanded* acts of will" (*HBLN* 9). Commanded acts count as free only because they spring from free volitions caused directly by the will (*HBLN* 48).

The will, Bramhall says, has "dominion over its own acts, to will or nill [i.e. will *not* to do something] without extrinsical necessitation" (*HBLN* 63).[5] The will is both a self-determining power and a "two-way" power. Each of these claims drives Bramhall toward incompatibilism.

For Bramhall, the will has "liberty to do or not to do" (*HBLN* 1): with respect to any given course of action A proposed by the intellect, the will can either elicit a volition to undertake A or refrain from eliciting such a volition. It can refrain either by producing some other volition (e.g. the decision not-to-A, or the decision to B) or by producing no volition at all. The will's ability to produce a volition or do nothing is its *liberty of exercise*, and its ability to produce this or that volition is called its *liberty of specification* (*HBLN* 1).[6] Though some agents (e.g. God, good and bad angels) do not have liberty of specification (*HBLN* 1), *every* free agent enjoys liberty of exercise over her volitions. Bramhall thus endorses a version of what philosophers now call the *principle of alternative possibilities* (PAP): a person did something freely only if she could have done otherwise.[7]

As Bramhall understands PAP, it leads quite directly to incompatibilism. He agrees with Molina's definition of freedom: "A free agent is that which, when all things are present that are needful to produce the effect, can nevertheless not produce it" (*HBLN* 63).[8] Let A stand for "the action that the agent actually performed." According to Bramhall, to say that the agent "could have done otherwise" means that the causally *necessary* conditions for A are not also *sufficient* for A: it is possible for those very same conditions to be present without A occurring – that is, they do not necessitate or determine A to occur. So, if the agent could have done otherwise, her action cannot have been causally determined. Free actions require "a universal immunity from all inevitability and determination to one" (*HBLN* 1).

Bramhall also claims that a free agent is "determined by himself" because the will has the power to "move itself" (*HBLN* 56). Free agents must be the sources or initiators of their own actions. But if the agent's action were causally determined by a prior cause outside the agent's control, then the true source of the action would be the prior cause, not the agent. Therefore, free actions cannot be subject to "extrinsical necessitation" (*HBLN* 63). This self-determination requirement adds nuance to Bramhall's understanding of the relationship between freedom and moral responsibility. Bramhall suggests that a diseased person can be appropriately blamed for having the inevitable symptoms of his disease, provided he contracted the disease through earlier bad free choices (*HBLN* 10–11; see also 52).[9] Similarly, an agent can be morally responsible for her causally necessitated actions, *provided* that the causes of those actions are not outside her control. We can be responsible for actions that are not free (because they do not satisfy PAP) if these actions flow in an appropriate way from prior free choices (which *did* satisfy PAP).

According to Bramhall, freedom is not compatible with determinism. But divine revelation, reason, and experience all teach us that we are free. Therefore, Bramhall concludes, determinism is false. He explicitly considers and rejects several purported sources of determinism, including "the concatenation of causes" (physical or natural determinism), "the last dictate of the understanding" (intellectual determinism), and "the decree of God" (theological determinism) (*HBLN* 3). Bramhall's rejection of these latter two forms of determinism deserves further scrutiny.

Many of Bramhall's Scholastic opponents (following Aquinas)[10] taught that "the will . . . necessarily follow[s] the last dictate of the understanding" (*HBLN* 12). On this intellectual determinist view, choice cannot occur until the intellect reaches a judgment about which possible course of action is best. The will then must choose the course of action that the intellect judges optimal. Against this view, Bramhall claims that when the agent is weighing several good (but not equally good) options, "the will . . . may accept that which the understanding judges to be less expedient" (*HBLN* 46). As witness to the reality of such weakness of will, he quotes the famous line spoken by Ovid's Medea: "*video meliora proboque, deteriora sequor*" ("I see and approve of the better, but I follow the worse").[11]

But what about when the intellect can find good only in one option? In such a case, Bramhall insists, the will retains its liberty of exercise: the agent can refrain from eliciting any choice at all. Therefore, the will is not strictly determined by the intellect. But even if the will were determined in such a case, this would not remove the will's power of (indirect) self-determination (*HBLN* 12–13, 47). For the will freely determines what comes up for deliberation in the intellect by controlling how attention is directed. Therefore, "whatsoever obligation the understanding does put on the will, is by the consent of the will, and derived from the power of the will, which was not necessitated to move the understanding to consult" (*HBLN* 46).[12]

Bramhall believes that God (and God alone) has the power to determine the human will to a specific act, and does so on rare occasions to control particular human decisions (*HBLN* 48, 62). But it cannot be true, according to Bramhall, that God *always* determines humans to choose as they do. For humans do many things contrary to God's command. If God were determining them to these sins, then God would be simultaneously *making* them sin and commanding them not to, which would be for God to engage in "plain mockery and derision" of human beings (*HBLN* 3). Thus in Bramhall's view, the doctrines that God loves humans and that humans have sinned together prove that theological determinism is false. Bramhall derives further proof for his position from the doctrine that some will be punished for their sins in hell. Anticipating Kant's famous "ought implies can" principle,[13] Bramhall says, "No man can be justly punished for doing that which was not in his power to shun" (*HBLN* 4, see also 51). Therefore, if humans were necessitated to sin, it would be unfair for God to damn them. Because (Bramhall believes) some people are damned, they must not have been determined to sin.

Bramhall's denial of theological determinism allows him to construct a free-will theodicy against the problem of evil. As a perfectly good being, God cannot be the active causal source of evil. Evil and sin arise from human misuse of free will: "The general power to act is from God, but the specification of the general and good power to . . . any particular evil, is not from God but from the free-will of man" (*HBLN* 50). Bramhall maintains, "God *causes* all good" but "*permits* all evil" (*HBLN* 50, my emphasis). The permitted evils are not necessary, because humans could have made better choices.

In their published controversy, Hobbes criticizes Bramhall's idea that the will is a self-mover. Hobbes invokes a long-cherished causal axiom: "nothing takes beginning from itself" (*HBLN* 38). Whatever begins to exist must have an external cause for its existence. Hobbes seems to take this axiom to imply that an agent's volitions must be predetermined by something outside the agent. Bramhall responds by agreeing that nothing can begin to *be* without a cause but insisting that a thing "may begin to *act* of itself without any other cause." Free agents, in Bramhall's view, can elicit volitions without being caused to do so. Hobbes responds that if the agent can begin to act without being caused to do so, then "the action . . . begins to be without any cause" (*HBLN* 87). If we assume that only events can cause events, then Hobbes's point seems correct, for in Bramhall's picture, the coming-into-existence of a volition is not determined by any prior event. However, Bramhall thinks that the volition does have a cause for its existence: it takes its beginning "from the power of willing, which is in the soul" (*HBLN* 61). The soul itself causes the volition. Not only events, but also substances, can be causes. Bramhall thus seems to implicitly endorse the 'agent-causation' account of libertarian freedom later made famous by Thomas Reid and Roderick Chisholm.[14]

An agent is a 'free cause' of her volition, because though she is causally necessary for the occurrence the volition, her mere existence is not sufficient for it (she might have refrained from causing it). Bramhall thus believes in nondeterministic or nonnecessitating causation, a possibility that (as we shall see) Hobbes rejects out of hand.

Hobbes offers another objection that reveals a fundamental difference between his modern approach to explanation and Bramhall's Aristotelian approach. As we have seen, Bramhall is comfortable with explaining events (in this case, the occurrence of volitions) in terms of the preexisting powers of substances (in this case, the wills of agents). Hobbes appears to reject this whole explanatory model. He says, "But as it is absurdly said, that to dance is an act allured or drawn . . . out of the ability to dance; so it is also to say, that the will is an act allured and drawn out of the power to will" (*HBLN* 33). Hobbes's statement reflects a common modern dissatisfaction with Scholastic explanations of natural events. The moderns complained that if we explain someone's dancing by appeal to her power to dance, we reason in a circle and have no real explanation at all. Instead, we should seek to uncover the underlying mechanisms (events and laws) that produced the dancing. For Hobbes, an object's present "power" to cause something is nothing "but those motions and present acts from which" a certain specific future act "necessarily proceeds" (*HBLN* 75). Hobbes has no room in his metaphysics for metaphysically basic powers – that is, powers that cannot be analyzed as necessary causal relations among specific events – and so will not countenance the existence of a two-way power called "the will."

2. Hobbes (1588–1679)

Hobbes is both a determinist and a compatibilist. He is a determinist because he thinks that every event has a cause (*Treatise* sect. 30, *HBLN* 38)[15] and that causes always necessitate their effects – the causally necessary conditions for an event are always logically sufficient for its occurrence.[16] There can be no nondeterministic causation, or "free causes" in Bramhall's sense (*Treatise* sect. 32, *HBLN* 38–39). Hobbes spells out his determinism as follows:

> That which I say necessitates and determines every action . . . is the sum of all those things which, being now existent, conduce and concur to the production of that action hereafter. . . . This concourse of causes, whereof every one is determined to be such as it is by a like concourse of former causes, may well be called (in respect they were all set and ordered by the eternal cause of all things, God Almighty) the decree of God.
>
> (*Treatise* sect. 11, *HBLN* 20)

Hobbes's determinism is at the same time both natural and theological. Every event is determined by the prior history of nature, which was in turn determined by God. Because the causal relation is transitive, God, as well as the past, is the cause of every event. Voluntary human actions are no exception: God "works in us, both to will and do, by the mediation of second causes" (*Questions* sect. 38, *HBLN* 89; see also *L* 21.4, *HBLN* 95).

Hobbes says that the will is "the necessary cause" of voluntary actions, which means that the will, in turn, "is also caused by other things whereof it disposes not" (*Treatise* sect. 30, *HBLN* 38). By the will, Hobbes does *not* mean a power, but rather an event of decision or choice, the same sort of event that Bramhall called a "volition" (*Questions* sect. 27, *HBLN* 82). But whereas for Bramhall an agent elicits a volition *in response* to her desires, for Hobbes the will *just is* a desire or appetite (*Questions* sect. 8, *HBLN* 75). The will is the inclination "which is immediately followed by the voluntary action" (*Questions* sect. 27, *HBLN* 82; see also *L* 6, *HBLN* 93–94). Hobbes thus seems to understand 'will' most fundamentally as "effective desire."[17]

Hobbes also describes volition as the last appetite in a process of deliberation. "When a man deliberates" concerning an action, Hobbes says, "he does nothing else but consider whether it be better for himself to do it or not to do it." So deliberation is "the alternate imagination of the good and evil [consequences] of an action," or the experience of alternating hope and fear concerning the action (*Treatise* sect. 26, *HBLN* 37). In this alternation of opposing appetites, "the last is that which we call the will" (*Treatise* sect. 27, *HBLN* 37). Hobbes sometimes speaks as if it is essential to volition that it be preceded by deliberation (*Treatise* sect. 8, *HBLN* 18), but he also says that actions not preceded by deliberation are still voluntary (*Treatise* sect. 25, *HBLN* 36–37). So, his considered view is probably that volition *often* terminates a process of deliberation but need not always do so.

According to Hobbes, the will always "follows the last opinion or judgment immediately preceding the action, concerning whether it be good to do it or not" (*Treatise* sect. 32, *HBLN* 34). Hobbes denies Medea's claim to see the better but follow the worse: "though Medea saw many reasons to forbear killing her children, yet the last dictate of her judgment was that the present revenge on her husband outweighed them all, and thereupon the wicked action necessarily followed" (*Treatise* sect. 23, *HBLN* 34–35; see also sect. 6, *HBLN* 17).

Hobbes's view is therefore similar to the intellectual determinism Bramhall opposed. However, for Hobbes, the will is determined not by a distinctively human rational faculty (the intellect), but by the imagination (*Questions* sect. 26, *HBLN* 81), or what Scholastics called the "sensitive appetite," a faculty we share with other animals (*Questions* sect. 28, *HBLN* 83). Hobbes's action theory is naturalistic, in the sense that it treats the human mind as just another part of nature, rather than something that functions in a fundamentally different way from other species.[18] For Hobbes, "appetite and will in man or beast" are "the same thing" (*Questions* sect. 29, *HBLN* 83). This naturalism derives from Hobbes's metaphysical materialism – his belief that all things, including the mind, are ultimately reducible to matter in motion, and therefore are caused in the same way.[19]

To sum up, then, on Hobbes's deterministic picture of human action, God determines the history of nature, which in turn determines certain objects to be present to an agent at a certain time. "External objects," Hobbes says, "cause conceptions, and conceptions appetite and fear, which are the first . . . beginnings of our actions" (*EL* 12.1, *HBLN* 91). One of these emotions terminates deliberation and becomes the will, which our actions always then follow (*EL* 12.6, *HBLN* 92). Human actions are thus determined by desire (the will), by opinion, by present external objects, by past history, and ultimately by God.

Hobbes says that liberty (i.e. freedom) is "the absence of external impediments" to action (*L* 14.2, *HBLN* 94).[20] Though inanimate creatures can enjoy liberty in this sense, in creatures with appetite, freedom consists in absence of impediment to *willed* action. So "a *free man* is he, that . . . is not hindered to do what he has a will to do" (*L* 21.2, *HBLN* 95). In this definition of freedom, any action that an agent both *wills* to do and *succeeds* in doing is a free action. Hence, all voluntary actions are free (*Questions* sect. 28, *HBLN* 82).[21]

Therefore, to determine whether an agent is responsible for a certain action, we need only determine whether she *willed* to perform it. The causal history leading up to her will is *irrelevant* to the question of moral responsibility. As Hobbes says, "he that does evil willingly, whether he be necessarily willing or not necessarily, may be justly punished" (*Questions* sect. 14.d, *HBLN* 76). With this remark, Hobbes flatly rejects Bramhall's "ought implies can" reasoning. He also articulates what is sometimes called a "supercompatibilist" understanding of freedom: a view according to which freedom is compatible with both the truth and the falsehood of determinism, so that we can be sure that we are free even if we cannot be sure whether determinism is true.[22] So though Hobbes believes in determinism, and thinks it compatible with freedom, he does not think it is *required* for freedom.

Hobbes thinks that the freedom to act as one wills is the only conceivable freedom (*Leviathan* ch. 5, *HBLN* 93). *Willing itself* cannot be free: "When desiring, one can, in truth, be free to *act*; one cannot, however, be free to *desire*" (*De homine* ch. 11.2, *HBLN* 97; see also *Elements of Law* ch. 12.5, *HBLN* 92). Hobbes seems to reach this conclusion through the following reasoning: "Whenever we say that someone has free-will to do this or that, or not to do it," Hobbes insists, "it must always be understood with this necessary condition: *if he wills*" (*De homine* ch. 11.2, *HBLN* 97). Actions are free only insofar as they accord with a prior volition. Therefore, a "free volition" would require a further volition to make it free. But this is impossible, in Hobbes's opinion. As we shall see, Locke further developed this line of reasoning against the possibility of free volitions.

Based on the texts considered so far, it may seem that for Hobbes, freedom requires only the absence of impediments to the will and does not require a two-way power to do otherwise than we do. This "one-way compatibilism"[23] is sometimes attributed to Hobbes,[24] and indeed it may be the position that he *ought* to have held. But his actual view is somewhat more complicated. Hobbes says that "a free agent is he that can do if he will and forbear if he will; and . . . liberty is the absence of external impediments" (*Treatise* sect. 33, *HBLN* 39; see also *Questions* preface, *HBLN* 69). Here Hobbes suggests that freedom does after all require some kind of ability to do otherwise. He seems to have thought that this requirement is consistent with his official "no impediments" account. However, it is not entirely clear that this two-way power requirement can be interpreted so as to truly cohere with the rest of what Hobbes says about freedom.

Perhaps Hobbes invokes the two-way power language to require not only that the agent be unimpeded in doing what she actually willed but also that she *would have been* unimpeded *if* she had willed otherwise. If so, then Hobbes anticipates one of the more famous parts of Locke's view of freedom. However, as Locke himself clearly showed, this kind of two-way power requirement rules out Hobbes's claim that all voluntary actions are free. So, on this reading, the two-way power requirement introduces incoherence into Hobbes's account of freedom.

A more plausible interpretation focuses on the fact that Hobbes usually associates two-way power with ongoing deliberation. Hobbes says that we retain "the liberty of doing or omitting, according to our own appetite or aversion" until deliberation ends (*L* 6.49, *HBLN* 93; see also *EL* 12.1, *HBLN* 91), and that "of a voluntary agent, it is all one to say he is free, and to say he has not made an end of deliberating" (*Treatise* sect. 28, *HBLN* 38). As Bramhall pointed out, this "deliberation account" of freedom seems to conflict in two ways with Hobbes's official absence-of-impediments account. First, Bramhall says, "there may be outward impediments even whilst [a person] is deliberating," so that the person is unfree on the official account and free on the deliberation account. Second, "after a man has ceased to deliberate, there may be no outward impediments," so that the person is unfree on the deliberation account and free on the official account (*HBLN* 59). Hobbes responds to the first problem by denying that there can be impediments to action until after the person has finished deliberating and willed to act in a certain way. But he says nothing to address the second problem, and so the difficulty remains. Perhaps Hobbes considers freedom before volition to be fundamentally different from freedom after volition. Distinguishing two different kinds of freedom for two different times would render his overall account consistent with itself,[25] but it is far from clear that Hobbes himself would be willing to draw such a distinction.[26]

Bramhall raises many interesting objections to Hobbes's compatibilist position, most of which beg the question against Hobbes in some way or other. One particular objection, however, is worthy of note. Bramhall imagines a manipulation counterexample to Hobbes's sort of compatibilism: "Whether one ravish Lucretia by force . . . or by amatory potions and magical incantations . . . necessitate her to satisfy his lust and . . . draw her inevitably and irresistibly to follow him spontaneously, Lucretia in both these conditions is to be pitied" (*HBLN* 10). When given a potion, Lucretia is the victim of what some contemporary philosophers call *covert nonconstraining control*.[27] She acts without constraint according to her will, and so would be free in Hobbes's view. However, intuitively she does not seem responsible for her actions, because her will does not seem to be truly her own. Hobbes does not respond to this objection.

3. Descartes (1595–1650)

Descartes once wrote that "[f]ree will is in itself the noblest thing we can have, since it makes us in a way equal to God . . . and so its correct use is the greatest of all the goods we possess" (AT V 85; CSMK 326). In addition to considering freedom of the utmost practical importance, Descartes also gave it an important theoretical role in his *Meditations*. Descartes agrees with Bramhall that we are free and that determinism is false, but it is far from clear that he is a libertarian—one who considers freedom to *require* indeterminism. Indeed, how Descartes understood the nature of freedom is a vexed question among scholars: there are several plausible, but incompatible, interpretations of his view.

Like Bramhall, Descartes rejects theological, physical, and intellectual determinism. He says that "everything that happens comes *entirely* from [God]" (AT IV 314; CSMK 272, my emphasis) and that "all the reasons that prove that God exists and is the first and immutable cause of all effects that do not depend on human free will prove similarly . . . that he is also the cause of all the effects that do so depend" (AT IV 314; CSMK 272). But though caused by God, our choices are not necessitated or determined. All events are necessitated "*except* for those things that [providence] has willed to depend on our free will" (AT XI 439; CSM I 380, my emphasis), and that God's power "*leaves the free actions of men undetermined*" (AT VIII 20; CSM I 206, my emphasis). For Descartes, humans are what Bramhall would call 'free causes' of their choices, and their freedom is not undermined by the fact that God via his ordinary concurrence (AT VII 60; CSM II 42) also causes their choices.

Descartes believes that deterministic laws of nature govern the motions of bodies (AT VIIIA 61–66; CSM I 240–243), including the human body (AT XI 341–242; CSM I 335). However, these laws govern only "purely corporeal causes, *i.e. those devoid of thought and mind*" (AT VIIIA 315; CSM I 279, my emphasis). Because the will is part of the incorporeal mind, its choices (and their immediate physical effects)[28] are not determined by the laws of nature.

Like Bramhall and the Scholastics, Descartes took human action to arise from the interaction of intellect and will.[29] And like Bramhall, he seems to reject intellectual determinism. Descartes may think that the contents of the intellect *sometimes* determine the will (more on this later), but he does not think they *always* do so: when intellectual perception is less than fully clear and distinct, the will has "the freedom to direct itself, without the determination of the intellect, towards one side or the other" (AT VII 378; CSM II 260).[30]

So, Descartes believes both that we are free (AT VIIIA 19–20; CSM I 205–206) and that determinism is false. But what if determinism *were* true? Would that necessarily destroy our freedom? Does Descartes take the incompatibilist position that we can be free *only if* determinism is false? To this question, Descartes's writings seem to give different answers in different places.

Descartes's remarks about divine providence seem to point toward incompatibilism. According to Descartes, God has a providential plan that "extends to all the most particular actions of men" (AT IV 315; CSMK 273) so that "the least thought cannot enter the mind of man if God has not wished and willed from all eternity that it enter therein" (AT IV 313–314; CSMK 272). "Nothing can possibly happen other than as it has been determined from all eternity by this Providence," Descartes says, "so that providence is like a fate or immutable necessity" (AT XI 438; CSM I 380). Now if Descartes were a compatibilist like Hobbes, he would see no difficulty in reconciling this doctrine of providence with human freedom: if freedom is compatible with determinism in general, then it must also be compatible with this specific sort of theological determinism. But instead Descartes declares, "We can easily get ourselves into great difficulties if we attempt to reconcile . . . divine preordination with the freedom of our will, or attempt to grasp both these things at once" (AT VIII 20; CSM I 206). Descartes considers divine providence a *problem* for human freedom, and this strongly suggests that he is an incompatibilist. Furthermore, in some of his correspondence he seems to attempt to resolve this problem in roughly the same way as did Jesuit incompatibilists like Molina and Suárez.[31]

A second factor pointing toward incompatibilism is Descartes's apparent use of free will theodicy. In the Third Meditation, Descartes offers a proof that God exists and is not a deceiver. Because he was made by a veracious creator, Descartes reasons, he can trust that whatever he clearly and distinctly perceives is true, thereby escaping his most radical skeptical doubts. However, at the opening of the Fourth Meditation, Descartes worries that if he were really created by an all-perfect God, he would be immune not just to error about what is clear and distinct but to *all* error: "Certainly, so long as I think only of God . . . I can find no cause of error or falsity. But when I turn back to myself, I know by experience that I am prone to countless errors" (AT VII 54; CSM II 38). If God causes everything in us, then how can there be error in us?

Descartes resolves this worry by appealing to human freedom. In a significant break from his Scholastic predecessors, Descartes claims that judgment is an act not of the intellect alone, but of the will and intellect together: the intellect proposes propositions for affirmation or denial, and the will passes judgment on them (AT VII 56; CSM II 39).[32] Our freedom enables us to affirm, deny, or suspend judgment concerning propositions that the intellect does not yet perceive clearly and distinctly. From an epistemic point of view, we ought to suspend judgment about such obscure propositions, but we often choose to go ahead and either affirm or deny them, and that is why we often err (AT VII 58–61; CSM II 40–41). Error is caused by misuse of human freedom, and therefore, Descartes concludes, God is not "in the strict and positive sense the cause of the errors to which . . . we are prone" (AT VIIIA 16; CSM I 203; see also AT VII 60; CSM II 42). In reasoning that if our errors are caused by bad free choices, then they are *not* caused by God, Descartes seems to assume that it is impossible for God to cause or determine our bad choices. And this may well be because he thought, as incompatibilists normally do, that "free" just *means* "undetermined."[33]

Although many of his texts smack of incompatibilism, Descartes also made two important claims concerning freedom that together seem to entail compatibilism. First, he affirmed a thesis of "clear and distinct determination" (CDD): clear and distinct perceptions in the intellect always determine the will's assent. He says that "[m]y nature is such that so long as I perceive something very clearly and distinctly I cannot but believe it to be true" (AT VII 69; CSM II 48) and that "[t]he will of a thinking thing is drawn voluntarily and freely (for that is the essence of will), but nevertheless infallibly, towards a clearly known good" (AT VII 166; CSM II 117, my translation).[34]

Second, unlike most advocates of free-will theodicy, who teach that evil or error are an inevitable risk for God in creating free creatures, Descartes believed that God could have given us freedom without such risk. He says,

> God could easily have brought it about that without losing my freedom, and despite the limitations in my knowledge, I should nonetheless never make a mistake. He could, for example, have endowed my intellect with a clear and distinct perception of everything about which I was ever likely to deliberate.
> (AT VII 61; CSM II 42)

If the intellect were always clear and distinct, then the will would never go wrong but would still be free.

Given CDD, if human intellectual states were always clear and distinct, then the intellect would always determine the will. So, the previous passage seems to imply that God could have made intellectual determinism true without undermining freedom of the will. In the actual world, where we often perceive things obscurely, our freedom requires intellectual indeterminism, but there are possible worlds in which freedom coexists with intellectual determinism. If Descartes held this view, then he is not a standard incompatibilist, for he does not think that the nature of freedom itself requires indeterminism.

But neither is he a standard compatibilist like Hobbes, for he clearly thinks that we would not be free if we were determined to bad behavior. Instead, Descartes probably thought of freedom as most fundamentally the ability to make the right choice. In the actual world, where obscure perceptions enable us to use the will badly, we count as free only if we are also able make the right choice (so in our circumstances, freedom requires two-way power of choice). But if we were to enjoy constant, clear perceptions, we would still be able to – and indeed, *would* – freely make the right choice even if we had no alternatives. Understood in this way, freedom is "asymmetrical": it is compatible with our being determined to do right, but incompatible with our being determined to do wrong.[35]

The passages considered previously are not the only ones to suggest that Descartes holds the asymmetrical view. Descartes's official definition of freedom may do so as well:

> [I] the will, or freedom of choice . . . simply consists in this: that we are able to do or not do (that is, to affirm or deny, to pursue or avoid); [II] or rather [*vel potius*], simply in this: that we are carried in such a way toward what the intellect proposes for affirmation or denial or for pursuit or avoidance, that we do not feel ourselves determined to it by any external force.
> (AT VII 57; CSM II 40)

The "or rather" here may signal that Descartes intends to retract the first part of the definition, to indicate, in effect, that two-way power is not truly essential to freedom. The essence of freedom consists rather in not being determined by external forces. Freedom is self-determination, which need not (though it may) involve choice amongst alternatives.[36] Descartes may think that clear and distinct perceptions in the intellect are not "external forces" (AT VII 58–59; CSM II 41). Therefore, they cannot threaten freedom even though they remove the will's two-way power of choice.

On the other hand, Descartes may have intended the "or rather" in his definition to mean something like "or in other words," so that the definition equates two-way power with self-determination (or absence of external determination).[37] Descartes sometimes says that the will *always* enjoys two-way power of choice, even in the face of clear and distinct perceptions (see AT VIIIA 19; CSM I 205 and AT IV 173; CSMK 245); and in one passage, he suggests that our praiseworthiness for good action depends on our being able to go wrong: "when we embrace the truth, our doing so voluntarily is much more to our credit than would be the case if we could not do otherwise" (AT VIIIA 19; CSM I 205). This claim does not fit with the asymmetrical view, according to which we can deserve praise for good actions even if we could not have done otherwise. So, Descartes's definition of freedom is also amenable to a more standard incompatibilist interpretation.

If Descartes is an incompatibilist after all, he must have a more nuanced understanding of CDD than is at first apparent. This may be the case, for in one place, he says,

> when a very evident reason moves us in one direction, although *morally speaking* we can hardly move in the contrary direction, *absolutely speaking* we can. For it is always open to us to hold back from pursuing a clearly known good, or from admitting a clearly perceived truth, provided we consider it a good thing to demonstrate the freedom of our will by so doing.
>
> (AT IV 173; CSMK 245, my emphasis)

Invoking a distinction from Bramhall and the Scholastics, we might take this to mean that in the face of a clear and distinct perception, the will is always determined with regard to its specification, but not with regard to its exercise: if it acts, it must assent to the perception, but it retains the power to do nothing at all. In this way, agents enjoying a constant stream of clear perceptions could never go wrong, but would retain libertarian two-way power.[38]

Alternatively, this passage may mean simply that in some circumstances (such as when we wish to demonstrate our freedom), clear perceptions do not determine the will, whereas in other circumstances it does. Again, like Bramhall, Descartes may have held that our freedom in the latter circumstances derives from our freedom in the former: when the will is determined by clear perceptions, it remains indirectly self-determining because it somehow brought about those clear perceptions through prior free decisions concerning how to direct or focus attention (see AT IV 117; CSMK 234).

We have considered several different possible interpretations of Descartes's views on freedom. None of these interpretations are without difficulty. This may be because Descartes's scattered remarks about freedom are not entirely consistent with one another. Texts dated up through 1641 lend themselves much more easily to a compatibilist interpretation, whereas texts from 1644 on tend to take a much more incompatibilist line. So, it may be that that Descartes simply changed his mind about freedom sometime in the early 1640s.[39]

4. Spinoza (1632–1677)

In part I of his *Ethics*, Spinoza argues for hard determinism: he thinks that all human actions are externally determined and so cannot be free. However, later in the *Ethics*, Spinoza describes an ideal "free man" (*E* 4p66–73, C 583–588)[40] and explains "the method or way leading to freedom" (preface to *E* 5 opening, C 594–597). Thus Spinoza uses the word "free" in two different (though, as we shall see, intimately related) senses.

According to Spinoza, there is only one substance: God. What a more traditional thinker like Descartes would call "created substances"[41] – rocks, trees, humans – Spinoza calls "modes" (i.e. features) of God. Spinoza believes further that there is a cause or reason for every truth, whether about God or the modes of God (*E* 1p11dem2, C 417; *E* 1a3, C 410). From this it follows that every individual thing or "finite mode" is determined to exist and to act in a definite way by a prior finite mode (*E* 1p28, C 432–433), so that for any finite mode there is an infinite series of prior modes that determine its existence and action. This whole infinite series of modes follows necessarily from God's own necessarily existing nature (*E* 1p16, C 424–425), so that "[t]hings could not have been produced by God in any other way or in any other order than is the case" (*E* 1p33, C 436–439). So, it seems that Spinoza is a "necessitarian," one who holds that our world exists necessarily, or, in other words, one who believes that the actual world is the only possible world.

There is some scholarly controversy about whether Spinoza is truly a necessitarian,[42] but he is clearly a determinist, and his determinism extends to his understanding of human action. Like Hobbes, Spinoza takes human action at a time to be caused by the mind's strongest desire at that time. He says, "mental decisions are nothing more than the appetites themselves" (*E* 3p2s; C 497), so that "every man necessarily seeks what he judges to be good and avoids what he judges to be evil" (*E* 4p19, C 556–557; *E* 2p28, C 470; see also *E* 4p7, 4p15, and *Short Treatise* II.17.4). For Spinoza, each of our beliefs, desires, and actions is determined by past history and by God's nature.

According to Spinoza, a free thing "exists solely from the necessity of its own nature, and is determined to action by itself alone" (*E* 1d7, C 409). God exists necessarily, and there is no other substance outside God to determine God's action. God's actions are determined solely by the divine nature. Therefore, God is free. This does not mean, however, that God could have done otherwise than God has in fact done. God's actions are not chosen by an indifferent divine will (*E* 1p33s2, C 436–439) but rather follow necessarily from God's nature. For example, "God freely understands himself and all things . . . because it follows solely from the necessity of his own nature that he should understand all things"; this example shows that Spinoza places freedom "not in free decision, but in free necessity" (Ep.58, M&S 290).[43] It appears, then, that Spinoza's concept of free action is very similar to one of the views that Descartes may have held: free actions must not be determined from outside the agent, but those that originate from within the agent may do so necessarily (two-way power is not required).

Finite modes are determined both to exist and to act by prior finite modes (*E* 1p28, C 432–433). Finite things, including human beings, are thus determined by things outside themselves, and so neither exist nor act freely. "Men are deceived," Spinoza says, "in thinking themselves free" (*E* 2p35s, C 473). We often do what we desire to do (Ep. 58, M&S 289–292), but this does not render us free, for our desires are determined by prior external causes. However, because we are often unaware of these prior causes, we succumb to the illusion that we act as we do "for no other reason" than that we so wish (Ep. 58, M&S 290).

In the twentieth century, Peter Strawson noted that we adopt "reactive attitudes" such as resentment and anger only toward those whom we regard as free and responsible agents.[44] Spinoza seems to have grasped this point quite clearly. He notes that we feel love toward things that cause us pleasure and hatred toward things that cause us pain. These feelings of love or hatred are amplified insofar as we believe that the things affecting us are produced freely (*E* 3p49, C 521); therefore, "deeming themselves to be free, men feel more love and hatred toward one another than toward other things" (*E* 3p49s, C 521).

Once we realize that all human actions are determined, this amplification effect is canceled, and we are freed from reactive attitudes: "He who rightly knows that all things follow from the necessity of the divine nature and happen in accordance with the eternal laws and rules of Nature will surely find nothing deserving of hatred, derision, or contempt nor will he pity anyone" (*E* 4p50s, C 574). Other emotions from which we can be freed include praise, blame (see *E* 1, appendix, C444; *Short Treatise* II.12.2, C117), repentance, and self-esteem (*E* 3d3, C 536–537). Spinoza views the loss of such emotions as a wholly salutary result of belief in determinism, for emotions like hatred and pity are bad for us (*E* 4p45, C 571–572; *E* 4p50, C 574). More generally, he believes that an appreciation of determinism gives the mind greater power over the emotions (*E* 5p5–6, C 599–600).

Though Spinoza does not think that humans are morally responsible in the ordinary sense, he still thinks that it is legitimate for society, and its agents such as judges, to reward or punish good or bad behavior. Punishment of a criminal is justified not so much by the backward-looking consideration that the criminal has done something to deserve such punishment as by the forward-looking considerations that he or she will be helped or improved by the process (*Short Treatise* 18.5, Curley 128), and that the general welfare depends on having a uniform system of rewards and punishments to encourage good behavior (*E* 4p63c and 4p63s, C 582–583).[45]

In part IV of the *Ethics*, Spinoza says that a slave is "guided only by emotion or belief" (*E* 4p66s, C 584). He cannot "control and check the emotions," so that "he is often compelled, although he sees the better course, to pursue the worse" (*E* 4, preface, C 543). In contrast to such an internally divided person, a "free man" who is "guided by reason . . . does only what he knows to be of greatest importance in life, which he therefore desires above all" (*E* 4p66s, C 584). Spinoza here seems to anticipate the views of Locke and Leibniz, as well as of some contemporary authors who view freedom as the ability to act in accord with one's deepest desires or with one's values.[46] This primarily normative notion of freedom seems entirely distinct from the descriptive notion (absence of external determination) that Spinoza discusses in part I of the *Ethics*. However, though the meaning of "free" changes from the earlier to the later parts of the *Ethics*, the two different meanings are connected by Spinoza's account of activity and passivity.

According to Spinoza, we act when we are the adequate (complete or total; *E* 3d1, C 492) cause of some event, that is when the event "can be clearly and distinctly understood through [our nature] alone" (*E* 3d2, C 493). We are passive "when something takes place in us, or follows from our nature, of which we are only the partial cause" (*E* 3d2, C 493). Activity and passivity thus defined appear to be a matter of degree: a horse from a team of four seems to be less active with respect to pulling a wagon than it would be if it had the help of only one other horse. In general, a thing would seem to be more active insofar as its causal contribution explains a greater proportion of the given effect. Spinoza seems to acknowledge that activity comes in degrees, for he says that the human body and mind's "power of activity" are capable of being increased or diminished (*E* 3d3, C 493; *E* 3p12, C 502; *E* 3p49, C 521). When he says that a thing can increase its power of activity, Spinoza seems to mean that it can increase its ability to be active with respect to the production of some effect (e.g. as one can sometimes through training develop the ability to lift a weight alone which one could previously only lift with help).[47]

Notice that a perfectly active being, as Spinoza defines it, would be one whose action followed from its own nature alone, without the influence of external causes. Such a being would be free or self-determining. Spinoza's notion of activity and his notion of freedom are both defined in terms of independence from external causes. Because such independence comes in degrees, freedom also can come in degrees, a fact which Spinoza explicitly acknowledges (see *E* 4p73pr, C 587; see also *Tractatus politicus* 2.7–11). Insofar as a person increases her power of acting, she increases her freedom.

We can now see how the "normative" notion of freedom in the latter part of the *Ethics* is connected to Spinoza's original definition of freedom. Reason demands that we act so as to benefit ourselves (*E* 4p24dem, C 558; *E* 4p63c, C 582; *E* 4p66s, C 584), and whatever benefits us increases our power of acting (see *E* 3p39s and 3p11s). Those who follow reason thus increase their power of acting, and hence increase their degree of freedom. This is why Spinoza's says that the "free man . . . lives solely according to the dictates of reason" (*E* 4p67pr, C 584).

Spinoza is not saying that a rational person is completely self-determining, as God is. Rather, he is saying that the rational person *more closely approximates* divine self-determination, or enjoys a greater *degree* of freedom and activity, than does the person driven by passions. "Free" in part I of the *Ethics* means completely free, whereas "free" in the later parts of the *Ethics* means relatively free, or better, more nearly completely free. In both parts, however, the central notion of freedom as self-determination or independence from external causes remains the same.

For Spinoza, ironically, we can maximize our *degree* of freedom only by acknowledging that we cannot be *perfectly* free. We must admit that the "free man" or perfectly rational agent is merely an ideal that we should try to approximate, for humans are inevitably determined by passions to some extent (*E* 4p4 and 4p4c, C 548–549). Indeed, Spinoza sometimes speaks of the free man as one who "strives *as far as he can*, to act well and rejoice" (*E* 4p73s, C 587; see also *E* 4p50s, C 574). It is only by accepting the truth of determinism – and hence our own moral limitations – that we can eradicate our harmful reactive attitudes toward ourselves and others, thereby achieving the greatest degree of freedom of which we are capable.

5. Locke (1632–1704)

John Locke sets out his understanding of human freedom in a chapter called "Of Power" in his *Essay Concerning Human Understanding*. Interpreting "Of Power" is difficult because Locke revised the chapter substantially as it moved from its first edition (1689/1690) to its fifth (published 1706). It is clear that Locke believed in human freedom throughout this period, but his position on determinism is less clear. Unlike Hobbes, he does not explicitly argue for a thesis of universal causal determinism.[48] However, in the first edition of the *Essay*, he seems to teach that *human choices* are all predetermined (so that he must be a compatibilist). In later editions, Locke may have given up determinism in an effort to preserve free will (thus endorsing libertarianism), but this is far from clear.

According to Locke, the will is the mind's "power to begin or forbear, continue or end" a mental or bodily action "barely by a thought or preference of the mind ordering, or . . . commanding the doing or not doing" of the action (*Essay* 2.21.5). The command is a volition and is the actual exercise of the power of willing. So, Locke seems implicitly to grant the Scholastic distinction between elicited acts of will (volitions) and commanded acts of will. Commanded acts, that is those caused by volitions, are *voluntary*; any other bodily or mental activity is involuntary (or *non*voluntary).

For Locke, we are free with respect to an action just in case we are able to (1) do the action if we will to do it and (2) refrain from doing the action if we will to refrain (*Essay* 2.21.8). Condition (1) entails that free actions must be voluntary and (2) requires that free agents possess "indifferency of ability" (*Essay* 2.21.10) or a kind of two-way power: as Locke says, "where-ever doing or not doing, will not equally follow upon" an agent's volition, "there he is not free" (*Essay* 2.21.8). So (2) entails that – contrary to Hobbes's view – not all voluntary actions are free. Locke illustrates this with a famous example. Imagine a man sitting in a room with his friend. Unbeknownst to him, he has been locked into the room. Wishing to visit his friend, he stays in the room and does not try the door. According to Locke, the man stays in the room voluntarily, but not freely. For if he were to wish to leave (i.e. *not* to stay), he would be unable to do so (*Essay* 2.21.10). He satisfies condition (1) but not condition (2).

Whatever his position on freedom ultimately turns out to be, Locke does not understand this two-way power requirement in a typical libertarian fashion. The two-way power he requires for freedom is "an indifferency of the operative powers of the man," which remains even when the will has determined those powers to act (*Essay* 2.21.71). For example, suppose that I choose to write something down, and so begin to write. I write freely because even as I write, I am able to refrain from writing, and because I could have refrained from writing to begin with. But as Locke understands it, to say that I could have refrained means *only* that *if* I had willed to refrain, I would have done so: it does *not* entail that I might have willed to refrain. Therefore, I can be able to write or not write, in the sense necessary for freedom, even if I have been causally determined to choose to write (see Letter 2979, VII: 409).[49] What threatens freedom is not causal determinism as such but rather forms of causal determinism that break the counterfactual dependence of our actions on our volitions – for example a convulsion (*Essay* 2.21.71) that would cause one's hand to move even if one chose for it to be still. Locke thus appears to adopt two-way compatibilism: freedom requires alternative possibilities, but such possibilities are compatible with determinism.

A libertarian like Bramhall would insist that we are able to *do* otherwise only if we are also able to *will* otherwise: "If the will be determined, the writing or not writing is likewise determined; and then he should not say, 'He may write or he may forbear' " (*HBLN* 45). Bramhall would doubtless complain that Locke, with his compatibilist interpretation of the two-way power requirement, is suggesting that we can have freedom of action without freedom of will (i.e. freedom of choice). But to talk of free action without free will is in Bramhall's view to engage in a "miserable subterfuge" (*HBLN* 8).

Locke is aware that in the minds of many, "a Man is not free at all, if he be not as free to will, as he is to act" (*Essay* 2.21.22). However, Locke, like Hobbes before him, believes this view is deeply confused, because willing or choice – unlike other kinds of action – cannot be free. Initially, Locke says that liberty is "as little applicable to the *Will*, as swiftness of Motion is to Sleep, or squareness to virtue," because "*Liberty*, which is but a power, belongs only to *Agents*, and cannot be an attribute or modification of the *Will*, which is also but a power" (*Essay* 2.21.14). The will is a *property* or *attribute* of a human being. Because it is not a substance, it cannot have properties of its own. Those who speak of free will mistakenly treat a property as if it were a substance (*Essay* 2.21.16).

Locke sees, however, that his argument does not really lay the central question to rest. For his opponents can turn the (nonsense) question "whether the will is free" into the (sensible) question *"Whether a Man be free to will"* (*Essay* 2.21.22) – that is whether agents are free in eliciting volitions. Locke responds to this reformulation of the question with a two-stage argument. First, he argues that agents cannot enjoy liberty of exercise with respect to volition. Then he argues that they cannot enjoy liberty of specification with respect to volition. Therefore, he concludes, agents are not free at all with respect to volition. It will be useful to consider the two stages of this argument separately.

First, Locke says that whenever an agent considers a possible action, "he cannot avoid willing the existence or not existence of that Action," because "one of them must necessarily follow; and that which does follow, follows . . . by his willing it" (*Essay* 2.21.23). Locke seems to be arguing as follows:

1. For any action that an agent considers performing, necessarily the agent must either perform it or fail to perform it.
2. For any action, the agent performs it (or fails to perform it) only if he first wills to perform it (or wills not to perform it).

Therefore,

3. For any action, it is necessary that the agent either will to perform it or will not to perform it.

This is not a sound argument. The second premise is false, for an agent could refrain from performing an action without first *choosing* to so refrain. For example, suppose I am trying to decide whether to order another drink, and pass out before reaching a decision. I would then fail to order another drink, but would not have *chosen* not to order another drink. Similarly, I might fail to perform certain actions simply by suspending judgment about whether I will perform them or not. It is especially surprising that Locke did not see this flaw in the argument, because in the later editions of the *Essay*, he places great importance on our ability to suspend judgment.

Locke's second-stage argument, however, looks much more promising. Locke says,

> To ask, whether a Man be at liberty to will either Motion, or Rest; Speaking or Silence; which he pleases, is to ask, whether a Man can *will*, what he *wills*; or be pleased with what he is pleased with. A Question, which, I think, needs no answer: and they, who can make a Question of it, must suppose one Will to determine the Acts of another, and another to determinate that; and so on *in infinitum*.
>
> (*Essay* 2.21.25)

Recall that for Locke,

1. Any free action A must be voluntary – that is, caused by a prior volition to perform A. Call this prior volition V.

Recall further that Locke is attempting to refute opponents who believe that

2. An action A is free only if the volition V that causes it is also free.

Locke supposes (2) is true in order to show that it leads to absurdity, as follows. Given (1), if A is a free action, then it must be caused by V, which we can illustrate as follows:

$A \leftarrow V$

Given (2), A is free only if V is also free. But notice that V itself is also an action, and so if it is free it must be, by (1), preceded by V2, a second-order volition – a choice to elicit choice V, like this:

$A \leftarrow V \leftarrow V2$

And by (2), V2 must also be free, which requires a volition V3, and so on. If (1) and (2) are both true, then to perform a single free action, an agent must first make infinitely many free choices. This, Locke believes, is absurd. Therefore, either (1) or (2) must be false. And (1) is true. So (2) is false: there *can* be free action without free volition.

Notice that though Locke offered this as an argument only against liberty of specification, its conclusion is actually more general than that. It would also work against liberty of exercise. So, this argument, if it works, is really all that Locke needs to show that free volitions are impossible (the failure of his earlier argument would not matter much). An argument of this sort was further refined by the American compatibilist Jonathan Edwards,[50] and is still regarded as a formidable criticism of the libertarian position on freedom.

If, as Locke argues, agents do not elicit volitions freely, then it is natural to conclude that they are determined to do so. And Locke goes on in the first edition to say explicitly that the will is determined (*Essay* 2.21.29, first edition). So, it seems that when he wrote the first edition of the *Essay*, Locke was, like Hobbes, a *soft determinist* – a compatibilist who believes that determinism is true. However, Locke may have backed away from this position in later editions.

In the first edition, Locke says that volition "*is* nothing but the *preferring* the doing of anything, to the not doing of it" (*Essay* 2.21.28, first edition). As in Hobbes, a choice is a kind of desire. It is determined by the greatest apparent good (*Essay* 2.21.29 and 2.21.38, first edition); that is, the agent is determined to choose the course of action that appears to be the best available option. But this determination of the will in no way impairs freedom:

> But though the preference of the Mind be always determined by the appearance of . . . greater Good; yet the Person who has the Power . . . to act, or not to act according to such preference, is nevertheless free, such determination abridges not that Power. He that has his Chains knocked off, and the Prison-doors set open to him, is perfectly at liberty, because he may either go or stay, as he best likes. . . . He ceases not to be free; though that which at that time appears to him the greater Good absolutely determines his preference, and makes him stay in his Prison.
>
> (*Essay* 2.21.33, first edition)

Locke's friend William Molyneux, a libertarian, grasped that Locke's view was a form of intellectual determinism and complained in a letter,

> you seem to make all Sins to proceed from our Understandings . . . and not at all from the Depravity of our Wills. Now it seems harsh to say, that a Man shall be Damn'd, because he understands no better than he does.
>
> (Letter 1579; IV, 601)

Apparently in response to this criticism, Locke substantially revised and expanded the chapter "Of Power" for the second edition of the *Essay* and says there that he has changed his opinion (though about what exactly, he does not indicate; *Essay* 2.21.72).[51]

In the new edition, Locke no longer identifies a volition with a desire, and indeed repudiates this earlier claim (*Essay* 2.21.30). He also redescribes the determination of the will as follows:

> To the Question, what is it that determines the Will? The true and proper Answer is, The mind. For that which determines the general power of directing, to this or that particular direction, is nothing but the Agent it self Exercising the power it has, that particular way.
>
> (*Essay* 2.21.29)

Locke seems to have moved from a Hobbesian event-causal picture, in which a certain kind of cognitive event (a grasping of such and such as the best available option) causes volition, to an agent-causal picture, in which volitions are produced directly by the substances whose acts they are. Locke is aware, however, that we can still ask, "What moves the mind, in every particular instance, to determine its general power of directing, to this or that particular Motion or Rest?" To which he answers, "The motive to change, is always some *uneasiness*. . . . This is the great motive that works on the Mind to put it upon Action, which for shortness sake we will call the *determining of the Will*" (*Essay* 2.21.29).

According to one form of intellectual determinism, we always choose the option that we judge to be best. Locke rejects this view in the new edition. For the uneasiness that determines the will is desire (*Essay* 2.21.31), and we desire only those objects that we judge necessary to our own happiness (*Essay* 2.21.41–43). We can see that a certain course of action is best without feeling that it would make us happy, and so we can fail to choose it (*Essay* 2.21.35). But though the will is not determined by disinterested judgments of goodness, it still seems (in Locke's new view) to be determined by intellectual judgments concerning what is necessary for happiness.

However, in section 47, Locke appears to repudiate intellectual determinism by introducing his "doctrine of suspension."[52] He says that the greatest or most pressing uneasiness determines the will "for the most part, but not always." He continues,

> For the mind having in most cases, as is evident in Experience, a power to *suspend* the execution and satisfaction of any of its desires . . . is at liberty to consider the objects of them; examine them on all sides, and weigh them with others. In this lies the liberty Man has; and from the not using of it right comes all that variety of mistakes, errors, and faults which we run into . . . whilst we precipitate the determination of our *wills*, and engage too soon before due *Examination*.
>
> (*Essay* 2.21.47)

Locke seems to be saying here that agents enjoy liberty of exercise over their volitions: though at a given moment they may be unable to choose against their prevailing desire, they retain the ability to refrain from willing anything at all. For Locke, this ability to hold back (analogous to Descartes's ability to suspend judgment in the face of obscure evidence) is "the source of all liberty," and "that, which is (as I think improperly) call'd *Free will*" (*Essay* 2.21.47). Whether the "last determination of the Judgment" will be "upon a hasty and precipitate view, or upon a due and mature *Examination*, is in our power" (*Essay* 2.21.52) in most cases, and so we are to blame for our mistakes. But in cases where an "extreme disturbance" such as "the pain of the Rack" removes our "liberty of thought," "God, who . . . requires of us no more than we are able to do . . . will judge as a kind and merciful Father" (*Essay* 2.21.53). With this last remark, Locke seems to endorse the incompatibilist "ought implies can" principle.

Locke's doctrine of suspension seems to contradict his position in section 23 that there is no liberty of exercise with respect to volitions. But when Locke introduced the doctrine of suspension, he did not alter or remove section 23. There seem to be two basic ways to interpret this puzzling situation. A determinist reading takes as basic Locke's denial that volitions can be free and then tries to render the doctrine of suspension compatible with this denial. An indeterminist reading privileges the passages on suspension and insists that Locke, at least in later years, gave up his "no free volition" doctrine. Let us examine each of these readings a bit more closely.

The most forceful argument for a determinist reading of Locke rests on the following consideration. Locke says, "the motive to change, is always some *uneasiness*" (*Essay* 2.21.29). This is a perfectly general statement, suggesting that when an agent decides to suspend the execution of one of her desires, her decision must be itself motivated by a further desire (call this a "second-order" desire). Locke never says anything explicitly about these second-order desires, but his view may well be that their strength always necessitates the outcome of deliberations concerning suspension. If this is correct, then Locke is still, basically, an intellectual determinist, though the doctrine of suspension has given his account considerably more nuance and sophistication. Locke certainly continued (in later editions) to speak in ways that appear to endorse intellectual determinism: "Man is put under a necessity by his constitution, as an intelligent Being, to be determined in *willing* by his own Thought and Judgment, what is best for him to do" (*Essay* 2.21.48).

However, there is also a good case for an indeterminist reading of Locke. For in 1701–1702, Locke corresponded with the libertarian Philippus van Limborch, who pressed Locke for clarification about whether he was a determinist. As a result of their correspondence, Locke inserted some passages into the fifth edition of his *Essay* to make his meaning clearer (see Letter 3043; VII, 504). In one such passage, he says that though "*in most cases* a Man is not a Liberty to forbear the act of volition . . . yet there is a case wherein a Man is at Liberty in respect of willing"; in this case, "a Man may suspend the act of his choice from being determined for or against the thing proposed, till he has examined, whether it be really of a nature . . . to make him happy" (*Essay* 2.21.56, my emphasis). In this passage, Locke seems to acknowledge the conflict between his doctrine of suspension and his earlier "no free volition" doctrine and to explicitly reject the latter in favor of the former. If this is correct, then for Locke, there are cases in which the strongest desire inclines – but does not determine – the agent to elicit a certain volition. Indeed, (second-order) deliberation about whether or not to suspend a (first-order) act of will may be just such a case. Furthermore, Locke says in a letter to Limborch that a man was free in willing "where he was able to will or not to will" (3192; VII, 680). This certainly looks like an endorsement of an incompatibilist position regarding freedom of will.

So, it may be that Locke was in the end a libertarian, despite the soft determinism evident in the first edition of the *Essay*. However, Locke's decision to retain many of his original arguments (even as he revised) casts serious doubt on this libertarian interpretation. Locke's reception into the eighteenth century bears witness to the puzzling nature of his position: as a recent commentator puts it, "just as [eighteenth century] necessitarians like to believe that Locke was really a confused member of their party, so libertarians hold that Locke was, despite some unfortunate phrasing, one of them."[53] "Of Power" proved to be as ambiguous as it was profound and influential.

6. Leibniz (1646–1716)

Leibniz once characterized "the great question of the free and the necessary" as a labyrinth "where our reason quite often goes astray" (*T* preface, H 53).[54] Though his views on this subject changed somewhat over time,[55] Leibniz's mature view seems to have been that people go astray primarily by imagining either that free choices are entirely undetermined (the error of Bramhall and Molina) or that all human actions occur of necessity (the error of Hobbes and Spinoza). The truth, Leibniz thought, lies in a mean between theses extremes: human actions are in some sense always predetermined but yet are not subject to a fatal necessity which would undermine freedom. Thus, it appears that Leibniz is some sort of determinist and compatibilist.[56]

Leibniz's rejection of libertarianism is straightforward. His metaphysical system is built, in part, on a strong form of the *principle of sufficient reason*, according to which "everything comes to pass as a result of determining reasons," reasons sufficient to explain "why the thing has happened and why it did not go otherwise" (*T* Reflexions sect. 2, H 394–395). This principle rules out the kind of freedom libertarians demand. For libertarians maintain that when we choose freely between two options A and B, the sum total of the reasons we consult in deliberation does not determine our action one way or the other. With our reasons held fixed, it is possible for us to choose either A or B. Therefore, our reasons can explain, at most, why we chose A. They cannot explain why we did *not* choose B, because we might have chosen B in light of those very same reasons. Leibniz believes that there must be a reason not only for why we chose as we did but also for why we did *not* choose as we did *not*, and so he thinks that libertarian freedom is a "chimerical notion" and a "false idea of freedom" (*T* sect. 320). He says, "I maintain absolutely that the power of determining oneself without a cause, i.e., without a source of the determination, implies a contradiction" (G II, 420; 1711 Letter to Des Bosses). Free actions, for Leibniz, are causally determined in some sense. Nevertheless, in Leibniz's view, *certain forms* of determinism would destroy freedom.

In a commentary on the Hobbes-Bramhall debate appended to his *Theodicy*, Leibniz reproves Hobbes for putting forth "exaggerated and odious conclusions and expressions, as if everything happened through an absolute necessity" (*T* Reflexions sect. 3, H 395). In Leibniz's terminology, something is absolutely necessary if its opposite implies a contradiction. So as Leibniz sees it, if Hobbes (along with Spinoza and Epicurus) were correct, then everything would be ruled by a

> blind necessity whereby ... things exist without intelligence and without choice, and consequently without God ... since in consequence of this necessity, all

would have existence through its own essence, just as necessarily as two and three make five.

(*T* Reflexions sect. 3, H 395)

In contrast to this necessitarian picture, Leibniz insists that the actual world is only one among infinitely many possible (i.e. noncontradictory) worlds, and that God freely chose to create it because it was the *best* of the options. God "could not fail to choose" the "best plan of the universe" (*T* Appendix Obj. VII, H 386), but this does not mean that God's choice was absolutely necessary. Rather, it was subject to what Leibniz calls "moral necessity," a "necessity which constrains the wise to do good" (*T* Reflexions sect. 3, H 395). For Leibniz, God's creative choice exemplifies a general truth about free choices: although they are always determined or "morally necessitated" by reasons, these reasons are not blind, mechanical causes but rather are considerations about the prospective value or goodness of the various possible courses of action open to the agent. In Aristotelian terminology, the reasons that determine us to act are *final*, rather than efficient, causes.

Unlike absolute necessity, Leibniz claims, moral necessity does not remove the will's ability to choose otherwise. Thus, Leibniz says in his *Discourse on Metaphysics*,

> by virtue of the decree which God has made that the will shall always seek the apparent good. . . . [H]e, without at all necessitating our choice, determines it by that which appears most desirable. For absolutely speaking, our will . . . is in a state of indifference, being able to act otherwise, or wholly to suspend its action, either alternative being and remaining possible.
>
> (*DM* sect. 30)

This passage suggests that Leibniz would agree with the "two-way" compatibilist account we saw earlier in the discussion of Locke: freedom requires the ability to do otherwise, but we can have this ability even when our actions are determined. Unlike Locke, Leibniz can insist that the will itself is free in this sense. For even when the will is determined by a certain reason to choose A, the will maintains a general power to do otherwise: if some other reason had been present instead, and had shown B to be the best option, then the will would have chosen B.

Unlike supercompatibilists (such as Hobbes), who think that freedom is compatible with both determinism *and* indeterminism, Leibniz does not think that freedom would be compatible with indeterminism. Being truly free depends, in his view, on being determined to choose what is best. He says, "It is an imperfection in our freedom that makes us capable of choosing evil instead of good . . . [or] the lesser good instead of the greater good" (*T* sect. 319). Thus he concludes that "the predetermination of events by their causes is precisely what contributes to" moral responsibility rather than destroying it (*T* Appendix Obj. III, H 382).

Leibniz's commitment to moral necessitation distinguishes his view both from standard libertarianism and from standard compatibilism. To better understand why Leibniz thought that freedom is compatible with – and indeed depends on – moral necessity, consider Leibniz's definition of freedom from section 288 of the *Theodicy*:

> Freedom . . . consists in intelligence, which involves a clear knowledge of the object of deliberation, in spontaneity, whereby we determine, and in contingency,

that is, in the exclusion of logical or metaphysical necessity. . . . The free substance is self-determining and that according to the motive of good perceived by the understanding, which inclines it without compelling it.

(*T* sect. 288)

Let us consider in turn Leibniz's notions of intelligence, spontaneity, and contingency.

According to Leibniz, agents always go for what they believe to be the *best* of their options. Unfortunately, he notes, what *appears* best to us is not always so: "what pleases us now is often a real evil, which would displease us if we had the eyes of the understanding open" (*T* sect. 289). Our perceptions of apparent goodness can be skewed because we experience "confused perceptions of the senses, and these beget passions and even imperceptible inclinations . . . [which] often thwart the judgment of the practical understanding" (*T* sect. 310). Insofar as we do not act in accord with our own reason, we are "slaves of passion" (*T* sect. 289). Thus, in an important sense we are *more free* "insofar as we act with a distinct knowledge," that is, with more *intelligence* (*T* sect. 289). Freedom in this sense comes in degrees. Perfect freedom requires perfect intelligence, and so "God alone is perfectly free."[57]

However, for Leibniz there is another sense of "free" in which freedom is opposed not to "bondage of the mind" but rather to "necessity."[58] In this sense, one is either free, or not; there are no degrees of freedom. And in this sense, our subjection to passion "does not prevent us . . . from making a free choice of that which pleases us most" (*T* sect. 289). Thus even the most wretched slaves of passion choose freely and are responsible for their choices.

Spontaneity is self-determination. We act spontaneously "in so far as we have within us the source of our actions" (*T* sect. 290). Leibniz often points out that in his metaphysical system, agents always act with spontaneity. Thus Leibniz declares that "each substance is the sole cause of all its actions, and . . . is free of all physical influence from every other substance, save the customary co-operation of God" (*T* sect. 300), so that "the soul has in itself a perfect spontaneity" (*T* sect. 291).

Unfortunately, Leibniz's appeal to metaphysical spontaneity seems inconsistent with some of his other claims about spontaneity and its opposite, constraint. In one place, he says that a man is constrained when he is "imprisoned against his will or thrown off a precipice."[59] However, speaking with metaphysical strictness, Leibniz must say that the man's remaining in the prison, or falling through the air, are not caused by other substances and so are just as spontaneous as any of the man's other actions. In some places, Leibniz seems to offer alternative accounts of spontaneity which allow that many human actions lack spontaneity.[60] Despite the frequency of his appeals to metaphysical spontaneity, these alternative accounts probably represent Leibniz's considered view on the matter, at least when moral responsibility is at issue.

As we have seen, Leibniz thinks that free actions must be contingent. "Freedom," he says, "must exclude an absolute and metaphysical or logical necessity" (*T* sect. 302). But if all of a person's actions are already contained in her complete concept, then it seems her actions would follow from her nature with logical necessity (as Leibniz acknowledges in *DM* sect. 13). Leibniz can respond to this difficulty by noting that properties can be contained in a creature's complete concept in more than one way. For example, a creature's existence is not contained in its concept directly (as three-sidedness is contained in a triangle's concept), but only insofar as the overall goodness of the creature's concept moves God to create it. Similarly, an agent's actions – like her existence – may not be built directly into her complete concept. Instead, her concept may contain *reasons for action*, from which the actions themselves follow by moral necessity. For example, Caesar crosses the Rubicon at a certain time not because it is part of his concept to so cross but because it is part of his concept to perceive crossing as the best of his available options at that time.[61]

Leibniz emphasizes that although free actions cannot be *metaphysically* necessary, they *can* be *morally* necessary. Final causes or considerations of goodness can render our actions certain, and in a way inevitable, without destroying the reality and significance of our choices. Leibniz's insistence on this connection between freedom and value develops themes implicit in many of the other philosophers we have examined, especially Descartes and Locke. Whether his view is truly coherent remains an open question, even as the labyrinth of freedom and determinism continues to lure today's philosophers into its depths.

Notes

1. See Suárez, *On Efficient Causality: Metaphysical Disputations 17, 18, and 19*, trans. A. J. Freddoso (New Haven: Yale University Press, 1994), 319. For Molina, see note 8.
2. See, for example, Robert Kane, *Free Will and Values* (Albany: State University of New York Press, 1986).
3. For a history of this debate and selections from the writings it generated, see Thomas Hobbes and John Bramhall, *Hobbes and Bramhall on Liberty and Necessity*, ed. Vere Chappell (Cambridge: Cambridge University Press, 1999), abbreviated in citations as *HBLN*. In-text references to Bramhall refer to page numbers in this work.
4. *HBLN*; see note 3.
5. As the next paragraph explains, whereas Bramhall thinks the free will often has the power to will or nill a course of action, all that is essential to freedom in his view is the ability to will a course of action or to refrain from so willing.
6. For the origins of this distinction and terminology, see Aquinas, *ST* 2.1q9a1 and *ST* 2.1q10a2.
7. Harry Frankfurt introduced this terminology in "Alternative Possibilities and Moral Responsibility," *Journal of Philosophy*, 66 (1969), 829–839.
8. For the original, see Molina's *Concordia* Bk I, Q14 A13 D2 n3, 14; Molina, Luis de, *Liberi arbitrii cum gratiae donis, divina praescientia, providentia, praedestinatione et reprobatione Concordia*, ed. J. Rabeneck (Oña and Madrid: Collegium Maximum S.J., 1953), 319.
9. There is a similar idea in Augustine: people are responsible for the effects of a disease (contracted through no fault of their own) if they freely refuse a medicine that would take away the disease. See *On Free Choice of the Will*, III.19, trans. Thomas Williams (Indianapolis: Hackett, 1993), 107.
10. See Aquinas, *ST* 2.1q13a1ad2, *ST* 2.1q13a6obj2, and *ST* 2.1q17a1.
11. *Metamorphoses* VII: 20–1; quoted by Bramhall in *Discourse* 23 (*HBLN*, 12).
12. Hobbes seems to offer something like the following criticism of this second response. If the will always followed the intellect's last dictate, then the will's earlier decisions about what to attend to would be externally determined by judgments concerning what things were best to attend to. To maintain that the will is the ultimate origin of its acts, then, Bramhall must claim that "the will affects a particular good before the man understands it to be good" (*HBLN*, 74), that is, he must believe that the will can choose a course of action that has not yet been represented in the intellect. Bramhall can avoid Hobbes's criticism here only if in granting that the will is determined by the intellect he means to grant that it is thus determined *in some types of cases, but not in all cases*.
13. See, for example, *Critique of Pure Reason* A807/B835, trans. Kemp-Smith (London, 1933), 637; and *Religion Within the Boundaries of Mere Reason* 6:50, in Immanuel Kant, *Religion and Rational Theology*, trans. and ed. Allen W. Wood and George di Giovanni (Cambridge: Cambridge University Press, 1996), 94.
14. See Thomas Reid, Knud Haakonssen, and James A. Harris, *Essays on the Active Powers of Man* (University Park, PA: Pennsylvania State University Press, 2010); and Roderick Chisholm, "Human Freedom and the Self," in Gary Watson (ed.), *Free Will* (2nd ed.; New York: Oxford University Press, 2003), 26–37.
15. In this section on Hobbes, in text citations start with the work and section by Hobbes, followed by the page numbers where this is found in *HBLN*.

16 See *Treatise* sect. 31, 38; Hobbes suggests that the connection between cause and effect is a conceptual or logical one when he says that with the cause posited, "it cannot be *understood* but that the effect is produced"; *De corpore* in W. Molesworth, ed., *The English Works of Thomas Hobbes of Malmesbury* (London: John Bohn, 1839–45), vol. I, 122, abbreviated hereafter *EW*.
17 These words are from Harry Frankfurt, "Freedom of the Will and the Concept of a Person," *The Journal of Philosophy*, 68 (1) (1971), 6. In defining "freedom" this way, Frankfurt clearly follows Hobbes.
18 He suggests that "appetite and will in man or beast" are "the same thing" (*Questions* sect. 29, 83).
19 See *L* 1–2, 6. This kind of materialism may seem odd for a theist (which Hobbes at least appears to have been), but in some places Hobbes suggests that God, too, is a body. See, for example, the appendix to the 1668 Latin edition of *L* 3.1–8 (translated in E. Curley (ed.), *Leviathan, With Selected Variants From the Latin Edition of 1668* (Indianapolis: Hackett, 1994), 538–542. See also *EW* IV, 306–313 and *EW* I, 10.
20 Hobbes illustrates the difference between internal and external impediments as follows: "we say he that is tied wants [i.e. lacks] the liberty to go, because the impediment is not in him but in his bands; whereas we say not so of him that is sick or lame, because the impediment is in himself" (*Treatise* sect. 29, 38).
21 See also *EW* III, 196; *EW* IV, 275; *EW* V, 365.
22 See Scott MacDonald, John Martin Fischer, Carl Ginet, Joseph Margolis, Mark Case, Elie Noujain, Robert Kane and Derk Pereboom, "Fischer's Discussion With Members of the Audience," *Journal of Ethics*, 4 (4) (2000), 413.
23 My terminology here follows Joseph Keim Campbell, "Descartes on Spontaneity, Indifference, and Alternatives," in Rocco J. Gennaro and Charles Huenemann (eds.), *New Essays on the Rationalists* (New York: Oxford University Press, 1999), 180. What Campbell here calls "two-way" compatibilism, he elsewhere refers to as "strong" compatibilism, applying the label "weak" to what he here calls "one-way" compatibilism. See his "A Compatibilist Theory of Alternative Possibilities," *Philosophical Studies*, 88 (1997), 319–330.
24 See, for example, Vere Chappell's introduction to *HBLN*, xviii.
25 For an argument that Hobbes distinguishes two different senses of freedom, see A. G. Wernham, "Liberty and Obligation in Hobbes," in Keith C. Brown (ed.), *Hobbes Studies* (Cambridge: Harvard University Press, 1965), 117–139.
26 For an argument that Hobbes acknowledges only one kind of freedom (manifested in different ways before and after deliberation ends), see Vere Chappell's entry on Hobbes in Robert Sleigh, Jr., Vere Chappell, and Michael Della Rocca, "Determinism and Human Freedom," in Daniel Garber and Michael Ayers (eds.), *The Cambridge History of Seventeenth-Century Philosophy* (Cambridge: Cambridge University Press, 1998), vol. II, 1223–1225.
27 See Robert Kane, *The Significance of Free Will* (New York: Oxford University Press, 1996), 65; see also Gary Watson, "Soft Libertarianism and Hard Compatibilism," in Monika Betzler (ed.), *Autonomes Handeln: Beitrage zur Philosophie von Harry G. Frankfurt* (Berlin: Academie-Verlag, 2000), 59–70.
28 For an example of such an action, see AT XI 343; CSM I 35.
29 AT VIIIA 17–18; CSM I 204. See also AT VIIIB 363; CSM I 307 and AT VII 377; CSM II 259.
30 See AT VII 61; CSM II 42, AT VII 377–78; CSM II 259–60, AT VIIIA 6; CSM I 194, and AT VIIIA 19–20; CSM I 205–06. For an important alternative interpretation to the one offered here, see Lex Newman, "Attention, Voluntarism, and Liberty in Descartes's Account of Judgment," *Res Philosophica* 92 (1) (2015), 61–91.
31 For an in-depth investigation of the relevant texts, see C. P. Ragland, "Descartes on Divine Providence and Human Freedom," *Archiv für Geschichte der Philosophie*, 87 (2) (2005), 159–188.
32 For a recent discussion of this aspect of Descartes's view, see Marie Jayasekera, "Responsibility in Descartes's Theory of Judgment," *Ergo* 3 (12) (2016): 293–319.
33 For discussions of Descartes's theodicy see C. P. Ragland, "Descartes's Theodicy," *Religious Studies: An International Journal for the Philosophy of Religion*, 43 (2) (2007), 125–144; Lex Newman, "The Fourth Meditation," *Philosophy and Phenomenological Research*, 59 (1999), 559–591; and Michael Latzer, "Descartes's Theodicy of Error," in E. Elmar and M. Latzer (eds.), *The Problem of Evil in Early Modern Philosophy* (Toronto: University of Toronto Press, 2001), 35–48.
34 Some other passages asserting CDD are AT III 64; CSMK 147, AT VII 58–59, 145; CSM II 41, 104, AT VIIIA 21; CSM I 207; AT IV 116; CSMK 233.
35 For similar conceptions of freedom, see Anselm, *De libertate arbitrii* in *Opera omnia*, ed. Schmitt (Edinburgh: Nelson, 1946), vol. I, 225; and Susan Wolf, "Asymmetrical Freedom," *Journal of Philosophy*, 77

(1980), 151–166. A sustained argument for the interpretation offered in this paragraph is given in C. P. Ragland, *The Will to Reason: Theodicy and Freedom in Descartes* (New York: Oxford University Press, 2016).
36 See Anthony Kenny, "Descartes on the Will," in R. J. Butler (ed.), *Cartesian Studies* (Oxford: Blackwell, 1972), 18–20. For similar readings see Michelle Beyssade, "Descartes's Doctrine of Freedom: Differences Between the French and Latin Texts of the Fourth Meditation," in John Cottingham (ed.), *Reason, Will, and Sensation: Studies in Descartes's Metaphysics* (Oxford: Clarendon Press, 1994), 194, 206; and Larmore, Charles, "Descartes' Psychologistic Theory of Assent," *History of Philosophy Quarterly*, 1 (1984), 67.
37 AT IV 118; CSMK 235 also seems to equate these two notions.
38 For this sort of reading, see Lilli K. Alanen, "Descartes on the Will and the Power to Do Otherwise," in Henrik Lagerlund and Mikko Yrjönsuuri (eds.), *Emotions and Choice From Boethius to Descartes* (Dordrecht; Boston, MA: Kluwer Academic Publishers, 2002), 279–298. For arguments against this suggestion, see section IV of C. P. Ragland, "Is Descartes a Libertarian?" in Daniel Garber and Steven M. Nadler (eds.), *Oxford Studies in Early Modern Philosophy, Volume III* (Oxford: Oxford University Press, 2006), 57–90; and Thomas Lennon, "No, Descartes is Not a Libertarian," in Daniel Garber and Donald Rutherford (eds.), *Oxford Studies in Early Modern Philosophy, Volume VII* (Oxford: Oxford University Press, 2015), 47–82.
39 For this view, see Alexander Boyce Gibson, *The Philosophy of Descartes* (London: Methuen, 1932), 332–339; and Michelle Beyssade, "Descartes's Doctrine of Freedom," 191–206. For an argument against it, see C. P. Ragland, "Descartes on Degrees of Freedom: A Close Look at a Key Text," *Essays in Philosophy*, 14 (2) (July 2013), 239–268.
40 C refers to page numbers in Edwin M. Curley (ed.), *The Collected Works of Spinoza, Volume I* (Princeton, NJ: Princeton University Press, 1985).
41 See AT VIIIA 24; CSM I 210.
42 For an excellent overview of interpretive issues surrounding Spinoza's apparent necessitarianism, see Newland's "Spinoza's Modal Metaphysics," *The Stanford Encyclopedia of Philosophy*. See also Edwin Curley and Gregory Walski, "Spinoza's Necessitarianism Reconsidered," in Rocco J. Gennaro and Charles Huenemann (eds.), *New Essays on the Rationalists* (New York: Oxford University Press, 1999), 241–262.
43 M&S refers to page numbers in M.L. Morgan and S. Shirley (eds.), *The Essential Spinoza: Ethics and Related Writings* (Indianapolis: Hackett, 2006).
44 Peter Strawson, "Freedom and Resentment," in Gary Watson (ed.), *Free Will* (Oxford: Oxford University Press, 1982), 59–80.
45 See also "Metaphysical Thoughts" ch. XIII (C 330), and the penultimate paragraph of Ep. 58 (M&S 291).
46 See, for example, Frankfurt, "Freedom of the Will and the Concept of a Person"; and Gary Watson, "Free Agency," in Gary Watson (ed.), *Free Will* (Oxford: Oxford University Press, 1983), 96–110.
47 On degrees of activity in Spinoza, see Michael Della Rocca, "Spinoza's Metaphysical Psychology," in Don Garrett (ed.), *The Cambridge Companion to Spinoza* (Cambridge: Cambridge University Press, 1996). See also Matthew J. Kisner, *Spinoza on Human Freedom: Reason, Autonomy and the Good Life* (Cambridge: Cambridge University Press, 2011).
48 For a contrary interpretation, see Vere Chappell's entry on Locke in the chapter "Determinism and Human Freedom," in Garber and Ayers, *The Cambridge History of Seventeenth-Century Philosophy*, vol. 2, 1250. But see also James A. Harris, *Of Liberty and Necessity: The Free Will Debate in Eighteenth-Century British Philosophy* (Oxford: Oxford University Press, 2008), 20, note 3.
49 References to letters include the letter number, followed by the volume and page number in E. S. de Beer (ed.), *The Correspondence of John Locke*, 8 vols. (Oxford: Clarendon Press, 1976–89).
50 Jonathan Edwards, *Freedom of the Will*, part II, section 1, ed. Kaufman and Frankena (New York: Irvington, 1982), 37–41.
51 But for a clearly signaled change of mind, see also *Essay* 2.21.31, 250–251.
52 This is Vere Chappell's name for the doctrine. See his "Locke on Freedom of the Will," in *Locke's Philosophy: Content and Context*, ed. G.A.J. Rogers (Oxford: Oxford University Press, 1994) 101–121.
53 James A. Harris, *Of Liberty and Necessity: The Free Will Debate in Eighteenth-Century British Philosophy* (Oxford: Clarendon Press, 2008), 39. For a book length study of Locke's conception of freedom, see Gideon Yaffe, *Liberty Worth the Name: Locke on Free Agency* (Princeton, NJ: Princeton University Press, 2000). Antonia LoLordo, *Locke's Moral Man*, (Oxford: Oxford University Press, 2012) argues that Locke wrote so ambiguously because he was agnostic about the metaphysics of freedom.

54 Citations from *Theodicy* refer to section numbers, sometimes with the addition of the page number in the edition translated by E. M. Huggard (La Salle, IL: Open Court Publishing, 1985). References to Huggard use the abbreviation "*H.*"
55 See the entry on Leibniz in "Determinism and Human Freedom," 1262.
56 See, for example, the relevant portions of Robert Adams, *Leibniz: Determinist, Theist, Idealist* (Oxford: Oxford University Press, 1998). However, Michael Murray argues that Leibniz's position has more in common with certain late Scholastic versions of incompatibilism than it does with most forms of compatibilism. See his "Spontaneity and Freedom in Leibniz," in Donald Rutherford and J. A. Cover (eds.), *Leibniz: Nature and Freedom* (Oxford: Oxford University Press, 2005), 194–216.
57 *NE* 2.21.8; Remnant and Bennett, eds. (Cambridge: Cambridge University Press, 1996), 174–175. See also *Theodicy* sect. 310.
58 *Ibid.*
59 *NE* 2.21.13, 170.
60 For a good discussion of this issue, see Donald Rutherford, "Leibniz on Spontaneity," in *Leibniz: Nature and Freedom*, 156–180.
61 See Adams, *Leibniz*, 189.

Part 3

EPISTEMOLOGY

6
SKEPTICISM

Gianni Paganini
(Translated by Antonio Russo)

1. The impact of Montaigne on modern skepticism: epistemology

Even though recent research has discovered a web of connections and uses of skepticism that preceded the reemergence of the work of Sextus Empiricus in Europe,[1] it is clear that the revival of Pyrrhonism, due to the manuscripts and the editions related to the Hellenistic philosopher, imparted new strength and original directions to early modern skepticism.[2] Whereas Academic skepticism's fundamental sources – Cicero's *Academica* and Augustine's *Contra Academicos* – were always, including during the Middle Ages, at people's disposal and known in the West, the few manuscripts of Sextus Empiricus's works that were available in European libraries apparently did not leave significant traces before the sixteenth century. Gianfrancesco Pico della Mirandola (1469–1533) was the first to make extensive use of Sextus Empiricus. In his *Examen vanitatis doctrinae gentium* (1520), Pico della Mirandola presented a Christianized and apologetic image of Sextus Empiricus.[3] Wider first-hand knowledge and a stronger impact of Sextus Empiricus's work on Western scholars became possible only later, by Henri Estienne's *Pyrrhoniae hypotyposes* (1562) and Gentian Hervet's *Adversus mathematicos* (1569), both Latin translations.[4] Finally, in 1570 Diogenes Laertius's edition was published. This was the primary source for Pyrrho's life and doctrines. Thus, in the case of skepticism, there is no question that the philological rediscovery preceded and made possible the philosophical reunderstanding of skepticism and especially Pyrrhonism.[5] This does not mean, however, that what happened was only an episode inside the *studia humanitatis* tradition. Once rediscovered, ancient skepticism was immediately exposed to a subtle enterprise of reinterpretation.

Michel de Montaigne (1533–1592) and Francisco Sanches (1551–1623) were the main authors that started this new interpretation. They made substantial contributions on the Pyrrhonian and the neo-Academic fronts respectively.

It is hard to underestimate Montaigne's importance as expounder of the "new" skepticism. Besides clearly distinguishing the real "skeptics" (namely the Pyrrhonists) from the "dogmatics" and the negative dogmatics (the "Academics"), the author of the *Essays* (first edition 1580) rethought and popularized fundamental notions such as "phenomenon," "criterion," "*epokhe*" or the suspension of judgment, "equipollence" (*isostheneia*), "ataraxy" or "apathy," the "vicious circle" (*diallelos*), and "infinite regress." For the first time, Montaigne translated all of Pyrrhonian skepticism's technical terminology into a modern language. More than that, skepticism was philosophically redirected to suit modern needs. With this reworking, Pyrrhonian skepticism passed from the register of philology (or, in certain cases, apologetics) to that of philosophy.

His first important contribution had to do with the notion of "appearance." Montaigne never used the word "phenomenon," which was not yet in use in modern languages. If not the word, however, the meaning was already present in Montaigne. Instead of the term "phenomenon," Montaigne usually spoke of "appearance" (*apparence*), which is a calque of the Latin *apparentia* (plural) used by Henri Estienne in his translation and commentary of Sextus's *Hypotyposes*. In Estienne's work, *apparentia* and *phainomena* are strictly equivalent.[6] This is not the only influence of Estienne's philological work on Montaigne's vocabulary. Another, no less important, concerns the notion of *phantasia*, which Estienne considered as equivalent to phenomenon. Estienne's Latin interpretation actually renders *phantasia* as "*persuasionem et coactam passionem*" ("assent and involuntary affection"), which largely overlaps the definition of phenomenon. The two influences (the one regarding *phainomenon*, the other connected to *phantasia*) tightly intertwine. In a crucial passage of the *Apology for Raymond Sebond*, Montaigne explains what a phenomenon is by appealing to the appearance, at the same time connecting it closely to the notion of *fantasie* (in French), which means to him "imagination," or more precisely "sensitive representation."[7]

These choices are not merely lexical but deeply influenced Montaigne's understanding of Pyrrhonian skepticism. They lead him to cast Pyrrhonian skepticism as a phenomenalism according to which (1) we know about reality only through the appearance and mainly the sensible appearance (these two phrases become almost synonymous), whereas according to Sextus there are also kinds of phenomena that are disclosed only to the intellect; they do not have sensible features but are rather *noumena*, and (2) the main scene of skepticism for Montaigne becomes the dichotomy between appearance and reality. The first is knowable. The second – because it includes essences and substances – is unknowable.[8] From the philological point of view, nowadays we can discuss whether this interpretation rightly fits the ancient sources. For example, a more radical and maybe also more correct reading of Pyrrhonian skepticism would consist most likely in what Conche called "the philosophy of pure appearance."[9] In fact, this avoided as dogmatic any discourse about independent realities that do not reveal themselves through phenomena.

On the other hand, it is certainly true that the dichotomy between appearance and reality suggested a dogmatic residue. As such, it was unfaithful to the original attitude of Greek Pyrrhonism. However, it is historically true that in this phenomenalistic version the ancient skepticism dressed in modern clothes and entered European culture – after the apologetic book of Gianfrancesco Pico. Then, on the basis of what we might call the main or primary scene of modern skepticism, Montaigne broke the link between reality and appearances and confined all of our knowledge to the latter. He stated Socrates's portrait dilemma in these terms: how can we be certain that the portrait is a picture of Socrates if we only have access to its representation, namely to appearances (phenomena and images), and do not have access to the original model?[10] It is in this scenario that Montaigne launched the search for the criterion. Because appearance and reality are now split, it is necessary to appeal to a "third" (the criterion) that guarantees one is similar to the other. In turn, this requires a new criterion, starting a sort of infinite regress. The vicious circle, as well as the dogmatic pretense to an alleged subjective evidence, will only be bad ways to avoid the aporia of the criterion and the regress.[11]

Montaigne adopted an epistemologically weak version of *phantasia* or *fantasie*, which is no longer a *phantasia kataleptike* (the apprehensive representation that, according to the Stoics, can provide a sure criterion for distinguishing between false and reliable representations of reality). Montaigne's skeptical *fantasie* is not able to fulfill this function any more, and that situation clears the way for the study of the subjective states of the mind in themselves and disconnected from reality. These subjective states of the mind are now rather connected to the organic equipment of the senses and are relative to circumstances, conditions, locations, frequency or rarity, habits, and so on. In the *Apology*, Montaigne closely follows the famous ten modes of Aenesidemus that had been expounded by Sextus. However, unlike the relativistic readings that betrayed the authentic skeptical meaning of these tropes, the author of the *Essays* really grasps their original content, which was calling into question the paradigm of normality on which Aristotelian epistemology was founded.

When Montaigne compares dreaming and being awake, being sober and being drunk, youth and old age, icterical and correct perception, health and illness, the author of the *Essays* points out that the real meaning of these opposite situations consists in calling into question the Aristotelian paradigm of normality. According to it, in a "normal" situation – with senses and intellect functioning according to nature – the subject's representation should give us an adequate and true representation of external reality. On the contrary, in the *Essays* not only are *species* (both sensible and intelligible) banished – *species* or *espèce* literally disappears from Montaigne's lexicon as a philosophical term – but also the complex Aristotelian psychology based on the relationship between matter and form is left behind. The *fantasies* are substituted for the *species*, whose function was to transmit the "form" of the object to the subject. Unlike *species*, "images" or *fantasies* are not copies but indirect effects of reality. In the light of these principles, Montaigne was then able to understand all subjective states within the single category of phenomena or appearances. Furthermore, although he recognized that from the point of view of ordinary life there are differences among them in degree of reliability, he could no longer justify a hierarchy of subjective states, either from an epistemological or from an ontological point of view. It is in this sense that one must read Montaigne's apparently paradoxical claim: "We are always with some sickness."[12] In other words, to perceive an object is always to be in a subjective state that reflects the quality of the subject rather than that of reality in itself. At the same time, perceiving a thing means accommodating and transforming the thing according to the self, giving it another form and appearance. Thus, this process of assimilation is also a process of falsification that prevents us from judging clearly what the thing is in and of itself: "Now, because our state accommodates things and turns them according to itself, we do not know what the actual things are anymore, as nothing comes to us but falsified and altered by our senses."[13]

Montaigne used exceptional states – dreaming and altered perception because of illness or age – simply to reveal something true of more "normal" states. This is that

> our imagination [*fantasie*] does not apply to external things, but it is conceived through senses. The senses do not grasp the external object but only what affects them. Thus, imagination is the passion and the affection of sense rather than the appearance of the object. But this passion and the object are different things. Therefore, those who judge through the appearances, judge on a different basis than the object.[14]

From this point of view, we always judge on the basis of "something different from the thing itself." Namely, we judge according to appearances that belong to the subject (they are states of the mind) and do not belong to the object (these appearances are not part of the object even in a formal sense). As a consequence, in the Pyrrhonian model of knowledge consisting of phenomena, perceptions are no longer guaranteed either epistemologically or ontologically, as was the case – thanks to the fact that the "form" applied on both sides of the knowledge relation – in the Aristotelian model of normality. Although phenomena differ with regard to pragmatic effectiveness in orienting everyday life, one can no longer distinguish them – as Stoics claimed – on the basis of their truth value as representations. Montaigne never arrived at an explicit statement of the "universal" doubt, which would appear at the end of Descartes's First Meditation. So as to be "universal," doubt should have both existential and essential consequences. In fact, it should suspend judgment not only as to the conformity of representations and things but also as to the very existence of things. Although we do not find in *Essays* a clear and explicit statement of this "universal" uncertainty, as will happen later in Descartes, it is fair to say that nearly all of its premises are already present in the *Apology for Raymond Sebond*, even if Montaigne hesitates to generalize this kind of doubt. Actually, the idea of a subject confined inside the representational sphere of its subjective states – appearances disconnected from reality – is not very far from the Cartesian ego of the First Meditation, which has lost contact with external reality. Some sentences from the *Essais* of which historians did not take sufficient note go in this direction and question the existence of external objects; we could say that it is a doubt as radical as the Cartesian one but in a way *local* rather than *global* because the doubt does not also apply to existence of the entire universe.[15] Sometimes Montaigne stops his investigation before questioning the "existence" level, therefore limiting the range of doubt to the essential features of the object (i.e. the conformity of the qualities as they are perceived with the thing-in-itself). However, it is also true that an object without any certain quality is always in danger of losing its existential stance.

2. Neo-Pyrrhonism, psychology, and self-reflexiveness

The third point for which Montaigne's mediation has been important is the conception of skepticism as philosophy of doubt. Benson Mates[16] showed us how unsatisfactory it is to translate simply as "to doubt" the term used by Sextus, *aporein*. Furthermore, whereas in the Greek tradition *ataraxia* and the mind's peace flow from assent's suspension – namely from *epokhé* – rather than from knowledge and judgment about things, Montaigne's attitude ends up making doubt, instead of *epokhé*, the climax of skeptic research. This is not without consequences, all the more because doubt is for Montaigne a state of restlessness and discomfort rather than of calm and liberation from emotion.[17] Through this double move, we see how the introduction of doubt in the modern ages as the main resource of skepticism affected our view of this philosophical movement, whereby skepticism and doubt become coextensional and synonymous. This was not true in the Greek tradition, and with his method of doubt, Descartes is the most prominent example of this change. Again, on the basis of Estienne's translation, it was the author of the *Essays* who was the first influential writer to state the idea that the main activity of the skeptic is that of doubting, in the exact meaning that this term takes in the theory of knowledge (an activity that basically concerns thoughts whose truth one evaluates); the doubter must examine the opposites before establishing which is the real one. The main activity of the modern skeptic turns out to be a mental exercise, whereas the ancient Pyrrhonist did a discursive practice: the former brings up doubts in his mind, the latter utters opposite statements, balancing each other until he reaches *isosthenia* or equipollence of the opposite sentences (e.g. "honey is sweet" vs "honey is bitter"). In the Greek Pyrrhonian tradition, doubting or wondering was not the main activity of the inquirer. In fact, the ancient skeptic used to compare conflicting propositions, so as to show that they were no more (*ou mallon*) asserted than denied. The proper stance of the Pyrrhonist was the suspension of judgment, rather than a fluctuating state of mind, like incertitude, doubt and hesitation. After Montaigne and under his influence, these mental and psychological aspects of skepticism, which are represented mostly by the activity of doubting, decidedly prevailed over the original Pyrrhonian linguistic formulations, and it contributed to render extremely problematic the ideal of living comfortably following appearances, according to the original Pyrrhonian project.

The pervasiveness of the new synonymy between skepticism and doubt can be seen in a crucial passage of the *Apology*. In fact, although Montaigne correctly retrieved the main *phonai* (mottos) of ancient skepticism and showed how they converge into the *epokhé*,[18] nonetheless, when he had to briefly summarize and defend them from the accusation of being self-contradictory, he drastically reduced their range to only two sentences: on the one hand, the formula of Socratic ignorance ("*J'ignore*"); on the other hand, the activity of doubt ("*Je doubte*").[19] One should note that both formulas are more of a betrayal than a faithful transmission of the genuine meaning of the *epokhé*; as a matter of fact, both imply a state quite different from the mere suspension of judgment, substituting a balanced neutrality with either a dogmatic denial ("I do not know") or a statement of wavering perplexity ("I doubt").

The fourth point concerns something lacking in Montaigne's reflection rather than something present in it; here, we allude to the lack of a theory of the subject able to oppose the supremacy of doubt, as will happen by contrast in Descartes with the discovery of the *cogito*. At first sight, to speak of a lack of a theory of the subject in an author like Montaigne, who is unanimously seen as a father of the modern subjectivity, may seem paradoxical and provocative. However, the observation proves itself to be grounded when one distinguishes between the actual examination of the subject, of which Montaigne was an unattainable master and a wonderful painter, and its proper philosophical theory, of which no early signs are to be found in the *Essays*. The point is that the Pyrrhonian model was more an obstacle than a help to the theoretical, as opposed to experiential, formulation of the role of the subject. It was in accordance with his practice of the "self" (*moi*), that Montaigne avoided a strong doctrine of the subject. Portraying himself as the main topic of *Essays*, he ended up by characterizing the subject in the forms of mutability, inconstancy, and multiplicity.

The result is even clearer if one looks at the doctrines of the soul as they appear in Montaigne's work. Within the sort of counter encyclopedia that is the *Apology*, besides the demolition of physics, metaphysics, and philosophical theology, there is also the demolition of philosophical psychology, examined in its main different schools. First, following the skeptical method of disagreements (*diaphonia*), Montaigne highlights the hopeless contradictions of psychology. He writes that treating this topic we find ourselves in the middle of the "Tower of Babel."[20] Furthermore, the checkmate given by Montaigne to any "strong" theory of the subject is already implicit in the form he chose for the treatment of this problem. Far from grounding the *esprit*'s prerogative, centrality, and activity, the extensive doxology Montaigne put together depicts the subject and the soul as parts of nature. He seems to place his trust especially in the crude materialism of Stoics and Epicureans, whereas he considers Platonism, with its complex doctrine of the psyche, to be a fairy tale and poetic philosophy. About Aristotle, Montaigne emphasizes that he was intentionally obscure in this respect to hide his tendency toward mortality of the intellect.[21] In conclusion, instead of appearing as an undiscussed chief character, the subject enters into the psychology section of the *Apology* as "an instable, dangerous and daring instrument" ("*un outil vagabond, dangereux et temeraire*"), upon which one cannot rely too much and to which it is better to assign "the tightest possible constraints" ("*les barrieres le plus contraintes qu'on peut*").[22]

Nor could Pyrrhonian tradition have helped Montaigne to make wider room for the subject. It is true that for Montaigne the "sacramental formula" of skeptics is *epekho* ("I suspend [the judgment]"), that is, it seems, a first-person point of view. However, this philosophy is defined more by impersonality than by subjectivity. Knowing, feeling, and evaluating are recordings of appearances that do not need a strong, substantial definition of the subject, even though they are always related to it. Experiencing phenomena are mostly described using the impersonal form *phainetai*, that is "it seems" or "it appears," so that there is no need to make explicit the role of the perceiving or thinking subject. Even when in Enesidemus's ten modes it comes to the relation between subject and object, the tone of the treatment is in general abruptly naturalistic. The human subject is a piece of nature, as are the humors, organs, and membranes in which the knowledge process – presented as a "combination" of these different contributions – is realized. From this point of view, the difference between humans and animals is not so significant and it is notable that, according to the first mode, all the living beings, as well as man, provide strong support to this "naturalization" of phenomena. If we want to risk a comparison, this is not far from Hume's idea of a "bundle of perceptions" to which the ego is anonymously reduced. In sum, especially for an author like Montaigne who attempted at a high level the *peinture* of the *moi*, Pyrrhonian tradition constituted an insurmountable obstacle not to practicing this exercise of writing but to rethinking that practice within a coherent theory that could define the ontological status of the subject and not simply its phenomenological status.[23]

A fifth aspect of the lesson Montaigne left to the moderns concerns skepticism's self-reflexiveness. In the *Essays*, in fact, we find both the Augustinian theme of ignorance aware of itself[24] and the Socratic *topos* of knowledge of not knowing.[25] But above all, we find the Pyrrhonian theme of the "extreme of doubt that subverts itself" ("*extremité de doubte qui se secoue soy-mesme*").[26] One should note that this formulation seems to get close to the situation Descartes will describe at the beginning of the Second Meditation, where he shows that a first certainty – the existence of the thinking ego as thinking – flows from the most radical uncertainty.

However, the correspondence to Descartes can be maintained only up to a certain point. In fact, in the *Apology*, Montaigne tries to get away from the paradox of skepticism and to avoid its transformation into a categorical formulation – although negative – as "nothing is certain except that there is nothing certain" ("*solum certi nihil esse certi*"). This formula had already been used against skeptics in ancient times but Montaigne finds a new way out from the paradox. In accordance with his famous device ("what do I know?"; "*que sais-je?*"), the author of the *Essays* is interpreting the Pyrrhonians' "eternal profession of ignorance" ("*perpetuelle confession d'ignorance*")[27] as a continuous quest. Their ignorance is not declared in a categorical form. On the contrary, to be "a complete ignorance" ("*une entiere ignorance*"), "that should ignore itself" ("*il faut qu'elle s'ignore soy-mesme*").[28] Pyrrhonians' ignorance leads to the *epokhé* and to a continuous quest rather than to dogmatic, albeit negative, conclusions: "They use their reason to seek and discuss, but not to define and decide."[29] The image of Socrates that surfaces in these pages of the *Apology* – although under some strain – is a character very similar to Pyrrho rather than to the master of neo-Academic skeptics like Cicero, Arcesilaus, and Carneades.[30] With Sextus Empiricus and Montaigne, we could say that doubt is similar to the "catarthic." Namely, it is like the purgative remedy that expels itself together with the illness: dogmatism.

It is in this way that Pyrrhonians "save" themselves, when "one takes them by the throat" and pushes them to "recognize that at least they assert and know this, that they doubt."[31] Avoiding self-contradiction, however, they also interrupt the argumentation process that will lead from doubt to certainty in Descartes's *Meditations*. In Montaigne, we find many of the procedures that Descartes will use to amplify doubt, although the former lacks the latter's thesis of the so-called deceiving God.[32] Furthermore, in Montaigne we do not find the brilliant move that is the Archimedean point of the *Meditations*, namely the move from the knowledge of not knowing to the certainty of thinking and, therefore, of being. For the very same reason that Montaigne withdrew into his "eternal ignorance" as a "continuous quest," Descartes thought, on the contrary, that the exercise of the *dynamis* of the skeptical mind would be just an ineffective doubt. In this way, he displayed in a unique formula both the acceptance of Montaigne's misunderstanding – the doubt instead of the *epokhé* – and the rejection of his major intuition – the *zetesis* instead of the dogma, even of the negative dogma of *akatalepsia* (incomprehensibility).

3. A new theory of skeptical subjectivity: Sanches's internalism and Charron's active skepticism

Pyrrhonism was not the only option available to skeptics during the late Renaissance and at the beginning of the seventeenth century. Although most of the commentators neglected him – following Brunschvicg[33] and Gilson[34] who paid more attention to Montaigne – Francisco Sanches was the other available option. The major influence on him was the neo-Academic *akatalepsia* – as one can tell from the title of his work, *Quod nihil scitur* (1581). Nowadays, some contemporary interpreters of skepticism have wondered whether this other tradition is a more likely background for the birth of Descartes's *cogito*. To some extent, the answer is affirmative. It is not a coincidence that Sanches's work too, like Descartes's, is clearly indebted to Augustine's method of refuting the Academics, as can be seen from his famous "if I am wrong, then I exist" ("*si fallor sum*"). This "motto proposition" ("*vexillum propositio*") itself, at the beginning of *Quod nihil scitur*, is a radicalization of knowledge of not knowing. Sanches starts his work with the sentence "I do not even know this, that I know nothing" ("*Nec unum hoc scio, me nihil scire*"). He goes on to show the advantages of his argumentative strategy. If he is able to prove the initial premise, then he is right to infer that "nothing is known" ("*nil sciri*"); if on the contrary he does not prove the initial premise, so much the better: total ignorance is confirmed. Actually, the initial assertion will revel true.[35] Either way, the *akatalepsia* will be verified. Moreover, in Sanches's work the distinction between Academics and Pyrrhonians seems to be erased in favor of the more general and indifferent category of "skeptics."

I believe, however, that to understand the real point of connection between Renaissance skepticism and Descartes's overcoming of skepticism one has to leave behind the logical-dialectical point of view – the analysis of what we call "the paradox of skepticism," which is similar to "the liar paradox" – and to adopt instead a more "meditative," in a Cartesian sense, or reflective, in Sanches's sense, approach. After all, Sanches's discovery is grounded neither in Pyrrhonism nor in the new academy but goes back to late Scholastic disputes about reflective knowledge of the soul.[36] From these debates Sanches inherited a conception of internal states for which there is no elusive distinction between representation and reality or appearance and reality. This was the distinction to which the skeptical doubt appealed in order to start the never-ending search for the criterion or to show the "bad" circularity of the vicious circle ("*diallelos*").

If one leaves aside Sanches's really tragic tones – for example when he evokes the dramatic experience of the labyrinth or the ruinous encounter with the Minotaur – one could say that his remarks about the "variety" ("*varietas*") of things, about the "multitude" ("*multitudo*") and "confusion" ("*confusio*") of opinions – "where there is multitude, here is confusion" ("*Ubi multitudo, ibi confusio*") – are directly in the background of the *Discours de la méthode*. In it, Descartes describes his desperate route through "the diversity of our opinions" ("*la diversité de nos opinions*"). Analogously, the sense of fallibility that affects the senses and from there spreads to the mind, producing a state of complete uncertainty in the form of a real deception ("What will the mind do when misled by senses? Will it more misled?"; "*Quid faciet mens sensu decepta? Decipi magis?*"), suggests the subsequent Cartesian enterprise of liberating the mind from all its prejudices. Sanches's procedure paradoxically gives the evidence of the worth of a genuine antiempiricist perspective.

One might extend the comparison of Descartes with Sanches[37] to the details, too, in particular to the need for the method of doubt, to the difficulty of using it, and to the fact that few are able to practice it. The differences between the achievements of different men mainly derive from the absence, or from the abuse, of method. These concepts are already clearly outlined in *Quod nihil scitur*. Analogously, on another front, Sanches, like Descartes, holds that one should reject authority. In the first place, this is because it is difficult to choose one among those on the market. But more than that, it is because in relying on others' opinions, the disciple becomes "a slave rather than a learned man." Descartes will say the same in a famous passage about the impossibility of sticking to one opinion once one meets different teachers and is acquainted with different opinions and customs without thinking them barbaric. This passage is not only a repetition of Enesidemus's tenth trope or of a famous passage of Montaigne about savages and "cannibales." It flows from a well-defined literary model already established by Sanches when he describes the loneliness of the disciple who cannot appeal to the judgment of others when searching for the truth.

The idea of doubting resulting in despairing ("*Despero*"), after a passionate searching through the knowledge of learned men, lies at the base of the Portuguese doctor's work. This is research that does not surrender to authorities; keeps on investigating nature ("I keep on [asking]"; "*Persisto tamen*"), sticking only to rational investigation about nature ("*Solam sequar ratione Naturam*"); and ignores the deceptive suggestions of rhetoric and dialectic. It is from this perspective that the dispute with Aristotle takes place; Aristotle, Sanches says, was a human being like us ("*Homo erat ut et nos*"), and although he presented himself as "one of the sharpest scrutinizers of nature," sometimes he was wrong and unaware of many things. In general, in the "Republic of Truth" it is better to doubt, to follow experience and reason than to "swear on authorities" ("*iurare in verba magistri*"). One can understand how influential Sanches could have been at a time in which the primary aim of skepticism was to free oneself from the Aristotelian method and the concept of "science" as "perfect knowledge of the thing" ("*rei perfecta cognitio*").[38]

However, and despite the title, *Quod nihil scitur* is not only an acataleptic work. It also contains ingredients that lean toward the overcoming of doubt. From the beginning, beside the profession of ignorance, Sanches develops another theme, that of the return to oneself after the disappointment of not knowing and the generalization of the doubt: "I am going to return to myself, calling everything into question" ("*Ad me proinde memetipsum retuli; omnia in dubium reuocans*"). This is the second thing Sanches inherits from Socrates, the Delphic demand to know oneself. This theme has a more precise – technical, as it were – meaning in Sanches and it is explicitly connected to his classification of human knowledge. Human knowledge is organized in accordance with the diversity of things that "the mind knows in different ways." The Portuguese doctor distinguishes between external (therefore sensible) and internal (therefore only intellectual) knowledge. Above all, he reconceives "internal" knowledge. According to him, the mind has all its internal knowledge by itself without the mediation of sensitive or imaginative *species*. As a consequence, the mind assigns all internal knowledge a special status.[39] This is a form of internalism that lays the foundations for Descartes's theory of mind.

In this way, Sanches seems to succeed in giving an affirmative answer to the question at the center of his research, namely whether one can say "something which would not be suspected of falsity." The philosopher starts with the "maker's knowledge" principle. This principle applies to whatever has been made by our intellect and also to what happens therein. It applies following a criterion of self-transparency according to which our certainty about our own thinking, willing, and desiring is more perfect than our certainty about what comes from outside:

> For I am more sure that I possess both inclination and will, and that I am at one moment contemplating this idea, at another moment shunning at abominating that idea, than that I see a temple, or Socrates. I have said that we are certain about the real existence of those things that either exist, or else originate, within ourselves.[40]

However, what keeps making "our condition unhappy" is that there is some sort of inverse proportion between the "understanding" ("*quod comprehendere possit*") and the "certainty" ("*certitudo*") of knowledge. The more the mind is certain of a thing, the less the mind is able to understand it and vice versa. It follows that we are absolutely certain that "we think, we want to write" and so on, but "we do not know what this thought, this will, this desire is." From the point of view of understanding, "the knowledge of external things through the senses is greater than the knowledge of internal things without the senses." The contrary happens regarding certainty. In this case, knowledge "of things that are either in us or made by us" is in the first place in the rank of undoubtful certainty. The knowledge we get through "discourse and reasoning" is even more unreliable.[41] One should note that the description Sanches gives of the certainty of internal states ("*quae in nobis aut sunt, aut a nobis fiunt*") will reappear almost literally the same in a passage of Descartes, where he defines the "cogitations" as "everything that happens/is made in us" ("*omnia quae in nobis fiunt*"), adding the claim that thoughts "taken in themselves and not referring to something else, cannot be considered false, if one speaks properly."[42] There is therefore quite a strong evidence to see in Sanches's doctrine of the certainty of internal states of the mind a skeptical "antecedent" of Descartes's thesis that the mind is transparent and that the ideas are evident when they are considered in themselves.[43]

Obviously, Descartes's different metaphysical attitude will allow him to assign a foundational value to internal facts of the mind that for Sanches were strong in certainty but poor in understanding or comprehension. However, this qualification should not make us forget the original contribution that Sanches made to the discovery of the self and therefore to the *cogito*. It was a result of great importance for modern thinking when the authors of the Renaissance harmonized the Delphic precept of knowing the self with the activity of doubt. Therefore, they viewed Socrates as a skeptic. In this way, they not only considered Socrates as an ancestor of skepticism, but they went also much beyond the Augustinian thesis ("*si fallor sum*"), which was too straightforward in refuting skepticism on the basis of the knowledge of the self. By distinguishing between internal and external states and explaining how it is possible to acquire much knowledge without going outside of oneself, Sanches enriched the tradition of early modern skepticism with an aspect that was absent from the Pyrrhonian tradition and was not that developed in the neo-Academic theory. The comparison with Descartes and his statement on the fecundity of the self is worth quoting. In the dialogue on the *Recherche de la vérité*, the character of Poliandre echoes Sanches's approach to the internal states of the mind: "There are so many things in the idea of a thinking being that to develop them all we would need whole days."[44]

At the beginning of the seventeenth century, the key figure of skepticism, at least with regard to popularity and influence, was neither Montaigne nor Sanches but a disciple of Montaigne, Pierre Charron (1541–1603). In his treatise *De la Sagesse* (1601, 1604 second edition modified), he succeeded in summarizing and rearranging Montaigne's thought, bringing forth that treatise of wisdom that was already implicit in the *Essays* but still needed to be explicitly and systematically expounded. Charron's work was such a success that it became a cornerstone for the new culture of the *honnête homme* that spread all throughout the seventeenth century, influencing both the skeptical-libertine *milieux* and Cartesian morals. In Charron's book various philosophical trends converge and cooperate: the Stoic reevaluation of the autonomy of virtue goes together with an argument against superstition and subordination of morality to faith. At the same time, the drive to an entirely mundane *preud'homie* ("human wisdom") appears to be full of Epicurean suggestions and contains daring references to an unscrupulous political prudence.

From the point of view of the history of skepticism, Charron's work is a landmark that separates modern forms from the ancient ones. *De la Sagesse* uncovers a new face of skepticism, which had deep impact on the common image of this movement during the early modern period. In Charron's work, the skeptical sage not only is an active and important character but also, what is more, breaks away from the classical Pyrrhonian pattern, as well as from its more recent reenacting in Montaigne's *Essays*. Regarding the ancient pattern, the attainment of *epokhē* was basically the result of a process of "detachment from the self," the fruit of an "accentuated passivity" of sensations and thoughts, "a paralysis of reason by itself,"[45] as Myles Burnyeat has put it. According to Jonathan Barnes, *epokhē* was a *pathos*, some sort of passivity or passion, that happened to inquirers (*skeptikoi*) at the end of their investigations.[46] Nearly the same can be said about Montaigne, except that this latter added a sense of pessimism and human frailty that was unknown to the ancient skeptics. When one reads Montaigne, it seems that skepticism inflicts a heavy blow not only to human arrogance but also to the value of the intellect and the senses themselves. Not by chance, reason is defined in the *Essays* as "an instrument of lead and wax, which one can lengthen, bend, and adapt to any direction and extent."[47]

From this point of view, Charron's skepticism is quite different. First, the author of *De la Sagesse* stresses the strength of reason, emphasizing at the same time the positive feature of skeptical examination. It is true that reason, and mostly skeptical reason, does not have "jurisdiction" on all subject matters: for example, Charron proclaims that skepticism makes no metaphysical claims and that it relies on revelation in theological matters. Nevertheless, in the mundane domain of "human wisdom," reason preserves its complete right "to judge about everything" and to "restrain assent" when faced with inadequate reasons. In his own field, the sage shows full "universality of spirit"; he is not narrowed by the "municipal law" that rules closed systems of beliefs, whether these beliefs be the elementary, sociological beliefs of the village or the more sophisticated beliefs of nations, philosophical schools, religions (i.e. actual religious rites and behaviors), and churches.

For the first time in the modern age, Charron's skeptical sage is someone who *fights* against an entire corpus of beliefs, someone who *decides to doubt* and *seeks* for arguments to this effect. Far from being the passive effect produced by the unresolved *diaphōnia* of appearances that are simply registered by the observer, Charron's art of doubting requires a conscious and voluntary decision from the subject. This is the main Charronian achievement: *epokhē* or suspension of judgment becomes with him a vigorous and voluntary liberating move from a system of beliefs rather than an imponderable point of balance between different opinions, as it was before in the ancient idea of equipollence. Skepticism demands a whole set of epistemic virtues that preserve the wise from precipitancy, prejudices, and mistakes. After Charron, the modern skeptic is someone who *wants* to cast into doubt almost everything, whereas the ancient Pyrrhonian *was cast* in doubt by different phenomena. From passive, skepticism becomes active; it is no longer the position of an impartial observer but the pose of a conscious protagonist who does not want to be enslaved to prejudices or opinions devoid of any rational justification. With *De la Sagesse*, one can see the author initiate the typical modern attitude of negative suspicion against any belief whose sole justification is habit, authority, or tradition.[48]

We can understand now why the value of *isostheneia* (equipollence) is no longer central in this new perspective. By challenging the cautious advice of "general indifference," Charron firmly sticks to the rational basis of skepticism. He declares that "the search for truth" is the real and explicit aim of any skeptical investigation, and that its instrument ("*outil*") is reason. Human dignity is now based on using reason in order to "judge" about everything:

> The real prerogative of humans, their proper and more natural practice, their worthier activity, is that of judging. Why are human beings that speak, reason, and intend? Because they have perhaps the mind to build castles in the air or to fill to bursting with silliness and trifles like most people? Whoever had eyes for darkness? Certainly, humans are made to see, to understand, to judge all things to such a point that they are called the guardian, supervisor, controller of nature, world, God's works. To deprive them of this right is the same as willing them not to be anymore humans but beasts.

This recourse to the "prerogative of judging" is all the more crucial, because humans are immerged in that condition of uncertainty that the skeptical crisis has revealed. This situation of doubt demands from the sage the most attentive practice of rational discernment:

> Since there is only one truth among a thousand lies and of a thousand opinions about the same subject, only one is the true one, why shouldn't I investigate which one is best, the most reasonable, good, useful, and convenient using reason? Is it possible that among so many laws, habits, beliefs, different and opposite customs, only those we practice are the good ones?

Charron's conclusion is univocal: "The sage will judge everything. Nothing will escape him that he lays on the table and on the scale to investigate."[49]

It is essential to notice that this kind of "judging" is neither dogmatic nor strictly Pyrrhonian. Concerning the former, Charron explains that the sage does not "judge" in the sense of "establishing, affirming, determining," but in the sense of a continuous quest that never ends ("to examine, evaluate, weigh and balance reasons on one side and on the other, and thus search for truth"). With regard to the latter, he admits that the sage can opine (contrary to the Pyrrhonian injunction against neo-Academics), even though "without any determination, decision, affirmation." This is a kind of having "weak" opinions, which brings Charron nearer to Academic probabilism.[50] In so doing, he inaugurates the typical modern *koinē* of skepticism, which is some sort of eclecticism in the art of doubting. Blending together both trends (Pyrrhonism and neo-Academicism), Charron goes much further than Montaigne, who had rather stressed the novelty of the former and rejected probabilism of the latter. The author of *De la Sagesse* opens the way to considering both traditions as belonging nearly to the same body of philosophy, because the theory and praxis of *epokhé* are largely common to these two skeptical trends. Among the neo-Academic features that are recognizable in *De la Sagesse*, there are (1) the emphasis on the ideal of intellectual integrity, which comes from Cicero; (2) the overt profession of Socratic ignorance, as the device of the wise man is the famous Socratic motto "*je ne sais*" ("I do not know"); (3) the stable intellectual and moral position ascribed to the sage, instead of the Pyrrhonian irresolution mostly practiced by Montaigne; (4) the leaning toward a more favorable assessment of probability, according to Carneades's doctrine; and (5) the emphasis put on the value of self-knowledge, which develops into a true philosophical anthropology, without losing all of its skeptical approach. In reality, this knowledge starting from the self and ending with humanity is basically aimed at fighting dogmatic presumption and ignorance. Charron's skeptical anthropology is mainly a doctrine about the moral and epistemic limits of anyone's self.[51]

Like Montaigne before him, Charron refrains from transforming this right to criticism into public expression. In fact, the author of *Sagesse* restrains the emancipation deriving from the skeptical doubt to "spirits well born, strong and vigorous" ("*esprits bien nez, forts et vigoureux*"). He is well aware of the necessity of institutions, and is pessimistic about the ability of self-determination of common people and of all "not too well talented men." With this split between internal and external, private and public, the reasons of the ego and the constraints induced from praxis and power, the space of modern skepticism becomes an internal region, whereas action is confined to an exterior conformism. This is a radical split that authorizes the extreme of simulation and dissimulation.

This is also a major innovation in comparison to the ancient Greek sources that ignored this dramatic divide. Faced with the constraints imposed by external requirements, the modern Charronian sage feels free to recur to pretense and reticence in order to keep his own interiority safe and free. Nevertheless, and despite this apparent conformism, the modern skeptic becomes the bearer of a new sense of intellectual emancipation that was unknown to the ancients. Actually, the relationship between the sage and society has completely changed with respect to antiquity. The moderns are confronted with schools of thought, political and religious bodies of beliefs that are organized, and compelling systems requiring from the subject the performance of precise behaviors, but also requiring him to take sides in the course of the ideological struggles that tear the commonwealth, the church, and their institutions. Thus, the modern skeptic has to experience the strength and the coercion of ideological systems that were almost unknown to antiquity.

In order to face this new and troubling situation, the modern skeptical sage, according to Charron, should adopt a cold and detached conception of acting that is tightly connected to the distinction between the external and the internal. The skeptic must give to the institutions just the minimum of his external commitment, the minimum that is absolutely necessary for the needs of *praxis* and for the functioning of the social body. By contrast, he ought to preserve for the internal and individual sphere his intimate beliefs. The modern skeptic can feel free to criticize in his internal sphere the common wisdom and the values of the city, which were not cast into doubt by the ancient skeptic. The main target of the criticism of the latter were not so much the beliefs and the rites of the city, but only the moral and political theories elaborated by the dogmatic philosophers. Among the moderns, instead, the basis for assent to the received wisdom is implicitly compromised, even though the dissent is not overly expressed. At least the skeptic's choices become more and more pragmatic, independent of any partisan dogmatism. Furthermore, the sage denounces the "mystical ground" (i.e. mysterious and arbitrary) of laws and customs: "laws and customs keep their credit not because they are right and good, but for being laws and customs: this is the ground of their authority."[52] As is well known, the sentence echoes a famous claim of Montaigne and expresses skepticism regarding the official motivations that are given to support ethics and politics.[53] This is another effect of the new protagonist pose that Charron's sage takes, at least in his internal sphere, toward the whole body of public opinions. Whereas the ancient Pyrrhonists usually stressed the perfect conformity of the skeptic to the customs and beliefs that make up not only ordinary life but also political life, Charron emphasizes the complete autonomy of the sage, who conceives himself as an independent subject, even while seeking refuge in the sphere of private consciousness.[54]

More than in Montaigne, scholars have spotted in Charron one of the best candidates for the forerunner of certain Cartesian themes.[55] In particular, the *cogito* would be nothing but a metaphysical subversion of the *epokhé*, because Descartes's principle has a more general significance than the self-awareness in Charron, which mainly has a moral import. These considerations regarding the importance of late Renaissance skepticism for the birth of modern skepticism can be extended to other figures, like Sanches and Campanella. Today it is no longer possible to agree with Gilson's negative judgment about "philosophers of the Renaissance that were engaged in doubting" and would have failed because of their basic empiricism.[56] In fact, their skeptical positions brought new themes that went far beyond the empiricist culture in with they nonetheless grew up. As we have already seen, whereas Stoicism supported the autonomy of the sage in Charron, the debate about certainty of the internal states of the mind deeply influenced Sanches.

On both these sides, late Renaissance skepticism recovered a strong theory of subjectivity that was lacking in ancient Pyrrhonism, as well as in Montaigne, and contributed to the birth of the modern subject with Descartes. Campanella, as we are going to see, represented self-criticism of late Renaissance empiricism, and at the same time the project of using skepticism to reform metaphysics.

4. Reappraisal and overcoming of skepticism before Descartes: Campanella's *Metaphysica*

Tommaso Campanella (1568–1639) dedicated the whole of the first book of his *Metaphysica* to the investigation of skeptical doubts. In the Inquisition's prison, he wrote and rewrote this work many times. The first time was in 1602, the second in 1611, the third in 1624, and only in 1638 was the work finally published in its entirety in Paris.[57] It is without question one of the seventeenth century's largest studies of the problem of skepticism, although neither the publication of Sextus Empiricus's works nor Pyrrhonism's renaissance seems to have influenced it. Basically, Campanella's text is a critical analysis of Aristotelian epistemology and the demonstration that Aristotelian theory leads to a skeptical impasse because it is based on an idea of scientific knowledge completely unattainable by human beings. The central topic in fact is "the question of whether science exists and how limited and partial it is to an extent realized only by those who know that they do not know anything perfectly and completely."[58] Campanella spends a large part of the beginning of the first book of *Metaphysica* reviewing the fourteen *dubitationes* of the skeptics. This may be the first and the largest compilation written in the seventeenth century about skepticism. Actually, it was composed prior to Gassendi's and Mersenne's analogous writings and prior to Descartes's *Discourse on Method*.

In the first book, we find many of the "commonplaces" of ancient and modern skepticism. The senses grasp only the "surface," the "accidents" or the "effects," whereas the "internal parts," the "substance" and the "essence" ("*quidditas*") are unknown to us.[59] Even with these qualifications, the principle that one knows differently depending on how one is affected holds. What we know, we only know "according to our measure, and not to that of being and truth." For an author that made the senses primary and the test of any kind of knowledge,[60] these arguments were especially tricky and would be further developed in a sort of *crescendo* in the third *dubitatio*, where it is shown that skeptics do not consider even partial and superficial knowledge to be really possible. A thorough investigation of the five senses and the usual examination of perceptual illusions (the bent oar, the glass cut into facets, the apparent movement of the land but not of the boat, etc.) lead him to conclude that "no sense perceives things as they are but only in the way it is affected."[61] Furthermore, because sensations are at the basis of the entire edifice of knowledge, each of us would end up having "his own philosophy depending on the perception of his senses."[62]

Concerning philosophical sources, it is interesting to note that Campanella pays particular attention to those sections of Plato's *Thaetetus* in which the problematic and uncertain character of sensible knowledge is emphasized for reasons of principle having to do with the phenomenal character of perception. Even the perfect knowledge will only be able to keep track of sensible appearances.[63] Before penetrating the soul of the sentient being, "images" are "deformed by the contamination of the organ and the medium through which we perceive"; thus, sensible appearances will always be "inexact and adulterated."[64]

Even though it differed from Platonism, Aristotelian epistemology also was grounded on universal and permanent elements as "the species and the whole, rather than on matter and the single parts." The obvious consequence for the Stagirite was that "science is about species" rather than individual entities, which are involved in aporias Heraclitus, Socrates, and Protagoras brought to light. To this abstractionist point of view, Campanella reacts together with the skeptics and as Sanches already did. He confirms the need for a kind of knowledge able to attain concrete and individual things, denouncing the Aristotelian science of universals: "it is not wisdom but a confused, common and external one, which does not attain the inside of the thing."[65] To the model of knowledge by abstraction,[66] the second *dubitatio* already opposes – to declare it unattainable – a kind of total knowledge that cannot be reduced to "the common things, without peculiarities," on the example of God's knowledge that attains all the "peculiarities."[67] Campanella thinks in conformity with the theses of a radical nominalism according to which "universals exist only in particulars."[68] But precisely for this reason, the reevaluation of the particular would have led to the skeptical heavy blow because in that hypothesis "in order to know something, which is impossible, we would need to know infinite things and the perishable ones too, which is impossible."[69]

Some of Campanella's passages deal with topics that were already present in Sextus and Cicero, but will have new life thanks to the Cartesian revival in the *Discours de la méthode*. These passages discuss doubting whether one can distinguish between dreaming and being awake, the comparison between being a sage and being mad, as well as the more dramatic comparison, taken from Euripides, between life and death.[70] Being amplified and deriving from the principle that knowledge is a "passive state" ("*passio*"), these topics have a particular meaning in the *Metaphysica*. In fact, according to Campanella's skeptics, a real transmutation, almost an alienation, would occur in knowledge: "the knower is transformed into what is known; therefore to know is tantamount to an alienation." Cleverly, the skeptics emphasize how this alienation is close to madness. In this way, the skeptics cast the shadow of a radical doubt on the constitutive structure of human knowledge. The eleventh, twelfth, and thirteenth *dubitationes* return to the topic of human "folly" ("delirium"). One can derive "that we sleep, are delirious, and are in the death's region"[71] from many signs. First, from the philosophical "deliriums,"[72] but also from the equally crazy contrasts that one can notice regarding doctrines of "principles," including the foundations of morality and religion. The pages Campanella devotes to this especially insidious topic offer a beautiful synthesis of the arguments produced by moral skepticism (including Carneades's discourse already recalled in the "Prolegomena" to Grotius's *De jure belli et pacis*). At the same time, the colorful annotations about the differences among religions and their odd beliefs seem to repeat famous arrows from libertines or from the first deists, who derived a lesson of disenchanted skepticism from theological disputes. To cite the questions Campanella put on the table,

> All believe they will save themselves with their own religion and that all the rest of the world will be condemned. This seems disgraceful of a God. Therefore either God likes all religions or does not care about these things. Also in this case delirium unfurls the sails.[73]

Other important metaphors flow from Campanella's platonic readings. The soul imprisoned in the body, locked up "like a craftsman in a dark cave,"[74] comes from the famous myth of Plato's *Republic* ("as if we were placed in a cave so that we might see only the shadows of the things that flow"). From the "Platonists and Augustine," he draws the conclusion that "all things we see are images of other real things that exist in the angelic world and in God."[75] All these themes are spread across Campanella's pages and clearly reveal something of the metaphysical background that underlies the skeptical *dubitationes*. The frequent references to the Socratic model, with its wisdom of "knowing that one knows nothing," also serve to emphasize his Platonic background. On the other hand, Campanella is not inclined to taking up the antiskeptical strategy that Socrates adopted in the *Thaetetus*. Rather, the author of the *Metaphysica* opposes the Platonic pretense of attaining the "stable and intelligible kind" using only "reason,"[76] and the primordial character of sense which even reason cannot ignore or give up: "No sane person will say that science begins from intellect. Science begins from sense; therefore one needs to philosophize from sense as the Creator of things established."[77] Whereas skepticism has good arguments to stress the boundaries and uncertainties of sense, Platonism is wrong in going further and denying that sensible knowledge is necessary, because there is no doubt that "the intellect does not know anything if not starting from sense."[78]

To paraphrase the core of Campanella's remarks, one could say that the problem of sensible knowledge must find an answer and that it cannot be ignored or simply dissolved by appealing to ideas. This is the first major skeptical lesson to be found in the *Metaphysica*. In this sense, although they clearly rely on some Platonic suggestions, Campanella's *dubitationes* have on the whole a strong anti-Platonic aim.

The author of the *Metaphysica*, on the other hand, finds his way out of this condition of uncertainty through his metaphysical and psychological program. It is a program that takes from sensationalism the awareness of the fact that any entity, and in particular the soul – *spiritus, sapit* – has "taste" and "knowledge" of itself. As the tendency to self-preservation is innate in any being, so there must exist in us a latent faculty ("*notitia indita et abdita*"; "innate and hidden notice") through which we can grasp ourselves in the interior: "The being of the soul, as of any other subject that knows, is self-knowledge."[79]

If we examine the final part of book I, which contains detailed replies to all the *dubitationes*, it is clear that, in each reply, Campanella takes hold of various aspects of skepticism, correcting and integrating them into a positive and constructive view of human knowledge: a limited view of course, but it is one that is effective and adequate within its own framework. Right from his first reply, Campanella stresses both the partiality and the operative nature of knowledge: human science is "nothing compared to what has been said about it, but it is something in itself providing enough for human life." Even when it is limited to sensible things, we still may go a little further and say that knowledge at least grasps the essence ("*quidditas*") "for those things that of themselves move sense, such as heat, cold, light."[80]

The Third *Dubitatio* encapsulates another important truth: if it is true that everyone suffers in different ways, nevertheless we may be equally certain that the interaction between objects and sentient being is a reality. Whereas the skeptic stubbornly insists on an impossible objectivity or neutrality, the metaphysician, on the contrary, comes to terms with reality:

> it is useless to blame the senses for the fact that they do not perceive except thus. Nor can the nature of things be blamed for the fact that they are not capable of presenting themselves only thus to those senses.[81]

This "science suited to us" will certainly be "slight and weak" ("*modica et exilis*"), as the author repeatedly stresses. Nevertheless, it will make available a precise confirmation of reality. If we determine the factors that cause appearance to vary, even that variation will lend itself to verification and correction, following the principle that "although the senses err in many things, they nevertheless correct themselves through other sensations."[82]

Ernst Cassirer, who recognized in Campanella's work "a complete theory of skepticism," believed skepticism to be the result of the "conflict" between sensualist Telesian gnoseology and Platonic-Augustinian metaphysics, centered around the doctrine of ideas and of primalities of being, which integrates and corrects the former without ever achieving a true fusion with it.[83] However, Campanella's antiskeptical strategy is more complex and innovative. Against Telesio, he clarifies that sensation is not only passion but "*passionis perception*" ("perception of passion"), and that therefore sensation is accompanied by an element of self-consciousness ("an act that judges about the perceived passion"), because sensation grasps the other only through a change of oneself. The step from here to regaining the basic certainty of his own existence was short. Campanella did it following the path of Augustine and his famous warning: "I cannot be wrong indeed, if I do not exist. In actual fact, what is nothing neither really knows nor is mistaken." Actually, regarding Augustine's inference, Campanella is interested much more in its metaphysical implication than in its epistemological importance, which on the contrary will be emphasized in Descartes's *Discours*. To underlie the self certainty is the reflection about the primalities of being, because the knowledge that implies itself naturally extends also to the power and willing:

> we can do things, know, and want other things because we can, know, and want ourselves . . . and it never happens that an entity Can, Knows, and Wants something, except because it can, knows, and wants itself to be affected by something.[84]

As the tendency to self-preservation is innate in any being, so it must exist in us a latent awareness ("innate and hidden notice") through which we can grasp ourselves in the interior: "The being of the soul, as of any other subject that knows, is self-knowledge."[85]

A contemporary of Gassendi and Mersenne, Campanella was not a "mitigated or constructive skeptic," in the *scientific* meaning that Popkin gave this qualification, despite his appeal to be satisfied with a "slight and weak science." In fact, the author of *Universalis philosophia* wants to go far beyond the horizons of physics and natural phenomena to include in knowledge the area of metaphysics. The "metaphysical" skeptic of his *dubitationes* does indeed correct Platonism with sensualism, but at the same time he opens the door to a new kind of research that heads in another, more ambitious direction: he moves from sensible data to derive judgments, and then reaches "reason" ("*ratio*") that, as he warns, "is not an abstract being" ("*non est ens rationis*").[86] This new perspective paves the way to the properly metaphysical parts of *Universalis philosophia*, with its theory of the three primalities of being (power, wisdom, love; "*pon, sin, mor*").

With his doubts, the skeptic brings to light truths that the simple empiricist ignores: he questions sensible knowledge and so helps reach a higher level of certainty, which is provided by metaphysical reason. In fact, skepticism is for Campanella only a preliminary, but necessary, stage to be overcome in his reform of metaphysics that would also include sciences, which are still in need of a deeper philosophical foundation than that that could be afforded simply by "mitigated skepticism."

Unfortunately, Descartes refused to read Campanella's *Universalis philosophia*, which Mersenne proposed to send him right after its publication in 1638. He already knew

De sensu rerum et magia and was negatively struck by the sensualism contained in this work. However, if he had read *Metaphysica*, he probably would have changed his negative opinion about Campanella's philosophy and possibly he would have appreciated both the foundational role assigned to skepticism and the attempt to overcome it by a new kind of metaphysics, even if Descartes's metaphysics was to be more scientific and definitely dualistic.[87] Anyway, Campanella's major work had a posterity, albeit a hidden one, in France, right in the Cartesian inner circle. In fact, Mersenne read *Metaphysica* when it was still in manuscript; what is worse, he plagiarized some significant portions of the first book on skepticism. Campanella sent the manuscript of his work to Mersenne in 1624, just a year before the publication of *La Vérité*. Because it was impossible to publish the *Metaphysica* in Italy because of the Inquisition's sentence, Mersenne promised Campanella that he would publish an edition in France. In reality, he did not keep his promise (the book was published only in 1638, when Campanella went to Paris, and apparently without any intervention from Mersenne), but the friar borrowed large sections from the *Metaphysica* in order to build his own character of the "Pyrrhonian" in *La Vérité des sciences*. Thanks to this plagiarism, we can claim that Campanella really influenced the French skeptical revival immediately prior to Descartes.

5. Skepticism and theory of science: the different approach of Mersenne and Gassendi

La vérité des sciences: Contre les Septiques ou Pyrrhoniens (1625) by Marin Mersenne (1588–1648) has been considered one of the most important documents before Descartes in the debate about skepticism in France. To Campanella's arguments Mersenne added the skeptical objections that he had got by reading Sextus Empiricus, namely the ten tropes of Enesidemus and "the five tropes of most recent skeptics," which were about dialectical procedures of proof. Not even the *pars construens* of Mersenne's work can be said to be more original. Whereas Campanella's solution to the problems of skepticism opened the path to a "new metaphysics," Mersenne's replies are much less ambitious, only reaching a compromise between the needs of the new mechanical sciences and a pragmatic version of Aristotelian theory about the most favorable conditions for acquiring empirical and intellectual knowledge. In truth, the solution of pursuing a science just fitted to the needs of human life, if not to the truth of the substance, had been already formulated in book I of Campanella's *Metaphysica*, on the basis of practical needs of everyday reality stressed by skeptics.

On the other hand, some antiskeptical moves made by Mersenne seem to prefigure similar arguments in Descartes's epistemology, with whom the friar was very familiar. In particular, to exorcize the danger of an infinite regress in the search for the criterion, the author of *La Vérité* appeals to a sort of intellectual evidence that is self-justifying: "the reason or the intellect is similar to the ruler which is used to judge of the straight line and of itself." The argument is clearly indicated in the margin by the caption "natural light of the intellect" that recalls the Cartesian "natural light."[88] Mersenne also returned to the theme of the self-confutation of doubt, although he did not venture so far as to formulate the principle of the *cogito*. He instead deploys against skeptics the old objection of being in contradiction. Thus, after having evoked the "natural desire" that pushes one "to know something true" and having shown the discontent of the spirit involved in the *epokhē* ("a suspension that the entire nature seems to go against"), the "Christian philosopher" (one of the three characters of *La Vérité des sciences* beside the

"Pyrrhonian" and the alchemist) claims that an exit strategy from Pyrrhonism could result in hurling back against the skeptics their own doubts. In so doing, he outlines the self-confirming figure of reflexivity, which cancels the effects of skepticism:

> if you doubt of it, I ask you whether you really know that you doubt of it; if you know it, confess then that you know something and therefore that you do not doubt of everything. If you doubt also of doubting, I will force you to admit the infinite progress that you yourself deny. Thus, no matter where you look, you must confess that there is something true and therefore you must say goodbye forever to your Pyrrhonism.[89]

This "good-bye" notwithstanding, in Mersenne's view the best confutation of skepticism is represented instead by the mathematical truths developed in books II, III, and IV of *La Vérité des sciences*. The effective acquisition of certainty, in mathematics as in mechanics, is the strongest argument for the impossibility of total doubt. In any event, the efficacy of science follows, in Mersenne's works, awareness that this knowledge is always within the boundaries of phenomena and it is not about "essences" or "substances." In *Les questions théologiques*, the author states,

> [W]e only see the external, the surface of nature, without being able to penetrate inside it. We will never be able to acquire any science beside that relative to its exterior effects, without being able to find their reason and to know how they function.[90]

Outside this theological context, in the *Questions inouyes*, Mersenne clarifies that the epistemological boundary is different depending on whether one deals with physics or mathematics. In the first case (Mersenne refers to Galileo's law of falling bodies), the principle that there is no science – in the classic sense of *episteme* – holds at least "according to the laws and notions of science given by Aristotle and the other philosophers," because the Aristotelian criterion implies that "one must prove to be impossible for a cause not to have the proposed effect." In this way, Mersenne establishes an equivalence between "*scire per causas*" ("to know through causes") and the demonstration of impossibility of the contrary effect. The conclusion cannot be but the impossibility to achieve this kind of science in the domain of physics. The case of mathematics seems very different. It is true that this science can reach its conclusions with absolute certainty. However, it is constrained to proceed in a conditional way because its objects must be postulated and one cannot prove their real existence.[91]

Split between factual knowledge that is empirically certain, but lacking rational justification, on the one hand, and the impeccable apodictical structure of mathematics, which lacks real referents, on the other, Mersenne still adheres to the practical importance and pragmatic efficacy of knowledge. Although "the fundamental differences between individuals and species" are unknown to us and the intellect cannot understand "the nature of substance," however – the "Christian philosopher" claims – "this knowledge is enough to guide our actions," because "to have science of something it is enough to know its effects, its operations and its use, through which we distinguish it from any other individual or distinguish its species from other species."[92]

Pierre Gassendi's (1592–1655) reflections also left their mark upon the search for a "middle path" between skepticism and dogmatism. However, one must distinguish two different stages of his thinking regarding this problem. The *Exercitationes paradoxicae adversus Aristoteleos* are representative of the first phase. Gassendi wrote them between 1620 and 1624, but published only the first book while he was alive. He may have been frightened of the uproar created by his attacks on Aristotle, as this was the time in which the Sorbonne confirmed the truth of Scholastic metaphysics as the foundations of knowledge against anti-Aristotelian and atomistic theses supported by Jean Bitaud, Etienne de Claves, and Antoine Villon. In reality, Gassendi's *Exercitationes* addressed much less Aristotle himself than the Aristotelians blamed for having suppressed *libertas philosophandi*. Gassendi actually inherits from the humanistic and Renaissance polemic against dogmatism. Combining in an eclectic way different skeptical trends, he praises not only the ancient "Academic and Pyrrhonian *akatalêpsia*"[93] but also the modern protagonists of the anti-Scholastic movement, like Erasmus, Vives, Pierre de la Ramée, Gianfrancesco Pico (Giovanni Pico's nephew and author of *Examen vanitatis doctrinae gentium*, the first comprehensive work based on Sextus Empiricus's writings), and Charron.[94] Sanches is not mentioned, but he was most probably another important reference, even if Gassendi contrasted with his excessive epistemological pessimism.

It is not a case that one of the culminating chapters of the work (*Exercitationes*, II, vi) re-echoes the title of Sanches's polemic, adding, however, a qualification that better depicts the author's goal: "That there is no science and mostly the Aristotelian one." Gassendi does not attack science or knowledge in general, like Sanches, but specifically the Aristotelian notion of science. Therefore, the fulcrum of the argument is an attempt to refute the deductive and syllogistic paradigm of demonstration. Gassendi, however, is more careful than his Renaissance predecessors to distinguish between two different conceptions of science.

On one conception science is "certain and evident knowledge of the object, gained through the notion of necessary cause or in a demonstrative way." As such, this conception suffers from the same aporias about universals, definitions, and the syllogistic method already illustrated by Sanches, Campanella, and Mersenne. The other conception, more modest and adequate to the real possibilities of empirical knowledge, only proposes "an experimental and appearance-relative notion" of science. Thus, it is an investigation programmatically grounded in experience, giving up the pretense of grasping the essences or natures of objects in themselves.[95]

If after an accurate analysis the results of the first kind of science come to be fruitless, the second model appears to Gassendi viable and more useful. It is more apt to satisfy the "natural desire" of humans to know. Its limitations should not lead to "desperation":

> Those that wish to philosophize do not fall into desperation because they see that the great philosophers recognize that one cannot know anything: I refer to the deep nature of things, about which they profess themselves ignorant, while from another point of view they know a lot, because of the knowable things, almost nothing is hidden to them.[96]

The conclusion is that only the alternative model of knowledge seems to Gassendi viable and useful. "It is possible to know only how one thing appears to one or another," as the title of the sixth section says.[97] Gassendi, however, does not hesitate to call this kind of phenomenal knowledge "science,"[98] stressing the fact that appearances can be collected, compared, and corrected by each other, according to the "historical" (i.e. descriptive) model of observational astronomy. Empirical knowledge can be cumulative and progressive, even while giving up searching for causes and therefore without any pretense of demonstration. Of course, this "science" is bound by the epistemological weak status of *phaenomena*, up to the point – as he says – that it is almost impossible to distinguish between "science" and "opinion."[99] Apparently, this word "opinion" is taken from the neo-Academic vocabulary, especially Carneades's. This latter, contrasting the Stoics, had granted the wise to hold "opinions," as long as they are not dogmatically assumed as a criterion of truth; the skeptic's "opinions" are always open to revision at any moment. Giving into opinions, the wise should not give up being aware of their fallibility. However, whereas Carneades gave the "persuasive opinion" (*pithanon*), mainly the practical function of discerning between *doxai* in ordinary life, Gassendi raises instead the epistemic aspect of "opinion," matching, as he often does, this latter and "science" or "knowledge." Furthermore, drawing on Cicero that had translated *pithanon* as *probabile* or *verisimile*, he claims that, due to the weakness of human intellect, we can state only "probable conjectures"[100] All this clears the way to a more ratiocinative status of *opinio*, or to a practice of rational inference starting from the sensible appearances and developing into "opinions." This is just an inchoative prospective, because the author of *Exercitationes* does not expound the complex and detailed theory of degrees of probability that Carneades had formulated and Sextus had reported. Anyway, science cannot reach beyond the domain of sensible appearances, not even through inferences made by the intellect.[101]

Thus, in this first work, skepticism becomes a powerful offensive instrument in the dispute against the abstract metaphysics of Scholastics. However, skepticism also risks jeopardizing some relevant aspects of the new science, challenging the status of mathematics, hypotheses, generalizations, and other theoretical ingredients of physical laws. In short, all the elements of the scientific enterprise that cannot be directly verified exceed – from the perspective of *Exercitationes* – the limit of phenomena, within which fruitful and effective knowledge is only possible. This narrow and almost exclusively empiricist approach was too high a price to pay for a supporter of the new science, such as Gassendi.

It will be mainly in *Syntagma philosophicum*, the work published only posthumously in 1659, but largely anticipated in *Animadversiones in decimum librum Diogenis Laertii* (1649), that the philosopher-scientist will go back again to the issue of skepticism and outline a path leading beyond this minimal solution of "scientia apparentialis." Unlike ancient skeptics (especially Sextus Empiricus) who drew a sharp line between "things concealed by nature" and "things momentarily concealed," Gassendi shows that a shrewd and critically controlled use of rational inference allows us to move in a legitimate way from phenomena to *adela* (unknown things), in both meanings of this word (things concealed either by nature or only momentarily). Reflection about the logical instrument of the "sign" (*semeion*)[102] is central here. Sextus Empiricus constrained the range of valid inference only to "commemorative" inference. These signs only keep track of the causal association of events that are in principle observable, although one of them is not actually observed yet; for instance, smoke is a sign of the temporarily unseen fire. Departing from Sextus, Gassendi does not hesitate to claim the veridicality and utility of so-called indicative signs too. This different kind of sign postulates the existence of causes or conditions that cannot be directly experienced apart from observable effects. For instance, sweat lets us infer the existence of invisible pores, and by observable actions we realize the existence of the soul, although neither pores nor the soul can ever be seen. After all, for Gassendi, Epicurean atomic theory, on which *Syntagma philosophicum* is founded, represents the result of a rational inference to the truth "that lies behind the surface" of things. Based on empirical data, that is the phenomena of the physical world, motion, and so on, the existence of realities such as the atom and empty space, which cannot be empirically verified, are hypothesized. In this way, the possibility arises of going beyond the "surface" or the "bark of things" and grasping a deeper level than that of phenomenal qualities. However, Gassendi continues to be critical of the pretense of reaching the "latent nature, the essence and almost the source, the root, the principle and the cause of these properties and specific functions." This is because the philosopher, in addition to his empiricist caution, continues to maintain a skeptical suspicion about theoretical constructions presented in terms of the definition of essences and substances.[103]

Far from falling under the categories already attacked in the *Exercitationes paradoxicae* in the tearing down of science in the Aristotelian sense, the atomistic schema instead becomes a hypothesis apt to "save phenomena," a rational excogitation to account for the perceived appearances. Therefore, skeptical objections do not prevent the transition from the description to explanation as long as the explanation stays within the boundaries of a hypothesis that is provisory and revisable in light of experience. One can understand, then, how Gassendi's initial agnosticism toward reality in itself tends to change into various forms of probabilism advocated by academic skeptics. The modality of knowing accessible to us has the probable characteristic of hypothetical knowledge rather than the necessary characteristic of apodictic knowledge. The more modest quest for verisimilitude replaces the pretense of attaining a definitive truth; the reasonable certainty that is always open to further verification takes the place of the illusion of evidence.

6. Descartes and the modern skeptics: how to reply to "skeptics that go beyond any boundary of doubt"

In the last few years, an increasing number of essays have compared the work of René Descartes (1596–1650) with major currents in ancient skepticism and, in particular, with Pyrrhonism.[104] However remarkable the results of this work have been from an analytical point of view, these investigations ultimately have disregarded philosophical information Descartes himself offered to frame correctly the context within which his attitude toward skepticism must be situated.

In fact, the first question to address should be about Descartes's actual knowledge and use of the texts of ancient skepticism. In this regard, investigation of Descartes's writings yields rather disappointing results, because his explicit references to his sources are quite generic. In most cases, he talks in general of "skeptics," more rarely of "Academics," and in a few other places of "Pyrrhonians."[105] It is striking that on these themes Diogenes Laertius is never explicitly mentioned – although it is easy to recognize his influence in the accusations of *apraxia* ("impossibility to act" according to their principles) addressed to the skeptics. Neither Sextus Empiricus nor Plutarch are quoted. Galen, too, receives little mention. In fact, although Descartes cites him regarding medical matters, the philosopher never refers to his *De optimo genere docendi*, which was printed in Erasmus's Latin translation as an appendix both to *Hypotyposes* edited by Estienne and Hervet's edition of *Adversus mathematicos*, as an important source for the knowledge of skepticism. Apparently, the Academic trend had a better fortune, but this is due especially to the refutation of Augustine and to the role played there by an argument – "*si fallor, sum*" – that could be considered an ancestor of *cogito*, as contemporaries like Arnauld immediately noted and indicated to Descartes.

Even where Descartes makes a more explicit acknowledgment of his debt to the texts of ancient skeptics, the avowal has an ambivalent meaning. Replying to the *Second Objections*, the author of the *Meditations* (1641) confesses to having read "many writings of Academics and Skeptics" (these latter being, presumably, Pyrrhonian skeptics), but he immediately adds to have done this without any enthusiasm, almost as an official duty: "and though it was not without distaste that I reheated this cabbage, still, I could not avoid devoting one whole Meditation to it."[106] Discussing with the Jesuit Bourdin (the author of *VII Objections*) and Hobbes (the author of *III Objections*), Descartes emphasizes only the "therapeutic" aim of his work on the skeptics. As Galen and Hippocrates had first to investigate diseases in order to be able to cure them, so Descartes thinks himself to have been the first and only philosopher to really refute skeptical arguments, precisely because he studied them carefully.[107] Therefore, although Descartes seems not to care for philological knowledge of ancient texts, their themes, that is the "reasons to doubt," nonetheless seem to him extremely important because the truths discovered in *Meditations* will be "safe and tested" only inasmuch as they turn to be unshakable by doubts, not even those that can be devised by going beyond ancient sources, doubts which Descartes will call "metaphysical doubts."[108]

The text of the dispute with Bourdin is especially useful for bringing to light the fact that Descartes's important confrontation is much more with "moderns," and "libertines" in particular, than with ancient "Pyrrhonists." Within the long discussion with the Jesuit, Descartes goes back to the *vexata quaestio* of what is a good use of skepticism. Wishing to reply to the accusation of having pushed the doubt too far, the philosopher develops more accurately his famous comparison between the search for the foundations of knowledge and the digging of a foundation for a building. Whereas Bourdin thought the pretense of finding a foundation "firmer" than anything else to be exaggerated and suggested keeping to a basis as firm as "the ground that sustains us," the author of *Meditations* instead claims that the firmness of the foundations must be proportional to the importance of the building one aims to erect on them. This is the development of a comparison between different kinds of knowledge already pointed out in the *Discours de la méthode* (1636): "*la terre mouvante et le sable*" ("moving soil and sand"), on the one hand, and "*le roc ou l'argile*" ("rock or clay"), on the other hand, respectively stand for only probable knowledge and indubitable certainty.[109] In the *Replies* to Bourdin, however, the gradation takes the place of a contraposition. If sand is considered enough to hold a hut, nothing less than rock is enough for erecting a tower. Outside the metaphor, it would be "absolutely false" ("*falsissimum*") if, in the enterprise of laying the "foundations of philosophy," the doubt – which has the duty of digging until it hits rock – stopped before "supreme certainty," that is before the firmest certainty that one can get.[110]

Compared to previous works, new elements emerge from the passage that follows:

> Neither must we think that the sect of the sceptics is long extinct. It flourishes today as much as ever, and nearly all who think that they have some ability beyond that of the rest of mankind, finding nothing that satisfies them in the common Philosophy, and seeing no other truth, take refuge in Scepticism.[111]

Here, in fact, Descartes looks at skepticism as something alive in the present day rather than only the reflex of ancient philosophies or an inheritance of previous generations, as in the passage quoted previously.[112] It is, he writes, a philosophical movement still at work, more vigorous and fashionable than ever. Therefore, it is not a theoretical fiction, something like a *jeu d'esprit*, but it has an existence that is independent, outside Descartes's system, and even a threatening one. In this polemic with Bourdin, skepticism appears as an actual challenge to which one has to reply convincingly, lest all metaphysical enterprises will fail. Therefore, it is not a "sect abolished today" to which one might refer with mockery and invective, as Bourdin and many others usually do, as if they were dealing with "desperate and incurable men" not deserving serious consideration.

Due to the actuality of the problem, most of the debate with Bourdin is about the strategy to adopt toward these skeptics, who are as alive as ever. Whereas the Jesuit is afraid that following them too far on the terrain of doubt will eventually show the impossibility of replying, Descartes instead thinks that any arbitrary stop in the dynamics of doubt is a sign of weakness and represents an implicit admission of defeat: "what will he answer to the skeptics that go beyond any boundary of doubt?"[113] According to him, refutation will only come after amplifying the doubt to its maximum level. This much is the methodological kernel of the debate.[114] Yet the philosophical background is also important, and Descartes's replies are revelatory of it. In fact, the point of view of the skeptics touches the metaphysical cornerstones of his system, because the "mistakes" of the "sect" which is "in fashion more than it ever was" are – Descartes claims – "the mistakes of the skeptical atheists" ("*Atheorum scepticorum errores*"). "Today's skeptics" call for "the demonstration of God's existence and the immortality of souls." The description that follows is even more precise:

> all those that today are modern skeptics [*omnes hodierni Sceptici*] do not doubt in practice [*in praxi*] that they have a head, that two plus three equals five, and other similar things. They only say that they treat them as true things because they appear so. But they do not believe them with certainty because they are not entirely convinced of them by certain and invincible reasons. And since it does not similarly appear to them that God exists and the human mind is immortal, they do not think they should deal with them as if they were real, not even in the praxis, unless it is previously proven by more certain reasons than any for which all the appearances are accepted.[115]

As is well known, the position of ancient skeptics regarding religious matters was quite different; neither Pyrrhonians nor Academics were really atheists. On the contrary, they introduced themselves as those that, in accordance with the rule of the *ou mallon* ("no more this than that") and the attitude of the *epokhé*, suspended judgment between the thesis that God and gods exist and that they do not exist. Furthermore, far from being impious, ancient skeptics complied with the religious traditions of their *polis*, according to the pragmatic criterion of following laws and customs without dogmatizing, neither positively nor negatively. Pyrrho was a very respected minister of his *polis* Elis; in Cicero's *De natura deorum*, the skeptic Cotta was assigned the role of an important officer of the atheists religion.

Descartes's picture is not even suitable to the skeptics of the previous generation. Although they were skeptics, neither Montaigne nor Charron ever directly questioned God's existence. At most, they pointed out the limits of any dogmatic representation of divinity and the serious harms done when religion degenerates into superstition. In their texts, the contrast (*diaphonia*) between philosophical opinions was an argument for the fact that divinity was not understandable, rather than an argument for its nonexistence. Furthermore, according to Montaigne, Pyrrhonian traditionalism should have acted as a barrier to the temptation of atheism, which he saw emerging from the rebellion of the Reformation rather than from the free inquiry of skeptics.

In conclusion, Descartes's reference to "the skeptics of today" ("*sceptici hodierni*") must be put in quite a different context, neither of the ancients nor of Montaigne or Charron. We believe he mainly referred to François de La Mothe Le Vayer (1588–1672), the most "Pyrrhonian" of the four "*libertins érudits*" (besides him, Guy Patin, Pierre Gassendi, and Gabriel Naudé) René Pintard wrote about in his already classical study.[116]

7. Descartes, La Mothe Le Vayer, and the French Libertines

In 1630, Le Vayer published the *Quatre Dialogues faits à l'imitation des anciens*, under the pseudonym Orasius Tubero and with the false date of 1506. This was followed in the next year by the *Cinq autres Dialogues du mesme autheur*.[117] In these dialogues, which renew the Socratic and Lucianic classic model in the light of the influential Erasmian precedent of *Colloquia*, Le Vayer illustrates with subtle irony the contradictory theses that the "dogmatic" philosophies produced in physics, ethics, and logic. Then, amplifying the potentialities already inherent in the tenth trope of Enesidemus, he compares the habits, customs, beliefs, and moral and political systems of different peoples and times to yield a lesson in skepticism. Thus, he argues for the conclusion that reason is not able to discover incontrovertible truths. Far from being the product of an anti-intellectualist nihilism, Le Vayer's inquiry is the result of an intellectual curiosity open to the new scene of seventeenth century knowledge. Against this background, the skeptical doubts have a new and original substantial character. The sense of the vastness of nature is constantly contrasted with the narrowness of perspectives typical both of commonsense and of old-fashioned philosophies misled by the cult of authority. "Dogmatism" gives expression to "the arrogance and recklessness of human spirit"; dogmatists usually think "as if, nature," Le Vayer continues, "had no other range than that of human knowledge" or "as if its range of action had no limits other than those of the intellectual sphere" that is delimited by the "conventional wisdom."[118] In his effort to break the stifling circle of traditions and philosophical sects, Le Vayer does not hesitate to evoke Lucretius's and Brunus's scandalous hypothesis of the immense plurality of worlds or to project the perspective of infinity onto the dimension of time.[119]

Therefore, according to him, an intellectual revolution must follow the astronomical revolution produced by the Copernican system – to which the author often refers – and the "discoveries of new worlds" like the Americas. This intellectual revolution should be able to reorient the point of view of humans according to the coordinates of the new cosmos. As Le Vayer says in recalling a telling formula of Francis Bacon, human knowledge must be harmonized "with the orbits of the mind concentric to the universe."[120] The skeptic of *Dialogues* is exactly the one who is able to "travel far and make spiritual navigations" leading him, as a new "Columbus in this ocean of the spirit," to discover "Americas and new worlds, full of riches and wonders unknown so far."[121]

Among the new features of this "modern" skepticism, the criticism of religion is one of the most interesting for our purpose. In Le Vayer's whole work one can find many assertions ascribable to "Christian Pyrrhonism" (the apologetic use that Gianfrancesco Pico inaugurated).[122] However, especially in these juvenile *Dialogues*, we see at work the "pagan," more or less explicitly antireligious attitude that skepticism came to assume in the libertine circle in the Paris of the 1630s. In particular, the dialogue *De la philosophie sceptique* contains an important revival of the notion of phenomenon, for which Le Vayer looks directly at the works of Sextus Empiricus. On the one hand, the skeptic adapts himself to the phenomenon or appearance, considered as passive affection within the domain of ordinary life – "life without dogmas." Yet, on the other hand, the skeptic rejects the attempts of dogmatics to go beyond the phenomenon toward what is "concealed by nature." With the dialogue *De la divinité* this notion of phenomenon is directly applied to the body of religious facts. Le Vayer explains that as astronomical systems, formulating their "hypotheses," try to "save the phenomena" of celestial movements, religions do the same regarding the facts of human moral life:

> All that we apprehend about Gods and religions is nothing but what the sharpest humans conceive to be most reasonable in their speaking of moral, economic and civil life, as to explain the phenomena of customs, actions and thoughts of common mortals, and to give them rules for a safe life devoid of any absurdity as much as is possible.

In fact, the dialogue concludes, "a religion so conceived is nothing but a particular system that accounts for moral phenomena [*phainomenes morales*] and all the appearances of our doubtful Ethics."[123]

As one can see, the position of skeptics regarding God and in general the *adela* ("hidden," "nonevident things") is described in the exact way that Descartes, replying to Bourdin, will outline it. Religious beliefs concern only appearances for which we have no compelling demonstrations, but just "phenomena." To this skeptical explanation, Le Vayer adds the famous libertine narrative according to which lawgivers are the real "inventors" of religions. Only the formal and explicit avowal of atheism (more precisely, in Descartes's words, "skeptical atheism") is missing. Paradoxically, it will be in his most official work, written under the impulse of Richelieu to rebut the Jansenist doctrine of "false virtues" of the pagans, rather than in his semiclandestine *Dialogues*, that Le Vayer will make explicit this point of his discourse. In *La vertu des payens* (1641), he assigns to most thinkers of antiquity a sort of "implicit faith," so that "the doors of salvation" are open to almost all of them. Only Pyrrho and Diogenes the Cynic are explicitly condemned to "hell." He acknowledges that Pyrrhonism in fact would have led philosophers to a "skeptic" rather than a "dogmatic" form of atheism:

> Beside the fact that Pyrrhonians never decided to recognize a first cause that made them disdain the idolatry of their time [the allusion to Aristotle's first mover is clear] it is certain that they believe in something about divine nature but only suspending their judgment, and they do not profess anything of what we said except for doubting and in order to conform to laws and customs of their time and country.

It follows that, quite independently of their ostentatiously displayed traditionalism, "Pyrrho's salvation and the salvation of all his disciples that held the same views on divinity" is ultimately "desperate," as Le Vayer claims.[124] This is the same kind of atheism that Descartes will condemn as among the "mistakes" of "skeptics of his time." Considering only phenomena and refusing to admit entities one can neither verify nor prove (such as God and the soul), libertines offered an original application of the skeptical attitude to religious matters. They went beyond the conformist caution of their ancient predecessors and at the same time escaped the accusation of returning to a kind of, even negative, dogmatism.

Against this background, Descartes's metaphysical choice and his effort to neutralize skepticism only after having brought it to its extreme consequences may be better understood. Holding against the cautious Bourdin that it is urgent to follow "those skeptics that doubt without limitations," Descartes does a very complex maneuver. In the "quarrel of ancient and modern skeptics," he takes sides with the moderns, because they left behind the prudent equidistance of ancient *isostheneia* and suspension of judgment. On the other hand, in outlining his own precept, "one should doubt of everything," the author of *Meditations* seems to approve the decision of modern libertines to go far beyond the limits accepted both by the ancients and Montaigne or Charron, but at the same time he accuses the contemporary skeptics of being unfaithful to their own program. Namely, according to Descartes, they did not really doubt without limitation, instead hey stopped at the simple level of the phenomena, and therefore did not succeed in reaching the supreme certainty that the true philosopher is looking for.

In fact, we witness a double radicalization of doubt, in comparison with ancient Pyrrhonism: the libertine and the Cartesian one. The former hits the metaphysical level (God, the soul) but only to include it in the range of phenomena or contradictory *noumena*; the latter casts in doubt even the appearances and clears the way to the overcoming of doubt, yet only after pushing it to the extreme consequences. The impact of Descartes's attitude is remarkable. Sentences like those relative to the existence of the body and the world, as sentences relative to appearances, were not investigated by either ancient or modern skeptics but were accepted on the modality of the Pyrrhonian formula *phainetai* ("it seems"). Instead, they become in the Cartesian philosophy subject to a further level of doubting, the doubt that Descartes calls "metaphysical." In this respect, Descartes's distinction between "practice of life" and "contemplation of truth" is only apparently similar and coextensive with the distinction found in the writings of Le Vayer between two different kinds of "criterion": the pragmatic and the theoretical one. At the beginning, for Descartes, only practice justifies beliefs, such as the belief in the existence of the external world, which are then put into doubt by the philosophical meditation. According to Sextus and Le Vayer, on the one hand, we have the criterion that "judges in the last instance and gives certainty to the objects of knowledge" and that is rejected by Pyrrhonists as dogmatic; on the other hand, instead, they follow the criterion "that conforms itself to the verisimilitudes without establishing anything, called *to phainomenon*, that is that which appears: this is the criterion of skepticism."[125] This doctrine corresponded exactly to the distinction, which Descartes described, made by the "skeptics of today" between the domain of "praxis" – the ordinary life for which phenomena in the nondogmatic sense of the word are enough – and the domain of the "demonstrations," with the corollary that the latter, unlike the former, are shown to be inadequate and subject to doubting rather than certainty. First, one should note that in Le Vayer's discourse, life "without dogmas" was open to the likely and probable, with a mixture of Pyrrhonian and Academic themes, whereas a feature of Descartes's more radical attitude concerns the rejection of probability, which is assimilated, at least theoretically, to falsity because it lacks infallible certainty. Second, Le Vayer's discourse was coherent with "modern" and especially French interpretations of ancient skepticism. Although accentuating the dichotomy between appearances and reality, the libertine assigned empirical connotations to the former, stressing its positive, although limited, contents.

On the contrary, behind the pragmatic defense of the certainties of ordinary life (such as that which one can find in the "provisional moral" of *Discours*), we find in Descartes's *Meditations* a program of deepening doubt, which is much more radical than the ancient and modern non-Cartesian skeptics, such as Le Vayer, would have accepted. In the *Meditations*, the doubt does not stop where ordinary life begins, like it happens in Pyrrhonian skepticism. It ultimately involves the domain of phenomena as well, including everything that appears, not only to the senses but also to the mind, such as mathematical truths. For a theory that has the ambitious aim of indubitability, the skeptical distinction between two kinds of criteria does not hold, except for the very limited aims of practical behavior, without involvement in any kind of "weak" belief. Because of this, Descartes's philosophical doubt stretches to subjects that an ancient skeptic would have considered exempt from investigation, such as the empirical evidence of one's own body and the existence of the external world.

Before deepening this peculiarity, let us follow the skeptical route of Descartes, referring to the *Discours* and the *Meditations*. The experience of "disparity," in the customs of people as in the opinions of philosophers, is for Descartes,[126] as for the "new Pyrrhonians," an initial source of doubt. Then, all the reasons that fed the skeptical tradition, from Sextus to Montaigne, to Charron and the erudite libertines, return. These include mistakes of the senses, about which Descartes advises "not to entirely trust those that have once deceived us"; the ascertainment that some "fall into errors and paralogisms" even about "the simplest argument of geometry"; and the illusions of dreaming and the doubt that there are not "definitive clues nor enough certain signs to distinguish neatly between dreaming and being awake."[127]

The next step in the method of doubt illustrates well the peculiarities of Descartes's antiskeptical strategy. It involves an amplification of the doubt (of a "hyperbolic" and "metaphysical" character) that was unknown to the ancient tradition. This amplification represents the radicalization of uncertainty until one finds the evidence afforded by *cogito ergo sum*. The doubt that not only the ideas coming from the senses but also those coming from the intellect are deceiving fictions finds support in the hypothesis that at the origin of our being there is

> a God who can do anything and by whom I have been created and produced as I am. Now, who can certify that such a God did not do things in such a way that there is no earth, no sky, no extended body, and however I perceive all these things which seem to exist exactly as I see them?

This argument projects uncertainty also onto mathematical truths that do not depend on experience: "it might be that He willed that I deceive myself any time I add two and three, or any time I enumerate the sides of a square."[128]

In this Cartesian version, the doubt in fact concerns the origin of the human subject and the nature of the cause he comes from. The arguments coming from sense deceptions, hallucinations of lunatics, and oneiric illusions left untouched mathematical truths and general truths, such as the independent existence of the simplest and most universal things. Although features of these things might be molded according to the liberty of one's imagination, their elementary constituents are not "fictitious." On the contrary, the hypothesis of the so-called deceiving God – an omnipotent divinity that constantly brings us into error or that created us in a way that we always are wrong – pushes the skeptical doubt much further. Besides projecting a halo of uncertainty on the reliability of our mathematical reasoning, this hypothesis questions the metaphysical cornerstones of the doctrine of common sense, that is that our ideas at the end come from the experience of external objects whose existence is independent of us. In his hyperbolic hypothesis – Descartes conjectures – the less fictitious ideas might also be put into our mind by an omnipotent divinity, even if no material reality corresponds to them. In the last part of the First Meditation, as an extreme support to doubt, the representation of a "God that can do anything" will be replaced by the figure of an "evil genius, no less clever and deceptive than he is powerful. This evil genius employed all his industry to deceive me." The final result is the complete derealization of the physical world: the sky, the earth, and "all external things" will be reduced, on this hypothesis, to "illusions and deceptions." In the same way, the subject himself will be deprived of any exterior material feature, because even the body ends up being in the sphere of deception.[129]

In the so-called *Conversation With Burman*, Descartes is aware of the fact that his strategy is peculiar compared to the classic antecedents.

> Here – the writer of the record refers to the passage in which the existence of the evil genius is postulated – the author makes humans as uncertain as he can, pushing them to the maximum doubt. Therefore, he does not only propose the usual doubts of skeptics, but he proposes all possible doubts, so as to destroy doubt at its root.[130]

Therefore Descartes's doubt is not a closed-off one, like the doubt of skeptics who "doubt only in order to doubt" and refuse to recognize evidence when they see it, just "to be rooted in their heresy of universal doubt, but only nominally, and sometimes because of a voluntary choice and on purpose." For Descartes, these are the examples to avoid. He wants to dismantle a mannered skepticism that fails to arrive at any positive result precisely because it lacks method and engagement. Notice, however, that according to the philosopher the shallowness of certain skepticism is caused by the fact that it does not really take seriously its aims of *skepsis* (i.e. of investigation) and *zetesis* (research). If skeptics had maintained their doubt long enough and with the proper intention, then precisely because of this they would have reached some certain truths. It is this reason that allows the philosopher to go back to skeptical arguments and delve into them: "Although Pyrrhonians did not get any certainty at the end of their doubting, this does not mean that it is impossible to succeed."[131]

Therefore, one must say that books such as *Meditations* contributed decisively not only to provide a solution but also to outline in original terms the theme of skepticism and thereby to the production of a new image for it in subsequent periods. In Descartes, we are presented with a turning point in the millenary history of this philosophical movement.

8. The Cartesian standard of modern skepticism

Starting from some important remarks of M. F. Burnyeat, these Cartesian peculiarities have been combined into what has been defined as the "standard modern verdict" on skepticism. According to this "verdict", the fundamentals points of modern skepticism are (1) the raising of the question about the existence of the external world, with the consequent crisis of direct realism and the dualistic implications that derived from this move; (2) the subjective conception of knowledge and truth, connected with the theory of ideas as internal objects of knowledge, distinct from – and, in later interpretations, opposite to – external reality; and (3) the asserted impossibility to practice the skeptical attitude and the need to confine it to theoretical questions, thus "isolating" it from the practices of ordinary life.[132]

At first, we will assess these three points and then add a fourth one, concerning (4) the different connotation that the state of *epokhé* takes on in Descartes and in the moderns, being a condition of doubt and instability rather than of imperturbability and peace of mind. In relation to each of these points of the "verdict," our investigation brings both confirmations and changes or additions, especially in connection with the modern and above all libertine sources we had pointed out. Here, we will try to summarize this complex interplay of continuities and discontinuities between Descartes, his ancient sources, and his modern interlocutors.

Regarding point (1), the *issue of realism*, Burnyeat and those that followed him held that ancient skeptics never questioned the realistic presupposition. They only would have criticized the validity of "criteria" the "dogmatic" philosophies proposed in different times, without questioning the assumption of the objective existence of the world. Nowadays, this view of ancient skepticism has been questioned, and according to some interpreters, ancient skepticism is credited with the doubting of external existence.[133] We cannot resolve the question concerning Greek sources here. On the other hand, it is correct, with Burnyeat, to describe modern skepticism as much more advanced in the progress of derealization of the world. The "crescendo" of Descartes's *Meditations*, from the hypothesis of the generalized dream to the conjecture of a deceiving God, all the way to the hyperbolic doubt produced by the hypothesis of the evil genius, is enough to establish that the realist assumption comes to a crisis. The realist assumption leaves in its place a thesis of the total and – in this phase – indomitable subjectivity of *all* our knowledge, including the supposed existence of a world outside the subject and including in this illusory domain the reality of the subject's own body. In contesting the "severity" of this doubt, Gassendi continued to support a "classic" and pre-Cartesian skeptical framework. He wrote against the author of the *Meditations* that it seems "that not only do you doubt that some ideas come from things outside us, but also that you doubt the existence of things outside us." In this regard, Gassendi objected that it is impossible "seriously to doubt the existence of these things" and to ignore that "they are something outside us." Therefore, it would be better, he concludes, "to treat things seriously and in good faith and to become accustomed to talking of things as they are."[134] It should also be noted that Montaigne and Sanches had already doubted that we could ascertain the existence of a correspondence between phenomenon and external object. Thus, they opened the door to a more radical skepticism, although they did not make explicit its antirealistic import. In this respect, the comparison with modern skepticism rather than ancient skepticism allows us to focus more closely on the features of Cartesian *epokhé* and to see how it is continuous with the reflections of its time about the extension of doubt. The Cartesian doubt is willing to impose a further and more radical turn to the phenomenalism of the "skeptics of today."

Regarding point (2), *internalism*, Descartes not only draws a clear line between "internal" and "external," between the domain of ideas and the world of material things outside, whose existence is not subject to immediate knowledge and depends on divine veracity. He includes in the external world, as susceptible to being revoked in the course of *epokhé*, even the thinking subject's own body. A new and more consistent conception of interiority derives from that. This conception is clearly distinct from the material world considered as entirely external. This is what is said, with vivid incisiveness, at the beginning of the Third Meditation, where the philosopher claims, "entertaining only myself and considering my inner sphere, I will attempt to make myself little by little more known and more familiar to myself."[135] No ancient skeptic ever went so far as to include the existence of his own body in the domain of subjective and possibly illusory phenomena. Although the discourse of Sextus Empiricus had some margin of ambiguity in relation to the "external" object, it should nonetheless be recognized that in works such as *Pyrrhoniae Hypotyposes* and *Adversus Mathematicos* the line of demarcation between the "internal" and the "external" does not go between minds and bodies but between the man and things "outside" him (*exothen*).[136] Hyperbolic doubt, internalism, the questioning of the existence of the external world, and dualism are instead tightly interwoven in Descartes's philosophy, whereas the less radical skepticism of his predecessors and contemporaries – like Gassendi – combined with a more traditional realistic thesis. Furthermore, one must emphasize that Cartesian dualism contains both the thesis that the mind can directly access its subjective states and a theory of ideas that in this way it is possible to develop without going "outside" the borders of the mind. This theory of ideas opens a domain of truths not at all dependent on experience and free of the existence of material objects. On the other hand, the presupposition of mental entities (ideas) as internal objects of knowledge will lead – once it is freed from the systematic concatenation of Cartesian metaphysics – to a representation of the cognitive process that ignores the correspondence with external objects. It will make the passage from cognition to external objects quite problematic, if not illegitimate and superfluous. This in fact will happen in the subsequent development of eighteenth century British empiricism – from Berkeley to Hume – and will lead to the setting up of that "veil of ideas," to be about to close around the subject. The subject will be the prisoner of his own representations, because access to a reality independent of ideas is forbidden to him. One should note however that the reference to the interiority of the subject has been previously advanced not only in the Augustinian line (which extends until Campanella) but also in Sanches's work, as we saw previously. Sanches clearly drew the distinction between "certainty" and "understanding," parallel to that between internal and external states. From a skeptical point of view, the distinction was close in tone to Cartesian reflections. Also, some of Montaigne's observations about "appearances" as "subject's passions," which therefore cannot be referred to the objectivity of an "external" thing, were along the same lines.

Point (3) of Cartesian innovation regards the way the philosopher rethinks the traditional accusation of *apraxia*, that is that it would be impossible to live in accordance with the skeptical doctrine. Descartes shows he trusts the ancient doxology which assigned to Pyrrho such a level of indifference that friends had to intervene to save him from dangers and precipices. It is also to avoid such inconvenience that Descartes accurately distinguished between "*usus vitae*" and "*contemplatio veritatis*." Doubting makes sense only from the second perspective, whereas in the practices of life one will adhere to commonsense beliefs, in accordance with those rules of the "provisional moral code" (*Discours de la méthode*) that recommend conformism and moderation and advise us to adhere to the probable, because, as Descartes explains, "when the matter is the conduct of life, it would be ridiculous not to trust one's senses."[137] It is important to emphasize that in addition to having consequences for the modern "fortune" of skepticism, from Gassendi to Hume, all the way to Moore and the present day, the Cartesian distinction is also responsible for a twofold transformation in the setup of the classical tradition.

Because it limits the *epokhē* attitude to theory, the Cartesian *distinguo* does not do justice to the concept of "life without dogmas." In Sextus's writings and also in Le Vayer's, this concept had a markedly practical value, acting as therapy and liberating one's life from the distorting power of beliefs. That doubt should be isolated from the domain of moral values (as is claimed by a precept of the "provisional moral code," which prescribes that we must follow customs and traditions) represents a considerable attenuation of skepticism. It is such that it deprives *skepsis* of its original "eversive" character.[138] Furthermore, apart from the issue of moral values, the discourse about "beliefs" is more complicated than it might seem, both on the ancient side and on the Cartesian side. On the first side, historians' opinions are divided between those who think that the *dogmata* rejected by Pyrrhonists are mainly the scientific ones and those about nonevident objects (M. Frede), and those (Annas, Burnyeat, and Fine) who hold that ancients' *epokhē* had a greater range, hitting all kind of beliefs. In addition, there is Barnes's proposals of distinguishing between the "rustic Pyrrhonist," who is more radical, and the "urbane Pyrrhonist," who is more moderate.[139] Regarding the other side of the issue, whether the "modern" doubt of the *Meditations* lets the beliefs of ordinary life subsist or not, Descartes scholars are similarly divided. With Burnyeat, some hold that the confinement of the doubt within the domain of "metaphysics," and the outlining of the "provisional moral code," means that Descartes's skepticism does not involve the nondogmatic beliefs of ordinary life. As the French philosopher said vividly in one passage, no one sane would doubt that his body and the world exist. Therefore, among the beliefs, the merely doxastic beliefs of the practical life would not be touched by the doubt of the *Meditations*. By the way, this is how the "*athei sceptici*" or "*sceptici hodierni*," which Descartes describes in the passage we looked at previously, read skeptical themes. Other scholars hold an opposite thesis. According to these latter, the fact that we need to protect the beliefs of ordinary life from the attack of the "metaphysical" doubt presupposed the idea that, when taken seriously, the authentic position of the skeptic is equivalent to a "no beliefs" view, whence the requirements of isolating the meditator's attitude from the *praxis*.

On this point, the reading we gave of the replies to Seventh Objections supports the second alternative, therefore goes *pro* G. Fine (though with different arguments from hers) and *contra* M. F. Burnyeat. In fact, our reading claims that Descartes felt it necessary to radicalize the doubt in order to give an answer to "modern," rather than to "ancient," skeptics. Descartes's skepticism is much less "isolated" than Descartes held. The "skeptics of today," discussed in the Seventh Replies, would not have accepted the First Meditation's conclusion of the doubt and the derealization of the world of ordinary experience. This is a peculiar and "radical" feature of skepticism in the new Cartesian version.

To make explicit the consequence of this radicalization to all beliefs, we would like to add point (4) to the "verdict" (doubt instead of *epokhē*). The consequence regards the different connotation that the state of *epokhē* assumes in Descartes. He calls the *epokhē* "suspension of judgment," accepting in this case Bourdin's terminology. For the ancients, the *epokhē* was directly connected to *ataraxia*, to the liberation from anxiety and therefore to a condition of interior confidence entirely opposite to the uncertainty and emotions that are characteristic of the life of the "dogmatic." By contrast, for moderns, especially with and after Descartes, it is a condition of doubt and uncertainty rather than apathy and imperturbability that embodies, from a psychological point of view, the situation of the skeptic. In the moral domain, skepticism is presented by the moderns as rejecting stable and firm determinations whereas, as Descartes pointed out many times, it is especially in the domain of praxis that perseverance and resoluteness concerning action are needed. In this way, as we saw previously, Descartes was rather the heir of Montaigne than of Sextus, interpreting skepticism as a condition of uneasiness as doubt replaces *epokhé* as its distinguishing feature; and he delivered his successors an image of skepticism very different from the one coming from more authentic and ancient historical coordinates.

Thus, an inversion was effected that had important consequences in the modern age. In Descartes, the idea of skepticism as practical wisdom *par excellence* declines. The attempt to elaborate skepticism in a coherent praxis is viewed as "eccentric" and nonsensical, if not banished as a preconceived fiction. As a matter of fact, the program of an entire "life without dogmas," that is as a durable stance, becomes an incomprehensible notion, because skepticism is recognized as having, at best, only a provisional and temporary legitimacy, just for the lapse of time when research has not attained its end yet.[140]

9. Debating on the "warrant" of natural beliefs: Malebranche, Arnauld, and Bayle

Whereas evidence (or certainty) and truth were dissociated in the skeptical dichotomy of appearance and reality, in the Cartesian metaphysics they are finally reconciled. However, it should be noted that this reconciliation had a high metaphysical and theological cost. It needed nothing less than the proof of the existence of God and His veracity. Merely relying on the criterion of truth (clarity and distinctness), Descartes did not have the instruments to claim as "true" what is supposed to be the cause of representations, that is the existence of things outside the *cogito*. Therefore, the entire Cartesian metaphysics, including the distinction between the soul and the body and the "rehabilitation" of sensible knowledge in the Sixth Meditation, is needed in order to really overcome skepticism. The evidence of the *cogito* alone is not enough. Although the *cogito* is an Archimedean point, it is limited to the awareness of the existence of the ego as and insofar as it is a thinking being.

Ultimately, Descartes's entire theory of knowledge depends on two factors: (1) a "*phenomenology*" and (2) a "*theodicy*," to use two terms now clear to us but still anachronistic relative to the time of Descartes. The first factor, what we call "*phenomenology*," aims to accurately distinguish in the actual content of the representation what is clear and distinct from what is obscure and confused. This distinction also enables us to separate the idea from the sensation, and the contribution of the intellect from that of the will – that is the perception of ideas from the judgment. More generally, in this way we become able to distinguish what belongs to the soul as *res cogitans* from what belongs to the body and functions not directly for the acquisition of knowledge but for the conservation of the body. Therefore, we have the means to separate the intellectual content of an idea from sensibility. The method Descartes practices consists in a form of "intellective" attention. This method makes evident what emerges at each level of analysis and distinguishes contributions and layers of meaning that are easy to confuse because they manifest themselves simultaneously.

Once this phenomenological analysis is done, the second factor, a rule of what we called "*theodicy*," applies to its results. Those things that we are inclined to believe without being able to resist and that we could not, even if we wished to, correct in any way, cannot be given to us by God, the author of our being, in such a way that we are systematically deceived by these beliefs without any possibility of discovering the illusion.

This warrant applies in the first place to clear and distinct ideas. Beginning with this principle, clear and distinct ideas are a source not only of certain but also true knowledge. On the contrary, the same principle does not immediately apply to the contents of sensibility as such. Actually, these contents can be purified by the intellect, which discovers the illusion separating what is clear from what, although useful for the *usus vitae*, is confused. Furthermore, this warrant applies to some of our natural inclinations – in particular, those we cannot resist. Among these, the tendency to believe in the external and real existence of material things as causes of our ideas is prominent. Descartes discusses this in the Sixth Meditation,[141] where many of the beliefs he doubted in the First Meditation are, although amended, restored. In particular, sensitive knowledge is gradually reinstated in its validity by the new course of reasoning. To begin, Descartes writes, "Now I do not think we should admit without prudence anything that seems to come from senses." The critique of sensible mistakes, like the role of the idea regarding the clear and distinct knowledge of bodies, is something already established. "However," he continues, "we should not doubt of everything."

More precisely, that bodies exist outside us, as the senses vouch, is true because it can be proved starting from God's veracity. In fact, if sensations did not really come from bodies, we would not have any way to realize it. Therefore, our mistake would be incorrigible, representing us a real deception. Yet God, of whom in the previous *Meditations* the existence and veracity has been proved, cannot deceive us. Then we are authorized to exclude that sensations are produced, not by bodies, but by our or other minds, even though this is theoretically possible. One must remember the hypothesis of the evil genius, who was supposed to send us false images of nonexistent bodies. They were real "dream delusions," Descartes said. That God does not deceive us is the solution to the immaterialistic doubt, which depended on the deceiving God. In the Third Meditation, the path of "adventitious ideas" was explored to see whether it would lead us to ascertain some reality other than that of our mind. At that time, however, the two arguments used by Descartes to rely on adventitious ideas – their involuntariness and the natural inclination to trust them – were taken not to be sufficient, because they were not assumed in conjunction with divine veracity.[142] Thus, the warrant given by the true God is crucial to overcoming skepticism and this is why the natural inclination, criticized in the Third Meditation, can then be restored in the Sixth Meditation. Without this metaphysical-theological support, skepticism, with all its doubts about the "external" existence of things, would still be a possible option and could not be excluded.

On the other hand, it is not the case that our senses tell us how bodies are made and which properties they really have. Realism, but not naïve realism, is true.[143] In particular, Descartes addresses the question of the objectivity of sensible qualities. He holds that the variations we are aware of in the sensations of sound, colors, heat, and so forth correspond to something really different in the bodies but that what is different is not as it appears in the sensible qualities. It is the famous distinction between primary qualities (extension, form, size), which correspond to objects, and secondary qualities (colors, smells, sounds, etc.) which do not "copy" as such the reality of bodies. Secondary qualities are a "teaching of nature," which is useful in orienting our behavior. However, the belief that bodies are exactly as their qualities describe them only derives from a "judgment." Therefore, according to the Cartesian theory of judgment, it comes from the will and very often from "the habit of judging in a thoughtless way." This habit, however, can be corrected. This is why the warrant of divine veracity does not apply to it: this tendency is not irresistible, and we can correct it through a proper use of our will.

It is regarding all these questions – that is questions about belief in the external existence of bodies and about the relationships between primary and secondary qualities – that Descartes's successors (especially Malebranche and Arnauld) asserted their criticisms. This continued until Pierre Bayle reestablished the conditions for the skeptical doubt. Actually, Bayle put the Cartesian theodicy, and therefore the metaphysical certainties that depended on this theodicy, into crisis.[144]

Pierre Bayle (1647–1706) presents a new kind of skepticism, which Popkin called "superskepticism"[145] to distinguish it from more limited and moderate forms of doubt. He started with the difficulties facing *a priori* notions of reason. The entry "Xenophanes" in the *Historical-Critical Dictionary* is exemplary. There Bayle traces the genealogy of skepticism back to Eleaticism, which is a hyperrationalist philosophical school. According to Bayle, in fact, Eleaticism contained the representation of the clearest and most distinct ideas of the intellect, carried out to their extreme consequences. Melissos, Parmenides, and Xenophanes grounded their systems on "*a priori* reasons" and on the notions of logical and metaphysical order. These notions require that nothing comes from nothing and that "the necessary Being is not limited." The consequence is that this latter is "infinite, omnipotent, and therefore one." The first of the two principles is common to all of ancient philosophy and looks like an indubitable truth of reason. The second principle is characteristic of modern philosophy and, as such, Christian theologians accept it. From there it is a short step to denying any becoming, change, or plurality of entities. The point of contact with skepticism is the Eleatic division of things between objects and phenomena, external things and things internal to consciousness, and the affirmation of the stability of the former and the illusion of the latter.[146] As is well known, this division will be at the core of what Hume will describe as the peculiarity of "modern philosophy." Hume rebukes modern philosophy because it leads to the most "eccentric skepticism" and "to the annihilation of external objects." This is because it is impossible, using the principles of modern philosophy, to move from simple perceptions to the "real, continuous, and independent existence of things."[147] We recognize in this statement the conclusive effect of the modern reappraisal of the skeptical distinction between appearance and reality as it is relaunched by Bayle.

For him, the "bad fall" into skepticism by Xenophanes is the paradigm result of metaphysical realism. The Eleatic, "since he cannot sustain the point that reason led him to, lets himself fall off of a precipice. He blames Reason which captured him in its nets and claims Reason is not able to understand anything."[148] More generally, Bayle's dialectic illustrates well the conflict between "skeptical reason" and "dogmatic reason." According to Hume, skeptical and dogmatic reason each foster and eventually annihilate one other. In other entries of the *Dictionary* ("Rimini," "Pyrrho," "Zeno Eleatic"), Bayle addresses the question of skepticism in the typical Cartesian context. He claims that Cartesianism implicitly suggests extending the status of phenomena or "appearances" from secondary qualities to primary qualities, and therefore brings new "advantages" to Pyrrhonists. In reality, Bayle notices that the only proof one could give of the real existence of bodies "must be derived from the fact that God would deceive me if he would impress in my soul the ideas I have of bodies without them existing in reality." Clearly, this is the Cartesian proof deduced from the veracity of God. However, immediately afterward Bayle qualifies it, adding that "this proof is very weak. It proves too much."[149] To understand this last judgment, we must examine the debate that took place immediately after Descartes among his followers.

Nicolas Malebranche (1638–1715) already attacked the demonstrative value of the Cartesian principle of God's veracity. In the *Sixième Eclaircissement* on the *Recherche de la vérité*, he holds "that it is very hard to prove the existence of bodies." The philosopher thought that Descartes did not really prove the existence of bodies. What we see could be a merely intelligible "world" without God being a "deceiver": "Why should we judge positively that outside us there is a material world similar to the intelligible world that we see?" For Malebranche only faith and reading of the Holy Writ let us ascertain that God created a world and that bodies really exist "outside us."[150] In contrast to Malebranche and more faithful to Cartesian orthodoxy, Antoine Arnauld (1612–94) replied to these remarks. He noticed that to doubt the existence of bodies and deny that this depends on the veracity of God may lead to "a very dangerous Pyrrhonism,"[151] which would shake from the foundations the reliability of all human knowledge.

In relation to this debate, Bayle's position is quite peculiar. Largely, he follows Malebranche's reasoning, but he takes advantage of it only to arrive at the same conclusion as Arnauld. At first, we must remark that the philosopher of Rotterdam does not seem interested in the proof "by faith" of external existence. Against this last attempt, he claims, with Arnauld, that it is a circular proof, because first one needs to believe in the existence of an external thing, in this case the biblical books and their contents, to derive thereby the warrant that there are external things. On the other hand, agreeing this time with Malebranche, Bayle holds that, although we have "a very strong inclination to believe that there are bodies," however strong, such an opinion "does not give us this result clearly or distinctly. We are inclined in this way only because of an impression." In this regard, as Malebranche remarked, "[i]f we consent, we do it freely since we can also not consent."[152] This tendency is not so irresistible that it be warranted by the veracious God, as Descartes believed.

Malebranche already claimed a sort of analogy between the impression leading us to believe in the existence of the body and that which pushes us to judge of sensible qualities, in particular the so-called secondary qualities. This analogy is strongly emphasized by Bayle's "Pyrrhonian abbot" in rem. B of the entry "Pyrrho" in the *Dictionary*:

> I ask: does God deceive human beings as regards colours? If He deceives them as regards colours, nothing prevents him from deceiving them with regard to extension. This second illusion is no less innocent or less compatible than the former with the most perfect Being. If he does not deceive them with regard to colours, this is because he does not inevitably lead them to say, *these colours exist outside my soul*, but only, *it seems to me that there are colours over there*. One can say the same about extension. God does not inevitably lead you to say, *it exists*, but only to judge that you feel it and that it *seems* that it exists. For a Cartesian it is no harder to suspend judgement about the existence of extension, than it is for a peasant not to affirm that the sun shines, that the snow is white, etc. Thus, if we deceive ourselves in asserting the existence of the extension, God is not the cause of the deception, since according to you He is not the cause of the mistakes of that peasant. Here are the advantages that these new philosophers can bring to Pyrrhonians.[153]

The link that Descartes had established between the divine warrant and the alleged existence of an invincible and incorrigible tendency of our mind is here resolved in favor of a phenomenalistic understanding of knowledge, which no longer implies the absolute or dogmatic positing of existence. One should note that in Bayle's text the approach is positively skeptic, whereas in Malebranche the existence of invincible tendencies that are metaphysically not warranted was presented in a more theological light. For him, the existence of this proclivity was "a consequence of the laws of the union of the soul and the body," especially after the "[original] sin which occasioned this union in the dependence" of the soul on the body.[154]

Bayle's point of view is very different. He is interested in emphasizing the total skeptical potential implicit in Malebranche's conclusion, independently of any theological assumption. This danger was already stressed by Arnauld in his reply to Malebranche. According to Arnauld, to weaken "the absolute evidence" of the principle of divine veracity by imposing on it conditions that take strength away from it is equivalent to "overturning divine faith and all human sciences." Besides introducing in the reasoning an unintelligible "quibble," to evoke the hypothesis of the sin which could have justified the existence of incorrigible erroneous tendencies is to make the principle of divine veracity "useless," because it becomes subject to too many restrictions. "The consequences of introducing these quibbles into the reasoning are so horrible and impious that it is even dangerous to emphasize them enough," wrote Arnauld.[155] In fact, the skeptical consequences that Bayle inferred from Malebranche's reasoning were good proof that Arnauld's fears were grounded.

Simon Foucher (1644–96) understood some of these consequences ahead of time. Going back to the neo-Academic tradition, he built his polemics against Malebranche noticing that one could apply with the same justification to primary qualities (extension and change, which are the constituents of the Cartesian *true* world) the subjective reduction applied to secondary qualities. Furthermore, Foucher developed a close criticism of the idea of "representation." He remarked that in Cartesian terms the direct object of the mind is not the thing itself but only the idea. This is "something which is known directly; that is, it is known for itself without any representation as intermediary."[156]

All these discussions came to a new astonishing result when Bayle placed them in the controversial entries background of his *Dictionary* about the question of moral badness and the theme of theodicy. Entries like "Pauliciens," "Manichéens," and "Marcionites" show clearly and at length the contradictions which our reason and, in particular, theology encounter when they try to reconcile the *a priori* notions of God and the *a posteriori* data about the existence of evil and sin. Once again, Bayle's positions take a hint from remarks of the "famous" Arnauld. Alarmed, like him, about the danger of "placing arbitrary constraints on the freedom of God,"[157] the philosopher of Rotterdam magnified at first the resources of the theme of divine omnipotence. He took away all those forms of "subjugation" to reason that had gained some importance with the rationalistic theology of Malebranche, Jaquelot, and Le Clerc. However, unlike Arnauld, Bayle argued in this way only to show that doing so eventually makes one run into the opposite danger. That is, one ends up with a conception of God according to which He "arbitrarily established good and bad." This omnipotent God, who is free from any constraint of reason, would be "the author of sin." In the same way, Bayle established a very close connection between the tradition of rigid predestinationism, according to which God is above any moral evaluation and the majority of humanity is condemned to damnation, on the one hand, and the Cartesian conception of God as free creator of the eternal truths, on the other hand. From a theological point of view, the Cartesian conception of God is, according to Bayle, the equivalent of the most rigid predestinationism. In both traditions, theological speculation opens the path to "the most extreme type of Pyrrhonism."[158] Furthermore, claiming that "God is not subject to the rules of human virtues" means, according to Bayle, facing insuperable difficulties. This is because "one no longer has the certainty that God's justice encourages Him to punish the bad and one is not able to confute those who claim that He is the author of sin."[159] In conclusion, for Bayle, moral skepticism was the consequence of theological themes developed by authors as different as Descartes, Arnauld, and Pierre Jurieu (1637–1713), who despite their diverse orientations nonetheless converged in placing God above all the categories of our moral judgments.[160]

In parallel, the skeptical abbot of the entry "Pyrrho" in Bayle's *Dictionnaire* showed from a speculative point of view that dogmatic theology, which contradicted reason with its beliefs about the Eucharist, the Incarnation, and the Trinity, offered "even more unsolvable arguments" than those of ancient skeptics. Verifying the systematic contradiction between rational evidence and religious dogmas, the abbot inferred a very general conclusion. This went quite beyond the topics of theology in a strict sense up to the point of casting doubt on the truth value of evidence:

> I conclude in the following way: if there were a sign that would allow us to know for sure the truth, such a sign would be the evidence. Yet evidence is not a sign of such a kind since it suits also false things.[161]

By dismissing the epistemological role and the metaphysical import of intellectual evidence, Bayle's discourse ideally finishes the Cartesian season. It shows how problematic and counterproductive it was to attempt to deduce from theological notions a warrant for human knowledge. This meant entering into the labyrinths of theodicy and possibly discovering that God could not be at the same time omnipotent and good, and therefore veracious. After having dismantled in this way the subtle structure of Cartesian metaphysics, human errors turned again to be what they were for the skeptics: the simple effect of the relativity or the constraints of human knowledge. As Popkin wrote, after Bayle skepticism could blossom anew on the earth "in the fallibility and failings of mere mortal earth-bound men,"[162] without invoking theological notions now considered embarrassing.[163]

10. Providential skepticism: limits and reality of knowledge in Locke and the British culture

The author of the *Dictionary* brought to its last consequences the skeptical implications of Cartesianism and made a contribution by fixing an image of "extreme" skepticism or Pyrrhonism that remained valid until Hume and beyond. On the contrary, John Locke (1632–1704) continued that form of "mitigated" or constructive skepticism which was inaugurated in France by Gassendi, an author who is mentioned in Locke's notes. This continuity is especially evident inasmuch as, in the case of knowledge of complex ideas of substance, the author of *An Essay Concerning Human Understanding* (1689) distinguishes the knowledge of sensitive qualities, to which we have access, from that of the real essences of things, which we cannot grasp. These latter are "only a Supposition of *an unknown support* of qualities that are capable of producing simple *Ideas* in us."[164] Usually, they are ideas of secondary qualities (sounds, flavors, colors, etc.) which are not in the objects in the same way that we know them. They are rather "powers" able to produce in us determinate sensations. In general, our idea of substance is "the confused *Idea of something* to which they [the simple ideas] belong, and in which they subsist."[165] This complex idea is necessary; however, Locke warns, it is basically the projection of a subjective need that lacks objective correspondence in the experience of things:

> yet because we cannot conceive, how they [the ideas] should subsist alone, nor one in another, we suppose them existing in, and supported by some common subject; which Support we denote by the name Substance, though it be certain, we have no clear, or distinct Idea of that thing we suppose a Support.[166]

The nature of the mind also poses difficult skeptical problems. In this regard, Locke suggests the famous hypothesis that the mind can think or better that God can "super-add to it another Substance with a Faculty of Thinking."[167] As such, the hypothesis cannot be totally discharged because we do not know what constitutes the substance of matter and of the mind respectively. It is better, then, to abandon speculation about essences and focus instead on the knowledge of observable qualities. In the chapter "On the Extension of Human Knowledge" (*Essay*, IV, iii), which is fundamental with regard to the question we are interested in, Locke, after having distinguished three grades of knowledge (intuitive, by proof, and by senses),[168] focuses on the knowledge of the "coexistence" of ideas: "in this consists the greatest and most material part of our Knowledge concerning Substances."[169] However, he must admit how limited our knowledge is in that regard.

Certainly, the author of the *Essay* shares the corpuscular hypothesis about the composition of matter. If not precisely the atomistic theory that Gassendi outlined, Locke's theory is a similar doctrine that is less ontologically committed.[170] Locke holds that the secondary qualities of substances depend ultimately "upon the primary Qualities of their minute and insensible parts; or if not upon them, upon something yet more remote from our Comprehension." Not knowing the "ground" of the qualities, it is impossible for us to "know which have a necessary union or inconsistency one with another."[171] Furthermore, "there is no discoverable connection between any *secondary Quality, and those primary Qualities* that it depends on."[172]

According to Locke a "useful and *experimental* Philosophy *in physical Things*"[173] is possible and desirable. However, it should limit itself to keep track of "a constant and regular connexion, in the ordinary course of Things."[174] It is impossible, instead, to have a real "scientific" philosophy because we lack "perfect and adequate ideas" even about the bodies closest to our experience. In sum, Locke follows the "corpuscularian hypothesis" because he thinks that this hypothesis cannot be substituted by another "which will afford us a fuller and clearer discovery of the necessary Connexion, and *Co-existence*, of the Powers, which are observed united in several sorts of them [bodies]."[175] However, he recognizes that this hypothesis does not go beyond the boundary of probability and that "the major probability is not certainty." In fact, we do not know "the real constitution of the minute Parts, on which their Qualities do depend; nor, if we did know them, could we discover any necessary *connexion* between them, and any of the *secondary Qualities*."[176] The corpuscular hypothesis about the structure of bodies, no matter how reasonable it is, is a conjecture one can assert only in terms of major probability.[177]

The idea of substance, to the extent that the human intellect can grasp it, coincides with the idea of a collection of observable qualities that compose the object, although we are not able to grasp the intrinsic link that connects them and explains the coexistence of the observable qualities.[178] Our knowledge only extends to "nominal essences" and does not grasp what Locke calls "real essences." To attain only nominal essences is to reach a combination of qualities that allow us to classify things under a certain species. To grasp the real essence instead would entail knowing the intrinsic constitution or real structure of things. However, this, as we saw, is impossible.[179]

Skepticism especially concerns the limits of science and affirms that ignorance exceeds knowledge. To some extent then the experimental philosopher is also a "skeptic." This kind of skepticism is quite different from the absolute skepticism proposed by Descartes in the First Meditation and that Bayle proposed as "Pyrrhonism." Regarding "the real existence" of things, Locke distinguishes between intuitive knowledge of one's own existence, demonstrative knowledge of the existence of God, and "merely sensitive" knowledge of other things.[180] About the last kind of knowledge, the British philosopher is very far from sharing "Pyrrhonian" doubts. In the *Essay*, the real existence of things can be considered certain as there are no reasonable grounds to doubt of it. Locke writes, "I think nobody can, in earnest, be so skeptical as to be uncertain of the existence of those things which he sees and feels." Perceiving a real object is very different from imagining it. Furthermore, whoever doubts the real existence of those things and pushes this doubting so far could not discuss with an interlocutor because he would have to doubt the existence of that interlocutor. Namely, he could not argue for his skepticism.[181] For Locke, the total doubt cannot be expressed, unless it contradicts itself.

The situation for mathematics and morality is profoundly different from that regarding the real knowledge of substances. In the *Essay*, mathematics and morality rise to the role of demonstrative sciences. The complex ideas they deal with are "archetypical ideas," which are created by the mind. These ideas therefore do not need to refer to an external reality as a copy does to the original.[182] As the mathematician considers the truths and the properties of a figure "only as they are in an *Idea* in his own Mind,"[183] so morality "is as capable of real Certainty as Mathematicks." This is because the complex ideas of "mixed modes" (e.g. the moral ideas) are produced by us without any pretense of conformity with external reality:

> Our moral Ideas, as well as mathematical, being Archetypes themselves, and so adequate, and complete Ideas, all the Agreement, or Disagreement, which we shall find in them, will produce real Knowledge, as well as in mathematical Figures.[184]

Therefore, it is not possible to be skeptical about morality because the relations between the ideas that compose its "mixed modes" are perfectly intelligible and exhaust their content.

To conclude on this point, at least with regard to physics and metaphysics, Locke's skepticism is more rigorous than that of Gassendi, from whom Locke took many ideas including the corpuscular hypothesis. Unlike the author of the *Syntagma*, Locke does not attempt to delineate a "scientific" theory of matter, for which he thinks there were not enough epistemological instruments and observable data. His corpuscular hypothesis is a rough schema, as compared to the more detailed atomism of Gassendi. However, Locke is persuaded of the "regularities" of the universe. In this regard, he maintains the validity of the cause-effect relationship, and in this sense, his limited skepticism is quite different from Hume's more radical one. This latter will question the order of the universe and make of it a subjective projection of beliefs and habits. The "regularity" of the universe is much firmer in Locke than in his Scottish successor, which is also evident in the *Essay*'s frequent references to the idea of the organizing power of God as "Wise Architect." God has arranged things with an "arbitrary will," Locke says.

However, He has done so with a providential design that favors human beings. God himself decided the degree of conformity, for instance, between secondary and primary qualities, consequently limiting our power of knowledge in a way that could also be useful and convenient for our life in the world. He judged a macroscopic rather than a microscopic vision of nature to be better for our lives; then He considered that we should have a greater knowledge of secondary rather than primary qualities. In fact, the simple ideas have that extent and degree of conformity that, according to God, is more apt to us: as such, He guarantees them. The simple ideas

> represent to us Things under those appearances which they are fitted to produce in us: whereby we are enabled to distinguish the sorts of particular Substances, to discern the states they are in, and so to take them for our Necessities, and apply them to our Uses.

Therefore, there is a regular and unchanging "correspondence" between the idea (e.g. the idea of being white) and the power, unknown to us, that produces it. In addition, an idea of a secondary quality "has all the real conformity it can, or ought to have, with Things without us."[185]

Despite all of this providentialism, Locke certainly felt the dramatic problem of the seventeenth century skepticism and formulated it in the clearest way with the following question:

> Our Knowledge therefore is real, only so far as there is a conformity between our Ideas and the reality of Things. But what shall be here the Criterion? How shall the Mind, when it perceives nothing but its own Ideas, know that they agree with Things themselves?[186]

However, at the end, Locke's answer to this problem is a recourse to the idea of divine providence that in its turn explains world regulation. Actually, divine providence guarantees that "the *certainty* of Things existing *in rerum naturâ*," when we have evidence of them from the senses, "is not only *as great* as our frame can attain to, but *as our Condition needs*."[187] As for Descartes, for Locke, too, we have God as a "guarantee." However, in Locke's case, the guarantee is in quite different terms. Instead of grounding the validity of a metaphysical comprehension of reality, Lockean providence only functions as a principle of accommodating knowledge to our pragmatic needs within the world. Our faculties respond "not to the full extent of Being, nor to a perfect, clear, comprehensive Knowledge of things free from all doubt and scruple," as Descartes claimed after having introduced the true and veracious God, "but to the preservation of us, in whom they [the faculties] are." At the end of Locke's long journey through the provinces of skepticism, the positions are in a way inverted compared to Descartes's point of view. Not full evidence but only "limited" knowledge is divinely "warranted." Although it might seem paradoxical to a Cartesian, for a Lockean some degree of reasonable or mitigated skepticism is the result of the divine action itself. We should not mind asking for more than this, "beyond which we have non concernment, either of Knowledge or Being." In fact, Locke claims that

> [s]uch an assurance of the Existence of Things without us, is sufficient to direct us in attaining the Good and avoiding the Evil, which is the important concernment we have of being made acquainted with them [things].[188]

In providing a remedy from the disastrous outcomes of excessive Cartesian speculative pretenses, at the same time this wise and cautious attitude saves Locke from the extreme skepticism to which Bayle had been led by the disappointment toward Descartes's metaphysics.

Locke's reflections happened in the English context, which was always impervious to Descartes's metaphysical research. In that context, people made a distinction between the kind of "excessive" doubts raised by Sextus and the French philosophers, on the one hand, and those reasonable doubts dealt with by probable information, experience, and common sense, on the other. Francis Bacon (1561–1626) is without any doubt at the origin of this positive and limiting tradition. According to him, the abandonment of the dogmatic ambitions, with their unreachable idea of science as "*scire per causas*," had to involve an analogous and parallel limitation of the range of doubting, because "before reaching truth in itself, an immense field opens to human activity." It would be "proper of a disturbed and confused mind to disregard – for the worry of searching immediately for the borders of the field – all those useful things that one can find in the middle of the field." To search for the "borders of the field" is what both dogmatics and skeptics do. They have opposite intentions but paradoxically get to the same result: the despair in real knowledge.[189] In Royal Society circles, it is *The Vanity of Dogmatizing*, by Joseph Glanvill (1636–80), that will make a clear distinction between infallible knowledge, which is not at man's disposal, and undoubtable knowledge, which can be reached. Based on this distinction, both Glanvill and John Wilkins (1614–72) built a theory of empirical science as a means of finding useful knowledge and solving human problems within the limits of a "reasonable doubt."[190]

Notes

1 For the skeptical situation during the Renaissance, see Gianni Paganini and José R. Maia Neto (eds.), *Renaissance Scepticisms*, Dordrecht, Springer, 2009; G. Paganini, the entry "Renaissance Skepticism," in M. Sgarbi (ed.), *Encyclopedia of Renaissance Philosophy*, Dordrecht, Springer, forthcoming, vol. I.

2 For a general overview of early modern skepticism, see Richard H. Popkin, *The History of Scepticism: From Savonarola to Bayle*, 3rd rev. and expanded ed., Oxford, Oxford University Press, 2003. More recently, Paganini has innovated this field of historical research: Gianni Paganini, *Skepsis. Le débat des modernes sur le scepticisme. Montaigne – Le Vayer – Campanella – Hobbes – Descartes – Bayle*, Paris, Vrin, 2008 (awarded by the French Academy).

3 See Gian Mario Cao, *Scepticism and Orthodoxy. Gianfrancesco Pico as a Reader of Sextus Empiricus*, Pisa/Roma, Fabrizio Serra Editore, 2007.

4 A complete edition, Greek and Latin, of Sextus Empiricus's works was not available until 1621.

5 Cf. Luciano Floridi, *Sextus Empiricus. The Transmission and Recovery of Pyrrhonism*, Oxford, Oxford University Press, 2002.

6 For this interpretation of Montaigne's skepticism and its drawing on Estienne's translation of Sextus, see Paganini, *Skepsis*, 15–60. On the difference with Sanches's case, cf. Paganini (2004). For example, when translating Sextus's main chapter about *epokhe* limitations ("Whether skeptics reject phenomena," *PH* I 19–20), Estienne felt it necessary to interpolate the text to explain better the sense of the Greek word *phainomena*. To this aim, he used all the variations on the verb "to appear" in the lexicon. In the next chapter (*PH* I 21–23), Sextus established an equivalence between phenomena – Estienne's *apparentia* – and *phantasia*.

7 As was first pointed out by Jean-Paul Dumont (*Le Scepticisme et le phénomène. Essai sur la signification et les origines du pyrrhonisme*, Paris, Vrin, 1972, pp. 44–45), the entire long passage from the *Apology for Raimond Sebond* (*Essays*, II, 12) is a brilliant paraphrase of Sextus Empiricus's text. Cf. Montaigne (*Essais*, II, 12, ed. P. Villey, Paris, P.U.F., 1999, pp. 600–601).

8 Charles Larmore ("Scepticism," in Daniel Garber and Michael Ayers (eds.), *The Cambridge History of Seventeenth-Century Philosophy*, Cambridge, Cambridge University Press, 1998, p. 1148) distinguished two other meanings of "appearance": (1) the observable qualities of things and (2) how things appear

(their apparent qualities) as opposed to how things can be in themselves. As to why the third meaning – the one pointed out in our text – prevails, at least in the *Apologie de Raimond Sebond*, cf. our volume: G. Paganini, *Skepsis*, op. cit., p. 35ff.

9 Conche, Marcel, *Pyrrhon ou l'apparence*, Paris, P.U.F., 1994.
10 *Essais*, II, 12, p. 601.
11 *Ibid.*, p. 600.
12 *Ibid.*, p. 569.
13 *Ibid.*, p. 600. Cf. p. 562, 587, 599, 603.
14 *Ibid.*, p. 601.
15 See, for instance, the following passages from the *Essais*: p. 541, 563, 603. Note that at p. 571 Montaigne uses a formula of Sextus Empiricus to emphasize that skeptics also question the data coming from common experience.
16 Benson Mates, *The Skeptic Way: Sextus Empiricus's Outlines of Pyrrhonism*, New York/Oxford, Oxford University Press, 1996, p. 30. About skepticism's reception in Montaigne through Estienne, cf. Paganini, *Skepsis*, p. 56ff.
17 See G. Paganini, "The Quarrel Over Ancient and Modern Scepticism: Some Reflections on Descartes and His Context," in Jeremy Popkin (ed.), *The Legacies of Richard Popkin*, Dordrecht, Springer, 2008, pp. 166–169.
18 *Essais*, II, 12, p. 505.
19 *Ibid.*, p. 527.
20 *Ibid.*, p. 553.
21 *Ibid.*, p. 552.
22 *Ibid.*, p. 559. On the problems raised by Montaigne's naturalism see Thierry Gontier, *De l'homme à l'animal. Montaigne et Descartes ou les paradoxes de la philosophie moderne sur la nature des animaux*, Paris, Vrin, 1998.
23 For a similar conclusion, see L. Eva, *A Figura do Filosofo. Ceticismo e Subjetividade en Montaigne*, op. cit., pp. 487–497.
24 *Essais*, II, 12, pp. 449–450.
25 *Ibid.*, p. 501.
26 *Ibid.*, p. 503.
27 *Ibid.*, p. 505.
28 *Ibid.*, p. 502.
29 *Ibid.*, p. 505.
30 Cf. on these topics: José R. Maia Neto, "Epoche as Perfection: Montaigne's View of Ancient Skepticism," in R. H. Popkin and J. R. Maia Neto (eds.), *Skepticism in Renaissance and Post-Renaissance Thought New Interpretations*, Amherst, Humanity Books, 2004, pp. 13–42.
31 *Essais*, II, 12, p. 527.
32 In Montaigne we only find the equivalent of the theme of divine omnipotence. To constrain God's creations by the laws of our limited intelligence would be to put limits on his will and potency (cf. *Essais*, II, 12, p. 527).
33 Cf. Léon Brunschvicg, *Descartes et Pascal lecteurs de Montaigne*, Neuchâtel, La Baconniere, 1945 (nouv. éd., Paris, Pocket, 1995).
34 See note 56.
35 Francisco Sanches, "*Quod nihil scitur*," in F. Sanches (ed.), *Opera philosophica*, Nova edição, precedida de introdução, publicada por Joaquim de Carvalho, Coimbra, 1955, p. 4. There is also an edition with an English translation that unfortunately omits the very important marginalia: *That Nothing Is Known (Quod nihil scitur)*. Introduction, notes, and bibliography by Elaine Limbrick. Latin text established, annotated, and translated by Douglas F. S. Thomson, New York/New Rochelle/Melbourne /Sydney, Cambridge University Press, 1988.
36 Cf. Yriökonsuuri Mikko, "The Scholastic Background of *Cogito ergo sum*," in Tuomo Aho and Mikko Yriökonsuuri (eds.), *Norms and Modes of Thinking in Descartes*, Acta Philosophica Fennica, vol. 64, 1999, pp. 47–70.
37 See G. Paganini, "Descartes and Renaissance Skepticism: The Sanches Case," in J. R. Maia Neto, G. Paganini, and J. C. Laursen (eds.), *Skepticism in the Modern Age: Building on the Work of Richard Popkin*, Leiden/Boston, Brill, 2009, pp. 249–267.
38 For an analysis of Sanches's work, see our *Skepsis*, chapter I. Cf. Agostino Lupoli, "*Humanus Animus Nusquam Consistit*: Doctor Sanchez's Diagnosis of the Incurable Human Unrest and Ignorance," in G.

Paganini and J. R. Maia Neto (eds.), *Renaissance Scepticisms*, Dordrecht, Springer, 2009, pp. 149–181; Claudio Buccolini, "The Philosophy of Francisco Sanches: Academic Scepticism and Conjectural Empiricism," in P. J. Smith and S. Charles (eds.), *Academic Scepticism in the Development of Early Modern Philosophy*, Dordrecht, Springer, 2017, pp. 1–24.

39 For Sanches, moreover, the principle of the maker's knowledge holds: "*Nec enim perfecte cognoscere quis potest, quae non creavit*" (*Quod nihil scitur*, p. 30).
40 *Quod nihil scitur*, pp. 32–33.
41 *Ibid.*, p. 33.
42 R. Descartes, *Principia philosophiae* I, 9 (AT VIII A, p. 7, l. 20–22). Cf. also I^{ae} *Responsiones* (AT VII, p. 107 l. 13–14); IV^{ae} *Responsiones* (AT VII, p. 246 l. 10–17). Clearly, the main reference is to the Second Meditation: "*Numquid me ipsum non tantum multo verius, multo certius, sed etiam multo distinctius evidentiusque, cognosco?*" (AT VII, p. 33 l. 4–6).
43 See G. Paganini, "Sanches et Descartes. Subjectivité et connaissance réflexive au temps des sceptiques," *Bulletin de la Société internationale des amis de Montaigne*, 64 (2016–2), pp. 173–185.
44 R. Descartes, *Recherche de la vérité* (AT X, p. 527): "*Tot res sunt, quæ in ideâ rei cogitantis continentur, ut integris diebus ad eas explicandas opus esset.*" Cf. p. 526 : "*Omnes enim veritates se invicem consequuntur, & mutuo inter se vinculo continentur.*"
45 Myles F. Burnyeat, "Can the Skeptic Live His Skepticism?" in M. F. Burnyeat (ed.), *The Skeptical Tradition*, Berkeley/Los Angeles/London, University of California Press, p. 133.
46 Jonathan Barnes, "The Beliefs of a Pyrrhonist," *Elenchos*, IV (1983), reprinted in *The Original Skeptics: A Controversy*, ed. by M. F. Burnyeat and Michael Frede, Indianapolis/Cambridge, Hackett, 1997, pp. 59–60.
47 Montaigne, *Essais*, II, 12, p. 565.
48 On this peculiar feature of Charron's skepticism, see Popkin, *The History*, op. cit., pp. 57–63, 68–70, 100–107; and Paganini (2009) "Charron et le scepticisme des modernes," *Corpus* 55 (2009), pp. 231–250.
49 From *Toutes les Oeuvres de Pierre Charron . . . Dernière édition. Revues, corrigées et augmentées.* A Paris, chez Jacques Villery, 1635: *Sagesse*, II, ii, vol. I, pp. 12–14.
50 Cf. F. Bahr, "La sagesse de Pierre Charron et le scepticisme académique, » in *Academic Scepticism*, op. cit., pp. 45–64.
51 For the emphasis on neo-Academic features in Charron's work, see José Maia Neto, *Academic Scepticism in Seventeenth-Century French Philosophy: The Charronian Legacy 1601–1662*, Heidelberg/New York/Dordrecht, Springer, 2016, pp. 11–44. See also Tullio Gregory, *Genèse de la raison classique de Charron à Descartes*, Paris, P.U.F., 2000, pp. 115–155.
52 Pierre Charron, op. cit., II, viii, § 2, p. 88.
53 See G. Paganini, "*Sages, spirituels, esprits forts*. Filosofia dell' *esprit* e tipologia umana nell'opera di Pierre Charron," in Vittorio Dini and Domenico Taranto (eds.), *La saggezza moderna. Temi e problemi dell'opera di Pierre Charron*, Napoli, Edizioni Scientifiche Italiane, 1987, pp. 113–156.
54 On the moral and political impact of skepticism on early modern philosophy, see John Christian Laursen, *The Politics of Skepticism in the Ancients, Montaigne, Hume, and Kant*, Leiden/New York/Köln, Brill, 1992; *Skepticism and Political Thought in the Seventeenth and Eighteenth Centuries*, ed. by John Christian Laursen and Gianni Paganini, University of Toronto Press, Toronto, 2015; *Pour et contre le scepticisme. Théories et Pratiques de l'Antiquité aux Lumières*. Textes recueillis et édités par Élodie Argaud, Nawalle El Yadari, Sébastien Charles et Gianni Paganini, Honoré Champion, Paris, 2015.
55 J.R. Maia Neto, "Charron's *Epoché* and Descartes' *Cogito*: The Sceptical Base of Descartes' Refutation of Scepticism," in G. Paganini (ed.), *The Return of Scepticism From Hobbes and Descartes to Bayle*, Dordrecht/Boston/London, Kluwer, 2003, pp. 81–113.
56 René Descartes, *Discours de la méthode*. Texte et commentaire par Etienne Gilson, 4th ed., Paris, Vrin, 1967, p. 288.
57 Except for other indications, we quote the first book of the *Metaphysica* from the recent edition of the Latin text, with Italian translation: *Metafisica*, liber I, edited by Paolo Ponzio, with a preface of Ada Lamacchia, Bari, Levante Editore, 1994. For a general presentation of Campanella's thought, see Germana Ernst, *Tommaso Campanella: The Book and the Body of Nature*, Dordrecht, Springer, 2010; Germana Ernst. "A Story in the History of Scholarship: The Rediscovery of Tommaso Campanella," in Cecilia Muratori and Gianni Paganini (eds.), *Early Modern Philosophers and the Renaissance Legacy*, Dordrech, Springer, 2016, pp. 277–292.
58 Campanella, *Metaphysica* I, proem, p. 42.
59 *Ibid.*, I, I, i, pp. 46–48.

60 *Ibid.*, I, I, iii, p. 74.
61 *Ibid.*, I, I, iii, p. 74.
62 *Ibid.*, p. 86.
63 *Ibid.*, I, I, v, p. 100.
64 *Ibid.*, I, I, vi, p. 102.
65 *Ibid.*, I, I, vii, p. 108.
66 *Ibid.*, I, I, ii, p. 56 and refuted at p. 58.
67 *Ibid.*, I, I, ii, p. 52.
68 *Ibid.*, I, I, ii, p. 54.
69 This is the title of *dubitatio* II (*Ibid.*, I, I, ii, p. 52).
70 See especially *dubitatio* X (*Ibid.*, I, I, x, p. 132ff.) However, the topic was already dealt with in *dubitatio* VIII (I, I, viii, p. 126).
71 *Ibid.*, I, I, xi, p. 146.
72 It is the topic of *dubitatio* XI (*Ibid.*, I, I, xi, p. 146ff.).
73 *Ibid.*, I, I, xii, p. 170.
74 *Ibid.*, I, I, x, p. 134.
75 *Ibid.*, I, I, vi, p. 104.
76 *Ibid.*, I, I, vii, p. 122.
77 *Ibid.*, I, I, vii, p. 124.
78 *Ibidem*.
79 T. Campanella, *Universalis philosophiae, seu metaphysicarum rerum, iuxta propria dogmata, partes tres, libri 18*. Ph. Burelly, Parisiis, 1638 (repr. Bottega d'Erasmo, Turin, 1961) II, p. 64.
80 Campanella, *Metafisica*, I, 1994, pp. 406–408.
81 *Ibid.*, p. 424.
82 *Ibid.*, p. 422.
83 Ernst Cassirer, *Das Erkenntnisproblem in der Philosophie und Wissenschaft der neueren Zeit*. Erster Band. B. Cassirer, Berlin, 1922, pp. 240–257.
84 *Metaphysica* (1638 ed.) I, p. 35 e 32. Cf. Augustine, *De civitate Dei*, XI, 26.
85 *Ibid.*, II, p. 64.
86 *Ibid.*, p. 344. On Campanella and skepticism, see G. Paganini, *Skepsis*, pp. 101–129; on the relations with Mersenne and Descartes, see pp. 129–170. Cf. also G. Paganini, "Tommaso Campanella: The Reappraisal and Refutation of Scepticism," in Gianni Paganini and José R. Maia Neto (eds.), *Renaissance Scepticisms*, Dordrecht, Springer, 2008, pp. 275–303.
87 The evidence is in G. Paganini, "Mersenne plagiaire: les doutes de Campanella dans la *Vérité des sciences*," *Dix-septième siècle*, 57 (2005), pp. 747–767. The classic work about Mersenne is that of Robert Lenoble, *Mersenne ou la naissance du mécanisme*, 2nd ed., Paris, Vrin, 1971. See also Peter Dear, *Mersenne and the Learning of the Schools*, Ithaca and London, Cornell University Press, 1988, pp. 42–43, 203–206, 224–227.
88 M. Mersenne, *La Vérité des sciences. Contre les septiques ou Pyrrhoniens*, A Paris, chez Toussainct du Bray, 1625 (anastatic reprint Stuttgart-Bad Cannstatt, Frommann, 1969) I, 15, p. 192.
89 *Ibid.*, p. 204.
90 M. Mersenne, *Les Questions theologiques, physiques, morales, et mathematiques. Où chacun trouvera du contentement, ou de l'exercice. Composées par L.P.M*. A Paris, chez Heny Guénon, 1634: question II.
91 M. Mersenne, *Questions inouyes ou recreation des sçavans. Qui contiennent beaucoup de choses concernantes la Theologie, la Philosophie et les Mathematiques*. A Paris, chez Jacques Villery, 1634: question XVIII ("Peut-on sçavoir quelque chose de certain dans la Physique, ou dans les Mathematiques?"), pp. 71, 73.
92 M. Mersenne, *La Verité des sciences*, op. cit., p. 15.
93 P. Gassendi, *Exercitationes paradoxicae adversus Aristoteleos*, Praefatio, in P. Gassendi, *Opera omnia in sex tomos divisa*. . . Lugduni, Sumptibus Laurentii Anisson et Ioann. Bapt. Devenet, 1658 – ristampa anastatica, con introd. di Tullio Gregory, Stuttgart-Bad Cannstatt, Frommann, 1964 (OO III, p. 99). Gassendi explicitly connects the ideal of "freedom of philosophizing" and Cicero's "integra iudicandi potestas" not only to Academic probabilism, but also to the Pyrrhonian suspension of judgment and subsequent *ataraxia* (*Exercitationes* I, ii, 7; OO III, p. 113a–b). The importance of the neo-Academic sources has been emphasized by Delphine Bellis, "Nos in Diem Vivimus: Gassendi's Probabilism and Academic Philosophy From Day to Day," in S. Charles and P.J. Smith (eds.), *Academic Scepticism in the Development of Early Modern Philosophy*, Dordrecht, Springer, 2017, pp. 201–240.
94 *Exercitationes*, Praefatio (OO I, p. 99).

95 For an interpretation of the relations between skeptical tendencies and the methodology of scientific knowledge in Gassendi, see Tullio Gregory, *Scetticismo ed empirismo. Studio su Gassendi*, Bari, Laterza, 1961; Olivier R. Bloch, *La philosophie de Gassendi. Nominalisme, matérialisme et métaphysique*, La Haye, M. Nijhoff, 1971 (especially chapter III: "Les ambigüités de l'agnosticisme," pp. 77–109); R. H. Popkin, *The History of Scepticism*, op. cit., pp. 120–127; Margaret J. Osler, *Divine Will and the Mechanical Philosophy: Gassendi and Descartes on Contingency and Necessity in the Created World*, Cambridge, Cambridge University Press, 1994; Saul Fisher, *Pierre Gassendi's Philosophy and Science. Atomism for Empiricists*, Leiden/Boston, Brill, 2005, pp. 19–42; Antonia Lolordo, *Pierre Gassendi and the Birth of Early Modern Philosophy*, Cambridge, Cambridge University Press, 2007. On the connections between skepticism and empiricism, see G. Paganini, "Gassendi's Interplay Between Skepticism and Empiricism," in D. Garber, D. Bellis, and M. R. Palmerino (eds.), *Pierre Gassendi, Routledge Studies in Seventeenth Century Philosophy*, forthcoming. On the fortune: Thomas M. Lennon, *The Battle of the Gods and Giants: The Legacies of Descartes and Gassendi, 1655–1715*, Princeton, Princeton University Press, 1993.

96 *Exercitationes* (OO III, p. 207b).

97 *Exercitationes* II, vi, 6 (OO III, p. 203a ff.).

98 *Ibid.*, p. 192a.

99 *Ibid.*, p. 206b.

100 *Exercitationes*, I, ii, 7 (OO III, p. 113b).

101 See *Exercitationes* II, vi (OO III, pp. 192–207). There is a critical edition of this work with French translation: Pierre Gassendi, *Dissertations en forme de paradoxes contre les Aristotéliciens*. Texte établi, traduit et annoté par Bernard Rochot, Paris, Vrin, 1959 (see pp. 435–505).

102 About the importance of the theory of signs in Gassendi, Jean-Charles Darmon, "Sortir du scepticisme: Gassendi et les signes," in P.-F. Moreau (ed.), *Le scepticisme au XVIe et au XVII ^{e}siècles*, Paris, A. Michel, 2001, pp. 222–238.

103 For the themes dealt with in the text, see P. Gassendi, *Syntagma Philosophicum*, Pars prima quae est Logica. liber II ("De Logicae fine"), chapt. V ("Posse aliquam veritatem signo aliquo innotecere et criterio diiudicari"), OO III, pp. 79b–86a. On the same topic see also Ralph Walker, "Gassendi and Skepticism," in *The Skeptical Tradition*, op. cit., pp. 319–336.

104 Among the recent literature in this wake, see Gail Fine, "Descartes and Ancient Skepticism: Reheated Cabbage?" *The Philosophical Review*, 109 (2000), pp. 195–234; Gail Fine., "Subjectivity, Ancient and Modern: The Cyrenaics, Sextus, and Descartes," in Jon Miller and Brian Inwood (eds.), *Hellenistic and Early Modern Philosophy*, Cambridge, Cambridge University Press, 2003, pp. 192–231; Marjorie Grene, "Descartes and Skepticism," *Review of Metaphysics*, 52 (1999), pp. 553–571; Casey Perin, "Descartes and the Legacy of Ancient Skepticism," in Janet Broughton and John Carriero (eds.), *A Companion to Descartes*, London, Blackwell, 2007, pp. 52–65. The same topic is discussed in Janet Broughton's book *Descartes's Method of Doubt*, Princeton/Oxford, Princeton University Press, 2002, pp. 33–41. Denis Kambouchner, *Les Méditations métaphysiques de Descartes*, vol. I: *Introduction générale*. Première Méditation, Paris, P.U.F., 2005, pp. 102–105, 217–226, 240–241, suggests that Descartes dealt especially with the neo-Academic tradition. This was due to the revival of the neo-Academic tradition within the moderate or scientific skepticism. In the same vein, cf. Leo Groarke "Descartes' First Meditation: Something Old, Something New, Something Borrowed," *Journal of the History of Philosophy*, 22 (1984), pp. 281–301, especially pp. 282–288. R. Davies's book *Descartes: Belief, Scepticism and Virtue*, London/New York, Routledge, 2001, is centered on the comparison with ancient Pyrrhonism (see especially pp. 153–155).

105 See the results of the survey made by Franco Meschini, "Descartes e gli Antichi," in Ettore Lojacono (ed.), *Socrate in Occidente*, Firenze, Le Monnier, 2004, pp. 283–323.

106 *Secondae Responsiones* (AT VII p. 130).

107 *Objectiones tertiae cum responsionibus authoris* (AT VI pp. 171–172).

108 *Ibid.* This new approach, connecting Descartes to the skeptics of his time, and especially the libertines, has been suggested and developed by G. Paganini, "The Quarrel Over Ancient and Modern Scepticism: Some Reflections on Descartes and His Context," in Jeremy Popkin (ed.), *The Legacies of Richard Popkin*, Dordrecht, Springer, 2008, pp. 173–194, and in a more extensive form G. Paganini., *Skepsis*, op. cit., chapter V ("Du bon usage du doute. Descartes et les sceptiques modernes"), pp. 229–348.

109 *Discours de la méthode* (AT VI p. 29).

110 *Obiectiones septimae cum notis authoris* (AT VII p. 548).

111 This is the Latin text of Descartes's reply to the Jesuit: "*Et verò, quid respondebit Scepticis, qui omnes dubitationis limites transcendunt? Quâ ratione ipsos refutabit? Nempe desperatis aut damnatis annumerabit.*

SKEPTICISM

Egregie certe; sed quibus illi eum interim annumerabunt? Neque putandum est eorum sectam dudum esse extinctam. Viget enim hodie quàm maxime, ac fere omnes, qui se aliquid ingenii prae caeteris habere putant, nihil inventientes in vulgari Philosophiâ quod ipsis satisfaciat, aliamque veriorem non videntes, ad Scepticam transfugiunt" (AT VII, p. 548 l. 24 – p. 549 l. 3). This passage is rightly evoked also by Popkin, *The History of Scepticism*, op. cit., p. 144.

112 See above, p. 167.
113 *Ibid.* (AT VII, p. 548).
114 For a comparison between the skeptical doubt and the Cartesian one, see J.-L. Marion, *Sur la théologie blanche de Descartes*, Paris, P.U.F., 1981, p. 314ff. On the scientific connections of the Cartesian doubt, cf. Daniel Garber, *Descartes Embodied. Reading Cartesian Philosophy through Cartesian Science*, Cambridge, Cambridge University Press, 2001, pp. 222–223, 235–242, 279–280.
115 *Ibid.* (AT VII 549).
116 René Pintard, *Le Libertinage érudit dans la première moitié du XVIIe siècle*, nouv. éd., Genève, Slatkine, 1983. Among the more recent studies about the libertine phenomenon, see T. Gregory, G. Paganini, G. Canziani, *Ricerche su letteratura libertina e letteratura clandestina nel Seicento*, Firenze, La Nuova Italia, 1981; Lorenzo Bianchi, *Tradizione libertina e critica storica. Da Naudé a Bayle*, Milano, Franco Angeli, 1988, in particular chapter I, pp. 11–58; T. Gregory, *Genèse de la raison classique de Charron à Descartes* cit., pp. 13–114; Jean-Pierre Cavaillé, *Dis/simulations. Jules-César Vanini, François La Mothe Le Vayer, Gabriel Naudé, Louis Machon et Torquato Accetto. Religion, morale et politique au XVIIe siècle*, Paris, Champion, 2002; G. Paganini, *Les philosophies clandestines à l'âge classique*, Paris, P.U.F., 2005. Isabelle Moreau, '*Guérir du sot*': *les stratégies d'écriture des libertins à l'âge classique*, Paris, Champion, 2007; the series *Libertinage et Philosophie*, ed. A. McKenna and P.-F. Moreau, Saint-Etienne, Presses de l'Université de Saint-Etienne, 1996ff.; G. Paganini, *Skepsis*, op. cit., ch. II (on Le Vayer).
117 F. La Mothe Le Vayer, *Dialogues faits à l'imitation des anciens*, edited by André Pessel, Paris, Fayard, 1988.
118 F. La Mothe Le Vayer, *Opuscule ou petit traité sceptique sur cette façon de parler*, "*N'avoir pas le sens commun*," in *Œuvres de François de La Mothe le Vayer*, 3rd rev. ed., Paris, chez Augustin Courbé, 1662 t. II, vol. I, pp. 370–71.
119 *Ibid.*, p. 371. Cf. G. Paganini, "Temps et histoire dans la pensée libertine, *Archives de philosophie*, 49 (1986), pp. 583–602.
120 F. La Mothe Le Vayer, "*De la philosophie sceptique*," in *Dialogues*, op. cit., p. 24.
121 F. La Mothe Le Vayer, "*De la vie privée*," in *Dialogues*, op. cit., p. 148; "*De la politique*" (*Dialogues*, op. cit., pp. 449–450).
122 The reading of R. H. Popkin (*The History of Scepticism*, op. cit., pp. 82–89) focuses on features that allow a fideistic reading of Le Vayer. In our view, Popkin's interpretation is unbalanced toward the so-called Christian Pyrrhonism, although he recognizes that Le Vayer's position is "a two-way street" and that therefore it would leave open the path to the "reasonableness of the Enlightenment." The same kind of reading has been explored by José R. Maia Neto, *The Christianization of Pyrrhonism: Scepticism and Faith in Pascal, Kierkegaard, and Shestov*, Dordrecht, Kluwer, 1995.
123 F. La Mothe Le Vayer, "*De la divinité*" (*Dialogues*, op. cit., pp. 330–331).
124 F. La Mothe Le Vayer, "*De la Vertu des Payens*," in *Œuvres*, op. cit., t. I, vol. II, part II, "De Pyrrhon et de la Secte Sceptique," p. 663.
125 F. La Mothe Le Vayer, *De l'Ignorance loauble* (*Dialogues*, op. cit., p. 242).
126 R. Descartes, *Discours* I (AT VI p. 10).
127 Descartes, *Meditationes de prima philosophia* I (AT VII, pp. 18–19); *Discours* IV (AT VI, pp. 31–32). For an accurate investigation of Descartes's attitude toward typical themes of the skeptical tradition, see (besides R.H. Popkin, *The History of Scepticism*, chapters IX–X, pp. 143–173) Edwin M. Curley, *Descartes Against the Skeptics*, Cambridge, MA, Harvard University Press, 1978; Harry G. Frankfurt, *Demons, Dreamers and Madmen: The Defence of Reason in Descartes's Meditations*, Indianapolis/New York, Bobbs-Merrill, 1970; Elisa Angelini, *Le idée e le cose. La teoria della percezione di Descartes*, Pisa, ETS, 2007.
128 *Meditationes* I (AT VII, p. 21).
129 *Ibid.*
130 Descartes, *Entretien avec Burman* (AT V, p. 147). The comment of Harry G. Frankfurt, *Demons. . .*, op. cit., p. 69ff. is useful. He distinguishes the "epistemological import" of the dreaming argument from the "essentially metaphysical" character of the hypothesis concerning an omnipotent deity. The theological background behind the hypothesis of a "deceiving God" goes back to Ockhamistic conceptions *de potentia Dei absoluta*. Cf. T. Gregory, *Genèse de la raison classique*, op. cit., pp. 293–350.

131 Descartes to Hyperaspistes, August 1641 (AT III, p. 434); to *** March 1638 (AT II, p. 38).
132 The peculiarities that distinguish skepticism *after* Descartes from classical skepticism have been pointed out by M. F. Burnyeat: "*The Sceptic in His Place and Time*," in Richard Rorty, J. B. Schneewind, and Quentin Skinner (eds.), *Philosophy in History: Essays on the Historiography of Philosophy*, Cambridge, Cambridge University Press, 1984, pp. 225–254; M. Burnyeat, "Idealism and Greek Philosophy: What Descartes Saw and Berkeley Missed," *The Philosophical Review*, XCI (1982), pp. 3–40, especially pp. 32ff.; M. Burnyeat, "Can the Skeptic Live His Skepticism?" in *The Skeptical Tradition*, op. cit., pp. 117–148). Regarding in particular the questions of moral skepticism, they have been studied by Julia Annas, "Doing Without Objective Values: Ancient and Modern Strategies," in M. Schofield and G. Striker (eds.), *The Norms of Nature: Studies in Hellenistic Ethics*, Cambridge, Cambridge University Press, 1986, pp. 3–29 (see, in the same direction, the introduction to Julia Annas and Jonathan Barnes, *The Modes of Scepticism*, op. cit., pp. 7–9).
133 Cf. the papers of G. Fine quoted previously, footnote 93 and also G. Fine, "Sextus and External World Scepticism," *Oxford Studies in Ancient Philosophy*, 24 (2003), pp. 341–385. For an antirealistic reading of ancient scepticism, see Leo Groarke, *Greek Scepticism: Anti-Realist Trends in Ancient Thought*, Montreal & Kingston/London/Buffalo, McGill-Queen's University Press, 1990.
134 P. Gassendi, *Obiectiones quintae* (AT VII, p. 282). On the hyperbolic doubt, see Giulia Belgioioso, "The Hyperbolic Way to the Truth From Balzac to Descartes," in *Skepticism in the Modern Age*, op. cit., pp. 269–293.
135 Descartes, *Meditationes* III (AT VII, p. 34).
136 Cfr. M. F. Burnyeat, *Idealism and Greek Philosophy*, op. cit., p. 29. About ambiguities in the realism behind the skeptical *epokhé*, cf. Charlotte L. Stough, *Greek Skepticism: A Study in Epistemology*, Berkeley/Los Angeles, University of California Press, 1969, pp. 76ff. To evaluate the vaster and deeper influence of Cartesian doubt compared to classical skepticism it is enough to consider the following fact: if appealing to oneiric images or hallucinations of madmen is a recurring *topos* in the ancient disputes that aimed to show that it is a mistake to assume a particular kind of sensible representation (as the Stoic *phantasia kataleptike*) as a criterion (cf., e.g., M. T. Cicero, *Lucullus*, pp. 88–89, on dreaming, madness, and drunkenness; Sextus Empiricus, *Adversus Mathematicos*, VII, pp. 61–63 and 404–405 on madness), it is also true that in no case are the examples of oneiric and hallucinatory states used, as they are in *Meditations*, to doubt the subject's whole perception and even the reality of his own body. Still useful are the warnings of Arne Naess, *Scepticism*, London, Routledge, 1968, pp. 17ff. He attributed to Sextus Empiricus a position of "neutrality towards subjectivist phenomenalism," distinguishing correctly his own notion of "exteriority" from that which will be affirmed afterward in Descartes's philosophy. Even regarding the passage more inclined to phenomenalism (*Pyrrhoniae Hypotyposes*, I, 15), Naess notices that the word *exothen* ("outside") of Sextus "occurs in a context which does not imply that philosophical distinction" (between the mind and the external world, as in Descartes): "There is no implication of externality in the sense of an external versus an introspected world" (*ibid.*, p. 17).
137 Descartes, *Quintae responsiones* (AT VII, pp. 349–50). Cf. also *Secundae Responsiones* (AT VII, p. 149), where Descartes mentions his *Discours*.
138 Annas, *Doing Without Objective Values* . . . , op. cit., p. 22.
139 For the reading of M. Frede, "Des Skeptikers Meinungen," *Neue Hefte für Philosophie*, 15–16 (1979), pp. 102–129 (Frede came back to the issue of the "life without beliefs" in "The Sceptic's Two Kinds of Assent and the Question of the Possibility of Knowledge," in *Philosophy in History*, op. cit., pp. 255–278). For Barnes's distinction, see "The Beliefs of a Pyrrhonist," in *Elenchos*, IV (1983), pp. 5–43, esp. pp. 8–9. Barnes holds that the first figure ("rustic Pyrrhonist") is the one closest to the spirit, if not to the letter, of Pyrrhonian texts: even though ordinary beliefs cannot be considered properly as *dogmata*, by denying to have at disposal the criterion of truth, the Pyrrhonian, according to Barnes (op. cit., p. 28), also abolishes all beliefs.
140 About the problem of *apraxia* in ancient skepticism, in particular with references to the different attitudes of neo-Academics and Pyrrhonists, cf. Gisela Striker, "Sceptical Strategies," in Malcolm Schofield, Myles Burnyeat, and Jonathan Barnes (eds.), *Doubt and Dogmatism. Studies in Hellenistic Epistemology*, Oxford, Clarendon Press, 1980, pp. 54–83 (esp. p. 63ff.). A convincing response to the objection of *apraxia* from the point of view of ancient skepticism can be found in the article of J.C. Laursen, "Yes, Skeptics Can Live Their Skepticism and Cope With Tyranny as Well as Anyone," in *Skepticism in Renaissance and Post-Renaissance Thought*, op. cit., pp. 201–234.
141 Descartes, *Meditationes* VI (AT VII 71–90).

142 Sergio Landucci, "Introduction to: Descartes," in R. Descartes and S. Landucci (eds.) *Meditazioni metafisiche*, Roma-Bari, Laterza, 1997, pp. LV–LVI.
143 *Ibid.*, p. LVII.
144 On this general topic, see Plinio Junqueira Smith, "Skepticism, Belief, and Justification," in *Skepticism in the Modern Age*, op. cit., pp. 171–190.
145 R. H. Popkin, *The History of Scepticism*, op. cit., ch. XVIII, p. 283ff. For an investigation of Bayle's skepticism, cf. G. Paganini, *Analisi della fede e critica della ragione nella filosofia di Pierre Bayle*, Firenze, La Nuova Italia, 1980, pp. 274–81, 312–31; G. Paganini, *Skepsis*, op. cit., pp. 349–384. For a different point of view, see Gianluca Mori, *Bayle philosophe*, Paris, Champion, 1999. For an overview of recent research (Mori, Lennon, Brogi), see G. Paganini, "Towards a 'critical' Bayle. About Three Recent Studies," *Eighteenth-Century Studies*, 37 (2004), pp. 510–520. Cf. the reassessment made by T. Ryan of the relationship between Bayle and Descartes's *Metaphysics*: Todd Ryan, *Pierre Bayle's Cartesian Metaphysics: Rediscovering Early Modern Philosophy*, New York/London, Routledge, 2009.
146 P. Bayle, *Dictionnaire Historique et Critique*, 5th ed., Amsterdam, Leyde etc.; P. Brunel, 1740, 4 vol., art. "Xénophanes," rem. A, t. IV, p. 516a.
147 D. Hume, *Treatise of Human Nature*, I, IV, 4. In "Xénophanes," rem. L, Bayle develops an even more radical form of skepticism "against reason," which puts rational "evidence" and the phenomena originating within a subject's consciousness into contradiction.
148 Art. "Xénophanes," rem. L, p. 524b.
149 Art. "Pyrrhon," rem. B, t. III, p. 732b.
150 N. Malebranche, *Eclaircissement VI* appended to *Recherche de la vérité*, in A. Robinet (ed.), Malebranche, *Œuvres complètes*, Paris, Vrin-CNRS, 1958–1964, t. III, pp. 59–64.
151 A. Arnauld, *Traité des vraies et des fausses idées*, ch. XXVIII (*Œuvres complètes de Messire Antoine Arnauld*, t. XXXVIII, Paris/Lausanne, chez Sigismond d'Arnay, 1780, p. 354).
152 Malebranche, op. cit., p. 62–63.
153 P. Bayle, art. "Pyrrho," rem. B, t. III, p. 732b.
154 Malebranche's reply is from the *Réponse au livre des vraies et des fausses idées* (ch. XXVI, § iv–v: OC VI, pp. 184–185), quoted by Bayle in "Zénon d'Elée," rem H, t. IV, p. 543b. On this see Frédéric Brahami, *Le travail du scepticisme. Montaigne, Bayle, Hume*, Paris, P.U.F., 2001, p. 132 ff.
155 Arnauld, *Défense contre la Réponse au Livre des vraies & des fausses idées* (*Œuvres* cit., t. XXXVIII, pp. 653–654).
156 S. Foucher, *Réponse pour la critique, à la préface du second volume de la Recherche de la vérité. Où l'on examine le sentiment de M. Descartes, touchant les Idées*, Paris, chez Charles Anget, 1686, p. 39. Cf. Emanuela Scribano, "Foucher and the Dilemmas of Representation: A 'Modern' Problem?" in Gianni Paganini (ed.), *The Return of Scepticism: From Hobbes and Descartes to Bayle*, Dordrecht/Boston/London, Kluwer, 2003, pp. 197–212.
157 A. Arnauld, *Reflexions sur le systême de la nature et de la grâce* (*Œuvres* cit., t. XXXIX, p. 603).
158 Cf. Bayle, *Réponses aux questions d'un provincial*, II, lxxxix (Bayle, *Œuvres diverses*, La Haye, chez P. Husson, 1727, 4 vol.) III, p. 675b. On this topic, see G. Paganini, "Bayle et les théologies philosophiques de son temps," in W. van Bunge and H. Bots (eds.), *Pierre Bayle (1647–1706), le philosophe de Rotterdam: Philosophy, Religion, and Reception*, Leiden/Boston, Brill, 2008, pp. 103–120.
159 Bayle, *Dictionnaire Historique et Critique*, "Éclaircissement sur les Manichéens," t. IV, p. 635.
160 About these topics in the literary, philosophical, and theological context, see Antony McKenna, *De Pascal à Voltaire: le rôle des Pensées de Pascal dans l'histoire des idées entre 1670 et 1734*, Oxford, Voltaire Foundation, 1990; G. Paganini and A. McKenna (eds.), *Pierre Bayle dans la République des lettres. Philosophie, religion, critique*, Paris, Champion, 2004. A new enriched and updated intellectual biography of P. Bayle, after the classical work of Elisabeth Labrousse (*Pierre Bayle*, 2 vols., The Hague, M. Nijhoff, 1963–1964; new ed., Paris, A. Michel, 1996) is provided by Hubert Bost, *Pierre Bayle*, Paris, Fayard, 2006.
161 Bayle, art. "Pyrrho," rem B, t. III, p. 733a.
162 R. H. Popkin, "For a Revised History of Scepticism," in G. Paganini (ed.), *The Return of Scepticism*, op. cit., p. xxv.
163 On academic features of Bayle's doubt, see Michael W. Hickson, "Disagreement and Academic Scepticism in Bayle," in *Academic Scepticism*, op. cit., pp. 293–318.
164 John Locke, *An Essay Concerning Human Understanding*, ed. Peter H. Nidditch, Oxford, Clarendon Press, 1975, II, xxiii, 2, p. 295. Regarding the presence of skeptical themes in the British context, we refer the reader to G. Paganini, "Hobbes Among Ancient and Modern Sceptics: Phenomena and Bodies," in G. Paganini (ed.), *The Return of Scepticism*, op. cit., pp. 3–35; G. Paganini, "Hobbes and the

Continental Tradition of Skepticism," in R. H. Popkin and J. R. Maia Neto (eds.), *Skepticism in Renaissance and Post-Renaissance Thought*, op. cit., pp. 65–105.
165 Locke, *Essay* II, xxiii, 3, p. 297.
166 *Essay* II xxiii 4, p. 297.
167 *Essay* IV iii 6, p. 541.
168 *Essay* IV ii 14, p. 537.
169 *Essay* IV iii 9, p. 544.
170 Regarding Locke's knowledge of Gassendi's books, cf. Maurice Cranston, *John Locke: A Biography*, London, Longmans, 1957, pp. 169–170; Richard I. Aaron, *John Locke*, Oxford, Clarendon Press, 1971, pp. 31–35; Walter Euchner, *Naturrecht und Politik bei John Locke*, Frankfurt a. M., Europäische Verlagsanstalt, 1969, chap. II.
171 *Essay* IV iii 11, p. 544.
172 *Essay* IV iii 12, p. 545.
173 *Essay* IV iii 26, p. 556.
174 *Essay* IV iii 28, p. 559.
175 *Essay* IV iii 16, p. 547–548.
176 *Essay* IV iii 14, p. 546.
177 Regarding the relationship between skepticism and probability in the British context, see Barbara J. Shapiro, *Probability and Certainty in Seventeenth-Century England: A Study of the Relationships Between Natural Science, Religion, History, Law, and Literature*, Princeton, Princeton University Press, 1983. On Locke see esp. G.A.J. Rogers, "John Locke and the Sceptics," in *The Return of Scepticism*, op. cit., pp. 37–53; G.A.J. Rogers, *Locke's Enlightenment: Aspects of the Origin, Nature, and Impact of His Philosophy*, Hildesheim, Olms, 1998.
178 Cf. Locke, *Essay*, II, xxiii, 3, pp. 296–297.
179 Cf. Locke, *Essay*, III, vi, 2, p. 439.
180 *Essay* IV iii 21, pp. 552–553.
181 *Essay* IV xi 3, p. 631; cf. IV ii 14, p. 537; IV xi 8, pp. 634–635.
182 *Essay* IV iv 5, p. 564.
183 *Essay* IV iv 6, p. 565.
184 *Essay* IV iv 7, p. 565; cf. IV iii 18, pp. 548–549.
185 *Essay* IV iv 4, p. 564.
186 *Essay* IV iv 3, p. 563.
187 *Essay* IV xi 8, p. 634.
188 *Essay* IV xi 8, p. 635.
189 F. Bacon, *Scala intellectus sive Filum Labyrinthi*. Cf. Silvia Manzo, "Certainty and Facts in Francis Bacon's Natural Histories. A Double Attitude Towards Skepticism," in *Skepticism in the Modern Age*, op. cit., pp. 123–137.
190 On Glanvill, see R.H. Popkin, "Joseph Glanvill Precursor of Hume," *Journal of the History of Ideas*, 14 (1953), pp. 292–303, re-edited in his volume *The High Road to Pyrrhonism*, ed. by Richard A. Watson and James E. Force, San Diego, Austin Hill Press, 1980, pp. 181–196. For a more general view, see Henry G. Van Leeuwen, *The Problem of Certainty in English Thought 1630–1690*, The Hague, M. Nijhoff, 1963.

7
THEORIES OF IDEAS
Lex Newman

Descartes's transformation of the notion of *ideas* deeply influenced subsequent thinking about their nature and epistemic significance in philosophical inquiry. By 1662, the transformation had become so fundamental in some quarters that Arnauld and Nicole would write, "Some words are so clear that they cannot be explained by others, for none are more clear or more simple. 'Idea' is such a word" (Arnauld 1964, 31). By the end of the seventeenth century, Locke was pleased to have his philosophy characterized as an example of the "way of ideas," notwithstanding his considerable disagreements with Descartes – a way he took to encompass every human effort to "employ our minds in thinking upon something" (W 4:72). The developing new understanding of *ideas* was part and parcel of a broader philosophical transformation underway.

This chapter develops three main themes deriving from three widely discussed characterizations of ideas offered by Descartes. He likens ideas to *images*: "Some of my thoughts are as it were the images of things, and it is only in these cases that the term 'idea' is strictly appropriate" (AT VII 37; CSM II 25). He says ideas are the items *immediately perceived* by minds: "I am taking the word 'idea' to refer to whatever is immediately perceived by the mind" (AT VII 181; CSM II 127). And he distinguishes ideas according to *three kinds of sources*: "I distinguish three kinds [of ideas]. Some are adventitious . . . others are constructed or made up . . . and others are innate" (AT III 383; CSMK 183).

What follows is organized around these three characterizations. Section 1 addresses the imagistic nature of ideas. Section 2 addresses the conception of ideas as objects of immediate perception, including the related topics of objective being, act and act-object theories, and conceptions of perceptual immediacy. Section 3 considers issues related to the origins of ideas, including the topic of innateness, and a look at Locke's influential theory of how all ideas derive from experience.

1. Ideas as images

In the Third Meditation, Descartes writes (in what I'll refer to as the "*tanquam* images" passage),

> Some of my thoughts are as it were [*tanquam*] the images of things, and it is only in these cases that the term "idea" is strictly appropriate – for example, when I think of a man, or a chimera, or the sky, or an angel, or God.
>
> (AT VII 37; CSM II 25)

In conveying some form of *imagism* about ideas, this passage raises questions. In what sense are *ideas*, in the strict sense of the term, properly likened to images? *All* ideas? And why the "*tanquam*" qualification?

One way to understand imagery is on the model of pictures. In some texts, Descartes likens sensory ideas to picturelike images – they are "like portraits drawn from nature," the senses being likened to an artist (AT X 507; CSM II 406).[1] Indeed, a number of passages imply that sensory ideas portray their objects in a way analogous with picturing (cf. AT VIIIA 11; CSM I 199, AT VII 42; CSM II 29, and AT III 567; CSMK 214). Are pictorial images therefore the way to understand the nature of ideas as *images*? Arguably yes, for ideas of external sensation.[2] But this understanding of the *tanquam* images passage, using sensory images as the model, creates problems for other sorts of ideas.

Hobbes understands the passage in this way and therefore raises the following objection. If ideas are understood in this way, then because we cannot represent God with sensory images, it follows that we have no idea of God (cf. AT VII 179f.; CSM II 126f.) – obviously an unacceptable result for Descartes. In his reply, Descartes writes,

> Here my critic wants the term "idea" to be taken to refer simply to the images of material things which are depicted in the corporeal imagination; and if this is granted, it is easy for him to prove that there can be no proper idea of an angel or of God.
>
> (AT VII 181; CSM II 127)

To help clarify that ideas are not restricted to sensory images, Descartes adds, "I used the word 'idea' because it was the standard philosophical term used to refer to the forms of perception belonging to the divine mind, even though we recognize that God does not possess any corporeal imagination" (AT VII 181; CSM II 127). Descartes wants the term *idea* to apply not only to sensory images, but to ideas of the intellect.[3]

On what understanding of images is the idea of God properly likened to an image? Presumably, there *is* such an understanding, for among the examples of "strictly appropriate" uses of the term *idea* offered in the *tanquam* images passage is the idea of God. Moreover, in a Third Meditation passage encompassing the clear and distinct idea of God, Descartes writes: "it is clear to me, by the natural light, that the ideas in me are like <pictures, or>[4] images [*imagines*]" (AT VII 42; CSM II 29); a roughly parallel passage of the *Principles* (likewise encompassing the idea of God) uses the language of the "idea or image [*imaginem*]" within us (AT VIIIA 12; CSM I 199). And in the Fifth Meditation, again, in a context apropos of the idea of God, Descartes writes, "There are many ways in which I understand that this idea is not something fictitious which is dependent on my thought, but is an image [*imaginem*] of a true and immutable nature" (AT VII 68; CSM II 47). The implication emerging from these texts is that ideational images need not take a sensory form.

How then should we understand the relevant nonsensory nature of imagery? Distinguish two aspects of sensory images: (1) the fact that they involve various sensory forms – some being *visual*, others *tactile*, and so on; and (2) the fact that those forms *depict* something – they are *of* or *about* some object. Suppose we read the *tanquam* images passage to refer not to aspect (1), but only to (2). That is, suppose Descartes's point is that ideas exhibit *intentionality* by their very nature. There is good reason to hold this. To Hobbes – in the context of discussing the *tanquam* images passage – Descartes writes that "I count volition and fear among my ideas" (AT VII 181; CSM II 127),[5] yet neither involves the sensory forms associated with external sensation. Indeed, in the continuation of the *tanquam* images passage itself, Descartes clarifies that volitions do *therefore* count as ideas (as I read the passage): "when I will, or am afraid, or affirm, or deny, there is always a particular thing *which I take as the object of my thought*," though these "have various additional forms" over and above the fact that they are *of* some object (AT VII 37; CSM II 25f., my emphasis).[6] I take the point to be that volitions take a very different form than nonvolitional ideas, and yet what all of them have in common – what makes all of them *ideas* – is their being directed at an object. Later in the Third Meditation, Descartes writes that "there can be no ideas which are not as it were *of* things [*tanquam rerum*]" (AT VII 44; CSM II 30, my emphasis). The French edition of this remark reads, "ideas, being like images, must in each case appear to us to represent something [*semble représenter quelque chose*]" (CSM II 30, note 2).

This later Third Meditation passage suggests an answer to the related question of why Descartes includes the *tanquam* qualification. The suggestion arises from what this passage and the original *tanquam* images passage have in common. Both discuss ideas that fail to represent successfully the objects of which they purport to be images. The original *tanquam* images passage includes in the list of examples the idea of a *chimera*. The later passage occurs in the context of discussing material falsity – a special notion of falsity, writes Descartes, that "occurs in ideas, when they represent non-things as things" (AT VII 43; CSM II 30). Suppose one thinks of *imaging* as a success notion, such that "*x* is an image of *y*" only if there *is* a *y* that *x* images; then, in cases in which there is no appropriate *y* – as with chimeras, and more general cases of material falsity – we might say of *x* that it is *as it were* an image of *y*, even if not an image, strictly speaking. From the point of view of the mind that is having such ideas, they certainly *appear* to be *of* an object. Again, as the French edition has it, "ideas, being like images, must in each case *appear* to us to represent something." I'm not prepared to make a blanket statement that Descartes always invokes *imaging* as a success notion, in this way. But this seems a plausible explanation of these two uses of the *tanquam* qualification. On the account of the *tanquam* images passages that emerges, ideas in the strict sense are likened to images in that they are always *of* something – at least, they always purport to be of something, whether or not the purported object actually exists.

The suggestion that Descartes's imagism centers on an aspect of intentionality helps explain some of the texts concerning the idea of God, but it does not explain every difficult passage. Some texts seem to draw a sharp distinction between images, on the one hand, and ideas of the intellect, on the other. To Mersenne, Descartes says that "whatever we conceive without an image is an idea of the pure mind, and whatever we conceive with an image is an idea of the imagination" (AT III 395; CSMK 186). The Second Meditation adds, "I now know that even bodies are not strictly perceived by the senses or the faculty of imagination but by the intellect alone" (AT VII 34; CSM II 22). Moreover, Descartes thinks his Sixth Meditation chiliagon discussion "clearly shows the difference between imagination and pure understanding" (AT VII 73; CSM II 51). How are we to reconcile such passages with the proposed reading of the *tanquam* images passage, as being concerned with intentionality?

I suggest the reconciliation lies again in our distinction of (1) the sensory aspect of images, and (2) their intentional aspect. Whereas I have been arguing that the *tanquam* images passage focuses on (2), these other passages are concerned with both (1) and (2); they are concerned with not only the intentionality of images but also the sensory aspect of ideas associated specifically with the faculty of imagination. That is, in some contexts Descartes is discussing the intentionality exhibited by all ideas; in other contexts, he is more narrowly focused on the sensory aspects of sensory images. The broader passage containing the remark to Mersenne (quoted previously) – "whatever we conceive without an image is an idea of the pure mind, and whatever we conceive with an image is an idea of the imagination" – is especially helpful. For that passage elaborates, as Descartes writes, on "what I mean by the idea of God," clarifying that his own use of "the word 'idea'" does not "restrict it to the images *of material things formed in the imagination*" (AT III 393; CSMK 185, my emphasis). This helps to clarify the spirit, even if not the letter, of all the problematic passages. In passages implying that ideas of the intellect count as images, he is using *image-talk* in a broad sense to include any idea in virtue of its intentionality – this would include the *tanquam* images passage. In passages implying that ideas of the intellect are distinct from images, he is using *image-talk* in a narrow sense that involves not only an idea's intentionality but also a sensory aspect encompassed by the faculty of imagination – as, for example, in Descartes's reference to "images *of material things formed in the* [faculty of] *imagination*."

Arguably, some such interpretive strategy applies also to Leibniz. He holds that all ideas exhibit intentionality. He too weighs in on the chiliagon example, concluding that it shows that the distinct idea of the chiliagon should be distinguished from the *image* of it:

> The upshot is that I have this idea of a chiliagon, even though I cannot have the image of one: one's senses and imagination would have to be sharper and more practised if they were to enable one to distinguish such a figure from a polygon which had one side less. But knowledge of figures does not depend upon the imagination, any more than knowledge of numbers does. . . . The point of this example is to bring out the difference between ideas, or rather between ideas and images.
>
> (*NE* II.29; 261f.)

In context, it is clear that Leibniz means to be distinguishing the distinct idea of the chiliagon from sensory images of it formed in the imagination – thus invoking images in the narrow *sensory* sense. Whereas if imagism is construed in the expansive way I have suggested for Descartes, then Leibniz too will be an imagist. For the distinct idea of a chiliagon is *about* something.

Locke's influential theory of ideas does, of course, not countenance ideas of the pure intellect. Even so, it owes much to Descartes on the imagist nature of ideas. Locke writes that ideas "are, as it were, the Pictures of Things" (this being one verbatim translation of Descartes's *tanquam* images passage) and goes on to call them "mental Draughts" (*Essay* 2.29.8); elsewhere, Locke adds that they are "just like that Picture, which the Painter makes" (*Essay* 4.7.16).[7] Locke indeed likens the mind to "a Looking-glass, which constantly receives variety of Images, or *Ideas*" (*Essay* 2.1.15).[8] As with Descartes, the texts in Locke present us with a prima facie tension. For the ideas in Locke's category of *reflection* lack the sensory forms associated with external sense and most naturally associated with pictures. Notice, however, that even ideas of reflection bear the mark of intentionality – they are *of* something. More generally, Locke understands ideas as playing a representational role:

> For since the Things, the Mind contemplates, are none of them, besides it self, present to the Understanding, 'tis necessary that something else, as a Sign or

Representation of the thing it considers, should be present to it: And these are *Ideas*.

(*Essay* 4.21.4)

Ideas can play the stated role only if they are *of* the things the mind contemplates. Entirely optional to *this* characterization is that ideas take the sensory forms characteristic of external sensation.

There are further texts in Locke that would need to be reconciled with the thesis that all ideas are properly likened to images. In some places, Locke makes clear that *not all* ideas count as images: not all simple ideas "are exactly the Images and *Resemblances* of something inherent in" the body producing them (*Essay* 2.8.7); not all are "the Images, or Representations of what does exist, the contrary whereof, in all but the primary Qualities of Bodies, hath been already shewed" (*Essay* 2.30.2). I suggest that the apparent problem in these passages resolves when we consider their context. Locke is alluding to differences between his own mechanist account of sensation and the Aristotelian account. On the latter, the respect in which all sensations are images of the qualities producing them is of *images* understood as *resemblances*. By contrast, mechanist doctrine denies such resemblance except in the case of primary-quality ideas. In this very narrow content of *image-talk* – a context incorporating the additional element of resemblance – Locke denies that all ideas are images. But this denial is compatible with holding that in the broader intentional sense, all ideas are properly likened to images.[9]

Thus far, our discussion has focused on rendering various texts compatible with an imagist account of ideas – imagism being characterized in terms of intentionality. We have taken for granted that all sensory ideas fit easily with that characterization. Not all commentators accept this. According to one view, some sensations do not exhibit intentionality. For example, insofar as pain sensations do not even purport to be about anything, they would not qualify as "*tanquam*" images under the interpretation I have suggested. Expressing the view, Richard Rorty writes, "The obvious objection to defining the mental as the intentional is that pains are not intentional – they do not represent, they are not about anything" (Rorty 1979, 22). Yet if pains thus lack intentionality, then Descartes and Locke face a dilemma. Either they are mistaken in categorizing pains as ideas or mistaken in characterizing all sensory ideas as images (or *tanquam* images, at any rate).

A line of reply is suggested by our earlier discussion. We may distinguish an intentionality aspect of the idea – its appearing to be about an object – from the issue of whether it successfully represents any such object.[10] On one view, pain experiences *do* exhibit the relevant sense of intentionality – always appearing to be *of* something, even if only confusedly or obscurely. Descartes explains that with sensations of pain and pleasure, "we generally regard them not as being in the mind alone, or in our perception, but as being in the hand or foot or in some other part of our body" (AT VIIIA 32f.; CSM I 216f.) – even if only mistakenly thus regarding them. For instance, even a faint physical ache – one seeming not to derive from any particular bodily location – is nonetheless directed at one's body; nor need the bodily parts at issue even exist, as in phantom limb cases. Indeed, a primary function of pain and pleasure requires that they seem to be about some part of the body. Descartes writes that "the proper purpose of the sensory perceptions given me by nature is simply to inform the mind of what is beneficial or harmful for the composite of which the mind is a part" (AT VII 83; CSM II 57–58).

Locke similarly holds that "the great Business of the Senses [is] to make us take notice of what hurts, or advantages the Body" (*Essay* 2.10.3). But of course, the function of indicating the presence of bodily benefits and harms depends on sensation seeming to be *about* that part of the body.

Malebranche takes a different tack in his theory of ideas, by dissociating sensations and ideas. According to his Vision in God doctrine, we see all things in God – a doctrine deeply influenced by Augustine's theory of divine illumination. The proper locus of ideas is the divine mind. In perception, our minds are (somehow) united with God's mind, thereby enabling our apprehension of ideas: "through His presence God is in close union with our minds, such that He might be said to be the place of minds as space is, in a sense, the place of bodies" (*Search* 3.2.6). On Malebranche's view, sensations do not represent external bodies; only ideas do. On one interpretation of him, ideas exhibit intentionality but not sensations (cf. Jolley 1990, 60). As argued previously, however, intentionality and representation should not be conflated. It is by no means clear that Malebranche conflates them. In Elucidation VI, he elaborates a series of Cartesian doubts about the senses, making clear their susceptibility to being about the wrong objects, or of wrongly portraying their objects; but notice that this susceptibility presupposes that they purport to be *about* objects. As for sensations of pain, Malebranche writes, "The most lively sensation and the one that seems to have the most necessary relation to some actually existing body is pain" (*Eluc.* VI/LO 570).[11] Moreover, like Descartes, Malebranche holds that our judgments about the existence of external bodies arise from sensory inclinations *about* those bodies. Putting terminological differences to the side, it would appear that Malebranche falls in line with Descartes in holding that even sensations count as *tanquam* images, under the intentionality interpretation here developed.

2. Ideas as objects of immediate perception

In the geometric exposition (Second Replies), Descartes offers this definition of *ideas*: "I understand this term [*idea*] to mean the form of any given thought, immediate perception of which makes me aware of the thought" (AT VII 160; CSM II 113). Descartes offers relevantly similar characterizations in two other passages: "Considering the ideas of all these qualities which presented themselves to my thought, although the ideas were, strictly speaking, the only immediate objects of my sensory awareness" (AT VII 75; CSM II 52); "I make it quite clear in several places . . . that I am taking the word 'idea' to refer to whatever is immediately perceived by the mind" (AT VII 181; CSM II 127). The perceptual immediacy characterization would prove influential. Indeed, some version of the thesis that ideas are the objects of immediate perception is adopted widely by subsequent seventeenth century philosophers:

> [B]y the word *idea*, I mean here nothing other than the immediate object, or the object closest to the mind, when it perceives something.
> (Malebranche, *Search* 3.2.1)

> [I]t is our ideas that we see immediately and which are the immediate object of our thought.
> (Arnauld, *VFI* 72)

By the term *idea* I understand any form of thought of which we are conscious through immediate perception.

(Spinoza, *Descartes' Principles* I def 1)

Whatsoever the Mind perceives in it self, or is the immediate object of Perception, Thought, or Understanding, that I call *Idea*.

(Locke, *Essay* 2.8.8)

[A]n idea is an immediate inner object [of thought].

(Leibniz, *NE* 2.1)

Beyond this apparent verbal agreement, it is less clear how to understand these statements. The characterization suggests two subclaims. First, ideas are in some fundamental sense *perceived*, thus counting as perceptual *objects*. Second, in being the *immediate* such objects of perception, they mediate our perception of some other objects. The discussion that follows is organized around these two subclaims.

2.1. Ideas as perceptual objects

In what sense do ideas – that is images, as it were – count as perceptual *objects*? An analogy may help. Think of a hall with portraits of United States presidents. The portraits are similar to each other insofar as being the same size, having a similar frame, and consisting of oil on canvas. Regarded *simply* as framed canvases, there would seem no difference between them. Regarded instead in terms of what each painting portrays, they are quite different. In the same vein, Descartes distinguishes two ways of regarding our ideas:

> In so far as the ideas are <considered> simply <as> modes of thought, there is no recognizable inequality among them. . . . But in so far as different ideas <are considered as images which> represent different things, it is clear that they differ widely.
>
> (AT VII 40; CSM II 27–28)

The doctrine of *objective being* arises for the sense in which ideas "differ widely" – the sense in which they are regarded as images representing different things.

Does the "objective being" of ideas constitute a genuine sort of *being*? Note that in addition to the way Obama is, in himself, is the way he is, *in* the painting. If, while standing in that hall of portraits, you were to point at the one of Obama and remark, "That's President Obama," you would be saying something true. The doctrine of objective being concerns the analogous sort of being that arises with ideas, namely the being of the objects of those ideas, as they exist *in* the ideas – that is, *as* represented.

That portraits and ideas introduce beings in need of explanation is suggested by consideration of their causes. Portraits have causal stories, as do ideas. Neither the portrait of Obama, nor our ideas of him, can have derived from nothing – "the mode of being by which a thing exists objectively <or representatively> in the intellect by way of an idea," writes Descartes, "is certainly not nothing, and so it cannot come from nothing" (AT VII 41; CSM II 29). A full explanation of the portrait of Obama would involve factors over and above a full explanation of merely a framed canvas; and it would involve factors over and above a full explanation of Obama, himself. Indeed, from details about a painting, we might be able to deduce facts about its painter. In a similar vein, Descartes famously argues for the existence of God from details about the clear and distinct idea of God. He argues, in effect, that the idea represents a being with so much perfection that it could only have been painted by a comparably perfect being. To explain the very existence of the clear and distinct idea of God, therefore, God itself must exist – or so argues Descartes, in the first of his Third Meditation proofs. Our present interest is not with this argument for God, but with the underlying doctrine of objective being.

Whatever the ontological status of these ideational beings, there seems a clear sense in which they can count as perceptual *objects*. With the portrait of Obama, it is one thing for the object of my attention to be the framed canvas, as such – perhaps noticing that it is an oil on canvas. It is quite another, for the object of attention to be Obama himself. And it seems a third scenario for the object to be Obama as he is *in* the painting.

Moving beyond analogies, how does Descartes understand the doctrine? Inconsistent use of terminology presents readers with interpretive puzzles.[12] But in the geometric exposition, Descartes defines the "*objective reality of an idea*" as follows: "By this I mean the being of the thing which is represented by an idea, in so far as this exists in the idea" (AT VII 161; CSM II 113). In a much-discussed passage of the First Replies, Descartes explains the doctrine to his objector, Caterus. Caterus had complained that our ideas present no additional beings to account for; and that the way to understand "objective being in the intellect" is as "simply the determination of an act of the intellect by means of an object" (AT VII 92; CSM II 66f.). In reply, Descartes clarifies that the way to understand "objective being in the intellect" is that the objects of perception are, in a sense, *in* our ideas of them:

> "Objective being in the intellect," he [Caterus] says, "is simply the determination of an act of the intellect by means of an object, and this is merely an extraneous label which adds nothing to the thing itself." Notice here that he is referring to the thing itself as if it were located outside the intellect, and in this sense "objective being in the intellect" is certainly an extraneous label; but I was speaking of the idea, which is never outside the intellect, and in this sense "objective being" simply means being in the intellect in the way in which objects are normally there.
> (AT VII 102; CSM II 74)

Descartes illustrates his point with our idea of the sun, explaining what he means in saying that the sun has objective being in the intellect:

> By this I mean that the idea of the sun is the sun itself existing in the intellect – not of course formally existing, as it does in the heavens, but objectively existing, i.e. in the way in which objects normally are in the intellect.
> (AT VII 102f.; CSM II 75)

How should we understand this alleged "way in which objects are normally in the intellect"? The portrait analogy helps. We have noted that with a portrait of the president there is a sense in which the president is *in* the painting; it is indeed the sense in which "objects normally are *in*" the pictures portraying them. The analogy is of the right sort. In the *Principles*, Descartes explicitly compares what is "contained in the idea merely objectively" to what is contained "in a picture" (AT VIIIA 11; CSM I 199; cf. also AT III 567; CSMK 214). And in the *Meditations*, he makes clear that this "objective mode of being belongs to ideas by their very nature" (AT VII 42; CSM II 29), a claim that helps us to appreciate the continuity between the doctrine of objective being and the contention that ideas are, by their very nature, *tanquam* images.[13]

Interpretive disagreements abound in connection with the doctrine of objective being. One way of situating the differences is in the terms of competing theories about the nature of ideas. According to so-called *act* theories of ideas, ideas are conceived as acts or operations of mind, but not as perceptual objects. In normal sense perception of the sun, the only perceptual *object* is the sun itself – in the heavens. Act theories deny not that in the perceiving mind there is an idea of the sun, but that the mind's perception is *of* the idea. In contrast are so-called *act-object* theories of ideas. Act-object theories concur that ideas function as perceptual acts and operations. But act-object theories allow, in addition, that ideas function as perceptual objects. In the context of a realist philosopher like Descartes, the view is not that in perceiving the sun, the idea of the sun is the ultimate object of perception; rather, the sun itself is. The view is instead that the idea functions as a *mediating* object of perception. Pictures do again provide a helpful analogy, and, as we have seen, Descartes encourages the analogy. Suppose in viewing a portrait of Obama, my attention is directed toward the object portrayed – the man himself, not the painting. In that case, I am perceiving Obama. But it is also the case that I am perceiving Obama *via* my perception of another object, the one *in* the portrait. Obama is the ultimate object of perception; the portrait of him is a mediating object of perception. If, in Descartes's theory, we understand sensory ideas on the model of mental pictures, they function as mediating perceptual objects in an analogous sense.

Both act and act-object theory interpretations must reckon with the doctrine of objective being. Act theory interpretations must either identify the objective sense of an idea with the idea *qua* act or operation (as we saw Caterus doing), or with the object perceived – for example the sun itself. Act-object theory interpretations can identify the objective sense of an idea with the sense in which the idea counts as a perceptual object: roughly, the sense suggested by the earlier analogy to the hall of presidential portraits. I favor an act-object interpretation of Descartes, and I take that analogy to shed light on his meaning.

Because Descartes holds that ideas are always acts and operations of mind, only act theory and act-object theory interpretations of him make any sense. But seventeenth century theories of ideas encompass two further options – *object* theories and *dispositional* theories.

The theory at play in Malebranche's Vision in God doctrine is best described as an object theory of ideas. Accordingly, ideas function as perceptual objects, but not as perceptual acts – at least, not where perceptual *acts* are understood as modifications of our minds, or particular datable mental events.[14] On Malebranche's theory, when we have normal sense perception of a body, say the sun, the idea of it is located in the divine mind; sense perception is of course accompanied by *sensations*, and these are acts of our minds. In Malebranche's theory, unlike Descartes, sensations do not count as ideas:

> When we perceive something sensible, two things are found in our perception: *sensation* and pure *idea*. The sensation is a modification of our soul, and it is God who causes it in us. . . . As for the idea found in conjunction with the sensation, it is in God, and we see it because it pleases God to reveal it to us. God joins

the sensation to the idea when objects are present so that we may believe them to be present and that we may have all the feelings and passions that we should have in relation to them.

(*Search* 3.2.6/LO 234)

The result is a full ontological dissociation of act and object, locating them in different minds.

Leibniz embraces a dispositional theory, whereby ideas need not be realized either as perceptual acts or as objects of conscious perception. Consequently, his theory counts as none of the above: "*an idea consists, not in some act, but in the faculty of thinking*, and we are said to have an idea of a thing even if we do not think of it, if only, on a given occasion, we can think of it" (*PPL* 207). We'll return to dispositional theories in section 3.

Commentators are split over whether to interpret Descartes as holding an act theory of ideas or instead an act-object theory, with regard to normal sense perception. A survey of the literature reveals not only that there are significant numbers of scholars on both sides of the debate but also that neither side is without weighty arguments. Though I hold an act-object interpretation, this chapter does not aim to settle the debate. I do, however, want to debunk one influential line of argument that is regularly made, and that is taken as establishing that the philosopher in question holds an act theory of ideas.

Call this the *identity-entails-act-theory* argument. The reasoning is supposed to establish a commitment to an act theory, based on the relationship between (1) the mind's *ideas* and (2) its corresponding *acts of perception*. If the relation between (1) and (2) is one of identity – that is, ideas are understood as being numerically the same ontological entities as their corresponding acts of perception – then, goes the reasoning, this shows that one is committed to an act theory of ideas. Versions of this argument are made for Descartes, Arnauld, Locke, and others.[15] Descartes and Locke sometimes use the term *idea* for both (1) and (2), perhaps even seeming to strengthen the argument. I'll therefore refer to ideas in the first sense, noted in (1), as "ideas/objects," and in the second sense, noted in (2), as "ideas/acts." As I want now to argue, the problem with the identity-entails-act-theory argument is that it is invalid.

To help clarify the argument's invalidity, distinguish two versions of the act-object theory. Call the one version the *tertium quid* view. On the *tertium quid* rendering, the idea/object counts as a third ontological entity in the perceptual chain: one item is the act of perception (the idea/act); a second item is the ultimate object of perception (say, the sun itself); a third item is the idea/object which functions as an ontological middleman, standing, as it were, between the act of perception and the ultimate object of perception. Though Malebranche's theory of ideas does not count as an act-object theory, it illustrates the notion of an idea/object (in the divine mind) functioning as a *tertium quid*, standing between the act of perception (in our minds) and the ultimate object of perception (the sun in the sky). In contrast with the *tertium quid* version of the act-object theory is what I'll call the *identity* version of the theory. Accordingly, the idea/object and its corresponding idea/act are, ontologically speaking, numerically the same mental item.[16] The idea/object is not a third entity over and above the act of perception and the ultimate object of perception. In Descartes's scheme of distinctions, the idea/object and its corresponding idea/act are only rationally distinct.[17] The analogy with pictures is again helpful. Consider a painting of the sun. In one sense, we can regard the painting in terms of the kinds of materials constituting it – for example oil on canvas. In another sense, we can regard the painting in terms of what it portrays – that is, the sun (as portrayed). Importantly, these are different ways of regarding *numerically the same object*. The sun-as-portrayed is a mediating perceptual object, but it is not ontologically distinct from the canvas. Likewise with ideas, on the identity version of the act-object theory. An idea can be regarded in terms of what constitutes it – regarding it as an act or modification of mind. Alternatively, the very same idea can be regarded in terms of what it portrays – regarding it as the sun (not, of course, the sun in the sky). Something comparable holds for other representational media. Michelangelo's *David* can be regarded as a hunk of stone, or as a representation of David; either way, it is numerically the same object.

The identity version of the act-object theory clarifies the invalidity of the identity-entails-act-theory argument. From the mere fact that a philosopher affirms the relevant identity of *ideas*, and their corresponding *acts of perception*, it does not follow that the philosopher holds an act theory. Other textual and doctrinal considerations would have to be marshaled to establish this conclusion.[18]

One might attempt to defend the reasoning of the identity-entails-act-theory argument by maintaining that the identity version of the act-object theory does not really count as an act-object theory. Such a defender might have in mind that to identify the idea with the act of perception just *is* to hold an act theory. But this is to ignore the difference between how the act and act-object theories understand the notion of ideas/objects. On act theories, the *only* perceptual object in play in normal sense perception is the external object – the sun itself, in our example. By contrast, on act-object theories there are *dual* perceptual objects: the idea of sun, which is the mediating perceptual object, and the sun itself, which is the ultimate object of perception. This difference between act and act-object theories has significant epistemic implications. For where ideas function as mediating objects of perception, they impose a "veil-of-perception."[19] That is, even in veridical sense perception, the objects of immediate awareness are the mind's own ideas. Not so, however, on act theories.[20]

Much ado has been made over Arnauld's contribution to the debate, in his *On True and False Ideas*. For he purports to be clarifying a Cartesian theory of ideas. What one finds in some of the literature on Arnauld is, again, an appeal to the identity-entails-act-theory argument. For example, some commentators attribute to Arnauld an act theory of ideas, based on the following passage:[21]

> I also take the *idea* of an object and the *perception* of that object to be the same thing. . . . [I]t is certain that there are *ideas* in this sense, and that they are attributes or modifications of our mind.
>
> (VFI 65)

Departing somewhat from Descartes's broad use of the term *idea*, Arnauld prefers to use the term *perception* for the mental act. The main point of this passage is made repeatedly by Arnauld, as when he writes that the idea and the perceptual act are not "two different entities, but rather a single modification of our soul" (VFI 66).

Such passages are exemplary of texts which – when properly understood – are *neutral* as to act and act-object interpretations. From the mere fact that Arnauld identifies the idea and its corresponding act of perception, it does not follow that he holds an act theory of ideas. In the broader context of Arnauld's work, he is trying to distance himself from Malebranche's theory whereby the ideas existing in the divine mind are *really distinct* from the perceptual acts in our minds. Arnauld indeed writes that the *only* representative ideas he rejects "as superfluous entities" are those that are "imagined to be really distinct from ideas taken as perception" (VFI 66). That he explicitly distances himself *only* from Malebranche's rendering of representative ideas suggests that Arnauld means to leave room for other conceptions of representative ideas. I contend that Arnauld's point is not to distance himself from all manner of act-object theories, but only *tertium quid* versions. Indeed, if we check other passages, we find Arnauld writing the following:

> [I]f I think of the sun, the objective reality of the sun, which is present to my mind, is the immediate object of this perception; and the possible or existing sun, which is outside my mind, is so to speak its mediate object. It is clear from this that, without invoking *representations* distinct from perceptions [as Malebranche does], it is true in this sense that, not only in the case of material things but generally in regard to all things, it is our ideas that we see *immediately* and which are *the immediate object of our thought*.
>
> (VFI 71f.)

This passage reads well as an affirmation of the identity version of the act-object theory. Arnauld makes clear that ideas function as mediating perceptual objects – the representing idea is "the immediate object" of the perception, what "we see *immediately*." And he distances himself from theories (like Malebranche's theory) rendering the representing ideas as being ontologically distinct from the corresponding perceptual act.[22]

2.2. Ideas as immediately perceived

We saw at the outset of section 2 that there is wide agreement in characterizing ideas as the objects of immediate perception. There are, however, multiple notions of *immediacy* arising in connection with perception. Malebranche, for example, embraces this characterization, even while placing ideas in the divine mind. Of particular interest are notions of immediacy arising in debates concerning *direct* versus *indirect* realism. The position called *direct realism* results from combining a direct theory of perception with metaphysical realism – the latter being the view that material objects have mind-independent existence. By contrast, *indirect realism* results from combining an indirect theory of perception (one popular version of which is called a representational theory of perception) with metaphysical realism. Commentators are split over whether to interpret the likes of Descartes, Arnauld, and Locke as direct realists or instead as indirect realists. I suggest that some of the dispute arises from ambiguity in the terms. What notion of *directness* or *immediacy* is at play in such views? And is this the sense in which ideas are said to be the objects of immediate perception?

Elsewhere,[23] I clarify multiple notions of perceptual directness or immediacy (I treat these terms as synonymous). For present purposes, I'll briefly summarize three of these notions.

First, what I call *epistemic directness* concerns the perception or apprehension of the truth of propositions – for example *that* there is a sun in the sky, *that* it is very bright in color, and so forth. This may be apprehended via inference, or without it. Inference introduces *epistemic* mediation rendering indirect one's perception of whether the proposition is true. Where the proposition is instead apprehended without inference, that is self-evidently, the perception of it is epistemically direct. In latter such cases, writes Locke, the mind considers the constituent ideas making up the proposition "by themselves, without the *intervention* of any other" – that is, "by their *immediate* Comparison" (*Essay* 4.2.1–2, my emphasis).[24] Directness and immediacy, on this notion, is a function simply of whether inference is involved.[25] My perception is epistemically direct if noninferential, epistemically indirect if inferential.

Second, what I call *phenomenological directness* concerns whether in normal sense perception our perception of external objects is *experienced* as direct. While engrossed in an event I am watching – say, a State of the Union Address – I may cease to notice that I am watching the president via the mediation of a television. If, in this case, the only perceptual objects that are a *noticed* part of my experience are those represented by the medium – but not the medium itself – then my perception is phenomenologically direct. Where instead the mediating role of another perceptual object – whether a television, photograph, sculpture, walking stick, and so forth – is a noticed part of the experience, then the perception is phenomenologically indirect.[26] Of present interest is not whether external-world material objects play a noticed mediating role, but whether internal world *ideas* do. There is general (perhaps universal) agreement that normal sense perception is, in this sense, phenomenologically direct, precisely because no mental entities are a *noticed* part of normal experience. As Hume writes, of ordinary experience, "men are carried, by a natural instinct or prepossession" to suppose – incorrectly, in Hume's view – "the very images, presented by the senses, to be the external objects, and never entertain any suspicion, that the one are nothing but representations of the other" (*Enquiry* 12.1).

Third, what I call *objectual* directness is perhaps best understood in an analogy with how pictures mediate our awareness of the objects they portray. In such cases, dual perceptual objects are in play. The portrait of Obama is a perceptual object in its own right, as is Obama himself. Having never seen Obama in person, my perception of him has always been via the mediation of some other physical medium – whether a photograph, a portrait, or a television. If I am perceiving Obama via my perception of some other object – material or immaterial – and that other object is, itself, a perceptible object in its own right – then my perception of Obama is *objectually* mediated; and, importantly, it is mediated in a manner independent of whether I *employ inferences* and independent of whether I *notice* the mediating role. That is, this notion of mediation is distinct from the epistemic and phenomenological notions. I call it *objectual*, because the medium is itself a perceptual object.[27]

I suggest that the notion of objectual directness and immediacy provides the correct understanding of Descartes's characterization of ideas – as being the objects of immediate perception. The similar characterizations we quoted from other seventeenth century philosophers deserve careful treatments of their own, and in the broader context of those philosophical systems. But consider, again, quotations from Descartes and Locke: that ideas are "the only immediate objects of my sensory awareness" (AT VII 75; CSM II 252); and that "*the Mind*, in all its Thoughts and Reasonings, hath no other immediate Object but its own *Ideas*" (*Essay* 4.1.1). According to act-object theories of ideas, ideas function as perceptual objects. Such theories conceive of ideas as perceptual media the immediate perception of which is involved in our mediated perception of external bodies. The resulting understanding of ideas fits well with these quotations from Descartes and Locke. And it fits well our notion of objectual directness and immediacy. The notion of immediacy in these quotations cannot be that of *epistemic* immediacy, unless one is prepared, thereby, to conclude that the point of these passages is to convey that our perception of bodies is indirect; for these quotes entail that only ideas, but not bodies, are directly perceived. (I do hold that these passages convey that our perception of bodies is indirect, but not *because* of reading these quotations to be invoking epistemic directness.) Neither is *phenomenological* directness the notion at play in these quotes. For it is bodies, not ideas, that are *experienced* as being the objects of immediate awareness – unlike what these quotations claim. Some other notion of directness is at play in these quotes. I contend that it is the notion of objectual directness and immediacy.

Returning to the question of whether the likes of Descartes, Arnauld, and Locke are direct realists, it turns out that that question can be ambiguous. For claims about the directness of perception can only be understood *relative* to some notion of directness. There is not much debate about whether normal sense perception is phenomenologically direct. Philosophical and interpretive debates tend to center around whether it is also epistemically or objectually direct. Interesting interpretive work on these questions is ongoing. For instance, in his direct realist interpretation of Descartes, John Carriero argues that the point of the Sixth Meditation proof concerning the external world has been systematically misunderstood: Descartes is not trying to argue *from* facts about his own ideas *to* facts about the external world *causes* of those ideas – as if conceding that a veil of perception must be overcome; rather, the point of the proof is to show "that there is no veil of ideas" (2009, 148):

> The argument (as I understand it) is not intended to get us from a realm of inner mental objects ("sensory ideas") to some other realm of outer, physical objects ("bodies"); rather, it is to confirm our instinctive feeling that we have been receiving information ("directly") from outer objects, bodies, all along.
> (2009, 26)

On this issue, and others, Carriero makes substantive arguments to support his interpretation – an account whereby sense perception is direct relative to (what I call) the epistemic and objectual notions. On my own more orthodox interpretation, Descartes holds that sense perception is direct relative to the phenomenological notion, but indirect relative to both the epistemic and objectual notions.[28] Though my primary aim has not been to argue for my interpretation, I believe we should understand statements by Descartes, Arnauld, and Locke – to the effect that ideas are the objects of immediate perception – in terms of the objectual notions of immediacy and directness.

3. Origins of ideas

To Mersenne, Descartes draws a threefold distinction of ideas based on the manner of their reception:

> I distinguish three kinds [of ideas]. Some are adventitious, such as the idea we commonly have of the sun; others are constructed or made up, in which class we can put the idea which the astronomers construct of the sun by their reasoning; and others are innate, such as the idea of God, mind, body, triangle, and in general all those which represent true, immutable and eternal essences.
> (AT III 383; CSMK 183)[29]

On this division, so-called *rationalists* and *empiricists* differ primarily on whether any ideas are innate, with empiricists maintaining that sense experience, the adventitious category, is our only basic ideational source. The "invented" or "constructed" category includes the further ideas minds generate from their existing ideas.

In what follows, section 3.1 discusses problems in understanding the criterion of innateness. Section 3.2 considers the debate about innate ideas. Section 3.3 develops key aspects of Locke's influential empiricist account.

3.1. *The criterion of innateness*

Alluding to Plato's doctrine of recollection, Descartes writes in his Fifth Meditation:

> [O]n first discovering them [various true and immutable natures] it seems that I am not so much learning something new as remembering what I knew before; or it seems like noticing for the first time things which were long present within me although I had never turned my mental gaze on them before.
> (AT VII 64; CSM II 44)

In an open letter, Descartes is more explicit in his approval of Plato's view:

> [A]ccording to Plato, Socrates asks a slave boy about the elements of geometry and thereby makes the boy able to dig out certain truths from his own mind which he had not previously recognized were there, thus attempting to establish the doctrine of reminiscence. Our knowledge of God is of this sort.
> (AT VIIIB 167; CSMK 222f.)

Such passages reveal a commitment to some form of innateness. But questions arise. How are we to understand the claim that there are ideas innate within us?[30]

One potential problem in understanding Descartes's notion of innateness arises from his understanding of ideas as *items of conscious awareness*.[31] If there were innate such ideas, then *ipso facto*, we would have ongoing awareness of them; but because there is nothing of which we have such ongoing awareness, there are no innate ideas. In the Third Objections, Hobbes puts the point this way: "It follows that no idea is innate; for what is innate is always present" (AT VII 188; CSM II 132). In his reply to Hobbes, Descartes adopts a dispositional characterization of innate ideas:

> [W]hen we say that an idea is innate in us, we do not mean that it is always there before us. This would mean that no idea was innate. We simply mean that we have within ourselves the faculty of summoning up the idea.
> (AT VII 189; CSM II 132)

This dispositional account is similar to a view held by Leibniz, who writes, "we are said to have an idea of a thing even if we do not think of it, if only, on a given occasion, we can think of it" (*PPL*, 207). The problem for Descartes, unlike Leibniz, is that his understanding of ideas seems to preclude such a view. If ideas are *actual* – not merely potential – items of awareness, he must either give up that there are innate ideas (for roughly Hobbes's reasons), or else say that what is innate is not strictly speaking the idea but the ability to summon it. The latter option provides a way of understanding his reply to Hobbes. Accordingly, when we *say* that an idea is innate, we *mean* that we have an innate disposition to have the idea; that is, the sense in which so-called innate ideas are *in* the mind is as an ability to be perceived. Ideas "always exist within us potentially," writes Descartes (AT VIIIB 361; CSM I 305), adding that the things "said to be naturally implanted in us are not for that reason expressly known by us" (AT VIIIB 166; CSMK 222) – an account allowing Descartes to maintain, with Leibniz, that we need not actually be aware of what is innate.

Some commentators have worried that a dispositional account of innate ideas is at odds with Descartes's doctrine of the transparency of mind.[32] The doctrine has it that there is nothing in the mind of which it is unaware. This doctrine is a consequence of defining the *whole* essence of mind in terms of thought, while defining *thought* so as "to include everything that is within us in such a way that we are immediately aware [*immediate conscii*] of it" (AT VII 160; CSM II 113). But if there is nothing in the mind of which we are unaware, it would seem to follow that there are no innate dispositions of which we are unaware. A version of the Hobbes objection therefore repeats itself. But Descartes has a reply. To Arnauld he clarifies that the transparency doctrine extends to innate faculties only on occasions when they are actually operating, but not when they remain unactualized:

> As to the fact that there can be nothing in the mind, in so far as it is a thinking thing, of which it is not aware, . . . we cannot have any thought of which we are not aware at the very moment when it is in us. . . . But it must be noted that, although we are always actually aware of the acts or operations of our minds, we are not always aware of the mind's faculties or powers, except potentially.
> (AT VII 246; CSM II 171–172)

On the dispositional account of innate ideas that has emerged, the mind is hardwired with various "ideas" *in that* it is has various dispositions or faculties or capacities which, when summoned, are realized as actual ideas – that is items of conscious awareness. We should add, however, that not just any summoning will do. *Proper* reflection is required in order to reveal these hardwired ideas, and that is one of the principal reasons why a proper method is needed in order to discover these ideas.[33] Absent proper method, important innate ideas might remain unactualized dispositions. In one place, Descartes states this in terms of implicit versus explicit ideas:

> I do not doubt that everyone has within himself an implicit idea of God, that is to say, an aptitude to perceive it explicitly; but I am not surprised that not everyone is aware that he has it or notices that he has it. Some people will perhaps not notice it even after reading my *Meditations* a thousand times.
> (AT III 430; CSMK 194; cf. AT IV 187)

The dispositional account of innateness would appear susceptible to a serious objection. The problem is that it fails to exclude any possible ideas. If the innateness of an idea is understood simply in terms of our minds having a disposition or capacity to have that idea, then every possible idea – including each possible adventitious idea – counts as innate. For every idea the mind can have is an idea it has the *capacity* to have. Putting the objection in terms of the empiricist tabula rasa metaphor, even an entirely smooth tablet has the *capacity* to take on whatever forms imprint it. Therefore, the dispositional account of innateness fails to distinguish innate ideas from experiential ideas.[34] In his *Essay*, Locke articulates this objection – here targeting a dispositional account of innate *truths*:[35]

> So that if the Capacity of knowing be the natural Impression contended for, all the Truths a Man ever comes to know, will, by this Account, be, every one of them, innate; and this great Point will amount to no more, but only to a very improper way of speaking; which whilst it pretends to assert the contrary, says nothing different from those, who deny innate Principles. For no Body, I think, ever denied, that the Mind was capable of knowing several Truths. The Capacity, they say, is innate, the Knowledge acquired. But then to what end such contest for certain innate Maxims? If Truths can be imprinted on the Understanding without being perceived, I can see no difference there can be, between any Truths the Mind is capable of knowing in respect of their Original: They must all be innate, or all adventitious: In vain shall a Man go about to distinguish them.
>
> (*Essay* 1.2.5)

The objection would appear devastating. As thus far characterized, the dispositional account of innateness does not offer a coherent way of distinguishing innate and non-innate ideas.

Enter Leibniz. Like Descartes, he accepts the rationalist doctrine of innate ideas. Yet, as we have seen, he characterizes ideas – all ideas – in terms of dispositions or capacities. This is promising. For because he holds that all ideas are dispositions, although not all are innate, he presumably has some other account of innateness than simply as dispositions. Indeed, Leibniz makes a distinction between two sorts of dispositions. Writing in his *New Essays* – a virtual point-by-point rebuttal to Locke's *Essay* – Leibniz responds to Locke's critique of the dispositional account of innateness. Leibniz agrees with Locke that the dispositional account of innateness would be fruitless if it entailed only "the mere capacity to receive those items of knowledge – a passive power to do so, as indeterminate as the power of wax to receive shapes or of a blank page to receive words" (*NE* 79). But when properly understood, the account entails more. To help clarify the proper understanding, Leibniz distinguishes two sorts of dispositions via an analogy to a sculptor's block of marble:

> I have also used the analogy of a veined block of marble, as opposed to an entirely homogeneous block of marble, or to a blank tablet – what the philosophers call a *tabula rasa*. For if the soul were like such a blank tablet then truths would be in us as the shape of Hercules is in a piece of marble when the marble is entirely neutral as to whether it assumes this shape or some other. However, if there were veins in the block which marked out the shape of Hercules rather than other shapes, then that block would be more determined to that shape and Hercules would be innate in it, in a way, even though labour would be required to expose the veins and to polish them into clarity, removing everything that prevents their being seen. This is how ideas and truths are innate in us – as inclinations, dispositions, tendencies, or natural potentialities.
>
> (*NE* 52)

Both blocks of marble have a capacity or disposition to be sculpted into the bust of Hercules. Only the veined block is *preformed* to take on this shape. But a preformation in the relevant sense "is not a bare faculty, consisting in a mere possibility of understanding those truths," adds Leibniz (*NE* 80). Because the terminology can be confusing, I'll mark the intended distinction using the terms *disposition* and *predisposition* (my terminology, not Leibniz's). The tabula rasa mind is disposed to have whatever ideas can be impressed on it. By contrast, concept nativism holds that the mind is *pre*disposed toward some ideas more so than others, whether or not the favored ideas are actually ever realized. Leibniz's distinction answers Locke's objection. And it restores definitional credibility to the dispositional account of innateness – though we should perhaps now refer to it as the *predispositional* account.

It is worth asking whether the predispositional account marks a correction of Descartes's account, or a clarification of it. Nowhere does Descartes explicitly draw the kind of distinction Leibniz makes. In some passages, the most natural reading suggests a mere disposition of the sort Locke decisively critiques. For example, in the *Comments on a Certain Broadsheet*, while characterizing innate ideas in terms of a faculty or disposition, Descartes writes,

> Consequently, these ideas, along with that faculty, are innate in us, i.e. they always exist within us potentially, for to exist in some faculty is not to exist actually, but merely potentially, since the term "faculty" denotes nothing but a potentiality.
> (AT VIIIB 361; CSM I 305)

But even here, if we bring to bear the broader context of the paragraph, it is clear that Descartes means to be invoking what is somehow *pre*formed in the mind, rather than a mere disposition. This commitment to the predispositional view comes more clearly in other passages. Elsewhere in the *Comments*, Descartes writes that the sense in which ideas are innate,

> is the same sense as that in which we say that generosity is "innate" in certain families, or that certain diseases such as gout or stones are innate in others: it is not so much that the babies of such families suffer from these diseases in their mother's womb, but simply that they are born with a certain "faculty" or tendency [*dispositione*] to contract them.
> (AT VIIIB 358; CSM I 303f.)

Though Descartes uses the language of a mere disposition, his example – of some families being more disposed to certain traits than others – entails what we are calling the predispositional view. More generally, Descartes's position that there are true and immutable natures innate to our minds makes clear that the veined block of marble provides the better metaphor for his account of innateness.[36]

What is less clear is how to fit this understanding of the mind – as having deep structure, or veining, in the form of innate predispositions – with Descartes's more general understanding of the nature of minds. As we have seen, he holds that we need not be aware of the mind's faculties, but only of the actual operation of those faculties – a view which entails that the predispositions are not themselves thoughts. But then it is unclear how his doctrine of innate predispositions squares with the doctrine that the *whole* essence of minds consists in *thought*.

3.2. The debate about innate ideas

How does one make a winning case on the innate ideas debate? One straightforward strategy involves rebutting unimpressive arguments. For example, in reply to popular accounts reasoning from the existence of principles "universally agreed upon by all Mankind" to the conclusion that those principles are innate, Locke points out what should have been obvious:

> This Argument, drawn from *Universal Consent*, has this Misfortune in it, That if it were true in matter of Fact, that there were certain Truths, wherein all Mankind agreed, it would not prove them innate. . . .
>
> But, which is worse, this Argument of Universal Consent, which is made use of, to prove innate Principles, seems to me a Demonstration that there are none such: Because there are none to which all Mankind give an Universal Assent.
>
> (*Essay* 1.2.2–4)

Dispositional accounts are more difficult to refute. Addressing why innate common notions are "not equally well perceived by everyone," Descartes explains that "they are capable of being clearly and distinctly perceived" by everyone, and that the reason they are not is because such notions "are in conflict with the preconceived opinions of some people"; whereas, these notions *are* perceived by those "who are free from such preconceived opinions" (AT VIIIA 24; CSM I 209).

I suggest that the most powerful and influential arguments in support of innate ideas take the form of (what have come to be called) *poverty of stimulus* arguments.[37] Such arguments reason from the premise that we have ideas that sense experience is too impoverished to give rise to, to the conclusion that those ideas derive from a nonexperiential source – namely an innate source. The reasoning is valid, assuming that our ideas either derive from the senses or are innate to our minds. Empiricists must therefore attempt to block the premise. One blocking strategy involves denying that we have the claimed idea.[38] An alternative blocking strategy involves denying that the senses are too impoverished to give rise to the claimed ideas.

Descartes's most famous such argument for innate ideas comes in his Second Meditation discussion of the wax. Imagine a melting hunk of wax, along with the ensuing transformation of all its sensory features. Appropriate contemplation is supposed to reveal a distinct conception of the wax, itself, as enduring the sensory changes:

> So what was it in the wax that I understood with such distinctness? Evidently none of the features which I arrived at by means of the senses; for whatever came under taste, smell, sight, touch or hearing has now altered – yet the wax remains.
>
> (AT VII 30; CSM II 20)

Descartes goes on to argue that our sensory and imaginative faculties are too impoverished to give rise to this distinct idea. The upshot is that the distinct idea of the wax must be innate. More generally, with regard to our distinct ideas of bodies, Descartes concludes "that this perception derives not from their being touched or seen but from their being understood" (AT VII 34; CSM II 22).

Descartes and other nativists offer further such poverty-of-stimulus-style arguments for ideas in metaphysics, mathematics, and logic. As already noted, empiricists are not without resources in their effort to block such arguments. The one blocking strategy involves denying that we have any such distinct idea, upon stripping away everything relevant to the senses; the other blocking strategy involves showing that sense experience can, after all, account for the content of the alleged idea.

Malebranche brings an interesting perspective to the anti-nativism side of the debate. He is no empiricist, but neither does he accept that we have innate ideas, for he denies that there are any ideas in *our* minds, at all. The locus of ideas is God's mind. Of particular interest is that Malebranche's theory undercuts an assumption at play in poverty-of-stimulus-style arguments – namely the assumption that our ideas either derive from the senses or are innate to our minds. Without this assumption, such arguments fail to support their intended conclusion. From the premise that we perceive ideas which do not derive from sense experience, it does not follow that such ideas are innate to our minds. Malebranche nonetheless offers his own series of arguments against innate ideas, including an appeal to parsimony. God always acts in the simplest way. And it is simplest, argues Malebranche, for there to be a single set of ideas, rather than replicating these beings – ideas understood as "representative beings" – in each created mind:

> Now, I ask whether it is likely that God created so many things along with the mind of man. My own view is that such is not the case, especially since all this could be done in another, much simpler and easier way, as we shall see shortly. For as God always acts in the simplest ways, it does not seem reasonable to explain how we know objects by assuming the creation of an infinity of beings, since the difficulty can be resolved in an easier and more straightforward fashion.
> (*Search* 3.2.4/LO 227)

I suggested that poverty-of-stimulus-style arguments have made the most effective case in support of innate ideas. I would likewise suggest that the most powerful and influential case for the other side derived from showing the explanatory power of experience. We can indeed view the bulk of book II, of Locke's *Essay*, as an extended argument showing that experience is rich enough to ground the gamut of concepts we have, including difficult philosophical notions. Let's now turn our attention to that project.

3.3. Locke on the origin of ideas

Empiricists at least as far back as Aristotle have likened the mind to a tabula rasa waiting to be impressed upon by the senses. As Locke explains the metaphor,

> Let us then suppose the Mind to be, as we say, white Paper, void of all Characters, without any *Ideas*; How comes it to be furnished? Whence comes it by that vast store, which the busy and boundless Fancy of Man has painted on it, with an almost endless variety? Whence has it all the materials of Reason and Knowledge? To this I answer, in one word, From *Experience*.
> (*Essay* 2.1.2)

Empiricism does in theory acknowledge just two of Descartes's three kinds of ideas – namely *adventitious* and *constructed*. The twofold distinction here is between the ideas originally presented in sensation and the further ideas the mind generates from those originals.

A number of issues arise in connection with the origins of experiential ideas. One issue concerns the causes of those original sensations. There is general agreement among major seventeenth century philosophers – both rationalists and empiricists – that sensations are caused by something external to the mind.[39] Another issue – our issue – concerns the mind's work in generating its further ideas from the originals. Related to the latter is the taxonomic division of labor between adventitious and constructed ideas. Prima facie, the bulk of our ideas about objects in the world would fall in the adventitious category. Consider, for example, our ideas of such ordinary objects as tables, trees, horses, and so forth. Are these ideas among the originals impressed on our minds by the world? Or are these constructed by our minds from some other ideas – the *others* being originally impressed on our minds by the world? The answer will depend on one's theory. Recall that Descartes places the ordinary idea of the sun in the adventitious category – "some [ideas] are adventitious, such as the idea we commonly have of the sun" – a placement that initially *seems* right. Locke's theory has the perhaps counterintuitive result that our ideas of such objects as tables, trees, horses – and stars – are constructions of the mind's own making. They are not among the original sensations imposed on us by the world.[40]

My aim in section 2.3 is to clarify the main features of Locke's account leading to this counterintuitive result. I'll first clarify his account of the distinction between adventitious and constructed ideas. I'll then develop the implications of the account for the status of ordinary objects.

Well known is that Locke distinguishes *simple* and *complex* ideas. Simples are the original sensations impressed on our minds; complexes are the further ideas the mind constructs from its simples. Locke's terminology has proven misleading, suggesting – wrongly (as will emerge) – that the original ideas always have simpler content than the further ideas constructed from them.

Simple ideas divide into two basic sorts. Those produced when the mind is directed outward, at bodies, Locke calls ideas of *sensation*; those produced when the mind is directed inward, at its own operations, he calls ideas of *reflection*.[41] A third category includes simples produced in either of the two basic ways – "other simple *Ideas*, which convey themselves into the Mind, by all the ways of Sensation and Reflection" (*Essay* 2.7.1).

Locke catalogues the various simple ideas of sensation in relation to the sensory inputs with which they are linked. Some "*have admittance only through one Sense*": for example "Light and Colours . . . come in only by the Eyes: All kinds of Noises, Sounds, and Tones only by the Ears: The several Tastes and Smells, by the Nose and Palate" (*Essay* 2.3.1). Other simples enter the mind via "*divers Senses*": for example our ideas of "*Space*, or *Extension, Figure, Rest*, and *Motion*: For these make perceivable impressions, both on the Eyes and Touch" (*Essay* 2.5.1).

Whereas simple ideas of sensation represent the qualities of external bodies, simple ideas of reflection represent states of the mind itself. That is, ideas of reflection are those "the Mind gets by reflecting on its own Operations within it self" – such operations as "*Perception, Thinking, Doubting, Believing, Reasoning, Knowing, Willing*" (*Essay* 2.1.4).

In book 2, chapter 2 ("*Of simples* Ideas"), Locke develops two main criteria for counting ideas as simple rather than complex – a *content* criterion and a *causal* criterion. The content criterion of idea simplicity explains his use of the terminology of *simple* and *complex*. Simple ideas are simple in the sense of having "uncompounded" content. Locke elaborates this by saying that each simple idea "contains in it nothing but *one uniform Appearance*" and "is not distinguishable into different *Ideas*" (*Essay* 2.2.1).

Some readers have worried that this characterization of *uncompoundedness* presents distinct conditions – what I'll call the *uniform-appearances* condition and the *not-further-distinguishable* condition. The worry is that these conditions yield different outcomes (cf. Stroud 1977, 20f.). For example, colors and sounds seem to meet the uniform-appearances condition but not the not-further-distinguishable condition. Consider that sounds are a *complex* of timbre and pitch – that is, ideas of sounds can be further distinguished into these component ideas. But in that case (goes the worry), the not-further-distinguishable condition entails that ideas of sounds should be treated as complex ideas, not simples. (Versions of this problem extend to other cases as well.)

I think Locke can avoid the problem if we regard his characterization as clarifying a *single* condition, rather than two. The section heading of *Essay* 2.1.1 is "*Uncompounded Appearances*," suggesting the following merging of the two conditions: simple ideas are uncompounded in being uniform appearances, that is they are not distinguishable into different component appearances. An idea of pitch cannot be a sensory appearance in the mind without it having some timbre or other; neither can an idea of timbre be a sensory appearance in the mind without it having some pitch or other. Neither of these component ideas could count, singly, as an *appearance* in the mind – the pitch-timbre complexity amounts to a minimum sensible. Therefore, neither idea counts as simple, because neither is an uncompounded appearance. As will emerge, the causal criterion of simplicity yields this same result – that ideas of pitch and timbre count as complex ideas.

The causal criterion of idea simplicity concerns the causes of an idea, not its content. The mind does not actively produce simple ideas in the same manner as it produces complex ideas. The simples are "those *Ideas*, in the reception whereof, the Mind is only passive" (*Essay* 2.12.1); complex ideas are produced *by* the mind, from its simples – "but as the Mind is wholly Passive in the reception of all its simple *Ideas*, so it exerts several acts of its own, whereby out of its simple *Ideas*, as the Materials and Foundations of the rest, the other are framed" (*Essay* 2.12.1). One difficulty is that the causal criterion seems better suited to ideas of external sense than to ideas of reflection – a problem Locke does not address. Focusing on its application to external sense, that simple ideas are passively received has two corollaries. First, simple ideas cannot be voluntarily refused.[42] Second, they cannot be voluntarily formed:[43] "it is not in the Power of the most exalted Wit, or enlarged Understanding, by any quickness or variety of Thought, to *invent or frame one new simple* Idea in the mind" (*Essay* 2.2.2). Like the content criterion, the causal criterion also entails that ideas of sounds are simple, whereas the ideas of pitch and timbre are complex. A person born deaf would be unable to frame an idea of sound, whereas those with fully functioning senses would be unable to avoid ideas of sound. And in persons already having such ideas, the mind produces the further ideas of pitch and timbre by the mental operation of abstraction.

One might worry that the causal criterion gets some ideas wrong. In mature minds, typical complex ideas – for example ideas of horses – seem to be formed not by the mind, but from the world imposing on the mind. Here, I suggest we understand the spirit of Locke's causal criterion to be that the formation of complex ideas necessarily involves mental operations, but not necessarily that it arises from voluntary effort.[44] I'll return to further reasons Locke is convinced that such complex ideas cannot be formed entirely by the world.

In book 2, chapter 12 ("Of *Complex* Ideas"), Locke explains three main ways that complex ideas are formed – "the Acts of the Mind wherein it exerts its Power over its simple *Ideas* are chiefly these three":

> 1. Combining several simple *Ideas* into one compound one, and thus all Complex *Ideas* are made. 2. The 2d. is bringing two *Ideas*, whether simple or complex, together; and setting them by one another, so as to take a view of them at once, without uniting them into one; by which way it gets all its *Ideas* of Relations. 3. The 3d. is separating them from all other *Ideas* that accompany them in their real existence; this is called *Abstraction*: And thus all its General *Ideas* are made.
>
> (*Essay* 2.12.1)

The first kind of operation – combining existing ideas to form something new – is the one most commonly associated with complex ideas; indeed, some such combining is arguably at play in the formation of all complex ideas.[45] The second and third operations also contribute to vast proportions of our ideas. The three kinds of operations are not exclusive. Complex ideas routinely involve more than one of these mental operations. Noteworthy is that in introducing these three operations, Locke says there are "chiefly" these three, implying that the threefold list might not be exhaustive. His point seems to be to highlight the main kinds of operations contributing to complex ideas.

In whatever ways the mind combines its ideas to form new complex ones, Locke thinks "they may be all reduced under these three Heads": ideas of *modes*, of *substances*, and of *relations* (*Essay* 2.12.3).

We are now in position to appreciate why, on Locke's account, our ideas of such objects as tables, trees, and horses fall into the category of complex ideas – a result entailed by both the content and causal criteria. Such ideas are made by the mind, rather than by the world. They are made "by collecting such Combinations of simple *Ideas*, as are by Experience and Observation of Men's Senses taken notice of to exist together. . . . Thus we come to have the *Ideas* of a Man, Horse, Gold, Water, etc." (*Essay* 2.23.3).

Recall the earlier worry that such ideas can seem to be formed entirely by the world. On a related worry, it might even seem that the sensory contents originally imposed on the mind have the complexity of, say, the idea of a horse. Locke thinks that decisive considerations dispel these worries. Consider that my complex idea of a horse may include simples from multiple senses – visual (e.g. its color, size, and shape), tactile (e.g. the feel of its mane), auditory (e.g. the sound of its neigh), olfactory (its smell), and so on. Because these simples are occasioned in the mind by different sensory inputs, the bundling of them into a single complex idea cannot have been the work of the world – "'tis plain," writes Locke, "the *Ideas* they [objects in the world] produce in the Mind, enter by the Senses simple and unmixed" (*Essay* 2.2.1). The world's contribution is to produce in the mind not a complex idea but rather a complexity of unbundled simple ideas. Minds do the bundling.

Related is that the work of bundling simples into complex ideas typically involves general ideas. In perceiving and recognizing an object as a horse, the mind collects the simple ideas presented in experience, noticing their agreement with its general idea of horses. "For when we say, this is a *Man*, that a *Horse*," explains Locke, "what do we else but rank Things under different specifick Names, as agreeing to those abstract *Ideas*, of which we have made those Names the signs?" (*Essay* 3.3.13). But the process of making general ideas is itself the "*Workmanship of the Understanding*," not the world. On Locke's view, "*General and Universal*, belong not to the real existence of Things; but *are the Inventions and Creatures of the Understanding*, made by it for its own use, *and concern only Signs*, Whether words or *Ideas*" (*Essay* 3.3.11). The contents of my ideas of *horses* and *humans* – and by which I rank things as one, rather than the other – are determined not by the world, but by my own mind.

One might object to this account of general ideas, arguing that if Locke's view were correct, then people would have differing conceptions of the objects in the world. Interestingly, Locke concurs; however, he cites this implication as support for his account of how general ideas are formed:

> For were they Nature's Workmanship, they could not be so various and different in several Men, as experience tells us they are. . . . It could not possibly be, that the abstract *Idea*, to which the name *Man* is given, should be different in several Men, if it were of Nature's making.
>
> (*Essay* 3.6.26)

In forming general ideas, most people "content themselves with some few obvious, and outward appearances of Things, thereby readily to distinguish and sort them for the common Affairs of Life" (*Essay* 3.6.30); the determination of which simples the mind selects for a general idea "*depends upon the various Care, Industry, or Fancy of him that makes it*" (*Essay* 3.6.29). Among Locke's favorite illustrations are the differences in how people conceive of gold:

> In some, this complex *Idea* contains a greater, and in others a smaller number of Qualities; and so is apparently such as the Mind makes it. The yellow shining Colour, makes *Gold* to children; others add Weight, Malleableness, and Fusibility; and others yet other Qualities, which they find joined with that yellow Colour, as constantly as its Weight and Fusibility: for in all these, and the like Qualities, one has as good a right to be put into the complex *Idea* of that Substance, wherein they are all join'd, as another. And therefore *different Men* leaving out, or putting in several simple *Ideas*, which others do not, according to their various Examination, Skill, or Observation of that subject, *have different Essences of Gold*; which must therefore be of their own, and not of Nature's making.
>
> (*Essay* 3.6.31)

Importantly on Locke's view, our conceptions often differ even in cases where they "pass well enough in ordinary Conversation" (*Essay* 3.6.31).

It emerges that on Locke's theory of ideas, the world – as perceived – owes more to construction than to the passive reception suggested by tabula rasa metaphors. That his philosophy anticipates aspects of Berkeley's immaterialism is well discussed. An important such anticipation is on display. On Locke's theory, the qualities causing our simple ideas are assumed to be *real*, though the uniform appearances of them are *ideas* in the mind. (They are indeed constructed appearances, at least in cases of secondary-quality ideas, which fail to resemble any real qualities in the world.) More to our present concerns, such objects as tables, trees, and horses are *ideal*; they are constructions of the mind's own making. In line with other seventeenth century transformations, the emerging understanding of our ideas of objects marks a step in the direction of the view whereby objects *conform to our cognition*, rather than the other way around.

Notes

1. The quoted passage is from the *Search for Truth*. Though the remark is from Epistemon, Eudoxus (Descartes's mouthpiece) approves of the characterization.
2. I argue this in Newman (2009).
3. Some commentators take this passage to show, further, that Descartes's choice of the term *idea* is linked specifically to nonsensory ideas. Ayers writes that Descartes is here stating that he chose the term "because its Scholastic employment for God's concepts of his creatures associated it clearly with intellect rather than with sense" (1991, 1:45). But this is not what the passage says. It says the term was chosen "because [*quia*]" of its standard reference to forms of divine perception, "although [*quamvis*]" we recognize no imagination in God (AT VII 181). That is, Descartes comes closer to saying he chose the term in spite of, rather than because of, its association with the intellect.
4. Words in angle brackets are part of the CSM translation and reflect additions found in the French edition.
5. On one kind of reading, volitions are not themselves ideas, though we are aware of them via ideas. But this remark to Hobbes implies something stronger – not just that we are aware of volitions via ideas, but that volitions *are* ideas. This stronger view finds support also in Descartes's remark to Mersenne – in the context of discussing our ideas of our acts of volition: "but I do not claim that the idea is different from the act itself" (AT III 295; CSMK 172). I take the point to be that ontologically the same mode of mind can be regarded either as an idea or as a volition. The upshot of this stronger reading is, ontologically speaking, that volitions *are* ideas – there is a mere "distinction of reason" between them (cf. AT VIIIA 30–31; CSM I 214–215).
6. Vere Chappell takes a different view, writing of the broader *tanquam* images passage: "That some thoughts are not ideas is clearly indicated in Meditation III" (1986, 195 note 13). Chappell cites also Descartes's 1649 letter to Clerselier (AT V 354; CSMK 376f.).
7. One finds many further passages implying that sensory ideas portray their objects in a way analogous with picturing (cf. *Essay* 2.24.1, 2.32.6, and 3.3.7). This way of reading Locke is not without controversy.
8. He extends the analogy, adding that the mind can "no more refuse to have, nor alter" its simple ideas "than a mirror can refuse, alter, or obliterate the Images or *Ideas*, which, the Objects set before it, do therein produce" (*Essay* 2.1.25), adding that over time those same ideas, if not refreshed, are lost from the memory – "the Imagery moulders away" (*Essay* 2.10.5).
9. On the resemblance conception of representation – not Locke's own official conception, but the one often at play in the context of contrasting Aristotelian and mechanist accounts of sensation – secondary-quality ideas *mis*represent the objects producing them. Locke may well have adopted the *tanquam* qualification – that is, that ideas "are, as it were, the Pictures of Things" – for reasons similar to those I have attributed to Descartes. Like Descartes, Locke also catalogues chimerical ideas *as* ideas (cf. *Essay* 2.30.1).
10. Cf. Wilson's influential discussion (1978, 102f.).
11. Jolley takes a different view. He writes, of the tendency "to ascribe intentionality to all mental phenomena":

    > Malebranche, like Rorty, believes that this tendency is fundamentally mistaken. In the first place, Malebranche wishes to draw our attention to a class of mental phenomena which have no objects or content at all; these phenomena he calls *sentiments*. The paradigm of a *sentiment*, for Malebranche, is a pain sensation, for pains are perhaps the clearest case of mental events which do not represent, which are not about anything.
    >
    > (1990, 60)

12. Descartes sometimes contrasts ideas in the *objective* sense with their *formal* reality sense, other times with ideas in the *material* sense, and other times contrasting the formal and the material senses. Jolley (1990, 14f.) and Smith (2013) offer helpful discussions of these inconsistencies.
13. With one exception, the various passages present a consistent account whereby the objective sense of an idea concerns the being of the object represented, *as* it is represented in the idea. The exception arises in the

preface to the *Meditations* where Descartes writes that the term *idea* can be taken, on the one hand, "as an operation of the intellect," or it "can be taken objectively, as the *thing represented* by that operation" (AT VII 8; CSM II 7, my emphasis). He does not say, here, the thing represented as represented, but just "the thing represented." Prima facie, this text identifies the objective sense of an idea with the formal reality of the cause of the idea. Not only does this prima facie reading conflict with other clear passages, it makes nonsense of the Third Meditation argument for God. I suggest that there is a better reading than the prima facie reading – one that anticipates what readers eventually find when they read the reply to Caterus. Accordingly, Descartes's phrase – the idea "can be taken objectively, as the thing represented by that operation" – is best read as elliptical; the fully articulated version is explained in his reply to Caterus. Recall, in explaining *objective being in the intellect* to Caterus, Descartes writes that "by this I mean that the idea of the sun is the sun itself existing in the intellect." Of course, he then offers the following further explanation: "not of course formally existing, as it does in the heavens, but objectively existing, i.e. in the way in which objects normally are in the intellect." Importantly, the further explanation does not negate the claim that the objective being of the sun "is the sun itself"; it simply expounds on the sense in which to take that phrase. I am suggesting that Descartes's preface remark – that the idea "can be taken objectively, as the thing represented" – is the abbreviated version, and that the comparable fully articulated version is this: the idea "can be taken objectively, as the thing represented" – *not of course the thing itself, but as it exists in the intellect, that is in the way in which objects normally are in the intellect.* Thus read, the preface remark is consistent with other passages regarding the objective sense of an idea. For a rather different take on this issue, see David Clemenson (2007).

14 Malebranche views ideas in God as abstract and eternal and denies that they count as modifications of God. The ideas of the external bodies we perceive are, in God, "only His essence, insofar as it is participable" (OC III, 149; *Eluc.* 10/LO 625).

15 Cf. Mackie (1998, 67), Yolton (1993, 90ff.), and Nadler (1989, 108ff. and 128ff.). Hoffman makes a similar observation of Nadler, namely "that he seems to conclude at one point that Descartes is a direct realist simply on the grounds that Descartes thinks of ideas as acts of perception" (2002, 172).

16 Terminology varies. In those systems in which the term *idea* is used only for perceptual objects, but not for the perceptual act, we may describe the identify version of the act-object theory by saying that the idea and the perceptual act are identical.

17 On the identity version, the mind's awareness of its idea/object is not via some distinct act of awareness (as would take us down the path of a regress); rather, the awareness of it is via the idea/act with which it is identical.

18 A similar mistake arises in arguing against act-object interpretations on the grounds that they *reify* ideas (cf. Woozley 1964, 25), or that they entail new "ontological entities" (Yolton 1970, 134). The mistake is of a piece with that in the identity-entails-act-theory argument, because such reasoning presupposes the *tertium quid* version of the act-object theory.

19 Jonathan Bennett coined the term "veil of perception" precisely to help express, in his view, "what is wrong with the theory" (1971, 69) where one's theory takes the form of an act-object view of ideas.

20 Writes Yolton, whose interpretation of Locke fits into our characterization of an act-theory account: "The way of ideas . . . does not place the perceiver in some vale of ideas forever trying to break out into the world of physical objects" (1970, 132).

21 Cf. Nadler (1989, 108ff.) and Yolton (1993, 90ff.).

22 Nadler is forced to explain away this passage, for he is convinced that the most natural reading of Arnauld's references to ideas as mediating objects conflicts with Arnauld's identification of ideas and perceptual acts – an implicit appeal to the identity-entails-act-theory argument. Nadler concludes that Arnauld's talk of ideas as mediating objects of perception is no more than a *façon de parler* (1989, 115ff.).

23 See Newman (2009).

24 In his *Elements of Natural Philosophy* (ch. 12), while addressing our "perception of the truth of affirmative or negative propositions," Locke writes,

> This perception is either immediate or mediate. Immediate perception of the [truth of propositions] is called intuitive knowledge. . . .
>
> The truth of these and the like propositions we know by a bare simple intuition of the ideas themselves, without any more ado; and such propositions are called self-evident.
>
> The mediate perception of the agreement or disagreement of two ideas is, when, by the intervention of one or more other ideas, their agreement or disagreement is shown. This is called demonstration.

25 This is a *descriptive* account, whereby the concern is with whether inference *is* involved; on a *normative* account, the concern is instead with whether inference *ought* to be involved in order to justify the proposition affirmed.
26 In his *Optics*, Descartes describes a scenario in which a blind person's tactile perception of the ground – via a walking stick – becomes (using our terminology) phenomenologically direct: "one might almost say that they see with their hands, or that their stick is the organ of some sixth sense given to them in place of sight" (AT VI 83f.; CSM I 153).
27 I offer a more detailed analysis of the notion of objectual immediacy in Newman (2009).
28 Newman (2011) offers a rebuttal to Carriero's direct realist interpretation.
29 In the *Meditations*, Descartes frames the distinction in terms of an *apparent* division: "Among my ideas, some appear [*videntur*] to be innate, some to be adventitious, and others to have been invented by me" (AT VII 37–38; CSM II 26). Bear in mind that at this juncture of the Third Meditation, the meditator has yet to establish the existence of an external world, or to exclude the existence of unknown mental faculties – outcomes relevant to the distinction.
30 I understand the main seventeenth century debate about innateness to be focused on general ideas (concepts), not sensations. This point is often overlooked. Descartes writes, of sensations, including "ideas of pain, colours, sounds and the like," that they must be innate, because "there is no similarity between these ideas and the corporeal motions" that produce them in the mind (AT VIIIB 369; CSM I 304). Locke would agree. What his concept empiricism requires is not that the materials forming sensory qualia are transported in, from outside the mind, but that all general ideas of pain, colors, sounds, and the like are formed from our sensations of them. Hume is explicit about this. He writes,

> As to those impressions, which arise from the senses, their ultimate cause is, in my opinion, perfectly inexplicable by human reason, and it will always be impossible to decide with certainty, whether they arise immediately from the object, *or are produced by the creative power of the mind*, or are derived from the Author of our being.
> (Treatise 1.2.5.2, my emphasis)

He adds that "it is probable, that no more was meant by those, who denied innate ideas, than that all ideas were copies of our impressions" (*Enquiry* 2). Bear in mind that Hume, unlike Locke, does not count sense impressions as ideas.
31 In Descartes's early writings he refers to corporeal images as "ideas" (cf. *The Rules* AT X 419; CSM I 44–45). In this chapter, however, I am interested in his fully mature doctrines, as are expressed for example in the *Meditations*, where he writes, "in so far as these images are in the corporeal imagination, that is, are depicted in some part of the brain, I do not call them 'ideas' at all" (AT VII 160f.; CSM II 113).
32 Wilson concludes "that Descartes does not provide a coherent account of how we are both 'conscious of all that is in us' and possibly ignorant of mathematics and metaphysics" (1978, 164). Bennett makes the point that in Leibniz the dispositional account of innateness is parasitic on his doctrine of subconscious perception (2001, 40f.) – a doctrine anathema to Descartes, given his own commitment to the transparency of the mental.
33 In Newman (2006), I develop this theme more fully in connection with Descartes's method of doubt.
34 Kenny (1968, 102f.) and Jolley (1990, 39f.) provide useful discussions of this problem.
35 See Rickless (2007) for a helpful discussion of Locke's handling of dispositional theories of innateness.
36 See Nelson (2008) for a helpful discussion of Descartes's account of innate ideas.
37 Cf. Cowie (1999, 31ff.).
38 Hume regularly invokes this strategy, arguing that we lack such alleged ideas as of the *self*, *necessary connection*, *substratum*, and so on.
39 In his Sixth Meditation argument, Descartes narrows the field of possible external causes of sensation, to these three: it is "either a body, that is, a corporeal nature . . . or else it is God, or some creature more noble than a body" (AT VII 79; CSM II 55). He goes on to argue, further, that the correct option is that external bodies cause our sensations. As he reveals in the synopsis to the *Meditations*, he thinks that "no sane person has ever seriously doubted" such conclusions as this one (AT VII 16; CSM II 11). It would therefore have surprised him to know that a series of quite distinguished philosophers would, instead, embrace the option that "it is God" that causes our sensations – including Malebranche and Leibniz (and in the eighteenth century, Berkeley).
40 Of course, the depth of this apparent disagreement between Descartes and Locke, on the common idea of the sun, depends on how one characterizes the adventitious-constructed distinction.

41 Acknowledging that both count as *sensations* broadly construed, Locke says that the category of reflection "might properly enough be call'd internal Sense" (*Essay* 2.1.4).
42 That is, under normal perception conditions – the person has normally functioning sense organs, the object is observable, and so on (cf. *Essay* 2.9.4ff.).
43 Barring such cases as when voluntary movements enable the senses to operate – for example opening one's eyes.
44 Note also that some elements of Locke's theory are, arguably, less a result of what introspection reveals than of their explanatory power. In conversation, Alan Nelson has suggested that simple ideas might be regarded as theoretical entities, much as are *atoms* on Locke's view (cf. *Essay* 2.2.2). Strictly speaking, we do not experience atoms; but their postulation helps to explain what we do experience. Neither do mature minds notice simple ideas, as such – as in ideas that "enter by the Senses simple and unmixed" (*Essay* 2.2.1). Rather, what we call *simple* are ideas noticed by abstracting them (via selective attention) from the complex ideas of which they are constituents. Postulating that some such original ideas enter the senses unmixed helps Locke to explain the ideas that we do notice.
45 This is perhaps Locke's point in remarking that "thus all Complex *Ideas* are made." On an alternative reading of the remark, only ideas resulting from this first operation count as complex ideas, but not those resulting from the second or third operations. This reading has the unexpected result that some ideas made by the mind are neither simple nor complex. Jolley holds such a view, writing that "the ideas of relation and abstract ideas which had formerly been subsumed under the heading of complex ideas now constitute two distinct categories" (1999, 45). In conversation, Jolley has conveyed that a further basis of his view is the opening remark of the quotation – and "thus all Complex *Ideas* are made." But as I have suggested, we can instead take that remark to imply that every complex idea involves, in some manner or other, the operation of *combining other ideas*. I suggest further that Locke's addition of new material to the fourth edition (including the block-quoted passage from *Essay* 2.12.1) serves to make explicit what is already implied by his treatment of relations and abstraction in the prior chapter: namely that these additional mental operations produce complex ideas – doing so in line with the earlier-discussed *causal criterion*, itself reiterated in *Essay* 2.12.2.

Bibliography

Arnauld, Antoine. 1990. *On True and False Ideas*. Stephen Gaukroger, trans. Manchester: Manchester University Press.
———. 1964. *The Art of Thinking*, trans. by James Dickoff and Patricia James. Indianapolis: Bobbs-Merrill.
Ayers, Michael. 1991. *Locke: Epistemology and Ontology*. Vol. 1. London: Routledge.
Bennett, Jonathan. 1971. *Locke, Berkeley, Hume: Central Themes*. Oxford: Oxford University Press.
———. 2001. *Learning From Six Philosophers: Descartes, Spinoza, Leibniz, Locke, Berkeley, Hume*. Vol. 2. Oxford: Clarendon Press.
Carriero, John. 2009. *Between Two Worlds: A Reading of Descartes's Meditations*. Princeton: Princeton University Press.
Chappell, Vere. 1986. "The Theory of Ideas." In A.O. Rorty, ed., *Essays on Descartes' Meditations*. Berkeley: University of California Press, 177–221.
———. 1994. "Locke's Theory of Ideas." In V. Chappell, ed., *The Cambridge Companion to Locke*. Cambridge: Cambridge University Press, 26–55.
Clemenson, David. 2007. *Descartes' Theory of Ideas*. London: Bloomsbury Academic.
Cowie, Fiona. 1999. *What's Within? Nativism Reconsidered*. Oxford: Oxford University Press.
Curley, E.M. 1978. *Descartes Against the Skeptics*. Cambridge, MA: Harvard University Press.
Hoffman, Paul. 2002. "Direct Realism, Intentionality, and the Objective Being of Ideas." *Pacific Philosophical Quarterly* 83, 163–179.
Hume, David. 1978. *A Treatise of Human Nature*. L.A. Selby-Bigge, ed., revised by P.H. Nidditch. Oxford: Oxford University Press.
———. 2000. *An Enquiry Concerning Human Understanding*. Tom Beauchamp, ed. Oxford: Clarendon Press.
Jolley, Nicholas. 1990. *The Light of the Soul: Theories of Ideas in Leibniz, Malebranche, and Descartes*. Oxford: Oxford University Press.
———. 1999. *Locke: His Philosophical Thought*. Oxford: Oxford University Press.
Kenny, Anthony. 1968. *Descartes: A Study of His Philosophy*. New York: Random House.
Mackie, J.L. 1998. "Locke and Representative Perception." In Vere Chappell, ed., *Locke*. Oxford: Oxford University Press, 60–68.

Nadler, Steven M. 1989. *Arnauld and the Cartesian Philosophy of Ideas*. Princeton: Princeton University Press.

Nelson, Alan. 2008. "Cartesian Innateness." In Janet Broughton and John Carriero, ed., *Companion to Descartes*. Oxford: Blackwell Publishing.

Newman, Lex. 2006. "Descartes' Rationalist Epistemology." In A. Nelson, ed., *Companion to Rationalism*. Oxford: Blackwell Publishing, 179–205.

———. 2009. "Ideas, Pictures, and the Directness of Perception in Descartes and Locke." *Philosophy Compass* 4, 134–154.

———. 2011. "Sensory Doubts and the Directness of Perception in the *Meditations*." *Midwest Studies in Philosophy* xxxv, 205–222.

Rickless, Samuel C. 2007. "Locke's Polemic Against Nativism." In L. Newman, ed., *Cambridge Companion to Locke's Essay*. Cambridge: Cambridge University Press, 33–36.

Rorty, R. 1979. *Philosophy and the Mirror of Nature*. Princeton: Princeton University Press.

Smith, Kurt. 2013. "Descartes' Theory of Ideas." In Edward N. Zalta, ed., *The Stanford Encyclopedia of Philosophy* (Spring 2013 Edition) <http://plato.stanford.edu/archives/spr2013/entries/descartes-ideas/>

Stroud, Barry. 1977. *Hume*. London: Routledge & Kegan Paul.

Wilson, Margaret Dauler. 1978. *Descartes*. London: Routledge & Kegan Paul.

Woozley, A.D. 1964. Introduction to his abridged edition of Locke's *An Essay Concerning Human Understanding*. London and Glasgow: Wm. Collins Sons and Co. Ltd.

Yolton, John W. 1970. *Locke and the Compass of Human Understanding*. Cambridge: Cambridge University Press.

———. 1993. *A Locke Dictionary*. Oxford: Blackwell Publishers.

8
LOGIC AND KNOWLEDGE
Alan Nelson

1. Introduction

When we think of elementary logic today, the science of such purely formal properties of inference as validity and soundness come to mind. And elementary metalogic studies the formal properties of systems of logically distinguished items. Aristotle's logic and its various developments already had these foci, but they were meant to accomplish even more. They were also meant to structure knowledge of the natural world by deducing phenomena from causes. Throughout the early modern period, this venerable logic still had many authoritative, well-placed adherents. A second intellectual tradition that shaped early modern thinking about logic and knowledge came from mathematics. Geometry, especially, stood as a shining example of human learning and ingenuity. In the early modern period, the twin hegemony of these classical influences came to be threatened. Striking advances in algebra and analytic geometry raised questions about the applicability of classical mathematical techniques to newly discovered problems. And the new, mechanical science exposed fatal inadequacies in the framework for empirical science set up two millennia earlier. There was, moreover, some tension between the logic of classical geometry and the logic of science. It had always been fairly obvious that practical mathematical reasoning rarely fit into the formal straightjacket of Aristotelian syllogistic logic.[1]

The growing dissatisfaction with the Aristotelian framework led to a search for a logic that would do more than impose an artificial structure on knowledge that had already been accumulated. Greater stress was laid on logic as a *method*, for guidance in the development of the new kinds of knowledge emerging during the scientific revolution. It became a goal to combine what we would now call a scientific method or philosophy of science with an epistemological and, eventually, metaphysical theory of the foundations and ordering of items of knowledge delivered by the method. Consequently, a useful logic could be only a description of our cognitive best practices arrived at through a metaphysical investigation of the nature of the mind and the objects of the mind's knowledge (Descartes), or else a more purely psychologistic examination of the objects of knowledge (Locke).

Descartes was a central figure, perhaps the most central figure, in this early modern project. Accordingly, the plan of this chapter is to trace how Descartes's distinctive and immeasurably influential theory of logic and knowledge grew in scope and sophistication as it came under increasing pressure from critics and from Descartes's own demands on it. After arriving at the final form of Descartes's theory, we will be in a position to understand some of the most important alternatives that emerged in reaction to it.

2. Descartes's basic logic

Let us then trace the chronological development of Descartes's theory through some of his major works: *Rules for the Direction of the Mind* (left unpublished in 1628), *Discourse on the Method of Rightly Conducting One's Reason and Seeking the Truth in the Sciences* (1637), *Meditations on First Philosophy* (1641/2), and *Principles of Philosophy* (1644).[2] In the *Rules*, we can find the core of Descartes's full, mature theory of logic and knowledge. Some important aspects of the theory do not make their appearance this early, but the basic theory of logic is here worked out in more detail than in any other place.

Descartes explains how in his system there are two sources of knowledge which he calls, following tradition, intuition and deduction.[3] Intuition, the fundamental member of the pair, is

> the conception of a clear and attentive mind, which is so easy and distinct that there can be no room for doubt about what we are understanding. Alternatively, and this comes to the same thing, intuition is the indubitable conception of a clear and attentive mind which proceeds solely from the light of reason.
> (*Rules*, AT X 368; CSM I 14)[4]

The objects of intuitions are called *simple natures*, and, as we shall see, the simplicity of intuitions is crucial to their grounding of knowledge. Deduction involves the unbroken mental transition from an initial intuition (or sometimes multiple initial intuitions) to another item. This transition must cover a connection so tight that the deduced item is itself intuited and, therefore, itself a simple nature. In this way, the epistemic status of the intuition is, at least in part, passed along to the conclusion. The process can be repeated so that the metaphor of links in a chain is apt:

> [Deduction] is similar to the way in which we know that the last link in a long chain is connected to the first: even if we cannot take in at one glance all the intermediate links on which the connection depends, we can have knowledge of the connection provided we survey the links one after the other, and keep in mind that each link from first to last is attached to its neighbor.
> (*Rules*, AT X 369–70; CSM I 15)

This is how knowledge and logic are integrated. Intuitions of simple natures are intrinsically epistemically privileged and logic deduction from them enlarges the class of privileged items. But how is it that a number of intuitions are linked into a structure that yields further, deductive, knowledge? One must perceive a necessary connection between the links but, again, what constitutes this connection? It would not do to say that the linkage is itself another item that is intuited because that would initiate a regress. What would link the linked items to the link? Moreover, the link cannot consist in any formal properties of the linked items because of Descartes's insistence that inference is a matter of content (i.e. natures) and not of form. Descartes has been read as making the intuition of linkage primitive and inexplicable,[5] but an explanation can be teased from the text. To find it, we need to learn more about what goes into the linking of deductive steps.

Descartes makes a further terminological distinction between the first intuition or premise in a deduction (let us for now assume that there is only one) called "absolute" and the intuition that succeeds it, which is called "relative" with respect to the first. The second item is then absolute with respect to the third and the third, which is relative to the second, is absolute with respect to the fourth, and so on. This relativity is also, as it were, transitive so that the nth intuition in a deduction is considered relative to the first. This terminology is not entirely apt because the absolute and the relative are, in this way, themselves relative. There is one exception. Every deduction begins with the intuition of a simple nature that is absolute in the highest degree (*maximè absolutum*; AT X 382; CSM I 22). Such a nature is also simple in the highest degree (*maximè simplices*; AT X 383; CSM I 22). What is important here is that Descartes does in fact explicate the absolute-relative linkages:

> I call "absolute" whatever has within it the pure and simple nature in question; that is, whatever is viewed (*consideratur*) as being independent, a cause, simple, universal, single, equal, straight, and other qualities of that sort. . . . The "relative", on the other hand, is *what shares the same nature*, or at least something of the same nature, in virtue of which we can relate it to the absolute and deduce it from the absolute in a definite series of steps. The concept of the "relative" involves other terms besides, which I call "relations": these include whatever is said to be dependent, an effects, composite, particular, many, unequal, dissimilar, oblique, etc.
>
> (AT X 381–2; CSM I 21, my emphasis)

So, what is relative in a deduction shares the same nature with what is absolute. I propose to interpret this as saying that the initial intuition is in some way identically present in every step because every step is relative to the stop that is absolute in the highest degree and not only to the next, immediately absolute step. This sharing of content between the absolute and relative is exactly what is needed to insure the necessary connection between the steps. As one transitions from an absolute step to a relative step, part of what is intuited does not change at all; this grounds the connection in the necessity of identity, so to speak. This also explains how deductions in some measure preserve the special certainty of the most absolute intuition. That very intuition is part of what is subsequently intuited in the relative steps. Another important consequence of this passage is that the simplicity of "simple natures" is relative in the same way as are the absolute and relative. Consider that every step in a deduction is an intuited simple nature. Because relative simple natures contain the most absolute, simplest nature, it must be that the relative steps have additional content that renders each of these steps as a whole nonidentical to the initial, most absolute step. In other words, when going from step to step there must be *something* that is different if steps are not to be repeated. So, the relative steps are actually composites, and intuiting them involves understanding *as if* simple what is actually complex.

This is certainly confusing. What might excuse using the term 'simple nature' for complexes? For one thing, the nth step of a deduction is simpler than the n+1th step; in fact, in some contexts it will suffice to have a truncated deduction in which the nth step is now made the first step and is treated (with respect to the truncated deduction) as absolute in the highest degree. This happens in geometry when we begin a demonstration with a previously demonstrated theorem. Recall the similar example of the cause-effect pair in the last quotation. The effect, call it *e*, is complex relative to the cause, but the deduction might continue by introducing an effect of *e*. Then *e* could be a cause of this further effect and, therefore, absolute and simple with respect to it. Another reason for thinking of some complexes as "simple" natures is that they can be intuited as wholes within subsequent steps that are thus relative to them. So, for example, an intuition of the simple nature *triangle inscribed in a square* can be grasped as having the simple nature *triangle* as a component without grasping that the triangle itself is composed of lines and angles. Finally, as we have seen, every step in a deduction shares the absolutely simple nature in the first step. So, one might see a derivative sense in which relative steps borrow a kind of simplicity from the "pure and simple" nature that is absolute in the highest degree.

So far, we have seen that every deduction begins with an intuition of a simple nature that is absolute in the highest degree. We have not yet been given a reason to suppose that there *are* any simple natures that are perfectly simple with no restrictions or qualifications whatsoever. In the last quotation, the examples are of things "viewed" as independent, a cause, and so forth. But they would be viewed otherwise if we found them to be deduced from other natures in a different deduction. Or, one might think that natures decompose into simpler natures without end. So, are there any utterly pure and simple natures that are not relative to any others, and if so, how can they be discovered?

Of course, in his mature philosophical system Descartes does isolate some ultimate natures or essences that serve as ultimate principles.[6] Thought, extension, and God are not in any way composed of even more basic and simple natures. We find some of this scheme is already present in the *Rules*. Intuiting is an operation of the "intellect." In Rule 8, Descartes repeatedly insists that the seeker of knowledge must, at least once in life (*semel in vita*) carefully investigate the intellect itself.[7] This simple nature, the intellect, is in an important sense the most basic item of knowledge because knowledge of everything else depends on it (AT X 395). In Descartes's mature system, knowledge of God will come to function as the singular item on which all other knowledge depends, but that is not in play here in the *Rules*. So, the intellect here turns out to be one of the items that are utterly absolute *principles*. Considered as pure, however, the intellect is limited as a basis for deductions. Its capacity is greatly enhanced when it is "aided" by imagination, sense perception, and memory (AT X 398, 411; CSM I 32, 39). The intellect requires the aid of these partly corporeal faculties for specific deductions involving natural phenomena in the extended world. It is no surprise then that extension is another utterly absolute, simple nature. Although Descartes does not here broach the metaphysics of mind-body union, in Rule 12 he does explain the great comprehensiveness of this dualism.[8] The extended world consists of shapes and motions, and any motion that can mechanically affect the sense organs can transmit other motions to the brain. The intellect can then "read" these signs in the brain and thereby encompass all knowledge of the extended world of which humans are capable (AT X 413–17).[9]

In Rule 12, Descartes identifies a third class of principles: "Lastly, those simples are to be termed 'common' which are ascribed indifferently, now to corporeal things, now to spirits – for instance, existence, unity, duration, and the like." He also here adds "common notions" such as "things that are the same as a third thing are the same as each other" (AT X 419; CSM I 45). The first group comprises what he will later call *attributes* in the *Principles*, where they get a special treatment that makes them dependent on the more basic natures of thought, extension, and God (see Nolan 1997). Here in the *Rules* it may be that they get their own category because their being common to bodies and minds seems to make them natures from which body and mind might both be deduced. That would yield the unsatisfactory result that these common natures would be the simplest and most absolute natures of all. Descartes could plausibly block that result by putting the common natures into their own, third category.

A convincing enumeration of the natures forming the ultimate basis of knowledge would have some obvious benefits.[10] One important benefit is a kind of definite limning of the bounds of rational knowledge. Aside from the principles themselves, any other item of knowledge will be ultimately deducible from them. Related to this definition of the scope of knowledge is the prospect of knowledge that is, in its essentials, complete. Any composite nature that is ever encountered can be either intuited (recall that means that it shares a nature with something absolute with respect to it) or exposed as a false construction of the imagination.[11] Perhaps chief among the benefits accruing to Descartes's theory of logic and knowledge in the *Rules* is that it provides the unified method for gaining knowledge that he found to be so sorely lacking in earlier theories. It was wrong of his Aristotelian predecessors to separate sharply various sciences according to their subject matter.

> For the sciences as a whole are nothing other than human wisdom, which always remains one and the same, however different the subjects to which it is applied, it being no more altered by them than sunlight is by the variety of the things it shines on.
>
> (Rule 1, AT X 360; CSM I 9)

In Rule 4, Descartes calls the science (*scientiam*)[12] of this unified method *mathesis universalis* (i.e. "universal mathematics"; AT X 378; CSM I 19).[13] It is universal because it includes ordinary mathematics as a special case as it brings all the other sciences (*scientiae*) together under a single framework of order and connection. The big idea here is that this framework is none other than the structure of deduction as discussed previously. It is for this reason that the "finest" (*nobillissimum*) example of this *scientia* is the study of the capacity of the intellect itself, namely its capacity for intuiting and deducing, both alone and with the aid of the sensory faculties.[14]

This method, or universal mathematics, casts a very surprising light on ordinary mathematics, including geometry, arithmetic, and algebra. The received Descartes familiar to scholars and students is besotted with love for mathematics and seeks to "mathematicize" nature and model all knowledge on the certainty and precision of mathematics. This common picture might seem to be reinforced in the *Rules* where the point is for universal wisdom to be pursued by a generalized *mathesis universalis*. A quite different picture emerges when we carefully consider how the most important application of *mathesis universalis* is not in ordinary mathematics, or even in mathematics applied to the natural world, but it is instead to the knowing subject itself and the most fundamental natures it intuits. Ordinary mathematics, then, turns out to be a mere special case of *scientia* and by no means the most significant part.

> I would not value these rules so highly if they were good only for solving those pointless problems with which arithmeticians and geometers are inclined to while away their time, for in that case all could credit myself with achieving would be to dabble in trifles with greater subtlety then they. I shall have much

to say below about figures and numbers, for no other disciplines can yield illustrations as evident and certain as these. But if one attends closely to my meaning, one will readily see that ordinary mathematics is far from my mind here, that it is quite another discipline I am expounding, and that these illustrations are more its outer garments than its inner parts. This discipline should contain the primary rudiments of human reason and extend to the discovery of truths in any field whatever.

(AT X 373–4; CSM I 17)

The importance of mathematics, therefore, does not derive from its enjoying any intrinsically exalted status. Instead, the practice of mathematics serves to train the intellect for the job of attaining *scientia* limited only by our stock of careful sensory observations. The method, after all, notoriously does not provide an algorithm for generating particular truths from principles. We need "to cultivate two special mental faculties, viz. perspicacity in the distinct intuition of particular things and discernment in the methodical deduction of one thing from another" (Rule 9, AT X 400; CSM I 33). In line with this injunction, Rule 10 directs us to "methodically survey even the most insignificant products of human skill, especially those which display or presuppose order." Furthermore,

[W]e must not take up the more difficult and arduous issues immediately, but must first tackle the simplest and least exalted arts, and especially those in which order prevails – such as weaving and carpet-making, or the more feminine arts of embroidery, in which threads are interwoven in an infinitely varied pattern. Number-games and any games involving arithmetic, and the like, belong here.

(AT X 403–4; CSM I 34–5)

All of this is compatible, of course, with Descartes's proceeding to say quite a lot about ordinary mathematics and even later publishing his *Geometry*, an entire book on the subject.[15] Naturally, it is true that mathematics and rigorously constructed games and arts are distinguished by the clarity and readily apprehended certainty of deductions constructed within them. The appreciation of deductions of more complicated phenomena requires more developed skills of "perspicacity and discernment."[16] It will emerge that this is crucial for understanding Cartesian empirical science.

We have seen that in the *Rules* much of Descartes's mature system is strongly foreshadowed. It is in the treatment of the ultimate, foundational principles that his theory of knowledge is most significantly developed in his later writings. In Rule 12, we had three foundational principles, or perhaps three classes of principles, laid out: intellect, extension, and what is common to both intellect and extension. Clearly, much of the attractiveness of the overall scheme depends on our *scientia* being interconnected thanks to its grounding in exactly these principles. This raises two pressing concerns that are hardly touched on in the *Rules*. The first is the initial determination of the principles. Descartes often claims that they are "easy" to intuit by unprejudiced intellects, but obviously many philosophers do not find them thus and others will not even accept Descartes's characterization of intuition. As we shall see, Hobbes is a good example of that. We might biographically speculate that Descartes arrived at these principles by first regarding them as hypotheses and subsequently confirming them by appeal to their explanatory power. In the text, however, Descartes presents the method as a tool for the discovery of important knowledge. This, he thought, was one of the principal advantages his system enjoyed over Scholastic logic and science. *Mathesis universalis* is meant to be a clarification, refinement, and extension of what was supposed to be the ancient mathematical technique of *analysis*.

The term 'analysis' and its complement 'synthesis'[17] had accumulated considerable flexibility by the time Descartes was writing.[18] In the *Rules* the process of analysis begins with an object of study which is then broken into component natures. The results are further analyzed, resolved, or decomposed whereupon those results are again analyzed and so on. The process can stop when we are satisfied that we have arrived at intuitions of simple natures. If, however, these simple natures are not ultimate principles, the process might continue until we arrive at one of those. Synthesis resembles this process in reverse; simple natures are recombined to arrive at a composite simple nature (recall the explanation of that awkward terminology). If the natures are carefully tracked during the synthesis, then the nature or natures that are absolute in the highest degree will be intuitively known to be shared in the successive compositions. Synthesis, therefore, is very closely related to deduction. Synthesis is not exactly the reverse of analysis because the analysis of the original object can involve discarding some residues that are confused and therefore not immediately intuitable. This means that a good synthesis will usually be a cleaned-up version of the corresponding analysis.

An important addition to the theory is the role that memory plays in deduction. As one moves along the links in a deductive chain, the more that one relies on memory of earlier links, the less certainty one will have of the later links and the final conclusion. Descartes held that the remedy for this was careful rehearsal of deductions:

> So I shall run through them several times in a continuous movement of the imagination, simultaneously intuiting one relation and passing on to the next, until I have learnt to pass from the first to the last so swiftly that memory is left with practically no role to play, and I seem to intuit the whole thing at once. In this way our memory is relieved, the sluggishness of our intelligence redressed, and its capacity is some way enlarged.
>
> (*Rules*, AT X 388; CSM I 25)

This seems to mean that a well-practiced deduction enables one to sweep from the intuition of what is most absolute to the least, simultaneously sweeping up the way in which the most absolute is shared throughout the links. If so, then there is a sense in which the conclusion of the deduction includes the intuition of the most absolute nature.[19]

One might think that Descartes is insinuating here in the *Rules* that someone skilled in the method can discover simple natures and, indeed, the ultimate principles by performing an analysis on more relative simple natures or even on initially confused sense perceptions. The problem with that suggestion is that Descartes realizes that analysis typically requires what he calls *enumeration* (AT X 388–91; CSM I 25–7). Enumeration guides analysis by specifying how an object of analysis is going to be decomposed into objects for further analysis. To take a non-Cartesian example, if we are analyzing a chocolate cake we might begin by distinguishing ingredients from procedures. Then we distinguish ingredients into the wet, dry, and decorative and the procedures into measuring, mixing, baking, and decorating. Next the dry ingredients are decomposed, and so forth. This shows that a good analysis of chocolate cake requires us to already have the categories of ingredients and procedures. And an analysis of ingredients requires us to have at hand the categories of wet and dry, and so on. By analogy, if we take as our object of analysis the Pythagorean theorem, we must already have at hand the simple natures of square, triangle, proportion, and so on. The point is that although analysis ultimately tops out at principles, we will often need to know what the principles (or the relevant simple natures) are so that we can guide the analysis with an appropriate enumeration.[20] And this is something that the *Rules* does not help us with except, perhaps, for the encouragement to think long and hard about games, embroidery, and the like until our intellects pick out the correct principles as effortlessly as Descartes himself does.[21]

A second large lacuna in the basic method of the *Rules* is in the characterization of the significance of the simple natures and principles themselves. It is being intuited by the intellect that distinguishes them. But how are they connected with extramental reality? Are the simple natures (especially those relative to extension) natures of really extended things, and if so, how is *that* known?[22] These two large issues must have become particularly salient for Descartes when he felt compelled to withhold from publication his scientific treatise, *The World*. Galileo's advocacy of the earth's movement had just been condemned and Descartes did not see how to excise Copernicanism from his own work. It is hard not to think that this was very significant in his coming to think it important and worthwhile to enlarge his epistemological project. He wanted to make his ultimate principles irresistible to open-minded readers. So, his problem was to make them both intellectually compelling (i.e. intuitive) and indubitably representative of reality (i.e. true).

3. Descartes's extended logic

It is possible to see Descartes's solution to this problem in the *Discourse* and especially in the *Meditations* as featuring a distinctive extension of his version of the traditional method of analysis and synthesis. The notorious method of doubt is that extension:

> But since I now wished to devote myself solely to the search for truth, I thought it necessary to do the very opposite and reject as if absolutely false everything in which I could imagine the least doubt, in order to see if I was left believing anything that was entirely indubitable.
> (*Discourse*, AT VI 31; CSM I 126–7)[23]

The method of doubt is multilayered and proves to be an extremely flexible. Among its virtues are its enabling us to (1) set aside prejudices that obscure the truth from the intellect; (2) withdraw from the senses, so that the intellect can perceive the natural light that shines on the principles; (3) induce a highly determined narrative order for educating oneself to intuit the principles; and (4) establish a "more than ordinary" certainty for the principles so that they come to serve, via analysis and synthesis, as the ground for *scientia*. Let us call this the "extended method of analysis and synthesis," or just the "extended method."

Why does this amount to an *extension* of the basic analytic-synthetic method? In ancient geometry, the basic procedure is most briefly described as beginning with what is to be demonstrated and then working backward or "regressing" to what is given as axiomatically true. If one wished, one could then reverse the procedure to obtain a synthetic demonstration. In Descartes's method as laid out in the *Rules*, there was little help to be found for establishing the "givenness" of his principles. In order to enumerate sufficiently and then analyze or regress, one must *first* have established principles. The genius of the method of doubt, then, is in analyzing arbitrary, commonsensical starting points into principles with absolutely no prior assumptions about what the principles will turn out to be or, indeed, whether principles can be discovered by the extended method at all.

The extended method begins with the firm resolution to doubt as much as possible, even when the reasons for doing so are very slight, hyperbolic, metaphysical, and so forth. The famous key move comes when the follower of the method, the "meditator" let's say, recognizes that doubting itself reveals an intuition of the existence of meditator's own thought. At a stroke, the *cogito* delivers the most central principle of the scheme presented in the *Rules* – the knowing subject itself. And as we proceed through the new extended method we learn about how the intellect is aided by the sensory faculties. In the highly developed treatment in the *Meditations*, the meditator proceeds to intuit extension as the simple nature to which all corporeal things are relative, and then the simple nature of the human being (which is somehow simple despite its being in a way composite). The terminology of 'simple natures' and the 'absolute' and 'relative' is replaced – more on this anon. After the intuition of mind and before those of extension and human nature,[24] there is the crucial interpolation of the intuition of God which entails God's necessary existence. This is completely absent in the *Rules*, and its role in the extended method requires a detailed explanation.

First, there are two large considerations that can only be touched upon here. One is that when Descartes came to apply the method to physics in a focused way in the preparation of *The World*, it emerged that God was a crucial principle in the deduction of the phenomena. God's immutability, for example, is a ground of the laws of motion. This already meant that the framework of the *Rules* was incomplete. Another looming concern already mentioned was Descartes's own desideratum that the science issuing from his method be compatible with or, even better, depend on fundamental theological requirements. The subtitle of the second edition of the *Meditations* emphasizes that one finds demonstrated therein "the existence of God and the distinction between the human soul and the body," whereas the work as a whole is dedicated to "the Dean and Doctors of the sacred Faculty of Theology at Paris" (AT VII 1, 17; CSM II 3, 12). And if God's existence is absolute, perfectly independent, and necessary, then the existence of minds, bodies, and humans is relative, dependent, and contingent. It would seem, therefore, that a complete system of knowledge cannot omit knowledge of God.

Important as these considerations were, there is a reason for including God that is more integral to the extended method that Descartes employs in his most mature works. The rigorous application of doubt calls into question even intuitions: "God could have given me a nature such that I was deceived even in matters which seemed most evident" (Third Meditation; AT VII 36; CSM II 25). Of course, the "most evident" matters are the ones that are intuitively grasped. Intuition was the entire basis for *scientia* in the *Rules*, so if God were to "deceive" us, then matters that *seemed* supremely evident might be quite otherwise in reality. Let us call this form of doubt the "maximal doubt" because it provides a hyperbolic means of making doubt absolutely universal – at least for a meditator who does not initially intuit what Descartes himself claims to intuit.[25] The entire framework for knowledge set up in the *Rules*, on the hypothesis of maximal doubt, is regarded as no more than a strictly idealist or psychologistic scheme lacking secure connection to reality. Maximal doubt must, therefore, somehow be conclusively silenced by reason if the right kind of knowledge is obtainable at all. The maximal doubt is supposed to be defeated by knowledge of a God whose infinite attributes include perfect power and benevolence. Such a God would give the meditator a nature such that it did *not* go wrong when it achieved its cognitive best, that is intuition. This then is "[t]he sense in which knowledge of all other things depends on the knowledge of God" (*Principles*, AT VIIIA 9; CSM I 197).

Here we have the deep internal reason that knowledge of God is the foundation of knowledge and that this knowledge must itself be established in the extended method. At this point matters become notoriously vexed, and the threat of a Cartesian circle must be confronted. Once one attains absolutely indubitable intuitive knowledge of God, it is easy to deduce from God's nature that intuitions are true representations of reality. But attaining an intuition of God seems to require that it be deduced from other intuitions. This is the procedure adopted in the Third Meditation. And how can the intuitions from which the intuition of God is deduced themselves be secure from doubt *prior* to having intuitive knowledge of God? That is a small, tight circle: the perfect reliability of intuitions depends on the knowledge of God, but the knowledge of God depends on its being intuited.

The tool that straightens the circle is the intuition of God, but only when deployed in a very special way.[26] Maximal doubt is distinctly perceived to be a manifest contradiction if the meditator considers it *simultaneously* with the intuition of God. Maximal doubt is the thought that God creates minds deceptively. But the intuition of God contradicts that; God is no deceiver. There is still a problem with applying this tool if it is difficult to make the intuition occurrent. For once the occurrent intuition is lost, the extended method requires reconsideration of maximal doubt, and it will remain in force until it can again be directly confronted with the occurrent intuition of God. If, for example, the meditator takes a rest at the end of the Third Meditation and then reconsiders maximal doubt, the doubt can be dispelled only by rehearsing the "proof" of God's existence. It is not sufficient to keep a written or remembered record of having had the clear and distinct perception of God in the past, for these records or memories are still dubitable. It has been suggested by some scholars that the intermittent *reproducibility* of the divine guarantee is the best that Descartes could offer. The full solution of the circle, therefore, requires that one have clear and distinct access to the idea of God without the prosthesis of a proof. If the reader of the *Meditations* can attain this skill, as Descartes believes he will by the end of the Fifth Meditation, then maximal doubt can be completely discharged.[27] Suppose that the careful consideration of maximal doubt itself makes one easily and spontaneously intuit God. After all, when examined, the maximal doubt involves the thought that the source of one's being, one's creator, creates defectively and deceptively. In this case, no matter how conscientiously one attempts to entertain maximal doubt, it will immediately and invincibly be shown to be incoherent. In other words, adhering conscientiously to the resolution to apply maximal doubt is the trigger that spontaneously produces the intuition of God.[28]

Having taken special pains in the *Meditations* to establish his fundamental principles for any careful reader, Descartes returned to his earlier project of building on those foundations.[29] The result was the fullest development of his entire system of knowledge in the *Principles of Philosophy*, first published in 1644. The explicit treatment of method in his earlier works was a propaedeutic to the development of *scientia* with utility for normal living. In the *Principles*, Descartes meant to deliver. In the preface to the work, we find the familiar plan for acquiring knowledge. After devising a provisional code for regulating life's activities, the student should learn logic:

> I do not mean the logic of the Schools, for this is strictly speaking nothing but a dialectic which teaches ways of expounding to others what one already knows or even of holding forth without judgement about things one does not know. Such logic corrupts good sense rather than increasing it. I mean instead the kind of logic which teaches us to direct our reason with a view to discovering the truths of which we are ignorant. Since this depends to a great extent on practice, it is good for the student to work for a long time at practicing the rules on very easy and simple questions like those of mathematics. Then when he has acquired some skill in finding the truth on these questions, he should begin to tackle true philosophy in earnest.
> (*Principles*, AT IXB 13–14; CSM I 186)

After developing one's native capacity for discernment with mathematical exercise, one moves on to matters of real importance. The text continues with the famous image of the tree of knowledge:

> The first part of philosophy is metaphysics which contains the principles of knowledge, including the explanation of the principal attributes of God, the non-material nature of our souls and all the clear and distinct notions which are in us.... Thus the whole of philosophy is like a tree. The roots are metaphysics, the trunk is physics, and the branches emerging from the trunk are all the other sciences which may be reduced to three principal ones, namely medicine, mechanics, and morals.

Descartes makes extravagant claims for his tree of *scientia*. Everything in the branches is to be demonstrated with the same certainty found in mathematics.

> I will admit as true only what has been deduced from indubitable common notions so evidently that it is fit to be considered as a mathematical demonstration. And since all natural phenomena can be explained in this way, as will become clear in what follows, I do not think that any other principles are either admissible or desirable in physics.
> (*Principles*, AT VIIIA 79; CSM I 247)[30]

Passages like these are often misread as implying that ordinary mathematics itself plays a prominent role in *scientia*. It is clear that everything will, at some level, have the same degree of certainty as mathematical demonstrations and be demonstrated in the same way. But mathematics itself is no part of the botanical description of the tree of knowledge. This echoes the remarks from the *Rules* about the value of trivial mathematical puzzles.[31] Recall the potential explanation of this kind of misunderstanding about the place of mathematics developed previously. At question is the status of the extended method as a realization of Descartes's earlier conception of *mathesis universalis*. Ordinary mathematics is a special case of the more general principles in that all-encompassing, universal science. The more general principles include the nature of the knowing subject (mind), God, and extension (the principle and subject matter of both physics and ordinary mathematics). So, it is true that physics (the trunk of the tree of *scientia*) and mathematics are deduced from the same principle – extension. It does not follow, however, that physics follows from ordinary mathematics or that physical natures must be explicitly dealt with by ordinary mathematical techniques.[32]

More needs to be said here about the emphasis being placed on the ultimate principles or, in the earlier terminology, "natures" that are ultimately absolute. In the preface to the *Principles* we find him recalling the results of the *Meditations*,

> Accordingly I took the being or existence of this thought as my first principle, and from it I deduced very clearly the following principles. There is a God who is the author of everything there is in the world. . . . [These] are all the principles that I make use of with regard to immaterial or metaphysical things, and from them I deduce very clearly the principles of corporeal or physical things, namely that there are bodies which are extended. . . . [H]ere in total are all the principles which I use to deduce the truth of other things.
> (AT IXB 10; CSM I 184)

Here the principles are identified as the metaphysically basic items revealed by the extended method: mind, God, and extension.[33] Later in the *Principles* they are characterized as finite and infinite substances (AT VIIIA 25–6; CSM I 211). There is a terminological infelicity left over from Descartes's use of "simple nature" and "absolute-relative" in the *Rules*. Descartes used the terms 'simple' and 'absolute,' even 'absolute in the highest degree,' for natures that could be deduced from other natures yet more absolute and simple. Nevertheless, Descartes seems to have regarded a small set of natures to be ultimately and unqualifiedly simple and absolute. In the *Principles*, Descartes lays the same metaphysical and epistemological foundation as in the *Meditations*, as we see in the last quotation. Again, however, he will sometimes use the term 'principle' for items that are deduced from the ultimate principles. For instance, he sometimes refers to the laws of motion as principles even though they are deduced from God and extension and, strictly speaking, relative to them.[34]

Another centrally important feature of the principles is that they are innate to the mind. Their innateness is repeatedly referred to in the *Rules* and *Discourse*.[35] In the Fifth Meditation, the principles, now cast as "true and immutable natures," are famously treated as innate ideas "brought forth from the treasure house of the mind" (AT VII 67; CSM II 46).[36] Such texts again raise the issue of how to count the ultimate principles. In the Fifth Meditation, Descartes marks the idea of God as the "first and most important" of the innate ideas, but there he also gives triangles and other geometrical figures as examples. If all and only principles are innate, it might seem to follow that triangles have true and immutable natures that are unanalyzable principles. We should instead conclude that innateness is also subject to the relativity of the absolute-relative distinction.[37] So a triangle is analyzable into lines, angles, the number three, and finally extension, just as *triangle inscribed in a square* can be "viewed" as having its own true and immutable nature despite its being a composite of triangle and square.[38]

4. Descartes's extended logic in practice

Having considered some aspects of the all-important Cartesian *principles*, we are finally ready for Descartes to show us in some detail the system of useful knowledge based upon them. Our expectations are high because Descartes reaffirms the extravagant claims that were made for his *scientia* in the early *Rules*. First, the passage quoted previously from the preface insists that the intuitive certainty of the principles will be transmitted to everything else by a chain of deductive links. The claim is repeated at the end of the book.

> Besides, there are some matters, even in relation to the things in nature, which we regard as absolutely, and more than just morally, certain. This certainty is based on a metaphysical foundation, namely that God is supremely good and in no way a deceiver, and hence that the faculty which he gave us for distinguishing truth from falsehood cannot lead us into error, so long as we are using it properly and are thereby perceiving something distinctly. Mathematical demonstrations have this kind of certainty, as does the knowledge that material things exist; and the same goes for all evident reasoning about material things. And perhaps even these results of mine will be allowed into the class of absolute certainties, if people consider how they have been deduced in an unbroken chain from the first and simplest principle of human knowledge.
> (*Principles*, AT VIIIA 328; CSM I 290)

Second, the extended method is supposed to make good on the promise of a *mathesis universalis*; in particular, the *scope* of *scientia* reaches all observable phenomena.

> By means of our senses we apprehend nothing in extended objects beyond their shapes, sizes, and motions.
> (AT VIIIA 321; CSM I 284)

> A simple enumeration will make it clear that there is no phenomenon of nature which I have omitted to consider in this treatise. For a list of natural phenomena cannot include anything which is not apprehended by the senses.
> (AT VIIIA 323; CSM I 285)

The point is that Descartes's dualism ensures that nothing can affect the sense organs except for bodies in motion. Therefore, anything that the senses can deliver to the intellect can be analyzed into the principle of extension.[39]

Descartes does temper his boasts about the scope of his accomplishments. He admits that there are many things pertaining to the fruit-bearing branches of the tree of knowledge (medicine, mechanics, and morals)[40] that are not dealt with. He blames the expense of collecting appropriate observations and appeals to posterity for the completion of the project (AT IXB 17; CSM I 188). Moreover, the boast about demonstrating his results in mathematical style is not as stretched as it might at first seem. In Newton's *Principles of Mathematical Philosophy*, we do find ordinary mathematics being used to deduce numerically quantified phenomena. Descartes is instead employing his universal method which subsumes mathematics but construes deduction more generally as intuiting the shared natures that link the deductive steps. Theoretically, that project could succeed without "mathematizing" the derivation of the phenomena in the Newtonian sense.

Having thus lowered the bar a bit, we can ask how well Descartes succeeds on his own terms with the items for which he actually does offer explanations in the *Principles*. The answer is that it takes much work to see how Descartes can meet expectations even when they are scaled back. Consider the treatment of magnetism which is showcased with about fifty articles devoted to its explanation (gravity, in contrast, gets only seven). Magnetic phenomena are particularly difficult to explain. Gilbert, who recorded particularly careful observations, was obliged to conclude in 1600 that it involved a nonmechanical occult form. Descartes was therefore very proud of his thoroughly mechanical explanation that appealed only to what can be deduced from his principles. That meant that the many curious phenomena could be explained in terms of only bodies and their motions. Descartes idea, in short, was that pervasive, invisibly small, screw-shaped particles circulate in vortexes through and around the earth. As these particles flow through the spiraled windings in tiny pores in magnets, iron, and steel, their screwing action moves the pieces of metal. In light of later, fully mathematicized explanations of electromagnetic phenomena this all seems hopelessly speculative, qualitative, and "unscientific" in our contemporary sense of the term. The contrast with Newton's treatment of gravitation, to take one example, is razor sharp. Let us see if we can reconstruct how Descartes could have thought he triumphed with his story about magnetism.

Descartes's general strategy had already been outlined in the *Rules*:

> take someone who thinks that nothing in the magnet can be known which does not consist of certain self-evident, simple natures. . . . [H]e carefully gathers together all the available observations concerning the stone in question; then he tries to deduce from this what sort of mixture of simple natures is necessary for producing all the effects which the magnet is found to have. Once he has discovered this mixture, he is in a position to make the bold claim that he has grasped the true nature of the magnet, so far as it is humanly possible to discover it on the basis of given observations.
>
> (Rules, AT X 427; CSM I 49–50)

If we can enumerate the mixture of natures that compose the magnetic phenomena, then we can analyze those all the way to the appropriate principles. This would entitle us to say that we have a demonstration of the mixed nature because we could produce the reversed synthesis should the occasion present itself. The goal, as we saw in our initial discussion of deduction, is to be able to intuit the same nature at the beginning, in the principle, and then in the conclusion of the deduction. If we are in this way able to form an unbroken chain of steps each of which contains the intuition of extension, then we have succeeded. At this point, we know already what the appropriate principle is – extension. So we somehow have to link that up with our enumerated phenomena.

We use our eyes and see, suppose, the scattered iron filings forming patterns when the magnet is placed in their midst. That is, we see bodies and their relative positions and motions. We are not immediately able to link deductively extension (the principle) with the particular motions of the iron filings. Our vision informs us of no mechanism pushing them from their scattered state into their characteristically ordered pattern. Our problem is to find the missing links. We allow our imagination to supply images of screw-like particles pushing against the windings in the pores in particles of iron with the result that the aggregates of these iron particles, the filings, are pushed into the motions that we observe. Our imagining is, perhaps, made more distinct and vivid by some previous results in the *Principles* about the origin of the grooved particles in unrelated processes. And this story fits nicely with his general cosmological picture of matter everywhere being in vortical motions. The "mixture" of natures – the shapes, relative sizes, and motions of the imagined particles – is all easily conceived as various determinations of extension, so they are easy to link intuitively to that ultimate principle. And if we can then intuitively link the imagined microscenario to the observed motions, we are done. We have not used any ordinary mathematics, but we have what Descartes regards as the same kind of demonstration as we find in mathematics. If we then allow our intellects to sweep from an intuition of extension to our sense perception of the phenomena, we can intuit these phenomena *as extended*. That is the required "shared nature" linking our deductive steps. There remains a question about whether Descartes has, in fact, used his brand of deduction to explain the phenomena. Is it really possible to move easily from the intuition of extension to intuiting extension *in* the nature of a distinctly imagined grooved particle? That will initially seem highly implausible, but for a graduate of the extended method, it is an easy task.[41]

Because the microparticles and their behavior in the story are neither observed nor produced from principles by some calculus, it is natural to think of them as *hypotheses*. As usual with scientific hypotheses, there are difficult problems about their epistemic status.[42] More specifically, if we are supposed to intuit the microparticles as simple natures, we must be certain of their nature and behavior. But is the story supplied by Descartes certain, keeping in mind that he invented the story outright? Must Descartes admit that regardless of how well his explanation holds up over time, that God nevertheless might have used some other mechanism to bring about the observed phenomena?

These questions are considered in the very last articles of the *Principles*.[43] Descartes begins by referring to the epitome of contemporaneous applied mechanics: clockwork. An expert clockmaker can achieve the same observed timekeeping with quite different mechanisms that can be invisible to the casual user. By analogy, it seems one must conclude that the "supreme craftsman" could bring about magnetic phenomena in a way undreamed of in Descartes's philosophy. Descartes freely admits this, but the admission is ambiguous. One reading is that God might, for all we know, have actually brought about the phenomena with entirely different kinds of microstructures. A second reading is that God might have done this, but most assuredly did not. There is a third reading that renders the texts most consistent. Descartes assumes in the *Principles* that the universe evolved into its present form after being created by God in an initially chaotic state. He believes this "fable" enhances the clarity of his explanations (*Principles*, AT VIIIA 101–2). Despite that, Descartes adheres to the theological doctrine that the universe was created largely in its present form. So, the supreme craftsman might have (and in fact did) bring about Descartes's grooved particles via a process quite unlike the one Descartes describes, but there is no doubt about the details of Descartes's explanation of the phenomena as they are *now* observed. Descartes's readers need not worry about the discrepancy between reality and his fictitious story about the origin of the micromechanism because it has no effect on how the phenomena are to be understood now. He hastens to add that his explanations of how things work now are nonetheless "morally certain," meaning that they can be unreservedly counted upon in the conduct of real-life affairs.

Referring to moral certainty in this way raises another issue. Items that are "merely" morally certain can still be uncertain in "relation to the absolute power of God." At this point, Descartes uses an analogy with a long message written in some code. If one hits on a code that yields a plausible message, it is morally certain the code is correct. It hardly seems possible that there is another code that would reveal an even more plausible message, but there is an absolute sense in which it is possible. Now think of the phenomena as like the message and Descartes's principles as like the code. And now, by the extreme standard of more-than-moral-certainty, it might seem there is an attenuated sense in which even the perfectly known principles are regarded as uncertain.[44] In the next article Descartes recovers by recalling the result of the extended method; God is the ultimate principle and the guarantor of our intuitions of the other principles. He concludes that the principles and whatever is actually deduced from them should be regarded as "absolutely, and more than just morally, certain." This, of course, does not conflict with the weaker claim that his explanations are also morally certain.

Before moving on to compare this theory of logic and knowledge with some other early modern theories, there is a last global objection to be considered. It is, quite bluntly, that Descartes succeeds because it is ridiculously easy to achieve success as he has defined it. One first comes to intuit a very few basic principles. One then carefully observes and enumerates the phenomena to be brought under the umbrella of *scientia*. Finally, one imagines explanations that deductively link these (keeping in mind that deductive links involve intuiting shared natures). This seems uncomfortably close to Leibniz's famous disparaging paraphrase: "take what is necessary, do as you ought to do, and you will get what you wanted." Descartes's response is to embrace as a virtue the ease with which *scientia* is generated. In the preface of the *Principles*, he confidently asserts that almost none are too "dull and slow" to be able to grasp his most advanced science: "For since the principles in question are clear, and nothing is permitted to be deduced form them except by very evident reasoning, everyone has enough intelligence to understand the things that depend on them" (AT VIIIA 12; CSM I 12).[45] Earlier, in the *Rules*, he explains at some length why his competitors have presented matters as involving complex details:

> On the other hand, whenever they have the luck to discover something certain and evident, they always present it wrapped up in various obscurities either because they fear that the simplicity of their argument may depreciate the importance of their finding, or because they begrudge us the plain truth.
> (Rule 3, AT X 367; CSM I 13)

> It is however a common failing of mortals to regard what is more difficult as more attractive. . . . But let us note that those who really do possess knowledge can discern the truth with equal facility whether they have derived it from a simple subject or from an obscure one. For once they have hit upon it, they grasp each truth by means of a single and distinct act which is similar in every case.
> (Rule 9, AT X 401; CSM I 33)[46]

The hard part is learning to deploy skillfully the intellect's intuition. And that, as we have seen, is best done with practice on puzzles, games, and mathematical problems.

5. Metaphysical objections: Spinoza and Malebranche

We are now prepared to consider briefly the views of some other important early modern thinkers in light of the framework erected by Descartes. In his early, incomplete work, *Treatise on the Emendation of the Intellect*, Spinoza takes up a position that has much in common with Descartes. By the time his finished his masterwork, *The Ethics* (finally published in 1677), large parts of the Cartesian framework of logic and knowledge remain, but we can also find his characteristic attempts to deal with difficulties left by his predecessor. We have seen that God is not mentioned in Descartes's exposition of his version of the analytic-synthetic method in the *Rules*, but in the extended method all *scientia* depends on God. In the *Ethics*, the highest grade of knowledge is called *intuitiva scientia* (intuitive knowledge). The term recalls Descartes and, as in Descartes, this kind of knowledge depends on knowledge of God. Spinoza makes clear that the right kind of dependence is very awkward for Descartes to bring off. Although it gets him the desired theological result that thought and extension stand in an effect-cause relation to God, it threatens to get the undesired logical result that they stand in the relative-absolute relation. This is bad for Descartes because the relative *shares a nature* with what is absolute and Descartes obviously cannot say that human minds and extension share God's nature; they are finite and God is infinite. Similarly, in Descartes's extended method, the meditator can analyze his own existence to arrive at God's existence, but one cannot say without qualification that the meditator's existence can be deduced from the premise that God exists. Spinoza cuts this Gordian knot by allowing that finite things logically follow from God. He also allows a strong sense in which finite things share a nature with God – they are "conceived through" God. This means they cannot be distinctly conceived at all, except insofar as they exist *in* God as modes of substance. This is rather close to saying that the concept of a finite thing is ultimately *analyzed* as crucially including the concept of God. And to say that finite things follow from God is rather close to saying that their concepts can be *synthesized* from the concept of God. Needless to say, this is all unorthodox theology. Another interesting consequence of this difference is that Spinoza's *scientia* does not engage a Cartesian circle. Recall that the circle results from the requirements of the extended method. Maximal doubt calls for something external to the intellect to ground its intuitions, and it requires a subtle trick to bridge that gap. In Spinoza's system, there is no such gap to bridge and hence no ground for intuitions – "truth is its own standard." The philosophical cost of this is that there can be no extended method of specially eliciting intuitions of principles. Spinoza can only demand that his readers have what he takes to be the appropriate intuitions, and there is no recourse for those that do not share them.

In Malebranche, we find an interesting attempt to split the difference between Descartes and Spinoza on these matters. Malebranche, like Spinoza, wants human knowledge to depend even more intimately on God than does Descartes. But like Descartes, he requires more than a modal distinction between the intellect and God. The key move is to deny that intuitive knowledge of principles is innately available; instead, the ideas are in the divine intellect whence they illuminate the human mind. This "vision in God" makes *scientia* possible without giving the human mind too much credit for it. Malebranche's account of geometry then can closely parallel Descartes's because God makes his idea of extension available for human knowledge. In a further twist, Malebranche maintains that God withholds from human minds his idea of the human mind itself. Because this idea does not illuminate created minds, they cannot intuit themselves as a principle. This means that nothing deductively follows about the mind (at least nothing accessible to humans), so there is no *scientia* to be had in that subject matter – there is no science of "psychology."

In some of Malebranche's polemics against Descartes, he takes it as a premise that there is no *scientia* of the soul and then concludes that there can be no intuition of the soul. Although the converse of that argument is an interesting consequence of the curious doctrine of vision in God, the polemical situation is embarrassing for Malebranche.

Descartes *does* hold that *scientia* of the mind is possible, so Malebranche's gainsaying that does not amount to an internal criticism. To see this, note that in Spinoza's dual-aspect monism, any item of *scientia* for extension is exactly paralleled by an item of *scientia* for thought. There is an analogue of that in Descartes. Anything known about extension is something (deductively) known about the knowing subject and therefore an item of *scientia*. Furthermore, for Descartes (unlike Spinoza), there is further *scientia* for the mind that has no parallel in extension. A particular volition, for example, can be analyzed into the faculty of will which in turn analyzes into the principle of thought. That analysis can then be reversed into a *scientia-yielding* deduction.[47]

6. Epistemological objections: Locke

The rationalist philosophers notably connected logic with metaphysical knowledge. Locke can be read as moving back to something very close to the spirit of Descartes's basic method and away from his extended method. For Locke, intuition and deduction operate in a way that is very close to what Descartes described in the *Rules*; metaphysical claims are minimal whereas logic studies the epistemological limits of human understanding. Locke defines knowledge as "the perception of the connection and agreement, or disagreement and repugnancy of any of our Ideas" (*Essay* 4.1.2).[48] Knowledge comes in three "degrees," two of which correspond to a now-familiar distinction drawn in Descartes. In Locke's version of *intuitive* knowledge, the perception of agreement or disagreement of ideas is utterly clear and unmediated by any other ideas (*Essay* 4.2.1). *Demonstrative* knowledge results when the mind cannot intuitively perceive agreement or disagreement but can, by considering other ideas in intervening steps, come to the requisite perception. In each of the intervening steps, the perception of agreement or disagreement must be intuitive (*Essay* 4.2.2–4.2.7). One difference from the account in the *Rules* is that Descartes thought that a carefully rehearsed demonstration could result in a sort of intuition of the conclusion, whereas for Locke the categories of intuitive and demonstrative knowledge are mutually exclusive. But that is a minor difference.

A more interesting difference emerges when Locke goes on to define *sensitive* knowledge, which is for him the third degree of knowledge. Locke introduces this by contrasting it with intuitive knowledge: "There can be nothing more certain, than that the *Idea* we receive from an external Object is in our Minds; this is intuitive Knowledge" (*Essay* 4.2.14). That is so far still Cartesian, but Locke continues: "we may add to the two former sorts of *Knowledge*, this also, of the existence of particular external objects, by that perception and Consciousness we have of the actual entrance of *Ideas* from them." Descartes will not allow that sensation unaided by reason can deliver any knowledge about what is external to the mind. On the other hand, we have seen that Descartes does think that all natural phenomena are subject to demonstration. For Locke, sensitive knowledge does not extend beyond what is immediately available to consciousness, nor are our ideas sufficient to establish the intuitive links that would be needed for demonstrations concerning the external world (excepting the special case of God). Scientific knowledge about the external world, therefore, can be no more than probable. What explains this difference of opinion?

Descartes's intuitive knowledge is of single, simple natures or principles innate in the mind which it can intuit perfectly distinctly or else embedded in composite natures. Moreover, these rationalist intuitions constitute knowledge of existing substances: mind, body, and God. Demonstrations, therefore, can penetrate to the essences of things. Locke drops talk of natures, principles, and innateness in this context. All of Locke's simple ideas, in contrast, need to be conveyed into the mind via external or internal sense. The latter delivers ideas of reflection which are gotten by the mind's taking notice of its own operations (*Essay* 2.1.4). Locke's simple ideas do not themselves constitute knowledge of substances. They do, however, delimit the scope of knowledge. This role for simple ideas brings out the way in which Locke makes use of something like the method of analysis or synthesis. All ideas are either simple or complex, and complex ideas are produced by the mind's operation on simples.[49] Ultimately, then, human knowledge (the perceived agreement or disagreement of ideas) can be constructed only from the stock of simples made available to the mind in experience. So, by using these versions of enumeration and analysis, Locke arrives at a fairly exhaustive list of the simples from which the mind has synthesized our actually experienced, complex ideas. This enables the mind to construct *nominal essences* for things based on appearances; knowledge of *real essences* exceeds the scope of human understanding because there is no way to synthesize complex ideas of them from simple ideas. This means that Locke is not proffering a logic of discovery – methodology is left to the scientists. Nor is he describing how a mind consciously goes about synthesizing complex ideas. His project is the purely epistemological one of determining the structure and extent of knowledge.

7. Formal objections: Hobbes and Leibniz

We have seen that most of the now-canonical early modern thinkers did not have much use for formal logic. This does not mean that the schools stopped teaching it or that popular textbooks were not in use. Nevertheless, the most famous and influential textbook, the so-called Port-Royal *Logic*, is a virtual compendium of Cartesianism.[50] In the section of the book that is devoted to rules of formal logic, the authors remind us that they are not so useful as was often supposed but, "Be that as it may, here is what is usually said about them, and even a bit more than is usually said" (Arnauld and Nicole 1996, 135). In their comprehensive history of logic, Kneale and Kneale write of the Port-Royal *Logic*, "although it is a source of a bad fashion of confusing logic with epistemology, it contains some novelties that are worth study" (1962, 316). Against this dominance of nonformal logic in the theories of progressive early modern philosophers, Hobbes and Leibniz stand as exceptions. To them we now turn.

Taking a chronological step back from Locke, we find in Hobbes a more uncompromising empiricism. Hobbes does not allow anything like Locke's ideas of reflection; everything in thought derives exclusively from sensations of material things. So, *reasoning* itself is nothing more than trains of successive traces of sensations. Of course, the representational power of thought is enhanced by the ability to use words as signs for previous sensations and their derivatives. Hobbes then emphasizes the fact that almost all reasoning depends on operations on linguistic signs for ideas. In "right reason" or deduction, the relevant operations reduce to addition and subtraction; deduction thus requires *computations* with linguistic signs. So 'human,' for example, might be a sum of 'speech using,' 'self-moving,' 'living,' and 'creature.' Science is defined as the knowledge of "consequences" which amount to trains of inferences in which the steps are linked by computation. This clearly puts much importance on clear definitions of words. Sums and differences will not be accurately computed unless it is perfectly clear how the components of the words are to be counted. This gives some idea of how morals and politics can be demonstrative sciences – all that is required is that the significance of such words as 'good' and 'justice' be carefully stipulated. Hobbes believed that even politics could be a demonstrative moral science (Locke similarly thought that there could be a demonstrative moral science) because it is possible precisely to define important theoretical ideas like *property*.

There is a huge philosophical gulf between Hobbes's extreme empiricism and the intellectualist metaphysics of Leibniz. But Leibniz was with Hobbes and against his great rationalist predecessors regarding formal logic. Leibniz took great interest in refinements of Aristotelian syllogistic logic, but more importantly he had a grand vision for a computational logic. For one thing, Leibniz disapproved of Hobbes's nominalist and conventionalist stance on definitions and truth. Leibniz sought *real definitions* such that deductions from them would prove the metaphysical possibility of the result. And instead of working in Hobbes's vaguely materialistic framework, Leibniz wanted primitive predicates that were metaphysically connected with divine attributes. Furthermore, whereas Hobbes seemed happy to take it for granted that honest, tedious labor could show that actual, practical scientific reasoning reduces to computations, Leibniz undertook these labors. He was rewarded with some results that prefigure nineteenth century advances by Boole and others. Leibniz, therefore, stands out as a truly transitional figure. Like Descartes, he believed that logic was, in principle, extremely important for the development of knowledge. The vision, however, included a plan for the kind of highly sophisticated, purely formal manipulation of symbols that characterizes fully modern logic.

8. Notes on secondary sources

These are mostly recent works in English in addition to those cited in the main body of the chapter. Many of them include extensive bibliographies of older works and scholarship in other languages. This chapter is about the early modern conception of logic as the science of how to think properly to arrive at knowledge. In this period, formal Aristotelian logic was disparaged by many of the figures we now regard as canonical, but it was not entirely ignored by them. And it remained dominant in the universities. A good general history of formal logic is Kneale and Kneale (1962). Beck (1952) is a close reading of Descartes's *Rules* that remains very valuable. Schuster (1980) discusses the voluminous controversy about how to interpret *mathesis universalis* in Descartes. Garber's seminal works (1992, 2001) are essential reading for the interpretation of Descartes on scientific knowledge. Unlike the present chapter's emphasis on large continuities, Garber argues that Descartes's thought divides into sharply separated stages. Gaukroger's intellectual biography of Descartes (1995) makes a detailed case for seeing Descartes's general theory of knowledge as driven by his scientific work, whereas his *Cartesian Logic* (1989) is one of the most extended treatments Descartes on logic. Schouls (1980) usefully compares Descartes and Locke on method and the foundations of knowledge with some special attention to analysis and synthesis. Smith (2010) is a detailed study of analysis and synthesis in Descartes and Leibniz and how their views are related to some ancient treatments of those techniques. A standard treatment of Spinoza that raises interesting questions on logic and reason is Curley (1969). Hobbes's views are best summarized in the first few chapters of his classic, *Leviathan*. Watkins (1973) focuses on the importance of logic and the theory of knowledge in Hobbes's thought. Hume combined a Lockean conception of logic with Hobbesian strictures about ideas; Owen (1999) is the main source for Hume and also includes useful chapters on Descartes and Locke. For an account of Hobbes and Leibniz's work on syllogistic logic, see Nuchelmans (1998); and Kneale and Kneale (1962, 320–44) is a general account of Leibniz on logic, whereas Rutherford (1995) explains the philosophy behind Leibniz's general program for a logical calculus. Parkinson's 1966 edition of selected works in formal logic by Leibniz has a substantial introduction. Finally, Easton (ed., 1997) collects a number of specific essays on the general topic of this chapter.

Notes

1. See for example Mancosu (1996, ch. 1).
2. Each will be referred to by the first word of the title. The *Rules* and *Principles* are divided into numbered sections and the latter has four parts. The *Discourse* has six parts and there are six meditations in the *Meditations*. Citations are from the standard English translation (Cottingham et al. 1984–5, vols. 1 and 2) and the standard edition (Adam and Tannery 1974–89, 11 vols.), giving first the Adam and Tannery edition and then the edition by Cottingham and colleagues by volume number and page.
3. Useful treatments of this background can be found in Jardine (1988) and Dear (1998). Descartes did not, however, see himself as adopting the traditional philosophy connected with the terminology:

    > In case anyone should be troubled by my novel use of the term "intuition" and of other terms to which I shall be forced to give a different meaning from their ordinary one, I wish to point out here that I am paying no attention to the way these terms have lately been used in the Schools.
    >
    > (AT X 369; CSM I 14)

4. This characterization of intuition corresponds perfectly with what Descartes will later refer to as clear and distinct perception:

    > I call a perception "clear" when it is present and accessible to the attentive mind. . . . I call a perception "distinct" if, as well as being clear, it is so sharply separated from all other perceptions that it contains within itself only what is clear.
    >
    > (AT VIIIA 22; CSM I 207–8)

    To emphasize this, and because many of Descartes's contemporaries use the term "intuition," I shall use the term "intuition" throughout this chapter.
5. For example, in Gaukroger (1989, 51).
6. I shall use the term "principles" to refer to natures that are perfectly simple and, therefore, not capable of being deduced from any others. Descartes later settles on the term as well (e.g. in the AT IXB 2–3; CSM I 179).
7. Garber (1992, 39–43) points out that the *semel in vita* theme is picked up in later works.
8. Descartes does, however, refer to the mind and body forming a composite whole which has its own faculties (AT X 411; CSM I 39–40). See also notes 24 and 33.
9. This consideration is worked out in more detail in the *Principles*. There Descartes first notes that "[o]ur next task is to examine whether these principles alone enable us to explain all natural phenomena [i.e. the effects which we perceived by means of our senses]" (AT IXB 103; CSM I 248). He next notes that "[b]y means of our senses we apprehend nothing in extended objects beyond their shapes, sizes, and motions" (AT VIIIA 321; CSM I 284). And he finally concludes that, "A simple enumeration will make it clear that there is no phenomenon of nature which I have omitted to consider in this treatise. For a list of natural phenomena cannot include anything which is not apprehended by the senses" (AT VIIIA 323; CSM I 285).
10. Here the word "enumeration" is being used in the familiar sense. This is related to Descartes's technical sense which is explained in what follows.
11. Because "it is possible to have . . . knowledge which is certain only of things which are entirely simple and absolute" (AT X 394; CSM I 29), we can be maximally certain about the nature of simple ideas. To the extent that an idea is composite, it is subject to doubt. Because "simple natures are all self-evident and never contain any falsity" (AT C 420; CSM I 45), this means that falsity and uncertainty in perceptions are products of a confused nature, for "we can go wrong only when we ourselves compose in some way the objects of our belief" (AT X 423; CSM I 47).

12 *Scientia* is the Aristotelian term for knowledge that is certain and explanatory because it is deduced from first principles. Descartes means to extend a similar status to anything falling under *mathesis universalis*. In later works, as we shall see, Descartes extends his method so that *scientia* also require the right kind of knowledge of God.

13
> When I considered the matter more closely, I came to see that the exclusive concern of mathematics is with questions of order or measure and that it is irrelevant whether the measure in question involves numbers, shapes, stars, sounds, or any other object whatever. This made me realize that there must be a general science which explains all the points that can be raised concerning order and measure irrespective of the subject-matter, and that this science should be termed *mathesis universalis* – a venerable term with a well-established meaning – for it covers everything that entitles these other science to be called branches of mathematics.
> (AT X 377–8; CSM I 119)

14
> If someone sets himself the problem of investigating every truth for the knowledge of which human reason is adequate – and this, I think, is something everyone who earnestly strives after good sense should do once in his life – he will indeed discover by means of the Rules we have proposed that nothing can be known prior to the intellect, since knowledge of everything else depends on the intellect and not vice versa.
> (AT X 395; CSM I 29–30)

15 Later in the *Principles*, Descartes explains his purpose thus:
> Finally in the *Geometry*, I aimed to demonstrate that I had discovered several things which had hitherto been unknown, and thus to promote the belief that many more things may yet be discovered, in order to stimulate everyone to undertake the search for truth.
> (AT IXB 15–6; CSM I 187)

It would seem he regarded his advances in geometry primarily as advertisements for the more important applications of the method. In a letter to Mersenne in 1630, Descartes responds to a wide range of questions about science, theology, and metaphysics but shows hardly any interest in Mersenne's mathematical questions (AT VII 195–210; CSM I 137–47).

16 The standard reading of the texts being discussed here is quite different. It has been argued that by *mathesis universalis* Descartes was referring either to something like the analytic geometry he goes on to develop or else to an abandoned project to produce a kind of supergeneralized mathematics. On either of these readings, it is hard to see why the mind itself provides the best example of it. Schuster (1980) contains a useful account of traditional interpretations. Some apparent infelicities in the text of the *Rules* have been attributed to the fact that Descartes wrote it in stages (see Gaukroger 1995, 99–181). A reading that downplays the appearance of infelicities is Sepper (1996).
17 These English words are cognates with the Greek. They were later translated into Latin as *resolutio* and *composito*, so methods of analysis and synthesis are sometimes referred to as resolutive-compositive.
18 A standard source is Randall (1961).
19 This point is elaborated and connected with a general interpretation of Descartes on intuition and deduction in Rogers and Nelson (n.d.).
20 Similar problems with the method of analysis and synthesis were discussed by Zabarella and others in the sixteenth century. For an overview, see Jardine (1988).
21 Smith (2010) works through some examples of the connection between enumeration and analysis.
22 For further discussion of this point and additional references, see Marion (1992).
23 This passage is paralleled in the *Meditations* (AT VII 12; CSM II 9, AT VII 17; CSM II 12), *Principles* (AT VIIIA 5; CSM I 193), and the *Search* (AT X 509–514; CSM II 406–09).
24 For discussion of whether human nature can be made intuitive, and therefore a principle, see Nelson (2008). There is a substantial literature on the different but related question of whether the human being is a substance, a recent treatment of which is Kaufman (2008).
25 When applying the extended method, the meditator must carry through the resolution to confront even genuine intuitions with maximal doubt. It is possible to do this despite the fact that an occurrent intuition is indubitable. The trick is that once one ceases to attend to the intuition, one can again doubt in general whether one's cognitive best is false. The maximal doubt therefore renders even one's own existence as intermittently doubtful and therefore not *scientia* until such time as maximal doubt is

26 discharged. For a full development of these points and for opposing views in the literature, see Newman and Nelson (1999). The present account of the extended method makes it possible to see the maximal doubt as a purely methodical device instead of as a direct confrontation with traditional skepticism.
26 The literature on Descartes is dominated by arguments that the program of securing knowledge against hyperbolic doubt fails. Some argue instead that it gains some strictly limited measure of success. The treatment in this chapter coheres with the general interpretation of logic and knowledge in Descartes developed in this chapter. For more details see Newman and Nelson (1999) and Nolan (2005).
27 There is still a puzzle about the status of the intuition of God. In extended analysis, we must first arrive at the intuition by a "proof" from intuited premises. This would appear to make those premises absolute and God relative – not at all the right picture for having the whole of *scientia* depending on God. The puzzle is solved if the Third Meditation's proof of God's existence is understood as an analysis. The meditator begins with such intuitions as her own existence as a thinking thing and the common notion that a cause must have at least as much reality as its effect. These are then broken down until the absolute nature, God, is intuited. Concerning the notion of proof as a means of revealing truths, see Hacking (1980) and Nolan (2005). Hacking's article begins with two memorable sentences: "Leibniz knew what a proof was. Descartes did not."
28 Newman and Nelson (1999) contains details on the operation of the *cogito-like* device that makes the thought of maximal doubt a trigger for the intuition of God.
29 The insufficiency of these pains was immediately apparent in the sets of *Objections* published along with the *Meditations*.
30 Cf. "in seeking the right path of truth we ought to concern ourselves only with objects which admit of as much certainly as the demonstrations of arithmetic and geometry" (*Rules*, AT X 366; CSM I 12).
31 Also in the *Discourse*, Descartes speaks of the defects of geometrical analysis and algebra in comparison to the systematic knowledge that would be delivered by the method he is there seeking (AT VI 17–18; CSM I 119–20).
32 We can now see this view expressed, for example, in this passage from the *Principles*: "The only principles which I accept, or require, in physics are those of geometry and pure mathematics; these principles explain all natural phenomena and enable us to provide quite certain demonstrations regarding them" (AT VIIIA 78; CSM I 247). Physics, geometry, and pure mathematics share the same natures, deriving from extension, but considered in different ways. It is not that mathematics is absolute and physics relative in deductions of natural phenomena.
33 Descartes seems to have been ambivalent about whether there is a principle corresponding to the unified human being. It is not hard to understand that the human being can be *regarded* as having its own principle or nature, just as an inscribed geometrical figure can be so regarded for some purposes. There are some texts that seem to make stronger claims: in the Sixth Meditation the meditator considers what *his* nature teaches him about his "whole self, insofar as I am a combination of body and mind," suggesting that he is deducing things from his human nature (AT VII 81; CSM I 56). Again, in correspondence with Princess Elizabeth, Descartes enumerates "primitive notions," which look very much like innate ideas. The list includes three items in the 28 June 1643 letter: the soul or intellect, extension, and the union of the soul and body (AT III 691–92). When Descartes is producing *scientia* about the human being (in some places in his last work, *The Passions of the Soul*, for example), it is very difficult to tell whether or not the analyses terminate in union as a principle, from which the phenomena are in turn synthetically deduced. This ambivalence is perfectly expressed in the *Principles*, where he seems first to insist on exactly two ultimate finite principles and then immediately take it back:

> But I recognize only two ultimate classes of things: first, intellectual or thinking things, i.e. those which pertain to mind or thinking substance; and secondly, material things, i.e. those which pertain to extended substance or body. . . . But we also experience within ourselves certain other things which must not be referred either to the mind alone or to the body alone. These arise . . . from the close and intimate union of our mind with the body.
> (AT VIIIA 23; CSM I 208–09)

34 For example, he writes, "the *various* principles of material things that we have so far discovered" (AT VIIIA 80; CSM I 248, my emphasis), where he seems to be referring to laws of collision and motion in fluids. Regarding laws, it is relevant that he calls them "secondary causes" (AT VIIIA 62; CSM I 240) to contrast them with God, the primary cause. Because causes are absolute relative to effects, it seems to follow that the laws are principles in only a relative sense.

35 In the *Rules* we have for example "innate principles" (*ingenitis principijs*; AT X 373; CSM I 17), "primary rudiments of human reason" (AT X 374; CSM I 17), "primary seeds of truth implanted innately in human minds" (AT X 376, my translation), and in the *Discourse*, "I derived these principles only from certain seeds of truth which are naturally in our souls" (AT VI 64; CSM I 144).

36 The device of true and immutable natures involves various subtleties. See Cunning (2003) for a discussion of the literature and an interpretation consistent with the present discussion.

37 Descartes's theory of innate ideas poses a number of textual problems. An interpretation in line with the treatment in this chapter, along with a discussion of the literature, can be found in Nelson (2008).

38 In Rule 12 we find, "a triangle is composed of these other natures ... [which] are better known than the triangle [itself]" (AT X 422; CSM I 46). The inscribed figure is discussed in the First Set of Replies (AT VII 118; CSM II 84). The number three gets a similar treatment; a detailed treatment of such examples can be found in Nolan (1998). When we then consider the contribution of "plus," "four," and "equals," it becomes obvious that whereas "2 + 2 = 4" ranks very high on a complex-simple scale, and although it is not the kind of thing that one would ever doubt outside of a meditational procedure, it is *not* a nature simple in the maximal degree, nor is it itself a principle. Note also that nothing of interest follows from "2 + 2 = 4" except the particular cases (involving apples, oranges, etc.) from which it has been abstracted. Here the particulars are prior to the generalization.

39 This point is already developed in Rule 12 where Descartes discusses the theory of sense perception (see also AT VIIIA 80; CSM I 248 and AT VIIIA 315; CSM I 279). The theory is also summarized at the end of the *Principles*. The summaries are in lieu of fifth and sixth parts which were at one time projected for treating human and animal biology in detail.

40 "By 'morals' I understand the highest and most perfect moral system, which presupposes a complete knowledge of all the other sciences, and is the ultimate level of wisdom" (AT IXB 14; CSM I 186). Descartes does go on to vaguely indicate how some of this is gained by reading the *Principles*, but a deductive account of how to live virtuously had to await his last book, *The Passions of the Soul*.

41 This recalls what is written about bodies in the extended method of the Sixth Meditation. After establishing that they exist, there is this clarification:

> They may not all exist in a way that exactly corresponds with my sensory grasp of them, for in many cases the grasp of the senses is very obscure and confused. But at least they possess all the properties which I clearly and distinctly understand, that is, all those which, viewed in general terms, are comprised within the subject-matter of pure mathematics.
>
> (AT VII 80; CSM II 55)

42 The main problems concerning hypotheses in Descartes are clearly formulated in Garber (1992, chs. 5 and 6). Garber presents a more pessimistic evaluation of the cogency of Descartes's claims about knowledge in these passages.

43 I shall be referring to *Principles*, part IV, articles 204–206 (AT VIIIA 327–29; CSM I 289–91).

44 This engages Descartes's notorious doctrine of the creation of the eternal truths which might seem to imply, for example, that God was not constrained to make the law of noncontradiction true. For discussion and references, see Nelson and Cunning (1999).

45 The rest of the book is sprinkled with remarks about how the proceedings are easy to demonstrate (*facile demonstratur*; AT VIIIA 137; CSM I 261), clearly perceived (*clare percipitur*; AT VIIIA 142; CSM I 262), "clearly" or "easily" understood (*clare intelligur*; AT VIIIA 145; CSM I 262), and so forth. See also the next note.

46 Also,

> Throughout this treatise, we shall try to pursue every humanly accessible path which leads to knowledge of the truth. We shall do this very carefully, and show the paths to be very easy, so that anyone who has mastered the whole method, however mediocre his intelligence, may see that there are no paths closed to him that are open to others, and that his lack of further knowledge is not due to any want of intelligence or method. As often as he applies his mind to acquire knowledge of something, either he will be entirely successful, or at least he will realize that success depends upon some observation which is not within his power to make.
>
> (AT X 399; CSM I 32)

47 For textual citations, a discussion of the literature, and some different arguments, see Nolan and Whipple (2005).

48 As is customary, I refer to Locke (1975) by book, chapter, and section separated by periods, so 4.1.2 refers to book 4, chapter 1, section 2. I have not changed the spelling, capitalization, and so forth.
49 Of course, most of our ideas are ramified as the mind operates on complex ideas to produce ideas of greater complexity. Some Locke scholars think that abstract ideas do not fit into the simple-complex dichotomy; that difficult issue need not concern us here.
50 This work (Arnauld and Nicole 1996) was first published in 1662 and went into a fifth edition in 1683. It was widely read in Britain and was used as a textbook at Cambridge and Oxford as late as the nineteenth century.

Bibliography

Adam, C. and Tannery, P. (eds.) (1974–89) *Oeuvres de Descartes*, 11 vols. Paris: Vrin.
Arnauld, A. and Nicole, P. (1996) Buroker, J.V. (trans. and ed.) *Logic or the Art of Thinking*. Cambridge: Cambridge University Press.
Beck, L.J. (1952) *The Method of Descartes*. London: Oxford University Press.
Clarke, D. "Descartes' Philosophy of Science and the Scientific Revolution," in Cottingham (ed.) 1992: 258–85.
Cottingham, J. (ed.) (1992) *The Cambridge Companion to Descartes*. Cambridge: Cambridge University Press.
———. Stoothoff, R. and Murdoch, D. (trans. and eds.) (1984) *The Philosophical Writings of Descartes*, vols. 1 and 2. Cambridge: Cambridge University Press.
Cunning, D. (2003) "True and Immutable Natures and Epistemic Progress in Descartes's Meditations," *British Journal for the History of Philosophy*, 11: 235–48.
Curley E. (1969) *Spinoza's Metaphysics*. Cambridge: Harvard University Press.
Dear, P. "Method and the Study of Nature," in Garber and Ayers (eds.) 1998: 147–77.
Easton, P. (ed.) (1997) *Logic and the Workings of the Mind*. Atascadero: Ridgeview Publishing.
Garber, D. (1992) *Descartes' Metaphysical Physics*. Chicago: Chicago University Press.
———. (2001) *Descartes Embodied*. Cambridge: Cambridge University Press.
———. and Ayers, M. (eds.) (1998) *The Cambridge History of Seventeenth-Century Philosophy*. Cambridge: Cambridge University Press.
Gaukroger, S. (ed.) (1980) *Descartes*. Sussex: The Harvester Press.
———. (1989) *Cartesian Logic*. Oxford: Oxford University Press.
———. (1995) *Descartes: An Intellectual Biography*. Oxford: Oxford University Press.
Hacking, I. "Proof and Eternal Truths: Descartes and Leibniz," in Gaukroger (ed.) 1980: 169–80.
Hobbes, T. (1994) Curley, E. (ed.) *Leviathan*. Indianapolis: Hackett Publishing Company.
Jardine, N. (1988) "Epistemology of the Sciences," in Schmitt, C., Q. Skinner, and E. Kessler (eds.) *The Cambridge History of Renaissance Philosophy*: 686–93. Cambridge: Cambridge University Press.
Kaufman, D. (2008) "Descartes on Composites, Incomplete Substances, and Kinds of Unity," *Archiv für Geschichte der Philosophie*, 90: 39–73.
Kneale, W. and Kneale, M. (1962) *The Development of Logic*. Oxford: Oxford University Press.
Locke, J. (1975) Nidditch, P. (ed.) *An Essay Concerning Human Understanding*. Oxford: Oxford University Press.
Mancosu, P. (1996) *Philosophy of Mathematics and Mathematical Practice in the Seventeenth Century*. New York: Oxford University Press.
Marion, J.-L. "Cartesian Metaphysics and the Role of the Simple Natures," in Cottingham (ed.) 1992: 115–39.
Nelson, A. (1997) "Descartes' Ontology of Thought," *Topoi*, 16: 163–78.
———. (2008). "Cartesian Innateness," in Broughton, J. and Carriero, J. (eds.) *A Companion to Descartes*: 319–33. Oxford: Blackwell.
———. and Cunning, D. (1999) "Cognition and Modality in Descartes," *Acta Philosophica Fennica*, 64: 137–54.
Newman, L. and Nelson, A. (1999) "Circumventing Cartesian Circles," *Nous*, 33: 370–404.
Nolan, L. (1997) "Reductionism and Nominalism in Descartes' Theory of Attributes," *Topoi*, 16: 129–40.
———. (1998) "Descartes' Theory of Universals," *Philosophical Studies*, 89: 161–80.
———. (2005) "The Ontological Argument as an Exercise in Cartesian Therapy," *Canadian Journal of Philosophy*, 35: 521–62.
———. and Whipple, J. (2005) "Self-Knowledge in Descartes and Malebranche," *Journal of the History of Philosophy*, 43: 55–81.

Nuchelmans, G. "Deductive Reasoning," in Garber and Ayers (eds.) 1998: 132–46.
Owen, D. (1999) *Hume's Reason*. Oxford: Oxford University Press.
Parkinson, G. (trans. and ed.) (1966) *Leibniz: Logical Papers*. Oxford: Oxford University Press.
Randall, J. (1961) *The School of Padua and the Emergence of Modern Science*. Padua: Antenore.
Rogers, B. and Nelson, A. (nd) "Descartes's Logic and the Paradox of Inference." Unpublished.
Rutherford, D. (1995) "Philosophy and Language in Leibniz," in Jolley, N. (ed.), *The Cambridge Companion to Leibniz*: 224–69. Cambridge: Cambridge University Press.
Schouls, P. (1980) *The Imposition of Method*. New York: Oxford University Press.
Schuster, J. (1980) "Descartes' *Mathesis Universalis* 1619–28," in Gaukroger (ed.) 1980: 41–96.
Sepper, D. (1996) *Descartes's Imagination*. Berkeley: University of California Press.
Smith, K. (2010) *Matter Matters*. New York: Oxford University Press.
Watkins, J.W.N. (1973) *Hobbes' System of Ideas*, 2nd ed. London: Hutchinson.

Part 4

MIND AND LANGUAGE

9
MIND-BODY PROBLEMS
David Cunning

There are a number of interlocking themes in the seventeenth-century discussion of the relationship between mind and body. One concerns the relative value of minds and bodies, as some philosophers inherit from the ancient and medieval tradition the view that minds are more exalted than bodies and are more than merely physical. Opponents of this view counter that minds are exalted *and* material and thus that body has been the victim of severe misrepresentation. A second theme is that substances have an underlying nature in terms of which of their modifications can be explained and understood. On this view, if we cannot understand how modifications like ideas and volitions can arise in a substance with modifications like size, shape, and motion, then ideas and volitions are to be attributed to a substance of a different kind. An opposing view is that there are independent and compelling arguments for the view *that* minds arise from matter, and our inability to understand *how* matter thinks is a fact about us and what we do and do not understand. A third theme is that minds and bodies appear to interact and that there is some difficulty in understanding their interaction if they are mutually exclusive substances with nothing in common. Some philosophers will neutralize the difficulty by arguing that minds and bodies do not interact, and others will argue that because minds and bodies do interact, minds must be physical as well. A final theme is that the behavior of bodies in the natural world is orderly and purposive and that it could not be orderly or purposive without some kind of intelligence guiding the way. Some philosophers will argue that because bodies are not intelligent, the guide must be immaterial, but others will argue that bodies are intelligent and are capable of exhibiting order on their own.

1. The relative value of mind and body

A number of ancient and medieval philosophers subscribed to the view that minds are more exalted than bodies. The motivations that generate the view center around the apparent indivisibility and intangibility of minds – and their consequent indestructibility and eternality – and also the ontological proximity of immaterial creatures to their supremely perfect and wholly immaterial creator. The view also arises from an appreciation of the value of certainty and from a widely held understanding that there is a significant difference between the kind of certainty that we can achieve when we attend to matters that are abstract and insensible and the kind of certainty that can be obtained through the senses. Things that are known perfectly are worthy of our attention, as are the apparently indivisible and intangible faculties by which we know them.

For example, in Plato we find the view that "the true philosopher despises" physical things.[1] The body is a distraction that "keeps us busy in a thousand ways because of its need for nurture" (66b); it "makes us too busy to practise philosophy" (66d), and so "the philosopher frees the soul from association with the body as much as possible" (64e–65a). On the Platonic view, souls are invisible and intangible and hence indivisible and divine. Bodies are their exact opposite (78b–80b). We know from our analysis of the concept of body, and from our observation of the sudden inactivity of things that die, that animated bodies have a soul and that bodies on their own are inert (105c–e). A soul is obviously what activates and enlivens a body, and the opposite of a soul, its body, is "death" (105e). The true philosopher thus despises bodies, because they are unimpressive in their own right, and in addition they distract us from things that are more worthy of our attention. They are not the source of any certainty, and they interfere with the faculties by which we can arrive at certainty (65a–67a). Our embodiment and our ensuing physical needs incline us to pursue sensible objects, but these are beneath us, and they interfere with our ability to attend to the things that are not.

Philosophers of the medieval period also endorse the view that body is a low-grade kind of being. In "On Beauty," Plotinus offers an extended discussion of "the darkness inherent in matter" and insists that sensible things are detestable except insofar as they imitate immaterial ideas and minds:

> This is why fire glows with a beauty beyond all other bodies, for fire holds the rank of idea in their regard. Always struggling aloft, this subtlest of elements is at the last limits of the bodily. . . . It sparkles and glows like an idea.[2]

Fire is still material, of course, and material things are no substitute for things that are immaterial and (hence) divine (40). We would do much better to turn our attention away from sensible bodies and attend instead to ideas. Plotinus continues,

> [A]n ugly soul . . . is friend to filthy pleasures, it lives a life abandoned to bodily sensation and enjoys its depravity. . . . If someone is immersed in mire or daubed with mud, his native comeliness disappears; all one sees is the mire and mud with which he is covered. Ugliness is due to the alien matter that encrusts him. If he would be attractive once more, he has to wash himself, get clean again, make himself what he was before. Thus we would be right in saying that ugliness of soul comes from its mingling with, fusion with, collapse into the bodily and material.
> (39)

In a word, Plotinus thinks that we should do everything that we can to mitigate the unfortunate fact of our embodiment and instead engage in philosophical reflection. His disciple Augustine continues in the same vein:

> How highly do you value th[e] will? You surely do not think it should be compared with wealth or honours or physical pleasures, or even all of these together. . . . Then should we not rejoice a little that we have something in our souls – this very thing that I call a good will – in comparison with which those things we mentioned are utterly worthless?[3]

For Augustine, body is so bad that sin consists in turning our attention away from eternal things to things that are temporal and corporeal (27).

This kind of thinking finds its way into the seventeenth century as well. In the Cartesian (and very Augustinian and Platonic) philosopher Nicolas Malebranche, we find the view that bodies are "inferior things" that are essentially passive and inert.[4] Malebranche indeed brings together the whole spectrum of themes that are advanced by his body-hating predecessors. In *Dialogues on Metaphysics and on Religion*, his spokesperson Theodore says to his opponent Aristes that our embodiment is a burden and that we should neutralize it to whatever extent we can:

> You are now ready to make thousands and thousands of discoveries in the land of truth. Distinguish ideas from sensations, but distinguish them well. . . . Your modalities are only darkness, remember that. Silence your senses, your imagination and your passions, and you will hear the pure voice of inner truth, the clear and evident responses of our common master. Never confound evidence, which results from the comparison of ideas, with the vivacity of the sensations which affect and disturb you. The more vivid our sensations, the more they spread darkness. . . . In a word, avoid all that affects you and quickly embrace all that enlightens you. We must follow Reason despite the seductions, the threats, the insults of the body to which we are united, despite the action of the objects surrounding us.
>
> (*Dialogues* III, 8)

For Malebranche, the search for truth is very literally a matter of retreating to the study, where the possibility is minimized that we will be distracted by the lures of the sensible world. It is a seduction and a threat, and the only contexts in which we are advised to attend to its advances are ones in which damage to our bodies would lead us to have yet additional modalities that would distract us further still.

In Malebranche's contemporary Ralph Cudworth we find a similar contempt for the body. Cudworth argues that there is a hierarchy of being that applies to creatures and that minds are at the top. Bodies are dead and lowly and are squarely at the bottom:

> There is unquestionably, a *Scale* or *Ladder* of *Nature*, and Degrees of *Perfection* and *Entity*, one above another, as of *Life*, *Sense*, and *Cogitation*, above Dead, Sensless and *Unthinking Matter*; or *Reason* and *Understanding* above *Sense*, &c.[5]

Cudworth is certainly aware that the bodies that surround us are active and engage in behaviors that are orderly and (at least apparently) teleological, but none of this is evidence that matter is not dead. Cudworth concludes that because matter *is* dead, its orderly and purposive behavior can only be explained on the assumption that it is accompanied by a (necessarily immaterial) guide.[6]

We might of course start to wonder why God would create matter at all if it is such a truly terrible thing. Interestingly, some seventeenth-century philosophers who emphasize the lowliness of bodies are prepared to admit that bodies might not exist after all. For example, Malebranche emphasizes that matter does not have to exist in order for us to have the sensory perceptions that we do, and indeed in the final analysis he thinks that our sensory perceptions are caused by God. Matter might happen to exist, says Malebranche, but for all we know it does not.[7] In Cudworth we find a statement of the view that on the ladder of being there is a "gradual descent" from immaterial minds to bodies (556), and then immediately afterward a discussion of earlier "panpsychist" views according to which everything is immaterial and divine (557–589), but Cudworth does not himself take the step of concluding that matter does not exist. He comes close to doing so, and presumably he should, but to be sure almost every mention of matter in his corpus includes a rejoinder to the effect that matter is an abomination and that we are stuck with it. Later in the century, Leibniz argues (in *Monadology*) that the fundamental elements of reality are wholly immaterial.[8] He offers numerous arguments for his idealism, but he is also just following through on an assumption that goes back to the *Discourse on Metaphysics* of 1686. Minds are the most perfect kind of thing,[9] and so if a benevolent and omnipotent being would create the finest universe possible, bodies would presumably be left out of the mix.[10]

There are other philosophers in the seventeenth century who are just as insistent that there is no such thing as matter. In Anne Conway, we find the view that matter is so terrible that God would not, and did not, create it:

> how can any dead thing proceed from him or be created by him, such as mere body or matter. . . ? It has truly been said that God does not make death. It is equally true that he did not make any dead thing, for how can a dead thing come from him who is infinite life and love? Or, how can any creature receive so vile and diminished an essence from him (who is so infinitely generous and good)?[11]

For Conway, God only creates souls, and so the everyday objects that surround us are something other than what we thought. As for Leibniz, the fundamental elements of reality for Conway are immaterial minds. Where Leibniz wants to do justice to the obvious intuition that immaterial things do not have features like motion and spatial location, however, Conway wants to deny that anything material exists but to do justice to the obvious intuition that things really have motion and spatial location.[12] Where Leibniz makes the inference that things do not really have these features, Conway insists that the denial of the existence of matter is just the denial of the existence of anything that meets all of the marks of the traditional Platonic conception of matter. There is nothing that is extended *and* dead *and* worthless, and so there is no matter.[13] We find a similar ontology in Margaret Cavendish. If God would not create anything that is lowly and worthless, then He would not create anything that answers to the Platonic conception of matter.[14] However, He did create the things that surround us and that we identify as material – and that we invented the term "matter" to pick out – and so the traditional conception of matter is misrepresentational. If matter is what we are talking about when we talk about solar systems and plants and cells and organs, and these are all active and wondrous and amazing, then Platonic matter is a chimera and a fiction. Cavendish finally embraces the view that minds are material, but a mind is not thereby "composed of raggs and shreds, but it is the purest, simplest and subtillest [sic] matter in Nature."[15] She agrees that nothing answers to the traditional conception of matter, but she does not want to draw the (potentially misleading) conclusion that immaterial minds are the only things that exist.[16]

Clearly, the predominant view in the seventeenth century is that matter does not have the resources to think. A concomitant of this view is that it would be a terrible disappointment if we were merely material, but fortunately we are not. On the opposite end of the spectrum is the view that everything is material and that matter is wonderful in part because it can think. *Most* thinkers in the period are at one end of this spectrum or other. Descartes occupies an interesting middle position and is in a category of his own. On the one hand, he supposes that the mind and its activities are more exalted than the activities of the body. For example, he writes that

> because nobody except God knows everything perfectly, we have to content ourselves with knowing the truths most useful to us. The first and chief of these is that there is a God on whom all things depend. . . . The second thing we must know is the nature of our soul. We must know that it subsists apart from the body, and is much nobler than the body, and that it is capable of enjoying countless satisfactions not to be found in this life.[17]

At the end of the Third Meditation he remarks that one of these satisfactions is achieved through (our eventual) disembodied reflection upon the greatness of God (AT VII 52; CSM II 35–6). He says also that if our mind did not have the ability to experience passions, it "would have no reason to wish to remain joined to its body for even one minute."[18] Descartes regards the mind and its pursuits as more noble than those of the body. However, he allows that the body has *some* value, as presumably he should if he is also going to hold that the extended universe is a creature of God. He says that we would have no reason to wish to remain joined to our bodies if we did not have the ability to experience passions, but of course we do have the ability to experience passions, to good effect: "the pleasures of the body are minor. . . . However, I do not think that they should be altogether despised, or even that one should free oneself altogether from the passions."[19] Indeed, he says that there are benefits to having passions and that a person is better off taking advantage of these: "[T]he pleasures common to it [the soul] and the body depend entirely on the passions, so that persons whom the passions can move most deeply are capable of enjoying the sweetest pleasures of this life."[20] The pleasure that accompanies a passion is not the qualitative equal of the pleasure of a disembodied mind, but in this life, we are not disembodied. We might regret that we can only get so much distance from our embodiment, and that we cannot engage in more philosophical reflection, but as a stoic, Descartes thinks that we should adjust our wants and desires to the reality in which we find ourselves.[21] Descartes thus occupies something of a middle position in the period. He does not think that bodies are darkness and death, but he does posit a qualitative difference between mind and body. He does recommend that we be in touch with our thinking *I*, but we ideally should do this just once in a lifetime (or *semel in vita*, AT VII 17). For the most part we should just live and express our embodiment.[22]

2. The intelligibility of thinking matter

A second issue that is of central concern to philosophers in the seventeenth century is whether there are any ontological implications that can be derived from the fact that we cannot understand how modifications like ideas and volitions would arise in an extended substance. We can understand how such a substance would have properties like size and motion and shape, and presumably that is the reason why these are properly described as extensive properties. But to some thinkers it seems wholly inconceivable and hence impossible that extensive properties in any configuration would be enough to bring about thought.

For example, Malebranche argues that one of the reasons that we know that bodies do not think is that we cannot conceive of thought as standing in relations of distance:

> Can a thing extended in length, width, and depth reason, desire, sense? Undoubtedly not, for all the ways of being of such an extended thing consist only in relations of distance; and it is evident that these relations are not perceptions, reasonings, pleasures, desires, sensations – in a word, thoughts. Therefore this *I* that thinks, my own substance, is not a body, since my perceptions, which surely belong to me, are something entirely different from relations of distance.[23]

For Malebranche, "the ways of being" of a body are restricted to what can be understood as bearing relations of distance to other things. It is impossible to conceive of a thought as having a size, or as being a certain distance from another thought or from a body, so a thought is not a body or the property of a body. In a similar vein, Leibniz weighs heavily on the datum that there is no way to explain how thought could arise from the figures and motions of bodies. He writes that

> [i]t must be confessed, moreover, that perception and what depends on it are inexplicable by mechanical reasons, that is, by figures and motions. If we pretend that there is a machine whose structure enables it to think, feel and have perception, one could think of it as enlarged yet preserving its same proportions, so that one could enter it as one does a mill. If we did this, we should find nothing within but parts which push upon each other; we should never see anything which would explain a perception.[24]

For Leibniz and Malebranche, bodies do not think under any circumstances. Locke takes a slightly different position, though one that is almost as restrictive. For Locke, the only way that bodies could think is if God superadded mental properties to them.[25] Absent a miracle, matter would never come around to thinking on its own, in virtue of the properties that are essential to it.

Descartes also puts an intelligibility constraint on the kinds of properties that a substance can have. Probably the most well-known proponent of substance dualism, he offers two central arguments for the view: the Sixth Meditation argument for the conclusion that mind and body are ontologically independent, and the famous (and also infamous) "argument from doubt." Here the focus will be on the first of these, though in the end the arguments may be very similar.[26]

The Sixth Meditation argument presupposes a significant amount of background in the form of epistemic progress that the meditator makes in the first five Meditations. In particular, Descartes assumes that in the Third Meditation the meditator arrives at a proper understanding of substantiality and the ontological dependence of modes upon a substance and that in the Second Meditation he arrives at a proper understanding of the difference between thinking and extendedness. Pretheoretically we have some understanding of these, but the detached reflection of the *Meditations* is supposed to emend our ideas of metaphysical objects and to bring them more into line.[27]

Descartes assumes for example that unless we are totally dense, we are able to notice that if we have ideas or volitions or any other mental modifications, these entail the existence of a substance on which they depend:

> We can ... easily come to know a substance by one of its attributes, in virtue of the common notion that nothingness possesses no attributes, that is to say, no properties or qualities. Thus, if we perceive the presence of some attribute, we can infer that there must also be present an existing thing or substance to which it may be attributed.[28]

To posit the existence of a shape is in effect to posit the existence of a substance, and to posit the existence of an idea or volition is to posit the existence of a substance. But that is not the only thing that we are positing when we posit the existence of a modification (and thereby a substance). We are also positing the existence of a nature or principal attribute through which the modification is understood:

> A substance may indeed be known through any attribute at all; but each substance has one principal property which constitutes its nature or essence, and to which all of its other properties are referred. Thus extension in length, breadth and depth constitutes the nature of corporeal substance; and thought constitutes the nature of thinking substance. Everything else which can be attributed to body presupposes extension, and is merely a mode of an extended thing; and similarly, whatever we find in the mind is simply one of the various modes of thinking. For example, shape is unintelligible except in an extended thing; and motion is unintelligible except as motion in an extended space; while imagination, sensation and will are intelligible only in a thinking thing.[29]

For Descartes, shape is a property of bodies because something cannot be a shape unless it is the shape of an extended thing. Motion is a property of bodies because something cannot have motion unless it has a location and so cannot have motion unless it is extended.[30] Our thoughts and volitions, however, cannot be conceived as having length, breadth, or depth. In positing or granting the existence of any of his ideas, Descartes is positing the existence of modes of thinking, but also a principle attribute or nature through which those modes are intelligible, and also an underlying substance. In positing the existence of an underlying substance, he is positing the existence of a thing that is ontologically independent in the sense that (unlike a modification) it does not depend on any other creature for its existence.[31]

If we grant the existence of all of these, there is just one final question to consider: is something enough to constitute a complete thing[32] or substance if all that it has is mental modifications and the principal attribute of thought? Descartes thinks that we can answer in the affirmative. Something is not a complete thing if it is just a thing that has a modification (for example an idea), for it must also have a principal attribute through which all its modifications are intelligible. But something *is* a complete thing if it has the nature of thinking, for it has modifications that depend on it, but it does not itself depend on or inhere in any other creature.[33] Descartes clearly thinks that we can recognize whether something is too dependent to be a substance, and he clearly thinks that we can recognize whether something is sufficiently independent to be a substance. For things that are in fact substances, we notice that they are substances when we are able to (successfully) think of them as "things which subsist on their own" (AT VII 222). We are in a position to think of mind and body in this manner:

> Now the mind can be perceived distinctly and completely (that is, sufficiently for it to be considered a complete thing) without any of the forms or attributes

> by which we recognize that body is a substance.... And similarly a body can be understood distinctly and as a complete thing, without any of the attributes which belong to the mind.
>
> (AT VII 223)

In recognizing the completeness or substantiality of a thing that has the principal attribute of thinking, and any accompanying mental modifications, Descartes is recognizing the existence of a substance that is mental throughout, for its preset boundary is the principal attribute or nature of thinking. All that he has left to do is to consider whether this nature is identical to the nature of extension:

> To say that thoughts are merely movements of the body is as perspicuous as saying that fire is ice, or that white is black; for no two ideas that we have are more different than those of black and white, or those of movement and thought. Our only way of knowing whether two things are different or identical is to consider whether we have different ideas of them, or one and the same idea.[34]

Descartes appears to hold that if we think carefully about what is involved in positing the existence of a mental item like an idea, we end up appreciating that we have posited the existence of a substance that is immaterial.

With all the relevant background in place, we can consider Descartes's Sixth Meditation argument and also the argument from doubt. In the Sixth Meditation argument, Descartes has already made a lot of epistemic progress in the *Meditations* and so has done the philosophical and conceptual footwork that allows him to recognize that minds are immaterial substances. He writes,

> simply by knowing that I exist and seeing at the same time that absolutely nothing else belongs to my nature or essence except that I am a thinking thing, I can infer correctly that my essence consists solely in the fact that I am a thinking thing.
>
> (AT VII 78)

Earlier in the Second Meditation, Descartes had posited the existence of his mind just insofar as it is a thinking thing. Now he is recognizing that something that has ideas and volitions and the nature of thinking is a substance if it has just these things, and so even if this thing is attached to something that has other kinds of features, its boundary as a substance starts and stops with the nature of thinking and mental modifications. He is recognizing that he is "solely ... a thinking thing." In the very next sentence, he remarks that "it is true that I may have (or, to anticipate, that I certainly have) a body that is very closely conjoined to me" (AT VII 78), but that "nevertheless" his mind is an immaterial substance. Like many philosophers in the tradition, Descartes holds that our embodiment stands in the way of our ability to grasp philosophical truth, and he is aware in particular that the intimate union between our mind and body might interfere with our ability to appreciate the result that minds and bodies are so different as to have nothing in common.[35] Accordingly, he prefaces the Sixth Meditation argument with the reminder that God's power is such that He can make the universe to be exactly as we clearly and distinctly perceive it (AT VII 78). So, if we clearly and distinctly perceive that minds are immaterial substances, it is true that they are immaterial substances, even if the fact of mind-body union might incline us to think otherwise.[36] As Descartes says just before he announces his clear and distinct perception of his mind as a wholly immaterial substance, "it is enough that I can clearly and distinctly understand one thing apart from another thing to be certain that the one is distinct from the other: because it can – at least by God – be posited separately."[37] God can make a universe in which immaterial minds and nonthinking bodies are united, and he has.[38]

Descartes argues that we cannot understand modifications like ideas and volitions in terms of extendedness. Cavendish agrees that we cannot understand how matter thinks, but she insists that we can understand that it thinks. Her smoking-gun argument for the view that minds are material is that minds move and that things move only if they are material. She writes, "Though Matter might be without Motion, yet Motion cannot be without matter; for it is impossible (in my opinion) that there should be an Immaterial Motion in Nature."[39] Mental items like ideas and volitions are the ideas and volitions of a mind, and because a person's mind moves along with his or her body when the body travels from place to place, the ideas and volitions of a mind are thereby the ideas and volitions of a material thing. Here Cavendish is anticipating a line of argumentation that we later find in Locke:

> No Body can imagine, that his Soul can think, or move a Body at *Oxford*, whilst he is at *London*; and cannot but know, that being united to his Body, it constantly changes place all the whole Journey, between *Oxford* and *London*, as the Coach, or Horse does, that carries him; and, I think, may be said to be truly all that while in motion.[40]

Here Locke is only hinting at (and perhaps trying to downplay or avoid) the conclusion that minds are material, but Cavendish is happy to draw the conclusion explicitly.[41] She takes as axiomatic that a thing can move only if it is material, and she takes it as obvious that if a person's body in any sense houses his or her mind, his or her mind is physical:

> Place [is] an attribute that belongs onely to a Body. . . . .[42]

> I would ask those, that say the Brain has neither sense, reason, nor self-motion, and therefore no Perception; but that all proceeds from an Immaterial Principle, and an Incorporeal Spirit, distinct from the body, which moveth and actuates corporeal matter; I would fain ask them, I say, where their Immaterial Ideas reside, in what part or place of the Body? . . . [I]f it [the spirit] have no dimension, how can it be confined in a material body?[43]

To the opponent who argues that it is naïve to appeal to the premise that minds move, and that the use of the language of bodies to speak of minds is at best metaphorical, Cavendish replies that if such language is even the slightest bit illuminating, it is to some degree descriptive.[44] If there is any sense in which minds move, they are material if there can be no immaterial motion. Cavendish is in effect asking us what we think we are engaging when we engage the mind of another person. If the person is before us, his mind is before us as well. If the person moves from one place to another, his mind is carried along with him. A mind is collection of bodies in a human body, and among its properties are the same ideas and volitions that the substance dualist would regard as immaterial.

For Cavendish, the first order of business is to establish *that* minds are material. Only then does she address the question of whether we understand how matter thinks. She argues that we do not and that it is not surprising that we do not, as we know the answer to hardly any of the how and why questions about the processes that we encounter in nature. For example,

> we have only found that Effect of the Load-stone, as to draw Iron to it, but the Attracting motion is in obscurity, being Invisible to the Sense of Man, so that his reason can only Discourse, and bring Probabilities to Strengthen his Arguments, having no Perfect Knowledge in that, nor in any thing else; besides, that Knowledge we have of several things, comes as it were by Chance, or by Experience, for certainly, all the Reason man hath, would never have found out that one Effect of the Load-stone, as to draw Iron, had not Experience or chance presented it to us, nor the Effect of the Needle.[45]

For Cavendish, there is "Natural Magick,"[46] even in the case of things that we take to be wholly unmysterious:

> the Load-stone may work as various effects upon several Subjects as Fire, but by reason we have not so much Experience of one as the other, the Strangeness creates a Wonder, for the Old saying is, that Ignorance is the Mother of Admiration, but Fire, which produces greater Effects by Invisible motions, yet we stand not at such Amaze, as at the Load-stone, because these Effects are Familiar unto us.[47]

Action at a distance is mysterious, Cavendish insists, but so is the power of fire, and the "Knowledge we have of several things" is on a par with it. This is a sustained theme throughout her corpus.[48] For example, we do not understand why the bodies that are involved in digestion would work together to digest rather than to do something else.[49] Nor do we know why the bodies that compose water and ice are transparent, when the bodies that come together to form other beings are not.[50] We can speculate on these, but in the end "Natures actions are not onely curious, but very various; and not onely various, but very obscure."[51] Thinking matter is no exception: "you might as well enquire how the world, or any part of it was created, or how the variety of creatures came to be, as ask how Reason and sensitive corporeal Knowledg [sic] was produced."[52] Bodies in the natural world clearly have capacities, Cavendish is maintaining, and it is by such capacities that they do what they do. We do not understand why a particular body or configuration of bodies would have the particular capacities that it does, and there is no special problem posed by the fact that we cannot understand how matter thinks.

Another important figure to consider in the discussion of the intelligibility of thinking matter is Kenelm Digby. We have seen that Cavendish defends the view that if we do not understand much of what happens in the natural world, our inability to understand how matter thinks is no evidence that minds are immaterial. Digby accepts the conditional that Cavendish is putting forward, but as a substance dualist he goes to great lengths to falsify the antecedent:

> what hope could I have, out of the actions of the soul to convince the nature of it to be incorporeall; if I could give no other account of bodies operations, than that they were performed by qualities occult, specificall, or incomprehensible?

> Would not my adversary presently answer, that any operation, out of which I should presse the soules being spirituall, was performed by a corporeall occult quality? and that, as he must acknowledge it to be incomprehensible, so must I likewise acknowledge other qualities of bodies to be as incomprehensible: and therefore could not with reason presse him, to shew how a body was able to doe such an operation, as I should inferre must of necessity proceede from a spiritt: since that neyther could I give account how the loadestone drew Iron, or looked to the north; how a stone, and other heavy thinges were carried downwards; how sight or fantasie was made; how digestion or purging were effected, and many other such questions, which are so slightly resolv'd in the schools?[53]

For Digby, a proof of the immateriality of the soul depends on the success of explanations of natural phenomena in terms of qualities like size, shape, and motion.[54] Undaunted, he attempts to offer a complete explanation of even the most intractable of natural phenomena, for example cohesion and action at a distance. As we will see, his explanations are elucidating to some extent, but there is an important sense in which he does not explain much at all.

Digby explains the apparent phenomenon of action at a distance in terms of the behavior of an insensible chord of atoms that connects the interacting bodies. According to Digby, there can be no real action at a distance, for an object cannot act where it is not, and "cannot work otherwise th[a]n by local motion."[55] It may seem implausible that attraction works by way of "subtle emanations from the agent body, to be the immediate workers of these effects [attraction]" (Digby), but action at a distance is more than implausible: "this is impossible; whereas the other can appear difficult at the worst, and therefore must be admitted, when no better and more intelligible solution can be found."[56] When two bodies attract, each emanates a series of atoms that form a tether by which the objects can be drawn toward each other:

> it is evident, that when they meet with such a stone as we have described, the helps by which they advance in their journey are notably encreased by the flood of atomes which they meet coming out of that stone; . . . they seize greedily upon them, and thereby do pluck themselves faster on: like a ferryman that draweth on his boat the swiftlier, the more vigorously he tuggeth & pulleth at the rope that lyeth thwart the river for him to hale himself over by.
>
> (183)

Digby is certainly offering a partial explanation of apparent action at a distance here. Bodies act on each other by local motion only, and there is nothing but the local motion and interaction of atoms from one end of the tether to the other. What Digby does not explain, of course, is why the atoms of the tether would cohere – why they would "seize greedily" upon each other. He does say that it is in the nature of bodies to be divisible and that bodies would not be divisible unless their default situation was to be united:

> For the nature of division is *the making of many*; which implyeth, that what is to be divided must of necessity be not *many* before it be divided. . . . And therefore, although we may seeke causes why some one thing sticketh faster together then some other, yet to ask absolutely why a body sticketh together,

were prejudiciall to the nature of quantity; whose essence is to have partes sticking together, or rather to have such unity, as without it all divisibility must be excluded.

(35)

But again, Digby is not so much offering an explanation of the cohesion of bodies as he is saying that it is in the nature of bodies to cohere. He does say elsewhere that when bodies stick together, "the reason hereof is the resemblance and Sympathy they have one with the other."[57] But for obvious reasons he is nervous about stopping here.[58] He attempts to offer an explanation as to why bodies would have this sympathy. One is (an experiential argument to the effect) that bodies of the same degree of rarity and density tend to cohere:

For proof whereof, we find that water doth unite and incorporate itself strongly and easily with water, oyle with oyle, the spirit of wine with the spirit of wine; but water and oyle can hardly unite, nor mercury with the spirit of wine, and other bodies of differing density and rarity.

(*Late Discourse*, 71)

Another is that bodies of a similar figure tend to cohere.[59] We can almost hear Hume objecting from afar: "Digby has confused his familiar experience of the cohesion of similar bodies and the repugnance of bodies that are different with an understanding of why similar bodies cohere."[60]

Digby's attempts to explain other cause-and-effect relationships in nature also fall short.[61] As a result, his opponent can argue that Digby has done little to block the hypothesis of thinking matter. Digby's opponent can argue that some of Digby's own accounts of natural phenomena entail that minds are material. For example, there is his argument for the view that light is material even though it is by no means a run-of-the-mill body:

But to settle us more firmly in the perswasion of light his being a body (and consequently fire); let us consider that the properties of a body are perpetually incident to light; . . . light is broken like a body; as when it is snapped in piece by a tougher body. It is gathered together into a little room by looking or burning glasses; as water is, by ordering the gutters of a house so as to bring into one cistern all that raineth dispersedly upon the whole roof. It . . . is to be wrought upon, and cast hither and thither at pleasure; all by the rule of other bodies.[62]

A mind can be broken or injured; in cases of Alzheimer's disease and other ailments, it is "wrought upon" by the workings of other bodies. At least one commentator has argued that Digby came to see his substance dualism as strained.[63] In the treatise on soul, he admits that the soul is subject to corruption and mutation.[64] In his best attempts to describe the soul, he uses physical predicates – reporting that we survey our thoughts "up and downe" (Digby, 386), that apprehension is "inward" (367), that when we deliberate we are "touch[ing]" reasons (381), and that thoughts are composed (356–7). Nowhere does Digby offer an argument for the view that minds are material, but one can be assembled from assumptions that he employs for other purposes.

At the very least it appears that Digby came to see that the explanations of the first part of the *Two Treatises* are not so explanatory as to rule out that minds are corporeal.[65] The failure is momentous. Like other philosophers in the tradition in which he is working, he considers material things to be entities of the lowest grade. He decries the "seely [silly] lumpe of flesh" to which we are attached, the "vileness of that heavy lumpe of flesh."[66] He speaks of the "overflowing reward" of a disembodied soul, "for thy enduring and patienting in this thy darksome prison."[67] The result that souls are corporeal would be a terrible disappointment, Digby thinks. His conception of matter is such that the result that souls are corporeal is to be avoided at all costs.

A final figure to consider in the discussion of the intelligibility of thinking matter is Thomas Hobbes. Like Cavendish, Hobbes is not particularly worried about the question of whether we can understand how matter thinks, but he instead focuses on the question of whether we can know that it thinks. He writes,

> The World, (I mean not the Earth onely, that denominates the Lovers of it *Worldly* men, but the *Universe*, that is, the whole masse of all things that are) is Coporeall, that is to say, Body; and hath the dimensions of Magnitude, namely, Length, Breadth, and Depth: also every part of Body, is likewise Body, and hath the like dimensions; and consequently every part of the Universe, is Body; and that which is not Body, is no part of the Universe: And because the Universe is All, that which is no part of it, is *Nothing*; and consequently *no where*. Nor does it follow from hence, that Spirits are nothing: for they have dimensions, and are therefore really Bodies.[68]

What is particularly interesting about Hobbes, though, and what makes his view distinctive in the seventeenth century, is that his understanding of thinking is so reductive that the question of our ability to understand thinking matter is almost too easy to require an explicit treatment. For Cavendish and Descartes and the rest of the figures that we have considered, modifications like ideas and volitions are very different from modifications like size, shape, and motion, and if matter does think, at least some of its activities leave us entirely in the dark. For Hobbes, however, mental states are simply motions: "These words, *appetite* and *aversion*, we have from the *Latins*, and they both of them signify the motions, one of approaching, the other of retiring" (*L* 6.2, 28). For Cavendish, minds and their mental states move along with the bodies that have them, and so minds are physical, and matter thinks. We may not understand thinking in terms of modifications like size, shape, and motion, but matter thinks nonetheless. For Hobbes, mental states just *are* motions. As motions, they are as straightforwardly physical as can be:

> And although unstudied men do not conceive any motion at all to be there, where the thing moved is invisible, or the space it is moved in is (for the shortness of it) insensible, yet that doth not hinder, but that such motions are. For let a space be never so little, that which is moved over a greater space whereof that little one is a part must first be moved over that. . . . [N]ature itself does often press upon men those truths which afterwards, when they look for somewhat beyond nature, they stumble at. For the schools find in mere appetite to go, or move, not actual motion at all; but because some motion they must acknowledge, they call it metaphorical motion, which is but an absurd speech; for though words may be called metaphorical, bodies and motions cannot.
> (*L* 6.1–2, 27–8)

Hobbes agrees with Cavendish that only physical things move. He finds himself more aligned with twentieth century philosophers, however, in his complete reduction of mental states to physical states.[69] His view is satisfying (or unsatisfying) to the extent that it is not an elimination of phenomena that we are setting out to capture at the start.

3. Mind-body union and interaction

Another critical juncture in the thinking of seventeenth century philosophers is the question of mind-body union and interaction. Some philosophers embrace the view that if minds and bodies are united and come into contact then both must be material. Cavendish has the view,[70] and it is in play in the thinking of some of her contemporaries:

> must not every union occur by means of close contact? And, as I asked before, how can contact occur without a body? How can something corporeal take hold of something incorporeal so as to keep it joined to itself? And how can the incorporeal grasp the corporeal to keep it reciprocally bound to itself, if it has nothing at all to enable it to grasp or be grasped?[71]

Here Gassendi is objecting to Descartes's substance dualism by appealing to the intuition that things with nothing in common cannot interact.[72] Descartes's reply to Gassendi is that there is no obvious reason that grounds the intuition, and that Gassendi hasn't provided one.[73] But Descartes's considered view on mind-body interaction is more difficult to corner still. He denies that things with nothing in common cannot interact, but he also appears to hold that mind-body interaction and union are a kind of illusion. He defends the view that God's preservation of creatures is really just a matter of constant creation and that ultimately neither minds nor bodies causally interact with each other, but instead that God is constantly creating them in their entirety at each and every moment.[74]

We find the same view in Malebranche, and less ambiguously. In *The Search After Truth* he argues that no creatures stand in causal relations and that only God is a real cause:

> We have only two sorts of ideas, ideas of minds and ideas of bodies; and as we should speak only of what we conceive, we should only reason according to these kinds of ideas. Thus, since the idea we have of all bodies makes us aware that they cannot move themselves, it must be concluded that it is minds which move them. But when we examine our idea of all finite minds, we do not see any necessary connection between their will and the motion of any body whatsoever. On the contrary, we see that there is none and that there can be none. . . . But when one thinks about the idea of God, i.e., of an infinitely perfect and consequently all-powerful being, one knows that there is such a connection between His will and the motion of all bodies, that it is impossible to conceive that He wills a body to be moved and that this body not be moved. We must therefore say that only His will can move bodies if we wish to state things as we conceive them and not as we sense them.
>
> (*Search* 6.2.3/LO 448)

The argument in this passage is not that no finite creature is a cause and that, because God is a cause, only God is a cause.[75] Malebranche indeed makes a case for the premise that neither finite minds nor finite bodies are causes, and he motivates the premises elsewhere,[76] but he does not assume that the only creatures that exist are minds and bodies:

> We should not claim . . . that all that exists are minds and bodies, thinking beings and extended beings, because we might be mistaken in this. For though it suffices to explain nature, and consequently we can conclude without fear of being mistaken that the natural things we have some knowledge of should depend on extension or thought, yet absolutely speaking it is possible that there are others of which we have no idea and see no effect.
>
> (*Search* 3.2.9/LO 250)

Malebranche repeats this again and again.[77] Although he subscribes to the thesis that all our ideas are in the mind of God, and although he holds that God cannot create an entity unless He has an idea of it (*Search* 3.2.6/LO 230), he does not hold that we have access to ideas of all the entities that God might have produced. There may be some entities of which we have no idea, as "it is possible that God has reasons we do not know for concealing them from us."[78]

The argument for the view that only God is a cause requires an additional premise, and Malebranche makes sure to provide it. The additional premise is that if God is omnipotent, then a sufficient condition for the occurrence of any Y is God's volition to bring about Y: "God needs no instruments to act; it suffices that He wills in order that a thing be, because it is a contradiction that He should will and that what He wills should not happen" (*Search* 6.2.3/LO 450). Malebranche then proceeds to argue that if God's volition to bring about a Y is sufficient to bring about Y, no creature is a cause. He continues,

> I see two wills concurring when an angel moves a body; that of God and that of the angel; and in order to know which of the two is the true cause of the movement of this body, it is necessary to know which is efficacious. There is a necessary connection between the will of God and the thing He wills. God wills in this case that, when an angel wills that this or that body be moved, it will be moved. Therefore, there is a necessary connection between the will of God and the movement of the body; and consequently it is God who is the true cause of its movement, whereas the will of the angel is only the occasional cause.
>
> (*Search* 6.2.3/LO 450)

Here Malebranche is not (yet) taking a stand on the nature of the divine concurrence that is at work in cases of creaturely activity. We know that eventually he will offer the metaphysically loaded view that divine concurrence is a matter of constant creation, but for now he is showing how we can use premises that are less controversial and still generate the result that only God is a cause. For now, he is assuming that for any Y that occurs, God wills that Y occur, and that in addition there is a creaturely antecedent X, but he is not yet making any claim as to the nature of divine concurrence or the nature of the concurrence of X.[79] But a claim about creaturely concurrence follows almost immediately. We consider the example of a finite volition and its intended effect, and we notice that the finite volition is not sufficient to guarantee the occurrence of its intended effect and thus that it does not necessitate it. Malebranche elaborates:

> *But to show this still more clearly*, let us suppose that God wills to produce the opposite of what some minds will, as might be thought in the case of demons or some other minds that deserve this punishment. One could not say in this case

> that God would communicate His power to them, since they could do nothing they willed to do.... Thus, all the volitions of minds are only occasional causes.
>
> (*Search* 6.2.3/LO 450, my emphasis)

For any Y, if a finite volition were the cause of Y, it would bring about Y, and God's volition to bring about something other than Y would not be sufficient to bring about its object.[80] The same applies for any creaturely antecedent to Y. No creature is efficacious, and only God is a cause.[81]

Malebranche also offers a second argument for the view that only God is a cause. In *Dialogues on Metaphysics and on Religion*, he writes that what it means for God to preserve creatures in existence is to constantly create them:

> If the world subsists, it is because God continues to will its existence. Thus, the conservation of creatures is, on the part of God, nothing but their continued creation.... [I]n essence the act of creation does not cease, because in God creation and conservation are but a single volition.
>
> (*Dialogues* VII, 112)

Some commentators have argued that in his identification of divine preservation and constant creation, Malebranche accepts the thesis that what it is for God to preserve a creature from moment to moment is for God to re-create the creature in its entirety from moment to moment.[82] If God re-creates a creature in its entirety from moment to moment, it is clear why only He would be a cause. The correct description of any scenario in which creatures C and E appear to stand in causal relations is not that C does something but that God creates C and then creates E.

Malebranche certainly appears to hold that what it is for God to preserve a creature in existence from moment to moment is for God to create the creature in its entirety from moment to moment. But if he does, a couple of interpretive problems arise. One is that Malebranche wants to say that finite minds and bodies are substances,[83] and it is extremely difficult to see how something that comes in and out of existence from moment to moment would be substantial,[84] just as it is difficult to see how something that is re-created from moment to moment would be the same thing re-created from moment to moment and not a new thing that is qualitatively identical to what preceded it. Malebranche himself says that "I believe and feel I must believe that after the soul's action there remain in its substance certain changes that really dispose it to this same action" (*Eluc.* 7/LO 578). As the famous Leibnizian objection intimates, Malebranche *should* say that something remains of a substance from moment to moment, and he does.

A second reason for rejecting the view that Malebranche subscribes to the thesis that God re-creates each and every thing in its entirety from moment to moment is that he insists that finite minds are free in a way that makes them accountable for what they do. Malebranche does not fail to see that if God re-creates a finite mind from moment to moment in its entirety, He also creates that finite mind insofar as it wills the courses of action that it pursues:

> If a man perceives and tastes an object, God creates him perceiving and tasting this object; and if he consents to the impulse that is excited in him, if he rests with this object, God creates him stopping at and resting with this object. God

creates him such as he is at that moment. He creates him in his consent in which he has no greater role than do bodies in the motion that moves them.[85]

If God re-creates a finite mind in its entirety from moment to moment, we would not be responsible for sin. Instead, "we would sin through no fault of our own, and God would truly be the cause of our disorders, because they would not be free but purely natural."[86] Religion would be an "illusion and a phantom" if we were punished for doing things over which we have no control (*Eluc.* 16/*LO* 669). Of course, religion is not an illusion or phantom for Malebranche. We are punished for some of what we do, and appropriately so: "Because God is just, He cannot help but one day punish the violence we do Him when we oblige Him to give us pleasure as a reward for the criminal actions we commit against Him."[87] Malebranche is aware of the problem here. On the one hand, he wants to emphasize the dependence of creatures on God.[88] On the other hand, he wants to say that there is a degree to which finite minds are independent.

When pressed, Malebranche rejects the view that God creates finite minds in their entirety from moment to moment. As we have seen, he holds that finite minds are substances and that there is something that remains in them from moment to moment. God does not constantly re-create the substance of a finite mind, and he does not create our free acts of consent:

> [O]nly the consent of our will depends wholly on us.... [O]nly our consent is truly ours.
>
> (*Search* 5.4/*LO* 357)

> [E]verything real in the natural determinations of our impulses also comes solely from God's action in us; for I am not speaking here about our consent to these determinations.
>
> (*Eluc.* 15/*LO* 679)

> I deny that God creates us as consenting precisely insofar as we are consenting or resting with a particular good.... God creates us, then, not precisely insofar as we are consenting or withholding our consent, but insofar as we are able to give or withhold it.
>
> (*Eluc.* 1/*LO* 554)

Malebranche does not hold that God re-creates finite substances in their entirety from moment to moment, but as we have seen he does say that the conservation of creatures is nothing but their continued creation. What would be helpful, then, is a model for understanding what Malebranche might mean when he says that conservation is just continued creation, when he does not mean the re-creation of a substance in its entirety from moment to moment. One thing to note in this regard is that when Malebranche speaks of God's constant creation of a corporeal object, he speaks specifically of God's creation of the corporeal modes that make the object the particular object that it is. For example, he says that "He cannot will that this chair exist, without at the same time willing that it exist either here or there and without His placing it somewhere."[89] Like Descartes, Malebranche is committed to the view that what it is that makes a material object a chair or piece of wax rather than some other thing is not its underlying substance but instead the modifications that it has. The underlying substance of any given material object is capable of infinitely many modifications, but if its modifications are not specified, it is too indeterminate to constitute a particular thing.[90] The suggestion that I want to make here is that on Malebranche's view what it means for God to produce particular things like tables and chairs at each and every moment is for God to produce modifications. As Malebranche says in Dialogue VII,

> the motive force of a moving body is simply the will of the creator who conserves [or creates] it successively in different places. It is not a quality that belongs to this body. *Nothing belongs to it except its modalities*, and modalities are inseparable from substances.
>
> (*Dialogues* VII, 117, my emphasis)

Malebranche of course cannot mean here that a body is merely a collection of modifications, for as he notes a modality cannot exist in separation from its substance. He presumably *does* mean that what belongs to a body that makes it the determinate particular body that it is and that differentiates it from other bodies is its modifications. If so, his view of the individuation of material objects runs parallel with his view of our perceptions of these objects. When we have a perception of a table, for example, we are interfaced with the mind of God, but we are not thereby accessing an ideational table in the mind of God: God's mind does not contain ideas of tables, but instead contains intelligible extension, and what it is for us to perceive a table (as opposed to some other physical object) is for us to have sensations that demarcate that intelligible extension in the form of a table.[91] It is of course beyond the scope of this chapter to defend an account of Malebranche's view of the individuation of bodies. However, if he holds that there are such things as material substance and thinking substance, and if he thinks that God does not create our acts of consent, then his doctrine of constant creation is the doctrine that God is constantly creating the modifications of creatures and that modifications do not include acts of consent.[92] Malebranche's God creates substances, and some of these substances are free.[93]

A final figure to consider in the seventeenth century debate about mind-body union and interaction is Benedict Spinoza. On the one hand, mind-body union and interaction should not be a special problem for Spinoza because he subscribes to the view that minds and bodies are identical.[94] This view is a bit of a conundrum, however, in that Spinoza is also quite insistent that minds and bodies do not interact in any way because they have nothing in common.[95]

The interpretive situation becomes even trickier when we attempt to make sense of both of these views on their own. The first (that united minds and bodies are identical) might seem to follow straightforwardly from Spinoza's larger metaphysics: there exists a maximally real substance (*E* 1p10), and so that substance has all the reality that is possible to be had, because if it lacked some reality it would not be maximally real (*E* 1p14–16); thus there exists only that substance. Furthermore, for any physical modification that exists in the substance, that modification also exists objectively (or as an idea), because if a modification of X exists in physical form, it exists in mental form also if thinking (or mentality) is a possible way of being; but individual ways of being (or attributes, like being extended or being mental) constitute the essence of a substance, and are different ways of conceiving its essence (*E* 1d4), and so are identical in reality. If so, then X existing physically is just X existing objectively, and minds and bodies are identical. A problem with this "straightforward" interpretation though is that commentators have shown that Spinoza is committed to the view that attributes are not identical.[96] For example, he says that a substance is more real to the extent that it has more attributes (E 1p9), and it is difficult to understand how something would be more real just because finite minds think of it in different ways.

The second view (that minds and bodies do not interact because they have nothing in common) also presents an interpretive conundrum. Spinoza is clearly committed to this view in *Ethics*. However, in a work that is clearly an initial version of *Ethics*, Spinoza says that our minds and bodies do interact:

> the soul in the body, as has already been remarked, can well bring it about that the [vital] spirits, which would otherwise move in one direction, should nevertheless move in the other direction; and since these [vital] spirits can also be made to move, and therefore directed, by the body, it may frequently happen that, when the body directs their movements towards one place, while the soul directs them towards another place, they bring about and occasion in us those particular fits of depression which we sometimes feel without knowing the reasons why we have them. . . . Furthermore, the power which the soul has to move the [vital] spirits may well be hindered also either because the motion of the [vital] spirits is much diminished, or because it is much decreased. Diminished, as when, having run much, we bring it about that the [vital] spirits, owing to this running, impart to the body much more than the usual amount of motion, and by losing this [motion] they are necessarily that much weakened; this may also happen through taking all too little food. Increased, as when, by drinking too much wine or other strong drink, we thereby become either merry or drunk, and bring it about that the soul has no power to control the body.[97]

Here (in *Short Treatise on God, Man, and His Well-Being*) we have an unambiguous expression of the view that our minds are affected by such physical processes as the intake of alcohol, and that minds make bodies move. We might interpret Spinoza as simply having changed his view by the time of *Ethics*, but very interestingly, in *Short Treatise* he also puts forward the view that minds and bodies do not interact, and in almost the same breath. Just a couple of paragraphs before he discusses the ways in which our minds can move our bodies and be affected by alcohol, he says that a given modification can only be caused by a modification of the same kind and that "no mode of thought can bring motion or rest into a body" (88). We might throw up our hands at this point and conclude that Spinoza *must* have changed his view by the time of the *Ethics*, because his earlier view is hardly a view at all. Alternately, we might argue that in the earlier text Spinoza holds that there is a sense in which minds and bodies interact and a sense in which they do not. More specifically, we might note that in *Ethics* part 1, axiom 4 Spinoza says that "[t]he knowledge of an effect depends on, and involves, the knowledge of the cause" (E 1p4a). Commentators have understood the axiom to mean that something is not strictly speaking the cause of something else unless it is in principle possible to understand how the existence of the first thing entails the existence of the second.[98] If this is Spinoza's view, then it is clear the sense in which he wants to deny mind-body interaction: for reasons already laid out by Cavendish, Digby, Malebranche, Leibniz, and Descartes, there is no way to understand how modifications like size, shape, and motion could result in modifications of thinking, and so any account of mental events in terms of physical events would not be *explanatory*. But at the same time it is clear why Spinoza would want to allow that there is a sense in which minds and bodies interact: physical modifications are in some sense identical to mental modifications, and so any case in which two physical modifications are causally interacting is a case in which a mental modification and a physical modification are interacting, even though they would not be interacting in a way that would allow us to explain the occurrence of the one in terms of the occurrence of the other.

There still remains the issue of the sense in which physical modifications are identical to mental modifications, for Spinoza, if he also holds that ways of being (like physicality and mentality) are not identical, but are objectively different. To repeat, one view is that for Spinoza there is no objective distinction between the attributes, and so a given physical mode of X would always just be identical to an idea of X. If in reality what it is to be a body is just the same as what it is to be an idea, an X that exists in physical form is also an X existing objectively. But another option is to argue that Spinozistic modifications are ontologically thick and exhibit multiple ways of being: that is, that one component of a modification of X is X in physical form, and another is X in mental form.[99] On such a view, modifications have every way of being because they are modifications of the maximally real substance, but a modification of X is not maximally real unless it manifests itself on the physical spectrum, the mental spectrum, and any other spectrum that might exist. To use an everyday analogy, Spinozistic modes are physical and mental in something like the way in which a thing could have multiple features like color and sound and taste, if having as many different kinds of features was a sign of having more reality. We could add color to an object, but it still would not be as real as possible if it did not have a sound, and if we gave it any amount of sound, that would not take away from its color, and it would not overlap with or dip into the taste compartment that we might fill later on. For Spinoza, a given mode of X exists objectively as an idea in God's omniscient mind, but that same mode is even more real if it is extended. *It* is extended, and so Spinoza's view is not just that an idea of X is identical to some physical modification, but instead the same modification is X both physically and objectively. Indeed, if the ideas in God's mind are not arranged in the exact same order as the physical bodies that they represent, then God's mind is not a perfect representation of physical reality.

Spinoza is committed to the view that there is a sense in which modes that are physical interact with modes that are mental. But he is clear that minds and bodies have nothing in common and strictly speaking do not interact causally. The suggestion here is that for Spinoza minds and bodies are identical in the sense that the same modes that are physical are also mental, that a body that causally interacts with another body is in fact an idea interacting with another body, but that strictly speaking minds and bodies do not causally interact in the sense that causal explanations are always fully explanatory and there are no intelligible explanations of mental events in terms of physical events or vice versa.[100]

4. Intelligent behavior in the natural world

Another focus of attention for philosophers in the seventeenth century is the question of how bodies are able to behave in an orderly manner. An obvious response to the question of course is that bodies exhibit order because there are laws of nature and because bodies obey them. For example, Descartes says that if we think with "the poets and the painters" that God "employs his own hands to open and close the portals of the winds, to cover flowers with dew, to hurl lightning upon rocks,"[101] we need to think again. He concludes the first section of *Meteorology* hoping to have established therein that explanations of natural phenomena should not be in terms of God's constant activity or the activity of other immaterial beings but instead in terms of matter and its law-governed motions.[102] Descartes's final position on the orderly behavior of bodies is not entirely clear, however, for as we have seen he also appears to subscribe to the Malebranchean view that only God is a real cause.[103] Other philosophers are less ambiguous in their response to the question of the orderly behavior of bodies. Cavendish takes bodies to be intelligent, and so she will argue that that their orderly and purposive behavior is no more inexplicable than the orderly and purposive behavior of a human body that is guided by a mind. For Malebranche, only God is a cause, and His intelligence and power are easily sufficient to account for any order anywhere. For Cudworth, God certainly has enough power to account for the orderly behavior of bodies, and matter is inherently inert, but because bodies are unworthy of God's constant attention, the order that we encounter in nature is due to creatures, and to creatures that are immaterial.

Cudworth arrives at his view after considering a trilemma:

> since neither all things are produced Fortuitously, or by the Unguided Mechanism of Matter, nor God himself may reasonably be thought to do all things Immediately and Miraculously; it may well be concluded, that there is *a Plastick Nature* under him, which as an Inferior and Subordinate Instrument, doth Drudgingly Execute that Part of his Providence, which consists in the Regular and Orderly Motion of Matter.
>
> (*TISU*, 150)

If matter is inherently passive, then bodies do not account for any sort of activity, and *a fortiori* they do not account for orderly activity.[104] But Cudworth also finds absurd the view that

> God himself [would do] all *Immediately*, and as it were with his own Hands, Form the Body of every Gnat and Fly, Instinct and Mite, as of other Animals in Generations, all whose Members have so much of Contrivance in them.
>
> (*TISU*, 147)

Cudworth's objection to the view is not, as some of his own remarks might seem to indicate, that it would have God's activity be laborious and strained.[105] Instead, he appreciates that God is omnipotent and that

> it may well be thought to be as Easie, for God, or an Omnipotent Being, to Make a Whole World, Matter and all, *Out of Nothing*, as it is for us to Create a Thought, or to Move a Finger.
>
> (*TISU*, 747)

He also says that an "Omnipotent Agent . . . could dispatch its work in a Moment" (*TISU*, 150). In the few places where Cudworth does entertain the view that God would have to labor to do each and every thing, he is speaking in the voice of common understanding.[106] His own view is that "it is so decorous in respect of God . . . [to] immediately do all the Meanest and Triflingest things himself Drudgingly, without making use of any Inferior and Subordinate Instruments."[107] Matter for Cudworth is dead – a "mere Heap of Dust"[108] – and so is not worthy of God's attention. As we have seen, many of the philosophers of the seventeenth century regard matter as a lowly and degenerate being, and Cudworth is among them. A systematic move for a subscriber to such a view is to say that God creates immaterial subordinates so that He can attend to higher things: "the *Chief Concernment* and Employment of *Divine Providence* in the World . . . is [instead] the *Oeconomy* of *Souls*, or *Government of Rational Beings*" (*TISU*, 885). God would be drudge if He did each and every thing because He would be attending to tasks that are beneath His attention.[109]

Cudworth appreciates that a third option for making sense of the orderly behavior of bodies is to posit laws of nature that are in place and that bodies obey. But here he argues that Descartes and the rest of the "Mechanick Theists" are just being disingenuous:

> These men (I say) seem not very well to understand themselves in this. Forasmuch as they must of necessity, either suppose these their *Laws* of *Motion* to execute themselves, or else be forced perpetually to concern the Deity in the Immediate Motion of every Atom of Matter throughout the Universe, in Order to the Execution and Observation of them. . . . [W]e cannot make any other Conclusion than this, That they do but unskillfully and unawares establish that very Thing which in words they oppose; and that their *Laws* of *Nature* concerning *Motion*, are Really nothing else, but a *Plastick Nature*.
> (*TISU*, 151)

For Cudworth, mechanists are confused when they deny the existence of immaterial forms and claim that the phenomena that such forms are intended to explain can be explained by positing laws in their stead.[110] Backed into a corner, the mechanist must say either that God does each and every thing or that He doesn't and that something else does. If the mechanist rejects the former, he must identify the entities that guide matter in its orderly behavior. As these entities are active, they must be immaterial. If they are immaterial but not God, they must be immaterial created beings. That is, they are just immaterial forms that are misleadingly dubbed "laws."

A final argument that Cudworth offers for the existence of plastic natures brings us full circle and back to the issue of the value of body and the quality of the things that God would create. In particular, God would not create the Malebranchean world of beings that are fully inert and dead:

> it seems not so agreeable to Reason neither, that Nature, as a Distinct thing from the Deity, should be quite Superseded or made to Signifie nothing, God himself doing all things Immediately and Miraculously; from whence it would follow also, that they are all done either *Forcibly* and *Violently*, or else *Artificially* only, and none of them by any *Inward Principle* of their own.[111]

Echoing Cavendish, Cudworth insists that because being that is alive is better than being that is dead, the world of God's creation will be full of life. He therefore opposes those mechanists who would have God "make a kind of Dead and Wooden World, as it were a Carved Statue, that hath nothing neither *Vital* nor *Magical* at all in it" (*TISU*, 148). These mechanists conceive of the universe as barren in a way that is inconsistent with the greatness of its creator, and they are thereby impious (*TISU*, 54). Plastic natures are minds, and they abound. They are not conscious thinkers,[112] but a lot of intelligent human behavior is performed unthinkingly as well.[113] A constraint on Cudworth's conception of plastic natures is that they must be lower on the chain of being than humans but higher than matter, and one way in which they secure this position is by being immaterial nonthinkers.[114] Plastic natures have to exist given everything else that we know, and in fact they fit quite nicely into the world with which we are familiar. *Qua* agents, plastic natures are similar to human beings who engage in habitual behavior, but unlike humans they are like this all the time.

Cudworth is not the only early modern figure to see the options for the mechanist in the terms that he specifies. Newton considers all of them, but he opts to feign no hypotheses.[115] Most of the time, Boyle is happy saying that laws of nature account for the orderly behavior of bodies, but when pressed to explain what it is that makes bodies behave in accordance with these laws, he rejects the view that there is any "vicegerent called nature" and concludes instead that God does all things directly.[116] As we have seen, Malebranche comes to the same conclusion. The supremacy of Malebranche's God is of course reflected in the range of His activity; it is also reflected in the manner of His activity:

> if God has not predestined all men to conform to the image of His son, who is the model and exemplar of the elect, it is because in this God acts in the simplest ways in relation to His intentions, which all favor His glory; it is because God is a universal cause and must not act as do particular causes, which have particular volitions for everything they do.[117]

One difference between divine activity and human activity is that humans are occasional causes and God is a real cause. Yet another difference is that human beings have a separate volition for each thing that they do. God's simplicity guarantees that His volitions are very few in number, and it also guarantees that they are less composite than those of creatures, or that they are general:

> God being obliged to act always in a manner worthy of Him, by means that are simple, general, constant, and uniform – in a word, means that are in conformity with the idea that we have of a general cause whose wisdom has no limits – He had to establish certain laws in the order of grace, as I have proved that He did in the order of nature. And yet these laws, on account of their simplicity, necessarily have unhappy consequences with respect to us: but these consequences do not warrant that God change these laws into more *composite* ones [*composées*]. For His laws have a greater proportion of wisdom and fecundity to the work that they produce than all others which He could establish for the same design, since He always acts in the most wise and perfect manner. It is true that God could remedy these unhappy consequences by an infinite number of particular volitions: but His wisdom, which He loves more than His work, and the immutable and necessary order which is the rule of His volitions do not permit this.[118]

Malebranche insists that one of God's attributes is generality. Accordingly, the view that God's volitions have a highly composite structure is not properly reflective of His greatness. Malebranche also holds that God's attributes include simplicity, constancy, and order. His activity exhibits constancy in that the effects of His volitions are constant in time.[119] His activity exhibits simplicity in that His volitions are few in number. He acts by a small number of general volitions, and because His activity exhibits order always, He acts by these volitions alone.[120] Malebranche does not speak with much precision about the exact number of God's volitions or about exactly how composite they are. Nor does he explain exactly how an atemporal being can have volitions that have effects that are in time. When pressed on the difficulties in all of these issues, Malebranche concedes that "[a]ll the divine ways are incomprehensible."[121] Malebranche's vague descriptions of the volitions of God (as general, orderly, simple, constant, and few in number) are presumably intended to gesture at His supremacy while still acknowledging our distance from Him.[122] His doctrine of constant creation ends up being the view that God is constantly creating the modifications of things by volitions that are general and noncomposite in character.[123]

Malebranche and Cudworth insist that bodies are inert and unintelligent and thus that they cannot be the source of their own activity. Cavendish of course argues that bodies are capable of thinking and that there is no greater mystery to the organization exhibited in particles and molecules and cells and plants than there is to the organization exhibited in the purposive behavior of minded human beings. Cavendish echoes Cudworth but of course come to a different conclusion:

> though the Opinion of Atoms is as Old as from the Time of Epicurus, yet my Conceptions of their Figures, Creating and Disposing, are New, and my Own. . . . It is not probable that the Substance of Infinite matter is only Infinite, Small, Senseless Fibres, Moving and Composing all Creatures by Chance, and that Chance should produce all things in such order and Method, unless every Single Atome were Animated Matter, having Animated Motion, which is Sense and Reason, Life and Knowledge.[124]

> If nature were not Self-knowing, Self-living, and also Perceptive, she would run into Confusion: for there could be neither Order, nor Method, in Ignorant motion.[125]

According to Malebranche and Cudworth, what God creates when He creates matter is a being that is dead and senseless and inert. Cavendish wonders why anyone would think that God would create such a thing when He could account for the orderly behavior of bodies more efficiently:

> I cannot imagine why God should make an Immaterial Spirit to be the Proxy or Vice-gerent of his Power, or the Quarter-master General of his Divine Providence, as your Author is pleased to style it, when he is able to effect it without any Under-Officers, and in a more easie and compendious way, as to impart immediately such self-moving power to Natural Matter, which man attributes to an Incorporeal Spirit.[126]

Cavendish is thereby reluctant to say that the reason why bodies behave in an orderly manner is that they obey laws of nature. Like Cudworth, Cavendish argues that if we take seriously what such laws would have to be, we will appreciate that in positing them we are positing more than we would like to admit. For Cavendish, the laws would have to be knowledgeable and perceptive. As part of nature, they would be material. They would not be anything in addition to the knowledgeable and perceptive bodies that Cavendish has already included in her ontology.[127]

5. Conclusion

Philosophy in the seventeenth century is extremely systematic. A figure will start out with fundamental axioms and intuitions and follow them wherever they lead. In some cases, the results will be counterintuitive, but if they do not conflict with the fundamental axioms and intuitions – and they will not if they are derived from the fundamental axioms and intuitions – then they are to be accepted as well. They may be counterintuitive, but only against the background of commonsense assumptions that themselves are in need of examination and that clearly are to be rejected if they conflict with truths that entail that they are false. Philosophers of course disagree on what these truths are, and Cavendish and Conway and Cudworth and Descartes and Digby and Leibniz and Malebranche and Spinoza are not going to yield ground in a head-to-head confrontation of metaphysical tenets. A consideration of their varying positions is still extremely fruitful, however, for it will isolate the different sets of premises that entail the whole spectrum of available views about the nature of minds and bodies, the place (if any) of God in our everyday lives, and the value of the things that surround us. The philosophers of the seventeenth century have done most of our work for us, if we can uncover additional considerations that entail that some of these premises are not only intuitive but also true.

Notes

1. Plato, *Phaedo*, in G.M.A. Grube (ed. and trans.), *Five Dialogues*, Indianapolis and Cambridge: Hackett Publishing Company (1981), 64d–e. Note that a small amount of material from this section is a development of material in David Cunning, "*Semel in Vita*: Descartes' Stoic View on the Place of Philosophy in Human Life," *Faith and Philosophy* 24 (2007), 164–83. I include this material with the permission of the editor and publisher.
2. *Essential Plotinus: Representative Treatises From the Enneads*, trans. and ed. Elmer O'Brien, Indianapolis, IN: Hackett Publishing Company (1975), I.6, 37.
3. Augustine, *On Free Choice of the Will*, ed. and trans. Thomas Williams, Indianapolis and Cambridge: Hackett Publishing Company (1993), 19.
4. Nicolas Malebranche, *The Search After Truth*, ed. and trans. Thomas M. Lennon and Paul J. Oscamp, Cambridge: Cambridge University Press (1997); *Search* 6.2.3/LO 447, 448.
5. Ralph Cudworth, *The True Intellectual System of the Universe*, Stuttgart-Bad Cannstatt: F. Fromann Verlag (1964), 858. (Note that this was first published in 1678.) See also 156, 157, 648, 857, and 858; and Sarah Hutton, "Cudworth, Boethius and the Scale of Nature," in G.A.J. Rogers, J.M. Vienne, and Y.C. Zarka (eds.), *The Cambridge Platonists in Philosophical Context*, Boston, MA: Kluwer Academic Publishers (1997), 96–9.
6. There is a discussion of Cudworth's immaterial "plastic natures" in section 4.
7. *The Search After Truth* (*Search* 1.10, 2.6); and Nicolas Malebranche, *Elucidations of the Search After Truth*, ed. and trans. Thomas M. Lennon, in Thomas M. Lennon and Paul J. Oscamp (eds. and trans.), *The Search After Truth* (Cambridge: Cambridge University Press, 1997); *Eluc.* 6/LO 568–76. Hereafter I use *Search* to refer to *The Search After Truth* and *Eluc.* to refer to the *Elucidations*.
8. *Monadology*, sections 1–11 in AG 213–214.
9. DM §5.
10. There is an interpretive debate about whether Leibniz is a full-blown idealist by the time of 1686. See, for example, Daniel Garber, "Leibniz and the Foundations of Physics: The Middle Years," in K. Okruhlik and J.R. Brown (eds.), *The Natural Philosophy of Leibniz*, Dordrecht: D. Reidel Publishing (1985), 27–130; and Robert M. Adams, *Leibniz: Determinist, Theist, Idealist*, Oxford: Oxford University Press (1998), 308–77. One thing to note for now is that in *Discourse on Metaphysics* Leibniz resolves the problem of mind-body interaction in terms of the harmonized activity of minds and (seemingly nonideal) bodies, but he also thinks that bodies are inherently passive, and so it is difficult to understand how a body's activity would be harmonious with that of a mind unless it was also active – that is to say mental.

11 Anne Conway, *The Principles of the Most Ancient and Modern Philosophy*, eds. Alison P. Coudert and Taylor Corse, Cambridge: Cambridge University Press (1996), 45. Note that this was first published in 1690.
12 Conway, 49, 51–2.
13 See also Leibniz, "On Nature Itself," in Leroy E. Loemker (ed.), *Gottfried Wilhelm Leibniz: Philosophical Papers and Letters*, 2nd edition, Dordrecht and Boston: D. Reidel Publishing Company (1969) (*PPL* 504). He writes that "it is consistent neither with the order nor with the beauty or the reason of things that there should be something vital or immanently active only in a small part of matter, when it would imply greater perfection if it were in all."
14 See, for example, Margaret Cavendish, *Philosophical Letters*, London (1664), 215, 518–9, 162–3, 186–7; Margaret Cavendish, *Observations Upon Experimental Philosophy*, ed. Eileen O'Neill, Cambridge: Cambridge University Press (2001), 209; and Margaret Cavendish, *Grounds of Natural Philosophy*, ed. Colette V. Michael, West Cornwall, CT: Locust Hill Press (1996), 47.
15 *Philosophical Letters*, 180.
16 Sarah Hutton argues that the monism of Conway is significantly different from that of Cavendish in that the former is a monism of spirit. See Sarah Hutton, "Anne Conway, Margaret Cavendish and Seventeenth-Century Thought," in Lynette Hunter and Sarah Hutton (eds.), *Women, Science and Medicine 1500–1700*, Stroud: Sutton (1997), 227. I am arguing that the views are not nearly as different as they might seem.
17 "To Princess Elizabeth, 15 September 1645," AT IV 291–2. Unless otherwise indicated, I use the translations in John Cottingham, Robert Stoothoff, and Dugald Murdoch, *The Philosophical Writings of Descartes, Volume I*, Cambridge: Cambridge University Press (1985); Cottingham, Stoothoff, and Murdoch, *The Philosophical Writings of Descartes, Volume II*, Cambridge: Cambridge University Press (1984); and Cottingham, Stoothoff, Murdoch, and Anthony Kenny, *The Philosophical Writings of Descartes, Volume III*, Cambridge: Cambridge University Press (1991). I use "AT" to refer to the pagination in Charles Adam and Paul Tannery, *Ouevres de Descartes, Volumes I–XII*, Paris: Vrin (1996).
18 "To Mersenne, 23 November 1646," AT IV 538.
19 "To Princess Elizabeth, 1 September 1645," AT IV 287.
20 *Passions of the Soul*, AT XI 488.
21 See especially "To Princess Elizabeth, 6 October 1645," AT IV 307; but see also "To Princess Elizabeth, 15 September 1645," AT IV 291–2, and "To Chanut, 1 February 1647." In the latter, Descartes says that

> [i]n my view, the way to reach the love of God is to consider that he is a mind, or a thing that thinks; . . . we must also take account of the infinity of his power, by which he has created so many things of which we are only a tiny part. . . . Finally, we must weigh our smallness against the greatness of the created universe. . . . If a man meditates on these things and understands them properly, he is filled with extreme joy. . . . Joining himself willingly entirely to God, he loves him so perfectly that he desires nothing at all except that his will should be done. Henceforth, because he knows that nothing can befall him which God has not decreed, he no longer fears death, pain or disgrace. He so loves this divine decree, deems it so just and so necessary, and knows that he must be so completely subject to it that even when he expects it to bring death or some other evil, he would not will to change it even if, *per impossible*, he could do so. He does not shun evils or afflictions, because they come to him from divine providence; still less does he eschew the permissible goods or pleasures he may enjoy in this life, since they too come from God. He accepts them with joy, without any fear of evils, and his love makes him perfectly happy.
>
> (AT IV 608–9)

22 See "To Princess Elizabeth, 28 June 1643," AT III 692–3.
23 Dialogue I, 6. Note that a small amount of material from this section is a development of material in David Cunning, "Cavendish on the Intelligibility of the Prospect of Thinking Matter," *History of Philosophy Quarterly* 23 (2006), 117–36. I include this material with the permission of the editor and University of Illinois Press.
24 G. W. Leibniz, *Monadology*, section 17, AG 215.
25 John Locke, *An Essay Concerning Human Understanding*, ed. Peter H. Nidditch, Oxford: Clarendon Press (1975); *Essay* 4.3.6, 540–1.
26 Descartes's infamous argument from doubt appears most prominently in *Discourse on the Method*, AT VI 32–3. The argument appears to run as follows: I am certain that my mind exists, but I can doubt

that anything material exists; therefore my mind is immaterial. After laying out an interpretation of the Sixth Meditation argument, I offer a suggestion for reading the argument from doubt, and one that allows Descartes to avoid some obvious objections. For example, in most cases we do not think that just because we can doubt that something has a feature, it does not have that feature. The thing might have the feature even if we do not know that it does.

27 See, for example, *Second Replies*, AT VII 155–7; *Principles* I: 70–74, AT VIIIA 34–8; and David Cunning, "Rationalism and Education," in Alan Nelson (ed.), *A Companion to Rationalism*, Oxford: Blackwell Publishing (2005), 61–81.

28 *Principles* I: 52, AT VIIIA 25. See also *Fourth Replies*, AT VII 222. Descartes writes, "We do not have immediate knowledge of substances, as I have noted elsewhere. We know them only by perceiving certain forms or attributes which must inhere in something if they are to exist; and we call the thing in which they inhere a 'substance.' "

29 *Principles* I: 53, AT VIIIA 25. See also *Principles* I: 64, AT VIIIA 31, and "To Regius, June 1642," AT III 567.

30 See also *Principles* II: 25–7, AT VIIIA 53–5.

31 *Principles* I: 51–2, AT VIIIA 24–5.

32 See also *Fourth Replies*, AT VII 221–3.

33 For more on Descartes's notion of a complete thing, see David Cunning, *Argument and Persuasion in Descartes' Meditations*, New York: Oxford University Press (2010), 81–92; and Marleen Rozemond, *Descartes's Dualism*, Cambridge, MA: Harvard University Press (1998), chapter 1.

34 "To Mersenne, 21 January 1641," AT III 285. See also "To [De Launay], 22 July 1641," AT III 421. Descartes writes,

> after the idea we have of God, which is very different from all those we have of created things, I do not know any other pair of ideas in the whole of nature which are as different from each other as these two.

35 *Fourth Replies*, AT VII 228–9; "To Elizabeth, 21 May 1643," AT III 664–5; "To Princess Elizabeth, 28 June 1643," AT III 693.

36 *Fourth Replies*, AT VII 226. See also "To Regius, June 1642," AT III 567, where Descartes says,

> You agree that thought is an attribute of a substance which contains no extension, and conversely that extension is an attribute of a substance that contains no thought. So you must also agree that a thinking substance is distinct from an extended substance. For the only criterion we have enabling us to know that one substance differs from another is that we understand one apart from the other. And God can surely bring about whatever we can clearly understand. . . . But we can clearly understand a thinking substance that is not extended, and an extended substance that does not think, as you agree.

See also "To Gibieuf, 19 January 1642," AT III 475–6; and "To [De Launay], 22 July 1641," AT III 421. See also Descartes's mention of God's power to make sure that we do not doubt our freedom just because we recognize the truth of the doctrine of divine preordination (*Principles* I: 40–1, AT VIIIA 20). See also *Second Replies*, AT VII 164; and *Principles* II: 35, AT VIIIA 60.

37 AT VII 78, my translation.

38 Descartes also offers the "argument from doubt" to establish that minds are immaterial substances. A charitable way to read the argument is as positing the existence of ideas and other mental modifications and then (as in the case of the Sixth Meditation argument) drawing the conclusion that these entail the existence of a thing that has the principal attribute of thinking and is a complete thing on its own. The next step of the argument would be to ask if we know that there exists anything material just by positing the existence of a thing that has the principal attribute of thinking and that is a complete thing on its own. If we have clear ideas of both thinking and extension, then if thinking substance were extended, we would know that something material existed just by virtue of positing a substance with the principal attribute of thought. If we posit the existence of such a substance and are still in doubt about the existence of material things, then a thinking substance is not material. Descartes's argument thus appears to be that principal attributes and the modes that are understood in terms of them are such that if minds were material, we would know that they were material, and so if we do not know that they are material then they are not. This kind of argument is not so unusual given that we sometimes say that if something were the case, we would know it, and so if we do not know it then it is not the case. What is crucial for Descartes's argument is that we do not need to consider all of the individual modifications of a thinking

substance to know that it is immaterial. Because modifications always have to be intelligible through a principal attribute, all we have to do to recognize the immateriality of mind is notice that a thing with just the principal attribute of thinking is substantial and that the principal attribute of thinking and the principal attribute of extension are different. What is conceived through one cannot be conceived through the other, and so a consideration of individual modifications can be bypassed and set aside.

39 Margaret Cavendish, *Grounds of Natural Philosophy*, ed. Colette V. Michael, West Cornwall, CT: Locust Hill Press (1996), 2. See also *Philosophical Letters*, 77, 402, 421; and Margaret Cavendish, *Philosophical and Physical Opinions*, London: printed for William Wilson (1663), 86.
40 *Essay* 2.23.20.
41 Nicholas Jolley has argued that the doctrine of thinking matter is lurking throughout Locke's corpus, and that one of Leibniz's central concerns in *New Essays on Human Understanding* is to expose and then undermine it. See Nicholas Jolley, *Leibniz and Locke: A Study of the New Essays on Human Understanding*, Oxford: Clarendon Press (1984), 18–25.
42 *Philosophical Letters*, 8.
43 *Philosophical Letters*, 185–6. See also 197, 225–6.
44 Leibniz argues that because the fundamental elements of reality are immaterial, and because predicates like contact and transposition do not apply to immaterial things, these predicates do not apply to the fundamental elements of reality (*Monadology* 7, AG 213–214). But he proceeds to flesh out the nature of a monad with the metaphorical language of windows (*Monadology*, section 7), dizziness (21), ponds (67), and spatial perspective on a city (57). Cavendish agrees that the language of contact and position applies only to bodies, but she concludes from this that minds are material. For a related discussion of the difficulty that the substance dualist encounters in attempting to describe thought without using the language that we use to describe bodies, see Tad Schmaltz, *Malebranche's Theory of the Soul*, New York and Oxford: Oxford University Press (1996), 127–62.
45 *Philosophical and Physical Opinions*, 191.
46 *Philosophical Letters*, 299, 302.
47 *Philosophical and Physical Opinions*, 194. See also 140.
48 See *Philosophical Letters*, 362, 367, 415; Margaret Cavendish, *The World's Olio*, London: printed for J. Martin and J. Allestrye (1655), 160–1, 176; Margaret Cavendish, *Poems and Fancies*, London: printed by T.R. for J. Martin and J. Allestrye (1653), 84–5; *Grounds of Natural Philosophy*, 176–7; and *Philosophical and Physical Observations*, 140, 196. In an almost Kantian vein, Cavendish writes,

> To give us Sense, and Reason too, / Yet know not what we're made to do. / Whether to Atomes turne, or Heaven up hye, / Or into new Formes change, and never dye. / Or else to Matter Prime to fall againe, / From thence to take new Formes, and so remaine. / Nature gives no such knowledge to Man-kind, / But strong Desires to torment the Mind . . . / O Nature! Nature! Cruell to Man-kind, / Gives Knowledge none, but Misery to find.
> ("A Dialogue Betwixt Man, and Nature," in *Poems and Fancies*, 58)

49 *Philosophical Letters*, 358–9.
50 *Philosophical Letters*, 472. There is an obvious similarity between the views of Cavendish and some of the views of Hume in *An Enquiry Concerning Human Understanding*. See Cunning 2006.
51 *Philosophical Letters*, 362. See also 272, 367.
52 *Philosophical Letters*, 526. See also 107.
53 Kenelm Digby, *Two Treatises in the One of Which, the Nature of Bodies; in the Other, the Nature of Mans Soule; is Looked Into: in Way of Discovery, of the Immortality of Reasonable Soules*, Paris: printed by Gilles Blaizot (1644), preface, third page. He also says,

> my desire and intent . . . is onely, to shew from what principles, all kinds of corporeall operations doe proceed; and what kinds of operations all these must be, which may issue out of these principles: to that end, that I may from thence, make a step to raise my discourse to the contemplation of the soule; and shew, that her operations are such, as cannot proceed from those principles; which being adequate and common to all bodies, we may rest assured, that what cannot issue from them, cannot have a body for its source.
> (preface, fifth page)

54 Note that Cavendish was writing with an eye to Digby (among many others). She interacted with Digby at meetings of the Cavendish Circle and read some of his work. See Eileen O'Neill, "Introduction," in O'Neill 2001, 15.

55 *Two Treatises*, 139. See also 35–6.
56 *Two Treatises*, 139. See also 163–5.
57 Kenelm Digby, *A Late Discourse Made in a Solemne Assembly of Nobles and Learned Men at Montpelier in France*, trans. R. White, London: printed for R. Lowndes and T. Davies (1658), 68.
58 He writes,

> If I should not explicate wherein this resemblance consisted, I should expose myself to the same censure and blame, as that which I taxed at the beginning of my Discourse, touching those who speak but lightly and vulgarly of the Powder of Sympathy, and such marvels of nature.
>
> (*Late Discourse*, 68)

59 Digby offers numerous observations along the same lines (*Late Discourse*, 72–75).
60 David Hume, *An Enquiry Concerning Human Understanding*, ed. Tom L. Beauchamp, Oxford: Clarendon Press (2000), section IV, part 1, paragraph 8, 26.
61 For example, he argues that the reason why fire makes gold swell, but does not have the same effect on asbestos, is that the latter "is of a very dry substance," whereas gold "aboundeth so much in liquidity" (*Two Treatises*, 132–3). Digby can point to differences between asbestos and gold to account for differences in the effects of fire on asbestos and gold, but he does not thereby explain why things react with fire as they do. There are many other such explanations in Digby's corpus. See, for example, *Two Treatises*, 92 (on why some bodies sink and others float), and *Two Treatises*, 136 (on why water dissolves salt). For Digby's fascinating attempt to explain the curative powers of various kinds of medicine, see *Two Treatises*, 163–5; and *Late Discourse*, 139–52.
62 *Two Treatises*, 45. See also *Late Discourse*, 19.
63 See R.T. Petersson, *Sir Kenelm Digby: The Ornament of England 1603–1665*, London: Jonathan Cape (1956), 208–9.
64 *Two Treatises*, 433.
65 See, for example, *Two Treatises*, 340. Digby says,

> And I am perswaded, that by this summary discourse (short indeed, in regard of so large a scope . . .) it appeareth evidently, that none of natures greatest secrets, whereof our senses give us notice in the effects, are so overshaded with an impenetrable veile, but that the diligent and wary hand of reason might unmaske them, and shew them to us, in their naked and genuine forms, and delight us with the contemplation of their native beauties; if we had as much care and constancy in the pursuit of them, as wee daily see men have in heaping up of wealth.

He says of the mixing of gold and mercury in particular that "the mysteries of this art" should be left "to those who professe it" (133). It should be noted that, as a result of his interactions with Nicolaus le Fevre, in the last years of his life (1660–1665) Digby flirted with the view that part of nature is an immaterial "universal spirit" that accounts in part for the behavior of bodies. See Betty Jo Dobbs, "Studies in the Natural Philosophy of Sir Kenelm Digby: Part II, Digby and Alchemy," *Ambix* 20 (1973), 156–61.

66 *Two Treatises*, 453. The word "seely" is changed to "silly" in the 1645 edition. See Kenelm Digby, *Two Treatises*, London: printed for John Williams (1645), 127.
67 *Two Treatises*, 453. See also preface, iii–v, and 433. See also Kenelm Digby, *Private Memoirs of Kenelm Digby*, London: Saunders and Otley, Conduit Street (1827), 235–9; and Kenelme Digby, "A Conference With a Lady About Choyce of Religion," in Kenelme Digby (trans.), *Albert the Great, Adhering to God*, London: Printed for Henry Harringman at the Anchor the New-Exchange (1654), 76–8.
68 Thomas Hobbes, *Leviathan*, ed. Edwin Curley, Indianapolis, IN: Hackett Publishing Company (1994), L 46.15, 459. Here Hobbes and Cavendish are almost intersecting. See Sarah Hutton, "Cudworth, Boethius and the Scale of Nature," in G.A.J. Rogers, J.M. Vienne, and Y.C. Zarka (eds.), *The Cambridge Platonists in Philosophical Context*, Boston: Kluwer Academic Publishers (1997), 426–7.
69 See for example J.J.C. Smart, "Sensations and Brain Processes," *The Philosophical Review* 68 (1959), 141–56.
70 *Philosophical Letters*, 197.
71 *Fifth Objections*, AT VII 344. Note that a small amount of material from this section is a development of material in David Cunning, "Malebranche and Occasional Causes," *Philosophy Compass* (2008). I include this material with the permission of the editor and Blackwell Publishing.
72 Other philosophers (in addition to Cavendish and Gassendi) find compelling the intuition that contact and penetration are physical notions and so would not apply to things that are immaterial. See, for

example, Leibniz, *Monadology*, section 7 (AG 213–214), and also Lucretius, *On the Nature of Things*, trans. and ed. Anthony M. Esolen, Baltimore and London: The Johns Hopkins University Press (1995), Book III, ll. 160–76, 95–6.

73 *Fifth Replies*, AT VII 388–9. Descartes says,

> Even though the mind is united to the whole body, it does not follow that it is extended throughout the body.... [I]t is not necessary for the mind itself to be a body, although it has the power of moving the body.

74 See, for example, Gary Hatfield, "Force (God) in Descartes' Physics," *Studies in History and Philosophy of Science* 10 (1979), 113–40; Steven Nadler, "Malebranche on Causation" in Steven Nadler (ed.), *The Cambridge Companion to Malebranche*, Cambridge: Cambridge University Press (2000), 119–20; and Kenneth Clatterbaugh, *The Causation Debate in Modern Philosophy, 1637–1739*, New York and London: Routledge (1999), 98–100.

75 See, for example, Nadler 2000, 117–8, 125–6. A similar interpretation is in Charles McCracken, *Malebranche and British Philosophy*, 99.

76 See *Search* 6.2.3/LO 448; *Eluc.* 15/LO 660; and *Search* 3.2.6/LO 232. For additional support for the premise that a cause is such that there is a necessary connection between it and its effect, see *Search* 5.1/LO 338; and *Search* 6.2.3/LO 450. Note that some commentators have assumed that Malebranche holds that if creatures were causes, the necessary connection obtaining between them and their effects would be weaker than the necessary connection that would obtain between God's volitions and their effects. (See, for example, Nicholas Jolley, "Introduction," in Jolley and Scott 1997, xxiv.) In the passages cited in support of the premise that there is a necessary connection between a cause and its effect, Malebranche is very clear that for any being to be a cause there would have to be an absolutely necessary connection between it and its effect.

77 See, for example, *Search* 3.2.9/LO 249; *Search* 3.2.7/LO 240; and *Search* 6.2.6/LO 484.

78 *Search* 3.2.9/LO 250. In the context of defending the doctrine of vision in God, Malebranche reaches a bit farther and suggests that we can think of anything. He argues (1) we can desire to think of anything, (2) we would not be able to do this unless we had ideas of all things, and (3) only God has ideas of all things; therefore, (4) we can access any idea in God's mind (*Search* 3.2.6/LO 232). Malebranche actually retreats from (1) at *Search* 3.2.9/LO 249. I am therefore disagreeing with Professor Nadler. See Steven Nadler, *Malebranche and Ideas*, Oxford: Oxford University Press (1992), 132.

79 Many of Malebranche's opponents would have held that God concurs in each and every thing that happens, and that when a creature brings about an event, the creature and God are both playing a causal role. For a discussion of standard Scholastic accounts of divine concurrence, see Alfred Freddoso, "God's General Concurrence With Secondary Causes: Why Conservation Is Not Enough," *Philosophical Perspectives* 5 (1991), 553–85.

80 Note that a very similar line of reasoning appears in one of Malebranche's predecessors, Al-Ghazali. The argument there is that if there were a necessary connection between, for example, the burning of a piece of cotton and its contact with fire, it would not be possible for God to prevent a piece of cotton from burning upon its contact with fire; but this is absurd. See Al-Ghazali, *The Incoherence of the Philosophers*, trans. Sabih Ahmad Kamali, Lahore: Pakistan Philosophical Congress (1963), 185. Al-Ghazali had a strong influence on Malebranche, if only indirect. See Steven Nadler, " 'No Necessary Connection': The Medieval Roots of the Occasionalist Roots of Hume," *The Monist* 79 (1996), 448–66; Alfred J. Freddoso, "Medieval Aristotelianism and the Case Against Secondary Causation in Nature," in Thomas V. Morris (ed.), *Divine and Human Action: Essays in the Metaphysics of Theism*, Ithaca, NY: Cornell University Press (1988), 94–6; and Majid Fakhry, *Islamic Occasionalism, and Its Critique by Averroes and Aquinas*, London: George Allen & Unwin Limited (1958), chapter 2.

81 Note that Jolley argues that Malebranche has to allow that if there exists the possibility of causal overdetermination, creatures could still be causes ("Introduction," xxiii). Jolley concludes that Malebranche must just be assuming the premise that there is no causal overdetermination. But this is not quite right, as Malebranche has no use for the premise. If there was any causal power in addition to the power of God's will, there would be a necessary connection between it (the finite causal power) and its effect, and God would not be omnipotent.

82 See Andrew Pyle, *Malebranche*, London and New York: Routledge Publishing Company (2003), 111–2, 209–10; Nadler, "Malebranche on Causation," 128–9; Robert Sleigh, Jr., Vere Chappel, and Michael Della Rocca, "Determinism and Human Freedom," in Daniel Garber and Michael Ayers (eds.), *The Cambridge History of Seventeenth-Century Philosophy*, Cambridge: Cambridge University Press (1998),

1244; and Andrew Pessin, "Malebranche's Doctrine of Freedom/Consent and the Incompleteness of God's Volitions," *British Journal for the History of Philosophy* 8 (2000), 21–53, 41–6.
83 Malebranche speaks of finite thinking substances and finite extended substances in a number of passages. See, for example, *Search* 1.1/LO 2; *Search* 3.2.8/LO 244–5; *Search* 3.2.9/LO 249–50; and *Dialogues* I, 6–7.
84 Here we might recall the Leibnizian objection that the Malebranchean "seems rather, like Spinoza, to make out of God the nature of the world itself, by causing created things to disappear into mere modifications of the one divine substance" (*On Nature Itself*, PPL 507).
85 *Eluc.* 1/LO 554. See also Elmar Kremer, "Malebranche on Human Freedom," in Nadler 2000, 210–4; Tad Schmaltz, *Malebranche's Theory of the Soul*, 227–8; David Scott, "Malebranche on the Soul's Power," *Studia Leibnitiana* 28 (1996), 37–57; Chappel Sleigh, Jr., and Della Rocca, "Determinism and Human Freedom," 1244; Pessin 2000, 41–6; and Ginette Dreyfus, *La volonté selon Malebranche*, Paris: J. Vrin (1958), 273–5.
86 *Eluc.* 1/LO 553. See also LO 553–4, and *Eluc.* 2/LO 560.
87 *Search* 4.10/LO 308–9. See also *Search* 1.2/LO 8–11; *Search* 1.14/LO 67–70; and *Search* 4.11/LO 312.
88 See also *Search* 5.2/LO 341; *Search* 6.2.3/LO 452; *Eluc.* 15/LO 657; and *Search* 2.3.4/LO 178–83.
89 *Dialogues* VII, 112. See also 116, where Malebranche fleshes out the apparent interaction of creatures in terms of God's constant creation of their modifications. He writes,

> This is what must be explained to you, in order to have reason agree with experience and provide you with the understanding of the greatest, the most fruitful and most necessary of all principles: namely: God communicates His power to creatures and unites them with one another, only because He establishes their modalities, occasional causes of the effects which He produces Himself.

90 See, for example, *Search* 3.1.1/LO 199. Of course, Descartes defends the view in his Second Meditation.
91 See, for example, *Dialogues* I, 17–18, and *Eluc.* 10/LO 621.
92 On Malebranche's view, God is constantly creating all modifications, but strictly speaking something is not a modification unless it is an occasional cause – that is to say unless it is followed by a change in a substance. See Nicolas Malebranche, "*Réflexions sur la prémotion physique*," in *Oeuvres de Malebranche*, OC XVI, 40; *Eluc.* 1/LO 551; and Kremer 2000, 211–4. Prefiguring Kant, Malebranche takes acts of consent to have no bearing whatsoever on the inclinations that we have; instead, they are simply the stances that we take toward the inclinations that we are going to have anyway. For more on this, see Cunning 2008 and Kremer 2000, 203–5.
93 An important objection to this interpretation is that in a number of passages Malebranche says that our sinful acts of consent are nothing. If sinful acts of consent are nothing, then they are not anything that God produces, but they are not anything that we produce either. The right view here, I think, is that Malebranche accepts the Augustinian position that sinful acts of consent are nothing in the sense that sin is a matter of what we do *not* do rather than what we in fact do. A sinful act of consent is sinful because it is a matter of not endorsing our inclination to love God, and we should endorse that inclination over inclinations toward transient things. (See, for example, *Eluc.* 1/LO 548, 549, 550, 551; and the preface to *Search*/LO 4–5.) For more on the influence of Augustine on Malebranche, see Tad Schmaltz, "Malebranche on Ideas and the Vision in God," in Nadler 2000, 61–8; and Nicholas Jolley, "The Relation Between Theology and Philosophy," in Garber and Ayers 1998, 371–3. Note that Professor Pessin (in Pessin 2000) defends an ingenious view according to which Malebranche holds that God is constantly creating each and every thing in its entirety, and in each case by a fully determinate particular volition, but that God is not accountable for causing all of the terrible things that happen in the universe because He creates things under a description that makes no reference to the ways in which they are terrible. On Pessin's view, God is not responsible for sin, but not because there are acts of consent that are independent of God. Instead, He is constantly creating our minds in their entirety, along with our acts of consent to things like murder and so forth, but under a description that is more neutral. God is constantly creating our minds in their entirety, but we are still punished for eternity for sin. Perhaps God punishes under a different description still, but this would be small consolation for the offender. Pessin's view is problematic on other grounds as well (and these are discussed in section 4).
94 E 2p7. All quotations from Spinoza will be taken from Samuel Shirley (trans.) and Michael L. Morgan (ed.), *Spinoza: Complete Works*, Indianapolis, IN: Hackett Publishing (2002).
95 E 2p5, E 2p6, E 3p2, E 1p3.
96 Bennett 1984, 147; Michael Della Rocca, *Representation and the Mind-Body Problem in Spinoza*, New York: Oxford University Press (1996), 157–71.

97 *Short Treatise on God, Man, and His Well-Being*, II.xix, 88–9.
98 See for example Della Rocca 1996, 3–17.
99 Bennett offers a version of this view. See Jonathan Bennett, A *Study of Spinoza's Ethics*, Indianapolis, IN: Hackett Publishing (1984), 141.
100 As Bennett points out, a problem that arises on this reading is that Spinoza appears to hold that modes can only be specified in terms of an attribute like thinking or extension, and so he appears to not allow talk of modes *simpliciter*.
101 AT VI 231; my translation. Note that a small amount of material from this section is a development of material in David Cunning, "Systematic Divergences in Malebranche and Cudworth," *Journal of the History of Philosophy* 41 (2003), 343–63. I include this material with the permission of the editor and the Johns Hopkins University Press.
102 AT VI 239. See also *Principles* IV: 198, AT VIIIA 322–3; "To Regius, January 1642," AT III 500; *Principles* II: 36–52, AT VIIIA 61–70; *Principles* IV: 187–188, AT VIIIA 314–5; and also *The World*, AT XI 34–35. Cudworth cites the passages from *Meteorology* as evidence that Descartes would not want to say that God's constant activity secures the orderly behavior of material things (*TISU*, 672). As already noted, Gary Hatfield makes a compelling case for the view that Descartes *is* committed to the view that God is directly responsible for all motion. Henri Carteron and Martial Gueroult defend the weaker claim that Descartes has tendencies toward this position but that some of the texts show that he is inclined to reject it. See Henri Carteron, "L'idee de force mecanique dans le systeme de Descartes," *Revue Philosophique* 94 (1922), 243–77, 483–511; and Martial Gueroult, "Metaphysique et physique de la force chez Descartes et chez Malebranche," *Revue de Metaphysique et de Morale* 59 (1954), 1–37, 113–34. I grant that Hatfield's texts are unambiguous, but I think that the contrary texts make it difficult to decide once and for all what Descartes actually thought.
103 Perhaps in the final analysis Descartes holds (with Malebranche) that only God is a cause, but that for pragmatic reasons it is crucial that we speak in terms of scientific laws and particulars. See, for example, *Eluc.* 15/LO 661–77.
104 See, for example, *TISU*, 28 and 668–669.
105 *TISU*, Preface to the Reader, x; *TISU*, 80–81, 884–885.
106 *TISU*, Preface to the Reader, x; *TISU*, 80–81, 884–885. Lydia Gysi argues that Cudworth does not really hold that God's greatness would be compromised if He did each and every thing. See Lydia Gysi, *Platonism and Cartesianism in the Philosophy of Ralph Cudworth*, Switzerland: Herbert Lang Bern (1962), 23. As evidence for her view, she points to some of the passages I have cited and also to a passage in which Cudworth speaks of the "*supposed* encumberment" (*TISU*, 884) that would burden God if He did each and every thing. I think that Gysi is right to note that in these passages Cudworth is distancing himself from the view that God would have to struggle to do each and every thing. However, as I argue later, Cudworth holds that such activity would compromise His greatness in other ways. Most commentators do not appreciate that Cudworth is often not speaking in his own voice when he describes God's activity. See, for example, Alan Gabbey, "Cudworth, More, and the Mechanical Analogy," in Richard Kroll, Richard Ashcraft, and Perez Zagorin (eds.), *Philosophy, Science, and Religion in England 1640–1700*, Cambridge: Cambridge University Press (1992), 120; J.A. Passmore, *Ralph Cudworth: An Interpretation*, Cambridge: Cambridge University Press (1951), 24–5; and Meyricke H. Carre, "Ralph Cudworth," *Philosophical Quarterly* 3 (1953), 329. J.L. Mosheim says that Cudworth *should* have said that it would be easy for God to do all things but that he does not. See Ralph Cudworth, *The True Intellectual System of the Universe*, ed. J.L. Mosheim, London: printed for Thomas Tegg (1845), volume I, 222, note 9.
107 *TISU*, 149. See also 149–50. Of course, Cudworth has to disagree with Malebranche that causality is such that there is a necessary connection between a cause and its effect. See Cunning 2003.
108 *TISU*, 147. See also 194–5.
109 Thus, Cudworth is working with one of the senses in which a thing can be a drudge. *The Oxford English Dictionary* defines "drudge" as "one employed in mean, servile, or distasteful work; a slave, a hack; a hard toiler." It defines "to drudge" as "to perform mean or servile tasks; to work hard or slavishly; to toil at laborious and distasteful work." See *The Oxford English Dictionary*, 2nd edition, prepared by J.A. Simpson and E.S.C. Weiner, Oxford: Oxford University Press (1989), volume IV, 1079–80. For Cudworth, if God did each and every thing, He would be a drudge in the first sense of each definition. It is worth noting that, in its explication of "drudgingly," the *OED* cites one of the *TISU* passages in which Cudworth claims that God would act drudgingly if He did all things (*OED*, 1080; *TISU*, 149).
110 See also Sarah Hutton, "Lord Herbert and the Cambridge Platonists," in Stuart Brown (ed.), *British Philosophy and the Age of the Enlightenment*, Routledge History of Philosophy, volume V, London and New York: Routledge (1996), 28.

111 *TISU*, 150. See also 151 and 54.
112 A plastic nature

> is not *Master* of that *Reason* and *Wisdom* according to which it acts, nor does it properly *Intend* those *Ends* which it acts for, nor indeed is it Expressly Conscious of what it doth, it not *Knowing*, but only *Doing*.
>
> (*TISU*, 162)

See also 679: Cudworth says that a plastic nature "hath no *Animal-Sense* or *Consciousness*, no *Understanding* or *Appetite*."

113 Cudworth writes,

> But because this may seem strange at the first sight, that Nature should be said to Act *for the sake of ends*, and *Regularly* or *Artificially*, and yet be itself devoid of *Knowledge* and *Understanding*, we shall therefore endeavour to persuade the *Possibility*, and facilitate the Belief of it, by some other Instances; and first by that of *Habits*, particularly those Musical ones of Singing, Playing upon Instruments, and Dancing.
>
> (*TISU*, 157)

See also 158–9.

114 See also Passmore 1951, 23–4, and W.C. DePauley, *The Candle of the Lord*, New York: The MacMillan Company (1937), 107.
115 Isaac Newton, *Mathematical Principles of Natural Philosophy*, eds. and trans. I. Bernard Cohen and Anne Whitman, Berkeley: University of California Press (1999), 943. This is not to say that Newton was not at times strongly inclined to one hypothesis over the others. See, for example, Howard Stein, "Newton's Metaphysics," in I. Bernard Cohen and George E. Smith (eds.), *The Cambridge Companion to Newton*, Cambridge: Cambridge University Press (2002).
116 Robert Boyle, *A Free Inquiry into the Vulgarly Received Notion of Nature*, in *Works* IV, 363; and Robert Boyle, *Christian Virtuoso*, in *Works* IV, 46. See also J.E. McGuire, "Boyle's Conception of Nature," *Journal of the History of Ideas* 33 (1972), 523–42; and Guido Giglioni, "Automata Compared: Boyle, Leibniz and the Debate on the Notion of Life," *British Journal for the History of Philosophy* 3 (1995), 271–2. For some of the wrinkles in this view, see Edwin McCann, "Was Boyle an Occasionalist?" in A.J. Holland (ed.), *Philosophy, Its History and Historiography*, Dordrecht: D. Reidel Publishing Company (1985), 229–31.
117 *Eluc.* 15/LO 667. See also *Dialogues* XIII.3, 244, and *Dialogues* XIII.12, 257–64.
118 Nicholas Malebranche, *Traité de la Nature et de la Grace*, OC 5: 49–50; my emphasis and translation. See also *Eluc.* 6/LO 568–569; *Dialogues* XI.3, 196–197; *Dialogues* XII.11, 230; and OC V 147.
119 *Dialogues* 7.5, 132.
120 For the view that Malebranche regards miracles as purely epistemic, see Cunning 2003. Steven Nadler has argued that Malebranche's God does each and every thing by a discrete and fully detailed particular volition and that what it is for Him to act by a general volition is to act by a particular volition that is in accordance with general laws. See "Occasionalism and General Will in Malebranche," *Journal of the History of Philosophy* 31 (1993), 41–6. There are a number of problems with Nadler's view. One is that the two texts he provides to support it are mistranslated: Nadler has Malebranche saying that God acts in accordance with general laws, but in the original French Malebranche's God is acting "*en consequence*" of general laws. See *Réponse aux Réflexions*, OC 8: 651, cited in Nadler 1993, 43; and *TNG*, OC 5:147, cited in Nadler 1993, 43–4. Also, immediately following the text that Nadler cites in *Réponse aux Réflexions*, Malebranche says that "This is not at all the view that God acts in me by a particular volition [*Ce n'est donc point que Dieu agisse en moi par une volonte particuliere*]." He goes on to explain that although God brings about each and every particular, He does this by general and noncomposite volitions. Nadler's final argument for his view is that Malebranche accepts "the axiomatic assumption" that if God moves an object on a particular occasion, God must have a particular volition to move the object on that occasion (Nadler 1993, 42). However, Nadler offers no evidence that this is an axiom for Malebranche. He might be attributing the axiom to Malebranche simply because he (Nadler) finds it inconceivable that a general volition could bring about any particular state of affairs; indeed, Nadler offers this very argument in response to an objection to his view from Desmond Clarke. See Nadler, "Malebranche's Occasionalism: A Reply to Clarke," *Journal of the History of Philosophy* 33 (1995), 507. However, Nadler himself admits that this kind of interpretive move is illegitimate: one of Clarke's objections was that we should reject the view that Malebranche's God always acts by particular volitions because we cannot conceive of God as atemporal and as executing particular volitions that cause temporal events to happen *at the*

same time that they happen. See Desmond Clarke, "Malebranche and Occasionalism: A Reply to Steven Nadler," *Journal of the History of Philosophy* 33 (1995), 501–4. Nadler rightly responds to Clarke that if a systematic reading of Malebranche shows that he holds a certain view, and if there is evidence that this view was coherent for him and his contemporaries, then its incoherence to us should not constrain us in our historical project of determining what Malebranche thought and why (Nadler 1995, 506). Previous attempts have been made to refute the view that Nadler defends, but they are unsuccessful. See, for example, Charles McCracken, *Malebranche and British Philosophy*, Oxford: Clarendon Press (1983), 100–1; Nicholas Jolley, *The Light of the Soul*, Oxford: Clarendon Press (1990), 106–7; and Andrew G. Black, "Malebranche's Theodicy," *Journal of the History of Philosophy* 35 (1997), 40.

121 *Dialogues* VII.10, 140. Malebranche sometimes refers more specifically to laws of the communications of motions, but he admits that we do not know what these are. See *Dialogues* X, esp. 188.

122 Malebranche is thus echoing Descartes's view that our grasp of God's nature is like our grasp of a mountain that we cannot nearly embrace. See "To [Mersenne], 27 May 1630," AT I 152. Some commentators have attempted to be more specific about the content of the general volitions of Malebranche's God. For example, Andrew Black offers the following schema: for all created substances x and y and for every time t_1, if x is G at t and x bears relation R to y then there is a time t_2 such that t_2 bears relation T to t_1 and y is F at t_2 (Black 1997, 34). See also Robert G. Sleigh, *Leibniz & Arnauld: A Commentary on their Correspondence*, New Haven, CT: Yale University Press (1990), 154–8. One of the problems with any such attempt, however, is that it is inevitably speculative. Black acknowledges this; he says that Malebranche's conception of God's general volitions is only "something like" the one that Black offers, that God's general volitions are "akin" to his schema (Black 1997, 39). See also Nadler 1993, 44–6.

123 See also Cunning 2008.

124 *Philosophical and Physical Opinions*, "Another Epistle to the Reader," ii. See also *Philosophical and Physical Opinions*, 293–4, and *Philosophical Letters*, 108, 151, 378, 417, 514–5.

125 *Grounds of Natural Philosophy*, 7. See also *Philosophical Letters*, 531. Cavendish might have come across this view in her reading of Henry More's *Antidote Against Atheism*. See Susan James, "The Philosophical Innovations of Margaret Cavendish," *British Journal for the History of Philosophy* 7 (1999), 222–3; and Henry More, *Antidote Against Atheism*, London (1653), 51–2.

126 *Philosophical Letters*, 215. Cavendish thinks that, strictly speaking, we cannot arrive at a view of the nature of matter by appealing to the nature of God, so she will always revert to her independent arguments. She thinks that the divine nature is beyond us, but she also insists rhetorically that if her *opponents* want to generate a view about the nature of matter from the nature of its creator, they should accept that matter is wondrous (and intelligent). See *Philosophical Letters*, 107, 139–142, 221, 230–1, 322, 462, 503–5. For example, she says of William Harvey that

> he doth speak so presumptuously of Gods Actions, Designs, Decrees, Laws, Attributes, Power, and secret Counsels, and describes the manner, how God created all things, and the mixture of the Elements to an hair, as if he had been Gods Counsellor and Assistant in the work of Creation; which whether it be not more impiety, then to say Matter is Infinite, I'le let others judg [sic]. Neither do I think this expression to be against the holy Scripture; for though I speak as a natural Philosopher, and am unwilling to cite the Scripture, which onely treats of things belonging to Faith, and not to Reason; yet I think there is not any passage which plainly denies Matter to be infinite, and Eternal, unless it be drawn by force to that sense. . . . [A]lso the Scripture says, *That Gods ways are unsearchable, and past finding out.*
>
> (*Philosophical Letters*, 462)

See also Londa Schiebinger, "Margaret Cavendish," in Mary Ellen Waithe (ed.), *A History of Women Philosophers*, Boston: Kluwer Academic Publishers (1991), 8. Cavendish thinks that we are mistaken if we think that we can say anything about God and His ways, but she adds that it follows from what her opponents *do* want to say about God that matter thinks. See also *Philosophical Letters*, 518–9, where she argues that it follows from her opposition's premise that God is good and just that He would make sure that all of His creatures would be able to worship Him, and so would make sure that all of His creatures had knowledge and perception. See also James 1999, 230.

127 See also Leibniz, "On Nature Itself," PPL 500–502, and "Letter to Arnauld, July 14, 1686," PPL 331–5. For more on Cavendish's view on the orderly behavior of bodies, see Cunning 2006; Karen Detlefsen, "Atomism, Monism, and Causation in Margaret Cavendish's Natural Philosophy," *Oxford Studies in Early Modern Philosophy* 3 (2005); and Karen Detlefsen, "Margaret Cavendish on the Relation Between God and World," *Philosophy Compass* (2009).

10
THEORIES OF SENSE PERCEPTION

Antonia LoLordo

1. Introduction

There is a bewildering diversity among seventeenth century theorists of perception. They do not always agree on what questions should be asked, let alone the answers or the methodology that should be used to find those answers. However, a few central questions arise within almost all seventeenth century theories of perception. The first such question concerns the nonmental aspects of perception. Some early modern philosophers paid a great deal of attention to the workings of the human perceptual apparatus. But even those who are not interested in the physiology of perception – like Leibniz and Locke – confront a more fundamental metaphysical question:

1. What must the external world be like for human beings to know it through sense perception?

This is a question faced by all theories of perception. But it is particularly salient for the mechanical philosophers of the seventeenth century. A central theme in the neo-Aristotelian theories that mechanism was intended to replace is that perception involves – indeed, requires – resemblance. Perception, neo-Aristotelians hold, occurs when the perceiver's soul comes to resemble the external object or quality it represents. This resemblance typically consists in shared form, and it is guaranteed by the transmission of intentional species. The philosophers I discuss next all reject this picture out of hand, because they reject the forms and species involved. Thus, they owe us another account of the metaphysics of the external world, one that makes it perceptible in their terms.

Because they reject the resemblance between perception and object, the philosophers discussed next also owe us an answer to a second question:

2. In virtue of what does a mental entity, state, or act represent something existing in the external world?

Many of the philosophers we shall discuss retain the Aristotelian notion that resemblance is the ideal mode of representation. They hold that our perceptions of size, shape, and motion do resemble the qualities they represent. However, they cannot claim that *all* perceptual representation occurs through resemblance. For on their view, secondary qualities do not exist in bodies, at least not as we perceive them.[1] Heat as we perceive it does not exist in the fire any more than the pain produced by standing too close to it does.

A further way in which the rejection of Aristotelianism complicates theories of perception is this. Hylomorphism suggests a view of the external world as intrinsically intelligible: because external objects have forms, they are intrinsically ready to be understood. The philosophers discussed next cannot think this and hence must explain:

3. How can a causal process that begins with nonintentional entities issue in mental states with representational content?

Of course, this question presupposes that some content *is* acquired in perception. Someone who claims that all mental content is innate can avoid it. But they face a different question:

4. How can innate ideas be brought to bear in the process of perception?

And because several of the philosophers we shall discuss hold that some content is innate and some is acquired, they must answer both (3) and (4).

Another set of questions derives from considering the relationship between perception, perceptual judgment, and knowledge:

5. How much of what we ordinarily consider perception is really judgment?

For instance, do we actually *perceive* that the body in front of us is a tower? That it is a body? That is roughly cubical and a few dozen feet away? Or are all these really judgments? And is any psychological work involved in coming to see it as cubical and a hundred feet away, or is this information given to us, just like the gray color of the tower?

Delineating the border between perception proper and perceptual judgment is of independent interest. So is the closely related issue of determining which aspects of perception are active and which passive. But it is also important because it connects to something more practically valuable:

6. To what extent is perception reliable?

Are there certain kinds of perception that are always true or always form the basis for true judgments, for instance, or certain classes that are systematically unreliable? And are there techniques we can use to make our perceptions more reliable?

Almost all the philosophers we shall discuss hold that the faculty of sense perception is, in general, reliable. However, to the extent that perception involves human activity – whether this is the activity of judgment or some other type of processing – it can issue in error. The less activity perception involves, the easier defending its reliability is.

Questions about where perception leaves off and perceptual judgment begins are closely related to questions about how much of the human perceptual process is active and how much passive. But they are not identical. Everyone agrees that judgment is an active process, even when the faculty of judgment is more or less compelled by the content presented to it. But not all the philosophers we discuss are committed to the claim that all perception is passive or that the distinction between activity and passivity maps perfectly onto the distinction between perception and perceptual judgments.

Lying behind the general insistence on the reliability of perception is not only a prevalent antiskepticism but also a virtually universal assumption that the human perceptual faculties are given to us by an omnipotent, omniscient, omnibenevolent God. Thus, they must be reliable when properly used. This suggests one final question:

7. What does proper use of the human perceptual apparatus consist in?

Sometimes this is coupled with a further, more practical question: how can we come to use our perceptual faculties better than we currently do?

This sketch of the central questions early modern theorists of perception face makes clear that their theories involve a combination of epistemological, metaphysical, and psychological elements. In what follows, I shall trace out the way that a number of different theories of perception answer these seven questions and the relative weights they assign to epistemological, metaphysical, and psychological factors. The main figures I will consider are Hobbes, Gassendi, Descartes, Malebranche, Locke, and Leibniz. However, because they are all reacting against the background of Aristotelianism, I shall begin with a very brief account of neo-Aristotelian theories of perception.

2. Neo-Aristotelianism

The vast majority of theorizing about perception in the first half of the seventeenth century was done by roughly Aristotelian philosophers. This is not because the vast majority of philosophers writing then were Aristotelians. Various forms of neo-Platonism and humanism were extremely widespread. However, perhaps because Aristotelians hold that all mental content ultimately originates in perception, they seem to have had particular interest in perception. Moreover, the first generation of philosophers discussed next – Hobbes, Gassendi, and Descartes – present their theories in opposition to Aristotelianism.

The crucial explanatory entities in Aristotelian theories are *intentional species*, representations transmitted from objects to perceivers' sense organs. All the philosophers discussed next reject species, but positing them is extremely helpful in explaining perceptual representation. If perception is mediated by species, then perceptual states can represent their objects by resembling them or even by being formally identical to them. Thus, species provide the theoretical underpinnings for what the early moderns saw as the commonsense view that perceptual states represent by resembling. Hobbes, for instance, grasps the motivation for admitting intentional species even while insisting that they are metaphysically illegitimate:

> [I]t is no hard matter for a man to fall into this opinion, that the same colours and shape are the very qualities themselves. . . . [T]his opinion hath been so long received, that the contrary must needs appear a great paradox; and yet the introduction of species visible and intelligible (which is necessary for the maintenance of that opinion) . . . is worse than any paradox, as being a plain impossibility.
>
> (EL 2.4)

Any controversy surrounding the theoretical role that intentional species are designed to fill is unimportant for our purposes. However, disagreements about the precise nature of species are more important. Opponents of Aristotelian theories of perception tend to treat intentional species as little pictures or images. Descartes, for example, mockingly refers to "all those little images flitting through the air, called *intentional species*, which so worry the imagination of Philosophers" (AT VI 85; CSM I 153–4). This is an accurate representation of the textbook view,[2] although more sophisticated writers made a point of insisting that species are not pictures or images.[3] And not everyone accepted the need for intentional species at all.[4]

One line of argument in favor of intentional species runs as follows. Start with two intuitively plausible premises: all action is through contact, and sensation is fundamentally passive.[5] It follows from the first premise that sight, smell, and hearing – the distance senses – need a medium of perception (typically, the air). And all five senses need a means whereby direct action or action through that medium occurs. From the second premise, it follows that the means must derive from the object perceived, not from the perceiver, thus ruling out the Platonic or Stoic theory that vision involves rays emitted from the eyes. Thus, sense perception requires some entity transmitted through the medium from objects to perceivers. This entity is the species, and it is conveyed or propagated from the sense organ to the brain, where the common sense is located. When the species – and hence the form – is instantiated in the common sense, we apprehend the object sensed.

Given the standard Aristotelian assumption that knowledge requires the soul to become like the object known, the intentional species must somehow make the soul like the object sensed. It does this by conveying the form of the object or quality to the soul, or at least allowing the soul to reconstruct that form. Hence, it is trivial that the reception of a given species causes us to apprehend the object it came from.

Hobbes, Gassendi, and Descartes all accept that action at a distance is impossible and thus that sense perception requires a kind of contact.[6] They also all accept that sense perception is mostly, if not entirely, passive. Thus, in some sense they all accept the first step of the argument sketched previously: sense perception requires that some entity is transmitted from objects to perceivers. But they diverge from the Aristotelian theory in denying the existence of forms and hence cannot accept the second step. This complicates their task significantly, because it requires them to provide an alternate account of what it is that is transmitted and an alternate account of how that thing engenders mental content.

3. Hobbes

Hobbes's alternate account is radically minimalist. There is a resemblance between sensation and the thing sensed, on Hobbes's view, although it is not the resemblance the Aristotelians had in mind. For – in keeping with his overarching view that all that exists is matter in motion – both the object sensed and the act of sensing it are mere motions. Hobbes dispenses not only with the intentional species so useful in neo-Aristotelian theories but also with the immaterial thinking substance that most of the seventeenth century philosophers we will discuss rely on.

Sensible qualities such as light, color, and sound "are, in the object, that causeth them, but so many several motions of the matter.... Neither in us... are they any thing else, but divers motions" (*L* 1.4). Thus, for instance,

> SOUND is *sense generated by the action of the medium, when its motion reacheth the ear and the rest of the organs of sense.*... [T]he motion of the medium is

not the sound itself, but the cause of it. For the phantasm which is made in us, that is to say, the reaction of the organ, is properly that which we call *sound*.

(*DCo* 19.1)

The similar claim that there is nothing outside us that can properly be called a color or image – only motion – is made in the earlier *Elements of Law* (*EL* 2.4). Here Hobbes's argument for the claim that sensible qualities are mere motions relies heavily on cases of perceptual error. Consider a blow to the head that causes its victim to see a flash of light. *This* flash of light cannot be anything other than motion in the brain; so, Hobbes concludes, *all* light must be just motion in the brain (*EL* 2.7). This argument assumes that normal perception should be explained in just the same terms as various divergent cases of error, hallucination, and the like. Hobbes is clearly committed to giving a unified account of veridical perception and illusion, but he does not, as far as I know, provide an argument for this. Perhaps he thinks that if only motions can be causes, no disjunctive account is possible.[7] However, almost all the philosophers we shall discuss give unified accounts of veridical and nonveridical perception; Gassendi is the only clear exception.

The claim that qualities are reducible to matter and motion is, of course, common among the early moderns. But the claim that *sensations themselves* are mere motions is so radical as to be worth repeating: sensation "can be nothing else but motion in some of the internal parts of the sentient" (*DCo* 25.2).[8] This radical reductionism is, unsurprisingly, accompanied by an almost total lack of attention to the intentional and qualitative aspects of sensation.

In contrast, throughout his works Hobbes has a great deal to say about the physical and physiological aspects of perception. The majority of this concerns vision in particular.[9] *De Corpore* and *Leviathan* present roughly the same account of the motion that constitutes sensation, although the former is much more detailed. I shall give just a rough sketch of Hobbes's view, because I am not chiefly concerned with the physiology of perception in this chapter.

External objects press on the sense organ either immediately (as in the case of the contact senses, touch and taste) or mediately (as in the case of the distance senses). The pressure thus produced is transmitted inward to the internal sense organ, which has its own motion and hence reacts against the pressure applied to it.[10] This creates conscious sensation: "from the reaction . . . a phantasm or idea hath its being; which, by reason that the endeavour is now outwards, doth always appear as something situated without the organ" (*DCo* 25.2).

This is more or less the end of Hobbes's account of sensation. He provides some explanation of why objects appear to us to be in the external world, when the relevant motion is internal: it is because the "endeavor" underlying that motion is directed outward. This is not a terribly plausible explanation, but it is an explanation nonetheless. In contrast, Hobbes gives no explanation at all for why such motions constitute representation. I suspect this is less because he sees no need to explain this than because he sees no possible way of doing so, but the text is ambiguous: "Of all the phenomena or appearances which are near us, the most admirable is apparition itself . . . namely, that some natural bodies have in themselves the patterns almost of all things, and others of none at all" (*DCo* 25.1). On another translation, intentionality is the most *wonderful* or *marvelous* natural phenomenon. Hobbes does not try to explain how motions in the brain can constitute intentional content. Nor does he try to explain the relation between the content and its cause. In this respect, Hobbes is radically different from both the Aristotelians and the philosophers discussed next. There is some reason to count this difference in Hobbes's favor. Most of the philosophers we shall discuss do not explain how motion in the brain constitutes content because they think perceptual states inhere in an immaterial substance. Then, to explain how mental states succeed in representing external objects, they fill in the explanatory gap Hobbes marvels at by appealing to arbitrary psychophysical laws.

Let us turn to the epistemological aspects of Hobbes's theory of perception. He insists that "there is no conception in a man's mind, which hath not . . . been begotten upon the organs of sense" (*L* 1.2) and that "all knowledge of fact . . . is originally sense" (*L* 7.3). This suggests that it is rather important to acquire the best conceptions possible – which, in turn, suggests that Hobbes should have something to say about the epistemology of perception. However, his account of perception actually contains very little epistemology. This may stem from the fact that perception, on his view, is an entirely passive process.

In fact, on Hobbes's view, even what most philosophers count as perceptual judgment rather than perception proper is passive. "By sense," says Hobbes, "we commonly understand the judgment we make of objects by their phantasms" (*DCo* 25.4). Correlating the data of the various senses does not require any mental activity:[11] no judgment or reasoning is required, and nothing like the Aristotelian common sense. It is simply a matter of memory:

> observation of differences is not perception made by a common organ of sense, distinct from sense or perception properly so called, but is memory of the differences of particular phantasms remaining for some time; as the distinction between hot and lucid, is nothing else but the memory both of a heat, and of an enlightening object.
>
> (*DCo* 25.8; 399)

Thus, even perceptual judgments, for Hobbes, do not appear to require any real activity on the part of the perceiver. This leaves little room for the sort of admonishments on how to avoid perceptual error common in philosophers like Descartes and Gassendi.

4. Gassendi

Like Hobbes, Descartes, and other early moderns, Gassendi rejects intentional species as metaphysically illegitimate fictions. The theory he intends to replace Aristotelianism is, like Hobbes's, broadly mechanistic: it is supposed to operate solely in terms of the size, shape, and motion of material corpuscles. And like Hobbes's, it is supposed to be materialist in another sense as well. It explains perception as an ability of a material human soul no different in kind than the souls of animals. Whether or not an immaterial soul exists – and Gassendi seems to have changed his mind about this over time – it plays no role in perception.[12]

Gassendi's metaphysics thus exert an important influence on the theory of perception he develops. Another important influence is his view that all sensory appearances are true or that the senses do not lie.[13] When we perceive a square tower as round from a distance, for instance, this perception is true, just as the perception of that tower as square from close up is true. The truth of the appearances influences Gassendi's theory of perception in two quite different ways. First, it motivates distinguishing perception from perceptual judgment and assigning a great deal of what looks like perception to judgment. Second, it requires an account of perceptual representation that has nothing to do with resemblance. Descartes, Locke, and Malebranche deny resemblance for ideas of secondary qualities but hold on to it for ideas of primary qualities, thus retaining the assumption that resemblance is the ideal form of representation. In contrast, Gassendi holds that neither ideas of secondary qualities nor ideas of primary qualities represent their objects by resembling them.[14] For if representation required resemblance, it would be difficult to see how both the perception of the distant tower as round and the perception of the nearby tower as square could successfully represent the tower.

Commitment to the truth of the appearances is obvious from the first of the canons of logic that appear throughout Gassendi's work: "Sense is never deceived, and hence every sensation and all Phantasies or appearances are true perceptions" (1.53a). Three different lines of argument support this claim. The first is pragmatic: if you allow that some appearances are false, Gassendi suggests, you will be led into skepticism. Reason is entirely dependent on the senses and hence cannot correct sensory error. All the senses are epistemically equal, so one sense cannot correct another. Finally, different sensations from the same sense modality cannot correct each other because there is no way to determine which is true.

The second line of argument holds that sense perceptions cannot be false because they do not affirm or deny anything. They just passively receive information, whereas affirming or denying that objects correspond to their appearances is the task of judgment. I find the first line of argument unsatisfying, as both the claim that reason cannot correct the senses and the claim that the senses cannot correct each other require more defense than they receive. I find the second line unsatisfying for a rather different reason: the truth of the appearances does real epistemic work for Gassendi and hence must amount to something more than that the senses make no truth claims at all. All sense perceptions must be true in some nontrivial sense.

The third line of argument is intended to ground such nontrivial truth. It starts with the claim that all sense perceptions convey real information about their causes and infers that examining the physical causes of these appearances provides empirical knowledge of the world. All sense perceptions are true because all provide the basis for true knowledge, if analyzed properly. Whether the tower looks round or square, for instance, is the result of a comprehensible chain of causes. Sight has received a round or square impression "for causes that have to be investigated by physics" (1.53b). A key part of that investigation is investigating how the human perceptual faculties work.

All the philosophers discussed here say far more about vision than any other sense modality. On Gassendi's view, vision results from *simulacra*: composites of light rays that provide the basis for reconstructing images of objects without being objects themselves (2.377b). When they hit the eye, they cause a chain of changes in the eye, nerves, and brain. At this point, "a certain trace or, as it were, mark or image is impressed on the brain" and "the person perceives the sensible thing from which the blow came" (2.403b). The trace in the brain is a fortunate by-product of the perceptual process; perception could occur without it. Its role is to make cognition of absent objects possible. Gassendi sometimes refers to this material trace as an idea; more commonly, though, "idea" refers to the act that this material trace makes possible. But either way, perception does not require ideas. This is a crucial difference between Gassendi's account and the others I discuss. It is also crucial for understanding the aspect of direct realism in his theory.

How does the motion of the nerves and the changes it produces in the brain cause us to perceive anything at all? Gassendi seems to recognize the importance of this question, asking rhetorically, "How could things capable of sense . . . arise from insensible things" (2.343a)? But his answer is unsatisfactory. He replies that although we do not know what "magnitude, figure, motion, situation and order of atoms" is required, he is sure that "non-sensing and inanimate things can be joined together in such a way that animate and sensing things result, just as non-igneous and non-hot things are joined together so that igneous and hot things result" (2.347b). This is an attempt to assimilate explaining how sensation arises from dumb matter to what Gassendi suggests is a much larger problem: how new properties can emerge from atomic composition. But on Gassendi's theory, such new properties are typically properties of perceptual states, not of bodies. Heat, for instance, exists only as a perceptual state: there is nothing in bodies resembling that state, only the motion of atoms. Hence, Gassendi's larger problem is really just the original problem all over again.[15] His account of the explanatory gap is no more satisfactory than Hobbes's. We shall see that none of the philosophers discussed later do much better.

Thus, let us turn to another issue in his theory of perception: the nature of the objects of perception. The object of perception plays a dual role in Aristotelian theories, as both what we are directly aware of and what exists in the external world. Denying resemblance precludes this answer, so Gassendi requires a new account of the object of perception.

Consider an example. When we perceive the sun through the unaided senses, perception represents it as about a foot in diameter. When we perceive the sun in the context of astronomical observation and reasoning, perception represents it as vast (3.316b–317a). Gassendi's explanation of why both perceptions are true depends on thinking of the objects of perception as the *simulacra* rather than their ultimate causes. But a number of factors push him toward saying that the object of perception is the real external object as well. The commonsense view of perception requires it. So does the individuation of perceptions; both ideas are ideas *of the sun* because the sun is their object.

Finally, it's important for Gassendi's epistemology that although both ideas are true, one is more "evident," and this requires that the object of perception is the sun itself. Evidence plays both a psychological and an epistemological role, like Cartesian clear and distinct perception and Stoic *kataleptic* impressions. Psychologically, evident perceptions compel assent; this provides the criterion for evidence. Epistemologically, evident perceptions provide the criterion for judgments about external objects. Some perceptions carry more information about the object sensed (and less about the perceptual process) than others, and they are the evident perceptions. Evident perceptions, in other words, present their objects as they really are. This again suggests a dual notion of the object of perception: in one sense, the object of perception is what the perception presents, that is what we are aware of in having it; and in another sense the object of perception is what the perception represents.

Understanding perceptual content as dual in this way helps us make sense of an otherwise puzzling assumption that runs through Gassendi's discussions of skepticism: that we can suspend judgment about the nature and intrinsic qualities of bodies but not about their existence. That an appearance is presented to us guarantees the existence of some external cause. But there is no guarantee that the appearance corresponds to its distal cause in any obvious way. Thus, it is reasonable to suspend judgment about the nature of objects but not their existence. Gassendi recognizes, of course, that hallucinations and dreams can be introspectively indistinguishable from appearances. But they are not appearances and cannot compel assent in the way that evident appearances do. Gassendi's theory of perception is, in effect, disjunctivist. It is notable that none of the other early modern theorists of perception we will discuss are tempted by disjunctivism or by the claim that we cannot suspend judgment about the existence of the objects that appear to us. I suspect this is because they all hold that perceptual and nonperceptual cognition use the same sort of mental representations: ideas. For if both perceptions and hallucinations are ideas, it is rather difficult to maintain that they are intrinsically different rather than merely causally different.

5. Descartes

Descartes's argument in the *Meditations* that knowledge is founded on the perceptions of the intellect, not the senses, is justly famous. But he wrote far more about the nature and mechanics of sense perception than about the intellect. Unlike the philosophers discussed previously, Descartes's interest in sense perception does not stem from the view that it is the sole – or even most important – source of mental content. Instead, he provides a theory of sense perception as part of his overarching program of replacing Aristotelianism with his own philosophy. In the *Discourse on Method*, Descartes's theory of sense perception and its relatively minimalist ontology serve as examples of how we can do without the metaphysically extravagant theories of the Aristotelians. In the *Meditations* and *Principles*, Descartes presents roughly the same theory of sense perception as part of an integrated system of physics.

Moreover, the theory of sense perception presented in the *Meditations* is necessary to rebut an obvious objection. Even setting aside the impact of the First Meditation's skeptical hypotheses, Descartes's metaphysical system implies that the senses are not accurate guides to the nature of the world around us. Nothing like the colors presented to us in sensation, for instance, really exists in external objects. Doesn't this make our God-given sensory faculties deceptive? Descartes has two replies. First, the senses are intended as guides to help us preserve the mind-body union rather than as tools for achieving scientific knowledge. Thus, if we use the senses properly we will not be led into false beliefs like the belief that external objects are really colored. Second, Descartes – like Gassendi – minimizes the extent of human sensory error by distinguishing sensation from judgment and placing much apparent sensory error on the side of judgment.

Descartes draws this distinction while delineating "three grades of sensation" in the Sixth Replies (AT VII 436–9; CSM II 294–6) The first, purely physiological, grade comprises the changes that sense perception produces in the sense organs, nerves, and brain. In the case of vision, for instance, the first grade of sensation occurs when the round globules that constitute light according to Cartesian physics hit the eye and move the animal spirits and ultimately the brain (AT VI 81–93; CSM I 152–7). At this point, the psychophysical laws governing the mind-body union come into play, and the second grade of sensation is produced. This second grade is purely mental: it includes "everything in the mind that results immediately from the fact that it is united to a corporeal organ thus affected" by external bodies (AT VI 437; CSM II 294–5).

When I speak of Cartesian sense perception from now on, I mean the second grade. For whereas the first grade of sensation is purely physiological, the third grade is really a species of judgment. In fact, it comprises two quite different kinds of judgment. One kind is involved in perception of size, shape, and distance.[16] These judgments are irresistible and truth conducive.[17] In contrast, the second sort is typified by the judgment that an external object has a color resembling the color our perception represents it as having. These judgments are false and derive from bad habits acquired in childhood that we can, with some effort, refrain from making. Because these childhood habits are deeply entrenched, we are not typically aware of making the second sort of judgments. However – as introspection shows – with practice we can become aware of them. Because of his claim that consciousness is essential to the mind,[18] Descartes must also hold that the judgments involved in perceiving size, shape, and distance are conscious, although he grants that we are not aware of having performed the relevant calculations. Hence, he makes the somewhat implausible claim that although we do these calculations consciously, they happen so quickly that they leave no traces in the memory (AT VII 438; CSM II 295–6). This leaves Descartes with a clear distinction between sense perception and judgment. Perception proper is passive, whereas the judgments involved in the third grade of sensation are active. Judgment yields claims about the qualities of external objects, some of which are true and some of which are false. Perception yields sensations such as the sensations of heat, color, and odor.

Sensations of heat and color are not in themselves false: strictly speaking, only judgments can be false. But they do provide the material for false judgments, and hence Descartes speaks of them as "materially false": if I judge that there is really something in bodies resembling my perceptions of heat and color, I will be judging falsely (AT VII 38; CSM II 26–7). How could a nondeceiving God give us materially false sensations? Descartes's answer is that, first, the bad habits acquired in childhood can be resisted. Judgment, after all, is an activity of the will and – when the perceptions in question are not clear and distinct – the will can either judge or refrain from judging. Second, although sensations provide the material for false judgments, they *also* provide the material for true judgments. When I judge that external objects are by nature as my senses represent them, I judge falsely – but I am also using the information provided by my senses incorrectly. The senses are intended to guide us in preserving the union of mind and body, not in acquiring scientific knowledge:

> without a doubt sensory perceptions are given to me by Nature in order to signify to the mind what things would be beneficial or harmful to the composite of which it is a part.
> (AT VII 83; CSM II 57–8)

> And when I use the senses as guides to which external objects should be sought and which avoided, they are generally reliable.
> (AT VII 81; CSM II 56)

Two difficult interpretive questions arise with respect to the status of Cartesian sensations. First, do Cartesian sensations have intentional content, or are they mere *qualia*? On one hand, Descartes insists that sensations represent nothing outside thought (AT VIIIA 35; CSM I 218–9). On the other, he describes sensations as confused modes of thought (AT VII 80; CSM II 55–6), and this seems to imply that there is something that they represent in a confused manner. Second, are there both sensations of primary qualities and sensations of secondary qualities? The two questions are closely related:

if you deny content to sensations, it is natural to deny the existence of primary-quality sensations; and if you accept primary-quality sensations, you should allow that sensations have content.

Part of the reason these questions are difficult is that it is difficult to say precisely what representation consists in for Descartes. It is clear that representation does not require resemblance, so it is no obstacle to sensations representing that they do not resemble their causes. It is also clear that sensations co-vary with the qualities of bodies in a lawlike manner. For there are laws that govern the relationship between mind and body in general, and between sensations and physical changes in the brain in particular. Thus, sensations can serve as signs of the qualities of bodies. However, the laws of the mind-body union are instituted by God, and God could have instituted a different set of laws if he had wanted. Of course, the laws instituted by God are intended to help preserve the mind-body union – but there are multiple different sets of laws that could serve this function equally well. No survival benefit accrues from the sensation of red being correlated with tomatoes and the sensation of green with grass rather than the other way around. Thus, the connection between sensations and the qualities that caused them is fundamentally arbitrary: we cannot read off the causally relevant quality from the sensation, as we can in the case of mental representations of primary qualities. Given all this, the question of whether sensations are representational amounts to the question of whether Descartes is willing to count the relevant sort of signification as representation. In any case, the questions about the intentionality of sensations and the existence of primary-quality sensations that lurk in the background of Descartes's account are brought to the fore by Malebranche.

6. Malebranche

Malebranche's theory of perception has a great deal in common with Descartes's. Both hold that the physical world is constituted solely of matter in motion, without forms, species, or anything that might resemble ideas of secondary qualities. Both have far more to say about vision than the other senses, and both rely heavily on geometrical optics. Both consider it important to distinguish perception from judgment and establish the reliability of different classes of perceptual judgments.

But in place of the three Cartesian grades of sensation, Malebranche has four, dividing Cartesian perceptual judgments into two classes – natural judgments and free judgments. Consider the example of a man looking up at the night sky. He sees the stars as existing at some distance outside him in the external world, thereby making a natural judgment. Then, in a free judgment, he forms the belief that they are located at some distance from him. The natural judgment – which Malebranche also describes as "a judgment of the senses or a compound sensation" – is unavoidable. We cannot help seeing the stars as external and distant. Natural judgments occur within us, but we are not agents of their production: a natural judgment "occurs independently of us, and even in spite of us" (*Search* 1.14.1/LO 68; cf. *Search* 1.9.3/LO 46). For they are inevitable given the nature of the human perceptual system. In contrast, the free judgment that the stars are located at some distance away – which is a matter of belief rather than appearance – is voluntary.

Natural judgments have a somewhat different status in the first and second editions of the *Search*. In the first edition, they have roughly the same status as the judgments Descartes holds are involved in size and distance perception. But in the second edition,

Malebranche denies that we play any role in the production of natural judgments. The paradigmatic natural judgments are these same calculations of size and distance,[19] and Malebranche insists that the finite human mind is not capable of making such complex calculations in the time available. The conclusion derived from this is a happy one from the point of Malebranche's overarching metaphysics: God's active intervention is necessary for even the simplest perceptions. I cannot see the coffee cup in front of me, for instance, without God's assistance.[20]

On Malebranche's view, both free and natural judgments are typically false. The distinction between judgments about primary qualities and judgments about secondary qualities – which is orthogonal to the distinction between free and natural judgments – plays a crucial role in Malebranche's explanation of the falsity of perceptual judgments. Descartes held that the judgments we habitually make about secondary qualities are false, at least when considered as guides to the intrinsic nature of the bodies around us as opposed to their desirability from our point of view. Malebranche more or less agrees with this verdict, although he places much less emphasis on the usefulness of sensation for preserving the mind-body union than Descartes does.

However, Malebranche disagrees sharply with the Cartesian account of primary-quality perception, insisting that almost all judgments about primary qualities are false as well. Visual perception of size, for instance, is systematically inaccurate because "sight ... does not represent extension to us as it is in itself, but only as it is in relation to our body" (*Search* 1.1.6/LO 28). And because distance perception depends on size perception and the perception of motion depends on distance perception, the errors ramify. Thus, the senses neither provide knowledge of the primary qualities of bodies as they are in themselves nor as they relate to us.

However, primary-quality perception remains epistemically superior:

> The judgments we form on the testimony of our eyes concerning extension, figure and motion are never exactly true. Nonetheless, it must be agreed that they are not altogether false: they include at least this truth, that outside us there are figures, motion, and extension, whatever these may be.
> (*Search* 1.10/LO 48)

Unlike the secondary qualities, size, shape, and motion in general "have a real existence, independent of our mind" (*Search* 1.10/LO 48).

Although almost all natural judgments are false, they are also, for Malebranche, inevitable. We cannot avoid seeing the sun as roughly the size of a dinner plate; all we can do is refrain from making the corresponding free judgment. The systematic falsity of natural judgment raises a serious problem from the Cartesian point of view. How can our perceptual faculties be systematically misleading when they have been given to us by an omnipotent, omnibenevolent God? Malebranche has essentially three different lines of response to this. First, he notes that we are particularly liable to err because of original sin (*Search* 1.5.1/LO 22). It is not intrinsic to natural judgments that they compel belief; it is a consequence of our fallen state that we cannot refuse assent to them. Second, he notes that in many cases of error – although *not*, it is important to note, irresistible natural judgments – error is the product of free will (*Search* 1.5.1/LO 23). Finally, Malebranche also suggests that some natural judgments are false only if construed as guides to the nature of things rather than that which is conducive to bodily survival (*Search* 1.12.5/LO 60). The last two suggestions are, of course, Cartesian.

We saw that it is a difficult interpretive question whether Cartesian sensations have intentional content and whether there are sensations of primary qualities. Malebranche is clear on this topic. Ideas of primary qualities – like all ideas – are located in God's mind, whereas the sensations occasioned by secondary qualities are in human minds. Thus, what we typically think of as sense perception is actually a compound of two very different mental states: "two things are found in our perception: *sensation* and *pure idea*" (*Search* 3.2.6/LO 234). The content of primary-quality perception is a partial view of intelligible extension, the idea of extension in God's mind. The sensation is a mental entity whose occasional cause is a set of movements in the sense organs, nerves, and brain. Sensations have no intelligible content: they are mere signs, like Gassendi's impressions.

Malebranche explains how our secondary-quality sensations and primary-quality ideas relate as follows:

> When you conceive it, intelligible extension is applied to your mind. . . . And when you sense or see it, a determinate part of this extension sensibly touches your soul and modifies it by the sensation of some color. For intelligible extension becomes visible and represents a certain body in particular only by means of color. . . . All the intelligible parts of intelligible extension are of the same nature insofar as they are ideas, just as all the parts of local or material extension have the same nature as a substance
>
> (*Dialogues* 1, 17)[21]

When we sense bodies, then, some part of intelligible extension "sensibly touches the soul." The presence of a perceptible body occasions God to simultaneously do two things. First, he makes us aware of the idea of extension that is in him, at least temporarily. Second, he modifies our mind with a certain sensation (*Dialogues* 12, 18).

Both divine acts are governed by the laws of the mind-body union, although in slightly different ways. In the case of sensations, the nature of the object sensed determines certain movements in my brain, which, in turn, determine the sensation in my mind:

> The modalities of a certain part of the brain . . . are always followed by the modalities or sensations of our soul, and this occurs solely as a consequence of the continually efficacious laws of the union of these two substances, that is . . . the constant and continually, efficacious volitions of the author of our being.
>
> (*Dialogues* 4, 59)

Just as in Descartes, these laws are intended to preserve the mind-body union. God gives us sensations that motivate us to seek bodies beneficial to us and shun those harmful to us. Aside from this motivational force, the laws are fundamentally arbitrary. There is no reason that a given movement in the brain occasions the taste of strawberries rather than the taste of wine.

In the case of our awareness of ideas in God, the determination runs through our sensations. Every secondary-quality sensation is accompanied by, and "makes visible," the idea of extension. The sensation of red, for instance, makes extension visible because it appears to us as spread out on an extended surface. God has instituted laws allowing me to see the idea of extension, in various ways, when I have various color sensations.

What Hobbes described as the most wonderful of all natural phenomena becomes in Malebranche the direct workings of God in his creation.

The most fundamental question theories of perception face is simply, how is perceptual representation possible? That is, how does the mind come to represent external objects in general, and how are particular representations hooked up with their objects? Malebranche's ultimate – and elegantly simple – answer is that perceptual representation is *not* possible, at least not for finite human minds. We do not represent external objects at all. Mental representation depends on two things: awareness of intelligible extension and the natural judgments that lead us to externalize our sensations in accordance with it. Because both awareness of intelligible extension and natural judgment depend on God, sensory representation would be entirely impossible without God. Of course, the conclusion that sense perception requires God is an obvious consequence of occasionalism. But as we have seen, Malebranche has independent arguments for why sense perception in particular requires divine agency.

7. Locke

Locke's interest in sense perception comes from a very different philosophical orientation than Descartes's or Malebranche's. For Locke, as for Gassendi and the Aristotelians, sense perception is necessary for gaining knowledge: without sense perception, we would lack the ideas out of which judgments are constructed. Fortunately, Locke thinks, we can take it for granted that sense perception is an accurate guide to the world. He reiterates the familiar Cartesian theme that because the faculty of sense perception is given to us by an omnipotent, omnibenevolent God, it must be truth conducive when used properly. Proper use may not, of course, include *scientific* use. In this, Locke agrees with Descartes. However, there is no other faculty superior to sense for achieving scientific knowledge: if sensation cannot ground science, this is because God did not design us with an eye toward scientific knowledge. Locke's account of what proper use of the human sensory faculties consists of goes substantially beyond the Cartesian view that the senses are intended solely to preserve the mind-body union. In the *Essay*, Locke is quite concerned to emphasize that God has fitted our faculties for the discovery of moral truths above all else: "Our Business here is not to know all things, but those which concern our Conduct" (*Essay* 1.1.6).

Locke's theory has far more in common with Gassendi's than with those of Descartes and Malebranche. But four differences are significant. First, for Locke sense perception *uses* ideas as well as producing them as fortunate by-products. He defines an idea as "whatsoever is the object of the understanding, when a man thinks" (*Essay* 1.1.8), and thinking includes perceiving (*Essay* 2.8.8). Perception and nonperceptual cognition, then, involve the same kind of mental representation. Although this simplifies his account of mental content significantly and makes it very easy to see why perception and hallucination are often indistinguishable, it also precludes the sort of disjunctivist treatment Gassendi favored. Second, Locke – here unlike Descartes, Malebranche, and the Aristotelians as well – has no interest in the "the Physical Consideration of the Mind," including the physiology of sense perception. Third, like Descartes and Malebranche, Locke distinguishes the representationality of primary and secondary qualities. Indeed, his account of mental representation is far clearer than Gassendi's (although that is not saying much). Finally, Locke is almost entirely unconcerned with sensory error. Indeed, it would be hard to discover, from reading the *Essay*, that sense perception is ever misleading.

On Locke's view, all mental content is built up from simple ideas. Simple ideas of sense represent those qualities that cause them under normal conditions.[22] Exactly how this representative function is performed is a little different for ideas of primary qualities and ideas of secondary qualities. On Locke's view, "the *Ideas of primary Qualities* of Bodies, *are Resemblances* of them, and their Patterns do really exist in the Bodies themselves" (*Essay* 2.8.15), whereas an idea of a secondary quality is "a bare effect of power" (*Essay* 2.8.25). Thus, my idea of the color of a tomato is the idea of red because it is the sort of idea typically acquired from red things, that is things with the appropriate primary-quality constitution. Locke can offer precisely the same explanation for the content of primary-quality ideas. My idea of the tower is the idea of a square thing because it is the sort of idea typically acquired from square things. But he can also say that ideas of primary qualities represent qualities in bodies via resemblance, so that the idea of the tower is the idea of something square because it resembles square things.

Simple ideas, then, represent those qualities of bodies they typically co-vary with. In some cases, they also resemble those qualities. In what initially looks like a weaker version of Gassendi's Epicurean claim that all appearances are true, Locke insists that simple ideas always represent successfully. But we shall see that Locke's claim is actually much stronger.

Locke takes it to be indisputable that the senses are at least largely accurate:

> I can no more doubt, whilst I read this, that I see white and black, and that something really exists, that causes that sensation in me, than that I write or move my hand; which is a certainty as great, as human nature is capable of, concerning the existence of anything, but a man's self alone, and of God.
> (*Essay* 4.11.2)

Our natural belief that sense perceptions derive from the external world needs no defense. It is more basic – and more certain – than any argument to the contrary. Nevertheless, Locke also offers arguments supporting it, two of which involve rather different appeals to God.

First, Locke argues, simple ideas of sensation must be adequate because we are entirely passive in acquiring them.[23] For "in simple *Ideas* . . . the mind is wholly confined to the Operation of things upon it; and can make to it self no simple *Idea*, more than what it has received" (*Essay* 2.30.2). Because we do not use our faculties in acquiring simple ideas, we cannot misuse them; and because God gave us those faculties, they cannot be misleading unless misused. Locke is careful to explain how this is consistent with the fact that our senses provide only limited knowledge:

> were our senses altered, and made much quicker and acuter, the appearance and outward scheme of things would have quite another face to us; and, I am apt to think, would be inconsistent with our being, or at least well-being, in this part of the universe which we inhabit . . . if by the help of such microscopical eyes (if I may so call them) a man could penetrate further than ordinary into the secret composition and radical texture of bodies, he would not make any great advantage by the change, if such an acute sight would not serve to conduct him to the market and exchange; if he could not see things he was to avoid, at a convenient distance; nor distinguish things he had to do with by those sensible qualities others do.
> (*Essay* 2.23.12)

This would be a natural place for Locke to discuss the fact that the senses occasionally misrepresent their objects, as well as represent them less than perfectly, but no such discussion occurs.

A second argument for the adequacy of all simple ideas involves God again. Ideas of sensation, Locke writes, are "designed to be the Marks, whereby we are to know, and distinguish Things, which we have to do with" (*Essay* 2.30.2). Simple ideas mark their causes because they "must be suitable to those Powers, [God] has placed in external Objects, or else they could not be produced in us" (*Essay* 2.32.14). Again, "being nothing but the effects of certain Powers in Things, fitted and ordained by GOD, to produce such Sensations in us, simple ideas cannot but be correspondent, and adequate to those Powers" (*Essay* 2.31.1).

As I have argued elsewhere,[24] Locke runs into difficulties here. Divine guarantee cannot underwrite the reliability of perception anywhere near as robustly as Locke suggests it can. The claim that simple ideas must correspond to their causes is ambiguous. If Locke means that simple ideas of red, as a type, correspond to the quality of redness because to mark something just *is* to be caused by it, then his claim is false. We do on occasion have simple ideas of red that are not caused by red things. On the other hand, if he means that a particular simple idea must correspond to the particular quality that caused it because for an idea to correspond to a quality just *is* to be caused by it, the claim is indisputable – but it will not do the philosophical work Locke needs it to do.

It is easiest to see what philosophical work the marking function of simple ideas does for Locke by example. Consider a man who is regularly caused to see yellow by objects that cause others to see blue. Locke explains that his idea of the color of that object successfully marks its object, and hence is adequate, because the man

> would be able as regularly to distinguish Things for his Use by those Appearances ... as if the Appearances, or *Ideas* in his Mind, received from those two Flowers, were exactly the same, with the *Ideas* in other Men's Minds.
> (*Essay* 2.32.15)

The idea type that steadily corresponds with an object type for me need not be the same as the idea type that steadily corresponds with that object type for you. We can "distinguish Things for [our] use," whether or not interperceiver correspondences are identical. But it *is* necessary for intraperceiver correspondences to be stable. We would not be able to navigate the world successfully if the flower that sometimes produced the idea of purple other times produced the idea of green, of the smell of gasoline, or the taste of soap. For the only way secondary-quality ideas can tell us about the qualities of things is via patterns of correspondence. To know that snow has a quality that produces an idea of whiteness in me tells me nothing (other than that an external world exists) if it does not tell me about the relations between that quality and qualities of previously encountered bodies. The sweetness of sugar, to choose another example, helps me distinguish it as edible only because *previous* sweet things have been edible. And the claim that simple ideas serve as guides for everyday life is central to the *Essay*. God has given us faculties that suffice for "the comfortable provision for this life and the way that leads to a better" (*Essay* 1.1.5). This cannot involve merely the trivial claim that all simple ideas of sensation do indeed have causes.

Further difficulties, and a reason to question the claim that sense perception is entirely passive, emerge when we look at Locke's most famous discussion of sense perception – the

Molyneux problem. This discussion occurs in chapter 2.9 of the *Essay*, titled "Of Perception," and almost at the very beginning Locke remarks that "in bare naked *perception*, the mind is, for the most part, only passive" (*Essay* 2.9.1). The bulk of the chapter addresses, albeit indirectly, the exceptions.

Locke's answer to the Molyneux problem is widely considered puzzling. Ideas of shape are simple ideas that can be received by more than one sense. Thus, his obvious answer to the Molyneux problem would be that the newly sighted blind man can immediately tell which is the cube and which the globe. But this is not what he says. Rather, Locke says that even assuming that the newly sighted blind man could distinguish the cube and the sphere by touch, he would not be able to identify them by sight without some training (*Essay* 2.9.8). This is because "the *Ideas we receive by sensation, are often* in grown People *alter'd by the Judgment*, without our taking notice of it" (*Essay* 2.9.8). For instance, because we are "accustomed to perceive, what kind of appearance convex Bodies are wont to make in us," our judgment transforms the idea of "a flat Circle variously shadow'd" into the idea of a sphere. More generally, "Judgment . . . by an habitual custom, alters the Appearances into their Causes" (*Essay* 2.9.8). This suggests something like the Cartesian view that a great deal of mental processing is required to get us from the two-dimensional information received on the retina to the perception of the size, shape, and distance of external objects. But unlike Descartes and Malebranche, Locke has no story to tell about how this works.

The Molyneux problem is important for understanding Locke because it threatens two of his central claims. First, it threatens any reading of the claim that simple ideas are real, true, and adequate on which it can do the epistemic work Locke needs it to do. For if the ideas involved in conscious sensation have been altered by judgment, we are not passive in acquiring them and hence they are not simple ideas. I see no good way to deal with this problem. Second, it threatens the transparency of the mental – the claim that it is "near a contradiction, to say that there are truths imprinted on the soul, which it perceives or understands not" (*Essay* 1.2.5). And this claim is crucial for his attack on innate knowledge. The literature contains a number of suggestions about this, but the important point for our purposes is that here Locke encounters a problem structurally similar to one found in Descartes. Both hold that all mental activity is *ipso facto* conscious, and both hold that perception involves a fair amount of mental activity. Both must also admit that we are not typically aware of having carried out all this activity. Locke does not address the problem as explicitly as Descartes, but it seems that he must give a similar answer. We can in principle be conscious of both the data acquired by perception and the habit that alters our judgments into their causes, although we are not typically aware of them.[25] We shall see that Leibniz – who alone of our philosophers is happy to allow for unconscious perception – is on much firmer ground here.

8. Leibniz

Leibniz stands apart from the philosophers discussed previously in ways that make him hard to integrate into any story. His metaphysical account of the world that is perceived by human minds is radically different from the roughly mechanist picture shared by Hobbes, Gassendi, Descartes, Malebranche, and Locke. This requires some explanation. Leibniz is a mechanist about the material world: that is, he holds that the material world obeys deterministic laws and that all causation in it is the collision of material bodies. However, for him the material world is ideal, and the ultimate objects of perception are not things that can have mechanical properties. And his account of the nature of the human mind differs just as radically. Descartes and Malebranche insist that consciousness is essential to the mind. And whereas Locke allows that minds might exist without thinking, he is just as suspicious as Descartes about the possibility of unconscious mental activity.[26] In contrast, Leibniz argues that the vast majority of mental activity is unconscious. Instead, for him, it is representation that is essential to cognitive activity.[27]

We began by looking at a neo-Aristotelian theory on which resemblance is the key component of representation. Some neo-Aristotelian theories, in fact, make the stronger claim that a kind of identity is required for representation. All the later philosophers we have discussed drop the identity claim, and all drop the claim that resemblance is necessary in the case of secondary-quality perception. Gassendi, at least, drops the claim that resemblance is required for the perception of size, shape, and motion as well.

Now, it seems clear that Leibniz should not claim that perceptual representation requires resemblance. For at the level of his deep metaphysics, there is no material world to possess the various primary and secondary qualities our perceptions purport to represent. And even at the level of the phenomena, Leibniz denies that bodies have qualities beyond extension, motion, and resistance – thus denying that there is anything in bodies resembling our secondary-quality sensations.[28] However, instead of abandoning the claim that perceptions represent their causes, Leibniz offers a reconstruction of it. In the course of an attack on the Cartesian, Lockean, and Malebranchean claim that the relation between sensations and their causes is arbitrary, Leibniz insists that

> there is a resemblance of a kind – not a perfect one which holds all the way through, but a resemblance in which one thing expresses another through some orderly relationship between them. Thus an ellipse . . . has some resemblance to the circle of which it is a projection . . . since there is a certain precise and natural relationship . . . there is a resemblance, i.e. a precise relationship, in the case of secondary qualities as well as of primary . . . pain does not resemble the movement of a pin; but it might thoroughly resemble the motions which the pin causes in our body, and might represent them in the soul.
>
> (*NE* 2.8)

This is not resemblance as we ordinarily understand it. Rather, what Leibniz is getting at is that the relationship between sensations and their causes is *intelligible*. It is governed by the principle of sufficient reason and hence cannot consist in a set of arbitrary psychophysical laws.

Elsewhere, Leibniz describes this relationship as one of expression. Expression does not require resemblance, as it is ordinarily understood. It may not even require isomorphism. However, it clearly *does* require that one can derive the state expressed from the state expressing it via some intelligible law. In a letter to Arnauld, for instance, Leibniz describes expression as "a constant and regular relation between what can be said about one and about the other."[29]

Expression is a much more general notion than perception, either in Leibniz's sense of the term or our own. For expression "is a genus of which natural perception, animal feeling, and intellectual knowledge are species."[30] In Leibniz's metaphysics, all the representative states of a substance are perceptions, whereas the underlying conative causes of transitions between states are appetitions.[31] In perception, each monad "mirrors" all the rest: more precisely, the states of each monad express the state of all other monads at that moment.[32] Perception and appetite are the two attributes essential to substance, so all substances have perceptions.

However, because Leibniz does not want to conclude that all substances are conscious – indeed, he thinks that consciousness is limited to humans – he denies that perceptions need be conscious. Indeed, on Leibniz's view, we are not conscious of the vast majority of our perceptions.[33] Even among the class of perceptions peculiar to individuals with sense organs – namely sensations – the vast majority are unconscious. But as well as distinguishing perception from sensation, Leibniz also distinguishes perception – "the inner state of the mind representing external things" – from *apperception* – "consciousness or the reflective knowledge of this inner state itself."[34] The distinction between perception and apperception is crucial to Leibniz's diagnosis of the Cartesian error of thinking that only human beings have sense perception. Descartes failed to distinguish perception from apperception, and hence failed to notice that although only humans are conscious of their sensations, they are not the only beings capable of sensation.

Perception, sensation, and intellectual knowledge are species of expression – but not all forms of expression are mental representations. The ellipse expresses the circle and the map expresses the terrain, but neither represents anything. What is crucial for mental representation is that it is the expression of many in one: many things – indeed, all the states of the universe – in one unified substance.[35] Leibniz writes,

> In natural perception and feeling it suffices that what is divisible and material and is found dispersed among several beings should be expressed or represented in a single indivisible being or in a substance which is endowed with a true unity. The possibility of such a representation of several things in one cannot be doubted, since our soul provides us with an example of it.[36]

Of course, in sensation we are not always conscious of the many that are expressed. Indeed, we are very rarely aware of the multiplicity expressed in a sensation even when we are conscious of the sensation itself. Sensations are not simple for Leibniz, as they are for Locke. Rather, they are composed of a vast multitude of *petites perceptions*: "a perception of light or colour of which we are aware is made up of many minute perceptions of which we are unaware" (*NE* 2.9). In most – if not all – cases, we cannot clearly distinguish the various members of this multitude.

Sensations are *relatively* distinct, as compared to the larger class of perceptions. When "perception is more distinct and accompanied by memory," it counts as sensation.[37] And we can make our sensations more distinct – that is isolate the *petites perceptions* they are composed of – through mental effort. Speaking of the perceptions of animals, Leibniz remarks that

> [w]e too have minute perceptions of which we are not aware in our present state. We could in fact become thoroughly aware of them and reflect on them, if we were not distracted by their multiplicity, which scatters the mind, and if bigger ones did not obliterate them or rather put them in the shade.
>
> (*NE* 2.9)

However, complete distinctness is only possible for God, who is uniquely aware of the fact that each of his singular representations is a singular representation and does not have sensation.[38] Some confusion will always remain in human sensation, and it is that confusion that explains why a certain sensation presents to us, say, the feeling of a painful pinprick rather than the collection of monadic states it really expresses.[39]

It is important to Leibniz to deny that the relationship between the sensation of pain and what it expresses is arbitrary. We may not be able to understand what the relationship is, but this does not mean that it is unintelligible; it means merely that we are unable to make the sensation sufficiently distinct. For God does not institute laws arbitrarily. However, Leibniz's theory seems to introduce arbitrariness at another point. Why is it that a state that confusedly expresses motions presents to us the feeling of pain, rather than something else? In other words, why does confused expression generate qualitative experience at all – and why do certain confused expressions constitute the qualitative experiences they do?[40] The notion of confusion does a great deal of work for Leibniz. As well as being supposed to explain the qualitative nature of experience, it explains why we seem to perceive unified objects like tables and chairs, when really each monad composing the table is represented individually; why we know some things better than others; and why some people have more knowledge than others, when we all represent everything that exists.[41]

I began by noting a series of questions that early modern theories of perception are designed to answer. It may be helpful to summarize Leibniz's answers to these questions, because he addresses them somewhat more obliquely than the other philosophers we have discussed. His metaphysics precludes any resemblance theory of representation, even one confined to ideas of primary qualities. In place of resemblance, Leibniz offers expression in a single, unified substance as the way in which representation occurs.

Due to his deep metaphysics, Leibniz is not required to answer our third question: how does a causal process with nonintentional starting points yield representational mental states? For sensations are not genuinely caused by external objects. Nor does he need to explain – as Descartes and Malebranche do – how innate ideas can be brought to bear on perceptual data. For there is no useful distinction to be drawn between innate mental content and content acquired in perception. Whatever the distinction between innate and acquired content exactly amounts to for Leibniz, it has something to do with the distinction between abstract or universal concepts and singular representations. There is no room for the sort of causal distinction Descartes, Locke, and Malebranche had in mind.

Our remaining two questions are these. Which aspects of perception are active, and which passive? To this, Leibniz can reply that *all* perception is active. In perception, the content perceived arises from our own soul, not the external world. One reason previous philosophers were concerned to delineate the extent to which perception is passive and the extent to which it is active is that insofar as perception is passive, it can be counted on not to mislead. But Leibniz is not terribly concerned with the possibility of perceptual error. Although he is deeply concerned with establishing a genuine distinction between well-founded phenomena and mere illusions, he has very little interest in explaining how we tell which is which in any particular case. In "On the Method of Distinguishing Real from Imaginary Phenomena," Leibniz provides a fairly standard and uninteresting set of criteria for distinguishing veridical perceptions from nonveridical ones: those perceptions that are more forceful and vivacious, and that cohere with the rest of experience, should be treated as veridical.[42] These criteria provide us with, at best, moral certainty rather than metaphysical certainty.[43] Nevertheless, over the course of a long life, there is no need to be concerned that the senses are unreliable.[44] This is roughly the answer Descartes provided at the end of the Sixth Meditation.[45]

9. Conclusion

The account I have presented here is not a simple linear progression. The six philosophers I have discussed are all attempting to explain how the perceptual representation of a mechanist and intrinsically unintelligible world is possible (although Leibniz is an outlier because he concludes that such perception would be impossible). But they do so in very different ways. They differ about the ontological basis of the ability to perceive: Hobbes, Gassendi, and perhaps Locke holding that it belongs to a material thing, and Descartes, Malebranche, Leibniz, and again perhaps Locke holding that it belongs to an immaterial substance. They differ about what representation consists in and about the extent to which mental representations have their genesis in perception. They differ about where the boundary between perception and judgment should be drawn and – in part as a result – about the extent to which perception is reliable and about what proper use of the human perceptual apparatus consists in. These differences reflect larger differences in their philosophical outlooks. For although theories of perception do influence the philosophical systems of their adherents to some extent, for the most part they are designed with an eye toward the larger metaphysical and epistemological goals of their authors.

Notes

1 Galileo, for instance, says that "tastes, odors, colors and so on . . . reside only in the consciousness" (ed. Stillman Drake: *Discoveries and Opinions of Galileo*. Garden City, NJ: Anchor Books, 1957, p. 257, from *The Assayer*). Locke holds the more sophisticated view that secondary qualities are really in bodies as powers to produce ideas but that ideas do not resemble the powers.

2 See, for example, Eustachius, *Physics* 3.1.2, who treats "species" and "image" as synonyms. Eustachius a Sancto Paolo. *Summa philosophiae quadripartita: de rebus dialecticis, moralibus, physicis, & metaphysicis*. Paris: Pierre Bilaine, 1620.

3 See, for example, Suárez, *De anima* 3.2.21, ed. Salvador Castellote. Madrid: Editorial Labor, 1981.

4 Eustachius, for instance, defends intentional species, thus suggesting that the need for them is at least in question. See *Physics* 3.1.2, which gives the rudiments of the argument from my next paragraph.

5 That is, we are passive with respect to the *content* of sense perception. Aristotelians need not deny that sensation is a form of activity.

6 At least, they all hold this with respect to the physiology of sense perception; Descartes, of course, would deny that contact is involved in its mental aspect.

7 I owe this suggestion to Stewart Duncan.

8 The earlier *Elements of Law* is not so obviously reductionist. There, Hobbes writes, "the said image or color is but an apparition unto us of that motion, agitation, or alteration, which the object worketh in the brain, or spirits, or some internal substance of the head" (*EL* 1.2.4). That is, color is an apparition of motion rather than motion itself. Here, Hobbes says nothing of interest about the relation between the motion and the apparition.

9 For more on this, see Ian Prinz, "Hobbes on Light and Vision," in Tom Sorell (ed.), *The Cambridge Companion to Hobbes*. New York: Cambridge University Press, 1996.

10 One respect in which *De corpore* and *Leviathan* differ is that *Leviathan* emphasizes the heart as the relevant internal organ: there Hobbes speaks of an "endeavour of the heart to deliver itself" (*L* 1.4). In contrast, although *De corpore* does refer to the heart it also makes clear that the brain "is a common organ to all the senses" (*DCo* 25.10).

11 One might dispute this on the grounds that because Hobbes argues that memory and imagination are two different names for the same thing, correlating the data of the various senses requires imagination and hence involves mental activity. However, I am inclined to go the other way and say that for Hobbes, even imagination does not involve genuine mental activity. Thanks to Stewart Duncan for this suggestion.

12 That the soul is entirely material – or at least, that we can only know the immaterial soul by faith – is suggested in the *Disquisitio Metaphysica*, Gassendi's *Objections* and *Counter Objections* to the

Meditations. See, for example, 3.369a, 3.386a. The posthumous *Syntagma Philosophicum* argues that there must be an immaterial soul because the mind performs three functions a material thing could never perform: it reflects on itself, entertains ideas of genuine universals, and has ideas of immaterial substances (2.440b–451b). None of these three functions, of course, are involved in perception. For more on this, see my "Gassendi on Human Knowledge of the Mind." *Archiv für Geschichte der Philosophie* 87.1 (2005), 1–21. All references to Gassendi's work are to his *Opera Omnia* (Lyon, 1655), 6 volumes.

13 The theory of perception is logically prior to the truth of the appearances. However, the truth of the appearances appears earlier in Gassendi's work and so must be the influence.
14 In fact, nothing like the primary quality–secondary quality distinction does any real work for Gassendi. See my "Primary and Secondary Qualities: Gassendi, Charleton and Seventeenth-Century Atomism," in Larry Nolan (ed.), *Primary and Secondary Qualities: The Modern Debate*. Oxford and New York: Oxford University Press, 2011.
15 This is not entirely fair. Composite bodies do possess some qualities – for instance gravity, magnetism, and electricity – that are not sensible qualities, and hence cannot be located in perceivers. However, the vast majority of the qualities Gassendi discusses are sensible.
16 Perception of size and distance requires judgment because the size of the retinal image is a product of object size and object distance jointly. Perception of shape requires judgment because perceived shape corrects for perspectival distortion.
17 Given that they are irresistible, they *must* be truth conducive; otherwise, God would be a deceiver.
18 See, for example, AT VIIIA 7; CSM I 194–5: "By the term 'thought' I understand all the things that we are conscious of happening in us, insofar as we are conscious of them."
19 Malebranche also thinks that there are much simpler natural judgments, such as when we feel pain as in our bodies: "men not only judge through a natural judgment that pain, for example, is in their hand, they also judge it by a free judgment; not only do they feel it there, they also believe it to be there" (*Search* 1.14.2/LO 69). Parsimony, together with Malebranche's broader ontological commitments, suggests that these judgments should be attributed to God as well. But Malebranche offers no reason to believe that we are incapable of making this simpler sort of natural judgment ourselves.
20 This requires some qualification. Sensations occur in us in accordance with the laws of the mind-body union instituted by God, but they do not require the active intervention of God performing "natural judgments" for us. If I made no natural judgment, all I would see when I looked at the coffee cup is variously colored light, located nowhere in particular – not even outside me.
21 Nicolas Malebranche, *Dialogues on Metaphysics and on Religion*. Ed. Nicholas Jolley and David Scott. Cambridge: Cambridge, 1997.
22 Locke is, I think, committed to giving a somewhat different account of how simple ideas of reflection represent, but that is outside the scope of this chapter.
23 Adequacy, for Locke, is a technical term: ideas are adequate just in case they "perfectly represent those Archetypes, which the Mind supposes them taken from; which it intends them to stand for, and to which it refers them" (*Essay* 4.31.1). He also offers technical definitions for the truth and reality of ideas, but adequacy is the core notion: all simple ideas are adequate, and adequacy implies truth and reality.
24 See my "Locke's Problem Concerning Perception," *Philosophy and Phenomenological Research* 77.3 (November 2008), 705–24.
25 One might add that Malebranche is pushed by this into the unappealing conclusion that such natural judgments are actually the result of God's causal activity, not our own. However, this would be somewhat unfair because in Malebranche's case, the move he makes to allow apparently unconscious perceptual processing fits in very well with his overarching schema.
26 See, for example, *Essay* 2.1.10.
27 This point is emphasized by Alison Simmons, "Changing the Cartesian Mind: Leibniz on Sensation, Representation and Consciousness." *The Philosophical Review* 110.1 (January 2001), 331–75. I say "cognitive activity" rather than "thought" because for Leibniz, thought is something over and above perception and apperception.
28 "On the Elements of Natural Science," in Gottfried Wilhelm Leibniz, *Philosophical Papers and Letters*. Ed. Leroy E. Loemker. Dordrecht, Holland: D. Reidel, 1969. PPL 277.
29 Letter to Arnauld of 9 October 1687; *PPL* 339.
30 Letter to Arnauld of 9 October 1687; *PPL* 339.
31 *Principles of Nature and Grace* 2; *PPL* 636.
32 Monads also express all their own past and future states, but this is not relevant for our purposes.

33 *Monadology* 14; *PPL* 644.
34 *PNG* 4; *PPL* 637.
35 *PNG* 2; *PPL* 636. Because all substances are mental for Leibniz – material substances are impossible – it is unnecessary to say *one unified thinking substance*.
36 Letter to Arnauld of 9 October 1687; *PPL* 339.
37 *Monadology* 19; *PPL* 644.
38 *Monadology* 13; *PPL* 640.
39 This is not Leibniz's only way of explaining how perception misrepresents, but it is an important one. Another tactic is suggested in his discussion of the Molyneux question:

> when we are deceived by a painting . . . we substitute one cause for another and believe that what comes merely from a flat painting actually comes from a body. . . . This confusion of the effect with the real or putative cause frequently occurs in other sorts of judgments too. This is how we come to believe that it is by an immediate real influence that we sense our bodies and the things which touch them, and move our arms, taking this influence to constitute the interaction between the soul and the body; whereas really all that we sense or alter in that way is what is within us.
>
> (*NE* 2.9)

40 A roughly parallel question arises for Descartes on readings that take sensations to have representational content.
41 See Benson Mates, *The Philosophy of Leibniz*. Oxford: Oxford University Press, 1989, pp. 200–1.
42 G 7.319. C. J. Gerhardt (ed.), *Die Philosophichen Schriften von Gottfried Wilhelm Leibniz*. Vol. 7. Leipzig: Alfred Lorenz Buchhandlung, 1931.
43 G 7.321.
44 G 7.323.
45 I would like to thank Paul Lodge for extensive help with this section.

11
CONSCIOUSNESS
Steven Nadler

Let me begin this chapter with a bold but, I believe, justified claim: the problem of consciousness begins in the seventeenth century. To be sure, ancient philosophers (above all, Aristotle) addressed various topics in the philosophy of mind, including perceptual awareness. And medieval thinkers, in their investigations of the nature of cognition, sensation, and volition, had much to say about intentionality and other features of conscious states.[1] But what we now regard as the "hard problem of consciousness," to use a well-known phrase,[2] is something that did not occupy philosophers in a serious way until the early modern period.[3]

There are many issues that could be considered in a chapter on consciousness in seventeenth century philosophy: intentionality or the object-directedness of mental (representational) states, sensory versus intellectual awareness, the role of ideas in perception and cognition, and so on. Moreover, the philosophical investigation of consciousness in this period was recognized to have important metaphysical, moral, and even theological ramifications. In Locke's view, consciousness is right at the heart of a proper account of personal identity; it therefore also has bearing on moral identity and responsibility, as well as on questions regarding immortality and eschatology (because presumably eternal reward and punishment would be meaningless unless they are being meted out to the same person or consciousness who lived the virtuous or vicious life in the first place). However, as important as all these issues are – in fact, just because they are so important and complex – they will not be directly addressed in this chapter.

I also want to distinguish the problem of consciousness from the problem of self-consciousness. As we shall see, early modern philosophers themselves often do not sufficiently discriminate between what makes a mental state a *conscious* mental state and what explains my knowing that it is *my* conscious state – between being consciously aware of x and being conscious that I am aware of x. Therefore, sometimes what appears to be an account of consciousness *per se* is really an account of self-consciousness. My focus will be on the relatively narrow but extraordinarily complicated question of what is consciousness *per se*. When Chalmers says that "the really hard problem of consciousness is the problem of experience," and particularly its "subjective aspect," what he is referring to is the familiar but ineffable process of consciously experiencing something (1995: 202). It is the raw qualitative awareness or subjectivity that Nagel (1974) has called "what it is like to be" and what Burge (2007) has called "phenomenal consciousness" (to distinguish it from "access consciousness").

The hard problem is, how are we to explain phenomenal consciousness? What gives rise to it and accounts for the difference between a conscious mental state and a nonconscious one? And why are some beings conscious whereas others, apparently, are not? Although contemporary philosophers and neuroscientists continue to wrestle with these questions, they were, in fact, first isolated and addressed in a sustained and (sometimes) systematic manner by seventeenth century philosophers. Thus, Pierre Gassendi, in his tedious but, it must be said, sometimes insightful objections to Descartes's *Meditations*, wants to know what exactly is that thing that thinks, and what is the nature of its substance that allows it to be a thinking thing?

> When you go on to say that you are a thinking thing, then we know what you are saying; but we knew it already, and it was not what we were asking you to tell us. Who doubts that you are thinking? What we are unclear about, what we are looking for, is that inner substance of yours whose property is to think. Your conclusion should be related to this inquiry, and should tell us not that you are a thinking thing, but what sort of thing this "you" who thinks really is. If we are asking about wine, and looking for the kind of knowledge which is superior to common knowledge, it will hardly be enough for you to say "wine is a liquid thing, which is compressed from grapes, white or red, sweet, intoxicating", and so on. You will have to attempt to investigate and somehow explain its internal substance, showing how it can be seen to be manufactured from spirits, tartar, the distillate, and other ingredients mixed together in such and such quantities and proportions. Similarly, given that you are looking for knowledge of yourself which is superior to common knowledge (that is, the kind of knowledge we have had up till now), you must see that it is certainly not enough for you to announce that you are a thing that thinks and doubts and understands etc. You should carefully scrutinize yourself and conduct a kind of chemical investigation of yourself, if you are to succeed in uncovering and explaining to us your internal substance. If you provide such an explanation, we shall ourselves doubtless be able to investigate whether or not you are better known than the body whose nature we know so much about through anatomy, chemistry, so many other sciences, so many senses and so many experiments.
> (AT VII 276–7; CSM II 192–3)

It might seem easy to accuse Gassendi of making a category mistake here. After all, the dualist Descartes wants to say that, because of the essential differences between mind and body and thus the unbridgeable gap between mental and mechanical explanations, we cannot possibly provide a mechanistic or "chemical" investigation of the mind's activities. But this would be to miss Gassendi's point. Although his question is surely informed by his own materialist tendencies about the mind, what he is demanding from Descartes is not a mechanistic account of consciousness. Rather, he wants an account of consciousness that makes the cause and origin of consciousness and its properties as clear as a mechanistic or chemical account does for wine and its properties. Such an account of consciousness need not be framed in terms of matter and motion, but it must do the same kind of explanatory work and incorporate the study of consciousness into the domain of the natural (but not necessarily the physical) sciences. It is an important challenge that Gassendi issues here, a request for the scientific basis of consciousness, and it is a shame that Descartes does not take it more seriously.[4] As we shall see, the so-called father of modern philosophy did a better job of identifying what it was that needed explaining than recognizing what would count as a satisfying explanation of it.

1. Descartes

One of the most famous sentences in the history of philosophy, the fulcrum with which Descartes hopes to establish new and secure foundations for the sciences, also represents the beginning of the study of consciousness in the modern period. It is, in fact, a kind of discovery of the datum of consciousness itself. When Descartes, in the *Discourse on Method*, proclaims "I think, therefore I am" (*je pense, donc je suis* or, in the more famous phrase from the Latin translation of the work, *cogito, ergo sum*), he thereby takes as the starting point of philosophical inquiry what he believes to be the most evident, transparent, and accessible set of facts of all: his own thoughts. In the *Meditations on First Philosophy*, as he pursues his epistemological and ontological investigations more deeply and asks what exactly he, in the midst of his hyperbolic doubt, can conclude with certainty that he is, he confidently concludes, "Thinking . . . A thing that thinks. A thing that doubts, understands, affirms, denies, is willing, is unwilling, and also imagines and has sensory perceptions" (AT VII 27–8; CSM II 18–9).

Descartes's achievement in the Second Meditation is to direct our attention to the indubitable presence constituted by the contents of the mind, that is consciousness itself. For Descartes, thought is the principal attribute or property of the immaterial substance that is the soul, and the soul's thinking includes all the sensory phenomena, imaginings, beliefs, volitions, doubts, intellectual conceivings, and other immediately accessible data that fill the theater of the mind. Although he admits that it is quite hard to define just what thought is, he insists that it is the easiest thing in the world to experience, basically because it is experience itself and is right there before us. As Descartes has Eudoxus say in the dialogue *The Search After Truth*, "to know what doubt is, what thought is . . . we [do not] have to rack our brains." There are, he continues,

> some things which are made more obscure by our attempts to define them: since they are very simple and clear, they are perceived and known just on their own, and there is no better way of knowing and perceiving them.

The only way, in fact, in which we can learn about such things is "by ourselves: what convinces us of them is simply our own experience or awareness – that awareness or internal testimony which everyone experiences within himself when he ponders on such matters" (AT X 523–4; CSM II 417–8).

Descartes does, in fact, define thought and identifies it with that "awareness or internal testimony" itself. That is, thinking, for Descartes, is defined by consciousness: "By the term 'thought', I understand everything which we are aware of [*nobis consciis*] as happening within us, in so far as we have awareness [*conscientia*] of it" (AT VIII 7; CSM I 195). There are no thoughts that are not episodes of conscious awareness, no nonconscious mental events: "There can be nothing in the mind, in so far as it is a thinking thing, of which it is not aware [*conscia*] . . . we cannot have any thought of which we are not aware at the very moment when it is in us" (AT VII 246; CSM II 171). And because, for Descartes, the essence of mind (as *res cogitans*) is thinking, it follows that the mind is always thinking and, therefore, always consciously active and having conscious thoughts.

Descartes does not have much more to say about the nature of consciousness. As we have seen, he rejects Gassendi's demand for a "chemical investigation" or explanation of consciousness. He does note, however, that what consciousness involves is basically thought thinking about itself. In his conversation with Frans Burman, he reportedly claimed that "to be conscious [*conscium esse*] is both to think and to reflect on one's thought." Moreover, this reflection on a thought or mental event is simultaneous with the mental event itself; it is not a subsequent memory of an earlier thought: "It is false that this reflection cannot occur while the previous thought is still there." The way Descartes continues his remarks here suggests that the reflection that constitutes the awareness accompanying a conscious thought involves a concomitant but second-order, even voluntary, thought directed at a primary thought distinct from it:

> This is because . . . the soul is capable of thinking of more than one thing at the same time, and of continuing with a particular thought which it has. It has the power to reflect on its thoughts as often as it likes, and to be aware of its thought in this way.
> (AT V 149; CSMK 335)

However, other comments by Descartes suggest that phenomenal consciousness should be distinguished from an explicit, higher-order reflection directed at one's thinking, in part because such a second-order thought would indeed occur subsequent to the original thought that is its object. Knowing what thought is, he says,

> does not require reflective knowledge or the kind of knowledge that is acquired by means of demonstrations; still less does it require knowledge of reflective knowledge, i.e., knowing that we know, and knowing that we know that we know, and so on ad infinitum. . . . It is quite sufficient that we should know it by that internal awareness [*cognitione illa interna*] which always precedes reflective knowledge. This inner awareness of one's thought and existence is so innate in all men that . . . we cannot fail to have it.
> (AT V 422; CSM II 285)

Although much remains obscure here – particularly regarding whether in this passage Descartes, when he refers to knowing "what thought is [*quid sit cogitatio*]," is talking about the immediate awareness of or acquaintance with one's thinking that characterizes phenomenal consciousness, or about a more cognitive grasp (or implicit, even propositional knowledge) of what thought is[5] – it does seem to be the former that he has in mind. Consciousness, then, appears primarily to be a kind of immediate self-relation that is an essential feature of any mental state; it does not require the effort of forming a second thought directed at a first thought.[6] My conscious awareness of an external object (an apple, for example) would involve both my perception of that object and the perception's own reflection on itself. The mind is thereby "thinking of more than one thing at the same time" insofar as it is thinking of both the apple and its own thinking of the apple, and doing so by the same act of thinking. That is, each act of thought directed at an external object would also be directed at itself and thus have both its external object (in this case, the apple) and an internal object (itself, the act of thinking of the apple). Or, as one scholar puts it, "whenever I think of object x . . . there is [for Descartes] only one act, the act of thinking of x, which has x as its primary object and itself as its secondary object" (Radner 1988: 446). Writing about the conscious awareness that accompanies all acts of volition, Descartes says that

> we have ideas not only of all that is in our intellect, but also of all that is in the will. For we cannot will anything without knowing that we will it, nor could we know this without an idea; but I do not claim that the idea is different from the action itself.
>
> (AT III 295; CSMK 172)

Descartes makes this same point in his *Passions of the Soul*: "It is certain that we cannot will anything without perceiving *by the same means* [*par mesme moyen*] that we are willing it" (AT XI 343; CSM I 335–6, my emphasis).[7]

This distinction between phenomenal consciousness as first-order awareness involving a mental act reflecting on itself and explicit reflection as a second-order act of thinking directed at a first-order act will form the core of what is the most important discussion of consciousness among the Cartesians in the seventeenth century.

2. Arnauld

Antoine Arnauld was a Catholic theologian and the intellectual leader of the embattled Jansenist movement in France. He was also one of the most talented and analytically gifted philosophical minds in the second half of the century. Although committed to many aspects of the Cartesian philosophy, Arnauld was not much of a system builder. Rather, most of his philosophizing took place as a critic in polemical encounters with the thought of others, most prominently Malebranche and Leibniz. And it was in his opening attack on Malebranche's major treatises, *The Search After Truth* and *Treatise on Nature and Grace*, and particularly in opposition to Malebranche's theory of ideas and the doctrine of the Vision in God, that Arnauld presents his views on consciousness.

The key to Arnauld's account of consciousness lies in his notion of "virtual reflection [*réflexion virtuelle*]." In *On True and False Ideas* (1683), Arnauld insists that every perceptual act (taken broadly to mean not only acts of perception *per se* but also any thought activity whatsoever) is a conscious act, that is it is accompanied by awareness. There are no nonconscious mental states. One cannot perceive or think of something without being aware that one is perceiving or thinking of something. "The thought that our soul has of itself" is a constant feature of mental life, because

> whatever it is that I am knowing, I know that I know it, by means of a certain virtual reflection which accompanies all my thoughts. . . . I thus know myself while knowing other things. And, in effect, it is principally this which, it seems, distinguishes intelligent beings from those which are not intelligent – the former *sunt conscia sui et suae operationis*, the latter are not.
>
> (Arnauld 1775: 184–5)

Adding a bit more explanatory detail, he says that

> our thought or perception is essentially reflective on itself, or, as it is said more aptly in Latin, *est sui conscia*. For I never think without knowing that I am thinking. I never know a square without my knowing that I know it; I never

see the sun, or, to put the matter beyond all doubt, I never seem to see the sun without my being certain that I seem to see it. . . . [A]t the same time that I conceive [something], I know that I am conceiving it.

(Arnauld 1775: 204)

More explicitly than Descartes, Arnauld accounts for consciousness by insisting that every mental act is reflective upon itself and thus accompanied by awareness. Every perception, in addition to being the perception of some external object, is also turned in upon itself and has itself (an act of the mind) as its (internal) object. Virtual reflection does not involve a second perceptual act distinct from the first and directed at it; rather, it is the self-awareness possessed by the first-order perception itself. Self-reflection is an essential part of any mental act, identical with the act, and the immediate awareness of a perception is not an experience distinct from simply having a perception. Whenever one perceives, no special effort is required to be aware *that one is perceiving* and thus for the perceiving to be a *conscious* experience. Arnauld thus, like Descartes albeit in clearer terms, distinguishes the virtual reflection that accompanies every perceptual act from what he calls "explicit reflection [*réflexion expresse*]," a second-order act of perception directed at the first and having it as its primary object: "Besides this reflection which can be called virtual, which is found in all perceptions, there is another, more explicit reflection by which we examine our perception by means of another perception" (Arnauld 1775: 204). Virtual reflection necessarily and involuntarily accompanies every perception; explicit reflection is a deliberate act performed upon one's first-order perception and has the latter as its intended object. With virtual reflection, I am (consciously) perceiving the world; with explicit reflection, I am (consciously) perceiving my perceiving of the world (the act of explicitly reflecting on another act of perception, because it is itself an act of perception, would have to be characterized by virtual reflection as well).

In the previous passages, Arnauld seems to stress the first-person content of awareness ("I know that I know it") and the presence therein of the self ("I thus know myself"). This might seem to suggest that the process of virtual reflection is meant to explain *self-*consciousness. This may be misleading, however. It is not clear that Arnauld believes that the "I" or self is explicitly a part of the content of first-order consciousness. Possibly, virtual reflection only lays the foundation for self-consciousness, which itself occurs at the level of explicit reflection. The proper content of virtual reflection when I am perceiving a table would thus be only "Here is a table presentation" (or "table awareness is taking place"), but not "*I* am perceiving a table"; the latter would be the content of an explicit reflection.[8] Be that as it may, even if virtual reflection does account for some low-level kind of self-consciousness, it is intended primarily to explain phenomenal consciousness.

Cartesians like Arnauld, following their philosophical master, focus on consciousness solely as a mental phenomenon, something belonging to the human mind independently of what may or may not be happening in the human body. For Descartes and his followers, there is no organic basis for consciousness. Although there are many conscious mental states that the mind would not have were it not united to a body – sensations, memories, imaginations, passions – the fact that they *are* conscious states bears no relationship to the kind of body with which the mind is united. This is a result of Cartesian dualism's ontological divide between mind and body. Although Descartes allows for a causal relationship between the mental and the physical and a divinely instituted providential correlation between type-states of the mind and type-states of the body, he does not envision any aspect of the *nature* of a mental state *qua* mental state – such as its being a conscious state – as having its explanation in or being the expression of any aspect of the nature of the body. Moreover, for Cartesians human beings are the only conscious beings in nature. This is because nonhuman animals lack souls. They are only machines, purely material automata that, although capable of sensory and affective responses to the world around them, are not endowed with consciousness proper. Both of these assumptions will be questioned in a serious way by Spinoza and Leibniz, erstwhile admirers of the Cartesian philosophy who, in their own mature systems, offer profound corrections to it.

3. Spinoza

It is generally believed that Spinoza, although he has much to say of value regarding the nature of the mind itself and its relationship to the body, even foreshadowing contemporary neuroscientific accounts of certain types of mental states,[9] nonetheless fails miserably to offer a coherent account of consciousness. As a matter of fact, although Spinoza may not explicitly offer an account of consciousness – it is not the subject of any proposition in the *Ethics* – he does appear to have at hand an explanation of consciousness, indeed a rather sophisticated one that depicts consciousness, like all elements of the mind for Spinoza, as deeply grounded in certain functional aspects of the body.

First, a brief review of Spinoza's conception of the human mind itself and its relationship to the human body: in Spinoza's metaphysics, there is the one, infinite, eternal, necessarily existing substance ("God, or Nature"). This substance has infinitely many attributes, but we have knowledge of only two of them: thought and extension. Whatever else exists is either an infinite or a finite mode of substance – or, more specifically, an infinite or finite mode of one of the attributes of substance.

Every finite mode of every attribute has a corresponding mode under the attribute of thought. This is the upshot of *Ethics* 2p3: "In God, there is necessarily an idea, both of his essence and of everything that necessarily follows from his essence" (*E* 2p3). For our purposes, what this means is that for every finite mode of the attribute of extension – that is every individual material body – there is a corresponding finite mode – or "idea" – in thought. That idea has that body as its object and is its "mind." This is true of macrobodies and their corresponding ideas, but it is also true of the constituent material parts of any macrobody, each of which is itself a body and thus will have a corresponding idea within the macroidea (or mind) of the macrobody. (Note that this doctrine also implies that for every finite mode of the attribute of thought, there is a corresponding finite mode or idea in thought; or, in other words, for every idea, there is an idea that has that first idea as its object.) The explanation for this correlation between bodies and states of bodies, on the one hand, and minds and states of minds, on the other hand, is Spinoza's monism:

> A mode of extension and the idea of that mode are one and the same thing, but expressed in two ways. . . . For example, a circle existing in nature and the idea of the existing circle . . . are one and the same thing, which is explained through different attributes.
>
> (*E* 2p7s)

What this means is that every single body in nature has a corresponding idea or mind. As Spinoza says, referring to the propositions he has established about the basics of the human mind-body relationship,

> the things we have shown so far are completely general and do not pertain more to man than to other Individuals, all of which, though in different degrees, are nevertheless animate. For of each thing there is necessarily an idea in God.
>
> (E 2p13s)

And any events in any particular body will be expressed modally by affections in that body's mind. Or, to paraphrase Spinoza, whatever happens in the object of the idea constituting a mind will be perceived by that mind, or there will necessarily be an idea of that thing in the mind. All bodies, in other words, have representational states associated with them; and what those representational states are of – at least in the most immediate sense, what they are expressions or reflections of – are the corresponding states of the correlative body.

It follows from this that the human mind is nothing but the mode in thought that corresponds to the mode in extension that is the human body. Or, more simply, the human mind is nothing but the idea of the human body (E 2p11; E 2p13). It is constituted by being the idea of a particular kind of extended entity, one that is generically – as a parcel of extension and a certain relatively stable pattern of motion and rest among its parts – no different from any other kind of extended entity. And given the parallelism, what is true of the individual considered as a body under extension will also be true of that individual considered as an idea or mind under thought. We thus have the following setup: all physical bodies in nature are animate in the sense of having associated minds or representational states. And the human mind is simply an expression in thought of the same thing that expresses itself in extension as a human body.

The first thing that is clear is that being conscious for Spinoza is not identical to simply having or being an idea. Merely having an intentional state is not *ipso facto* to have a conscious state. This is true even if, for Spinoza, all intentional states, all mental states, are indeed conscious states; even if they are all *necessarily* conscious states; and even if every individual in nature is, by virtue of having a mind corresponding to its body, not only animate but also conscious. Many things that Spinoza says appear strongly to support this distinction between idea and conscious idea.[10]

The most natural reading of Spinoza's view of consciousness – the one that is almost unanimously found in the scholarly literature (or at least among those writers who do think that Spinoza does indeed have an account) – is that according to which consciousness is tantamount to having an idea of an idea.[11] Given the terms of Spinoza's ontology, this aspect of his system does indeed seem perfectly well suited for making sense of the awareness of our mental states (as well as the awareness of the objects of those mental states) in which consciousness consists.

Spinoza first introduces the notion of ideas of ideas (*ideae idearum*) in Ethics 2p20d and 2p21 as yet another consequence of the universal parallelism. It is something that follows from the fact that (according to E 2p3) there is an idea in God for every affection or mode of every attribute, including the attribute of thought. Just as there is an idea for every mode of extension, every body, so too is there an idea, or a mode of thought, for every idea or mode of thought, with the former having the latter as its object:

> E 2p20: There is also in God an idea, or knowledge [*cognitio*], of the human mind, which follows in God in the same way and is related to God in the same way as the idea, or knowledge, of the human body.
>
> Dem.: Thought is an attribute of God (by 2p1), and so (by 2p3) there must necessarily be in God an idea both of [NS: thought] and of all its affections, and consequently (by 2p11) of the human mind also. Next, this idea, or knowledge, of the mind does not follow in God insofar as He is infinite, but insofar as He is affected by another idea of a singular thing (by 2p9). But the order and connection of ideas is the same as the order and connection of causes (by 2p7). Therefore, this idea, or knowledge, of the mind follows in God and is related to God in the same way as the idea, or knowledge, of the body, q.e.d.

In the scholium to E 2p21, after demonstrating that "this idea of the mind is united to the mind in the same way as the mind is united to the body," Spinoza notes that

> the idea of the mind ... and the mind itself follow in God from the same power of thinking and the same necessity. For the idea of the mind, i.e., the idea of the idea, is nothing but the form of the idea insofar as this is considered as a mode of thinking without relation to the object.

And what is true of the mind *qua* idea of the body is also true of every idea within (or constitutive of) the mind: each is also attended by an idea of an idea (i.e. an idea of itself). In *E* 2p22, we are told that "the human mind perceives [*percipit*] not only the affections of the body, but also the ideas of these affections"; but the ideas of the affections of the body just are the constitutive ideas of the mind, and so for the mind to perceive them is just for each of them to be the object of an idea. Finally, *E* 2p23 states that "the mind does not know itself, except insofar as it perceives the ideas of the affections of the body."

Sometimes the ideas-of-ideas doctrine is interpreted as meaning that every idea is the object of a distinct, second-order idea. But this cannot be right. Spinoza claims that there is, at some level, an identity between the idea of an idea and the idea that is its object. Just as an extended body and the idea of that extended body are one and the same thing conceived under two different attributes, so too the idea of the mind or of any other idea and the idea that is its object "are one and the same thing [*una eademque*] which is conceived under one and the same attribute, viz. Thought" (*E* 2p21s). This does not necessarily mean that the idea of an idea and its idea-*ideatum* are numerically identical as modes of thinking. But Spinoza does explicitly say that an idea of an idea and its idea-*ideatum* are "united"; the idea of an idea is nothing but the "form of the idea," and thus is in one sense inseparable from it. This is certainly an obscure element of Spinoza's thought, but it seems to mean that the occurrence of an idea of an idea is part of the same event as the occurrence of the idea, that one cannot exist without the other insofar as they both constitute essential elements of the idea event – in short, there cannot be an idea without an idea of an idea. By contrast, a second-order idea would presumably be distinct from the idea that is its object, with the latter capable in principle of existing without the former. Perhaps, if Spinoza's ideas of ideas are to explain consciousness, they will have more in common with the first-order self-reflection or virtual reflection of an idea found in Descartes and Arnauld rather than the explicit reflection that requires a second-order idea directed at the first. However, according to the ideas-of-ideas doctrine, there presumably still is a second idea involved, albeit one that occurs at the same level or order as the original idea and is inseparable from it (just as the mind and the body, although identical and inseparable, are still two different modal expressions).

There is some highly suggestive evidence that Spinoza sees the ideas-of-ideas doctrine as an account of consciousness. Perhaps the most explicit of these appears in *Ethics* 4p8. In this proposition, Spinoza argues that "the knowledge of good and evil is nothing but an affect of Joy or Sadness insofar as we are conscious of it [*ejus sumus conscii*]." The affects of joy or sadness are, respectively, increases or decreases in an individual's striving or power of acting; and we call an external thing good or evil insofar as we perceive that it affects us with joy or sadness. Knowing that something is good or evil, then, is a matter of cognizing the affect that it brings about – or, in Spinoza's words, having an idea of the joy or sadness in the mind that is the correlate of the affect in the body caused by the external thing. To explain what this idea of a mental affect is – which he here identifies with being *conscious* of the affect – he refers the reader back to E 2p21, where he explains the notion of an idea of an idea.

Much of the discussion over Spinoza's ideas-of-ideas doctrine as an account of consciousness has orbited around the question of the extent of consciousness for Spinoza. Whether one is willing to accept the ideas-of-ideas doctrine as his account of consciousness has often depended on whether one is also willing to attribute to Spinoza two particular theses: first, the thesis that every thing in nature is a conscious being, or that all minds or all ideas correlated with all bodies are conscious minds; and second, the thesis that all states or ideas in the human mind are conscious states or ideas. Descartes, we know, rejects the first thesis but accepts the second. But what about Spinoza?

There is a great deal of debate on this set of issues. Some commentators believe that Spinoza does indeed intend to distinguish between conscious and nonconscious minds and between conscious and nonconscious ideas in the human mind; and some of these further believe that Spinoza successfully establishes that distinction, whereas others think that, although he intends to maintain it, he fails to offer a coherent way of doing so. Others argue that Spinoza does not intend any such distinction and is perfectly willing to accept the universality of consciousness.

The reason why this is relevant to the issue at hand is that if Spinoza does indeed want a distinction between conscious and nonconscious minds, and between conscious and nonconscious ideas in the human mind, then the ideas-of-ideas doctrine will not serve him well as an account of consciousness. The ideas-of-ideas doctrine is universally valid: it applies equally to all ideas in thought, regardless of whether the corresponding bodies of these ideas are human bodies or some other variety. Every idea in thought is associated with an idea for which it is the *ideatum*.

If one believes that the ideas-of-ideas doctrine is the closest that Spinoza comes to offering an account of consciousness, then one must accept that for Spinoza all minds, all beings in nature are conscious, and that all ideas or mental states in the human mind are conscious. But perhaps this conclusion, as odd as this may seem, can be given an acceptable and harmless interpretation, similar to the way in which Spinoza's claim about everything in nature having a mind and therefore being animate is often rendered palatable.

However, there is a further, more serious problem for this approach to consciousness in Spinoza. For even if Spinoza *is* willing to recognize consciousness throughout all of nature, well beyond the human domain, surely he will want at least to distinguish between degrees of consciousness, at least among different kinds of individuals. Not only would it be extremely counterintuitive to deny such differences in consciousness – could he really want to say that a tree is *as* conscious as a human being? – but that Spinoza wants such a distinction is clear from *Ethics* 5p31s and 5p39s, where he speaks of individual human beings achieving a greater or lesser degree of consciousness. If there can be a difference in degree of consciousness within and among human beings, should there not also be a difference in degree of phenomenal consciousness between human beings and other things? Indeed, Spinoza does speak of the human mind "surpassing" other minds (E 2p13s), and presumably one of the ways in which it does so is because of the nature of its consciousness. Thus, it would seem that if any interpretation of Spinoza's account of consciousness leads to the conclusion that all beings are equally conscious and in the same way, and that all ideas in the human mind are equally conscious, then so much the worse for that interpretation.

But that is precisely where the ideas-of-ideas account leads. Just as every body in extension has a corresponding idea in thought in the same way and to the same degree, so every mind, insofar as it is an idea, is accompanied by an idea of an idea, equally and to the same degree, as is every idea in every mind. It is hard to see how the ideas-of-ideas doctrine can account for differences in degrees of consciousness throughout nature; but this would seem to be precisely one of the things it must do.

In the light of these problems and confusions, a number of scholars have been driven to conclude that there is simply no coherent account of consciousness in Spinoza, and especially that he does not distinguish between being conscious and simply having an idea.[12] This would be a premature conclusion, however. In fact, there are some very suggestive remarks in the *Ethics* that represent a naturalistic account of consciousness that is precocious insofar as it points the way to just the kind of empirical, scientific inquiry into consciousness that characterizes contemporary neuroscience and (some) recent philosophy of mind.

To make sense of Spinoza's understanding of consciousness, one must look beyond the ideas-of-ideas doctrine and toward a couple of remarks scattered in various parts of the *Ethics*. Two passages, especially, are crucial. The first occurs at E 2p13s and takes as its starting points the already established parallelism between the human body and the human mind – which guarantees that insofar as the human body has certain properties and capacities, so does the human mind – and the additional claim that the human body is indeed "more excellent" than any other kind of body in nature. Here is what Spinoza says in the first passage:

> In proportion as a body is more capable [*aptius*] than others of doing many things at once, or being acted upon in many ways at once, so its mind is more capable than others of perceiving many things at once. And in proportion as the actions of a body depend more on itself alone, and as other bodies concur with it less in acting, so its mind is more capable of understanding distinctly.
> (E 2p13s)

This, Spinoza concludes, will help us understand the way in which the human mind "surpasses" other minds in nature and the "excellence" of this one kind of mind over all others.

The second passage is at *E* 5p39s:

> Because human bodies are capable [*apta*] of a great many things, there is no doubt but that they can be of such a nature that they are related to minds which have a great knowledge of themselves and of God.... He who, like an infant or child, has a body capable of very few things and very heavily dependent on external causes, has a mind which considered solely in itself is conscious [*conscia*] of almost nothing of itself, or of God, or of things. On the other hand, he who has a body capable of a great many things, has a mind which considered only in itself is very much conscious of itself, and of God, and of things.

The second passage tells us not only that the human mind is "more excellent" than other minds because its body surpasses other bodies in its own aptitudes or capacities but also that the mind of any individual human being becomes more excellent as its body becomes more active and develops greater aptitudes or capacities.

But what exactly is this higher "excellence" of the mind that so depends on the greater capabilities of the body? The second passage itself tells us: it is consciousness or self-awareness – or, rather, a higher degree of consciousness. Here is an alternative to the ideas-of-ideas doctrine as the locus of Spinoza's account of consciousness. Human or higher consciousness, on this reading, is for Spinoza nothing but the mental correlate of the superlative complexity of the human body.

Any body for Spinoza is individuated by the particular and stable ratio of motion and rest among the particles and collections of particles of matter composing it. It is the body it is because its parts, although perhaps in motion relative to each other (or to groups of each other), nonetheless maintain the same basic kinetic relations:

> Definition: When a number of bodies, whether of the same or of different size, are so constrained by other bodies that they lie upon one another, or they so move, whether with the same degree or different degrees of speed, that they communicate their motions to each other in a certain fixed manner, we shall say that those bodies are united with one another and that they all together compose one body or individual, which is distinguished from the others by this union of bodies.
>
> (Geb. II 99–100; Spinoza 1984: 460)

The human body is no different from any other kind of body in this regard. However, as the previous passages indicate, it does surpass other bodies by its superior capacities. And these greater capacities of the human body are to be understood as (or reducible to) that body's greater number of kinds of parts and greater number of kinds of motion-rest relationships among those parts – in short, greater complexity – relative to other kinds of bodies. The human body is a magnificent machine with a wide variety of parts and motions. And this variety goes deep, because the body's largest parts are themselves richly and intensively composite, constituted out of further composite parts, and so on. Above all, the human body is endowed with a brain and neurological system more intricate, multifaceted, adaptable, active, and responsive than what is found in any other physical existent. In short, the human body is simply a more complex parcel of extension than any other finite mode of that attribute. Or, at least, this is how I think Spinoza regards it.

Now the passages quoted previously (*E* 2p13s and *E* 5p39s) make no direct mention of complexity; they refer primarily to what a body is "more apt" or "more capable" of. But for Spinoza, a body's aptitudes are a function of the constitutional makeup of the body: its material parts and the ratios of motion and rest between them (i.e. their structures and motive relationships). Thus, the human body's greater aptitude relative to other types of body amounts to its greater complexity. This is why Spinoza insists in introducing the so-called Physical Digression of part 2 that to understand the difference between the human body and other kinds of bodies and just *how* the former surpasses the latter, it is necessary to investigate its greater aptitudes, and that to understand *these* it is above all necessary to understand what a body is and what it is about one kind of body's extended nature that distinguishes it from another kind of body. In the *Short Treatise*, he says that "the differences between [one body and another] arise only from the different proportions of motion and rest, by which this one is so, and not so, and this and not that" (Geb. I 52; Spinoza 1984: 95). In the *Ethics*, this approach is subtly manifest in Spinoza's insistence that an individual body "retains its nature . . . so long as each part retains its motion, and communicates it, as before, to the others," adding – in a clause that seems to draw a direct connection between the constitutive complexity of a body and its passive capabilities – that "by this we see how a composite individual can be affected in many ways, and still preserve its nature" (*E* 2lem.7). The upshot, then, is that the references of *E* 2p13s and *E* 5p39s to the human body's superior aptitudes or capacities should be understood as references to its superior complexity as a parcel of extension.

Turning now to consciousness, on this account, consciousness is simply the reflection within thought of a body's internal relations in extension (just as the mind itself is the reflection in thought of the body's basic reality). It is a matter of complexity, flexibility, and responsiveness in an individual's thinking – in essence, the thinking turned upon itself and its objects in a particular way – reflecting or expressing (in a different attribute) the complexity, flexibility, and responsiveness of that individual's body. More to the point, the human being's greater degree of consciousness (relative to other finite beings), in turn, is nothing but the correlate within a finite mode of thought (i.e. the human mind) of the greater complexity, flexibility, and responsiveness in extension of the human body. Just as the human body is composed of a rich diversity of parts and relations among those parts – compositionally deeper and relationally richer than what is found in any other kind of body – so too the human mind is composed of a rich diversity of ideas corresponding to those bodily parts and motions, and an equally rich diversity of relations among those ideas also corresponding to the relations among the bodily parts. And any individual idea in that mind holds within itself a superbly rich concatenation of subideas and relations (corresponding to the body's subparts and their relations). Consciousness, on this view, just *is* that rich tangle of idea relationships found within the human mind and within any particular idea in the mind, a mental reflection of the rich tangle of material relationships found in the human body. This complexity that makes an idea conscious occurs within the first-order idea itself; it does not require a second-order idea directed at the first. Whereas the ideas-of-ideas account apparently does not require a second-order idea either, this second approach does not even require an "idea of an idea," that is an idea that has another idea as its object. The complex of ideas and of idea relationships that, on this reading, Spinoza offers as an explanation of consciousness is not necessarily the relationship of intentionality that characterizes the idea-of-an-idea relation (although that may indeed be one of the many kinds of relationships among ideas that make up consciousness).

To add some more detail, consider what Spinoza says in the passage from E 2p13s: the more capable the body is, the more the mind is "capable than others of perceiving many things at once." One way of looking at this is that the mind's increased ability to perceive many things at once *is* consciousness in the sense that consciousness is a kind of perceiving many things at once. To return to the example used earlier, take one's conscious awareness of an apple. Is it not, at the same time and through the same act, both the perception of the apple and an awareness of the perception of the apple? As with the accounts in Descartes and Arnauld, it is a way in which thinking is turned upon itself in a certain way.

This account of consciousness in Spinoza does not require that only human beings are conscious. All bodies have some degree of complexity, and this will be reflected in the corresponding complexity of their correlate minds. So, if consciousness is just the correlate complexity in thought of the body's complexity in extension, then there may certainly be a continuum of consciousness among minds in nature and a sense in which all minds have some degree of consciousness. But the increased consciousness that Spinoza should – and does – admit characterizes mature human minds is a function of the increased complexity, initiative, motions, and activity and responsiveness that characterizes the mature human body. So, unlike the ideas-of-ideas account, this interpretation, although possibly implying that all minds in nature are conscious to some degree, does not imply that all minds are conscious to the same degree.

On the other hand, maybe Spinoza, although he is willing to attribute minds to all things in nature, does not want to attribute consciousness to them as well. In this case, we can regard consciousness as an emergent property that certain mental systems take on only when their correlate bodies possess a particular minimal level of complexity and activity. Perhaps there is a threshold level of complexity in the body for which, once reached, the corresponding level of complexity in the mind is consciousness. In this way, Spinoza can consistently claim that only human beings have consciousness without violating either the parallelism or the universality of animateness in nature. This, however, would not fit well with what one scholar has called Spinoza's "incremental naturalism," or the view that there are no leaps in nature, that important explanatory properties and relations are not simply present or absent, but rather are pervasively present throughout all of nature in greater or lesser degrees (Garrett 2008: 18). For that reason, it may be that any talk of emergence for Spinoza should ultimately be rejected. This complexity account of consciousness also explains Spinoza's remark about infants having lesser degrees of consciousness of self than adults, because their bodies, although possessing much of the right neurological hardware, have not yet quite activated all of the human body's motions and capacities or realized all of its relational potentialities.[13]

4. Cudworth

Before turning to Leibniz, there are two English philosophers of the seventeenth century whose considerations of consciousness warrant discussion here. The first is the Cambridge Platonist Ralph Cudworth, primarily because he seems to have been the first philosopher writing in English to make extensive use of the term "consciousness" and to employ it in a particular, philosophically considered way: "Cudworth should be credited with having introduced 'consciousness' as a philosophical term into English" (Thiel 1991: 79).

Cudworth's discussion of consciousness occurs in the context of an investigation not of the human mind but of a certain incorporeal causal agent operating in the material world of bodies. In his *The True Intellectual System of the Universe* (1678), Cudworth offers an extended argument through which "all the Reason and Philosophy of Atheism is confuted; and its Impossibility demonstrated." The key to refuting atheism, he believes, lies in undermining its materialist assumption about the universe. If the Epicureans were right and there was nothing but matter, there would be no life, no order, and no lawlike behavior in nature: "*Life* and *Understanding* are not Essential to Matter . . . [and] they can never possibly rise out of any *Mixture* or *Modification* of *Dead* and *Stupid Matter* whatsoever" (Cudworth 1678: 145). The structures and teleological features of the world around us could never come about by the blind operations of inanimate bodies. They require intelligence, goal-oriented intentions, and active power, and these can be found only in souls or minds: "*Life, Cogitation* and *Understanding* do not Essentially belong *to Matter*, and all *Substance* as such, but are the peculiar *Attributes* and *Characteristics* of *Substance Incorporeal*" (Cudworth 1678: 146). Cudworth's conclusion is that "there is something in Nature besides Mechanism, and consequently Substance Incorporeal. . . . [T]here is a *Mixture* of *Life* or *Plastic Nature* together with *Mechanism*, which runs through the whole Corporeal Universe" (Cudworth 1678: 148).

This "Plastic Nature" is an immaterial agent within the material realm and is causally responsible for the characteristic ways in which bodies behave and organize themselves. It acts teleologically, "for the Sake of Something," and carries out the plan that has been ordained by the superior intelligence that has placed it in the world, that is God. The plastic nature is an "inward Principle in Matter" that acts upon it and causes it to move according to laws: "Nature is *Art* as it were *Incorporated* and *Imbodied* in matter, which doth not act upon it from without *Mechanically*, but from within *Vitally* and *Magically* . . . as an *Inward* and *Living Soul* or *Law* in it" (Cudworth 1678: 156). It is a "*Mental Causality* in the world" (Cudworth 1678: 155). Without such an immaterial agent mediating between God and matter, only two options remain: blind materialism ("mechanical necessity"), which cannot explain the order of things; or ubiquitous divine causality, whereby "every thing in Nature should be done immediately by God Himself," which is unworthy of God's majesty.

Although Cudworth's plastic nature is soul-like and causally responsible for the regular and orderly motion of bodies, it does not itself act intelligently, neither "*electively* nor with *discretion*." It does not understand the ends for which it acts nor does it intend them. Rather, it is programmed to carry out ("execute") God's plan but without knowing anything about that plan. It is "but a certain Power of moving Matter, which doth not *Know*, but *only Do*" (Cudworth 1678: 156).

But how can something act for the sake of ends in nature but not understand those ends nor the reasons for its actions? This is where the issue of consciousness enters Cudworth's discussion. Cudworth compares the actions of the plastic nature to habitual or instinctive actions in animals, the things performed by living creatures without any explicit intentions. Although such actions come from a vital and immaterial principle, the agent is not conscious of doing them. Likewise, the plastic nature acts without consciousness: it does not know what it is doing or even that it is doing it. (Unlike humans and animals, the plastic nature does not even have the capacity to become conscious of what it is doing.)

> There is in the next place another *Imperfection* to be observed in the *Plastic Nature*, that as it doth not comprehend the *Reason* of its own Action, so neither is it *Clearly* and *Expressly Conscious of what* it doth; in which Respect, it

doth not only fall short of *Human Art*, but even of that very Manner of Acting which is in Brutes themselves, who though they do not Understand the Reason of those Actions, that their Natural Instincts lead them to, yet they are generally conceived to be Conscious of them, and to do them by *Fancy Plastic Nature* in the *Formation* of Plants and Animals, seems to have no *Animal Fancy*, no Express *Synaisthesis*, *Con-sense* or *Consciousness* of what it doth.

(Cudworth 1678: 158)

Cudworth defines consciousness as "Self-Perception." It is thought turned upon itself, a

[d]*uplication*, that is included in the Nature of *Synaisthesis, Con-sense* and *Consciousness*, which makes a Being to be Present with it self, Attentive to its own Actions, or Animadversive of them, to perceive it self to Do or Suffer, and to have a *Fruition* or *Enjoyment* of it self.

(Cudworth 1678: 159)

The term that Cudworth uses for consciousness, "synaisthesis" (which he takes from Plotinus), is a kind of awareness or perception – or, to put it less cognitively, a feeling – of one's mental activities, both sensations and intellectual thoughts, while one is having them, as well as of one's actions while one is doing them.[14] It is this that is lacking in the incorporeal plastic nature. Consciousness is essential to what Cudworth calls "cogitation," which includes both sense perception and intellectual conceiving. But not all immaterial beings are cogitative (and thus conscious) souls.

Cudworth explicitly distinguishes the presence to self that consciousness or synaisthesis involves from self-consciousness. Self-consciousness arises from synaisthesis but is not identical with it. The consciousness or awareness in perception and intellection is also distinct from and independent of explicit reflection, or what Cudworth calls "Expressly Conscious Cogitation" or "Express Consciousness" (Cudworth 1678: 159). For Cudworth, consciousness is simultaneous with the action of which one is aware; reflection is subsequent to it. In this regard, Cudworth is in agreement with the Cartesian account.

Unlike the Cartesians, however, Cudworth attributes consciousness or synaisthesis not just to human beings but to animals as well. Moreover, Cudworth rejects Descartes's view that human souls are always conscious and that all their thoughts are conscious thoughts. He insists that in sleep, for example, the mind is active but there is no synaisthesis. At such times, as well as during habitual and instinctive activities, when that presence of conscious awareness is lacking or deficient, a human being functions more like Cudworth's plastic nature than like an intelligent being.

5. Locke

Consciousness is central to John Locke's account of personal identity. It is what unifies the variety of thoughts and actions that take place in a thinking being into a single mental domain and, thus, into one self. States of past and present awareness, linked by memory, are bound together into one stream of conscious activity; and as long as that stream of consciousness remains unbroken, there is one person persisting through time:

Tis plain consciousness . . . unites Existences, and Actions, very remote in time, into the same Person, as well as it does the Existence and Actions of the

immediately preceding moment: So that whatever has the consciousness of present and past Actions, is the same Person to whom they both belong.
(*Essay Concerning Human Understanding* [henceforth, *Essay*] 2.27.16)

Correlatively, any break in consciousness – such as a gap in memory between one series of conscious states and a later series – represents a break in personal identity; two independent series of conscious states unrelated by memory, even if they belong to the same thinking substance, constitute two consciousnesses and thus two persons: "If it be possible for the same Man to have distinct incommunicable consciousness at different times, it is past doubt the same Man would at different times make different Persons" (*Essay* 2.27.20).

Whereas Locke has much to say about how consciousness binds up mental events into persons, he is more reserved on the question as to the nature of consciousness itself. This may be because he takes it as introspectively obvious what consciousness is, something that should be evident to anyone who experiences it and is capable of reflecting on it. He does insist, like most of the philosophers discussed in this chapter (except Leibniz and Cudworth), that all thoughts are conscious; there are no mental states that are not conscious states. Consciousness is the immediate awareness that accompanies *all* acts of thinking. It is

> inseparable from thinking, and . . . essential to it: It being impossible for anyone to perceive, without perceiving that he does perceive. When we see, hear, smell, taste, feel, meditate or will any thing, we know that we do so. Thus it is always as to our present Sensations and Perceptions.
>
> (*Essay* 2.27.9)

Locke sometimes seems willing to suspend judgment over the question of whether it is in principle impossible for there to be unconscious thoughts (or, in a related vein, over the question as to whether the soul is always thinking). Reason alone cannot decide the issue; and because such thoughts would not be accompanied by awareness, experience provides no evidence as to whether or not they occur. At the same time, Locke's considered view is that "men think not always," and he insists that at least the empirical fact of the matter is that "[no one can] think at any time waking or sleeping, without being sensible of it" (*Essay* 2.1.10). In fact, he appears at times to regard this as a necessary truth:

> If they say, The Man thinks always, but is not always conscious of it; they may as well say, His Body is extended, without having parts. For 'tis altogether as intelligible to say, that a body is extended without parts, as that any thing thinks without being conscious of it, or perceiving, that it does so. They who talk thus, may, with as much reason, if it be necessary to their Hypothesis, say, That a Man is always hungry, but that he does not always feel it: Whereas hunger consists in that very sensation, as thinking consists in being conscious that one thinks.
>
> (*Essay* 2.1.19)

Locke explains consciousness as the perception of one's thinking: "Consciousness is the perception of what passes in a Man's own mind" (*Essay* 2.1.19). It is different from the perception that consists in the reception of ideas through the senses or through introspection, however: "External Objects furnish the Mind with the Ideas of sensible qualities, which are all those different perceptions they produce in us: And the Mind furnishes the Understanding with Ideas of its own operations" (*Essay* 2.1.5). In perception understood as the reception of ideas, the mind is mostly passive, whether it is attending to external things or its own states. The perception that constitutes consciousness, however, whereby the mind's perceiving turns on itself, is an action; it is something the mind does rather than undergoes. No new ideas result from it; rather, it is the reason why the ideas arising from sensation or introspection enter awareness.

What this shows, moreover, is that consciousness is not, no more than it is for Descartes and the other philosophers examined so far, a second-order act of perception directed at another act of the mind. Rather, it is once again the product of a *self*-reflective awareness that simultaneously accompanies each act. The reflection that constitutes consciousness must be distinguished from explicit reflection or attentive introspection on what is happening in the mind (whereby "the Mind furnishes the Understanding with Ideas of its own operations"). This latter, for which Locke usually reserves the term "reflection," does demand a second-order act of thinking and requires some effort. Thus, children enjoy full conscious awareness and, no less than adults, have the phenomenal experience of things that composes their subjectivity. But

> 'tis pretty late, before most Children get *Ideas* of the Operations of their own Minds; and some have not any very clear, or perfect *Ideas* of the greatest part of them all their Lives. Because, though they pass there continually; yet like floating Visions, they make not deep Impressions enough, to leave in the Mind clear distinct lasting Ideas, till the Understanding turns inward upon it self, *reflects* on its own *Operations*, and makes them the Object of its own Contemplation.
> (*Essay* 2.1.8)

The immature attention of children is drawn to "outward Sensations," and they "seldom make any considerable Reflection on what passes within them." But their conscious lives are no less rich because of this.

6. Leibniz

No philosopher in the seventeenth century gave more thought to the nature and extent of consciousness than Leibniz. It is a matter of concern in many writings throughout his long career, particularly as he struggles with the question of who exactly is a moral agent in God's "most perfect republic." The question of consciousness really comes to the fore, however, in a number of works from his later period: in particular, the *New Essays on Human Understanding* (1703–05, henceforth *NE*), *Principles of Nature and Grace* (1714, henceforth *PNG*), and the *Monadology* (1714).[15]

One of the bedrock principles of Leibniz's philosophy is the law of continuity. There are no gaps in nature, no sudden and unprecedented emergent properties: "Nothing takes place suddenly, and it is one of my great and best confirmed maxims that nature never makes leaps" (*NE* preface, Ak VI.6: 56).[16] All natural development and change occurs by degrees. There is, therefore, no hard boundary between those creatures that have conscious states and those that do not, nor between those states of the mind that are conscious and those that are not. Rather, there is a continuum in nature among grades of consciousness, both among creatures and within any given mind. It extends from the minutest and nonconscious perceptions to those that are accompanied by full awareness, or what Leibniz calls "apperception."

Leibniz's universe in his late writings is made up of "monads" – simple, immaterial substances that are the atoms or building blocks of all complex things. A monad is a mind-like entity; it has no extension and does not literally occupy space. It can aggregate with other monads, however, and collections or "aggregates" of monads constitute "composite" beings. The human body, for example, is an aggregate of monads unified by a dominant monad, the human soul. A monad has "no windows through which something can enter or leave." Although causally isolated and devoid of parts because of its metaphysical simplicity, a monad does have qualities and an internal principle of change for its succession of states; these are what differentiate one monad from another. Because it is a mind, the states that constitute the diversity within a monad are its "perceptions" (*Monadology* §§1–12).

Leibniz defines a perception as "the passing state which involves and represents a multitude in the unity or in the simple substance" (*Monadology* §14),[17] or "the internal state of the monad representing external things" (*PNG* §4). The content of a perception – its manifold of represented elements – is the multiplicity, whereas the singularity of the monad and the uniqueness of its perspective contributes the unity. Leibniz explicitly claims, however, that not all perceptions in a monad – including those in the human mind – are conscious states. Perception is one thing, conscious awareness is another. The mind is filled with many unconscious perceptions, which Leibniz calls *petites perceptions*. Only a subset of these are accompanied by apperception and, thus, rise to the level of conscious awareness:

> We always have an infinity of minute perceptions without being aware of them. We are never without perceptions, but necessarily we are often without *awareness*, namely when none of our perceptions stands out.
> (*NE* 2.19.4, Ak VI.6: 161–2)

> It is good to distinguish between *perception*, which is the internal state of the monad representing external things, and *apperception*, which is *consciousness*, or the reflective knowledge of this internal state, something not given to all souls, nor at all times to a given soul.
> (*PNG* §4)

The minute perceptions that make up much of the mind's contents are present both when there are no conscious states at all and during conscious episodes. A mind or monad for Leibniz is always thinking, even if no conscious thoughts are momentarily occurring. This is because thinking, although not the essence of the soul, is its "essential action." The difference between a nonconscious thought and a conscious one is apperception, which Leibniz sometimes also calls reflection.

In certain contexts, Leibniz describes the reflection that, when added to perception, makes for consciousness as a form of "attention" to what is there already in us. "At every moment," he says, "there is in us an infinity of perceptions, unaccompanied by awareness or reflection," but these for the most part are "too minute and too numerous" to attract our attention or be noticed: "When we are not alerted, so to speak, to pay heed to certain of our own present perceptions, we allow them to slip by unconsidered and even unnoticed" (*NE* preface, Ak VI.6: 53–4). On other occasions, reflection is described as a kind of immediate memory:

> A present or immediate memory, the memory of what was taking place immediately before – or, in other words, the consciousness or reflection which accompanies inner activity – cannot immediately deceive us. If it could, we would not even be certain that we are thinking about such and such a thing.
> (*NE* 2.27.13, Ak VI.6: 238)

That is, the testimony of present consciousness understood as memory is incorrigible. As we shall see, by using the terms 'consciousness' and 'reflection' interchangeably, and describing them as either attention or memory, Leibniz creates some difficulty in determining just what kind of activity apperception is. Still, this much is clear so far: consciousness is identified with reflection or apperception – or, more precisely, a conscious state of awareness (which Leibniz sometimes calls "thought") of some object *x* is the result of reflection or apperception added to a (previously unnoticed) mental representation or perception of *x*.[18]

> Beasts have perception, and . . . they don't necessarily have thought, that is, have reflection or anything which could be the object of it. We too have minute perceptions of which we are not aware in our present state. We could in fact become thoroughly aware of them and reflect on them, if we were not distracted by their multiplicity. . . . I would prefer to distinguish between perception and *being aware*.
> (*NE* 2.9.1–4, Ak VI.6: 134).

The more difficult question, when trying to make sense of Leibniz's views on consciousness, is what exactly it is that gets added to a "mere perception" that transforms it into a conscious state. What is that reflection or apperception (or "immediate memory") of which Leibniz speaks?

Leibniz sometimes treats apperception as a matter of a second-order perception being directed at a first-order perception. When a perception is sufficiently distinct in the mind, it attracts a higher-order attention and thereby becomes conscious. Because this attention comes (immediately) after the original act, it is a form of memory. Thus, Leibniz (as we have seen) speaks in the *New Essays* of "a present or immediate memory, the memory of what was taking place immediately before – or in other words, the consciousness or reflection which accompanies inner activity." In the *Monadology* (§19), he insists on the difference between a bare monad, which has only "simple perceptions," and a soul, which has sensation. A sensation is "something more than a simple perception. . . . [W]e should only call those substances *souls* where perception is more distinct and accompanied by memory."[19]

However, Leibniz also seems to want to distinguish the reflection that is identical with apperception and that makes for conscious awareness from a second-order reflection that consists in explicitly attending to a first-order perception (and thus presumably involves memory, to keep that first-order perception in view):

> We are aware of [*nous nous appercevons*] many things, within ourselves and around us, which we do not understand; and we *understand* them when we have

distinct ideas of them accompanied by the power to reflect and to derive necessary truths from those ideas.

Nonhuman animals can have consciousness or apperception but not understanding, because they cannot reflect on their perceptions to derive truths from them:

> Beasts have no understanding, at least in this sense; although they have the faculty for awareness [*s'appercevoir*] of the more conspicuous and outstanding impressions – as when a wild boar is aware of someone who is shouting at it, and goes straight at that person, having previously had only a bare perception of him. . . . So "understanding" in my sense is what in Latin is called *intellectus*, and the exercise of this faculty is called "intellection", which is a distinct perception combined with a faculty of reflection, which the beasts do not have.
> (*NE* 2.21.5, Ak VI.6: 173)

Passages like this suggest that the reflection that constitutes apperception is not in fact the product of a second-order act but simply a self-reflection accompanying a first-order act, much like Arnauld's virtual reflection.

There is yet another reading of Leibniz's account of consciousness, one that also treats it as a first-order phenomenon. It views apperception as a remarkable qualitative feature of the conscious perceptions themselves, namely the distinctness of a perception. The difference between a conscious perception and an unconscious one is simply the fact that the former enjoys a higher degree of distinctness than the latter. Distinctness raises a "bare perception" or idea to the level of awareness, whereby it becomes "noticeable." This is the case, for example, in *Monadology* §§23–24:

> 23. Since on being awakened from a stupor, we apperceive our perceptions, it must be the case that we had some perceptions immediately before, even though we did not apperceive them; for a perception can only come naturally from another perception, as a motion can only come naturally from a motion.

> 24. From this we see that if, in our perceptions, we had nothing distinct or, so to speak, in relief and stronger in flavor, we would always be in a stupor. And this is the state of bare monads.

In the continuation of a passage from the *New Essays* quoted previously, Leibniz insists that the reason why so many of those minute perceptions pass through us "unaccompanied by awareness or reflection" is that "they are not sufficiently distinctive on their own" and thus "we pay no heed to [them]. . . . [W]e are unable to pick [them] out from the crowd." He compares this to

> the roaring noise of the sea which impresses itself on us when we are standing on the shore. To hear this noise as we do, we must hear the parts which make up this whole, that is, the noise of each wave, although each of these little noises makes itself known only when combined confusedly with all the others, and would not be noticed if the wave which made it were by itself.
> (*NE* preface, Ak VI.6: 53–4)

On this reading, consciousness or apperception just is the greater distinctness (or, as he sometimes calls it, "forcefulness") of a perception. It is not that the distinctness attracts some additional, second-order mental activity or notice and consciousness is accounted for by that higher-order event. Rather the heightened distinctness or strength of the perception *is* awareness. It has been alleged that the advantage of seeing apperception as a first-order qualitative feature of perceptions in this way is that, unlike any interpretation that relies on a higher-order perception, it allows Leibniz to draw the distinction between conscious and nonconscious mental events without violating the law of continuity. Distinctness apparently can come in degrees, but higher-order thought makes a sudden appearance: it is either there or it is not.[20] This appears to be something that Leibniz himself is careful to preserve: "Noticeable perceptions arise by degrees from ones which are too minute to be noticed" (*NE* preface, Ak VI.6: 57).

Such a reading also seems to allow Leibniz to claim that nonhuman animals have conscious awareness. Although they are not capable of higher-order reflective thinking, their sensations (as is clear from the passage about the wild boar) can certainly enjoy distinctness. On the other hand, in the *Principles of Nature and Grace* (§4), after saying that animals are only "sometimes" in the condition of simple living things and their souls "in the condition of simple monads" (which suggests that at other times they *do* rise to the level of conscious beings), Leibniz goes on to chide the Cartesians for failing to see that not all monads are conscious minds – that there is a difference between a simple perceiving substance and a thinking substance that also enjoys apperception: "This is what leads [them] to believe that only minds are monads, that there are no souls in beasts." This would seem to imply that although animals do not have "apperception, which is consciousness, or the reflective knowledge of [perceptions], something not given to all souls," they do have perceiving souls. Thus, whether or not Leibniz actually does believe consciousness to extend in nature beyond human minds remains a rather vexed question.[21]

Notes

1 Aquinas, for example, seems interested in both conscious awareness and self-consciousness (as in ST q78a4). On the other hand, as Pasnau reminds us, Aquinas "never explicitly takes up" the topic of consciousness (2002: 197).
2 Chalmers (1995).
3 Pasnau (2002) notes that "premodern philosophers do not generally talk about consciousness per se." He suggests, however, that this may be because "they never clearly saw that there might be a problem about the mind other than the problem of consciousness" – that in their efforts to explain the various forms of cognition "they take for granted that they are trying to explain what we call consciousness. There was no need for a special word to describe the problem, because consciousness was the whole problem" (197).
4 Descartes does, it seems, miss Gassendi's point and accuses him of making a category mistake; see AT VII 359–60; CSM II 248–9.
5 Compare, for example, Wilson (1978: 160–1) with Radner (1988: 451).
6 Beyssade (1979: 244–9) agrees that there is a distinction in Descartes between conscious awareness and reflective consciousness. See also McCrae (1976) and Glauser (2011). Not all scholars who agree on this, however, also agree that conscious awareness occurs through a first-order act reflecting on itself.
7 Lähteenmäki (2007) suggests, by contrast, that for Descartes consciousness within first-order adult (but not infant) perceptual awareness occurs through a "second perception" (albeit not a deliberately willed second-order act): "What we have here is an intellectual perception of a logically prior but temporally simultaneous perception which occurs as a byproduct of the intial perception" (189). On the other hand, the consciousness of volition for Descartes *does* occur, Lähteenmäki insists, by the reflexivity of the first-order act of volition itself; thus, on his reading, consciousness occurs differently in adult perception and volition.

8 In chapter 4 ("Arnauld on Cognition and Consciousness") of his Ph.D. dissertation, Matthias Somers persuasively argues that virtual reflection does provide some form of self-consciousness for Arnauld. Presumably, though, it is not the explicit self-consciousness that is required to formulate the *cogito*.
9 See Damasio (2001).
10 For example, in *Ethics* 3p11s, where it is suggested that an affect in the mind (i.e. an idea) may, at least in principle, not be attended by consciousness.
11 Curley (1969: 126–9), Curley (1988: 71–3), Matheron (1994), and Wilson (1999). Bennett (1984: 188), on the other hand, insists that the ideas-of-ideas doctrine is a theory of self-knowledge, but not a theory of consciousness or awareness.
12 For example, Wilson (1999) and Bennett (1984).
13 I argue for this interpretation at greater length in Nadler (2008). Garrett (2008), who also rejects the ideas-of-ideas doctrine as Spinoza's account of consciousness, offers yet another reading, one related to the central notion of power.
14 See Thiel (1991: 89).
15 For consciousness in Leibniz's earlier works, see Kulstad (1991, chapter 2).
16 The translations of the passages from *NE* are from Leibniz (1982), which uses the same pagination as the Akademie edition (Leibniz 1923).
17 The translations of the passages from the *Monadology* and the *Principles of Nature and Grace* are from Leibniz (1989). Because these works are organized and usually cited by numbered paragraphs, no explicit citation of any edition is given. Both are in Leibniz (1875–90), vol. 6: the *Monadology* 607–23; the *Principles* 598–606.
18 It is clear, at least, to most scholars. Russell, however, believes that for Leibniz consciousness is to be identified with perception *per se*, whereas apperception accounts for *self*-consciousness (1937: 156). McCrae, on the other hand, more properly distinguishes consciousness and apperception (which he calls "primitive awareness") from mere perception, although he also insists that primitive awareness includes some form of self-awareness (1976: 24–6).
19 This interpretation is found in Jorgensen (2011), Kulstad (1991), and Gennaro (1999), among many others. It is probably the standard way of reading Leibniz on consciousness.
20 See, for example, McCrae (1976), especially pp. 36–7, and Jorgensen (2009).
21 See Kulstad (1991).

Bibliography

Arnauld, A. (1775) *Oeuvres de Messire Antoine Arnauld*, 43 vols., Brussels: Sigismond d'Arnay.
Bennett, J. (1984) *A Study of Spinoza's Ethics*, Indianapolis: Hackett.
Beyssade, J.-M. (1979) *La philosophie première de Descartes*, Paris: Flammarion.
Burge, T. (2007) "Two Types of Consciousness", in Tyler Burge, *Foundations of Mind: Philosophical Essays*, vol. 2, Oxford: Oxford University Press, 383–4.
Chalmers, D. (1995) "Facing Up to the Problem of Consciousness," *Journal of Consciousness Studies* 2: 200–19.
Cudworth, R. (1678) *The True Intellectual System of the Universe*, London: Royston.
Curley, E.M. (1969) *Spinoza's Metaphysics: An Interpretation*, Cambridge: Harvard University Press.
—— (1988) *Behind the Geometric Method*, Princeton: Princeton University Press.
Damasio, A. (2001) *Looking for Spinoza: Joy, Sorrow, and the Feeling Brain*, New York: Harcourt.
Descartes, R. (1974–83) *Oeuvres de Descartes*, 11 vols., ed. Charles Adam and Paul Tannery, Paris: J. Vrin.
—— (1976) *Descartes' Conversation With Burman*, trans. and ed. John Cottingham, Oxford: Clarendon Press.
—— (1985) *The Philosophical Writings of Descartes*, 2 vols., trans. and ed. John Cottingham, Robert Stoothoff, and Dugald Murdoch, Cambridge: Cambridge University Press.
Garrett, D. (2008) "Representation and Consciousness in Spinoza's Naturalistic Theory of the Imagination," in Charles Huenemann (ed.), *Interpreting Spinoza: Critical Essays*, Cambridge: Cambridge University Press.
Gennaro, R. (1999) "Leibniz on Consciousness and Self-Consciousness," in Rocco J. Gennaro and Charles Huenemann (eds.), *New Essays on the Rationalists*, New York: Oxford University Press, 353–71.
Glauser, R. (2011) "Conscience et connaissance de la pensée chez Descartes," in Sébastien Charles and Syliane Malinowski-Charles (eds.), *Descartes et ses critiques*, Laval, Quebec: Presses de l'Université de Laval, 13–32.
Jorgensen, L.M. (2009) "The Principle of Continuity and Leibniz's Theory of Consciousness," *Journal of the History of Philosophy* 47: 223–48.

Jorgensen, L. M. (2011) "Leibniz on Memory and Consciousness," *British Journal for the History of Philosophy* 19: 887–916.

Kulstad, M. (1991) *Leibniz on Apperception, Consciousness, and Reflection*, Munich: Philosophia.

Lähteenmäki, V. (2007) "Orders of Consciousness and Forms of Reflexivity in Descartes," in Sara Heinämaa, Vili Lähteenmäki, and Pauliina Remes (eds.), *Consciousness: From Perception to Reflection in the History of Philosophy*, Dordrecht: Springer, 177–201.

Leibniz, G. W. (1875–90) *Die Philosophischen Schriften*, 7 vols., ed. C. I. Gerhardt, Berlin: Weidmann.

—— (1923) *Sämtliche Schriften und Briefe*, ed. Deutsche Akademie der Wissenschaften, Darmstadt, Leipzig, Berlin: Akademie Verlag.

—— (1982) *New Essays on Human Understanding*, trans. Jonathan Bennett and Peter Remnant, Cambridge: Cambridge University Press.

—— (1989) *Philosophical Essays*, trans. Roger Ariew and Daniel Garber, Indianapolis: Hackett Publishing.

Matheron, A. (1994) "Ideas of Ideas and Certainty in the *Tractatus de Intellectus Emendatione* and in the *Ethics*," in Yirmiyahu Yovel (ed.), *Spinoza on Knowledge and the Human Mind*, Leiden: Brill, 83–91.

McCrae, R. (1976) *Leibniz: Perception, Apperception, & Thought*, Toronto: University of Toronto Press.

Nadler, S. (2008) "Spinoza and Consciousness," *Mind* 117: 575–601.

Nagel, T. (1974) "What Is It Like to Be a Bat?" *The Philosophical Review* 83: 435–50.

Pasnau, R. (2002) *Thomas Aquinas on Human Nature*, Cambridge: Cambridge University Press.

Radner, D. (1988) "Thought and Consciousness in Descartes," *Journal of the History of Ideas* 26: 439–52.

Russell, B. (1937) *A Critical Exposition of the Philosophy of Leibniz*, London: George Allen & Unwin.

Spinoza, B. (1925) *Spinoza Opera*, 4 vols., ed. Carl Gebhardt, Heidelberg: Carl Winter.

—— (1984) *The Collected Works of Spinoza*. Vol. 1, trans. and ed. Edwin Curley, Princeton: Princeton University Press.

Thiel, U. (1991) "Cudworth and Seventeenth-Century Theories of Consciousness," in Stephen Gaukroger (ed.), *The Uses of Antiquity: The Scientific Revolution and the Classical Tradition*, Dordrecht: Kluwer, 79–98.

Wilson, M. (1978) *Descartes*, London: Routledge & Kegan Paul.

—— (1999) "Objects, Ideas and 'Minds': Comments on Spinoza's Theory of Mind," in Margaret Wilson (ed.), *Ideas and Mechanism: Essays on Early Modern Philosophy*, Princeton: Princeton University Press, 126–40.

12
POWER AND PASSION IN HOBBES, DESCARTES AND SPINOZA

Deborah Brown

1. Introduction

It is tempting to view references to the potentialities and powers of bodies in mechanical treatises of the early seventeenth century as vestigial traits of a natural philosophy not yet fully distinguished from its Aristotelian progenitors. Such references seem at odds with an assumption, widely held among early critics of the new mechanical philosophy, that in its insistence that all material things are configurations of inertial bits of matter colliding aimlessly with one another, mechanism eradicated all inherent powers and activity from nature.[1] The alleged erosion of active and passive powers from physics was part of a general undermining of the influence of Aristotle and of the idea that each kind of thing could be characterized by its *potentiae*, powers to cause change and potentialities to undergo change. One problem that the Aristotelian notion of active powers was designed to solve – accounting for the starting point and direction of change – remained, however, and the mechanists' idea that bodies exhibit law-governed tendencies or "strivings" (*conatus*) to move in a certain direction restored something of this original idea. As the natural expression of these strivings in organic systems, the passions held the key to ousting Aristotelianism from the one domain of natural philosophy where its authority appeared unquestionable – biology. Theories of the passions proliferated in the seventeenth century less from a natural curiosity in the subject than from a pressing need to demonstrate the completeness of mechanism as a science of nature.

I begin by outlining why traditional accounts of the passions could not easily be incorporated into the new mechanical philosophy. Without understanding the contours of that tradition, we will be hard pressed to understand what was so shocking in Hobbes's insistence that justice and public policy belong in the science of human nature rather than in the "rules or infallibility of reason"[2]; why Descartes's declaration that he will approach the passions *en physicien*[3] would have indicated anything new; and how Spinoza could unblinkingly propose a *geometrical reduction* in which human actions and desires are treated "exactly as if [we] were dealing with lines, planes, and bodies."[4] I focus on these three figures as early adopters of mechanism who recognised the importance of reconceiving the relationship between passion and natural power, on the one hand, and passion and reason, on the other. The differences between these three thinkers are as important as their similarities for understanding the tensions within the new philosophy. Whereas Descartes holds on to the preeminence of reason and will – that "kingdom within a kingdom," as Spinoza comments derisively[5] – Hobbes and Spinoza develop more complex accounts of human behaviour in which deliberation and will are explained in terms of fluctuations among opposing passions. The inversion of will and appetite as the principal determinants of human action had profound ramifications for how self-knowledge, self-mastery and the social order were subsequently understood. There would henceforth be no quick fix for the human condition.

2. The traditional backdrop

It is fair to say that at the beginning of the seventeenth century there was no single, dominant theory of the passions. Treatises written in the seventeenth century continued to bear the marks of Aquinas's influence, in particular, by conceiving of passions as movements of the sensitive appetite, one part of a quadripartite division within the soul. But a range of other influences – Aristotelian, neo-Platonic, Galenic, Augustinian, Stoic, Epicurean and Sceptical – also left their marks on the philosophical landscape. In attempting to develop a new account of human nature consistent with the new physics, philosophers of the seventeenth century could not theorize in a vacuum. Whether cognizant of doing so or not, they cherry-picked from the rich store of ancient and medieval ideas in developing their own.

In neo-Aristotelian approaches, passions were classified among the "natural inclinations" of an organism and governed by "final causes" – the ends or outcomes that direct an organism's development and behaviour. Most ancient and medieval theories viewed the passions as both *cognitive* – involving representations of things as good or evil for the organism – and *conative* – motive powers towards or away from that which the organism apprehends as good or evil for it. These two features of the passions were reflected in the ways in which they were taxonomized and the various therapies that were developed for controlling them. Although there existed great differences between the various taxonomic schemes that appeared between antiquity and the later middle ages, there were common themes in how passions were differentiated. What defined a passion was whether its "formal object"[6] – the type of object or situation in relation to which the passion is an appropriate (or, indeed, even possible response) – was good or evil, present or future, surmountable or insurmountable and so on. The Stoics operated with a modest fourfold distinction according to whether the passion was directed at present or future good or evil (delight, distress, desire and fear) and regarded passions as false judgements that could continue through their "first motions" to agitate the body of even the most sagacious person, even one inclined to dismiss the judgemental aspect of the passion. Rejecting the conflation of passions and sensitive judgements, Aquinas produced an elaborate scheme involving five pairs of passions and one with no opposite (anger) classified into two general kinds – concupiscible (love, desire, joy; hatred, aversion, sadness) and irascible (hope, courage, despair, fear and anger) – depending upon whether the passion is directed at sensible good or evil as such or at good or evil perceived as arduous or difficult to attain or avoid.[7] From well before Aquinas, taxonomic approaches produced classification schemes that resembled Porphyrian trees, with two genera (concupiscible and irascible) and multiple species, but although the approach was not new in Aquinas,[8] Aquinas's taxonomy became mainstream and the most influential point of departure for the early moderns.

On the Thomistic picture, the soul is composed of two subordinate sensitive faculties (apprehension and appetite) and two superordinate rational faculties (reason and will). Aquinas conceives of this as a real distinction between powers of the soul and necessary to account for intrapsychic conflict. Despair, an irascible passion, for example, impedes the operation of desire, a concupiscible one. The appeal of the Thomistic account lay in its organisational simplicity and clarity, with each role neatly and hierarchically defined, but by the end of the sixteenth century, the neat divisions of this faculty psychology were beginning to erode. When Descartes rejects the idea of intrapsychic conflict in favour of conflict between the body and soul, rejecting in the process the distinction between concupiscible and irascible passions, he is picking up on a line of criticism already operative within late Scholastic debates.[9] It is evident, for example, in the nominalists' critique of tendencies to treat what are really just conceptual distinctions between faculties of the soul as real distinctions. If the soul is indeed unitary, lacking in parts, then the distinction between passions and other motive forces like the will must also be "less than real." Such arguments, as Peter King has shown,[10] opened the door for thinkers like Ockham and Scotus to talk about "active emotions of the will" – active liking (*complacentia*) or disliking (*displacentia*) – rendering the distinction between concupiscible and irascible passions merely conceptual. Suárez too is adamant that the passions constitute one power, which, by turning the soul this way and that, creates only the illusion of a soul divided against itself.[11] There are interesting parallels as well between Suárez's view of a single power switching direction and Hobbes's account of deliberation, as we shall see.

Although Thomism was a dominant force leading into the seventeenth century, it was not, therefore, the only game in town. Galen's humouric physiology, tripartite division of the soul and identification of the brain as the seat of sensation were also widely accepted ideas, particularly in medical faculties.[12] The Stoics and their Augustinian opponents too influenced seventeenth century thinking, an outcome of the popularity Hellenistic philosophy had regained towards the end of the sixteenth century in France.[13] The impact of Stoic thought can be detected in the general undermining of the faculty-psychology model favoured by Aristotelians and through their alternative "cognitivist" approach to the passions. Whereas Thomists regarded passions as essentially motive forces (movements of the sensitive appetite) occasioned by sensory apprehensions, neo-Stoics regarded passions as species of false, intellectual judgement (or as primarily constituted by such judgements). As essentially irrational judgements about the values of things, passions, according to the Stoics, were prone to misrepresentation, exaggeration and error. Seventeenth century accounts typically maintained some version of cognitivism while rejecting the general antipathy towards passions demonstrated by the Stoics themselves.

Stoicism aligned the passions (*pathê*) with passivity – with being subject to fortune through forces beyond reason – and with falsehood and vice. In representing as absolute what is only good or evil relative to contingent and particular circumstances, all passions are vicious and impede the natural end of all human activity – tranquillity of the soul (*apatheia*) and independence from fortune.[14] Because each passion contains an involuntary component (a "first motion," *propatheiai*) and a voluntary component (an act of assent to an expressed proposition), direct mastery of the passions was thought to be possible, but only to the extent that the soul can withhold assent to the second component. Control of the latter was deemed sufficient for a life of virtue.

Despite their general antipathy to the passions, the Stoics acknowledged a handful of "good" emotions (*eupatheiai*) – joy, wish, caution and their derivatives – which originated in the intellect and assisted in the struggle for self-mastery.[15] Descartes's distinction between passions that originate in the body and "internal emotions" that originate in the soul bears the marks of this Stoic distinction between good and bad affects.[16] But Stoicism had few medieval adherents. Augustine, an influential opponent of Stoicism, rejected the idea that a person could attain happiness in this life through self-discipline alone. In our postlapsarian state, happiness can only be achieved through the gift of divine grace.[17] *Apatheia*, moreover, is an impossible goal for humans. Passion is unavoidable because love is the basis of all human motivation and fundamental to our union with God. Love for possession of an object is desire; love for an object possessed is joy; love that shuns what opposes it is fear; love that feels that opposition is grief.[18] Although few medieval and early modern accounts accepted the ideal of *apatheia*, however, many Stoic techniques for reducing the effects of a passions – for example cognitive exercises to offset one passion by its contrary – were standard remedies for debilitating passions.[19]

Although the tradition argued, therefore, about whether virtue required freedom from passion and about the functions of the passions in a well-ordered soul, the arrival of mechanism added a new twist to the story. Mechanism left little room for natural inclinations and final causes. Descartes countenances three reasons for denying final causes and natural inclinations in the Aristotelian sense: (1) God's intentions are inscrutable (AT 7: 55; AT 8A: 81; AT 4: 292); (2) the category of efficient causality suffices to understand all causal operations, including God's (AT 8A: 15–16); and (3) bodies devoid of cognition cannot represent the direction or end towards which they move (AT 7: 442; AT 3: 667–8). Spinoza adds to this list the (medieval)[20] objection that final causes implausibly render God's efficacy dependent upon finite ends and imply a desire for something lacking.[21] But if the passions were not to be thought of as natural inclinations in the Aristotelian sense, the question arose as to whether they were natural inclinations in some other sense.

3. Mechanism and *conatus* in Hobbes and Descartes

Hobbes's treatment of the passions is offered as a continuation of his physics. The first developed account appears in the *Elements of Law* (1640) and again, with some modifications,[22] in *Leviathan* (1651), *De corpore* (1655) and *De homine* (1658). In many ways, the most interesting discussion appears in his comments on Thomas White's *De mundo*, most likely written between 1642 and 1643. Hobbes is thus writing extensively about the passions immediately prior to the point in time at which Descartes's attention is drawn to the subject. Descartes's *Les Passions de l'âme*, drafted at the behest of Princess Elisabeth of Bohemia between 1645 and 1646, was completed in 1649. Although Descartes and Hobbes are working on the same set of issues at roughly the same time, it is hard to establish any clear lines of influence between the two. Where they do intersect is in debating the nature of the *conatus* or inertial tendencies of bodies. In 1641, there is an indirect exchange through Mersenne (AT 3: 354; CSMK: 178) over the interpretation of the first law of mechanics – in particular, over what constitutes a body's striving (*conatus*; "endeavour" in English) to remain in the same state. Indirectly, this dispute reveals much about how each understood the mechanical foundations of the passions.[23]

For Hobbes, the passions are the driving force behind all animal action, constitute whatever understanding of good and evil is possible and define the degree of happiness an animal possesses (DME 462ff). For Descartes, although "all the good and evil in this life depends upon the passions" (PS, a.212; AT 11: 488; CSM 1: 404), the autonomy of reason and will always remains a complicating factor. But for both, the passions capture an important (and for Hobbes, complete) source of power that an animal has to obtain what it needs and resist what hinders it pursuit of happiness.

The difference between Descartes and Hobbes on the subject of the *conatus* can be summarized in one sentence: where Hobbes identifies the *conatus* or endeavour of a body with its motion, Descartes uses other terminology – "action," "cause," "force," "potentiality" – none of which are coextensional with motion. Hobbes cannot envisage any kind of change which does not consist in motion because all change involves continual progression – a continual mutation in the agent and patient – which, being divisible into parts, requires us to think of each part, including the beginning as an action and cause of motion and so motion itself (EP 123–4): "For let a space be never so little, that which is moved over a greater space, whereof that little one is part, must first be moved over that" (L 119). The conflation of action, first cause of change and first motion may appear question begging – a conclusion Hobbes attempts to subvert by arguing that because we do not perceive change except as something is affected in our sense and we only sense change by sensing motion, the idea of a change not involving motion is, therefore, incoherent (EP 126; 131). Because a body at rest – that is one that remains in one and the same place relative to contiguous bodies – is nonetheless striving to move in a certain direction, even a body at rest must be in motion. The proof of this is that when the obstacle to its moving is removed, the body moves and in a certain direction without the application of any additional force. The *conatus* that initiates such movement must, Hobbes concludes, itself be motion for only something in motion can be a cause of motion. But because it is imperceptible, it must be *infinitesimal motion* – "motion made in less space and time than can be given; that is, less than can be determined or assigned by exposition or number; that is motion made through the length of a point and an instant of time" (EP 206).

Although Descartes at one point refers to "force" as "the first preparation of motion," it is not itself motion (AT 8A: 115). At *Principles of Philosophy* II, 43, the terms "force," "action," "power" and "striving" are conceptually linked: the force of each body to act against another or to resist the action of another consists "in the single fact that each thing strives, as far as it is in itself [*quantum in se est*], to remain in the same state" (AT 8A: 66). Through several examples, Descartes outlines how a body can have a tendency to move in a certain direction without being in motion, or how it can be altered in its directional tendencies without its motion being altered, or how a body can exhibit several tendencies according to the diverse causes acting upon it (AT 8A: 108–9). A striving to move "passes through" a body even at rest. For example, wine in the bottom of a vat has a tendency to move downwards (AT 1: 451; AT 6: 86–7), and a stone in a sling has tendencies to move away from the centre of a circle and to be deflected on tangents from points along the arc upon which it actually travels (AT 8A: 108–10).

Although in rejecting the identification of *conatus* with motion, Descartes could be accused of treating *conatus* as an occult quality, Hobbes's analysis is not without its own puzzling features. One must accept a peculiar account of infinitesimals as having different and potentially conflicting properties – for example when a body at rest exhibits tendencies to move in opposite directions at once on account of the variety of forces operating upon it. We cannot here pursue these technical issues surrounding the comparative uses of *conatus* but note the differences so as to better understand why the different theorists approached the passions as they did. Descartes uses the independence of "action" and "motion" to support his claim that incorporeal substances can act on corporeal ones. Thus, he writes to More (5 Feb. 1649) that "we clearly conclude that no incorporeal substances are in any strict sense extended. I conceive them as sorts of powers or forces, which although they can act upon extended things, are not themselves extended" (CSMK: 361). Volitions and "internal emotions" which originate in the soul similarly act on the body and are an important source of the soul's resilience to capricious fortune (PS. a.147; CSM 1: 381), though strictly speaking they are not motions. Because there is no force independent of motion, on Hobbes's view, all the soul's operations must instead be explained in terms of motions of the body. In a fairly fundamental way, the dualism of Descartes and materialism of Hobbes are dependent on the different ways in which these forces that determine the direction in which matter moves are understood.

4. Descartes and Hobbes on the passions

The new physics provided an occasion for a revolutionary approach to human nature and the human condition. According to Hobbes and in contrast to ascetic and Stoic approaches to the passions, desire belongs to the essence of animal and human existence. Without desire, there is only death. Hence, *apatheia* – freedom from passion – is a ridiculous and impossible ideal. While we live, we never cease to strive for things we need or to avoid things that threaten our survival. Nature has value for us only insofar as it increases our power and power is measured by the capacity we have to procure what we need. The world is not full of independently valuable objects; we seek things we need because we cannot do otherwise, and we mistakenly think that what we seek is, therefore, intrinsically good. But even the idea of projected or relative value is misleading; what is good for us is only the gradual increase in our power over nature, including others. Rejecting the *summum bonum* of the ancients, Hobbes notes that no one can live whose desires are at an end. Happiness (felicity) consists in nothing but the continual succession of desires. The "grounds of good, and hence of happiness, consist in seeking" (L 160). There is no happiness in possessing objects, only to lose, seek and possess them again – as if we could be made happy by scratching a perpetual itch. Happiness consists only in advancing from one kind of good, which we retain, and are not, therefore, plagued by fear of losing it, to another:

> Happiness is the joy noticed in a prolonged and serene progress of searching from [power] to the next power; and that peace of mind the moral philosophers speak of is not rest or inactivity or the deprivation of desire, but a gentle motion from a good that has been acquired to one that must be acquired.
> (DME 465)

For Hobbes, the centrality of desire in defining the human (and animal) condition is connected to his understanding of *conatus* and the dynamic conception of matter that it affords:[24]

> Also, if the name be given for such form as is the beginning of motion, then, as long as that motion remains, it will be the same individual thing; as that man will always be the same, whose actions and thoughts proceed all from the same

> beginning of motion, namely, that which was in his generation; and that will be the same river which flows from the same fountain, whether the water be the same water, or other water, or something else than water, flow from thence; and that the same city, whose acts proceed continually from the same institution, whether the men be the same or no.
>
> (EP 138)

To seek *apatheia* would thus be equivalent to seeking death. What is "natural" for a human body is striving to increase its power, which is equivalent to the motion that defines it from its earliest moment. Every body has a *conatus* (endeavour); the difference for sentient bodies is that they are made conscious of their endeavour through the passions.[25] The striving of each is "*a perpetuall and restlesse desire of Power after Power, that ceaseth onely in Death, because we cannot be assured of the power and means to live well without the acquisition of more*" (L.I.xi). Deliberately self-destructive behaviour (e.g. suicide) is thus paradoxical, a conclusion Hobbes and Spinoza both embrace, explaining away all apparent cases of deliberate self-harm as the product of unknown external causes.[26]

Descartes begins his "little treatise" on the passions in a similarly naturalistic spirit with a lengthy description of how all movements of the body, including those that originate from the actions of the soul (volitions), are mediated by movements of the animal spirits, and how these spirits are capable, without the intervention of the soul, of moving the animal in ways that serve to preserve it. Passions are a species of perception, which occur in the soul but originate from things outside it and yet are "*referred to the soul itself.*" This language of "referring" is a little mysterious, but one way to understand it is in terms of the different kinds of predication we make with our sensory terminology: perceptions that are referred to some part of the body (e.g. pains) tend be predicated of those parts – we say that *the foot is in pain*, not that the soul is. Those referred outside are predicable of external things (e.g. perceptions of light, colour, sound, etc). And those referred to the soul itself (passions and emotions) are said of the soul – we say that *the soul is angry, afraid, proud*, and so forth. Passions indicate the utility or disutility that objects have for the union by, in other words, representing the specific effects of these objects on the soul.[27] Their "principal function" is to determine, move and strengthen the will towards obtaining what is useful for the body or avoiding what is harmful to it.

Descartes's physiological account of the passions grounds their operations in the operations of the laws of nature. The various ways in which external bodies impinge upon the senses and affect the flow of the blood explain all the variety of symptoms and effects of the passions. The heating of the blood in the heart produces vaporous matter that is then filtered in the brain into the animal spirits, the finest particles of matter that course through the nerves and are responsible for every movement of the muscles. In accordance with the second law, fluid parts of the body travel in a straight line, being diverted this way or that only when encountering an obstacle. Of particular note is the way in which the coarser parts of the animal spirits meeting no resistance in the spongy parts of the brain create deep channels which subsequently dispose the organism to react in similar ways to similar circumstances. This is memory (AT 4: 310; CSMK: 270; AT 4: 114–15; CSMK: 233). The formation of these channels enables the brain to be to some extent predictive, anticipating effects before they occur, initiating fast reflex responses and reducing the element of surprise for the soul, promoting the chances of more successful interventions. The dispositions that define one's temperament are grounded in the actual arrangements of matter that are produced in the body through its earliest encounters with the world (AT 4: 604–5; CSMK: 307).

For Descartes, there are six principal passions: wonder, love, hatred, desire, joy and sadness (PS a.69; AT 11: 380; CSM 1: 353). From those basic six, many others develop through combination or as variations that depend on different kinds of objects and associated thoughts. Anger, for example, is "a kind of hatred or aversion towards those who have done some evil or who have tried to harm . . . us in particular," whereas indignation is directed at "those who do some evil, whatever it may be." Further precisifications of anger and indignation depend on whether they are joined to pity, derision, wonder, joy, fear, self-love or the desire for revenge (PS aa. 195–200; AT 11: 475–9; CSM 1: 397–9). The taxonomy does not, therefore, produce anything resembling a Porphyrian tree but is rather a highly nuanced account of our emotional reality.

With the exception of wonder, passions involving a perception of things external to the soul as affecting the body in a determinate way presuppose a prior experience of the object that is associated with pleasure or pain. Wonder is the "first of all passions" and is evoked by things that are novel or extraordinary (PS a.70; AT 11: 380–1; CSM 1: 353). Wonder is critical for focusing attention and is thus an important aid in the process of acquiring knowledge (PS a. 74; AT 11: 383; CSM 1: 354). Depending on how a new experience unfolds – whether it turns out to be pleasurable, painful or neutral – wonder eventually gives way to esteem, contempt or indifference towards the object in question. Although each passion corresponds to a dedicated movement of the animal spirits and may involve other effects in the body produced through the agitation of the blood, each passion is principally differentiated by the kind of thought associated with its "first cause," which is typically an external object (PS a.51; AT 11: 371; CSM 1: 349).

Descartes's taxonomy of the passions is, in this respect, quite traditional. It aligns with medieval practices of differentiating passions by their formal objects. Fear is a response to a perceived threat. Envy is directed at a desirable object possessed by another. Hope is for a desirable outcome perceived as probable; despair for a desirable outcome perceived as improbable. The taxonomic criteria are many and varied but they include considerations of whether the object is a perceived good or evil; novel or familiar; probable or improbable; possessed or not; attainable or unattainable; past, present or future; deserved or undeserved; caused by oneself or by another; and so on.[28] Desire has a special place in the system, being the last passion in any affective series, the passion that acts directly upon the will, and the immediate impetus to action (PS a.101; AT 11: 403; CSM 1: 363).

In Descartes's dualistic system, the passions have a foot in both the mind and the body. They are passions of the soul but "one and the same thing" as the actions in the body that are their proximal causes (PS a.1; AT 11: 327; CSM 1: 328). What is less clear is how a passion is in turn a cause of action in the body. The corresponding movements of the animal spirits are sufficient on their own to produce an appropriate bodily movement; indeed, this is how animals survive. But is the passion itself then causally relevant or simply epiphenomenal?

Despite Descartes's avowal that the will is impotent to change the course of any passion that disturbs the heart and blood (PS a. 45–6; AT 11: 362–4; CSM 1: 345), because the will alone is the motive force of the soul, the process by which any passion of the soul produces action must be mediated by the will. Descartes speaks of passions as "inclining" the will – presumably inclining it to assent to the appearance of good or evil it represents. But then the power to act appears to reside ultimately either with the autonomous will or, if the will is indisposed, with the involuntary movements of the animal spirits in the body.

Because of Hobbes's identification between *conatus* and motion, the control a passion exerts over action is more direct. The will is nothing other than the endeavour of the body under the guise of appetite or aversion. "Appetite is the first *conatus*, i.e., an invisible motion of animals' nerves or spirits towards an object they perceive or imagine," and aversion is "a conatus or motion towards the [bodily] parts that feel distaste for the object felt or imagined . . . commonly called avoidance" (DME 447). Every passion is, therefore, Janus-faced. It is both the motion or endeavour of the body and a self-awareness of that endeavour. Hence, there is no threat that passions are epiphenomenal to the process by which an animal responds to a situation. In *Elements of Law*, Hobbes writes that all passions proceed from the glory that depends upon an imagination or conception of one's power.[29] If the imagination is pleasurable, it produces an aspiration to increase one's power, inducing either (vicious) pride or a justified self-evaluation leading possibly to courage; if displeasure attends the imagination, humility or dejection are produced, creating the potential for fear or shame (EL c.9). All subsequent passions revolve around the experience of power involved in glory or its lack. The crowning passion, *magnanimity*, is simply glory well grounded in the experience of possessing sufficient power to attain one's ends in an overt manner. Magnanimity differs from pusillanimity, which is based on self-doubt, and from every other kind of glory, including those relying on fame, fallacy, art, enmity or contention. Magnanimity is thus associated with a range of socially useful emotions, such as charity, and the absence of negative passions produced by the lack of something valuable, such as anger and envy.

Although this emphasis on glory is absent in *Leviathan* and later works, Hobbes retains the connection between passions and the experience of power or powerlessness. The passions are equivalent to one of two kinds of motion in animals, those we call "voluntary" and those we call "vital," that begin in generation and continue throughout the whole of an animal's life (L 118). All voluntary motions depend upon a prior thought of "whither, which way and what" and hence upon the imagination, the first internal beginning of voluntary action. What we experience when we are moved by a passion just is the body's movement towards or away from some object, even if the movement is infinitesimal (L 119). The passion is the first moment of change and is motion itself:

> This motion, in which consisteth pleasure or pain, is also a solicitation or provocation either to draw near the thing that pleaseth, or to retire from the thing that displeaseth; and this solicitation is the endeavour or internal beginning of animal motion, which when the object delighteth, is called appetite; when it displeaseth, it is called aversion, in respect of the displeasure present; but in respect of the displeasure expected, fear. So that pleasure, love, and appetite, which is also called desire are divers names for divers considerations of the same thing.
>
> (HN, 32)

All the variety among the passions amounts to the different ways in which the endeavour of a human body expresses itself according to differences in its circumstances. The two basic forms are desire and aversion which, when connected to different thoughts, are referred to as different passions. Thus, desire differs from love by signifying the absence rather than presence of the object sought; aversion and hate by the absence or presence of the object to be avoided. A third passion – contempt (which seems to include indifference) – is identified with immobility, resulting from the fact that the heart's movements are occupied with other "more potent" objects or because it has had no experience of the object in question. Contempt thus performs some of the functions that wonder performs for Descartes, enabling the body to resist being drawn either towards or away from the object long enough for it to be investigated (L 120).

Because the body is continually undergoing change, we need not expect any constancy in our passions, according to Hobbes; the same objects will not affect different individuals in the same way or the same individual in the same way on different occasions. From these considerations, Hobbes argues that there is no good or evil *per se*, no common "Rule of Good and Evil" in objects themselves, only that which has utility or disutility for an individual person if residing in the state of nature (i.e. where there is no civil society), or as established by the sovereign, the person representing the commonwealth, or by the arbitrator or judge established therein to mediate disagreements among people (L 120–1). The experience of our passions constitutes either delight or trouble of mind, which accompanies all appetite, desire, love, aversion and hatred. Pleasure is the appearance or sense of something good, pain, the sensing of something bad; and are such as to assist or hinder the vital motions in performing their functions (L 121–2). Pleasures and pains arise from the sensation of present objects (sensual pleasures or pains) or from the expectations of objects or their consequences (pleasures of the mind or grief). The basic movements towards or away from objects tinged with either pleasure or pain produce six simple passions: appetite, desire, love, aversion, hate, joy and grief. These are so named according to whether the object of desire is attainable or not, whether it is loved or hated ("good" or "evil"), whether several passions occur together, and what alteration or succession among the passions takes place.

Differences in the way particular passions are defined aside, Hobbes's strategy is much the same as Descartes's. Passions are taxonomised according to their associated thoughts concerning the utility or disutility of objects. As for Descartes, the very same motion in the body can constitute different passions depending on differences among the associated thoughts. *Appetite* with an opinion of hurt from the object is *fear*; with a thought of avoiding hurt, *courage*; sudden courage, *anger*; anger for a great hurt done to another, *indignation*. Fear of an invisible power feigned by the mind but publicly allowed is *religion*; if publicly disavowed, *superstition*; and if based on the truth, *true religion* (L 124).

One of the most fascinating aspects of Hobbes's account of the passions is his analysis of deliberation. Deliberation just is the *alternation* among the passions in regard to one and the same thing and is rational or irrational as the passions themselves are fitting in the circumstances or not (EL c.12; DME 447–8). When we alternate between appetite and aversion, hope, fear, desire and despair, as when we consider the pros and cons of a certain course of action, the good or evil consequences, probability or improbability of attaining what we desire, "the whole summe of Desires, Aversions, Hopes and Fears, continued till the thing be done, or thought impossible, is that we call Deliberation" (L 127). It is so called, Hobbes notes, because it puts to an end the liberty we have of performing or omitting the action. Deliberation terminates either in an action or a thought that the end is impossible (L 127; DME 449). Rejecting the Scholastic idea of the will as a rational appetite, Hobbes thus identifies the will as the last appetite in the deliberative series, this being the defining consideration in determining whether an action is voluntary or involuntary (L 128; DME 448).[30] Given these deflationary concepts of deliberation and will, it is not surprising that Hobbes is prepared to accept that "beasts" also deliberate (L 128; DME 127). Where they differ from us emotionally is in lacking the *curiosity* (a species of *admiration*, wonder) that enables us to philosophise and acquire knowledge about the world (EL c.9).

Where Descartes retains the Scholastic idea of an autonomous realm of reason and will, Hobbes regards what we think of as definitively human and free action as subjected to the same kind of mechanical explanation as any other natural phenomenon. This fundamental difference between the two thinkers is grounded in part in their different approaches to the *conatus*. Where Hobbes sees the *conatus* of the human body as *exhausting* the explanation of all the choices and actions a person performs, Descartes does not. It is Hobbes's reductionist approach and the methodology behind it rather than Descartes's which sets the stage for the work of figures like Spinoza and Hume who too would see little merit in the idea of an autonomous realm of human freedom, preferring instead the idea of human nature thoroughly immersed in and continuous with the rest of nature.

5. Spinoza, *conatus* and passion

There is no way to understand Spinoza's contribution to debates in the seventeenth century about the nature and function of the passions outside the framework of his complex and unique metaphysical system. The passions make their formal entrance at the beginning of part III of the *Ethics*, along with a discussion of the *conatus* and only after Spinoza has taken himself to have established that God is necessary, one with nature and the only substance that exists. That one substance has, however, two principal attributes – thought and extension – through which all things must be conceived. Individual things are in the category of modes – bodies are individuated as distinct ratios of motion and rest and minds as the ideas of particular human bodies. Every change that occurs can be conceived under the attribute of either thought or extension. Causal descriptions are closed under a single attribute. Given the distinction in attributes or natures, we cannot understand how things that fall under one attribute could be causes or effects of things that fall under the other (E IP3). Thus, Spinoza rejects as completely unintelligible the kind of causal interaction between mind and body Descartes takes for granted (E IIIP2). Whereas Descartes suggests that a particular human body is individuated by its relationship to a persisting and independent human mind,[31] Spinoza argues that any particular mind, constituted as it is by certain modes of thinking or ideas in God, must have an actual, existing thing other than itself as its object. And because there can be no idea which does not have an object (E IIP11), by a process of elimination, Spinoza concludes that the only candidate object for the mind is the human body. In this framework, the passions play a central role not just in the account of self-knowledge but also in the account of our knowledge of all other bodies around us. Because I have ideas of the modifications of my own body and no others, were something other than my body to be the object of my mind, I would have an idea of the effects of it rather than of my own body (E IIAx4); but clearly, I do not (E IIP13). I have ideas of the effects of other bodies only insofar as I have ideas of the modifications of my own body they produce, and the ideas of such modifications are my passions. The passions are, therefore, the principal source of our knowledge of our own minds and bodies, and through them of other bodies as well (E IIp23).

All this seems to make the mind dependent upon the human body for its individuation. But the matter is more complex. As an object of the idea of the mind, "the human body exists according as we feel it" (E IIP13c; E IIp19), which suggests that the limits of the human body are defined by what the mind can sense, through, for example, sensations like pain and pleasure, proprioception and the passions. Whether this is an adequate test for identifying the boundaries of a particular body need not delay us here. The point is that being one and the same substance, neither the mind nor the body takes metaphysical priority. As a monist, Spinoza regards the power of the mind as the same as the power of the body, and this, he claims, is indicative of a true union (E IIP21n). Spinoza uses "power," "power of acting," "essence," "desire" and "virtue" interchangeably and defines the power of acting of a being in terms of its *conatus* or endeavour to persist in being (E IIIP7–9; 54; 57; E IV, Def. 8). The power of acting of mind and body operate in tandem. As a body is more apt for performing many actions at the same time, so too will the mind be more apt for perceiving many things at once. And as the body acts more independently, so too will the mind be more apt for distinct understanding (E IIP13n). Increases in the power of thought also correspond to increases in the power of acting. It is only by understanding our place in the whole of nature *sub specie aeternitatis* that one can be liberated from impulses for things that enslave the body and cause pain and distress – to wit, riches, honour and pleasure.[32]

Part II of the *Ethics* closes with the promise that this picture of nature will help with the regulation of life.[33] The closer we come to understanding ourselves as participants in the divine nature, the more we will be able to perfect our actions and understand God. The *Ethics* instructs us to seek happiness and virtue in that which is within our power to enact, namely that which follows from our nature and the understanding of our relationship to God, and to bear what happens to us beyond our control as part of the providential order. Part III, *On the Nature and Origin of Emotions*, is framed around the rejection of the tradition according to which human agents have absolute power over and autonomy from nature, including their own. In thinking that he could attain complete control over his emotions, Descartes supposedly "showed nothing but the greatness and ingenuity of his intellect" (E 83). "Nature is always the same and one everywhere," and passions follow by the same necessity from natural causes as any other thing (E 84). Spinoza does in due course have things to say about how the passions can be moderated, but this too is explained through the forces of nature, in particular through the natural striving of human beings to persist in being. Virtue consists in acting according to the laws of nature to preserve oneself (E IV, Def. 8; E IVP18). There is no alternative source of power, action or virtue to subvert the course of nature.

Emotion (*affectus*) is defined as any modification of the body whereby its power of acting is increased or decreased and the concomitant idea of such a modification. This bears an obvious affinity with Hobbes's Janus-faced account of the passions as self-aware endeavours. Affects fall into two types. To the extent that one is an "adequate cause" of some modification of the body – that is, a cause whose effect can be clearly and distinctly seen through it (E III, Def. I) – one's emotion is an *action*. Where one is instead only a partial or "inadequate cause" – where the effect cannot be clearly and distinctly understood (E III, Def. I) – one is subject to a *passion*. The connection between being an inadequate cause and having inadequate ideas sets the stage for Spinoza's story about how human life naturally regulates itself through an increased understanding of nature.[34]

One of Spinoza's working assumptions is that every way in which the body is affected either increases or diminishes its power of acting (E III. Post. I; E IIP13). What this "power of acting" amounts to is not entirely clear. John Carriero notes that Spinoza uses the expression interchangeably with talk of increases in perfection and reality; hence, in striving to increase its power of acting, a being is striving for a greater degree of perfection or reality.[35] What an individual is under the attribute of extension is a certain ratio of motion and rest, but increasing one's power of acting does not seem to be simply a matter of increasing one's motion, as if one would necessarily be more powerful by going faster or moving more often. The only hints we have as to what it might be are those offered previously: being able to do more things at once and, simultaneously, being able to perceive more things at once, are marks of perfection (E IIP13s).[36] On this formulation, increasing one's power of acting is a matter of increasing the ratio of actions to passions. The more that what we do depends on things outside us, the more passive we are and the fewer clear and distinct ideas we have.[37] But "perfection" in Spinoza's framework is not an intrinsically normative notion – "perfection" and "imperfection" are inventions of the mind that are used to compare different individuals of the same kind. Nature herself does not make any such discriminations (E IV, Preface).

The autonomy to which we can aspire is, therefore only relative, and as Hobbes had previously argued, much of what we think of as autonomous behaviour is really driven by passions that only decrease our autonomy.[38] We think, for example, that we speak freely when instead we

> cannot put a stop to the desire to talk, just as experience teaches as clearly as reason that men think themselves free on account of this alone, that they are conscious of their actions and ignorant of the causes of them; and moreover that the decisions of the mind are nothing save their desires, which are various according to various dispositions of the body.
>
> (E IIIP3; pp. 88–9)

What we think are determinations of the will are nothing other than the effects of our strongest desires (*cupiditas*). Indecision or wavering of the mind (*animi fluctuatio*) is not essentially different, but only the sign of conflicting emotions or not knowing what one wants (E IIIP2; cf. E IIIP17). Spinoza's analysis of what we think of as "free" choices and actions is reminiscent of Hobbes's analysis of deliberation.

If what we think of as being in the realm of choice and decision, acts of the mind, belong instead in the realm of desire, what then is desire? Desire is the counterpart under the attribute of thought of modifications of the body. More precisely, desire is the consciousness of the *conatus* of the body to persist in being. In E IIIP7–9, *conatus* is identified with the essence, the power of acting and the power to persist in being of an individual thing. All our actions and passions of the mind are expressions of our *conatus*. *Voluntas* (will) is *conatus* referred solely to the mind. Appetite is *conatus* referred simultaneously to mind and body. As for Hobbes, objects lack intrinsic value: "We endeavour, wish, desire, or long for nothing because we deem it good, but on the other hand, we deem it good because we endeavour, wish for, desire or long for it" (E IIP9n). The passions introduce us to ideas of good or evil, but these ideas represent things we deem useful or deleterious to our survival because they cause pleasure or pain (E IV Preface; P8).

According to Spinoza's "general definition" (E III Def; pp. 139–40), a passion of the mind is a confused idea by which the mind affirms a greater or lesser power of existing of its body in comparison with a previous state and is determined thereby to think of one thing rather than another. The passions draw one's attention, in other words, to a change in the state of the body and to something that affects its power of existing, and in this way mind and body contribute to the same act of self-preservation. The passions fall into three basic kinds: desire, pleasure (the experience of moving to a higher state of perfection or increased power of acting) and pain (the experience of diminishing perfection). All others are derived from these (E IIIP9–10; P57–8). The imagination is a source of both pleasure and pain. Pleasure is the feeling of the transition to a greater state of power and perfection; pain, the feeling of the transition to a lesser state. Hence, emotions like love that help the mind in its *conatus* or endeavour are important, and the mind will strive to keep images of beloved things in mind (E IIIP20–1). When we imagine something, an external body is present in the mind which can affect it in a mode which either increases or diminishes its power of acting. The mind will endeavour to imagine those things which increase its power of acting, or if it is conscious of something diminishing its power of acting, to remember something that cuts off the existence of that thing (E IIIP7; P37; P39). We experience love when pleasure accompanies the idea of an external cause, and we endeavour to preserve it. We hate something when we experience pain accompanying the idea of it and endeavour to remove or destroy it (E IIIP13; 39; 43). Sometimes a mere association with other ideas colours our experience. When we suffer two passions at once, the two will likely recur together whenever one or the other is evoked (E IIIP14; 52). If we come across something that resembles a previous cause of love or hate, whether real or imagined, we may similarly be affected with pleasure or pain (E IIIP15–18; 46). Because we can be moved by the images of things (E IIIP18), we are able to experience an inconstant pleasure of an imagined future outcome about which we have some doubt – hope – or an inconstant pain involving some doubt – fear (E, p. 98). Joy and sadness are responses to events past in which we continue to imagine ourselves involved (E IIIP18n2; P19).

So far, Spinoza's account seems exclusively focused on the self and its self-preservation, but there is, he thinks, a straightforward mechanical process by which we are affected by the increasing or diminishing power of others. Because we are capable of imagining others whom we love or hate to be affected by pleasure or pain, we will accordingly be pleased or distressed. The increase or decrease in others' power of acting is a factor that can influence our own degree of perfection. From this "imitation of the affects" (E IIIP27, n.1), a host of socially oriented emotions – pity, favour, indignation, envy, pride (*superbia*), partiality, disdain, compassion and emulation – are evoked (E IIIP21–7). The reason why we tend to be affected by an image of another human and the signs of their pleasure or pain is that in forming an image of them, which is a modification of our own body, we have an idea that involves both the nature of our own body and that of the other, represented as being the same or similar. Noting the similarity in our natures is not sufficient, however, to determine how we will react emotionally to others – there is also the question of whether they (or things like them) have been associated in our past with pleasure or pain. How exactly we are affected depends then on whether we are disposed to love or hate the other. Loving a being external to us tends to produce emotions in us similar to those it experiences; hating tends to produce contrary emotions. Through such mechanisms, our *conatus* extends itself to promote the well-being of everything conducive to our pleasure and *felicitas* and to destroy everything contrary to it (E IIIP28–9).

Lest we think that nature is rife with competition between individuals and unrestrained passions, it should be noted that there are forces that lead us as much towards social harmony. We cannot experience pure joy at the destruction of our enemies because regarding them as similar in essence to us naturally produces pain at the thought of their destruction (E IIIP47). Coming to understand the necessity of things lessens our feelings of love but also hatred and all their derivatives (E IIIP49). Reflection on the mind, its adequate ideas and its power of acting produces joy and a more distinct image of the self, which is naturally pleasurable, and because what is pleasurable always increases a thing's power of acting, the reflective mind is self-rewarding (E IIIP53; P58). The more active we are, the more resilient we are in the face of capricious fortune. Given that we cannot survive without the cooperation of external things (E IVP3; P18), however, the most we can hope to attain is a state where the balance of emotions is in favour of those that involve only desire and pleasure and refer to us insofar as we are active, and this, Spinoza deems, is *fortitude*. Fortitude is composed of spiritedness (*animositas*, or the desire by which each strives for self-preservation through reason) and nobility of mind (*generositas*, or the desire by which each strives to help and befriend others). Fortitude is Spinoza's equivalent of the "master passion" of previous traditions, for example, Descartes's notion of *générosité*, and the cornerstone of his moral psychology (E IIIP58–9).

6. Passions to politics

Although we cannot do justice here to the complex political philosophies that emerged in connection with the burgeoning interest in the passions in the seventeenth century, we can see how thinking about the relationship between power and passion would naturally lead to an interest in the concept of political power. Descartes, Hobbes and Spinoza each conceive of the passions as a manifestation of the law of inertia. In each account, the power of a thing to obtain what it needs in order to persist in being is measured by the power it possesses to obtain what it desires or loves or hopes for, and so on. For each of our thinkers, civil society emerges in the story as a solution to the coordination problem that individuals must collectively face or perish. The political problem is how to reconcile the fundamental duty of care towards oneself that is by nature our *conatus* or endeavour with the obligations of citizenship.

Despite their differences, each of our thinkers came to think that there was a natural solution to this problem. In striving for self-preservation, a person naturally comes to feel and identify with being a part of a larger, more powerful whole – the state or commonwealth. Hobbes assumes that combining one's power with others is always in one's rational self-interest, just as a larger stone will have a greater impact on the ground than a smaller one (EL 150–1). Spinoza too points to an obvious truth: "there is nothing more useful to man than man" (E IVP18n). But it is not just that joining forces with others is prudent; what passions like generosity and fortitude reveal to us is the fundamental moral equality between individual persons.

Whereas, for Descartes and Spinoza, passions such as love and generosity encourage the soul to join in union with others, Hobbes develops a complicated story about how social interaction produces passions that temper excessively egoistic desires. Whether from fear or love, humans cannot but progress towards the creation of civil society. It is true that for Hobbes power is measured by the capacity to procure what one needs to satisfy one's desires: "The Power of a Man, (to take it Universally,) is his present means, to obtain some future apparent Good" (EL 150). But there are natural constraints on the unbridled accumulation of power. Riches are a source of power but also provoke envy and resentment; hence, riches combined with liberality or a reputation for providing protection or love of man or wisdom or nobility or eloquence constitute a more secure way of increasing one's power (EL 150–1).

The transition to civil society is for Hobbes a necessity and anything but smooth. Hobbes's starting point – the state of nature – is rife with competition and conflict and the struggle for power, a zero-sum game (DME 469). We are repelled by things that lower our opinion of our own power; we are grieved by the loss of riches and friends because this threatens our power to obtain future goods; we are easily insulted because barbs remind us of our weakness; and we are pained by others' success because this causes us to doubt our own power. One's increase in power cancels out another's. Joy is nothing but pride or boasting of one's power in comparison with another (DME 465–6). Among the virtues, prudence, which consists of the power to increase one's power and secure the means for satisfying future desires, is unsurprisingly elevated above all others (DME 469). Whatever socially useful emotions emerge in the ordinary course of nature, they are never sufficient to eliminate the deleterious effects of competition.

Part of the difficulty for Hobbes in conceiving of social harmony lies in his conception of the way the *conatus* expresses itself – as a war of everyone against everyone and as a right to everything and everyone. There is, in other words, no distinction between right and power. For Descartes and Spinoza, by contrast, although our desires may put us in competition with others, we are also primitively moved by love towards others and this makes us perceive their endeavours as extensions of our own. Love, according to Descartes, is the first awakening of consciousness in the developing foetus (AT 4: 604–5; CSMK 307), and through love we are disposed to form unions in which we identify ourselves as parts of wholes greater than ourselves. As he writes to Princess Elisabeth:

> After one has recognised the goodness of God, the immortality of our souls and the grandeur of the universe, there is still one truth the knowledge of which seems to me especially useful and that is that although each of us is a person separated from others, whose interests consequently are in some fashion distinct from those of the rest of the world, one ought always to think that one could not subsist alone and that one is, in effect, one of the parts of the universe, and more particularly still, one of the parts of this earth, and of the state, of this society and of this family, to which one is joined by one's domicile, one's solemn oath, and by birth. And it is necessary to prefer always the interests of a whole of which one is a part to those of his person in particular, though always with measure and discretion, for one would do wrong to expose oneself to a great evil to procure only a little good for his parents or his country.
> (AT 4: 293; CSMK: 266, trans alt.)

Love incites the soul "to join itself in volition to the objects that appear to be suitable to it" (AT 11: 387) and its principal function is to render the union – whether that be a union of mind and body or a family or a nation – more perfect (AT 11: 430; 432). Through love, a passion rooted in the primal movements of the animal spirits but involving explicitly the assent of the will, the boundaries of the self are extended to include others as parts of one's moral self, structuring individual preferences in the service of these greater wholes. If we get a lucky start, the *conatus* of our bodies will be channelled in these socially useful paths. The unnatural state is one in which, through some analogue of disease, socially destructive passions, like envy, anger and hatred, gain the upper hand. The path back towards self-preservation lies for Descartes in the triumph of love, the mastery of "vain desires" and the development through reflection on the unlimited power of the will and resolve to use it well – *generosity* – Descartes's master passion and highest virtue. (AT 11: 446)

On Hobbes's view, the idea that we can overcome the destructive force of competition in nature without the artifice of civil society is simply naïve. In sustaining the state, however, institutions that help us identify ourselves as parts of a larger whole are of critical importance. The main function of the "body politic" is to align the interests of individuals with those of the commonwealth. As if recognising that power cannot be completely alienated from individuals no matter how great the force of the commonwealth, Hobbes seeks to explain how it may at least be redirected through gentler pressures. The unity of the commonwealth depends particularly on the existence of civil laws about which citizens must be educated:

> And the grounds of these Rights, have the rather need to be diligently, and truly taught; because they cannot be maintained by any Civill Law, or terrour of legal punishment. For a Civill Law, that shall forbid Rebellion, (and such is all resistance to the essentiall Rights of Soveraignty,) is not (as a Civill Law) any obligation, but by vertue onely of the Law of Nature, that forbiddeth the violation of Faith; which naturall obligation if men know not, they cannot know the Right of any Law the Soveraign maketh. And for the Punishment, they take it but for an act of Hostility; which when they think they have strength enough, they will endeavour by acts of Hostility, to avoid.
>
> (L 377)

It is "the duty and the benefit" of the sovereign to instruct the populace in the essential rights of sovereignty in order to prevent a return to the state of war or rebellion against the commonwealth. Education is required "for the will of another, cannot be understood, but by his (the subject's) own word, or act, or by conjecture taken from his scope and purpose" (L 319). Given the inevitability of desires geared towards the self-interest of individuals and their own preservation, legal and educational institutions help to direct individual tendencies in more socially useful ways. Properly managed, the *conatus* of individuals can succeed in preserving them without destroying others:

> For the use of Lawes . . . is not to bind the People from all Voluntary actions; but to direct and keep them in such motion, as not to hurt themselves by their own impetuous desires, rashnesse or indiscretion, as Hedges are set, not to stop Travellers, but to keep them in the way.
>
> (L 388)

Where Hobbes sees a sharp dichotomy between the natural state and the civil state, Spinoza sees only continuity. To repeat, "Nature is always the same and one everywhere" and civil society must, therefore, be as much the product of natural law as anything else. Spinoza agrees with Hobbes, however, that civil society and its institutions are necessary to create conditions for human freedom, wherein individuals "give up their natural right and render themselves reciprocally secure" (E IVP36–7, p. 168).[39] The transition to civil society does not involve a rupture from the state of nature but emerges from the ordinary course of our emotional exchanges.[40] In the state of reason, we understand how it is that we agree in nature with others and can, as a result, judge what is objectively good and bad for beings of our kind (E IVP35). Under these conditions, pursuing what is good for others is no different from pursuing what is good for one's self – *each person can be a God to others* (E IVP35–7). The creation of civil society signals the emergence of normativity in nature, for here alone are things decreed good or bad by common consent and the rule of law justified (E IVP37).

7. Conclusion

Early seventeenth century debates about the passions are not peripheral to our understanding of the major scientific and metaphysical shifts in the period. In many respects, these debates offer the clearest insight into the challenges mechanism presented to our understanding of nature and our place within it. The conflation of passion and the power of organisms to persevere in existence opened up the theoretical possibility of a truly universal science of nature, one that left no realm of activity beyond the reach of the laws of mechanics. The radical consequences of this shift should not be underestimated, for although it did much to free philosophical thinking from the shackles of Aristotelian natural philosophy, the closer human action came to being conceived of as the product of brute forces of nature, the more reason's grip on our self-determination began to erode. What resulted were some ingenious, if not entirely edifying, attempts to reconceive power and autonomy in ways consistent with the idea that we do not stand above nature but are simply the part put on this earth to understand it.

Notes

1 This was certainly the view of the Cambridge Platonists. See, for example, Ralph Cudworth, *The True Intellectual System of the Universe*. 2nd ed. London, 1678/1743: 147ff.
2 Epistle, *Elements of Law*. References to Hobbes's texts are as follows: *Thomas White's De Mundo Examined* (hereafter, DME) (1976), Harold Whitmore Jones, trans. Bradford University (unearthed from among Mersenne's papers and first published in Latin by Jacquot and Jones in 1973, Paris: J. Vrin); *Elements of Law* (hereafter, EL), *De Corpore* (hereafter, DC) and *Elements of Philosophy* (hereafter, EP) from *The English Works of Thomas Hobbes of Malmesbury*, Sir Thomas Molesworth, ed. Aalen, Germany: Scientia, 1962; and *Leviathan* (hereafter, L) C. B. Macpherson, ed. Penguin edition, 1968.
3 "As a physicist" (i.e. natural philosopher). Descartes writes this in a prefatory letter to his "little treatise" – *The Passions of the Soul* (hereafter, PS) (AT 11: 326; CSM 1: 327). All references to Descartes's texts are from Descartes, René. 1897–1913/1996. *Oeuvres de Descartes* (AT). 12 volumes, Charles Adam and Paul Tannery, eds. Paris: J. Vrin; and *The Philosophical Writings of Descartes* (CSM/CSMK; 1984–91). J. Cottingham, R. Stoothoff and D. Murdoch, eds., vols 1–2, and J. Cottingham, R. Stoothoff, D. Murdoch, and A. Kenny, eds., vol. 3. Cambridge: Cambridge University Press. Descartes's intention is to align his work with one of two mainstream approaches to the passions – that of the physicist as opposed to that of the dialectician – as defined by mentioned by Aristotle in his *De Anima* (403a29–b9). Despite this comment and like Aristotle, Descartes ends up combining both approaches, defining passions physiologically, by their associated thoughts and by their cognitive and moral roles. See my *Descartes and the Passionate Mind*. Cambridge: Cambridge University Press, 2006: ch.2.
4 Benedictus de Spinoza, *Ethics* (hereafter E). Boyle ed. London: Heron Books, n.d., preface: p. 84.
5 *Ibid.*, p. 83.
6 For a discussion of the traditional notion of a formal object, see Anthony Kenny, *The Anatomy of the Soul*. Oxford: Blackwell, 1962: 189 ff.
7 *Summa Theologica* (hereafter, S.T.). Blackfriars edition, vol. 1. New York: Benziger Brothers, 1946: I–II. q.22.
8 It can be seen, as Peter King has argued, as deriving from Plato's account of the irrational element of the soul (*Republic* 436A–441C), reproduced by Aristotle (N.E. 1.13 and *Rhetoric* 1.10) and passed down through Augustine, Nemesius of Emesa, John Blund and Jean de la Rochelle. See King, *Medieval Affective Psychology*, pp. 1–2 (unpublished, 16 July 2015: http://www.colorado.edu/neh2015/sites/default/files/attached-files/king.affective_psychology.pdf; accessed 19 February 2017).

9   Descartes instead explains all apparent intrapsychic conflict in terms of the soul and body pushing the pineal gland in opposite directions (PS, a.47; AT 11: 345; CSM 1: 345–6).
10 King, "Medieval Affective Psychology," p. 3.
11 Suárez, *Tractatus*, vol. iv.4, 762b. The distinction is at best conceptual and useful for practical purposes.
12 Claudius Galen, *On the Passions and Errors of the Soul*. Trans. Paul W. Harkins, intro. Walter Riese. Columbus, OH: Ohio State University Press, 1963.
13 For an overview of debates in France over the passions in the late sixteenth and early seventeenth centuries, see Anthony Levi's *French Moralists: The Theory of the Passions 1585–1649*. Oxford: Clarendon Press, 1964.
14 Amy Schmitter notes that in attempting to Latinize the Greek term "pathos," Cicero (*De Finibus Bonorum et Malorum* 255) considers how the passions are not commonly described as diseases and settles on "*perturbationes*," which connotes a vicious disturbance. See Amy M. Schmitter, 2010. "17th and 18th Century Theories of Emotions," in Edward N. Zalta, ed. *The Stanford Encyclopedia of Philosophy* (Winter 2016 edition), https://plato.stanford.edu/archives/win2016/entries/emotions-17th18th. In the *Tusculan Disputations*, J. E. King, trans. Loeb Classical Library, 1989: IV, 35 (Cambridge, MA: Harvard University Press), Cicero uses erotic love as an example of the irrational partiality of emotional judgements. The inconstancy of love with respect to persons with the same qualities or the same person at different times is taken to be evidence of its irrationality.
15 See Simo Knuuttila, *Emotions in Ancient and Medieval Philosophy*. Oxford: Clarendon Press, 2004, 68–70.
16 PS, a.147; CSM 1: 381.
17 De civitate Dei, 14.9.
18 Ibid., 14.7.
19 See my 2006: ch.2.
20 The argument can be found in Buridan's *Quaestiones super octo libros Physicorum Aristotelis (secundum ultimam lecturam)*, M. Streijger and P.J.J.M. Bakker, eds. Leiden: Brill, 2015: II.q.7: "Whether the end is a cause?"
21 E 1. Appendix, Boyle: p. 33.
22 The *Elements of Law* (c.9) places glory, the passion proceeding from the imagination or conception of one's power, at the center of its taxonomy, whereas in the *Leviathan* (c.6), desire and aversion are the two principal passions.
23 There is, of course, also Hobbes's objections to the *Meditations* and Descartes's replies, first published in 1641, but the subject of the *conatus* does not arise there. Hobbes's sixth objection relates to Descartes's comments about the passions, but given Descartes's abrupt reply, the exchange yields little of interest compared to what can be gleaned from examining what the texts each separately devote to the subject of the passions (AT 7: 181–2; CSM 2: 128).
24 David van Mill, in his "Rationality, Action and Autonomy in Hobbes's Leviathan," *Polity*, 27.2 (1994), 284–306, argues from these passages and others against the tendency to view Hobbes as determining all human action as mechanistic responses to external pressures and thus as establishing the foundation for human autonomy. I agree that for Hobbes not all human actions are reactions to external stimuli but argue that there are mechanical foundations for the internal striving for power and the very autonomy van Mill thinks is irreducible.
25 The clearest explication of this idea that the pleasure we derive from our experience of our own power is what spurs us on to future desires and actions can be found at DME pp. 463–8.
26 DME, 463–8; EIIIP4; EIIIP10; EIVP18s; EIVP20.
27 See my *Descartes and the Passionate Mind*, c.4 for an analysis of "referring."
28 *Descartes and the Passionate Mind*, pp. 52–3, contains a fuller description of Descartes's taxonomy in comparison with medieval taxonomies.
29 The idea of glory as a principal driver of human behaviour and as connected to one's sense of power is prominent also in Machiavelli. See, for example, Niccolò Machiavelli, *Discourses on Livy*. Harvey Mansfield and Nathan Tarcov, trans. Chicago, IL: University of Chicago Press, 1966: I.58.
30 In his commentary on White's *De mundo*, Hobbes denies that deliberation could be syllogistic, for given that it pertains to future events, it must instead rely on memory of similar events, and thus it is a matter of what the mind can picture and expect rather than what it can derive from the meanings of terms (DME 448).
31 See Descartes's 9 February 1645 letter to Mesland (AT 4: 166–7; CSMK: 242–3).
32 See Spinoza's *Treatise on the Emendation of the Intellect* (hereafter, TEI). A. Boyle, trans. London: Heron Books: 228–9; 230–1.

33 E, p. 80.
34 TEI 227–263; E IV, preface. The distinction between adequate and inadequate ideas has bearing on the question of why for Spinoza deliberate self-harm is impossible. Because individual things are modes that express the power of God to exist and act, anything contrary to an individual that could destroy it is contrary also to the idea of that individual. Hence, it cannot be an act of the one destroyed, something which follows from an adequate idea of itself, to terminate its being, although it may be something it does from passion or an inadequate idea of itself (E, pp. 90–1). But then its apparent self-destruction is always rooted in external causes.
35 John Carriero, "Conatus and Perfection in Spinoza," *Midwest Studies in Philosophy*, 35 (2011): 69–92, at p. 71.
36 *Ibid.*, pp. 71–2.
37 There is something reminiscent of Descartes's notion of "objective perfection" or "objective reality" (AT 7: 134–5; CSM 2: 96–7) in Spinoza's suggestion that perfection increases with increases in complexity and independence. Just as a complex machine or automaton has more perfection than a simpler tool, so too will the idea of a complex machine have more objective reality or objective perfection than the idea of a simpler tool.
38 The influence of Hobbes on Spinoza and his milieu, particularly in political philosophy, was substantial. See, for example, Michael Petry, "Hobbes and the Early Dutch Spinozists," in C. De Deugd, ed. *Spinoza's Political and Theological Thought*. Amsterdam: North-Holland Publishing, 1984: 63–72.
39 See also Spinoza's *Tractatus Politicus*, P 2.15 and 6.1. Translated into English as *Political Treatise*, Samuel Shirley, trans. Indianapolis, IN: Hackett, 2000.
40 For an illuminating account of the differences between Hobbes and Spinoza on how the passions contribute to the formation of civil society, see Aurelia Armstrong, "Natural and Unnatural Communities: Spinoza Beyond Hobbes," *British Journal for the History of Philosophy*, 17.2 (2009): 279–305.

13
PHILOSOPHY OF LANGUAGE
Walter Ott

[T]he light of human minds is perspicuous words, but by exact definitions first snuffed, and purged from ambiguity; *reason* is the *pace*; increase of *science*, the *way*; and the benefit of mankind, the *end*. And on the contrary, metaphors, and senseless and ambiguous words, are like *ignes fatui*; and reasoning upon them is wandering among innumerable absurdities; and their end, contention, and sedition, or contempt.

– Thomas Hobbes[1]

How language works – its functions, mechanisms, and limitations – matters to the early moderns as much as it does to contemporary philosophers. Many of the moderns make reflection on language central to their philosophical projects, both as a tool for explaining human cognition, and as a weapon to be used against competing views. Even in philosophers for whom language is less central, we can find important connections between their views on language and their other philosophical commitments.

This is not to say that language matters to the moderns for the same reasons it matters to us. In what follows, I begin by asking why reflection on language occupies the privileged place it does in so many of their works. In the second section, I consider the possibility of language in nonhuman animals, partly to discover just what the moderns think counts as a language. If we can find out why some philosophers think that animals that clearly produce articulate sounds in response to their environments nevertheless fall short of being language users, we shall have a good idea of just what these thinkers take language to be. Here I shall say something briefly about what some moderns thought language could *become*: a perfect instrument for the communication and discovery of truths.

In the third and fourth sections, I explore how these philosophers think human languages actually work. The modern period is what Ian Hacking calls "the heyday of ideas": most philosophers defend a broadly mentalistic picture, according to which words have meaning only to the extent that they are associated with mental objects or events. Language as such contributes nothing to thought and inherits whatever meaning it has from thought. I shall argue that, on the whole, the philosophers of the period do not believe that words refer at all, whether to things or ideas; neither do words have ideas as their (Fregean) sense. Instead, words *indicate* ideas in the mind of the person using them.

Quine calls the claim that words get their meaning by being associated with private mental contents "the museum myth" (1969, 27). Frege and Wittgenstein, each in his own way, critique this general picture on the grounds that it makes meaning publicly inaccessible. But objections to the dominant view on the basis of the privacy of the mental are hardly news; Locke's indefatigable critic, John Sergeant, attacked him on these same lines. As we shall see, the moderns are not without their defenses.

With this as background, we can then (in section 5) trace out the consequences of the moderns' views on language. Thus, I proceed to the question of definitions, so central to the Scholastic conception of *scientia*. I shall argue that in some cases the moderns' understanding of how language functions reins in the aspiration to real definitions. It is here that we shall see distinctive conceptions of the signification of words put to work in attacking Scholastic views. And we shall also find defenders of real definitions, such as Leibniz and Sergeant, fighting back.

In section 6, we turn to the problem of universals. Even the most rabid nominalist must account for one obvious linguistic phenomenon: the applicability of a single name to multiple individuals.[2] More turns on this question than might at first appear. For the Scholastics, the mind's ability to use universals in thought – in Aquinas's jargon, to abstract the intelligible species from its material conditions – is indicative of the intellect's immateriality.[3] Thus it is particularly important for a materialist like Hobbes, and for anyone who, like Locke, wishes to remain agnostic about the materiality of the mind,[4] to offer another explanation.[5]

Having dealt with the signification of individual words, we can turn to propositions (section 7). The issue is interesting in its own right, because the moderns confront recognizably contemporary problems, such as the unity of the proposition. But it also has implications for the further development of empiricism in particular. By making room for syncategorematic terms – terms such as 'is,' 'if,' and 'but' – some philosophers believe we can sensefully talk about that which lies beyond all experience. At the end of this chapter (section 8), I hope to indicate how otherwise obscure questions about the nature of the proposition lie at the heart of some core issues in early modern philosophy generally.

1. Why does language matter to the moderns?[6]

In the early modern period, reflection on language is undertaken not so much as a worthy endeavor in its own right but as a means of diagnosing the errors of one's competitors. What spurs most of these figures is not disinterested curiosity but a need to wrest control of the intellectual climate from the schools. Thus, the most obvious way in which language matters to the moderns is as a danger and, correspondingly, as a possible means of cognitive "therapy." Having recognized a family of errors as flowing from some mistaken assumption about how words work, one is then cured of the desire, say, to suppose that each thing is possessed of its own nature or essence, or that each quality for which we have a word must correspond to some real quality in the object.

Some of the dangers on which the moderns fixate are thoroughly pedestrian. The constant injunctions one finds to avoid ambiguity and metaphor in philosophical or scientific contexts are hardly new. Nor is it particularly hard to see why such injunctions should be so common. As the Aristotelian view[7] crumbles, so many competitors arise that even the simplest words no longer have an agreed upon meaning. In 1629,

Descartes writes, "[a]s it is, almost all our words have confused meanings, and men's minds are so accustomed to them that there is hardly anything which they can perfectly understand."[8] When there is no universally accepted worldview to take the place of the old, even a word like 'weight,' let alone 'gravity,' takes on different meanings, depending on which of the available theories the speaker happens to hold.[9]

Replacing the Aristotelian view means uprooting common ways of speaking. Bacon, for example, says that unless "men are forewarned and arm themselves against them," the idols or illusions[10] enshrined in the old philosophy will infect the new.[11] At a deeper level, then, we find the worry that a major barrier to the acceptance of the new philosophies is ordinary language itself. Both Aristotelianism and ordinary speech are shot through with ontological assumptions many of the new philosophers wish to brand as false. Indeed, despite their technical sophistication (or, as most moderns prefer, their predilection for "insignificant speech"),[12] the Scholastics are seen as simply codifying the errors embedded in ordinary language.

Consider the doctrine of secondary qualities. Galileo, Descartes, Locke, and others agree that qualities such as color and taste are either bare powers or nothing at all in the bodies themselves. There are no real, nondispositional feature of bodies that we report with words like 'fuchsia' or 'tangy.' How were the Scholastics led to think otherwise? Partly, the moderns think, because they took ordinary language as a good guide to metaphysics. When we have meaningful words for a quality, we are tempted to think that they must correspond to a genuine quality in the objects of which we predicate them.[13]

This is no mere misstep on the part of the Scholastics but an instance of a pervasive tendency, common to the schoolmen and to the rest of us, to fall under the spell of language. In his *Treatise on the Emendation of the Understanding*, Spinoza writes that "words, no less than imagination, can bring about many grave errors unless we exercise great caution." For Spinoza, words are "a part of the imagination," and, having been instituted by human beings according to the imagination and not the intellect, must be used with care.[14]

In giving a diagnosis of the tendency to take ordinary language as our guide to metaphysics, the moderns typically point to the danger of focusing on words rather than things. To put it somewhat hyperbolically, their worry is that words will usurp the place that ideas should properly play in thought.[15] "Words," Hobbes writes, "are wise men's counters; they do but reckon by them; but they are the money of fools."[16] As Arnauld and Nicole put it in their *Logic*:

> [O]ur need to use external signs to make ourselves understood causes us to connect our ideas to words in such a way that we often pay more attention to the words than to the things. Now this is one of the most common causes of confusion in our thoughts and discourse.[17]

But why were the moderns so worried about this particular pitfall? One answer comes from their attitude toward Scholastic natural philosophy. In its simplest form, Aristotelian science is classificatory. One begins with a set of definitions arrived at through experience. These *per se* or essential predications are intended to capture the essence of the thing.[18] One then uses these definitions in syllogisms that are not just formally valid but that show why something *must* be the case. To give a hackneyed example, the definition of man as a rational animal, plus the premise that Socrates is a man, allows us to infer that Socrates is rational. More than this, however, the syllogism is also supposed to *explain* why Socrates is rational, namely by showing that he shares in the essence of man. This admittedly simplified example nevertheless captures the basic form a completed Aristotelian science would take: a set of demonstrations, based on real or *de re* definitions, that allows us to explain why things happen as they do.[19]

Although Aristotle and the Scholastics agree that empirical observation is essential for discovering real essences, the moderns worry that syllogistic logic depends too much on definitions generated not even from the armchair but from the classroom. One's conclusions will be only as good as the definitions with which one starts. The general attitude is that the Scholastic program for science is a garbage in–garbage out system.

However useful syllogisms might be for stating one's results, most of the figures I shall discuss agree that they are not a useful tool for discovery.[20] More than this, syllogisms cozen philosophers into thinking they are making genuine progress when all they are doing is manipulating elements in a formal system. This kind of worry is no doubt partly responsible for the low esteem in which formal approaches were generally held. In Locke's *Essay*, for example, we find an insistence on the mind's capacity to detect errors in reasoning without the help of Scholastic textbooks and, more generally, without the aid of any kind of formal analysis.[21] Such hostile attitudes toward syllogistic logic are admirably expressed by Joseph Glanvill, a friend of Locke's, who dismisses Scholastic natural philosophy as a "flatulent vacuity."[22]

But this is not to say that there were not philosophers pushing in the other direction. Arguing against Locke, Leibniz claims that the invention of the syllogism is "one of the finest, and indeed one of the most important, to be made by the human mind."[23] Harking back to his own ambitions for a universal characteristic, a numerical system that would form the perfect language, Leibniz speaks of syllogistic logic as a kind of "universal mathematics."[24] And Hobbes devotes part of his treatment of logic to syllogisms. As we shall see, these philosophers' divergent attitudes toward the formalism of the Scholastics can be traced back to their own approaches to definition. If one begins with real definitions, definitions that capture the essence or, in Hobbes's case, the causes of a thing, the products of one's syllogistic reasoning might be correspondingly more valuable. The disagreement illustrates the complex relationship between the Scholastics and the moderns: even when they are dismissed, Scholastic ideas or methods percolate through modern texts.[25]

2. Languages, animal and perfect

In his *Discourse on Method* of 1637, Descartes argues that we have "two very certain means" of distinguishing beings that have souls from everything else, including nonhuman animals and machines.[26] Having explained the body and nearly all its motions and functions in purely mechanical terms, Descartes must now find some way of distinguishing ensouled beings from others.[27] The best evidence we can have for the presence of a soul is the presence of reason, the "universal instrument,"[28] and language. Though the operations of reason extend more widely, they include their most obvious manifestation, language. Descartes argues that only a human being is able to "produce different arrangements of words so as to give an appropriately meaningful answer to whatever is said in its presence."[29]

Descartes later drops the reference to reason or subsumes it under the heading of language. In his 1646 letter to the Marquess of Newcastle, Descartes claims that

> [i]n fact, there are none of our external actions that could assure those who examine them that our body is not simply a machine that moves itself, but

contains a soul that has thoughts, were it not for words or other signs made in reference to topics that present themselves without any relation to any passion.[30]

Each of the qualifications Descartes makes here is important. First, to avoid begging the question, he allows that signs other than words can constitute a language. (Descartes does not want to deny that mutes can in a sense "speak.") Second, it is vital that the signs produced not have "any relation to any passion" simply because signs so used can be explained purely mechanically. This excludes not only grunts and cries of pain but, Descartes thinks, any signs a being or machine can be taught to produce on command. When your parrot tells you that Wellington won at Waterloo, it does so only in response to some stimulus. By contrast, even a madman's disjointed and irrational speech is generated spontaneously and not simply in response to external stimuli.[31]

What lessons can we draw from these arguments? At a minimum, a language speaker must use signs to indicate to others her own mental states. But this is not sufficient. Language use requires the deployment of signs in such a way as to indicate thoughts that are not tied to the being's immediate surroundings or passions. This is a very vague criterion, but Descartes's general point seems clear. More controversially, Descartes's talk of our ability to produce different "arrangements of signs" suggests a criterion of compositionality: one must be able to use the same signs, differently arranged, to indicate different thoughts.[32]

Given that the chief use of a language is to express our thoughts, what, under ideal conditions, would language look like? Having looked at one end of the spectrum – sounds and marks that do not rise to the level of language use – we can now pause to look at the other. The intense awareness of the arbitrary nature of words in the modern period made the prospect of a perfect language seem at once intensely desirable and, in some minds, achievable. Criticizing such a proposal passed on to him by his friend Mersenne, Descartes sketches how such a language would have to be developed, namely on analogy with mathematics. Given a limited number of primitives, one can understand any integer. So, order is what is needed; all possible thoughts would have to be arranged on analogy with the order of natural numbers. If such an order could be discovered, it would enable a recursive generation and comprehension of any possible thought. Such a perfect language depends on the true philosophy that would separate out all the simple ideas in the human imagination out of which all thoughts are made.[33] Descartes is pessimistic about the prospects for a perfect language: it would be tantamount to a "terrestrial paradise." Leibniz, for his part, is more sanguine, and drew up plans for what he calls the "universal characteristic."[34] For Descartes, mathematics is a model or analogy for the perfect language; for Leibniz, the perfect language just is mathematics, with the addition of a semantics that joins each number to an idea. Once in possession of such a language, we could settle any dispute simply by calculation. Leibniz seems never to have abandoned his hopes despite never making any real progress toward achieving them.[35]

Neither of the ideal languages contemplated by Descartes or Leibniz would represent a return to the language of Adam, who (some thought) possessed a mystical language whose words expressed the true natures of things. Jacob Boehme is perhaps the most prominent figure of the era to hanker after an Adamic language and to accord it a quasi-mystical status. Kabalistic thinkers of the era also exhibit similar tendencies.[36] Instead, an ideal language would be a purely conventional system for formulating any possible thought.

Nearly all parties to the debate accept that words are signs imposed purely arbitrarily. Leibniz might seem to be the exception, and in a sense, he is. In response to Locke's assertion that words are arbitrarily chosen, Leibniz argues that, although our selections of sounds are not determined by any natural necessity, nevertheless, "they are settled by reasons – sometimes natural ones in which chance plays some part, sometimes moral ones which involve choice."[37] (Leibniz devotes his single lengthiest response to Locke in all of the *New Essays* to this issue.) Leibniz tries to establish two interconnected points: that all European languages have a "primitive root-origin"[38] and that this language in some cases was formed in imitation of the sounds of nature. The latter point is designed to support the former. Thus, for example, Leibniz thinks that the Latin *coaxere* and the German *couaqen* or *quaken* were derived from a common word intended to mimic the croaking of frogs. However prescient Leibniz's hypothesis of an ur-language might be, it is far from the mystical view of Boehme: there is no suggestion that this primitive language somehow grasps the natures of things, though of course it might have been more convenient for expressing certain thoughts, or easier to learn.[39]

These reflections on languages, animal and otherwise, reveal the key background assumption of most modern thinking about language: words are signs, established by convention, whose primary purpose is to allow others to discern our thoughts. This sounds like a truism; as we shall see, it is more controversial than first appears. Moreover, it is only the scaffolding on which a completed view might be erected. Much will turn, as we shall see, on just how one understands the claim that words are *signs*.

3. Signs and names

It is not an exaggeration to say that all modern thinking about language stems from a single paragraph in Aristotle:[40]

> Now spoken words are symbols of affections in the soul, and written marks symbols of spoken sounds. And just as written marks are not the same for all men, neither are spoken sounds. But what these are in the first place signs of – affections of the soul – are the same for all; and what these affections are likenesses of – actual things – are also the same.
> (*De interpretatione* 16a3–8)[41]

Spoken words are signs (*semeia* in Greek; in Latin, *notae*) of passions in the mind. By "affections" (*pathemata*) Aristotle means not affections in our contemporary sense but mental representations or concepts. A word itself is an arbitrarily chosen symbol or sign that is in no way tied to things in the world; the work of intentionality is done wholly at the level of mental representations. These affections, Aristotle says, resemble or are likenesses of real things. On this view, the difference between parrot-speak and language lies in the subjective experience of the speaker. However astutely one might mimic the speech of a Richard Feynman, unless one has the relevant mental acts and objects, one is merely parroting him. Thus, a language speaker must not only be able to produce a variety of articulate sounds; as Locke puts it, she must also "*be able to use these sounds, as signs of internal conceptions.*"[42]

Each of us, on the dominant modern view, has her own idiolect, what we might call thoughtish. This is composed of the ideas and acts of her mind. Given our shared mental structures and capacities, and the fact that we inhabit a single world, all humans can in principle share the same language of thought.[43] But each person's thoughts are her own, accessible to others only indirectly. The role of language, then, is to turn isolated minds into a community of mutually intelligible beings. As Hobbes writes, "the general use of speech, is to transfer our mental discourse, into verbal."[44]

How this transference is effected is controversial. The Scholastics typically use 'signify' in a broad sense to mean "express," "reveal," or "make known."[45] Taken in this sense, it is natural to say that words can also signify things, qualities, or extramental states of affairs. Precisely how the moderns understand signification is something we shall have to discover. I shall now argue that they typically construe signification in a much-narrower way, so that only ideas or mental acts can be signified by words.

Note that Aristotle's text speaks of two relations: (R1) word–mental object and (R2) mental object–thing in the world. The first is signification; the second is, on Aristotle's view, resemblance. A mental object represents a thing in the world in virtue of resembling it. We can begin to understand signification if we contrast it with this second relation.

As we have seen, the moderns in general wish to reject the Aristotelian's assumption that each phenomenal quality we experience is a real quality in the object itself. (This remains the case, even though there is an exception to the rule: ideas of primary qualities, some philosophers such as Locke believe, do indeed resemble those qualities in objects themselves.)[46] But what then is the relation between an experience of redness and the object itself? That is, in the case of secondary qualities, what is R2? If the real features of bodies are just size, shape, and movement, R2 cannot, in this case, be resemblance, because there is nothing in the object that our idea of yellow or sour resembles. Perhaps reflecting on R1 can provide a solution. Presenting his views on light in the early *Le Monde*, Descartes exploits the Aristotelian's use of linguistic signification in R1 to argue that R2 need not be understood in terms of resemblance. Addressing an imaginary Scholastic interlocutor, Descartes writes,

> Words, as you well know, bear no resemblance to the things they signify, and yet they make us think of these things. . . . Now if words, which signify nothing except by human convention, suffice to make us think of things to which they bear no resemblance, then why could nature not also have established some sign which would make us have the sensation of light, even if the sign contained nothing in itself which is similar to this sensation? Is it not thus that nature has established laughter and tears, to make us read joy and sadness on the faces of men?[47]

Descartes goes on to use an example from Galileo's *The Assayer*: we experience tickling when certain motions occur, but there is nothing in the experience that resembles these motions.[48] So far, we know only that signification is not resemblance. But what is it? Descartes's text offers a minimal characterization: for x to signify y is for x to make us think of y. As Arnauld and Nicole put it in their *Logic*, "the nature of the sign consists in prompting in the senses the idea of the thing symbolized by the idea of the symbol."[49] This can happen either by convention (as in words, R1) or by nature (as in sensations, R2).

As it stands, this Cartesian view of signs is pretty clearly flawed. Most obviously, it suffers from what we might call the conjunction problem.[50] Any given utterance can make me think of almost anything at all: 'rain' can make me think of the stuff that falls from the sky, but it can also make me think of the Teutonic songbirds Milli Vanilli or of the grass withering in my yard. If this is all it takes to be a sign, then almost everything is a sign of almost everything else. The point is not that words are ambiguous, but rather even a single, univocal word can call to mind any number of things, only one (or some) of which is plausibly construed as its meaning in the pretheoretical sense. The same goes for natural signs; lactation, to use another of Aristotle's examples, can make me think of pregnancy, but it can also call to mind the practice of wet-nursing or the antibiotic properties of mother's milk.

More important, the Cartesian view focuses on only one of the jobs the moderns as a whole expect words to do. Locke speaks for the moderns when he claims that, because a person's ideas lie hidden in his own mind and are not directly accessible to others, he must "be *able to use these Sounds, as Signs of internal Conceptions*; and to make them stand as marks for the *Ideas* within his own Mind, whereby they might be made known to others."[51] So we need now to look for an understanding of signification that focuses on this second role: not merely causing ideas in the hearer but serving as signs of ideas in *the speaker*. Discovering just how this second role is satisfied will also allow us to answer the conjunction problem, both with regard to R1 and R2.

Because speech requires that we be able to use sounds as signs of our internal conceptions, it also requires that the speaker *intend* to use signs in a certain way. An intention to reveal one's thoughts, then, is at least a prerequisite for accomplishing the core purpose of language. But how is this intention to be satisfied?[52]

Let us return to the Port-Royal text. A sign in general is just anything that makes us think of something other than itself. There are many ways of causing people to form thoughts, however, and lumping them all together is misleading. Consider some of the examples the Port-Royalians use: some signs, such as maps and paintings, bring about the thought of what they signify by resembling, or in some way being isomorphic to, their objects. But this cannot be the sense of 'sign' in linguistic contexts. Neither the sound 'map' nor the shape of its letters resembles or maps the idea *map*. (We have already seen Descartes exploit this fact.) We need, then, a different notion, which will also fall under the genus of signification. Now, Arnauld and Nicole also say that facial expressions are signs of emotions, that a hot cinder is a sign of a fire, and that symptoms indicate a disease. These things cause us to think of what they signify not by resembling them but by *indicating* them. I suspect this is also what Aristotle means when he calls words *semeia*; in any case, it is pretty clearly what the moderns mean.[53]

Hobbes makes all of this considerably clearer. He writes,

> Now, those things we call SIGNS are the *antecedents of their consequents, and the consequents of their antecedents, as often as we observe them to go before or follow after in the same manner*. For example, a thick cloud is a sign of rain to follow, and rain a sign that a cloud has gone before, for this reason only, that we seldom see clouds without the consequence of rain, nor rain at any time but when a cloud has gone before. And of signs, some are *natural*, whereof I have already given an example, others are *arbitrary*, namely, those we make choice of at our own pleasure, as a bush hung up, signifies that wine is to be sold there; a stone set in the ground signifies the bound of a field; and words so and so connected, signify the cogitations and motions of our mind.[54]

In this famous passage, Hobbes offers a clear account of just how words function to reveal our thoughts to others. Natural signs can be said to mean what they signify: to use an example of H. P. Grice's, it is natural to say such things as "these spots mean measles." Conventional signs are arbitrary but, when used by people intending to participate in those conventions, can equally well function as indicators. This is the role of words.

As we have seen, the Scholastics typically use 'signify' in a broad sense to mean express, reveal, or make known. It is a matter of debate among the Scholastics whether words signify the matter or form of things, or the substance generated by their combination. I am suggesting that most of the moderns use a considerably narrower sense: indication. A word does indeed make known or reveal the speaker's ideas, but only by virtue of indicating them. Armed with his notion of signification, Hobbes addresses the Scholastic debate directly:

> But seeing names ordered in speech (as is defined) are signs of our conceptions, it is manifest they are not signs of the things themselves; for that the sound of this word *stone* should be the sign of a stone, cannot be understood in any sense but this, that he that hears it collects that he that pronounces it thinks of a stone. And, therefore, that disputation, whether names signify the matter or form, or something compounded of both, and other like subtleties of the *metaphysics*, is kept up by erring men, and such as understand not the words they dispute about.[55]

The argument couldn't be simpler: because stones do not appear whenever I say the word 'stone,' it is obvious that 'stone' does not signify stones, but only our idea of them.[56] It is pointless, then, to wonder whether words signify form, matter, or substance; the answer is, none of the above.

To sum up: words play at least two roles. They cause the hearer to think of an idea, and they indicate an idea in the mind of the speaker. (They can also serve as what Hobbes and Locke call marks, reminders to oneself of what one has been thinking. In this respect, they need not have any public use attached to them.)[57] These two roles are easily conflated: it is by first serving as an indication that a word attains its power to cause in the hearer the idea it indicates in the mind of the speaker.[58]

Locke is the first figure I have found to explicitly separate these roles. Locke famously says that "words, as they are used by Men, can properly and immediately signify nothing but *Ideas*, that are in the Mind of the Speaker" (3.2.4: 406). (We will come back to the "properly and immediately" later.) It is only in their role as indications of ideas that words can be said to be signs. This is clear from Locke's stipulation that they are not just signs of ideas but signs of ideas *in the mind of the speaker*. Whether they cause the right ideas in one's audience or not, words are not signs of *their* ideas, but only of the speaker's.

Locke of course recognizes that we hardly ever explicitly infer from a speaker's words to her ideas and instead simply allow them to raise up ideas in our own minds.[59] We suppose that our words are indications not only of our own ideas but also of ideas in the minds of others. And this, Locke thinks, is simply a mistake:

> [Men] *suppose their Words to be Marks of the* Ideas *in the Minds also of other Men, with whom they communicate*: For else they should talk in vain, and could not be understood, if the Sounds they applied to one *Idea*, were such, as by the Hearer, were applied to another, which is to speak two Languages. But in this, Men stand not usually to examine, whether the *Idea* they, and those they discourse with have in their Minds, be the same: But think it enough, that they use the

Word, as they imagine, in the common Acceptation of that Language; in which case they suppose, that the *Idea*, they make it a sign of, is precisely the same, to which the Understanding Men of that Country, apply that name.[60]

To be sure, successful communication requires that the interlocutors associate the same ideas with the same words. But we cannot simply assume this; given the conventional nature of language, it is all too common for speakers to talk past each other.

It is by using words as indications of, or grounds for inference to, our own thoughts that we make ourselves understood. How, though, does any of this help with the conjunction problem? Having replaced the broad characterization of 'sign' provided by the Port-Royalians with the more particular concept of a sign as an indication, it might seem that this is a problem no longer. Not so. A spoken word might indicate an idea in the mind of the speaker, but it also indicates the presence of oxygen, that the speaker has a larynx, and so on. The same is true of our second relation, R2, that between an idea and what it signifies. An occurrence of the visual idea of a toad on a toadstool in my visual field indicates the presence of a toad, but it also indicates that I am not in outer space, that gravity is behaving itself, and so on.

There is a flip side to this objection: a spoken word does not always indicate the same idea on every occasion, as Locke is at pains to point out. Similarly, I do not token the sensory idea *frog* when and only when I am in the presence of frogs: any number of things, from poorly seen crabs to shadows, can trigger this idea. So, what then does this idea signify? It seems we have to say that it signifies a disjunction: in the case of 'frog,' it signifies the disjunction of all those ideas in the minds of speakers using them, and in the case of the idea *frog*, it signifies the disjunction of everything that causes it. This is the disjunction problem.

The clearest answer to these problems comes from Locke. Let's begin with the case of ideas and their objects, relation R2. Now, some ideas – ideas of primary qualities – resemble what they represent, namely qualities of bodies. But *all* ideas of sensation signify what causes them:

> Our *simple* Ideas *are all real*, all agree to the reality of things. Not that they are all of them the Images, or Representations of what does exist, the contrary whereof, in all but the primary Qualities of Bodies, hath been already shewed. But though Whiteness and Coldness are no more in Snow, than Pain is; yet those *Ideas* of Whiteness, and Coldness, Pain, *etc.*, being in us the Effects of Powers in Things without us, ordained by our Maker, to produce in us such Sensations; they are real *Ideas* in us, whereby we distinguish the Qualities, that are really in thing themselves. For *these several Appearances, being designed to be the Marks, whereby we are to know, and distinguish Things*, which we have to do with; our *Ideas* do as well serve us to that purpose, and are as real distinguishing Characters, whether they be only constant Effects, or else exact Resemblances of something in the things themselves: the reality lying in that steady correspondence, they have with the distinct Constitutions of real Beings.[61]

The sensation of cold resembles nothing in the snow that caused it. What, then, is the use of having such a sensation, if inspecting it offers no guide to the real qualities of the object? Although not resembling the object, the idea of cold, we might say, causally co-varies with the power in the object to produce it. So, all simple ideas of sensation, whether resembling anything in bodies or not, indicate those qualities that cause them. This is good evidence that Locke takes words to be indicators as well, assuming he uses 'sign' univocally.

On its own, of course, the fact that some ideas represent their objects by being caused by them does not help with the problems we have been looking at. But Locke's story is not a purely causal one: recall that ideas are "designed" or intended by God to serve as signs or marks of qualities in objects. So, what an idea signifies is not just anything that happens to cause it but what God *intended* to cause it. These usually, though not always, overlap. Thus, given the teleological element, the disjunction problem disappears.[62] The conjunction problem vanishes as well: although the occurrence of an idea of white indicates many things about the environment, it is only intended by God to indicate one thing: the presence of an object endowed with the appropriate qualities and powers.[63]

The case is not so different with words. Remember that, by participating in a complex set of conventions, we can use words to indicate what passes in our minds. Although a spoken word also indicates that the speaker has a larynx, this is not what the word is *intended* to do, considered from the point of view of this convention.

To make this clearer, consider another of Hobbes's examples of a conventional sign, one that does not involve spoken or written language. Although a pile of stones might indicate anything at all, when I have reason to believe that my neighbor is aware of the conventions of marking the boundary of a field, I can legitimately infer that the stones are there for that purpose. Notice that this attributes a precise set of intentions to my neighbor, as well as an ability to predict mine.

Although few writers in the period develop this picture of language to the same degree as Locke, it seems to be what we might call the default setting for the moderns. The word-thing relation is broken into two: word-idea (R1) and idea-thing (R2). The analysis of R1 requires a notion of signification as indication, and at least in the case of secondary qualities, so does R2.

4. Complications and objections

As I have indicated, the broad outline sketched previously is filled out in different ways among the moderns. In this section, I want to discuss Hobbes's picture in more detail before moving on briefly to Locke and then to some of the most important objections lodged against these sorts of views. Although first articulated in the modern period, these objections will be familiar to readers of twentieth century philosophy, where they resurface, though usually without any awareness of their antiquity.

Every noun is what Hobbes calls a "name." Now, Hobbes is clear that some names, such as "man," "tree," and so on, are names "of the things themselves."[64] Other names, like 'nothing,' are the names of, well, nothing. What is this relation of naming? Names themselves fall into two categories: marks and signs. A mark is a word taken by a single user as a means of recalling what he has previously thought. This use is logically and temporally prior to its use as a sign: once a speaker uses a name as a mark, he is then able to use it in such a way as to allow others to infer what he is thinking.[65]

So far, so good; but none of this helps explain how it is that 'dogs' can name dogs. These sounds or inscriptions either mark a speaker's own previous thoughts or signify those thoughts to others. Hobbes says nothing at all about the relation of naming, leading some to think that he takes it as a primitive.[66]

This might be the case, but I suspect there is a more charitable answer. Recall Hobbes's previous claim that the only sense in which 'stone' can signify a stone is "that he that hears it collects that he that pronounces it thinks of a stone."[67] If we want a way to explain how 'stone' can *name* a stone, this is it: the word-object relation of naming must run through the word-idea relation (signification as indication) and from there to the idea-thing relation (representation, however that is accomplished).

We find a similar conundrum in Locke. For as often as Locke says that words signify, or primarily signify, nothing but ideas in the mind of the speaker, he also speaks of words naming or designating things. One might think that he is appealing to some further and primitive word-thing relation, not reducible to R1 and R2. But the text is quite puzzling, because Locke also says that words "are names of *Ideas*."[68] Although this is controversial, I find it overwhelmingly likely that Hobbes and Locke are both acquiescing in common ways of speaking and using the naming relation as a shorthand. This is only to be expected, because stating the two-part relation between word and object is rather cumbersome.

A second puzzle is generated by Locke's talk of primary signification. Sometimes Locke says not that words signify nothing but ideas in the mind of the speaker but that they *primarily* do so, implying that in some secondary sense they signify things themselves.[69] Unfortunately, Locke never so much as uses the phrase "secondary signification," or anything remotely like it. It was fairly common in late Scholasticism to distinguish between the primary signification of words, namely ideas, and their secondary signification, namely things. But Locke clearly intends his claim about words to tell against these same Scholastics, as we shall see later. Why, then, would he be helping himself to some of their jargon?

Again, I think the answer is convenience. We have seen Hobbes claim that there is indeed a sense in which words signify things. It would be natural enough for Locke to have this same sense in mind – words secondarily signify things in the sense that they signify ideas, which in turn represent things. Even if Locke's occasional talk of "primary signification" implies a notion of secondary signification, he need not be read as introducing an irreducible and novel category of linguistic function.[70]

Before moving forward, we should note just how foreign this picture of language is to many twentieth century philosophers. Ian Hacking (1975) goes so far as to deny that any of these figures, particularly Hobbes, actually *has* a theory of meaning. Though hyperbolic, Hacking's point is a useful guard against anachronism: the Fregean notions of sense and reference really have no place in the moderns. A stone at the edge of a field is just not the right sort of thing to refer, or have a sense; it merely indicates. Nor do words, in and of themselves, carry with them any mode of presentation or reference. This is hardly surprising, given the use the moderns think words must be put to: words serve only as the means by which we make our thoughts known to one another. It is the thoughts themselves that present things in a given way and refer to or pick out individuals in the world. Indeed, if one is determined to find an analogue for *Sinn* and *Bedeutung* in the modern period, the best place to look is not words but ideas.[71] The Port-Royal *Logic*, for instance, speaks of an idea's comprehension– "the attributes that it contains in itself" – and its extension– "the subjects to which the idea applies."[72]

Before going on to show how this picture gives the moderns some tools with which to attack their opponents, we should consider three fairly obvious objections.

First, this indicator approach to language can seem hopelessly myopic. Even if it is suited to explaining the fact-stating uses of words,[73] it seems to ignore a wide variety of linguistic acts. Words can be used to embarrass, attack, promise, and so on, and on, and on. Although it is common to associate this sort of insight with J. L. Austin in the twentieth century, George Berkeley in the eighteenth was to make this a core issue in his debate with Locke.[74] And recognition of such other uses of words comes early on in the modern period. We have already looked at Descartes's discussion of the use of sounds to indicate emotions or pain (though of course he does not think these uses amount to a use of *language per se*.) Hobbes, too, makes a point of discussing the use of speech to express emotions.[75] Hobbes also is keenly aware that people sometimes speak in order to please others; he lists this among the uses of language, alongside its role as signifier of ideas. (Hobbes lists the use of language to injure or "grieve" others among its abuses.) Given the driving forces behind the moderns' interests in language, it should hardly be surprising that they largely neglect the non-fact-stating uses of language. What is more, many of these other uses of language are parasitic on its role as a means of communication. No one could use the phrase 'Sellars said so' as a means of intellectual intimidation if it did not straightforwardly signify a set of ideas and mental acts.

Second, even when we confine ourselves to these fact-stating uses of language, it seems absurd to say that words signify ideas. Don't we also need words to talk about *things*? J. S. Mill writes that "[w]hen I say, 'the sun is the cause of the day,' I do not mean that my idea of the sun causes or excites in me the idea of the day."[76] But this criticism misses the mark by assuming that if words *signify* ideas, they are about or *refer to* those ideas. Nothing could be further from the sense in which the moderns understand linguistic signification.[77]

Our final objection is more fundamental, and stems from the privacy of the ideas and acts the moderns think words are used to signify. If my mental life is never open to inspection by others, how can I use words to reveal it to them? This is really two points: (1) because ideas are, as Locke says, "all within [a man's] own Breast, invisible, and hidden from others,"[78] there is no way to check whether we are speaking the same language or merely using homonyms. Moreover, (2) it is impossible to ever get the conventions necessary for communication off the ground, because there is no way for us to agree to use a word as a sign of a given idea. To do *that*, we would have to have some other convention already in place. Although these criticisms are most often associated with Wittgenstein and Frege, they were first pressed by John Sergeant, the maverick Catholic priest who in 1694 published a lengthy critique of Locke's *Essay*. Sergeant writes,

> Our words are *ad placitum*, and have no *Natural* Connexion with the Things they signifie, but are order'd to express them by the *Agreement* of Mankind: Therefore what's signified by them, must be *fore-known* to that Agreement. But the *Ideas* . . . we have, cannot be *fore-known* to this Agreement, since they could not be at all known, (*being in the Mind*,) but by the *Words*; which, not being yet agreed on, can make known, or signifie, nothing.[79]

How can we, as a group, decide that 'tree' will signify the idea of a tree, when we have no public means of pointing to the idea?

To see Locke's answer, we must note that Sergeant assumes that it is *only* by means of words that make our ideas known to others. This is the point Locke will deny. On his view, language first gets going by means of ostensive definition (and indeed any word for a simple idea can *only* be defined by ostension). One says 'tree,' points to a tree, and hopes the other person cottons on. There is no guarantee that she will, but given our very similar cognitive and perceptual equipment, plus a good deal of trial and error, it seems to work. Thus, ostensive definition is necessary at the start of language. It also provides an answer to (2): how can I check that my interlocutor understands me? Only by using other words and ultimately, in the limiting case, "*by presenting to his Senses that Subject, which may produce it in his Mind*, and mak[ing] him actually have the *Idea*, the word stands for."[80] This move is hardly uncontroversial, of course; philosophers from Augustine to Wittgenstein have argued that ostensive definition, used in this way, is problematic. Answering their critiques would take us too far afield, but it does seem to me that the difficulties have been exaggerated.

It is worth pausing to examine Sergeant's own positive view, because he represents one of the few dissenting voices to what I have represented as the dominant view among the moderns. Sergeant rejects the way of ideas in part because he thinks our speech is directly about real things; for him, words reach right out to the world, as it were. But this is not to say that he anticipates Frege or Kripke. On the contrary, his claim is founded on the puzzling doctrine that numerically the same thing can have what Sergeant calls two "manners of existence": in the body, materially, and in the mind, immaterially. When I think of a cathedral, the cathedral itself, on Sergeant's view, exists in my mind. Whether this is a clever anticipation of John McDowell's doctrine of object-dependent thought or a hopeless muddle, or both, is an open question.[81]

5. Definitions

With this sketch of the dominant modern conception of signification in place, we can begin to look at some of its consequences. Undoubtedly the modern philosopher to make the most hay of the nature of signification is Locke. Locke did not set out to include in the *Essay* a book on language. Having finished his account of the origin of ideas in book 2, Locke had intended to proceed straightaway to a discussion of knowledge. But he found that "there is so close a connexion between *Ideas* and *Words*" that he was unable to treat knowledge until he had first considered the nature of language.[82] By far the largest portion of book 3 is negative; it takes its place in Locke's project as "under-labourer" for the sciences, clearing away the rubbish of Scholasticism.

Nowhere is this more evident than in his chapter on the abuse of words. The fifth abuse Locke discusses is "*setting them in the place of Things, which they do or can by no means signify.*"[83] Although words like 'man' or 'gold'

> signify nothing truly but a complex *Idea* of Properties, united together in one sort of Substances: Yet there is scarce any Body in the use of these Words, but often supposes each of those names to stand for a thing having the real Essence, on which those properties depend.[84]

It is natural, though quite mistaken, for us to assume that our words directly reach out to things. Locke recognizes that his readers will likely be chagrinned to learn that they can at best use words to signify their own thoughts.[85] When I say "nitrate fertilizers are explosive," I don't want simply to say that the idea of explosivity is contained in my idea of nitrate fertilizers; I "tacitly suppose," to use Locke's phrase, that I am referring to the stuff itself, the fertilizer, and saying that its real essence produces its explosive powers.[86] But this supposition is always false.

Recall that a completed Aristotelian science would be a network of definitions and other propositions connected by syllogisms. These definitions have the status of first principles, starting points from which the rest of the network is derived. If Locke is right, however, any definition is nothing but a report of the contents of one's own ideas. Why? Simply because the words used in those definitions can, like all words, only signify mental contents.[87]

On Locke's view, an awareness of this fact about language would put a stop to the vast majority of disputes, in philosophy and out of it. Is a bat a bird or not? Is this *really* gold or isn't it? Is this a particularly hirsute baby or a monster?[88] The only thing you can do is consult your abstract idea of these kinds, what Locke calls their nominal essences, and figure it out. There just is no further fact of the matter.[89] The tendency to think that these questions are important – that answering them would tell us something, not about our own ideas, but about the world – is just another unhappy result of the tendency to think that words signify the things themselves.

In addition to these nominal essences, Locke acknowledges that there are real essences: "the real internal, but generally in Substances, unknown Constitution of Things, whereon their discoverable Qualities depend."[90] It is a serious mistake to think of Lockean real essences as substitutes for Aristotelian essences, suitably rigged up for the mechanical philosophy. Among other things, Aristotelian essences are supposed to be what they are regardless of anyone's conceptual activity.[91] A man is a man and not a duck no matter how anyone conceives of the two kinds. Now, at the level of tokens, this is quite true of a Lockean real essence: there is some hidden arrangement of corpuscles that gives this particular thing we call a duck its observable qualities. But it is not true at the level of types, or kinds: there is nothing out there that really marks off one such arrangement from another. As Locke says, "*Essence*, even in this [i.e. the real] sense, *relates to a sort*, and supposes a *Species*."[92] Even if all our epistemic limitations were lifted and we had a God's-eye view of the corpuscles of a body, we would still be deploying our abstract idea *duck* when we asked after the real essence of this species. What is more important, there is no reason to suppose that for each set of properties we track with our nominal essences there corresponds a unique *real* essence.[93]

Here it is instructive to look at Leibniz's critique of Locke in the *New Essays*.[94] In response to Locke's assertion that words signify nothing but thoughts, Leibniz simply asserts that "things as well as ideas are indicated [*marquées*] by words."[95] Thus when Locke inveighs against the practice of putting words in the place of things they cannot signify, Leibniz replies that "it [is] obviously wrong to criticize this common usage."[96] Having simply rejected Locke's claims about the limits of the signification of words, Leibniz, as a result, turns a deaf ear to the strictures Locke would infer from them. What is more striking, Leibniz provides no account of how it could be that *things* are signified or indicated (*marquées*) by words.

On Locke's view, then, definitions are of words, not of things, and these definitions, even under epistemically idealized conditions, yield only the constituent ideas that we associate with the word. The limits of language are the limits of our ideas. Now, Locke thinks that recognizing this requires one to give up the Aristotelian project of natural philosophy as confused.[97] But of course it is open to the Aristotelian to simply identify a thing's essence with our idea of it, a trick we have seen Sergeant turn with his doctrine of "notions." Indeed, Locke sometimes presents his opponents' view as the claim that the essences of things *just are* our ideas.[98]

In a similar vein, Cartesians like Arnauld and Nicole, although abandoning the framework of Aristotelian hylomorphism, hold that some definitions of ideas capture an eternal essence. 'Triangle,' on their view, can be given either a nominal definition, in which case it is merely stipulative,[99] or a real definition, which expresses the constituent parts of the idea we have agreed to signify by the term 'triangle.'[100] Real definitions, on their view, can be true or false, and require argument. Unlike nominal definitions, they cannot simply be assumed at the outset of a demonstration. It is no surprise, then, to find Cartesian critics of Spinoza's *Ethics* arguing that he begs the question by offering no argument for the definitions on which his system depends.[101]

It is hard to know, however, precisely what the Port-Royalians are asking for when they demand an argument for a purportedly real definition. Leibniz makes this much clearer when he says that a real definition must reveal the possibility of the thing defined.[102] When this is done *a priori*, a real definition of, for example, a triangle shows how the properties of a triangle can be combined without contradiction.[103] A real definition is also, for Leibniz, a causal definition, in the sense that it "contains the possible generation of the thing" (1989, 57).

This last remark signals yet another notion of definition in the modern period, one that also has Aristotelian roots. On this view, definitions should, as Hobbes puts it, capture the "cause and generation" of anything that has them. Hobbes here takes his cue from geometry, "the only science that it hath pleased God hitherto to bestow upon mankind."[104] The proper definition of a circle, for example, is the circumduction of a straight line in a plane.[105] Definitions should embody a kind of maker's knowledge, a recipe for bringing about the thing defined. Similarly, we find Spinoza claiming that definitions of created things must include their proximate causes.[106]

6. Reasoning and universals

The moderns as a whole are united, as we have seen, in the view that the role of language is to make publicly available the private goings-on of one's mind. Although this is Hobbes's official view, he also suggests a quite different picture according to which some reasoning can be done only with words. This violates the typical two-tiered structure, with mental discourse serving as the primary bearer of intentionality and meaning, and verbal, whether written or spoken, imperfectly mirroring thought. Hobbes makes the radical suggestion that language use might be in some way constitutive of reasoning itself.[107]

Reasoning, for Hobbes, is nothing more or less than "*reckoning*, that is, adding and subtracting, of the consequences of general names agreed upon for the *marking* and *signifying* of our thoughts."[108] On Hobbes's computational theory of the mind, reasoning proceeds by quite literally adding and subtracting either words or concepts. But, as we shall see, Hobbes thinks that only words are universal. That is, as far as the subject's interior life goes, only particulars are the objects of thought. Note that this is quite different from a view that says that ideas themselves can be universal, or at least that their immediate intentional objects can be general in the sense that they pick out a class of particulars. On Hobbes's view, only words themselves can range over particulars.

This feature of Hobbes's view puts him squarely in the bull's-eye of Descartes and his fellow travelers. In an admittedly odd objection to Descartes's wax argument, Hobbes writes,

> Now, what shall we say if it turns out that reasoning is simply the joining together and linking of names or labels by means of the verb "is"? It would follow that

> the inferences in our reasoning tell us nothing at all about the natures of things, but merely tell us about the labels applied to them; that is, all we can infer is whether or not we are combining the names of things in accordance with the arbitrary conventions which we have laid down in respect of their meaning.[109]

Descartes finds this so silly he cannot believe anyone even entertained it. For Descartes, reasoning is "not a linking of names but of the things that are signified by the names."[110] Like Leibniz in his objection to Locke, Descartes does not bother to explain how *things* can be joined together. Obviously, he does not have in mind physically connecting things, as if building an Erector set were reasoning; at most he can mean that the things themselves are linked in the sense that our ideas represent them, and the ideas are joined in a proposition or judgment. As Descartes goes on to point out, it is not clear where precisely Hobbes disagrees: after all, Hobbes himself holds that phantasms or ideas represent bodies and their accidents, and that our ideas are signified by words. To this extent, then, reasoning can indeed be about things.

This passage of Hobbes's has often been taken to mean that he endorses a "Humpty-Dumpty" theory of meaning and truth. Hobbes's emphasis on the arbitrary nature of linguistic convention seems to indicate that what makes a proposition true is simply whether it accords with these conventions. Thus, Leibniz famously calls Hobbes a "super-nominalist," who believes that "the truth of things itself consists in names and what is more, that it depends on the human will, because truth allegedly depends on the definitions of terms, and definitions depend on the human will."[111]

We have already seen that Hobbesian definitions do not depend on the human will, in any interesting sense. So, Hobbes cannot consistently mean what Leibniz, Descartes, and the Port-Royalians think he means. Moreover, as Arnauld and Nicole point out, the claim that truth is arbitrary does not follow from the fact that the imposition of words is arbitrary. Once the signification of the relevant words is settled, whether a proposition is true or not is as objective as anything could be.

What, then, is Hobbes getting at it in his objection to Descartes? To answer this question, we need to look at the consequence Hobbes infers:

> If this is so, as may well be the case, reasoning will depend on names, names will depend on the imagination, and imagination will depend (as I believe it does) merely on the motions of our bodily organs; and so the mind will be nothing more than motion occurring in various parts of an organic body.[112]

The real point of Hobbes's claim that reasoning depends on names, which in turn depend on imagination, is to counter Descartes's dualism. As we have seen, Descartes takes reason, the universal instrument, to be one of the features that separates man not just from other animals but from *any* corporeal being. Nothing can at once reason and be merely corporeal. Hobbes's objection is a direct challenge to this view: Hobbes promises to explain the phenomena of reasoning purely through words and imagination. The imagination, which includes memory, is conceded by all parties to the debate to be purely corporeal. Thus, no Cartesian intellect need apply.[113]

Seen in this materialist light, Hobbes's position comes into focus. A true proposition, he thinks, is one in which the predicate contains or comprehends its subject – for example 'mammal' contains or encompasses 'whale.'[114] This is a purely extensional theory of truth: what makes "whales are mammals" true is the fact that the word 'mammals' has been applied to a certain class of beings, and 'whale' has been applied to a subset of this class. In one sense, why *these* names (and not others) have been applied has no good answer: we could just as well have spoken of 'shwales' and 'shmammals.' In another, it has a perfectly good answer: we have applied these names in such a way as to track the resemblances and differences in the phantasms caused by these things.[115] It is then misleading to say that, for Hobbes, reasoning about kinds consists in the mere manipulation of words. And it is this further story – one spelled out in the vocabulary of phantasms and objective resemblances – that prevents his view from falling into supernominalism.

7. Propositions

If the questions of definition and reasoning occasioned debate in the modern period, the question of propositions generated something like consensus. The intriguing issue is just what the object of this consensus amounts to. As we shall see, in its baldest statements, it seems vulnerable to a fairly obvious objection. Although the moderns as a whole have a good answer to one question about propositions, namely what elevates a mere string of words to the status of a proposition, this answer seems to commit them to a wildly implausible view of the attitudes (e.g. belief, dissent, supposition, doubt) we adopt toward them.

One useful way into the question of propositions is afforded by an influential objection to Hobbes's view. Hobbes holds that the copula is superfluous: there might be "some nations" that have no word that corresponds to our word 'is.'[116] Peter Geach writes, "we might very well object that it [the copula] is necessary, because a pair of names is not a proposition but a list."[117] 'Whales mammals,' for example, does not assert anything, nor does it admit of a truth value. Add the copula ('whales are mammals') and you get something with both these features. So, the copula, for Geach, is an essential element in any proposition: it unites the subject and predicate into a complex that admits of a truth value.

But Hobbes in fact endorses Geach's point: Hobbes thinks that a proposition "*is a speech consisting of two names copulated, by which he that speaketh signifies he conceives the latter name to be the name of the same thing whereof the former is the name.*"[118] What, then, is going on? Hobbes, I suggest, is pointing out that there is nothing essential in the grammatical form: we might indicate how we conceive of the names in question by our tone of voice rather than by 'is,' 'est,' or what have you. Hobbes and Geach agree that the job of the copula must get done; Hobbes simply denies that it needs to be done by a distinct syntactic unit.

This concern with what unites words or ideas in a proposition and distinguishes propositions from lists can be found as far back as Aristotle's *De interpretatione* (16a10–19) and runs right through the modern period. But where Hobbes focuses on names, and makes speech essential to the formation of a proposition, most of his fellow travelers take the more traditional line that there are purely mental, as well as verbal, propositions, and that the role of a verbal proposition is to mirror the mental proposition.

Thus, a more typical pronouncement is to be found in the Port-Royal *Logic*:

> [a]fter conceiving things by our ideas, we compare these ideas, and, finding that some belong together and others do not, we unite or separate them. This is called *affirming* or *denying*, and in general *judging* . . . [and] this judgment is also called a *proposition*.[119]

As with Hobbes, it is crucial that a judgment or proposition consists not merely of a pair of ideas or words but of these items combined or taken in a certain way. Similar pronouncements can be found in Locke.[120] 'Is' signifies not another idea but rather a mental act. To this extent, Locke departs from his blanket claim that all words signify ideas in the mind of the speaker. Some of them must signify mental acts.[121]

The problem with this dominant view is not hard to see. Take the proposition "[i]f a creature's will can obstruct the absolute will of God, God is not omnipotent." The antecedent here is itself a proposition: a creature's will can obstruct the absolute will of God. And yet when I assert the conditional, I am not, of course, asserting the antecedent.[122] Nor am I asserting the consequent, namely that God is not omnipotent. And yet each is itself a proposition, which entails that I find that the constituent ideas agree or disagree. To even think "God is not omnipotent" is, it seems, to assent to this proposition: I have to *find* that the ideas *God* and *omnipotent* disagree. The very nature of a judgment or a proposition, it seems, precludes any attitude toward that proposition other than assent. And this is absurd.[123]

It is not as if the moderns are somehow blinkered to the obvious fact that not every proposition we entertain, whether in the context of a conditional or not, is not an object of assent. In fact, the previous example is drawn from the Port-Royal *Logic* itself.[124] But providing for the unity of the proposition as the moderns do seemingly makes it impossible to account for propositional attitudes.

What, then, are we to conclude? Could the Port-Royal logicians and Locke have been so inconsistent as to insist on the possibility of entertaining a proposition without assenting to it and in the same breath offering an analysis that makes this flatly impossible? One possible move is to claim that the subpropositional use of 'is' is not equivalent to assertion. That is, an affirmation is not necessarily an assertion. There are two acts that need to be performed: a union of subject and predicate, and then the adoption of an attitude toward the resulting proposition. The skeptic can argue that such a reading is precluded by the Port-Royalians' talk of *finding* that the subject and predicate agree or disagree. But if *finding* entails assent, it has an even more dire consequence: one cannot find that two ideas agree, for example, when those ideas *do not* agree. 'Find,' like 'see,' is a success term. Taken at face value, then, the Port-Royalian view makes it impossible not only to entertain a proposition without assenting to it but also to assent to a proposition that it is not in fact true. Considerations of charity must be played off textual considerations to achieve some kind of equilibrium, and it is plausible to read the Port-Royalians, and Locke, as holding that the affirmation involved in constructing any proposition is only provisional, and can be canceled by further acts of the mind.[125]

Not all the moderns agree that a judgment or proposition requires a further act of the mind beyond that of conceiving of an idea alone. Some think that to entertain the proposition that x is F, for example, is just to have a single idea. In other words, the traditional distinction between conceiving and judging is collapsed. This doctrine has its source in Descartes and comes to fruition, if one wants to call it that, in Spinoza. It lives on in the next century in the work of Hume.[126]

Here again we can begin with a contemporary objection. Descartes is often painted as an epistemic voluntarist, that is someone who thinks that the will is always free to affirm or deny any proposition at all.[127] Judgment, for Descartes, is an act of the will, and so, the objection goes, he thinks that the mind can either affirm or deny any proposition. This is obviously false: I cannot will myself to disbelieve 2 + 2 = 4, no matter how hard I try.

That the objection is wrongheaded can be seen from Descartes's analysis of will:

> [T]he will ... consists simply in the fact that when the intellect puts something forward for affirmation or denial or for pursuit or avoidance, our inclinations are such that we do not feel we are determined *by any external force*.[128]

This leaves open that we can be determined by an *internal* force, namely the light of reason. The more clearly I understand a true proposition like 2 + 2 = 4, the more I find affirming it irresistible, and the more free my will is in affirming it.

Spinoza takes this as his starting point in analyzing propositions. For him, what most moderns take to be distinct acts – forming an idea and then combining it with others to generate a proposition – are conflated. Any act of the will just is an affirmation or negation, and these are identical to the ideas most moderns would take as their objects. His argument is roughly as follows: because conception and affirmation (or negation) are always, and necessarily, found together, there can be no real distinction between them. As Spinoza writes, "[t]here is in the mind no volition, that is, affirmation and negation, except that which an idea, insofar as it is an idea, involves."[129] Take the claim (P) that the three angles of a triangle are equal to two right angles. Now, we cannot affirm (P) without having the idea of a triangle. Conversely, and more controversially, we cannot, Spinoza thinks, have the idea of a triangle without affirming (P). So, affirming (P) "belongs to the essence of the idea of a triangle."

Although not directly an influence on later philosophers, like Hume, who also reduce judgment to conception, Spinoza's position represents a novel and radical departure from the Aristotelian tradition. But if the traditional view faces the problem of propositional attitudes, Spinoza's is undone by it. However plausible as an account of *a priori* necessary propositions, Spinoza's view cannot make sense of any other.

8. Definite descriptions and the limits of thought

Syncategorematic terms – words like 'is,' 'of,' 'and,' and 'but' – are crucial not just in constructing propositions but in expressing their connection. Locke gives an astute analysis of 'but,' tracing its different roles in indicating postures that the mind adopts toward propositions. As we have seen, it is not clear whether the tradition in which Locke stands can offer an analysis of the proposition consistent with these postures.

What concerns us in this section, however, is the role of syncategoremata in constructing what contemporary philosophers call definite descriptions. Syncategoremata are subpropositional elements that are nevertheless not just noun, or noun-adjective, combinations. 'That tapir over there' includes not just a sign of the idea of a tapir but words indicating further mental acts. As we shall see, they play an indispensable role in extending the bounds of sense.[130]

The best starting point is the exchange between Hobbes and Descartes. Hobbes argues that we have no ideas of God or substance; these are established by inference but not given in any idea.[131] Substance, for example, "is something that is established solely by reasoning; it is not something that is conceived, or that presents any idea to us."[132] The Port-Royalians, endorsing what I have called the default modern view of signification, draw the obvious conclusion: "if we had no idea of God, in uttering the name 'God' we would conceive only these three letters, 'G,' 'o,' 'd.' "[133] Using language to communicate requires that we have a single idea for each categorematic word we utter.

What has Hobbes to say for himself? To establish that x exists by means of inference or reasoning obviously requires that I first have some way to think and talk about x. Moreover, it is hard to see how Hobbes could deny that we "conceive" of substance and yet claim that we know it exists. For a coherent development of Hobbes's insights in his exchange with Descartes, we have to look to Locke.

Consider Locke's own analysis of substance. Construed as an ultimate substratum or underpinning of qualities, substance is not a possible object of experience.[134] It is not a macroscopic quality that can cause ideas in us, but the cushion in which the pins of qualities stick. Thus, Locke's own index entry for "substance" reads "S. no idea of it."[135] At the same time, Locke clearly thinks that we *do*, in some sense, have an idea of substance; otherwise the word would be nonsense. Locke's ambivalence can be accounted for by seeing the difference between thinking of x in virtue of having a single idea that represents x and in virtue of having a string of ideas and acts that jointly represent x. Only in the latter sense can we have an "idea" of substance. "That which underlies and supports qualities" does not signify a single idea in the mind of the speaker but rather a complex of ideas and mental acts, much as a proposition must include words that signify ideas and the mental act of combination or separation.[136] "Substance" is an abbreviated definite description.

Bertrand Russell takes definite descriptions to be the only means by which an empiricist avoids idealism.[137] In the same way, Locke uses them to extend the limits of thought beyond ideas and even the objects they represent. By structuring ideas and mental acts in the right way, we can transcend the narrow limits imposed by the veil, or better, the window, of ideas. For the very same reason, Locke's use of descriptions makes him the target of later empiricists.

Although Berkeley ultimately goes on to endorse a substance view of the mind, he entertains in his notebooks a Humean picture, on which the mind is nothing more than an aggregate of ideas. Arguing against the Lockean view, Berkeley writes, "Say you the Mind is not the Perceptions. but that thing wch perceives. I answer you are abus'd by the words that & thing these are vague empty words wthout a meaning."[138] Here, Berkeley zeroes in on precisely the syncategorematic terms so vital to Lockean definite descriptions. The words 'that' and 'thing' are denied a meaning because they cannot be correlated with any ideas. Having taken over what he (mis)takes as Locke's philosophy of language, namely the view that all words signify ideas, Berkeley can accuse Locke of inconsistency: 'that' does not signify any idea at all (it is "empty" and "without a meaning").[139] But on Locke's real view, 'that' can nevertheless be significant, because it indicates an act of the mind.

The issue of definite descriptions has clear ramifications for later thinkers. One of the most striking features of Hume's emaciated empiricism is its refusal even to entertain Lockean definite descriptions as a means of thinking about that which is permanently hidden from experience. Might this not be a result of his view of the nature of the proposition, and his rejection of syncategorematic terms as signifying anything over and above one's ideas?

Because this topic is the most obvious link to the debates of the eighteenth century, it makes an appropriate place to end this sketch of philosophy of language in the seventeenth.

9. Conclusion

If this chapter licenses any lesson, it is that philosophy of language in the seventeenth century is a vast and lively battlefield, distinguished by skirmishes and sometimes routs. Its front lines extend to many of the core issues in metaphysics. And if the background assumptions that structure the debate are foreign to us, if it is fought on terrain we find difficult to map, that makes it all the more instructive. For throwing our own assumptions into stark relief is surely one of the ways in which the history of philosophy matters to philosophy.[140]

10. Further reading

The best place to start is Ian Hacking's classic *Why Does Language Matter to Philosophy?* (1975). In a lucid and accessible style, Hacking argues for some intriguing positions and makes the first sustained foray into the history of the philosophy of language, all the while keeping one eye on contemporary debates.

More recently, Michael Losonsky's *Linguistic Turns in Modern Philosophy* (2007a) covers much the same territory, though in a very different way. Losonsky's theme is the split between those approaches to language that treat it as a formal system and those that treat it as a practical tool for communication. Like Hacking, Losonsky begins in the seventeenth century and continues through the twentieth.

Finally, two special issues of journals are well worth reading. *Synthese* (1988), titled "Thought and Language in the Philosophy of the Enlightenment," contains a number of important pieces, particularly on Locke, Descartes, and Berkeley. And *Philosophia* (2009) includes the proceedings of a 2008 conference titled "Meaning and Modern Empiricism."

Notes

1 *Leviathan* (hereafter, "Lev"), I.v: 36–7. References to Lev are in the following form: part.chapter: page number in Hobbes (1839–45), vol. 3.
2 It is important not to be misled by the moderns' wide use of "name." This encompasses not just what we think of as proper names but nearly any noun or noun-adjective complex.
3 Note that, in the typical case, the mind uses, rather than thinks of, universals. On Aquinas's view, for example, the intelligible species is not itself the object of thought. It can, of course, become so, when the mind reflects on its own activity. But for the most part the intellect uses the abstracted species to think of individuals, though not *qua* individuals.
4 This is Locke's official position. His argument for God's existence in *Essay* 4.10, however, creates problems for this agnosticism. For more on this, see Downing (2007). References to Locke's *Essay* are to Locke (1975) and are in the following form: book.chapter.section: page number, if applicable.
5 The connection between universality and immateriality runs throughout many of the early moderns. For example, at least early in his career, Gassendi argued that, being material, our minds cannot entertain genuine universals. For more on this, see LoLordo (2007: 234f.).
6 In this opening section, I run roughshod over many differences among the moderns; these will emerge in the following sections.
7 I do not wish to underestimate the degree to which Aristotelianism is heterogeneous. It is misleading, though extremely convenient, to speak of "the" Aristotelian view. Many views we think of as distinctive of the early modern period were prefigured in the tremendous array of positions flying under the banner of Aristotelianism. Nevertheless, this particular "ism" does point to a family of views that have some common commitments.
8 1629 Letter to Mersenne (CSM III 10f). References are to Descartes (1984) and in the following form: volume, page number.

9 For another example, see the Port-Royal *Logic* I.11: 58f. References are to part, chapter, and page number in Arnauld and Nicole (1996).
10 "Idol" is the standard translation for Bacon's *idola*; Michael Silverthorne (in Bacon 2000) makes a good case for translating it as "illusion," and indeed this seems to be how the English cognate of the word was understood at the time. Hobbes, for example, writes that demons are "idols or phantasms of the brain, without any real nature of their own" (Lev IV.44: 605.)
11 *The New Organon* I.xxxviii in Bacon (2000: 40).
12 See Hobbes, Lev I.i: 3.
13 As Galileo puts it in *The Assayer*, "[j]ust because we have given special names to these qualities, different from the names we have given to the primary and real properties, we are tempted into believing that the former really and truly exist as well as the latter" (in Matthews 1989: 57).
14 Spinoza (2002: 24); see *Theological-Political Treatise* (2002: 505) for the claim that words acquire meaning through their use. In an intriguing article, David Savan (1973) argues that Spinoza's views on language entail that the true philosophy is unstatable: given Spinoza's view that words are a part of the imagination, Savan claims, they cannot mirror the intellect, as truth requires. But see the rejoinder by G.H.R. Parkinson in the same volume.
15 For more on this, see esp. Dawson (2007), though I think she tends to exaggerate the moderns' anxiety about these issues.
16 Lev I.4: 25.
17 Port-Royal *Logic* I.11: 58.
18 For some Scholastics, such as Aquinas, "definition" means only the definiens, not the entire proposition. I ignore this complication here.
19 See Aristotle's *Posterior Analytics* and esp. Aquinas's commentary (1970).
20 See esp. Descartes's appendix to Fifth Replies, CSM II 271; see also *Rules for the Direction of the Mind*, CSM I 36, 51.
21 See esp. Nuchelmans (1998c: 133f.)
22 Glanvill (1665: 143).
23 *New Essays Concerning Human Understanding* (hereafter, "NE") III.xvii: 478. Page numbers refer to the Akademie edition (Leibniz 1990) and are followed by Bennett and Remnant (Leibniz 1996). Translations of NE are those of Bennett and Remnant unless noted. See also Nuchelmans (1998c: 133f.)
24 NE III.x.xvii: 478.
25 It is also worth noting that the structure of a Scholastic textbook in logic – beginning with individual terms, then moving to propositions, to formal reasoning, and finally to general remarks about logical method – lives on in many modern works. This is explicit in the Port-Royal *Logic* and in Hobbes's logic, book I of his *De Corpore*; it is perhaps implicit in the structure of Locke's *Essay*. Book 1 aside, we can think of book 2 as focusing on the mental counterparts of categorematic words, book 3 on propositions, and book 4 on method.
26 CSM I 139–40.
27 John Cottingham calls this problem "the disappearing soul": if everything from nutrition to locomotion to pain avoidance can be explained mechanically, what is left for the Cartesian soul to do? See Cottingham (1992).
28 CSM I 140.
29 CSM I 140.
30 CSM III 303.
31 This is an intriguing point in Descartes's argument. Although the use of signs in the ways specified seems to be set up here as an indication of both reason and thought, the madman's speech "does not follow reason," and yet still counts as an indication of thought. That Descartes distinguishes between reason and thought is evident in the 1649 *Passions of the Soul*, Descartes's last work, where he says that beasts "have no reason, nor perhaps any thought" (CSM I 348). So, although language use is a sufficient condition for thought, it is not one of reason.
32 Compositionality as a criterion of languagehood becomes explicit in Berkeley: "[i]t is the articulation, combination, variety, copiousness, extensive and general use and easy application of signs . . . that constitute the true nature of language," *Alciphron* Dialogue IV, section 12, in Berkeley (1949–58, vol. 5: 157).

In taking language use to be the primary means of discerning reasoning (or at least thinking) beings from those that are not, Descartes is unusual in the period we are examining. The debate that ensues focuses squarely on the attribution of thought, whether the animal is a language user or not. See, for

example, Locke, *Essay* 2.11.5: 157–8. Locke locates the main difference between humans and animals in the ability to abstract, not in the possession of thought, ideas, or language. See also the exchange between Philalethes (Locke's spokesman) and Theophilus (who represents Leibniz's own views) in the latter's NE: 142–5.
33 CSM III 10; cf. Descartes's talk of true colors in the Third Meditation.
34 Earlier writers, such as Ramon Lull, hoped for such a language in part because it would enable proselytizers of the true religion to convince infidels more readily.
35 See Leibniz's "Preface to a Universal Characteristic" and "Samples of the Numerical Characteristic" in Leibniz (1989: 5–18). In a short dialogue from 1677, Leibniz (1969: 182–5) suggests that, whereas the characters of such a language, and indeed all languages, are arbitrarily chosen, the truths constructed out of them depend only on their relations to each other and to things. For discussion, see Losonsky (2007a: 57f.)
36 For more on this, see Eco (1997). Hans Aarsleff (1964) has made much of the Adamic thought of the period, even reading book 3 of Locke's *Essay* as a response. For a corrective, see Ian Hacking (1988). Although Aarsleff reads Leibniz as taking up the Adamic cause in his *New Essays*, there is little evidence for this. Indeed, Leibniz himself says of Boehme, "he neither understood himself, nor have others understood him" (quoted in Hacking 1988: 144).
37 NE III.ii: 278.
38 NE III.ii: 281.
39 *Pace* Aarsleff (1964). When Leibniz says that "there is something natural in the origin of words – something which reveals a relationship between things and the sounds and motions of the vocal organs" (NE III.ii: 283), he has in mind not just onomatopoeia but the psychological concomitants of making certain vocalizations. For example, Leibniz thinks *r* "naturally signifies a violent motion" (NE III.ii: 283) and hence comes to be used in words signifying such motion.
40 Or, more precisely, the Latin translation of this paragraph by Boethius. See Ashworth (1981, 300).
41 In Aristotle (1984, vol. 1: 25).
42 Locke, *Essay* 3.1.2: 402.
43 The extent to which this is true depends on each philosopher's conception of the origin of ideas. Descartes's God could in principle create a mind without one or more innate ideas; such a mind would be operating without a full stock of mental materials from which to form thoughts. Similarly, Locke holds that a person born blind will have no way of representing color, except perhaps indirectly.
44 Lev I.4: 19; cf. Locke, *Essay* 3.1
45 See Ashworth (1981; 1984). On Ashworth's reading, signification in the late Scholastic sense includes "aspects" of both sense and reference, though it is not to be identified with either. Ashworth argues that this sense of signification carries over into Locke; here we disagree.
46 Although this is controversial, I agree with Michael Jacovides's claim that Locke means "resemblance" literally; see Jacovides (1999).
47 CSM I 81. Note that the motions of the brain that signify light are not themselves perceived, even though they make us think of light. Descartes thus rejects the traditional requirement that the sign itself be perceivable. Descartes might have in mind the notion of formal signs, commonly deployed by Scholastics such as John Poinsot, according to which a sign need not itself be perceived (see Ashworth 1988). In this, Descartes has very few fellow travelers among the moderns; possible exceptions are the Cambridge Platonists, such as Ralph Cudworth. For more on this, see Slezak (2000) and Yolton (2000).
48 CSM I 82.
49 *Logic* I.4: 36.
50 This is the flip side of what is known as the disjunction problem in contemporary philosophy of mind.
51 *Essay* 3.1.2: 402. Cf. the Port-Royal *Logic*:

> On this topic we can generally say that words are distinct and articulated sounds that people have made into signs to indicate what takes place in the mind. Since what takes place in the mind consists in conceiving, judging, reasoning, and ordering, as we have already said, words function to indicate all these operations.
>
> (II.i: 74)

52 Correspondingly, our intentions as hearers or readers ought to be to interpret the words as their author intended. For more on this, and for criticism of the indicator reading of Locke, see Winkler (2009).
53 This is controversial. For different views, see Ashworth (1984) and Kretzmann (1968). For a defense, see chapter 2 of Ott (2004) and E. J. Lowe (2007), chapter 4.

54 *De Corpore* (henceforth "DC") I.ii.2: 14–15. References to DC are in the following form: part.chapter.section: page number in Hobbes (1839–45), vol.1.
55 DC I.ii.5: 17.
56 Trivially, one *could* set up a convention by which 'stone' signifies stones, namely by uttering the sound only when in the presence of stone. But this is not the purpose of language, according to Hobbes (or Locke, or the Port-Royalians, for that matter). In such a case, words would not be able to fulfill their function of unfolding one's mind to another.
57 See Lev I.4: 19–20:

> So that the first use of names, is to serve for *marks*, or *notes* of remembrance. Another is, when many use the same words, to signify, by their connexion and order, one to another, what they conceive, or think of each matter; and also what they desire, fear, or have any passion for. And for this use they are called *signs*.

Locke does not bother to distinguish between marks and signs in this way, even though he clearly thinks words have both uses.
58 If they construe the relationship between signs as causes and signs as indications as one of genus to species, the Port-Royalians can escape my charge of having conflated the two uses.
59 See esp. *Essay* 3.2.7–8: 407–8.
60 *Essay* 3.2.4: 406.
61 *Essay* 2.30.2: 372–3, my emphasis; see 4.11.12: 631.
62 For more on this, see Sally Ferguson (2001). Contemporary philosophers of mind have developed similar stories by replacing God with natural selection. These issues are very complicated; for doubts about reading Locke as a proponent of teleosemantics or any externalist theory of the meaning of ideas, see Ott (2012).
63 See, for example, *Essay* 2.32.14: 388.
64 DC I.ii.6: 17.
65 DC I.ii.4: 16.
66 See Watkins (1973: 102). Watkins claims that Hobbes says nothing about the naming relation because he cannot accommodate it within his causal psychology.
67 DC I.ii.5: 17.
68 *Essay* 3.7.1: 471.
69 "The use then of Words, is to be sensible Marks of *Ideas*; and the *Ideas* they stand for, are their proper and immediate Signification" (*Essay* 3.2.1: 405); "[W]ords, as they are used by Men, can properly and immediately signify nothing but *Ideas*, that are in the Mind of the Speaker" (3.2.4: 406). But Locke often leaves off the restriction to primary or immediate signification; for example, he writes, "[words'] signification [in a man's use of them] . . . is limited to his *Ideas*, and they can be Signs of nothing else" (3.2.8: 408).
70 Once again, I should note that this is controversial. For criticism of my view, see Losonsky (2007b).
71 Losonsky (2007b) rather puzzlingly lumps my view in with Hacking's. Because I do not think that Lockean signification is sense, reference, or any combination thereof, Losonsky claims that I deny that Locke has a theory of meaning. This is trivially true if one means by "a theory of meaning" a *Fregean* theory of meaning, that is one that explains the sense and reference of words. It is false if one simply means "a theory that purports to explain how words function in communication."
72 *Logic* I.6: 39–40. Nuchelmans (1998a) argues that Leibniz employs a similar distinction.
73 By "fact-stating," I mean something broader than the term strictly implies, to include not just declarative statements but questions, conditionals, and so on. The line between fact-stating and non-fact-stating uses is a fluid one.
74 See, for example, *Philosophical Commentaries*, section 720; introduction to the *Principles*, section 19; *Alciphron* VII.5: 292.
75 See DC I.iii.1: 29. Hobbes and Descartes are thinking here of things like 'ouch' or perhaps profanity. Obviously, a word like 'joy,' as a sign, indicates an idea of joy, but it need not, as my own present experience attests, indicate that the person using it is experiencing joy at that moment.
76 Mill (1867: 15). In 1694, John Sergeant (1984: 33–5) made a similar criticism.
77 Thus Alston (1964) is wrong to call this sort of view "linguistic idealism."
78 *Essay* 3.2.1: 405.
79 Sergeant (1984: 34).
80 *Essay* 3.11.14: 515.

81 For amusing critiques of "Mr. J. S." on this point, see Locke's letter to Stillingfleet (1812, vol. 4: 390–1) and the anonymous pamphlet *A Dialogue Between Mr Merriman, and Dr Chymist: Concerning Sergents Paradoxes, in His New Method to Science, and His Solid Philosophy* (London, 1698).
82 *Essay* 2.33.19: 401.
83 *Essay* 3.10.17: 499.
84 *Essay* 3.10.18: 500. Note that Locke, as elsewhere in book 3 and throughout the *Essay*, does not include the limitation to primary or immediate signification. This is another reason to deny that secondary signification, if Locke believes in such a thing, is a new category, irreducible to primary signification.
85 See Winkler (2009).
86 See *Essay* 3.10.17–18: 500, where Locke uses the examples of gold and malleability.
87 Cf. Hobbes, DC I.v.7: 60, where Hobbes argues that it is false to say that "*the definition is the essence of the thing.* . . . For definition is not the essence of anything but a speech signifying what we conceive of the essence thereof."
88 For bats and birds, see *Essay* 3.11.7: 511; for the baby, see 3.6.26: 452–4.
89 I mean, no fact of the matter beyond the contents of those ideas. Now, if our abstract ideas captured Aristotelian real essences, then in an indirect way the world would be settling these questions.
90 *Essay* 3.3.15: 417.
91 These other things include acting as migration barriers: once a thing exists with a certain essence, it cannot then change that essence without being destroyed. On Locke's view, there are no such barriers in nature.
92 *Essay* 3.6.6: 442.
93 *Essay* 3.6.8: 443–4; 3.10.20: 501–2.
94 Here, I shall not delve into the details of Leibniz's defense of the Aristotelian picture, except to the extent that it's directly relevant to the question of language. For more on this debate, see Jolley (1984), chapter 8.
95 NE III.ii: 287. I depart slightly from Bennett and Remnant's translation here.
96 NE III.x: 345.
97 This is the main point of *Essay* 3.10 and, arguably, 3.6.
98 Against this permutation of the Aristotelian view, Locke argues that, if our ideas of substances just were their real essences, we would be able deduce all their other properties. See 3.10.18: 500 and 3.10.21: 502. It is not clear how effective this is, because both Leibniz and Sergeant point out that it is no part of the opposing position that our grasp of these essences is complete.
99 Nominal definitions can be individually stipulative, as when I say that 'mongfy' is to mean 'square,' or collectively so, as when a convention is in place that associates a word with a given idea. What I am calling individually stipulative definitions cannot be challenged and are neither true nor false; ascertaining the truth of a collectively stipulated definition requires looking to the linguistic practices of one's community.
100 See *Logic* II.12–14: 111–123.
101 See, for example, Pierre-Sylvain Régis, *Refutation de l'opinion de Spinosa* in Régis (1996) (first published 1704).
102 See *Discourse on Metaphysics*, section 24, in Leibniz (1989: 57).
103 This is the core of Leibniz's objection to Descartes's ontological argument for the existence of God. That argument begins with the definition of God and immediately infers His existence, from the fact that He is a perfect being. For Leibniz, however, one cannot simply assume that just because one knows the meaning of the word 'God' that one has in fact secured a real definition of God. One must prove that the constituent ideas – here, the ideas of God's attributes – are logically consistent. Only by doing so can one prove that God is even a *possible* being, let alone actual and necessary. See Leibniz's letter to Countess Elizabeth (1989: 238f.)
104 Lev I.4: 23–4.
105 See DC VI.13.
106 *Treatise on the Emendation of the Intellect* in Spinoza (2002: 26).
107 At least where general terms are concerned; Pettit (2008) goes much further and argues that, for Hobbes, language use is *constitutive* of thought. That this claim is mistaken will emerge as we go. Although Hobbes thinks reasoning about universals requires language – because universals are names – he does not think that all thought (or even all reasoning) concerns universals.
108 Lev I.5: 30.

109 Third Objections in CSM II 125.
110 Third Replies in CSM II 126.
111 "Preface to an Edition of Nizolius" (1670), in Leibniz (1969: 128). For discussion, see Watkins (1973).
112 Third Objections, CSM II 126.
113 Similar concerns prompt Locke's dismantling of the Sixth Meditation argument for the intellect: the intellect is supposed to be immaterial, and so allowing for it would be inconsistent with Locke's official agnosticism about the ultimate nature of the mind. See *Essay* 2.29.13–14: 368.
114 See DC I.iii.7. Note that Leibniz inverts this; for Leibniz, a true proposition is one in which the (concept of the) subject contains the (concept of the) predicate. See "Primary Truths" (in Leibniz 1989: 30–4). The difference between Hobbes and Leibniz here can be accounted for, I suspect, by noticing that Hobbes's definition of a true proposition is extensional, whereas Leibniz's is intentional. That is, Leibniz is worried about the relations between concepts, whereas Hobbes is worried about the extensions of the subject and predicate.
115 See esp. DC I.iii.3: 31 and DC I.ii.9: 20.
116 DC I.iii.2: 31.
117 Geach (1980: 60).
118 DC I.iii.2: 30.
119 *Logic* II.3: 82.
120 See esp. *Essay* 3.7. Note that Locke does not use "judgment" to refer to the act of the mind by which ideas are united in a mental proposition, but rather to a propositional attitude falling short of assent but nevertheless with some presumption of positive epistemic status (4.18.17: 685).
121 This point provides indirect support for the indicator reading; the copula, if it is doing its job, cannot be a referring term, nor can it have Ashworthian "aspects" of both sense and reference while being reducible to neither.
122 The problem of conditionals vexed many of the most acute thinkers of the era. Leibniz wanted to reduce all conditional judgments to categoricals: thus, you can read "if something is a whale, it is a mammal" as "all whales are mammals." This is a popular strategy in the period, also deployed by Arnold Geulincx. For more on this, see Nuchelmans (1998b: 123f.) But it is hard to believe that all conditionals are reducible to categorical claims.
123 For another statement of this argument, see Buroker's introduction to Arnauld and Nicole (1996).
124 *Logic* II.9: 100.
125 I experiment with different ways to accommodate a distinction between proposition and attitude in Locke in chapter 2 of Ott (2004). David Owen (2007) makes a powerful argument that none of these will work. This issue strikes me, though perhaps no one else, as an open question.
126 See Hume (2000), book I, part III, section 7, paragraph 5.
127 By "free" here I mean that the mind is able to judge otherwise than it in fact does.
128 The Fourth Meditation in CSM II 40; my emphasis.
129 *Ethics*, part II, proposition 49 in Spinoza (2002: 272).
130 Here I mean "sense" as opposed to nonsense, not *Sinn*.
131 Hobbes, of course, takes ideas to be images, which Descartes and the Port-Royalians deny. But this disagreement is orthogonal to the issue I am examining here.
132 CSM II 130.
133 *Logic* I.i: 27.
134 This is controversial. Although Locke uses "substance" in many ways, one of these is substratum, which I believe means the ultimate particular in which qualities inhere. I thus endorse the pin-cushion reading of Locke, in opposition to, for example, Michal Ayers (1991).
135 In Locke (1975: 745).
136 Cf. The Port-Royal *Logic*'s treatment of descriptions, which they treat as "less exact" definitions. See *Logic* II.16: 126.
137 See Russell (1912: 46f.).
138 *Philosophical Commentaries*, section 581.
139 In the *Commentaries*, Berkeley does eventually acknowledge that Lockean particles signify acts instead of ideas (section 667). This realization is no doubt an important force in the development of Berkeley's doctrine of notions. But throughout his published works, he mischaracterizes Locke as holding that all words signify ideas.
140 I am indebted to Antonia LoLordo for helpful comments.

Bibliography

Aarsleff, Hans. 1964. "Leibniz on Locke on Language." *American Philosophical Quarterly* 1: 165–88.
Alston, William. 1964. *The Philosophy of Language.* Englewood Cliffs, NJ: Prentice Hall.
Anonymous. 1698. *A Dialogue Between Mr Merriman, and Dr Chymist: Concerning Sergents Paradoxes, in His New Method to Science, and His Solid Philosophy.* London: n.p.
Aquinas, Thomas. 1970. *Commentary on the Posterior Analytics.* Trans. by F. R. Larcher. New York: Magi Books.
Aristotle. 1984. *The Complete Works of Aristotle.* 2 vols. Ed. by Jonathan Barnes. Princeton, NJ: Princeton University Press.
Arnauld, Antoine and Pierre Nicole. 1970. *La Logique, ou L'art de Penser.* Paris: Flammarion.
———. 1996. *Logic or the Art of Thinking.* Trans. and ed. by Jill Vance Buroker. Cambridge: Cambridge University Press.
Ashworth, E. J. 1981. "Do Words Signify Ideas or Things?" *Journal of the History of Philosophy* 19: 299–326.
———. 1984. "Locke on Language." *Canadian Journal of Philosophy* 14: 45–73.
———. 1988. "The Historical Origins of John Poinsot's *Treatise on Signs*." *Semiotica* 69: 129–47.
———. 1990. "Domingo de Soto and the Doctrine of Signs." In *De Ortu Grammaticae.* Ed. by G. L. Bursill-Hall, Sten Ebbesen, and Konrad Koerner. Philadelphia: John Benjamins.
Ayers, M. R. 1991. *Locke: Epistemology and Ontology.* London: Routledge.
Ayers, M. R. and Daniel Garber, eds. 1998. *The Cambridge History of Seventeenth-Century Philosophy.* 2 vols. Cambridge: Cambridge University Press.
Bacon, Francis. 2000. *The New Organon.* Ed. by L. Jardine and M. Silverthorne. Trans. by M. Silverthorne. Cambridge: Cambridge University Press.
Bennett, Jonathan. 1971. *Locke, Berkeley, Hume: Central Themes.* Oxford: Clarendon Press.
Berkeley, George. 1949–58. *The Works of George Berkeley.* Ed. by A. A. Luce and T. E. Jessop. 8 vols. London: Thomas Nelson.
Boyle, Robert. 1991. *Selected Philosophical Papers of Robert Boyle.* Ed. by M. A. Stewart. Indianapolis: Hackett.
Cottingham, John. 1992. "Cartesian Dualism." In *The Cambridge Companion to Descartes.* Ed. by J. Cottingham. Cambridge: Cambridge University Press.
Dawson, Hannah. 2007. *Locke, Language and Early-Modern Philosophy.* Cambridge: Cambridge University Press.
Descartes, René. 1984. *The Philosophical Writings of Descartes.* Vols. 1 and 2. Ed by John Cottingham, Robert Stoothoff, and Dugald Murdoch; Vol. 3. Ed. by Cottingham, Stoothoff, Murdoch, and Anthony Kenny. New York: Cambridge University Press.
Digby, Sir Kenelm. 1657. *Two Treatises: In the One of Which, the Nature of Bodies, in the Other the Nature of Mans Soule Is Looked Into: In Way of Discovery of the Immortality of Reasonable Soules.* Paris: Gilles Blaizot.
Downing, Lisa. 2007. "Locke's Ontology." In *The Cambridge Companion to Locke's Essay.* Ed. by Lex Newman. Cambridge: Cambridge University Press.
Dretske, Fred. 1990. "Misrepresentation." In *Mind and Cognition.* Ed. by William G. Lycan. Oxford: Blackwell.
Eco, Umberto. 1997. *The Search for the Perfect Language.* London: Blackwell.
Ferguson, Sally. 2001. "Lockian Teleosemantics." *Locke Studies* 1: 105–22.
Fodor, Jerry. 1984. "Semantics, Wisconsin Style." *Synthese* 59: 231–50.
Geach, Peter. 1980. *Reference and Generality.* Ithaca: Cornell University Press.
Glanvill, Joseph. 1665. *Scepsis Scientifica: Or, Confest Ignorance, the Way to Science; In An Essay of The Vanity of Dogmatizing, and Confident Opinion.* London: E. Cotes.
Hacking, Ian. 1975. *Why Does Language Matter to Philosophy?* Cambridge: Cambridge University Press.
———. 1988. "Locke, Leibniz, and Hans Aarsleff." *Synthese* 75 (2): 135–54.
Hobbes, Thomas. 1839–45. *The English Works of Thomas Hobbes.* Ed. by William Molesworth. 11 vols. London: Richards.
Hume, David. 2000. *A Treatise of Human Nature.* Ed. by D. F. Norton and M. Norton. Oxford: Oxford University Press.
Jacovides, Michael. 1999. "Locke's Resemblance Theses." *Philosophical Review* 108: 46–96.
Jesseph, Douglas. 1996. "Hobbes and the Method of Natural Science." In *The Cambridge Companion to Hobbes.* Ed. by T. Sorrell. Cambridge: Cambridge University Press.
Jolley, Nicholas. 1984. *Leibniz and Locke.* Oxford: Oxford University Press.

Kretzmann, Norman. 1968. "The Main Thesis of Locke's Semantic Theory." *Philosophical Review* 77: 175–96. Reprinted in *Locke on Human Understanding*. Ed. by I. C. Tipton. Oxford: Oxford University Press, 1975.

Leibniz, G. W. 1969. *Philosophical Papers and Letters*. Ed. by L. Loemker. Dordrecht: Reidel.

———. 1989. *Philosophical Essays*. Ed. by R. Ariew and D. Garber. Indianapolis: Hackett.

———. 1990. *Nouveaux Essais sur L'entendement*. Ed. by André Robinet and Heinrich Schepers. In *Philosophische Shriften*, vol. 6. Berlin: Akademie-Verlag.

———. 1996. *New Essays on Human Understanding*. Trans. and Ed. by Jonathan Bennett and Peter Remnant. Cambridge: Cambridge University Press.

Locke, John. 1812. *The Works of John Locke*. 11th ed. 10 vols. London: Thomas Tegg.

———. 1975. *An Essay Concerning Human Understanding*. Ed. by P. H. Nidditch. Oxford: Clarendon.

LoLordo, Antonia. 2007. *Pierre Gassendi and the Birth of Early Modern Philosophy*. Cambridge: Cambridge University Press.

Losonsky, Michael. 2007a. *Linguistic Turns in Modern Philosophy*. Cambridge: Cambridge University Press.

———. 2007b. "Language, Meaning, and Mind in Locke's Essay." In *The Cambridge Companion to Locke's Essay*. Ed. by Lex Newman. Cambridge: Cambridge University Press.

Lowe, E. J. 2007. *Locke*. London: Routledge.

Matthews, Michael R., ed. 1989. *The Scientific Background to Modern Philosophy*. Indianapolis: Hackett.

Mill, J. S. 1867. *A System of Logic*. New York: Harper.

Nuchelmans, Gabriel. 1980. *Late Scholastic and Humanist Theories of the Proposition*. New York: North Holland.

———. 1983. *Judgment and Proposition From Descartes to Kant*. New York: North Holland.

———. 1998a. "Logic in the Seventeenth Century." In Ayers and Garber (1998).

———. 1998b. "Proposition and Judgment." In Ayers and Garber (1998).

———. 1998c. "Deductive Reasoning." In Ayers and Garber (1998).

Ott, Walter. 2002. "Propositional Attitudes in Modern Philosophy." *Dialogue* 41: 1–18.

———. 2004. *Locke's Philosophy of Language*. Cambridge: Cambridge University Press.

———. 2012. "What Is Locke's Theory of Representation?" *British Journal for the History of Philosophy* 20, 6: 1077–1095.

Owen, David. 2007. "Locke on Judgment." In *The Cambridge Companion to Locke's Essay*. Ed. by Lex Newman. Cambridge: Cambridge University Press.

Pettit, Philip. 2008. *Made With Words*. Princeton, NJ: Princeton University Press.

Quine, W.V.O. 1969. *Ontological Relativity and Other Essays*. Columbia, NY: Columbia University Press.

Régis, Pierre-Sylvain. 1996. *L'usage de la raison et de la foi*. Paris: Fayard.

Russell, Bertrand. 1912. *The Problems of Philosophy*. Oxford: Oxford University Press.

Savan, David. 1973. "Spinoza and Language." In *Spinoza: A Collection of Critical Essays*. Ed. by Marjorie Grene. New York: Anchor.

Sergeant, John. 1984. *Solid Philosophy Asserted Against the Fancies of the Ideists*. New York: Garland.

Shields, Christopher. 2003. *Order in Multiplicity: Homonymy in the Philosophy of Aristotle*. Oxford: Oxford University Press.

Slezak, Peter. 2000. "Descartes' Startling Doctrine of the Reverse-Sign Relation." In *Descartes' Natural Philosophy*. Ed. by Stephen Gaukroger, John Schuster, and John Sutton. London: Routledge.

Spinoza, Baruch. 2002. *Complete Works*. Ed. by Michael Morgan. Indianapolis: Hackett.

Watkins, J.W.N. 1973. *Hobbes's System of Ideas*. London: Hutchinson.

Winkler, Kenneth P. 1989. *Berkeley: An Interpretation*. Oxford: Oxford University Press.

———. 2009. "Signification, Projection, Intention." *Philosophia* 37 (3): 477–501.

Yolton, John. 2000. "Response to My Fellow Symposiasts." In *Descartes' Natural Philosophy*. Ed. by Stephen Gaukroger, John Schuster, and John Sutton. London: Routledge.

Part 5

NATURAL PHILOSOPHY AND THE MATERIAL WORLD

14
NATURAL PHILOSOPHY
Andrew Janiak

1. What exactly was natural philosophy?

We take it for granted that the natural sciences use mathematics to understand a wide range of phenomena. The mathematics employed by scientists is often used to express the laws of nature in the form of equations – it seems obvious to us not only that there are laws of nature but also that it is a task of science to discover them. We think that many scientific disciplines are focused on discovering, modeling, and studying the fundamental forces of nature. And certainly, we think it obvious that scientists should use experiments and observation to study all aspects of nature. We might even say that the following is constitutive of natural science as we know it: nature can be understood using mathematics, experiments, and observation; it has laws governing it; and there are basic forces operating in it.[1] This notion of science's project was shaped by a series of profound developments during what is often called the "scientific revolution," a period of tremendous intellectual ferment that began sometime before the seventeenth century and ended sometime after its close. But each of these three aspects of the scientific project was hotly contested throughout the era of the scientific revolution. Anyone who sought to understand nature in 1600, or 1650, or even 1700, could not take these matters for granted.

Another aspect of developments in the seventeenth century may confuse the contemporary reader. Scientific investigations today bear no obvious relation to *philosophy*, or to what religion or theology say about the creation. The debates about the relationship between religion and the sciences that rage today typically presuppose that these are separate kinds of inquiry into the world and its beginning. But the intellectual landscape that a figure like Galileo, Descartes, or Boyle encountered in his own day was fundamentally different from ours, despite the fact that their mathematical, empirical, and scientific work led to our own in myriad ways. The study of the natural world in the era of Galileo and of Newton involved what was then called "natural philosophy," a fascinating and often confusing discipline that flourished throughout the medieval and early modern periods and that has no clear analogue in the twenty-first century understanding of the structure of knowledge.[2] Yet it would be highly misleading to think that the practitioners of natural philosophy formed an intellectual movement or an ideology. There was no consensus then about the proper methods or techniques that the natural philosopher ought to employ. Happily, the contemporary reader can begin to grasp the very idea of natural philosophy precisely by considering the plethora of debates in which all of the major figures in the seventeenth century became embroiled. It is much more profitable to analyze these debates than to try to weave a grand narrative describing the many views of the main figures of the seventeenth century. Grand narratives, even when they are not Whiggish, tend to mislead.

During the seventeenth century, there was something approaching consensus about the methodological parameters of natural philosophy. But here, too, the contemporary reader is bound to be perplexed. From our point of view, natural philosophy seems to be an odd mélange: it encompasses what we would consider to be fundamentally distinct intellectual endeavors, including philosophy (especially metaphysics and epistemology) the natural sciences (especially physics), theology, and perhaps even religion.[3] Thus the danger of anachronism – and of conceptual confusion – looms large. If a text in natural philosophy – such as Descartes's *Principia*, first published in 1644, or Newton's *Principia mathematica*, first published in 1687 – mentions God or the divine, we tend to think that natural philosophy must have *included* theology. Similarly, if Descartes or Newton discusses the distinction between space and body, or the essence of matter, we tend to think that natural philosophy must have included metaphysics. But this is not quite right. Despite their numerous disagreements – many of which animate the development of natural philosophy throughout the century – Cartesians and Newtonians agreed that natural philosophy is *distinct* from both theology and metaphysics. In this period, it is common to speak of the two great books: the book of nature and the Bible; each was seen as the work of God. The theologian's discussion of the divine is often guided by faith, and is always guided by an interpretation of Scripture, especially the Bible. In contrast, the natural philosopher's discussion of the divine is centered on the book of nature – hence he will interpret nature as the work of a creator, employing it as his sole guide.[4] As is the case now, metaphysics in the seventeenth century was understood in disparate ways: it might be an analysis of *being qua being*; it might be thought of as "first philosophy," a philosophical inquiry that is (logically) prior to any other; or it might be conceived of as an analysis in particular of nonphysical entities such as God and the human soul. But however it was conceived, it was typically distinguished from natural philosophy, with its sole focus on nature and *natural* beings, like rocks, planets, and stars. So, for starters, we can conceive of natural philosophy as an attempt to understand all of nature, including its creator. But why did great mathematicians and scientists like Descartes or Newton think that a mathematical analysis of a planetary orbit, or an experimental investigation of heat, could be connected in some way to a study of the creator of the world? This question will help animate this chapter.

2. Applying mathematics to nature

Throughout the century, a debate raged about whether the natural philosopher could legitimately employ geometric and arithmetic methods to model and understand phenomena. But if natural philosophy is the precursor to natural science as we know it, why should it have been controversial to think that one could employ mathematics to understand the world? As the seventeenth century began, many thinkers – such as Galileo in the Italian-speaking world, and Descartes, a bit later, in the French- and Dutch-speaking regions of Europe – came to maturity at a time when Scholastic, or "neo-Aristotelian," thinking dominated natural philosophy (Blair 2006). It is impossible to do justice here to this rich and varied tradition, which spans many centuries, many texts, and many debates, but one thing seems clear: according to what I will call the Scholastic natural philosophy that was often predominant at the beginning of the century, the study of nature was often separated from mathematics. More specifically, natural philosophy was understood as a distinct discipline, one separate from the mathematical disciplines, such as geometry and arithmetic, on the one hand, and from the so-called mixed mathematical disciplines, such as music or optics, on the other. Thus a figure like Galileo or Descartes certainly could not take it for granted, for example, that geometry might be employed to understand natural phenomena. Indeed, Isaac Beekman, who met Descartes in 1618 and who had a crucial formative influence on his later work, wrote an entry in his diary after meeting the future author of the *Meditations*. He writes of Descartes that he

> says he has never met anyone other than me who pursues his studies in the way I do, combining physics and mathematics in an exact way. And for my part, I have never spoken with anyone apart from him who studies in this way.[5]

It is in this context that we ought to interpret Galileo's famous pronouncement that the book of nature is written in the language of mathematics. In 1623 Galileo proclaimed that "philosophy is written in this most grand book . . . (I am speaking of the universe) . . . [which] is written in the language of mathematics, and its characters are triangles, circles, and other geometrical figures" (quoted by Mahoney 1997, 703). Hence this slogan was not expressing a widely shared view among natural philosophers – it was an expression of a particular side of a long-standing debate that would continue throughout the rest of the century.

Despite Galileo's immense importance, the question of whether natural philosophy could legitimately – or perhaps fruitfully – employ mathematical principles and methods was brought to center stage by the subsequent work of René Descartes. It is probably safe to say that by the middle of the century, Descartes had set the agenda of natural philosophy for philosophers throughout Europe (Heilbron 1982; Henry 2013). As Beekman already recognized in the early part of the century, Descartes would become a great champion of employing mathematical methods in order to understand nature and its parts. Just as significantly, Descartes invented analytic geometry and was widely regarded as one of the great geometers of the first half of the seventeenth century. His *Géometrie* (1637) was translated into Latin and widely read as the most advanced text in that field. The influence of the *Géometrie* was not limited to Holland or France: a young Isaac Newton read it and profited greatly from it a generation later. So, if we conceive of this century as involving a grand struggle between the traditional conception of natural philosophy espoused in the schools – the so-called Scholastic conception – and the great "moderns" of the day, Descartes was firmly, and self-consciously, on the side of the new movement.

But as with many narratives involving grand struggles, the historical facts are more complicated. As it turned out, Descartes actually pursued a program in natural philosophy that exhibited a much more vexed relationship with the modern mathematics that he himself had invented and promulgated. During his early years, from the time he worked with Beekman in 1618 through the 1620s, Descartes's plan may have been to follow through on his promise to establish a fully mathematical approach to understanding problems in natural philosophy, especially the motions of material bodies. Part of his conception may have been to follow Aristotle in one crucial respect: working out the details of an (admittedly anti-Aristotelian) physics first, and worrying about various metaphysical questions later. And as the decade of the 1620s came to a close, Descartes wrote and prepared to publish a grand text in natural philosophy titled *Le Monde*. However, he stopped the presses in 1633 after he learned of Galileo's house arrest by the Vatican for his advocacy of a Copernican orientation toward the question of the earth's place within the universe, for Descartes had endorsed a similar view in *Le Monde*.[6] The withdrawal of *Le Monde* from the press had a dramatic impact on Descartes's literary life, serving to invert his Aristotelian plan by leading him to write a text in metaphysics, the *Meditations* (1641), first and follow it with his work in physics, the *Principles* (1644). This had three profound effects. First and foremost, Descartes would forever after be known for developing a strong conception of the metaphysical foundations of physics – indeed, he has been described as propounding a "metaphysical physics" (Garber 1992). Second, Descartes would also become known for failing to live up to his original promise of articulating a mathematical physics in detail. And third, Descartes avoided the problems that ensnared Galileo by presenting a conception of motion according to which one can effectively skirt the question of whether the earth moves or is stationary.

Why did Descartes's promulgation of a metaphysical foundation for physics prevent him from articulating a mathematical orientation toward natural philosophy? There is an irony to the story. First and foremost, as other entries in this companion indicate in depth, Descartes's metaphysics takes there to be two substances in the world: extended substances, like tables and chairs, and thinking substances, like the human mind. Descartes thought in particular that the essence of extended substances is exhausted by their extension, by their three-dimensionality. Hence tables might be blue or green, they might be wooden or plastic, they might be expensive or cheap, but these are all accidental features of them: their only essential feature lies in being extended. (And in fact, Descartes would say that the other features of a table are merely modes of its principal attribute or essence, namely its extension.) Hence as Daniel Garber has put it, for Descartes, material bodies like tables are "the objects of geometry made real" (Garber 1992, 63). In that sense, one might think that Cartesian metaphysics paves the way for the employment of mathematical methods, especially geometric methods, within natural philosophy: if an object like a rock is essentially an extended thing, we can treat it like an object in geometry and then understand its motion using geometrical techniques. As Lisa Shabel very nicely indicates, the classic early modern problem of the applicability of mathematics to nature and its quantities is, in a sense, easily solved by Descartes, for he contends that the essence of material bodies is the very extension of which we have a clear and distinct idea when we consider our representations of geometric objects. We know that geometry, and the rest of pure mathematics perhaps, applies to natural objects because the essence of those objects is just extension (Shabel 2005, 38).

But this is not the end of the story. For Descartes, it is indeed possible to think of ordinary material bodies as geometric objects, and if we consider them in abstraction from the rest of nature, then we can understand their changes mathematically. However, natural philosophy does not consider objects in abstraction from the rest of nature: it considers them as participants in the great system of objects that constitutes the natural world. So, to do natural philosophy, we have to embed our little rock in the world in which it actually exists. When we do so, however, we encounter a further problem generated by Descartes's metaphysics. As it turns out, Cartesianism is not exhausted by the view that the essence of material bodies is extension: it also includes the related claim that extension itself is indistinct from matter or substance. For Descartes, in other words, it is a conceptual confusion to adopt the idea of empty space: extension for Descartes is a property, and as such, it must be regarded as a property of *some substance*. Hence the idea of an empty space – an empty extension – is incoherent because it presents a property without anything having that property. It is sort of like saying, I walked down the street yesterday and saw redness – not a red car, or a red bicycle, but just redness itself. So, for Descartes, the whole of nature consists of an indefinite multitude of extended substances. When we look across a lawn, or stare into space, it may *appear* to us as if space can be empty, but in fact, all of space is full of objects big and small. Hence Descartes presents the idea that nature is a plenum.

If nature is a plenum, the motion of our little rock, which seemed so straightforward in the abstract, becomes incredibly complex. Suppose, for instance, that I am standing on the main quad at my college and I throw a rock across the lawn. When the rock leaves my hand, it immediately becomes ensnared in a vast network of other objects on its trajectory toward the grass. To get a basic grasp on the Cartesian view, we might think of the rock as entering a kind of conveyor belt of tiny particles as it sails through the air: it pushes the numerous particles in front of it and is also perhaps pushed along by the particles behind and surrounding it. But the complexity of the situation exceeds even this picture, for we must also conceive of the rock as bearing some weight toward the earth – hence there are also numerous particles flowing downward toward the ground that impede the rectilinear motion of the rock, giving it a classic parabolic trajectory, and eventually bringing it to rest on the lawn. The complexity is overwhelming. We are obviously very far from thinking of a point generating a curved line through its motion.

Descartes took his metaphysical commitments seriously. In part 2 of his *Principles* (1644), where he discusses space, time, and motion in detail, he presents what is clearly a qualitative physics. So Descartes's legacy is twofold and filled with tension: on the one hand, he followed in Galileo's (and Beekman's) footsteps by strongly opposing Aristotelian natural philosophy, advocating the use of mathematical methods to understand motion and natural change, and presenting an austere metaphysics that would be welcome to geometers; on the other hand, his plenist view of nature presented a picture in which the motion of ordinary objects like rocks and balls is fantastically complex, exceeding the capacity of even the greatest mathematicians.[7]

That was the state of affairs when a young Isaac Newton picked up the *Meditations* and the *Géometrie* in the early 1660s in Cambridge. He also read Descartes's *Principles* in depth, and it is safe to say that he considered Descartes the greatest natural philosopher, if not the greatest mathematician, in the previous generation. (A young Leibniz, working far away on the Continent, may have felt similarly.) When Newton gave some lectures in the early 1670s as part of his charge as Lucasian professor of mathematics, he lamented the state of natural philosophy, noting in particular that the profound developments in geometrical techniques had thus far exhibited little impact on the discipline. His inaugural Lucasian professor lectures in 1670 included the following:

> the generation of colors includes so much geometry, and the understanding of colors is supported by so much evidence, that for their sake I can thus attempt to extend the bounds of mathematics somewhat, just as astronomy, geography, navigation, optics, and mechanics are truly considered mathematical sciences even if they deal with physical things: the heavens, earth, seas, light, and local motion. Thus although colors may belong to physics [*ad Physicam pertineant*],

> the science of them must nevertheless be considered mathematical, insofar as they are treated by mathematical reasoning. Indeed, since an exact science [*accurata scientia*] of them seems to be one of the most difficult that philosophy is in need of, I hope to show – as it were, by my example – how valuable mathematics is in natural philosophy. I therefore urge geometers to investigate nature more rigorously, and those devoted to natural science to learn geometry first.[8]

From Newton's point of view, then, the Cartesian program in natural philosophy had not lived up to its rhetoric. Intriguingly, Newton would eventually write an extensive critique of Cartesian metaphysics. Whether he did so because he recognized that Descartes's views in metaphysics, especially his advocacy of a plenum, ultimately undermined the employment of mathematics by natural philosophers, remains an intriguing open question.

These developments set the stage for Newton's own magnum opus, the *Principia mathematica* (London, 1687). In a famous exchange with Edmond Halley – the discoverer of the comet, and the person often credited with encouraging Newton to write and publish his work – Newton explains that for his *Principia mathematica* to be considered a work in *natural philosophy*, he must include what would become its third book, with its focus on the motions of falling bodies on earth and on the motions of the heavenly bodies. Without the application of Newton's mathematical methods and conclusions from books one and two of *Principia mathematica* to the natural objects in our solar system, we would have instead a book more aptly titled, *De motu corporum*, or *On the motion of bodies*.[9] Hence the natural philosopher, from Newton's point of view, is not concerned with the motion of any body whatsoever in any medium, under any physical conditions we might be able to conceive; he is concerned with the motions of bodies within nature. It is no surprise, then, that for Newton, as for many natural philosophers in this period, one of the great outstanding questions is how to understand the earth-sun system, including the question of whether the earth is at the center of the solar system and is moving or at rest.

For a committed Cartesian reader, one might say, this move from the first two books of *Principia mathematica*, in which we consider the motions of bodies in abstraction from various factors involving nature as we find it, to the third book, in which those factors are explicitly invoked, would be problematic. As we have seen, a Cartesian would regard the actual motions of material bodies as occurring within a plenum with a huge multitude of moving parts; this would render those motions intractable from a geometrical point of view. And it seems plausible that a Cartesian reader would understand Newton's book III as committing him, explicitly or implicitly, to the falsity of the plenist conception of nature found in Descartes.[10]

In any event, there is no doubt that Newton's *Principia mathematica* was designed to signal a break with Descartes, for Newton always emphasized that *his* principles were mathematical in character, unlike the principles that Descartes had followed in part two of his *Principles*, where geometry played little if any role. Newton even titled his magnum opus to establish a replacement for Descartes's *Principles of Philosophy*, first published in Amsterdam in 1644, a text that Newton kept in his personal library.[11] The differences between the two works are stark. Whereas Descartes's *Principia* attempts to account for an immense range of phenomena – tackling everything from global skepticism about human knowledge; to God's immutability; to the nature of heat, light, weight; and so on – Newton's text focuses specifically on the mathematical analysis of motion and the forces that cause it. The audiences of the two works differed accordingly: Descartes was comprehensible to anyone with a decent education in the codified Aristotelian corpus, or late Scholastic natural philosophy. In contrast, Newton's *Principia mathematica* was comprehensible only to the most sophisticated mathematicians, such as Huygens and Leibniz, and probably incomprehensible even to some of its prominent (if anonymous) reviewers, such as Locke. To find an example of how a seventeenth century natural philosopher employed mathematics to understand something about nature, we turn briefly to an example in Newton.

The famous opening of *Principia mathematica* can indicate, *very briefly*, how Newton employed geometry in order to make inferences about the forces in nature that cause certain kinds of motion. In book I, propositions 2 and 3, Newton intends to discuss the relationship between Kepler's so-called area law, which deals with the actual motions of the planetary bodies, and his new notion of a centripetal force, which he has just introduced in the definitions that precede book I. This relationship will then be crucial in book III, where Newton argues for what will later be known as the law of universal gravitation.

In figure 14.1, reproduced from book I, Newton begins by connecting Kepler's area law with his own First Law (the law of inertia) in an ingenious way. He informs us that we should think of a body as moving rectilinearly (inertially) from points A to B, and as then struck by an instantaneous force at B, which knocks the body into a new trajectory from B to C. Newton seems comfortable here with the counterfactual claim, associated with his Second Law, that the body would have traveled from C to c if it had not been struck by the force. Similarly, the body travels from B to C, and is then struck by an instantaneous force that propels it along the new trajectory from C to D, and so on. In each case, we are to conceive of the body as following a trajectory that deviates from the tangent along the polygon with center S, where the tangential trajectory represents the path that the body would have taken, in accordance with the First Law, if it had not been struck by a force at B, C, D, E, and so on. (We are to think of these forces as impacting on the body in equal intervals of time, such that the time elapsed from A to B is equivalent to the time elapsed from B to C, etc.)

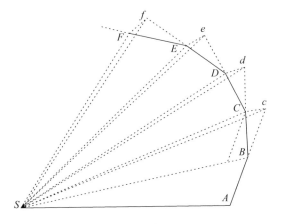

Figure 14.1 Proposition I in Newton, *Principia mathematica*

Newton then begins to capture Kepler's area law by comparing the areas of the triangles *SAB* and *SBc*: these triangles have equal areas by virtue of the fact that they have equal bases and equal heights. This means that the orbiting body sweeps out equal areas from *A* to *B* to *C*. And we know that it does so in equal times, in turn, because we have taken the Second Law to govern the body's motion, which means that it is moving uniformly from *A* to *B* to *C*, and these line segments are equal *ex hypothesi* (because they are taken to be radii of the circle *S*). So, the orbiting body sweeps out equal areas in equal times, which is precisely what Kepler's area law states.

There can be no doubt that Newton made astonishing progress in using mathematical, especially geometric, methods in answering questions about the motions of bodies and the forces that cause them in *Principia mathematica*. But it would be highly inaccurate to suggest that by century's end, Newton's approach had garnered universal support. Indeed, the use of mathematical methods and principles within natural philosophy remained highly contentious even at the end of the seventeenth century. The contested nature of mathematics, in fact, even hampered understanding of Newton's idea of employing mathematical principles of natural philosophy (at least from his point of view). The first edition of Newton's *Principia mathematica* was met with four reviews in England and on the Continent (Cohen 1992). One of these reacted to Newton's mathematical approach by contending that in fact Newton had failed to provide a work in natural philosophy at all. According to the reviewer, he had merely provided a mathematical treatise that does not characterize the motions of bodies in nature. It is a sure measure of the contentious nature of the use of mathematics in this context that the reviewer simply did not view book III of *Principia mathematica* as Newton did, namely as providing a characterization and analysis of the motions of bodies on earth and in the solar system. The reviewer could not see past Newton's immense mathematical apparatus to recognize that the theory of universal gravity concerns the motions of bodies in nature and is therefore an essential component in Newton's work within natural philosophy (Cohen 1992, 145–58). This conception of Newton's work continued into the next century, even among leading philosophers. For instance, in a letter from 1707, Malebranche writes, "Although M. Newton is not a physicist, his book is very curious and very useful to those who have good principles of physics; he is, moreover, an excellent geometer."[12]

3. Space, time, and motion

If any concept occupied the center of natural philosophy in this century, it was *motion*. Why so? There are several reasons. The question of whether the earth moves in an orbit as other heavenly bodies do was at the center of Galileo's strife with the Catholic Church in 1616 and 1633, which raises general questions about natural philosophy's relationship with theology and with religious doctrine. The question of how to understand the curvilinear motion of a projectile on earth or of a heavenly body such as the moon was at the center of attempts to employ mathematical methods to the study of nature, so this raises general questions about natural philosophy's relationship with mathematics. The study of motion was one of the central points of contention between Descartes on the one hand, and his various critics, including especially the Newtonians and the Leibnizians, on the other, so this raises general questions about the development of natural philosophy in the seventeenth century. And finally, for many philosophers – including especially Descartes, Leibniz, Newton, and their interlocutors and critics – nature is governed by a small set of laws that fundamentally characterize the motions of bodies.

One of the most important figures to study motion in the early part – or indeed, in any part – of the century was obviously Galileo. He played a crucial role in promulgating the anti-Aristotelian sentiments that drove much of the rhetoric, if not the substance, of natural philosophy in this period, especially on questions about motion. Galileo argued against the Aristotelian, or Scholastic, notion that a moving body must have a mover at every instant of its motion. He thereby promoted key aspects of what would eventually become known as the principle of inertia by century's end. Many different, although related, notions are often characterized as expressing the principle of inertia – for clarity, we can distinguish three separate ideas that led eventually to this principle. First, a body remains in any state of motion unless impinged upon by some external cause; second, a body remains at rest unless impinged upon by some external cause; and third, a body in motion will move rectilinearly unless impinged upon by some external cause. It is sometimes said – by no less a figure than Newton himself – that Galileo played a key role in developing the principle of inertia, but it might be more historically accurate to claim that he worked especially on the first two ideas.[13] He did so in an explicit move against the prevailing Aristotelian notions of his day. For his part, it is not clear that he fully endorsed the third idea, because he may have thought that the curvilinear motions of the planetary bodies were "natural" in the precise sense that they required no external cause, although he also contended that in the sublunary realm, projectiles that move curvilinearly do require such as cause. Just as significantly, Galileo provided a hugely influential study of free fall, which helped to establish the (surprising) result that all bodies fall with the same acceleration, regardless of their material properties. His anti-Aristotelian ideas about motion, and his study of free fall, each had a major impact on later work in natural philosophy, especially on that of Descartes and Newton.

For various reasons, Descartes is often unjustly neglected in discussions of the laws of motion in general, and of the principle of inertia in particular. It was Descartes, and not Newton or any subsequent thinker, who first articulated the importance of the third idea of motion listed previously: a body in motion will move rectilinearly unless impinged upon by an external cause. Hence it was Descartes who took any curvilinear motion, even of the planetary bodies, to require an external cause, a crucial conceptual step for future developments in celestial mechanics. Descartes was also the first philosopher to speak of the laws of nature in a modern sense.[14] He introduces his first two laws of nature in his *Principles* (AT VIIIA 62–62; CSM I 240–241) as follows:

> The first law of nature [*lex naturae*]: that each and every thing, in so far as it can [*quantum in se est*], always perseveres in the same state, and thus what is once in motion always continues to move. . . . The second law of nature: that all motion is in itself rectilinear; and hence any body moving in a circle tends always to move away from the center of the circle it describes.[15]

These two notions are extremely fertile for future research in physics. For instance, if we take the planets to be orbiting the sun in circles – or in ellipses, as Kepler suggested – then the laws tell us that the planets tend to move away from the centers of their orbits. This implies, in turn, that some cause is hindering this tendency, thereby maintaining the planetary orbits around the sun. The question is, what is that cause?

Although Descartes's laws are central to his conception of space, time, and motion, especially to his understanding of where to look in nature for the causal factors that alter the motions of bodies, they do not exhaust that conception. He also provided a fruitful distinction between what we might call an ordinary – or *vulgare* – idea of motion, and a philosophically precise, or true, idea. The distinction enables Descartes to further distance himself from what he took to be prevailing "Scholastic" or neo-Aristotelian ideas concerning motion and also to present a view in his physics that connects closely with his metaphysical views of body and space.

Descartes tells us (Latin: AT VIII-1: 53; French: AT IX-2: 75) that motion in the ordinary sense is "nothing other than *the action by which a body passes from one place to another*."[16] This ordinary idea of motion in Descartes is problematic because it includes the "Scholastic" idea that motion must have a mover at every instant. Hence it says that motion consists in *the action* whereby one material thing is transferred from one place to another. The notion of a place may not be rigorous, or may be unphilosophical, but the deeper problem may be that this view of motion is inconsistent with Descartes's laws, because it requires a mover to continually cause any motion.[17] Thus on the proper (*propria*) view, we jettison the Scholastic notion, and attempt to employ a view of motion that is consistent with the three laws of nature found in the *Principles*. Motion does not require a mover at all – in fact, any object in motion will continue to move unless impeded by some object.

In light of these problems, Descartes jettisons the notions of *place* and *action*, defining true motion as follows:

> If, on the other hand, we consider what should be understood by *motion*, not in common usage but in accordance with the truth of the matter, and if our aim is to assign a determinate nature to it, we may say that *motion is the transfer of one piece of matter, or one body, from the vicinity of the others which immediately touch it, and which we consider to be at rest, to the vicinity of others* [*ex vicinia eorum corporum, quoe illud immediate contingent & tanquam quiescentia spectantur, in viciniam aliorum*].
>
> (AT VIIIA 53–4; CSM I 232–4)

This true or "proper" conception of motion may be demanded by Descartes's metaphysics. The *vulgare* conception presumably reflects our ordinary ideas about motion and can employ notions that are imprecise or inherently problematic. But if one thinks that extension is the essence of body, and therefore that there cannot be any empty space, then wherever there is a place, there is a body (or bodies). Any travel from place to place will necessarily involve a change in the traveling body's relation to other bodies. And any body will necessarily be surrounded by other bodies – its "vicinity" – at every instant.

The Cartesian conception of space, time, and motion, it is fair to say, set the stage for nearly all later discussions of these topics within natural philosophy in the seventeenth century. They certainly did so for the three leading natural philosophers after midcentury, Isaac Newton in England and Gottfried Leibniz and Christiaan Huygens on the Continent. One of the most sustained critiques of the Cartesian conception occurs in a now famous unpublished manuscript written by Newton, *De Gravitatione*. Many of Newton's objections to *Principia Philosophiae* in *De Gravitatione* reflect an overarching attitude toward Cartesian proper motion, namely that it fails to reflect facts about motion expressed by Descartes's own laws of nature. Hence Newton presents in particular a systematic *internal* critique of Cartesian natural philosophy. Newton claims, for instance, that Descartes is inconsistent regarding the ever-important issue of the earth's motion. On the one hand, Descartes's conception of "proper" motion implies that a body B moves if two conditions are met: first, B is transferred from one group of surrounding bodies to another group; and second, B's original group of surrounding bodies is regarded as not moving. Because the earth is carried around its solar orbit by a vortex that entirely surrounds it, Descartes concludes that the earth does not *truly* move. On the other hand, Descartes says that the earth has a tendency to recede from the sun (Newton cites the *Principles*, part 3 §140). But by Descartes's laws, if the earth were at rest, it would remain at rest and would *not* tend to recede from the sun – it would only have such a tendency if it were following a curvilinear trajectory.

According to Newton (2014, 29–30), Descartes's view that each body has only one "proper" motion also conflicts with his definition of such motion. Imagine two observers in separate spacecraft watching the earth and its vortex flow through the solar system (imagine, for the sake of argument, that the vortex is perceptible). One observer maintains an unchanging position external to the vortex surrounding the earth, and regards the vortex as being at rest. From her point of view, if the earth remains surrounded by the vortex, it *does not move*, properly speaking; but if the earth is transferred away from this vortex, it *does move*, because she regards the vortex as being at rest. If a second observer is placed such that he regards the vortex surrounding the earth at time t_1 as moving, then given the definition above, *he cannot regard the earth as moving, even if it is transferred to the vicinity of other bodies at t_2*. The reason is that the earth cannot move beginning at t_1 if at t_1 the vortex surrounding it is *not* regarded as at rest. So, these observers will disagree if they each take the earth to be transferred away from the vicinity of the vortex that surrounds it at t_1.

Newton also objects to the fact that Descartes renders a body's proper motion *relative* to its position with respect to other bodies. Newton makes his case as follows: suppose that the vortex surrounding the earth were moving according to Descartes's view of proper motion – that is, the vortex is transferred from the bodies surrounding it, which we regard as being at rest. This means the earth must be at rest. If God were to render the vortex surrounding the earth motionless, without interacting with the earth in any way, then a formerly stationary earth would begin moving (as long as we regarded the vortex as being at rest). God could therefore move the earth without applying a force to it or causally interacting with it. Once again, we find a tension with Descartes's laws, because the first law indicates that a body at rest will remain at rest unless acted upon – to explain the first law, Descartes writes, "If it is at rest, we hold that it will never begin to move unless it is pushed into motion by some cause" (AT VIIA 62–3; part 2: §37). From Newton's point of view, it is a mistake to sever the tie between true motion and external action, *a tie implied by Descartes's own laws*. Otherwise put, Cartesian proper motion does not involve a connection between a body's true motion and some external cause acting on that body.

Newton's critical attitude toward Cartesian natural philosophy sheds considerable light on his extremely influential discussion of space, time, and motion in the opening scholium of *Principia mathematica*. The scholium follows the definitions at the text's beginning, before book I. Newton notes that he will not *define* space, time, and motion, as he did with the quantity of matter (i.e. mass), the quantity of motion, and certain concepts of force:

> Thus far it has seemed best to explain the senses in which less familiar words are to be taken in this treatise. Time, space, place, and motion are familiar to everyone. But it must be noted that these quantities are commonly conceived not otherwise

than in relation to the perceivable. And this is the origin of certain prejudices; to eliminate them it is useful to distinguish these quantities into absolute and relative, true and apparent, mathematical and common.
(Newton 1972, vol. 1: 46; cf. Newton 1999, 408)

Although Newton thinks the common conception of space, time, and motion leads to problematic "prejudices," the fact that he does not define space, time, and motion here is crucial, for he begins with the common understanding of these quantities and then introduces the idea that the common point of view actually presents us with measures of the quantities that are presented directly within the mathematical point of view. For instance, from the common point of view, we take some (relative) space delimited by object relations to be space itself: we might, say, take the space of our air to be space itself, which could be reasonable for practical purposes. This is a *measure* of space itself, as if one were measuring a college campus by walking through one of its buildings, just as a clock's ticking away the hours will give us a measure of the quantity, time. The mathematical point of view, however, considers these quantities themselves, rather than their *measures*.

After distinguishing absolute and relative space, Newton distinguishes between absolute (or true) and merely relative motion: "Absolute motion is the translation of a body from absolute place to absolute place; relative motion is the translation from relative place to relative place" (Newton 1972, vol. 1: 47; Newton 1999, 409). But isn't it sufficient to think of each body's motion as involving changes in its relations to other bodies, or perhaps to relative places that are defined in terms of such relations? Newton provides us with at least four salient reasons to jettison the view that we can understand a body's true motion in terms of changes in its relations to other bodies (Descartes gives one construal of this view). First, he notes an empirical fact, namely that there may be no body that is truly at rest anywhere in the universe to which we could refer the relative motions of all other bodies (Newton 1972, vol. 1: 48–9; Newton 1999, 411). Second, he notes that although there may in fact be a body that is truly at rest, it is perfectly possible that we will be unable to determine *which* body is at rest, and that some other body within the reach of our senses – say within our solar system, if we count astronomical observation – maintains a fixed position with respect to the truly resting body.

With his third point, Newton echoes the idea in *De Gravitatione* that if we take true motion to involve a change in object relations, we will sever the tie between motion and its causes. He writes in the scholium,

> The causes which distinguish true from relative motions are the forces impressed on bodies to generate motion. True motion is neither generated nor altered except by forces impressed on the moving body itself, but relative motion can be generated and altered without forces impressed on this body.
> (Newton 1972, vol. 1: 50; Newton 1999, 412)

The idea is that a body's relations to other bodies do not bear the right relationship to external causes – what Newton calls "impressed forces" – for as he indicates in *De Gravitatione*, we can alter the relations of a body *without impressing any force on it*; and even if we impress a force on a given body, if we impress forces on the bodies that bear a relation to it, their relations might remain unchanged. Therefore, in order to understand the relation between true motion and impressed force, we should not understand true motion in terms of a body's relations with other bodies. This helps to place Newton's move to absolute space in the right light: in order to understand the relationship between true motion and impressed force, we construe true motion in terms of a body's relation to places within absolute space, rather than in terms of its relation to other bodies.

Newton's fourth reason for rejecting the Cartesian conception of true motion involves his famous rotating bucket example. The example is extremely clever, bringing Newton's response to Descartes to a higher level than what we find in *De Gravitatione*. Newton asks us to imagine that we have an ordinary bucket suspended from a rope and filled with water. If we twist the rope and then release it, the bucket will begin to rotate; as it does so, the water in the bucket will eventually rotate as well. The bucket surrounds the water – it is what Descartes would call the "vicinity" of the water. When the water and the bucket are rotating synchronously, they do not change relations with one another, and parts of the water do not change their relations with the corresponding parts of the bucket: for Descartes, that means the water is not moving, according to the "proper" concept of motion. But the concavity of the water indicates that it is actually rotating (it is accelerating), which means that it does have a true motion. Newton concludes that we should not understand true motion as involving a change in relations between bodies. The example is a powerful reply to Cartesian physics.

Descartes's rhetoric suggests that natural philosophy, or physics, must rest on a metaphysical foundation – its trunk must be held up by metaphysical roots.[18] Newton does not react to this viewpoint as some twentieth century commentators have said; in particular, he does not focus primarily on the claim that it is dangerous or unwise to rest physics on a metaphysical foundation. He has a much more decisive rejection in mind: Descartes's problem is that his metaphysical views push him to adopt ideas about space, time, and motion that are in fact inconsistent with what his own laws tell us about space, time, and motion. Thus Newton's analysis indicates a kind of bifurcation of Cartesian views in physics into two distinct sectors, one of which is indeed founded on metaphysical notions and the other of which is relatively autonomous. On the one hand, in part two of the *Principles*, Descartes articulates basic concepts of space, time, and motion that reflect, or are demanded by, his metaphysical commitments, especially his plenist view and his identification of body and extension. On the other hand, in the same section of the text, Descartes articulates three laws that are relatively autonomous from these concerns, for what they indicate about space, time, and motion is inconsistent with the explicit discussion of these concepts in the part of physics that rests on a metaphysical foundation.

Newton's criticism of Descartes points to a *prima facie* difficulty inherent within Descartes's project of resting physics, or natural philosophy, on a metaphysical foundation. To see this problem, consider, first of all, the structure of part 2 of the *Principles*. After ten sections that consider various issues, including the nature of body and of rarefaction, section 10 begins a broad discussion of space – one that includes discussions of various issues, such as the vacuum – that continues until section 23, when the issue of motion is introduced; the discussion of motion continues until section 33. After section 36, which presents the idea that God is the "primary cause" of motion, preserving the quantity of motion in the universe, the three laws of nature are introduced and discussed in the next eight sections. Of course, Descartes thinks that the three laws of nature articulated in part two of the *Principles* rest on the metaphysical views that undergird the notions of space, time, and motion found within that same text. Descartes argues, in particular, that the laws are derived from God's immutability and from the identification of space and body. It is possible that whereas Descartes's view of true or proper motion rests specifically on his identification of space and body, his *first two* laws rest specifically on the notion of God's immutability (here I bracket the third law). If these two aspects of Cartesian metaphysics entail mutually incompatible ideas of motion, they may be in some tension with one another. Or more precisely, the specific way in which Descartes understands the implications of God's immutability seems to conflict with the specific way in which he understands the implications of his identification of body and space.

One might also adopt a slightly different perspective on these issues. As we saw previously, one reason for Descartes to jettison the (ordinary) idea that motion is the *action* by which a body travels from place to place is that this may conflict with the first two laws of nature. These laws tell us that a body will remain in its state of motion – whether it is at rest or moving rectilinearly – unless acted upon by something external. Hence the laws seem to imply that a body moving rectilinearly need not be thought of as acted upon by anything at all. This may conflict with the ordinary idea that motion *just is an action*. So, in this specific sense, Descartes's definition of true motion captures an important aspect of the view of motion expressed in the first two laws of nature. From Newton's point of view, however, it did not capture enough.

Descartes's struggle to rest his physics on a secure metaphysical foundation, and Newton's reaction to it, sheds light on Newton's own metaphysical views, limited as they are (see Janiak 2008). Newton seeks specifically to distinguish between space and body, contending that space can be empty, at least within certain regions. This allows us to think of the space of the real world as akin to the space of geometry, and we can think of motion through the world as akin to a geometric figure moving within geometric space. For Descartes, motion in the real world occurs in a plenum and therefore is entirely distinct from motion within geometric space. In this specific regard, we can see that Newton has some reason to contend that Descartes's metaphysics – which includes the view that the void, or empty space, is incoherent and indeed metaphysically impossible – hampers his physics by making it difficult to see how we can treat the motion of a real object in nature as we would understand the motion of a geometrical figure. For Newton, that is no problem. In that sense, *De Gravitatione* sets up *Principia mathematica*'s use of mathematics by rejecting Cartesian metaphysics, distinguishing rigorously between extension and body. This might be connected, in turn, to Newton's comment in *De Gravitatione* that he rejects Descartes's "fictions" in order to lay "truer foundations of the mechanical sciences." In tandem, it may be misleading to contend that Newton achieves mathematical progress within natural philosophy by rejecting the Cartesian requirement that we obtain a secure metaphysical foundation for our understanding of the motions of bodies within nature. We have seen that Descartes's metaphysics may lead him to the view that the world is a plenum, which leads, in turn, to his pessimism that we can achieve any mathematical progress in understanding the motions of bodies within nature. In response, Newton develops a picture of the world according to which we can think of nature as an infinite Euclidean space with both empty regions and other regions filled with finite bodies of various configurations. This is a distinct metaphysical conception, one that enables Newton to conceive of the motion of bodies in a mathematically tractable way.

Just as Newton was one of Descartes's most profound critics within natural philosophy, Leibniz was one of Newton's. Although it is anachronistic to understand the first edition of *Principia mathematica* (1687) as inaugurating or contributing to a debate between Newton and Leibniz concerning the concepts of space, time, and motion, there is little doubt that Newton had Leibniz primarily in mind when he substantially altered his text in its second edition (1713). By that time, he was engaged in a multipronged philosophical – and sometimes political – debate with Leibniz and his followers. Despite their vociferous disagreements about natural philosophy and the invention of the calculus, however, Leibniz's perspective on the failures of Cartesianism actually coheres nicely with Newton's in several respects. From Leibniz's point of view, at least in his mature thinking (circa 1695 and later), Descartes is wrong to think of bodies as merely extended because then we cannot envision how they bear forces – how there can be causation in nature. But note also that for Leibniz, we cannot really have a mathematical physics in a straightforward way, at least in the sense that mathematics, and especially geometry, is not a sufficient guide for understanding motion within nature, because we need a causal notion within natural philosophy when we attempt to understand motion. And so to our mathematical toolbox we must add a causal notion – employing the principle of sufficient reason – in order to make any progress within, or perhaps even to be doing, natural philosophy. Once we have that causal notion we can analyze the motions of bodies within nature. We see this point at the beginning of Leibniz's second letter to Clarke in their famous correspondence from the early eighteenth century.

Descartes obviously never encountered Newton's bucket experiment, but Leibniz did and took it seriously. How might he respond? Leibniz believes in the equivalence of hypotheses, a view that supports the relativity of motion in the sense that it indicates that it is arbitrary to contend that any particular body is moving. The reason is that motion involves a change in relations between two or more bodies, so one can attribute the motion in question to either (or to any) of the bodies. The hypothesis that one body is moving is "equivalent" to the hypothesis that its neighbor is moving. Leibniz indicates that this view definitely holds for any rectilinear motion. But he was aware that from Newton's point of view, rotational motions are special because they must be accelerations. (Rectilinear motions *can* be accelerations, but they need not be because they can be inertial.) And he was aware, in particular, that Newton tried to argue that the bucket example involves an inertial effect – including the concavity of the water's surface – that enables us to infer that this is a true motion. Hence for Newton, we can legitimately attribute the motion to the water, and not to some other body in the vicinity. This would break the equivalence of hypotheses: if the stars, or indeed, everything else in the universe, were rotating (backward, as it were) around the water, it would not render its surface concave. So, the hypothesis that the water is moving is not equivalent to the hypothesis that other objects are moving.

Ironically, despite his numerous disagreements with the Cartesian view of space, time, and motion, Leibniz might reply that all motion, including rotational and any curvilinear motion, is actually rectilinear in the sense that it is composed of an infinite number of minute – one might say "infinitesimal" – motions. (Such a view is obviously connected to the idea – employed in book I of Newton's *Principia* – that we can obtain a circle if we take a many-sided polygon and infinitely increase the number of its sides.) Descartes had expressed exactly this same view of motion in part 2 of his *Principles*, as we saw previously. So, his first point might be that even if the water is rotating, its motion is actually rectilinear, in the proper analysis. His next point might be that a complete dynamical explanation of this imagined physical setup would indicate the causes of the bucket's solidity and of the water's fluidity. And then he might conclude the following: these points indicate that, *contra* Newton, we cannot infer any true motion of any particular object from the phenomena involved in this physical situation.[19]

More generally, Leibniz served as one of Newton's most vociferous critics, wielding an allegiance to some form of mechanism when denouncing Newton's apparent postulation of "action at a distance" between material bodies, such as the earth and the moon, in his theory of universal gravity in *Principia mathematica*. From that point on, discussions of "mechanism" took on a slightly new character, as Newton's defenders and critics attempted to reconcile the new theory of gravity, on the one hand, with the mechanist commitment to surface impacts among material bodies as the principal or sole agent of change within nature, on the other.[20] The challenge that Newton bequeaths to the eighteenth century is evident already in these discussions: is there some way of maintaining a firm commitment to the mechanical philosophy, and the picture of matter, motion, and causation it expresses, in the face of a new theory of nature in which a fundamental causal interaction (namely gravitation) has been described by a new law of nature? This is clearly a live issue already for Leibniz and Clarke in their correspondence from 1715–16 (ended only upon Leibniz's death in November of 1716), and it remains a live issue, for example, for Kant in 1786, when he presents a thoroughgoing criticism of the mechanical philosophy in his *Metaphysical Foundations of Natural Science*. It is in this sense that Newton's theory of universal gravity, first articulated in the late seventeenth century, helps shape the philosophical agenda of the eighteenth.

4. Theology and natural philosophy

Galileo's house arrest in 1633, together with Descartes's decision later that year not to publish *Le Monde* because of its Copernican perspective, suggest the conclusion that theology and religion impinged upon natural philosophy in the seventeenth century, hampering it in various ways. Descartes's and Newton's discussions of God within natural philosophy can also make it tempting to conclude that they are parroting well-worn theological points. But the actual historical relationship between theology and natural philosophy is more complicated than these points suggest (Harrison 2005).

When the contemporary reader thinks about natural philosophy in the seventeenth century, there is a serious danger that anachronistic preconceptions will hamper her understanding. For us, it might seem natural to think that if Descartes or Newton discusses God in some context, then he is engaged in a "theological" discussion. In contemporary discourse, the term "theological" is often used rather generally to refer to any discussion that includes mention of the divine. But in the seventeenth century, theology was understood in a narrower, or perhaps a more technical, sense. A text was not theological merely by virtue of containing some mention of the divine being; rather, it was theological if its treatment of the divine was largely, or entirely, based on a reading of certain specific texts, especially the Bible and the writings of the prophets. Or it could be theological by virtue of making specific reference to faith, or to the beliefs expressed in what we might now call a particular faith tradition.[21] Various thinkers understood this basic point in various ways. But the basic distinction between theology and natural philosophy shared by many thinkers is relatively clear: natural philosophy can study nature as God's creation, treating God, for example, as the first cause, but it does so without reference to faith or to Holy Writ. Thus, Descartes can contend that the first two laws of nature are derived from God's property of immutability without in any way rendering his physics *theological*.[22]

It was precisely the basic distinction between theology and natural philosophy that was one of the most fundamental disputes of the century. For if natural philosophy studies nature without considering what the Hebrew or Greek Bibles teach about nature, how can anyone guarantee that their conclusions will be consistent? If one reads in Scripture that the earth was created in six days, or that there was once a day when the sun stopped moving, and so on, how can these characterizations be made to cohere with the view of nature that philosophers develop? This kind of question captured the attention of numerous philosophers and theologians working in numerous institutional and political contexts throughout the century.

Perhaps the most famous attempt at accommodating religion and natural philosophy was Galileo's 1615 letter to the Grand Duchess Christina, written just one year before the Church officially censured Copernican astronomical doctrine.[23] One of Galileo's overarching points in the letter is that genuine truths cannot conflict. So if the Copernican conception of the earth-sun relationship is correct, it cannot conflict with the account of such matters found in Holy Writ. We can resolve any tension between the two by adopting a second fundamental attitude: namely the idea that Scripture – unlike mathematical astronomy – is written in the common language. Thus, we can always search for a deeper, "*hidden*," meaning of any biblical passage if we seek to resolve its tension with a conclusion reached by natural philosophy. This indicates that for Galileo, there is an intriguing and useful consequence of insisting that natural philosophy must employ mathematical methods: it studies nature by using a language that differs fundamentally from the language employed by Christianity.

Working in the generation after Galileo, and especially in the wake of Descartes's achievements in natural philosophy, the great British philosopher Robert Boyle articulated an especially detailed conception of the relationship between theology and natural philosophy. In 1674, Boyle published his *Excellency of Theology Compared With Natural Philosophy*, a book which attempts to indicate the details of the distinction between these two fields (Boyle, *Works* 8: 12–28). Boyle seems to think that nature can disclose aspects of the divine being, and that these can be learned by the natural philosopher, but he also contends that Scripture discloses much more about God's attributes than one can discover from studying the natural world as he does. To know the nature and will of God, we require revelation. And in tandem, he claims that it is revelation, and not nature or its philosophical interpreters, which provides us insight into crucial topics like the immortality of the soul, the concept of sin, heaven and hell, and so on.[24] Unlike the topics of natural philosophy – the nature of the "spring" of the air, the possibility of creating a vacuum, and so on – these topics are of universal interest and import. So in this text, Boyle's project is not so much to seek accommodation between theology and natural philosophy but to indicate the superiority of the former over the latter in certain limited, yet central, respects. Elsewhere, he made the familiar point that Aristotelianism, which teaches that nature is eternal and which enables one to conceive of nature as autonomous from the divine, is a poor candidate for natural philosophers working within the context of early modern Christianity. He took the new natural philosophy, the new corpuscularianism, to be much better suited for the project of accommodation.

Boyle was certainly the most important natural philosopher in England in the middle of the century, so everyone else, including the young Isaac Newton, worked in his wake. In both his early years, and in the period when he wrote *Principia mathematica*, Newton expended considerable energy on his own version of the project of accommodation. Newton's solution to what he regards as the fundamental problem facing natural philosophy is unique, differing from Galileo's approach and from Boyle's. Newton placed great importance on these issues, as evidenced by the fact that he mentions his strategy of accommodation at the very beginning of the *Principia*, in the scholium on space and time:

> Relative quantities, therefore, are not the actual quantities whose names they bear but are those sensible measures of them (whether true or erroneous) that are commonly used instead of the quantities being measured. But if the meanings of words are to be defined by usage, then it is these sensible measures which should properly be understood by the terms "time", "space", "place", and "motion", and the manner of expression will be out of the ordinary and purely mathematical if the quantities being measured are understood here. Accordingly those who there interpret these words as referring to the quantities being measured do violence to the Scriptures. And they no less corrupt mathematics and philosophy who confuse true quantities with their relations and common measures.
> (Newton 1999, 413–14)

For Newton, space and time are "quantities," and relative spaces and times are "measures" of them: when you look at your watch, for instance, you measure the quantity, *time* (with varying degrees of accuracy). But Newton's suggestion is confusing: why does one do violence to Scripture if one conflates the *measures* of space and time with those *quantities themselves*?

The first answer to this question is obvious. For Newton, as for Galileo and others, Scripture is written in the language of the "common person," so in interpreting its descriptions of space or motion, we ought to understand these as claims concerning *relative spaces*. To understand these descriptions as holding of absolute space, according to Newton, does "violence" to the Scriptures because it undermines their veracity. Thus, if Scripture proclaims that the sun once miraculously stopped moving, we should not understand this as a change in what Newton calls its "true" motion, which would obviously have to be accompanied by various effects, but rather as a change in its *relative* motion, which need not be accompanied by such effects, for it merely involves a change in its relations to other bodies.

But in presenting this view, Newton is not merely parroting the strategy of accommodation articulated by Galileo in his letter to the grand duchess – he is employing his distinction between absolute and relative space in a novel way. Remarkably, this is evident already in Newton's pre-*Principia* correspondence. Toward the end of 1680, one of Newton's acquaintances from Cambridge, the author Thomas Burnet, wrote him to discover his opinion of some ideas in Burnet's soon-to-be-famous book *Telluris theoria sacra*, or *Sacred Theory of the Earth*. On Christmas Eve in 1680, Newton presented Burnet with some criticisms of his attempt to accommodate the Biblical description of the creation of the earth with the current teachings of what Burnet, in original English, simply calls "philosophy." On 13 January 1681 – the new year, by the new calendar – Burnet wrote a lengthy reply from his London home. One of his essential claims is that the Mosaic description of the creation – according to which, of course, the world itself was created within six days – cannot be squared with the teachings of philosophy, and that we must therefore regard Moses as providing us not with a description of what Burnet calls "physical reality" but rather with a *metaphorical* description. The business of philosophy, of course, is to provide a description of physical reality.

One might expect Newton to endorse this point of view. After all, it enables Burnet to dissolve the deep tension between the biblical view of the world and the philosophical one, and Burnet, who later became a doctor of divinity, certainly shows the kind of respect for the Hebrew Bible that someone like Newton (who was extremely devout) would find *de rigeur*. Later that month, however, Newton strongly rejected Burnet's method of accommodation. He writes,

> As to Moses I do not think his description of the creation either philosophical or feigned, but that he described realities in a language artificially adapted to the sense of the vulgar. Thus where he speaks of two great lights I suppose he means their apparent, not real greatness. So when he tells us God placed those lights in the firmament, he speaks I suppose of their apparent not of their real place, his business being not to correct the vulgar notions in matters philosophical but to adapt a description of the creation as handsomely as he could to the sense and capacity of the vulgar.
> (Newton to Burnet, January 1681, in Newton 1959–1977, vol. 2: 331)

Later in the same lengthy letter, Newton elaborates:

> Consider therefore whether any one who understood the process of the creation and designed to accommodate to the vulgar not an Ideal or poetical but a true description of it as succinctly and theologically as Moses has done, without omitting any thing material which the vulgar have a notion of or describing any being further than the vulgar have a notion of it, could mend that description which Moses has given us. If it be said that the expression of making and setting two great lights in the firmament is more poetical than natural: so also are some other expressions of Moses, as where he tells us the windows or floodgates of heaven were opened Gen 7 and afterwards stopped again Gen 8 and yet the things signified by such figurative expressions are not Ideal or moral but true. For Moses accommodating his words to the gross conceptions of the vulgar, describes things much after the manner as one of the vulgar would have been inclined to do had he lived and seen the whole series of what Moses describes.
> (Newton to Burnet, January 1681, *Correspondence*, vol. 2: 333)

Newton thus forcefully argues that we cannot resolve the tension between the teachings of the Bible and those of philosophy by simply declaring the former to be written in a common language that employs various poetical or metaphorical descriptions. Instead, he makes the surprising claim that Moses gives us a description of the creation that is not metaphorical or poetical, but *true*.

Newton's scholium helps to explicate this potentially confusing claim. Newton's distinction between the mathematical (or absolute) perspective and the common (or relative) perspective should not be collapsed into the distinction between the true and the false. If we understand Moses to be referring to apparent space, time, and motion – or, equivalently, *relative* space, time, and motion – then the truth of his descriptions can be rescued. So, sacred texts are neither false nor metaphorically true – as Newton tells Burnet, they are neither "philosophical" nor "feigned" – but rather literally true, if understood in the right way. To see this point, take a simple statement, say, "The sun set last night in Durham at 7 p.m." This is not a metaphorical claim, for Newton, but rather a literal claim about the apparent, or relative, motion of the sun vis-à-vis some earthly location. When I say that the sun set last night, I am not characterizing the true (mathematical, absolute) motion of the sun – I know very well that the sun does not revolve around a stationary earth. Moreover, we can distinguish between true and false statements concerning true or apparent motions: hence it is false (say) that the sun set last night in Durham at midnight.

Thus from Newton's point of view, natural philosophy attempts to uncover the true motions of the objects that constitute our world; Scripture describes those same objects – the moon, the sun, the earth, the stars – but characterizes how they *appear to us*. Because it certainly *appears* as if the earth is a stationary body circled each day by the sun, the Bible describes this appearance. It is the natural philosopher who discovers the true motions of the earth and the sun. What is more surprising, however, is this: it is not merely the case that Newton thinks of the natural philosopher as legitimately investigating the nature of the divine being when he analyzes the *phenomena*. If Newton were to limit himself to the kind of design argument we find in many authors in this period – the kind of argument he himself makes in the first edition of the *Principia* and in his correspondence with Bentley six years later – he would be simply implying that the natural philosopher can add *further arguments* for the existence of God. This would not alter the *knowledge* of the divine available to theologians. *Instead*, Newton transcends that familiar point of view in a fundamental way. He implies that even the most sophisticated interpretation of *all of Holy Scripture* will leave us *without* a complete understanding of the creator. For as we have seen, Holy Writ is always limited in its description of the creation to discussions of *apparent* motions, *common* measures of time, and *relative* ideas of space. For Newton, there is a crucial aspect of the divine that we *cannot understand* if we limit ourselves to these resources of theology and of the interpretation of religious texts. It is the natural philosopher who fully understands God's relation to the creation. God does not inhabit any merely apparent or relative or common space: God is an infinite being who inhabits an infinite and eternal mathematical space. One cannot learn that fact from reading the Bible. Perhaps it is only the natural philosopher who knows the true nature of God. A surprising conclusion indeed.

Notes

1 According to Daston and Stolleis, it was "an innovation of the first magnitude to connect natural laws with causal explanations" (2008), for natural philosophy was taken to be focused on the search for causes within nature, but it was seen as fundamentally distinct from those disciplines, such as astronomy and optics (so-called mixed mathematics), that employed mathematical techniques and that searched for what were sometimes called *laws*. So, one could tell the story of seventeenth century natural philosophy by emphasizing its expansion into areas, such as the explanation of astronomical phenomena, which were traditionally handled by separate disciplines, or by emphasizing that it came to provide nomological investigations of nature that were traditionally the province of other areas. Daston and Stolleis also rightly contend that the elements of these two stories intersect.

2 For an erudite discussion of natural philosophy in the late medieval period, especially the fourteenth century, see Murdoch 1982, and for a discussion focused on the thirteenth century, see French and Cunningham 1996. French and Cunningham later argue that natural philosophy was created in the thirteenth century when the Latin West wished to reintroduce Greek philosophy into the world of Christianity. They focus their attention on the work of Dominican and Franciscan friars, seeing the former as largely Aristotelian in orientation and the latter as Platonic.

3 For varying conceptions of natural philosophy, see French and Cunningham (1996), Grant (2007), Stein (1993), and Funkenstein (1986).

4 For an influential pre-Newtonian conception, see the Cartesian treatise by Rohault, *System of Natural Philosophy*, vol. I: 20–1. Rohault is especially concerned to indicate that natural philosophy analyzes objects within their natural state, where the contrast class is not the quasi-Aristotelian "violent" state

of a thing, but rather some state that God creates against the ordinary course of nature. Hence Rohault explicitly brackets miracles, and what he calls "the mysteries of faith."
5 Quoted by Gaukroger (2008, 4–5); see also Garber 2000.
6 *Le Monde* was published only posthumously, in Paris in 1664. This description of the historical record is actually somewhat simplified, although it is the description one will often find, and it may be the best characterization of Descartes's own understanding of the events in question. However, many scholars would now argue that Galileo was not placed under house arrest in 1633 for advocating a Copernican view but rather for abrogating to himself the authority to pronounce opinions on various issues with theological import, issues that many theologians and officials in the Vatican took to fall under their own purview (cf. Heilbron 2010).
7 The other great post-Cartesian natural philosopher, Leibniz, had his own metaphysical commitments that led him to intriguing views of the application of mathematics. One intriguing aspect of Leibniz's conception of the relation between mathematics and metaphysics bears mentioning here, as it distinguishes his view from those of his most important predecessor, Descartes, and his most important interlocutor, Newton. From Leibniz's point of view, reality consists of an infinite series of nonspatial, noninteracting, simple substances called monads. The objects of our experience – tables, chairs, and the like – are merely the "appearances" of these monads when viewed from the human perceptual point of view. Given this metaphysical distinction between the appearances and the reality that underlies them, the question of how mathematics applies to the world takes on a new meaning: we might ask this of the natural world, the realm of our scientific or physical investigations, but we might also ask this of the reality discovered and described by fundamental metaphysics. It seems clear that for Leibniz, the monadic realm is not describable mathematically: he insists that monads lack spatial properties, thereby limiting any geometric characterization of them, and he denies that monads are mathematical points, thereby preventing any arithmetic characterization of them. So in a special Leibnizian sense, mathematics does not apply to *reality* (see Shabel 2005, 42–3), but it does apply to nature.
8 *Optical Papers*, vol. I: 86–7. Isaac Barrow preceded Newton as the Lucasian professor at Cambridge; for a helpful discussion of his influence on Newton's conception of the role of mathematics within natural philosophy, see Shapiro (1993, 30–40).
9 On 20 June 1686, Newton wrote to Halley as follows:

> I designed the whole to consist of three books. . . . The third I now design to suppress. Philosophy is such an impertinently litigious lady that a man had as good be engaged in law suits as have to do with her. I found it so formerly [he presumably means the 1670s optics disputes] & now I no sooner come near her again but she gives me warning. The two first books without the third will not so well bear the title of Philosophiae naturalis Principia Mathematica & therefore I had altered it to this De Motu corporum libri duo: but upon second thoughts I retain the former title. Twill help the sale of the book which I ought not to diminish now tis yours.
>
> (*Correspondence*, vol. II: 437)

This was written in response to Halley, who had written to Newton two weeks earlier that he ought to include book III because "the application of this mathematical part, to the system of the world; is what will render it acceptable to all naturalists, as well as mathematicians, and much advance the sale of the book" (*Correspondence*, vol. II: 434). Without the third book, in which Newton discusses what he calls "the system of the world," the first two books of *Principia mathematica* could not very accurately be called natural philosophy; rather, they would be better described as two books on the motion of bodies. For Newton, as for Halley, natural philosophy was not principally concerned with just any motion of bodies that was tractable through mathematical analysis; rather, it was concerned with the mathematical analysis of the motions of the bodies within our solar system – within nature as we perceive it in our vicinity of the universe. And that, of course, is part of a long tradition in natural philosophy. Newton's innovation is to provide a mathematical analysis of the motions of these bodies. On Halley's role in printing the *Principia*, see Cohen, "Introduction to Newton's *Principia*," 130–42.
10 For his part, Newton explicitly attempted to vanquish the Cartesian plenist, vortex-based, view of motion in book II of *Principia mathematica* by considering numerous cases in which bodies move through resisting media.
11 Nonetheless, Newton held Descartes in high esteem. When Newton wrote to Hooke in a famous letter, "If I have seen further it is by standing on the shoulders of giants," he included Descartes among them (1959–1977, vol. I: 416). Remarkably, Newton sometimes referred to the *Principia* as his "Principia Philosophiae" – for instance, in his (anonymous) "An Account," 180 and 198; cf. the notes of Cohen and

12 Malebranche, *Oeuvres*, 19: 771–72; I owe this reference to Tad Schmaltz.
13 Newton actually attributed his first two laws of motion to Galileo. This was certainly a sign of respect, as Newton's references to his predecessors are few and far between. (He also cited Huygens, Wren, and Wallis for their work on impact in the 1660s.) It may also have been a subtle indication that Newton sought to align his work with the mathematical tradition represented by Galileo, rather than with the powerful Cartesian tradition of that era.
14 Although it was common to speak of laws – *leges* – in thirteenth century optics and in early sixteenth century astronomy, Descartes was probably the first to speak of them within the context of natural philosophy. He took them to be what we would now call *a priori*, deriving them from God. Robert Hooke may have been the first philosopher to say that he had established a law of nature experimentally, in his unjustly neglected *Micrographia* of 1665. In any event, it was commonplace to speak of the laws of nature within natural philosophy by the 1670s. For instance, although Boyle apparently did not employ the concept of a law of nature in his early work, by the time of his "Excellency and Grounds of the Mechanical Hypothesis" in 1674, he was contending that God established the laws of nature (Boyle, *Works* 8: 103–4). See especially Steinle (2008) and Ruby (1986, 341–59).
15 Descartes's understanding of the laws of nature is complex. For instance, although he takes God to be the "primary" cause of motion (AT VIIIA 61; CSM I 240), he considers the laws to be secondary causes of it. For an illuminating treatment of this possibly confusing notion, see Schmaltz (2008, 105–16).
16 That is: "nihil aliud est quàm *actio, quâ corpus aliquod ex uno loco in alium migrat*." The italics are in the original Latin and in the original French.
17 For an illuminating discussion, see Garber (1992, 159–62). It may also conflict with section 26 of part 2, which indicates that despite appearances to the contrary, the motion of a body does not require more action than rest.
18 In the preface to the French edition of the text (1647), he writes (AT IXB 14): "*Ainsi toute la Philosophie est comme un arbre, dont les racines sont la Metaphysique, le tronc est la Physique, & les branches qui sortent de ce tronc sont toutes les autres sciences, qui se reduisent à trois principales, à scauoir la Medecine, la Mechanique & la Morale, j'entens la plus haute & la plus parfait Morale, qui, presupposant une entire connoissance des autres sciences, est le dernier degree de la Sagesse.*"
19 Thanks to Ori Belkind for discussion of related issues.
20 This can be seen, for instance, in Locke's correspondence with Stillingfleet, in which he indicates that *Principia mathematica* altered his opinion about the truth of mechanism as a picture of natural change. In a famous passage, he admits to Stillingfleet that Newton has demonstrated that bodies gravitate toward one another, and although he insists that this cannot be understood by considering the essence of matter (by which he means "solid extended substance"), nonetheless we might be forced to conclude that God has superadded gravity to matter in some way unknown, and perhaps unknowable, to us. See Janiak (2015, 109–110).
21 Here I am obviously bracketing what was sometimes called "natural theology" in the period, for its relation to natural philosophy is more complex and would take us far afield.
22 Descartes explores the distinction between theology and first philosophy – that is metaphysics – rather than natural philosophy in his dedicatory letter to the faculty of theology in Paris in his *Meditations* (AT VII 1–2; CSM II 3–4).
23 Although written in 1615, Galileo's letter to the grand duchess was not published until 1636 (through the Elzevier publishing house in Leiden) in both Latin and the original Italian (in parallel columns).
24 Boyle argues in particular that even if Descartes is right to think that the mind and the body are distinct in some sense, we cannot know that the soul is immortal unless we appeal to revelation, because immortality requires specific actions by God that cannot be known through the study of nature (*Works* 8: 23–5). For an illuminating discussion of Boyle's views on such matters, see Hunter 2009 (especially pages 82–4).

Bibliography

Anstey, Peter, and John Schuster, eds., 2005, *The Science of Nature in the Seventeenth Century*, Dordrecht: Springer.

Bentley, Richard, 1842, *The Correspondence of Richard Bentley*, edited by Christopher Wordsworth, London: John Murray.

Bertoloni Meli, Domenico, 1993, *Equivalence and Priority: Newton vs. Leibniz*, Oxford: Oxford University Press.

Bertoloni Meli, Domenico, 2002, "Newton and the Leibniz-Clarke Correspondence," in I. B. Cohen and G. Smith, eds.

Blair, Ann, 2006, "Natural Philosophy," in Katharine Park and Lorraine Daston, eds., *The Cambridge History of Science, Volume 3: Early Modern Science*, Cambridge: Cambridge University Press.

Blay, Michel, 1995, *Les "Principia" de Newton*, Paris: Presses universitaires de France.

Boas, Marie, 1952, "The Establishment of the Mechanical Philosophy," *Osiris* 10, 412–541.

Boyle, Robert, 1999, *The Works of Robert Boyle*, edited by Michael Hunter and Edward Davis, London: Pickering and Chatto.

Clarke, Samuel, and Gottfried Wilhelm Leibniz, 1717, *A Collection of Papers, Which Passed Between the Late Learned Mr. Leibnitz and Dr. Clarke, in the Years of 1715 and 1716*, London: Printed for James Knapton.

Cohen, I. Bernard, 1969, "Isaac Newton's *Principia*, the Scriptures, and the Divine Providence," in Sidney Morgenbesser, Patrick Suppes, and Morton White, eds., *Philosophy, Science and Method: Essays in Honor of Ernest Nagel*, New York: St. Martin's Press.

Cohen, I. Bernard, 1990, "Newton and Descartes," in Giulia Belgioioso et al., eds., *Descartes: il metodo e I saggi*, Rome: Istituto della Enciclopedia Italiana.

Cohen, I. Bernard, 1992, "The Review of the First Edition of Newton's *Principia* in the Acta Eruditorum, With Notes on the Other Reviews," in P. M. Harman and Alan Shapiro, eds., *The Investigation of Difficult Things: Essays on Newton and the History of the Exact Sciences in Honour of D. T. Whiteside*, Cambridge: Cambridge University Press.

Cohen, I. Bernard, and Alexandre Koyré, 1962, "Newton and the Leibniz-Clarke Correspondence," *Archives internationales d'histoire des sciences* 15, 63–126.

Cohen, I. Bernard, and George Smith, eds., 2002, *The Cambridge Companion to Newton*, Cambridge: Cambridge University Press.

Daston, Lorraine, and Michael Stolleis, eds., 2008, *Natural Law and Laws of Nature in Early Modern Europe*, reprinted 2016, London: Routledge.

Descartes, René, 1982, *Principia Philosophiae*, in *Oeuvres de Descartes*, edited by Charles Adam and Paul Tannery, volume VIII-1, Paris: Vrin.

Descartes, René, 1985, *The Philosophical Writings of Descartes*, translated by John Cottingham, Robert Stoothoff, and Dugald Murdoch, volume 1, Cambridge: Cambridge University Press.

Descartes, René, 1989, *Principes*, in *Oeuvres de Descartes*, edited and translated by Charles Adam and Paul Tannery, volume IX-2, Paris: Vrin.

Dobbs, Betty Jo Teeter, 1994, "Newton as Final Cause and First Mover," *Isis* 85, 633–643.

Domski, Mary, 2003, "The Constructible and the Intelligible in Newton's Philosophy of Geometry," *Philosophy of Science* 70, 1114–1124.

Domski, Mary, 2010, "Newton's Empiricism and Metaphysics," *Philosophy Compass* 5, 525–534.

French, Roger, and Andrew Cunningham, 1996, *Before Science: The Invention of the Friars' Natural Philosophy*, Brookfield: Scholar's Press.

Funkenstein, Amos, 1986, *Theology and the Scientific Imagination From the Middle Ages to the Seventeenth Century*, Princeton, NJ: Princeton University Press.

Gabbey, Alan, 2004, "What Was Mechanical About the Mechanical Philosophy?" in Carla Rita Palmerino and J.M.M.H. Thijssen, eds., *The Reception of the Galilean Science of Motion in Seventeenth-Century Europe*, Dordrecht: Kluwer.

Galileo, 2008, "Letter to the Grand Duchess Christina," in Maurice Finocchiaro, ed. and trans., *The Essential Galileo*, Indianapolis, IN: Hackett.

Garber, Daniel, 1992, *Descartes's Metaphysical Physics*, Chicago: University of Chicago Press.

Garber, Daniel, 2000, "A Different Descartes: Descartes and the Programme for a Mathematical Physics in His Correspondence," in Stephen Gaukroger et al., eds., *Descartes' Natural Philosophy*. London: Routledge.

Gaukroger, Stephen, 2005, "The Autonomy of Natural Philosophy," in Anstey and Schuster, eds.

Gaukroger, Stephen, 2008, "Life and Works," in Janet Broughton and John Carriero, eds., *A Companion to Descartes*, Oxford: Blackwell.

Goclenius, Rodolphus, 1613, *Lexicon Philosophicum*, Frankfurt.

Grant, Edward, 2000, "God and Natural Philosophy: The Late Middle Ages and Sir Isaac Newton," *Early Science and Medicine* 5, 279–298.
Grant, Edward, 2007, *A History of Natural Philosophy*, Cambridge: Cambridge University Press.
Guicciardini, Niccolò, 2009, *Isaac Newton on Mathematical Certainty and Method*, Cambridge, MA: MIT Press.
Harper, William, 2011, *Isaac Newton's Scientific Method: Turning Date Into Evidence About Gravity and Cosmology*, Oxford: Oxford University Press.
Harrison, Peter, 2005, "Physico-Theology and the Mixed Sciences: The Role of Theology in Early Modern Natural Philosophy," in Anstey and Schuster, eds.
Heilbron, J. L., 1982, *Elements of Early Modern Physics*, Berkeley: University of California Press.
Heilbron, J. L., 2010, *Galileo*, Oxford: Oxford University Press.
Henry, John, 2013, "The Reception of Cartesianism," in Peter Anstey, ed.
Hesse, Mary, 1961, *Forces and Fields: The Concept of Action at a Distance in the History of Physics*, London: Nelson.
Hunter, Michael, 2009, *Boyle: Between God and Science*, New Haven, CT: Yale University Press.
Hutton, Sarah, 1994, "More, Newton and the Language of Biblical Prophecy," in Force and Popkin, eds.
Iliffe, Rob, 2006, "Friendly Criticism: Richard Simon, John Locke, Isaac Newton and the *Johannine Comma*," in Hessayon and Keene, eds.
Jacob, Margaret, 1986, "Christianity and the Newtonian Worldview," in David Lindberg and Ronald Numbers, eds., *God and Nature: Historical Essays on the Encounter Between Christianity and Science*, Berkeley: University of California Press.
Janiak, Andrew, 2008, *Newton as Philosopher*, Cambridge: Cambridge University Press.
Janiak, Andrew, 2015, Newton, Boston and Oxford: Wiley Blackwell.
Janiak, Andrew, 2015, *Newton*, Boston and Oxford: Wiley Blackwell.
Kant, Immanuel, 1786/1997, *Metaphysische Anfangsgründe der Naturwissenschaft*, edited by Konstantin Pollok, Hamburg: Felix Meiner Verlag.
Kochiras, Hylarie, 2009, "Gravity and Newton's Substance Counting Problem," *Studies in History and Philosophy of Science* 40, 267–280.
Koyré, Alexandre, 1957, *From the Closed World to the Infinite Universe*, Baltimore, MD: Johns Hopkins University Press.
Koyré, Alexandre, 1968, *Newtonian Studies*, Chicago: University of Chicago Press.
Lüthy, Christoph, 2000, "What to Do With Seventeenth-Century Natural Philosophy? A Taxonomic Problem," *Perspectives on Science* 8, 164–195.
Mahoney, Michael, 1997, "The Mathematical Realm of Nature," in Daniel Garber and Michael Ayers, eds., *The Cambridge History of Seventeenth Century Philosophy*, Cambridge: Cambridge University Press.
Malebranche, Nicolas, 1991, *Oeuvres complètes*, edited by André Robinet, Paris: Librairie philosophique J. Vrin.
Mandelbrote, Scott, 1993, "A Duty of the Greatest Moment: Isaac Newton and the Writing of Biblical Criticism," *The British Journal for the History of Science* 26, 281–302.
Mandelbrote, Scott, 1994, "Isaac Newton and Thomas Burnet: Biblical Criticism and the Crisis of Late Seventeenth-Century England," in Force and Popkin, eds.
McGuire, J. E., 1972, "Boyle's Conception of Nature," *Journal of the History of Ideas* 33, 523–542.
Metzger, Hélène, 1938, *Attraction universelle et religion naturelle chez quelques commentateurs anglais de Newton*, Paris: Hermann et cie.
Murdoch, John, 1982, "The Analytic Character of Late Medieval Learning: Natural Philosophy Without Nature," in L. D. Roberts, ed., *Approaches to Nature in the Middle Ages*, Binghamton, NY: Center for Medieval and Early Renaissance Studies.
Nelson, Alan, 1995, "Micro-Chaos and Idealization in Cartesian Physics," *Philosophical Studies* 77, 377–391.
Newton, Isaac, unknown date, *De Gravitatione et Aequipondio Fluidorum*, MSS Add. 4003, University Library, Cambridge.
Newton, Isaac, 1959–1977, *The Correspondence of Isaac Newton*, edited by H. W. Turnbull, et al., Cambridge: Cambridge University Press.
Newton, Isaac, 1972, *Philosophiae Naturalis Principia Mathematica*, edited by Alexandre Koyré and I. Bernard Cohen, with Anne Whitman, 3rd edition with variant readings, Cambridge, MA: Harvard University Press.
Newton, Isaac, 1984, *The Optical Papers of Isaac Newton, volume 1*, edited by Alan Shapiro, Cambridge: Cambridge University Press.

Newton, Isaac, 1999, *The Principia: Mathematical Principles of Natural Philosophy*, translated by I. Bernard Cohen and Anne Whitman, Berkeley: University of California Press.

Newton, Isaac, 2014, *Newton: Philosophical Writings*, edited by Andrew Janiak, 2nd edition, Cambridge: Cambridge University Press.

Palmerino, Carla Rita, 2006. "The Mathematical Characters of Galileo's Book of Nature," in Klaus van Berkel and Arjo Vanderjagt, eds., *The Book of Nature in Early Modern and Modern History*. Leuven and Paris: Peeters.

Rohault, Jacques, 1723, *System of Natural Philosophy: Illustrated With Dr. Samuel Clarke's Notes, Taken Mostly out of Sir Isaac Newton's Philosophy*, translated by John Clarke, London: James Knapton.

Ruby, Jane, 1986, "The Origins of Scientific Law," *Journal of the History of Ideas* 47.

Schmaltz, Tad, 2008, *Descartes on Causation*, Oxford: Oxford University Press.

Shabel, Lisa, 2005, "Apriority and Application: Philosophy of Mathematics in the Modern Period," in Stewart Shapiro, ed., *The Oxford Handbook of Philosophy of Math and Logic*, Oxford: Oxford University Press.

Shapiro, Alan, 1993, *Fits, Passions and Paroxysms: Physics, Method, and Chemistry and Newton's Theories of Colored Bodies and Fits of Easy Reflection*, Cambridge: Cambridge University Press.

Smith, George, 2002, "The Methodology of the *Principia*," in Cohen and Smith, eds.

Snobelen, Stephen, 2005, " 'The True Frame of Nature': Isaac Newton, Heresy, and the Reformation of Natural Philosophy," in John Brooke and Ian Maclean, eds., *Heterodoxy in Early Modern Science and Religion*, Oxford: Oxford University Press.

Snobelen, Stephen, 2006, " 'To us there is but one God, the Father': Antitrinitarian Textual Criticism in Seventeenth and Early-Eighteenth Century England," in Hessayon and Keene, eds.

Stein, Howard, 1993, "On Philosophy and Natural Philosophy in the Seventeenth Century," in *Midwest Studies in Philosophy*, volume 18, Minneapolis: University of Minnesota Press.

Steinle, Friedrich, 2008, "From Principles to Regularities: Tracing 'Laws of Nature' in Early Modern France and England," in Daston and Stollheis, eds.

Westfall, Richard S., 1971, *Force in Newton's Physics*, New York: Wiley.

Wilson, Margaret, 1999, *Ideas and Mechanism*, Princeton, NJ: Princeton University Press.

15
THE THEORY OF MATTER
Andrew Pyle

1. Introduction

"The theory of matter" can mean many things, ranging from the most abstract metaphysical issues about persistence and change, identity and individuation, down to detailed empirical issues about the actual constitution of bodies. The metaphysician might enquire whether more than one form can coexist in the same portion of matter. The chemist might ask whether the so-called elements fire, air, water, and earth are indeed the ultimate constituents of all material things, and, if so, how they are present in compounds. At first sight, they are addressing very different questions, one informed by textual scholarship and hard thought, the other by hands-on experience in the laboratory. But the answer to the metaphysician's question has implications for the chemist and vice versa. Similarly, the metaphysician might investigate the actuality or otherwise of the parts of a body before division; the natural philosopher might seek an account of some of the properties of bodies in terms of the arrangement of their parts. Here the very intelligibility of a programme in natural philosophy depends on a particular answer to a deep and difficult question of metaphysics. Arguments in matter theory can clearly run both ways. We might start with first principles and use a set of accepted principles to set constraints and impose guidelines on empirical research. Or we could argue back from successful empirical work to the picture of nature that they presuppose. Philosophers of a "rationalist" persuasion such as Descartes and Leibniz will tend to favour the former approach; philosophers of an "empiricist" persuasion such as Boyle and Locke will favour the latter.[1]

In seventeenth century accounts of matter such as those of Descartes and Gassendi, Boyle and Newton we encounter a rich mixture of metaphysical arguments with empirical ones. Early modern philosophers sought an account of matter that would satisfy both reason and experience. Ideally, it would be perfectly intelligible and free from internal contradictions, and it would explain the phenomena both of common experience and of the emerging natural sciences.

2. The Scholastic background to early modern philosophy

Almost all the major figures of early modern philosophy[2] received a thorough grounding in Scholastic Aristotelianism. Most of them would later say that they learned nothing from "the schoolmen," and would dismiss their university studies as a complete waste of time. But this was unfair. As we shall see, the Scholastics provided a framework of technical terms, of set questions, and of stock arguments that could be redeployed by the new philosophers.[3] Are all forms merely *accidental*, capable of being generated or destroyed by mere rearrangement of parts, or are there also *substantial* forms, irreducible to the arrangement of parts? The Scholastics defended the latter view for organisms, whereas they accepted the former for artefacts such as machines. So, if a thinker such as Boyle can show that the distinction between natural and artificial products is indefensible, he has opened up an avenue to the conclusion that all forms may be accidental. Are the parts of a material thing all actually preexistent, prior to any process of division? Or does division create parts rather than merely revealing preexistent parts? In opposition to the Scholastics, most (but by no means all) of the "moderns" took the former view, arguing that the very possibility of division presupposes already distinct parts. But the question cannot be raised without the Scholastic notions of actuality and potentiality, and without raising deep questions of conceptual and ontological priority. And what becomes of the elements in a chemical compound? If they are destroyed, we have corruption and regeneration rather than mixture. If they continue to exist, can the mixture be perfectly homogeneous, as Aristotle thought? At this point, answers to traditional questions from Aristotelian natural philosophy have obvious implications for the emerging science of chemistry. In the next section, we will document in more detail some of the key issues of late Scholastic matter theory that provided the framework for seventeenth century natural philosophy.

3. Scholastic matter theory

Aristotelian natural philosophy is generally characterised as *hylomorphic*, emphasising the constitution of all bodies out of *hyle* (matter) and *morphe* (form). But what exactly did Aristotle and his followers mean by these two key terms? Here a concrete example or two may help both to introduce the key terms and to pose further questions. Suppose I am seeking to make a chair out of some beech wood, or a statue of Hercules out of a lump of bronze. Here the wood and the bronze provide the matter, and the craftsman seeks to impose a form. The wood and the bronze have no natural tendency to assume that form rather than any other; they possess only what the Aristotelian will call a "passive potency" to be informed (shaped) in various ways. A given form may *require* a certain type of matter rather than another (the carpenter would be ill-advised to make his chair of balsa wood), but the matter provides at best a necessary condition for the actualisation of a particular form. One cannot explain the properties of the chair or the statue in terms of its matter, as if the matter somehow determined the form. On the contrary, it is forms that provide the principles of intelligibility of things; it is always a form that is grasped by the mind when it seeks to answer the "what is it?" question.

But the "matter" in these examples – beech wood and bronze – is already informed matter. Beech wood differs in important respects from pine and oak; bronze consists of a characteristic mixture of copper and tin. For the Aristotelian, the matter-form distinction is not a simple, unequivocal, one-off affair. What is matter at one level (the beech wood, the bronze) may turn out at a lower level of analysis to be a matter-form complex. Beech wood is produced in the course of nature, as the vegetable soul of the beech tree takes in the elements fire, air, water, and earth (FAWE), mixes them, and imposes on the resulting mixture its specific form or nature. Bronze is produced by art (i.e. human craftsmanship), when determinate mixtures of copper and tin are smelted together. But the copper and the tin are themselves products of nature, "growing" in veins of ore in the "womb" of the earth. In the final analysis, they too must be the products of mixtures of FAWE, perhaps informed by something like a "seed" or a "seminal principle."[4] Copper and tin, iron and lead are distinct metals, with characteristic properties, and thus forms of their own.

Does this "ladder of nature" bottom out when we come at last to the elements FAWE? If so, we could identify the elements with matter itself, the ultimate substratum of the physical world. But the elements already seem to be "informed" at least by pairs of the Aristotelian primary qualities hot, cold, dry, and moist (HCDM). Fire is hot and dry, air is hot and moist, water is cold and moist, and earth is cold and dry. So FAWE are not entirely formless and undifferentiated, not merely a featureless stuff onto which forms are imposed. And according to Aristotle, the elements are transformed into one another in the course of nature. But this entails the existence of a common substratum, a featureless stuff materially prior even to the elements.[5] This is the notorious *prime matter* of the Scholastic tradition. Prime matter, it seems, is conceptually necessary to provide a rock bottom to the natural hierarchy we have been discussing. If we are to insist that water *changes* into air, rather than water ceasing to be and air coming to be, it seems we are committed to an underlying stuff that abides through the change. The problem is that we seem to be unable – for deep reasons of principle – to say anything positive about this supposed stuff. For the mind to grasp it and characterize it in any way would presuppose form, but prime matter is, *ex hypothesi*, prior to all forms.

One most fundamental problem concerns the quantification of prime matter. If a litre of water produces, on evaporation, ten litres of air (according to the Aristotelian), then one might expect, on condensation, to recover one litre of water again. Matter, it would appear, must observe a conservation principle. But prime matter has, according to Aristotle, no positive features whatsoever. The clearest statement of this comes in chapter 3 of *Metaphysics*, book Z:

> By matter I mean that which in itself is neither a particular thing nor of a certain quantity nor assigned to any of the other categories by which being is determined. . . . Therefore the ultimate substratum is of itself neither a particular thing nor of a particular quantity nor otherwise positively characterized; nor yet is it the negations of these, for negations also will belong to it only by accident.[6]

The point is repeated in the physical treatise *On Coming-to-Be and Passing-Away*:

> that which is not a substance or "this" cannot possess predicates drawn from any of the other Categories either – e.g. we cannot attribute to it a quality, quantity, or position.[7]

There is, it appears, a deep tension in Aristotle's thinking on this subject.[8] To serve as the ultimate substratum for natural change, matter must be quantified and space filling. But Aristotle's flat insistence that the other categories (quantity, quality, relation, etc.) are always dependent on *substance* (which always involves form) rules out the very intelligibility of asking how much prime matter is present in a given body, or whether prime matter is more densely packed in lead than in water. The concept of matter, it seems, is being asked to fill too many roles. For the natural philosopher, the notion of an independently quantified, space-filling, *actual* stuff is very appealing; for the metaphysician, prime matter is so utterly featureless as to be closely akin to "nonbeing."

Even if we were to agree on the need for an abiding and quantified stuff to serve as the underlying substratum of all natural changes, it would be hard to fix definite terms for the quantification. For the Aristotelian, the same amount of matter can occupy more or less volume: when water is transformed into air it becomes intrinsically thinner, and the same quantity of matter occupies perhaps ten times more space. So, matter cannot be quantified in terms of volume. Weight is also ruled out: fire is material, but absolutely light – adding fire to a body increases the quantity of matter but subtracts from the weight. The modern (Newtonian) concept of mass was still in its infancy.[9] So, if a Scholastic philosopher endorsed the notion of a "quantity of matter," this notion remained at a rudimentary and intuitive level, neither characterised with any precision in philosophical terms nor given any measurable empirical sense. Some Scholastics (e.g. Scotus and Ockham) were prepared to depart from Aristotelian orthodoxy far enough to admit a "matter" with at least some minimum degree of actuality of its own. Here, of course, they came into conflict with the influential Thomist tradition.

According to Thomas Aquinas and his followers, form is to matter as "act" to mere "potency" – form is the actualization of matter, which is in itself nothing more than the potential to acquire forms. Matter cannot even be said to *exist*, except insofar as it is informed by some form or other. Theory requires that we postulate matter, but we can never encounter or experience it except through its forms. On no account must we confuse matter with substance: "matter is not a thing's substance or else all forms would be accidental, as the early natural philosophers held; but matter is part of substance."[10] The "early natural philosophers" Aquinas refers to here are the Ionians and atomists, who had sought to explain forms in terms of matter, and who had been – in Aquinas's eyes – refuted by Aristotle in book Z of the *Metaphysics*. Aquinas admits that merely accidental forms such as those of artefacts can be explained in terms of the arrangement of independently existing material parts. The properties of our chair, for example, depended on the way in which the various pieces of beech wood were fastened together. These pieces of wood had characteristic sizes and shapes of their own, and could have been given other arrangements. But the properties of a cat cannot be explained in terms of the arrangement of *its* parts. If we divide a cat into its supposed parts (heart, lungs, liver, eyes, ears, etc.) we have, of course, killed it. And the parts of the corpse are *not* identical with the corresponding parts of the original living feline. We admittedly use the same names ("heart," "eye," etc.) for the parts of the organism and those of the corpse, but we do so, an Aristotelian will insist, only homonymously. The correct definition of a living organ is functional: to be an eye is to possess the power of sight; to be a heart is to possess the power of pumping blood. It follows that the corresponding parts of the corpse are *not* eye and heart respectively. There is no prospect of explaining the features of the living cat by putting together its parts because the bloody organs scattered around the butcher's slab are not even the parts of the cat. For living things, we need to posit a *substantial form* that is irreducible to any mere arrangement of material parts. Rather than explaining the formal properties of the organism "bottom up," in terms of the arrangement of independently real parts, the only intelligible course of explanation is "top down," starting with the substantial form of the organism and explaining the contribution of its *living* parts to the form of the whole.

The substantial forms (SFs) of the Scholastics were the target of severe and sustained criticism from almost[11] all of the "moderns" in the seventeenth century. Descartes and

Gassendi, Boyle and Locke were as one in dismissing the theory as useless and ultimately unintelligible verbiage, as making zero contribution to our understanding of nature. But before we dismiss the theory out of hand, we ought at least to understand what it was meant to explain.[12] A Scholastic philosopher might invoke SFs to explain the following:

1. Specificity. The different species of metals, plants, animals, and so forth are marked by highly specific properties and powers, which appear (at least on the face of it) to be irreducible to mere material arrangement.
2. Unity of essences. If we say that a given power or property is essential to a given thing, we are saying that that thing could not exist without that power or property. Suppose we list properties FGH as essential properties of some given natural kind – say a metal such as tin. It would then appear logically possible that the properties F, G, and H could come apart, and that there could be metals that are essentially F and G but not H, or G and H but not F, and so on. But in nature essential properties come in fixed and reliable clusters. This, according to the Scholastic, is because they all stem from a common SF.
3. Natural limits. If one is changing a thing, for example by heating it, there will be a natural limit to how far one can go before one crosses a boundary and the original thing is not altered but destroyed, and something new created. A mere alteration such as heating is naturally reversible (the water in the kettle will cool down again); coming to be and ceasing to be (which involve new SFs) are not.
4. Preferred (natural) states. The water in the kettle will spontaneously cool down again once it has been heated; a bent twig will spring back; a mammal that has been chilled (but not enough to kill it) will return to its normal body temperature. In these and many other such cases, there seems to a natural state that is somehow "preferred," and to which the system will return after disturbance. SFs are not just formal but also teleological principles – they explain the fact that natural processes generally seem to be directed towards ends or goals.

The theory of SFs was taken to have considerable explanatory power. The wisest of the schoolmen admitted that they couldn't give a clear account of what exactly SFs were, nor of how they served their various functions. But their existence was taken to be clear from nature. Those innovators who would consign SFs to the rubbish bin of discarded hypotheses were therefore obliged either to deny the phenomena or to provide better alterative explanations of them. As we shall see, the seventeenth century critics of Scholastic Aristotelianism pursued a mixed strategy in this regard, denying outright some of the supposed phenomena to be explained, and seeking to account for others in terms that require only accidental forms (arrangements of independently existing parts). In Descartes's *Principles of Philosophy*, Hobbes's *De Corpore*, Gassendi's *Syntagma*, and Boyle's *Origin of Forms and Qualities*, we can study the mechanical philosophers' responses to the above set of Scholastic arguments for SFs.

A closely related issue concerns the actuality or otherwise of the parts of a body, a topic that has received in-depth treatment in an admirable recent study by Thomas Holden.[13] One might think it self-evident that division cannot create distinct parts but only makes manifest the distinct parts that were already present. If I cut a cake into two halves, is not the distinct existence of the two halves a precondition of the possibility of division? If you share this intuition, you are an advocate of what Holden calls the "actual parts doctrine," along with the majority of early modern philosophers.[14] If you reject it, and insist that division creates parts rather than merely revealing them, you are an advocate of the "potential parts doctrine," along with the Aristotelians and a handful of early modern figures such as Kenelm Digby and Thomas Hobbes.[15] Neither position, as we shall see, is without its problems.

If you accept the actual parts doctrine, can you also accept infinite divisibility? Even a physically indivisible Democritean atom is an extended thing, with its own size and shape. It follows that, according to the actual parts doctrine, it is – at least in the eyes of the philosopher, if not those of the physicist – a compound thing, made up of its distinct, albeit physically inseparable, parts. Given the actual parts doctrine, it seems that infinite divisibility entails actually infinite dividedness – every body will be made up of an actually infinite aggregate of parts. Our minds inevitably search for the last or ultimate parts, parts which, according to the actual parts doctrine, must always be "there" waiting to be uncovered. But if these are extended, they cannot be ultimate parts, because anything extended consists of parts. Are our ultimate parts mere point atoms, themselves unextended? Galileo sketches such a matter theory in Day One of the *Two New Sciences*,[16] arguing that the only account of the continuum that satisfactorily combines the actual parts intuition with the geometrization of nature is that continuous magnitudes consist of actual infinities of unextended point particles. But even the genius of Galileo couldn't handle the obvious objections, or anticipate developments in nineteenth century mathematics. How does a collection of unextended point atoms fill space? Can one point atom be adjacent to another, or are there always point vacua between them? Are there more point atoms in a larger body than a smaller one? To avoid biting the bullet with Galileo and accepting actually infinite dividedness, actual parts theorists might find themselves obliged to reject infinite divisibility. But that, as Holden sees, would bring the actual parts theory into conflict with the geometrization of nature.

If you reject the actual parts doctrine, you can endorse infinite divisibility by drawing its teeth. For the Aristotelian, to say that something is infinitely divisible means no more than that it can be divided as many times as one chooses, or that no given finite number of cuts will ever exhaust its potency for further division. Infinite divisibility does not entail actually infinite dividedness, and the search for *ultimate* parts of the continuum can be dismissed as incoherent. The parts are not ontologically prior to the whole, so questions about their number (finite or infinite?) and nature (extended or unextended?) do not arise. Any given continuum may be divided as many times – in thought or in physical reality – as one chooses, but the idea that each such cut gets us one step closer to a bedrock level of ultimate constituents is illusory. The attractions of the theory are obvious: it provides an account of the continuum that is consistent with geometry while avoiding a lot of awkward and unanswerable questions of metaphysics. The problems are equally obvious. Many critics will simply repeat the intuition underlying the actual parts doctrine: how can one separate the left-hand part of the cube from the right-hand part unless they are really distinct? More precisely, mustn't there be an *actual* ground for the Aristotelian potency for further division? Positing a potency, critics of the potential parts doctrine will insist, can serve either a descriptive or an explanatory role. No one will object to saying that a magnet has the power to attract iron, or that salt has the power of dissolving in water, or that any extended object has the potency for division, so long as these are merely descriptive uses of the terms "power" and "potency." What we want to understand, of course, is what it is that provides the *actual ground* of these powers. And in the case of the potency for further division, it is the actual existence of distinct parts that – if true – would provide the most natural and obvious explanation.

The search for actual grounds for Scholastic "potencies" is, as we shall see, one of the most prominent themes of the mechanical philosophy of the seventeenth century.

Questions about "act" and "potency" are also at the heart of the debate about the status of the elements in a compound. In his influential treatise *On Coming-to-Be and Passing-Away* Aristotle had argued that chemical composition is not merely a matter of the mechanical aggregation of unaltered particles (like a mixture of grains of wheat and barley) but involves interaction between the elements FAWE, producing a new form.[17] A true combination (*mixis*) of the elements only occurs, he insists, when the resulting product is a *homoeomer*, that is when every part is of the same nature as the whole. So, when the elements FAWE are mixed to produce a compound such as iron, beech wood, or human flesh, that compound has its own specific form. This new form C, the form of the compound, so dominates the matter that any part of something with form C is itself C. Although FAWE have gone into the making of C, not even the eagle-eyed Lynceus could discern bits of FAWE within the resulting compound. Every part of iron is iron; every part of beech wood is beech wood; every part of flesh is flesh.

This doctrine of *mixis*, Aristotle saw, raises an obvious difficulty. It seems, on the face of it, as if the original elements FAWE have simply ceased to be in the formation of C.[18] But if this is so, we no longer have an account of chemical combination, and we can no longer speak of FAWE as the elements out of which all other material things are composed. On the face of it, Aristotle falls into contradiction at this point. If every part of C is C (not fire, or air, or water, or earth), then it seems that FAWE have been destroyed and not combined in the formation of C. But we were searching for a coherent account of combination that does not reduce it to ceasing to be and coming to be. Once again, the protean concept of "potency" is brought into play to evade outright contradiction:

> Since, however, some things are-potentially while others are-actually, the constituents combined in a compound can "be" in a sense and yet "not-be". The compound may be-actually other than the constituents from which it has resulted; nevertheless each of them may still be-potentially what it was before they were combined, and both of them may survive undestroyed.[19]

The elements survive potentially in the compound in two senses: they can be extracted from it, and some of their powers remain, albeit in tempered or weakened forms.[20] (Living flesh, for example, retains a little of the heating power of its component fire). But what becomes of the SFs of the elements in the compound? The great Islamic commentators on Aristotle provided idiosyncratic readings. According to Avicenna, the SFs exist but in an "unawakened" sense, that is without their characteristic properties, being "subordinated" to the form of the compound C. This gives Avicenna a pluralist view, allowing several distinct forms to inform the same matter. According to the rival account of Averroes, the forms themselves are attenuated in the mixture. In Thomas Aquinas's discussion of the issue, both of these positions are explicitly rejected in favour of what Aquinas sees as a more authentically Aristotelian position.[21] Forms, Aquinas urges against Averroes, are not the sorts of things susceptible to more or less – an SF is either present in some portion of matter or it is not. But neither can there be several forms present in the same matter in a relation of subordination, so Avicenna's pluralism is also rejected in favour of a strict monism.

Aquinas takes himself to be articulating an authentically Aristotelian account of the status of the elements in compounds. But it is easy to see how his argument can be turned to distinctly un-Aristotelian ends. He insists that the forms of FAWE cannot coexist in *the same* portion of matter either with one another or with the form of the compound C. Nothing can be both fire and water, or fire and flesh. It follows that if the forms of the elements do actually continue to exist in the compound, they must inform *different* portions of the compound body, which will therefore not be perfectly homogeneous. As we shall see later, seventeenth century chemists thought they could provide good empirical evidence for the *actual* existence of the elements (either FAWE, or some alternatives) in compounds, and thus in turn for a particulate matter theory.[22] If Aristotle defines a true "mixt" as perfectly homogeneous, it may simply follow that there are no such things in nature. Once again, the Scholastics provided the conceptual framework, the essential terminology, and the key questions that would drive seventeenth century developments in matter theory.

4. The Cartesian challenge

Educated at the prestigious Jesuit college of La Flèche, he was well versed in Scholastic Aristotelianism, but remained singularly unimpressed by the lack of clarity of central notions such as that of SF. The natural philosophers, he felt, were trying to explain the obscure (the phenomena of nature) by the still more obscure (SFs), and had no way of determining anything with certainty. The mathematical sciences, by contrast, offered both clarity and certainty. The application of mathematics to nature in so-called mixed mathematics (optics, acoustics, mechanics) offered the prospect of a style of explanation involving only clearly conceived notions (shape, motion, arrangement of parts), and as such clearly preferable to the forms and qualities of the schoolmen. Under the influence of such figures as Isaac Beeckman and Marin Mersenne, the young Descartes set out to show that the whole of nature could be explained in such purely mechanical terms. The resulting treatise, *Le Monde* (*The World*), was written between 1629 and 1633, but was to remain unpublished until 1664, long after Descartes's death.

In chapter 2 of *Le Monde*, Descartes discusses the heat and light of fire. For the Aristotelian, fire has its own characteristic SF, and Heat is one of the four most fundamental natural qualities (HCDM). Descartes insists, however, that all such forms and qualities are redundant:

> When flame burns wood or some other similar material, we can see with the naked eye that it sets the minute parts of the wood in motion and separates them from one another, thus transforming the finer parts into fire, air, and smoke, and leaving the coarser parts as ashes. Others may, if they wish, imagine the form of fire, the quality of heat, and the process of burning to be completely different things in the wood. For my part, I am afraid of mistakenly supposing there is anything more in the wood than what I see must necessarily be in it, and so I am content to limit my conception to the motion of its parts.[23]

The crucial claim here is that the manifest effects of fire on burning bodies can be explained in terms of a particular kind of local motion (a rapid agitation of the minute parts), and cannot be explained without it. The supposed forms and qualities of the schools are, in explanatory terms, both idle and redundant. They explain nothing, and all the phenomena can be explained without them. In chapter 5, Descartes goes on to introduce his own account of the elements, differentiating them from one another simply in terms of the sizes, shapes, and motions of their parts. He responds to the anticipated objection in the following terms:

> If you find it strange that in explaining these elements I do not use the qualities called "heat", "cold", "moisture" and "dryness" – as the philosophers do – I shall say to you that these qualities themselves seem to me to need explanation. Indeed, unless I am mistaken, not only these four qualities but all the others as well, including even the forms of inanimate bodies, can be explained without the need to suppose anything in their matter other than the motion, size, shape, and arrangement of its parts.[24]

Descartes goes on, in chapter 6, to describe an imaginary new world composed entirely of the matter he has described. Because this is a mere thought experiment, an exercise in "what if?" reasoning, we are free to set our own terms:

> Now since we are taking the liberty of fashioning this matter as we fancy, let us attribute to it, if we may, a nature in which there is absolutely nothing that everyone cannot know as perfectly as possible. To this end, let us expressly suppose that it does not have the form of earth, fire, or air, or any other specific form, like that of wood, stone, or metal. Let us also suppose that it lacks the qualities of being hot or cold, dry or moist, light or heavy, and of having any taste, smell, sound, colour, light, or other such quality in the nature of which there might be said to be something which is not known clearly by everyone.[25]

What is known "as perfectly as possible" and "clearly by everyone" is extension in three dimensions and the familiar modes of size, shape, and motion. The nature of the imagined matter of this imaginary world is through-and-through intelligible. Every peasant can grasp size and shape and local motion, although of course it will take a mathematician to articulate the more advanced parts of geometry and kinematics. This supposed matter, Descartes continues, is entirely *actual*, and thus quite distinct from the prime matter of the schoolmen:

> On the other hand, let us not also think that this matter is the "prime matter" of the philosophers, which they have stripped so thoroughly of all its forms and qualities that nothing remains in it which can be clearly understood. Let us rather conceive it as a real, perfectly solid body which uniformly fills the entire length, breadth and depth of this huge space in the midst of which we have brought our mind to rest. Thus, each of its parts always occupies a part of that space which it fits so easily that it could neither fill a larger one nor squeeze into a smaller; nor could it, while remaining there, allow another body to find a place there.[26]

The error of the schoolmen, he explains, and the source of their unintelligible notion of prime matter, was their attempt to distinguish matter from extension:

> Thus I may tell them at this point that, unless I am mistaken, the whole difficulty they face with their matter arises simply from their wanting to distinguish

it from its own quantity and from its external extension – that is, from the property it has of occupying space. In this, however, I am quite willing for them to think they are right, for I have no intention of stopping to contradict them. But they should also not find it strange if I suppose that the quantity of the matter I have described does not differ from its substance any more than number differs from the things numbered. Nor should they find it strange if I conceive its extension, or the property it has of occupying space, not as an accident, but as its true form or essence.[27]

Descartes tells his intended readers that he is writing a fiction, an account of a world that God could have created in the "imaginary" space beyond the Heavens. But if this fictitious world exhibits all the same phenomena as our world, readers will naturally be led to ask how we know that our actual world is a world of prime matter and SFs rather than the radically simplified world of Descartes's imagination. The argumentative strategy here is transparent. If the principles he employs to construct his new world are (1) superior in terms of their intelligibility (which can scarcely be denied) and (2) adequate to explain the phenomena of our experience (which would be denied by his opponents), then we ought to prefer his principles to those of his Scholastic opponents as an account of our own actual world.

But *Le Monde* remained unpublished during Descartes's lifetime. The condemnation of Galileo in 1633 shocked him, and he wrote to Mersenne in November of that year informing him that he had decided not to publish.[28] Descartes may have worried about *Le Monde*'s rejection of Scholastic matter theory. This was, given the centrality of the Eucharist to Christian theology, an obvious source of concern for the authorities of the Church, and it has been suggested in one recent study that Galileo got into trouble as much for his atomistic matter theory as for his Copernicanism.[29]

In any event, Descartes held back on publishing his matter theory for almost a decade. Inattentive readers of the *Meditations*, their minds occupied by the lofty topics of God and the soul, might not have noticed the claim in the Sixth Meditation to have a distinct idea of body, "in so far as this is simply an extended, non-thinking thing."[30] But of course Descartes's epistemological project of purging the mind of the prejudices of the senses is intended to provide the foundations of his mechanistic physics as well as of his metaphysics of God and the soul. This is explicitly acknowledged in a well-known letter to Mersenne of 1641:

> I may tell you, between ourselves, that these six *Meditations* contain the entire foundations of my physics. But it is not necessary to say so, if you please, since that might make it harder for those who favour Aristotle to approve them. I hope that those who read them will gradually accustom themselves to my principles and recognise the truth in them before they notice that they destroy those of Aristotle.[31]

Descartes favoured, at this period, an indirect attack on Aristotelian natural philosophy. He would advance his own views, based on a homogenous matter consisting of extension alone and differentiated only by size, shape, and local motion of parts and see how far he could take this explanatory programme. If it turned out that he could explain all the difficult phenomena of nature (e.g. heat, light, gravity, magnetism) in these purely mechanistic terms, readers would gradually realise that the SFs of the schoolmen were simply redundant. This strategy is made explicit in the *Meteors* of 1637, in which the qualitative homogeneity of Cartesian matter receives its clearest statement:

> I regard these particles as all being composed of one single kind of matter, and believe that each of them could be divided repeatedly in infinitely many ways, and that there is no more difference between them than there is between stones of various different shapes cut from the same rock. Bear in mind, too, that to avoid a breach with the philosophers, I have no wish to deny any further items which they may imagine in bodies over and above what I have described, such as "substantial forms" or their "real qualities" and so on. It simply seems to me that my arguments must be all the more acceptable in so far as I can make them depend on fewer things.[32]

In a letter to Regius in January 1642, Descartes rebukes his Dutch disciple for taking an unnecessarily confrontational tone:

> For example, why did you need to reject openly substantial forms and real qualities? Do you not remember that on p164 of my *Meteorology*, I said quite expressly that I do not at all reject or deny them, but simply found them unnecessary in setting out my explanations? If you had taken this course, everybody in your audience would have rejected them as soon as they saw they were useless, and in the mean time you would not have become so unpopular with your colleagues.[33]

On occasion, however, Descartes himself could still be provoked into going further and revealing more of his thought. In his replies to the Sixth Objections, he defends his arguments for mind-body dualism in the Sixth Meditation. After setting out his own conception of body as "something which has length, breadth and depth and is capable of various shapes and motions,"[34] he finds himself seeking to account for the commonsense (and Aristotelian) view that matter also possesses real qualities such as gravity. From our own immediate experience, he says, we know what it is for a mind to be united with a body and capable of moving it.[35] When we think of gravity as a real moving power in the heavy body, we are tacitly projecting this model outwards onto inanimate nature. We think of the power of gravity as coextensive with the heavy body, just as we naturally think of the human mind as wholly present in all of its associated living body:

> But what makes it especially clear that my idea of gravity was taken largely from the idea I had of the mind is the fact that I thought that gravity carried bodies towards the centre of the earth as if it had some knowledge of the centre within itself. For this surely could not happen without knowledge, and there can be no knowledge except in a mind.[36]

By replacing the Aristotelian notion of gravity as the inner striving of a heavy body towards its natural place with his own rival account of a purely external impulse by currents of subtle matter, Descartes marks a decisive shift in natural philosophy. How the human mind moves its own body is, he thinks, sufficiently well understood *from experience*, but we should not seek to use this particular primitive notion as a source for further generalization in natural philosophy. We should not seek to represent growing oak trees, flowing streams, and falling stones as significantly like our own intentional bodily movements. The SFs and real qualities of the Scholastics are rejected as products of anthropomorphism, stemming from the thoughtless prejudices of childhood. Once the intellect has been properly purged of the prejudices of the senses and the imagination, we will realise that such anthropomorphism is simply groundless, and will thus come to embrace the mechanical philosophy.

This new philosophy would receive its most detailed formulation in the *Principles of Philosophy* (1644). At *Principles* I.53, we are told that each substance has one principal attribute which "constitutes its nature and essence, and to which all its other properties are referred."[37] For corporeal substance or body, this essential attribute is extension in length, breadth, and depth. Every property of every material thing is a "mode" or modification of extension, and thus cannot be conceived to have any existence of its own distinct from extension. In part 2 of the *Principles* he develops the implications of this thesis for natural philosophy. The nature of body, he tells us, "consists not in weight, hardness, colour, or the like, but simply in extension."[38] This immediately entails that there can be no true vacuum or absolutely empty space, and that condensation and rarefaction occur by means of the inflow and outflow of currents of a very subtle and all-pervasive fluid.[39] The Aristotelians were wrong to think that the same amount of matter could fill more or less space: because matter just is three-dimensional extension, quantity of matter cannot be distinguished from bulk or volume. Instead of explaining condensation as the packing of more matter into a given volume, we must explain as the packing of more *gross* matter (characterised in terms of particle size), into a given volume, and the corresponding squeezing out of the *subtle* matter from between the particles of gross matter. This, Descartes insists, is the only intelligible account of condensation and rarefaction:

> I really do not see what has prompted others to say that rarefaction occurs through an increase in quantity, in preference to explaining it by means of this example of the sponge. It is true that when air or water is rarefied, we do not see any pores being made larger, or any new body coming to fill them up. But to invent something unintelligible so as to provide a purely verbal explanation of rarefaction is surely less rational than inferring the existence of pores or gaps which are made larger, and supposing that some new body comes and fills them.[40]

The Aristotelian account, he insists, depends too much on the prejudices of the senses, and ends up embracing the "complete contradiction" of assuming that a body could grow in size without the addition of new matter. But this argument looks too quick and may simply beg the question. We saw earlier that the Scholastics had both conceptual and empirical difficulties over the notion of "quantity of matter," but their thesis that *quantitas materiae* must be distinguished from bulk or volume, and that matter can fill space with greater or lesser intensity, is not manifestly self-contradictory. We can grant Descartes his claim that the geometer's concept of extended magnitude was the only clear and distinct concept of quantity he and his contemporaries possessed, and that the Scholastics' notion was much more vague and indeterminate; it does not follow that the Scholastic notion was incapable of being made precise, perhaps in dynamic terms.[41]

From the thesis that the essence of matter simply consists in three-dimensional extension, Descartes proceeds to derive a number of further theses. Let us list a few of the most important propositions of Cartesian matter theory:

1. A vacuum, that is space entirely void of material substance, is a contradiction in terms.[42]
2. Atoms are impossible.[43]
3. The extension of the world (i.e. of the physical universe) is indefinite.[44]
4. There is a single matter of the Heavens and the earth.[45]
5. All the variety and diversity in matter depends on motion.[46]

These theses can be seen as direct implications of the claim at *Principles* II.4, that the nature or essence of matter consists in extension alone. A broad picture is painted of an "indefinite" physical universe (Descartes prefers to reserve the positive term "infinite" for God), consisting of a single homogeneous matter, differentiated and diversified solely by the local motion of its constituent particles. These particles are, in principle, divisible *ad infinitum*: Descartes sees the rejection of atomism as straightforward:

> For if there were any atoms, then no matter how small we imagined them to be, they would necessarily have to be extended; and hence we could in our thought divide each of them into two or more smaller parts, and hence recognize their divisibility. For anything we can divide in our thought must, for that very reason, be known to be divisible; so if we were to judge it to be indivisible, our judgment would conflict with our knowledge. Even if we imagine that God has chosen to bring it about that some particle of matter is incapable of being divided into smaller particles, it will still not be correct, strictly speaking, to call this particle indivisible. For, by making it indivisible by any of his creatures, God certainly could not take away his own power of dividing it, since it is quite impossible for him to diminish his own power, as has been noted above. Hence, strictly speaking, the particle will remain divisible, since it is divisible by its very nature.[47]

Even if God were to exercise His omnipotent will in establishing a sort of cosmic "superglue" binding the parts of a given corpuscle together in such a way that no natural power could divide them, those parts would remain *really distinct* from one another. In *Principles* I.60, Descartes had earlier explained this notion of a real distinction, distinguishing it from a merely modal distinction or a distinction of reason. Two substances, he explains, are really distinct when each can exist without the other, as ascertained by the test of clear and distinct conceivability:

> For example, even though we may not yet know for certain that any extended or corporeal substance exists in reality, the mere fact that we have an idea of such a substance enables us to be certain that it is capable of existing. And we can also be certain that, if it exists, each and every part of it, as delimited by us in our thought, is really distinct from the other parts of the same substance.[48]

Descartes thus appears, in the terminology of Thomas Holden, to be a strict advocate of the *actual parts doctrine*, believing that the parts of every body are really distinct prior to and independent of any process of division.[49]

Does Descartes admit a plurality of material substances? If every part of every body is indeed a "complete substance," it would seem to follow that every material thing contains an actual infinity of distinct material substances. But this raises obvious difficulties. The actual parts doctrine seems – at least at first sight[50] – to entail the thesis of ultimate parts, the claim that every body has an actual ultimate constitution out of all the distinct parts into which it could ever be divided. These would then be candidates for substancehood, because each is capable of independent existence; the bodies composed of them will merely be aggregates out of these independent units, dependent for their existence on the existence and ordering of their parts. But these ultimate parts could not themselves be extended (because every extended thing is divisible, and hence composed of further parts), nor could they be mere unextended points (it was a commonplace that a continuum cannot be constituted out of points). Descartes himself seems content to leave this matter deeply mysterious, contenting himself with some dark utterances about the inability of our finite minds to understand the infinite. But the search for genuine substances in the material world could not lightly be set aside, and led, as we shall see, to some striking developments in post-Cartesian matter theory.

In Geraud de Cordemoy's *Six Discours sur la Distinction et l'union de Corps et de l'Ame* (1666), the first discourse marks a sharp distinction between *corps* and *matière*, arguing that *corps* (body) is best defined as "an extended substance," and *matière* (matter) as "an assemblage of bodies."[51] The division of a portion of matter must, Cordemoy argues, terminate after a finite number of steps. After n steps, he claims, one will have a portion of matter consisting of only two bodies, so division must terminate after $n + 1$ steps, because a body is a substance, and a substance is indivisible. The search for substances to serve as indivisible units thus leads Cordemoy to embrace – for metaphysical reasons rather than physical – a form of atomism. Every portion of matter, on this theory, contains some finite (albeit no doubt very large) number of atoms, and can thus be divided into just that many distinct parts. Although mainstream Cartesians dismissed this argument for atomism as blatantly question begging, and rejected Cordemoy's extended atoms as unintelligible, Leibniz praised him for demanding genuine units as a condition of intelligibility. In a letter to Arnauld in 1686, Leibniz writes as follows:

> I remember that Cordemoy, in his treatise *On the Distinction between Body and Soul*, thought he needed to admit atoms, or extended indivisible bodies, to save substantial unity in bodies, so as to find something fixed to constitute a simple being. But you rightly concluded that I am not of that opinion. It appears that Cordemoy recognized something of the truth, but he did not yet see what the true notion of substance consists in; but this is the key to the most important knowledge.[52]

In the *New System of Nature* (1695), Leibniz repeats this mixture of praise and criticism. Cordemoy, we are told, had a sound insight (the need for substantial units to serve as the metaphysical substratum of nature), but misunderstood its implications, and thus mistakenly opted for material atoms. The bodies of our experience, Leibniz reminds us, are all compound things:

> Yet if there were no true substantial unities, there would be nothing substantial or real in the collection. That was what forced Cordemoy to abandon Descartes and to embrace the Democritean doctrine of atoms in order to find a true unity. But *atoms of matter* are contrary to reason.[53]

The search for substance in the material realm thus led Cordemoy *down* to the level of the atoms. The same search led Spinoza *up* to the level of the material universe considered as a whole, or, in Spinoza's terms, God-conceived-under-the-attribute-of-extension. Descartes, we have seen, emphasised the real distinction of the parts of matter. But is this a distinction at the level of substance or only of modes? If God were to annihilate the contents of a closed vessel, Descartes claims in his arguments against the void, the walls of the vessel would come together.[54] But has any extended substance actually been annihilated here? The physical universe remains, presumably, as "indefinite" in extent as before. Where there was air before (half an inch to the right of the glass of the left-hand wall, say) there is now more glass (what had been the right-hand wall), but no recognizable portion of extension has ceased to be. A region of space that was airy has become glassy, and other such qualitative changes have occurred elsewhere to compensate (the glass of the vessel has moved but has not increased in volume), but these are mere modal changes. By identifying material substance with extension in three dimensions, Cartesianism seems to lend itself to this transformation. There is one and only one material substance (the physical universe), diversely modified to produce bodies of various kinds.[55]

5. Gassendi and the revival of Epicurean atomism

Throughout the Middle Ages, the texts of Aristotle provided the basis of the philosophy curriculum. It followed, of course, that Democritean atomism was never entirely forgotten, because generations of students were taught Aristotle's objections to Democritus in the *Physics* and the treatise *On Coming-to-Be and Passing-Away*. But such familiarity with ancient atomism would have been fragmentary and unsystematic. The work of humanist scholars in the fifteenth century helped to fill the gaps: a Latin edition of Diogenes Laertius's *Lives of the Most Eminent Philosophers* appeared in 1433 and provided much information (albeit heavily anecdotal) about Epicurus and his school. The publication in 1473 of Lucretius's great Latin poem *De Rerum Natura* gave evidence that Epicurean atomism provided a systematic body of natural philosophy to rival that of Aristotle. Philosophers such as Giordano Bruno in Italy and Thomas Hariot in England came to endorse versions of atomism, often mixing elements from different traditions.[56] Francis Bacon praises Democritus for some aspects of his natural philosophy such as the actuality of matter and the central causal role played by local motion, although ultimately rejecting the void and the immutability of atoms in the *Novum Organum*. By around 1600, it can safely be said, ancient atomism (whether Democritean or Epicurean in inspiration) was once again a living option for the natural philosopher.

One obvious problem, of course, was the long-standing association of atomism with irreligion. We don't know Democritus's views about the gods in detail, but given his materialism and the central role played in his system by the chance collisions of atoms, he seems far removed from mainstream theism. In the case of the Epicureans, we know that, although they admitted the existence of the pagan gods and goddesses of antiquity, they flatly denied that the gods had created our world, or cared about our doings, or would reward our virtues and punish our vices in an afterlife. The Epicureans' outright denial of creation, providence, and the immortality of the soul made them, in the eyes of Christian theologians, atheists in all but name. It was left to Pierre Gassendi (1592–1655) to "baptise" Epicurus, that is to detach the atomic theory from its association with irreligion. We need only suppose, Gassendi argues, that God has created a vast but finite stock of atoms, given to each its own motive force (*vis motrix, pondus*), and set them in motion in endless empty space, and we can reconcile atomism with the Christian doctrines of creation and providence. Immortality proves rather more difficult: Gassendi has to argue that the Epicurean theory of the soul as a "vapour" or "breath" that is dissipated at death captures only its "lower" aspects, and that an immaterial and immortal soul is needed to explain the "higher" aspects of human mentality.

In a series of weighty tomes, culminating in the posthumous *Syntagma Philosophicum* (1658), Gassendi set out this new version of atomism, seeking to reformulate Epicurean doctrines in such a way as to render them compatible both with Christian dogma and with the emerging natural sciences. Throughout the second half of the seventeenth century, his system was regarded as the main modern rival to that of Descartes. In England, Walter Charleton disseminated this system in his *Physiologia Epicuro-Gassendo-Charletoniana* (1654); in France, François Bernier's *Abrégé de la Philosophie de M. Gassendi* (1678) helped to spread the word. Charleton was an important source for both Boyle and Newton,[57] whereas Bernier was on friendly terms with Locke. Perceptive critic Leibniz even suggests, in his *New Essays*, that the character Philalethes (the Locke character) is a disciple of Gassendi and Bernier.[58]

In opposition to Descartes, who denied any real distinction between space and matter, or between a body and its "internal" place,[59] Gassendi draws a sharp distinction between the incorporeal dimensions of space and the corporeal dimensions of the bodies that fill it. Atoms are distinguished from empty space by their *antitypy* or complete mutual impenetrability, an all-or-nothing property that must be distinguished from the observable properties it will be invoked to explain. Along with impenetrable atoms, as part of the same explanatory package deal, go interstitial vacua. When mercury amalgamates with gold, or sweat oozes through our skin, we need to postulate invisibly small pores to explain the phenomenon without assuming any interpenetration of bodies. With regard to the precise ontological status of his void space – is it substance or accident? – Gassendi is studiedly careful, suggesting that space may not fit neatly into the traditional Aristotelian framework of the categories. Space and time, he writes in the *Syntagma*, are *res verae* (true things) and *entia realis* (real entities) that are nevertheless not substances in the Aristotelian sense.[60]

The atoms of Gassendi, like those of the ancient atomists, are all made of the same homogeneous and qualitatively undifferentiated stuff – atoms are not intrinsically fiery, airy, watery, or earthy. Atoms are differentiated by their sizes, shapes, and their innate endowments with motive force.[61] Each atom is physically indivisible for the reason given by the ancient atomists: division would require the presence of inner void, but an atom is perfectly solid, therefore without inner void, and hence indivisible, at least in the course of nature. But these atoms still possess sizes and shapes, and so consist of spatially distinct parts: each atom will still appear, when represented by either the intellect or the imagination, as a *compound* thing. The issue crops up in the course of the exchanges with Descartes prompted by Gassendi's Fifth Objections to the *Meditations*. Descartes claims that the infinite divisibility of matter simply follows from our clear and distinct idea of it as extension in three dimensions; Gassendi retorts that this idea of matter as infinitely divisible may be a mere abstraction, useful in mathematics but of no relevance to physics; Descartes explodes with a torrent of abuse and invective. If we cannot argue from our clear and distinct ideas to the properties of the corresponding things, he rages, we must "entirely close the door to reason and content ourselves with being monkeys or parrots rather than men."[62]

Gassendi's English disciple Walter Charleton goes one step further than his master on this issue. The natural philosopher, he argues in his *Physiologia*, need not trouble himself with the abstractions of the mathematicians. The geometer may assume infinite divisibility if he pleases. This in turn will entail an actual infinity of parts in every continuous magnitude – Charleton is quite explicit in his statements of the actual parts doctrine:

> Those things which can exist being actually separate; are really distinct: but Parts can exist being actually separate; therefore they are really distinct, even before division. For Division doth not give them their peculiar Entity and Individuation, which is essential to them and the root of Distinction.[63]

The geometer may assume infinite divisibility, Charleton admits, "not that he doth, or can really understand it so, but that many convenient conclusions, and no considerable incongruities, follow from the conclusions thereof."[64] Pressed on the question of whether the assumption is true or false, Charleton is blunt: "Our expedient is, that, though we should concede those suppositions to be false, yet may they afford true and necessary conclusions: every novice in logick well knowing how to extract undeniable conclusions out of the most false propositions."[65]

Charleton thus seems committed to the Epicurean theory of a granular space and atoms consisting of mathematically indivisible minimal parts.[66] If the "grain" of space is very fine, the geometers' assumption of infinite divisibility will be, as he suggests, literally false but useful for purposes of computation. There is, however, no need to assume that Gassendi would have endorsed such a radical position. He seems to have been content to regard the constitution of the atom and the unshakeable cohesion of its parts as simply a brute fact, established no doubt by inscrutable divine decree.

Given a stock of hard, rigid, immutable atoms, each with its characteristic size, shape, and endowment of motive force,[67] Gassendi sets out to explain the various qualities of observable bodies. Explanations might take us all the way down to the properties of the atoms themselves: there might be special atoms (qualified by size, shape, and motive force) for certain properties. Cold, for example, is not (as for Descartes) a mere privation of that rapid agitation of the particles of a body that constitutes heat; there are special "frigorific atoms," bulky and unwieldy atoms that inhibit this agitation.[68] Most atomistic explanations of qualities will not, however, take this form. More often, Gassendi and his disciples will appeal to the *textures* of compound bodies to explain their characteristic properties and powers. Here "texture" is a technical term, referring to the arrangements and internecine local motions of the parts of a compound body. "Parts," in this context, may refer either to atoms or to relatively stable complexes of atoms: there is no reason to suppose that every qualitative change or new generation in the course of nature requires a resolution of matter all the way down to the atoms. If we seek to explain colour, for example, we will find ourselves talking about the arrangement of the superficial parts of bodies and the effects such arrangements produce on incident light. But lots of very different substances can be red, or blue, or green, and colours are easily altered. The colour of a body might thus indicate merely the arrangement of relatively gross and compound corpuscles at its surface and tell us little or nothing about its component atoms.

The problems facing seventeenth century atomism were many and varied. There is, as we have already seen, a difficulty about the composition of the atoms themselves. They have a variety of sizes and shapes and so consist of distinct parts. Are they, in principle, divisible *ad infinitum*? Do we side with Charleton and deny the infinite divisibility even of space, or do we follow the more modest approach of Gassendi and say that the composition of the parts of the atom is simply a mystery to us? If mere lack of an inner void is to explain physical indivisibility, surely atoms should coalesce rather than rebound whenever they come into contact face to face? And even if this problem could be overcome, another would immediately loom. Perfectly rigid bodies must alter velocity *instantaneously* on collision – the laws of such collisions would have to be radically different from those of the colliding bodies of our experience, in which (to use modern terminology for the moment) some of the kinetic energy of their motion is turned into the potential energy of elastic deformation.[69] Arguments of this kind would be pressed by Leibniz when he claimed that atoms of matter are "contrary to reason."

6. Chemical atomism

Before going on to discuss the views of Boyle and Newton, we must at least say a few words about a type of particulate matter theory quite distinct from Epicurean atomism. Strange though it may sound, the sources for this theory can actually be found in the works of Aristotle. In book 1 of the *Physics*, Aristotle launches an argument against Anaxagoras that presupposes the existence of *natural minima* of organic materials such as flesh and bone.[70] Commentators would extend this theory to the elements FAWE, and the resulting theory of natural minima would receive extensive development in the Middle Ages.[71] And in book 4 of the *Meteorology*, Aristotle makes considerable use of explanations in terms of pores and corpuscles to explain phenomena such as the insolubility of terracotta and the combustibility of wood.[72] So although the authority of Aristotle could plainly be cited against Democritean (and, by extension, Epicurean) atomism, it by no means followed that he was hostile to all forms of particulate or corpuscular matter theory.

According to the theory of natural minima, there is a natural size limit beneath which a given type of stuff cannot exist as such but will undergo corruption, its matter being taken over the form of some surrounding body. (This natural limit need not be an absolute one, but may be environment dependent, as a number of the Scholastics insisted.) The existence of such limits, even if established, would not, of course, establish the actual existence of *bona fide* particles with distinct identities and histories, like Democritean atoms. But the natural minima tradition seems to have undergone a gradual transformation, over the centuries, from thinking of minima simply as natural limits to thinking of them as abiding and actual particles.[73] This remains, of course, a qualitative matter theory: atoms of fire remain hot and dry, atoms of water cold and wet, and bodies with these opposed qualities will necessarily *interact* when minima of FAWE combine to form compound bodies. The coming to be of a compound is no mere mechanical aggregation of abiding and unchanging atoms; it involves, characteristically, a new dominant form, to which the forms of the elements FAWE are subordinated.

In the Middle Ages, this Aristotelian theory of natural minima would become fused with certain chemical doctrines regarding the constitution of metals. According to the *Summa Perfectionis* of the Latin pseudo-Geber (late thirteenth century) the minima of the elements FAWE are held together in a "very strong composition" to make the least particles of the two "principles" of the alchemists, mercury and sulphur, and these in turn combine to form the higher-level particles of metals. If we regard the minima of the elements as effectively atomic or C_0 (level zero of composition), the particles of mercury and sulphur will be C_1 (first level of composition), the particles of gold and silver, copper and iron will be C_2 (second level of composition), and so on. We have here the beginnings of a hierarchic matter theory combining the elements of Aristotle, the mercury-sulphur theory of the alchemists, and the emphasis on aggregation and disaggregation characteristic of atomism. If each minimum of fire retains its identity in a particle of sulphur, and each particle of sulphur retains its identity in a particle of iron, we have a theory of mixture that implicitly denies Aristotle's insistence on the perfect homogeneity of the compound.[74] To be sure, every portion of gold will consist of C_2s each of which is gold, so in that sense it is homogeneous, but if we could penetrate more deeply into its constitution there is no reason to suppose that it is gold all the way down.

In the seventeenth century, this kind of chemical atomism would find many advocates, perhaps the most prominent being the German doctor Daniel Sennert (1572–1637).[75] In works such as the *De Chymicorum* (1619) and *Hypomnemata Physica* (1636), Sennert articulates and defends a subtle and sophisticated hierarchic theory of the nature of matter, borrowing elements of atomism, Aristotelianism, and contemporary chemistry. Sennert accepts the existence of physically indivisible minima of FAWE, which he is inclined to identify with the atoms of Democritus. These smallest particles, he writes, "are called the minima of nature, atoms, and indivisible corpuscles of bodies. They owe their name to the fact that they cannot be further divided through natural processes, and reversely form the building blocks of all natural bodies."[76]

These so-called atoms are far removed from the rigid, homogeneous, qualityless atoms of Democritus. Each of the minima of fire retains the form and distinctive qualities of fire. Although the minima have distinct sizes, their *shapes* are hardly mentioned and seem not to have been considered of explanatory significance. Sennert accepts the identification of coming to be and ceasing to be with aggregation and disaggregation of particles that was characteristic of the atomist tradition, but his conception of the nature of these particles is still far removed from that of Democritus.

A new compound C comes to be when the elements FAWE are combined *per minima*, that is in a form of combination that reaches down to the smallest parts. But what becomes of the forms of the elements FAWE in the compound? This, Sennert admits, is a very difficult question, one of "total darkness."[77] Juxtaposed minima of fire and water must of course interact in virtue of their opposed qualities, producing a resulting compound C that at least appears perfectly homogeneous. This new compound C will have its own dominant form, to which the forms of FAWE are subordinated. The SF of C somehow imposes itself on all the material constituents of C, organising them into a genuine unity. As Sennert says, "natural things do not come into existence through a casual cooperation of atoms – even if perhaps Democritus thought so – but through a dominating superior form."[78]

This chemical atomic theory was believed to rest on a firm empirical footing, grounded in laboratory experience. If one takes an alloy of gold and silver, one cannot discern distinct gold and silver particles in the compound. But one can dissolve the silver in *aqua fortis* (our nitric acid), leaving the gold behind. The resulting solution of silver in *aqua fortis* (our silver nitrate) can be passed through filter paper without any loss of the dissolved silver, which can be extracted from the salt by standard means, gram for gram, with only the minute losses of normal experimental error.[79] According to the chemical atomic theory, this extraction of the silver from the alloy is explained by the presence of actual silver particles, albeit invisibly small and hence indiscernible by sense. On the rival Aristotelian theory of total mixture, one would have an unexplained "potency" of the alloy (to yield silver) without any actual ground. Worse still, there would be no reason, on the theory of total mixture, for gold and silver to be extractable from the alloy rather than other metals, or even nonmetals.[80] Although by no means demonstrative, this argument from superior explanatory power was found overwhelmingly persuasive by many seventeenth century chemists.

7. Boyle's corpuscular philosophy

In the writings of Robert Boyle (1627–91) we find a systematic attempt to articulate a theory of matter that is studiedly neutral between those of Descartes and Gassendi, stressing their similarities and downplaying their differences.[81] "I write," Boyle tells his readers at the start of the *Origin of Forms and Qualities*, "rather for the corpuscularians in general than any part of them."[82] On controversial issues such as atoms and the void, Boyle is very reluctant to take sides. The Boylean vacuum produced by his famous air pump may not be a true vacuum: all that we can be confident of from experience is that it is (almost) empty of air, not that it is a space entirely devoid of matter. (If light requires an ethereal medium, then the transmission of light through the Boylean vacuum proves the existence of such a subtle fluid in the vessel.) As for indivisibles, Boyle is similarly guarded and noncommittal. There are, he says, a "great store" of invisibly small corpuscles, each of which is so *solid* that "though it be mentally, and by divine Omnipotence divisible, yet by reason of its smallness and solidity nature doth scarce ever actually divide it; and these may in this sense be called *minima* or *prima naturalia*."[83]

This is a very weak claim. Boyle does not even claim that these *prima naturalia* are forever undivided, far less that they are indivisible. The latter claim of the atomists, he reminds us in the *History of Fluidity and Firmness*, needs proof: "For to say that it is the nature of every such corpuscle to be indivisible is but to give me cause to demand how that appears; for so important an assertion needs more than a bare affirmation for proof."[84]

The atomists, he reminds us, have given no adequate explanation for the supposedly unbreakable cohesion of the constituent parts of their atoms. If they say that it is the lack of inner void that explains cohesion, they owe us an account of why two atoms do not coalesce when they come into contact face to face.[85] Ultimately, their account of cohesion is no less mysterious and no more enlightening than those of rival natural philosophies. Boyle thus remains sceptical of the existence of *indivisibles* in any strict sense. But as he sees, this is irrelevant to the adoption of atomism as an explanatory programme in natural philosophy. Given a stock of physically *undivided* corpuscles, we can construct explanatory accounts of the forms and qualities of bodies in terms of their sizes, shapes, motions, and changing arrangements.

In part 1 of the *Sceptical Chymist*, Boyle's spokesman Carneades sets out his own positive account of the constitution of matter, in opposition to those of Aristotelians and chemical philosophers. We begin with a single universal matter, diversified by size, shape, and local motion:

> It seems not absurd to conceive, that at the first production of mixt bodies, the universal matter, whereof they among the other parts of the universe consisted, was actually divided, into little particles, of several sizes and shapes, variously moved.[86]

These least particles readily combine to form relatively stable clusters:

> Neither is it impossible that of these minute particles divers of the smallest and neighbouring ones were here and there associated into minute masses or clusters, and did by their collation constitute great store of such little primary concretions or masses, as were not easily dissipable into such particles, as composed them.[87]

For example, gold can be alloyed with other metals, dissolved in *aqua regia*, and precipitated out of such solution in a variety of salts, but the same quantity of gold remains available for extraction. The most natural explanation for such phenomena, Carneades continues, is that the particles of metals retain their identities in bodies of a higher degree of composition. The corpuscles of gold and mercury, he writes,

> though they be not primary concretions of the most minute particles of matter, but confessedly mixed bodies, are able to concur plentifully to the composition of several very differing bodies, without losing their own nature or texture, or having their cohesion violated by the divorce of their associated parts or ingredients.[88]

Given a single undifferentiated and universal matter (the stuff of the "atoms") all the immense variety of naturally occurring bodies can be constructed in the course of nature, which is of course simply the artifice of God. Just as we humans can create more and more complex machines out of iron, so God can create ever more complex bodies by combining the least particles to form C_1s, then these relatively stable C_1s to form C_2s, and so on. The distinction between the products of nature (which require SFs) and those of art or human contrivance (whose forms are merely accidental) is illusory. In both nature and art, forms are created and destroyed merely by the mechanical rearrangement of corpuscles: the chemist is merely the mechanic of the microrealm.[89]

Can any material substance be made out of any other, merely by rearranging its corpuscles to produce a new characteristic texture? In the *Origin of Forms and Qualities*, Boyle is typically reluctant to commit himself, but comes very close to a positive answer:

> Though I would not say that any thing can immediately be made of every thing, as a gold ring of a wedge of gold; yet since bodies having but one common matter can be differenced but by accidents, which seem all of them to be the effects and consequences of local motion, I see not why it should not be absurd to think that (at least among inanimate bodies) by the intervention of some very small addition or subtraction of matter (which yet in most cases will not be needed) and an orderly series of transmutations, disposing by degrees the matter to be transmuted, almost of any thing may at length be made any thing.[90]

Although he hedges the claim around with hesitations and qualifications, Boyle is drawn to the thesis that the universal matter is universally transmutable. One might think, for example, that water cannot be transmuted into oil or salt. But Boyle took the experimental work of Van Helmont very seriously, and Van Helmont's famous willow-tree experiment had showed – to the satisfaction of most of his contemporaries – that plants take all their growth from water. And of course, the distillation of vegetable matter will generally produce some oils, and leave a salty residue behind. So, it appears that by "an orderly series of transmutations" one can derive both an inflammable oil and an alkaline salt from water. With the benefit of hindsight and the aid of later biology and chemistry, we can point to the flaws in Helmont's reasoning; we should not blame seventeenth century figures like Boyle from taking his results at face value.

Given a single universal matter and a complex and hierarchic matter theory, in which chemical species only arise a fairly high level of aggregation (perhaps C_3s or C_4s) we should not be surprised by Boyle's positive attitude to the alchemical project for the production of gold from base metals. Normal chemical operations, as Boyle says, leave the corpuscles of metals unaffected in alloys, solutions, and salts. But more penetrating analytical agents should be able to dissolve the textures characteristic of base metals such as lead, making transmutation possible. Although his discussions of the topic are hedged around with his habitual doubts and qualifications, he does seem to have believed both that a handful of genuine "adepts" had achieved the production of the philosophers' stone and the transmutation of base metals into gold and that he himself was not far from uncovering the secrets of their art.

In such a matter theory, Boyle explains in *The Origin of Forms and Qualities*, there is no place for the "substantial" forms and "real" qualities of the Aristotelians. The wisest of the schoolmen, he reminds us, "confess, that they do not well know them," that their nature and manner of operation are hidden from us.[91] But if this is correct, the postulation of SFs can serve no explanatory purpose: it cannot shed any light on a natural phenomenon to be told that it is due to an SF.[92] If the phenomena cannot be explained in terms of SFs, and can be explained without them, then the postulation of SFs is both unnecessary and useless. In this critique of SFs, Boyle had been anticipated, of course, by Descartes, Hobbes, Gassendi, and many others. What Boyle seeks to do is to buttress the empirical flank of the anti-Aristotelian argument by providing *experimental* evidence of the mechanical origin of forms and qualities. My chief aim, he writes, is

> to make it probable to you by experiments . . . that almost all sorts of qualities may be produced mechanically; I mean by such corporeal agents as do not appear . . . to work otherwise than by virtue of the motion, size, figure and contrivance of their parts (which attributes I call the mechanical affections of matter because to them men willingly refer the various operations of mechanical engines).[93]

Heat and cold may be explained either by the pure kinetic theory of Descartes or the mixed-kinetic theory of Gassendi and Charleton;[94] colours as they are in the objects may be simply surface textures; specific chemical properties such as affinities may be explained in terms of the lock-and-key model. Laboratory evidence shows us that we can alter the properties of bodies simply by mechanical means, that is by rearranging their constituent parts; in such cases, there is no need to posit an SF. The Aristotelians are happy to grant that the forms of artefacts are accidental, but still insist that natural substances possess SFs. But, Boyle retorts, there is no real distinction to be drawn here. Artificial "vitriol" (ferrous sulphate) can be readily manufactured in the laboratory from iron and sulphuric acid by "a convenient apposition of the small parts of the saline menstruum to those of the metal."[95] This "factitious" vitriol has exactly the same properties as those of the naturally occurring substance (produced by the weathering of iron pyrites): if the juxtaposition of corpuscles explains the properties of the synthetic material, why not also the natural one? There is, Boyle concludes, no real distinction between nature and art: the phenomena produced by the mechanical arts (which of course include chemistry) should "be looked upon as really belonging to the history of nature in its full and due extent."[96]

Boyle thus accepts from the Aristotelians the significance of form as an explanatory category, but insists that the term must be reinterpreted. Form is not a mysterious substance, capable in principle of distinct existence; rather, there is nothing more to form than an arrangement and motion of parts, a (dynamic) texture or microstructure. A form, he concludes, consists in

> such a convention of these ... mechanical affections of matter as is necessary to constitute a body of that determinate kind. And so, though I shall for brevity's sake retain the word Form, yet I would be understood to mean by it, not a real substance distinct from matter, but only the matter itself of a natural body, considered with its peculiar manner of existence; which I think may not inconveniently be called either its specifical or its demonstrating state, or its essential modification; or, ... in one word, its stamp.[97]

8. Newton's atomic theory

Isaac Newton (1642–1727) tended to think of the theory of matter as belonging to metaphysics rather than to physics proper, that is as taking us beyond what could be established by observation and experiment. For this reason, we must generally turn to unpublished manuscripts and to the so-called queries appended to the *Opticks* if we want to learn his views. We know that he was consistently hostile to Descartes's natural philosophy, and much more sympathetic to the atomism of Gassendi and Charleton, but he clearly does not wish to include speculative claims about the atoms and the void in the main body of either *The Principia* or the *Opticks*.[98] There is no evidence that Newton was a positivist in anything like the modern sense, but he did insist on a sharp distinction between propositions that can be, in his terms, "deduced from the phenomena," and more speculative claims that cannot be so deduced, and was quite clear that atomism lay – at least at the time he was writing – on the wrong side of this dividing line.

In an early manuscript, *De Gravitatone et Aequipondium Fluidorum*, Newton launched a vigorous critique of Descartes's views regarding space and matter, defending, against Descartes, a conception of space as ontologically absolute, independent of the bodies that fill it. Given the nature of space, Newton continues, we can proceed to discuss that of body:

> Of this, however, the explanation must be more uncertain, for it does not exist necessarily but by the divine will, because it is hardly given to us to know the limits of the divine power, that is to say, whether matter could be created in one way only, or whether there are several ways by which different beings similar to bodies could be produced. And though it scarcely seems credible that God could create beings similar to bodies which display all their actions and exhibit all their phenomena, and yet would not be bodies in essential and metaphysical constitution, as I have no clear and distinct perception of this matter I should not dare to affirm the contrary, and hence I am reluctant to say positively what the nature of bodies is, but I would rather describe a certain kind of being

similar in every way to bodies, and whose creation we cannot deny to be within the power of God, so that we can hardly say it is not body.[99]

God could simply decree that a given portion of space be impenetrable by bodies and even by the rays of light:

> If he should exercise this power, and cause some space projecting above the earth, like a mountain or any other body, to be impervious to bodies and thus stop or reflect light and all impinging things, it seems impossible that we should not consider this space really to be a body from the evidence of our senses (which constitute our sole judges in this matter); for it ought to be regarded as tangible on account of its impenetrability, and visible, opaque, and coloured on account of the reflection of light, and it will resonate when struck because the adjacent air will be moved by the blow.[100]

We still need, of course, an account of the mobility and of the enduring identity conditions of these "bodies," but there seems no reason of principle why the theory should not be extended in a perfectly intuitive manner:

> If we should suppose that that impenetrability is not always maintained in the same part of space but can be transferred here and there according to certain laws, yet so that the quantity and shape of that impenetrable space are not changed, there will be no property of body which it does not possess. It would have shape, be tangible and mobile, and be capable of reflecting and being reflected, and constitute no less a part of the nature of things than any other corpuscle.[101]

For all we know, it might be the case that *all* the bodies of our experience are merely local thickenings of space, produced and maintained by the almighty power of God, operating of course according to strict and universal laws. Neither reason nor experience counts against such a theory: it is internally coherent, economical in its assumptions, and perfectly consistent with the phenomena. Here in this unpublished manuscript, Newton thus comes close to embracing a pure "field metaphysics" of body – what exists in its own right (and hence qualifies as substantial) is space itself; bodies are merely modes or modifications of space.

In later works, however, both published and unpublished, Newton seems committed to a more traditional atomist picture. We know from his early notebooks that he made a serious study of Charleton's *Physiologia*, and that he favoured atomist over Cartesian explanations of a variety of natural phenomena.[102] After the publication of *The Principia* (1687) he launched into an intensive study of the surviving texts of the ancient atomists, notably of course Lucretius's *De Rerum Natura*, writing a number of "classical scholia" that were at one time intended for inclusion in the second edition of his magnum opus.[103] Although the "classical scholia" remained unpublished, allusions to atomism, and explicit borrowings from atomist arguments, surface from time to time in the published works. In query 28 of the *Opticks*, for example, Newton is arguing against the aether of the Cartesians. For rejecting such a medium, he writes, "we have the authority of those the oldest and most celebrated Philosophers of Greece and Phoenicia, who made a Vacuum, and Atoms, and the Gravity of Atoms, the first principles of their

Philosophy."[104] After going on to cite a number of optical and chemical phenomena that seemed to demand explanation in atomic terms, he concluded, in a famous passage from query 31:

> All these things being consider'd, it seems probable to me, that God in the Beginning form'd Matter in solid, massy, hard, impenetrable, moveable Particles, of such Sizes and Figures, and with such other Properties, and in such Proportion to Space, as most conduced to the End for which he form'd them.[105]

The passage continues with an argument for the hardness of the atoms that could have been derived directly from the verses of Lucretius:[106]

> these primitive Particles being Solids, are incomparably harder than any porous Bodies compounded of them; even so very hard, as never to wear or break in pieces; no ordinary Power being able to divide what God himself made one in the first Creation. While the Particles continue entire, they may compose Bodies of one and the same Nature and Texture in all Ages: But should they wear away, or break in pieces, the Nature of Things depending on them, would be changed. Water and Earth, composed of old worn Particles and Fragments of Particles, would not be of the same Nature and Texture now, with Water and Earth composed of entire Particles in the Beginning.[107]

Like Boyle, Newton espoused a hierarchic matter theory, in which chemical species emerge only at a fairly high level in the organization of matter. In book two of the *Opticks*, he sketches an account that involves an equal admixture of void at each level of the hierarchy.[108] If we take perfectly solid atoms or C_0s, and combine them with an equal volume of void, we obtain corpuscles of the first degree of composition or C_1s. Combining C_1s with equal amounts of void yields C_2s, and so on up the scale.[109] If at each stage of aggregation an equal volume of void is intermixed, a corpuscle of the nth grade of composition C_n will contain only one part in two to the nth power of solid matter. In the great thirty-first query, this account is developed further: the smallest corpuscles, he explains,

> cohere by the strongest Attractions, and compose bigger Particles of weaker Virtue; and many of these may cohere and compose bigger Particles whose Virtue is still weaker, and so on for divers Successions, until the Progression end in the biggest Particles on which the operations in Chymistry, and the Colours of natural Bodies depend, and which by cohering compose Bodies of a sensible magnitude.[110]

The atoms thus cohere very strongly to give C_1s; C_1s cohere more weakly to give C_2s, and so on up the scale. (Newton of course includes attractive and repulsive forces into his version of the atomic theory.) Newton thus provides an account both of the theoretical possibility of alchemical transmutation and of its practical difficulty. Suppose that the least particles of gold are C_5s. In salts, solutions, and alloys, these relatively stable C_5s remain entire and undivided: *aqua regia*, for example, can separate these least particles of gold from one another but cannot enter into their characteristic texture and decompose it. A more powerful reagent might, however, be capable of "opening the texture" of gold, breaking it down, perhaps, into the "philosophical" mercury and sulphur of the alchemists.[111] The dream of the alchemists – the transmutation of base metals into gold – is not theoretically absurd, but practically very difficult, owing to the strength of the interparticulate attractive forces that need to be overcome.

If we take from the ancient atomists their assumption of the inertial homogeneity of the atoms (no atom is intrinsically denser or rarer than any other), and add the central argument of *The Principia* for the proportionality of mass and weight, we have the makings of an argument for a very radical claim indeed – that all observed bodies are almost entirely composed of empty space. As early as his first notebooks, the *Quaestiones Quaedam Philosophicae* (1664–66) Newton had seen this implication of the atomic theory. Gold dissolves in *aqua regia* and will form an amalgam with mercury, indicating that it is not perfectly solid but contains pores. Suppose, says the young Newton, that it is half solid matter and half empty space. It will follow, assuming that specific gravity measures the quantity of solid matter per unit volume, that water is about one part in 40 of solid matter, and atmospheric air one part in 3,600. But atmospheric air retains its elasticity even when further rarefied in some of Boyle's air-pump experiments, a fact more readily explained in terms of interparticulate repulsive forces than mechanical models like Boyle's little springs.[112]

In the 1660s, of course, the use of specific gravity as a measure of quantity of matter per unit volume was simply an assumption Newton took from the atomists – both Aristotelians and Cartesians would simply have rejected that assumption, and hence the soundness of any arguments depending on it. In *The Principia*, however, Newton shows, "by experiments made with the greatest accuracy," that the quantity of matter (mass) in a body is proportional to its weight.[113] The Aristotelians are wrong to think that there is matter (fire) with mass but no weight (or even negative weight); the Cartesians are wrong to think that the weight of a body depends on its texture or arrangement of parts. On either the Aristotelian or the Cartesian theory, the period of a pendulum should depend on the material of the bob and not simply on the length of the string, but Newton's "experiments made with the greatest accuracy" demonstrate conclusively that it is only the length of the string that (at any given point on the earth's surface) determines the period.

The phenomena of the reflection and refraction of light, Newton teaches in the *Opticks*, have momentous consequences for matter theory:

> We may understand that Bodies are much more rare and porous than is commonly believed. Water is nineteen times lighter, and by consequence nineteen times rarer than Gold, and gold is so rare as very readily to transmit the magnetick Effluvia, and easily to admit Quicksilver into its Pores, and to let Water pass through it.[114]

If gold is less than half composed of solid matter, it will follow that

> Water has above forty times more Pores than Parts. And he that can find out an Hypothesis, by which Water may be so rare, and yet not capable of compression by force, may doubtless by the same Hypothesis make Gold, and Water, and all other Bodies, so much rarer as he pleases; so that Light may find a ready passage through transparent substances.[115]

We have here a powerful argument[116] with only one contentious premise:

1. We cannot account for the observed properties of gold unless we assume that it "abounds with pores," which pores must constitute *at least half* of its total volume.[117]
2. Weight is a measure of mass (established in *The Principia*). So, a given volume of gold contains roughly twenty times as much matter as the same volume of water.
3. There is a homogeneous matter of which the least particles of all things are made. This assumption of the inertial homogeneity of the stuff of the atoms is borrowed by Newton from the atomist tradition and is a crucial premise that might simply be denied by his opponents. Newton freely grants that it is a contingent assumption dependent on the divine will: in other worlds, he admits, there may be particles of "different Densities and Forces."[118]
4. If (1) and (2), we can infer that a given volume of water contains less than one-fortieth the matter that would be contained in a perfectly solid block of the same size. And if (3), we can further conclude from this that it consists of at least 97.5% of empty space.
5. But water is (all but) incompressible: it can be subjected to very great pressures without undergoing significant condensation. To explain this fact, we will find ourselves obliged to postulate powerful interparticulate repulsive forces.
6. But if the impenetrability of a body can be explained without assuming that its solid matter fills any significant proportion of its total bulk, we may take this "dematerialization" of matter as far as we wish. Gold might be one part in ten (or less) of solid matter, making water one part in two hundred (or less). The observed impenetrability of bodies becomes a function of the repulsive forces. Newton, we know, still believed in solid, space-filling atoms – he still thinks of the mass of an atom as a measure of its volume of solid matter[119] – but it is the forces that are now doing all the real explanatory work.

This is no mere speculative hypothesis, Newton insists; it is a model amply confirmed by optical evidence. Light, he reminds us in the *Opticks*, "is transmitted through pellucid Bodies in right lines to very great distances. How Bodies can have a sufficient quantity of Pores for producing these Effects is very difficult to conceive, but perhaps not altogether impossible."[120]

In another draft passage intended for *The Principia*, the conclusion is drawn quite explicitly. To explain the passage of a stream of light corpuscles through a transparent body with scarcely no loss, we must have recourse to

> a certain wonderful and exceedingly artificial texture of the particles of bodies by which all bodies, like networks, allow magnetic effluvia and rays of light to pass through them in all directions and offer them a very free passage: and by such a hypothesis the rarity of bodies may be increased at will.[121]

Solid, space-filing matter seems to be in danger fading away entirely, leaving minute centres of attractive and repulsive forces scattered across an infinite void. Some of Newton's immediate disciples delighted in the "immateriality" of the master's physics. In his Boyle Lectures for 1692, Richard Bentley asserted (after close consultation with Newton himself) that "the empty Space of our solar Region . . . is 8575 Hundred Thousand Million Million times more ample than all the corporeal substance in it."[122] This provides further evidence for the existence of God's providence: without divine guidance, the scattered atoms would never have come together to form our world. Samuel Clarke, replying to Leibniz's accusation that Newton's physics leads to materialism, retorts that Newton's principles "prove matter, or body, to be the smallest and most inconsiderable part of the universe."[123] All the solid matter in the universe, Joseph Priestley would later say in a memorable phase, might – for all we know – be condensed into the volume of a nutshell.[124] Take this line of reasoning to its ultimate conclusion, and we have the theory of Roger Boscovic, according to which atoms are merely point centres of alternating "spheres" of attractive and repulsive forces: solid matter has utterly disappeared.

9. Leibniz's critique of Cartesians and atomists – SFs revisited

Traditional accounts of the scientific revolution[125] often paint a picture of the triumphal progress of the mechanical philosophy, whether in Cartesian or atomist form, and a corresponding retreat of Scholastic Aristotelianism. In the natural sciences, there can be no doubt that spectacular progress was being made, and that Boyle's pneumatics and Newton's celestial mechanics were vastly superior to the accounts of the same phenomena offered by the schoolmen around the year 1600. But was there comparable progress in natural philosophy in general, or in matter theory in particular? Was the nature of matter any better understood in 1700 than in 1600? One of the most acute and perceptive thinkers of his age thought that neither the Cartesians nor the atomists could offer a coherent and intelligible account of matter, and that the much-derided Scholastics were right on some important points. In any account of seventeenth century matter theory, it seems proper to leave the last word to Gottfried Wilhelm Leibniz (1646–1716).

There was a time, Leibniz writes in his manuscript *On the Nature of Body and the Laws of Motion* (c. 1690) when he held the Cartesian view that "all the phenomena of motion could be explained on purely geometrical principles, assuming no metaphysical propositions, and that the laws of impact depend only on the composition of motions."[126] But this assumption had led Descartes to articulate a set of laws of motion and collision that were inconsistent with one another, incompatible with certain rational principles, and flatly contrary to experience. To explain the nature of colliding bodies, one needs to have recourse to certain *powers*, such as those that are manifest in elastic collisions. And these powers are not reducible to mere modifications of extension:

> over and above that which is deduced from extension and its variation or modification alone, we must add and recognize in bodies certain notions or forms that are immaterial, so to speak, or independent of extension, which you can call powers, by means of which speed is adjusted to magnitude.[127]

In the manuscript *Of Body and Force, Against the Cartesians* (1702) this criticism is taken to a more metaphysical level. The Cartesians think that the very essence of matter is three-dimensional extension; Leibniz retorts that he agrees with those thinkers who believe that "there is something passive in body over and above extension, namely, that by which body resists penetration."[128] In unravelling the nature of extension, he continues, he noticed that "it is relative to something which must be spread out, and that it signifies a diffusion or repetition of a certain nature.[129] What is this "something" that, by being diffused or spread out, constitutes a body? The answer must be sought in the set of distinctive *powers*, active and passive, that will form the subject matter of the new science of dynamics. The Cartesians are guilty of reifying a mere abstraction in thinking that mere extension could be the essence of a body. And because their notion of body contains no powers, they are forced into the dubious metaphysics of occasionalism when they seek to explain how bodies move and collide.

The Cartesians also struggle to accommodate the intuition that substances must be indivisible units. On a Cartesian view, it seems that every body is an aggregate of aggregates of aggregates *ad infinitum*. But an aggregate, intuition suggests, is ontologically dependent on the simples that constitute it. In modern terms, we might say that an atom of carbon is dependent on its protons, neutrons, and electrons; the electrons, protons, and neutrons are dependent on quarks; the quarks are dependent on – what? Can this regress go on for ever, or must we terminate with something absolutely simple? We have already seen Leibniz give qualified praise to Cordemoy for demanding an end to the regress. But if we identify extension as the very essence of matter, it seems that there is no principled way of blocking the regress *ad infinitum*. Cordemoy wanted to find a way of being both a Cartesian and an atomist, but by doing so he fell into inconsistency.

What of the atomists themselves? "When I was a young man," Leibniz admits in the fourth of his famous letters to Samuel Clarke, "I also gave in to the notion of a vacuum and atoms; but reason brought me into the right way."[130] The atomists' world picture, the mature Leibniz believed, pleases the imagination but fails to satisfy the demands of reason. Atomism, he writes in the *New System of Nature* (1695) is "contrary to reason."[131] The atomist is right to demand simples, but wrong to think that his theory satisfies this demand. The least corpuscle, Leibniz writes to Clarke, "is actually subdivided *in infinitum*, and contains a world of other creatures."[132] Atomists from Democritus to Gassendi have embraced the actual parts doctrine, but have failed to answer the obvious ensuing question about the parts of the atoms themselves. The absolute cohesiveness of the parts of a Democritean atom is, Leibniz writes to Huygens in 1692, something utterly inexplicable in natural terms, and thus "a kind of perpetual miracle."[133] The same point is repeated in a letter to Hartsoeker in 1711.[134] Cohesion in general, Leibniz thinks, can be explained either in terms of an inner *conatus* (striving) of the parts of a body towards one another, or of the external pressure of some surrounding medium. Neither of these causes, however, would produce an infinite and unshakeable cohesiveness; to account for this, atomists must invoke the will of God, which is to abandon natural philosophy altogether.

Leibniz's other main line of attack on atomism concerns the laws of motion, and especially the laws of colliding bodies. The Democritean atom is perfectly rigid, incapable of elastic deformation. The collision of such bodies, Leibniz argues, would violate two of the great principles of natural philosophy. In the collisions of such bodies, "living force" or *vis viva* (our kinetic energy) would always be lost, because, as Leibniz writes to Huygens, such bodies cannot be elastic and "it is only elasticity which makes bodies rebound."[135] But this would violate the principle of the conservation of *vis viva*, and allow the physical universe itself to be running down. (Committed atomists like Newton and his disciple Clarke were in fact happy to accept this consequence of their theory and did not regard it as any kind of *reduction*.)[136] The picture of the physical universe as winding down like a piece of old clockwork, needing occasional winding up by the clockmaker (God), was objectionable to Leibniz on philosophical and theological grounds and helped to prompt his famous exchange of letters with Clarke.

The other principle that the collision of hard bodies would violate is the law of continuity, often summed up in the Latin maxim *natura non fait saltum* (nature does not make jumps). In the collision of perfectly rigid bodies, the change in each body's motion would necessarily have to occur "through a leap or in a moment, for the direct motion becomes retrograde at the very moment of collision."[137] If the principle of continuity is true, there can be no perfectly rigid bodies, because the collisions of such bodies would involve velocities leaping instantaneously from $+v$ to $-v$, or from $+v$ to zero. Anyone familiar with a little differential calculus (of which, of course, Leibniz was cofounder with Newton) will see the problem here: there will be a change of velocity (ds/dt) with no assignable value for the acceleration or deceleration involved. If we assume that the motions of bodies can be represented in the terminology of the differential calculus, there can be no collisions between rigid Democritean atoms, and hence – to all intents and purposes – no rigid Democritean atoms.[138]

The ancients, Leibniz suggests in his *Discourse on Metaphysics* (1686), were right to see that the intelligibility of the material universe requires the existence of individual substances: "this is why they introduced and maintained the substantial forms which are so decried today."[139] This opinion, he argues, is "not so distant from the truth nor so ridiculous as the common lot of our new philosophers imagines."[140] The moderns, he continues, have been much too hasty to condemn the whole doctrine of SFs: "there is much more solidity than one imagines in the opinions of the Scholastic philosophers and theologians, provided that they are used appropriately and in their proper place."[141] Of course, SFs should not be invoked in the explanation of particular phenomena: they belong to metaphysics rather than to physics. We need to invoke them not to explain how individual bodies behave and move, but (1) to explain how there can be individual material substances at all and (2) to provide a metaphysical ground for the distinctive powers of bodies.

A genuine substance, he insists, must be an *unum per se*, a natural unity, as opposed to a mere being by aggregation.[142] The Aristotelians can meet this demand; atomist and Cartesian accounts of matter fail it, for reasons we have identified. And Aristotle was also right to think that the paradigm cases of genuine individual substances are organisms. A block of marble, a pile of stones, and the corpse of an animal are, Leibniz explains to Arnauld, mere "beings by aggregation" and cannot properly be called substances at all.[143] But such beings by aggregation are ontologically dependent on genuine individual substances, which possess SFs: "I assign substantial forms to all corporeal substances that are more than mechanically united."[144] If only organisms possess SFs, and the very existence of any being by aggregation presupposes a more fundamental level of genuine individual substances, it will follow that the entire physical universe is ultimately composed of organisms. These may, of course, be very remote from our perception: we don't see the constitution of a block of marble or a dead cat out of microorganisms, but reason demands that there must be such corporeal substances: if not, "bodies would only be true phenomena, like the rainbow."[145]

The *New System of Nature* (1695) repeats the claim that "it is impossible to find the principles of a true unity in matter alone."[146] To find such true unities we must have recourse to a "formal atom," because "a material thing cannot be both material and, at the same time, perfectly indivisible, that is, endowed with a true unity." This explains the need to "rehabilitate" the much-derided SFs of the Scholastics, but in a manner that would make them intelligible: "I found," he concludes, "that their nature consists in force."[147] More precisely, as he explains in the *Specimen of Dynamics* (1695), we need to distinguish the "primitive" forces (active and passive) inherent in each and every SF from the "derivative" forces (active and passive) that are their manifestation in the natural world.[148] The physicist thus needs to posit a range of forces to explain the phenomena of nature (e.g. the motions and collisions of bodies); the metaphysician explains these forces as the expression within the phenomenal world of the SFs constitutive of genuine individual substances (i.e. organisms).

The story of matter theory in the seventeenth century is rich and varied, but frustratingly inconclusive. To portray it simply in terms of the rejection of Scholastic Aristotelianism and its replacement by one version or other of the mechanical philosophy (Cartesian or atomist) would be oversimplified, to say the least. As Leibniz saw, neither the Cartesians nor the atomists had a satisfactory account of material substance. Cartesianism might well be forced to evolve in the direction of the "field metaphysics" of Spinoza; atomism can offer no account of the absolute cohesiveness and indivisibility of its atoms. We may find Leibniz's own rehabilitation of Aristotle, and his resulting pan-organismic theory of matter, wildly speculative and utterly implausible, but his insistence that matter can only be properly understood in terms of its characteristic powers (which cannot be reduced to mere modes of extension) paved the way for much eighteenth century thinking on the subject.[149] And the issues debated in the seventeenth century by Scholastics, atomists, Cartesians, and Leibnizians are very much alive and still with us, albeit perhaps in somewhat different terminology.

Notes

1 The old textbook distinction between rationalists and empiricists in early modern philosophy has come in for a lot of criticism in the recent literature, including the editor's introduction to this *Companion*. It is, of course, easy to discern elements of "empiricism" in textbook "rationalists" such as Descartes and Leibniz, and elements of "rationalism" in textbook "empiricists" such as Locke and Berkeley. But the old terminology may still be of some use if, instead of dividing early modern philosophers into two opposed schools, we ask instead, of any given thinker, how much he thinks can be proved from first principles and how much must be left to the authority of experience. When Boyle seeks to provide empirical evidence for the truth of his "corpuscular philosophy" (and is rebuked for it by Spinoza), we can see that the labels of "empiricist" and "rationalist" are neither entirely useless nor entirely anachronistic.
2 The striking exception is of course Spinoza, who for obvious reasons could never have pursued a normal course of study at any university of his period.
3 See Charles Schmitt (1973).
4 Some Renaissance thinkers took this analogy between vegetation and the growth of metals in the earth very seriously; for others, it may have been no more than a *façon de parler*.
5 The most explicit statement of this claim is in the *Meteorologica* (book 1, ch. 3, 339a36–b1). Here Aristotle states that "[f]ire, air, water, earth, we assert, originate from one another, and each of them exists potentially in each, as all things do that can be resolved into a common and ultimate substrate."
6 Aristotle, *Metaphysics*, book 7, ch. 3, 1029a20–26.
7 Aristotle, *On Coming-to-Be and Passing-Away*, book 1, ch. 3, 317b9–12.
8 I document this tension in appendix 2 of my *Atomism* (pp. 663–73). For much more detailed and scholarly discussion, see the papers in Ernan McMullin, ed. (1963).
9 For details of this story, see Jammer (1961).
10 Aquinas, ST 2q54. Quoted from Mary Clark, ed., p. 58.
11 The striking exception is of course Leibniz, who thought that the notion of SF – properly understood – was essential to a sound metaphysics, although the Scholastics had mistakenly tried to use it as a contribution to empirical science.
12 The best explanation of the role(s) of SFs is in Dennis des Chene, pp. 70–4.
13 Holden (2004). The great merit of Holden's book is that he distinguishes the metaphysical issue (actual vs. potential parts) from merely mathematical issues (e.g. the sum of an infinite series) and insists – rightly – on the primacy of the former.

14 See Holden, pp. 84–8, for statements of the actual parts doctrine and a list of its adherents.
15 See Holden, pp. 95–9, for statements of the potential parts doctrine and a list of its adherents.
16 Galileo, *Two New Sciences*, pp. 26–35.
17 Aristotle, *De Gen et Corr*, book 1, ch. 10, 328a10–16.
18 Aristotle, *De Gen et Corr*, book 1, ch. 10, 327a35–b7.
19 Aristotle, *De Gen et Corr*, book 1, ch. 10, 327b23–27.
20 For this notion of a V-potency, see McMullin in McMullin, ed., 306.
21 For Aquinas's commentary on this part of *De Gen et Corr*, see Edward Grant, ed., pp. 603–5.
22 See Hooykaas and Pyle, *Atomism*, pp. 307–11.
23 AT XI 7; CSM I 83.
24 AT XI 25–26; CSM I 89.
25 AT XI 33; CSM I 90–91.
26 AT XI 33; CSM I 91.
27 AT XI 35–36; CSM I 92.
28 AT I 270–272; CSMK 40–41.
29 See Pietro Redondo, *Galileo Heretic* (1988).
30 AT VII 78; CSM II 54.
31 AT III 297–8; CSMK 173.
32 AT VI 239; CSM II 173.
33 AT III 492; CSMK 205.
34 AT VII 440; CSM II 297.
35 AT III 691–2; CSMK 226–7.
36 AT VII 442; CSM II 298.
37 AT VIIIA 25; CSM I 210.
38 AT VIIIA 42; CSM I 224.
39 AT VIIIA 43; CSM I 225.
40 AT VIIIA 44; CSM I 225–6.
41 It is of course the intuitive precursor of the modern (Newtonian) concept of mass.
42 AT VIIIA 49; CSM I 229–30.
43 AT VIIIA 51–2; CSM I 231–2.
44 AT VIIIA 52; CSM I 232.
45 AT VIIIA 52; CSM I 232.
46 AT VIIIA 52–53; CSM I 232–3.
47 AT VIIIA 51–2; CSM I 231–2.
48 AT VIIIA 28–29; CSM I 213.
49 See Holden, p. 86.
50 Holden discusses this argument – from the actual parts doctrine to the thesis of ultimate parts – in his chapter 3 (pp. 141–7), rejecting it as invalid in the case of infinitely divisible bodies.
51 Cordemoy, pp. 95–6.
52 Leibniz to Arnauld (1686), from AG 80–1.
53 Leibniz, *New System*, from AG 142.
54 AT VIIIA 50; CSM I 231.
55 For a recent defence of this interpretation, see Kurt Smith and Alan Nelson (2010). "Divisibility and Cartesian Extension." *Oxford Studies in Early Modern Philosophy*, vol. 5. For a recent defence of a "pluralist" interpretation of Descartes, see Dan Kaufman. (2014). "Cartesian Substances, Individual Bodies, and Corruptibility." *Res Philosophica* 91.1 (Special Issue: Modern Philosophy).
56 See Robert Kargon (1966), pp. 6–40.
57 For evidence of Charleton's influence on Boyle and the young Newton, see Kargon (1964) and Westfall (1962) respectively.
58 Leibniz, *NE* 1.1. Philalethes says to Theophilus (Leibniz) that "[y]ou sided with Descartes, and with the opinions of the famous author of the *Search After Truth* [Malebranche]; and I found the views of Gassendi, as expounded by M.Bernier, more plausible and natural."
59 AT VIIIA 45; CSM I 227.
60 For discussion, see LoLordo, pp. 106–8.
61 Gassendi is not as clear as one might wish on this point, but does seem to think that the finer atoms of fire and air that constitute animal souls have a particularly high endowment of *pondus* or motive force, and that the bulky "frigorific atoms" that explain cold are particularly resistant to being set in motion.

62 AT IXA 212; CSM II 275.
63 Charleton, p. 108. See Holden, pp. 114–5.
64 Charleton, p. 95.
65 Charleton, p. 96.
66 For a fuller account of this theory, see Pyle, *Atomism*, ch. 1, pp. 30–6.
67 Whether Gassendi thinks of the motive force of a given atom as fixed, or whether atoms can push each other around by transfer of motion, is not altogether clear from the texts. For discussion, see LoLordo, pp. 149–52.
68 For an enlightening account of the relative merits of Descartes's kinetic and Gassendi's mixed-kinetic accounts of cold, see Robert Boyle's *New Experiments and Observations Touching Cold* (*Works*, vol. 2, pp. 462ff.).
69 The terminology here is of course anachronistic. But the worry expressed – that the collision of perfectly rigid bodies would violate the laws of nature – is not. It was voiced by Leibniz and many others. Or detailed discussion of the issues raised, see Scott.
70 Aristotle, *Physics* 1, 4, 187b14–22.
71 For more details, see Murdoch, "The Medieval and Renaissance Theory of Minima Naturalia," in Lüthy, Murdoch, and Newman, eds. For the transformation of the *minima naturalia* tradition into something more akin to atomism proper, see Van Melsen.
72 See Newman, *Atoms and Alchemy*, pp. 66–8.
73 See Van Melsen, pp. 68–9.
74 See Newman, pp. 27–31.
75 For Sennert, see Van Melsen, and Newman, ch. 4, pp. 85–125.
76 Quoted from Van Melsen, p. 80.
77 Quoted from Van Melsen, p. 83.
78 Quoted from Van Melsen, p. 84. Although he admits that the question is a difficult one, Sennert favours Avicenna's theory of the status of the forms of the elements in the compound: the forms of FAWE are still present, but in an "unawakened" state, not manifest to sense until the compound body is dissolved. The minima of F remain F, and the minima of W remain W, even though to our senses C is an Aristotelian homoeomer, that is every part of C is C. The minima of FAWE combine to form *prima mixta*, the first compound principles, the least particles of the substances they compose. The simplest of these *prima mixta* are those of Paracelsus's three chemical principles, mercury, sulphur, and salt. Sennert thus develops an explicitly hierarchic chemical atomic theory: the atoms (C_0s) are the minima of FAWE; the C_1s are the least particles of mercury, sulphur, and salt; C_2s are the least particles of more compound bodies such as the metals; and so on. On this theory, there can be no transmutation of the elements FAWE (every minimum of fire remains forever fire), but the transmutation of metals looks to be possible in principle (it would only require the dissolving of C_2s into C_1s and then assembling new C_2s).
79 For a detailed account, see Newman, ch. 4.
80 See Pyle, pp. 308–9; Newman, pp. 113–4.
81 The best recent study of Boyle's natural philosophy is Anstey (2000).
82 Boyle, OFQ, *Works*, vol. 3, 7.
83 Boyle, *Works*, vol. 3, 29.
84 Boyle, *Works*, vol. 1, 412.
85 Boyle, *Works*, vol. 1, 412–3.
86 Boyle, *Works*, vol. 1, 474.
87 Boyle, *Works*, vol. 1, 475.
88 Boyle, *Works*, vol. 1, 475–6.
89 Boyle, *Works*, vol. 1, 571.
90 Boyle, *Works*, vol. 3, 35.
91 Boyle, *Works*, vol. 3, 11.
92 Boyle, *Works*, vol. 3, 38.
93 Boyle, *Works*, vol. 3, 13.
94 I call it a "mixed-kinetic" theory because it acknowledges that heat is an agitation of the particles of a body, but then posits special "calorific" and "frigorific" atoms which, in virtue of their sizes, shapes, and motions, are especially prone to excite or inhibit such agitation. For discussion, see Pyle, pp. 565–70.
95 Boyle, *Works*, vol. 3, 45.
96 Boyle, *Works*, vol. 3, 435–6.
97 Boyle, *Works*, vol. 3, 28.

But just how mechanical was Boyle's "Mechanical Philosophy"? This has been a topic of lively dispute in the recent literature. In my *Atomism* (1995), I painted a traditional picture of Boyle as fully committed to the reductionist programme of the mechanical philosophy, which in turn provided a fruitful heuristic for the development of his scientific work in pneumatics and chemistry. This old picture has since been challenged by a number of later authors. Here is a very brief sketch of the state of the current debate.

Antonio Clericuzio has argued that Boyle was not a committed mechanist at all, pointing out that in many contexts – but most notably in his chemistry – he posits special properties and powers of bodies without showing how these are to be reduced to the sizes, shapes, motions, and arrangements of the smallest undivided particles of matter (Clericuzio 1990 and 2000, ch. 4). This argument is inconclusive against the traditional interpretation of Boyle. So long as the properties in question are found only in complex bodies, and so long as we bear in mind that "unreduced" does not entail "irreducible," we can freely admit that Boyle's mechanical philosophy is gappy and programmatic, without seeing any need to retract our original reading. A number of Boyle's lesser works provide supporting evidence for this response. In works such as "The Great Effects of Even Languid and Unheeded Motion," "Notes ... About the Atmospheres of Consistent Bodies Here Below," and "Experiments and Considerations About the Porosity of Bodies," he outlines a programme for the explanation of so-called occult qualities in terms of effluvia, pores and figures, and unheeded motions – that is in purely mechanistic terms (see Pyle 1995, appendix 6). The accounts offered in these works are admittedly mere explanation sketches, or suggestions for where a proper explanation might be found, but they do support the traditional picture of Boyle as a mechanist.

Alan Chalmers grants that Boyle is committed to mechanism, but thinks that the mechanical philosophy played no useful role in guiding and shaping the science (Chalmers 1993). In his best science, says Chalmers, Boyle makes free use of properties such as weight and elasticity, properties that no one had successfully reduced to size, shape, and local motion. The mechanical philosophy famously likens the physical universe to a pendulum clock or a pocket watch, but a pendulum clock is driven by a falling weight and a pocket watch by the elasticity of its spring. In Boyle's scientific work, Chalmers argues, he posits the properties he needs to explain the phenomena; the supposed commitment to a particular philosophy of nature is a mere idle wheel. In my reply to Chalmers (Pyle 2002) I granted parts of his case, while seeking to defend what I could of my own reading of the texts. Boyle frequently posits a division of intellectual labour between the experimentalists and the people he calls "speculative wits." An experimental philosopher (Boyle himself) will discover the weight and spring (elasticity) of the air; the "speculative wit" (e.g. Descartes or Gassendi) will seek to account for these properties in purely mechanistic terms. At times the experimentalists will outrun the speculators, leaving the latter struggling to catch up. On such occasions, it will seem that Chalmers is right and the science is entirely independent of the philosophy. But this does not follow: the mechanical philosophy might still be playing a heuristic role in framing questions, helping to direct experimental design, and integrating work in different sciences.

William Newman, in his recent book, *Atoms and Alchemy*, takes all three of us (Clericuzio, Chalmers, and myself) to task for asking the wrong questions, and foisting onto Boyle an anachronistic and overprecise conception of mechanism (Newman, pp. 175–182). He suggests that Boyle can properly be described as a mechanist because he thinks that forms and qualities are generated and lost by the aggregation and disaggregation of corpuscles in a hierarchic matter theory that owes a major debt to the chemical atomism of Sennert. That Boyle held *this* position is clear from the texts. But what Clericuzio, Chalmers, and I wanted to know is whether Boyle also thought that it was possible in principle to explain all the properties of compound bodies in terms exclusively of the sizes, shapes, motions, and arrangements of their simpler parts. Is Boyle committed to the reductionist programme of the ancient atomists, or would he be happy to admit that complex bodies have "superadded" or "emergent" properties that cannot be accounted for in this way? Newman refuses to answer, and suggests that the question is ill-posed. The self-denying austerity of his approach will surely frustrate many readers.

98   It is clear from the *Opticks* that Newton favours a corpuscular theory of light (as opposed to the wave theory of Huygens), but he does not regard this theory as established by his experiments, and even suggests a way in which the rival wave theory could be modified to accommodate his results.
99   From Janiak, ed., p. 27.
100 From Janiak, ed., p. 27–8.
101 From Janiak, ed., p. 28.

102 For the texts of these early notebooks, see McGuire and Tamny. For an illuminating overview, see Westfall (1962).
103 For the story of these "classical scholia," see McGuire and Rattansi.
104 Newton *Opticks*, query 28, p. 369.
105 Newton *Opticks*, query 31, p. 400.
106 See *De Rerum Natura*, book 1, especially lines 584–598, where Lucretius argues that the constancy of nature requires that the atoms must be immune to change.
107 Newton, *Opticks*, query 31, p. 400.
108 Newton, *Opticks*, book 2, part 3, proposition 8, p. 268.
109 For commentary, see Thackray (1970), p. 24.
110 Newton, *Opticks*, query 31, p. 394.
111 For a heroic attempt to make chemical sense of Newton's alchemy, see Betty Jo Dobbs.
112 See Westfall (1962), pp. 180–1.
113 Newton, *Principia*, book 2, proposition 24, corollary VII, p. 304.
114 Newton, *Opticks*, book 2, part 3, proposition 8, p. 267.
115 Newton, *Opticks*, book 2, part 3, proposition 8, p. 267.
116 I borrow this statement of the argument from my own *Atomism* (pp. 503–4).
117 Elsewhere, in a draft passage intended for *Principia*, Newton estimates the ratio of pores to solid matter in gold to be 5:2. See Hall and Hall, eds., p. 317.
118 Newton, *Opticks*, query 31, p. 404.
119 See McGuire (1968), p. 161.
120 Newton, *Opticks*, book 2, part 3, proposition 8, p. 268.
121 From Hall and Hall, eds., p. 317.
122 Bentley, in Burnet, ed., vol. 1, p. 48.
123 Samuel Clarke, "First Reply," from H.G. Alexander, ed., p. 12.
124 See Thackray (1968) for the development of the "nut-shell" theory of matter in eighteenth century discussions of the implications of the doctrines of Newton's *Opticks*.
125 See, for example, Dijksterhuis and Pyle (1995).
126 AG 245.
127 AG 250.
128 AG 250.
129 AG 251.
130 From H.G. Alexander, ed., p. 43. The same thought – that atomism satisfies the imagination but not the intellect – is also expressed in the *New System* (AG 139)
131 AG 142.
132 From H.G. Alexander, ed., p. 43.
133 From *PPL* 132. For conflict between atomism and conservation theory more broadly, see Scott.
134 For enlightening commentary, see Koyré (1965), p. 141.
135 From *PPL* 416.
136 See Newton, *Opticks*, query 31, p. 398, Clarke's *Fifth Reply* to Leibniz, in H.G. Alexander, ed., 112.
137 From *PPL* 446.
138 One could of course devise an account in which Democritean atoms exist but never collide, but what would be the purpose of such a theory? What role would the rigid atoms be playing?
139 AG 42.
140 AG 42.
141 AG 43.
142 AG 65.
143 AG 78.
144 AG 80.
145 AG 80. Whether Leibniz in the end came to abandon the "Aristotelianism" of his middle period and to embrace a form of phenomenalism continues to divide the scholars. For contrary views on this question, see Adams (who thinks that Leibniz's late metaphysics was a form of idealism) and Phemister (who doubts whether the middle-period "Aristotelianism" was ever really abandoned).
146 AG 139.
147 AG 139.
148 AG 119.
149 For the continuation of some of these lines of thought in Kant, see Rae Langton's wonderful book, *Kantian Humility*.

Bibliography

Adams, Robert (1994), *Leibniz: Determinist, Theist, Idealist* (Oxford and New York, Oxford University Press).
Alexander, H.G. ed. (1956), *The Leibniz-Clarke Correspondence* (Manchester, University of Manchester Press).
Anstey, Peter (2000), *The Philosophy of Robert Boyle* (London and New York, Routledge).
Anstey, Peter (2002), "Robert Boyle and the Heuristic Value of Mechanism," *Studies in History and Philosophy of Science* 33, 161–174.
Aristotle (1941), *The Basic Works*, edited with an introduction by Richard McKeon (New York, Random House).
Bacon, Francis (1862–1874), *Works*, 14 volumes, edited by J. Spedding, R.L. Ellis, and D.D. Heath (London, Longmans).
Bennett, Jonathan (1984), *A Study of Spinoza's Ethics* (Indianapolis, Hackett).
Boyle, Robert (1772), *Works*, 6 volumes, edited by Thomas Birch (London).
Burnet, Gilbert, ed. (2000), *A Defence of Natural and Revealed Religion, Being an Abridgement of the Sermons Preached at the Lecture Founded by Robert Boyle*, 4 volumes, with a new introduction by Andrew Pyle (Bristol, Thoemmes).
Chalmers, Alan (1993), "The Lack of Excellency of Boyle's Mechanical Philosophy," *Studies in History and Philosophy of Science* 24, 541–564.
Chalmers, Alan (2002), "Experiment Versus Mechanical Philosophy in the Work of Robert Boyle: A Reply to Anstey and Pyle," *Studies in the History and Philosophy of Science* 33, 187–193.
Charleton, Walter (1654), *Physiologia Epicuro-Gassendo-Charletoniana* (London).
Clark, Mary, ed. (1974), *An Aquinas Reader: Selections From the Writings of Thomas Aquinas* (London, Hodder and Stoughton).
Clericuzio, Antonio (1990), "A Redefinition of Boyle's Chemistry and Corpuscular Philosophy," *Annals of Science* 47, 561–589.
Clericuzio, Antonio (2000), *Elements, Principles and Corpuscles: A Study of Atomism and Chemistry in the Seventeenth Century* (Dordrecht, Kluwer).
Cordemoy, Géraud de (1968), *Oeuvres Philosophiques*, edited by P. Clair and F. Girbal (Paris, Presses Universitaires de France).
Costabel, Pierre (1973), *Leibniz and Dynamics*, translated by R.E.W. Maddison (Paris, Hermann).
Des Chene, Dennis (1996), *Physiologia: Natural Philosophy in Late Aristotelian and Cartesian Thought* (Ithaca and London, Cornell University Press).
Descartes, René (1897–1910), *Oeuvres de Descartes*, 12 volumes, edited by Charles Adam and Paul Tannery (Paris, Cerf).
Descartes, René (1985–1991), *The Philosophical Writings of Descartes*, edited and translated by John Cottingham, Robert Stoothoff, and (for volume 3) Anthony Kenny (Cambridge and New York, Cambridge University Press).
Dijksterhuis, E.J. (1961), *The Mechanisation of the World Picture*, translated by C. Dijkshoorn (Oxford, Clarendon).
Dijksterhuis, E.J. (1961), *The Mechanisation of the World View*, translated by C. Dikshoorn (Oxford, Clarendon).
Dobbs, Betty-Jo (1975), *The Foundations of Newton's Alchemy* (Cambridge, Cambridge University Press).
Galilei, Galileo (1954), *Dialogues Concerning Two New Sciences*, translated by Henry Crew and Alfonso de Salvo (New York, Dover Publications).
Garber, Daniel (1992), *Descartes' Metaphysical Physics* (Chicago and London, Chicago University Press).
Garber, Daniel (2001), *Descartes Embodied: Reading Cartesian Philosophy Through Cartesian Science* (Cambridge and New York, Cambridge University Press).
Garber, Daniel (2009), *Leibniz: Body, Substance, Monad* (Oxford, Oxford University Press).
Gassendi, Pierre (1972), *Selected Writings*, edited and translated by C.B. Brush (New York, Johnson Reprints).
Grant, Edward, ed. (1974), *A Source Book in Medieval Science* (Cambridge, MA, Harvard University Press).
Hall, A.R., and Hall, M.B., eds. (1962), *Unpublished Scientific Papers of Isaac Newton* (Cambridge, Cambridge University Press).
Holden, Thomas (2004), *The Architecture of Matter: Galileo to Kant* (Oxford and New York, Oxford University Press).
Hooykaas, R. (1949), "The Experimental Origin of Chemical Atomic and Molecular Theory before Boyle," *Chymia* 2, 65–80.
Jammer, Max (1961), *Concepts of Mass* (Cambridge, MA, Harvard University Press).

Kargon, Robert (1964), "Walter Charleton, Robert Boyle, and the Reception of Epicurean Atomism in England," *Isis* 55, 184–192.
Kargon, Robert (1966), *Atomism From Hariot to Newton* (Oxford, Oxford University Press).
Koyré, Alexander (1965), *Newtonian Studies* (London, Chapman and Hall).
Langton, Rae (1998), *Kantian Humility: Our Ignorance of Things-in-Themselves* (Oxford and New York, Oxford University Press).
Leibniz, Gottfried Wilhelm (1989), *Philosophical Essays*, edited by Roger Ariew and Daniel Garber (Indianapolis and Cambridge, Hackett). [cited as 'AG'].
Loemker, L, translated and edited, *Gottfried Wilhelm Leibniz: PhilosophicalPapers and Letters*, 2nd edition, Dordrecht, D. Reidel, 1969.
LoLordo Antonia (2007), *Pierre Gassendi and the Birth of Early Modern Philosophy* (Cambridge and New York, Cambridge University Press).
Lucretius (1947), *On the Nature of Things*, text, translation, and Commentary in 3 volumes, edited by C. Bailey (Oxford, Clarendon).
Christoph Lüthy, John E. Murdoch, and William R Newman., eds. (2001), *Late Medieval and Early Modern Corpuscular Matter Theories* (Leiden, Boston, and Köln, Brill).
McGuire, J. E. (1968), "Force, Active Principles, and Newton's Invisible Realm," *Ambix* 15, 154–208.
McGuire, J. E., and Rattansi, P. M. (1966), "Newton and the Pipes of Pan," *Notes and Records of the Royal Society of London* 21, 108–143.
McGuire, J. E., and Tamny, Martin, eds. (2008), *Certain Physiological Questions: Newton's Trinity Notebook* (Cambridge and New York, Cambridge University Press).
McMullin, Ernan, ed. (1963), *The Concept of Matter in Greek and Medieval Philosophy* (Notre Dame, IN, University of Notre Dame Press).
Newman, William (2006), *Atoms and Alchemy: Chymistry and the Experimental Origins of the Scientific Revolution* (Chicago and London, University of Chicago Press).
Newton, Isaac (1934), *Mathematical Principles of Natural Philosophy*, 2 volumes, translated by A. Motte (1729), revised translation by F. Cajori (1934) (Berkeley, University of California Press).
Newton, Isaac (1952), *Opticks*, 4th London edition (1730) (New York, Dover).
Newton, Isaac (2004), *Philosophical Writings*, edited by Andrew Janiak (Cambridge and New York, Cambridge University Press).
Osler, Margaret (1994), *Divine Will and the Mechanical Philosophy: Gassendi and Descartes on Contingency and Necessity in the Created World* (Cambridge and New York, Cambridge University Press).
Pasnau, Robert (2011), *Metaphysical Themes 1274–1671* (Oxford, Clarendon).
Phemister, Pauline (2005), *Leibniz and the Natural World: Activity, Passivity, and Corporeal Substance in Leibniz's Philosophy* (Dordrecht, Springer).
Principe, Lawrence (1998), *The Aspiring Adept: Robert Boyle and His Alchemical Quest* (Princeton, NJ, Princeton University Press).
Pyle, Andrew, *Atomism and its Critics*, Bristol, Thoemmes, 1995.
Pyle, Andrew (1995), *Atomism and Its Critics: From Democritus to Newton* (Bristol, Thoemmes).
Pyle, Andrew (2002), "Boyle on Science and the Mechanical Philosophy: A Reply to Chalmers," *Studies in History and Philosophy of Science* 33, 175–190.
Redondi, Pietro (1987), *Galileo Heretic*, translated by Raymond Rosenthal (London, Penguin).
Redondi, Pietro, *Galileo Heretic*, translated by Raymond Rosenthal, Harmondsworth, Penguin, 1988.
Schmitt, Charles (1973), "Towards a Reassessment of Renaissance Aristotelianism," *History of Science* 11, 159–193.
Scott, Wilson L. (1970), *The Conflict Between Atomism and Conservation Theory, 1644–1860* (London, MacDonald).
Secada, Jorge (2000), *Cartesian Metaphysics: The Scholastic Origins of Modern Philosophy* (Cambridge and New York, Cambridge University Press).
Spinoza, Benedict (1994), *A Spinoza Reader*, edited and translated by Edwin Curley (Princeton, NJ, Princeton University Press).
Thackray, Arnold, 'Matter in a Nut-Shell: Newton's *Opticks* and Eighteenth-Century Chemistry', *Ambix* 15, 1968, 29–53.
Van Melsen, A. G. (1960), *From Atomos to Atom* (New York, Harper).
Westfall, R. S. (1962), "The Foundations of Newton's Philosophy of Nature," *British Journal for the History of Science* 1, 171–182.

Part 6

MORAL PHILOSOPHY AND POLITICAL PHILOSOPHY

16
MORAL PHILOSOPHY
Michael LeBuffe

Dramatic changes in the understanding of nature and turbulent debates in religion marked seventeenth century moral philosophy. Many of the most important works of the century were attempts to defend new moral concepts or to recast old ones, as a way of responding to new doctrines in religion, epistemology, and metaphysics. Many others were attempts to show that traditional conceptions of value, or elements of them, did not after all require revision. Moral concepts depend, or might be taken to depend, upon our conception of the world in various ways. The first section of this chapter presents a basic form of a challenge to traditional views arising from new conceptions of God and the world in the seventeenth century together with four basic questions that arise out of this challenge. The second and third sections present responses to these questions drawn from the most revisionary and systematic moral doctrines of the century, those of Thomas Hobbes (1588–1679) and Benedictus Spinoza (1632–1677). The final section uses these philosophers as points of reference for the understanding of major trends of seventeenth century moral philosophy. Very roughly, moral philosophy in the century presents an arc of radicalism, with earlier figures such as Grotius and Descartes building toward a criticism of traditional views, Hobbes and Spinoza presenting the most biting and direct revisions, and later figures such as Cumberland, Pufendorf, and Locke working to reconcile traditional views and new scientific and theological doctrines.

1. The challenge of modernity: Descartes and Aquinas

Seventeenth century moral philosophers responded to a wide variety of sources, including sacred texts; Aristotle, Cicero, Augustine, and other ancient Greek and Roman authors; Luther, Calvin, and Suarez, towering figures of the sixteenth century; Maimonides, Aquinas, Scotus, and other high medieval philosophers; and of course each other. Aquinas's views, although tremendously influential, serve primarily a heuristic purpose here. Aquinas held, confidently and in a relatively clear, systematic form, versions of many of the views which came most heavily under attack and debate in the seventeenth century.

Aquinas held that there is a highest good, which is God. God acts with a purpose, which is the promotion of the good; and He gives all of His creations a purpose also, which is to seek the good (I.6.1). Human beings know our good. Practical reason in us is knowledge of God's law, which directs us to pursue our end (Ia.IIae.90.1, 2). We all possess such knowledge, although it can be more or less perfect (Ia.IIae.94.4, Ia.IIae.99.2R2). Whereas lower creatures act according to God's plan as a matter of course, we human beings do so, when we do so, by free decision (I.83.1). If we follow God's law, we attain our good, which just is union with God (Ia.IIae.3.7), and our happiness consists in this union (Ia.IIae.4.4). By its nature God's law also promotes the good for all in common (Ia.IIae.90.4), so whatever promotes one's own good is no different from what promotes *the* good.

For Aquinas, all things in the world alike are governed by God's purposes, and moral concepts such as goodness, law, and reason fit smoothly into the system of final causes. Central questions for early modern moral philosophy arise from the disruption to this systematically unified conception of morality in the world presented by new approaches to science and theology. A principal element of the challenge presented to this view by the new science will be familiar to many students of philosophy from their study of Descartes's works. Although Descartes does not deny that God has purposes and even seems to make some understanding of them do work, as where, at critical points in the argument of the *Meditations* he relies on an understanding of God on which God could not be a deceiver, he is also generally skeptical of our ability to know God's purposes. He insists, notably, that the business of investigating natural things requires us to understand efficient and not final causes:

> We should investigate not the final but the efficient causes of created things.
>
> We will arrive at no explanations related to natural things from the purpose that God or nature had in view in fashioning them. For we should not be so arrogant as to suppose that we can share in his plans. But we should consider him to be the efficient cause of all things instead.
>
> (*Principles of Philosophy* 1.28)

As stated, Descartes's concern is epistemological: God has plans, or may have, but we cannot "share in them" and will be able to produce no explanations from trying to do so. The statement is so strong, however, that it verges on a metaphysical denial of final causes: as a matter of convention we should in dealing with natural things consider God as an efficient cause. Such a restrictive conception of our ability to understand final causes in natural things raises questions for Thomistic confidence about human beings. We, after all, are also created things. If we cannot share in God's plans for other created things, can we be confident in our ability to know our own ends? On the other hand, if we do have an ability to understand things through efficient causes, might it be within reach to understand ourselves in such terms?

Very generally, the emphasis on an understanding of the natural world exclusively in terms of efficient causation raises the question of how the investigation of ourselves and of value relates to the investigation of the natural world. Suppose that moral law and value are teleological and based upon our own knowledge of our purposes. If attention to purpose in nature is ruled out for other things, then in an important sense a single systematic understanding of the world is no longer possible. The separation of the human from the rest of creation is suspicious. If we reject such a separation, on the other hand, our status as created things governed by accounts of efficient causation in the world may cast suspicion on any claim about us that incorporates teleological explanation. Four related, more specific issues were the subject of heated debate throughout the seventeenth century and will be of particular interest.

First, how do we understand *value*? On a traditional conception, our good is our end, the purpose that God gives to us. If God's purpose for me is still something that I can know even though I cannot know God's purpose for other things, this special kind of knowledge will have to be explained. If, on the other hand, we come to deny that we have a purpose or that our purpose can be known, will we be sceptics about value? Or will we conceive it in some new way without reference to God's purposes?

Second, how do we understand *moral law*? Traditionally, laws are dictates of practical reason, evident from our understanding of God's will or of our own natures, which require us to pursue the good. If value itself is understood in some different way, then this understanding of law will have to change as well. Because moral law and practical reason are closely associated, we may also have to arrive at a new understanding of practical rationality. Just as Descartes's objection to the search for final causes wavers between the epistemological and the metaphysical, so too this question may arise in two different ways. Lacking the relevant knowledge of God's commands, can we know moral law in some other way? Alternatively, does moral law consist in something other than God's command or plan?

Third, are we *free*? The compatibility of human freedom and our aspiration to understand the causes of all things is a perennial problem for philosophy. Aquinas's own views on free choice are notoriously unclear, for example, and a metaphysics that emphasizes teleology, while it shapes the possible accounts of free choice that one might defend, does not make the task of explaining freedom easy for him. The new emphasis on efficient causation in explanation in the seventeenth century does however recast the challenge of explaining human freedom. The new science proposes to explain all change in a body by reference to the prior states of the body and universal causal laws. We have bodies. Are we somehow exempt from these laws? Or is there a sense of human freedom under which our bodies are indeed governed by these laws but we are nevertheless sometimes free?

Fourth, what is the relation between *self-interest and morality*? On the Thomistic conception, because our happiness is attained in the attainment of our end and our end is part of the good, there is not a strong distinction between what is good for me and what is good *simpliciter*. Individuals may have an imperfect understanding of what their good consists in, so they may perceive a conflict between self-interest and the good, but such a perception will always be mistaken. New conceptions of value and of law need not incorporate the assumption that there is never a conflict between self-interest and value. If they do not, then the association of practical reason with the demands of morality may no longer be plausible. Why should we say that it is unreasonable to pursue one's interest when that conflicts with the requirements of morality?

2. Hobbes

Hobbes rejects many of the principal bases of traditional conceptions of value explicitly and directly. His tasks are to give an account of morality that is robust without making use of the conceptions that he rejects and to define and defend those moral concepts he retains – including notably law, goodness, and freedom – in a way that is both plausible and also consistent with that rejection.

Hobbes's clearest comprehensive rejection of tradition may be found in the opening of the chapter of *Leviathan* (1651) explicitly dedicated to morality, "Of the Difference of Manners":

> BY MANNERS, I mean not here Decency of behavior; as how one man should salute another, or how a man should wash his mouth, or pick his teeth before company, and such other points of the *Small Morals*; but those qualities of mankind that concern their living together in Peace and Unity. To which end we are to consider that the Felicity of this life consisteth not in the repose of a mind satisfied. For there is no such *Finis ultimus* (utmost aim) nor *Summum Bonum* (greatest Good) as is spoken of in the books of the old Moral Philosophers. Nor can a man any more live whose Desires are at an end than he whose Senses and Imaginations are at a stand. Felicity is a continual progress of the desire from one object to another, the attaining of the former being still but the way to the latter. The cause whereof is that the object of man's desire is not to enjoy once only, and for one instant of time, but to assure forever the way of his future desire. And therefore the voluntary actions and inclinations of all men tend not only to the procuring, but also to the assuring of a contented life, and differ only in the way, which ariseth partly from the diversity of passions in diverse men, and partly from the difference of the knowledge or opinion each one has of the causes which produce the effect desired.
> (*Leviathan* 150: 3–20)

Here Hobbes dismisses without argument the notion there is a human end, a highest good that our end is a part of, or any happiness to be found in its attainment. Whereas Descartes expresses skepticism about our ability to know God's purpose, Hobbes simply asserts that there is no final end and no greatest good. Whatever accounts he offers of freedom, natural law, value, and its relation to self-interest, then, will have to be conceived and defended without the resources provided by the "old Moral Philosophers." He does offer an alternative account of happiness (i.e. "felicity," the cognate of the Thomistic term *felicitas*) in terms of desire: attaining the object of one's desire – continually, because new desires always arise when old desires are satisfied or defeated – makes one happy. This solution, however, raises more explicitly an issue that already arises once the highest good is dismissed. The highest good, traditionally conceived, unifies each person's happiness and the happiness of all: my mind is satisfied, finally, when it attains a unity with God. Where this easy identification of individual and universal welfare is dismissed, the moral philosopher faces the challenge of describing the relation of self-interested and moral goods. Hobbes identifies an individual's happiness with the satisfaction of desire in this passage, and he suggests that, where two desires conflict, the attainment of happiness for one person might be inconsistent with such attainment for another. Where he admits a "diversity of passions in diverse men," Hobbes seems to acknowledge quickly that such conflict is possible.

In addition to the challenges for an account of morality that arise from the rejection of traditional resources, Hobbes also seems to accept the constraints imposed by the new science, one of which he takes to be universal determinism. The many references to causal language in the new accounts of desire and felicity in chapter 11 may already seem to suggest this view. However, terms such as "assuring" and "procuring" show that, as in many of Hobbes's discussions of human passions and desire, he acknowledges the directedness of human desire and many passions, a feature of them that is perhaps most naturally accommodated by teleological language. (The opening of chapter 17 of *Leviathan*, which refers to the final end that we have in forming a commonwealth, is perhaps the strongest such example.) Strong, general evidence of determinism in Hobbes may be found in *De Corpore* (1655) or *Concerning Body*:

> in whatsoever instant the cause is entire, in the same instant the effect is produced. For if it not be produced, something is still wanting, which is requisite for the production of it; and therefore the cause was not entire, as was supposed.
>
> And seeing a necessary cause is defined to be that, which being supposed, the effect cannot but follow; this also may be collected, that whatsoever effect is produced at any time, the same is produced by a necessary cause.
>
> (EW 1, 123)

If by "whatsoever effect," Hobbes means whatsoever there is, then this passage commits him to universal determinism. (Note that Hobbes's term "necessary" seems here to refer to what today is usually called "hypothetical necessity" and is synonymous with determinism.) As bodies among other bodies, human beings move and change in ways that, at least in principle, can be known from a knowledge of nature and previous states and that could not be otherwise. So, in his defense of moral theses, beyond avoiding traditional doctrines that he finds unsatisfactory, Hobbes must accommodate determinism.

Supposing that Hobbes is a universal determinist, that position is not inconsistent with the admission of some final causes, which Hobbes might appear to invoke in his theories of desire, passion, and the state. Indeed, despite his rejections of the final end and the *summum bonum*, Hobbes does accept some explanation in terms of final causes. In *Concerning Body*, he restricts such explanations to treatments of sense and will, however, and also requires that such causes reduce to efficient causes: "A *final cause* has no place but in such things as have sense and will; and this also shall prove hereafter to be an efficient cause" (EW 1, 132).

Hobbes's account of *value* begins with an individual's own desire. He identifies an individual person's good, in some sense, with the object of their desire. What might have seemed, then, to be a pressing problem of coordination – how do we get people to look past individual self-interest in order to attain true goods which are to be had in peace and unity? – now looks like a problem of moral conflict. Individuals with conflicting desires would seem to make one and the same end both good and evil. Even peace and unity in society, when those come at the cost of some citizens' desires, might be evil as a result. Here are the initial accounts of good and evil from chapter 6 of *Leviathan*:

> But whatsoever is the object of any man's appetite or desire, that is it which he for his part calleth good; and the object of his hate and aversion, evil; and of his contempt, vile and inconsiderable. For these words of good, evil, and contemptible are ever used with relation to the person that useth them: there being nothing simply and absolutely so; nor any common rule of good and evil to be taken from the nature of the objects themselves; but from the person of the man, where there is no Commonwealth; or, in a Commonwealth, from the person that representeth it; or from an arbitrator or judge, whom men disagreeing shall by consent set up and make his sentence the rule thereof.
>
> (80: 29–82: 4)

Scholars disagree about the meaning of this passage. Some take Hobbes to defend a relativistic conception of value, on which any object that I desire is good for me, any object you desire is good for you, and so on. Others take Hobbes's account of good and evil here to be projective. That is, they take Hobbes here to describe the circumstances in which people find things to have value: whatever I desire, I also find good; whatever you desire, you also find good, and so on. Such an interpretation does not require Hobbes himself to have any position at all on what the good actually is or on whether anything has value. However, it is natural to take his claims that there is nothing simply and absolutely good nor anything in the nature of objects that makes them good or evil to imply that there is nothing that really has value. The relativist thinks, then, that there is value but that it is a function of desires. The projectivist thinks that there are judgments about what has value, which track our desires, and this view naturally (although not ineluctably) leads to the conclusion that those judgments are mistaken and that there is no value in the world.

The problem of coordinating *self-interest and morality* arises under either reading, although in slightly different forms. In each case, Hobbes has the burden of showing that "good" is univocal across individual and social contexts, or if it is not, of spelling out the two different senses and their relation to one another. In his initial account of good and evil at chapter 6 of *Leviathan*, Hobbes may seem to solve the problem by fiat, declaring that individual welfare and the moral good do not conflict by simply and impossibly allowing the commonwealth to determine individual desires. (The function of the commonwealth is probably more complex, really, and involves Hobbes's intricate theories of authorization, reason, and performative utterance.) The argument of *Leviathan* offers a number of other rich resources, however, for explaining the relation between self-interest and morality. Even without reference to God's purposes for human beings or to positive law, Hobbes has reasons for suggesting that morality requires what is certainly in one's own interest and what is commonly known to be so.

We may start by examining what is in some sense the source of the good, human desire and its source, passion. Very generally, Hobbes offers an account of human passion on which several passions – fear, glory, and pride – are very common and powerful. Fear is the most common and powerful: "The Passion to be reckoned upon, is Fear" (*Leviathan* 216: 7–8). Together with the fear of invisible powers, the fear of death, and principally death at the hands of others, is for Hobbes the most powerful human motive. As a result, it is a matter of fact about human desire that many of our most powerful desires are those by which we seek to avoid the objects that we fear and find evil, a point that explains Hobbes's emphasis on the desirability and value of a secure and contented life at the beginning of chapter 11.

Hobbes's account of *moral law* reveals the relationship between accounts of the human good in self-interest and in morality. Many of the most important moral goods – such as peace, promise keeping, justice, gratitude, and so on – Hobbes presents as known means to the preservation of life. The main steps of the argument may be found in chapters 14 and 15 of *Leviathan*. Hobbes defines a right of nature as

> the Liberty each man hath, to use his own power, as he will himself, for the preservation of his own nature: that is to say, of his own life; and consequently, of doing any thing, which in his own Judgement, and Reason, he shall conceive to be the aptest means thereunto.
>
> (*Leviathan* 198: 4–8)

Then he defines "Law of Nature":

> a Precept, or general Rule, found out by Reason, by which a man is forbidden to do, that, which is destructive of his life, or taketh away the means of preserving the same; and to omit, that, by which he thinketh it may be best preserved.
> (*Leviathan* 198: 14–17)

For the laws of nature that Hobbes introduces corresponding to traditional virtues, he offers arguments that invoke the ends – aversion of death, love of life and contented life – emphasized in his account of human passion and desire. At the end of his account of the laws of nature, he brings individual desire and the laws of nature together explicitly:

> *Good* and *Evil*, are names that signify our Appetites and Aversions; which in different tempers, customs, and doctrines of men, are different. . . . And consequently all men agree on this, that Peace is Good, and therefore also the way, or means of peace, which (as I have shown before) are Justice, Gratitude, Modesty, Equity, Mercy and the rest of the Laws of Nature, are good; that is to say, moral virtues; and their contrary Vices, Evil. Now the science of Virtue and Vice, is Moral Philosophy; and therefore the true Doctrine of the Laws of Nature, is the true Moral Philosophy.
> (*Leviathan* 242: 3–5, 13–19)

The interpretation of this argument, including both the relation between Hobbes's psychology and the laws of nature and also the meaning of the laws of nature, is still a matter of considerable debate among scholars. It is clear under any interpretation, however, that Hobbes takes his account of human passions and desires, and the definitions of "good" and "evil" that he offers in the course of that account, to be a basis of some kind for his laws of nature. In doing so, he offers a way in which we can know the laws and appreciate an important kind of force in them, without knowing that they are commanded by God. You and I will be similar, no matter what our other differences, in that we will both find peace good, and, because finding a thing good just is a matter of desiring it, we will both want to seek it. In this way, Hobbes finds a kind of motivation associated with moral law.

Hobbes's also recasts his invocations of practical reason in terms of our desires and our agreement. On the traditional, Thomistic view, practical rationality is possessed by human beings as a means to help them to understand God's plans. It can, perhaps, be interpreted that way in Hobbes as well, but it can also and more readily be interpreted in terms of common desires and a common understanding of the means toward attaining ends commonly desired. Thus, one might argue that Hobbes takes avoiding death always to be rational just because the fear of death is so powerful: whatever are the most dominant objects of human desire are also and therefore rational to desire. In addition, Hobbes takes his laws of nature to be dictates of reason just because they are conclusions concerning what conduces to our conservation and defense (*Leviathan* 242: 26–28), and because they are known by all, a point that Hobbes indicates in the previous passage by writing that "all men agree" about value of peace and the means to peace. So, Hobbes's account of practical reason emphasizes common passions and common prudential reasoning rather than God's purpose and a standard of reason external to human psychology.

The laws of nature secure the univocity of "good" in its self-interested and moral uses, or something very close to it, and Hobbes defends his adherence to the traditional identification of one's own good and the good *simpliciter* by arguing that adherence of a certain kind to the laws of nature is always what reasonable people will find to be in their own interest. He takes up the issue most directly by raising an objection to the identification of self-interest and morality in the central case of justice:

> The Fool hath said in his heart, there is no such thing as Justice, and sometimes also with his tongue; seriously alleging that every man's conservation and contentment being committed to his own care, there could be no reason why every man might not do what he thought conduced thereunto: and therefore also to make, or not make; keep, or not keep, Covenants was not against Reason when it conduced to one's benefit. He does not therein deny that there be Covenants; and that they are sometimes broken, sometimes kept; and that such breach of them may be called Injustice, and the observance of them Justice: but he questioneth whether Injustice, taking away the fear of God (for the same fool hath said in his heart there is no God), may not sometimes stand with that Reason which dictateth to every man his own good; and particularly then, when it conduceth to such a benefit as shall put a man in a condition to neglect not only the dispraise and revilings, but also the power of other men.
> (*Leviathan* 222: 1–14)

The fool contests Hobbes's characterization of rationality, making self-interested behavior but not moral behavior (i.e. just behavior) always rational. So, the fool directly attacks the strategy that Hobbes uses to bring self-interest and morality together. In response, Hobbes defends the view that it is always rational to be just, that is, to keep covenants that one makes and also consistently publicly and privately maintain that it is rational to do so: those who are, and are known to be, keepers of covenants, are just and rational, and (at least as far as we can predict before the action in question) they are also going to be better off. Hobbes's insistence that all ordinary people *know* that the laws of nature dictate the means to contented life is indicated by his use of the label "Fool": it is only a person lacking reason who would raise such an objection in the first place.

Hobbes's revisionary accounts of value, rationality, and natural law work together as components of his solution to the problem of reconciling self-interest and morality. He presents them so that they may be known at least independently of any knowledge of God's plan. The account of the fool shows this I think. Hobbes's response to the fool is a response to someone who, beyond denying the consistency of self-interest and justice, also denies that there is a God, so his arguments are supposed to be sound and recognizably sound to an atheist.

Hobbes revision of received morality requires more of him than making do without a providential God, however. It also restrains him within the bounds of the new science of body. In his response to the question of whether human beings are sometimes *free*, Hobbes maintains the traditional association of freedom with responsibility, and he argues that the position that we are sometimes free does not conflict with universal determinism. Here are Hobbes's definition of "liberty" and an assertion of the compatibility of freedom and determinism from chapter 21 of *Leviathan*:

> LIBERTY, or FREEDOM, signifieth properly the absence of Opposition (by Opposition, I mean external Impediments of motion); and may be applied no

less to Irrational and Inanimate creatures than to Rational. For whatsoever is so tied, or environed, as it cannot move but within a certain space, which space is determined by the opposition of some external body, we say it hath not Liberty to go further.

(324: 3–8)

Liberty and necessity are consistent; as in the water, that hath not only *liberty*, but a *necessity* of descending by the Channel; so, likewise in the Actions which men voluntarily do, which, because they proceed from their will, proceed from *liberty*; and yet because every act of man's will and every desire and inclination proceedeth from some cause, and that from another cause, in a continual chain (whose first link is in the hand of God, the first of all causes), proceed from *necessity*. So that to him that could see the connexion of those causes, the *necessity* of all men's voluntary actions would appear manifest.

(326: 9–17)

Whereas traditional views take human beings to be unlike many other created beings precisely in having free choice, Hobbes builds a definition of liberty that applies explicitly to all creatures. We – and squirrels and waterfalls – are free whenever our motion is not impeded. His compatibilism follows easily from this conception of liberty. Our actions, like the actions of all bodies, are the effects of precedent causes. Indeed, it is with respect to some effect that might (in different circumstances) have followed but does not that one is not free.

Hobbes's account of freedom is clearly consistent with determinism. It is also politically important: under a specialized and revised definition, the artificial chains that are impediments to action in the laws of states impede us artificially. It is not clear, however, whether it is successful as a means of securing the moral notions traditionally associated with free action. More important to the interpretation of Hobbes's moral philosophy, the extent to which such notions enter into his moral thought is also not clear. Hobbes does occasionally invoke the idea of just punishment in connection with voluntary action, as he does in this passage from his dispute with John Bramhall (1594–1663), *Of Liberty and Necessity* (1654):

These actions I call VOLUNTARY my Lord, if I understand him aright that calls them SPONTANEOUS. I call them *voluntary*, because those *actions* that follow immediately the *last* appetite, are *voluntary*, and here where is one only appetite, that one is the last. Besides, I see it is reasonable to punish a *rash* action, which could not be justly done by man to man, unless the same were *voluntary*. For no *action* of a man can be said to be without *deliberation*, though never so sudden, because it is supposed he had time to *deliberate* all the precedent time of his life, whether he should do that kind of action or not.

(EW 4, 272)

Just punishment is, however, a political concept as it concerns Hobbes in chapter 21 of *Leviathan*, and it seldom enters his writings as it does in this passage from Bramhall. Likewise, responsibility seems to be of little interest to Hobbes as a moral concept.

Perhaps the moral concept the understanding of which most requires an understanding of freedom in Hobbes is obligation. In chapter 13 of *Leviathan*, for example, he writes,

> Covenants entered into by fear, in the condition of mere Nature, are obligatory. For example, if I Covenant to pay a ransom, or service for my life, to an enemy, I am bound by it. For it is a Contract, wherein one receiveth the benefit of life; the other is to receive money, or service for it, and consequently, where no other Law (as in the condition of mere Nature) forbiddeth the performance, the Covenant is valid.
>
> (*Leviathan* 212: 15–20)

Whereas many of us might think that coercion excuses us from keeping our promises, Hobbes relies upon his notion of liberty to extend the scope of possible obligation. Fear, recall, is for Hobbes the passion to be reckoned on. It determines most of our free actions. There is not then, for Hobbes, a morally significant difference to be found among obligations that we undertake in other circumstances and those that arise under coercion. They are undertaken freely in the same sense. If responsibility and punishment outside of the context of civil laws are not central moral concepts for Hobbes, obligation certainly is. The theory of obligation in *Leviathan* derives a great deal of its revisionary character from Hobbes's naturalized and permissive definition of freedom.

3. Spinoza

Spinoza rejects final causation in God or in nature more clearly and forcefully than Hobbes. He characterizes the view not as an old philosophical doctrine, but as a kind of belief that people commonly and naturally, but also falsely and harmfully, come to hold. The explanation of this natural tendency is the central task of a long appendix that follows his account of God in part 1 of the *Ethics*. (The *Ethics* was published after Spinoza's death in 1677 but circulated in various forms much earlier.)

> All the prejudices that I undertake here to reveal depend upon this one, that evidently men commonly suppose that all natural things act, as they themselves do, on account of an end. Indeed, they judge it to be certain that God himself directs everything to some certain end: they say that God has made all things for man but man so that he might worship God. I will consider first, therefore, this prejudice, asking first why most people rest satisfied with it and, next, why all are so inclined by nature to embrace it. Next, I will show that it is false and, finally, how from this prejudice others have arisen concerning good and evil, merit and sin, praise and blame, order and confusion, beauty and ugliness, and other things of this kind.
>
> (GII/78, 1–12)

It is possible that, like Hobbes, Spinoza accepts final causation in human behavior. Students of Spinoza dispute this question still, and the debate turns principally perhaps on the phrase "as they themselves do" in this passage. If all of men's suppositions are suspect, then their supposition that they themselves act on account of end is no evidence that they do. If the phrase indicates an account of knowledge rather than mere supposition in ordinary people, however, or if it is meant to arise outside the context of the supposition and in Spinoza's own voice, then it is evidence that Spinoza takes there to be final causation in human desires.

In either case, Spinoza also resembles Hobbes in the restrictions that he imposes upon himself by adopting universal determinism:

> 1p28: Every singular thing, or anything that is finite and has a determinate existence, cannot exist or be determined to act unless it is determined to exist and act by another cause, which is also finite and has a determinate existence; and, again, this cause also cannot exist or be determined to act unless it is determined to exist and act by another, which is also finite and has a determinate existence, and so on to infinity.

Spinoza recognizes the implication of his endorsement of determinism for a contracausal conception of free choice (the demonstration to this proposition cites 1p28):

> 2p48: In the mind there is no absolute, or free, will; but the mind is determined to will this or that by a cause, which is itself determined by another, and this again by another and so on to infinite.

So, morality, in Spinoza's presentation of it, can permit no final causes in nature and must include no doctrines inconsistent with universal determinism.

Although Spinoza is like Hobbes in adopting metaphysical commitments that constrain his moral theory, Spinoza is in a way much more ambitious in the moral doctrine that he hopes to defend. Surprisingly, Spinoza preserves many of the doctrines of the "old Moral Philosophers" that Hobbes rejects. Unlike Hobbes, for example, he does argue that there is a highest good:

> 4p28: The mind's highest good [*summum bonum*] is the knowledge of God; its highest virtue is to know God.

Spinoza also takes there to be a final end, in which a mind rests content, and, as the proposition that the mind's highest good is the knowledge of God suggests, he even adopts those elements of the traditional view that make God in some sense the thing with which we seek union (see especially 5p40s) and find happiness and contentment in attaining. The clearest general statement of his view is part 4, appendix 4:

> In life, therefore, it is especially useful to perfect, as far as we can, the intellect, or reason, and in this one thing consists man's greatest felicity, or blessedness. Indeed, blessedness is nothing but that self-contentment of mind that arises from the intuitive knowledge of God. And perfecting the intellect is nothing other than understanding God and the attributes and actions of God which follow from the necessity of his nature. Therefore, the final end [*finis ultimus*] of a man who is led by reason, that is, the highest desire by means of which he tries to regulate all the others is that by which he is moved to an adequate conception of himself, and also of all things that can fall under his understanding.

Spinoza, then, does break sharply with teleological metaphysics and does adopt universal determinism, but he also aspires to capture – or to recast – a great deal of what Hobbes rejects entirely.

Spinoza's account of *value* starts, as Hobbes's does, from accounts of human desire and ordinary human value judgments. Desire has its origins in a perfectly general account of the action of singular things:

> 3p6: Each thing, as far as it is in itself, strives to persevere, in its being.

At 3p7, Spinoza argues that this striving is the essence of each thing. Human affects are changes in a person's power of acting, virtue, or perfection (these are nearly equivalent terms for Spinoza). A scholium to 3p11 includes a definition of human passions in terms of such changes:

> We see, then, that the mind can undergo great changes, and can pass now to a greater, now to a lesser perfection, passions that certainly explain to us the affects of happiness [*laetitia*] and sadness [*tristitia*]. By "happiness", therefore, I shall understand in what follows a passion by which the mind passes to a greater perfection. By "sadness", however, a passion by which it passes to a lesser perfection.

"Desire" (*cupiditas*) is a synonym for "striving" (*conatus*) emphasizing the human consciousness of striving: " 'Desire' may be defined as appetite together with the consciousness of appetite" (3p9s). So, forms of happiness and sadness change our desires and subsequently our behavior. Most frequently, as Spinoza understands it, human life consists in a vulnerability to passion in the form of the present, changeable influence of external objects. The result is, typically, a kind of inconstancy in our desires and a lack of real control over our lives: "we are driven about in many ways by external causes and, like waves on the sea driven by shifting winds, we toss about, ignorant of our fortune and fate" (3p59s, Spinoza 1972, 2/189, 4–7). The moral theory of the *Ethics* makes the understanding and control of passion and thereby the regulation of desire its principal tasks.

In his account of the psychology of desire, Spinoza identifies our judgments of value with the objects that we desire and in which we experience or anticipate happiness or sadness:

> 3p9s: It is established from all this, then, that we strive for, will, want, or desire nothing because we judge it to be good; rather, we judge something to be good because we strive for it, will it, want it, and desire it.

> 3p39s: By "good" here, I understand every kind of happiness, and whatever leads to it, and especially this: what satisfies any kind of longing, whatever that may be. By "evil", however, I understand here any kind of sadness and especially this: what frustrates longing.

If these accounts describe ordinary use – and their appearance in Spinoza's account of the human affects suggests that they do – Spinoza holds a view of ordinary use similar to Hobbes's on which it is a fixed fact about human beings that whatever we desire we find to be good, whether or not we understand value to consist in being desired. I might, for example, think of value in an object to consist in the fact that it was made for my use by a benevolent God. Nevertheless, it will be true of me that I will call "good" only those things that bring me joy; so, when I experience joy in a warm fire, I will call it good in accordance with 3p39s but I will regard the fire as something produced for me by divine providence.

Although the scholia of part 3 of the *Ethics* suggest that it is a fixed fact about us that we *find* the objects that we desire and enjoy good, Spinoza does not suggest that it is a fixed fact about us that we *understand* value in any particular way. Indeed, it is our ability to understand value in different ways that provides Spinoza with a resource that helps him to recast traditional ethical notions such as the final end and the highest good. In the appendix to part 1, Spinoza explicitly picks out for criticism the idea that people ordinarily understand value in terms of God's providence:

> After men persuaded themselves that everything that happens, happens on their account, they had to judge that what is most important in each thing is what is most useful to them and to rate as most excellent all those things that pleased them best. So they had to form these notions by which they explained natural things: good, evil, order, confusion, warm, cold, beauty, ugliness. And, because they suppose themselves free, these notions have arisen: praise and blame, sin and merit. I will examine the latter notions after I discuss human nature. The former I will explain briefly here. They have called whatever conduces to health and the worship of God, "good," but what is contrary to these things, "evil." . . . It is no wonder, then, that (as we note also in passing) we find so many controversies and from them, finally, scepticism to have arisen among men. For although human bodies agree in many ways, they vary in even more. So what seems good to one, to another seems evil; what seems orderly to one, to another seems confused; what is pleasing to one, to another is displeasing.

The ordinary understanding of value that Spinoza criticizes builds upon false beliefs about an anthropomorphic God and harms us by giving rise to controversy and skepticism. However, the human understanding of value is not fixed. In a preface to part 4, Spinoza begins to construct a new understanding of good and evil, and also a new basis on which to understand traditional ethical notions, by emphasizing the point that, as beings that do act purposively, we can construct our goals for ourselves and conceive of value in terms of those goals:

> because we want to form an idea of man as a model of human nature to which we can refer, it will be useful for to us retain these same words with the sense that I have described. By "good" therefore in what follows I shall understand this: what we certainly know to be a means by which we may move closer and closer to the model of human nature that we set before us. By "evil," though, this: what we certainly know impedes us, so that we are less like that model. Next, we shall say that men are more perfect, or less perfect, to the extent that they move closer to or further from this model.

In the first definitions of part 4, Spinoza presents formal accounts of good and evil that draw upon the discussion of the preface:

> 4d1: By "good" I shall understand this, what we certainly know to be useful to us.
>
> 4d2: By "evil", however, I shall understand this, what we certainly know prevents us from being masters of some good.
>
> On these definitions, see the end of the preceding Preface.

The moral sage, as much as the ordinary person, will find the objects of desire and the sources of happiness to be good. It is a fixed fact about human psychology that this is where we find value. How we understand value, however, is not fixed. The moral sage will operate with an understanding of good and evil better than that of the ordinary person, one that is not based on false beliefs and that is more productive of value.

Because Spinoza emphasizes a kind of goal directedness – a model of human nature that we set before ourselves – that he takes to survive his criticism of teleology in nature, he is able to use a strategy for the reconciliation of *self-interest and morality* similar to traditional strategies on which any perceived conflict between one's own interest and the good generally is mistaken. The strategy is perhaps best seen, as it is in Hobbes, in relation to reason; that is, Spinoza attempts to show that there is no conflict between the view that it is reasonable to pursue one's own interest and the view that is it reasonable to pursue the moral good.

Self-interest is prominent in Spinoza's moral theory, but its role is difficult to characterize. There is substantial textual evidence suggesting that Spinoza is a psychological egoist. The clearest passage may be found in the appendix to part 1 of the *Ethics*: "all men in all things act for the sake of an end, namely, their advantage, which they want." There is also substantial textual evidence complicating any interpretation of Spinoza's psychology, including 4p20 and its scholium, where Spinoza writes that people can neglect what is useful to them and admits that people even act to end their own lives, and 4p44s, where Spinoza characterizes those afflicted by monomania as having no other goal besides the object of greed, ambition, or lust. The clearest such passage may be found in an early work, unpublished but probably completed by 1662, the *Treatise on the Emendation of the Intellect*:

> The pursuit of honors and wealth distract the mind not a little, especially when the latter is sought only for itself, because it is supposed to be the highest good. However, honor distracts the mind in this way to a far greater extent: indeed it is always supposed to be good through itself and the ultimate end toward which all things are arranged.
>
> (GII/6, 7–12)

It is not clear whether or in what way, in interpreting Spinoza's psychology, critics ought to try to reconcile the claims that all men seek their own advantage and that some people seek other ends, including ends contrary to their own advantage, exclusively and for their own sake. It is better perhaps not to describe the most important drive toward self-interest as psychological at all. An alternative might be, emphasizing 3p6 and 3p7, to characterize Spinoza as a kind of metaphysical egoist, for whom our natures are (even if our psychologies are not) characterized by a kind of drive that, unimpeded, secures our own good. Another or a complementary strategy is to emphasize the place of reason in Spinoza. The fact that those who seek something other than their own interest are also those most in the grip of passion suggests that Spinoza is a rational egoist. The claims at 4p18s that reason requires self-love, the pursuit of one's own advantage, and the preservation of one's own being support this interpretation. In some sense that must be reconciled with his criticism of teleology, Spinoza takes our natures and therefore also our conscious desires to aim at our own advantage, and, most clearly, he characterizes practical rationality in these terms.

Indeed, in arguing that self-interest and morality do not conflict, Spinoza's intellectualism in ethics is most evident. At 4p26 he argues that reason requires nothing but the striving for understanding, a claim that forces readers to reconstrue all of the items listed in 4p18s – advantage, preservation, self-concern – in intellectualist terms. Then, from this characterization of human interest, Spinoza proceeds to argue, most clearly at 4p35 and 4p36, that my pursuit of understanding does not conflict with but aids and is aided by your own pursuit. At 4p36, for example, he argues that "[t]he greatest good of those who seek virtue is common to all and can be enjoyed equally by all." The appeal of such a conception of the good is clear. Many of the circumstances that concern Hobbes – in which it might seem rational for me to violate the common good in the pursuit of my own – are those in which you and I clearly compete for material goods. Spinoza does occasionally invoke the same kind of arguments that Hobbes uses to show that material goods, such as food, clothing, and company, are best secured through cooperation, and that all ordinary people can recognize this point. In the *Ethics*, at 4p40 he offers such an argument; the theme is clearest, however, in the *Theological-Political Treatise* (1670), where he writes,

> Society is very useful not only for securing one's life against enemies, but also for lightening the many tasks that must be done. Indeed, it is necessary for this. For unless men were willing to give work to each other, anyone would lack both the skill and the time to be able to provide for his own sustenance and survival. Indeed, all are not equally suited to all tasks, and no one alone could provide the things which he most needs. Each alone would lack both the strength and the time, I say, to plow, to sow, to reap, to grind, to cook, to weave, to sew, and to do all the many things which must be done to sustain life – not to mention, the arts and sciences, which are absolutely necessary to the perfection of human nature and to blessedness. We see, then, that those who live barbarously without a state lead a miserable and almost brutish life.
> (GIII/59, 13–27)

In the *Ethics*, however, Spinoza emphasizes the pursuit of understanding and characterizes rationality and morality – including especially cooperation – in terms of the pursuit of knowledge. We are very useful to one another, but only insofar as we live according to the guidance of reason (4p35c). Those among us who remain ignorant, on the other hand, are dangerous; they may require guidance from certain forms of passions that are harmful in themselves but which will render them safe and more easily led to knowledge (4p54s); and we should avoid accepting favors from them (4p70). Spinoza unites self-interest and morality, then, by emphasizing in both a good that is easily shared, knowledge. It is conceivable of course that you and I might compete for scarce resources in our pursuit of knowledge. Unlike food or clothing, though, knowledge is not an item that I take and consume in such a way that you cannot use it, and it is plausible to think that, at least in many circumstances, you and I indeed can be a great help to one another in the pursuit of knowledge. Spinoza argues that people led by reason seek nothing for themselves that they do not also seek for others (4p18s). An emphasis on intellectualism, on which the sole complete good of a rational person is understanding, makes that strong claim seems more plausible.

Spinoza's account of *moral law* also incorporates a strong conception of rationality. Because Spinoza's moral philosophy emphasizes bondage to and freedom from passion, an account of the morality of actions is less prominent in the *Ethics* than an account of passion and its control. Indeed, he argues at 4p59 that actions do not hold inherent value for him:

> To every action to which we are determined by an affect that is a passion, we can be determined, without that affect, by reason. . . .
>
> Alternative Dem: Any action is called evil insofar as it arises from this: that we have been affected by hate or some other evil affect (see 4p45c1). But no action, considered in itself, is good or evil (4 Preface), but one and the same action is now good, now evil; therefore, to the same action that is now evil or that now arises from some evil affect, we may be led by reason.
>
> (4p59)

An action is right only if it arises in the right sort of way, that is from reason. Nevertheless, there are a few kinds of actions that Spinoza does recommend because of their close relationship to reason: reason always requires such actions, even if one might perform them, irrationally and so wrongly, from the wrong motives. Such actions include, most generally, the item that Spinoza lists at 4p18s: loving oneself, and seeking one's own advantage, what is useful, what leads to perfection, and to preserve one's being. Other prominent actions demanded by reason include that strongly intellectualist requirement that we pursue only understanding (4p26) and prudential maxims requiring indifference to the time at which we attain certain goods (4p62, 4p66) and a focus solely on the degree of good to be attained or evil to be avoided (4p65).

On Aquinas's view, practical reason and moral law are also closely related: we understand that we are to perform a certain action because we understand God's will and, in particular, our own natures. Hobbes is ambivalent about the relationship of moral law to God's will; at the very least, he takes all of those of who are sane to know the laws of nature insofar as we recognize their usefulness for our ends. In Spinoza's moral theory, the idea of an understanding of God's will disappears entirely. (It does play an important role in his political theory.) Spinoza does, however, maintain a close association between practical rationality and moral law. He also maintains a version of the doctrine that practical reason arises from a kind of knowledge that we all possess. At 2p38c, Spinoza characterizes ideas of reason as a kind of knowledge that all human minds possess. The dictates of reason just are those ideas of reason that relate to particular kinds of actions; in the deductive form of the argument of the *Ethics*, the dictates typically derive from 2p38c or related propositions. The label "reason" suggests, then, for Spinoza, that all human minds possess knowledge of the dictates.

Although Spinoza rejects any notion of contracausal free will and indeed rejects any notion of human will entirely, a sense in which we can be *free* is prominent in his moral theory. Spinoza's notion of freedom is a compatibilist one. All actions are determined, of course, but a thing's actions may be determined either by the thing itself or by external causes. Spinoza defines freedom as self-determination (1d7). A human being, like any singular thing, has an essence that consists in its striving to persevere in being, by 3p7, so our freedom will consist in the extent to which we act from our nature and do persevere.

What is more important in distinguishing Spinoza's account of freedom from most contracausal accounts is that freedom for Spinoza is itself valuable rather than being a condition of the attainment of value. Freedom, traditionally conceived, gives me an opportunity to do good or to do evil. For Spinoza, freedom is expressed in action itself. The more free I am, the more my actions are good. More importantly, however, my freedom is itself what holds value; it is my perfection and virtue.

The only completely free being is God (1p17 and, especially, c2). In constructing a model of human nature, it would be foolish of us to aim at complete freedom. Indeed, in the preface to part 5, Spinoza explicitly criticizes Descartes and the Stoics for maintaining this possibility. We should, rather, conceive of a being that is limited in power and position in the ways that we are and conceive of moral progress in those terms. The free human being, then, is one for whom death is inevitable, but who has the correct attitude toward it (4p67); who faces dangers, but is able to avoid many (4p69); who avoid favors from the ignorant just because doing so has dangerous consequences (4p70); and who lives in a state in order to get the benefits of cooperation (4p73). Although free human beings remain susceptible to the harmful influence of external objects, especially in the form of harmful passions, they nevertheless are the causes of their own actions to a greater extent than other, similarly finite people. Spinoza dedicates part 5 of the *Ethics* to an account of the means that we have of attaining the degree of freedom that human beings are able to attain, and he characterizes human salvation as the possession of this degree of freedom.

4. An arc of radicalism

Hobbes and Spinoza both reject teleology in nature as a basis for an explanation of value. Each also, although in different ways, rejects traditional conceptions of value, moral law, freedom, and self-interest founded in an understanding of God's purposes. Very roughly, their views may be seen as high points in an arc of radicalism in the seventeenth century, with authors preceding them offering steps toward the rejection of traditional moral views and authors following them either defending tradition or attempting to reconcile traditional conceptions of morality with a commitment in science to efficient causation and a new variety of doctrines in religion and theology.

4.1. A step toward Hobbes: Grotius (1583–1645)

Grotius makes important steps toward Hobbesian doctrine by raising in a difficult form the question of the relation between *self-interest and morality*, and his doctrine of *moral law* makes it largely independent of God. Grotius is not clearly a consistently revolutionary figure. He certainly presents himself as a traditional one, for example, in frequent references to classical Greek and especially Roman authors. His most important contributions to moral philosophy are his accounts of law, and even these are frequently, self-consciously traditional. All of Grotius's discussions of natural law develop traditional themes, including theories of practical reason, human desire, and even divine providence. In one of his works, *Commentary on the Law of Prize and Booty* (composed in or shortly after 1603 and then lost until 1864), Grotius associates natural law explicitly with God's plan and so supports a traditional understanding of it. In chapter 2 of that work, he characterizes law, generally, as what God has shown to be his will and contends, citing Cicero as an authority, that we come to know natural law by coming to understand God's purpose in the design in nature.

The Law of War and Peace (1625) is the source of a number of political and moral arguments of enduring importance, including notably a seminal account of international law. It is also the source of a challenge to traditional conceptions of moral law, and it provides something of a basis for the kind of theory of moral law that one finds in Hobbes: a theory on which the law, in some form, can be known without knowledge of God's purposes and on which it can in a way be binding even if God has no purposes.

In *The Law of War and Peace*, Grotius suggests in two ways that the law of nature is in some sense independent of God. First, he suggests that laws of nature are laws of reason that are independent of God's will. Notably, at I1.10, he writes,

> Now the Law of Nature is so unalterable, that it cannot be changed even by God himself. For although the power of God is infinite, yet there are some things, to which it does not extend. Because the things so expressed would have no true meaning, but imply a contradiction.

Of course, reason can be construed as a faculty that human beings possess by which they can understand what God wills. Under such a conception, the view that reason gives us the ability to understand the law of nature is not a significant development. In this passage, however, Grotius clearly places the law of reason beyond the power of God to alter and so distinguishes it from God.

Second, Grotius constructs a list of necessary conditions for natural law that includes no reference to God at all and emphasizes the importance of self-interest in our theories of morality and its requirements. In the prologue to *The Law of War and Peace*, he presents an objection in the voice of the ancient skeptic, Carneades:

> there is no law of nature, because all creatures, men as well as animals, are impelled by nature toward ends advantageous to themselves; that, consequently, there is no justice; or, if such there be, it is supreme folly, since one does violence to his own interests if he consults the advantage of others.

The objection anticipates the concerns that move Hobbes's fool. Rather than taking the more radical Hobbesian approach and attempting to respond to the objection while accepting the premise of a largely egoistic psychology, Grotius rejects Carneades's conception of human desire. He argues in response to this objection that we desire society in addition to selfish ends, a feature of our psychology which separates us from animals. In addition, we also have a power of discrimination and judgment, and, if it is different, a power of knowing and acting in accordance with principles. He concludes,

> in such things it is meet for the nature of man, within the limitations of human intelligence, to follow the direction of a well-tempered judgment, being neither

led astray by fear or the allurement of immediate pleasure, nor carried away by rash impulse. Whatever is clearly at variance with such judgment is understood to be contrary also to the law of nature, that is, to the nature of man.

(prologue)

Such a conception of the law of nature does not clearly reject any view on which laws of nature are God's commands: it is not clear that human conative psychology and practical judgment are sufficient for natural law on this view. However, Grotius by any account provides a strong basis for such a view. Moreover, if one were to argue that God's command cannot be known (or not agreed upon) or even that God's existence cannot be known, the conditions that Grotius sets up may stand as an account of the best way that we have of knowing natural law. Grotius himself makes this point:

What we have been saying would have a degree of validity even if we should concede that which cannot be conceded without the utmost wickedness: that there is no God, or that the affairs of men are of no concern to Him.

(prologue)

The prologue's emphasis on human psychology and reason as a basis for the characterization of moral law is a notable break with traditional views, which many of Grotius's successors noticed, debated, and developed. It includes steps toward a questioning of teleology, a concern about the relationship between self-interest and morality, and a conception of moral law that is independent of God's plans or commands.

4.2. *A step toward Spinoza: Descartes (1596–1650)*

Together with other major physical scientists of the early modern period, Descartes makes significant contributions to the development of an account of nature that emphasizes efficient causation and de-emphasizes final causation. As we have seen, Descartes's aversion to appeals to teleology in physics raises the question of the place of final causes in moral philosophy: why should a kind of explanation that is not acceptable in one domain be acceptable in another, or, as Spinoza asks (3 preface), why should humanity be a kingdom within a kingdom? It is an indirect but extremely important spur to the development of moral theories with similar emphases.

The new interest in a thoroughgoing explanation in terms of efficient causation contributed in a positive way to moral philosophy during the seventeenth century as well, however. Hobbes and Spinoza both draw upon such theories of desire, passion, and freedom in building their accounts of human interest and morality. Beyond his central importance as a champion of the new science, Descartes also contributes to the development of these theories. Most clearly, Descartes's emphasis on knowledge as a source of *value* and his contributions to new compatibilist understandings of ways in which we can become *free* are important steps toward Spinoza's views. This second point is somewhat ironic. Descartes remains committed in all of his writings to the view that the human will resembles the divine will in its freedom, a view that threatens to complicate the use of mechanistic psychology in his moral theory. Nevertheless, Descartes's emphasis on knowledge and the control of passion was an important influence on Spinoza.

Notably, Descartes's hesitancy to make claims about moral law shows a tendency to rely more strongly on human psychology and epistemology in moral theory and less strongly on a knowledge of God purposes.

Although human will is, in some contracausal sense, free on Descartes's view, it functions correctly when it is guided steadily by a well-conceived plan or, in the best case, by knowledge. The plan need not always be founded upon knowledge, as the provisional morality that Descartes recommends in the third part of his *Discourse on the Method* (1637) makes clear:

1. To obey the laws and customs of my country, holding constantly to the religion in which by God's grace I had been instructed from my childhood, and governing myself in all else according to those opinions that were the most moderate and the furthest from excess.

2. To be as firm and resolute in my action as I was able, and to follow even the most doubtful of my opinions, once I had put faith in them, with no less constancy than if they had been quite certain.

3. To try always to conquer myself rather than fortune, and to change my desires rather than the order of the world.

4. To make a review of the various occupations that men have in this life in order to choose the best. . . . I thought that I could do no better than . . . to direct my whole life to the cultivation of reason, and to advance as far as I could in the knowledge of the truth.

(AT VI 23–27, excerpted)

Descartes seems to conceive of a typical case of a bad human life, as Spinoza does later, as one in which a person is inconstant and irresolute. The commitment to adhering to a plan, even before the attainment of knowledge, is perhaps something the mature Spinoza would not think possible. (The young Spinoza does propose something similar to the plan of the *Discourse*; see the *Treatise on the Emendation of the Intellect*, GII/9–10.) Here perhaps, Descartes's doctrine of the freedom of will has practical consequences. He takes it to be possible and recommends that we decide to pursue a certain way of living with constancy before we attain knowledge. Spinoza, by contrast, takes greater constancy in living to be a mark of the attainment of knowledge.

This difference between Descartes and Spinoza is less pronounced in their accounts of virtue. Spinoza, as we have seen, takes virtue just to consist in power, perfection, or action from understanding. Descartes takes this at least to be the typical case, although his account leaves open the possibility that a person who acts from a constant plan and who happened to strike upon the right plan might act virtuously as well. In a letter to his most important correspondent on moral questions, Elisabeth of Bohemia (1618–1680), Descartes argues that the virtuous person is one who is constant just because of understanding and adherence to the commands of reason:

[Each person] should have a firm and constant resolution to carry out all that reason recommends without being turned away by his passions or his appetites; and it is in the firmness of this resolution that, I believe, virtue consists.

(4 August 1645, AT IV 265)

In the same letter, he also acknowledges that constancy that does not accompany such understanding (although it is presumably better than simply to be driven this way and that by shifting winds) is not reliably virtuous, although he seems to leave open the possibility that it could be:

> virtue alone is sufficient to make us content in this life. But this point notwithstanding, if it is not enlightened by understanding, virtue can be false, that is to say, will and the resolution to do well can bring us to evil things, when we think them good; happiness which comes in this way is not solid.... [T]he right use of reason, by giving a true knowledge of the good, prevents virtue from being false.
> (4 August 1645, AT IV 267)

Descartes moves toward Spinoza's view, then. He makes action from reason typical of the virtuous and he makes knowledge of the good and right reason sufficient for virtue in one who resolves to act well.

Descartes's *Passions of the Soul* (1649), a work dedicated to Elisabeth, is his most fully developed account of moral psychology. There, in articles 48 and 49, he moves closer to a view associating knowledge in a mind with its ability to act with constancy:

> 48. What I call [the soul's] proper weapons are firm and determinant judgments concerning the knowledge of good and of evil, which guide a soul that is resolved to manage the actions of its life.
>
> 49. The power of the soul is not sufficient without knowledge of the truth.
> (AT XI 367–368)

These passages, and many of the discussions of particular passions in the book, show a degree of commitment to understanding moral psychology and the value of persons and actions in terms that move away from an understanding of God's providence and toward a theory of morality that finds value in understanding alone.

Like Grotius, however, Descartes is a transitional figure in ethics. In the *Passions*, he explains human passions, most broadly, by reference to their purpose and the purposes of nature:

> 52. The function of all of the passions consists in this alone, that they dispose the soul to want those things that nature says are useful for us and to persist in this volition; and the same agitation of the spirits that customarily causes them also disposes the body toward those movements which serve the fulfillment of the desires.
> (AT XI 372)

So, his commitment to banishing final causes from physics does not extend to accounts of human psychology. Nor does his universal commitment to determinism in bodies. Indeed, his emphasis on free will endures in the *Passions* where it is an essential component of his account of the best state of the soul, generosity (*generosité*):

> 153. I believe that true Generosity which makes a man's self-esteem as great as it can legitimately be, consists entirely in this: in part, in his knowledge that

nothing truly is his but this free control of his own will, and that he should be praised or blamed for nothing except its good or bad use; and, in part, in his feeling in himself a firm and constant resolution to use this same thing well.

(AT XI 445–446)

Descartes builds toward ethical doctrines that do not rely upon final causation in nature and that are consistent with, and make use of, causal determinism. His views nevertheless incorporate many of the commitments that Spinoza and Hobbes reject.

4.3. A step back from Hobbes: Cumberland (1631–1718)

Hobbes's writings faced varied and strong criticism, especially from established English-language philosophers and theologians. Among these, Richard Cumberland is notable for the enduring importance and originality of his criticisms of Hobbes's accounts of *value* and the relation between *self-interest and morality*. Cumberland's *On the Laws of Nature* (1672) addresses Grotius and, principally, Hobbes. He introduces there a universal law of nature, to which all other laws may be reduced:

> The Endeavour, to the utmost of our power, of promoting the common Good of the whole System of rational Agents, conduces, as far as in us lies, to the good of every Part, in which our own Happiness, as that of a Part, is contain'd. But contrary Actions produce contrary Effects, and consequently our own Misery, among that of others.
>
> (introduction, §9)

As we have seen, Hobbes takes my good to consist, in some sense, in what I desire. Frequently, he takes the object of desire to be a contented life and the means to it. Felicity, or happiness, is also closely connected to desire: the continual satisfaction of desire brings felicity. Cumberland criticizes Hobbes's association of good with desire directly:

> I *own*, therefore, "That to be call'd *Good*, which *agrees* with another, and, consequently, that the *Term* is *Relative*"; but it is not always *referr'd* to the *Desire*, nor always to that *one Person only*, who desires it. In these *two* Points *Hobbes* has often *err'd* grosly, (tho he sometimes comes out with the Truth, in Contradiction to himself;). . . . I, on the *contrary*, am of *Opinion*, "That things are *first judg'd* to be *Good*, and that they are *afterwards desir'd*, only so far as they *seem Good*: That any thing is therefore *truly* judg'd *Good*, because its *Effect* or Force *truly helps Nature*: That a *Private* Good, is that which profits *One*; *Publick*, which is of advantage to *Many*; *not* because it is *desir'd* from *Opinion*, whether true or false; or *delights*, for this or that Moment of time."
>
> (*On the Laws of Nature*, ch. 3, §2)

As his universal law of nature shows, Cumberland conceives of value in terms of happiness. The view is not far from one that emphasizes desire, and, as Cumberland himself suggests here, it can be easily confused with Hobbes's view. However, Cumberland's emphasis on the notion that judgments of the good drive desire and his subsequent association of practical rationality with *correct* judgments of the good move Cumberland away from any projective or relativist analysis of value and back toward a traditional, realist conception.

Cumberland also disagrees with what he takes to be Hobbes's characterization of desire, on which each person pursues only private good (*On the Laws of Nature*, ch. 3, §4). Although Cumberland's interpretation is open to question, he does offer an account of the relation between self-interest and the common good that is closer to the Thomistic view than it is to that of Hobbes. As his account of the universal law of nature makes clear, Cumberland takes one's own happiness to provide the "sanction" for a law which requires the happiness of all, a means to the greatest individual happiness. Hobbes, or so Cumberland understands him, takes all desire to be self-interested, so that we follow the laws of nature in order to secure further ends that we want, such as a contented life, and Hobbes does, in his accounts of laws of nature, tend to take the rationality of law keeping to be instrumental and prudential. Cumberland emphasizes the point that we may and frequently do desire the happiness of others and rightly take our happiness to consist in the greater happiness:

> This *Reason*, by which we have prov'd the *Happiness of the Will to consist in the most extensive Benevolence*, is greatly confirm'd by *Experience*, which gives us vast *Pleasure* in the acts of *Love*, *Hope* and *Joy*, whether employ'd about our own Good, or that of others. *These Affections are Essential Ingredients of Happiness*; they bring *Pleasure* along with them, and we find *them* continually mov'd by the *Happiness of others*. He, therefore, robs Man of great part of his Happiness, who deprives him of that most pleasant affection of *Love* and *Benevolence* towards others, and of that *Joy*, which arises from their Happiness. *Our own* Advantages can afford but *small matter of Joy*; the Subject will be exceedingly *inlarged*, if we are delighted with the Happiness of *every other person*.
> (*On the Laws of Nature*, ch. 5, §15)

Cumberland, then, defends a more traditional conception of the relationship between self-interest and morality, on which the human good and the good of all are not distinct.

4.4. A step back from Hobbes and Spinoza: Pufendorf (1632–1694)

In distinctive and influential ways, Samuel Pufendorf also resuscitates elements of traditional conceptions of morality, especially teleology, in defending conceptions of freedom, value, the relation between self-interest and morality, and natural law against the kinds of views held by Grotius and Hobbes, whose views he addresses frequently, and Spinoza, a less frequent direct target.

Pufendorf defines law in his most important work, *On the Law of Nature and Nations* (1672): "In general, a law may conveniently enough be defined 'a decree by which a sovereign obliges a subject to conform his actions to what he prescribes. . . . [T]he term 'decree' here is equivalent to 'command' " (I.6.4). Pufendorf's emphasis on command establishes the importance of will to his moral philosophy. The possession of a free will separates those who can create laws, including human beings and God, from the rest of creation; moreover, relation to a commanded action separates genuinely moral goods from natural goods, such as those that might relate to human well-being but whose pursuit is not commanded. Natural law is commanded by God and requires human beings to do what is always good for them, "that which is exactly fitted to suit with the rational and social nature of man, that human kind cannot maintain an honest and a peaceful fellowship without it" (I.6.18). It also, as in Hobbes, is known "by ordinary sagacity of men" (I.6.18). Men create positive law, Pufendorf writes in the same paragraph, and it can vary by circumstance. Because both forms of law arise from will in the right way, however, both oblige in the same sense.

It is will, in other words, that for Pufendorf, makes a thing moral. Beings with understanding and will, including human beings and God alike, can create "moral entities" that reflect ends:

> For whatever is endued with understanding, can from the reflex knowledge of things, and from comparing them with one another, form such notions as may prove very serviceable in the direction of an agreeable and consistent faculty. *Moral entities* are of this kind; the origin of which is justly to be referred to almighty God, who would not that men should pass their life like beasts, without culture and without Rule; but that they and their Actions should be moderated by settled maxims and principles; which could not be effected without the application of such terms and notions. But the greatest part of them were afterwards added at the pleasure of men, as they found it expedient to bring them in, for the polishing and the methodising of common life. And from hence the end of them is plainly to be discovered, which is not, like that of natural beings, the perfection of the universe, but the particular perfection of human conduct: as superior to brutal, in being capable of regular beauty and grace: that thus in so inconstant a subject as the motions of men's minds, an agreeable elegance and harmony might be produced.
>
> (I13)

Certainly, Pufendorf here rejects views that make value relative or projective. He takes value to be real, even if it is created; those with will and understanding create moral entities in order to guide the will. Pufendorf makes it clear in other passages that moral entities help us, moreover, because each of us possesses a free will that is not limited by causal determinism, a "[l]iberty of exerting, suspending, or moderating his Actions, without being confin'd to any necessary Course and Method" (I12). So, like Aquinas, he takes human free choice to be essential to morality and takes the point of morality to be the pursuit of a final end. Pufendorf, then, retreats both from the rejection of teleology in nature and from the universal determinism that characterize the moral theories of Hobbes and Spinoza.

Pufendorf, is however, like Grotius and Descartes on the other side of the arc, a mixed figure. A notably original element of his view may be found at the end of the previous passage. Whereas traditional conceptions of the end of human beings make it part of the end of all of creation, Pufendorf makes the human good distinctive: it is the perfection of human conduct.

4.5. A step back from Hobbes: Locke (1632–1704)

Locke endorses a traditional conception of the law of nature as a command of God that we know by means of practical reason. This view is to be found frequently in an early work, *Essays on the Law of Nature* (1664; see especially ch. 5) in which Locke frequently refers to divine purpose. It may also be found, in a somewhat more subtle form, later in his *Two Treatises of Government* (1690):

> The State of Nature has a Law of Nature to govern it, which obliges every one: And Reason, which is that Law, teaches all Mankind who will but consult it, that being all equal and independent, no one ought to harm another in his Life, Health, Liberty, or Possessions. For Men being all the Workmanship of one Omnipotent, and infinitely wise Maker; All the Servants of one Sovereign Master, sent into the World by his order and about his business, they are his Property, whose Workmanship they are, made to last during his, not one another's Pleasure.
>
> (II.2.6)

So, Locke takes our moral obligation to arise from divine God's command, and he understands it in terms of our end. In that sense, his moral theory is traditional. These views are stated briefly, however, and Locke does not devote a great deal of argument to them. His accounts of how human beings understand and use moral concepts are much more fully developed, and his contributions to moral philosophy may principally be found there, and, in particular, in his accounts of liberty.

In his accounts of liberty, Locke works to reconcile the new, clear commitment to causal determinism and a form of the traditional commitment to free choice. In *An Essay Concerning Human Understanding*, he defines the term:

> Where-ever doing or not doing, will not equally follow upon the preference of his mind directing it, there he is not Free, though perhaps the Action may be voluntary. So the *Idea* of *Liberty* is the *Idea* of a Power in any Agent to do or forbear any particular Action, according to the determination or thought of the mind, whereby either of them is preferr'd to the other.
>
> (II.21.8)

A notable restriction on Hobbes's definition is a requirement in Locke that action be voluntary. On Hobbes's account of liberty, recall, the label "may be applied no less to Irrational and Inanimate creatures than to Rational." Locke, by contrast, defines "liberty" as a power in an agent and as an idea that applies only to voluntary action. So, Locke distinguishes rational creatures from others. He does so, moreover, in a way that does not require a commitment to a theory of will that is as strong as those defended, for example, by Descartes or Pufendorf. So, he is free to understand human agency in a way that is compatible with commitments of the new science, including determinism. (How Locke does understand human agency and the extent to which his account is successful remain hotly debated topics.)

Locke also makes an important addition to Hobbes's account of freedom. He emphasizes the condition that agents have a power "to forbear any particular Action" in which they are free. That an action be voluntary, then, is a necessary but not a sufficient condition for its freedom. Locke emphasizes this point with an example of a willing prisoner:

> Suppose a Man be carried, whilst fast asleep, into a Room, where is a Person he long to see and speak with; and be there locked fast in, beyond his power to get out; he awakes, and is glad to find himself in so desirable Company, which he

stays willing in, *i.e.*, preferrs his stay to going away. I ask, Is not this stay voluntary? I think no Body will doubt it: and yet being locked fast in, 'tis evident he is not at liberty not to stay, he has not freedom to be gone. So the *Liberty is not an* Idea *belonging to Volition,* or preferring; but to the Person having Power of doing, or forbearing to do, according as the Mind shall chuse or direct.

(II.21.10)

Like his emphasis on volitional action, the notion of power enriches the concept of an agent. Locke again owes his readers an account of the ways in which the attribution of such power to any human action is consistent with our understanding of nature. The attribution of voluntary actions and of powers to human agents, however, suggests that Locke thinks that there are resources, within the constraints of our best understanding of the world, for offering rich explanations of the features of human beings in virtue of which we may be able to explain moral reasoning and related notions such as responsibility and punishment.

Further reading

Darwall, S. (1995) *The British Moralists and the Internal "Ought": 1640–1740.* Cambridge: Cambridge University Press.
Kavka, G. (1986) *Hobbesian Moral and Political Theory.* Princeton: Princeton University Press.
Kisner, M. (2011) *Spinoza on Human Freedom: Reason, Autonomy, and Good Life.* Cambridge: Cambridge University Press.
LeBuffe, M. (2010) *From Bondage to Freedom: Spinoza on Human Excellence.* Oxford: Oxford University Press.
Lloyd, S.A. (2009) *Morality in the Philosophy of Thomas Hobbes: Cases in the Law of Nature.* Cambridge: Cambridge University Press.
Schneewind, J.B. (1988) *The Invention of Autonomy: A History of Modern Moral Philosophy.* Cambridge: Cambridge University Press.
Yaffe, G. (2000) *Liberty Worth the Name: Locke on Free Agency.* Princeton: Princeton University Press.

Bibliography

Original dates of publication for all works are given parenthetically in the main text. Editions listed here are those quoted or cited. I have sometimes changed the spelling or punctuation of English language texts for the sake of clarity. Translations of Latin and French texts are my own unless otherwise noted.

Cumberland, R. (1727) *Of the Laws of Nature,* translated by John Maxwell. London: R. Phillips. (This edition is widely available both scanned and online).
Grotius, H. (1814) *On the Law of War and Peace,* translated by A.C. Campbell. London. (References cite book, chapter, and section. This edition is widely available online).
———. (1950) *Commentary of the Law of Prize and Booty,* translated by Gwladys Williams and Walter Zeydel. Oxford: Clarendon Press.
Hobbes, T. (1966) *The English Works of Thomas Hobbes,* edited by Sir William Molesworth. 11 vols. London: John Bohn. (References abbreviated EW with volume and pages numbers).
———. (2012) *Leviathan,* edited by Noel Malcolm. 3 vols. Oxford: Clarendon Press. (All references to *Leviathan* use this work, refer to volume 2, and cite page and line number).
Locke, J. (1960) *Two Treatises of Government,* edited by Peter Laslett. Cambridge: Cambridge University Press.
———. (1975) *An Essay Concerning Human Understanding,* edited by Peter Nidditch. Oxford: Oxford University Press.
Pufendorf, S. (1710) *Of the Law of Nature and Nations,* translated by Basil Kennett and others. Oxford: L. Lichfield. (This edition is available as a Google Digital Copy from the library of Princeton University. References are to book, chapter, and section).

Spinoza, B. (1972) *Spinoza Opera*, edited by Carl Gebhardt. 4 vols., Heidelberg: Carl Winter. (References are abbreviated "G," with volume, page, and line numbers or refer to elements of Spinoza's texts. For example, "1p28" is *Ethics*, part 1, proposition 28).

Aquinas, Thomas (1888) *Summa Theologiae. 9 vols. In Sancti Thomae Aquinatis doctoris angelici opera omnia iussu impanseque Leonis XIII P. M. edita*, vols. 4–12. Rome: Typographia Polyglotta S.C. de Propaganda Fide, 1888–1906. (References are to part, question, and article).

17
POLITICAL PHILOSOPHY
Susanne Sreedhar

1. Europe in the seventeenth century: the political and philosophical backdrop

It was once common to describe the seventeenth century as the period during which modern Western liberalism was born. Scholars have pointed to the emergence and subsequent rise of liberal notions of freedom, equality, individual rights, popular sovereignty, limited government justified by the consent of the governed, and separation of church and state as concepts central to the discourse of seventeenth century political philosophy. But it is easy to overstate this point and, with hindsight, see seventeenth century political philosophy as a series of moments in an inevitable progression toward the Enlightenment and toward the American and French Revolutions of the next century. In reality, the texture of seventeenth century political thought is both more complicated and more interesting than this view suggests. The so-called liberal concepts neither originated in nor dominated seventeenth century political philosophy; many of these concepts have precursors in medieval philosophy, and some of the most important theorists of the seventeenth century advanced views that were decidedly nonliberal (at least in the contemporary sense of the word). This chapter presents an overview of some of the major figures and debates in seventeenth century political philosophy.

To begin, an understanding of the particular historical character of seventeenth century Europe is critical to understanding the political philosophy that it spawned. The Continent witnessed enormous conflict and instability during this time. The roots of this conflict can be found in the previous centuries with the religious schisms of the Reformation and Counter-Reformation, which caused considerable social and political unrest. Although the French wars of religion ended officially with the Edict of Nantes in 1598, tension and clashes between Protestant Huguenots and Catholics continued throughout the seventeenth century, and the edict was revoked in 1685. England, the locus of much of the best-known political theorizing during this period, experienced a series of momentous events, including a civil war culminating in the trial and public execution of the sitting monarch, an interim dictatorship under Oliver Cromwell, the subsequent restoration of the monarchy, and the so-called Glorious Revolution of 1689. Moreover, as the emerging nation-states of Europe wrestled with internal divisions, they were also forced to defend against threats of attack from external enemies. The Thirty Years' War raged on the Continent during the first half of the century, and there was regular fighting, or the threat of fighting, in and between many of the various countries and provinces in Europe. Periodic episodes of plague, famine, religious persecution, and rebellion were the norm, making life for many in the seventeenth century uncertain in a multitude of ways.

One of the most distinctive features of this period is the high degree of involvement in *actual* politics by the people who were writing and publishing the great works of political theory. Many political theorists worked closely with those who held public office. As a result, they were deeply involved in the controversies of the day. Many were persecuted for their political beliefs; some were imprisoned or forced to flee their countries. Indeed, it is striking just how many of the most important works of seventeenth century political philosophy were written while their authors were in exile or in jail. To give a few examples, Hugo Grotius was secretary and advisor to Johan von Oldenbarnevelt, who occupied something close to the role of prime minister in the Dutch Republic. When Oldenbarnevelt was executed after his rivals gained power in 1618, Grotius was imprisoned. After making a daring escape in a cart of books and dirty laundry, he fled to France and then Germany, eventually serving as the Swedish ambassador to France. Thomas Hobbes was in the employ of some of the most prominent royalist families in England and went into exile in Paris in 1641 when the tide of the civil war began to turn against the king. Hobbes had even made an unsuccessful bid for a seat in the English House of Commons, and though he never actually served in office, he was never far from the debates about English politics. Samuel von Pufendorf composed his first major work of political theory in a Danish prison in 1658–59, and he spent much of his later life as the royal historiographer to the Swedish and German courts. Finally, John Locke was the secretary of the Board of Trade, and participated in the writing of the Constitution of the American Carolinas. Locke was forced into exile in Holland in 1683, and was able to return to England only at the end of the Glorious Revolution.

There is no doubt that the tumultuous political environment in which these thinkers lived influenced the ways in which they approached philosophical questions about the origin, purpose, and limits of the state. Hobbes explicitly acknowledges as much, describing his most famous work as "occasioned by the disorders of our present time" (*L*, "Review and Conclusion" 17). In an important sense, the whole century was *disordered*, precipitating some changes in people's philosophical and political commitments while leaving other commitments unscathed. We can understand their philosophies, at least in part, as efforts both to accommodate disorder and to propose more resilient forms of order. A number of the most striking differences among the political theories of the seventeenth century can be understood in part as disagreements about the root causes of political unrest and how best to eliminate or at least manage it.

The specific philosophical questions asked and the specific philosophical issues engaged were largely products of this particular historical context. The frequent bids for power from competing civil, political, and religious factions meant that at many points during this century, it was unclear *to what degree* and *to whom* one's obedience was owed. As a result, questions about the legitimacy of a ruler's power, as well as the legitimacy of resistance to that power, were at the forefront of political action and political theory. Given this historical situation, it is unsurprising that many of the philosophical debates centered on questions of *political authority* and *political obligation*. Faced with the question, "What is the source and nature of the state's authority (i.e. its *rightful* power to rule)?" one common view held that the power of rulers over their subjects was ordained by God; another suggested that the right to rule could only be derived from the consent of the people, who were by nature free and equal. Political theorists disagreed about the form government should take (monarchy, aristocracy, democracy, or some combination of these), and they disagreed about whether the state's power of government was subject to any limits, and who, if anyone, was in a position to enforce those limits. Faced with the question, "Why are subjects obligated to obey the commands of the state, and when, if ever, are they permitted to disobey or even rebel against those in power?" some argued for unconditional obedience; others found justifications for disobedience in claims of self-defense, breach of contract, or appeals to conscience. Closely related to these issues were questions about the relationship between ecclesiastical law and secular law, including the matter of religious toleration, which also occasioned their share of dispute.

The answers to these basic questions about authority and obligation were often, though not always, connected in important ways. If God granted a king power, one could plausibly understand the king's power as both absolute and irresistible. But, if the ruler's power derived from the transfer of authority by free and equal people, it seems prima facie more plausible to conceive of that power as limited and the people as entitled to resist or depose their ruler if he violated the conditions upon which this authority had been transferred to him. Defenders of royal power tended to invoke a divine sanction for political rule; proponents of popular sovereignty frequently appealed to a contractual relationship between ruler and ruled in order to justify organized resistance to the king. But political theorists also combined these ideas in surprising and unique ways. For example, some (most famously, Hobbes) used the idea that free and equal people contract to form a government as part of a defense of an extreme theory of absolute monarchy with a strict prohibition on rebellion. In contrast, others used the idea of monarchy as a divinely ordained institution to ground a claim that subjects have both the right and the duty to resist their king under certain circumstances. Many more permutations were espoused, and there were important nuances in – and differences among – the ways in which concepts like "freedom," "equality," and "rights" were used. A chapter such as this cannot hope to do justice to the rich complexity of political thought in the early modern period; however, I aim to give the reader a sense of this complexity as I trace the twin concerns about political authority and political obligation through some of the most important, influential, and enduring political philosophies of the seventeenth century.

2. The divine right of kings

These questions of political authority and obligation come to the forefront in particular because of the waning of notions of God-given authority and the waxing of secular, or at least nondenominational, theories of politics. A natural place to begin, then, is with a theory known as "the divine right of kings" (or sometimes "the divine right theory of monarchy"), which holds that kings are appointed by God to rule over their subjects.[1] As the century opens, the reigning king of England, James I, publicly espouses this theory, declaring in a speech to Parliament that "[t]he State of MONARCHIE is the supremest thing upon earth: For kings are not onely GODS Lieutenants upon earth, and sit upon GODS throne, but even by GOD himself they are called GODS" (James I 1994, 181). Though there are a number of variations on the theme, there are three general tenets of divine right theory. First, *only* the king has the authority to govern; that is, the king has a monopoly on the rightful use of political power. Of course, the king is not personally and directly responsible for every exercise of state power; but those who pass legislation and adjudicate controversies do so at his pleasure (i.e. all other exercises of state power are either explicitly delegated or legitimate only so long as the king does not object). Often cited as evidence for this proposition is Romans 13: 1–7, which states that "[e]veryone must submit himself to the governing authorities, for there is no authority except that which God has established." This idea was originally put to use in order to refute the claims of clerics that the church has dominion over spiritual matters, and later to establish the supremacy of the monarchy over competing bids for power from its rival in civil society, namely parliament.

The second tenet is that the king is accountable only to God. The king is entrusted with the care of his subjects like a shepherd with his flock, and just as the sheep (either individually or collectively) cannot rightly accuse or punish their shepherd, subjects in a kingship cannot rightly accuse or punish their king. When Parliament finally won the long and bloody civil war in England, they charged King Charles I with treason. At his trial, Charles simply said, "Princes are not bound to give an account of their actions but to God alone" (quoted in Sommerville 1986, 34). He would not recognize the legality or legitimacy of the proceedings, refusing even to enter a plea. Unfortunately for him, his refusal to take the trial seriously did not stop Parliament from finding him guilty and beheading him.

Third, divine right theory is usually taken to include a doctrine of nonresistance, according to which any and all resistance to royal power is wrongful, no matter how incompetently or tyrannically the king behaves. Because the authority of kings is not only likened to but also supposed to be derived from the authority of God, then disagreeing with the king is akin to disagreeing with God, and at the very least shows profound disrespect for God's choice of rulers. The obligations of subjects to obey their rulers are subsumed under their obligations of obedience to God and, like their obligations to God, should be inviolable. James I draws this comparison saying, "That as to dispute what God may doe, is Blasphemie. . . . So is it sedition in Subjects, to dispute what a King may do in the height of his power" (James I 1994, 184). If one's duty to God requires universal submission to all aspects of a king's rule, then the only solution to even the worst tyranny is prayer.

Given how closely royal authority was tied to its divine origin, a common concern was what to do in the event that the king issued an order in direct opposition to a person's understanding of the will of God. This happened quite frequently, given the proliferation of various sects of Christianity with their different and conflicting interpretations of God's will. Some versions of divine right theory deny royal heresy as a possibility; after all, the king is supposed to be God on earth and so cannot act against God. But other versions accept that a king may indeed act heretically and recommend that in those cases subjects disobey the heretical command but only on the condition that they passively submit to the punishment for their disobedience. Almost never was *active* resistance – explicit or organized protest or out-and-out rebellion – permitted.

The theory of divine right was endorsed by various monarchs (who clearly had a stake in the matter) and was presumed to require no corroboration beyond Scripture, but it also enjoyed a few attempts to provide it with philosophical support. The most famous and most valiant of these attempts was written by Sir Robert Filmer in his defense of the royalist cause against the parliamentary rebellion in England. Filmer (1588–1653) intended to discredit the appeals to the natural freedom and equality of mankind, and the contract between ruler and ruled, that were central to Parliament's case against the king. His argument begins with the observation that no person is ever born free because each was born to a father who ruled him. Relations of domination and subordination (i.e. relations of *rule*) were, on Filmer's account, natural – part of the structures of nature that God had ordained for human beings. Building on these patriarchal foundations, Filmer proceeded to make a case for royal absolutism. The ideology of natural and divinely ordained hierarchies, whether in the family or between social classes, was widely accepted in early modern England, making the starting points of Filmer's argument appear to be particularly familiar and compelling at that time.

Filmer's crucial step was his contention that the rule of a king over his subjects is analogous to the rule of a father over his family; both are aspects of the natural, divinely ordained hierarchy set out in the first book of the Bible. As Filmer reads it, the book of Genesis tells the story of the first instance of political authority – the grant of power from God to Adam to rule over his descendants and to use and control the natural resources of the earth. Armed with the premise that the Bible provides an accurate account of history, Filmer constructed a narrative to explain how Charles I came to possess a godly right to rule England in the first half of the 1600s. He posited that the divine grant of authority to Adam has been handed down by primogeniture through the generations such that any present king enjoys his reign as a result of and at the pleasure of God. Unlike James I, who thought that God *directly* conferred the authority to rule England on himself and subsequently on his son Charles, Filmer held that the divine warrant enjoyed by Charles I was *indirect*. God did not directly appoint Charles to rule England; rather, Charles inherited from his father the right to rule that had been passed down through the generations of English kings.[2]

Filmer's particular brand of divine right theory included a commitment to absolutism modeled on Jean Bodin's famous theory of absolute sovereignty from the sixteenth century. In his widely read work, *Six Books of the Commonwealth* (1576), Bodin argued that sovereignty must be *absolute*; that is, the supreme power in any state must be *undivided* and *unlimited*. The power to make, interpret, and enforce laws is indivisible and so must be held by one body or institution, whether that be a single monarch, an aristocratic council, or a democratic assembly. For Bodin and many who followed him, this entails that sovereign power cannot be limited by a system of laws, because any person or institution in a position to judge whether a law had been broken would itself be the real sovereign. In this respect, Bodin, Filmer, and other absolutists were writing not only against Aristotle, who thought that there could be mixed forms of government, but also in opposition to any theory of limited or constitutional government. Filmer and the divine right theorists were not the only ones to adopt a Bodinian conception of sovereignty, though it suited their purposes especially well.

Because Filmer's patriarchal case for the divine right of kings was the most systematic, reasoned, and influential defense of the position, many of the tracts on political theory in the seventeenth and eighteenth centuries devoted space to refuting it. The most famous and most extensive of these refutations was Locke's; other well-known rebuttals were given by Edward Coke and John Milton. Locke dedicated the whole of the first treatise of his *Two Treatises of Government* to a step-by-step rebuttal of Filmer's view, attacking both the content and the logic of Filmer's argument in a sustained critique. Locke not only rejects what he takes to be all of the major assumptions but also argues that, even if those assumptions are granted, Filmer's conclusions still do not follow. For example, Locke argues that begetting a child does not confer authority over that child, but points out that, even if it did, then the mother would have a claim to rule the child, as well as the father (a thesis clearly incompatible with patriarchalism). Furthermore, even if the notion of paternal authority were defensible, it would not be inheritable; the eldest son cannot hold power over his siblings because he did not beget them. Locke also takes issue with Filmer's interpretation of the book of Genesis, arguing that God did not grant Adam exclusive title to the earth's natural resources; God gave those resources to all of mankind (a claim that plays a significant role in the theory of property Locke offers in the *Second Treatise*).

In my view, the most interesting part of Filmer's legacy was not his *alternative* to social contract theory but his *critique* of it. Against theories that favored government formed by agreement between naturally free and equal people, Filmer argued that no person was born free from subordination nor had there ever existed a society of free people. His strategy had two parts. First, he insisted that, as a matter of historical fact, there was never a state of freedom and equality, nor was there ever any actual contract establishing a government or actual consent given by those governed to their governors. Second, he accused those who invoked such concepts of hypocrisy; they proclaimed that everyone was free and equal, subject only to that authority to which they voluntarily agreed, while at the same time excluding women and children from the political arena. It is indeed true that virtually all political theorists of the seventeenth century excluded women and children from their analyses, and to the extent that they did engage this issue, they struggled to provide a compelling account of how women and children agreed to their subordination. Filmer pointed out that if they were true to their word, proponents of consent-based theories of government would include *all* people, including women and children, in their analyses, and because they failed to do so, they betrayed their own principles (Filmer 1991, 142). To be sure, Filmer was not making any kind of feminist statement here; rather, he meant the appeal to women and children to serve as a *reductio*, showing that his opponents' views must be false, because following them to their logical conclusion leads to the absurd idea that women and children are equal and so must consent to be ruled.

Writing at the end of the century, Mary Astell, one of the best-known female British philosophers of the early modern period, similarly calls attention to the hypocrisy of contract-based theories of government. Punning on the inclusive and exclusive meanings of the word "man," she asks, "If *all Men are born free*, how is it that all Women are born slaves?" (Astell 1996, 18). Unlike Filmer, Astell arguably *was* making protofeminist claims, and her place in the history of philosophy depends in part on this fact. Even so, her goal was not to argue for women's equal inclusion in political society but to improve the conditions of their lives and, especially, to promote better education for them. Astell is an interesting example of the way in which various and even seemingly incompatible commitments were combined in the seventeenth century; she was a divine right royalist who strongly rejected social contract theory, but she nonetheless made some of the most famous protofeminist claims of the century.

Finally, attention should be paid to the logic of the ideas that form the backbone of divine right theory. Independent of how convincing or unconvincing one might find it, there seems to be a fairly coherent story to be told if one starts with the assumption that monarchs derive their power from God (and thus their power, like God's, is absolute), and one's obligation to those monarchs (like one's obligation to God) requires unqualified obedience and total submission. But whereas Filmer and others linked divine sanction for political rule with royal absolutism and duties of nonresistance, the concepts are logically distinct. To briefly illustrate this, consider two theories that combine the concepts in different ways. First, Philip Hunton, one of the most articulate and effective defenders of Parliament in its struggles with the Crown during the English civil wars, argued that the coercive power of the state can only be derived from God. But unlike Filmer, Hunton put this claim to use in an overall justification for mixed monarchy, an idea ruled out by the Bodinian absolutism that Filmer adopted. Second, Francisco Suárez, an important figure in the tradition of Catholic resistance theory, invoked the divine origins of political power in order to validate – and indeed encourage – active resistance to particular Protestant kings. Both Hunton and Suárez combined a commitment to a God-given royal prerogative with ideas about the necessity for contractual agreements between rulers and those ruled. Both insisted that the power of kings could only come from God, but instead of seeing this as opposed to ideas about freedom, equality, consent, and resistance, they constructed theories in which the divine establishment of monarchy and the elements of contract theory were not only consistent but also mutually reinforcing.

Filmer's account of divine authority depends on the premise that divine right is necessarily *royal* right, but not everyone shared this presupposition. Many in the more radical Protestant camp accepted the truth of the same biblical passages (e.g. Romans 13: 1–7) about all power being ordained by God, but they rejected the view that God ordained it *via* the king; moreover, they held that the passage is about the source of *all* power, not just monarchical power. For them, Romans left open what *form* of government was appropriate, legitimate, and just. And there have been other attempts to reinterpret the Romans passage and the Pauline doctrine in general. One of the reasons divine rightists like Filmer argued for the grant of sovereignty to Adam and for the centrality of patriarchy was to answer the challenge that God did not ordain any particular form of government. However, this claim did not originate with Filmer or the seventeenth century; the question of whether God had granted sovereignty, or rather dominion, to Adam was hotly debated by William of Occam, Marsilius de Padua, and others who were engaged in the Franciscan poverty debate in the thirteenth and fourteenth centuries. In the end, then, the notion of a divine sanction for political rule turns out to be a somewhat promiscuous idea, used with equal ease in service of radically different and opposing ends. Its usefulness and persuasiveness waned in the face of disagreements about the nature of the divine, disagreements whose intractable nature became more and more evident in the course of the seventeenth century.

Whatever its philosophical merits or shortcomings, the theory of the divine right of kings played an important role in the development of early modern political thought, and the various ways in which it was rejected played a role in the development of late modern political thought. It also played a central role in persistent political controversies in England about the status of the monarchy and the future of the Crown. Obviously important in the context of the civil wars of the 1640s, notions of the divine right were revived, albeit temporarily, during the restoration of the monarchy with Charles II in 1660; but though the monarchy has endured in England since the Restoration, English kings and queens since the Glorious Revolution have never again claimed anything approaching the power of God. In France, appeals to monarchical divine right persisted into the eighteenth century, when they were invoked as a political claim by King Louis XIV and forcefully defended as a theoretical position by French bishop and theologian Jacques-Bénigne Bossuet. But the doctrine of divine right was critiqued in France during the Enlightenment and eventually abandoned with the French Revolution.

Thus, the seventeenth century was the beginning of the end for the theory of divine right. Although political theorists, most notably Pufendorf and Locke, built a minimalist notion of God (and thus, the notion of a divinely structured order) into their theories, these theories nonetheless represented a shift toward a secular notion of political authority that gained force throughout the early modern period. Growing religious divisions and profound scientific discoveries made it increasingly difficult to defend any position, political or otherwise, on the basis of purely theological premises. Interpretations of Scripture and confessional doctrines were the source of a great deal of violent conflict and could no longer support a stable, publicly shared conception of political legitimacy.

3. The birth of modern social contract theory

The impossibility of establishing a shared religious basis for political authority and obligation opens up a number of fundamental questions in political philosophy. If the authority to rule over others does not come from God, then where does it come from? If the obligation that people have to obey those in charge cannot be reduced to or explained by some higher obligation, then how do they come under that obligation at all? And if the natural condition of man is not one of subordination, then what is it?

The idea that government is a product of the voluntary agreement of the governed, deriving its authority from a contract or some other form of consent, arguably has a history as old as Western political philosophy itself, having been suggested by Glaucon in Plato's *Republic*, as well as by Epicurus. Indeed, notions of consent trace their roots back to Roman law. But the "modern social contract tradition" is usually thought to originate in the seventeenth century and claims, as its most famous proponents, two seventeenth century philosophers: Hobbes and Locke.[3] This tradition is set apart from its predecessors by its use of the following concepts and strategies. First, social contract theorists reject the idea that political authority is naturally or divinely ordained, instead positing that people are naturally free and equal. Second, given that this is the case, the agreement to be ruled – which is secured when would-be subjects enter into some sort of contract, or give their consent in some other fashion – provides the *only* legitimate source for a system of political power. Finally, political authority and obligation are thus conceived from the "bottom up," as opposed to the "top-down" approach of divine right. In spite of these shared concepts and strategies, however, each theorist spelled out the details of such a contract, and what kind of government would result, differently.

In this chapter, I focus primarily on four of the most significant, most systematic, and most philosophical proponents of seventeenth century social contract theory – Grotius, Hobbes, Pufendorf, and Locke. I conclude with a brief discussion of Spinoza, whose place in the social contract tradition is contested.[4] Part of my goal is to show how these theories can be fruitfully understood in light of the century's increasing religious and cultural discord, and in response to failed attempts to base political authority and obligation on contested principles, theological or otherwise.[5] Furthermore, in focusing on the work of four main theorists, my primary interest lies in developing the *philosophical* relationships among their respective accounts of the social contract. Although we will see that there are significant and extensive differences, it is worth highlighting first their common structural and methodological starting points.

Early contract theorists were concerned with two key questions; namely the *origin* and the *limits* of political authority and obligation. They also shared a basic methodological approach to these questions. In broad terms, social contract theorists start with a picture of human nature (described partly in terms of principles of natural law or natural right) and from there derive claims about what human life would be like without government – that is in some kind of natural, or precivil, condition, usually called a "state of nature." They conclude that this would be unpleasant, impoverished, perhaps even violent, and therefore – they argue – people would take action to escape it by agreeing to institute a government. Social contract theorists then tend to ask, "In that context, what kind of government would people agree to form?"; "What natural rights could or would people give up in such a contract?"; and "Given such an agreement, could resistance or rebellion ever be legitimate?" Theorists provide widely divergent answers to these questions, and these answers determine what each thinks about the nature and limits of political authority and obligation. Thus, all of the theorists develop different versions of the same theoretical elements, namely (1) a conception of natural law and right, (2) a conception of the state of nature, (3) a conception of the social contract and the move to civil order, (4) an account of the proper form or forms of government, and (5) implications for the duties of government and for rights of resistance.

Seventeenth century social contract theory can be seen as a series of attempts to provide political theories derived from principles that did not presuppose controversial or contested moral or religious ideas and could therefore – in principle – be rationally acceptable to all. This feature is one of the most philosophically important aspects of the modern social contract tradition, and it is part of what makes the seventeenth century so significant from the point of view of the history of political theory.

Hugo Grotius (1583–1645) is a logical starting point for this discussion, both because of his chronological precedence and because of his influence over subsequent seventeenth and eighteenth century writers.[6] Grotius is widely credited with one of the most crucial shifts in the emergence of social contract theory and the modern theory of natural law. He is best known for his contributions to debates about the relations *between* states, what Grotius and his contemporaries called the "law of nations" and what we now know as international law and international relations.[7] Nevertheless, in his account of political relations *within* the state, Grotius addressed the twin questions of political authority and obligation that would come to define subsequent contract theories.

The Grotian project begins with an account of the law of nature, conceived as the set of principles that are true for all peoples at all times.[8] For Grotius, these universally valid principles could be identified by examining human nature. Human beings, like all other beings, desire self-preservation. Human beings also desire to live in a peaceful and rational social order.[9]

Self-preservation is broadly construed to include things that promote or protect physical survival, even if they are not strictly necessary for it, so it is perhaps more accurate to speak of advantage or self-interest. For Grotius, the claim that we desire our own preservation and advantage is both a descriptive and a normative claim. He believes it is uncontroversial not only that people *do*, in fact, behave in these ways but also that by nature they are *allowed* to seek their own advantage. But self-preservation has ultimate priority, so that one is permitted to put one's own advantage before the needs or interests of others, especially when it is a matter of life or death. Thus, he holds that people are allowed to seek their own advantage as long as they do not unnecessarily injure others; they are permitted what Grotius calls "the pursuit of innocent Profit" (*DJB* II.II.2). By nature, he claims, we are subject to moral rules and principles: not to steal from others, to provide restitution if we do, to keep promises, and to impose punishment when it is merited. However, although we are obligated not to hurt or steal from others (unless our lives depend on doing so), he does not claim that we have natural obligations to *assist* others in their pursuit of self-preservation. That is, there are no natural duties of mutual aid. Grotian natural law, then, is constituted by both permissions and injunctions; we are permitted to seek our own advantage but we are obliged to do so only in a certain way. Moreover, when these rules are violated, nature calls for such wrongdoings to be avenged.

Grotius made two important and innovative claims on the basis of his initial picture of natural law. First, he framed key components in the language of *natural rights* and developed natural rights in connection with his account of man's natural desires. On his view, we have natural rights to self-preservation and to pursue "innocent Profit." We also have natural rights not to be injured by others, and to demand restitution or inflict punishment on those who violate our rights. Historically speaking, such language is now so familiar that it is easy to overlook the degree of conceptual innovation involved. Very briefly, according to the medieval view, one could only speak of right actions or "the right"; one could not see *rights* as powers that individuals have. In contrast, though he used the term in a wide variety of ways, Grotius developed the more familiar view that rights are moral powers that people can possess.[10] These powers provide moral permissions and responsibilities, and they are the kinds of things that could be retained or given away. Importantly, rights hold independent of states; they are not granted by states. Although there are precursors to this conceptual shift in Suárez, Vitoria, and others, Grotius is often credited with giving the first account of rights as we know them now.

His second innovative claim concerned the metaphysical and epistemic status of natural law. As we have seen, Grotius argues that the principles of natural law (and, for him, natural rights) are determined by human nature and discoverable by means of a rational examination of human nature as such. They are "*the Rule and Dictate of Right Reason*" (*DJB* I.I.X.1) and are "engrafted in the minds of all."[11] This means that the same principles he identifies can and would be affirmed by anyone else who conducts such an examination. But, crucially, Grotius also claims that the principles of natural law *are in fact* agreed upon. For Grotius, then, the agreement is not only hypothetical but also actual (if implicit). So, for example, with regard to the priority of the right of self-preservation, he says that Christianity might oblige people to sacrifice themselves, but no one (presumably Christians included) would claim that natural law itself demands such actions (*DJB* I.II.VI.2; Tuck 2005, xxii.). Moreover, he makes it clear that he is offering an account of natural law as agreed upon by all nations and peoples, irrespective of religion, creed, and other beliefs (e.g. *DJB* I.II.III). These claims are important in the context of his endeavor to provide a basis for international law; such a system could not be dependent on the doctrines, beliefs, or values of any particular culture or region. Both the Dutch and the Indians should, by force of rational consideration, accept his principles, and, further, they actually do.

Grotius's strong universal-agreement view is present elsewhere in his writings. First, Grotius took his opponent to be Carneades, the famous skeptic (and he presumably took himself to be victorious against this opponent).[12] This shows that he sees his account as impossible to reject, even for the most skeptical of skeptics. Second, Grotius holds that the principles of natural law would be true even if there were no God or if God did not concern himself with human affairs. This last claim is one of the most infamous in his vast corpus of writings on political theory, and he retreated from it in later editions of his work. But the point remains: Grotius took the principles of natural law or right that he set out to be *acceptable* and, even more significant, to be *accepted* by everyone capable of rational thought. And a large part of why he held this to be true is that his principles were deliberately thin, meaning that he intentionally made their content rather sparse. It is no wonder that Richard Tuck, one of the best-known contemporary writers on Grotius, talks about his "minimalism" (Tuck 2005, xviii). In order to appeal to the widest possible audience, Grotius is trying to lay a foundation that depends on as few premises as possible, a sensible strategy given the deep and widespread disagreements that characterized seventeenth century political life.

The conception of natural rights as powers or entitlements that are transferrable allowed Grotius to construct a novel explanation for the origin of political authority. People give up their natural rights in an act of voluntary consent in order to form a government.[13] The question of whether *all* natural rights are transferrable, or only some of them, is one that Grotius also considers. In his view, the entirety of one's natural rights can be transferred, giving a government absolute and indisputable power over its subjects; he reasons that communities of people, like individuals, can thus voluntarily enter conditions of slavery (*DJB* I.III.VIII.1). He does not claim that governments *must* be constituted along these lines, only that it is possible and has, in fact, occurred. However, there are points where Grotius seems to waver on these issues. With regard to both tyranny and necessity, he states that natural rights were either not given up or somehow returned to peoples or individuals. Specifically, he says that people living under tyrannical governments cannot be supposed to have consented to such rule and that, in conditions of necessity (e.g. starving, imminent death), the natural right of property is restored. So, people are allowed to steal and so forth if they need to do so to save their lives (*DJB* II.VI.V). But the passages in which he makes these claims are in tension with his general claim that all rights are transferrable and people can rightfully enslave themselves. Moreover, Grotius advocates monarchy and denies that rulers have obligations to their subjects. He does encourage rulers to treat their subjects well and describes those who do as "praiseworthy," but he denies unequivocally that there is a right of resistance (*DJB* I.IV.II). Regrettably, he never renders this denial consistent with his remarks on tyranny and necessity.

Grotius, then, developed some of the most fundamental and eventually most widely held elements of social contract theory – individuals as the bearers of natural, or pre-political, rights; the authority of the state as a product of a willful transfer of those rights – but it was Thomas Hobbes who took those ingredients and developed them into a fully fledged theory. Hobbes is not unreasonably thought of as the father of modern social contract theory, but his debt to Grotius should not be underestimated.

Influenced by the new science, Hobbes (1588–1679) took it upon himself to create a science of politics. He set out to produce a geometric-style proof that his theory of the state was correct (*L* 4–5; Jesseph 1996, 86–107). He describes feeling awed by his encounter with the proof for the Pythagorean theorem: he was attracted to the idea that if one accepts the definitions and axioms with which one begins, one could derive (using deduction) a conclusion not susceptible to logical rejection (Martinich 2005, 6; Grant 1996, 111). Although political philosophy (unlike geometry) does not admit of valid deductive arguments for any interesting conclusion, Hobbes intended to convince people of the truth of his conclusion by offering a theory that began with uncontroversial starting points and proceeded as logically as possible. It was necessary because he knew his conclusion – that absolute monarchy is the best form of government, and that subjects are permitted to disobey only under the rarest of circumstances – was one that people would want to reject.

The Grotian influence is evident in Hobbes's starting points, as well as his method. Beginning with a general claim about human psychology, namely that there is a natural impulse to avoid death (comparable to the force of gravity), he infers that it would be particularly unreasonable to blame people for acting on it (*DC* 1.7). Thus, people have a natural right to seek self-preservation. Hobbes describes this, saying,

> The Right of Nature, which writers commonly call *jus naturale*, is the liberty each man hath to use his own power, as he will himself, for the preservation of his own nature, that is to say, of his own life, and consequently of doing anything, which in his own judgment and reason, he shall conceive to be the aptest means thereunto.
>
> (*L* 14.1)

The "liberty" in this case is a freedom from blame, a moral permission. And the claim that people naturally have such a moral permission is, for Hobbes, a claim that no one could reasonably reject (Lloyd 2009).

Natural law, the corollary to natural right, Hobbes defines as a dictate of reason requiring each person to preserve herself. In this way, Hobbes represents the most decisive break with the Scholastic natural law tradition. He rejected the Scholastic-medieval-Aristotelian conceptions of natural law, with their theological and teleological views of the universe. Starting from a materialist, mechanist metaphysics, he thought that the nature of reality was no more than matter in motion and the principles therein, and hence human behavior was no exception. He famously denied the existence of a final or highest good (*summum bonum*) for people, instead claiming that the greatest we can hope for is the satisfaction of desire after desire, ceasing only in death. There are places in which he references connections between natural law and divine law, but Hobbes's canonical and foundational formulation of natural law bespeaks a clear secularity – namely it is

> a precept of general rule, found out by reason, by which a man is forbidden to do that which is destructive of his life or taketh away the means of preserving the same, and to omit that by which he thinketh it may be preserved.
>
> (*L* 14.2)

Because Grotius was severely criticized for suggesting that natural law might be true even if there were no God, it is unsurprising that Hobbes was charged with atheism, a charge that followed him his entire life.[14]

In the state of nature, then, even people who lie, steal, or attack others do so "with right," as long as they sincerely believe that doing so contributes to their self-preservation. But because Hobbes's account of what that right means is limited – it simply grants permission and removes blame from the actor – it does not give others any corresponding obligation to respect it. Indeed, according to Hobbes, there can be no obligations at all in the state of nature. For him, obligations can only arise from a covenant or contract, and there can be no covenants or contracts without an external authority to enforce them, and it is precisely the absence of this kind of external authority that defines the state of nature as such. This reflects another contrast with Grotius: for Hobbes, all obligations are contractual whereas, for Grotius, some obligations come from natural law. Moreover, Hobbes explicitly rejects Grotius's claim about natural sociability, even in the minimal form Grotius gives it. Indeed, Hobbes offers an extended argument for the fundamental differences between humans and naturally social animals, bees and ants. It is not that Hobbes thinks that people are naturally *anti*social, *per se*; rather, for human beings, social interaction is not something that comes easily or without great cost and effort. Unlike Grotius, Hobbes does not include a desire to live in a peaceful, rational social order with others as a fundamental part of human nature; in fact, he suggests that, to the extent that natural individuals want contact with one another, such contact is motivated by a desire to compete, rob, dominate, or exterminate the other.

A central part of Hobbes's account of human nature is the claim that people are more or less equal, at least in the sense that no person is so much stronger or smarter than another that they can entirely dominate them or enjoy safety from the attempts of others to dominate them in return. As a result, the state of nature is frightening and violent – a state of war. But the condition of war is not a condition of constant fighting; rather it obtains when there is a "known disposition" to fight (*L* 13.8). This known disposition is ensured by the fact that what Hobbes calls "anticipation" (preemptive strike) is a rational strategy, even for those who prefer to be left alone – the "diffident," as Hobbes calls them (*L* 13.4). As a result, the inhabitants of the state of nature cannot rely on future stability or security and must be constantly ready to defend their lives and property; in that context, there is no point trying to pursue long-term projects; make complex tools or objects; or do any of the things that provide comfort, improve standards of living, or create wealth. Hobbes famously declares that human life in the state of nature is "solitary, poor, nasty, brutish, and short" (*L* 13.9).

Because the state of nature is antithetical to self-preservation, people will, according to Hobbes, be desperate to escape from it; and the way they do this is by agreeing with one another to institute a sovereign to rule over them and provide the peace and security that is impossible in their natural (i.e. precivil) condition. The goods of safety and hope for a more contented life are only possible if people give up their natural rights and authorize a sovereign to rule over them. The social contract is how this happens. It is a contract of each with all; the sovereign is not a party to it.

According to Hobbes, the sovereign instituted by the social contract is unlimited and undivided – that is it is absolute in the Bodinian sense. Thus, first, the people's authorization of the sovereign is total, meaning that he cannot be judged by, or held accountable to, any other person or body. Second, the sovereign power must also be entirely unified, because divisions give rise to discord or disagreement. For Hobbes, limited and divided government serves to invite the causes of social unrest. Hobbes also argues that monarchy is the most desirable form of government, but his argument here is a pragmatic, not a principled, one. Like Bodin, however, he accepts that other forms of government, such as democracy and aristocracy, can be relatively effective as long as they are absolute and undivided. Finally, the fact that unlimited authorization need not – and in Hobbes, does not – necessitate unlimited political obligation is crucial for appreciating the nature of Hobbes's social contract theory.

For many subsequent contract theorists, the importance of consent in authorizing and legitimizing government implied that government remained accountable to the people, whose consent could, at least in principle, be withdrawn. It is therefore striking to modern eyes that a social contract theory grounds a justification for unlimited, undivided monarchy, and it is equally surprising that it was used to undercut the possibility of justifying rebellion. However, Hobbes rules out any possibility of a legitimate *collective* resistance to a sitting monarch, or to any established government. Attempts at rebellion, he argues, are not only prohibited by the social contract, but perhaps equally significant is the fact that they are pragmatically foolish, even if they are successful (*L* 15.4–9). Indeed, Hobbes famously claims that any government is better than no government on the grounds that political dissent or discord, by destabilizing the conditions of the social contract, risks a return to state-of-nature-like conditions (*L* 18.20).

It might be thought that Hobbes's position on *individual* resistance would be similarly unequivocal, given that the social contract places no limits on the authorization of the sovereign. However, he allows that in certain rare circumstances, subjects do have rights of resistance. The starting point is that subjects retain the right of self-defense, so that if one's life, person, or liberty is endangered, one may resist – even if the threat comes from the sovereign himself. As a result, prisoners facing capital punishment have the right to fight their captors. Hobbes expands this right to include the right to resist punishment more generally (for yourself and particular loved ones) and the right to refuse to go to war (*L* chs. 14 and 21).

Although Hobbes himself is less than clear on what basis these rights are retained, it is possible to reconstruct an argument for why – on his account – these extended resistance rights make sense. Each person's obligation to obey the sovereign is limited by the very reasons they agree to submit themselves in the first place, namely to protect their life, limbs, and property. Though the sovereign power is not limited, according to the Hobbesian social contract, the extent of each subject's *obligation* is, and must be. In the end, though, Hobbes is able to admit these rights only because doing so will not pose a risk to the stability of the commonwealth. They are mere permission rights and confer no obligation on others to respect them; the condemned man may fight back without injustice, but he is unlikely to escape the scaffold (Sreedhar 2010).

Critics – in Hobbes's time and now – have taken issue with virtually every step in his argument. Notable criticisms include the charge of atheism, the picture of human nature as seemingly (inherently) selfish and atomistic, the justification for absolute monarchy, the coherence of Hobbes's retained rights, his response to the fool, and on it goes. Pufendorf and others have criticized Hobbes for mischaracterizing human nature and for ignoring the inescapable social element of human existence. Locke gives a convincing argument that Hobbes was wrong to think that the best way to escape the state of nature was to give up (almost) all of one's rights to an absolute monarch. Locke charges that it would be foolish to subject oneself to the whims of a lion when one's natural enemies are foxes and polecats, whom one is much better suited to handle. Locke also points out the corrupting nature of vast power concentrated in a single individual or institution, pointing to history as a guide to what happens when rulers are given the amount of power Hobbes recommends. Contemporary scholars and readers throughout the ages have raised these points and others and Hobbes has earned a significant place in the canon of the history of political thought, though his place is usually that of a foil – an interesting and provocative foil, but a foil nonetheless.

Samuel von Pufendorf (1632–1694) is, in many ways, a victim of the contingent and occasionally arbitrary ways in which the Western canon took shape. He was a dominant intellectual figure in his own time – indeed, his *On the Duty of Man and Citizen* (*DOH*) was the standard textbook of natural law for a century after it was published[15] – yet, much like Grotius and *unlike* fellow contract theorists Hobbes and Locke, Pufendorf rarely finds a place on contemporary reading lists for the history of political thought.[16] Despite his failure to maintain a more notable place in the standard canon, Pufendorf is a crucial figure in understanding the arc of social contract theory in the seventeenth century.[17]

Certainly, he studied both Grotius and Hobbes and directly responded to them, accepting some of their claims, refuting others, and modifying or trying to improve on various aspects of their theories. He was also read by Locke and influenced him greatly.[18] For the purposes of this chapter, it is useful to concentrate on a few of Pufendorf's most significant contributions to seventeenth century political thought: (1) his insistence that natural law both depends on God and the foregrounding of human sociability; (2) his longer, more complex, and more sophisticated account of human life without government, which distinguishes *precivil* life from *presocial* life; (3) his employment of a two-stage contract, whereby people first agree to form a political entity and then the political entity institutes a government (a device that is taken up and further developed by Locke); and (4) his argument that, though government *can be* absolute, it *should* be limited as to prevent abuses of power.

Understood against the background of Hobbes and Grotius, one of the most notable differences is that Pufendorf gives a primacy of place to a voluntarist God in his theory of natural law. Whereas Hobbes's description of natural law does not include God, and Grotius asserts that natural law would be true in the absence of God, Pufendorf grants God a central role in the story. But, Pufendorf does not intend that this move be a *partisan* one. Although it might seem like including God contradicts the idea of a secular basis to avoid doctrinal differences, Pufendorf's God is minimal.[19] Nevertheless, God is needed to make natural law genuinely law, because laws are defined as rules propagated by someone with the authority to make rules and attach punishments and rewards to them (*DJN* I.6.9). According to a then-dominant (and still familiar) account of law, the very existence of law presupposes a *lawgiver*, to create and bestow it with authority.[20] Pufendorf agrees that if there exist natural laws, there must be a natural lawgiver, and the only appropriate candidate is God (*DOH* I.2.6). He also has a doctrine of positive law, in which the lawgivers are people. Moreover, we know that there are natural laws by the "natural light" of "any adult of sound mind"; in general, Pufendorf thinks that the principles he gives about human nature, and what follows from those principles, are self-evident, given how God created our minds (*DOH* I.1.4; I.2.4). Whereas Pufendorf's metaethics is a voluntarist one, he maintains that there are three fundamental types of duties – duties to self, duties to others, and duties to God.

In addition to this divine component, Pufendorf's account of human nature and the laws associated with it give primacy of place to a strong conception of human sociality, the desire and need to come together to live in some socially organized way. The idea of inherent human sociality is one that Hobbes adamantly denied. Grotius acknowledged it but conceived of it in minimal terms: we have natural duties not to hurt or steal from each other unnecessarily, but there are no natural duties of mutual aid or cooperation. Yet Pufendorf argues that human sociality is such that it gives rise to a wide and meaningful set of natural duties to others; although he recognizes the centrality of the desire for self-preservation, he claims that the "fundamental natural law is: every man ought to do as much as he can to cultivate and preserve sociality" (*DOH* I.3.9). Subsequent natural laws prescribe those things that lend themselves to peaceful and cooperative social life and forbid those things inimical to it. Central to this line of reasoning is the idea that human beings are weak and dependent (*DJN* II.1.8). Fulfillment of even their most basic needs for survival requires interpersonal cooperation and association.

Given the primacy of place afforded to sociality, it is unsurprising that Pufendorf's account of the state of nature is much richer than his predecessors', both in substance and in quality. Not only do we learn more details about the state of nature in Pufendorf, but the details he provides leave the reader with a far more appealing impression than, for example, Hobbes's state of nature as a war of all against all. This comes out in stark relief when one juxtaposes their respective views on strangers in the state of nature; Hobbes insists that strangers are enemies (every person is enemy to every other person); Pufendorf explicitly denies Hobbes's claim, instead characterizing strangers as "friend[s] we cannot wholly rely on" (*DOH* II.1.11). He posits the existence of interpersonal relationships and small group associations that can exist in precivil life, including both families and master-servant relationships. In his reconstruction of the hypothetical (and semihistorical) narrative of state formation, Pufendorf describes the male heads of households coming together to form a government. A number of things are assumed in this discussion. First, that there are households in the state of nature; Pufendorf thinks that women voluntarily subordinate themselves to men in marriage (and that the institution exists outside the state) and so their children will be under the rule of the father. There are also servants, or wage earners, who can contribute to the growth and flourishing of households. Patriarchal families can provide a number of goods – a limited amount of security, cooperation, division of labor, and so forth. Aware of their weakness and mutual interdependence, people voluntarily act in ways that fulfill their natural social tendencies without the imposition of coercive measures. In other words, in Pufendorf's picture there are substantial voluntary associations that form "naturally," and all are based in contract and consent. If those associations are sufficiently small and recourses are sufficiently available, no state is needed.

However, in his reconstruction of human history, Pufendorf says that eventually there will be a need for more security than such small households can provide. In large part, his argument rests on the idea that although people have more substantive natural duties of sociality, they cannot be trusted to fulfill them, even with the threat of God's punishment. Consequently, they need both a state and the prospect of temporal sanctions for trespass. Marriage, households, property, and commerce are all possible without civil laws, though the latter two might not be as efficient as they are in a state. But it is not all rosy. People cannot be trusted to follow natural law, even though it is dictated not only by God but also by reason. Some people are simply wicked, others are lazy; and even those who desire to follow natural law might not always have the knowledge or inclination to do so. As a result, they need sanctions of the kind that can be provided only by a government. Moreover, there are coordination problems. The state, then, is needed for security. Families and households can provide food and basic goods, but, ultimately, security and a stable, lasting peace require civil institutions (*DOH* II.5.8–9; *DJN* VII.2.7–8).

Pufendorf's idea of the social contract itself is also more complex than his predecessors, and it serves as a precursor to the Lockean social contract. In his account, the social contract consists of "two agreements and one decree." For Hobbes, the idea that there could be a political entity without a sovereign was incoherent. The unity of the commonwealth was provided by the unity of the sovereign. Pufendorf and Locke following him saw that individuals in the state of nature could be thought of as forming a political unit and then deciding on a particular form of government. According to Pufendorf's account, there is an agreement of the heads of household – each with every other – to form a "single and perpetual union [in order to] administer the means of their safety and security by common counsel and leadership" such that they become "fellow citizens." There is then a decree on the form of government, which is determined by majority vote, followed by a second agreement in which the particular ruler or rulers are granted authority. The ruler(s) "bind" themselves to provide for the common peace and security and the ruled "bind themselves to obedience" (*DOH* II.6.7–9; see also *DJN* 7.2.7). The voluntarist foundation of covenant in Pufendorf's account means that it is up to people to decide for themselves which form of government they wish to implement. He expresses a preference for monarchy but allows that aristocracy and democracy can be legitimate forms of government, as long as state power is supreme and undivided. Divided, mixed, or balanced governments are "irregular" states, to be avoided if at all possible (*DOH* II.8.12; *DJN* 7.5.12–15).

No matter its form, however, government is "unaccountable" to its subjects, and Pufendorf denies the legitimacy of political resistance, urging those living under harsh political rule to patience; the "severity [of sovereign authority] must be patiently borne by citizens in exactly the same way that good children must bear the ill temper of their parents" (*DOH* II.9.2–4; see also *DJN* 7.8.4–6). So, although Pufendorf gives an extended discussion of the duties of sovereigns to rule well, he provides little recourse if they fail to do so. Pufendorf accepts the Hobbesian idea that sovereignty must be unified (i.e. undivided) and supreme; he rejects the idea that it must be unlimited. In fact, he argues in favor of limitations of government power. Those limitations, however, do not, on Pufendorf's account, license rebellion; and, in this sense, they are similar to the duties of the sovereign to rule well. Finally, like Grotius, Pufendorf both seems to recognize a right to resistance in rare, extreme circumstances of tyranny and fails to reconcile this exception with his more general claims about the supremacy of sovereign power and the requirement of obedience to "severe" governments.

Influenced by the works of Grotius, Hobbes, and Pufendorf, John Locke (1632–1704) offered what is plausibly seen as the most famous (and well-liked) social contract theory of the seventeenth century. It was Locke's ideas (or, more specifically, how Locke's ideas were taken up by his later readers) that so influenced the French and American Revolutions. Most famous are (1) his account of the naturalness and inviolability of private property rights and (2) his arguments for the necessity of limited government and the existence of a right of revolution again governments who transgress their limits.

In keeping with the traditions in which he was writing, Locke's political philosophy begins with an account of natural law and natural rights. According to Locke, natural law requires that people pursue not only their own self-preservation but also the preservation of their fellow human beings. Preservation is understood broadly to include "life, health, liberty, [and] possessions." Like Grotius, he gives lexical priority to one's self-preservation; the duty to preserve others is contingent upon it not endangering one's own preservation. So, I have a duty to help you preserve yourself but not if doing so endangers my own preservation. It is not exactly clear how much we should make of this caveat, because circumstances in which multiple individuals' self-preservation are mutually exclusive occur only rarely. Nevertheless, the claim is foundational to Locke's view; natural law permits me to hurt you or steal from you but *only* if doing so is necessary to save my own life or is punishment for violating natural law. Otherwise I am obligated to aid in your preservation with the emphasis being on people's natural rights to life, liberty, and property.

A basic premise in Locke's account of natural law is the claim that people are God's creation. He says,

> For men being all the workmanship of one omnipotent, and infinitely wise maker; all the servants of one sovereign master, sent into the world by his order,

and about his business; they are his property, whose workmanship they are, made to last during his, not one another's pleasure.

(*Treatise* 2.2.6)

The "made to last" phrase is key. God made me and so he (and not you) gets to decide how long I get to last. That is why you are not allowed to kill me; it is not your decision (you do not have standing to decide when my life ends). Locke invokes the idea that we are creations of God to explain why it is impermissible to sell oneself into slavery – a person is not his own to sell; he is also the property of God. Were someone to sell himself into slavery, he would be selling something that did not entirely belong to him (*Treatise* 2.2.2).

The Lockean state of nature is a state of equality and a state of liberty (within the guidelines of natural law), but it is not a state in which people would wish to remain. Locke denies that it is equivalent to a state of "war"; rather he claims that it is, as he says, "inconvenient." Three things account for the inconvenience of the state of nature: the lack of a publicly known set of laws, the absence of fair and unbiased judges, and the lack of enforcement power. Although a substantive natural law exists – one that requires each to respect and promote one another's natural rights to life, liberty, and property – this is insufficient to ground a tolerable or prosperous social order. Locke's natural law is quite general, and people need more specific rules in order to engage in peaceful and productive social cooperation. In many cases, people can have differing interpretations of what natural law requires and whether it has been violated. Because people tend to be biased in favor of themselves and they are not always rational, it will be difficult if not impossible to adjudicate disputes over natural law. Finally, because everyone has the power to enforce natural law and punish what they see as violations of it, there cannot be an institution with a monopoly on enforcement power, which for Locke is a necessary condition for peaceful and orderly social life. It is clear that the three inconveniences Locke identifies in the state of nature are solvable by civil institutions; in fact, they are precisely the things with which the state is created to deal. The state provides publicly known specific laws for people to follow, appoints fair and unbiased judges to adjudicate disputes, and enforces the rulings of those judges.

On Locke's account, the emergence of the state is a two-stage process. First, people in the state of nature, recognizing the inconveniences of their condition, agree to come together to form an independent political entity, the commonwealth. This agreement must be unanimous. Then, by majority vote, the members of the commonwealth authorize a particular government (Locke recommends a constitutional monarchy with a parliamentary legislature). The commonwealth entrusts the government with the power and right to enforce natural law. Crucial to this picture is the idea that if the government fails in its duty, the people – the commonwealth – can revoke its grant of authority. In turn, this serves to ground a right of revolution. For Locke, government is empowered for the sake of the protection of natural rights and the enforcement of natural law, and it is limited by the scope of that empowerment. If it exceeds that mandate, its acts are no longer justified or legitimate. Locke recognizes that, in any given case, it is impossible for people to know whether natural law has in fact been violated or whether the government has actually exceeded its mandate. In that case, he admits that "the only appeal is to heaven," meaning God is the ultimate judge. This epistemic uncertainty is inescapable and makes it the case that people can never be sure in any given situation whether or not their revolution is justified. But they must nevertheless act in the face of that uncertainty, and one of the most enduring aspects of Locke's legacy is simply the fact that he institutionalizes a right of revolution. Finally, imposing taxes on the people without their consent constitutes a paradigmatic violation of Lockean natural law (it fails to respect people's natural right to their own property) and so can also ground a right of revolution. In light of Locke's particular views on the limitations of the state and his account of the proper response to possible transgressions of those limits, it is unsurprising that the revolutionaries of the eighteenth century found Locke's theory to be so appealing.

As we have seen, seventeenth century social contract theory emerged in large part as a philosophical response to the very real and immediate political problem of *difference*, and ensuing problems of conflict and intolerance. Although the political landscape had shifted, somewhat, by Locke's time, the sense of urgency remained. Thus, no account of Locke's *political philosophical* project and its place in contract theory is complete without a brief discussion of his very famous views on religious toleration.

After the restoration of the English monarchy and the Church of England in 1660, a new series of measures called the Clarendon Code were passed. These provided for the enforcement of an Anglican religious orthodoxy by requiring Anglican Communion of all municipal officials, by compelling the use of the Anglican prayer book, the *Book of Common Prayer*, by preventing the assembly of dissenting religious groups, and by forbidding nonconformist ministers from coming within five miles of incorporated towns or teaching in their schools.[21]

Locke's general claim is that religion cannot be the justification for or basis upon which the force of law may affect one's civil interests (life, liberty, and property) – "the religious sphere" of one's life (concern for the salvation of souls) is given completely over to "churches."[22] Thus, in the same way that the civil magistrate has no jurisdiction over one's *spiritual* interests (e.g. interests in salvation), churches have no jurisdiction over one's *civil* interests. Nor, he contends, can states legitimately use their power (the force of law) to coerce religious belief or practice.

Locke gives a number of arguments for the strict separation of church and state, some directed at Christians in general, some at what he calls "zealots," some at magistrates, some at established churches, and some at individuals. *A Letter Concerning Toleration* consists in a series of such arguments, and though some are tailored to one audience more than another, there are recurring themes. First and foremost, he emphasizes the *impossibility* and *irrationality* of coercing genuine religious beliefs. The state's tool is coercion – the use of force or the threat of the use of force – and force is incapable of affecting a "genuine inward persuasion of the mind," which is necessary for salvation. Coercion, thus, simply *cannot* be employed for salvation – it offends against the very nature of religious faith and doctrine in *every* sense. Quite obviously, compelling people to profess what they do not believe is simply overtly forcing them to lie.[23] Moreover, Locke argues that, from the perspective of the persecuted, it is irrational to follow the directives of another on religious matters, for they could be wrong about what is or is not pleasing to God. But in either case, if one does not believe sincerely, then following another in action (even if they are "right" about what Locke calls the "true religion") is a patently illegitimate path to "the mansions of the blessed" (Locke 1983, 38).

Obviously, one could give a much more robust discussion of the precise details of Locke's arguments, their respective interpretive debates, and the trenchant criticisms that have been offered against them, but doing so would stray far from the central issues that I wish to address. I will mention only two of the most damning objections to Locke's defense of toleration. First, Locke explicitly denies that Catholics and atheists need to be tolerated; and, second, his defense of toleration seems to proceed from exclusively *prudential* grounds rather than from any *genuine* respect for religious freedom.[24] The first objection is more easily explained, if not excused, by appeal to the issues that were in the air during the time in which Locke was writing. Most of the famous seventeenth century English defenders of toleration did not defend the claim that atheists should be tolerated – the issue was simply not on the table politically or philosophically.[25] Again, this in no way *excuses* Locke on this issue but is rather an explanation.[26] The second objection is more problematic. From a contemporary perspective – in which basic respect for religious freedom is a defining feature of the ideology of liberal democracy *and* human rights – it remains true that Locke's defense of toleration seems to draw on what some have called the "wrong kinds of reasons." So, whereas there is good reason to treat Locke as a seminal progenitor of contemporary theories of toleration, there is also an important sense in which he (like all influential historical figures) was a product of his time, and in hindsight the shortcomings of his view are brought into sharp relief.

During the seventeenth century, then, a series of thinkers consolidated various strands of thought into a tradition we now know as social contract theory. Grotius formulated a secular basis for natural law and reenvisioned rights as entitlements that could be transferred as the basis of a conception of political authority. Subsequent philosophers developed comprehensive theories, including accounts of natural law or right, the state of nature, the social contract, the best form of government, and the possible legitimacy of rebellion. However, as we have seen, these key elements of a broadly contractarian approach were developed in different ways: Hobbes depicted the state as a Leviathan, with an absolute ruler; Pufendorf encouraged limited government, focusing on the duty of the ruler to rule well; and Locke insisted on the necessary limitations on government power and emphasized the existence of a right to rebellion if those limits were exceeded.

The political thought of Baruch Spinoza (1632–77) shares many key features of social contract theory. Moreover, he seems to be a natural historical companion to Locke, because he offers an impassioned defense of toleration, which appears to be similar to Locke's strategy for answering the political problem of cultural and religious diversity. Yet, a close look at Spinoza's philosophy reveals that these attributions are at least misleading, and perhaps mistaken. Both his political theory and his views on toleration differ from contractarian approaches in important respects. Although Spinoza often writes about the issues that concerned social contract theorists, he does so from a perspective that denies the possibility of transcendent moral values, rights, or justifications. So, although Spinoza is an important figure in our narrative, he is so both for his departures from the social contract tradition and for his place within it.

Spinoza is most well known for his *Ethics*, but his political philosophy is developed in his less-studied works, the *Tractatus Theologico-Politicus* (*TTP*) and the unfinished *Tractatus Politicus* (*TP*). Although it caused an uproar in the seventeenth century, Spinoza's political philosophy has received comparatively little scholarly attention.[27] This is due to several factors. First, there is the contentious nature of his philosophical commitments. Second, his political views are difficult to interpret because the arguments in the *TTP* were written primarily as a commentary on the Calvinist theocrats who controlled the Dutch provinces. Third, his accounts of natural right, the state of nature, the social contract, forms of government, and the legitimacy of rebellion are strikingly different from the broader contractarian tradition because of his thoroughgoing denial of transcendental standards of right action and good conduct. To see just how different

Spinoza's approach to these issues is, let us briefly consider some of his starker divergences from the social contract tradition.

To begin with, consider Spinoza's conception of natural right, which he identifies with power. For him, one has the *right* to do something if one has the *power* to do it:

> By the right and established order of Nature I mean simply the rules governing the nature of every individual thing, according to which we conceive it as naturally determined to exist and to act in a definite way. For example, fish are determined by nature to swim, and the big ones to eat the smaller ones. Thus it is by sovereign natural right that fish inhabit water, and the big ones eat the smaller ones. For it is certain that Nature, taken in the absolute sense, has the sovereign right to do all that she can do; that is, Nature's right is co-extensive with her power.... But since the universal power of Nature as a whole is nothing but the power of all individual things taken together, it follows that each individual thing has the sovereign right to do all that it can do; i.e., the right of the individual is co-extensive with its determinate power.
>
> (*TTP* 173)

Spinoza holds that human beings are part of this "right and established order of nature," and that philosophy must be thoroughly naturalized. In effectively rejecting a central tenet of much of the entire natural law tradition, Spinoza argues that the same laws govern both human beings and the rest of nature (*E* 3 preface; *TP* 2.5).[28] As we have seen, the social contract theorists distance themselves from theological premises, though they do so in varying degrees. But they all presuppose an external *normative* order that differs from the *actual* order of things. For all of them – Grotius to Locke – people can be said to act *against* nature.[29] But, Spinoza denies the existence of a natural order – or any order – that can offer a normative and transcendental standard against which action can be measured.[30]

Similarly, Spinoza offers a discussion of contracts that abstracts away from transcendental standards of normativity. He offers a utility-based account of obligation according to which "the validity of an agreement rests on its utility, without which the agreement automatically becomes null and void" (*TTP* 176). To think otherwise would violate his naturalistic view of human psychology by demanding that people refrain from acting in the way they think best – from picking the greater evil over the lesser evil or the lesser good over the greater good, as Spinoza puts it. Of course, according to Spinoza, if people were always guided by reason, then they would all forswear deceit. But because he sees that people are not all rational, and because he sees that they are all guided by immediate pleasure and pain, we should assume that people will not be honest unless there are external conditions in place that make it less pleasant to deceive than to stand by their commitments.

Spinoza's discussion of sovereignty and the relationship between ruler and ruled is similarly derived from his thoroughgoing naturalism. Both sovereign and subjects have the right to do whatever is in their power; specifically, "the sovereign power in a State has right over a subject only in proportion to the excess of its power over that subject" (Ep 50). So, when asked questions like "does the government have the right to raise taxes however it likes?" or "do subjects have the right to rebel in an attempt to usurp a sitting ruler?" Spinoza's answer must always be "it depends." If a government has the power to enact and enforce a piece of legislation, it has the right to do so. If a group of subjects is powerful enough to usurp the leader, then its members cannot be said to act against right in carrying out a rebellion. In short, nothing can be said to be done against right. However, it may still be irrational or pragmatically ill-advised to carry out a rebellion or to enact a particular piece of legislation. But whether or not this is the case will depend on the features of the particular action, and the implications for the people who live within a society. Spinoza's answers to the fundamental questions of political authority and obligation thus seem to be fundamentally opposed to those of his predecessors (as well as those who came after him).

But although Spinoza seems to simply collapse normative questions into nonnormative or descriptive ones, the story is not so simple. Spinoza decidedly rejects the claim that "might makes right." Even if Cortez had the right to conquer the Aztecs, this does not *mean* that it was good for him to do so – the rightness or wrongness of this action critically depends on the particular increases and decreases in power that resulted from this action. In short, although Spinoza denies the existence of a transcendental standard of right and wrong, he nonetheless has resources for making evaluative claims about the structure of political action (Curley 1996). So, he does offer political claims that deserve attention. For example, he insists that the sovereign is responsible for ensuring political stability (and so for preventing rebellion or seditious activity). He grounds this claim in the recognition that the power of the sovereign is diminished in proportion to the number of subjects who are ready to join a conspiracy against it. So, for the sovereign to retain power, it must avoid doing things that will incite insurrection. Moreover, he argues for the superiority of democracy over other forms of government, overtly rejecting the Hobbesian justification for monarchy; and he does so on the basis of the claim that "in a democracy there is less danger of a government behaving unreasonably, for it is practically impossible for the majority of a single assembly, if it is of some size, to agree on the same piece of folly" (*TTP* 178). So, although Spinoza does not argue for limited government or accord subjects a right to revolution properly speaking, he does attempt to offer naturalistic equivalents that are grounded on his claim that the right or power of the state is essentially limited by the right or power of the people.

Turning to the other key aspect of his political philosophy, his defense of toleration and free speech, Spinoza, like Hobbes, asserts that the state has the right to dictate public religion. He adopts the same Erastian position that subordinates all other authorities (and specifically ecclesiastical authorities) to the state; indeed, the title of chapter 19 of the TTP reads, "It is shown that the right over matters of religion is vested entirely in the sovereign, and that the external forms of worship should be as accord with the peace of the commonwealth, if we would serve God aright." However, unlike Hobbes, Spinoza recommends that the government refrain from exercising substantial control over speech and religion, claiming that a stable political order should generally allow for freedom in both areas. Unlike Locke, however, Spinoza's account of toleration is not at bottom a freedom to worship. He draws a strict separation between outward expressions of faith and inner thoughts or worship of God. Like Locke, Spinoza thinks the latter are simply outside the control of the state because it is strictly impossible to legislate belief. But he recommends allowing various forms of outward worship on the grounds that attempting to curb such worship is impracticable and likely to backfire. Although Spinoza's reasons tend to be pragmatic rather than principled, and he emphasizes that the sovereign always has the power to limit speech and expressions of religious faith, it is not clear how wide the scope of toleration is meant to be on Spinoza's account. On the one hand, Spinoza argues that the essence of the state is to preserve the freedom to philosophize (as he puts it in the epigram to the *TTP*):

> By means of which it is shown not only that Freedom of Philosophising can be allowed in Preserving Piety and the Peace of the Republic: but also that it is not possible for such Freedom to be upheld except when accompanied by the Peace of the Republic and Piety Themselves.

In fact, Spinoza notes in the preface that the goal of the *TTP* is to demonstrate the truth of this biconditional.[31] But although his notoriously deep republican commitments make it seem as if Spinoza should offer an unlimited defense of free speech, he is not unequivocal on the issue. For example, later on in the *TTP*, he says that granting full freedom of speech "could have the most disastrous consequences" (*TTP* 223). So, although he provides a compelling argument against oppressive rule – it is unstable and imprudent – he does not provide resources for defending limited government, toleration, or civil rights on the basis of an appeal to rights or liberty (or the value thereof).[32] This could be read as either an advantage or a disadvantage of Spinoza's account, depending on one's other commitments, and commentators have taken both positions.

As this brief overview indicates, Spinoza's political philosophy shares several elements that are central to the social contract approach. However, his views differ fundamentally from Grotius, Hobbes, Locke, and Pufendorf. Each of those thinkers wanted to explain political authority, and legitimacy, and obligation, as well as which forms of state are morally better or worse, by reference to a transcendental, nonnormative standard. The questions they answer arise only once you accept that power does not always entail authority and that there are things a ruler ought not to do, even if he can. Spinoza's naturalism precludes asking these questions *in the same way* as other social contract theorists; however, he still hopes to answer these questions in terms that are grounded in natural facts about human behavior and human psychology. The explanations offered by other social contract theorists depend fundamentally on the idea that human beings are the sort of creatures that can create enduring obligations to each other by means of consent or agreement, but Spinoza thinks that people will not uphold their obligations if they conflict with their interests and so suggests that obligations only remain binding to the extent that there are social institutions in place to ensure that our interests line up with the obligations that we have taken on.

To the extent that Spinoza is part of the social contract tradition, he is so only in an idiosyncratic way. But, regardless of how we classify Spinoza's views, the question of most interest concerns the viability of these views and the soundness of his arguments. Many people have wondered whether Spinoza offers a genuinely normative political theory; and if not, we must ask whether those of us who wish to do so can nevertheless learn something from him. I suggest that the sort of normative project that is common to the social contract theorists that we have discussed is thrown into sharp relief by considering Spinoza's naturalizing approach. But it is the normative project that persists throughout the eighteenth century and that has come to structure the vast majority of contemporary political philosophy. Of course, as it developed, social contract theory became more democratic, eventually more participatory, with basic rights being protected. And this is the form we find it in today – a far cry from Hobbes's *Leviathan* though, in an important sense, rooted in the basic commitments that gave rise to it.

Notes

1 For an excellent discussion of the divine right of kings, see Sommerville (1986: 9–46).
2 For extended discussions of Filmer's philosophy, see Sommerville's introduction to his edition of Filmer's *Patriarcha and Other Political Writings* (Cambridge: Cambridge University Press, 1991); Gordon J. Schochet's *Patriarchalism in Political Thought: The Authoritarian Family and Political Speculation and Attitudes Especially in Seventeenth-Century England* (Oxford: Basil Blackwell, 1975); and James Daly, *Sir Robert Filmer and English Political Thought* (Toronto: University of Toronto Press, 1979).
3 Note that the "modern social contract tradition" is also sometimes confusingly called the "classical social contract tradition." Both need to be differentiated from the contemporary social contract tradition of the twentieth and twenty-first centuries most famously espoused by John Rawls. In general, contemporary social contract theory also attempts to offer political principles that could, in some sense, be rationally acceptable to all.
4 Interestingly, a number of other philosophers, most of whom were known for their work in other areas of philosophy, also explicated or defended some sort of contract views (e.g. Gassendi). An interesting exception is Leibniz, who explicitly argued against the idea that humans lived as equals in a prepolitical state and criticized Locke's contractarianism. Leibniz's political theory, to the extent there was one, is sometimes characterized as Platonist, given that he supported the rule of the wisest (see Nicholas Jolley, *Leibniz*, New York: Routledge, 2005, pp. 176–198).
5 Ian Hunter and David Saunders put this nicely, saying,

> Even at their most theoretical – indeed, especially at their most theoretical – seventeenth-century natural law doctrines represented a series of attempts, made in desperate times, to provide political authority with a normative basis capable of withstanding the shattering impacts of confessional division and civil disorder.
>
> (*Natural Law and Civil Sovereignty*, Palgrave MacMillan, 2002, p. 5)

6 For a useful overview of Grotius's political thought, see Tuck's introduction (pp. xviii–xxxiii) to the three-volume set of Grotius's masterpiece *De Iure Belli ac Pacis* or *The Rights of War and Peace* (DJB) (Indianapolis: Liberty Fund, 2005).
7 For a useful discussion of this, see David Armitage's introduction to *The Free Sea* (2004) Indianapolis: Liberty Fund.
8 It is important to note that Grotius's account of natural law and natural right is both detailed and internally ambiguous, and it is not possible within the constraints of this essay to address its complexities or alleged inconsistencies in full; the aim, here, is to indicate its most central and influential features. For a useful discussion of this, see Knud Haakonssen's section on Grotius in his "The Moral Conservatism of Natural Rights," in Hunter and Saunders, eds., pp. 28–34.
9 See *De Iure Praedae Commentarius* or *Commentary on the Law of Prize and Booty* (DJP), ed. Martine Julia van Ittersum (Indianapolis: Liberty Fund, 2006); chapter 2, and DJB, The Preliminary Discourse, paragraphs 6–8.
10 Grotius uses the term "right" in a number of different ways, including the medieval way, though I cannot discuss the richness or the ambiguities in this term. In his discussion of the right of war, Grotius claims that *ius* (plural *iura*) can have three distinct meanings: first, it can mean simply what is just; second, it can signify the kind of law that makes *ius naturale* a dictate of reason; and, third, he used it in the way that I am pointing out here. At the center of this third meaning is the individual or person, and *ius* is conceived of as "a moral Quality annexed to the person, enabling him to have, or do, something justly" (I.I.III–IV). He goes on to suggest that, in this third sense, a moral quality may be deemed to be a faculty that each person has signifying a power over oneself, namely liberty, or a claim on or power over other persons or things; and he thus argues that a right is something we have. Because he focuses on the individual subject as rights-bearer, Grotius is sometimes credited with offering a theory of "subjective" rights, as opposed to the "objective" notion of right found in medieval philosophy. For useful discussions of the meanings of *ius* in Grotius, see Brian Tierney's *The Idea of Natural Rights: Studies on Natural Rights, Natural Law and Church Law 1150–1625* (Atlanta: Scholars Press, 1997), pp. 316–42; and Richard Tuck's *Natural Rights Theories* (Cambridge: Cambridge University Press, 1979), pp. 58–81.
11 *The Free Sea*, p. 8. See also the prolegomena to DJP where he claims that all philosophers who have entertained this question have agreed on his fundamental principles.
12 DJP II:10–11. See Robert Shaver (1996), "Grotius on Scepticism and Self-Interest," *Archiv für Geschichte der Philosophie*, 78, pp. 27–47; and Richard Tuck (1983), "Grotius, Carneades and Hobbes," *Grotiana*, N.S., 4, pp. 43–62.

13 Although some scholars have disputed whether Grotius should be viewed as a contractarian or even a protocontractarian, many of the core elements of contractarianism – voluntary consent, the transfer of natural rights as the basis for political power – can be found in Grotius's theory. Moreover, whether Grotius is a contractarian or not, the framework within which contractarians theorize about how a contract comes into existence and what it's supposed to do is one of his central legacies.

14 There is a great debate over whether or not Hobbes was in fact an atheist, and, although he denied the charge himself, his formulation of natural law is famously one that includes no mention of God at all.

15 The *DOH* was a greatly abridged version of his much longer work *De Jure Naturae et Gentium Libri Octo* or *On the Law of Nature and of Nations in Eight Books* (*DJN*) and was commissioned with the intention of using it as a textbook for students of natural law.

16 This may in part be due to the fact that, like Grotius, Pufendorf's major work is very long. *DOH* is not particularly edifying if it is not read it alongside *DJN* (as was the teaching practice).

17 For useful discussions of Pufendorf's political theory, see Craig L. Carr and Michael J. Seidler (1996), "Pufendorf, Sociality and the Modern State," *History of Political Thought*, 17, pp. 354–78; Michael Nutkiewicz (1983), "Samuel Pufendorf: Obligation as the Basis of the State," *Journal of the History of Philosophy*, 21, pp. 15–29; and J. B. Schneewind (1987), "Pufendorf's Place in the History of Ethics," *Synthese*, 72, pp. 123–55.

18 In *Some Thoughts Concerning Education* (1693), Locke listed *DJN* at the top of his reading list for students saying that it "instructed in the natural rights of men, and the original and foundations of society, and the duties resulting from thence."

19 Though minimal, Pufendorf's God seems to be recognizably Christian. It is important to see that Pufendorf was attempting to give a theory that would be acceptable to the various warring factions within Christianity, and he was acutely aware of the damage that the factions had done to political stability and civil order. Scholars disagree about the role and importance of God in Pufendorf's overall philosophy, but it is clear that he wanted to separate our religious duties from our personal and civic duties in an attempt to deescalate the violence and antagonisms that had come as a result of their combination.

20 For representative examples of early modern philosophers who say (more or less) that laws are decrees and that there has to be a decree maker, see Leibniz, *On Nature Itself*, 501, in *Gottfried Wilhelm Leibniz: Philosophical Papers and Letters*, 2nd ed., Leroy E. Loemker, ed. (Dordrecht and Boston: D. Reidel Publishing Company, 1969); Malebranche, *Dialogues* IV.11, 59–60, the Jolley and Scott translation; and, finally, Ralph Cudworth, *The True Intellectual System of the Universe* (Stuttgart-Bad Cannstatt: F. Fromann Verlag, 1964), 161, who claims that laws are made by God and implanted into creatures.

21 Locke developed his theories regarding toleration during this period. His ideas exhibited an evolution over a twenty-year period moving from opposition to religious toleration in his early works to his remarkable defense of toleration in *A Letter Concerning Toleration* written in the 1680s. There is no doubt that his experience of the imposition of intolerance was in part responsible for the change in his views. See Wotton's introduction to his edition of *Locke's Political Writings* for an excellent analysis of the transformation of Locke's views.

22 Locke understands "churches" to be "voluntary Societ[ies] of Men, joining themselves together of their own accord in order to the publick worshipping of God, in such a manner as they judge acceptable to him and effectual to the Salvation of their Souls" (Locke 1983, 28). What Locke calls the "Duty of the Civil Magistrate" extends only to "civil interests," which include "Life, Liberty, Health, and Indolency of Body; and the possession of outward things, such as money, Lands, Houses, Furniture, and the Like." This duty "neither can nor ought in any manner to be extended to the Salvation of Souls. . . . [T]he Magistrate's Power extends not to the establishing of any articles of Faith, or Forms of Worship, by the force of his Laws" (Locke 1983, 26–27).

23 In an especially perspicuous and pointed passage, Locke addresses those who argue in favor of forcing nonbelievers to profess the "true religion." Locke says,

> A sweet religion, indeed, that obliges men to dissemble and tell lies, both to God and man, for the salvation of their souls! If the magistrate thinks to save men thus, he seems to understand little of the way of salvation. And if he does it not in order to save them, why is he so solicitous about the articles of faith as to enact them by a law?

24 As Jeremy Waldron (1988) notes, echoing a claim made by one of Locke's contemporary critics, Jonas Proast, Locke offers only "instrumental" reasons to respect religious difference. As a result, this approach

may appear to be unpalatable today, even to those who share Locke's overall commitment to religious toleration.
25 Rare exceptions can be found in the writings of members of a minority of radical Protestant groups such as the Seekers and the Levelers; here, Peter Bayle is perhaps the most notable example.
26 The exclusion of Catholics is harder to make sense of. Locke justifies excluding them on the grounds that they ultimately owe their obedience to a foreign power, namely the Pope in Rome. On this point, it is worth noting that many in England at this time were (and perhaps not unreasonably) afraid that England might soon become a Catholic country. Again, this does not excuse Locke's refusal of toleration to Catholics, it is only a possible explanation of why he held such a position. And again, there was the rare exception. John Foxe, an Anabaptist, articulated a sweeping doctrine of tolerance, even toward Catholics, even though he "detested their doctrines with every fibre of his being." And the radical Protestant groups who sometimes advocated for toleration that included atheists also sometimes included Catholics.
27 The essays in the recent book, *Spinoza's "Theological-Political Treatise": A Critical Guide*. Eds. Yitzhak Melamed and Michael Rosenthal (Cambridge: Cambridge University Press, 2010), are a welcome exception to this trend.
28 On the relation between Spinoza and Hobbes in particular, see D.J. Den Uyl and S. Warner "Liberalism and Hobbes and Spinoza" in *Studia Spinozana* 3 (1987), 261–318; and, more recently, D. Garrett. " 'Promising' Ideas: Hobbes and Contract in Spinoza's Political Philosophy" in Melamed and Rosenthal (2010).
29 Strictly speaking, the story is more complex. For Spinoza, people can – in an important sense – act in a way that is contrary to their nature; they do so when they act on the basis of bare affect, mere opinion, or hearsay that represents the world in a confused and fragmentary way. For Spinoza, even when people act on the basis of confused and fragmented representations, they act out of necessity; however, Spinoza does believe that it is possible for our mistaken ideas to be emendated in a way that can yield actions that are more free. A clear articulation of this point depends on an understanding of Spinoza's metaphysics and epistemology, which is beyond the scope of this chapter. For a good discussion of the role of affect and imagination in Spinoza's thought, see Susan James (2009), "Freedom, Slavery and the Passions," in Oli Koistinen (ed.) *Cambridge Companion to Spinoza's Ethics*, Cambridge: Cambridge University Press, pp. 223–41.
30 As I discuss later, the fact that Spinoza rejects transcendental norms and transcendental standards of the sort that other social contract theorists hoped to establish does not mean that he rejects normativity *simpliciter*. As Curley (1996, 322) puts the point, "to say that Genghis Khan acts in accordance with natural right is compatible with saying that he acts contrary to the law of reason, and I take this also to be a normative claim." Edwin Curley (1996), "Kissinger, Spinoza, and Genghis Khan" in D. Garrett (ed.) *Cambridge Companion to Spinoza*, Cambridge: Cambridge University Press, pp. 315–42.
31 The import of this fact for Spinoza's political philosophy receives its most complete defense in Aaron Garrett (2012), "Knowing the Essence of the State in Spinoza's *Tractatus Theologico-Politicus*," *European Journal of Philosophy*, 20:1.
32 See Justin Steinberg's essay "Spinoza's Curious Defense of Toleration" in *Spinoza's "Theological-Political Treatise": A Critical Guide*. Eds. Yitzhak Melamed and Michael Rosenthal (Cambridge: Cambridge University Press, 2010).

Bibliography

Astell, M. (1996) *Mary Astell: Political Writings*, ed. P. Springborg, Cambridge: Cambridge University Press.
Grant, H. (1996) "Hobbes and Mathematics," in Tom Sorell (ed.) *The Cambridge Companion to Hobbes*, Cambridge: Cambridge University Press, pp. 108–128.
Hobbes, T. (1994) *Leviathan*, ed. Edwin Curley. Indianapolis: Hackett.
Jesseph, D. (1996) "Hobbes and the method of natural science," in Tom Sorell (ed.) *The Cambridge Companion to Hobbes*, Cambridge: Cambridge University Press, pp. 86–107.
King James VI and I (1994) *Political Writings*, ed. J.P. Sommerville, Cambridge: Cambridge University Press.
Lloyd, S.A. (2009) *Morality in the Philosophy of Thomas Hobbes: Cases in the Laws of Nature*, Cambridge: Cambridge University Press.
Locke, J. (1983) *A Letter Concerning Toleration*, ed. J. Tully, Indianapolis: Hackett Publishing.
Locke, J. (2003) *Two Treatises of Government*, ed. P. Laslett, Cambridge: Cambridge University Press.

Martinich, A. (2005) *Hobbes*, New York: Routledge.
Sommerville, J. P. (1986) *Politics and Ideology in England, 1603–1640*, Essex: Longman Publishing.
Spinoza, B. (2001) *Theological-Political Treatise*, 2nd ed., trans. S. Shirley, Indianapolis: Hackett.
Sreedhar, S. (2010) *Hobbes on Resistance: Defying the Leviathan*, Cambridge: Cambridge University Press.
Waldron, J. (1988) "Locke: Toleration and the Rationality of Persecution," in S. Mendus (ed.) *Justifying Toleration: Contemporary and Historical Perspectives*, Cambridge: Cambridge University Press, pp. 61–86.

Part 7

PHILOSOPHICAL THEOLOGY

18
ARGUMENTS FOR THE EXISTENCE OF GOD

Marcy P. Lascano

1. Introduction

Arguments for the existence of God play an important role in the systematic philosophies of the seventeenth century. Many thinkers from this period seek to show both that their philosophical positions harmonize with the new science of mechanism and that this new science is consistent with the existence of the Judeo-Christian God. These goals, at times, necessitate a partial reconstrual of God's nature and his role in the universe. Notably, in the thought of Descartes, Locke, and Leibniz, God features as the designer, conservator, and ruler of the mechanistic world that we see and of the moral ideals toward which we must strive.

Although a number of novel arguments for God's existence were introduced in this period, many of the arguments deployed by these early modern philosophers have precursors in medieval (and even ancient) sources. But even when reformulating traditional arguments, thinkers from this period introduce significant innovations. These innovations are, generally speaking, dictated by the particular philosopher's metaphysics and his or her assumptions about the nature of the physical world. In some cases, such presuppositions can be constraining, making it impossible for a philosopher to accept a traditional doctrine or argument. In other cases, these same presuppositions can be liberating and allow a philosopher to strengthen traditional forms of reasoning using clarifications, distinctions, and insights made possible by his or her own system. For this reason, each argument is best understood in terms of its place in its author's overarching philosophical system. That said, there is much to be gained by examining these arguments on their own terms, which is the aim of this piece.

Arguments for the existence of God generally fall into one of four categories: ontological, cosmological, teleological (including design), or moral. Ontological arguments attempt to show that God exists by using *a priori* reasoning concerning the concept of a perfect being. Cosmological arguments, sometimes called "first cause" arguments, begin with *a posteriori* claims (generally claims about what exists) and argue via a causal principle to the source of existence. Teleological arguments claim that certain features of the universe evince a design or purpose and from this we can, inductively, infer that there must be an intelligent being who created it. Finally, moral arguments attempt to show that morality and justice require a lawgiver or that the large degree of agreement concerning moral sentiments requires a singular source. In the seventeenth century, I believe it is fair to say that the ontological and cosmological arguments reign. However, we do see several interesting examples of design and moral arguments. Perhaps most interesting in this period is the development of arguments that attempt to show the existence of God is required as the ground of knowledge or truth. Examples of this type of argument are Leibniz's argument from the eternal truths, Malebranche's argument from mere sight, and Cudworth's argument based on knowledge of universals. All of these arguments will be discussed in more detail in what follows.

In this piece, I begin by reconstructing the arguments of several of the most influential philosophers of the seventeenth century. After discussing the canonical figures, I turn to the discussion of philosophers whose work – though less well known than the work of Descartes and Locke – merits our philosophical interest and attention. It is my hope that the inclusion of so-called minor figures will open the door to further study of their views. I begin the discussion of the canonical figures with Descartes.

2. René Descartes (1596–1650)

Descartes's arguments for the existence of God are perhaps the best known and most influential from the early modern period. Some see many of the later arguments for God's existence as refinements of Descartes's arguments. Descartes employs two types of arguments for God's existence – one *a priori* and one *a posteriori*. Kant dubbed the *a priori* argument "the ontological argument." The *a posteriori* argument is a version of the cosmological argument. The arguments are given in their most detailed form in the *Meditations*.[1] However, variations on these arguments are also presented in both the *Discourse on Method* and the *Principles of Philosophy*.[2]

2.1. The a posteriori *argument*

There is some debate among scholars as to whether there are actually two *a posteriori* arguments or only one.[3] Here, two arguments are provided and it is left to the reader to determine whether the second is merely a retelling or an expansion of the first.

Descartes tells us in the Third Meditation that it is "manifest by the natural light that there must be at least as much [reality] in the efficient and total cause as in the effect of that cause."[4] From this causal principle, which I will refer to as the "containment principle," two other causal principles follow deductively: first, that *nothing comes from nothing*, and second, that *the less perfect cannot cause the more perfect*.[5] We can see the relation between the two principles by considering that if an idea contained something that was not contained in its cause, this something would have to come from nothing.[6]

Descartes proceeds to examine his idea of God, which he tells us he understands as "a substance that is infinite, [eternal, immutable,] independent, supremely intelligent, supremely powerful, and which created both myself and everything else (if anything else there be) that exists."[7] He then proceeds to consider the cause of this idea. Descartes writes, "If I have an idea whose objective reality is so great that I am sure that the same reality does not exist in me, either formally or eminently, then I can know that other things exist."[8] Because it seems unlikely that Descartes is the cause of his own idea of God – for he lacks some of the perfections contained in the idea – Descartes concludes that God must necessarily exist.

The second proof is sometimes called the "continuous creation" proof. Descartes writes that without careful attention, one might wonder why the *idea* of a being more perfect than oneself must necessarily be caused by a being that *really is* more perfect than oneself. He then considers whether his own existence would be possible without such a being. Descartes wants to consider not only how he began to exist but also how he is preserved in being, which he takes to be merely conceptually different from the act of creation. That is, he thinks of preservation in being – *conservation* – as continuous creation. Descartes believes that if we consider the fact that we must be continually created, it will be much easier to see that God must be the total and efficient cause of our existence.

Descartes tells us that there are only four possible options for the cause of his existence: (1) himself, (2) his parents, (3) a being less perfect than God, and (4) God.[9] Descartes proceeds to argue by elimination. He says that he cannot be the cause of his own existence, for if he were the cause, he would have given himself all the perfections contained in his idea of God – perfections which he knows he lacks. Moreover, he observes in himself no power that would enable him to preserve himself in existence.[10] He next considers whether a being less powerful than God might have created him. He answers that because he knows that he is a thinking thing, and that he has in him the idea of a being with all the perfections, the cause of his existence (including his idea) must also be a thinking thing and it must contain all the perfections he attributes to God. Thus, the being that creates him (and it must be a single being, because the perfections of unity and simplicity are contained in his idea of a perfect being) cannot be anything less than a being with all the perfections. If this being with all the perfections derives its existence from itself, then it must be God. If it does not derive its existence from itself, but from something else, then we can ask the same question again about the being that is its cause until we arrive finally at the total and efficient cause, which is God. He finally considers his parents as the cause of his existence, and he concludes that in addition to what he has just said, it is incorrect to think that his parents generated him *qua* thinking thing or that they can preserve him in being.

2.2. The a priori *argument*

The *a priori* argument is quite simple in form. Descartes tells us in the Fifth Meditation, "the mere fact that I can produce from my thoughts the idea of something entails that everything which I clearly and distinctly perceive to belong to that thing really does belong to it."[11] Here, Descartes uses his "truth rule." The rule states that whatever is clearly and distinctly perceived is indubitably true. Descartes then claims he has a clear and distinct idea of God as a supremely perfect being.[12] Because existence is a perfection, he concludes that God exists.

2.3. Objections and replies

Descartes answers several objections to his arguments in the Objections and Replies to the Meditations.[13] Many objections to the *a posteriori* argument claim that the causal principle, which requires there to be at least as much reality in the cause as there is in the effect, is false.[14] Here, two objections to the *a priori* argument will be briefly considered, along with Descartes's replies.

The first objection is a restatement of Aquinas's objection to Anselm's version of the ontological argument.[15] The objection states that, although it makes sense to say that God is a supremely perfect being, it does not follow from this that there is anything in reality which answers to this description. Descartes attempts to address this objection in the Fifth Meditation.[16] He notes that there are some ideas which provide us with logically necessary truths about their objects, whether there be any such objects in reality or not. For instance, even if there were no actual triangles, it would still be logically necessary that the three angles of a triangle are equal to two right angles. To say that it is possible that there be a triangle that lacks this property is nonsensical. However, these truths tell us nothing about whether any triangle actually exists. But the case of the reality of a perfect being is importantly different from the triangle. The idea of a perfect being, according to Descartes, contains within it the idea of existence. So just as it is nonsensical to imagine a triangle without the property of having its three angles being equal to two right angles, it is nonsensical to think of a perfect being without the property of existence. It is logically necessary that a perfect being contain this property. So, Descartes's reply to Aquinas's objection is that, in the special case of God, we can know that our idea has an actual referent because in the idea of God, His existence is not separable from His essence.

The second objection to be considered here is one made famous by Leibniz. Leibniz notes that the *a priori* argument, as given by Descartes, only shows that if a being with all the perfections is possible, then such a being exists. However, Leibniz claims that Descartes has not shown that such a being is possible. How can we be certain that a being with all the perfections is possible, especially given Descartes's claim that we cannot grasp the infinite nature of God?

Descartes anticipates this objection in the Replies to the First Set of Objections.[17] He writes, "It must be noted that possible existence is contained in the concept or idea of everything we clearly and distinctly understand."[18] Descartes is famous for claiming that we cannot grasp the nature of an infinite being. But Descartes makes a distinction between grasping and understanding. Grasping is more robust than understanding. We can have an understanding of God's perfections that is in keeping with our finite nature, and this is sufficient for having a clear and distinct idea of God as an infinitely perfect being even though as finite beings we cannot grasp the infinite in its entirety. So, Descartes's reply to Leibniz would consist in saying that anything that we can clearly and distinctly perceive is possible. If I clearly and distinctly perceive a being with all the perfections, then that being is possible. And because existence is a perfection, that being must really exist.[19]

3. John Locke (1632–1704)

Locke provides a cosmological proof for the existence of God in *An Essay Concerning Human Understanding*. Locke's argument has been widely criticized, both by his contemporaries and by historians. Lockean replies to some of these objections will be provided by using materials from the *Essay* and from "Deus," a short piece where Locke criticizes Descartes's ontological proof and provides a rationale for Locke's own methodology.[20]

In 4.10 of the *Essay*, titled "Of Our Knowledge of the Existence of God," Locke gives his cosmological argument. He writes that, with "thought and attention" and "the application of a regular deduction from some part of our intuitive knowledge," he can demonstrate the existence of God from the "undoubted knowledge we have of our own existence."[21]

Locke starts from his awareness of his own thought, reasoning, and feelings and concludes from this that he exists. This reasoning is, of course, similar to Descartes's famous

cogito: I think; I exist. Locke writes, "I think it is beyond Question, that *Man has a clear Perception of his own Being*; he knows certainly, that he exists, and that he is something."
Locke then continues,

> In the next place, Man knows by an intuitive Certainty, that bare nothing can no more produce any real Being, than it can be equal to two right Angles. If a man knows not that Non-entity, or the Absence of all Being cannot be equal to two right Angles, it is impossible that he know any demonstration in Euclid. If therefore we know there is some real Being, and that Non-entity cannot produce any real Being, it is an evident demonstration, that from Eternity there has been something; Since what was not from Eternity, had a Beginning; and what had a Beginning, must be produced by something else.
>
> (*Essay* 4.10.3)

The first part of Locke's cosmological argument might be rendered as follows:

1. I exist.
2. Therefore, there exists some real being.
3. Nothing, or nonentity, cannot produce real being (*ex nihilo, nihil fit*).
4. Therefore, at all times from eternity, there must have existed something.

Then Locke continues:

> Next, it is evident, that what had its Being and Beginning from another, must also have all that which is in, and belongs to its Being from another too. All the Powers it has, must be owing to, and received from the same Source. This eternal Source of all being must also be the Source and Original of all Power; and so this eternal Being must also be the most powerful.[22]

The final two premises of the argument are as follows:

5. Whatever is caused to exist by another gets all its being and power from that cause.
6. Therefore, the eternal being is the cause of all real being and is also all powerful.

Locke has been accused of making three mistakes in his proof: (1) using "nothing" as the name of something, (2) making the fallacious logical move from "at every past time something existed" to "there is something which existed at every past time," and (3) making the fallacious move from there being one eternal thing that exists to there being one eternal thing that is the cause of everything else.[23]

Let us take each of these criticisms in order. The first criticism is that in claiming that nothing comes from nothing, Locke is not saying merely that nothing happens without a cause, but that it is logically impossible that something happens without a cause. However, though it might be true that all actual events are caused, it does not seem contradictory that they might not have been.[24] So Locke's claim that nothing can come from nothing is too strong. Moreover, it is claimed that Locke's mistake is the result of treating *nothing* as a substantive. However, there are two reasons for thinking that this is not Locke's intention. First, Locke is generally careful in the text to say "nothing, non-entity," which would seem to indicate that he is aware of the fact that "nothing" sounds as if it were the name of an entity and that he seeks to dispel this confusion. Second, Locke's acceptance of *ex nihilo, nihil fit* is not unqualified. In the cosmological argument, Locke is talking about a special type of existent, namely those that *begin* to exist. Locke holds that for any thing that begins to exist, there is a cause for that thing's beginning to exist. This still leaves room for something that always existed having no cause of its existence. An eternal being might exist uncaused. Nevertheless, according to Locke, our ideas concerning causation are such that for any effect we assume that there must have been a cause – even if we cannot discover this cause.[25] This is so because our notions of cause and effect are derived entirely from our ideas received from sensation and reflection, and we can have no clear idea of eternity. Locke writes, "For to have the Idea of Cause and Effect, it suffices to consider any simple Idea, or Substance, as beginning to exist, by the Operation of some other, without knowing the manner of that Operation."[26] As we can see from this passage, Locke's maxim is that *for every effect, which begins to exist, there is a cause*. Of course, the cause may not be discernible or knowable to us. Nonetheless, Locke holds that this maxim is intuitively certain because it is a relation between our ideas.

The second criticism of Locke's argument is that the move from premise 4 to premise 6 is fallacious. Locke appears to reason that because nothing can come from nothing, and something exists, there must have existed something always. However, from this, it does not follow there is *one* thing which has existed always, as the conclusion at 6 seems to indicate. We can only validly conclude that, at all times, there is something such that it exists. We cannot say that there is one thing, or two things, or infinitely many things. We cannot validly conclude from the proposition that *something exists at every time*, that *there is some particular thing that exists at every time*, just as we cannot conclude from the proposition that *everybody loves somebody*, that *there exists some one person whom everyone loves*. Thus, it seems Locke's argument for the existence of an eternal being is invalid. Here, it is useful to turn to Locke's essay "Deus" for a better understanding of Locke's thinking on this point. In "Deus," Locke tells us that the primary problem with Descartes's ontological argument is that the addition of the idea of necessary existence to our complex idea of God does not prove that there is any real being which answers to that description. Moreover, Locke points out that Descartes's move is equally available to the atheist materialist who wants to prove that mere "senseless matter" is the eternal cause of all that exists. Locke claims that *neither* the theist nor the atheist deny that something has been in existence from all eternity; rather the dispute is over the nature of the eternal thing – the theist claims that it is knowing, immaterial substance and the atheist claims that it is senseless, immaterial matter. Locke's aim in the cosmological proof is to give reasons for thinking that the eternal thing is knowing immaterial substance, or God, rather than senseless matter. Locke seems to have taken this context for granted in the *Essay*, assuming that his interlocutors would agree that some one thing – either God or the universe of senseless material substances – has always existed. He writes,

> The fallacy of his pretended great proof of a Deity appears to me thus: – The question between the Theists and Atheists I take to be this, viz. not whether there has been nothing from eternity, but whether the eternal Being that made, and still keeps all things in that order, beauty, and method, in which we see them, be a knowing immaterial substance, or a senseless material substance; for that something, either senseless matter, or a knowing spirit, has been from eternity, I think nobody doubts.[27]

Thus, if we understand Locke's argument in the context of the dispute between the theist and the materialist atheist, we can see that the crux of the argument is not whether something exists from eternity or not, but what the nature of the existing thing is. Of course, the problem of the number of immaterial knowing things remains an issue, but it was not Locke's primary concern in the rendering of the argument. This leads us to the third criticism.

The third criticism is given by Leibniz in the *New Essays on Human Understanding*. Here, Leibniz notes Locke's conclusion, that there is only *one* eternal being that is the cause of all other real beings, is contentious. Leibniz writes,

> Furthermore, there are those who, if they do admit eternal beings (as the Epicureans do with their atoms), will not regard themselves as committed to granting that there is an eternal being which is the sole source of all the others. For though they would acknowledge that whatever confers existence also confers the thing's other qualities and powers, they will deny that a single thing gives existence to the others, and will even say that for each thing the joint action of several others is required. Thus, we shan't be brought by that argument, unaided, to one source of all powers.[28]

Leibniz is objecting to Locke's formulation of the causal principle. Leibniz claims that even if we accept that the eternal thing is immaterial and knowing, there is argument given for the claim that all the powers in the world must come from one single source. It is perfectly consistent with Locke's principle, *ex nihilo, nihil fit*, that there be multiple causes of all the power and being that exists. However, it seems clear that Locke holds a stronger principle according to which there must be a single cause for all the power and being in the world. Locke's stronger causal principle states that *whatever begins to exist is caused to exist by another and gets all its being and power from that same cause*. Locke writes,

> And whatsoever is first of all Things, must necessarily contain in it, and actually have, at least, all the Perfections that can ever exist; nor can it ever give to another any perfection that it hath not, either actually in itself, or at least in a higher degree.[29]

However, Locke does not provide any supplemental argumentation for this stronger causal principle.

4. Benedict de Spinoza (1632–1677)

Spinoza's proofs for the existence of God are found in *Ethics*, part 1, proposition 11. The definitions and axioms needed for understanding these proofs are provided in the preceding sections of the *Ethics*. Here, the proofs are given, along with some supporting arguments and criticisms.

Proposition 11 is titled "God, or *a substance consisting of infinite attributes, each of which expresses an eternal and infinite essence, necessarily exists.*"[30] Here, Spinoza provides four demonstrations for the existence of God. All the demonstrations are grounded in Spinoza's definitions and axioms concerning substances and causation. The first two demonstrations are variations on the same idea and depend on the causation of substances. The second two demonstrations are *a posteriori* and *a priori* versions of a proof based on the concept of power.

Spinoza defines substance as "what is in itself and is conceived though itself, that is, that whose concept does not require the concept of another thing, from which it must be formed."[31] His account of substance resembles those given by the Scholastics and Descartes. However, Spinoza, unlike Descartes, is not a substance dualist. He believes that when we consider the identity conditions and causal relations of substances, we must conclude that there is – and can only be – one substance. This is so because substances must be distinguished from one another by either their attributes (or essences) or by their affections (or *modes* in Descartes's usage). Because affections are posterior to the existence of substances, they cannot be used to distinguish substances from each other. Therefore, substances must be distinguished by their attributes. However, this implies that for every substance, there must be a unique attribute or collection of attributes. Once Spinoza has argued that no two substances can share an attribute, he seeks to provide proofs for the existence of a substance with infinite attributes. In doing so, he secures his monism – there can be no substances other than God because he has all the possible attributes.

The first demonstration of an infinite substance is a version of the ontological argument. Spinoza reasons, if God, who is a substance consisting of an infinity of attributes, does not exist, then His essence does not involve existence. But it pertains to the nature of substance to exist (*E* 1p7). If it is part of a substance's nature to exist, it must necessarily exist. Therefore, God, an infinite substance, necessarily exists.

Spinoza's argument rests on two claims: (1) no two substances can share an attribute, and (2) existence is included in the essence of a substance. Here is the crucial *E* 1p7 reasoning for the conclusion that a substance cannot be produced by anything external to itself: in nature there are only substances, attributes, and affections. Affections are posterior to substances, and so they cannot be the cause of substances. If attributes are used to differentiate substances, then there must be a unique attribute for every substance.[32] Substances cannot cause one another because no two substances have attributes in common (*E* 1p5),[33] and therefore they cannot affect each other (*E* 1a4 and *E* 1a5).[34] Thus, a substance cannot be caused by anything external to itself. Therefore, a substance must cause itself, that is its essences must involve existence.

The second proof is based on the principle of sufficient reason (PSR). Spinoza states the principle as follows: "for each thing there must be assigned a cause, or reason, both for its existence and for its nonexistence."[35] If it were possible that there be a reason or cause for God's nonexistence, then He would not exist. In order for there to be a reason for God not to exist, either God's nature would have to be contradictory (like a square circle) or there would have to be some other substance that prevented God's existence. God's nature is not contradictory. There can be no other substance preventing God's existence, because if another substance existed, it would have a nature different from God's nature (otherwise the substance with God's nature would exist and so He would exist). However, a substance with a nature different from God's nature would have nothing in common with God and could not cause His existence or nonexistence (see previous argument). Therefore, there is nothing preventing God's existence. Therefore, God necessarily exists.

In response to the first two proofs, one might challenge the definition of God as a substance with infinite attributes. This objection seeks to show that the first proof is question begging, and that the term "infinite being" in the second proof should be understood as infinite *in kind* rather than absolutely infinite. According to Spinoza, each of the attributes of a substance must be conceived through itself (*E* 1p10), and the more being or reality a thing has, the more attributes it will have (*E* 1p9). However, the claim that an infinite being must be absolutely infinite, that is must have an infinite number of attributes rather than just a single attribute to an infinite degree (which he calls infinite *in kind*), is not convincing. It is true that given Spinoza's system, if a being with infinite attributes exists, then there is only one substance, but Spinoza has not shown that there must be such a substance. It is consistent with his claims that an infinite number of attributes exist, but that each of the attributes is had by a separate substance. If this situation obtained, then there would be infinitely many separate substances, each of which is infinite in kind and exists through itself.

The last two proofs for the existence of God rely on the notion of power. It is important to note that Spinoza is not speaking here of the power of substances, but the power of being in general (given that he has already shown in *E* 1p8 that all substances are infinite). Spinoza calls the first version of the second proof "*a posteriori*." Presumably, he does so because it contains one empirical premise – that finite beings exist. The *a posteriori* proof based on the idea of power runs as follows. To be able not to exist is to lack power, and to be able to exist is to have power. Finite beings exist. If there were only finite beings in existence, then finite beings would have more power than infinite beings. Finite beings do not have more power than infinite beings. Therefore, an absolutely infinite being necessarily exists.

Spinoza also gives what he calls an *a priori* version of this proof. The proof runs as follows: being able to exist is a power. The more reality belongs to the nature of a thing, the more power it has. An infinite being has in its nature an absolutely infinite power of existing. Therefore, an infinite being necessarily exists.

These proofs have implications which are controversial in at least three aspects. First, if Spinoza's arguments are sound, then God is the only substance. All other beings, including human beings, are attributes or affections of God; human beings are not real entities in themselves. Second, Spinoza's arguments are sometimes criticized as having naturalized God. Spinoza often uses the phrase *deus sive natura*, which translates as "God or nature," as if the two terms were interchangeable. Spinoza may be equating the will and intellect of God with the laws of nature, or he may be denying that God has any personal attributes at all. God is not the creator of the world, because all things that exist are part of God, who is the immanent cause of His own being. Finally, Spinoza's arguments are controversial because they entail necessitarianism. Because God is the necessarily existing substance and all things are part of that substance, all things that exist, exist necessarily.

5. Nicolas Malebranche (1638–1715)

Malebranche gives two related arguments for the existence of God. The first argument is a version of Descartes's ontological argument, which Malebranche claims is the simplest and best argument for the existence of God. In *The Search After Truth*, he gives a detailed account of Descartes's argument and responds to some objections. Although his ontological argument is not unique, his conception of God is. Malebranche supplements the Cartesian argument for God's existence with a second argument based on "mere sight." Malebranche claims that this argument has its roots in Thomas Aquinas's notion that God's knowledge is really knowledge of His own being or essence, so that all things must somehow be *in* God. In what follows, Malebranche's claim that God is "being in general" will be discussed first, followed by a discussion of the argument from mere sight.

Malebranche's ontological argument begins with his statement of Descartes's truth rule: "Here is the first principle: one should attribute to a thing what one clearly conceives to be included in the idea that represents it."[36] Malebranche refers to the truth rule as "the general principle of all the sciences."[37] He then goes on to say that we clearly conceive that necessary existence is included in the idea of an infinitely perfect being. Therefore, we know that God, or an infinitely perfect being, exists.

What is interestingly different about Malebranche's ontological argument is that he takes God to be "being in general." Most theologians, Descartes included, take God to be the being with the greatest reality or the most being. Malebranche's view is decidedly more radical. Some object to Descartes's argument on the grounds that one could use similar reasoning to define just about anything into existence. Malebranche responds by claiming that the reasoning only applies to God because He is essentially different from all other beings. He is different because all other beings are particular beings, or as Malebranche puts it, "such beings." He writes,

> But the idea of God or of being in general, of being without limit, of infinite being, is not a fiction of the mind. It is not a complex idea that includes some contradiction; there is nothing simpler, although it includes necessary existence; for it is evident that being (I do not say a *such being*) has its existence in itself, and that being cannot actually (or really) not be, since it is impossible and contradictory that true being be without existence. It could be that there were no bodies, because bodies are *such beings* that participate in being and are dependent upon it. But being without restriction is necessary; it is independent; it derives what it is from nothing but itself; everything that is comes from it. If there is anything, it is, since everything that is comes from it; but if there were nothing in particular, it would be, because it is in itself and because it cannot be clearly conceived as nonexistent, unless it is represented as a being in particular or as a *such being*, that is, unless it is considered as a completely different idea than its own. For those who do not see that God is [exists] usually do not consider being, but a *such being* and consequently a being that can be or not be.[38]

Necessary existence is contained within the concept of God because He is being in general. We cannot claim of any particular (or *such*) being that it exists, but being in general cannot fail to exist. Whether or not there were any particular beings at all, it would still be true that the general notion of being would exist. Because God is being in general, He necessarily exists.

Malebranche supplements the ontological argument with the argument that all ideas exist in, and come to us from, God. In order for us to have certain knowledge, Malebranche claims that ideas must be necessary and immutable. Finite beings cannot have direct access to such ideas from perception because perception only provides sensations of mutable particular finite things. Malebranche claims, "it is certain that nothingness or the false is not perceptible or intelligible," yet we certainly believe false things. However, we do not clearly and distinctly perceive false things. Malebranche writes,

> It is impossible to perceive a falsehood, a relation of equality, for example, between two and two, and five; for this or any like relation that does not exist

can be believed, but certainly cannot be perceived because nothingness is not perceptible. Properly speaking, this is the first principle of all our knowledge.... For the principle generally accepted by the Cartesians, that whatever is clearly conceived to be contained in the idea representing a thing can be asserted of that thing, depends on it; and this principle is true only if we assume that ideas are immutable, necessary, and divine.[39]

Ideas must be grounded in something necessary and immutable in order for the truth rule to hold; that is, in order for knowledge to be possible at all. The notion that all ideas are contained in God and that it is only through God's affecting our minds that we can have the idea of anything at all is the basis for the argument that our *mere sight* shows God's existence. Malebranche writes,

It is certain, and everyone knows this from experience, that when we want to think about some particular thing, we first glance over all beings and then apply ourselves to the consideration of the object we wish to think about. Now, it is indubitable that we could desire to see a particular object only if we had already seen it, though in a general and confused fashion. As a result of this, given that we can desire to see all beings, now one, now another, it is certain that all beings are present to our mind; and it seems that all beings can be present to our mind only because God; i.e., He who includes all things in the simplicity of his being, is present to it.[40]

Here, Malebranche argues that in order to see things – both particular things and general things – we must have contact with something that can affect our minds or souls. Because only something "higher" than the mind can affect it, material objects cannot affect the mind. Only God can affect the mind and He knows all things – general and particular – because He includes all things eminently. Malebranche also notes that we could not have the idea of general or universal things by perception, for we only perceive particular things – not general things. "The mind would be incapable of representing universal ideas of genus, species, and so on, to itself had it not seen all beings contained in one."[41]

Malebranche's claim that God is being in general allows him to ground all ideas in a necessary and immutable nature. However, the view does have some serious theological consequences. Most importantly, if God is being in general rather than a particular being, it seems that God is an abstract object. This, of course, is in direct conflict with the theological doctrine that God is a person.

Finally, although Malebranche claims that Aquinas held a view similar to his own, Aquinas did not think that God was being in general. Aquinas thought that the source of God's knowledge is His essence; that is, that God has ideas of all possible things contained in His essence. But this is so only because God knows His own will. According to Aquinas, God knows both what He wills and what He does not will. This is sufficient for giving Him knowledge of all possible things, without resorting to the claim that God is being in general.

6. Gottfried Wilhelm Leibniz (1646–1716)

Leibniz has four arguments for the existence of God. He offers an "improved" version of the ontological argument that is meant to address his criticism of Descartes's version of the argument. He also presents a cosmological argument, an argument based on the existence of the eternal truths and an argument based on preestablished harmony.

6.1. The ontological argument

Leibniz's criticisms of Descartes's ontological argument are found in a number of his works.[42] Leibniz argues that Descartes's proof only shows that if a being with all the perfections is possible, then he exists. However, Leibniz maintains that Descartes failed to show that a being with all the perfections is, in fact, possible. Here is a version of the criticism from "Meditations on Knowledge, Truth, and Ideas":[43]

> An argument for the existence of God, celebrated among the Scholastics long ago and revived by Descartes, once led me to consider this point more distinctly. The argument goes: whatever follows from the idea or definition of anything can be predicated of that thing. Since the most perfect being includes all perfections, among which is existence, existence follows from the idea of God (or the idea of a most perfect being, or the idea of that than which nothing greater can be thought). Therefore existence can be predicated of God. But one must realize that from this argument we can conclude only that, if God is possible, then it follows that he exists. For we cannot safely use definitions for drawing conclusions unless we know first that they are real definitions, that is, that they include no contradictions, because we can draw contradictory conclusions from notions that include contradictions, which is absurd.[44]

Leibniz maintains that there are two ways of resolving the problem. One is to presume God's existence. This is not sufficient for proof of God's existence, but he tells us that it will suffice in practical matters. Leibniz writes,

> For there is always a presumption on the side of possibility, that is, everything is held to be possible unless it is proven to be impossible. There is, therefore, a presumption that God is possible, that is, that he exists, since in him existence follows from possibility. This is sufficient for practical matters in life, but it is not sufficient for demonstration.[45]

The second way is to demonstrate God's existence by showing that a being with all the perfections is possible. Leibniz thinks that he succeeds in doing this. First, he defines "perfection" as "every simple quality which is positive and absolute and which expresses whatever it expresses without any limits."[46] A simple quality, Leibniz tells us, is one that is "unanalyzable or indefinable, for otherwise either it will not be one simple quality but an aggregate of many ... which is contrary to hypothesis, since it is assumed to be purely positive."[47] Next, he goes on to argue that no two such simple positive qualities can be contradictory. The argument is reminiscent of an argument in Plato's *Theaetetus* to the effect that, because simples are unanalyzable, they are also unknowable.[48] In the *Theaetetus*, this claim is taken as a problem for any combinatorial theory of language, but here, Leibniz uses it to show that no two simple properties can be incompatible. In his notes from a discussion with Spinoza, "That a Most Perfect Being Exists," Leibniz writes,

> For let us assume that there is a proposition of this kind: A and B are incompatible, understanding by A and B two simple forms or perfections of this kind. It makes no difference if more than two are assumed simultaneously. It is clear that this proposition cannot be demonstrated without an analysis of the terms

> A and B, either or both, for otherwise their nature would not enter into the reasoning, and incompatibility could be demonstrated equally well about any other things as about themselves. And by hypothesis they are unanalyzable. Therefore this proposition cannot be demonstrated about them.
>
> But it is certainly demonstrated about them if it were true, since this proposition is not true by itself. For all propositions which are necessarily true are either demonstrable or known *per se*. Therefore this proposition is not necessarily true, or it is not necessary that A and B should not be in the same subject. Therefore they can be in the same subject. And since this reasoning is the same for any other assumed qualities of this kind whatsoever, it follows that all perfections are compatible.
>
> Therefore there is, or can be conceived, a subject of all perfections or a most perfect being. Hence it is clear that this being exists, since existence is contained in the number of perfections.[49]

Here, Leibniz argues via reduction. He says, suppose any two unanalyzable simples or perfections are incompatible. In order to demonstrate that they are incompatible, it must be shown that they are contradictory in nature. But, in order to show two things to be contradictory in nature, we must be able to analyze their nature. However, by definition, the nature of perfections is unanalyzable. Therefore, it cannot be demonstrated that any two unanalyzable perfections are incompatible. We cannot know *per se* that any two unanalyzable perfections are incompatible because we cannot know their terms. Therefore, it is not necessarily true that any two unanalyzable perfections are incompatible. Therefore, it is possible that any two unanalyzable perfections are compatible. Therefore, it is possible that a being with all the perfections exists.

Leibniz thought that this proof of the compossibility of the perfections was sufficient to render the ontological argument sound, for he has shown that a being with all the perfections is possible. However, it seems unlikely that the traditional perfections of God – for example omnipotence, omnibenevolence, and omniscience – are unanalyzable. In fact, a great deal of philosophical ink has been spent analyzing these concepts and trying to avoid the apparent incompatibilities between them.

6.2. *The cosmological argument*

The clearest formulation of Leibniz's cosmological argument is given in his essay "On the Ultimate Origination of Things."[50] Leibniz begins the argument as follows:

> Beyond the world, that is, beyond the collection of finite things, there is some One Being who rules, not only as the soul is the ruler in me, or, better, as the self is the ruler in my body, but also in a much higher sense. For the One Being who rules the universe not only rules the world, but also fashions or creates it; he is above the world, and, so to speak, extramundane, and therefore he is the ultimate reason for things. For we cannot find in any of the individual things, or even in the entire collection and series of things, a sufficient reason for why they exist.[51]

Leibniz's argument makes use of the PSR. He claims that because everything that exists must have a sufficient reason or cause for why it exists as it does and not some other way, we must be able to give a reason for the existence of the world. Given that the world is a collection of contingent things, the sufficient reason for the whole world cannot be in the collection. Leibniz tries to support this claim with the following reasoning:

> Let us suppose that a book on the elements of geometry has always existed, one copy always made from another. It is obvious that although we can explain a present copy of the book from the previous book from which it was copied, this will never lead us to a complete explanation, no matter how many books back we go, since we can always wonder why there have always been such books, why these books were written, and why they were written the way they were. What is true of these books is also true of the different states of the world, for the state which follows is, in a sense, copied from the preceding state, though in accordance with certain laws of change. And so, however far back we might go into previous states, we will never find in those states a complete explanation for why, indeed there is any world at all, and why it is the way that it is.[52]

This portion of Leibniz's argument can be stated formally as follows:

1. A sufficient reason for the existence of the world will tell us why it exists and why it is the way that it is.
2. For every state of the world, we can give a reason for why that state exists and why it is the way that it is, if we know the previous state of the world and the laws.
3. The world is the collection of all of its states.[53]
4. But there is no state of the world that can provide a sufficient reason for why *all* the states of the world exist and why they are the way that they are.
5. Therefore, no state of the world can be a sufficient reason for the existence of the world.

The most common objection to the Leibnizian cosmological argument is that the PSR is false. The objector claims that there is no reason to believe that for everything that exists, there is a reason or cause for its existence. Contemporary commentators often look to physics, and in particular quantum mechanics, for exceptions to the rule. Because there is widespread disagreement concerning the principle and a robust literature which discusses it, it will not be discussed here.[54]

Instead, let us consider Leibniz's claim that a sufficient reason cannot be had from the world itself. The most famous criticism of this claim comes from Bertrand Russell.[55] Russell argued that to demand an explanation for the entire world is to commit a fallacy. It is similar to saying, *every man has a mother, therefore; all of humanity must have a mother*. Because there is no entity "humanity" over and above all the actual human beings, there is nothing more to explain once one has explained the mother of every individual human being. However, Leibniz thinks that other worlds were possible. That is, he thought that there are infinitely many worlds that might have obtained. Given that existence might have been quite different from the way that it is, one might think it is fair to ask why it is the way that it is. Thus, when Leibniz asks why this collection of contingent beings exists, he is asking a question, the answer to which requires a comparison between the existing collection and some other possible collection. "Why this one, or these, rather than some other one, or those?"[56]

6.3. The argument from the eternal truths

Leibniz's argument for the existence of God based on the eternal truths can be seen most easily in sections 43 through 45 of the *Monadology*.[57] There, he writes,

> It is also true that God is not only the source of existences, but also that of essences insofar as they are real, that is, or the source of that which is real in possibility. This is because God's understanding is the realm of eternal truths or that of the ideas on which they depend; without him there would be nothing real in possibles, and not only would nothing exist, but also nothing would be possible.
>
> For if there is reality in essences or possibles, or indeed in eternal truths, this reality must be grounded in something existent and actual, and consequently, it must be grounded in the existence of the necessary being, in whom essence involves existence, that is, in whom possible being is sufficient for actual being.[58]

Leibniz's commitment to the PSR comes through here as well. If the PSR is necessarily true, as Leibniz thought, then every possibility must be grounded in an entity that could make it actual. Leibniz holds that the only thing that could be the cause of all essences and possibilities is a necessarily existing being who has the power to make any essence or possibility actual. He believes that the possible worlds and the ideas of the essences of things are contained in the understanding of God. Thus, it is God that is the ground of all essences and possibilities. It should be noted that Leibniz did not believe that the eternal truths were subject to God's will. Leibniz did not think that God controls what is eternally true; He merely understands what is so and could not be otherwise.

6.4. The argument from preestablished harmony

The argument from preestablished harmony begins with Leibniz's assertion that created substances cannot affect one another, and that these substances are continually produced by the power of God. Thus, Leibniz holds that God creates souls in such a way that everything in them arises from their own nature. The soul is created, as he says, "with a perfect spontaneity as regards itself, and yet with a perfect conformity to things outside of it."[59] Thus, souls are completely independent of one another, yet they are in perfect correspondence with each other with respect to their perceptions of each other and the universe around them. The proof that is based on this thesis is that, were there no one source of the many substances that have no communication with one another, there would not be such a perfect and harmonious agreement between the perceptions of beings. Thus, because we have harmonious perceptions, we can know that God exists.

7. George Berkeley (1685–1753)

The argument for the existence of God in the *Treatise Concerning the Principles of Human Knowledge* is found in sections 25 through 33 and in sections 145 through 147 (with elaborations and replies to objections continuing to section 156), and in the second dialogue of the *Three Dialogues Between Hylas and Philonous*. The arguments in both texts are similar, but the argument given here is from the *Principles*.

In the first thirty-three sections of the *Principles*, Berkeley formulates an argument for idealism. After showing that no corporeal or material entities exist, he elucidates the cause of our ideas. We know from experience that we have ideas, and if there are no material things outside us causing them, then they must have a different source. The argument for the existence of God is a causal argument that seeks to show that all of our ideas of sense come from God. First, Berkeley argues that all our ideas are inactive. He writes,

> All our ideas, sensations, or the things which we perceive, by whatsoever names they may be distinguished, are visibly inactive, there is nothing of power or agency included in them. So that one idea or object of thought cannot produce, or make any alteration in another. . . . For since they [ideas] and every part of them exist only in the mind, it follows that there is nothing in them but what is perceived. But whoever shall attend to his ideas, whether of sense or reflexion, will not perceive in them any power or activity; there is therefore no such thing contained in them.[60]

Here, we see that our ideas cannot be the cause of themselves or of other ideas. Berkeley next divides our ideas into two types: ideas of imagination, which are subject to the will of the mind that has them, and ideas of sense, which are not subject to the will of the mind that has them. The cause of our ideas of imagination is evident. However, the cause of our ideas of sense is not evident. He writes,

> The ideas of sense are more strong, lively, and distinct than those of the imagination; they have likewise a steadiness, order, and coherence, and are not excited at random, as those which are the effects of human wills often are, but in a regular train or series, the admirable connexion whereof sufficiently testifies the wisdom and benevolence of its Author.[61]

Berkeley rules out the possibility of our ideas of sense being caused by other men, and argues that the harmony of our ideas indicates that there is one powerful source. He writes,

> Yet it is evident to every one, that those things which are called the works of Nature, that is, the far greater part of the ideas or sensations perceived by us, are not produced by, or dependent on the wills of men. There is therefore some other spirit that causes them, since it is repugnant that they should subsist by themselves . . . but if we attentively consider the constant regularity, order and concatenation of natural things, the surprising magnificence, beauty, and perfection of the larger, and the exquisite contrivance of the smaller parts of the creation, together with the exact harmony and correspondence of the whole, but above all, the never enough admired laws of pain and pleasure, and the instincts or natural inclinations, appetites, and passions of animals; I say if we consider all these things, and at the same time attend to the meaning and import of the attributes, one, eternal, infinitely wise, good, and perfect, we shall clearly perceive that they belong to the aforesaid spirit, *who works all in all*, and *by whom all things consist*.[62]

The argument is as follows: our ideas of sense might be caused by us, by other ideas, by other human minds, or by nonhuman minds. Berkeley then proceeds to eliminate ourselves, our ideas, and human minds as possible causes and concludes that our ideas of sense must be caused by nonhuman minds. He then claims that because our sensations are regular, orderly, and coherent, they must be caused by something powerful, wise, and good. Thus, our ideas of sense are caused by a powerful, wise, and good nonhuman mind, which is God.

There is not sufficient space here to discuss Berkeley's arguments for idealism here, so let us pass over that assumption. We can see that Berkeley still has a problem with the inference from our sensations as regular, orderly, and coherent to the claim that they are caused by a powerful, wise, and good being. Berkeley accepts the causal principle that a cause cannot transmit anything it does not have to an effect. So, he may infer that the cause of our ideas of sense is powerful, wise, and good enough to produce our orderly and coherent ideas. However, it does not follow from this that there must be a *singular* cause for all our ideas of sense.[63] It is perfectly consistent with the causal principle mentioned previously that there be a multitude of causes that work together to produce our orderly and coherent ideas of sensation.

8. "Noncanonical figures"

8.1. Pierre Gassendi (1592–1655)

Pierre Gassendi gives a design argument in the *Syntagma*. Like all design arguments, Gassendi's argument is probabilistic; that is, it is not a valid deductive argument but resembles an inference to the best explanation. Gassendi begins by showing that we receive through the senses a sign that may lead us via reasoning to truths that cannot be known by sense perception. He writes,

> Since it is well known that we perceive some things through the mind and some through the senses, and that all knowledge which we have in the mind had its beginning in the senses (even Plato, when he contends that knowledge is nothing more than recollection, teaches that it is aroused by things perceived through the senses), therefore a certain sensible sign must come before the mind by which it is led to the knowledge of the thing lying hidden unperceived by the senses.[64]

Next, Gassendi argues that we can (through this method) know of things hidden to the senses, such as the pores of the skin, the legs of mites, and the soul of man. Gassendi argues that the latter case should be counted as a truth as secure as the former cases. For it was only with the development of the microscope that it was possible to confirm such truths as the skin contains pores and mites have legs. He writes,

> But really, before they appeared to us, were they less true than they are now, however much less known they may have been? And were they not on the same footing as many things which are known now by reason alone, and I do not mean those that are defined as hidden only temporarily, to which some empirical sign is ascribed? Then why aren't so many of these things considered true with equal authority though they are perceived by the mind alone and can no more appear to the senses than those other truths could in the past?[65]

And so by similar reasoning, we can know from the sign of the order, harmony, and grandeur of the universe that God exists. He concludes,

> For when among other questions we hear it asked if God is or exists in the universe, that is a truth of existence which it would be a great service to establish firmly even if it is not proven at the same time what he is or what his nature is. Although God is such that he can no more come under the perusal of the senses than the soul can, still we infer that the soul exists in the body from the actions that occur before the senses and are so peculiarly appropriate to a soul that if one were not present, they would not be either. In the same way we deduce that God exists in the universe from his effects perceived by the senses, which could not be produced by anything but God and which therefore would not be observed unless God were present in the world, such as the great order of the universe, its great beauty, its grandeur, its harmony, which are so great that they can only result from a sovereignly wise, good, powerful, and inexhaustible cause.[66]

Gassendi is well aware of the leading objection to the design argument, namely that it does not prove the existence of the Christian God. In other words, the argument does not conclude with the claim that a necessary, omnipotent, omnibenevolent, and omniscient God exists. Rather, his argument only seeks to show that the world is created by a wise and powerful ruler or designer. However, Gassendi claims that even if we cannot know, because of our limited means of attaining knowledge, what God is like, we can be as certain of his existence as we can of any truth we gain knowledge of by means of the senses and reason:

> In the same way we do not know from those works, so great and so perfect, which are some sort of sign, just what God looks like or what his true nature is; but we understand with the greatest certainty that he is present in the universe, for the lines that he has traced in the universe, so to speak, are such that they can come only from an incomparable artisan.[67]

8.2. Benjamin Whichcote (1609–1683)

Whichcote, a Cambridge Platonist, provides a causal argument for the existence of God. In "The Use of Reason in Matters of Religion," he argues that there are many effects that we observe in the world which are not of our making and are beyond our understanding. These effects must have a cause, and the cause must be such that it is able to produce the effects that we see. Because these effects include intelligent beings, we can know that the cause is some higher intelligent being. He writes,

> There are *Effects* in the World natural; of Inanimates, of Vegetables, and Sensitives; and in the World moral, of spiritual Substances, and intelligent Agents, that shew there is a God. For they do far transcend Mind and Understanding in Man: Therefore they must be the Product of some higher Being. And if we bring a Man to acknowledge a Being that is abler and wiser than himself, he acknowledges *Deity*.[68]

It is in reasoning about the nature of the world – from effects to cause – that we can learn of God's existence. Whichcote argues that the nature of the stars, moon, and planets transcends our reason, and we are led to the conclusion that there must be an intelligence greater than our own that is responsible for these effects.

8.3. Henry More (1614–1687)

In More's "An Antidote to Atheism," he presents several arguments for the existence of God. In section VIII, he provides a version of Descartes's ontological argument and addresses some leading objections. In section IX, he argues that our innate idea of God is a sign that God exists, and in section X, he provides a moral argument for God's existence. The moral argument is given in what follows.

More's basic argument is simple: human beings share a natural conscience and this is evidence of God's existence. By "natural conscience," More means a propensity to feel fear and remorse for wrongdoing (even when a human being's acts are not punishable by men) and a hope or expectation of being successful and prosperous for doing what is good.[69] He claims that this natural conscience is shared by all human beings. From the fact that there is natural conscience, More concludes that there must be a "Superintendent Principle" which ensures that good will happen to those who deserve it – either in this world, or in a world to come. He writes,

> It is also very naturall for a man that follows honestly the dictates of his own Conscience, to be full of good hopes, and much at ease, and secure that all things at home and abroad will go successfully with him, though his actions or sincere motions of his Mind act nothing upon Nature or the course of the world to change them any way: wherefore it implyes that there is a Superintendent Principle over Nature, and the materiall frame of the world, that lookes to it so that nothing shall come to passe, but what is consistent with the good and welfare of honest and conscientious Men. And if it does not happen to them according to their expectations in this world, it does naturally bring in them a belief of a world to come.[70]

The argument is based on the claim that neither universal remorse for wrongdoing nor hope of reward for right actions would exist without a universal law and enforcer of that law. The best explanation for our moral or "natural" conscience, then, is that God has instilled in us a sense of the moral laws and an expectation of the punishment and rewards that will follow on our disobeying or obeying these laws, respectively.

More's argument is open to the criticism that, even if we grant that all humans do have a sort of moral conscience, there may be other explanations of its development, such as evolutionary processes or acculturation.

8.4. Ralph Cudworth (1617–1688)

Cudworth's *The True Intellectual System of the Universe* is an extended argument for the existence of God. This long book contains two general strands of argumentation. One is the attempt to undermine atheistic arguments against God's existence; the other is an attempt to show that throughout history, all men, including the so-called pagans, have believed in the existence of God. Because it is beyond the scope of this chapter, or any chapter, to discuss all of Cudworth's arguments, we shall focus on two.

The first argument is a reply to what Cudworth calls the "First Atheistic Argument." Here, Cudworth attempts to show that we can know God through the nature of knowledge and intellection.

According to Cudworth, we can have knowledge of things other than particulars. He writes,

> Wherefore, besides the phantasms of singular bodies or of sensible things existing without us (which are not mere passions neither), it is plain that our human mind hath other cogitations or conceptions in it; namely the ideas of the intelligible natures and essences of things which are universal, and by and under which it understands singulars.[71]

He supports the claim that we must have knowledge of universals with two examples. First, we understand abstract, universal notions which have no singular, perceptible units or instances, such as life, senses, reason, and knowledge. Second, we have ideas of properties that can never exist in reality, such as being a perfectly straight line or being a perfect circle. He writes, "Notwithstanding which, they are not absolute non-entities, since we can demonstrate things concerning them, and though they never were nor will be, yet are they possible to exist, since nothing can be conceived but it either is or else is possible to be."[72] If conceivability is our guide to possibility, then it seems that these entities are possible entities. Cudworth continues,

> But when from our conceptions, we conclude of some things, that though they are not, yet they are possible to be (since nothing that is not can be possible to be, unless there be something actually in being which hath sufficient power to produce it) we do implicitly suppose the existence of God or omnipotent Being thereby, which can make whatsoever is conceivable, though it yet be not, to exist; and therefore material triangles, circles, spheres, cubes, mathematically exact.[73]

Thus, Cudworth concludes that there must be an omnipotent being from our knowledge of the possibility of unactualized universals. His explanation of the origin and ground of our universal knowledge and understanding is that God, in considering His own power, eternally and immutably understands the extent of that power, and thus, of all possibility.[74]

The second argument we will consider is Cudworth's version of the "prime mover" argument. The argument has its roots in Aristotle, is repeated by Aquinas, and eventually evolves into versions of the cosmological argument that seek the first cause of the world. In book 1, chapter 5, of the *Intellectual System*, Cudworth considers the atheistic claim that there is no nonmaterial unmoved first cause of motion or action in the world because all motion is local motion and all things are moved by some other preceding thing. Thus, the atheist claims, the material world is, and has been always, in motion. Against this claim, Cudworth writes,

> Moreover it is certain from hence also, that there is another species of action, distinct form local motion, and such as is . . . self-activity. For since the local

motion of body is efficiently ... not caused by the substance itself moving, but by something else acting upon it, that action by which local motion is first caused, cannot be it self local motion, but must be ... self-activity, that which is not a passion from any other agent, but springs from the immediate agent it self; which species of action is called *cogitation*.[75]

Here, Cudworth argues that we must resort to a first cause of motion that is not caused by some other thing. Cudworth concludes that the first cause of all motion in the world is cogitation or a thinking being, an incorporeal and thinking substance. However, Cudworth's claim that local motion must be efficiently caused by another – and so cannot be the first and only cause of all motion in the world – is undermined by the possibility of an infinite chain of local motions.

8.5. *Isaac Newton (1642–1727)*

Isaac Newton puts forth a design argument for the existence of God in the general scholium of *The Principia* and in query 31 of the *Opticks*. In both places the argument is fairly brief and is based on the claim that the universe, although maintained in its current state by general laws of nature, could not have been originally formed by these general laws. Newton thought that in order for the universe to manifest the order and arrangement that it does, it must have not only a designer, but a ruler. In the general scholium he writes, "this most elegant system of the sun, planets, and comets could not have arisen without the design and dominion of an intelligent and powerful being."[76]

Newton explains that although the stars and planets can maintain their orbits by means of the law of gravity, they could not have obtained their original positions by gravity. That the stars and planets are so fortuitously arranged and that the other galaxies which we can observe are at such a distance that they do not collapse into one another can only be explained by reference to the purposeful actions of an intelligent designer. He writes,

> And if the fixed stars are the centers of similar systems, they will all be constructed according to a similar design and subject to the dominion of *One*, especially since the light of the fixed stars is of the same nature as the light of the sun, and all the systems send light into all the others. And so that the systems of the fixed stars will not fall upon one another as a result of their gravity, he has placed them at immense distances from one another.[77]

He expounds a similar argument in query 31 of the *Opticks*:

> Now by the help of these principles, all material things seem to have been composed of the hard and solid particles above mentioned, variously associated in the first creation by the counsel of an intelligent agent. For it became him who created them to set them in order. And if he did so, it's unphilosophical to seek for any other origin of the world, or to pretend that it might arise out of a chaos by the mere laws of nature; though being once formed, it may continue by those laws for many ages.[78]

In addition to the appeal to design that we find in the general scholium and query 31, Newton appeals to the symmetry of bodies and the origin of the sense organs, brains, and internal organs of animals as evidence of intelligent design:

> Such a wonderful uniformity in the planetary system must be allowed the effect of choice. And so must the uniformity in the bodies of animals. . . . Also the first contrivance of those very artifical parts of animals, the eyes, ears, brain, muscles, heart, lungs, midriff, glands, larynx, hands, wings, swimming bladders, natural spectacles and other organs of sense and motion; and the instinct of brutes and insects, can be the effect of nothing else than the wisdom and skill of a powerful ever-living agent, who being in all places, is more able by his will to move the bodies within his boundless uniform sensorium, and thereby to form and reform the parts of the universe, than we are by our will to move the parts of our own bodies.[79]

Newton was criticized for calling space "God's sensorium," and he went to great lengths to explain that space is not a part of God, nor is God identical with space. Immediately after presenting the design argument in *The Principia*, Newton goes on to explain some of God's attributes, as well as the relation between God and absolute space.

Another criticism that Newton faced was based on the continuation of the passage cited previously (*Opticks*, query 31). Newton writes,

> For while comets move in very eccentric orbits in all manner of positions, blind fate could never make all the planets move one and the same way in orbits concentric, some inconsiderable irregularities excepted, which may have risen from the mutual actions of comets and planets upon one another, and which will be apt to increase, till this system wants a reformation.[80]

Here, Newton seems to say that the universe is an imperfect machine that will eventually need repair or modification. In addition to implying that God did not adequately design the universe, it also seems to imply that God simply designed or created the universe and then left it to run according to general laws inadequate for its conservation.

8.6. *John Norris (1657–1711)*

Norris provides an argument for the existence of God from the "steady and immutable nature of truth." He begins by dividing truth into two categories: the truth of the object or thing, and the truth of the subject or understanding. His argument is based on the truth of the object, which is also divided into two sorts. First, there is simple truth. Simple truth, he writes, is "transcendental truth, which is convertible with *Ens* [being] and concerns all being whereby everything is really what it is."[81] Second, there is complex truth. Complex truth involves "certain relations and habitudes of things one towards another."[82] Truth, according to Norris, is "the composition or division of ideas according to their respective habitudes and relations." Norris gives examples of the relations between things to show that these relations are immutable and steady. He cites the logical proposition that *a cause must precede its effect*, the physical proposition that *all local motion is successive*, the metaphysical proposition that *nothing both is and is not at the same time and place*, and mathematical propositions such as that *all right angles are equal*.[83]

These propositions are not made true by human will or intellect, and would be true even if no human existed. Thus, he concludes they are immutable and steady truths. In addition, according to Norris, these truths must be based on the simple essences of things. The mathematical truth that *if two circles intersect, they do not share the same center* would not hold if there were no simple essence of circles or centers. From this he concludes that simple essences are eternal and immutable.

He then argues that simple essences are eternal and immutable either in nature or in ideas of the understanding. Because it is obvious that no thing in nature is eternal and immutable, he concludes that it is the idea of simple essences which must be eternal and immutable. But being ideas, these simple essences must exist in a mind. Therefore, he concludes that eternal and immutable simple essences exist in "an eternal mind or understanding, omniscient, immutable and endowed with all possible perfections, which we call God."[84]

8.7. Damaris Cudworth Masham (1659–1708)

Damaris Masham's proof for the existence of God is a combination of the cosmological and design arguments. It bears a strong resemblance to Cudworth's and Locke's arguments, but unlike them, Masham clearly states that her argument contains nondeductive elements. Masham introduces her demonstration of God's existence by offering some methodological remarks. She, like Cudworth (her father) and Locke, will use the knowledge gained immediately from ideas of sensation and reflection to support the existence of a first cause of the universe.[85] She writes,

> To see what light we receive from Nature to direct our Actions, and how far we are Naturally able to obey that Light; Men must be consider'd purely as in the state of Nature, viz. as having no extrinsick Law to direct them, but indu'd only with a faculty of comparing their distant Ideas by intermediate Ones, and Thence of deducing, or inferring one thing from another; whereby our Knowledge immediately received from Sense, or Reflection, is inlarg'd to a view of Truths remote, or future, in an Application of which Faculty of the mind to a consideration of our own Existence and Nature, together with the beauty and order of the Universe, so far as it falls under our view, we may come to the knowledge of a First Cause; and that this must be an Intelligent Being, Wise and Powerful, beyond what we are able to conceive.[86]

First, by means of reflection, we can consider our own existence and nature. From such reflection, we can infer that the cause of our existence is intelligent. Second, we can consider our ideas from sensation concerning the order and beauty of the universe. From this, we can infer that the first cause of the universe is wise and powerful. The wisdom of the first cause is manifest in the orderly nature of the universe, and the power of the first cause is manifest in the production of the universe out of nothing. She continues,

> And as we delight in our selves, and receive pleasure from the objects which surround us, sufficient to indear to us the possession and injoyment of Life, we cannot from thence but infer, that this Wise and Powerful Being is also most Good, since he has made us out of nothing to give us a Being wherein we find such Happiness, as makes us very unwilling to part therewith.[87]

Because we have been provided with those faculties and external objects which are necessary for our pleasure and happiness, we can infer that the first cause of the universe is good. Finally, she argues that the attributes which are manifest when we contemplate the universe – intelligence, wisdom, power, and goodness – must inhere in a substance. The substance that contains these attributes is the first cause, that is God. She writes,

> And thus, by a consideration of the Attributes of God, visible in the Works of the Creation, we come to a knowledge of his Existence, who is an Invisible Being: For since Power, Wisdom, and Goodnesss, which we manifestly discern in the production and conservation of our selves, and the Universe, could not subsist independently of some substance for them to inhere in, we are assur'd that there is a substance where unto they do belong, or of which they are the Attributes.[88]

Much of this argument is nondeductive in nature, which is in keeping with Masham's empiricist methodology. We can only attain knowledge (whether probabilistic or demonstrative) by means of reasoning from ideas gathered from reflection and sensation.

Masham's argument does not seem to guarantee the unity of God. Her inference that the attributes that are found in the world must inhere in *one* being rather than many is not substantiated. It is consistent with all that she writes that there be several different beings, each of whom manifests only one of the attributes, and who together cause the existence of all other things.

8.8. *Mary Astell (1666–1731)*

Mary Astell's argument for the existence of God combines elements of the ontological and cosmological arguments. She proceeds by first acknowledging that we have an idea of a perfect being, where this idea includes the attributes of wisdom, justice, holiness, omnipresence, and omnipotence. This idea of God also includes the idea of self-existence: such a being must be self-existent, because if it were caused, then there would be something greater – a being that causes itself and which is capable of giving God all the aforementioned perfections. However, no cause is possible for God, because He is a perfect being (there is no greater being). She then argues that a perfect being must exist in order to create all the perfections that are exhibited in the world; otherwise, some perfections would have no cause, which she holds is impossible.

Astell writes,

> And when I think of God, I can't possibly think of him to be any other than the most perfect being; a being infinite in all perfections. We need not be told wherein perfection consists, for let us be ever so skeptical, we must needs acknowledge that wisdom and goodness, justice and holiness, are perfections, and indeed the greatest perfections. So that an intelligent nature defective in these can't be perfect, but destitute of them must needs be miserable. Knowledge and power without them would not be beauties but blemishes; nor can a being be infinitely wise and good, just and holy, unless he be also omnipresent and omnipotent.[89]

Here Astell answers the objection that we cannot have the idea of a perfect being because we cannot, as limited and imperfect beings, fully understand what constitutes perfection. In her view, we do not need to know precisely what would constitute perfection, so long as we can establish that a perfect being must have certain attributes. These attributes are those such that any being who lacked them would be miserable. We can verify by observation which attributes make for miserable creatures, and so we can presumably extrapolate from this, and our experience of what makes a being well-off, to determine which attributes are good making. These are the attributes that can be perfections.

As already mentioned, Astell goes on to make the case that a being with all the perfections must be self-existent. She writes,

> For if God derived his being from any but himself, there must be something greater and more perfect than God, which is absurd since God is by supposition the most perfect being and consequently self-existing. Because there can be no absolute and infinite perfection but where there is self-existence; from whence should it be derived? And self-existence is such a perfection as necessarily includes all other perfections. That there is a self-existing being is evident to the meanest understanding, for without it there could have been no men, no world, no being at all. Since that which once was not, could never have made itself; nor can any being communicate that to another which it has not itself. Therefore the self-existing being must contain all other perfections; therefore, it must be an intelligent being, and therefore, it must be God.[90]

Because Astell's argument is a version of the ontological argument, it inherits many of the difficulties that face other versions of this argument. However, she makes an interesting addition to the argument when she claims that if there were no self-existent being with all the perfections we see exhibited in the world – wisdom, goodness, justice, and so forth – then these perfections would have had to come from nothing. Here she commits herself to the causal principle that no thing can exist without a cause (*ex nihilo, nihil fit*), and its corollary that no effect can have something that was not in its cause.[91]

8.9. Samuel Clarke (1675–1729)

Samuel Clarke offers an extremely detailed and tightly argued version of the cosmological argument in his *A Demonstration of the Being and Attributes of God*.[92] The first two sections of this work concern the cosmological argument, whereas the rest of the work is dedicated to demonstrating the attributes of God. Like all cosmological arguments, Clarke's begins with an empirical fact that something now exists. He writes at the beginning of section I,

> For, since something now is, it is evident that something always was, otherwise the things that now are must have been produced out of nothing, absolutely and without a cause, which is a plain contradiction in terms. For, to say a thing is produced and yet that there is no cause at all for that production, is to say that something is effected when it is effected by nothing, that is, at the same time when it is not effected at all.[93]

Clarke's argument, like Leibniz's, utilizes the PSR. He states the principle as follows:

> Whatever exists has a cause, a reason, a ground of its existence, a foundation on which its existence relies, a ground or reason why it does exist rather than not exist, either in the necessity of its own nature (and then it must have been of itself eternal), or in the will of some other being (and then that other being must, at lest in the order of nature and causality, have existed before it).[94]

He continues in section II to argue that if there has always been something from eternity, then either there is an infinite chain of finite beings or there is one necessary being:

> For, since something must needs have been from eternity, as has been already proved and is granted on all hands, either there has always exited some one unchangeable and independent being from which all other beings that are or ever were in the universe have received their original, or else there has been an infinite succession of changeable and dependent beings produced from one another in an endless progression without any original cause at all.[95]

Clarke then argues that an infinite chain of changeable and dependent beings can have no cause or reason for its existence. He says that the chain of dependent beings can have no cause or reason outside the chain; for by hypothesis, the chain includes all the dependent beings that exist. In addition, the chain can have no reason inside the chain because no being in the chain is self-existent or necessary. An infinite chain of changeable and dependent beings can have no cause or reason for its existence in itself; it must have its cause or reason in the will of some other being. Therefore, we can conclude that there has been from eternity one unchangeable and independent being. Clarke goes on to argue that the unchangeable and independent being is self-existent, infinite in power, intelligent, and has freedom of will and choice. Because Clarke's argument utilizes the PSR, it is subject to the objection that this principle is false.

9. Further reading

In addition to the primary sources listed in the bibliography, the reader is directed to the following sources for more information about the arguments discussed in this chapter.

Robert Merrihew Adams, *Leibniz: Determinist, Theist, Idealist* (Oxford: Oxford University Press, 1994). Adams's book is regarded as the most comprehensive and penetrating examination of Leibniz's philosophy. Chapter 5 is dedicated to the ontological argument. Here, Adams looks at Leibniz's criticisms of Descartes and Leibniz's various attempts at completing the proof. Chapter 7 examines the argument for the existence of God from the eternal truths.

Jean-Marie Beyssade, "The Idea of God and the Proofs of His Existence" in *The Cambridge Companion to Descartes*, edited and translated by John Cottingham (Cambridge: Cambridge University Press, 1992), 174–199. The author explicates the complicated relationship between the role that the idea of God plays in the proofs for the existence of God and how we come to have the idea of God.

Jonathan Bennett, "God and Matter in Locke: An Exposition of Essay 4.10" in *Early Modern Philosophy: Mind, Matter, and Metaphysics*, edited by Christia Mercer and Eileen O'Neill (Oxford: Oxford University Press, 2005), 161–182. Bennett provides detailed criticisms of Locke's cosmological argument and discusses Locke's suggestion that matter might think.

Alan Donagan, "Spinoza's Theology" in *The Cambridge Companion to Spinoza*, edited by Don Garrett (Cambridge: Cambridge University Press, 1996), 343–382. A comprehensive overview of Spinoza's natural theology and his views on revelation, imagination, and universal religious faith.

Douglas M. Jesseph, "Berkeley, God, and Explanation" in *Early Modern Philosophy: Mind, Matter, and Metaphysics*, edited by Christia Mercer and Eileen O'Neill (Oxford: Oxford University Press, 2005), 183–205. This chapter analyzes Berkeley's arguments for the existence of God in the *Principles of Human Knowledge*, *Three Dialogues*, and *Alciphron*. Against traditional interpretations which portray Berkeley as offering three distinct proofs of God's existence, Jesseph argues that these three proofs are actually all variations of a single proof that utilizes inference to the best explanation. He continues by showing how his interpretation of Berkeley's arguments connects Berkeley's conception of God to his views about causation and explanation.

Lawrence Nolan and Alan Nelson, "Proofs for the Existence of God" in *The Blackwell Guide to Descartes' Meditations*, edited by Stephen Gaukroger (Malden, MA: Blackwell Publishing, 2006), 104–121. The authors attempt to argue for a simpler view of Descartes's theistic proofs in the *Meditations*. They argue that the cosmological proof of the Third Meditation depends on the causal principle that nothing comes from nothing, rather than the more robust and controversial causal principle that the objective reality of an idea must have a cause with at least as much formal reality. They also attempt to show that the ontological proof of the Fifth Meditation is best understood not as a formal proof but as an axiom, revealed as self-evident by analytic meditation.

Antonia LoLordo, *Pierre Gassendi and the Birth of Early Modern Philosophy* (Cambridge: Cambridge University Press, 2007). A book-length treatment of Gassendi's philosophical system. Chapter 10 includes a discussion of our knowledge of God, as well as the role of the soul and reason in Gassendi's theology.

William Rowe, *The Cosmological Argument* (New York: Fordham University Press, 1998). This book is a comprehensive study of the cosmological argument for the existence of God that looks at the arguments from Aquinas, Duns Scotus, and Samuel Clarke. Rowe also examines the PSR and discusses both historical and contemporary criticisms of the argument.

Notes

1. For the *a posteriori* argument, see the Third Meditation, *The Philosophical Writings of Descartes*, translated by John Cottingham, Robert Stoothoff, and Dugald Murdoch (Cambridge: Cambridge University Press, 1984). For the *a priori* argument, see the Fifth Meditation, AT VII 64–68; CSM II 45–47.
2. AT VI 33–36; CSM I 127–129 and AT VIIIA 10–13; CSM I 197–200.
3. See Beyssade (1992) and Nelson and Nolan (2006).
4. AT VII 40; CSM II 28.
5. AT VII 40–41; CSM II 28.
6. AT VII 41; CSM II 29.
7. AT VII 45; CSM II 31.
8. AT VII 42; CSM II 29. In order to have a property formally, a substance must have it in virtue of its intrinsic nature. To have a property eminently, a substance must be powerful enough to cause the property in other things while not itself exemplifying the property.
9. AT VII 48; CSM II 33.
10. AT VII 49; CSM II 33–34. Here Descartes commits himself to the transparency of the mind.
11. AT VII 65; CSM II 45.
12. For an interesting discussion of how we perceive infinite substance, see Alice Sowaal's "Descartes Reply to Gassendi: How We Can Know All of God, All at Once, But Still Have More to Learn About Him," in *British Journal for the History of Philosophy* 19(3) 2011: 419–449.
13. See the First and Fifth Objections.
14. Recently, Alan Nelson and Lawrence Nolan have argued that the Third Meditation argument is actually based on the more acceptable causal principle that nothing comes from nothing, rather than the stronger containment principle used in my rendition of the argument. See "Proofs for the Existence of God," in *A Guide to Descartes' Meditations*, edited by Gaukroger (London: Routledge, 2005).
15. An attempt at giving this objection is made in the First Objections (AT VII 96–99; CSM II 70–2). However, Caterus confuses Aquinas's view and Anselm's view, making the objection unclear. For Aquinas's views, see ST I.q2.a3.
16. AT VII 66–68; CSM II 46–47.
17. AT VII 116–177, 119; CSM II 83, 85.
18. AT VII 116; CSM II 83.
19. Of course, Kant famously criticized the proof on the grounds that existence is not a predicate.

20 John Locke, *An Essay Concerning Human Understanding*, edited by Peter H. Nidditch (Oxford: Clarendon Press, 1975). "Deus," in *The Life and Letters of John Locke*, edited by Peter King (London: George Bell & Sons, York Street, Covent Garden, 1884), 306–316. All references to the *Essay* are given by book, chapter, and section. "Deus" is cited by page number.
21 *Essay* 4.10.1.
22 *Essay* 4.10.4.
23 Jonathan Bennett, "God and Matter in Locke: An Exposition of Essay 4.10," in *Early Modern Philosophy: Mind, Matter, and Metaphysics*, edited by Christia Mercer and Eileen O'Neill (Oxford: Oxford University Press, 2005), 162. For further contemporary criticisms of Locke's proof, see Nicolas Wolterstorf, "Locke's Philosophy of Religion," in *The Cambridge Companion to Locke*, edited by Vere Chappell (Cambridge, 1994), 189; and Michael Ayers, *Locke: Epistemology & Ontology* (London: Routledge, 1991), 182.
24 Of course, Leibniz holds that it is *impossible* for something to happen without a sufficient reason or cause.
25 *Essay* 2.27.20.
26 *Essay* 2.26.2.
27 "Deus," 306.
28 Leibniz, *New Essays on Human Understanding*, edited and translated by Peter Remnant and Jonathan Bennett (Cambridge: Cambridge University Press, 1981); *NE* 4.10.6, 436.
29 *Essay* 4.10.10.
30 References to the *Ethics* (E) will be by part (1–5), proposition (p), definition (d), scholium (s), and corollary (c).
31 E 1d3.
32 For a defense of Spinoza's reasoning, see Daniel Whiting's "Spinoza, the No Shared Attribute Thesis, and the Principle of Sufficient Reason," in *British Journal for the History of Philosophy* 19(3) 2011: 543–548.
33 E 1p5: if there were two or more distinct substances, they would have to be distinguished either by their attributes or by their affections.
34 E 1a4: the knowledge of an effect depends on, and involves, the knowledge of its cause. E 1a5: things that have nothing in common with one another also cannot be understood through one another, or the concept of the one does not involve the concept of the other.
35 E 1p7s2.
36 N. Malebranche, *The Search After Truth*, translated by T.M. Lennon and P.J. Olscamp (Cambridge: Cambridge University Press, 1997b; original copyright: Ohio State University Press, 1980), 4:11.2/LO 317. Hereafter cited as *Search*, book, part, and chapter, or Elucidation (*Eluc.*).
37 *Search* 4.11.2/LO 317.
38 *Search* 4.11.2/LO 318.
39 *Search* 4.11.3/LO 320.
40 *Search* 3.2.6/LO 232.
41 *Search* 3.2.6/LO 232.
42 See, for example, *PPL* 165f., 168, 211, 231, 292f, 386, and *NE* 437f.
43 AG 23–7.
44 AG 25.
45 Letter to Elisabeth (1678?), AG 235–40.
46 *PPL* 167; *De Summa Rerum: Metaphysical Papers 1675–1676*, 101–103.
47 *PPL* 167; *De Summa Rerum: Metaphysical Papers 1675–1676*, 101–103.
48 Plato, *Theaetetus*, translated by John McDowell (Oxford: Oxford University Press, 1963), 94–109.
49 *PPL* 167; *De Summa Rerum: Metaphysical Papers 1675–1676*, 101–103.
50 Versions of the argument can also be found in *Monadology* §36–39; see AG 217–8, and T §7.
51 AG 149.
52 AG 149.
53 AG 149.
54 See the further readings for more on PSR.
55 William Rowe discusses Russell's objection in his important article "Two Criticisms of the Cosmological Argument," in *The Monist* 54(3) 1970: 441–459.
56 Perhaps it will be objected here that premise (4) still does make a mistake because the world is all that there is, so there is nothing to compare it with. In other words, it cannot be that the question Leibniz is asking is "Why does this world exist rather than some other?" because there are no other worlds. However, Leibniz holds that this world is one of infinitely many possible worlds that could have been

actualized. Thus, we can ask the question, "Why this world rather than some other world that could have existed instead?"
57 Leibniz also refers his readers to T §§20, 184, 189, and 335.
58 Monadology, 43–44; see AG 218.
59 Leibniz, "New System of the Nature of Substances and Their Communication, and of the Union Which Exists Between the Soul and the Body," reprinted in *G. W. Leibniz: Philosophical Texts*, edited by Woolhouse and Franks (Oxford: Oxford University Press, 1998), 150 (NS §14).
60 *Principles*, §25.
61 *Principles*, §30.
62 *Principles*, §146. The italicized portions are found in the Bible at I Cor. 12: 6 and Col. 1: 17, respectively.
63 Berkeley does not give the causal principle explicitly in the *Principles*. However, it is stated explicitly in the *Second Dialogue*. He writes,

> Yes, it is infinitely more extravagant to say – a thing which is inert operates on the mind, and which is unperceiving is the cause of our perceptions, without any regard either to consistency, or the old known axiom, *nothing can give to another that which it hath not itself*.

64 Pierre Gassendi, "The Syntagma," in *The Selected Works of Pierre Gassendi*, edited and translated by Craig Bush (New York: Johnson Reprint Corporation, 1972), 333 (Syntagma, book II, ch. 5).
65 Gassendi, *Selected Works*, 335.
66 Gassendi, *Selected Works*, 336.
67 Gassendi, *Selected Works*, 337.
68 Benjamin Whichcote, "The Use of Reason in Matters of Religion," in *The Cambridge Platonists*, edited by C. A. Patrides (Cambridge: Cambridge University Press, 1969), 54.
69 Henry More, "An Antidote Against Atheism," in *The Cambridge Platonists*, edited by C. A. Patrides (Cambridge: Cambridge University Press, 1969), 235.
70 Henry More, "An Antidote Against Atheism," in *The Cambridge Platonists*, edited by C. A. Patrides (Cambridge: Cambridge University Press, 1969), 236.
71 Ralph Cudworth, *The True Intellectual System of the Universe* (London: Richard Royton, 1678; reprint, Stuttgart-Bad Cannstatt: Friedrich Frommann Verlag, 1964), 731 (*True Intellectual System*, book I, ch. IV).
72 Cudworth, *The True Intellectual System*, 732.
73 Cudworth, *The True Intellectual System*, 732.
74 Cf. Aquinas.
75 Cudworth, *The True Intellectual System*, 844.
76 Isaac Newton, "The Principia," in *Newton: Philosophical Writings*, edited by Andrew Janiak (Cambridge: Cambridge University Press, 2004), 90.
77 *Principia*, 90.
78 Isaac Newton, "Queries to the Opticks," in *Newton: Philosophical Writings*, edited by Andrew Janiak (Cambridge: Cambridge University Press, 2004), 138.
79 Query 31, 138.
80 Query 31, 138.
81 John Norris, "A Metaphysical Essay, Towards the Demonstration of a God, From the Steady and Immutable Nature of Truth," in *A Collection of Miscellanies: Consisting of Poems, Essays, Discourses and Letters, Occasionally Written* (London: W. Bowyer for S. Manship, 1717), 144.
82 Norris, 144.
83 Norris, 146.
84 Norris, 148.
85 Masham accepts the Lockean view of ideas, and the claim that all our ideas are grounded in sensory or perceptual experience. She also accepts the empiricist view that all of our most important knowledge comes from inductive reasoning, especially inference to the best explanation.
86 Damaris Masham, *Occasional Thoughts in Reference to a Vertuous or Christian Life* (London: A. and J. Churchil, 1705), 29–30.
87 Masham, *Occasional Thoughts*, 29–30.
88 Masham, *Occasional Thoughts*, 29–30.
89 Mary Astell, *The Christian Religion, As Profess'd by a Daughter of the Church of England. In a Letter to the Right Honourable, T.L.CI.* (London: for R. Wilkin, 1705; 1717), reissued as *The Christian Religion, As Profess'd by a Daughter of the Church of England Containing Proper Directions for the Due Behaviour of*

Women in Every Station of Life. With a Few Cursory Remarks on Archbishop Tillotson's Doctrine of the Satisfaction of Christ, &c. (London: for W. Parker, 1730), 5.
90. Mary Astell, *The Christian Religion, As Profess'd by a Daughter of the Church of England. In a Letter to the Right Honourable, T.L.CI.* (London: for R. Wilkin, 1705; 1717), reissued as *The Christian Religion, As Profess'd by a Daughter of the Church of England Containing Proper Directions for the Due Behaviour of Women in Every Station of Life. With a Few Cursory Remarks on Archbishop Tillotson's Doctrine of the Satisfaction of Christ, &c.* (London: for W. Parker, 1730), 7–9.
91. For a more in-depth study of this argument and Astell's views on God's nature, see my "Mary Astell on the Existence and Nature of God," in *Feminist Interpretations of Mary Astell*, edited by Penelope Weiss and Alice Sowaal (University Park: Pennsylvania State University Press, 2016), 168–187.
92. Samuel Clarke, *A Demonstration of the Being and Attributes of God and Other Writings*, edited by Ezio Vailati (Cambridge: Cambridge University Press, 1998).
93. *A Demonstration*, 8.
94. *A Demonstration*, 8.
95. *A Demonstration*, 10.

Bibliography

Adams, Robert Merrihew. *Leibniz: Determinist, Theist, Idealist*. New York: Oxford University Press, 1994.

Aquinas, Thomas. *Summa Theologiae*. Edited by P. Caramello. Turin/Rome: Marietti, 1950. Cited by part, question, and article numbers.

Astell, Mary. *The Christian Religion as Professed by a Daughter of the Church of England*. London: R. Wilkin, 1705.

Ayers, Michael. *Locke: Epistemology & Ontology*. London: Routledge, 1991.

———. "Mechanism, Superaddition, and the Proof of God's Existence in Locke's Essay." *Philosophical Review* 90:2 (1981), 210–251.

Bennett, Jonathan Francis. "God and Matter in Locke: An Exposition of Essay 4.10." In *Early Modern Philosophy: Mind, Matter, and Metaphysics*. Edited by Christia Mercer and Eileen O'Neil, 161–182. Oxford: Oxford University Press, 2005.

———. *Learning From Six Philosophers: Descartes, Spinoza, Leibniz, Locke, Berkeley, Hume*. 2 vols. Oxford; New York: Clarendon Press; Oxford University Press, 2001.

Berkeley, George. *Three Dialogues Between Hylas and Philonous*. Edited by Jonathan Dancy. Oxford: Oxford University Press, 1998.

———. *A Treatise Concerning the Principles of Human Knowledge*. Edited by Jonathan Dancy. Oxford: Oxford University Press, 1998. Cited by section number.

Beyssade, Jean-Marie. "The Idea of God and the Proofs of His Existence." In *The Cambridge Companion to Descartes*. Edited and Translated by John Cottingham, 174–199. Cambridge: Cambridge University Press, 1992.

Blumenfeld, David. "Leibniz's Ontological and Cosmological Arguments." In *The Cambridge Companion to Leibniz*. Edited by Nicholas Jolley, 353–381. Cambridge: Cambridge University Press, 1995.

Clarke, Samuel. *A Demonstration of the Being and Attributes of God and Other Writings*. Edited by Ezio Vailati. Cambridge: Cambridge University Press, 1998.

Cragg, Gerald R. *The Cambridge Platonists*. Oxford: Oxford University Press, 1968.

Cudworth, Ralph. *The True Intellectual System of the Universe: The First Part Wherein, All the Reason and Philosophy of Atheism Is Confuted; and Its Impossibility Demonstrated*. London: Richard Royton, 1678.

Descartes, René. *The Philosophical Writings of Descartes*. Translated by John Cottingham, Robert Stoothoff, and Dugald Murdoch. Cambridge: Cambridge University Press, 1984. Cited by volume and page.

Gassendi, Pierre. *The Selected Works of Pierre Gassendi*. Edited and Translated by Craig B. Bush. New York: Johnson Reprint Corporation, 1972.

Leibniz, G. W. *De Summa Rerum: Metaphysical Papers 1675–1676*. Edited and Translated by G.H.R. Parkinson. New Haven: Yale University Press, 1992.

———. *Gottfried Wilhelm Leibniz: Sämtliche Schriften und Briefe*. Edited by Deutsche Akademie der Wissenschaften zu Berlin. Series VI: Philosophical Writings. Berlin: Akademie-Verlag, 1923. Cited by volume and page number.

———. *New Essays on Human Understanding*. Edited and Translated by Peter Remnant and Jonathan Bennett. Cambridge: Cambridge University Press, 1981.

———. *Philosophical Essays*. Edited and Translated by Roger Ariew and Daniel Garber. Indianapolis: Hackett, 1989.

———. *Philosophical Papers and Letters*. Edited and Translated by Leroy E. Loemker. Dordrecht: D. Reidel, 2nd ed. 1969.

———. *Philosophical Writings*. Edited by G.H.R. Parkinson; Translated by Mary Morris and G.H.R. Parkinson. London: Dent, 1973.

———. *Theodicy: Essays on the Goodness of God, the Freedom of Man, and the Origin of Evil*. Edited by Austin Farrar; Translated by E. M. Huggard. La Salle, IL: Open Court, 1952.

Locke, John. "Deus." In *The Life and Letters of John Locke*. Edited by Peter King. London: G. Bell, 1829.

———. *An Essay Concerning Human Understanding*. Edited by Peter Nidditch. Oxford: Oxford University Press, 1975.

Lolordo, Antonia. *Pierre Gassendi and the Birth of Early Modern Philosophy*. Cambridge: Cambridge University Press, 2007.

Mackie, J. L. *The Miracle of Theism: Arguments for and Against the Existence of God*. Oxford: Oxford University Press, 1982.

Malebranche, Nicholas. *Dialogues on Metaphysics and on Religion*. Edited by N. Jolley; Translated by D. Scott. Cambridge: Cambridge University Press, 1997.

———. *The Search After Truth*. Edited and Translated by T. Lennon and P. Olscamp. Columbus: The Ohio State University Press, 1980.

Masham, Damaris Cudworth. *Occasional Thoughts in Reference to a Vertuous or Christian Life*. London: A. and J. Churchil, 1705.

Mates, Benson. *The Philosophy of Leibniz: Metaphysics & Language*. Oxford: Oxford University Press, 1986.

Mercer, Christia and O'Neill, Eileen. *Early Modern Philosophy: Mind, Matter, and Metaphysics*. Oxford: Oxford University Press, 2005.

Newton, Isaac. *Newton: Philosophical Writings*. Edited by Andrew Janiak. Cambridge: Cambridge University Press, 2004.

Nolan, Lawrence and Nelson, Alan. "Proofs for the Existence of God." In *The Blackwell Guide to Descartes' Meditations*. Edited by Stephen Gaukroger, 104–121. Malden, MA: Blackwell Publishing, 2006.

Norris, John. *A Collection of Miscellanies: Consisting of Poems, Essays, Discourses and Letters, Occasionally Written*. London: W. Bowyer for S. Manship, 1717.

Patrides, C. A. *The Cambridge Platonists*. Cambridge: Cambridge University Press, 1969.

Spinoza, Benedictus de. *The Collected Works of Spinoza*. Edited and Translated by Edwin Curley. Princeton: Princeton University Press, 1985. Cited by volume and page numbers.

———. *A Spinoza Reader: The Ethics and Other Works*. Edited and Translated by Edwin Curley. Princeton: Princeton University Press, 1994.

19
THE PROBLEM OF EVIL
Samuel Newlands

1. Introduction

As the other chapters in this volume show, the seventeenth century was an especially vibrant period of philosophical reflection, ushering in novel accounts in metaphysics, epistemology, philosophy of mind, natural science, philosophical theology, and even the methodology of philosophy itself. Many of these developments were shaped by a rich historical backdrop, and the same is true for the problem of evil. Philosophical reflections on evil in the form of Christian theodicies reached a high point in the late seventeenth century, but they weren't produced in a vacuum. The goal of this chapter is to shed fresh light on the context and content of the most influential early modern discussions of evil.

Before turning to the problem of evil in its historical clothing, it will be helpful to have a sense for what the problem is supposed to be. In its most general form, the problem of evil concerns the relation between God and the evils in our world. If God is all-powerful and perfectly good, whence evil? Of course, like the "problem of free will" and the "problem of skepticism," the so-called problem of evil is really a *host* of philosophical issues that have been lumped together as one of the great, transcendent problems of philosophy to be repeatedly clarified but never really solved. I will consider only a subset of the issues here.

Part of what has made philosophical reflection on God and evil so long-lasting is the way it draws deeply from many other branches of philosophy: theses from metaphysics, epistemology, ethics, and philosophical theology are all utilized in formulating the problems. Another reason for the perennial interest in the relation of God to evil is less sanguine. We are each intimately acquainted with evil, both as perpetrators and victims, and this personal closeness can make the problems seem more urgent. The previous century was marred by evil on an epic scale, one that as yet shows no signs of shrinking in the new millennium.[1]

The seventeenth century also witnessed its fair share of large-scale horrors: religious wars, genocidal conquests, tyrannical oppression, persecution, plagues, catastrophic natural disasters – not to mention the prosaic evils encountered and committed in everyday life. As Bayle put it in 1697,

> Man is wicked and miserable. Everyone is aware of this from what goes on within himself, and from the commerce he is obliged to carry on with his neighbor . . .

monuments to human misery and wickedness are found everywhere – prisons, hospitals, gallows, beggars. . . . Properly speaking, history is nothing but the crimes and misfortunes of the human race.[2]

Milton voices a similar view near the end of *Paradise Lost* (1667), as Adam is given a glimpse of the depths of human suffering in its many forms. The description concludes,

> Dire was the tossing, deep the groans. Despair
> Tended the sick busiest from couch to couch.
> And over them triumphant Death his dart
> Shook, but delayed to strike, though oft invoked
> With vows, as their chief good, and final hope.

Adam weeps in reply,

> O miserable mankind! To what fall
> Degraded, to what wretched state reserved!
> Better end here unborn.[3]

Although the tone and emphases of seventeenth century discussions of evil are similar to those in contemporary philosophy of religion, it is worth highlighting a few notable differences at the outset. First, contemporary discussions often focus on whether or not God *exists*, given the existence, distribution, or kinds of evil in the world, where "God" is usually taken in a generically monotheistic way as an omnipotent, omniscient, omnibenevolent personal being. Discussions about the problem of evil are usually between (real or imagined) atheists, on the one hand, and theists, on the other.[4]

By contrast, almost all of the early modern authors we will discuss in this chapter were committed monotheists of one stripe or another. "Atheism," as we use the term today, was then a charge leveled against one's intellectual enemies and never a label willingly embraced. Even the two great bogeymen of the seventeenth century, Hobbes and Spinoza, vociferously denied being atheists (though to little avail). Although there was much written in the period decrying the rising tide of atheism, the named targets were usually long-dead Epicureans and Stoics – though with intimations that their followers were alive and well in modern times. Even those, like Bayle, who emphasized the problem of widespread human suffering, did not openly proclaim that the evil in our world constituted a defeater for revealed religion.

A second major difference between then and now concerns how the problem of evil is framed. Contemporary discussions often present the issue in epistemological terms: is belief in the existence of God justified, given the facts about evil? The early moderns we will discuss were generally much more interested in metaphysical questions about the relation between God and evil. It was a guiding assumption in the Western world, powerfully defended but rarely doubted in public, that the God described in Jewish and Christian Scriptures exists and is perfect in power, knowledge, and goodness. (Exactly what those qualities amounted to and entailed was, of course, a matter of considerable debate.) Although confidence was generally high that satisfying answers could be given, seventeenth century philosophers raised many ontological and causal questions about evil. Given God's goodness, how is God causally involved in our evil-soaked cosmos? Given God's sovereignty, how is God not the author of sin? What greater goods explain and justify God's willingness to allow and sometimes cause so much pain and suffering? Could God have made a world that contained less evil, and if so, why didn't God? Most generally, what is the nature and source of evil?[5]

Early modern philosophers proposed a variety of answers to these questions in the form of what we now call "theodicies," a coin termed by Leibniz. For example, some argued that the good of a uniformly law-governed cosmos explains and justifies the existence of horribly disfigured creatures in a world created by God. Global, positive explanations like this for why some evils exist mark a final point of contrast with contemporary discussions. Attempts to provide comprehensive theodicies reached their peak in the late seventeenth and early eighteenth centuries. Today, most theistic philosophers of religion set a far more modest goal in addressing objections from evil: a "defense," rather than a theodicy.[6] They focus on what justifiable reasons God *might* have for allowing the evils of our world (or why we should expect not to know God's reasons), without trying to show what reasons God *in fact* has.

In addition to differences in orientation and goals, contemporary discussions also diverge in *content* from their seventeenth century counterparts. There was a dominant core of philosophical teaching about evil that originated in neo-Platonism, was embraced by early Christian church theologians, elevated to the status of orthodoxy by Augustine, flourished under the enriching of Aristotelian Scholastics, survived on both sides of the Reformation split, and remained deeply attractive to many well into the seventeenth century. This traditional set of ideas formed the backbone of Western philosophical reflections on the problem of evil for centuries.[7] Although some pieces of that traditional account survive today in fractured form, other elements have been eclipsed since the early modern period. What happened? As we will see, part of this neglected story lies in the developments of the seventeenth century.

2. Warm-up: some seventeenth century questions about God and evil

Premodern discussions of evil often assumed that one must understand the ontological nature of evil before trying to understand its source.[8] This "ontology-first" approach fueled elaborate taxonomies of evils in the medieval period. By and large, the early moderns tended to eschew such classification projects, and by the start of the seventeenth century, a simple threefold division of evil was quickly becoming standard. Evils were categorized as (1) evils of imperfection, or "metaphysical evils"; (2) physical evils, or "natural evils"; and (3) moral evils, or "sins."

Samuel Clarke nicely summarizes the basic categories:

> all that we call evil is either an evil of imperfection, as the want of certain faculties and excellencies which other creatures have, or natural evil, as pain death and the like, or moral evil, as all kinds of vice.[9]

Working backward through Clarke's list, *moral evil* is the familiar category of culpable misdeeds and omissions brought about by free rational agents, that is, sin. *Physical* or *natural evils* are states accompanied by pain and suffering that are brought about either by natural events (e.g. earthquakes and dog bites), or by rational agents (e.g. just punishments for committing moral evils or consequences of another's free action).[10] *Metaphysical evils* are probably the least familiar category, and exploring them in the next section will take us deep into the heart of the most prominent traditional account of God's relation to evil. For now, we should think of them as species-specific limitations in the way Clarke suggests: that I cannot fly, that my dog cannot compose a symphony, and so forth.[11]

Using this division, we can now consider some of the main questions about God's relation to evil that occupied seventeenth century philosophers. The following numbered propositions, which I will refer back to repeatedly in subsequent sections, were among the generally accepted tenets of Western Christian theism:

1. God exists and is perfect in power, knowledge, and goodness.
2. God created the world *ex nihilo*, preserves the world at each moment of its existence, and concurs[12] immediately in all secondary causal activity.
3. God does not cause any moral evils.
4. God causes some physical evils.
5. God causes all metaphysical evils.
6. God is entirely blameless for the existence of any moral, physical, or metaphysical evil.

Proposition (3) states that God doesn't cause sin, which was extended to exclude God's causing agents to sin. As it was often put, God is not the "author of sin." Propositions (4) and (5) may sound surprising until we recall what is meant by "evil" there. Typical examples of the physical evils that God causes would be the suffering of creatures to punish them for disobedience or to inculcate virtues like perseverance in them.[13] To say that God causes all metaphysical evil is just to draw out a consequence of (2), because being limited in various ways is part of what it is to be a creature instead of a god.[14] These close connections between God and evil is balanced by (6), the claim that God is in no way blameworthy for any evils, even those for which God has a direct role in bringing about.

The task of the theodicist was to explain how these premises were to be reconciled with the facts about evil that Bayle and Milton noted previously. After all, everyday experience strongly recommends (7):

7. Moral, physical, and metaphysical evils exist in abundance.[15]

There are tensions among these seven propositions. To see this, let's begin with moral evils. According to (3), moral evils are not brought about by God. But according to (2), God sustains the world in existence at every moment, which presumably includes sustaining the sinful states of the world. But how can God preserve the world at each moment without being at least partially responsible for the existence of its moral evils? After all, at least this much seems plausible: if God hadn't sustained the world in existence after 1652, the Huguenots would not have been persecuted under Louis XIV's reign.[16] If so, we might wonder how God can remain entirely blameless for subsequent moral atrocities. Matters become even murkier when we add with (2) the widely accepted thesis that God cooperates immediately in every creaturely action, including morally evil acts. For it is not clear how God can cooperate in the production of moral evil without being the partial cause of moral evil as well.

Furthermore, if God causes some nonmoral evils, (4) and (5), we may wonder how God remains blameless for them (6). Again, this seems at least initially plausible: God could have made a world free of at least some of our world's physical evils and limitations without thereby making more evil. But if so, it is difficult to see how God isn't blameworthy for not bringing about less physical and metaphysical evil than God could have.

There are, of course, quick replies that could be made to these concerns, though they only deepen the puzzles. For instance, perhaps (7) is overly strong: maybe the range and distribution of evils isn't as abundant as a quick glance at a history book would suggest. Leibniz sometimes pursues this tact, claiming that we readily ascent to (7) because we are not used to taking the entire universe into account when judging the distributions and amounts of evil. We tend to focus only on our little isolated portion of the cosmos, which generates far too small a sample size of rational creatures to make sound judgments about the overall balance or imbalance of evils and goods in the universe.[17] But even if one agreed with Leibniz that the world doesn't contain as much evil as Bayle and Milton claimed, the same sorts of questions about (1)–(6) could be raised with a weaker version of (7), such as (7*):

7*. There exist at least some moral, physical, and metaphysical evils.

Leibniz can't sensibly deny (7*), regardless of how isolated or uncommon those evils are.

Another quick reply to worries about (4) and (5) would be to advance the following moral principle:

8. An agent is not blameworthy for bringing about an evil if the bringing about of that evil also brings about a greater good that, necessarily, could not otherwise be had.

Proposition (8) is a strong moral principle that would need independent defense and refinement. But we use something like it in everyday moral reasoning. Think of the blamelessness of the parent who causes her child to suffer by giving him foul-tasting medicine, the only available remedy, in order to bring about the greater good of restored health. This suggests that there may be greater goods, tightly attached to certain evils, whose outweighing goodness justifies our causing or permitting those evils.

However, even if something like (8) were true, it isn't obvious that *God* could ever be in such a situation. It may seem like a perfectly powerful being could bring about *any* good it wanted, without being forced, as it were, to allow evils as a consequence. In the analogue to the parent case, surely God could get the good of a healthy creature without relying on medicine at all.

The tensions are quickly multiplying. As we will see, the seventeenth century abounded in replies. But first, let us consider what had been a dominant reply to these concerns for over a thousand years. As it happens, it is also the same basic reply given by one of the seventeenth century's greatest innovators: Descartes.

3. Descartes's (mostly) traditional answers

However we judge Descartes's pretensions for philosophical novelty, when it comes to the problem of evil, he is thoroughly and self-consciously conservative. In the *Meditations*, he focuses mostly on cognitive error and its source in our extending our wills beyond the clear and distinct deliverances of our intellects. But Descartes's account generalizes,[18] and his language and framework for explaining evil mostly repeats the main Scholastic account of evil. Indeed, in a few compact sentences in the Fourth

THE PROBLEM OF EVIL

Meditation, Descartes neatly summarizes the major conclusions of over a dozen centuries of Christian reflection on evil:

> In this incorrect use of free will may be found the privation which constitutes the essence of error. The privation, I say, lies in the operation of the will insofar as it proceeds from me, but not in the faculty of will which I received from God, nor even in its operation, insofar as it depends on him. . . . For insofar as these acts depend on God, they are wholly true and good; and my ability to perform them means that there is in a sense more perfection in me than would be if I lacked this ability. As for the privation involved – which is all that the essential definition of falsity and wrong consists in – this does not in any way require the concurrence of God, since it is not a thing; indeed, when it is referred to God as its cause, it should be called not a privation but simply a negation.

Shortly after this, Descartes adds,

> Had God made me [better able to align my will and understanding], I can easily understand that, considered as a totality, I would have been more perfect than I am now. But I cannot therefore deny that there may in some way be more perfection in the universe as a whole because some of its parts are not immune from error, while others are immune, than there would be if all the parts were exactly alike.[19]

Although some of the details may seem obscure at first glance, Descartes's reasoning in these paragraphs echoes the three main components of the most prevalent pre-seventeenth century theodicy: privation theory, creaturely freedom, and cosmic diversity. I will use Descartes as a guide through each of these traditional pieces before turning to the mounting criticisms this account faced in the seventeenth century.

3.1. Privation theory and moral evil

Let's begin with a bit of metaphysical background. According to a then-standard ontological picture, reality is stratified into what has been dubbed "the great chain of being."[20] At the top of (or even beyond) this variegated chain is God, who is the most real, the most perfect, the most intelligible, and the most good. Humans, somewhere lower down on the scale of being than God, are less real, less perfect, and less good. Rocks, somewhere yet lower on the chain than humans, are even less real, perfect, and good than both God and humans. Linking the members of the chain together are relations of dependence; the stuff lower on the chain is more dependent and hence less perfect than the stuff higher up. As Descartes reflects on his own ontological status in the Fourth Meditation, "I realize that I am, as it were, something intermediate between God and nothingness, or between supreme being and non-being."[21]

Two widely accepted corollaries to this account are important for the problem of evil. First, *goodness and being are coextensive.*[22] That is, to the degree to which something is real, to that degree it is good; *and* to the degree to which a thing lacks goodness, to that degree it lacks being or reality – and hence it lies farther down on the ontological chain. Call this the "coextensive principle."

541

Second, *the chain of being is plentiful*. Usually this meant that for any pair of creatures x and y that differ in some degree of being, there exists at least one thing (or one kind of thing) that is more real, perfect, good, and intelligible than x and less real, and so forth, than y.[23] Reality is as full as it can be, which means there are no jumps or gaps along the chain. Call this the "plentitude principle." The plenitude principle entails that the created order is smooth and continuous, a conclusion that led to extravagant and wonderfully imaginative cosmologies during the medieval period. Although many of the scientific beliefs and practices that had been used to fill out this plenum were challenged during the early modern period, the basic metaphysics of a plentiful chain of being and goodness remained enormously influential and vibrant throughout the seventeenth century.

Using this background, here is one possible account of the nature of evil. Everything that exists must exist somewhere on the chain of being, in which case everything that exists has some degree of reality. It follows, by the coextensive principle, that everything that exists also has some degree of goodness. Hence there does not exist anything that is purely evil; all creation is to some degree good.[24] But the chain of being is quite stratified, according to the plenitude principle. So, although everything that exists is to some degree good, perhaps things are more evil the more limited they are, that is the farther down they stand on the chain of being. That is, perhaps all evil is just an *absence of goodness*. Call this the "evil as limitation" view, a view that was held by some neo-Platonists.[25]

The *evil as limitation* view would satisfy monotheists' competing intuitions that (1) good and evil are correlated and interdefinable and (2) good and evil are asymmetrically dependent (i.e. goodness is prior to evil). On this view, things are evil just to the extent to which they lack goodness, which is just to the extent to which they lack reality, being, or perfection.

Despite its coherence and historical pedigree, the *evil as limitation* view was rejected by almost everyone in the Western Christian tradition since at least Augustine.[26] For one, the view entailed that all evil was due entirely to metaphysical limitations, which collapsed the distinction between moral and nonmoral evil. Christians vociferously denied that all evil was based entirely on creaturely weaknesses or limitations. Sometimes evils involve a perversion, a twisting, a turning away.[27] They conceded that although the explanation for moral evil will always involve creaturely limitations, those limitations could not bear all the explanatory weight.

Furthermore, if *evil as limitation* were correct, God would be causally responsible for all instances of evil. After all, in the monotheistic version, God created the chain of beings, in which case God would also be the creator of every evil. Just as this would put too much responsibility on God, it would also ascribe too little responsibility for evil to created moral agents. Talk about excuses. All our moral failures could be blamed on limitations that were built into our very natures.

Descartes briefly considers the *evil as limitation* view, but then follows the bulk of Christian tradition in rejecting it as inadequate. "For error is not a pure negation [i.e. limitation], but rather a privation or lack of some knowledge *which should be in me*" (my emphasis).[28] Descartes reasons that some evil involves a lack of goodness that a thing *ought to have*, goodness that it has been *deprived* from having. Some evil, in other words, involves a *privation of goodness*, not merely a lack of goodness. This echoes the dominant understanding of the nature of evil heading into the seventeenth century. According to the traditional view, moral and physical evils were privations of appropriate perfections. Call this the "evil as privation" view.

An underlying assumption of the *evil as privation* view is that there are independent standards built into the world that establish what degree of goodness and kinds of perfections each thing ought to possess. These "oughts" aren't established by human conventions or cultural standards. For Descartes, some of these standards concern how rational agents ought to use their wills and intellects: we ought not to assent to confused and obscure ideas.

Scholastics understood physical evils to be privative as well, and so they also needed a nonmoral source of natural "oughts." Within Scholastic Aristotelianism, the source of such natural oughts was found in the purposive natures of things: the intrinsic *telos* of a thing's nature determined the perfections it ought to have.[29] Take the classical example of blindness. The evil of blindness is not simply the absence of sight, or else it would follow that rocks suffer the plight of blindness. But it would seem highly inappropriate for us to bemoan the plague of blindness ravaging the world's mountains. According to privation theory, such lamentations are out of place because rocks aren't the sorts of things that are supposed to see in the first place. The evil of blindness is a *privation* of sight, an absence of sight in something that, by its nature, *ought to see*. As Aquinas explains,

> therefore, not every defect of the good is an evil, but the defect of the good *which is naturally due*. For the want of sight is not an evil in a stone, but it is an evil in an animal, since it is against the nature of a stone to see.
>
> (my emphasis)[30]

It follows that, for example, what is a physical evil for a fawn (being eaten by a lion) need not be an evil for a lion (eating a fawn).

So far, I have focused on the ontology of evil and claimed that Descartes follows the Scholastics in accepting the privation view of moral evil over the limitation view. Even if this ontology of moral evils is correct, however, we still need an account of the cause and justification of moral evils in a world blamelessly brought about by a perfectly good God.

Consider a (fictitious) example of moral evil: out of selfish anger, I push a man into a busy street where he is struck by a car. Creaturely limitations are part of what make that evil possible: that the man's body can be shoved against his will, that he is capable of experiencing pain and suffering, that I am susceptible to emotional outbursts, and so forth. Descartes acknowledges that God brings about those creaturely limitations, but he claims that God is blameless for doing so.[31] In fact, some of those limitations are based on perfections that other types of things lack. Descartes explains that "my ability to perform [these wrong acts] means that there is in a sense more perfection in me than would be if I lacked this ability."[32] That is, whereas my susceptibility to emotional outbursts is a prerequisite for my pushing the man in anger, my ability to experience emotions is a kind of excellence, one that lowly rocks fail to have.

This accounts for God's causal involvement in the *prerequisites* for moral evil. (For the *justification* of that involvement, see section 3.3.) But according to (2), God causally contributes to more than just the prerequisites for my pushing the man. God causally cooperates in the very act of pushing itself, a thesis Descartes would also accept: "For *insofar as these acts depend on God*, they are wholly true and good" (my emphasis).[33] That is, God causally cooperates in the very acts of moral evil, though in such a way that God is not at all responsible for the evil aspects of moral evils. However, it is not yet clear how God can cooperate in my pushing the man onto the street (the sinful *act*) without thereby being a partial cause of the moral evil of my angry shoving (the sinful *aspect* of the act).

Here is where privation theory truly earns its keep for Descartes: "As for the privation involved – which is all that the essential definition of falsity and wrong consists in – this does not in any way require the concurrence of God, *since it is not a thing*" (my emphasis).[34] He is even clearer in the *Principles*: "Moreover, errors are not things, requiring the real concurrence of God for their production."[35] And again, "When I say [God understands, wills, and accomplishes] 'everything' I mean all *things*: for God does not will the evil of sin, which is not a thing."[36]

Descartes's idea for reconciling (2) and (3) seems to be that God doesn't concur in the morally evil aspects of my sin because there isn't any*thing* there for God to cause. The traditional ontology of evil plays a significant role here. Moral evil is a *privation* of goodness, a kind of perverted absence. But God doesn't need to concur in absences; God, as the source of all and only good things, needs to concur only in the production of goodness and being. As Aquinas summarizes this strategy, "whatever there is of being and action in a bad action, is reduced to God as the cause; whereas whatever defect is in it is not caused by God, but by the deficient secondary cause."[37] Returning to my example: to the extent to which my shoving the man expresses being and goodness – as it surely does, being pushing at will isn't something rocks can do – God concurs in it. But God doesn't concur in the failing short of the goodness my action ought to express, for there isn't anything there with which God need concur.

There are a number of questions one might raise about this purported reconciliation.[38] Are the evil and nonevil aspects of a sin so neatly separable? If God doesn't cause the evil aspect of moral evil *because* God doesn't cause privations, who does cause the privative evil aspect, and how? How is God blameless for creating a world full of limitations in the first place? Descartes's answers to some of these questions involve the remaining two pieces of the traditional account: creaturely freedom and cosmic diversity.

3.2. Moral evil and the greater good of freedom

Descartes admits that God is responsible for the *possibility* of moral evil in virtue of having created limited creatures. In this section, we will look at who or what, according to Descartes, is responsible for the *actuality* of moral evil. His explanation is again a familiar one: God is responsible but blameless for creating free creatures capable of misusing their freedom, and free creatures are responsible and very blameworthy for actually misusing it.

Descartes's appeal to freedom in the problem of evil has three basic pieces, all of which echo the traditional free will theodicy. First, all moral evil is due to rational creatures misusing their freedom. Second, at least some kinds of free creatures cannot be free without possessing the ability to misuse their freedom and produce moral evil. Last, a world containing free creatures which possess the ability for misused freedom is better, all things considered, than a world without such free creatures.

Descartes emphatically affirms the existence of freedom in us:

> That there is freedom in our will, and that we have the power in many cases to give or withhold our assent at will, is so evident that it must be counted among the first and most common notions that are innate in us.[39]

Descartes also endorses the claim that all moral evil is the result of misused creaturely freedom: "In this incorrect use of free will may be found the privation which constitutes the essence of error."[40] Descartes emphasizes that because the source of moral error lies in our actual misuses of freedom, the blame lies squarely with us and not with our God-given natures: "The fact that we fall into error is a defect in the way we act or in the use we make of our freedom, but not a defect in our nature."[41]

The second step of the traditional free will theodicy helps explains *why* our misuses of freedom aren't due to a defective nature. According to Scholastic accounts of human freedom, a necessary condition on being free with respect to a moral action is the ability to either bring about that action or to refrain from doing so. Some in the late seventeenth century disagreed with this so-called indifference condition on freedom (see section 4.2).[42] Nonetheless, Descartes appears to affirm something like it, claiming that "the will consists in our ability to do or not do something (that is, to affirm or deny, to pursue or avoid)."[43] If so, then even God couldn't bring about the good of free creatures like us without allowing the possibility of error and sin.

The final step of the traditional free will theodicy makes a claim about the *value* of our freedom. According to free will theodicies, it is better that the world contains creatures who are capable of freely bringing about moral evil than that it not contain them, even if worlds without free creatures also contain no moral evil. The point is sometimes strengthened to cover actual misuses of freedom too: worlds like ours with actually abused freedom are better, all else equal, than worlds without any freedom and moral evil.

Putting it all together now, the existence of creatures with potentially, and perhaps even actually abused freedom, is the greater good that renders blameless God's creation of a world like ours. Furthermore, God couldn't realize this great good without allowing at least the possibility of evil. Finally, *actual* moral evil is caused entirely by creatures misusing that freedom. Together with privation theory (section 3.1), this account shows how God is neither the author of sin (3), nor blameworthy for allowing creatures to cause sins (6).

One could try to use the free will theodicy to cover the justification of physical evils as well. Augustine influentially argued that misused creaturely freedom was ultimately responsible for all physical evils: "a perverse will is the cause of all [moral and physical] evil."[44] According to this extended account, human and animal suffering involved in natural disasters, disease, and death are justly administered divine punishments for original and ongoing human sin. Hence, God's blamelessness in producing physical evils is also explained by creaturely freedom gone afoul.[45]

This extension of the free will theodicy won fewer adherents in the seventeenth century. Locke and others argued against the moral appropriateness of inherited guilt.[46] Even if we could make sense of how later human beings were "with" original sinners in sinning and so deserving of punishment prior to actually sinning, it is hard to see why the punishment of nonhuman animals would be justified as a consequence of original sin, especially given the millions of years of suffering endured by sentient, nonrational creatures that we now know occurred prior to the arrival of *homo sapiens*. Later, we will see how others in the seventeenth century, most notably Malebranche, provided an alternative explanation for the existence of physical evils and animal suffering that was not rooted in an extension of the traditional free will theodicy (section 5).

We have now seen how Descartes relies on privation theory and creaturely freedom to try to show that God is not the cause of moral evil and is blameless for its existence. But Descartes acknowledges a concern about his account. Even if a necessary condition on our freedom is the *ability* to err and sin, surely an omnipotent being could have acted in such a way that we sin and err much less – or even not at all: "I can see, however, that God could easily have brought it about that without losing my freedom, and despite the limitations in my knowledge, I should nonetheless never make a mistake."[47] God's failure to do so reraises concerns about God's blamelessness for the existence of moral evils. To put it bluntly, if God could have brought it about that free creatures "never make a mistake," why didn't God? To answer this, we need the final piece of the traditional theodicy: the great good of cosmic diversity.

3.3. Metaphysical evil and the great good of diversity

The previous two sections focused on God's relation to moral and physical evils. Parts of that discussion appealed to the inherent limitations of creatures. In this section, we will look at the traditional justification for these limitations. This issue is especially pressing in light of Descartes's admission that God could have given us natures such that we are free and yet never in fact err and sin. What justifies God's decision not to give us better natures?

Descartes rejects one way of understanding this question: "[God] did not bestow on us everything which he was able to bestow, but which equally we can see he was not obliged to give us."[48] That is, we shouldn't think that God was in any way *obliged* to give us more abilities or perfections than God has given us. Nonetheless, even if God wasn't *obliged* to do better for us, we can still wonder why God didn't, as a matter of fact, do better for us. This is an instance of a more general puzzle facing the traditional theodicy. If things like rocks and humans are so limited, why make them at all?

The classical answer involved a greater-goods appeal to something we've already encountered: plenitude. A world with a plentiful range of diverse creatures is better than a world of homogeneous excellence, even if creating diversity requires God to create more limited and deficient creatures. Variety isn't just the spice of life, it is an excellent-making feature of the universe. Aquinas reasons, "the universe would not be perfect if only one grade of goodness were found in things."[49] He then applies this insight:

> The perfection of the universe requires that there should be inequality in things, so that every grade of goodness may be realized. Now, one grade of goodness is that of the good which cannot fail. Another grade of goodness is that of the good which can fail in goodness, and this grade is to be found in existence itself.[50]

The basic idea is that God brings about lesser goods and beings because their existence contributes to a rich cosmic variety that could not otherwise be had. Whereas moral evil was justified by the greater good of creaturely freedom, metaphysical evil is justified by the greater good of cosmic diversity.

Appeals to the good of cosmic diversity continued into the late seventeenth century. The great Cambridge Platonist, Ralph Cudworth, argued that to think that God's goodness requires God to produce no metaphysical evils is to think that "God should either have made nothing at all, since there can be nothing besides himself absolutely perfect, or else nothing but the higher rank of angels, free from mortality and all those other evils that attend mankind."[51] But this, Cudworth disapprovingly warns, would be to become

> like those who would blame a comedy or tragedy because they were not all kings or heroes that acted in it, but some servants and rustic clowns introduced

also, talking after their rude fashion. Whereas the dramatic poem would neither be complete, nor elegant and delightful, were all those worser parts taken out of it.[52]

Hence, although metaphysically limited creatures (our "rustic clowns") are imperfect relative to other, less limited creatures, their existence contributes to a more perfect whole by making the world more diverse.

I have already quoted the passage in which Descartes appears sympathetic to the appeal to cosmic diversity (from AT VII 61; CSM II 42), in which Descartes claims that although God could have made me better by making me better disposed to make correct judgments, the world as a whole is better for containing creatures like me instead of containing only rational creatures whose wills and intellects never misalign. Descartes admits that God could have been better *to me*, though at the cost of bringing about a less perfect world as a whole. And because God has no obligation to be better to me than God already has been, God is justified in bringing about the greater good of a diverse world by creating limited creatures like me.

At least, that *would* be the traditional version of Descartes's point, but that isn't quite what he says. Descartes doesn't claim that the world *is* better as a whole for having limited parts like us in it. He claims it *might be*, or rather, that he *can't deny* that it might be, a double qualification where tradition asserts a simple indicative.

This is Descartes's second main departure from the traditional theodicy we've been considering. It is noteworthy mostly because it severely curtails the scope of the rest of Descartes's theodicy. If Descartes asserts that the world as a whole *is* more perfect in virtue of containing limited parts like us, he can explain God's blamelessness in creating metaphysical evils. But Descartes offers a more cautious, defensive conclusion: it hasn't been proven impossible that the cosmic diversity cited by Aquinas and Cudworth is a greater good that could not otherwise be had without the kinds and distributions of metaphysical evils in our world.

However, Descartes's sudden pullback from theodicy to mere defense undermines the explanatory force of the rest of Descartes's theodicy in the Fourth Mediation. For if limitations make moral evils possible, and if it is merely possible that God is blameless in creating those limitations, then it is likewise merely possible that God is blameless for the existence of moral evils. A merely possible explanation may be better than no explanation at all, but the explanatory force of Descartes's account of evil is weakened considerably.[53]

In later sections, we will see Spinoza and Leibniz offer justifications for metaphysical evils at full theodician strength. Yet, they will also conclude that there are good reasons to reject the first two parts of the traditional theodicy, the ones that Descartes had tried to keep at full strength.

4. Seventeenth century criticisms of the traditional answers

For all its influence, the three-part explanation of the relation between God and evil – privation theory, freedom, and diversity – faced increasingly sharp challenges in the seventeenth century. In this section, we will look at several criticisms of appeals to privation theory and freedom in theodicies.

4.1. Privation theory challenged

Although it occupied a central role for centuries, privation theory has largely fallen by the wayside in contemporary discussions of the problem of evil.[54] In the late seventeenth century, the abandonment of privation theory was already underway. This was partly due to larger intellectual shifts occurring in the early modern period. The main advocates of privation theory at the turn of the seventeenth century were Aristotelian Scholastics. These so-called schoolmen became a common target for progressive early modern philosophers. The laborious and prolix writing style of Scholastics was taken as good evidence for the intellectual darkness into which the West had plunged prior to the rebirth of humanism and the rise of modern natural science. Hobbes wonders of Scholastics, "When men write whole volumes of such stuff, are they not mad, or intend to make others so?"[55]

Hobbes's sharp-tongued criticism wasn't leveled only at Scholasticism in general. After outlining a version of traditional privation theory, Hobbes concludes, "So, where the Scholastics wanted to seem most subtle, they showed most their stupidity."[56] Even Leibniz, who was fairly sympathetic to Scholastic ideas and who later offered nominal support of privation theory, initially condemned it as tainted. He writes that privation theory is "a leftover from the visionary philosophy of the past; it is a subterfuge with which a reasonable person will never be satisfied."[57]

Making matters worse in the eyes of leading early moderns, privations were also entrenched in Aristotelian physics.[58] Aquinas even applied the language of privative *evil* to the natural world: heat is an evil for water when it deprives water of its naturally cold state.[59] Undoubtedly, the growing early modern belief in the triumph of mechanism over Aristotelian physics cast a dark shadow over the entire framework of explanation via privations, moral and natural alike. If privations were no longer needed for science in the natural realm (as even Descartes agreed), why think they are required for a science of the mind and morality?

Although this "guilt by association" charge explains some of the disappearance of privation theory, early moderns also raised more direct philosophical concerns in the context of the problem of evil. Malebranche, for instance, objects that "pain is a real and true evil . . . thus not every evil is an evil just because it deprives us of good," adding later that pain "is always a real evil to those who suffer it, as long as they suffer it."[60] That is, some physical evils like pain and suffering are not merely absences of an appropriate good; their evil is quite positive and real.[61] If so, privation theory is not an extensionally adequate account of the nature of evil.

Of course, medieval advocates of privation theory admitted that there was *something* real in all evil, namely the subject of the privation.[62] Privation theorists did not claim that there is nothing real to the evils of our world, though they are sometimes caricatured in this way. But they did think that our very real experiences of pain and suffering are not themselves evil. Rather, the evil of, say, a debilitating neurological disorder lies in the malfunctioning of the patient's nerves and the corresponding absence of proper function. In fact, the patient's experience of pain is an appropriate perfection that, coupled with a properly functioning set of nerves, would result only in goods, like desires to seek out food and to avoid touching hot sticks.

Malebranche rejects this account and claims that the evil of at least some pain is itself a real, positive quality that is opposed to the good of the sufferer, and not simply the absence of an appropriately functioning mechanism. Attempts by privation theorists to redescribe the cases are simply unconvincing, Malebranche thinks. Whether or not he's right, Malebranche's verdict on the intrinsic evil of some pains and suffering is now the dominant and mostly unquestioned view in contemporary discussions of evil.

Leibniz objected not so much to the ontology of privative accounts of evil,[63] but to Scholastic attempts to use privation theory to demonstrate that God is not the author of sin. In an early essay, Leibniz writes,

> For to say that God is not the author of sin, because he is not the author of a privation, although he can be called the author of everything that is real and positive in the sin – that is a manifest illusion.... I am amazed that these people did not go further and try to persuade us that man himself is not the author of sin, since he is only the author of the physical or real aspect, the privation being something for which there is no author.[64]

Leibniz's main objection in this passage is that if Descartes's "evil is not a thing" move absolves God from causal responsibility for moral evil, parallel reasoning will also absolve humans from causal responsibility for moral evil – a *reductio ad absurdum*.[65] For if evil has no divine cause because it is not real, then it isn't clear how there can be *any* cause of it.[66] Leibniz reasons that privation theory thus entails that all moral and physical evil is entirely uncaused, and one doesn't have to share his fondness for the principle of sufficient reason to find that conclusion troubling.

The obvious rejoinder is that although evil is a privation of goodness and being, *there is* a real subject of the privation that lacks the appropriate perfection. So even if nothing can cause a privation *per se*, humans *can* bring it about that subjects lack perfections they ought to have, and, in that sense, they can cause privative evils. But Leibniz could simply push his point a step further. If humans cause privative moral evil by producing changes in subjects that are thereby deprived of appropriate perfections, then the same could hold equally well of God. After all, God too has the power to cause real subjects to lack appropriate perfections (e.g. when in meting out punishments), and so if to cause a privation one has only to cause a subject to lack an appropriate perfection, it is no longer clear why God can't cause privative evils after all. Therefore, Leibniz concludes, if God is nevertheless not responsible for moral evil, it must be in virtue of something besides the fact that evil is a privation.

Spinoza offered a far more sweeping criticism of privation theory. In 1663, Spinoza published a book on the Cartesian system in which he repeated Descartes's account of error as "a privation of the proper use of liberty."[67] William Blyenbergh, a young Dutch Calvinist, wrote to Spinoza to express his dissatisfaction with this account. Blyenbergh presented Spinoza with a dilemma: "either Adam's forbidden act... is not evil in itself, or else God himself seems to bring about what we call evil." He added, "And it seems to me that neither you nor Monsieur Descartes solve this difficulty by saying that evil is a non-being with which God does not concur."[68]

In reply, Spinoza undercuts the very foundations of privation theory. Recall that the traditional distinction between mere negation and privation assumed the existence of human-independent norms of goodness and appropriate perfections. Spinoza rejects this supposition:

> Privation is not an act of depriving; it is nothing more than a state of want, which in itself is nothing. It is only a construct of the mind or a mode of thinking which we form from comparing things with one another.[69]

Rather than being based on the failure to conform to intrinsic "oughts," privations result from comparative human judgments: "a privation is nothing but denying something of a thing which *we judge* to pertain to its nature, and negation nothing but denying something of a thing because it does not pertain to its nature" (my emphasis).[70]

Spinoza even discusses the traditional example of blindness and denies that blindness in humans is a privation of a perfection that every human, by their shared natures, ought to have. According to Spinoza, the evil of blindness is instead based on an all-too-human judgment, not some unrealized natural *telos*:

> We say, for example, that a blind man is deprived of sight because we easily imagine him as seeing, whether this imagination arises from the fact that we compare him with others who see, or his present state with his past when he used to see. And when we consider man in this way, by comparing his nature with that of others or with his own past nature, then we affirm that seeing pertains to his nature, and *for that reason* we say that he is deprived of it.[71]

Hence, on Spinoza's view, *all privation is mere negation*, plus a bit of comparative judgment.

Spinoza rejects more than just traditional privative accounts of *physical* evils. In the appendix to his book on Descartes, Spinoza also denies the traditional account of moral evil: "Evil and sins are nothing in things, but are only in the human mind which compares things with one another."[72] Nor is his rejection limited to evils. According to Spinoza, claims about *goodness* also turn out to be based on subjective judgments of utility: "As far as good and evil are concerned, they also indicate nothing positive in things, considered in themselves, nor are they anything other than modes of thinking, or notions we form because we compare things to one another."[73]

Interestingly, by the time Spinoza reaches these sweeping heights (or lows), he has conceded Blyenburgh's original point. Blyenburgh had claimed that either God is the author of moral evil or else there is no moral evil. Spinoza embraces the second horn of the dilemma and admits that there is no such thing as moral (or physical) evil, if "evil" refers to the deprivation of an intrinsic excellence that is independent of human judgments.

To the extent to which he even retains the term, evil for Spinoza is only a kind of weakness or relative limitation.[74] Put positively, all evil for Spinoza is metaphysical evil, a return to the *evil as limitation* view. Spinoza does, however, follow the traditional account on one point. Like everyone else we've discussed, Spinoza explains the existence of metaphysical evils by appeal to cosmic diversity:

> But to those who ask, "Why did God not create all men so that they would be governed by the command of reason?" I answer only, "because he did not lack the material to create all things, from the highest degree of perfection to the lowest"; or, to speak more properly, "because the laws of his nature have been so ample that they sufficed for producing all things which can be conceived by an infinite intellect" (as I have demonstrated in 1p16).[75]

By the start of the eighteenth century, privation theory began to disappear from discussions of evil, even among those who otherwise continued to embrace the traditional account. Clarke, for instance, presents a standard version of the traditional theodicy in 1705, just sixty-four years after Descartes's *Meditations*:

> For liberty implying a natural power of doing evil as well as good; and the imperfect nature of finite beings making it possible for them to abuse this their

THE PROBLEM OF EVIL

liberty to an actual commission of evil; and it being necessary to the order and beauty of the whole and the for displaying the infinite wisdom of the creator that there should be different and various degrees of creatures whereof consequently some must be less perfect than others, hence there necessarily arises a possibility of evil, notwithstanding that the creator is infinitely good.[76]

Clarke's account is notable mostly for its complete lack of appeal to privation and its presumption that this absence needs no explanation.

4.2. Free will theodicy challenged

Privation theory wasn't the only aspect of the traditional theodicy under fire in the seventeenth century. Some early moderns objected to the broadly libertarian account of creaturely freedom in late Scholasticism. However, the two alternatives to libertarianism – compatibilism (Hobbes, Locke, and Leibniz)[77] and hard incompatibilism (Spinoza)[78] – could not as easily shift the burden for moral evils to misused creaturely freedom. For if we can act freely while being determined to do so (compatibilism), surely God could have determined us to commit much less moral evil. On the other hand, if there is no creaturely freedom (hard incompatibilism), tracing evils back to morally responsible creatures is a nonstarter.

There were also challenges to the free will theodicy that did not focus as directly on the viability of libertarianism. Bayle was a particularly sharp critic in this regard:

> Those who say that God permitted sin because he could not have prevented it without destroying the free will that he had given to man, and which was the best present he made to him, expose themselves greatly. The reason they give is lovely. It has a *je ne sais quoi*, an indefinable something that is dazzling. It has grandeur. But in the end, it can be opposed by arguments more easily understood by all men and based more on common sense and the ideas of order.[79]

Bayle's most penetrating criticisms focus on the metaphysics and the value of creaturely freedom.

In the first series of objections, Bayle questions why an omnipotent and omniscient God couldn't create free creatures who, in fact, perform only morally good actions, while still retaining the *capacity* to bring about moral evil. The cogency of Bayle's challenge on this point turns on larger issues of grace, foreknowledge, and freedom, so I will just mention two of Bayle's ideas under this topic.

First, Bayle thinks God could allow creatures to act freely just in cases in which God knows that they otherwise would use their freedom to perform morally good actions. Bayle likens this oversight to what we would expect of an effective guardian: "If [God] gives them free will, [God ought to] always efficiently watch over them to prevent their falling into sin."[80] By using such knowledge, God could override our freedom whenever God knows that we would otherwise use it to freely bring about moral evil.

One might object that this preventative oversight would undermine the excellence of our freedom. Bayle questions in reply why the greater good of creaturely freedom must involve *unconstrained* freedom. Why isn't an unrealized *capacity* for freely causing moral evil enough of a good?

> To have regard for man's free will, to abstain carefully from interfering with the inclination of a man who is going to lose his innocence forever and is going to condemn himself eternally, do you call that a legitimate observation of the privileges of freedom?[81]

In a different vein, Bayle suggests that God could bestow on each of us a sufficient amount of grace so that we invariably, though still freely, perform only good actions. He thinks theologians are already committed to the compatibility of praiseworthy human free actions and the gift of divine grace.[82] He reasons that God could therefore give creatures enough grace to ensure that they perform only good actions without undermining their freedom:

> All theologians agree that God can infallibly produce a good act of the will in the human soul without depriving it of its free functions . . . then they have to acknowledge that a proper assistance furnished by God to Adam, or some help that was so arranged that it would have infallibly prevented his Fall, would have been in complete accord with the use of his free will . . . and would have left him sufficient room to act meritoriously.[83]

Bayle's second main challenge focuses on the value claim of the free will theodicy. Bayle denies that the good of human freedom outweighs the costs of the moral evils of our world, in which case a truly good God would have created a world without free creatures at all. Bayle presents colorful examples from everyday life to support this judgment, such as the following:

> There is no good mother who, having given her daughters permission to go to a dance, would not revoke that permission if she were assured that they would succumb to temptation and lose their virginity there. And any mother who, knowing for sure that this would come to pass, allowed them to go to the dance and was satisfied with exhorting them to be virtuous and with threatening to disown them if they were no longer virgins when they returned home, would, at the very least, bring upon herself the charge that she loved neither her daughters nor chastity. . . . She would be told that . . . it would have been better to keep her daughters in her sight than to give them the privilege of freedom.[84]

In other words, Bayle thinks that a perfectly good God, faced with a choice between creating free sinners whom God knows will screw up in the ways we do or creating a world without free creatures at all, ought to choose no freedom and no moral evil: "If there be no other way of avoiding this result than by revoking his donation [of freedom], he would have to do this. This would better preserve his character as patron and benefactor than anything else he might do."[85]

Part of Bayle's point in using examples from human life is to remind his readers that we would surely judge *human* agents to be morally deficient if they acted in the ways that God is supposed to have acted according to free will theodicies. So, either the standards of human and divine goodness are different (an option Bayle rejects for other reasons), or else free will theodicies fail to demonstrate God's blamelessness. Bayle thinks this conclusion is even more obvious when we recall that the punishment for misused freedom is supposed to be eternal damnation: "But it follows necessarily that he should have deprived them of [freedom] at any cost rather than wait until it should result in their eternal damnation."[86]

Bayle's own solution – at least the one he officially gives – is to avoid seeking explanations altogether for why God allows evil. According to Bayle, theists should instead say,

> "I do not know; I only believe that He had some reasons for it that are really worthy of his infinite wisdom, but which are incomprehensible to me." By offering this answer, you will stop the most obstinate disputers short.[87]

Although appeals to faith without explanations resonated with some in the seventeenth century, the remaining figures we will look at defend the appropriateness of offering theodicies, even though they share some of Bayle's suspicions about the traditional account.

5. Malebranche and physical evil

So far, I have focused mostly on moral and metaphysical evils. In this section, I'll turn to physical evils and Malebranche's striking explanation for their existence and distribution in a world sustained by an omnipotent and omnibenevolent God.[88]

Malebranche is in a tight spot when it comes to the problem of evil. He is an occasionalist, which entails that he rejects proposition (2), but in a way that makes explaining God's blamelessness in evil even more difficult. For according to occasionalism, God is the *only* true cause. So not only does God cause *some* physical evils, per proposition (4), God is the sole cause of every change in the world.[89] This means that attempts to justify God's actions by claiming that God merely *allows*, but doesn't *cause*, physical evils won't work for Malebranche. God causes natural disasters and deformities, as well as any pain and suffering that attends them: "He does not allow monsters; it is He who makes them."[90] The problem of evil that Malebranche raises for himself is thus quite daunting: "Therefore, the universe is the most perfect God can create? What! So many monsters, so many disorders, the great number of impious people; does all this contribute to the perfection of the universe?"[91]

In reply, Malebranche concedes that God could have made a better world than ours: "God could, no doubt, make a world more perfect than the one in which we live."[92] In particular, God could have made a world with much less physical evil, including fewer natural disasters, diseases, and deformities and less pain and suffering. Malebranche explains that God didn't because

> God wills that His action as well as His world bear the character of his attributes. Not content that the universe honors Him through its excellence and beauty, He wills that His ways glorify Him through their simplicity, their fecundity, their universality.[93]

That is, God doesn't decide which possible world to create based only on the content of the world. God also wants to produce that content *in the best possible way*: "Thus, do not imagine that God willed absolutely to make the most perfect work possible, but only the most perfect in relation to the ways most worthy of Him."[94]

According to Malebranche, God acts in the most perfect ways when God acts through simple, constant, and uniform means – characteristics that reflect some of God's own attributes. In the physical world, Malebranche thinks God so perfectly acts through two fundamental laws of motion.[95] An unfortunate but unavoidable by-product of God's acting through such simple, constant, and uniform physical laws is the production of many physical evils:

> Now these laws, because of their simplicity, necessarily have unhappy consequences with respect to us: but these consequences do not make it necessary for God to change these laws into more complicated ones. . . . [I]t is true that God could remedy these unhappy consequences through an infinite number of particular wills: but order will not have it so.[96]

Malebranche here acknowledges that God could, of course, interrupt or complicate the physical laws and prevent many physical evils from occurring. For example, God could suspend the laws of motion whenever cars crash into each other. But doing so would require God to act in a less simple, constant, and uniform manner – in short, in a less perfect way. Because God is at least as concerned about acting in the most perfect way as He is about the excellence of the world these ways produce, God usually does not circumvent the natural order.[97]

Malebranche claims that God's intention to act in the most perfect way also explains why God is blameless for doing so, despite the bad consequences we suffer as a result: "And in consequence, God is not to be blamed for not distributing the order and simplicity of his laws by miracles which would be quite convenient to our needs, but quite opposed to the wisdom of God."[98] Behind Malebranche's justification is, I believe, an appeal to something like the "Doctrine of Double Effect."[99] God foresaw but did not intend the physical evils that result from God's praiseworthy effort to create and preserve the world in the best possible manner: "He has not established the laws of the communication of motion *with the design* of producing monsters. . . . [H]e willed these laws *because* of their fruitfulness, and not their sterility" (my emphasis).[100]

Malebranche's point is that God does not *use* physical evils as a means to achieve God's goals in creation, nor are the evils part of God's intended goals: "Thus, God does not will positively or directly that there should be monsters, but He wills positively certain laws of the communication of motion, of which monsters are necessary consequences."[101] Malebranche readily admits that if there had been a possible world with equally simple, uniform, and constant laws and fewer physical evils, God would have created it instead.[102] But, alas for us, there is no such possible world.[103]

Malebranche elegantly applies this strategy to the distribution of both physical evils and divine grace: "Here is why the world is filled with *impious people*, monsters, disorders of all kinds. *God could convert all people* and prevent all disorders. But He must not thereby upset the simplicity and uniformity of His action" (my emphasis).[104] Just as sometimes the simplicity and constancy of God's action in the physical world mean that rain falls uselessly in the ocean, so too God's simple and uniform distribution of grace to everyone may entail that it sometimes falls uselessly on those ill-disposed to consent to its taking root.

> Thus as one has no right to be annoyed that rain falls in the sea where it is useless, and that it does not fall on seeded grounds where it is necessary . . . so too one ought not complain of the apparent irregularity according to which grace

is given to men.... [T]he simplicity of general laws does not permit that this grace, which is inefficacious in this corrupted heart, fall in another heart where it would be efficacious.... For finally the order of grace would be less perfect, less admirable, less lovable, if it were more complex.[105]

Leibniz, our final seventeenth century theodicist, thought Malebranche was on the right track. Leibniz agrees that God takes into account the means of organizing and preserving the world when choosing which possible world to bring about. However, Leibniz denies that God is as singularly concerned with the uniformity and constancy of God's ways as Malebranche sometimes suggests. Leibniz thinks God seeks to maximize *both* the simplicity of means and the "variety, richness, and abundance" of effects.[106] In fact, according to Leibniz, our world is the best possible world partly because it best harmonizes these twin demands of perfection: simplicity of ways and diversity of effects.[107]

6. Leibniz and the best possible world

If there is a single philosopher most closely associated with the problem of evil in intellectual history, it is Leibniz. One of the unsurpassed geniuses of the seventeenth century, Leibniz wrestled throughout his philosophical career with understanding the relation between God and evil. He explores numerous and sometimes conflicting accounts, some traditional, others novel. Several of these explanations are pulled together in the only book he ever published, *Theodicy: Essays on the Goodness of God, the Freedom of Man, and the Origin of Evil*.[108]

The thesis at the heart of Leibniz's theodicy – indeed, much of his philosophical system – is that God freely created the best of all possible worlds, namely *our* world. There are a number of internal concerns one might have about this claim, as Leibniz himself recognized. He struggled throughout his writings to show how God's creation of the best possible world was free and contingent, while also maintaining that God, by God's very nature, couldn't have done less than the best. Leibniz also denied that God's choice of the best rendered our actions (including moral evils) necessary, a perpetual worry for Leibniz's philosophical system. For if God must choose the best possible world, and if our sins are part of the best possible world, it seems like our sins will be necessary too. And if our sins do follow as consequences of God's choice of the best possible world, it isn't clear how we remain morally responsible and God remains blameless for them. These are important concerns to which Leibniz regularly returned, though I will focus here on more general issues surrounding Leibniz's claim that this is the best of all possible worlds.[109]

Leibniz thinks he can prove that ours is the sole best of all possible worlds (BPW), at least assuming that God exists and is perfectly wise and reasonable (which are also provable, according to Leibniz).[110] Our world is the best along the three dimensions that we have been using for evil: "For perfection includes not only the moral good and the physical good of intelligent creatures, but also the good which is purely metaphysical, and concerns also creatures devoid of reason."[111] So our world, according to Leibniz, is morally, physically, and metaphysically the best and most perfect that God could create.

If Leibniz is right about this, then he will have an immediate explanation of God's blamelessness for the existence of evil, one that neatly circumvents all the previously discussed options. For if our world is the BPW, then God can hardly be blamed for bringing it about, at least on the assumptions that *ought* implies *can* and that bringing about nothing would be an inferior possibility. In other words, once we add that ours is the BPW, (6) follows from the conjunction of propositions (1) and (2) without needing further explanation of why God causes physical and metaphysical evils or allows moral evils:[112]

> It is true that one can imagine possible worlds without sin and without unhappiness . . . but these same worlds again would be very inferior to ours in goodness. I cannot show you this in detail. . . . But you must judge with me *ab effectu* [from the effect], since God has chosen this world as it is.[113]

Leibniz even takes his BPW claim on the offensive: if God had created a world with less evil, God wouldn't have been perfectly good:

> Wisdom only shows God the best possible exercise of His goodness: after that, the evil that occurs is an inevitable result of the best. I will add something stronger: To permit the evil, as God permits it, is the greatest goodness.[114]

Hence, God is actually *praiseworthy* for creating a world that contains evil:

> Since, in short, it was necessary to choose from all the things possible what produced the best effect together, and since vice entered in by this door, God would not have been altogether good, altogether wise if he had excluded it.[115]

Leibniz hastens to explain that this does *not* mean that God prefers sin and suffering. Like Malebranche, Leibniz admits that God would have preferred to create a world in which Judas doesn't betray Jesus (to use one of Leibniz's favorite examples), at least when that betrayal is considered in isolation. When deciding on which possible world to create, however, God doesn't consider events in isolation, because not all events are possible together. Instead, God considers entire worlds, complete series of compossible events.[116] Therefore, an event that is preferable in isolation may be part of an overall nonpreferable series. Thus, although God would prefer, say, a world without damned sinners, *all else being equal*, once everything else in such possible worlds is taken into account, God sees that those other worlds are undesirable, *all things considered*.[117]

One might respond that surely God could have made our world without at least some of the parts that, considered in themselves, are highly undesirable. Why not make our world, except without Hitler? Leibniz replies that the contents of possible worlds are so deeply intertwined that a world without Hitler would also be a world without us. Who we are is bound up with our relations to other people and events, including the horrors of the twentieth century.

Leibniz defends a very strong version of this idea, claiming that *every* part of a possible world is essentially connected to every other part: "Thus, if the smallest evil that comes to pass in the world were missing in it, it would no longer be this world," and, he adds elsewhere, none of us would have existed either.[118] Hence, wishing that God had created a different world, one free of any of the evils of our world, cuts against our own self-interests, at least if it is better for us to exist than never to have been born at all. More importantly, had God created a world with any less evil, God would have created a different, and therefore suboptimal, world. Leibniz concludes, "God, doing what his wisdom and his goodness combined ordain, is not answerable for the evil that he permits."[119]

Leibniz's claim that ours is the BPW offers a sweeping, concise, and decisive justification for why God made a world with as much evil as ours. But can it be taken seriously? The reply from many readers of the *Theodicy* was a firm "no." Indeed, the aftermath of this, the most famous early modern theodicy, represents a remarkable pivot in intellectual history. Within a generation, Leibniz's bold proclamation that our world (with all of its sin, misery, and deformities) is the best world that God could have made became the subject of parody and ridicule among Parisian intellectuals. In his famous reply, *Candide*, Voltaire wryly mocks what he takes to be Leibniz's unrealistic optimism: "Candide, stunned, stupefied, despairing, bleeding, trembling, said to himself: If this is the best of all possible worlds, what are the others like?"[120]

The individual suffering of Candide also presents a broader challenge for Leibniz and the others we have been considering. We have seen how seventeenth century theodicists appealed to a variety of greater goods to show how God's role in our evil-stricken world is blameless: cosmic diversity; unfettered creaturely freedom; simple, uniform, and fecund laws; the manifestation of divine justice; creaturely character development; and even goods beyond our ken.[121] Their appeals to these sorts of greater goods have not gone unchallenged – even by later theists. Some theists have pointedly asked, "*To whom or to what* do those greater goods accrue?"[122] The concern is that the greater goods of seventeenth century theodicies are good only for the world as a whole or only for a subset of individuals, such as the perpetrators of evil or the nondamned. This has raised fresh challenges for our seventeenth century theodicists, challenges that focus less on their explanations of God's blamelessness for evils and more on their assumptions about the focus and extent of God's goodness and love.[123]

Notes

1 A canvassing of the large-scale twentieth century horrors can be found in Glover, *Humanity: A Moral History of the Twentieth Century*.
2 Bayle, *Dictionary*, "Manicheans," rem. D.
3 Milton, *Paradise Lost*, XI.489–503.
4 For a recent sample of this kind of discussion, see Plantinga and Tooley, *Knowledge of God*.
5 Another issue that was treated as part of the problem of evil in the seventeenth century concerned the distribution and efficaciousness of divine grace. There were bitter divides within Catholic factions (e.g. Jesuits vs. Dominicans vs. Jansenists) and Protestant factions (e.g. Lutherans vs. Calvinists vs. Methodists) over grace. Leibniz highlights the divisiveness of these issues:

> It is here that people have principally divided; no comet, no earthquake, no plague has done more harm. It is here that laziness has found shelter, evil has found camouflage, and God himself has had to be a pretence for both. . . . [W]e [Christians] have awakened so many sects that rarely a rift has arisen among us in which predestination and election have not had a part.
> (Leibniz, CP 7)

Though we would now classify this as a theological dispute, the boundaries between philosophy and theology were more fluid in the early modern period. For reasons of space, I will mostly ignore this topic here.
6 The "defense" label was coined by Alvin Plantinga, a contemporary philosopher of religion who has developed several theistic defenses against objections from evil.
7 A few qualifiers: by "dominant," I mean that a sizable and influential number adhered to these views, not that there were no influential dissenters. By "traditional," I have in mind those who were heavily

influential in the Western Christian tradition. There are other theistic traditions, but in this chapter I will focus on the tradition most influential on the seventeenth century figures we will be discussing, namely the Christianity of the Latin West.

8 See, for instance, Augustine, *On Free Choice of Will*, 1 and 4; Aquinas, ST 1q48; Suárez, DM 9.1.
9 Clarke, *Demonstration*, 78–9; see also King, *De Origine Mali*, 37; and Leibniz, T §21.
10 I will use "physical" to keep us from thinking only of things like natural disasters when the category is invoked, though it should be kept in mind that mental suffering falls under this category too.
11 We shouldn't get hung up at this point on whether it is appropriate to call such limitations "evils" (Aquinas suggests no; ST 1q48a3). The more important issue will be the role these creaturely limitations play in explaining moral and physical evil.
12 Concurrence was a complex theory about how God's causal activity, over and above creation and preservation, relates to the causal activity of creatures, so-called secondary causes. The dominant Scholastic position was that God cooperates, or *concurs*, immediately in every effect that creatures bring about. This happens in such a way that the divine and secondary cause act by a single action and are each the immediate cause of a single, undivided, and non-overdetermined effect. The two main alternatives were *occasionalism*, according to which God is the sole causal agent, and *mere conservationism*, according to which creatures bring about some effects without the immediate causal cooperation of God. For a very lucid discussion of concurrence theory, see Freddoso "God's General Concurrence with Secondary Causes." Like any of these tenets, divine concurrence was not accepted by *everyone* in the seventeenth century, but dissenters (e.g. Malebranche) could expect to be accused of heterodoxy.
13 See Aquinas, ST 1q49a2, SCG IIIa.76.6; and Suárez, DM 11.3.24.
14 Aquinas, ST 1q47a1.
15 I will ignore the question of the appropriate bearers of evil: intentions, actions, persons, the states of affairs they bring about, or some combination of these. I will instead follow seventeenth century practice and loosely slide back and forth for readability.
16 In 1652, Louis XIV endorsed the Edict of Nantes, which granted political and religious liberties to the Protestant Huguenots; by the time he repealed it in 1685 (known as "the Revocation"), their widespread persecution in the Sun King's France was already well underway.
17 Leibniz, T §19 and §220.
18 Descartes describes his account in the *Meditations* as explaining "the source of my error *and sin*" (AT VII 58; CSM II 41, my emphasis), and he claims to avoid talking about good and evil only to avoid becoming embattled in a theological controversy (AT IV 117; CSMK III 234 and AT V 159; CSMK 342).
19 AT VII 60–61; CSM II 41–42.
20 The classical study on this background is Lovejoy, *The Great Chain of Being*, though I have reservations about some of the details of his analyses of early modern figures (especially Spinoza and Leibniz).
21 AT VII 54; CSM II 38.
22 In Scholasticism, this was known as the "convertibility of goodness and being." For a representative defense of this view, see Aquinas, ST 1q 5a1.
23 For simplicity, I will pass over questions about whether plentitude should be applied at the level of properties, individuals, species, and natural kinds, as these distinctions will not be relevant here. Many medieval accounts applied plentitude at the level of species.
24 Aquinas, ST q49a3.
25 See, for instance, Plotinus *Enneads* I.8; and Proclus, *The Nature and Origin of Evil*, sec. 51.
26 For a helpful summary of the most influential figures, see Suárez, DM 11.1.3.
27 Aquinas, SCG IIIa.x.11.
28 AT VII 55; CSM II 38. Though I think it amounts to a terminological difference, recall that Aquinas was hesitant to call purely metaphysical limitations "evil," whereas some early moderns accepted calling them "evil." Hence, in the Thomistic tradition, *all* evils are privations, and God is not blameworthy for nonevil limitations. But the same point holds for seventeenth century categories: all nonmetaphysical evils are privations, and God is not blameworthy for metaphysical evils.
29 The teleological nature of traditional privation theory is vividly displayed in Aquinas, SCG IIIa.iv.4; *On Evil* I, art 1, ad 10; and ST 1q49a1.
30 Aquinas, ST 1q48a5ad1.
31 AT VII 60; CSM II 41–42.
32 AT VII 60; CSM II 42.
33 AT VII 60; CSM II 42. See also *Principles* I.23 (AT VIIIA 14; CSM I 201) and I.41 (AT VIIIA 20; CSM I 206). Descartes is offering a version of Aquinas's claim that God causally contributes to the *acts* of sin, though not the sinful aspects of sins (see Aquinas, STae q79a2).

34 AT VII 60–61; CSM II 42.
35 *Principles* I.31 (AT VIIIA 17; CSM I 203–204).
36 *Principles* I.23 (AT VIIIA 14; CSM I 201).
37 Aquinas, ST 1q49a2ad2. One might ask Aquinas, "But what is the cause of the deficiency of the secondary cause?" Aquinas's basic answer is that the *nonsinful* deficiency or limitation arises from our ability to ignore the demands of reason and God's law in a given situation, whereas *actual sin* happens when we freely will without paying attention to those demands (see ST 1q49a2ad3; *On Evil* I, art 3; III, art 2; and III, art 3, ad 13). If one then asks for a prior cause of *that* free action, Aquinas claims that no further answer is needed: "And there is no need to seek a cause of this nonuse of the aforementioned rule, since the very freedom of the will, by which it can act or not act, is enough to explain the non-use" (*On Evil*, I, art 3; for an earlier version of this reply, see Augustine, *On Free Choice of the Will*, 104–105). As Suárez emphasizes (foreshadowing a version of Descartes's previous point), because the evil aspect of this free action is found in its *nonuse* of the appropriate rule, there is no need for divine concurrence, because "a secondary cause does not need God's cooperation insofar as it does not act, but only insofar as it does anything" (Suárez, *DM* 11.3.22).
38 For a fuller discussion, see Newlands, forthcoming.
39 *Principles* I.39 (AT VIIIA 19–20; CSM I 205–206).
40 AT VII 60; CSM II 41. Though Descartes focuses here on our will's free assent to confused and obscure perceptions as the source of culpable error, his account on this point generalizes to all moral fault.
41 *Principles* I.38 (AT VIIIA 19; CSM I 205).
42 Note that indifference does not require equipoise of reasons, although some early moderns uncharitably took it to. A canonical formulation of indifference coming out of late Scholasticism is something like all the temporally (and, according to the Jesuits, causally) prior requisites of the action having been posited, an agent can (1) either will or not will ("freedom of exercise") and (2) either will φ or will some other alternative to φ ("freedom of specification"). This condition *does not* mean that the agent must have no stronger reason for doing one rather than the other, as in the case of Buridan's ass.
43 AT VII 57; CSM II 40. See also AT IV 116–177; CSMK III 234 and AT IV 173; CSMK 245). Descartes's view on the necessary conditions for freedom is a notoriously difficult interpretive matter. Descartes continues in the previous passage, "or rather," and then goes on to write things that seem to undermine the point he has just made about the requirements for freedom. For more, see C. P. Ragland's chapter in this volume.
44 Augustine, *On Free Choice of the Will*, 104.
45 Aquinas emphasizes that God's intention in meting out punishment is not the suffering of creatures *per se*, but rather the establishing of God's justice in the world – a necessary (but unintended) consequence of which is the suffering of deserving creatures (Aquinas, *On Evil*, q I, art 3, ad 10).
46 For discussion, see Phillip L. Quinn, "Disputing the Augustinian Legacy."
47 AT VII 61; CSM II 42. According to Augustine, God *did* create free creatures who, by gifts of divine grace, are unable to sin (Augustine, *On Rebuke and Grace*, 99; for a weaker version that God created free creatures who, as a matter of fact, will never sin, see *Free Choice of the Will*, 80–81). Aquinas claims that although *by nature* all rational creatures can sin, by grace some may be unable to sin (ST 1q63a1).
48 *Principles* I.31 (AT IXB 39; CSM I 204), note added to French edition.
49 Aquinas, ST 1q47a2; see also a1. For Augustine's version, see *On Free Choice of the Will*, 79–80.
50 Aquinas, ST 1q48a2; see also SCG IIIa.71.3. Aquinas is speaking of corruptibility in general, not simply moral evil, though I think his point is supposed to apply to the goodness of morally corruptible creatures too. Aquinas sometimes goes further: "so the perfection of the universe requires that there should be some [things] which can fail in goodness, and *thence it follows that sometimes they do fail*" (ST 1q48a2). If applied to rational creatures, the italicized inference threatens the traditional account. But if we follow Leibniz and contemporary metaphysicians in sharply distinguishing the modal from the temporal, there is also little reason to follow Aquinas in making it.
51 Cudworth, *Intellectual System* II.338.
52 Cudworth, *Intellectual System* II.340; Leibniz makes similarly colorful appeals (Leibniz, T §124).
53 Descartes's qualified claim also raises tough questions from a contemporary perspective. Is it supposed to be *probable* that such diversity is the greater good? Merely *logically possible*? Or is it really just a claim about an open epistemic possibility, in which case Descartes's defense would answer only the most absurdly strong atheistic arguments from evil?
54 This section is a heavily condensed version of parts of Newlands, "Evils, Privations, and the Early Moderns," forthcoming, in *Evil* in the Oxford Philosophical Concepts series.

55 L 8.27. Hobbes even suggests that some of the religious strife in Christendom was due to the way Scholastics merged Aristotle and Christianity, "from whence there arose so many contradictions and absurdities as brought the clergy into a reputation both of ignorance and fraudulent intention, and inclined people to revolt from them" (L 12.31).
56 L 45.22.
57 Leibniz, CP 111.
58 See, for example, Aristotle, *Physics* V.6.
59 *On Evil*, I, art. 1, ad 1; see also Suárez, DM 11.3.12. For Descartes's reply, see AT I 485; CSMK III 79.
60 Malebranche, *Search* 5.3/LO 348 and *Search* 5.8/LO 392, respectively.
61 For a discussion of other places where Malebranche asserts a more positive ontology of evil, see Moreau, *Deux Cartesians*, 93–95. Not for nothing was Malebranche accused of being a Manichean.
62 *On Evil* I, art. 1; Suárez DM 11.3.6.
63 Though see Leibniz, Ak II.1.488, where he makes a similar point to Malebranche's.
64 CP 111.
65 For a fuller discussion of this passage, and Leibniz's views on privation theory more generally, see Newlands, "Leibniz on Privations, Limitations, and the Metaphysics of Evil."
66 Bayle makes a similar objection (Bayle, *Objections to Poiret* 161).
67 *Curley* 257.
68 Ep 18.
69 Ep 21.
70 Ep 21.
71 Ep 21, my emphasis.
72 *Curley* 328.
73 *Curley* 545.
74 *Curley* 546.
75 *Curley* 446.
76 Clark, *Demonstration* 78.
77 L 21.4; Locke, *Essay* 2.21; Leibniz, T §288.
78 *Curley* 425 and 483–484.
79 *Dictionary*, "Paulicians," rem. E.
80 *Dictionary*, "Manicheans," rem. D.
81 *Dictionary*, "Paulicians," rem. M.
82 In the background is the Scholastic idea that every praiseworthy creaturely act must be accompanied by a special concurring gift of divine grace that is over and above God's ordinary, general concurrence. There were sharp disputes at the start of the seventeenth century over exactly how this was compatible with human freedom, but *that they were compatible* was widely agreed upon (see note 50).
83 *Dictionary*, "Paulicians," rem. M.
84 *Dictionary*, "Paulicians," rem. E.
85 *Dictionary*, "Paulicians," rem. M.
86 *Dictionary*, "Paulicians," rem. M.
87 *Dictionary*, "Paulicians," rem. M.
88 For the sake of space, I will ignore Malebranche's appeal to the incarnation of Jesus Christ as the motive for God's creating anything in the first place and as part of the explanation for God's action in the world (cf. *Dialogues* 9, 154–160, 210–215; *TNG* 1.1–4, 32, 54.). For an overview of this strand in Malebranche, see Donald Rutherford, "Malebranche's Theodicy."
89 Like everyone else in the seventeenth century, Malebranche denies that God causes moral evil (*Eluc.* 1/LO 556). Somewhat brazenly, he too appeals to creaturely freedom as the true source of sins. However, it is very difficult to see how humans could ever be morally responsible under occasionalism. (For Malebranche's most succinct attempt to address this concern, see *Search* 547–558).
90 *Dialogues* 9, 164.
91 *Dialogues* 9, 161.
92 *TNG* 1.14.
93 *Dialogues* 9, 163.
94 *Dialogues* 9, 163.
95 *TNG* 1.15.
96 *TNG* 1.43.
97 Malebranche does allow for the possibilities of miraculous interventions in cases where God's other attributes (e.g. justice or benevolence) overrule the demands of simplicity, but these are exceptional

(cf. *Dialogues* 9, 199 and *TNG* 1.21.). In a throwback to Augustine's strategy, Malebranche also claims that prior to sinning, Adam had the ability to avoid physical evils by stopping the communication of pain from his body to his mind, but that part of his punishment for sin was losing that ability (*Eluc.* 8/LO 580–81).

98 *TNG* 1.43.
99 According to the doctrine of double effect, it may be permissible for an agent to act in a way that has both good and bad effects, so long as the bad effects meet certain conditions. The most important conditions are that the bad effects are neither the intended goal of the act nor part of the means for achieving that goal. The bad effects must also not be *so* bad as to disproportionately outweigh the good effects, a condition that is more difficult for Malebranche's theodicy to satisfy.
100 *TNG* 1.19; see also *TNG* 1.18.
101 *Eluc.* 8/LO 589; see also *Dialogues* 9, 164.
102 *TNG* 1.22.
103 Like Leibniz (and unlike Descartes), Malebranche denies that the contents of possible worlds are determined by God's volitions (Malebranche, *Search* 587, and *Dialogues* VII.111). Such is our bad modal luck: there is not a better possible world than ours that could be preserved by at least as perfect means. (For Malebranche's version of possible worlds, which is very similar to Leibniz's, see *Dialogues* 10,191, 199, 208 and *TNG* 1.12.)
104 *Dialogues* 9, 164.
105 *TNG* 1.44.
106 AG 38–39. Leibniz may be talking past Malebranche here, because Malebranche sometimes claims that God's means are perfect partly in virtue of their productivity and fecundity (*TNG* 1.17–18), although he most often emphasizes their simplicity and uniformity.
107 Malebranche too claims that God seeks to achieve "the most beautiful harmony possible" (*Dialogues* 11, 208). Hence, one might again wonder how deep Leibniz's disagreement with Malebranche over the bestness of our world really runs (cf. AG 36–37). If the means of God's actions are included as parts of possible worlds, Malebranche would agree that the actual world is the best possible world.
108 Virtually every substantive claim that Leibniz makes in his *Theodicy* also appears in writings he left unpublished. In the interests of accessibility, I will cite the *Theodicy* versions of his claims when possible.
109 For a brief overview of Leibniz's reply to some of the aforementioned concerns, see Michael Murray, "Leibniz on the Problem of Evil."
110 For a quick version of his proof that God exists and created the BPW, see Leibniz, *T* §7–9 and §224–228. He claims elsewhere that his view has the support of "a great many passages from Sacred Scripture and the holy fathers" (AG 37).
111 *T* §209.
112 Not that Leibniz shies away from offering such explanations. Indeed, he sometimes embraces the three main aspects of the traditional account: the good of plenitude explains metaphysical evils (*T* §124); the good of retributive justice explains at least some physical evils (*T* §§265–266); and misused creaturely freedom explains moral evil (*T* §273).
113 *T* §10. It is worth keeping in mind that despite Leibniz's bold claim that ours is the BPW, he does not think that we have much insight into what the compensating greater goods actually are that particular evils occasion.
114 *T* §121.
115 *T* §194.
116 *T* §9 and §225.
117 *T* §22, §122, and §222.
118 *T* §9 and CP 107.
119 *T* §120.
120 *Candide* 12.
121 For the last, see AG 115.
122 This is, for example, one way to understand Ivan Karamazov's challenge in Dostoyevsky, *The Brothers Karamazov*, 244. For a late twentieth century version, see Marilyn Adams, *Horrendous Evils and the Goodness of God*.
123 I am grateful to Sean Greenberg and Dan Kaufman for comments on an earlier draft. I wrote this paper for this volume back in 2007. Endless production delays mean that by the time it finally appears in print more than a decade later, it may be somewhat outdated. For an example of exciting new scholarship on this topic that I neglected back then, see Jill GraperHernadez, *Early Modern Women and the Problem of Evil*.

Bibilography

Primary

Aquinas, Thomas. *De Malo*. Translated by Richard Regan. Oxford: Oxford University Press, 2003.

Aristotle. *Physics* in *The Complete Works of Aristotle*, 2 vols., trans. and ed. by Jonathan Barnes (Princeton: Princeton University Press, 1984.

Augustine. 1993. *On Free Choice of the Will*, ed. and trans. Thomas Williams. Indianapolis and Cambridge: Hackett Publishing Company.

———, *On Rebuke and Grace*. In *Theological Anthropology*, trans. and ed. J. Patout Burns (Philadelphia: Fortress Press, 1981.

Bayle, *Historical and Critical Dictionary* [cited as 'Dictionary']. Bayle, Pierre. *Historical Critical Dictionary: Selections*, trans. by Richard H. Popkin (Indianapolis: Hackett Publishing Company, 1991).

———, *Objections to Poiret*. In *Oeuvres Diverses de M. Pierre Bayle*, vol. 4 (The Hague, 1727–1731). Reprinted by Georg Olms, 1968.

Clarke, S. 1998. *A Demonstration of the Being and Attributes of God and Other Writings*. Edited by Ezio Vailati. Cambridge: Cambridge University Press.

Cudworth, Ralph, 1678, The True Intellectual System of the Universe. 3 vols. London.

Dostoevsky, Fyodor. *The Brothers Karamazov*. Trans. By Richard Pevear and Larissa Volokhonsky. Farrar, Straus, and Giroux, 2002.

King, William. *De Origine Mali* (Dublin: Andreas Crook, 1702).

Leibniz, *Samtliche Schriften und Briefe*. Darmstadt and Berlin: Berlin Academy, 1923– present (cited by series. volume/page).

———, *Confessio Philosophi: Papers Concerning the Problem of Evil, 1671–1678*, trans. and ed. by Robert C. Sleigh, Jr. (New Haven: Yale University Press, 2005) [cited as 'CP'].

———, *Philosophical Essays*. Ed. by R. Ariew and D. Garber. Indianapolis: Hackett. [cited as 'AG'].

———, *Theodicy: Essays on the Goodness of God, the Freedom of Man, and the Origin of Evil*. Trans. by E.M. Huggard (La Salle: Open Court, 1990) [cited as 'T'].

Milton, *Paradise Lost*. Ed. by Gordon Teskey. New York: W.W. Norton and Co., 2004.

Plotinus, *Enneads*. Trans. Stephen McKenna (New York: Larson Publications, 1992).

Proclus, *The Nature and Origin of Evil* in *Neoplatonic Philosophy*. Trans. and ed. by John Dillon and Lloyd P. Gerson (Indianapolis: Hackett Publishing Company, 2004).

Spinoza, *The Letters*. Trans. by Samuel Shirley (Indianapolis: Hackett Publishing Company, 1995) [cited as 'Ep'].

Voltaire, *Candide*. Ed. by Robert M. Adams. New York: W.W. Norton and Co., 1992.

Secondary

Adams, Marilyn. *Horrendous Evils and the Goodness of God* (Ithaca: Cornell University Press, 1999).

Freddoso, Alfred. "God's General Concurrence With Secondary Causes: Why Conservation Is Not Enough." *American Catholic Philosophical Quarterly* 67 (1994): 131–156.

Glover, Jonathan. *Humanity: A Moral History of the Twentieth Century* (New Haven: Yale University Press, 2001).

Hernandez, Jill Graper. *EarlyModern Women and the Problem of Evil: Attrocity and Theodicy* (New York: Routledge-Taylor & Francis, 2016).

Lovejoy, Arthur. *The Great Chain of Being* (Cambridge, MA: Harvard University Press, 1934).

Moreau, Denis. *Deux Cartésiens* (Paris: J. Vrin, 1999).

Murray, Michael. "Leibniz on the Problem of Evil." *The Stanford Encyclopedia of Philosophy* (Spring 2011 Edition), ed. Edward N. Zalta. http://plato.stanford.edu/archives/spr2011/entries/leibniz-evil/.

———. *Nature Red in Tooth and Claw* (Oxford: Oxford University Press, 2008).

Newlands, Samuel. "Evils, Privations, and the Early Moderns." In *Evil*, eds. Scott MacDonald and Andrew Chignell (Oxford: Oxford University Press, forthcoming).

———. "Leibniz on Privations, Limitations, and the Metaphysics of Evil." *Journal of the History of Philosophy* 52 (2014): 281–308.

Plantinga, Alvin and Tooley, Michael. *Knowledge of God* (Oxford: Wiley-Blackwell, 2008)

Quinn, Philip L. "Disputing the Augustinian Legacy." In *The Augustinian Tradition*, ed. Gareth B. Matthews (Berkeley: University of California Press, 1998): 233–250.

Rutherford, Don. "Malebranche's Theodicy." In *The Cambridge Companion to Malebranche*, ed. Steven Nadler (Cambridge: Cambridge University Press, 2000): 165–189.

20
THE RISE OF RELIGIOUS SKEPTICISM

Michael W. Hickson and Thomas M. Lennon

1. Introduction

In James Joyce's *A Portrait of the Artist as a Young Man*, Stephen Dedalus expresses his rejection of religion with these words: "I will not serve." In so doing, he intentionally echoes the "*Non serviam*" of Lucifer which marked the fall of a third of the angels from God's sight. If we attempt to understand Stephen's, or Lucifer's, rejection of God, the search for the underlying reason might be endless, for in all likelihood, something other than reason is ultimately behind it. Cranly presses his friend Stephen: "Many persons have doubts, even religious persons, yet they overcome them or put them aside. Are your doubts . . . too strong?" Stephen responds, "I do not wish to overcome them."[1] Stephen's rejection is not based on reasons, but pure choice.

If every case of the rejection of religion is like Stephen's, then there is no hope of understanding the striking rise of atheism in the early modern period, because there is little to be understood, just documented. And to a certain degree, Stephen's case is paradigmatic. Religions neither gain nor lose the majority of their partisans by means of syllogisms. Yet, if there never had been an argument attacking the foundational claims of some or every religion, then it is hard to believe that any intelligent person would ever be attracted to atheism. On the other hand, if reasons began piling up suggesting that there is no God, or that the soul dies with the body, then one would expect to find an increase in boldness in those people who were aware of these arguments, perhaps even leading to a chorus of *non serviam*. Such a chorus can be found in the eighteenth century *philosophes*. Although there can be no enumeration of philosophical developments in the seventeenth century which is sufficient for explaining this rise of atheism, in the following pages we lay out several key developments which were instrumental for the rise of atheism.

The seventeenth century is the natural focus of historians of atheism because, in the century prior, a rational foundation for atheism was generally considered oxymoronic, whereas at the beginning of the eighteenth century, and continually throughout the Enlightenment, philosophical arguments undermining the existence of God, providence, the immortality of the soul, and other foundations of religion circulated, at first clandestinely, and later in the published works of some of Europe's most famous *philosophes*. A radical shift in thinking took place in the seventeenth century, giving rise to skepticism about the foundations of theology.

Formulating an atheistic philosophy was not merely a practical difficulty for thinkers of the sixteenth century, deriving from a temporary lack of metaphysical or scientific arguments, but was, in Lucien Febvre's view, a conceptual impossibility: atheism as a philosophical system, rather than as an immoral, libertine way of life, was literally unthinkable throughout the 1500s and early 1600s.[2] The sixteenth century was far too saturated in religion, far too restricted by the ecclesiastical Latin in which it communicated its ideas, and far too engrossed in the prejudice (supported by Scripture)[3] that only fools and sinners could deny God's existence, for it to conceive of the "speculative atheist" who would begin to cause such a stir in the following century. That said, and seemingly paradoxically, philosophers and theologians of the period devoted much effort toward defeating the specter of the threat of atheism, which they hazily imagined as a constant threat.

At the end of the seventeenth century, however, in the early Enlightenment, not only was the speculative atheist now concretely imaginable but also there were numerous instances of such atheists who were writing books and who had no shortage of ammunition to employ against their theistic counterparts. A study of the clandestine atheistic texts of the early 1700s has led Gianluca Mori to conclude that the earliest overt atheists had found in the previous century a myriad of strongholds for their attacks on religion.[4] No single philosopher or system had inspired all these atheists, no single target was their aim, and no single strategy was eventually adopted by them all. The rise of atheism was therefore not a case of a single Athena born from the head of a single Zeus. Rather, after centuries of philosophical and theological arguments aimed at drowning this indistinct threat, atheists distinctly emerged from the seventeenth century in full force like Pharaoh's army, frenzied and hostile, from the depths of the Red Sea. The question is therefore vital: what came about in the seventeenth century to breathe life and vigor into the previously unthinkable?

In the following we take numerous soundings in seventeenth century philosophy and find potential sources of the atheism of the next century lying at various depths of the works and trends we consider. We begin by considering individual philosophers: Descartes, Berkeley, Hobbes, Spinoza, Leibniz, and Bayle. Later, we consider a variety of themes related to atheism in diverse ways: Socinianism, theological disputes, idolatry, the secularization of ethics, the scientific revolution, skepticism, and biblical criticism. A word of caution is needed at the outset: Pierre Bayle inevitably figures in the story we have to tell, not only as a philosopher whose ideas were thought to give impetus to the later atheist cause, but also as a fellow commentator who documented the rise of atheism around him. His role in the story, therefore, occasionally changes.

2. The father of modern philosophy

The fundamental text for interpreting philosophy both in the seventeenth century and thereafter is Descartes's *Meditations* (1642). Certainly, insofar as philosophy has ever since taken the so-called epistemological turn, the basic problems of philosophy trace to the questions, distinctions, and arguments that Descartes deployed there. There have been many differing views on precisely what led Descartes to write and publish this work, but at least what he himself actually said about his motivation is very clear, and it gives the work a rather different cast from the usual depiction of it. In the dedicatory letter that begins the work, he draws attention to two topics on which he announces what he takes to be demonstrative proofs, the existence of God and the immortality of the soul.

Descartes allows that faith is sufficient to ground the belief of those who already accept the existence of God, but to appeal to faith through Scripture, he says, in order to convince the unbeliever would be circular, because Scripture is reliable only if it records the word of God. Thus, an independent demonstration relying on reason alone is necessary. The existence of God had long been held amenable to such treatment, based on Wisdom 13 and Romans 1, such that all ignorance of God was held to be culpable. The immortality of the soul, on the other hand, had been viewed by some as in a different category, knowable only on the basis of faith, because reason strongly suggests that the soul dies with the body. But at the Fifth Lateran Council (1513), the Church expressly condemned this view, and, as Descartes reports it, "enjoined Christian philosophers to refute [the view] and to establish the truth."[5]

The great irony was that in responding to these needs, Descartes may well have done more for the cause of atheism and materialism than if he had remained silent on the topic. For even among his followers, Descartes's arguments on these topics were not found convincing. Indeed, there were more than a few in his own time, and there are a few now, of the view that Descartes deliberately subverted with bad arguments the very views for which he only feigned support. Such conscious dissimulation is hard to credit, but the irony remains that Descartes's philosophical method, concepts, and overall project greased the skids to the obvious religious skepticism of the next century.

The *Meditations* deploys a very demanding version of the method of doubt first introduced in the *Discourse on the Method* four years earlier. In seeking the certainty that he craves after an education stuffed with too much falsehood, Descartes takes the apparently opposite course of doubting everything that can be doubted, even for the slightest conceivable reason. The premise is that if he finds something that cannot be doubted, then it can be accepted, indeed must be accepted, as certain. What he appears to know on the basis of the senses is easily set aside, ultimately on the basis that he might be dreaming. Even in dreams some things might be true, such as arithmetic and geometry, but they too are impugned by doubt on the basis that the omnipotent God could create him and the world such that even this putative knowledge might be false.

Only in the Second Meditation does Descartes take the next step in his application of doubt when with the *cogito* he finds that he cannot doubt his own existence. Before that, however, he exacerbates the skeptical crisis of the First Meditation by raising and answering an objection to his method in a way that has the effect of calling the existence of God into question. The objection is that constant and constrained deception about such obvious things as mathematics would be inconsistent with God's goodness, and hence doubt of mathematics is unreasonable. The reply is that the fact of any deception at all is no less inconsistent with divine goodness, and yet the fact that we are at least sometimes mistaken is undeniable. And to sustain this skeptical challenge, Descartes goes even further in his doubt:

> Perhaps there may be some who would prefer to deny the existence of so powerful a God than believe that everything is uncertain. Let us not argue with them, but grant them that everything said about God is a fiction.[6]

This concession, even just for methodological purposes, goes further than, for example, Aquinas did, whose preface to his own demonstration of the existence of God asks "whether God exists." But Descartes goes even further, for he finds that, even with the conscious intention to doubt all his former beliefs, some of the longer held of them continue to intrude upon him. To counterbalance their force, he pretends that they are not just dubitable but "utterly false," and to bring himself to this state, he pretends that "not God, who is supremely good and the source of truth, but rather some malicious demon of the utmost power and cunning has employed all his energies in order to deceive [him]."[7] The supposition is not just atheism, but diabolism.

Now, Descartes is prepared to invoke this hyperbolic doubt, as he calls it, because he is confident that beginning in the Third Meditation he can demonstrate the existence of God in a way that makes it more certain even than the *cogito* itself. But suppose that his attempt to do so fails, or is perceived to fail as it was even by his most devoted and gifted followers. Notably, Nicolas Malebranche thought that Descartes's argument needed correction (which he tried to supply, but with no greater success in convincing the philosophical world). Suppose further that Descartes thought that if his attempt failed, no other would succeed. The consequences for theism were immediately drawn by philosophers who were theists themselves. Pierre-Daniel Huet was one who criticized Descartes on this (and almost everything else in his system).

According to Huet, Descartes should consider

> whether he acted with sufficient modesty and prudence when he boasted with obvious pride that he had shown that God exists with arguments more certain than any geometrical theorem proved by the mathematicians, and that he had found the only way to arrive at certain knowledge of so great a thing, which, if sought by others hereafter in some other way, will perforce show them to be impious.[8]

That is, Descartes was so arrogant as to claim that unless he succeeded in proving the existence of God, no one else would, and that this was so obvious that any other attempt to do so would be an offense to religion. Such pride might goeth before the fall, in this case into atheism.

3. Berkeley's testimony

One sophisticated, and appalled, observer of the atheist development was George Berkeley, an ordained Anglican priest and, later, bishop, who tried to interrupt its continuation. Against materialism he argued for idealism, the view that nothing exists apart from the mind's perception, that the world we perceive through the senses exists only in the mind that perceives it. This apparently strange view, which Berkeley took to be actually closer to common sense than its competitors, was advanced as a "new and unanswerable proof of the existence of God" and of His providence. The view is found in his *Principles of Human Knowledge* (1710) and *Three Dialogues Between Hylas and Philonous* (1713), as well as in his first work, the *Essay Towards a New Theory of Vision* (1709), in which he tried to forestall the objection to his idealism that some things exist outside the mind because we perceive them at a distance. The tree on yonder hill cannot exist only in the mind because it is seen to exist out there. The rebuttal is that distance consists of relations between sensations, all of which exist only in the mind. Roughly, the idea is that vision is a language that God uses to communicate with us about what to expect through touch. Visual perceptions, such as an increasing size, are signs designed to advise us about the tactile, which in the form of hard objects might imperil our well-being. This semiotic relation between God and human perceivers is Berkeley's way of recognizing the intimacy expressed in Acts 17:28: "In him we live and move and have our being."

In the event, Berkeley's efforts to establish idealism and thwart religious skepticism failed miserably, and he was led to another attempt with his *Theory of Vision Vindicated* (1733), which is of interest here because of its assessment of what he was trying to refute and the causes of his failure, all of which he traced to the seventeenth century. As Berkeley sees it, there is a deliberate and mendacious progression during the first thirty years of the eighteenth century from the seeming rational defense of Christianity to its elimination in favor of natural religion, or deism, and then to outright atheism. He does not explicitly identify the villains, but Matthew Tindal might well have been one of them. The title of one of his works gives the game away: *Christianity as Old as the Creation*. The implicit message is that anything of truth in revealed religion could have been known by reason prior to any revelation, which is therefore superfluous, so that the putative defense of Christianity as rational is in fact revealed as a snake in its breast. The next step, as Berkeley saw it, was to subvert all religion by an ostensible defense of natural religion against Christianity. Because religion for Berkeley is founded on the recognition of a "watchful, active, intelligent, free Spirit," deism meant the elimination of religion. Deistic defenders of religion are thus a fifth column, whose motivations are castigated by Berkeley in no uncertain terms.

Of a piece with the perceived slide into atheism was an altered conception of the human soul, its governance, and its fate. The deists denied the existence of an immortal soul with the prospect of reward or punishment in an afterlife based on the performance or failure to perform duty in this life. They substituted taste for duty and denied that there were rewards or punishments for actions beyond those actions' natural consequences. The *bête noire* in this instance is clearly identified as Shaftesbury, in his *Characteristics* (1711).

These historical developments are explicitly found in the early eighteenth century. Their roots, according to Berkeley, span the previous century: "That atheistical principles have taken deeper root and are farther spread than most people are apt to imagine will be plain, he says, to whoever considers that pantheism, materialism, and fatalism are nothing but atheism a little disguised." From whom do these views spring? At this point, Berkeley names names. The spread of atheism will be plain to whoever considers "that the notions of Hobbes, Spinoza, Leibniz, and Bayle are relished and applauded."[9] Certain obvious connections suggest themselves – Spinoza with pantheism, for example; but none of those listed can be obviously connected with all three of the views, and at least one, Bayle, seems unconnected with any of them. Our view is that Berkeley's principal target is, though unmentioned, Descartes. As we see it, it was he whom Berkeley regarded as the main obstacle to be removed by his ground-clearing work, the *New Theory of Vision*. We now turn to a reading of Descartes that extends the obstacle he represents to the domain of religion.

4. Descartes

It is clear from Berkeley's notebooks (later published as *The Philosophical Commentaries*) both that Berkeley read Descartes's work and that he did not like what he found there. But like Newton, the philosophical implications of whose work also displeased Berkeley, Descartes is hardly mentioned by Berkeley. It may be that their undeniable achievements, particularly in the sciences, gave them a status of respect lacking in the case of Locke, who without such achievement is explicitly attacked by Berkeley. In any case, it was Descartes who can be read as both advancing the three views identified by Berkeley and as the source of them to the extent they appear in the four authors he names. His theory of vision, especially its metaphysical infrastructure, is certainly under attack both in the *New Theory of Vision* and the *Vindication*.

That the dualist Descartes should be read as a materialist perhaps seems hardly credible until it is recalled that by the term Berkeley means anyone who asserts not the strong view that everything is material but the weaker view that material substance exists. Descartes certainly falls under that description with his view that extension, space, and matter are all the same thing, a thing that answers to Berkeley's characterization of a material substance as inert, insensible (i.e. unsensing), and independent of mind.

Pantheism is also a view that at first seems hard to attribute to Descartes, who clearly asserts that God creates the world with a freedom of indifference. No Spinozistic deduction here of a world really identical to God. But when in his doctrine of substance Descartes tries to ground the distinction between God and creation, he fails to do so:

> By *substance* we can understand nothing other than a thing which exists in such a way as to depend on no other thing for its existence. And there is only one substance which can be understood to depend on no other thing whatsoever, namely God.[10]

Everything else depends on God not only for its initial existence (creation) but also for its continued existence (concurrence). To draw the distinction between God and creation, Descartes is led to distinguish, as Spinoza does not, between causal and ontological dependence. But even this distinction had been obscured when in the Sixth Meditation Descartes practically asserts verbatim Spinoza's later formula "*Deus sive natura*" (God or nature). There, in the context of a proof of the existence of body, Descartes discusses the teaching of nature. And what is this "nature"? He tells us, "if nature is considered in its general aspect, then I understand by the term nothing other than God himself, or the ordered system of created things established by God."[11]

Finally, fatalism also initially appears inimical to Descartes's system. For it recognizes not just freedom, but a freedom of indifference in both God and man. That is, both God and man are capable of alternative actions apart from any constraint whatsoever. But once again, there are other views that introduce a competing view. In his account of the formation of the world, Descartes claims that the world progresses through every possible state of which it is capable. That is, every possible state is eventually actualized. This claim was viewed, and criticized, as a form of fatalism.

Thus, might Descartes be read as a source of all three of the ills that Berkeley identifies? How accurate a reading is it? We think that although the reading is not wildly implausible, and although there were others beside Berkeley who subscribed to all or part of it, the reading is superficial and ignores many other texts that lead in a very different direction. But our concern is with the historical account of the rise of atheism, not its justification, and so we now turn to the authors that Berkeley explicitly mentions.

5. Hobbes

Hobbes was surely in mind when Berkeley worried about the rise of materialism in the age. One of the earliest thinkers to focus on Hobbes's materialism and its consequences for religion was Henry More. More belonged to the Cambridge Platonists who were known for a preoccupation with theology, a rigid mind-body dualism, a strong belief in the eternal existence of rational and moral principles, and an opposition to the mechanical science. They sought an alternative philosophical response to the downfall of Aristotelianism from the ones on offer from Hobbes and Descartes, who were frequently the targets of their criticism.

In chapter 3 of *The Immortality of the Soul, So Farre Forth as It Is Demonstrable From the Knowledge of Nature and the Light of Reason* (1659), More identifies the primary cause of doubts about the immortality of the soul to be the belief that the notion of "spirit" is nonsense. It is for this reason that he soon goes on to consider the views of Hobbes, whom he called "the Exploder of immaterial substances," for in *Human Nature*, to take just one of many possible examples, Hobbes writes, "to conceive a spirit, is to conceive something that hath dimension. But spirits supernatural commonly signify some substance without dimension; which two words do flatly contradict one another."[12] In Hobbes's view, spirits are extremely subtle bodies which do not work on the senses, a view More found equivalent to the denial of the existence of spirit altogether. Of the attribution of the word "spirit" to God, Hobbes wrote that we do not conceive of what we mean, but rather seek to show a sign of reverence to God by abstracting from "all corporeal grossness." For Hobbes, God is in every way incomprehensible, and so we can ascribe qualities to him only out of ignorance or a sense of reverence, a view which is compatible both with fideism (which seems to be Bayle's interpretation of Hobbes in the *Dictionary* article devoted to him) and with atheism, which was More's worry.

6. Spinoza

Spinoza is a far from unlikely target for Berkeley, for he was the target of just about everyone else in his time. Indeed, with not too much stretching, Spinoza might qualify under all three of Berkeley's specific complaints. He held what Bayle called the "hideous hypothesis" that there is only one substance in the universe and that is God, *Deus sive natura* (God or nature) as he called it. It is hard to find a clearer statement of pantheism in this or any other period. The one substance is the subject of an infinite number of attributes, of which two are known to us, the Cartesian pair of thought and extension. Because for the Cartesians extension and matter are one and the same, this would mean that Spinoza is a materialist – not in the sense that everything is only matter, for the one substance also has the attribute of thought, but in the sense that everything is at least material. In addition, although Spinoza ends by asserting a kind of human freedom in part 5 of his *Ethics*, it is of an entirely intellectual sort, with roots in the no less problematic views of the ancient Stoics. Moreover, earlier in the work, he made clear that the whole of the universe, and *a fortiori* God Himself, was subject to a strict determinism which ruled out the intelligibility of teleological explanations and thereby of any recognizable notion of providence.

7. Leibniz

Leibniz's appearance with Hobbes, Spinoza, and Bayle, is prima facie rather surprising. However unjustly, the latter were widely regarded as philosophically suspect, whereas the irenic, undogmatic diplomat Leibniz seems to be, and seems to have been regarded as, no threat to orthodoxy. It was he, after all, who was chosen to represent the Lutheran side in the effort to find reconciliation with Roman Catholicism, an effort that failed through no fault of his. As for the impending Enlightenment that Berkeley sought to forestall, Leibniz was regarded by it, not as a source of support, but as an antiquated object of ridicule.

Nonetheless, Leibniz's conception of the principle of sufficient reason might have given Berkeley cause for concern. If it's the case, as Leibniz thought, that every change in an individual substance, or monad, occurs as the expression of the concept of that individual, then it might be argued that everything we do is fated to be done just as we do it, and that we have no free will. Leibniz's efforts to distinguish himself from the fatalists might be successful, but his technical attempt to secure the compatibility seems rather less so. Even if the analysis that shows a given state to be part of the individual concept requires an infinite number of steps, the fact is that the state is a part, and our inability to complete the analysis shows only our ignorance of how we are determined, not that we are undetermined. Bayle was one who objected to Leibniz's monadism at the base of his determinism as making relations between humans, and between them and God, mechanical, with no room for genuine dialogue or responsibility.

8. Bayle

After the publication of the first edition of his *Historical and Critical Dictionary* (1697), Pierre Bayle spent the rest of his life replying to a variety of charges lodged on the basis of that work, mainly of Pyrrhonian skepticism and atheism. The *Dictionary* was to become the philosophical best seller of the eighteenth century, inspiring not only the works of the French deistic and atheistic *philosophes*, but also the likes of Hume and Kant. Early readers saw in the *Dictionary* a work of unparalleled erudition, but also the seeds, if not the very fruits, of religious skepticism. The articles mainly cited in this regard are "Manicheans," "Marcionites," and "Paulicians," all of which concern the Manichean sect and their claim that there is not one, single, benevolent God, but two warring first principles of all things – good and evil. Bayle's thesis throughout the *Dictionary* and his later works is that the Manicheans are able to explain the origin of evil better than Christians. His remedy for the inability of Christian theologians to offer an adequate solution to the problem of evil was faith. Because Scripture claims that God is one and that He is good, and because it also claims that He permitted evil in the world, the Manichean hypothesis must be incorrect, though we can know this only through faith in the Bible.

In the last years of his life, Bayle engaged in a lengthy war of words with Jean Le Clerc, which ultimately gave rise to Bayle's last book, *Dialogues of Maxime and Themiste* (posthumous, 1707). Le Clerc argued that Bayle's position on the problem of evil could lead only to the worst kind of Pyrrhonism, and possibly atheism, for it amounted to the claim that we have no rational basis for asserting that God is good, or that He is not a deceiver. Without these facts about God in place, God's very existence is questioned, as is the foundation of all knowledge. In recent years, Gianluca Mori has offered the best case, much like the one offered by Le Clerc, that Bayle's philosophy leads to atheism. Mori's argument is that throughout Bayle's works, particularly in his treatment of the problem of evil, "Christian theology only uselessly amplifies the difficulties of philosophy by condemning it to the most exaggerated irrationalism."[13] In other words, by showing the necessity of the appeal to blind faith in order to uphold the doctrines of Christianity, in Mori's view, Bayle was attempting to show the ridiculousness of those doctrines. Mori's interpretation is essentially the Enlightenment interpretation of Bayle, which has come in for heavy criticism.[14]

From a consideration of some of the major authors whose works were considered by Berkeley and others to be an important source of atheism, we turn now to various themes associated with the rise of atheism in the seventeenth century.

9. Socinianism

Berkeley's ruminations about incipient deism were not entirely a matter of rational reconstruction after the fact. A version of proto-deism had long been recognized under the term "Socinianism." The movement, if that is what it was, began with Fausto Sozzini (1539–1604). Sozzini was something of a religious reformer, who because of his views was chased from one European locale to another. His doctrine amounted to a systemic revision of Christianity based on what he took to be rational principles, beginning with the rejection of original sin, and with it the need for a divine redeemer. Instead, people save themselves through a moral life, without the need of grace. Those who do not save themselves are simply annihilated rather than condemned to eternal punishment, which also was contrary to Sozzini's rational principles.

Although there is a more or less continuous history of Socinianism throughout the seventeenth into the eighteenth century, there is a sense in which it was a movement without adherents. For Socinianism, and its cognates, was a term of abuse. No one of any respectability or standing admitted to being a Socinian. Nonetheless, the systematic significance of the doctrine was repeatedly articulated in what was thought to be a *reductio ad absurdum* of it. A good example, with later implications for religious skepticism, was Sozzini's conception of the deity. Again, on what he took to be rational principles, he addressed the problem of evil by arguing that no benevolent God would create the world knowing the evil that humankind would produce and hence that He did so in ignorance of what in fact came unpredictably from human free will. In short, God was surprised by the events of the Garden of Eden. This elimination of omniscience, in particular of divine foreknowledge, was, to say the least, the unraveling of a conceptual thread whose termination historically was for some the elimination of all divine attributes and outright atheism.

With varying degrees of plausibility, many in the seventeenth century were accused, and accused each other, of Socinianism. Locke is the best-known philosopher who came under such scrutiny, holding as he did views that were either heterodox or suspicious in Socinian terms. In a recently discovered text, Leibniz implicated him as at least a fellow traveler: Locke, said Leibniz, "inclined to the Socinians." In a philosophically very important debate, Edward Stillingfleet, Bishop of Worcester, found Locke's views on substance subversive of key doctrines such as the Trinity, which is to say the divinity of Christ, and the resurrection of the body at the Second Coming. Jonathan Edwards saw that Locke's rejection of original sin had unsettling implications for the doctrine of the redemption. Leibniz had many concerns, principally with Locke's apparent rejection of the natural immortality of the soul. In a text from book 4 of the *Essay*, Locke sought to illustrate how poor our ideas of matter and thinking are by supposing that, for all we know, God might have superadded to matter, "fitly disposed," the power of thinking. But if the mind is material, according to Leibniz, then it is divisible, and the best argument for its immortality, namely its simplicity, is upset. Whether Locke intended all these consequences is doubtful, but implications of his views were made explicit and were embraced in no uncertain terms by the deist John Toland, the title of whose main work gives the gist: *Christianity Not Mysterious* (1696).[15]

10. Kors's thesis

Alan Charles Kors's *Atheism in France* is likely to remain a reference book on the rise of atheism for some time.[16] Kors's thesis is that to explain the rise of atheism is not a matter of explaining how atheistic theses were first conceived and developed, because these had always been around, but rather it is a question of how the atheistic position came to be seen as stronger than the opposing theistic one. Eighteenth century atheists had only to look to the works of orthodox Christian theologians and philosophers of the previous century to find their weapons ready-made. In fact, the atheists hardly needed weapons; Kors's thesis is that the rise of atheism owes its success to "fratricide" among believers.

Kors begins with the paradox alluded to at the outset of this chapter. In the sixteenth century, the atheist was equated with the debaucher, and never with the calm, studious philosopher, yet arguments abounded against the possible objections of clever atheists. Theologians were attacking an "atheism without atheists." Kors argues that the reason for this was the style of Scholastic disputation common at the time, wherein the necessary first step was always to consider the objections of possible opponents to one's thesis. Hence the objections of atheists always preceded proofs of God's existence. In addition, the Thomistic notion of a "preamble to faith" suggested to many in the sixteenth and seventeenth centuries that all discussion of religion and morality had to be prefaced with rational proofs of God's existence, the immortality of the soul, and other such doctrines accessible to reason, upon which revelation was built. The upshot of the combination of these Scholastic traditions was that most orthodox theological works began with a statement and refutation of the views of atheists. In many such works, these atheistic views were developed quite strongly, and in some cases even more strongly than the refutations which followed them.

The fratricidal debate which is central to Kors's argument involves the Cartesians and Thomists of the mid- to late seventeenth century. Both groups were eager to prove God's existence, and both thought the other group's proofs were inadequate. The Cartesians, wary of sense knowledge, doubted that the Thomistic *a posteriori* proofs could ever lead to knowledge of the existence of a perfect being. Only *a priori* reason, which is far more perfect than the senses, could afford such knowledge. On the other hand, Thomists never ceased pointing out fallacies in Descartes's move from the idea of a perfect being to the reality of that being outside the mind. Each side accused the other of ruining the foundations of religion and abetting atheists, and in so doing, the two sides unwittingly laid the foundations of disbelief. Kors's thesis is not the strong view that these debates led participants or onlookers to atheism; rather, it is the mitigated claim that all that the later atheists would need to build up a philosophical refutation of religion could be found in the texts of these debates.

11. Idolatry

The issue of idolatry furnishes another example of how the logic of theistic internecine dispute paved the way to religious skepticism. Halbertal and Margalit have advanced the thesis that the charge of idolatry that was originally deployed by anthropomorphic, "folk" religion against its rivals was later redirected by philosophical religion against it and ultimately against religion itself. The logic was that if there is false worship, there is no guarantee that that there is any true worship. All religion might turn out to be a form of idolatry.[17] Moreover, one result of this philosophical religion was the disambiguation of the rabbinic formula for idolatry, namely "strange worship," which could mean a violation either of proper ritual or of the proper object of that ritual, namely God. Philosophical religion largely ignored ceremony and focused on the proper metaphysical conception of God. The abstract possibility of universal idolatry thus became the possibility of atheism.

Idolatry is, literally, the worship of idols, or, more generally, of false gods. But why would anyone ever engage in such a gravely punishable offense? To do so out of ignorance would not be punishable, as idolatry certainly was, and to do it deliberately would be suicidal, not to say just plain weird. Halbertal and Margalit have shown that the earliest Jewish model for the relation between God and His people was marriage: God as husband, and Israel as His wife.[18] In these terms, idolatry was conceived of as marital infidelity. The attraction of idolatry was twofold: freed of the strictures of her proper spouse, who is repeatedly described in Scripture as a jealous God, Israel was free to indulge in every sort of licentiousness, and, moreover, the act itself of idolatry came to have an erotic charge.[19] Not incidentally, we can here apply this work to a seventeenth century characterization of idolatry that otherwise seems strange. Locke in his *Letter on Toleration*, for example, cites Galatians 5, and takes idolatry to be "a work of the flesh" along with adultery and fornication. For him and for others in the period, the characteristics of the model were applied literally to the modeled well beyond the original metaphor.[20]

In the early modern period, difference between sects was often cast in terms of idolatry; the only reason a rival sect had different religious beliefs, about the Trinity for example, and worshiped with a different ritual, without the Eucharist for example, was that the object of the belief and ritual was different and, presumably, mistaken. That is, a false conception of the divinity leads to false religious belief, inappropriate religious ceremony, and inappropriate behavior generally. This drift is clear in an important text from Descartes. Gassendi had objected that the idea of God is not innate, as Descartes had claimed in the Third Meditation, but instead was constructed piecemeal from ideas derived from the senses, and therefore that it is not true, as Descartes had also claimed, that nothing can be added to or taken away from the idea of God. Descartes replied by deploying a stark version of the traditional theory of reference:

> An idea represents the essence of a thing, and if anything is added or taken away from the essence, then the idea automatically becomes the idea of something else. This is how the ideas of Pandora and of all false Gods are formed by those who do not have a correct conception of the true God.[21]

Descartes stops short of calling Gassendi an idolater, but others later in the seventeenth century, Bayle for example, were not so polite.

Bayle was, perhaps most of all in his various occupations, a defender of his fellow French Protestants' cause against their Catholic persecutors. Both sides were nominally Christian, but differed on two fundamental issues. One was the nature of grace, which determined their competing views on predestination, free will, and other philosophically interesting questions. It had been discussed ad nauseam by the time of Bayle, who instead concentrated on the second issue, the Catholic doctrine according to which Christ is "truly, really, and substantially present" in the Eucharist. Both sides agreed that if the doctrine is true, then Catholics are right to adore the sacrament on the altar, but that if it is false, and the Eucharist is, for example, only a symbol of Christ, then such adoration would be idolatrous, and Bayle explicitly drew this damning inference. Our interest in the debate is less for the arguments for and against the doctrine than for the philosophical issues they raised. For example, if Christ is divine, then he is omnipresent and the sacrament on the altar in any case would have no special status.[22] Such abstract issues went a long way in the direction of deism and eventually of outright atheism as the sensibility of a personal, intimately present God began to evaporate. An omnipresent deity who is never personally present in any particular place is essentially an absent deity and not far from a nonexistent one.

There is another connection between idolatry and atheism brought out in Bayle's writings which helps us understand more deeply the way in which religious infighting in the period led to a rise in atheism. In the *Pensées diverses*, chapter 117, Bayle argues that idolaters, those whose ideas of God and religion are false, are the true atheists. His point is a subtle one, given the reinterpretation of the term "atheist" on offer in that work. For Bayle's purposes, when he argues that atheists can be moral (a claim we will consider in greater detail later), he understands atheists to be those people who deny the existence of God on speculative grounds. He is aware, however, that the majority of his readers mean something entirely different by the word "atheist," namely "moral reprobate." When Bayle argues that idolaters are the "true atheists," he means that idolaters answer more closely to the term atheist as it is commonly used; that is, idolaters are the moral reprobates. There is a surprising reversal here: real atheists turn out not to be atheists at all (as this term is popularly understood), whereas the nominally religious can be, and often are, atheists. The charge is surely being targeted at Catholics, largely on account of their widespread persecution of fellow (Protestant) Christians, but his point is deeper than just this and transcends denominational boundaries.

Idolatry is motivated by what Bayle calls "false zeal," the unmistakable sign of which is that "men follow the morality of the Church very badly, while they fight like lions for the spread of its theory."[23] Idolaters acknowledge a God or gods, but this belief has no effect on their moral lives. Nothing is more scandalous in Bayle's view than intolerant theological disputes arising from the zeal of idolaters:

> When I see churchgoers exact revenge on their enemies, either through defamatory libel or through calumny secretly spread about, I do not hesitate to say that such a gentleman as had crippled a peasant with the blows of a stick offended God less than they would. The black bile and gall that are seen on every page of many books ... presuppose a disposition of the heart more removed from Christian charity than does the violence of a cavalier who beats his landlord and who throws his furniture out the window.[24]

The *Pensées diverses* aims to prove that one's intellectual principles can be independent from one's actions, such that atheists can be moral and religious believers can be immoral. Bayle's thesis is that such a separation between one's religious beliefs and one's actions is the surest cause of atheism in a community and, indeed, ought itself to be considered the true atheism.

12. Morality without salvation

As we have seen, Descartes dedicated his *Meditations* to the faculty of the Sorbonne with the promise of proving God's existence and the immortality of the soul. Equally important to recognize in that prefatory letter is the reason Descartes gives for why he will do this:

> since in this life the rewards offered to vice are often greater than the rewards of virtue, few people would prefer what is right to what is expedient if they did not fear God or have the expectation of an after-life.[25]

Descartes is merely repeating here a commonplace of his time concerning moral motivation: people are by and large incapable of acting morally without the aid of fear and expectation of an afterlife. This view was still widespread well after the seventeenth century (and has no shortage of proponents to this day), but it came in for interesting and systematic criticism for the first time in the decades following Descartes. These criticisms paved the way for the thoroughly secular moral theories of the eighteenth century, either deliberately or accidentally aiding the atheist's cause.

Moral thought in the seventeenth century remained tightly linked to religion in certain respects. On the metaphysical level, God was seen as necessary to ground the validity of moral principles. There was much debate concerning the way in which God grounded these principles, but little debate ensued about whether God's existence was in some way necessary as a foundation for morality. Voluntarists, such as Descartes, held that God creates moral precepts by an indifferent act of His will, whereas intellectualists, such as Malebranche, held that God's will, like ours, is constrained by law, often expressed in terms of God's knowledge of eternal truths; but both agreed that moral principles derived in some way from God. A possible exception to this was Hugo Grotius, who famously wrote of his version of the natural law, that

> what we have been saying would have a certain degree of validity even if we should concede that which cannot be conceded without the utmost wickedness, that there is no God, or that the affairs of men are of no concern to Him.[26]

J. B. Schneewind argues, however, that too much has been made of this comment, and downplays its role in the later history of the secularization of ethics.[27]

Although the existence of God remained a first principle of morality on the metaphysical level throughout the seventeenth century, it did not remain so on the epistemological level. That is, moral thinkers began to see moral action as independent of *belief* in God, whether or not they could imagine a theoretical system of morality independent of God's existence. This is important for our purposes, for as we have seen, atheism was virtually equated with immorality at this time, and one of the principal reasons for this, as Descartes mentions in his letter to the Sorbonne, is that atheists do not fear God or eternal damnation, and so they lack motivation for acting morally. Therefore, to the degree that living morally came to be seen as independent of the hope or fear of God and the afterlife, to that degree the traditional conception of the atheist was challenged. If one can live morally without holy fear, then atheists can live morally; but then what is an atheist if he is no longer necessarily vicious? Hence, the modern atheist's identity was in part shaped through developments in seventeenth century ethics. Three phases in that development will be considered immediately here.

It was commonly held throughout the seventeenth century that few people would be saved, and that the majority of people, including many believers, would remain forever corrupted by sin. The question arose therefore whether the unsaved could live morally, or at least peaceably in society, and if so, how, given their corruption? One positive response to this question invoked a providential theory of human passion. By following one's instinct of self-love, morally good action is not exactly attained, but can be imitated such that nobody can tell the difference. Building upon the moral thought of Blaise Pascal, Pierre Nicole forwarded such a view in his *Moral Essays* (1671), which were read well into the eighteenth century. By following self-interest in the form of servile fear, all the effects of divine charity can be mimicked such that neither we, nor anybody else, can tell what our true motive is. Because we desire and need the respect of others, we are kind to them, show gratitude toward them, practice patience with them, and so on.[28] Self-love can give rise not to true salvific morality which only flows from Christian charity, but to the appearance of virtue, and to all common customs needed for life in human society. Thus, with or without the fear of God, a peaceful society is within reach.

A similar line of thought is found in Bayle's discussion of the possibility of a society of atheists, in his 1682 *Various Thoughts on the Occasion of a Comet*. Bayle argues that atheists can have a sense of moral decency, that they can be motivated to perform good works for the sake of glory and praise, and that their vices are kept in check by human laws as much as those of believers. It follows that atheists possess all that is necessary to function in society. Bayle consequently asks an important question, marking a significant moment in the history of atheism: "Whence comes it, then, . . . that everyone supposes atheists to be the greatest scoundrels in the universe, who kill, rape, and plunder all they can?" His answer indicates the fundamental error he finds in most moral theories hitherto: "It is because one falsely imagines that a man always acts according to his principles, that is, according to what he believes in the matter of religion."[29] That people do not act according to their principles is what Bayle seeks to prove over the course of the rest of the *Various Thoughts*. One argument for this has a religious foundation, namely the fall of Adam, after which human beings were subject to their passions, and not their reason, in all that they do. But the fact of a radical separation between principles and actions is clear enough from myriad empirical examples, which Bayle relishes in providing. On the one hand, there have been virtuous atheists, such as Epicurus, Vanini, and Spinoza, whereas on the other hand, there has never been a shortage of vicious believers, as the crusades and religious persecution, mainly by Catholics, amply demonstrate.

In his *Various Thoughts*, after having challenged the myth of the vicious atheist, Bayle relates a story intended to illustrate why even Christians should desire a separation between morality and the hope or fear of an afterlife. This story points us to what is perhaps the most surprising chapter in the separation of morality and religious belief in the seventeenth century, that dealing with the Quietists. The story, well known at the time, runs thus:

> an ambassador from Saint [King] Louis to the Sultan of Damascus, having asked a woman whom he found in the streets what she had in mind in carrying a flame in one hand and water in the other, learned from this woman that she intended to burn paradise with the fire and extinguish the flames of hell with the water so that men would no longer serve the divinity for mercenary reasons.[30]

The story, which was first related in a life of Saint Louis, was frequently depicted by artists, and was meant to represent the ideal of living morally not for the sake of reward or out of fear of punishment, but from a pure motive of doing good for good's sake. The image of this woman aptly became the emblem of the Quietist cause.[31]

Quietism was given its impetus by Miguel de Molinos's *Spiritual Guide* (1675), a work on the topic of prayer that sought to free people from the restrictive Jesuit methods of meditation. It taught the prayer of quiet contemplation instead, which involved an abandonment of all intellectual acts, all imagination, even every act of the will, replacing these with an "obscure faith" and a "pure love." The importance of the *Spiritual Guide* cannot be exaggerated: it was written originally in Spanish, but within five years, it was already in its sixth edition in Italian (Molinos lived and taught in Rome) and was being translated into Latin, French, Dutch, English, and German. The spread of the work was halted after Molinos's 1687 condemnation by the Inquisition, which found sixty-eight heresies in the work. Among them, "the soul should neither reflect upon itself nor upon God: in the prayer of quiet all reflection is hurtful, even reflection upon one's own actions and sins"; "he who gives his free will to God is not concerned about heaven or hell, or about perfection, or about virtue, or about sanctity: he must do away with all hope of salvation too"; and "he who loves God by means of rational argumentation or intellectual understanding does not truly love God."[32]

Though Molinos's work was allegedly intended as an aid to Christian piety, it eliminated any role in the moral life for explicit thoughts about God, and especially for hope and fear of an afterlife. Molinos believed that virtue should not be practiced out of fear of hell or from the prospect of a reward, nor for any other explicitly religious motive; rather, it should be the quiet inspiration of the Holy Spirit that comes only to those who have no distinct religious thoughts in their mind. The sincerity of Molinos's religious beliefs has been questioned up to our own day for obvious reasons. In any case, his ideas ultimately led to one of the greatest theological battles of all time, between Jacques Bossuet and François Fénelon, both French bishops. The latter developed Molinos's insight that thoughts of the afterlife should be eradicated from the mind in order to live a truly moral life. Bossuet in turn argued that this destroyed the Christian virtue of hope. Bossuet ultimately won the debate, earning a condemnation of Fénelon's ideas by Pope Innocent XI in 1699. However, the damage was already done: the necessity of the afterlife as a motivation for acting morally was now seriously in question, and mainly because of the writings of Catholic theologians. Like many other theological debates, the Quietist controversy did not itself lead directly to atheism, but it inadvertently provided atheists with arguments with which to pursue their cause; in this case, it provided arguments that morality could and should be independent of the expectation of an afterlife.

13. The new science

It is tempting today to look at the scientific revolutions of the seventeenth century as the cause of the rise of atheism in the period. Most outspoken atheists today tend either to be scientists or to make their case on the basis of science. Indeed, the "new science" of the seventeenth century, especially due to its tendencies toward mechanism and materialism, which challenged any role for the soul in animal activity, was feared for its potential consequences for religion, especially for the doctrine of the immateriality and immortality of the human soul. However, the target of the new science was not religion, but the Aristotelian worldview. Some could not tell the difference, because much of theology, at least for Catholics, was based on the writings of Thomas Aquinas, which were in turn based on the philosophy of Aristotle; so, any threat to Aristotle was a threat to sound theology. But many scientists could tell the difference and found their scientific views compatible with a simpler, less dogmatic Christianity than the one Aquinas had offered. Rather than fitting their science and theology into a single, coherent, all-encompassing system, they viewed science and religion as "two Books," each with its own doctrines and methods, and a minimal amount of overlap. Such was the view of Robert Boyle.

Boyle, perhaps more than any other seventeenth century figure, worried about the effects of the new science upon religious beliefs. It is instructive to note that his main concern was not so much the threat of scientific discoveries for the perceived truth of religion, but rather the "scientific attitude" which the large number of such discoveries brought about. In his *Excellency of Theology* (1674), Boyle addresses scientists in an attempt to show them why theology is still worthy of study and, indeed, why it is immensely greater in value than experimental science. He denounces system building in science, having spent his own illustrious scientific career content with making numerous individual, concrete discoveries, such as the law of gases which bears his name. Without a totalizing system, science cannot be a threat to religion. He also denounces the unjustified pride he finds rampant among natural scientists, as well as their endless quest for worldly fame through novel discoveries. In the *Excellency and Grounds of the Mechanical Hypothesis* (1674), Boyle addresses the compatibility of scientific and religious claims, which he sums up as follows:

> the universe being once framed by God, and the laws of motion being settled and all upheld by his incessant concourse and general providence, the phenomena of the world thus constituted are physically produced by the mechanical affections of the parts of matter, and how they operate upon one another according to mechanical laws.[33]

Boyle left a large endowment to the Royal Society for a lecture series (which is ongoing to this day) devoted to the compatibility of science and religion.

14. Skepticism and biblical criticism

Kors's *Atheism in France* has been criticized in the literature for not giving enough of a role to the rediscovery of ancient skepticism in the sixteenth and seventeenth centuries in the rise of atheism in the period. The story of the rise of Pyrrhonian skepticism in modern Europe, and its relation to the religious thought of the age, has been most fully related by Richard Popkin in *The History of Scepticism: From Savonarola to Bayle*.[34] Popkin's thesis is that theological disputes in the time of the Reformation and Counter-Reformation centered on a religious variation of an issue at the heart of skepticism, namely the criterion of truth. Protestants objected to the Roman Catholic tradition of authority, especially that of the Pope, as the criterion of a proper reading of Scripture, and offered in its stead the "way of examination," which involved an individual reading of Scripture guided by conscience and the inspiration of the Holy Spirit. Catholics argued that the way of examination, considered as a criterion of what one ought to believe about Scripture, was utterly unreliable and could only lead to as many interpretations of Scripture as there were readers of it. Just as this debate was raging over the criterion of faith, the skeptical works of Sextus Empiricus were slowly being rediscovered and translated into modern languages, providing both sides of this theological debate with sophisticated machinery to debunk their opponent's arguments about the proper criterion.

In Popkin's view, these disputes were accompanied by a rise in fideism, the view that faith, unaided by human reason, is the sole means of arriving at religious truth. The skeptical arguments against any and every rationally grounded criterion of faith were found devastating, and so advocating a blind faith was, for most, the surest escape from the Pyrrhonians' sting. One of the virtues of Popkin's book is that it challenged the long-held belief that skepticism and atheism were interchangeable terms. In Popkin's view, both fideism and atheism are arbitrary choices, complete *non sequiturs*, once skepticism is accepted: "Complete scepticism is a two-way street, from which one can exit either into the 'reasonableness' of the Enlightenment or the blind faith of the fideist. In either case, the sceptical argument would be the same."[35] It appears that many in the seventeenth century took the fideist road, whereas the eighteenth century opted for the atheist one. An important element in this shift surely owes something to the application of skeptical arguments to a critical reading of the Bible in the mid- to late seventeenth century.

The "unholy trinity" (as Popkin calls them) of early Bible criticism consisted of Thomas Hobbes, Isaac La Peyrère, and Spinoza. Hobbes is usually credited in this regard with being the first to deny outright the authorship of the entire Pentateuch by Moses. The relevant text is *Leviathan*, part 3, chapter 33, "Of the Number, Antiquity, Scope, Authority, and Interpreters of the Books of the Holy Scripture," wherein Hobbes provides several concrete texts which Moses could not possibly have written. Foremost among them is Deuteronomy 34: 6, which states that nobody is aware of the location of Moses's sepulcher at the time the text is being written. Hobbes notes the obvious, which is that Moses could not have lived to speak of his own burial place in this way, and then makes the less obvious, though no less compelling point, that a prophecy concerning the lost location of his own tomb would be a strange prophecy indeed for Moses to make. Denying the Mosaic authorship of the Pentateuch was tantamount at the time to denying the divine inspiration of the text and opened the door to a new degree of religious skepticism.

Isaac La Peyrère (1596–1676) was infamous for his book, the *Prae-Adamite*, which called into question the historical accuracy of several anthropological claims of the Bible, especially that Adam was the first man, and then that all the people on earth descended from Noah and the other survivors of the great flood. The notorious "pre-Adamites" were postulated by La Peyrère mainly on account of then-recent contact made with other, non-European cultures, especially the Mexicans and Chinese, who had strong evidence to support their claim that they descended from a race of people dating further back than biblical times. La Peyrère's ideas were widely opposed by philosophers and theologians of many stripes, and he eventually abjured before Pope Alexander VII in 1657. By then, however, his ideas were well known and had been read by many, including Spinoza.

As we have seen, Cartesian philosophy had been feared as a system necessarily leading to atheism, and in Spinoza's use of that system, many believed they had their proof. In the *Tractatus Theologico-Politicus*, the Cartesian method of doubt is applied to Scripture, with a consequent elimination of most of it: "I hold that the method of interpreting Scripture is no different from the method of interpreting Nature, and is in fact in complete accord with it."[36] Spinoza argues that prophecy is based on imagination and not reason, and that what the biblical prophets set down contains no cognitive content beyond what is attainable by the natural light. Moreover, God did not force the minds of the prophets in order that they would grasp His truth perfectly, but adapted His revelation to their various prejudices and ignorance. Hence the many factual errors in the Bible, which Spinoza, following La Peyrère, points out. The holy book therefore becomes a human work like any other. It gets worse, however, for Spinoza argues at length that the text we possess is very unlikely to be the text as it was revealed to the prophets on account of the accumulated errors of copyists, and more importantly, on account of the evolution of Hebrew and Greek orthography. Whether or not Spinoza was an atheist has always been a charged question, but the potential usefulness of the *Tractatus* for the atheist cause cannot be disputed.

15. Conclusion

Our conclusion is largely a negative one, namely that the emergence of atheism in the early modern period was not dictated as the result of rational argument. This is not to say, however, that philosophical argument had no role to play. On the contrary, we have seen that philosophical arguments, concepts, distinctions, and so forth were repeatedly seized upon as vehicles, even pretexts, for heterodox views of every sort that were arrived at independently. Our citation of the case of Stephen Dedalus at the outset reflects the view of the seventeenth century Pyrrhonians that both theism and atheism are rationally unconstrained choices, not unlike Kierkegaard's leap of faith. Why choose, then, one way or the other? Believers of one sort would appeal to grace, others of another sort to circumstance, or as Berkeley disparagingly put it, to taste.

The struggle between faith and reason is intelligible only within a totalizing worldview such as the Scholastic Aristotelianism that was overthrown in the seventeenth century. The struggle continued only to the extent that there has been a replacement for it, but every subsequent rival has failed – the Enlightenment itself, Marxism, scientism, and so on. Another upshot of our study is that the apparent opposition between faith and reason has been overcome, not in favor of one over the other, but as a noncontest between separate realms, the character of which is beyond the scope of this chapter, but which has already been alluded to previously in the treatment of Boyle, who articulated such a view. But if this drift is at all plausible, then it should be no surprise to still find both theists and atheists on the contemporary scene, and, because the history of the opposition is so poorly appreciated, a debate, sometimes no less bitter than in previous times, between them.

Notes

1. James Joyce, *A Portrait of the Artist as a Young Man* (London/New York: Penguin Books, 1992), 260.
2. Lucien Febvre, *The Problem of Unbelief in the Sixteenth Century: The Religion of Rabelais*, trans. B. Gottlieb (Cambridge, MA: Harvard University Press, 1982).
3. "The fool hath said in his heart, 'there is no God' "; Psalm 14: 1.
4. Gianluca Mori and Alain Mothu (eds.), *Philosophes sans Dieu: Textes athées clandestins du XVIIIè siècle* (Paris: Honoré Champion, 2005).
5. AT VII 1–3; CSM II 3–4.
6. AT VII 21; CSM II 14.
7. AT VII 23; CSM II 15.
8. Pierre-Daniel Huet, *Against Cartesian Philosophy*, trans. Thomas M. Lennon (Amherst, NY: Humanity Books, 2003), 172.

9 George Berkeley, *Theory of Vision Vindicated*, sec. 6.
10 AT VIIIA 25; CSM I 210.
11 AT X 438; CSM I 56.
12 Thomas Hobbes, *Human Nature and De Corpore Politico*. Oxford World's Classics. Edited by J.C.A. Gaskin (Oxford: Oxford University Press, 1994), ch. 11, art. 4, 65.
13 Gianluca Mori, *Bayle Philosophe* (Paris: Honoré Champion, 1999), 309.
14 For a critique of the kind of argument on which Mori bases his case, see Michael W. Hickson and Thomas M. Lennon, "The Real Significance of Bayle's Authorship of the *Avis*," *British Journal for the History of Philosophy* 17:1 (January 2009), 191–206.
15 For the best account of the question of Socinianism in Locke's work, including discussion and references for the aforementioned, see Nicholas Jolley, *Locke and Leibniz: A Study of the New Essays on Human Understanding* (Oxford: Clarendon Press, 1984), ch. 2.
16 Alan Charles Kors, *Atheism in France, 1650–1729: The Orthodox Sources of Disbelief* (Princeton, NJ: Princeton University Press, 1990). This is supposed to be volume one of two, but the second volume has yet to appear.
17 Moshe Halbertal and Avishai Margalit, *Idolatry* (Cambridge, MA: Harvard University Press, 1992), 2–3. The principal target of philosophical religion is the reliance of folk religion on imagination and tradition. This critique is already underway with Maimonides, according to them, and is sustained later by Descartes and Kant; pp. 112–14.
18 Halbertal and Margalit, ch. 1.
19 Halbertal and Margalit, p. 24.
20 Locke, John, *Epistola de tolerantia: A Letter on Toleration*, ed. R. Klibansky, trans. J. Gough (Oxford: Oxford University Press, 1968), 116–19. The Calvinist Pierre Jurieu took cupidity to be the source of the Socinians' false conception of God, and traced Catholics' idolatrous practices to "culpable unregulated passion"; pp. 231–33. *Des droits des deux souverains en matière de religion*. . . . (Rotterdam, 1687).
21 AT VII 371; CSM II 256.
22 For an instance of such anti-Catholic reason, see David-Augustin Brueys (1640–1723), *Réponse au livre de Mr. de Condom* (Geneva: chez Jean Pictet, 1681), 193–4.
23 *Continuation des pensées diverses*, cxx, in Pierre Bayle, *Oeuvres diverses* (OD) III (Hildesheim: G. Olms, 1964–1982), 215a.
24 Pierre Bayle, *Various Thoughts on the Occasion of a Comet*, trans. Robert C. Bartlett (Albany: State University of New York Press, 2000), 208–9; *Pensées diverses*, 170 (OD III, 108a).
25 AT VII 2; CSM II 3.
26 *On the Law of War and Peace* (1625), prologomena, quoted from J. B. Schneewind, *The Invention of Autonomy: A History of Modern Moral Philosophy* (New York: Cambridge University Press, 1998), 67–8.
27 Schneewind, *ibid*.
28 See *ibid*., 275–9.
29 *Various Thoughts*, 220; *Pensées diverses sur la comète*, sec. 177 (OD III, 113b).
30 *Various Thoughts*, 221; *Pensées diverses*, sec. 178 (OD III, 114b).
31 Jacques Le Brun, *Le pur amour de Platon à Lacan* (Paris: Editions du Seuil, 2002), 107–16.
32 Molinos's condemnation is given in Pope Innocent XI's bull, *Caelestis Pastor*, of 3 September 1687, which can be found (in Latin) in appendix D of Paul Dudon, *Le Quiétiste Espagnol Michel Molinos (1628–1696)* (Paris: Gabriel Beauchesne, 1921), 292–9.
33 Robert Boyle, *Works* 8: 108, quoted from *The Excellencies of Robert Boyle*, edited by J. J. MacIntosh (Peterborough: Broadview Press, 2008), 57.
34 Richard H. Popkin, *The History of Scepticism: From Savonarola to Bayle* (Oxford/New York: Oxford University Press, 2003).
35 *Ibid*., 86.
36 Benedict de Spinoza, *Tractatus Theologico-Politicus*, trans. Samuel Shirley (Leiden: E. J. Brill, 1989), ch. 7, 141.

Bibliography

Febvre, Lucien. *The Problem of Unbelief in the Sixteenth Century: The Religion of Rabelais*, trans. B. Gottlieb (Cambridge, MA: Harvard University Press, 1982).

Halbertal, Moshe, and Avishai Margalit. *Idolatry* (Cambridge, MA: Harvard University Press, 1992).

Hazard, Paul. *The European Mind: 1680–1715*, trans. J. Lewis May (Cleveland, OH: World Publishing Co., 1963).

Kors, Alan Charles. *Atheism in France, 1650–1729: The Orthodox Sources of Disbelief* (Princeton, NJ: Princeton University Press, 1990).

Popkin, Richard H. *The History of Scepticism: From Savonarola to Bayle* (Oxford/New York: Oxford University Press, 2003).

Schneewind, J. B. *The Invention of Autonomy: A History of Modern Moral Philosophy* (New York: Cambridge University Press, 1998).

INDEX OF NAMES

Álvarez, Diego 18
Aquinas, Thomas 4, 5, 6; commentaries on 4; on existence of God 513, 515; moral philosophy 449–51, 464; on passions 335, 355; on religious skepticism 577–8; on substance 36; theory of matter 413, 416
Aristotle 3–5, 7, 13; on logic and knowledge 224; moral philosophy 449; natural philosophy 387; parameters for subsequent discussions of substance 35; on passions 356–7, 359–61, 371; on qualities 62–5, 67, 70, 74; on skepticism 150, 152, 164; on substance 36, 51; theory of matter 411, 412, 416, 424, 427–8, 440
Arnauld, Antoine: on consciousness 319, 323, 330; links to Baroque Scholasticism 17; on passions 356, 360, 361, 368; on skepticism 167, 179–82, 195; on substance 46; on theories of ideas 200, 205, 206, 208, 210; on theories on sense perception 304
Ashworth, Jennifer 16, 19
Astell, Mary 481, 528–9
Augustine 145, 151, 160, 166, 200, 255, 337, 449
Aureol, Peter 12
Austin, J. L. 366
Averroes (ibn Rushd) 5
Avicenna 4, 416

Bacon, Francis 15, 169, 186, 424
Barnes, Jonathan 154, 176
Bayle, Pierre: on evil 536–7, 539, 540, 551–3; on religious skepticism 564, 567, 569, 570–1, 573–4, 576; on skepticism 179–82, 184, 186
Beck, L. J. 243
Beeckman, Isaac 387, 417
Bentley, Richard 436
Berkeley, George: on existence of God 519–21; on passions 366, 374, 375; on qualities 81; on religious skepticism 564, 566–7, 568, 570, 571; on substance 47–8; on theories of ideas 218
Bernier, François 425
Blyenbergh, William 549, 550
Bodin, Jean 480, 488
Boehme, Jacob 358
Bononia, Joannes à 16
Boscovic, Roger 437
Bossuet, Jacques-Bénigne 482, 577
Bourdin, Jean 167–8, 170

Boyle, Robert: natural philosophy 385, 401; on qualities 69, 73, 74, 78; on religious skepticism 578; on substance 38; theory of matter 414, 427, 429–32, 434, 437
Bramhall, John 117–21, 123, 124, 127, 131, 136, 457
Brown, Stuart 19
Bruno, Giordano 424
Brunschvicg, Léon 151
Burge, Tyler 310
Burgersdijk, Franco 15, 16
Burman, Frans 313
Burnet, Thomas 402, 403
Burnyeat, Myles 154, 173–4, 176

Cajetan 5, 7
Calvin, John 449
Campanella, Tommaso 157, 158–62
Caramuel y Lobkowitz, Juan 18
Carneades 165
Carriero, John 208, 345–6
Cassirer, Ernst 161
Cavendish, Margaret 256, 261–2, 265–6, 271, 274, 276, 277
Chalmers, David 310
Charles I, King 479–80
Charles II, King 482
Charleton, Walter 66, 70, 72, 76, 425–6, 431, 432, 433
Charron, Pierre 154–8, 168, 169, 171, 172
Chisholm, Roderick 120
Cicero 159, 165, 168, 449
Clarke, Samuel 437, 438, 529–30, 538, 550–1
Clauberg, Johann 16, 19
Claves, Etienne de 164
Clemenson, David 5, 6
Coke, Edward 480
Combach, Johann 15, 16
Conche, Marcel 146
Conway, Anne 256
Cordemoy, Geraud de 423–4, 438
Couto, Sebastião do 14
Cromwell, Oliver 476
Cudworth, Ralph 255–6, 273–6, 277, 323–5, 523–5, 546–7
Cumberland, Richard 449, 470–1

Dedalus, Stephen 580
de Gruit, Huig 16

INDEX OF NAMES

De Kater, Jan 11–12
de la Ramée, Pierre 164
Des Bosses, Bartholomew 18, 48, 113, 136
Descartes, René 5, 9, 11–12, 19; on causation 87, 88, 90–9, 101, 108; on consciousness 311–14, 315, 319, 323; on evil 540–7, 549–51; on existence of God 505–8, 510, 512–14, 516, 523; on freedom and determinism 124–7, 135, 139; links to Baroque Scholasticism 13–15; on logic and knowledge 224–41; on mind-body problems 257, 258–61, 266, 271, 272–3, 277; moral philosophy 449–51, 465, 467–70, 473; natural philosophy 385–91, 392–4, 397–401, 410; on passions 334–5, 337–45, 348, 356, 357–8, 369, 370, 372–3; on qualities 66–72, 74, 76–7; on religious skepticism 564–9, 573, 574–5; on skepticism 148–52, 154, 157, 158, 161–2, 166–73, 175–9, 182, 185; on substance 35, 36, 38–43, 45, 46, 49; on theories of ideas 195–214; on theories on sense perception 289, 290, 292, 293, 295–7, 299, 300, 303–4, 306, 307; theory of matter 413–14, 417–21, 423, 424, 425, 429, 431, 432, 437
Des Chene, Dennis 19
de Vries, Simon 42
Digby, Kenelm 72–3, 74, 75, 262–4, 271, 277, 415
Di Liscia, D. A. 19
Doyle, J. P. 19

Easton, P. 244
Edwards, Jonathan 571
Elisabeth, Princess 88, 90–1, 96, 337, 349, 468, 469
Epicurus 64, 65, 67, 72, 576
Esparza y Artieda, Martin de 18
Estienne, Henri 145, 146, 148, 166

Febvre, Lucien 564
Fénelon, François 577
Ferrater Mora, J. 19
Fesaye, Philibert 17
Feynman, Richard 359
Filmer, Robert 479–82
Fonseca, Pedro da 5, 6–7, 8, 9–11, 18
Foucher, Simon 181
Frege, Gottlob 355, 366
Friedman, R. 19
Froidmont, Libert 18

Galen 166
Galilei, Galileo: on causation 87; natural philosophy 385, 386, 387, 389, 392, 393, 400, 401, 402; on passions 356; on qualities 69, 72, 75, 77–8, 78–9, 81; on skepticism 163; theory of matter 415, 419
Garber, Daniel 388
Gassendi, Pierre 13; on consciousness 311, 313; on existence of God 521–2; links to Baroque Scholasticism 17; on mind-body problems 266; on qualities 70, 72, 74, 76; on religious skepticism 573; on skepticism 161, 163–6, 169, 174, 175, 182, 183, 184; on substance 36, 49; on theories on sense perception 289, 290, 292–5, 299, 300, 301, 303–4, 307; on theories on sense perception 303; theory of matter 410, 414, 424–7, 429, 431, 432, 438
Gaukroger, S. 243
Geach, Peter 371
Geulincx, Arnold 104
Giacon, C. 19
Gilbert, William 237
Gilson, E. 15, 151
Glanvill, Joseph 186
Góis, Manuel de 4, 5, 14
Gracia, J. J. E. 19
Grice, H. P. 362
Grotius, Hugo: moral philosophy 465–7, 469; political philosophy 477, 483, 484–8, 490, 492, 495, 498; on skepticism 159

Hacking, Ian 365, 375
Harbertal, Moshe 572, 573
Hariot, Thomas 424
Heereboord, Adrian 16
Helmont, van 430–1
Heraclitus 159
Hervet, Gentian 145, 166
Hitler, Adolf 556
Hobbes, Thomas: on evil 537, 548, 551; on freedom and determinism 118, 120, 121–4, 125, 128, 130, 131, 132, 136; links to Baroque Scholasticism 15; on logic and knowledge 229, 242–3, 243–4; on mind-body problems 265; moral philosophy 449, 451–8, 459–60, 465, 466, 467, 470–1, 472, 473; on passions 334, 335, 337–44, 345, 348–50, 354, 355, 357, 360–2, 364, 365, 366, 369–74; political philosophy 477, 478, 483, 486–91, 497, 498; on qualities 67–8, 70, 72, 74–8; on religious skepticism 564, 567–9; on theories of ideas 209; on theories on sense perception 289, 290–2, 300, 303, 307; theory of matter 414, 415, 431
Hoffman, Paul 14
Holden, Thomas 414–15, 422
Huet, Pierre-Daniel 566
Hume, David 104, 175, 179, 182, 184, 243, 374
Hunton, Philip 481–2
Huygens, Christiaan 394, 438

Innocent XI, Pope 577
Izquierdo, Sebastián 18

James I, King 478–9
Jaquelot, Isaac 181
Joyce, James 563
Jurieu, Pierre 182

Kant, Immanuel 400
Keckerman, Bartholomew 16
Kepler, Johannes 391–2

INDEX OF NAMES

Kessler, E. 19
King, Peter 336
Kneale, M. 242, 243, 244
Kneale, W. 242, 243, 244
Kors, Alan Charles 572, 578
Kraye, Jill 19

Laertius, Diogenes 145, 166, 424
La Peyrère, Isaac 579
Le Clerc, Jean 181, 570
Leibniz, Gottfried Wilhelm von 38; on causation 87, 92, 108–14; on consciousness 314, 327–31; on evil 538, 540, 548, 549, 551, 555–7; on existence of God 505, 506, 508, 511, 515–19; on freedom and determinism 129, 136–9; links to Baroque Scholasticism 18–19; on logic and knowledge 242–3, 243–4; on mind-body problems 256, 258, 271, 277; natural philosophy 389, 391–4, 398–400; on passions 357, 358, 368, 369, 370; on religious skepticism 564, 567, 569–70; on substance 36, 45–8; on theories of ideas 198, 201, 204, 209–12; on theories on sense perception 287, 289, 303–6; theory of matter 410, 423, 427, 437–40
Leijenhorst, Cees 15
Le Vayer, François de La Mothe 169–73
Limborch, Philippus van 135–6
Locke, John: on causation 87, 98–102; on consciousness 325–7; on evil 551; on existence of God 505, 508–11, 527; on freedom and determinism 123, 129, 130–6, 139; links to Baroque Scholasticism 15–16; on logic and knowledge 241–2; on mind-body problems 258, 261; moral philosophy 449, 472–4; natural philosophy 391; on passions 355, 356, 359, 362–4, 365, 366, 367–8, 374, 375; political philosophy 477, 481, 482–3, 490, 492–5, 497, 498; on qualities 66–7, 70, 73, 76–81; on religious skepticism 571, 573; on skepticism 182–6; on substance 36, 49–51; on theories of ideas 198–9, 201, 206, 207, 209, 211–12, 214–19; on theories on sense perception 287, 289, 293, 300–3, 303–4, 305, 306, 307; theory of matter 414
Lohr, C. 19
Losonsky, Michael 375
Louis XIV, King 482, 539
Lucretius 64, 65, 67, 70, 72, 74, 433
Luther, Martin 449
Lüthy, C. 19
Lynch, Richard 18

Macedo, Francisco 18
Magirus, Johannes 17
Maimonides 449
Malebranche, Nicolas: on causation 87, 89, 92, 102–7, 108, 113; on consciousness 314; on evil 545, 548, 553–5, 556; on existence of God 513–15; links to Baroque Scholasticism 17; on logic and knowledge 239–41; on mind-body problems 255, 258, 266–70, 271, 273, 275–6, 277; natural philosophy 392; on qualities 68; on religious skepticism 566, 575; on skepticism 179, 180–1; on theories of ideas 200, 203, 205–6, 214; on theories on sense perception 289, 293, 297–300, 303–4, 306, 307
Margalit, Avishai 572, 573
Masham, Damaris Cudworth 527–8
Mates, Benson 148
Mendo, Andrés 18
Menn, S. 19
Mercer, C. 19
Mersenne, Marin 161, 162–3, 164, 197, 198, 208, 417, 419
Metheun, C. 19
Michelangelo 205
Mill, J. S. 366
Milton, John 480, 537, 539, 540
Mirandola, Pico della 145
Molina, Mario 118, 136
Molinos, Miguel de 577
Molyneux, William 134
Montaigne, Michel de 145–51, 152, 154, 156, 157, 158, 171, 172, 174
More, Henry 96–7, 523, 568
Mori, Gianluca 564, 570
Moses 403, 579
Murdoch, J. E. 19

Nagel, T. 310
Naudé, Gabriel 169
Newton, Isaac: on existence of God 525–6; on logic and knowledge 236; natural philosophy 385, 386, 389–92, 393–4, 396–404; on qualities 70, 73; on religious skepticism 567; theory of matter 427, 432–7, 436, 438, 439
Nicole, Pierre 17, 195, 356, 360, 361, 368, 576
Nielsen, L. 19
Norris, John 526–7
Novotny, D. 19
Nuchelmans, G. 19, 244

Obama, Barack 201–2, 203, 207
Oldenbarnevelt, Johan von 477
Osler, M. J. 17
Ovid 119
Owen, D. 243

Padua, Masilius de 482
Parkinson, G. 244
Pascal, Blaise 576
Patin, Guy 169
Patrizi, Francesco 15
Pendzig, P. 17
Pereira, Benito 16, 19
Pérez, Antonio 18
Philopnous, John 5
Pico, Gianfrancesco 146, 164, 169

INDEX OF NAMES

Pintard, René 169
Poinsot, Jean 13
Popkin, Richard 578–9
Pozzo, R. 19
Protagoras 159
Pufendorf, Samuel von 449, 471–2, 473, 477, 482–3, 489–92, 498
Pyrrho 145, 170, 175

Quine, Willard V. O. 355

Reefsen, Jakob 16
Reid, Thomas 120
Richardson, R. C. 90
Risse, W. 19
Rohault, Jacques 70, 72, 74
Rorty, Richard 199
Rubio, Antonio 5, 14, 18
Rutherford, D. 244

Sanches, Francisco 145, 151–4, 157, 159, 164, 174
Sanderson, Robert 15, 16
Scheibler, Christof 15
Schmitt, C. 19
Schmutz, Jacob 19
Schneewind, J. B. 575
Schouls, Peter 243
Schuurman, Paul 16
Scotus, John Duns 4, 17, 22, 36, 336, 413, 449
Sennert, Daniel 428
Sergeant, John 355, 366, 367
Sextus Empiricus 145, 146, 147, 151, 158, 159, 162, 164, 165, 166, 170, 171, 172, 175, 176, 578–9
Shabel, Lisa 388
Smiglecki, Marcin 15, 16
Smith, Samuel 15, 16
Socrates 3, 4–5, 146, 151, 153, 154, 159, 209, 356
Sommervogel, C. 19
Sozzini, Fausto 571
Spinoza, Benedict de: on consciousness 316–23; on evil 537, 550; on existence of God 511–13; on freedom and determinism 127–30, 136; links to Baroque Scholasticism 16–18; on logic and knowledge 239–41; on mind-body problems 271–2, 277; moral philosophy 449, 458–65, 467, 472; moral philosophy 467–8; on passions 335, 337, 344–51, 356, 369, 373; political philosophy 483, 495–8; on religious skepticism 564, 567, 568, 569, 576, 577, 579–80; on substance 35, 36, 41–5, 51; on theories of ideas 201; theory of matter 440
Stillingfleet, Edward 50, 51
Stone, M. F. W. 19
Strawson, Peter 128
Suárez, Francisco 9, 10, 18, 35, 36–9, 41–4, 46, 118, 449, 482

Themistius 5
Thomas, Jakob 18
Toland, John 571
Toledo, Francisco 5, 14
Tournemine, René-Joseph de 48
Trentman, J. A. 19
Trieu, Philippe du 15, 16
Tschirnhaus, Walther von 44–5
Tuck, R. 19

Valla, Paolo 18
van den Enden, Frans 16
Vanini, Lucilio 576
Vázquez, Gabriel 18
Villon, Antoine 164
Vives, Juan Luis 164
Volder, Burchard de 112–13

Wallace, William A. 19
Watkins, J. W. N. 243
Werenberg, Jakob 18
Whichcote, Benjamin 522–3
White, K. 19
White, Thomas 337
Wilkins, John 186
Winkelman, Steven 20
Wittgenstein, Ludwig 355, 366, 367

Yolton, John 16

Zabarella, Giacomo 5–6, 15, 16, 18

INDEX OF SUBJECTS

Abrége de la Philosophie de M. Gassendi 425
Academica 145
accentuated passivity 154
accidents 60–1
active power 334–5
active skepticism 151–8
actuality 6–11, 12
Aditus ad logicam 16
Adversus mathematicos 145, 166, 175
algebra 224
anger 343
Anselm 507
"Antidote to Atheism, An" 523
apatheia 337, 339, 340
Apologie de Raimond Sebond 146, 148, 150
apperception 328–9
appetite 343
Assayer, The 360
Atheism in France 572
atomic theory 432–7
atomism 64–5, 81, 437–40; chemical 427–9; theory of matter and revival of Epicurean 424–7

bare perception 330
Baroque Scholasticism: Bacon, Hobbes, and Locke and 15–16; Descartes' rejection of 13–15; further reading on 19; general metaphysics 6–11; Leibniz and 18–19; matter theory 411–17; philosophy of cognition: conceivability of individuals 3–6; philosophy of cognition: essentialist direct realism and beings of reason 11–13; 17th century philosophers' links to 13–19; Spinoza, Gassendi, Malebranche, and Arnauld and 16–18; theory of matter background 410–11
being as possibility 6–11
beings of reason 11–13
blackness 71
Of Body and Force, Against the Cartesians 437

Capreolus 5
Cartesians: dual substances of mind and bodies 90, 93; hylomorphism 14; interactionism 91; and primary-secondary quality distinction 75–6; radicalization of doubt 171; sense perception and 297–300; standard of modern skepticism 173–7, 178–9; substantial forms 413–14, 437–40; theory of matter 417–24
Categories 35, 45

Caterus 202
causation: Descartes on 92–8; general problem of divine action in nature and 88–90; intersubstantial 90–2; introduction to 87–8; Leibniz on 108–14; Locke on 98–102; Malebranche on 102–7, 255
chemical atomism 427–9
Christianity Not Mysterious 571
Clarendon Code 494
clear and distinct determinism 125–6
color, theory of 62, 63, 71–4, 79
On Coming-to-Be and Passing-Away 416, 424
Commentary on the Law of Prize and Booty 466
common sensibles 62–3
compatibilitism 117, 137, 457; Hobbes on 121–4
conatus 337–40, 342, 344–8
conceivability of individuals 3–6
concurrentism 89, 94
consciousness 310–12; Arnauld on 314–16; Cudworth on 323–5; Descartes on 312–14; law of continuity and 327–8; Leibniz on 327–31; Locke on 325–7; Malebranche 314; phenomenal 310–11; self- 325; Spinoza on 316–22
contempt 343
Contra Academicos 145
Conversations Chrétiennes 104
Conversation With Burman 173
corpuscular philosophy 429–32
Counter-Reformation, the 476
courage 343

De anima 4
debating on the "warrant" of natural beliefs 177–82
de Beauval, Basnage 110
De Chymicorum 428
De corpore 15, 291, 337, 453
De Gravitatione 394, 396–7, 432
De homine 337
De intepretatione 371
De jure belli et pacis 159
De La Sagesse 154–5, 156
deliberation 343–4
Democritus 64, 424, 428, 438
De Rerum Natura 424
desire 342–3
determinism 117; clear and distinct 125–6; doctrine of suspension and 134–5; freedom compatibility

INDEX OF SUBJECTS

with 119, 122–3, 133; Hobbes on 121–4; Locke on 130–6; self-determination 119; Spinoza on 127–30; theological 120; of the will 134; *see also* free will/freedom
Dialogues of Maxime and Themiste 570
Dialogues on Metaphysics and on Religion 102–3, 106, 255
Diogenes the Cynic 170
Discours de la méthode 159, 161, 172
Discourse on Metaphysics 45–8, 137, 439
Discourse on the Method of Rightly Conducting One's Reason and Seeking the Truth in the Sciences 225, 231, 295, 312, 357, 565
Disputations 15
On the Distinction between Body and Soul 423
diversity, greater good of 546–7
divine right of kings 478–83
doctrine of suspension 134–5
doubting 155, 171
dream delusions 178
On the Duty of Man and Citizen 489–90

Elements of Law 291, 337, 342
elicited acts of will 118
emergence of the state 493–5
empiricism and origins of ideas 208–9
enumeration 230
Epicurean atomism 424–7
epistemic directness 206
Erasmus 164, 166
Essay Concerning Human Understanding 49, 130, 132–4, 182, 185, 326, 357, 367, 473
Essays 150
Essay Towards a New Theory of Vision 566
esse-modes 8–12
essences 50–1
essentialist direct realism 11–13
Ethics 41–4, 45, 127, 129, 130, 239, 240, 271, 345, 458; consciousness and 316; moral philosophy and 460–4
Euripides 159
evil 536–8; Descartes' traditional answers on 540–7; greater good of freedom and 544–5; Leibniz on 555–7; Malebranche and physical 553–5; metaphysical 546–7; privation theory and 541–4; seventeenth century criticisms of the traditional answers on 547–51; seventeenth century questions about God and 538–40
Examen vanitatis doctrinae gentium 145; Berkeley on 519–21
Excellency and Grounds of the Mechanical Hypothesis 578
Excellency of Theology Compared With Natural Philosophy 401, 578
existence of God 505–6; Astell on 528–9; Benedict de Spinoza on 511–13; Clarke on 529–30; Cudworth on 523–5; Descartes on 506–8; Gassendi on 521–2; Leibniz on 515–19; Locke on 508–11; Malebranche on 513–15; Masham on 527–8; More on 523; Newton on 525–6; noncanonical figures on 521–30; Norris on 526–7; Whichcote on 522–3
extended logic 231–5; in practice 235–9
extension of power 96–7, 100

fear 343
Fifth Lateran Council 39, 565
finite substances 88–90
fire, air, water, and earth (FAWE) 411–12, 416–17, 427, 428
flavor 62
fortitude 348
free agents 119; Descartes on 124–7
free will/freedom 117; Bramhall on 117–21; Hobbes on 121–4; Leibniz on 136–9; Locke on 130–6; moral law and 451; Spinoza on 127–30; theodicy 551–3; *see also* determinism

Géometrie 387
geometry 224, 240, 387, 391
Giles of Rome 5
Glorious Revolution 476
God: arguments for existence of (*see* existence of God); as author of sin 181–2; causal power of 88–90, 95, 102, 105, 255, 272–3; conserving the world by continuously creating 106; divine providence 125, 257; generality 275–6; intelligent behavior in the natural world and 272–6; intuition of 233; knowledge of 240; law 450; modes of 128; as mover 45; perfection of understanding 43; power over human will 119–20; providential skepticism and 182–6; as self-determining 130; seventeenth century questions about evil and 538–40; skeptics on 168, 170, 172–3, 181–2, 182–6
gravity 62

hard determinists 117
hearing 74
Historical and Critical Dictionary 570
History of Fluidity and Firmness 429
human nature 488
hylomorphism 39
Hypomnemata Physica 428

ideas 49–50, 195, 362, 363; criterion of innateness and 209–12; debate about innate 213–14; of ideas doctrine 316–22; as images 195–200; as immediately perceived 206–8; Locke on origin of 214–16; as objects of immediate perception 200–8; origins of 208–19; as perceptual objects 201–6; *see also* consciousness
identity-entails-act-theory argument 204–5
idolatry 572–4
images, ideas as 195–200
imaginary space 15
Immortality of the Soul 569

INDEX OF SUBJECTS

On the Improvement of First Philosophy and on the Notion of Substance 47
incompatibilism 117
Index Scolastico-Cartésien 15
indignation 343
indirect realism 206
innate ideas, debate about 213–14
innateness 209–12
Institutionum Metaphysicarum libri duo 16
intellect 3–6; passive 3–4
intelligent behavior in the natural world 272–6
intelligibility of thinking matter 257–66
interaction and mind-body union 266–72
interactionism 91
internalism 151–8, 174–5
intersubstantial causation 90–2
intuition of God 233
isostheneia 155

Jesuits: on being as possibility 6–7; on intellect of individuals 6; on philosophy of cognition 4

language 354–5; animal and perfect 357–9; complications and objections among the moderns 364–7; definite descriptions and the limits of thought 373–4; definitions 367–9; importance to the moderns 355–7; propositions 371–3; reasoning and universals 369–71; signs and names 359–64
La sagesse 154
La Vérité 162
La vérité des sciences: Contre les Septiques ou Pyrrhoniens 162–6
law of continuity 327–8
Law of War and Peace, The 466
On the Laws of Nature 470–1
Le Monde 360, 388, 400
Les Passions de l'âme 337
Letter Concerning Toleration, A 494
Leviathan 291, 337, 342, 452–8, 579
libertarianism 117; Bramhall on 117–21; Leibniz' rejection of 136–9; *see also* free will/freedom
libertines 169–73
Of Liberty and Necessity 457
liberty of exercise 118
liberty of specification 118
light: color and 72; porphyry and 79–80; theory of 62–3, 69–71
limits of thought 373–4
Linguistic Turns in Modern Philosophy 375
Lives of the Most Eminent Philosophers 424
local motion 62
logic: Descartes' basic 225–31; Descartes' extended 231–5; Descartes' extended, in practice 235–9; epistemological objections 241–2; formal objections 242–3; introduction to 224–5; metaphysical objections 239–41; notes on secondary sources 243–4
Logic 356, 360, 371

Logica 16
Logicae artis comendium 16
Logique, ou l'art de penser 17
love 342–3

Maductio ad logicam 16
mathematics applied to nature 386–92
matter, theory of: Boyle's corpuscular philosophy 429–32; Cartesian challenge 417–24; chemical atomism and 427–9; Gassendi and revival of Epicurean atomism and 424–7; introduction to 410; Leibniz's critique of Cartesians and atomists 437–40; Newton's atomic theory 432–7; Scholastic 411–17; Scholastic background to early modern philosophy on 410–11
"Meaning and Modern Empiricism" 375
Meditations 11–12, 17, 38, 39, 49, 95–6, 260, 295, 311, 388, 389, 564, 565; skepticism and 151, 167, 172, 174, 176, 178; theory of matter and 419, 425; on understanding of God 450
Meditations on First Philosophy 225
mere perception 329
Metaphysica (Campanella) 158–62
Metaphysical Disputations 36
metaphysical evil 546–7
Metaphysical Foundations of Natural Science 400
Metaphysicla 45
Metaphysicorum libri duo 16
metaphysics 35–6, 388; Baroque Scholasticism and general 6–11; Leibniz on 45–8; Locke on 49–51; objections to Descartes' logic 239–41; sense perception and 292–4; Spinoza on 41–5; Suárez on 36–8
Metaphysics (Aristotle) 35
Meteorology 427
Meteors 420
mind and body 277, 295; consciousness and 316; intelligent behavior in the natural world 272–6; intelligibility of thinking matter 257–66; relative value of 253–7; union and interaction 266–72
modes 8–11; of God 128
Monadology 47, 327, 330
monads 47, 328
monism 316
morality without salvation 574–7
moral law 451
moral philosophy 449; arc of radicalism 465–70; challenge of modernity and 449–51; Cumberland on 470–1; Descartes on 467–70; Hobbes on 451–8; Locke on 472–4; Pufendorf on 471–2; Spinoza on 458–65
moral responsibility 117
motion: *conatus* and 342; local 62; natural 67; rest and 65–9; space, time, and 392–400

names and signs 359–64
natural beliefs, debating on the "warrant" of 177–82

589

INDEX OF SUBJECTS

natural conscience 523
natural law 487
natural motion 67
natural philosophy: applying mathematics to nature 386–92; space, time, and motion 392–400; theology and 400–4; what exactly was 385–6
natural rights as powers 485–6
nature: laws of 393–4; mathematics applied to 386–92; theories of 62
On the Nature and Origin of Emotions 345
On the Nature of Body and the Laws 437
necissitarianism 128
neo-Aristotelianism 289–90
neo-Pyrrhonism 148–51
New Essays Concerning Human Understanding 50, 327, 329, 359, 425
New System of Nature 47, 48, 423, 438, 439
New Theory of Vision 568
Novum Organum 424

objective-esse 11–12
objectivism 11
objectual directness 207
occasionalism 89, 91, 102
odor 62
ontology of power 45
Opera logica 16
Opticks 432, 434, 435
Opus metaphysicum 16
Origin of Forms and Qualities 37–8, 429, 431

pantheism 568
Paradise Lost 537
passions 334–5; Descartes and Hobbes on 339–44; mechanism and *conatus* in Hobbes and Descartes 337–9; to politics 348–51; as powers of the soul 336; taxonomy of 341; traditional backdrop for theories of 335–7; wonder as first of 341
Passions of the Soul 314, 469
passive intellect 3–4
passive power 334–5
passivity, accentuated 154
Pensées diverses 574
perception, ideas as objects of immediate 200–8; *see also* sense perception
petites perceptions 328
phantasms 3, 147, 371
phenomenal consciousness 310–11
phenomenological directness 207–8
phenomenology 177
Philosophia 375
Philosophiae Naturalis Principia Mathematica 87
Philosophical Transactions of the Royal Society 73
philosophy of cognition: conceivability of individuals 3–6; essentialist direct realism and beings of reason 11–13
physical evil 553–5

Physics 5, 14, 427
Physiologiae Peripateticae Libri Sex 17
Physiologia Epicuro-Gassendo-Chareltoniana 425, 426
"Plastic Nature" 324
Plato 158, 159–60, 209, 254, 483
Platonism 158, 254, 323
Plotinus 254
Plutarch 166
political philosophy: birth of modern social contract theory and 483–98; divine right of kings and 478–83; Europe in the seventeenth century and 476–8
politics, passions to 348–51
Portrait of the Artist as a Young Man, A 563
Port-Royalians 17, 242, 361, 363, 365, 369–73
power: active and passive 334–5; extension of 96–7, 100; natural rights at 485–6; ontology of 45
"Of Power" 130
Prae-Adamite 579
prerogative of judging 156
primary-secondary quality distinction 74–8, 98; arguments for 78–81
Principia mathematica philosophiae naturalis 71, 390–1, 395, 398, 401, 432, 436
Principia Philosophiae 394
principle of alternative possibilities (PAP) 118
Principles of Human Knowledge 566
Principles of Mathematical Philosophy 236
Principles of Nature and Grace 327, 331
Principles of Philosophy 14, 38, 39–40, 43, 45, 66, 93, 295, 338, 388, 389, 421; laws of nature in 393–4; on logic 225, 233–4, 235
privation theory and moral evil 541–4; challenge to 548–51
propositions 371–3
providential skepticism 182–6
Pyrrhoniae hypotyposes 145, 175

Quadeam Philosophicae 435
qualities 81; accidental 60; atomism 64–5, 81; color 62, 63, 71–4, 79; light 69–71; motion and rest 65–9; primary-secondary quality distinction 74–81, 98; sound 62, 74; of substances, Aristotle on 62–4
Quatre Dialogues faits à l'imitation des anciens 169

radicalism and moral philosophy 465–70
rationalism and origins of ideas 208–9
realism: essentialist direct 11–13; indirect 206
reason, beings of 11–13
reasoning and universals 369–71
Reformation, the 476
relative spaces 402
relative value of mind and body 253–7
religion 343; divine right of kings and 478–83; natural philosophy and 400–4
religious skepticism: Bayle on 570–1; Berkeley on 566–7; biblical criticism and 578–80; Descartes and 564–6, 567–8; Hobbes on 568–9; idolatry and

INDEX OF SUBJECTS

572–4; introduction to 563–4; Kors on 572; Leibniz on 569–70; morality without salvation and 574–7; new science and 577–8; Socinianism and 571; Spinoza on 569
Renaissance skepticism 157–8
Republic 159–60, 483
resemblance 77
rest and motion 65–9
Rules for the Direction of the Mind 225, 230–1, 232, 235, 240, 241

Sacred Theory of the Earth 402
salvation, morality without 574–7
Sceptical Chymist 429
Scholasticism *see* Baroque Scholasticism
Search After Truth, The 266, 312, 314
self-consciousness 325
self-determination 119, 465; spontaneity as 138
self-interest and morality 454, 462–3
self-perception 325
self-reflexiveness 148–51
sense perception 307; Descartes on 295–7; Gassendi on 292–4; Hobbes on 290–2; introduction to 287–9; Leibniz on 303–6; Locke on 300–3; Malebranche on 297–300; neo-Aristotelianism 289–90
sensible qualities 62–3
signs and names 359–64
simple nature 226–7
simpliciter 11
Six Books of the Commonwealth 480
skepticism: Campanella on reappraisal and overcoming of 158–62; Cartesian standard of modern 173–7; debating on the "warrant" of natural beliefs 177–82; Descartes, La Mothe Le Vayer, and French Libertines on 169–73; Descartes and modern 166–9; epistemology 145–8; impact of Montaigne on modern 145–8; neo-Pyrrhonism, psychology, and self-reflexiveness 148–51; new theory of skeptical subjectivity 151–8; providential 182–6; Pyrrhonian 145–6; rise of religious 563–80; super- 179; theory of science and 162–6
social contract theory 483–98
Socinianism 571
soul(s): and body extension of power 96–7, 100; immortality of 168; as mobile 100; passions occurring in the 340; powers of 336
sound 62, 74
space, time, and motion 392–400
Specimen of Dynamics 439–40
spontaneity 138
subjectivity, skeptical 151–8
substance(s) 81; accidents of 60; Aristotle on qualities of 62–4; atomism 64–5, 81; color 62, 63, 71–4, 79; finite 88–90; Leibniz on 45–8; light 62–3, 69–71; limits of thought on 373–4; Locke on 49–51; motion and rest 65–9; primary-secondary quality distinction 74–81, 98; "quasi-Aristotelian" corporeal 46; sound 62, 74; Spinoza on 41–5; Suárez on 36–8

substantial bond 48
substantial forms (SFs) 413–14, 437–40
substratum 49
Summa Perfectonis 427
superskepticism 179
Sylva sylvarum 15
synaisthesis 325
syncategoremata 373–4
Syntagma Philosophicum 17, 165–6, 425, 521
Synthese 375

tangible qualities of substances 62, 63–4
Telesian gnoseology 161
Telluris theoria sacra 402
Thaetetus 158
theodicy: challenge to free will 551–3; in theory of knowledge 177
Theodicy 18, 136, 137–8, 555
Theological-Political Treatise 463
theology and natural philosophy 400–4
theory of knowledge 177
theory of science and skepticism 162–6
Thirty Years' War 476–7
Thomism: on being as possibility 6; on passions 335–6
"Thought and Language in the Philosophy of the Enlightenment" 375
Three Dialogues Between Hylas and Philonous 520, 566
touch, sense of 63, 80
Tractatus Politicus 495
Tractatus Theologico-Politicus 495–8, 579
Treatise Concerning the Principles of Human Knowledge 519
Treatise of the Principles of Human Knowledge 47–8
Treatise on Nature and Grace 314
Treatise on the Emendation of the Intellect 239, 356, 468
On True and False Ideas 205, 314
True Intellectual System of the Universe, The 324
true religion 343
Two New Sciences 415
Two Treatises 264
Two Treatises of Government 480

Universalis philosophia 161–2
universals and reasoning 369–71

Vanity of Dogmatizing, The 186
Vindication 568

ways of being 258
whiteness 71, 72–3, 79–80
Why Does Language Matter to Philosophy? 375
William of Occam 482
World, The 66, 232

Xenophanes 179

zealots 494

Taylor & Francis eBooks

Helping you to choose the right eBooks for your Library

Add Routledge titles to your library's digital collection today. Taylor and Francis ebooks contains over 50,000 titles in the Humanities, Social Sciences, Behavioural Sciences, Built Environment and Law.

Choose from a range of subject packages or create your own!

Benefits for you
- » Free MARC records
- » COUNTER-compliant usage statistics
- » Flexible purchase and pricing options
- » All titles DRM-free.

Benefits for your user
- » Off-site, anytime access via Athens or referring URL
- » Print or copy pages or chapters
- » Full content search
- » Bookmark, highlight and annotate text
- » Access to thousands of pages of quality research at the click of a button.

REQUEST YOUR FREE INSTITUTIONAL TRIAL TODAY

Free Trials Available
We offer free trials to qualifying academic, corporate and government customers.

eCollections – Choose from over 30 subject eCollections, including:

Archaeology	Language Learning
Architecture	Law
Asian Studies	Literature
Business & Management	Media & Communication
Classical Studies	Middle East Studies
Construction	Music
Creative & Media Arts	Philosophy
Criminology & Criminal Justice	Planning
Economics	Politics
Education	Psychology & Mental Health
Energy	Religion
Engineering	Security
English Language & Linguistics	Social Work
Environment & Sustainability	Sociology
Geography	Sport
Health Studies	Theatre & Performance
History	Tourism, Hospitality & Events

For more information, pricing enquiries or to order a free trial, please contact your local sales team:
www.tandfebooks.com/page/sales

 | The home of Routledge books

www.tandfebooks.com